Desert Island Lists

Also by Roy Plomley

Days Seemed Longer (Autobiography)
Desert Island Discs
Desert Island Book (Editor)
Plomley's Pick (Editor)
French Dressing (Fiction)

Desert Island Lists

Roy Plomley
With Derek Drescher

Hutchinson
London Melbourne Sydney Auckland Johannesburg

Hutchinson & Co. (Publishers) Ltd
An imprint of the Hutchinson Publishing Group

17–21 Conway Street, London W1P 6JD

Hutchinson Publishing Group (Australia) Pty Ltd
16–22 Church Street, Hawthorn, Melbourne, Victoria 3122

Hutchinson Group (NZ) Ltd
32–34 View Road, PO Box 40–086, Glenfield, Auckland 10

Hutchinson Group (SA) Pty Ltd
PO Box 337, Bergvlei 2012, South Africa

First published 1984

© Roy Plomley 1984

Set in Linotron Plantin Light by Tradespools Limited, Frome, Somerset

Printed and bound in Great Britain by Anchor Brendon Ltd,
Tiptree, Essex

British Library Cataloguing in Publication Data
Plomley, Roy
  Desert Island lists.
  1. Desert island discs (Radio programme)
  I. Title   II. Drescher, Derek
  789.9′1   PN1991.77.D/

ISBN 0 09 151761 3

We are grateful to Derek Lewis, who is in charge of the BBC
Gramophone Library, for allowing us to check contentious points in their
index, and to two of his staff, Gillian Reichardt and Adrian Hindal-
Briscall, whose professional services were called upon to check our
amateur cataloguing.

To Leslie Perowne
– who was there at the beginning

LIST OF ABBREVIATIONS

CSO	Chicago Symphony Orchestra
LCO	London Chamber Orchestra
LPO	London Philharmonic Orchestra
LSO	London Symphony Orchestra
NPO	New Philharmonia Orchestra
RPO	Royal Philharmonic Orchestra

Foreword by Roy Plomley

I suppose the question I am asked most frequently by new acquaintances is, 'When did *Desert Island Discs* start?' – and, almost invariably, it is followed by, 'Which discs did so-and-so choose?'

Well, I can remember the answer to the first question – it was 29 January 1942, and it had been on 3 November 1941 that I had written to the BBC suggesting the idea, with the expectation of being offered a series of six programmes. But I can recall very few of the records chosen by my guests, which is hardly surprising since there have now been over 1700 of them – and that means nearly 14,000 records. So, when it was suggested that I should compile this book, my first reaction was that it would be very useful because, instead of racking my brains, I could refer inquirers to it.

My second reaction was that it was going to take a vast amount of work, so I invited Derek Drescher to collaborate with me. Derek has produced *Desert Island Discs* for the past eight years, knows more about music that I do and, as well as being a friendly and companionable man, has an orderly mind, which is something I don't lay claim to. We thought we were embarking on a project which would take us about three months: in fact, it has taken us about eight times as long.

First, all the material had to be dug out, some of it from BBC files dating back over forty years, much of it on flimsy and faded carbon copies. (I also have a set of the material myself, but we decided to use the BBC's set, because their attic is much better organized than mine! At this point, I would like to express my gratitude to the BBC.) We assembled 1700 transcripts and 1700 P-as-Bs.

P-as-B is an abbreviation of Programme-as-Broadcast, and it is a typed list of all the records used in each programme, giving the titles, composers, lyricists, soloists, orchestras, conductors, publishers, catalogue numbers and other pieces of information, some of them in foreign languages. It is typed after all the excitement of the preparation and recording of a programme is over, so it is not a job to be approached with great enthusiasm, which means that every fact on every P-as-B has had to be checked for accuracy.

We did not set out to give complete information about every record. For example, we have not included catalogue numbers because, after the first issue, manufacturers frequently republish discs under different numbers and on different labels, and it is impossible to keep track of all that. However, we have given sufficient information in every case to enable a reader to go to his local record dealer and say, 'Is this record currently available?', and the dealer can then consult his trade catalogues.

If the disc in question is no longer listed, one can always advertise for it. There are a number of magazines, notably the old-established *Gramophone*, which publish small advertisements asking for copies of out-of-print records.

When the series started, the only discs generally available were of the 78 rpm variety, which played for only three or four minutes each, and the repertoire of recorded music was limited; now it is vast, and the more recent lists in this book will show how much more knowledgeable people are about music than they used to be.

As well as giving each castaway's statutory ration of eight records, we have indicated with an asterisk (*) the one he or she would choose to keep if the other seven were to be lost in the surf or melted in the sun. We also list the one luxury chosen – that one article of no practical use which would give pleasure in adversity. The diversity of these is staggering, and they range from the Albert Memorial (Hermione Gingold) to a navel brush (Frank Muir).

Each castaway is allowed to take one book, other than *The Bible* and *The Complete Works of Shakespeare*, which are a standard issue to be found on every island. We assume that *The Bible* is placed there by The Gideon Society, but have no idea where the volume of Shakespeare comes from. The listing of the chosen extra volume is sometimes rather vague, because my guests seldom think to bring the chosen book to the studio, and sometimes cannot remember the exact title.

The luxury and the one book were late additions to the basic *Desert Island Discs* format; the luxury crept in after about a hundred programmes, and the book after about four hundred.

Another familiar question: have I ever visited a desert island myself? The answer is No, although I was once given the opportunity. Years ago, I was summoned to the office of a very senior BBC official, who waved me to an armchair and said, 'Sit down, Plomley, and have a glass of sherry.' It crossed my mind that this could only be a preliminary to the sack or to a vastly increased fee, but it was neither.

Having settled himself in an armchair opposite, my host said, 'Plomley, we're going to send you to a desert island.'

'Oh?' I said. It seemed an inadequate reply, but it was all I could think of at the moment. 'When?'

'As soon as you're free. We'll make arrangements with the government of a group of islands in the Indian Ocean to provide something suitable, and we'll send you out there for a week or two. Then we'll come over to you every evening after the 6 o'clock news and I'll ask you questions about how you've been getting on.'

'I've a better idea,' I said. 'I've had more experience of asking questions than you have, so I suggest that you go to a desert island and I come over to you after the 6 o'clock news.'

'Do you mean that you don't want to go?' He looked and sounded incredulous.

'To be honest, I don't. I've just finished compiling an anthology about desert islands –' (I won't bother you with the title, publisher and price, because it's now out of print) '– and I know quite a lot about them. For example, I know that there are about three hundred varieties of poisonous fish, and a vastly greater number of poisonous berries, and there are varieties of coral on which you just must *not* cut your foot, and there are land crabs that do dreadful things to you if you're not careful. I don't think I want to risk my life to boost the listening figures.'

He was obviously very disappointed in me, and I was not offered a second glass of sherry. I still have not been to a desert island. I may change my mind one day, but I don't think so.

The labours of the two compilers are now finished, and we are going out for a drink. We would like to make it clear that neither of us has any connection with the record industry, and for any further information on the recordings listed you should consult your local dealer.

29 January 1942

1 Vic Oliver

Comedian, actor and musician

¶ Chopin, Étude No. 12 in C minor (opus 10) (Alfred Cortot *piano*)

¶ Haydn Wood, 'Roses of Picardy' (New Light Symphony)

¶ 'Love is a Dancing Thing' (from *Follow the Sun*) (Hildegarde)

¶ Tchaikovsky, 'Marche Slav' (opus 31) (BBC Symphony)

¶ 'Happy Days are Here Again' (Jack Hylton's Orchestra)

¶ 'Parade of the Tin Soldiers' (New Light Symphony)

¶ 'I Give You My Heart' (Bebe Daniels)

¶ Wagner, 'The Ride of the Valkyries' (from *Die Walküre*) (Symphony/Coates)

5 February 1942

2 James Agate

Critic

¶ Handel/Beecham, *Origin of Design: Ballet* (LPO/Beecham)

¶ Rachmaninov, 'Rhapsody on a Theme of Paganini' (Benno Moiseiwitsch *piano*/LPO/Cameron)

¶ Duparc, 'Phidylé' (Maggie Teyte/LPO/Heward)

¶ 'I Hear You Calling Me' (John McCormack)

¶ J. Strauss, 'Tales from the Vienna Woods' (Philadelphia Orchestra/Stokowski)

¶ Walton, *Façade* (Orchestre Raymonde/Walter)

¶ Coates, 'By the Sleepy Lagoon' (Eric Coates Orchestra)

¶ Tchaikovsky, Symphony No. 4 in F minor (Boston Symphony/Koussevitzky)

12 February 1942

3 Commander Campbell

Mariner, explorer, 'Brains Trust' member

¶ German, *Merrie England* (selection) (New Mayfair Orchestra)

¶ Stanford, 'The Old Superb' (Peter Dawson)

¶ Elgar, 'Cockaigne Overture' (BBC Symphony/Elgar)

¶ Grieg, 'Anitra's Dance' (from *Peer Gynt Suite*) (LPO/Goossens)

¶ 'My Little Grey Home in the West' (Frances Langford)

¶ Gilbert & Sullivan, *The Gondoliers* (selection) (Band of HM Coldstream Guards)

¶ Coates, *Four Ways Suite* (New Light Symphony/Coates)

¶ *Gaiety Memories* (London Palladium Orchestra)

19 February 1942

4 C. B. Cochran

Showman

¶ 'C. B. Cochran Medley' (C. B. Cochran/Edward Cooper/Elisabeth Welch)

¶ Messager/Guitry, 'J'ai deux amants' (from *L'Amour Masqué*) (Yvonne Printemps)

¶ Granados, Spanish Dance No. 1 (New Light Symphony)

¶ Coward, 'Dear Little Café' (from *Bitter Sweet*) (Peggy Wood/George Metaxa)

¶ Mussorgsky, 'In the Town of Kazan' (from *Boris Godunov*) (Feodor Chaliapin)

¶ 'Flamingo' (Duke Ellington and his Orchestra)

¶ Massenet, 'L'amour est un vertu rare' (from *Thaïs*) (Maria Jeritza)

¶ Prokofiev, *The Love of Three Oranges* (Boston Symphony/Koussevitsky)

26 February 1942

5 Pat Kirkwood

Actress

¶ Porter, 'I Get a Kick Out of You' (from *Anything Goes*) (Ethel Merman)

¶ 'The Worm' (Arthur Askey)

¶ Schubert, 'Serenade' (Webster Booth)

¶ 'Dancing with My Shadow' (Elsie Carlisle)

¶ Offenbach, 'Barcarolle' (from *Tales of Hoffman*) (New Light Symphony)

¶ 'Thanks for the Memory' (from the film) (Shirley Ross/Bob Hope)

¶ Bach/Gounod, 'Ave Maria' (Gracie Fields)

¶ Rodgers & Hart, 'Where or When?' (from *Babes in Arms*) (Jack Hylton's Orchestra)

4 March 1942

6 Jack Hylton

Bandleader and impresario

¶ Tchaikovsky, Symphony No. 5 in E minor (opus 64) (LPO/Beecham)

¶ 'Rhymes' (Jack Hylton's Orchestra)

¶ 'I Kiss Your Hand, Madam' (Jack Hylton's Orchestra)

¶ 'Trains' (Reginald Gardiner)

¶ 'Sand in My Shoes' (RAF Squadronaires)

¶ 'Grinzing' (Jack Hylton's Orchestra)

¶ 'Cavalcade of Popular Songs' (Jack Hylton's Orchestra/Flanagan & Allen/Stanley Holloway, etc.)

¶ Rachmaninov, Piano Concerto No. 2 in C minor (opus 18) (Sergei Rachmaninov/Philadelphia Orchestra/Stokowski)

12 March 1942

7 Captain A. E. Dingle ('Sinbad')

Mariner and writer

¶ J. F. Wagner, 'Under the Double Eagle' (march) (Band of HM Coldstream Guards)

¶ 'The Floral Dance' (Peter Dawson)

¶ Kreisler, 'Caprice Viennois' (Fritz Kreisler *violin*)

¶ 'He Played His Ukelele as the Ship Went Down' (The Two Leslies)

¶ Kern & Hammerstein, 'Old Man River' (from *Show Boat*) (Paul Robeson)

¶ 'A Bunger-up of Ratholes' (Jack Warner)

¶ Beethoven, Sonata No. 14 in C sharp minor (opus 27, no. 2) (Wilhelm Backhaus *piano*)

¶ Offenbach, *Orpheus in the Underworld* (overture) (Bournemouth Municipal Orchestra/Godfrey)

19 March 1942
8 Joan Jay
**Glamour girl from London's
Windmill Theatre**
¶ Gershwin, 'Rhapsody in Blue'
(George Gershwin *piano*/Paul
Whiteman and his Concert
Orchestra)
¶ 'Tell Your Troubles to the
Breeze' (Mantovani and his
Orchestra)
¶ Chopin, Nocturne in E flat
major (opus 9, no. 2) (Artur
Rubinstein *piano*)
¶ 'My Blue Heaven'
(Whispering Jack Smith)
¶ 'Taboo' (Lecuona Cuban
Boys)
¶ Bach/Gounod, 'Ave Maria'
(Deanna Durbin)
¶ 'Frenesi' (Carroll Gibbons and
the Savoy Hotel Orpheans)
¶ Tchaikovsky, Piano Concerto
No. 1 in B flat minor (Artur
Rubinstein/LSO/Barbirolli)

26 March 1942
9 Rev. Canon W. H. Elliott
**Precentor of His Majesty's
Chapels Royal, Vicar of St
Michael's, Chester Square,
London**
¶ 'I'll Walk Beside You' (Peter
Dawson)
¶ Sibelius, 'Valse Triste' (LPO/
Harty)
¶ Chopin, Étude No. 3 in E
major (opus 10) (Eileen Joyce
piano)
¶ Vaughan Williams, 'Linden
Lea' (George Baker)
¶ 'Deep River' (Paul Robeson)
¶ Walford Davies, 'Solemn
Melody' (Hallé Orchestra/
Harty)
¶ 'Joshua Fit de Battle of
Jericho' (Paul Robeson/
Laurence Brown)
¶ Clarke, 'Trumpet Voluntary'
(Alex Harris *trumpet*/Harold
Dawber *organ*/Hallé Orchestra/
Harty)

2 April 1942
10 Arthur Askey
Comedian
¶ Coates, 'The Three Bears'
(Jack Hylton and his Orchestra)
¶ McDowell, 'To a Wild Rose'
(Victor Olof Sextet)

¶ 'Canoe Song' (from the film
Sanders of the River) (Paul
Robeson)
¶ Schubert, 'Serenade'
(Webster Booth)
¶ Mendelssohn, 'The Bees'
Wedding' (*Songs Without
Words*, no. 34) (Sergei
Rachmaninov *piano*)
¶ 'Sing as We Go' (from film)
(Gracie Fields)
¶ Tchaikovsky, Quartet in D
major: Andante Cantabile (opus
11) (Budapest String Quartet)
¶ *Band Waggon* (excerpt from
radio series) (Arthur Askey/
Richard Murdoch/company)

9 April 1942
11 Eva Turner
Soprano
¶ Wagner, *Tristan und Isolde*
(Prelude) (Berlin Philharmonic/
Furtwängler)
¶ Rachmaninov, 'Rhapsody on
a Theme of Paganini' (Sergei
Rachmaninov *piano*/
Philadelphia Orchestra/
Stokowski)
¶ Elgar, 'Nimrod' (from *Enigma
Variations*) (BBC Symphony/
Boult)
¶ Bach/Hess, 'Jesu, Joy of
Man's Desiring' (Myra Hess
piano)
¶ Szulc, 'Clair de lune' (Nellie
Melba)
¶ Chabrier, 'España' (LPO/
Beecham)
¶ Tchaikovsky, Piano Concerto
No. 1 in B flat (opus 23)
(Vladimir Horowitz/NBC
Symphony/Toscanini)
¶ Verdi, *Aida* (triumphal
march) (Boston Promenade
Orchestra/Fiedler)

16 April 1942
12 Harry Parry
**Jazz clarinettist, leader of
Radio Rhythm Club Sextet**
¶ 'I Surrender, Dear' (Artie
Shaw Orchestra)
¶ Bach/Gounod, 'Ave Maria'
(Deanna Durbin)
¶ 'Farewell Blues' (Benny
Goodman Orchestra)
¶ Brahms, Quintet in B minor
for clarinet and strings (opus
115) (Reginald Kell/Busch
Quartet)

¶ Berlin, 'Blue Skies' (Paul
Whiteman's Sax Socktette)
¶ 'Confessin'' (Louis Armstrong
and his Orchestra)
¶ 'Frenesi' (Woody Herman
Orchestra)
¶ Gershwin, 'Rhapsody in Blue'
(George Gershwin *piano*/Paul
Whiteman and his Concert
Orchestra)

23 April 1942
13 Tom Webster
Sports cartoonist
¶ 'When Day is Done' (Paul
Whiteman and his Concert
Orchestra)
¶ 'Underneath the Arches'
(Flanagan & Allen)
¶ 'Finckiana' (Herman Finck
Orchestra)
¶ Mendelssohn, 'Hear My
Prayer' (Ernest Lough/G.
Thalben-Bell *organ*/Temple
Church Choir, London)
¶ 'I Belong to Glasgow' (Will
Fyffe)
¶ 'Smoke Gets in Your Eyes'
(from *Roberta*) (Carroll Gibbons
and his Boy Friends)
¶ 'Wilkie Bard Medley' (Wilkie
Bard)
¶ Tchaikovsky, *The Sleeping
Beauty* (waltz) (Boston
Promenade Orchestra/Fiedler)

30 April 1942
14 Ivor Novello
Composer, playwright, actor
¶ Debussy, *Prélude à l'après-
midi d'un faune* (LPO/Beecham)
¶ 'The Garden Where the
Praties Grow' (John
McCormack)
¶ Bach, Suite No. 3 in D major
(Adolf Busch Chamber Players)
¶ Debussy, 'De fleurs' (from
Proses lyriques) (Maggie Teyte/
Gerald Moore *piano*)
¶ Hahn/Guitry, 'Air de la lettre'
(from *Mozart*) (Yvonne
Printemps)
¶ Delius, 'On Hearing the First
Cuckoo in Spring' (RPO/
Beecham)
¶ Brahms, 'Academic Festival
Overture' (Vienna
Philharmonic/Walter)
¶ 'Londonderry Air' (Lionel
Tertis *viola*)

7 May 1942
15 Roy Plomley
(interviewed by Leslie
Perowne)
¶ Mozart, *Il Seraglio* (overture)
(Vienna Philharmonic/Krauss)
¶ Gershwin, 'Bess, You is My
Woman Now' (from *Porgy and
Bess*) (Todd Duncan/Anne
Brown)
¶ 'Harmonising' (Fred Elizalde
piano)
¶ Borodin, 'Polovtsian Dances'
(from *Prince Igor*) (Leeds
Festival Choir/LPO/Beecham)
¶ 'Pour vous, j'avais fait cette
chanson' (Jean Sablon)
¶ Borodin, Quartet No. 2 in D
major (nocturne) (Lener String
Quartet)
¶ 'Creole Rhapsody' (Duke
Ellington and his Orchestra)
¶ J. Strauss, *Die Fledermaus*
(Act 2 finale) (Covent Garden
Opera Company)

9 July 1942
16 Beatrice Lillie
Actress and revue star
¶ Rachmaninov, Piano
Concerto No. 2 in C minor
(Sergei Rachmaninov/
Philharmonia Orchestra/
Stokowski)
¶ Tchaikovksy, 'None but the
Lonely Heart' (John
McCormack)
¶ 'Swanee River' (Bing Crosby)
¶ Waldteufel, 'The Skater's
Waltz' (Boston Promenade
Orchestra/Fiedler)
¶ Malotte, 'The Lord's Prayer'
(Webster Booth)
¶ Gershwin, 'Bess, You is My
Woman Now' (from *Porgy and
Bess*) (Helen Jepson/Lawrence
Tibbett)
¶ Fraser-Simson/Milne,
'Christopher Robin is Saying
His Prayers' (Turner Layton)
¶ Liszt, 'Hungarian Rhapsody
No. 2' (Seven Viennese Singing
Sisters)

23 July 1942
17 Leslie Howard
Actor and film producer
¶ Walton, 'Spitfire' (prelude
and fugue) (from film *The First
of the Few*) (Hallé Orchestra/
Walton)
¶ 'Say It with Music' (Paul
Whiteman and his Orchestra)
¶ 'The Folks Who Live on the
Hill' (Bing Crosby)
¶ Debussy, 'La fille aux cheveux
de lin' (Alfred Cortot *piano*)
¶ 'J'ai ta main dans ma main'
(Charles Trenet)
¶ Grieg, Piano Concerto in A
minor (opus 16) (Arthur de
Greef *piano*/Royal Albert Hall
Orchestra/Ronald)
¶ 'Phil the Fluter's Ball' (Peter
Dawson)
¶ Beethoven, Symphony No. 5
in C minor (opus 67) (NBC
Symphony/Toscanini)

6 August 1942
18 Nathaniel Gubbins
Humorous writer
¶ Boughton, 'Faery Song' (from
The Immortal Hour) (Webster
Booth)
¶ Brahms, Waltz No. 15 in A
flat (opus 39) (Fritz Kreisler
violin)
¶ Porter, 'You're the Top' (from
Anything Goes) (Victor Young
and his Orchestra)
¶ 'Passing By' (Alvar Liddell)
¶ 'June in January' (from film
Here is My Heart) (Bing Crosby)
¶ Coward, 'Mad Dogs and
Englishmen' (from *Words and
Music*) (Noël Coward)
¶ 'Medley of Negro Spirituals'
(Paul Robeson/Jack Hylton and
his Orchestra)
¶ Gay, *The Beggar's Opera*
(vocal selection) (Michael
Redgrave/company)

20 August 1942
19 Barrington Dalby
Boxing referee and sports
broadcaster
¶ German, 'The English Rose'
(from *Merrie England*) (Webster
Booth)
¶ Litolff, Concerto
Symphonique No. 4 (scherzo)
(Irene Scharrer *piano*/LSO/
Wood)

¶ Coward, 'The Stately Homes
of England' (from *Operette*)
(Original cast)
¶ 'At the Well' (Flora
Woodman/Eric Gritton *piano*)
¶ Walton, *Façade* (LPO/
Walton)
¶ Gounod, 'Nazareth' (Peter
Dawson)
¶ Debussy, 'Passepied' (from
'Suite Bergamasque') (LSO)
¶ Coates, 'Knightsbridge
March' (from *London Suite*)
(New Light Symphony/Lewis)

10 September 1942
20 Emlyn Williams
Actor and playwright
¶ Tchaikovsky, Symphony No.
5 in E minor (LPO/Beecham)
¶ 'Boum' (Charles Trenet)
¶ Shakespeare, *Hamlet* (excerpt)
(John Gielgud)
¶ 'The House is Haunted'
(Gracie Fields)
¶ Lalo, Symphonie Espagnole
for Violin and Orchestra (opus
21) (Yehudi Menuhin/Paris
Symphony/Enesco)
¶ 'The Very Thought of You'
(Ray Noble Orchestra)
¶ Hahn/Guitry 'Air de la lettre'
(from *Mozart*) (Yvonne
Printemps)
¶ Offenbach, 'Fantasia' (Marek
Weber Orchestra)

17 September 1942
21 Lord Elton
Author and broadcaster
¶ 'Were You There?' (Paul
Robeson)
¶ Ireland/Brook, 'Spring
Sorrow' (Stuart Robertson)
¶ 'Adeste Fideles' (John
McCormack/Choir)
¶ Foster, 'Drink to Me Only
with Thine Eyes' (Peter
Dawson)
¶ Dvořák, 'Humoresque' (opus
101, no. 7) (Fritz Kreisler
violin)
¶ Offenbach, 'Barcarolle' (from
Tales of Hoffmann) (LPO/
Beecham)

¶Handel, 'Comfort Ye, My People' (from *Messiah*) (Walter Widdop)

¶Clarke, 'Trumpet Voluntary' (Alex Harris *Trumpet*/Harold Dawber *organ*/Hallé Orchestra/Harty)

25 September 1942
22 Richard Tauber
Tenor

¶Beethoven, 'Egmont Overture' (NBC Symphony/Toscanini)

¶Kahn, 'Ave Maria' (Enrico Caruso)

¶'Falling in Love Again' (from film *The Blue Angel*) Marlene Dietrich)

¶Tauber, 'Symphonic Prologue and Epilogue to an Imaginary Play' (Vienna Philharmonic/Tauber)

¶Grieg, 'Spring' (from *Elegiac Melodies*) (LPO/Goossens)

¶'These Foolish Things' (from *Spread It Abroad*) (Greta Keller)

¶Tchaikovsky, Symphony No. 6 in E minor (Boston Symphony/Koussevitzky)

Wagner, *Tristan und Isolde* (Prelude and *Liebestod*) (Berlin Philharmonic/Furtwängler)

9 October 1942
23 Jonah Barrington
Musician and critic

¶Rachmaninov, 'Rhapsody on a Theme of Paganini' (Sergei Rachmaninov *piano*/Philharmonia Orchestra/Stokowski)

¶'Silversmith' (from *Spanish Choral Ballads*) (BBC Chorus/Cyril Dalmaine)

¶Coward, *Private Lives* (excerpt, Act 1) (Noël Coward/Gertrude Lawrence)

¶Stravinsky, *Le sacre du printemps* (Philadelphia Orchestra/Stokowski)

¶'Aloha Oe' (Bing Crosby)

¶Sibelius, 'The Swan of Tuonela' (Philadelphia Orchestra/Ormandy)

¶'Horrortorio' (from *Tell Her the Truth*) (Bobby Howes/Wylie Watson/Peter Haddon/Jack Lambert)

¶Elgar, Violin Concerto (Yehudi Menuhin/LSO/Elgar)

24 October 1942
24 Michael Powell
Film director

¶'The Campbells are Coming' (Glasgow Orpheus Choir/Roberton)

¶Bax, 'Tintagel' (NSO/Goossens)

¶Gershwin, 'I Got Plenty of Nuttin'' (from *Porgy and Bess*) (Todd Duncan)

¶'Without a Song' from the film *The Prodigal* (Victor Young Orchestra)

¶'Bessarabianka' (Peter Lescenco)

¶Mussorgsky, *Boris Godunov* (excerpt) (Feodor Chaliapin)

¶Tchaikovsky, Serenade in C major for String Orchestra (waltz) (BBC Symphony/Boult)

¶Vaughan Williams, *49th Parallel* (opening music) (from the film)

3 December 1942
25 Admiral Sir Edward Evans
Antarctic explorer

¶Grieg, 'Solveig's Song' (from *Peer Gynt Suite No. 2*) (New Light Symphony/Goossens)

¶Schubert, *Lilac Time* (selection) (New Light Symphony)

¶Tchaikovsky, 'Valse des fleurs' (from *Casse-Noisette Suite*) (Philadelphia Orchestra/Stokowski)

¶Bach/Gounod, 'Ave Maria' (Nellie Melba)

¶Mendelssohn, 'Spring Song' (from *Songs Without words*) (New Queens's Hall Orchestra/Wood)

¶'Road to the Isles' (from *Songs of the Hebrides*) (Robert Irwin)

¶Friml, 'Song of the Vagabonds' (from *The Vagabond King*) (Dennis King/Chorus)

¶'Abide with Me' (Clara Butt)

20 March 1943
26 Donald McCullough
Question Master of The Brains Trust

¶'I Belong to Glasgow' (Will Fyffe)

¶'Fantasia on English Melodies' (Georgian Singers)

¶'Parlez-moi d'amour' (Lucienne Boyer)

¶'Strip the Willow' and 'Dashing White Sergeant' (Scottish Dance Orchestra)

¶Tchaikovsky, *The Sleeping Beauty* (waltz) (Royal Opera House Orchestra, Covent Garden/Sargent)

¶Foster, 'The Old Folks at Home' (Fritz Kreisler *violin*)

¶'Road to the Isles' (from *Songs of the Hebrides*) (Polish Army Choir)

¶'Sousa Medley' (Band of HM Coldstream Guards)

12 April 1943
27 Ian Hay
Novelist and playwright

¶'The King is Still in London' (George Hancock)

¶'I'll Sing Thee Songs of Araby' (Ben Davies)

¶Handel, Largo in G (Arthur Meale *organ*)

¶'A Nightingale Sang in Berkeley Square' (from *New Faces*) (Vera Lynn)

¶'The Lion and Albert' (Stanley Holloway)

¶'Cherry Ripe' (Albert Sandler Trio)

¶HM King George V, Message to the Empire (Christmas Day broadcast, 1935)

¶Gilbert & Sullivan, *The Gondoliers* (selection) (Court Symphony Orchestra)

¶*Note: There is doubt as to whether the recording by HM George V was broadcast.*

8 June 1943
28 Tom Driberg MP
Politician and journalist

¶Beethoven, Symphony No. 8 in F major (opus 93) (Boston Symphony/Koussevitzky)

¶Mozart, Piano Concerto in D minor (K. 466) (Edwin Fischer/LPO/Fischer)

¶Bach/Walton, *The Wise Virgins* (Sadler's Wells Orchestra/Walton)

¶'Cockles and Mussels' (Maxine Sullivan)

¶'St Louis Blues' (Ethel Waters)

¶ 'Sing Me a Song with a Social Significance' from *Pins and Needles* (Kay Weber/Sonny Schuyler)
¶ Joyce, 'Anna Livia Plurabelle' (from *Finnegans Wake*) (James Joyce)
¶ Palestrina, *Missa Papae Marcelli* (Kyrie) (Westminster Cathedral Choir)

19 June 1943
29 Frank Swinnerton
Writer
¶ Rossini, *William Tell* (overture) (LPO/Beecham)
¶ Gilbert & Sullivan, 'If You Want to Know Who We Are' (from *The Mikado*) (Derek Oldham/Radley Flynn/Chorus)
¶ Sousa, 'The Stars and Stripes Forever' (Band of HM Coldstream Guards)
¶ Chopin, Ballade No. 3 in A flat major (opus 47) (Alfred Cortot *piano*)
¶ Saint-Saëns, 'Danse macabre' (Philadelphia Orchestra/Stokowski)
¶ Tchaikovsky, Serenade in C major (opus 48) (waltz) (Boston Symphony/Koussevitzky)
¶ Beethoven, Piano Concerto No. 5 in E flat major (opus 73) (Artur Schnabel/LSO/Sargent)
¶ J. Strauss, *Die Fledermaus* (Act 2 finale) (Covent Garden Opera Company)

26 June 1943
30 Beverley Baxter MP
Politician and drama critic
¶ Wagner, *Tristan und Isolde* (Prelude) (Berlin Philharmonic/Furtwängler)
¶ Tchaikovsky, 'Romeo and Juliet Fantasy Overture' (Boston Symphony/Koussevitzky)
¶ Rachmaninov, Piano Concerto No. 2 in C minor (Sergei Rachmaninov/Philadelphia Orchestra/Stokowski)
¶ Franck, Symphonic Variations for Piano and Orchestra (Alfred Cortot/LPO/Ronald)
¶ Bizet, 'Au fond du temple saint' (from *Les pêcheurs des perles*) (Edmond Clément/Marcel Journet)

¶ R. Strauss, *Der Rosenkavalier* (waltzes) (Dresden State Opera Orchestra/Böhm)
¶ 'Gonna Shout All Over God's Heaven' (Louis Armstrong/Lyn Murray Quartet)
¶ Elgar, 'Nimrod' (from *Enigma Variations*) (BBC Symphony/Boult)

16 July 1943
31 Herbert Hodge
Taxi-driver and writer
¶ 'The Lambeth Walk' (from *Me and My Girl*) (Lupino Lane/Teddie St Denis/Company)
¶ 'Water Boy' (Paul Robeson)
¶ 'In the Big Rock Candy Mountains' (Harry McClintock)
¶ Rimsky-Korsakov, 'Hymn to the Sun' (from *Le coq d'or*) (Fritz Kreisler *violin*)
¶ 'Leaning on a Lamp Post' (from film *Feather Your Nest*) (George Formby)
¶ Tchaikovsky, Serenade in C major (opus 48) (BBC Symphony/Boult)
¶ 'Lullaby of Broadway' (from film *Gold Diggers of 1935*) (Boswell Sisters)
¶ 'Sailing Up the Clyde' (Will Fyffe)

26 July 1943
32 C. A. Lejeune
Film critic
¶ 'The Old Refrain' (Fritz Kreisler *violin*)
¶ 'Roaming in the Gloaming' (Harry Lauder)
¶ Puccini, 'O My Beloved Father' (from *Gianni Schicchi*) (Joan Hammond)
¶ 'Turn Ye to Me' (Joseph Hislop)
¶ Crook, incidental music to *Peter Pan* (London Palladium Orchestra/Crean)
¶ 'Oh, Miss Hannah' (The Revellers)
¶ Gilbert & Sullivan, 'When the Night Wind Howls' (from *Ruddigore*) (Darrell Fancourt/Chorus)
¶ Berlin, 'White Christmas' (from film *Holiday Inn*) (Bing Crosby)

16 August 1943
33 Ivor Brown
Writer, editor and drama critic
¶ 'Tiger Rag' (Louis Armstrong Orchestra)
¶ 'Archibald Joyce Waltz Medley' (Viennese Waltz Orchestra)
¶ 'Eriskay Love Lilt' (Hugh McKay)
¶ 'The Dashing White Sergeant' (Strings of the BBC Scottish Orchestra)
¶ Shakespeare, *Richard II* (speech) and 'Sonnet' (John Gielgud)
¶ O. Straus, *The Waltz Dream* (selection) (Marek Weber Orchestra)
¶ *Max Miller in the Theatre*
¶ Mozart, *Eine Kleine Nachtmusik* (K. 525) (Vienna Philharmonic/Walter)

2 October 1943
34 Tom Harrisson
Anthropologist and founder of Mass Observation
¶ 'Shadrack' (Louis Armstrong/Lyn Murray Chorus)
¶ 'Underneath the Arches' (Flanagan & Allen/Henry Hall Orchestra)
¶ Walton/Sitwell, *Façade* (tango) (Constant Lambert *speaker*/Orchestra.)
¶ 'Ballad for Americans' (Paul Robeson/American People's Chorus)
¶ 'Mr Gallagher and Mr Sheen' (Bing Crosby/Johnny Mercer)
¶ Schubert, Impromptu in B flat major (opus 142, no. 3) (Edwin Fischer *piano*)
¶ 'Washboards Get Together' (Washboard Serenaders)
¶ Song of a skylark (recorded by Dr Ludwig Koch)

5 October 1943
35 Lady Eleanor Smith
Novelist and screenwriter
¶ 'Tango Flamenco' (La Nina de los Peines)
¶ Tchaikovsky, *Swan Lake* (LPO/Barbirolli)
¶ Debussy, *Prélude à l'après-midi d'un faune* (Philadelphia Orchestra/Stokowski)

¶ Stravinsky, *Petrushka* (Philadelphia Orchestra/ Stokowski)
¶ Hahn/Guitry, 'Air de la lettre' (from *Mozart*) (Yvonne Printemps)
¶ Falla, *The Three-Cornered Hat* (suite) (Boston Promenade Orchestra/Fiedler)
¶ Rossini/Respighi, *Boutique fantasque* (LPO/Goossens)
¶ Wagner, 'Forest Murmurs' (from *Siegfried*) (Berlin State Opera Orchestra/Blech)

11 October 1943
36 Sir Stephen Tallents
Administrator
¶ 'Oft in the Stilly Night' (David Wilson/Fred Mackey)
¶ Parry, 'Jerusalem' (Massed Choirs at Royal Command Concert, Empire Day, 1938)
¶ Foster, 'Drink to Me Only with Thine Eyes' (Paul Robeson)
¶ 'Transatlantic Lullaby' (from *The Gate Revue*) (Turner Layton)
¶ Excerpt from commentary on an international football match
¶ 'The Whiffenpoof Song' (Rudy Vallee/Vocal Quartet/ Carroll Gibbons Orchestra)
¶ 'The Holly and the Ivy' (Royal Choral Society/Sargent)
¶ 'Regimental March Medley' (HM Grenadier Guards Band)

16 November 1943
37 C. H. Middleton
Gardener and broadcaster
¶ 'Dear Old Home Songs' (BBC Chorus/Lewis)
¶ Schubert, 'Serenade' (John McCormack)
¶ 'The Old Sow' (Albert Richardson)
¶ Ketelbey, 'In a Monastery Garden' (Band of HM Coldstream Guards)
¶ 'Drinking' (Malcolm McEachern)
¶ Offenbach, 'Barcarolle' (from *Tales of Hoffmann*) (Jeanne Dusseau/Nancy Evans/Sadler's Wells Chorus and Orchestra)
¶ Suppé, *Poet and Peasant* (overture) (Band of HM Coldstream Guards)
¶ 'In an Old-fashioned Town' (Harold Williams)

23 November 1943
38 J. B. Morton
'Beachcomber' of the *Daily Express*
¶ 'Plaisir d'amour' (John McCormack)
¶ Chopin, Étude in E major (opus 10, no. 3) (Ignace Jan Paderewski *piano*)
¶ Franck, 'Panis Angelicus' (John McCormack)
¶ Grieg, 'Evening in the Mountains' (opus 68) (New Mayfair Chamber Orchestra/ Walter)
¶ Mozart, *Don Giovanni* (minuet) (Wanda Landowska *harpsichord*)
¶ Chopin, Prelude in A flat minor (opus 28, no. 17) (Alfred Cortot *piano*)
¶ Bizet, *L'Arlesienne Suite No. 2* (intermezzo) (Boston Promenade Orchestra/Fiedler)
¶ 'In the Shade of the Palm' (from *Floradora*) (Dennis Noble)

31 December 1943
39 Dr Charles Hill, later Lord Hill
'The Radio Doctor'
¶ 'Londonderry Air' (Fritz Kreisler *violin*)
¶ 'Always', 'When You and I Were Seventeen', 'What'll I Do?' (waltz medley) (Charlie Kunz *piano*)
¶ Gilbert & Sullivan, *The Mikado* (overture)
¶ 'Drinking' (Malcolm McEachern)
¶ 'Sweet and Lovely' (Layton & Johnstone)
¶ 'Live, Laugh and Love' (from film *Congress Dances*) (London Palladium Orchestra/Crean)
¶ 'Colonel Bogey' (Black Dyke Mills Band)
¶ 'Little Old Lady' (Sam Browne/Ambrose Orchestra)

8 January 1944
40 Alan Dent
Drama critic
¶ Berlioz, 'Absence' (*Nuits d'été*, opus 7, no. 4) (Maggie Teyte/LPO/Heward)
¶ 'Ca' the Yowes to the Knowes' (Isobel Baillie)

¶ Rossini, 'I'm the Factotum' (from *The Barber of Seville*) (Dennis Noble/Sadler's Wells Orchestra)
¶ Handel, 'Where'er You Walk' (from *Semele*) (Webster Booth/ Hallé Orchestra/Braithwaite)
¶ 'Tom Bowling' (Walter Widdop)
¶ Schubert, 'To Music' (Isobel Baillie)
¶ 'Round the Hay Wain' (Chauve Souris Company)
¶ 'Sur le pont d'Avignon' (Jean Sablon)

15 January 1944
41 Pamela Frankau
Novelist
¶ Palestrina, 'Sanctus' (from *Missa Papae Marcelli*) (Berlin State Choir and Orchestra/ Rudel)
¶ Purcell, 'When I am Laid in Earth' (from *Dido and Aeneas Suite*) (Philadelphia Orchestra/ Ormandy)
¶ Bach, Brandenburg Concerto No. 6 in B flat major (Busch Chamber Players)
¶ Mozart, *The Magic Flute* (overture) (BBC Symphony/ Toscanini)
¶ Beethoven, Piano Concerto No. 5 in E flat (opus 73) (Benno Moiseiwitsch/LPO/Szell)
¶ Brahms, Trio in A minor (opus 114) (Louis Kentner *piano*, Reginald Kell *clarinet*, Anthony Pini *cello*)
¶ Tchaikovsky, Symphony No. 5 in E minor (opus 64) (Philadelphia Orchestra/ Stokowski)
¶ Debussy, Nocturne No. 2: 'Fêtes' (Philadelphia Orchestra/ Stokowski)

12 February 1944
42 Squadron Leader Ralph Reader MBE
Producer and songwriter
¶ Gershwin, 'Rhapsody in Blue' (Alec Templeton *piano*/André Kostelanetz Orchestre)
¶ 'She's Funny that Way' (Ted Lewis and his Orchestra)
¶ Toye, 'The Haunted Ballroom' (Orchestre Raymonde)

¶ Tchaikovsky, *Swan Lake* (waltz) (LPO/Dorati)

¶ 'My Melancholy Baby' (Bing Crosby)

¶ 'Two Sleepy People' (from film *Thanks for the Memory*) (Bob Hope/Shirley Ross)

¶ 'Santa Barbara' (Joe Loss Orchestra)

¶ 'Bless This House' (Webster Booth)

19 February 1944
43 Wing Commander Guy Gibson VC, DSO, DFC
Leader of 'Dam Busters' raid

¶ 'Warsaw Concerto' (from film *Dangerous Moonlight*) (Louis Kentner *piano*/LSO/Matheson)

¶ Rodgers & Hart, 'Where or When?' (from *Babes in Arms*) (Adelaide Hall)

¶ J. Strauss, *Thousand and One Nights* (waltz) (Symphony Orchestra/Johann Stauss III)

¶ Wagner, *The Flying Dutchman* (overture) (Berlin State Opera Orchestra/Muck)

¶ 'If I Had My Way' (Bing Crosby)

¶ 'The Marines Hymn' (Fred Waring Pennsylvanians/Glee Club)

¶ 'The Royal Air Force March Past' (Band of HM Royal Air Force)

¶ Wagner, 'The Ride of the Valkyries' (from *Die Walküre*) (Queen's Hall Orchestra/Wood)

20 March 1944
44 Mabel Constanduros
Novelist, playwright, actress and variety artist

¶ Schumann, 'Traumerei' (Minneapolis Symphony/ Ormandy)

¶ 'Water Boy' (Paul Robeson)

¶ Granados, 'Andaluza' (Spanish Dance, opus 37, no. 5) (Yehudi Menuhin *violin*)

¶ Coward, 'The Stately Homes of England' (from *Operette*) (Quartet from original cast)

¶ Chopin, Étude in F major (opus 25, no. 3) (Solomon *piano*)

¶ Chopin, Prelude in D flat minor (opus 28, no. 15) (Ignace Jan Paderewski *piano*)

¶ Delius, 'Serenade' (from *Hassan*) (LPO/Beecham)

¶ 'The Road to the Isles' (from *Songs of the Hebrides*) (Stuart Robertson)

4 August 1945
45 Frederick Grisewood
Broadcaster

¶ Debussy, 'Les sons et les parfums tournent dans l'air du soir' (*Preludes*, Book 1, No. 4) (Walter Gieseking *piano*)

¶ Daybreak on a Surrey farm (sound effects)

'German Commissionaire Scene' (from *Seeing Stars*) (Leslie Henson/Fred Emney)

¶ 'Archibald Joyce Waltz Medley' (Debroy Somers Band)

¶ Byron/White, 'So We'll Go No More A-roving' (Gervase Elwes)

¶ Weinberger, *Schwanda the Bagpiper* (polka) (Minneapolis Symphony/Ormandy)

¶ Purcell, 'When I am Laid in Earth' (from *Dido and Aeneas*) (Elsie Suddaby)

¶ Delius, 'Summer Night on the River' (Royal Philharmonic/ Beecham)

11 August 1945
46 Peter Fettes
Light Programme announcer

¶ 'Vieni sul mar' (Enrico Caruso)

¶ 'Truro Maggot' (Frederick Thurston clarinet)

¶ 'Bohunkus' (Frank Crumit)

¶ Debussy, 'Minstrels' (*Preludes*, Book 1, No. 12) (Yehudi Menuhin *violin*)

¶ 'She Moved Through the Fair' (John McCormack)

¶ Chopin, Waltz in D flat minor (opus 64, no. 1) (Vladimir de Pachmann *piano*)

¶ Verdi, 'Cortigiani, vil razza dannata' (from *Rigoletto*) (Giuseppe de Luca/ Metropolitan Opera House Chorus and Orchestra/Setti)

¶ Elgar, 'Dream Children' (Hallé Orchestra/Harty)

18 August 1945
47 Jill Balcon
Actress and Light Programme announcer

¶ 'My Lagen Love' (Dennis Cox)

¶ Vaughan Williams, *The Wasps* (overture) (Hallé Orchestra/ Sargent)

¶ Schubert, Trio No. 1 in B flat (opus 99) (Alfred Cortot *piano*/ Jacques Thibaud *violin*/Pablo Casals *cello*)

¶ 'Sur le pont d'Avignon' (Jean Sablon)

¶ Mozart, Symphony No. 39 in E flat major (BBC Symphony/ Walter)

¶ Bach, 'My Heart Ever Faithful' (Cantata No. 68) (Isobel Baillie/Anthony Pini *cello*)

¶ Ravel, 'Jeux d'eau' (Eileen Joyce *piano*)

¶ Verdi, 'Bella figlia dell' amore' (from *Rigoletto*) (Nellie Melba/ Edna Thornton/John McCormack/Mario Sammarco)

25 August 1945
48 Michael Harrison
Soldier and Light Programme announcer

¶ Purcell, 'Nymphs and Shepherds' (Manchester schoolchildren's choir/Hallé Orchestra/Harty)

¶ Bach, Double Violin Concerto in D minor (Yehudi Menuhin/ Georges Enesco/Orchestra/ Monteux)

¶ Chopin, Ballade No. 2 in F major (Anatole Kitain *piano*)

¶ Vaughan Williams, 'Fantasia on Greensleeves' (Jacques Orchestra)

¶ Brahms, Symphony No. 1 in C minor (Vienna Philharmonic/ Walter)

¶ Handel, 'Silent Worship' (from *Ptolemy*) (Dennis Noble)

¶ Franck, Pièce No. 5 (Léon Goossens *oboe*/Gerald Moore *piano*)

¶ Handel, 'Hallelujah Chorus' (from *Messiah*) (Royal Choral Society/Royal Liverpool Philharmonic/Sargent)

1 September 1945
49 Joan Edgar
Light Programme announcer
¶Tchaikovsky, 'Rose Adagio'
(from *The Sleeping Beauty*)
(Sadler's Wells Orchestra/
Lambert)
¶'Bob White' (Bing Crosby/
Connie Boswell)
¶Puccini, *Madam Butterfly*
(love duet) (Joan Hammond/
Webster Booth)
¶'Chloe' (Spike Jones and his
City Slickers)
¶Debussy, 'Claire de Lune'
(from *Suite bergamasque*)
(André Kostelanetz Orchestra)
¶Porter, 'It's De-Lovely' (from
The Fleet's Lit Up) (Frances
Day)
¶Wood, 'Fantasia on British
Sea Songs' (LSO/Wood)
¶Wagner, *Lohengrin* (Act 3
prelude) (New York
Philharmonic/Toscanini)

8 September 1945
50 Roy Williams
Light Programme announcer
¶Puccini, 'Love and Music'
(from *Tosca*) (Joan Hammond)
¶Chopin, Ballade No. 1 in G
minor (opus 23) (Benno
Moiseiwitsch *piano*)
¶Verdi, 'La vergine degli
angeli' (from *La forza del
destino*) (Ezio Pinza/Rosa
Ponselle)
¶Donizetti, 'Chi mi frena'
(sextet from *Lucia di
Lammermoor*) Maria Gentile,
Dino Borgioli & others/La Scala
Orchestra)
¶'Sur le pont d'Avignon' (Jean
Sablon)
¶Verdi, 'Miserere' (from *Il
Trovatore*) (Joan Cross/Webster
Booth/Sadler's Wells Chorus
and Orchestra)
¶'The Lass of Richmond Hill'
(Dale Smith/Westminster
Singers)
¶Offenbach/Rosenthal, *Gaîté
Parisienne* (LPO/Kürtz)

15 September 1945
51 Alvar Lidell
Announcer and singer
¶Handel, 'Hallelujah Chorus'
(from *Messiah*) (Royal Choral
Society/LPO/Sargent)

¶Bach, Suite No. 1 in G major
(prelude) (Pablo Casals *cello*)
¶Mozart, 'Deh vieni alla
finestra' (from *Don Giovanni*)
(John Brownlee/Glyndebourne
Festival Orchestra/Busch)
¶Brahms, 'Waltz' (opus 39, no.
3) (Anatole Kitain *piano*)
¶'Trains' (Reginald Gardiner)
¶Ravel, 'Pièce en forme de
Habanera' (Yehudi Menuhin
violin)
¶'Oh, Beautiful Varmeland'
(Jussi Björling)
¶Wolf, Italian Serenade in G
major (Budapest String
Quartet)

22 September 1945
52 Pat Butler
Light Programme announcer
¶Wagner, *Lohengrin* (Act 3
prelude) (New York
Philharmonic/Toscanini)
¶Bizet/Horowitz, 'Variations
on Themes from *Carmen*'
(Vladimir Horowitz *piano*)
¶Mozart, 'Fin ch' han dal vino'
(from *Don Giovanni*) (Ezio
Pinza)
¶Zeller, 'Nightingale Song'
(from *Der Vogelhändler*)
(Elisabeth Schumann)
¶Vaughan Williams, 'Fantasia
on Greensleeves' (Hallé
Orchestra/Sargent)
¶Tchaikovsky, 'None but the
Lonely Heart' (opus 6, no. 6)
(Lawrence Tibbett)
¶'La Spagnola' (Beniamino
Gigli)
¶Bemberg, 'Un ange est venu'
(Nellie Melba/John Brownlee)

29 September 1945
53 Margaret Hubble
Light Programme announcer
¶Mendelssohn, Symphony No.
3 (overture) (LPO/Beecham)
¶'The Owl and the Pussy Cat'
(Stuart Robertson)
¶Beethoven, Symphony No. 7
in A minor (New York
Philharmonic/Toscanini)
¶Raff, 'La fileuse' (Yvonne
Arnaud *piano*)
¶'Pour vous j'avais fait cette
chanson' (Jean Sablon)
¶Bach, Suite No. 3 in D major
(Adolf Busch Chamber Players)

¶'The Pessimistic Character
with the Crabapple Face' (Bing
Crosby)
¶Rossini/Respighi, *La boutique
fantasque* (LPO/Goossens)

6 October 1945
54 Michael Redgrave
Actor
¶'Marechiare' (Tito Schipa)
¶Ravel, Quartet in F major
(Pro Arte Quartet)
¶'I Know Where I'm Goin''
(Barbara Mullen)
¶Gluck, 'Dance of the Blessed
Spirits' (from *Orfeo ed Euridice*)
(New York Philharmonic/
Toscanini)
¶Wordsworth, 'Upon
Westminster Bridge' (Edith
Evans)
¶Gay, 'Youth's the Season'
(from *The Beggar's Opera*)
(Michael Redgrave/Chorus)
¶Britten (arr.), 'Little Sir
William' and 'Oliver Cromwell'
(Peter Pears)
¶Handel, Sonata No. 5 in D
(Yehudi Menuhin *violin*/Marcel
Gazelle *piano*)

13 October 1945
55 Claire Luce
Actress
¶Rachmaninov, Prelude in G
flat minor (opus 32, no. 3)
(Sergei Rachmaninov *piano*)
¶Debussy/Verlaine, 'Le faune'
(Maggie Teyte/Alfred Cortot
piano)
¶Porter, 'Night and Day' (from
The Gay Divorce) (André
Kostelanetz Orchestra)
¶Debussy, Quartet in G minor
(opus 10) (Pro Arte Quartet)
¶Beethoven, Symphony No.6
in F major (opus 68) (BBC
Symphony/Toscanini)
¶Mussorgsky, 'Farewell of
Boris' (from *Boris Godunov*)
(Feodor Chaliapin)
¶Shakespeare, 'Let Me not to
the Marriage of True Minds'
(Edith Evans)
¶Sibelius, 'Valse triste' (opus
44) (Philadelphia Orchestra/
Stokowski)

20 October 1945
56 Dr C. E. M. Joad
Philosopher, writer and scholar

¶ Bach, Concerto for Two Violins in D minor (Yehudi Menuhin/Georges Enesco/Orchestra/Monteux)
¶ Mozart, Sinfonia Concertante in E flat (K. 364) (Albert Sammons *violin*/Lionel Tertis *viola*/LPO/Harty). *(Dr Joad chose the whole of this work on four 12-inch discs.)*
¶ Schubert, Quartet No. 14 in D minor (second movement) (Busch String Quartet)
¶ Beethoven, Symphony No. 3 in E flat major (NBC Symphony/Toscanini). *(The last movement was chosen, on two discs.)*

27 October 1945
57 Celia Johnson
Actress

¶ Elgar, 'Cockaigne Overture' (BBC Symphony/Elgar)
¶ Coward, 'I'll See You Again' (from *Bitter Sweet*) (Peggy Wood/George Metaxa)
¶ Chopin, Waltz in C sharp minor (opus 64, no. 2) (Ignace Jan Paderewski *piano*)
¶ O. Straus, 'Depuis trois ans passés' (from *Mariette*) (Yvonne Printemps)
¶ Weber, 'Invitation to the Waltz' (BBC Symphony/Toscanini)
¶ 'My Guy's Come Back' (Joe Loss Orchestra)
¶ 'I'm Going to See you Today' (Joyce Grenfell)
¶ Beethoven, Symphony No. 6 in F major (BBC Symphony/Toscanini)

3 November 1945
58 Valerie Hobson
Actress

¶ Butterworth, 'Rhapsody' (from *A Shropshire Lad*) (Hallé Orchestra/Boult)
¶ 'The Way You Look Tonight' (from film *Swing Time*) (Fred Astaire)
¶ 'Holiday for Strings' (André Kostelanetz Orchestra)

¶ 'Phil the Fluter's Ball' (Brian Lawrence)
¶ Rachmaninov, 'Rhapsody on a Theme of Paganini' (Sergei Rachmaninov *piano*/Philadelphia Orchestra/Stokowski)
¶ 'I'll Follow My Secret Heart' (from *Conversation Piece*) (Yvonne Printemps)
¶ Debussy, 'Claire de lune' (from *Suite bergamasque*) (André Kostelanetz Orchestra)
¶ Dvořák, Symphony No. 9 in E minor (Prague Philharmonic/Szell)

10 November 1945
59 Bobby Howes
Musical comedy actor

¶ Grieg, 'Anitra's Dance' (from *Peer Gynt Suite No. 1*) (LPO/Goossens)
¶ Debussy, 'Claire de lune' (from *Suite bergamasque*) (Harold Bauer *piano*)
¶ 'Sunday, Monday or Always' (Bing Crosby)
¶ Brahms, Sonata in E flat major for Clarinet and Piano (Frederick Thurston *clarinet*/Myers Foggin *piano*)
¶ 'Holiday for Strings' (David Rose Orchestra)
¶ Borodin, 'Polovtsian Dances' (from *Prince Igor*) (Leeds Festival Choir/LPO/Beecham)
¶ Mendelssohn, 'Hear My Prayer' (Ernest Lough/G. Thalben-Ball *organ*/Choir of Temple Church, London)
¶ Gershwin, 'Rhapsody in Blue' (George Gershwin *piano*/Paul Whiteman and his Concert Orchestra)

17 November 1945
60 Deborah Kerr
Actress

¶ Ravel, 'Pavane pour une infante défunte' (André Kostelanetz Orchestra)
¶ 'Je tire ma reverence' (Jean Sablon)
¶ Tchaikovsky, Serenade in C major (opus 48) (Boston Symphony/Koussevitzky)
¶ 'She Moved Through the Fair' (Sydney McEwen)

¶ Franck, 'Symphonic Variations' (Walter Gieseking *piano*/LPO/Wood)
¶ 'Mr Gallagher and Mr Sheen' (Bing Crosby/Johnny Mercer)
¶ Dvořák, Symphony No. 9 in E minor (Philadelphia Orchestra/Stokowski)
¶ Prokofiev, *Peter and the Wolf* (Richard Hale *narrator*/Boston Symphony/Koussevitzky)

24 November 1945
61 Signalman Henry Wheeler
Naval rating

¶ 'Danny Boy' (John McHugh)
¶ Porter, 'Begin the Beguine' (from *Jubilee*) (Joe Loss Orchestra)
¶ 'If You Were the Only Girl in the World' (from *The Bing Boys are Here*) (Webster Booth/Anne Ziegler)
¶ Schumann, Romance in F sharp minor (opus 28, no. 2) (Benno Moiseiwitsch *piano*)
¶ 'Beautiful Love' (Victor Young Orchestra)
¶ Herbert, 'Ah, Sweet Mystery of Life' (from *Naughty Marietta*) (Nelson Eddy)
¶ Vaughan Williams, 'Fantasia on Greensleeves' (Hallé Orchestra/Sargent)
¶ 'The Holy City' (Richard Crooks)

1 December 1945
62 Eileen Joyce
Concert pianist

¶ Purcell, 'Nymphs and Shepherds' (Manchester schoolchildren's choir/Hallé Orchestra/Harty)
¶ Bach, 'Ricercare a 6 voci' (from *Der Musicalischen Opfer*) (Edwin Fischer Chamber Orchestra)
¶ Mozart, Symphony No. 40 in G minor (NBC Symphony/Toscanini)
¶ Elgar, Violin Concerto in B minor (opus 61) (Yehudi Menuhin/LSO/Elgar)
¶ Beethoven, Quartet in C major (opus 59, no. 3) (Busch String Quartet)
¶ Mendelssohn, 'Hear Ye, Israel' (from *Elijah*) (Isobel Baillie/Robinson)

¶ Schubert, Quintet in A major (opus 114) (Artur Schnabel *piano*/members of Pro Arte String Quartet/Claude Hobday *double bass*)
¶ Brahms, Symphony No. 4 in E minor (opus 98) (BBC Symphony/Walter)

8 December 1945
63 Stewart Granger
Actor
¶ Paganini/Green, 'Romance' (from film *The Magic Bow*) (Yehudi Menuhin *violin*/Gerald Moore *piano*)
¶ 'The Three Caballeros' (Bing Crosby/Andrews Sisters)
¶ Beethoven, Piano Concerto No. 5 in E flat (opus 73) (Benno Moiseiwitsch/LSO/Szell)
¶ 'The Songs of the Black Hussars' (Chauve-Souris Company)
¶ Bach/Hess, 'Jesu, Joy of Man's Desiring' (Myra Hess *piano*)
¶ J. Strauss, 'Tales from the Vienna Woods' (Philadelphia Orchestra/Stokowski)
¶ Puccini, 'In quelle trine morbide' (from *Manon Lescaut*) (Hina Spani/La Scala Orchestra)
¶ Gretchaninov, 'Glory to Thee, O Lord' (from *Twofold Litany*) (Feodor Chaliapin/Choir of Russian Church of the Metropolitan of Paris)

15 December 1945
64 Richard Goolden
Actor
¶ *The Belle of New York* (selection) (Band of HM Coldstream Guards)
¶ 'Lily of Laguna' (Eugene Stratton)
¶ Lehár, *The Merry Widow* (selection) (London Theatre Orchestra)
¶ Mendelssohn, 'Oh, Taste and See' (Ernest Lough/R. Mallett/ Choir of Temple Church, London)
¶ 'If You Were the Only Girl in the World' (from *The Bing Boys are Here*) (George Robey/Violet Loraine)
¶ 'Im Prater Bluhn Wieder die Baume' (Richard Tauber)

¶ Beethoven, Sonata in C sharp minor (opus 27, no. 2) (Mark Hambourg *piano*)
¶ Haydn Wood, 'A Brown Bird Singing' (Reginald Foort *organ*)

22 December 1945
65 Nova Pilbeam
Actress
¶ Beethoven, Bagatelle No. 4 (opus 126) (Artur Schnabel *piano*)
¶ Mozart, Symphony No. 41 in C major (K. 551) (Vienna Philharmonic/Walter)
¶ Bach, Sonata No. 5 in F minor (Alfred Dubois *violin*/Marcel Maas *piano*)
¶ Schubert, 'Der Lindenbaum' (from *Winterreise*, opus 89) (Gerhard Husch/Hans Udo Muller *piano*)
¶ Bartok, 'Roumanian Folk Dances' (Yehudi Menuhin *violin*/Marcel Gazzelle *piano*)
¶ Handel, 'For Unto Us a Child is Born' (from *Messiah*) (Philharmonic Choir)
¶ Beethoven, Trio in B flat (opus 11) (M. Raucheisen *piano*/L. Kohl *clarinet*/J. Disclez *cello*)
¶ Bach, 'Dona Nobis Pacem' (from *Mass in B minor*) (Philharmonic Choir/LSO/ Coates)

29 December 1945
66 Sonia Dresdel
Actress
¶ Beethoven, Symphony No. 7 in A major (opus 92) (Vienna Philharmonic/Weingartner)
¶ Delius, 'A Walk to the Paradise Garden' (from *A Village Romeo and Juliet*) (RPO/ Beecham)
¶ Schumann, 'Ich grolle nicht' (from *Dichterliebe*, opus 48) (Gerhard Husch)
¶ Chopin, Étude No. 12 in C minor (Louis Kentner *piano*)
¶ Schumann, Piano Concerto in A minor (opus 54) (Myra Hess/ Orchestra/Walter Goehr)
¶ Debussy, 'Clair de lune' from *Suite bergamasque* (André Kostelanetz Orchestra)

¶ Elgar, 'Nimrod' (from *Enigma Variations*, opus 36) (BBC Symphony/Boult)
¶ Grieg, 'Last Spring' (*Elegiac Melody No. 2*) (Amsterdam Concertgebouw/Mengelberg)

5 January 1946
67 Barbara Mullen
Actress and singer
¶ Tchaikovsky, Piano Concerto No. 1 in B flat minor (opus 23) (Vladimir Horowitz/NBC Symphony/Toscanini)
¶ 'The Big Rock Candy Mountains' (Rocky Mountaineers)
¶ 'Kyrie Eleison' (plainsong) (Schola of Ampleforth Abbey)
¶ 'Loch Lomond' (Polish Army Choir)
¶ 'My Bonnie Lies Over the Ocean' (Ella Logan)
¶ 'Shadrack' (Louis Armstrong/ Lyn Murray Choir)
¶ Bach, 'Gigue' (from *French Suite No. 5*) (Myra Hess *piano*)
¶ Parry, 'Jerusalem' (Paul Robeson)

3 January 1951
68 Eric Portman
Actor
¶ 'Le fiacre' (Jean Sablon)
¶ Lehar, 'The Merry Widow Waltz' (Marek Weber and his Orchestra)
¶ 'Because' (Eva Turner)
¶ 'Cancoes de Criancas' (Peter Kreuder *piano*)
¶ Mendelssohn, *Midsummer Night's Dream* (intermezzo) (Amsterdam Concertgebouw/ Van Beinum)
¶ 'Cool Water' (Nellie Lutcher)
¶ 'Maladie d'amour' (Henri Salvador)
¶ 'A Voice in the Night' (from film *Wanted for Murder*) (Eric Harrison *piano*/Queen's Hall Light Orchestra/Williams)

10 January 1951
69 Monica Dickens
Novelist
¶ 'The Kerry Dance' (John McHugh/Grace Shearer *piano*)
¶ 'Once in Royal David's City' (King's College Chapel Choir/ Ord)

¶ 'Have I Told You Lately that I Love You?' (Gene Autry)
¶ 'Ballin' the Jack' (Danny Kaye)
¶ Martini, 'Plaisir d'amour' (Maggie Teyte/Gerald Moore *piano*)
¶ Coward, 'Shadow Play' (from *Tonight at 8.30*) (Gertrude Lawrence/Noël Coward/Phoenix Theatre Orchestra/Greenwood)
¶ 'I'll Follow My Secret Heart' (from *Conversation Piece*) (Yvonne Printemps/Noël Coward)
¶ Porter 'Just One of Those Things' (from *Jubilee*) (Dinah Shore)
¶ Adam, 'Mad Scene' (from *Giselle*) (Royal Opera House Orchestra, Covent Garden/Lambert)

17 January 1951
70 Robertson Hare
Character actor
¶ 'Bewitched' (Bill Snyder and his Orchestra)
¶ 'Bojangles of Harlem' (from film *Swing Time*) (Fred Astaire)
¶ Heuberger, *The Opera Ball* (overture) (Berlin State Opera Orchestra/Blech)
¶ 'Transatlantic Lullaby' (from *The Gate Revue*) (Turner Layton)
¶ Porter, 'Night and Day' (from *The Gay Divorce*) (André Kostelanetz Orchestra)
¶ Gershwin, 'Shall We Dance?' (from film) (Fred Astaire)
¶ Diana Hare *piano* (private recording)
¶ 'John Brown's Body' (Stuart Robertson)

24 January 1951
71 Yvonne Arnaud
Actress and concert pianist
¶ Delius, 'A Walk to the Paradise Garden' (from *A Village Romeo and Juliet*) (RPO/Beecham)
¶ 'Mademoiselle Hortensia' (Leo Marjane)
¶ Brahms, Violin Concerto in D major (Ginette Neveu/Philharmonia Orchestra/Dobrowen)

¶ Mozart, *The Marriage of Figaro* (overture) (Hallé Orchestra/Barbirolli)
¶ Schumann, 'Du Meine Seele' (from *Widmung*) (Herbert Janssen/Gerald Moore *piano*)
¶ 'La partie de bridge' (Pills/Tabet/Mireille/Jean Sablon)
¶ Beethoven, Symphony No. 9 in D minor (Elisabeth Schwarzkopf/Elisabeth Hoengen/Julius Patzak/Hans Hotter/Vienna Philharmonic/von Karajan)

31 January 1951
72 Donald Peers
Vocalist
¶ 'When Father Papered the Parlour' (Billy Williams)
¶ Puccini, 'Love and Music' (from *Tosca*) (Joan Hammond/Hallé Orchestra/Heward)
¶ 'Donald the Dub' (Frank Crumit)
¶ 'Wait for the Wagon' (march) (Band of HM Coldstream Guards)
¶ 'Behind the Clouds' (Gene Austin)
¶ 'Old Father Thames' (Peter Dawson)
¶ 'It's a Lovely Day Tomorrow' (Binnie Hale)
¶ Verdi, *La traviata* (Act 1 prelude) (Santa Cecilia Orchestra/de Sabata)

7 February 1951
73 Peter Scott
Naturalist, painter and traveller
¶ Gershwin, 'Love Walked In' (from film *Goldwyn Follies*) (Ambrose Orchestra)
¶ Mozart, Piano Concerto No. 27 in B flat (Robert Casadesus/New York Philharmonic/Barbirolli)
¶ 'Honky Tonkin'' (Teresa Brewer/Dixieland All Stars)
¶ Beethoven, Symphony No. 7 in A major (opus 92) (Vienna Philharmonic/Weingartner)
¶ Coward, 'Nina' (from *Sigh No More*) (Noël Coward)
¶ Schubert, Quintet in C major (opus 163) (Pro Arte Quartet/Anthony Pini *cello*)

¶ 'Forever and Ever' (The Skylarks/Russ Morgan and his Orchestra)
¶ Sibelius, Symphony No. 1 in E minor (Minneapolis Symphony/Ormandy)

14 February 1951
74 Constance Cummings
Actress
¶ 'Londonderry Air' (Fritz Kreisler *violin*/Franz Rupp *piano*)
¶ 'Girls Were Made to Take Care of Boys' (from film *One Sunday Afternoon*) (Rose Murphy)
¶ Puccini, 'Che gelida manina' (from *La Bohème*) (Beniamino Gigli/La Scala Orchestra/Berrettoni)
¶ 'Don't Believe Everything You Dream' (Flanagan & Allen)
¶ Ravel, 'Conversation of Beauty and the Beast' (from *Mother Goose Suite*) (LSO/Previtali)
¶ Boughton, 'The Faery Song' (from *The Immortal Hour*) (Glasgow Orpheus Choir/Roberton)
¶ 'Wanderings' (Josh White)
¶ Handel, 'Hallelujah Chorus' (from *Messiah*) (Huddersfield Choral Society/Liverpool Philharmonic/Sargent)

21 February 1951
75 Jack Buchanan
Actor and manager
¶ 'So Tell a Tree' (Bing Crosby)
¶ 'Limehouse Blues' (Duke Ellington and his Cotton Club Orchestra)
¶ 'The Dashing White Sergeant' (Glasgow Orpheus Choir/Roberton)
¶ 'For Every Man There's a Woman' (Peggy Lee/Benny Goodman Orchestra)
¶ 'Who?' (from *Sunny*) (Guy Lombardo and his Royal Canadians)
¶ 'Life Gits Tee-Jus, Don't It?' (Peter Lind Hayes)
¶ 'Donkey Serenade' (from film *Firefly*) (Melachrino Strings)
¶ 'Swing Low, Sweet Chariot' (Bing Crosby)

28 February 1951
76 Kay Hammond
Actress

¶ O. Straus, *Mariette* (Act 2 finale) (Yvonne Printemps/ Sacha Guitry)
¶ 'De Glory Road' (from film *Metropolitan*) (Lawrence Tibbett)
¶ Puccini, 'Love and Music' (from *Tosca*) (Joan Hammond/ Hallé Orchestra/Heward)
¶ Tchaikovsky, 'Dance of the Swans' (from *Swan Lake*) (LPO/Dorati)
¶ 'Cara Sposina' (Alfredo del Pelo)
¶ Chopin, Etude in A flat major (opus 25, no. 1) (Alfred Cortot *piano*)
¶ Verdi, 'O Terra, Addio' (from *Aida*) (Maria Caniglia/ Beniamino Gigli/Rome Opera House Orchestra and Chorus/ Serafin)
¶ Beethoven, Symphony No. 5 in C minor (NBC Symphony/ Toscanini)

7 March 1951
77 Peter Ustinov
Playwright, actor and film director

¶ 'À la Barcillunisa' (Giuseppe di Stefano)
¶ Meilhac/Halevy/Offenbach, 'O, mon cher amant, je te jure' (from *La perichole*) (Jennie Tourel)
¶ Prokofiev, Violin Concerto No. 2 in G minor (Jascha Heifetz/Boston Symphony/ Koussevitzky)
¶ Villa-Lobos, Bachianas Brasileiras No. 5 (aria) (Bidu Sayao/eight cellos/Villa-Lobos)
¶ Schubert, Quartet in A minor (opus 29) (Philharmonia String Quartet)
¶ Janáček, 'Co Chvila' (from *Jenůfa*) (Marie Podvalova)
¶ Janáček, 'Sinfonietta' (CPO/ Kubelik)
¶ Davidovsky, 'Prière de Saint-Simon' (Choir of Russian Church of the Metropolitan of Paris/Afonsky)

14 March 1951
78 Joan Hammond
Singer

¶ Wagner, *Tannhäuser* (overture) (LPO/Beecham)
¶ Sibelius, 'The Swan of Tuonela' (Philadelphia Orchestra/Ormandy)
¶ Chopin, Étude in G flat major (opus 10, no. 5) (Alfred Cortot *piano*)
¶ Tchaikovsky, Violin Concerto in D major (Jascha Heifetz/ LPO/Barbirolli)
¶ R. Strauss, *Der Rosenkavalier* (final trio) (Lotte Lehmann/ Elisabeth Schumann/Maria Olszewska/Vienna Philharmonic/Heger)
¶ Tchaikovsky, Symphony No. 5 in E minor (LPO/Beecham)
¶ Mozart, *Eine Kleine Nachtmusik* (Vienna Philharmonic/Walter)
¶ 'Abide with Me' (Choir of St Margaret's, Westminster/ Dawson)

21 March 1951
79 John Clements
Actor and manager

¶ Beethoven, Leonora Overture No. 3 (NBC Symphony/ Toscanini)
¶ Puccini, 'O soave fanciulla' (from *La bohème*) (Beniamino Gigli/Maria Caniglia/Goehr)
¶ Bach, Prelude and Fugue No. 1 in C major (Wilhelm Backhaus *piano*)
¶ Verdi, 'Caro nome' (from *Rigoletto*) (Amelita Galli-Curci)
¶ Puccini, 'E lucevan le stelle' (from *Tosca*) (Ferruccio Tagliavini/EIAR Symphony, Turin/Tansini)
¶ Saint-Saëns, 'Introduction and rondo capriccioso' (Jascha Heifetz *violin*/LPO/Barbirolli)
¶ Massenet, 'Death of Thaïs' (from *Thaïs*) (Dorothy Kirsten/ Robert Merrill/RCA Victor Symphony/Morel)
¶ Beethoven, Piano Concerto No. 5 in E flat major (Artur Schnabel/Philharmonia Orchestra/Galliera)

28 March 1951
80 Ted Kavanagh
Comedy writer and creator of *ITMA*

¶ 'Believe Me, if All Those Endearing Young Charms' (John McCormack)
¶ 'Our Village Concert' (Syd Howard/Vera Pearce/Leonard Henry)
¶ Borodin, 'Polovtsian Dances' (from *Prince Igor*) (Leeds Festival Choir/LPO/Beecham)
¶ 'Sweeney Todd, the Demon Barber of Fleet Street' (Tod Slaughter/Company)
¶ 'Forty-seven Ginger-headed Sailors' (Tommy Handley)
¶ Delibes, 'Bell Song' (from *Lakmé*) (Florence Foster Jenkins/Cosme McMoon *piano*)
¶ 'Blaydon Races' (Owen Brannigan/Gerald Moore *piano*)
¶ 'Berceuse pour une poupée' (Les Chanteuses de la Colombière/Boller)

4 April 1951
81 Anona Winn
Actress and singer

¶ 'Christopher Columbus' (Guy Mitchell)
¶ Puccini, 'Ah, Love Me a Little' (from *Madam Butterfly*) (Joan Hammond/Webster Booth/Royal Liverpool Philharmonic/Sargent)
¶ 'Le fiacre' (Jean Sablon)
¶ Porter, 'You're the Top' (from *Anything Goes*) (Anona Winn/ Billy Marlow)
¶ Shostakovich, Symphony No. 1 (opus 10) (Philadelphia Orchestra/Stokowski)
¶ 'Ballin' the Jack' (Danny Kaye)
¶ 'The Peanut Vendor' (Louis Armstrong Orchestra)
¶ Ellis, 'Table for Two' (from *Bless the Bride*) (Georges Guétary)

11 April 1951
82 Muir Mathieson
Conductor

¶ Lambert, 'The Rio Grande' (Hallé Orchestra/Lambert)
¶ Bliss, 'March' (from film *Things to Come*) (LSO/ Mathieson)

¶ Bax, 'The Garden of Fand' (RPO/Beecham)
¶ Coleridge-Taylor, 'When They Buried Minnehaha' (from *Hiawatha*) (Royal Choral Society/Sargent)
¶ Walton, Concerto for Viola and Orchestra (William Primrose/Philharmonia Orchestra/Walton)
¶ 'Warsaw Concerto' (from film *Dangerous Moonlight*) (LSO/Mathieson)
¶ 'Bonnie Dundee' (Kirkintilloch Junior Choir)
¶ Vaughan Williams, Symphony No. 6 in E minor (LSO/Boult)

18 April 1951
83 Peter Fleming
Writer and traveller
¶ 'The Clouds Will Soon Roll By' (Layton & Johnstone)
¶ 'Regimental March of the Rifle Brigade' (National Military Band/Robinson)
¶ 'As Time Goes By' (from film *Casablanca*) (Anne Shelton/Ambrose Orchestra)
¶ Shakespeare/Walton, 'St Crispin's Day' (from *Henry V*) (Laurence Olivier/Philharmonia Orchestra/Walton)
¶ 'Ashby de la Zouch' (Lew Stone and his Nova-Tones)
¶ 'Lili Marlene' (Lale Andersen)
¶ Mendelssohn, 'The Hebrides Overture' (LPO/Van Beinum)
¶ Coward, 'I'll See You Again' (from *Bitter Sweet*) (Hildegarde)

25 April 1951
84 Margaret Lockwood
Actress
¶ 'Eton Boating Song' (John Rorke/London Community Singers/Glyn Jones)
¶ Verdi, *La traviata* (Act 1 prelude) (Santa Cecilia Orchestra, Rome/de Sabata)
¶ Novello, 'Someday My Heart Will Awake' (from *King's Rhapsody*) (Vanessa Lee)
¶ Vaughan Williams, 'Fantasia on Greensleeves' (Halle Orchestra/Barbirolli)
¶ 'Skye Boat Song' (Luton Girls' Choir)
¶ Tchaikovsky, *Swan Lake* (finale) (LPO/Dorati)

¶ 'The Spinning Wheel' (Delia Murphy/Arthur Darley *guitar*)
¶ Wagner, 'The Ride of the Valkyries' (from *Die Walküre*) (Vienna Philharmonic/Furtwängler)

2 May 1951
85 Petula Clark
Actress and singer
¶ 'Aba Daba Honeymoon' (from film *Two Weeks with Love*) (Debbie Reynolds)
¶ 'Story of the Stars' (Jack Pleis)
¶ 'Dear, Dear, Dear' (Champ Butler)
¶ Ravel, 'La Valse' (Paris Conservatoire Orchestra/Ansermet)
¶ 'A Friend of Johnny's' (Jo Stafford)
¶ 'Gipsy Fiddler' (Ray Martin and his Concert Orchestra)
¶ 'Life's Desire' (Jimmy Young)
¶ 'Temptation' (Jo Stafford/Red Ingle and the Natural Seven)

9 May 1951
86 Larry Adler
Harmonica player
¶ Rachmaninov, 'Rhapsody on a Theme of Paganini' (Sergei Rachmaninov *piano*/Philadelphia Orchestra/Stokowski)
¶ Mozart, Quartet in F major (K. 370) (Leon Goossens *oboe*/J. Lener *violin*/S. Roth *viola*/I. Hartman *cello*)
¶ Mozart, Symphony No. 40 in G minor (LPO/Beecham)
¶ Bach, Double Violin Concerto in D minor (Yehudi Menuhin/Georges Enesco/Orchestra/Monteux)
¶ Brahms, Symphony No. 1 in C minor (Vienna Philharmonic/Furtwängler)
¶ Prokofiev, Violin Concerto No. 2 in G minor (Jascha Heifetz/Boston Symphony/Koussevitzky)
¶ Rachmaninov, Piano Concerto No. 2 in C minor (Sergei Rachmaninov/Philadelphia Orchestra/Stokowski)
¶ Beethoven, Violin Concerto in D major (Jascha Heifetz/NBC Symphony/Toscanini)

16 May 1951
87 Denis Compton and W. J. Edrich
Cricketers
¶ (Compton) Trenet, 'La mer' (Charles Trenet)
¶ (Edrich) Tchaikovsky, *Swan Lake* (waltz) (Hallé Orchestra/Barbirolli)
¶ (C) Rodgers & Hammerstein, 'If I Loved You' (from *Carousel*) Iva Withers/Stephen Douglass)
¶ (E) Verdi, 'Sanctus' (from *Requiem Mass*) (Rome Opera House Orchestra and Chorus/Serafin)
¶ (C) Porter, 'So in Love' (from *Kiss Me Kate*) (Bill Johnson)
¶ (E) 'Ballin' the Jack' (Danny Kaye)
¶ (C) 'Victory Test Match Calypso' (England *v* West Indies, Lord's, 1950) (Lord Beginner/Calypso Rhythm Kings)
¶ (E) 'Nature Boy' (Dick Haymes/The Song Spinners)

23 May 1951
88 Ann Todd
Actress
¶ Khachaturian, 'Sabre Dance' (from *Gayaneh Ballet Suite*) (New York Philharmonic/Kurtz)
¶ 'Munasterio è Santa Chiara' (Carlo Buti)
¶ Offenbach/Rosenthal (arr.) *Gaïté Parisienne* (ballet music) LPO/Kurtz)
¶ Bach/Gounod, 'Ave Maria' (Gracie Fields)
¶ 'Skye Boat Song' (Ian Macpherson)
¶ Ravel, 'Lever du jour' (from *Daphnis and Chloe Suite No. 2*) Boston Symphony/Koussevitzky)
¶ Rodgers & Hammerstein, 'People Will Say We're in Love' (from *Oklahoma*) (Alfred Drake/Joan Roberts)
¶ Rachmaninov, Piano Concerto No. 2 in C minor (Eileen Joyce/LPO/Leinsdorf)

30 May 1951
89 Maggie Teyte
Singer
¶Debussy, 'Clair de lune' (from *Suite bergamasque*) (Jascha Heifetz *violin*/Emanuel Bay *piano*)
¶Bach, Toccata, Adagio and Fugue in C major (Gina Bachauer *piano*)
¶Schubert, 'The Erl King' (Bernhard Sonnerstedt/Gerald Moore *piano*)
¶Barber, 'Adagio for Strings' (Boyd Neel Orchestra)
¶Wagner, 'Brünnhilde's Immolation' (from *Götterdämmerung*) (Kirsten Flagstad/Philharmonia Orchestra/Furtwängler)
¶Mendelssohn, 'The Hebrides Overture' (Hallé Orchestra/Barbirolli)
¶Handel, 'I Know that My Redeemer Liveth' (from *Messiah*) (Ernest Lough/G. Thalben-Ball *organ*)
¶Khachaturian, *Masquerade Suite* (waltz) (Boston Promenade Orchestra/Fiedler)

6 June 1951
90 Tommy Trinder
Comedian
¶ 'On the Sunny Side of the Street' (Ted Lewis and his Band)
¶ 'I'm a Vulture for Horticulture' (Jimmy Durante)
¶Ponchielli, 'Dance of the Hours' (from *La Gioconda*) (Paris Conservatoire Orchestra/Fistoulari)
¶Porter, 'So in Love' (from *Kiss Me Kate*) (Dinah Shore)
¶ 'The Whistler and His Dog' (Jerry Allen Trio)
¶ 'My Resistance is Low' (Hoagy Carmichael)
¶ 'How High the Moon' (Les Paul *guitar*/Mary Ford)
¶ 'Tiger Rag' (Duke Ellington Orchestra)

13 June 1951
91 Gracie Fields
Singer and actress
¶Meyerbeer, 'O Paradiso!' (from *L'africaine*) (Enrico Caruso)

¶Vaughan Williams, 'Fantasia on Greensleeves' (Hallé Orchestra/Barbirolli)
¶ 'Sam, Pick Up Tha' Musket' (Stanley Holloway)
¶Sarasate, 'Zigeunerweisen' (Jascha Heifetz *violin*/LSO/Barbirolli)
¶Kern & Hammerstein, *Showboat* (selection) (Geraldo and his Romance in Rhythm Orchestra/Olive Groves/George Baker/Chorus)
¶Delius, 'Intermezzo' and 'Serenade' (from *Hassan*) (Hallé Orchestra/Lambert)
¶Rossini, 'Una voce poco fa' (from *The Barber of Seville*) (Luisa Tetrazzini)
¶Tchaikovsky, 'Romeo and Juliet Fantasy Overture' (Vienna Philharmonic/von Karajan)

20 June 1951
92 Eric Coates
Composer
¶Elgar, 'Cockaigne Overture' (LPO/Van Beinum)
¶German, 'Pastoral Dance' (from *Nell Gwynn Dances No. 2*) (City of Birmingham Symphony/Weldon)
¶Wieniawski, Violin Concerto No. 2 in D minor (Jascha Heifetz/LPO/Barbirolli)
¶Debussy, *Prélude à l'après-midi d'un faune* (LPO/Beecham)
¶Brahms, Quintet in B minor (Reginald Kell *clarinet*/Busch Quartet)
¶Kreisler, 'Tambourin chinois' (opus 3) (André Kostelanetz Orchestra)
¶Chopin, Waltz No. 14 in E minor (Witold Malcuzynski *piano*)
¶Coates, 'Valse' (from *Four Centuries Suite*) (National Symphony/Coates)

27 June 1951
93 Bill Johnson
Actor and singer
¶Berlin, 'White Christmas' (from film *Holiday Inn*) (Bing Crosby)
¶Vaughan Williams, 'Fantasia on Greensleeves' (Hallé Orchestra/Sargent)

¶Puccini, 'E lucevan le stelle' (from *Tosca*) (Giuseppe di Stefano)
¶Debussy, 'La cathédrale engloutie' (*Preludes* Book 1, No. 10) (Solomon *piano*)
¶ 'The Last Round-up' (Bing Crosby)
¶Provost, *Souvenir de Vienne* (intermezzo) (from film *Escape to Happiness*) (Boston Promenade Orchestra/Fiedler)
¶Porter, 'Where is the Life that Late I led?' (from *Kiss Me Kate*) (Bill Johnson)
¶Verdi, 'Eri tu che macchiavi' (from *Un Ballo in Maschera*) (Giovanni Inghilleri/Philharmonia Orchestra/Erede)

4 July 1951
94 Stanley Holloway
Actor, singer and variety artist
¶ 'Ragamuffin' (Albert Sandler Trio)
¶ 'The Waiter, the Porter and the Upstairs Maid' (from film *The Birth of the Blues*) (Bing Crosby/Mary Martin/Jack Teagarden)
¶Litolff, Concerto Symphonique No. 4 (Irene Scharrer *piano*/LSO/Wood)
¶ 'Selling a Car' (Harry Tate/Company)
¶Elgar, 'Chanson de matin' (Philharmonia Orchestra/Collingwood)
¶ 'Memory Street' (from *The Co-optimists*) (Elsa Macfarlane/Stanley Holloway)
¶ 'Three Green Bonnets' (Gracie Fields)
¶Coleridge-Taylor, 'Farewell Said He, Minnehaha' (from *Hiawatha*) (Howard Fry/Royal Choral Society/Sargent)

11 July 1951
95 Cicely Courtneidge
Actress and comedienne
¶Coates, 'Halcyon Days' and 'Elizabeth Tudor' (from *The Three Elizabeths*) (National Symphony/Coates)
¶ 'I'll Be Around' (Mills Brothers)
¶Gershwin, 'Rhapsody in Blue' (Melachrino Orchestra)

¶Mendelssohn, *A Midsummer Night's Dream* (scherzo) (Philharmonia Orchestra/Kubelik)
¶'I'll Be Seeing You' (Bing Crosby)
¶Saint-Saëns, 'Carnival of the Animals' (Philadelphia Orchestra/Stokowski)
¶'The Laughing Policeman' (Charles Penrose)
¶Elgar, 'Pomp and Circumstance' March No. 1 in D major (Philharmonia Orchestra/Sargent)

18 July 1951
96 Leslie Henson
Comedy actor
¶'The Wheel Tapper' (Stanley Holloway)
¶Gershwin, 'My One and Only' (from *Funny Face*) (Fred Astaire)
¶'The Waltz in Swing Time' (from film *Swing Time*) (BBC Dance Orchestra/Hall)
¶Rodgers & Hart, 'On Your Toes' (from *On Your Toes*) (Jack Whiting/Carroll Gibbons/Savoy Hotel Orpheans)
¶'The Windsor Melody' (Mantovani and his Concert Orchestra)
¶'She's My Lovely' (from *Hide and Seek*) (Bobby Howes/London Hippodrome Theatre Orchestra)
¶Ivor Novello selection (Olive Gilbert/Helen Hill/Peter Graves/Webster Booth/Acres)
¶'A Little Co-operation from You' (from *Going Greek*) (Louise Browne/Roy Royston)

25 July 1951
97 Jean Kent
Actress
¶Offenbach/Rosenthal (arr.), *Gaîté Parisienne* (ballet music) LPO/Kurtz)
¶'A Little of What You Fancy Does You Good' (Marie Lloyd)
¶Lehár, 'Girls Were Made to Love and Kiss' (from *Paganini*) (Richard Tauber)
¶Debussy, Arabesque No. 1 (John Cockerill *harp*)
¶'Jubilee Stomp' (Duke Ellington and his Orchestra)

¶J. Strauss, 'Ach Wie So Herrlich' (from *Eine Nacht in Venedig*) (Erich Kunz/Vienna Volksoper Orchestra/Paulik)
¶Verdi/Liszt, *Rigoletto*: Concert Paraphrase (Egon Petri *piano*)
¶J. Strauss, *Die Fledermaus* (Act 2 finale) (Sieglinde Wagner/Julius Patzak/Kurt Preger/Hilde Gueden/Alfred Poell/Wilma Lipp/Vienna State Opera Chorus/Vienna Philharmonic/Krauss)

1 August 1951
98 Jimmy Edwards
Comedian
¶Coates, *Three Bears Suite* (Foden's Motor Works Band)
¶'The Carnival of Venice' (Harry James and his Orchestra)
¶'Little Bo(p) Peep' (Ray Ellington Quartet)
¶'The Policeman's Holiday' (The Keynotes)
¶'Stumbling' (Sid Phillips and his Band)
¶R. Strauss, Concerto No. 1 in E for Horn and Orchestra (Dennis Brain/Philharmonia Orchestra/Galliera)
¶'Sid Field Plays Golf' (Sid Field/Company)
¶Britten, 'Four Sea Interludes: No. 4, Storm' (from *Peter Grimes*) (Amsterdam Concertgebouw/Van Beinum)

8 August 1951
99 Joyce Grenfell
Writer and entertainer
¶Bach, Toccata in G (Myra Hess *piano*)
¶Dvořák, Cello Concerto in D minor (opus 104) (Pablo Casals/CPO/Szell)
¶Rachmaninov, Vocalise (opus 34, no. 14) (Boston Symphony/Koussevitzky)
¶'The Trolley Song' (from film *Meet Me in St Louis*) (Judy Garland)
¶Granados, 'El mirar de la maja' (from *Tonadillas*) (Victoria de los Angeles/Gerald Moore *piano*)
¶Bach, 'Ricercare a 6 voci (from *The Musical Offering*) (Kammerochester/Edwin Fischer)

¶O. Straus, 'Depuis trois ans passés' (from *Mariette*) (Yvonne Printemps)
¶Purcell, 'Nymphs and Shepherds' (Manchester schoolchildren's choir/Hallé Orchestra/Harty)

15 August 1951
100 A. E. Matthews
Actor
¶Coward, 'A Room with a View' (from *This Year of Grace*) (Noël Coward)
¶'British Guards March Medley'
¶Lehár, 'The Merry Widow Waltz' (Harry Davidson and his Orchestra)
¶A medley of songs including 'The Honeysuckle and the Bee' (Ellaline Terriss/Seymour Hicks)
¶'Monckton Melodies' (BBC Theatre Orchestra/Robinson)
¶'The Jewel of Asia' (from *The Geisha*) (Marie Tempest)
¶'The Invincible Eagle' (Band of HM Coldstream Guards)
¶'When We are Married' (from *The Belle of New York*) (Albert Sandler Trio)

22 August 1951
101 Phyllis Calvert
Actress
¶Purcell, 'Nymphs and Shepherds' (Manchester schoolchildren's choir/Hallé Orchestra/Harty)
¶'Lazy Day' (Bing Crosby)
¶Franck, Symphony in D minor (Philharmonia Orchestra/Galliera)
¶Wilde, 'The Happy Prince' (Frank Phillips)
¶Berlin, 'I Got Lost in His Arms' (from *Annie Get Your Gun*) (Ethel Merman)
¶Paganini/Green (arr.), 'Romance' (from film *The Magic Bow*) (Yehudi Menuhin *violin*/Gerald Moore *piano*)
¶Mozart, 'Vanish'd Are Ye' (from *The Marriage of Figaro*) (Isobel Baillie/Philharmonia Orchestra/Susskind)
¶Sibelius, Symphony No. 2 in D major (RPO/Beecham)

29 August 1951
102 Vivian Ellis
Theatre composer

¶ Rimsky-Korsakov, 'Scheherazade' (Paris Conservatoire Orchestra/Ansermet)

¶ Bach/Hess, 'Jesu, Joy of Man's Desiring' (Myra Hess *piano*)

¶ Stravinsky, *Petrushka* (Orchestre de la Suisse Romande/Ansermet)

¶ Hahn/Guitry, 'Air de la lettre' (from *Mozart*) (Yvonne Printemps)

¶ Bach/Gounod, 'Ave Maria' (Vivian Ellis *piano*/his mother *violin*)

¶ Arlen & Harburg, 'Over the Rainbow' (from film *The Wizard of Oz*) (Judy Garland)

¶ Chopin, Étude No. 27 in A flat (Alfred Cortot *piano*)

¶ Wagner, *Tristan und Isolde* (prelude) (Berlin Philharmonic/Furtwängler)

5 September 1951
103 Anne Crawford
Actress

¶ 'Please' (Bing Crosby)

¶ Coates, 'The Three Bears' (Coates)

¶ 'These Foolish Things' (Jean Sablon)

¶ Mozart, Symphony No. 40 in G minor (LPO/Beecham)

¶ 'Dancing in the Dark' (Carmen Cavallaro *piano*)

¶ Offenbach/Rosenthal (arr.), *Gaïté Parisienne* (ballet music) (LPO/Kurtz)

¶ 'Candy Kisses' (Danny Kaye)

¶ 'Seascape' (Queen's Hall Light Orchestra/Farnon)

12 September 1951
104 Freddie Mills
Light heavyweight boxer

¶ Fanfare used at White City before big fights

¶ 'Coronation Scot' (Queen's Hall Light Orchestra/Torch)

¶ 'You Can't Keep a Good Dreamer Down' (from film *London Town*) (Sid Field)

¶ 'I've Got a Lovely Bunch of Coconuts' (Danny Kaye)

¶ 'I'll Get By' (Johnny Green)

¶ 'Rock-a-Bye Your Baby' (from film *Jolson Sings Again*) (Al Jolson)

¶ Chopin, Fantasie-Impromptu in C sharp minor (opus 66) (Halina Stefanska *piano*)

¶ 'Beware' (Norman Wisdom)

¶ *RAF Choruses* (selection)

16 September 1951
105 Sally Ann Howes
Actress

¶ Vaughan Williams, 'Fantasia on Greensleeves' (Hallé Orchestra/Sargent)

¶ Rodgers & Hammerstein, 'Oh, What a Beautiful Morning' (from *Oklahoma*) (Howard Keel)

¶ Walford Davies 'God Be in My Head' (Templars Octet)

¶ Ravel, 'Jeux d'eau' (Eileen Joyce *piano*)

¶ Berlin, 'There's No Business Like Show Business' (from film) (Betty Hutton/Howard Keel)

¶ Ravel, *Daphnis and Chloe Suite No. 2* (Paris Conservatoire Orchestra/Munch)

¶ 'She's My Lovely' (from *Hide and Seek*) (Bobby Howes)

¶ Tchaikovsky, *Swan Lake Ballet Suite* (Hallé Orchestra/Barbirolli)

¶ LUXURY: Garlic

25 September 1951
106 George Robey CBE
Comedian

¶ Tchaikovsky, 'Dance of the Sugar Plum Fairy' (from *Nutcracker Suite*) (Philharmonia Orchestra/Malko)

¶ Coward, 'I'll See You Again' (from *Bitter Sweet*) (Peggy Wood/George Metaxa)

¶ Grieg, Piano Concerto in A minor (Artur Rubinstein/Philadelphia Orchestra/Ormandy)

¶ Gilbert & Sullivan, *The Gondoliers* (selection) (Richard Green Orchestra)

¶ Verdi, 'Falstaff's Monologue' (from *Falstaff*, Act 1) (Mariano Stabile/Erede)

¶ Kreisler, 'Liebesfreud' (Fritz Kreisler *violin*)

¶ Novello, *Glamorous Nights* (selection) (Drury Lane Theatre Orchestra/Prentice)

¶ Elgar, 'Land of Hope and Glory' (Gracie Fields)

2 October 1951
107 Mai Zetterling
Actress

¶ Tchaikovsky, '1812 Overture' (Philharmonia Orchestra/Malko)

¶ Sibelius, 'Sav Sav Susa' (Aulikki Rautawaara/Berlin Philharmonic/Schmidt-Isserstedt)

¶ Falla, 'Nights in the Gardens of Spain' (Jacqueline Blancard *piano*/Orchestre de la Suisse Romande/Ansermet)

¶ Schumann, 'Aufschwung' (from *Fantasiestucke*, opus 12) (Wilhelm Backhaus *piano*)

¶ Shakespeare/Walton, 'To Be or Not to Be' (from film *Hamlet*) (Sir Laurence Olivier/Philharmonia Orchestra/Mathieson)

¶ Bach, Sonata No. 4 in D minor (Gioconda da Vito *violin*)

¶ 'Ballad for Americans' (Paul Robeson)

¶ Beethoven, Symphony No. 3 in B flat major (Vienna Philharmonic/Furtwängler)

9 October 1951
108 Henry Kendall
Actor and director

¶ Puccini, 'O soave fanciulla' (from *La bohème*) (Enrico Caruso/Nellie Melba)

¶ 'Love Will Find a Way' (from *The Maid of the Mountains*) (Jose Collins)

¶ Berlin, 'Let's Face the Music and Dance' (from film *Follow the Fleet*) (Fred Astaire)

¶ Ravel, 'Pavane pour une infante défunte' (Boston Symphony/Koussevitzky)

¶ Delius, 'La Calinda' (from *Koanga*) (LPO/Beecham)

¶ Novello, 'My Dearest Dear' (from *The Dancing Years*) (Mary Ellis/Ivor Novello)

¶ Grieg, 'A Swan' (Kirsten Flagstad/Philharmonia Orchestra/Braithwaite)

¶ 'My Lucky Day' (from film *This Week of Grace*) (Gracie Fields)
¶ BOOK: *Who's Who in the Theatre*

23 October 1951
109 Gerald Moore
Accompanist
¶ Fauré, Piano Quartet in C minor (London Belgian Piano Quartet)
¶ German, 'O Peaceful England' (from *Merrie England*) (Gladys Ripley)
¶ Wordsworth, 'Upon Westminster Bridge' (Edith Evans)
¶ 'Will You Walk a Little Faster?' (from *Alice in Wonderland*) (George Baker/ Gerald Moore *piano*)
¶ Beethoven, Symphony No. 6 in F major (Vienna Philharmonic/Walter)
¶ Hahn/Guitry, 'Air de la lettre' (from *Mozart*) (Yvonne Printemps)
¶ Purcell, 'Nymphs and Shepherds' (Manchester schoolchildren's choir/Hallé Orchestra/Harty)
¶ Bach, 'Air' (from Suite No. 3 in D) (Royal Liverpool Philharmonic/Sargent)
¶ LUXURY: A double bass.

30 October 1951
110 Clemence Dane
Playwright and novelist
¶ Bach, Double Violin Concerto in D minor (Arthur Grumiaux/ Jean Pougnet/Philharmonia Orchestra/Susskind)
¶ Mozart, 'Voi che sapete' (from *The Marriage of Figaro*) (Irmgard Seefried/Vienna Philharmonic/von Karajan)
¶ Stravinsky, *Apollon Musagète* (Boston Symphony/ Koussevitzky)
¶ Coward, *Private Lives* (love scene) (Gertrude Lawrence/ Noël Coward)
¶ Addinsell, 'Tune in G' (Mantovani and his Orchestra)
¶ Acclamation and fanfare, Coronation of King George VI and Queen Elizabeth in Westminster Abbey

¶ Vaughan Williams, Symphony No. 5 in D major (Hallé Orchestra/Barbirolli)
*¶ Shakespeare, 'Shall I Compare Thee to a Summer's Day?' (John Gielgud)

6 November 1951
111 Ronald Shiner
Actor
¶ *Good Old Songs* (selection) (Jack Hylton and his Orchestra)
¶ 'My Blue Heaven' (Jack Smith)
¶ 'Serenade' (Alfredo Campoli/ Salon Orchestra)
¶ 'Home' (from *Something in the Air*) (Cicely Courtneidge)
¶ Mendelssohn, 'Hear my prayer' (Ernest Lough/G. Thalben-Ball *organ*/Choir of Temple Church, London)
¶ 'Tico-Tico' (Edmundo Ros and his Cuban Orchestra)
¶ 'Now is the Hour' (Gracie Fields)
¶ 'Maybe It's Because I'm a Londoner' (Billy Cotton and his Band)
¶ LUXURY: Any animal which he could train.

13 November 1951
112 Diana Wynyard
Actress
¶ Debussy, Estampe No. 3 'Jardins sous la pluie' (Claudio Arrau *piano*)
¶ O. Straus, *Mariette* (Act 2 finale) (Yvonne Printemps/ Sacha Guitry)
¶ Verdi, 'Libera me' (from *Requiem Mass*) (Maria Caniglia/ Chorus of Rome Opera House/ Serafin)
¶ Schubert, Symphony No. 9 in C major (LSO/ Walter)
¶ 'Cohen on the Telephone' (Tom Clare)
¶ Bach/Hess, 'Jesu, Joy of Man's Desiring' (Myra Hess *piano*)
¶ T. S. Eliot, 'Journey of the Magi' (John Gielgud)
¶ Gershwin, 'I've Got Rhythm' (Mary Martin)
¶ LUXURY: *El Medico*, oil painting by Goya.

20 November 1951
113 George Formby
Comedian and singer
¶ 'MacNamara's Band' (Bing Crosby)
¶ 'Hear My Song, Violetta' (Josef Locke)
¶ 'Be Like the Kettle and Sing' and 'After the Rain' (from *We'll Meet Again*) (Vera Lynn)
¶ 'The Shot Gun Boogie' (Tennessee Ernie Ford)
¶ 'Londonderry Air' (Philharmonia Orchestra/ Braithwaite)
¶ 'The Kerry Dance' (John McCormack)
¶ 'Never Trust a Woman' (Phil Harris and his Orchestra)
¶ 'I Was Leaning on a Lamp Post at the Corner of the Street' (George Formby Snr)
¶ LUXURY: His first ukelele.

27 November 1951
114 Kathleen Harrison
Character actress
¶ Street barrel organ selection
¶ Rodgers & Hammerstein, *Oklahoma* (selection) (André Kostelanetz Orchestra)
¶ Falla, 'Miller's Dance' (from *The Three-Cornered Hat*) (Philharmonia Orchestra/ Galliera)
¶ 'Gidi Ya Nar' (Muhammad al-Kahlawi and Chorus)
¶ 'Harry Lime Theme' (from film *The Third Man*) (Anton Karas *zither*)
¶ Porter 'Just One of Those Things' (from *Jubilee*) (Maurice Chevalier)
¶ Wilde, 'Lady Bracknell interviews John Worthing' (from *The Importance of Being Earnest*) (Edith Evans/John Gielgud)
¶ Rimsky-Korsakov, *Scheherazade* (Paris Conservatoire Orchestra/ Ansermet)
¶ BOOK: Charles Dickens, *The Pickwick Papers*

4 December 1951
115 Elisabeth Schumann
Singer
¶ Wagner, 'Meines Glückes Lacht' (from *Die Meistersinger*) Elisabeth Schumann/Lauritz Melchior/Friedrick Schorr/ Gladys Parr/Benn Williams/ LSO/Barbirolli)
¶ Schubert, Sonata in B flat minor (Artur Schnabel *piano*)
¶ R. Strauss, 'Marschallin's Monologue' (from *Der Rosenkavalier*) (Lotte Lehmann/ Vienna Philharmonic/Heger)
¶ 'Le fiacre' (Jean Sablon)
¶ Bach, 'Ich habe genug' (from Cantata No. 82) (Hans Hotter/ Philharmonia Orchestra/ Bernard)
¶ Humperdinck, 'Evening Prayer' (from *Hansel und Gretel*) (Elisabeth Schumann/Ernest Lush *piano*)
¶ Verdi, *La traviata* (Act 3 prelude) (NBC Symphony/ Toscanini)
¶ R. Strauss, *Der Rosenkavalier* (final trio) (Lotte Lehmann/ Elisabeth Schumann/Maria Olszewska/Vienna Philharmonic/Heger)

11 December 1951
116 John Mills
Actor
¶ Rachmaninov, Piano Concerto No. 2 in C minor (Cyril Smith/Royal Liverpool Philharmonic/Sargent)
¶ 'And the Angels Sing' (Bing Crosby)
¶ Coward, 'Twentieth-Century Blues' (from *Cavalcade*) (New Mayfair Novelty Orchestra)
¶ Adam, *Giselle* (finale) (Royal Opera House Orchestra, Covent Garden/Lambert)
¶ Novello, 'Someday My Heart Will Awake' (from *King's Rhapsody*) (Vanessa Lee)
¶ 'Blue Skies' (Benny Goodman and his Orchestra)
¶ Tchaikovsky, 'Romeo and Juliet Fantasy Overture' (Vienna Philharmonic/von Karajan)

18 December 1951
117 Vera Lynn
Vocalist
¶ 'Virgin of the Sun God' (Yma Sumac/Baxter)
¶ Debussy, 'Clair de lune' (from *Suite bergamasque*) (André Kostelanetz Orchestra)
¶ 'Very Good Advice' (from film *Alice in Wonderland*) (Doris Day/The Four Hits)
¶ Tchaikovsky, 'Dance of the Sugar Plum Fairy' (from *Nutcracker Suite*) (Philharmonia Orchestra/Malko)
¶ Rodgers & Hammerstein, 'Soliloquy' (from *Carousel*) (Frank Sinatra)
¶ 'Hymne à l'amour' (Edith Piaf)
¶ 'Tongue Twisters' (Danny Kaye)
¶ 'A Man and His Dream' (Artie Shaw and his Orchestra)
¶ LUXURY: Curling tongs.

1 January 1952
118 Jack Hulbert
Actor and producer
¶ Tchaikovsky, 'Aurora's Wedding' and 'The Bluebird' (from *The Sleeping Beauty*) (LPO/Kurtz)
¶ Wagner, 'Isolde's Narrative and Curse' (from *Tristan und Isolde*) Kirsten Flagstad/ Philharmonia Orchestra/ Dobrowen)
¶ 'Rock-a-Bye Your Baby' (from film *Jolson Sings Again*) (Al Jolson)
¶ 'Things are Looking Up' (from film) (Cicely Courtneidge)
¶ Mendelssohn, *A Midsummer Night's Dream* (overture) (RPO/ Beecham)
¶ Wagner, *Rienzi* (overture) (LPO/Knappertsbusch)
¶ Shakespeare, 'To Be or Not to Be' (from *Hamlet*) (Sir Laurence Olivier)
¶ 'Laughing Gas' (Cicely Courtneidge/Company)
¶ LUXURY: Cigarettes.

8 January 1952
119 Carroll Gibbons
Pianist and bandleader
¶ Tchaikovsky, Piano Concerto No. 1 in B flat minor (Solomon/ Philharmonia Orchestra/ Dobrowen)
¶ Chopin, Waltz in D flat major (opus 64, no. 1) (Vladimir de Pachmann *piano*)
¶ Rachmaninov, 'Rhapsody on a Theme of Paganini' (Benno Moiseiwitsch *piano*/LPO/ Cameron)
¶ 'Song of the Islands' (Bing Crosby)
¶ 'Charmaine' (Melachrino Strings)
¶ Rodgers & Hammerstein, 'Some Enchanted Evening' (from *South Pacific*) (Les Howard)
¶ 'Great Day' (Robert Farnon and his Orchestra/George Mitchell Choir)
¶ Puccini, 'One Fine Day' (from *Madam Butterfly*) (Joan Hammond)
¶ LUXURY: Music manuscript paper.

15 January 1952
120 Sybil Thorndike
Actress
¶ Bach, Brandenburg Concerto No. 5 in D (Boyd Neel String Orchestra)
¶ Bach, Toccata and Fugue in D minor (Albert Schweitzer *organ*)
¶ Delius, 'On Hearing the First Cuckoo in Spring' (RPO/ Beecham)
¶ Franck, 'Symphonic Variations' (Alfred Cortot *piano*/LPO/Ronald)
¶ Bach, Fantasia in C minor (Edwin Fischer *piano*)
¶ Beethoven, 'Kreutzer' Sonata in A major (opus 47) (Hephzibah and Yehudi Menuhin *piano and violin*)
¶ Shakespeare, 'Shall I Compare Thee to a Summer's Day?' (John Gielgud)
¶ Mozart, L'amero saro constante' (from *Il re pastore*) (Elisabeth Schwarzkopf/Vienna Philharmonic/Krips)
¶ LUXURY: A blue vase, which was an engagement present from her husband.

22 January 1952
121 Spike Hughes
Writer, musician and critic
¶ Mozart, Quintet in G minor
(K. 516) (Pro Arte Quartet/
Alfred Hobday *second violin*)
¶ J. Strauss, 'Emperor Waltz'
(Vienna Philharmonic/Walter)
¶ 'Elegy' (Spike Hughes and his
Orchestra)
¶ Porter, 'You'd be So Nice to
Come Home To' (from film
Something to Shout About)
(Dinah Shore)
¶ Verdi, 'La donna e mobile'
(from *Rigoletto*) (Enrico Caruso)
¶ 'Drop Me Off at Harlem'
(Duke Ellington and his
Orchestra)
¶ Ravel, 'Pièce en forme
d'Habanera' (Joseph Szigeti
violin/Nikita de Magaloff *piano*)
¶ Beethoven, Symphony No. 5
in C minor (NBC Symphony/
Toscanini)
¶ LUXURY: A barrel of wine.

29 January 1952
122 Jeanne de Casalis
**Actress, playwright and
comedienne**
¶ 'Qagela Lapa' (Zululand War
Dancers)
¶ 'Paris' (Yves Montand)
¶ Falla, 'Miller's Dance' (from
The Three-Cornered Hat)
(Philharmonic Orchestra/
Galliera)
¶ Puccini, 'Love and Music'
(from *Tosca*) (Joan Hammond/
Hallé Orchestra/Heward)
¶ 'Two Black Crows' (Moran &
Mack)
¶ Debussy, 'Jeux des vagues'
(from *La mer*) (Philharmonic
Orchestra/Galliera)
¶ 'Tabou' (Lecuona Cuban Boys)
¶ 'Mort de Don Quixote' (from
film *Don Quixote*) (Feodor
Chaliapin)
¶ LUXURY: A picture by Cézanne
or a large feather bed.

5 February 1952
123 Peter Brough and
Archie Andrews
Ventriloquist and his doll
¶ 'Beyond the Blue Horizon'
(Hans Carste and his Orchestra)
¶ 'Marine Medley' (Ernest
Butcher)

¶ 'Underneath the Arches'
(Flanagan & Allen)
¶ 'Blues in the Night' (Ronald
Chesney *harmonica*/George
Elliot *guitar*)
¶ Rodgers & Hammerstein,
'Some Enchanted Evening'
(from *South Pacific*) (Perry
Como)
¶ 'Mediterranean Concerto'
(Semprini *piano*)
¶ 'Raise Your Voices' (Tanner
Sisters/Hedley Ward Trio)
¶ Rodgers & Hart, *Words and
Music* (selection) (Melachrino
Orchestra)
¶ LUXURY: Golf clubs.

19 February 1952
124 Compton Mackenzie
Writer
¶ Sibelius, 'The Swan of
Tuonela' (Philadelphia
Orchestra/Ormandy)
¶ 'La Paloma' (Conchita
Supervia)
¶ Beethoven, Sonata No. 5 in F
major ('Spring') (opus 24)
(Jascha Heifetz *violin*/Emanuel
Bay *piano*)
¶ Mozart, Sonata in C major
(K. 296) (Lili Krauss *piano*/
Simon Goldberg *violin*)
¶ Verdi, *La traviata* (Act 3
prelude) (NBC Symphony/
Toscanini)
¶ 'Plaisir d'amour' (Tito Schipa/
Orchestra/Sabajno)
¶ Wagner, 'Du Bist der Lenz'
(from *Die Walküre*) (Lotte
Lehmann/Lauritz Melchior/
Vienna Philharmonic/Walter)
¶ Schubert, Quintet in C major
(opus 163) (Anthony Pini *cello*/
Pro Arte Quartet)
¶ LUXURY: Four pipes and
matches.

26 February 1952
125 Elizabeth Welch
Actress and singer
¶ Porter, 'Begin the Beguine'
(from *Jubilee*) (Peter Yorke and
his Orchestra)
¶ 'I'll Follow My Secret Heart'
(from *Conversation Piece*)
(Yvonne Printemps)
¶ J. Strauss, 'Emperor Waltz'
(Vienna Philharmonic/Walter)

¶ Ravel, 'Cat Duet' (from
L'enfant et les sortilèges)
(Marguerite Legouhy/Yvon le
Mac'hadar/French National
Radio Orchestra/Bour)
¶ 'Rincon de España' (Gracia de
Triana)
¶ Puccini, 'In questa reggia'
(from *Turandot*) (Eva Turner)
¶ 'La Golondrina' (Melachrino
Strings)
¶ Novello, 'Fold Your Wings'
(from *Glamorous Nights*) (Mary
Ellis/Trevor Jones)

4 March 1952
126 Roger Livesey
Actor
¶ Sinding, 'Rustle of Spring'
(Walter Gieseking *piano*)
¶ 'Kashmiri Song' (Mantovani
and his Concert Orchestra)
¶ Mendelssohn, *A Midsummer
Night's Dream* (overture) (RPO/
Beecham)
¶ Tchaikovsky, 'Hamlet
Overture' Hallé Orchestra/
Lambert)
¶ 'MCC *v* West Indies Calypso'
(Egbert Moore/Gerald Clark
and his Caribbean Serenaders)
¶ 'Warum' (from film *Student
von Prag*) (Miliza Korjus)
¶ 'The House is Haunted'
(Gracie Fields)
¶ Puccini, 'Sono andati?' (from
La bohème) (Licia Albanese/
Beniamino Gigli/La Scala
Orchestra/Berrettoni)
¶ LUXURY: Golf clubs.

11 March 1952
127 Hermione Gingold
Actress
¶ 'The Runaway Rocking
Horse' (Queen's Light
Orchestra/Williams)
¶ Britten, *Young Person's Guide
to the Orchestra* (Royal Liverpool
Philharmonic/Sargent)
¶ Bach/Hess, 'Jesu, Joy of
Man's Desiring' (Myra Hess
piano)
¶ 'Paris, tu n'a pas changé' (Jean
Sablon)
¶ Handel, *The Music for the
Royal Fireworks* (minuet) (LPO/
Boult)
¶ O. Straus, 'La ronde de
l'amour' (from film *La ronde*)
(Anton Walbrook)

¶Rodgers & Hammerstein, 'Some Enchanted Evening' (from *South Pacific*) (Paul Weston Orchestra)
¶Franck, 'Symphonic Variations' (Moura Lympany *piano*/Philharmonia Orchestra/Susskind)
¶LUXURY: A barrel of lipstick.

18 March 1952
128 Fred Emney
Actor and comedian
¶'Doll Dance' (Frankie Carle)
¶'Swing Low, Sweet Chariot' (Bing Crosby)
¶Rachmaninov, Piano Concerto No. 2 in C minor (Benno Moiseiwitsch/LPO/Goehr)
¶'A Million Tears' (Flanagan & Allen)
¶*Max Miller in the Theatre*
¶'Lover' (from film *Love Me Tonight*) (André Kostelanetz Orchestra)
¶'Where Flamingos Fly' (Carole Carr/Geraldo and his Orchestra)
¶'Jack Buchanan Medley' (Jack Buchanan with Orchestra)
¶LUXURY: A large box of cigars.

26 March 1952
129 Anna Neagle
Actress
¶Bach, 'Sanctus' (from *Mass in B minor*) (Philharmonic Choir/LSO/Coates)
¶'The Road to the Isles' (from *Songs of the Hebrides*) (Stuart Robertson/Herbert Dawson *piano*)
¶'Piccadilly 1944' (from film *Piccadilly Incident*) (Louis Levy and his Music from the Movies)
¶'When You Wish upon a Star' (from film *Pinnochio*) (Cliff Edwards)
¶Sibelius, Symphony No. 2 in D minor (Boston Symphony/Koussevitzky)
¶Dvořák, 'Songs My Mother Taught Me' (Nellie Melba)
¶'All the Things You Are' (from *Very Warm for May*) (André Kostelanetz Orchestra)

¶Gretchaninov, 'The Creed' (Choir of the Russian Church of the Metropolitan of Paris/Afonsky)
¶LUXURY: Tea.

1 April 1952
130 Richard Hearne
Actor and comedian
¶Delius, 'On Hearing the First Cuckoo in Spring' (RPO/Beecham)
¶Elgar, 'Nimrod' (from *Enigma Variations*) (Hallé Orchestra/Barbirolli)
¶Falla, 'Love the Magician' (from *Ritual Fire Dance*) (National Symphony/Jorda)
¶'Greensleeves' (Luton Girls' Choir)
¶Shakespeare, 'John of Gaunt's Speech' (from *Richard II*) (John Gielgud)
¶Coates, 'Valsette' (from *Wood Nymphs*) (Light Symphony Orchestra/Coates)
¶Grieg, Symphonic Dance No. 2 (LSO/Coppola)
¶Selection of favourite tunes (Peggy Cochrane *violin*)

8 April 1952
131 Wynford Vaughan-Thomas
Broadcaster and writer
¶Mozart, 'La ci darem la mano' (from *Don Giovanni*) (John Brownlee/Audrey Mildmay/Glyndebourne Festival Opera Company/Busch)
¶'Ridgeway's Late Joys' (actual performance in the Player's Theatre, Covent Garden)
¶Bach, Double Concerto in D minor (Jascha Heifetz *violin*/RCA Victor Concert Orchestra/Waxman)
¶'The Ash Grove' (Dowlais United Choir)
¶'Makin' Whoopee' (Eddie Cantor)
¶'Joyeux enfants de la Bourgogne' (Chanteurs du Vin de France)
¶'Buttons and Bows' (from film *Paleface*) (Dinah Shore)
¶Brahms, Piano Concerto No. 2 in B flat (Vladimir Horowitz/NBC Symphony/Toscanini)
¶LUXURY: Combined radio and television receiver.

15 April 1952
132 Delia Murphy
Folk singer
¶'Hannigan's Hooley' (The Four Ramblers)
¶'My Lagan Love' (John McCormack)
¶Puccini, 'O Tentatrice!' (from *Manon Lescaut*) (Margaret Sheridan/Auraliano Pertile/La Scala Orchestra/Sabajno)
¶'Knock'd 'em in the Old Kent Road' (Reg Grant)
¶Mozart, 'Wiegenlied' (Elisabeth Schumann)
¶Berlin, 'Top Hat, White Tie and Tails' (from film *Top Hat*) (Fred Astaire)
¶'Mrs Mulligan in Court' (Jimmy O'Dea/Harry O'Donovan)
¶Schubert, Symphony No. 8 in B minor (Vienna Philharmonic/Walter)
¶LUXURY: A still for making poteen.

22 April 1952
133 Richard Murdoch and Kenneth Horne
Comedians
¶(Murdoch) 'I'm Gonna Sit Right Down and Write Myself a Letter' (Fats Waller and his Rhythm)
¶(Horne) Bizet, 'Il fior che averi a me tu dato' (from *Carmen*) (Enrico Caruso)
¶(M) 'Cycling' (John Tilley)
¶(H) Porter, 'Night and Day' (from *The Gay Divorce*) (Fred Astaire)
¶(M) Rossini/Respighi, 'Can-Can' (from *La boutique fantasque*) (RPO/Kurtz)
¶(H) 'Melancholy Weeps' (Fred Elizalde *piano*)
¶(M) 'Boum' (from film *La route enchantée*) (Charles Trenet)
¶(H) 'Doin' the New Low Down' (Bill Robinson/Irving Wills and his Hotsy Totsy Gang)
¶LUXURIES: (M) A test-your-strength fairground machine; (H) a mah-jong set.

29 April 1952
134 Kirsten Flagstad
Singer

¶ R. Strauss, *Der Rosenkavalier* (final trio) (Lotte Lehmann/ Elisabeth Schumann/Maria Olszewska/Vienna Philharmonic/Heger)
¶ Mendelssohn, *A Midsummer Night's Dream* (overture) (RPO/ Beecham)
¶ Beethoven, Trio No. 6 in B flat major (opus 97) (Artur Rubinstein *piano*/Jascha Heifetz *violin*/Emanuel Feuermann *cello*)
¶ Verdi, 'Ingemisco Tamquam Reus' (from *Requiem Mass*) (Jussi Björling)
¶ Puccini, 'O! mio babbino caro' (from *Gianni Schicchi*) (Elisabeth Schwarzkopf/Vienna Philharmonic/von Karajan)
¶ Chopin, Sonata in B minor (Dinu Lipatti *piano*)
¶ Duparc/Baudelaire, 'L'invitation au voyage' (Maggie Teyte/LPO/Heward)
¶ Grieg, Piano Concerto in A minor (Walter Gieseking/ Philharmonia Orchestra/von Karajan)
¶ LUXURY: Knitting needles and wool.

13 May 1952
135 Fay Compton
Actress

¶ Sibelius, 'The Swan of Tuonela' (Philadelphia Orchestra/Stokowski)
¶ Rossini, 'Largo al factotum' (from *The Barber of Seville*) (Lawrence Tibbett)
¶ 'And the Angels Sing' (Bing Crosby)
¶ Arensky, *Suite for Two Pianos* (opus 15, waltz) (Vitya Vronsky/Victor Babin)
¶ Delius, 'To the Queen of My Heart' and 'Love's Philosophy' (Heddle Nash/Gerald Moore *piano*)
¶ Dukas, 'The Sorcerer's Apprentice' (New York Philharmonic/Toscanini)
¶ 'Si tu m'aimes' (Jean Sablon/ Garland Wilson *piano*)

¶ Dohnanyi, 'Variations on a Nursery Theme' (Cyril Smith *piano*/Royal Liverpool Philharmonic/Sargent)
¶ LUXURY: Her two dogs.

20 May 1952
136 Robert Beatty
Actor

¶ Beethoven, Sonata in C minor (opus 13) (Moiseiwitsch *piano*)
¶ J. Strauss, 'Frühlingsstimuen' (Erna Sack soprano/Orchestra of the Berlin Opera House/ Hans Schmidt)
¶ Sibelius, 'The Swan of Tuonela' (Eugene Ormandy/ Philadelphia Orchestra
¶ 'Eileen Oge' (Barbara Mullen/ Gerald Moore *piano*)
¶ Verdi, 'Requiem Mass' (Ebe Stignani *mezzo-soprano*/ Orchestra and Chorus of the Royal Opera House, Rome/ Tullio Serafin)
¶ 'The Funny Old Hills' (Bing Crosby with John Scott Trotter and his Orchestra)
¶ 'Sleigh Ride' (Percy Faith and his Orchestra with Chorus)
¶ Wood (arr.), 'Fantasia on British Sea Songs' Hornpipe: 'Jack's the Lad' (LSO/Wood)

27 May 1952
137 Dorothy Dickson
Singer

¶ Wagner, 'Isolde's *Liebestod*' (from *Tristan und Isolde*) (Kirsten Flagstad)
¶ Chopin, Nocturne in E flat major (opus 9, no. 2) (Artur Rubinstein *piano*)
¶ Messager, 'J'ai deux amants' (from *L'amour masqué*) (Yvonne Printemps)
¶ Mendelssohn, Violin Concerto in E minor (opus 64) (Jascha Heifetz/RPO/Beecham)
¶ Shakespeare, 'Let Me Not to the Marriage of True Minds' (Edith Evans)
¶ 'Paris sera toujours Paris' (Maurice Chevalier)
¶ Puccini, 'O! mio babbino caro' (from *Gianni Schicchi*) (Elisabeth Schwarzkopf/Vienna Philharmonic/von Karajan)
¶ Beethoven, Symphony No. 7 in A major (Vienna Philharmonic/Furtwängler)

3 June 1952
138 Gilbert Harding
Broadcaster and lecturer

¶ Clarke, 'Trumpet Voluntary' (Harry Mortimer *trumpet*/ Reginald Foort *organ*/London Brass Players/Weldon)
¶ 'I'm Knee Deep in Daisies' (Whispering Jack Smith)
¶ Handel, 'Hallelujah Chorus' (from *Messiah*) (Huddersfield Choral Society/Royal Liverpool Philharmonic/Sargent)
¶ Peel, 'In Summertime on Bredon' (Keith Falkner/Gerald Moore *piano*)
¶ 'La Paloma' (Emilio de Gogorza)
¶ 'Sussex by the Sea' (Band and Chorus of Royal Air Force)
¶ 'Rose of Tralee' (John McHugh)
¶ 'Veni Creator' (Le maîtrise de la Cathédrale de Soissons/ Doyen)
¶ 'Eton Boating Song' (Eton College Musical Society) (*Extra record played because of available time*)
¶ LUXURY: A Kelly Man (a toy with concentric men inside).

10 June 1952
139 Googie Withers
Actress

¶ 'Sang Rag a Bhairvai' (Music of the Orient)
¶ Porter, 'Just One of Those Things' (from *Jubilee*) (Sam Browne/Ambrose and his Orchestra)
¶ Rachmaninov, Piano Concerto No. 2 in C minor (opus 18) (Sergei Rachmaninov/ Philadelphia Orchestra/ Stokowski)
¶ Gretchaninov, 'The Creed' (Choir of the Russian Church of the Metropolitan of Paris/ Afonsky)
¶ Puccini, 'Love and Music' (from *Tosca*) (Joan Hammond/ Hallé Orchestra/Heward)
¶ Bach, Harpsichord Concerto No. 5 in F minor (Edwin Fischer *piano* and his Chamber Orchestra)
¶ Rodgers & Hammerstein, 'Some Enchanted Evening' (from *South Pacific*) (Ezio Pinza)

¶Vaughan Williams, 'Fantasia on Greensleeves' (Jacques Orchestra)
¶LUXURY: Her lucky charm – a jade amulet.

17 June 1952
140 Godfrey Winn
Writer
¶J. Strauss, 'Wine, Women and Song' (waltz) (Boston Promenade Orchestra/Fiedler)
¶Dvořák, 'O Silver Moon' (from *Rusalka*) (Joan Hammond/Philharmonia Orchestra/Tausky)
¶Porter, 'Begin the Beguine' (from *Jubilee*) (Hutch)
¶Elgar, 'Pomp and Circumstance' March No. 1 in D minor (Philharmonia Orchestra/Sargent)
¶Granados, 'The Lover and the Nightingale' (from *Goyescas*) (Artur Rubinstein *piano*)
¶'Whispering Grass' (The Ink Spots)
¶Puccini, 'Nessun dorma' (from *Turandot*) (Jussi Björling)
¶Elgar, Violin Concerto in E minor (Yehudi Menuhin/LSO/Elgar)
¶LUXURY: A pack of cards for bridge.

24 June 1952
141 Ellaline Terriss
Veteran actress and singer
¶'Kings of the Waltz' (medley of Strauss waltzes) (LPO/Goehr)
¶'On a Slow Boat to China' (Maurice Chevalier)
¶German, 'Morris Dance' (from *Henry VIII Dances*) (BBC Theatre Orchestra/Robinson)
¶O. Strauss, 'Depuis trois ans passés' (from *Mariette*) (Yvonne Printemps)
¶Bach/Gounod, 'Ave Maria' (Gracie Fields)
¶Elgar, 'Nimrod' (from *Enigma Variations*) (Hallé Orchestra/Barbirolli)
¶Berlin, 'Call Me Madam' and 'It's a Lovely Day' (from *Call Me Madam*) (Shani Wallis/Jeff Warren)
¶'I Leave My Heart in an English Garden' (from *Dear Miss Phoebe*) (Webster Booth)
¶LUXURY: A piano.

1 July 1952
142 Boyd Neel
Conductor
¶Mozart, Sinfonia Concertante for Violin and Viola (K. 364) (Albert Sammons *violin*/Lionel Tertis *viola*/LPO/Harty)
¶Gilbert & Sullivan, 'When the Buds are Blossoming' (madrigal) (from *Ruddigore*) (Muriel Dickson/Dorothy Gill/Derek Oldham/Stuart Robertson/D'Oyly Carte Chorus and Orchestra)
¶J. Strauss, 'Morgenblätter' (waltz) (RPO/Beecham)
¶Mozart, 'Der Höhe Rache' (from *The Magic Flute*, Act 2) (Florence Foster Jenkins/Cosme McMoon *piano*)
¶Hahn, 'Si mes vers avaient des ailes' (Maggie Teyte/Gerald Moore *piano*)
¶Scarlatti, Sonata in F (Kathleen Long *piano*)
¶Verdi, 'Sanctus' (from *Requiem Mass*) (Orchestra and Chorus of Rome Opera House/Serafin)
¶LUXURY: A gramophone operated by pedals for slow-speed records (in 1952, only a gramophone for 78s was provided).

8 July 1952
143 Fred Perry
Tennis champion
¶Bach/Gounod, 'Ave Maria' (John McCormack/Fritz Kreisler *violin*)
¶Elgar, 'Land of Hope and Glory' (Nancy Evans/Band and Chorus of HM Coldstream Guards)
¶Tchaikovsky, Piano Concerto No. 1 in B flat minor (opus 23) (Solomon/Philharmonia Orchestra/Dobrowen)
¶'By the Shores of the Balaton Lake' and 'Slowly Flows the River Maros' (Magyari Imre and his Hungarian Gypsy Orchestra)
¶Wagner, 'Pilgrims' Chorus' (from *Tannhäuser*) (State Opera Chorus and Orchestra/Blech)
¶Debussy, 'Clair de lune' (from *Suite bergamasque*) (Benno Moiseiwitsch *piano*)

¶Tchaikovsky, '1812 Overture' (Philharmonia Orchestra/Malko)
¶'The Lost Chord' (Webster Booth/Herbert Dawson *organ*)
¶LUXURY: Radio transmitter.

15 July 1952
144 Henry Hall
Dance band leader
¶'Miss Annabelle Lee' (from *Will-o'-the-Whispers*) (Whispering Jack Smith)
¶'Every Little Movement' (from film *On Moonlight Bay*) (Doris Day)
¶Rodgers & Hammerstein, 'Oklahoma' (from *Oklahoma*) (Alfred Drake)
¶'Underneath the Arches' (Flanagan & Allen/Henry Hall and his Orchestra)
¶Mozart, *The Magic Flute* (overture) (BBC Symphony/Toscanini)
¶Coward, *Private Lives* (love scene) (Gertrude Lawrence/Noël Coward)
¶Chopin, Berceuse in D flat major (opus 57) (Alfred Cortot *piano*)
¶'It's Time to Say Goodnight' (Ray Noble and his Orchestra)
¶LUXURY: A watch.

22 July 1952
145 Gladys Cooper
Actress and manager
¶Debussy, *Prélude à l'après-midi d'un faune* (LPO/Beecham)
¶Khachaturian, 'Sabre Dance' (from *Gayaneh*) (Philharmonia Orchestra/Malko)
¶Ravel, 'La Valse' (Paris Conservatoire Orchestra/Ansermet)
¶Grofé, 'On the Trail' (from *The Grand Canyon Suite*) (NBC Symphony/Toscanini)
¶'Baia' (from film *The Three Caballeros*) (Bing Crosby)
¶'Man Smart and Woman Smarter' (Cyril Blake Calypso Band)
¶Rachmaninov, Piano Concerto No. 2 in C minor (Sergei Rachmaninov/Philadelphia Orchestra/Stokowski)

¶'Love's Old Sweet Song' (John McCormack/Edwin Schneider *piano*)

¶LUXURY: The complete works of Shakespeare.

29 July 1952
146 Christopher Stone
Broadcaster

¶'When a Woman Smiles' (from *O Mistress Mine*) (Yvonne Printemps/Pierre Fresnay)

¶Parry, 'Jerusalem' (Peter Dawson)

¶Delius, 'La calinda' (from *Koanga*) (Hallé Orchestra/Lambert)

¶'I'll Walk Beside You' (John McHugh)

¶Beethoven, Piano Sonata No. 26 in E flat major (Artur Schnabel)

¶'Bird on the Wing is Passing' (Annette Mills)

¶'Silent Night, Holy Night' (Isobel Baillie/Muriel Brunskill/Heddle Nash/Norman Allin)

¶'When Everyone Else Has Passed You By' (Scovell & Wheldon)

¶LUXURY: A good soft bed.

5 August 1952
147 Joan Greenwood
Actress

¶Beethoven, Symphony No. 6 in F minor (BBC Symphony/Toscanini)

¶Leoncavallo, 'Vesti la giubba' (from *Pagliacci*) (Enrico Caruso)

¶J. Strauss, 'Voices of Spring' (waltz) (LPO/Beecham)

¶Racine, *Phèdre* (Sarah Bernhardt)

¶Rimsky-Korsakov, *Scheherazade*, (Paris Conservatoire Orchestra/Ansermet)

¶'L'ame des poètes' (Charles Trenet)

¶*Mass for the Coronation of Charles V, 1364* (Les Paraphonistes de St Jean des Matines Chorus and Brass Ensemble)

¶Beethoven, Symphony No. 5 in C minor (Vienna Philharmonic/von Karajan)

¶LUXURY: Cigarettes.

12 August 1952
148 Michael Denison and Dulcie Gray
Actor and actress

¶(Gray) 'Imagine My Surprise' (Fats Waller and his Rhythm)

¶(Denison) Rossini, *The Barber of Seville* (overture) (Philharmonia Orchestra/Galliera)

¶(G) Beethoven, Piano Concerto No. 5 in E flat (Artur Schnabel/Philharmonia Orchestra/Galliera)

¶(D) Mozart, 'Sull' aria!' (from *The Marriage of Figaro*) (Anlikki Rantawaara/Audrey Mildmay/Glyndebourne Festival Opera Company/Busch)

¶(G) 'She's Funny That Way' (Frank Sinatra)

¶(D) 'Zamba' (from *Mi santa tierra*) (Los Trovadores de Cuyo)

¶(G) Chopin, Polonaise No. 6 in A flat (opus 53) (Arthur Rubinstein *piano*)

¶(D) Gretchaninov, 'The Creed' (Choir of the Russian Church of the Metropolitan of Paris/Afonsky)

¶LUXURIES: (D) A raft (to fish from but not escape); (G) a large supply of insecticide.

19 August 1952
149 Trevor Howard
Actor

¶Elgar, 'Cockaigne Overture' (LPO/Van Beinum)

¶Rachmaninov, Étude in C major (opus 33, no. 2) (Sergei Rachmaninov *piano*)

¶Mozart, 'Ave Verum' (Choir of Strasbourg Cathedral/Hoch)

¶Borodin/Sargent, 'Nocturne for String Orchestra' (Philharmonia Orchestra/Sargent)

¶Walton, *Façade Suite* (waltz) (Philharmonia Orchestra/Lambert)

¶'Le grand café' and 'La polka du roi' (Charles Trenet)

¶'Swing Guitars' (Quintet of the Hot Club of France)

¶Franck, Symphony in D minor (Philharmonia Orchestra/Galliera)

¶LUXURY: One of his wife's cakes.

26 August 1952
150 Anne Shelton
Vocalist

¶'Jezebel' (Frankie Laine)

¶'Rock-a-Bye Your Baby' (from film *Jolson Sings Again*) (Al Jolson)

¶'Come Back to Sorrento' (Kingsway Symphony Orchestra/Camarata)

¶'Indian Love Call' (from *Rose Marie*) (Jeanette Macdonald/Nelson Eddy)

¶Schubert, 'Ave Maria' (Bing Crosby)

¶'Rustic Samba' and 'The Breeze and I' (Stanley Black and his Orchestra)

¶'Because of Rain' (Nat 'King' Cole)

¶Arlen & Harburg, 'Over the Rainbow' (from film *The Wizard of Oz*) (Judy Garland)

¶LUXURY: The little cross that hangs over her bed.

¶BOOK: Thor Heyerdahl, *Kon-Tiki*

2 September 1952
151 Richard Attenborough
Actor and director

¶'Bolton Wanderers *v* Chelsea, 2 June 1945' (commentary by Raymond Glendenning)

¶'Formidable' (Charles Trenet)

¶Handel, 'Haste Thee Nymph' (Glasgow Orpheus Choir/Roberton)

¶Shakespeare/Walton, 'Once More Unto the Breach' (from film *Henry V*) (Laurence Olivier/Philharmonia Orchestra/Walton)

¶R. Strauss, 'Don Juan: Tone Poem' (Boston Symphony/Koussevitzky)

¶Berlin, 'Blue Skies' (from film) (Art Lund/Benny Goodman and his Orchestra)

¶Villa-Lobos, Bachiana Brasileira No. 5 (Bidu Sayao/eight cellos/Villa-Lobos)

¶Schubert, Symphony No. 9 in C major (Vienna Philharmonic/von Karajan)

¶LUXURY: Set of record catalogues.

9 September 1952
152 Vivien Leigh
Actress

¶Sibelius, Violin Concerto in D minor (opus 47) (Ginette Neveu/Philharmonia Orchestra/Susskind)

¶O. Straus, *Mariette* (Act 2) (Yvonne Printemps/Sacha Guitry)

¶Beethoven, Symphony No. 9 in D minor (second movement) (Vienna Philharmonic/von Karajan)

¶Beethoven, Symphony No. 9 in D minor (fourth movement) (Georg Maiki/Vienna State Opera Chorus/Vienna Philharmonic/Weingartner)

¶'Ballin' the Jack' (Danny Kaye)

¶Ravel, 'Lever du jour' (from *Daphnis and Chloe Suite No. 2*) (Paris Conservatoire Orchestra/Munch)

¶'If the Heart of a Man' (from film *The Beggar's Opera*) (Laurence Olivier)

¶Walton, 'Valse and Tango-pasodoblé' (from *Façade Suite*) (Philharmonia Orchestra/Lambert)

¶LUXURY: A piano.

16 September 1952
153 Ted Ray
Comedian

¶Paganini/Green (arr.), 'Romance' (from film *The Magic Bow*) (Yehudi Menuhin *violin*/Gerald Moore *piano*)

¶'Thanks for the Memory' (from film) (Shirley Ross/Bob Hope)

¶'Trumpet Rhapsody' (Harry James and his Orchestra)

¶'Jack the Giant Killer' (Ted Ray and his son Andrew)

¶Chopin, Waltz No. 14 in E minor (Sergei Rachmaninov *piano*)

¶'Gone Fishin'' (Bing Crosby/Louis Armstrong)

¶Tchaikovsky, Symphony No. 5 in E minor (LPO/Beecham)

¶'Cry' (Johnnie Ray and the Four Lads)

¶LUXURY: A dozen hairnets.

23 September 1952
154 Winifred Atwell
Variety pianist

¶'Tain't Nobody's Biz-nezz If I Do' (Fats Waller and his Rhythm)

¶'Delicado' (Stan Kenton and his Orchestra)

¶'Deep River' (Marion Anderson)

¶Falla, 'Danse espagnole' (from *La vida breva*) (Jascha Heifetz *violin*/Emanuel Bay *piano*)

¶'How High the Moon' (Les Paul *guitar*/Mary Ford)

¶'Unforgettable' (Nat 'King' Cole)

¶Rachmaninov, Piano Concerto No. 2 in C minor (Sergei Rachmaninov/Philadelphia Orchestra/Stokowski)

¶'I'm the Guy Who Found the Lost Chord' (from film *This Time for Keeps*) (Jimmy Durante)

¶LUXURY: A comb (for combing hair and making music).

3 October 1952
155 Esmond Knight
Actor

¶Gluck, 'Dance of the Blessed Spirits' (from *Orfeo ed Euridice*) NBC Symphony/Toscanini)

¶'Shadrack' (Louis Armstrong/Lyn Murray Chorus)

¶'Ding Dong Ding' and 'I Saw Three Ships' (from *Festival of Nine Lessons and Carols*, King's College Chapel, Cambridge)

¶Bach, Brandenburg Concerto No. 5 in D major (Danish State Broadcasting Chamber Orchestra/Woldike)

¶Motor-car racing, Jersey, 28 April 1949 (commentary by Eric Findon/Max Robertson/Patrick Beech)

¶Weelkes, 'On the plains, fairy trains' (Cambridge University Madrigal Society/Ord)

¶Walton, Opening music from film *Henry V* (Philharmonia Orchestra with Chorus/Walton)

¶Handel, 'Allegro' (from *Water Music Suite*) (Hallé Orchestra/Sargent)

¶BOOK: Gombrich *The Story of Art*

10 October 1952
156 Binnie Hale
Musical comedy actress

¶Rachmaninov, 'Rhapsody on a Theme of Paganini' (Sergei Rachmaninov *piano*/Philadelphia Orchestra/Stokowski)

¶'She's My Lovely' (from *Hide and Seek*) (Bobby Howes)

¶'Fine Brown Frame' (Nellie Lutcher and her Rhythm)

¶Hahn, 'Si mes vers avaient des ailes' (Maggie Teyte/Gerald Moore *piano*)

¶O. Straus, *Mariette* (Act 2 finale) (Yvonne Printemps/Sacha Guitry)

¶*Columbia on Parade* (19 of Columbia's Greatest Artists and Bands)

¶Coward, 'Mrs Worthington' (Noël Coward)

¶Gretchaninov, 'The Creed' (Choir of the Russian Church of the Metropolitan of Paris/Afonsky)

¶LUXURY: A piano.

17 October 1952
157 Joy Worth
Home Service announcer

¶Gamelan, music from Java

¶'The Botany Class' (Arthur Marshall)

¶Tchaikovsky, *The Sleeping Beauty* (march, Act 3) (Royal Opera House Orchestra, Covent Garden/Lambert)

¶'Santa Lucia Luntana' (Beniamino Gigli)

¶'Kalamazoo' (from film *Orchestra Wives*) (Glenn Miller and his Orchestra)

¶Beethoven, Sonata in C sharp minor (opus 27, no. 2) (Solomon *piano*)

¶O. Straus, *Mariette* (Act 2 finale) (Yvonne Printemps/Sacha Guitry)

¶Debussy, 'La mer' (NBC Symphony/Toscanini)

¶LUXURY: A very expensive piece of jewellery.

24 October 1952
158 Florence Desmond
Actress and impersonator
¶ Tchaikovsky, 'Romeo and Juliet Fantasy Overture' (Vienna Philharmonic/von Karajan)
¶ 'Chant of the Weed' (André Kostelanetz Orchestra)
¶ Rodgers & Hart, 'The Lady is a Tramp' (from film *Words and Music*) (Lena Horne)
¶ 'Laura' (from film) (David Rose and his Orchestra)
¶ Dukas, 'The Sorcerer's Apprentice' (Paris Conservatoire Orchestra/Jorda)
¶ 'The Way You Look Tonight' (from film *Swing Time*) (Fred Astaire)
¶ Rodgers & Hart, 'Slaughter on Tenth Avenue' (from *On Your Toes*) (Paul Whiteman and his Concert Orchestra)
¶ Carmichael, 'Stardust' (Morton Gould and his Orchestra)
¶ LUXURY: Family photograph album.

31 October 1952
159 W. Macqueen-Pope
Writer and theatre historian
¶ Novello, *The Dancing Years* (selection) (Drury Lane Theatre/Prentice)
¶ Lehár, 'You are My Heart's Delight' (from *The Land of Smiles*) (Richard Tauber)
¶ 'Dawn Chorus' (Ludwig Koch recording, Sussex, March 1949)
¶ 'If You were the Only Girl in the World' (from *The Bing Boys are Here*) (Violet Loraine/George Robey)
¶ Mendelssohn, *A Midsummer Night's Dream* (scherzo) (Philharmonia Orchestra/Kubelik)
¶ 'God Rest Ye Merry, Gentlemen' (St Brandon's CDS Choir, Bristol)
¶ 'Monckton Melodies' (BBC Theatre Orchestra/Robinson)
¶ 'In the Shadows' (Tom Jones and his Orchestra)
¶ LUXURY: One of his lucky charms.

7 November 1952
160 Tessie O'Shea
Actress and variety artist
¶ Ketelbey, 'In a Persian Market' (Boston Promenade Orchestra/Fiedler)
¶ 'Sarie Marais' (Alec Benjamin)
¶ 'Down by the River' (from film *Mississippi*) (Bing Crosby)
¶ Tchaikovsky, *The Sleeping Beauty* (waltz) (Hallé Orchestra/Sargent)
¶ 'Waltzing Matilda' (Peter Dawson/Orchestra and Chorus)
¶ 'Outside of Heaven' (Eddie Fisher)
¶ 'Land of My Fathers' (Crowd at Wales *v* Ireland rugby match, Swansea, 12 March 1949)
¶ 'I Do Like to be Beside the Seaside' (Community singing)
¶ LUXURY: Her ukelele.

14 November 1952
161 Nigel Patrick
Actor and director
¶ Delius, 'Serenade' (from *Hassan*) (LPO/Beecham)
¶ Shakespeare, 'Now I am Alone' (from *Hamlet*) (John Barrymore)
¶ 'Ballad for Americans' (Bing Crosby)
¶ Liszt, Hungarian Rhapsody No. 2 (Viennese Seven Singing Sisters)
¶ 'Come Back to Sorrento' (Gracie Fields)
¶ Khachaturian, 'Sabre Dance' (from *Gayaneh*) (Philharmonia Orchestra/Malko)
¶ Weill, 'September Song' (from *Knickerbocker Holiday*) (Walter Huston)
¶ 'Santa Lucia' (Semprini)
¶ LUXURY: His 'useless' dog.

21 November 1952
162 Ada Reeve
Music-hall star and actress
¶ Coates, 'By the Sleepy Lagoon' (Eric Coates and his Symphony Orchestra)
¶ Gershwin, 'Do-Do-Do' (from *Oh, Kay!*) (Gertrude Lawrence)
¶ 'Motoring' (Harry Tate and Company)
¶ Kern & Hammerstein, 'Lonesome Road' (from film *Show Boat*) (Gene Austin)
¶ Liszt, Hungarian Rhapsody No. 6 (Mark Hambourg *piano*)

¶ 'Some of These Days' (Sophie Tucker)
¶ Ketelbey, 'In a Monastery Garden' (Albert W. Ketelbey and his Concert Orchestra)
¶ Donizetti, 'Chi mi frena' (from *Lucia di Lammermoor*) (Marcel Journet/Enrico Caruso/Antonia Scotti/Marcella Sembrich/Barbara Severina/Francesco Daddi)
¶ LUXURY: A workbox for embroidery.

28 November 1952
163 Sonnie Hale
Actor, director and playwright
¶ Mendelssohn, 'The Hebrides Overture' (Hallé Orchestra/Barbirolli)
¶ 'Tiger Rag' (André Kostelanetz Orchestra)
¶ 'De Glory Road' (from film *Metropolitan*) (Lawrence Tibbett/Stewart Wille *piano*)
¶ 'Avalon' (Benny Goodman Quartet)
¶ Puccini, 'Love and Music' (from *Tosca*) (Joan Hammond/Hallé Orchestra/Heward)
¶ Gershwin, Piano Concerto in F (Roy Bargy/Paul Whiteman and his Orchestra)
¶ Rodgers & Hart, 'Falling in Love' (from film *The Boys from Syracuse*) (Allan Jones)
¶ Elgar, 'Pomp and Circumstance' March No. 1 in D major (opus 36) (Royal Festival Orchestra and Choir/Sargent)
¶ LUXURY: Scented soap.

5 December 1952
164 Gordon Harker
Character actor
¶ Wagner, 'Siegfried Idyll' (Philharmonia Orchestra/Cantelli)
¶ Mozart, 'Deh vieni, non tardar' (from *The Marriage of Figaro*) (Elisabeth Schumann)
¶ Schumann, Piano Quintet in E flat major (Artur Schnabel/Pro Arte Quartet)
¶ 'The Cloths of Heaven' (John McCormack/Edwin Schneider *piano*)
¶ 'If a Grey-haired Lady Says "How's Yer Father?"' (Flanagan & Allen)

¶ Dvořák, Cello Concerto in B minor (opus 104) (Pierre Fournier/Philharmonia Orchestra/Kubelik)
¶ Verdi, 'Canzone del salce' (from *Otello*) (Elisabeth Rethberg)
¶ Wagner, 'Selig, wie die Sonne' (from *Die Meistersinger*) (Elisabeth Schumann/Lauritz Melchior/Friedrich Schorr/ Gladys Parr/Ben Williams/ LSO/Barbirolli)
¶ LUXURY: A camera and lots of film.

12 December 1952
165 Bill Greenslade
Home Service announcer
¶ Ravel, 'Lever du jour' (from *Daphnis and Chloe Suite No. 2*) (Paris Conservatoire Orchestra/ Munch)
¶ Charpentier, 'Depuis le jour' (from *Louise*) (Janine Micheau/ Paris Conservatoire Orchestra/ Desormière)
¶ R. Strauss, 'Da geht er hin' (from *Der Rosenkavalier*) (Lotte Lehmann/Vienna Philharmonic/Heger)
¶ Saint-Saëns, 'Introduction and Rondo Capriccioso' (Jascha Heifetz *violin*/LPO/Barbirolli)
¶ Lotti, 'Crucifixus' (Les Chanteurs de Saint-Eustache)
¶ Wagner, *Lohengrin* (Act 1 prelude) (New York Philharmonic/Toscanini)
¶ 'Paris' (from film *L'homme aux mains d'argile*) (Edith Piaf)
¶ Tchaikovsky, Piano Concerto No. 1 in B flat minor (Vladimir Horowitz/NBC Symphony/ Toscanini)

19 December 1952
166 Joy Nichols
Broadcaster and variety artist
¶ 'Sleigh Ride' (Bing Crosby)
¶ Ponchielli, 'Dance of the Hours' (from *La Gioconda*) (Columbia Symphony Orchestra/Beecham)
¶ 'When You Wish Upon a Star' (from film *Pinocchio*) (Cliff Edwards)
¶ J. Strauss, 'Nun's Chorus' (from *Casanova*) (Anni Frind/ Chorus and Orchestra des Grossen Schauspielhauses, Berlin)

¶ Heuberger, 'En chambre separée' (from *The Opera Ball*) (Richard Tauber)
¶ 'Jumping Bean' (Queen's Hall Light Orchestra/Farnon)
¶ Weill, 'Lost in the Stars' (from *Lost in the Stars*) (Walter Huston)
¶ *Roberta* (selection) (New Mayfair Orchestra)
¶ LUXURY: A mink sleeping bag.

2 January 1953
167 Wilfred Pickles
Broadcaster
¶ 'If I Should Fall in Love Again' (Josephine Bradley and her Strict Tempo Dance Orchestra)
¶ Handel, 'Comfort Ye, My People' (from *Messiah*) (Walter Widdop)
¶ Ponchielli, 'Dance of the Hours' (from *La Gioconda*) (Hallé Orchestra/Sargent)
¶ 'We'll Meet Again' (Vera Lynn/Arthur Young *novachord*)
¶ 'Bonnie Dundee' (Glasgow Orpheus Choir)
¶ 'Underneath the Arches' (Flanagan & Allen)
¶ 'Inka Dinka Doo' (from film *The Great Schnozzle*) (Jimmy Durante)
¶ 'Land of My Fathers' (David Lloyd/Band and Chorus of Welsh Guards)
¶ LUXURY: His yellow waistcoat.
¶ BOOK: *The Oxford Book of English Verse*

9 January 1953
168 Margaret Rutherford
Actress
¶ Debussy, 'La mer' (Orchestre de la Suisse Romande/ Ansermet)
¶ 'Land of Heart's Desire' (Andrew Macpherson)
¶ Macdowell, 'AD 1620' (from *Sea Pieces*, opus 55) (Myra Hess *piano*)
¶ 'Pedro the Fisherman' (from *The Lisbon Story*) (Richard Tauber)
¶ Smyth, *The Wreckers* (overture) (British Symphony Orchestra/Smyth)
¶ Debussy, 'La cathédrale engloutie' (*Preludes*, Book 1, No. 10) (Solomon *piano*)

¶ Elgar, 'Where Corals Lie' (from *Sea Pictures*, opus 37) (Gladys Ripley/Philharmonia Orchestra/Weldon)
¶ Mendelssohn, 'The Hebrides Overture' (LPO/Beecham)
¶ LUXURY: A bejewelled golden comb.

16 January 1953
169 Ralph Lynn
Farce actor
¶ 'Auf Wiedersehen' (Ursula Maury)
¶ 'On a Slow Boat to China' (Maurice Chevalier)
¶ Mendelssohn, *A Midsummer Night's Dream* (nocturne) (LPO/ Beecham)
¶ Berlin, 'Top Hat, White Tie and Tails' (from film *Top Hat*) (Fred Astaire)
¶ 'The Cuckoo in the Wood' (Minna Reverelli)
¶ 'I Love the Moon' (Richard Tauber)
¶ Sibelius, 'Valse triste' (from *Kuolema*) (Royal Liverpool Philharmonic/Sargent)
¶ 'Beyond the Blue Horizon' (from film *Monte Carlo*) (Jeannette MacDonald)
¶ LUXURY: His eyeglass.

23 January 1953
170 Belita
Actress, dancer and skater
¶ Gershwin, 'Rhapsody in Blue' (Oscar Levant *piano*/ Philadelphia Orchestra/ Ormandy)
¶ 'When We're Alone' (Shirley Ross/Bob Hope)
¶ Shakespeare, 'Now I am Alone' (from *Hamlet*) (John Barrymore)
¶ Coward, 'I'll See You Again' (from *Bitter Sweet*) (André Kostelanetz Orchestra)
¶ 'Mock Mozart' (Peter Ustinov/Anthony Hopkins *harpsichord*)
¶ 'You Belong to Me' (Wally Fryer and his Perfect Tempo Dance Orchestra)
¶ Racine, *Phèdre* (Sarah Bernhardt)
¶ 'Manhattan Tower' (Elliot Lewis/Beverly Mahr/Gordon Jenkins and his Orchestra and Chorus)
¶ LUXURY: An encyclopaedia.

30 January 1953
171 Duncan Carse
Actor and explorer

¶ Tchaikovsky, 'Romeo and Juliet Fantasy Overture' (Vienna Philharmonic/von Karajan)

¶ 'Thanks for the Memory' (from the film) (Shirley Ross/Bob Hope)

¶ 'Gunner Joe' (Stanley Holloway/Wolseley Charles *piano*)

¶ R. Strauss, 'Ständchen' (Elisabeth Schumann)

¶ 'Go Down Moses' (Paul Robeson)

¶ Debussy, 'Clair de lune' (from *Suite bergamasque*) (Benno Moiseiwitsch *piano*)

¶ Sibelius, Symphony No. 2 in D major (RPO/Beecham)

¶ Scriabin, Étude in D sharp minor (opus 8, no. 12) (Friedrich Wuhrer *piano*)

¶ LUXURY: A pin-up picture.

6 February 1953
172 Donald Wolfit
Actor-manager

¶ Bach/Stokowski, Toccata and fugue in D minor (Philadelphia Orchestra/Stokowski)

¶ 'All Creatures Now' (Cambridge University Madrigal Society/Ord)

¶ 'Roaming in the Gloaming' (Sir Harry Lauder)

¶ Tchaikovsky, Violin Concerto in D major (Ida Haendel/National Symphony/Cameron)

¶ Sibelius, 'The Swan of Tuonela' (Leopold Stokowski and his Symphony Orchestra)

¶ 'Lily of Laguna' (G. H. Elliott)

¶ 'Let Thy Merciful Ears, O Lord' (King's College Chapel Choir/Ord)

¶ Franck, Symphony in D minor (LPO/Beecham)

¶ LUXURY: A violin with instruction book.

¶ BOOK: The Bible.

13 February 1953
173 Jean Carson
Musical comedy actress

¶ Porter, 'I Get a Kick Out of You' (from *Anything Goes*) (Billy Daniels)

¶ Arlen & Harburg, 'Over the Rainbow' (from film *The Wizard of Oz*) (Judy Garland)

¶ 'Portrait of Jennie' (Nat King Cole Trio)

¶ 'My Heart Sings' (Kathryn Grayson)

¶ 'Pot Luck' (Johnny Brandon)

¶ Gershwin, 'It Ain't Necessarily So' (from *Porgy and Bess*) (Lawrence Tibbett)

¶ Coward, 'I'll See You Again' (from *Bitter Sweet*) (André Kostelanetz Orchestra)

¶ 'When Your Lover Has Gone' (Frank Sinatra)

¶ 'The Jitterbug' (from film *The Wizard of Oz*) (Judy Garland)

¶ 'Too Marvellous for Words' (Billy Daniels) (*Extra disc allowed for reasons of time.*)

¶ LUXURY: An umbrella.

20 February 1953
174 David Tomlinson
Actor

¶ 'La chanson des rues' (Jean Sablon)

¶ Verdi, 'Si pel, ciel marmoreo giuro!' (from *Otello*) (Enrico Caruso/Titta Ruffo)

¶ 'Some Other Bird Whistled a Tune' (Whispering Jack Smith)

¶ Shakespeare, 'To Be or Not to Be' (from *Hamlet*) (Sir Laurence Olivier)

¶ 'The Way You Look Tonight' (from film *Swing Time*) (Fred Astaire)

¶ *Famous Waltzes of the World* (Alfred Beres and his Orchestra)

¶ 'Gertrude Lawrence Medley' (Gertrude Lawrence)

¶ Puccini, 'O mio babbino caro' (from *Gianni Schicchi*) (Joan Hammond/Hallé Orchestra/Heward)

¶ LUXURY: Eddie Gray's juggling equipment.

27 February 1953
175 Sheila Sim
Actress

¶ Delibes, *Coppelia* (Paris Conservatoire Orchestra/Desormière)

¶ Puccini, 'Ah! Quai a chi la tocca' (from *Manon Lescaut*) (Mario del Monaco/Santa Cecilia Orchestra, Rome/Erede)

¶ 'Milk 'Em in the Morning Blues' (Tennessee Ernie Ford)

¶ Menotti, *The Consul* (Act 2, final aria) (Patricia Neway)

¶ Beethoven, Violin Concerto in D major (opus 61) (Yehudi Menuhin/Lucerne Festival Orchestra/Furtwängler)

¶ 'When Somebody Thinks You're Wonderful' (Fats Waller and his Rhythm)

¶ Wilde, 'Lady Bracknell Interviews John Worthing' (from *The Importance of Being Earnest*) (Edith Evans/John Gielgud)

¶ R. Strauss, 'Don Juan' (Boston Symphony/Koussevitzky)

¶ LUXURY: A clock.

6 March 1953
176 Richard Todd
Actor

¶ 'Anima e core' (Beniamino Gigli)

¶ Rachmaninov, Piano Concerto No. 2 in C minor (Cyril Smith/Royal Liverpool Philharmonic/Sargent)

¶ Coward, 'Mad Dogs and Englishmen' (from *Words and Music*) (Noël Coward)

¶ 'We'll Meet Again' (Vera Lynn/Arthur Young *novachord*)

¶ Wagner, 'The Ride of the Valkyries' (from *Die Walküre*) (Vienna Philharmonic/Furtwängler)

¶ 'The Road to the Isles' (from *Songs of the Hebrides*) (Polish Army Choir)

¶ 'Londonderry Air' (Philharmonia Orchestra/Braithwaite)

¶ 'Greensleeves' (Bill Johnson)

13 March 1953
177 Pamela Brown
Actress

¶ Rodgers & Hart, *On Your Toes* (selection) (Carroll Gibbons/Savoy Hotel Orpheans)

¶ 'Papaveri e papere' (Clelia Grisoni)

¶ Tchaikovsky, 'Romeo and Juliet Fantasy Overture' (RPO/Beecham)

¶ Gershwin, 'Embraceable You' (from *Girl Crazy*) (Judy Garland)

¶ 'Cole Porter Fantasy'
(Melachrino Orchestra)
¶ Rodgers & Hammerstein,
'People Will Say We're in Love'
(from *Oklahoma*) (Alfred
Drake/Joan Roberts)
¶ ''Deed I Do' (Lena Horne)
¶ Debussy, *Prélude à l'après-
midi d'un faune* (Philharmonia
Orchestra/Galliera)
¶ LUXURY: *Encyclopaedia
Britannica*

20 March 1953
178 Max Miller
Comedian
¶ 'I Used to Sigh for the Silvery
Moon' (G. H. Elliott)
¶ J. Strauss, 'Voices of Spring'
(Lily Pons)
¶ 'Smoke Gets in Your Eyes'
from *Roberta* (Larry Adler)
¶ 'Has Anyone Here Seen
Kelly?' (Florrie Forde)
¶ Dickens, 'Captain Cuttle'
(from *Dombey and Son*)
(Bransby Williams)
¶ 'Hey Neighbour!' (from
Knights of Madness) (Flanagan
& Allen)
¶ Berlin, 'Top Hat, White Tie
and Tails' (from film *Top Hat*)
(Fred Astaire)
¶ Berlin, 'Cheek to Cheek'
(from film *Top Hat*) (Fred
Astaire)
¶ 'In a Golden Coach' (Doreen
Stephens/Chorus/Billy Cotton
and his Band) (*Extra disc
allowed for reasons of time.*)
¶ LUXURY: A double pack of cards.

27 March 1953
179 Moira Lister
Actress
¶ 'Delicado' (Waldyr Azevedo
and his Orchestra)
¶ Weill, 'September Song'
(from *Knickerbocker Holiday*)
(Walter Huston)
¶ 'C'est d' la faute' (Edith Piaf)
¶ Chopin, Polonaise in A major
(Louis Kentner *piano*)
¶ 'Les feuilles mortes' (Yves
Montand)
¶ Rimsky-Korsakov,
'Scheherazade' (Paris
Conservatoire Orchestra/
Ansermet)
¶ 'Trois fois merci' (Jacqueline
François)

¶ 'Dance of the Moon Festival'
(Yma Sumac)
¶ LUXURY: A guitar.
¶ BOOK: A book about
astronomy.

3 April 1953
180 Webster Booth
Tenor
¶ Sibelius, 'Finlandia'
(Philharmonia Orchestra/
Malko)
¶ Berlin, 'You Can't Get a Man
with a Gun' (from *Annie Get
Your Gun*) (Ethel Merman)
¶ Liszt, 'Liebestraum' (no. 3)
(Tito Schipa/José Echaniz
piano)
¶ 'Chloe' (Spike Jones and his
City Slickers)
¶ 'The Lute Player' (Harold
Williams)
¶ Gilbert & Sullivan, *Yeoman of
the Guard* (overture) (Royal
Liverpool Philharmonic/
Sargent)
¶ Handel, 'Ombra mai fu' (from
Xerxes) (Kathleen Ferrier/LSO/
Sargent)
¶ Handel, 'Comfort Ye, My
People' (from *Messiah*)
(Webster Booth/LPO/
Braithwaite)
¶ LUXURY: An ivory pig – his
lucky charm.

10 April 1953
181 Yolande Donlan
Actress
¶ 'Gertrude Lawrence Medley'
(Gertrude Lawrence)
¶ 'Softly, as in a Morning
Sunrise' (from *New Moon*)
(Nelson Eddy)
¶ 'Jim' (Ella Fitzgerald)
¶ Paderewski, Minuet in G (José
Iturbi *piano*)
¶ Berlin, 'I'm Getting Tired so I
Can Sleep' (from *This is the
Army*) (Private Stuart Churchill
and Soldier Octet)
¶ Shostakovich, *The Age of Gold*
(polka) (National Symphony/
Kindler)
¶ 'San Fernando Valley' (Bing
Crosby)
¶ 'It's a Fine, Fine Night' (from
film *Penny Princess*) (Frank
Cordell's Chorus and
Orchestra)

¶ 'Ridin' Down the Canyon'
(from *Tumbling Tumbleweeds*)
(Bing Crosby)
¶ 'This Love of Mine' (Ella
Fitzgerald)
(*Extra discs allowed for reasons of
time.*)
¶ BOOK: A Mediterranean
cookbook.

17 April 1953
182 Norman Wisdom
Comedian
¶ 'Coronation Scot' (Sidney
Torch and his Orchestra)
¶ 'Dummy Song' (Max
Bygraves/Peter Brough and
Archie Andrews)
¶ 'The Three Trumpeters'
(Band of the Royal Military
School of Music/Roberts)
¶ Tauber, 'My Heart and I'
(from *Old Chelsea*) (Luton Girls'
Choir)
¶ Rimsky-Korsakov, 'Flight of
the Bumble Bee' (from *The
Legend of Tsar Saltan*) (Harry
James and his Orchestra).
¶ Sibelius, 'Valse Triste' (from
Kuolema) (Philharmonia
Orchestra/Kletzki)
¶ 'What is a Boy?' (Jan Peerce)
¶ 'Now is the Hour' (Gracie
Fields)
¶ LUXURY: Motor car and petrol.

24 April 1953
183 Isabel Jeans
Actress
¶ Mozart, *Il seraglio* (overture)
(Vienna Philharmonic/Krauss)
¶ Wagner, 'Brünnhilde's
Immolation' (from
Götterdämmerung) (Kirsten
Flagstad/Philharmonia
Orchestra/Furtwängler)
¶ Litolff, Concerto
Symphonique No. 4 (scherzo)
(Moura Lympany *piano*/
Philharmonia Orchestra/
Susskind)
¶ Gretchaninov, 'The Creed'
(Choir of the Russian Church of
the Metropolitan of Paris/
Afonsky)
¶ Handel, *Water Music Suite*
(Hallé Orchestra/Sargent)
¶ 'Santa Lucia' (Enrico Caruso)
¶ Beethoven, Symphony No. 6
in F (LPO/Kleiber)

¶Purcell, 'Ayres for the Theatre' (London Chamber Orchestra/Bernard)
¶LUXURY: Her St Christopher's medal.

1 May 1953
184 John Arlott
Writer, poet and cricket commentator
¶'Lord Lovell' (Robert Irwin)
¶'Land of My Fathers' (Crowd at Wales *v* Ireland rugby match, Swansea, 12 March 1949)
¶'These Foolish Things' (from *Spread It Abroad*) (Lew Stone and his Band)
¶Britten (arr.), 'The Foggy Foggy Dew' (Peter Pears/ Benjamin Britten *piano*)
¶Verdi, 'Bella figlia dell'amore' (from *Rigoletto*) (Amelita Galli-Curci/Louise Homer/ Beniamino Gigli/Giuseppe de Luca)
¶Britten (arr.), 'Little Sir William' (Peter Pears/Benjamin Britten *piano*)
¶'In Dulci Jubilo' (King's College Chapel Choir/Ord)
¶Beethoven, Symphony No. 7 in A major (Vienna Philharmonic/Furtwängler)
¶LUXURY: The biggest second-hand bookshop in the world.

8 May 1953
185 Jack Hawkins
Actor
¶Sibelius, 'The Swan of Tuonela' (Mitchell Miller *cor anglais*/Symphony Orchestra/ Stokowski)
¶Purcell, 'Hark the Echoing Air' (from *The Faery Queene*) (Isobel Baillie/Hallé Orchestra/ Heward)
¶Handel, 'The Arrival of the Queen of Sheba' (from *Solomon*) (LPO/Beecham)
¶Gershwin, Preludes Nos. 1 and 2 (George Gershwin *piano*)
¶Gershwin, 'Bess, You is My Woman Now' (from *Porgy and Bess*) (Todd Duncan/Ann Brown)
¶Stravinsky, *Le sacre du printemps* (Amsterdam Concertgebouw/Van Beinum)

¶Wagner, 'Der Männer Sippe' (from *Die Walküre*) (Lotte Lehmann/Vienna Philharmonic/Walter)
¶Handel, *Zadok the Priest* (from recording of the Coronation of King George VI and Queen Elizabeth in Westminster Abbey)

15 May 1953
186 Naunton Wayne
Actor
¶Wagner, *Die Meistersinger* (overture) (Philharmonia Orchestra/Dobrowen)
¶'Melville Gideon Medley' (Melville Gideon with Orchestra)
¶'Deep Purple' (Paul Weston and his Orchestra)
¶'Vi Ser For Lidt Til Hinanden' (Gaby Stenberg/ Hans Kurt)
¶'A Pretty Girl is Like a Melody' (from *Ziegfeld Follies of 1919*) (André Kostelanetz Orchestra)
¶Beethoven, Symphony No. 7 in A major (Vienna Philharmonic/Furtwängler)
¶'It's the Woman who Pays' (Chick Endor/Charlie Farrell)
¶Tchaikovsky, Symphony No. 6 in B minor (Philharmonia Orchestra/Malko)

22 May 1953
187 Arthur Wint
Athlete and double Olympic gold medallist
¶'Names of Funny Places' (The Jamaican Calypsonians/Hubert Porter *vocals*)
¶Falla, 'Danse Espagnole' (trans. Kreisler) (from *La Vida Breve*) (Heifetz *violin*/Emanuel Bay *piano*)
¶'Ma Curly-Headed Baby' (Paul Robeson with orchestra)
¶'In the Mood' (Glen Miller and his Orchestra)
¶Dvorak, Symphony No. 5 in E minor (Czech Philharmonic Orchestra/Georg Szell)
¶Saint-Saëns, 'Softly awakes my Heart' (Marion Anderson with orchestra/Lawrance Collingwood)

¶Friml, 'Indian Love Call' (from *Rose Marie*) (Jeannette MacDonald *soprano*/Nelson Eddy *baritone*/Orchestra/ Nathaniel Shilkret)
¶Handel, *Messiah: Hallelujah Chorus* (Huddersfield Choral Society/Liverpool Philharmonic Orchestra/Sargent)

29 May 1953
188 Pamela Kellino
Actress, writer and producer
¶'The Harry Lime Theme' (from film *The Third Man*) (Anton Karas *zither*)
¶'And the Bull Walked Around, Olay' (Richard Hayes)
¶'Tell Me You're Mine' (The Gaylords)
¶Lerner & Loewe, 'I Talk to the Trees' (from *Paint Your Wagon*) (Hutch)
¶'Half as Much' (Rosemary Clooney)
¶'Blue Tango' (Hugo Winterhalter and his Orchestra)
¶'Jealousy' (Hutch)
¶Ravel, 'Bolero' (Paris Conservatoire Orchestra/ Munch)
¶BOOK: Gustave Flaubert, *Madame Bovary*

12 June 1953
189 Sir Ralph Richardson
Actor
¶Bishop, 'Lo, Hear the Gentle Lark' (Amelita Galli-Curci)
¶Beethoven, Sonata in A flat major (opus 26) (Artur Schnabel *piano*)
¶'Dry Bones' (Fred Waring and his Pennsylvanians)
¶*No, No, Nanette* (medley) (Binnie Hale with Orchestra)
¶Humperdinck, *Hansel und Gretel* (dance duet) (Manchester schoolchildren's choir/Hallé Orchestra/Harty)
¶Shakespeare, 'Now is the Winter of Our Discontent' (from *Richard III*) (Sir Henry Irving)
¶'A Tisket-a-Tasket' (Ella Fitzgerald)
¶Brahms, Symphony No. 1 in C minor (NBC Symphony/ Toscanini)
¶LUXURY: His pipe.

19 June 1953
190 Robert Helpmann
Dancer, choreographer and actor
¶ Tchaikovsky, *The Sleeping Beauty* (Royal Opera House Orchestra, Covent Garden/ Lambert)
¶ 'La Cachimba de San Juan' (rumba) (Don Azpiazu and his Orchestra)
¶ Puccini, 'Io t'ho ghermita' (from *Madam Butterfly*) (Beniamino Gigli/Toti dal Monte/Orchestra of the Rome Opera House/de Fabritiis)
¶ 'J'ai deux amours' (Josephine Baker)
¶ Sibelius, 'The Bard' (LPO/ Beecham)
¶ Verdi, *La forza del destino* (excerpt from Act 2) (Maria Caniglia/Chorus/EIAR Radio Symphony, Turin/Marinuzzi)
¶ Gershwin, 'Embraceable You' (from *Girl Crazy*) (Judy Garland)
¶ Tchaikovsky, 'Hamlet Overture' (Hallé Orchestra/ Lambert)
¶ LUXURY: A box of paints.

26 June 1953
191 Leo Genn
Actor
¶ Debussy, 'La cathédrale engloutie' (*Preludes*, Book 1, No. 10) (Solomon *piano*)
¶ 'Water Boy' (Paul Robeson)
¶ 'What is This Thing Called Love?' (Hutch)
¶ 'Happy Days and Lonely Nights' (Layton & Johnstone)
¶ Tchaikovsky, 'Romeo and Juliet Fantasy Overture' (Philharmonia Orchestra/ Cantelli)
¶ 'J'attendrai' (Tino Rossi)
¶ 'The Whiffenpoof Song' (Bing Crosby)
¶ Beethoven, Sonata No. 14 in C sharp minor (opus 27, no. 2) (Solomon *piano*)
¶ LUXURY: A chess set with a book of problems.

2 July 1953
192 Lizbeth Webb
Actress and singer
¶ 'Bewitched' (Bill Snyder and his Orchestra)

¶ 'I'll Follow My Secret Heart' (from *Conversation Piece*) (Yvonne Printemps)
¶ 'April in Portugal' (Geraldo and his New Concert Orchestra)
¶ Loesser, 'If I were a Bell' (from *Guys and Dolls*) (Lizbeth Webb)
¶ Verdi, *La Traviata* (prelude) (Santa Cecilia Orchestra, Rome/ de Sabata)
¶ Puccini, 'Te Deum' (from *Tosca*) (Marko Rothmuller/ Philharmonia Orchestra/Erede)
¶ Debussy, 'La fille aux cheveux de lin' (*Preludes*, Book 1, No. 8) (Isidor Achron *piano*)
¶ Khachaturian, *Masquerade Suite* (waltz) (Boston Promenade Orchestra/Fiedler)
¶ LUXURY: Nicholas, her three-inch-tall boy mascot.

10 July 1953
193 Geraldine McEwan
Actress
¶ Coward, 'Nina' (from *Sigh No More*) (Noël Coward)
¶ Tchaikovsky, *Eugene Onegin* (waltz) (Hallé Orchestra/ Sargent)
¶ 'That's Why Darkies were Born' (Paul Robeson)
¶ 'Valentine' (from film *Innocents of Paris*) (Maurice Chevalier)
¶ Elgar, Cello Concerto in E minor (Pablo Casals/BBC Symphony/Boult)
¶ 'A Little of What You Fancy Does You Good' (Marie Lloyd)
¶ Puccini, 'Che gelida manina' (from *La bohème*) (Beniamino Gigli)
¶ 'Ma Curly-headed Baby' (Paul Robeson)
¶ LUXURY: A box of water-colours.

17 July 1953
194 Cecil Parker
Actor
¶ 'My Heart Stood Still' (from *One Damn Thing After Another*) (Edythe Baker *piano*)
¶ 'The Little Old Mill' (Carole Carr/Geraldo and his Orchestra)
¶ Coward, 'Mad Dogs and Englishmen' (from *Words and Music*) (Noël Coward)

¶ Tchaikovsky, 'March' (from *Nutcracker Suite*) Philharmonia Orchestra/Markevitch)
¶ 'Je sais que vous êtes jolie!' (Jean Sablon)
¶ 'Victory Test Match Calypso' (England *v* West Indies, Lord's, 1950) (Lord Beginner/Calypso Rhythm Kings)
¶ Rubinstein, 'Persian Love Song' (Feodor Chaliapin)
¶ 'Life is Nothing Without Music' (Albert Sandler and his Orchestra)
¶ BOOK: *Oxford Book of Quotations*

24 July 1953
195 Brian Reece
Actor
¶ Coward, 'A Room with a View' (from *This Year of Grace*) (Noël Coward)
¶ 'Let's Do It' (Hutch)
¶ Ellis, 'I was Never Kissed Before' (from *Bless the Bride*) (Georges Guetary/Lizbeth Webb)
¶ 'England is a Lovely Place' (from *Tough at the Top*) (Maria d'Attili)
¶ 'The Girl Without a Name' (from *Seven Year Itch*) (Roberto Inglez and his Orchestra)
¶ Verdi, 'Celeste Aida' (from *Aida*) (Beniamino Gigli)
¶ 'Memories of You' (Louis Armstrong and his Orchestra)
¶ Berlin, 'I Got Lost in His Arms' (from *Annie Get Your Gun*) (Dinah Shore)
¶ Ellis, 'This is My Lovely Day' (from *Bless the Bride*) (Georges Guetary/Lizbeth Webb) *(Extra record allowed for reasons of time.)*
¶ LUXURY: A ventriloquist's dummy.

31 July 1953
196 Cyril Ritchard
Actor, revue artist and director
¶ 'Le monsieur aux lilas' (Lucienne Boyer)
¶ 'Portrait of a Flirt' (David Rose and his Orchestra)

¶ Menotti, 'Shepherds' Dance' (from *Amahl and the Night Visitors*) (Rosemary Kuhlmann/Chet Allen/Andrew McKinley/Leon Lichner/David Aiken)
¶ Lehár, 'Vilja' (from film *The Merry Widow*) (Fernando Lamas)
¶ 'Tabou' (Renato/Pepe Nunez and his Rhythm Band)
¶ Scott, 'Lullaby' (Cedric Sharpe *cello*/Cecil Dixon *piano*)
¶ Rodgers & Hammerstein, 'Soliloquy' (from *Carousel*) (John Raitt)
¶ Bizet, Symphony No. 1 in C (LPO/Munch)
¶ LUXURY: A photograph of Madge Elliott, his wife.

7 August 1953
197 Nora Swinburne
Actress
¶ Tchaikovsky, *Swan Lake Ballet Suite* (Hallé Orchestra/Barbirolli)
¶ Puccini, 'E lucevan le stelle' (from *Tosca*) (Jussi Björling)
¶ Mendelssohn, 'Wedding March' (from *A Midsummer Night's Dream*) (BBC Symphony/Boult)
¶ Puccini, 'Bimba dagli occhi pleni di malia' (from *Madam Butterfly*) (Beniamino Gigli/Toti dal Monte/Orchestra of the Rome Opera House/de Fabritiis)
¶ 'La vita e rosa' (Carlo Buti)
¶ 'Three Kings' (Keith Miller/King's College Chapel Choir/Ord)
¶ Handel/Beecham, 'The Gods Go A-Begging' (minuet and hornpipe) (LPO/Beecham)
¶ J. Strauss, incidental music for the play, *A Woman of No Importance*
¶ LUXURY: Her make-up box and contents.
¶ BOOK: The Bible.

14 August 1953
198 Hugh Williams
Actor
¶ 'I'm Gonna Sit Right Down and Write Myself a Letter' (Fats Waller and his Rhythm)
¶ 'Abide with Me' (H. Briggs *boy soprano*)

¶ Gershwin, 'Rhapsody in Blue' (Oscar Levant *piano*/Philadelphia Orchestra/Ormandy)
¶ Shakespeare, 'How All Occasions Do Inform Against Me' (from *Hamlet*) (John Gielgud)
¶ 'Love in Bloom' (from film *She Loves Me Not*) (Bing Crosby)
¶ 'I Surrender, Dear' (Louis Armstrong and his All Stars)
¶ Offenbach/Rosenthal (arr.), 'Can-Can' (from *Gaîté Parisienne*) (LPO/Kurtz)
¶ 'Land of My Fathers' (Royal Welsh Male Choir)
¶ LUXURY: A corkscrew.

21 August 1953
199 Alfredo Campoli
Conductor and violinist
¶ Vieuxtemps, Violin Concerto No. 5 in A minor (opus 37) (Jascha Heifetz/LSO/Sargent)
¶ Verdi, 'Nile Scene' (from *Aida*) Santa Cecilia Orchestra, Rome/Erede)
¶ Verdi, *La traviata* (Act 3 prelude) (NBC Symphony/Toscanini)
¶ 'Ragging the Scale' (Paul Whiteman's Swinging Strings)
¶ Dohnanyi, Capriccio in F minor (opus 28, no. 6) (Vladimir Horowitz *piano*)
¶ Puccini, 'Che gelida manina' (from *La bohème*) (Beniamino Gigli)
¶ 'Exhibition Snooker, Albany Club: Joe Davis v Horace Lindrum' (commentary by Raymond Glendenning on a 100 break by Joe Davis, 19 February 1947)
¶ Lalo, 'Symphonie Espagnole' (Alfredo Campoli *violin*/LPO/Van Beinum)
¶ LUXURY: A football.

28 August 1953
200 Hutch (Leslie A. Hutchinson)
Singer at the piano
¶ Albéniz, 'Navarra' (Artur Rubinstein *piano*)
¶ 'Fisherman John' (Hutch)
¶ Puccini, 'Nessun dorma' (from *Turandot*) (Jussi Björling)

¶ 'Holiday for Strings' (David Rose and his Orchestra)
¶ 'I'm the Guy Who Found the Lost Chord' (from film *This Time for Keeps*) (Jimmy Durante)
¶ Tchaikovsky, 'Waltz of the Flowers' (from *Nutcracker Suite*) (Philharmonia Orchestra/Malko)
¶ 'Abide with Me' (Dr Osborne Peasgood *organ*/Bach Choir/Jacques)
¶ Novello, *Glamorous Nights* (selection) (Drury Lane Theatre Orchestra/Prentice)
¶ BOOK: An anthology of world poetry.

4 September 1953
201 Hugh Sinclair
Actor
¶ Weill, 'September Song' (from *Knickerbocker Holiday*) (Walter Huston)
¶ 'A Little White Room' (from *Floodlight*) (Frances Day/John Mills)
¶ Bach, 'Gavotte' (from Sonata No. 6 in E) (Andrés Segovia *guitar*)
¶ 'Jack Buchanan Medley' (Jack Buchanan with Orchestra)
¶ Chopin, Prelude in D flat (opus 28, no. 15) (Alfred Cortot *piano*)
¶ 'Menilmontant' (Charles Trenet)
¶ Mozart, Concerto for flute and harp in C (Lili Laskine *harp*/Réné le Roy *flute*/RPO/Beecham)
¶ Stanford, Nunc Dimittis in B flat (Dr Osborne Peasgood *organ*/Westminster Abbey Choir/Bullock)

11 September 1953
202 Peggy Cummins
Actress
¶ *Manhattan Tower: A Musical Narrative* (Elliot Lewis/Beverley Mahr/Gordon Jenkins and his Orchestra and Chorus)
¶ Debussy, 'La cathédrale engloutie' (*Preludes*, Book 1, No. 10) (Solomon *piano*)
¶ 'Again' (Joe Graydon and Chorus/Gordon Jenkins and his Orchestra)

¶ Grieg, 'Morning' (from *Peer Gynt Suite No. 1*) (Hallé Orchestra/Barbirolli)
¶ Rodgers & Hammerstein, 'If I Loved You' (from *Carousel*) (Jan Clayton/John Raitt)
¶ Novello, *Perchance to Dream* (selection) (Charles Shadwell and his Orchestra)
¶ 'The Way You Look Tonight' (from film *Swing Time*) (Fred Astaire)
¶ Rachmaninov, Piano Concerto No. 2 in C minor (Benno Moiseiwitsch/LPO/Goehr)
¶ LUXURY: A painting of circus horses by Toulouse-Lautrec.

18 September 1953
203 Jack Warner
Actor and comedian
¶ Fucik, 'Entry of the Gladiators' (Vienna Symphony/Stolz)
¶ 'The Garden Where the Praties Grow' (John McCormack)
¶ 'Sid Field Plays Golf' (Sid Field/Company)
¶ 'Blue Tango' (Leroy Anderson and his Concert Orchestra)
¶ 'She's My Lovely' (from *Hide and Seek*) (Bobby Howes)
¶ Loesser, 'Sit Down, You're Rocking the Boat' (from *Guys and Dolls*) (Stubby Kaye)
¶ 'Son Calypso' (from *Jamaica Way*) (Robert Inglez and his Orchestra)
¶ 'Melville Gideon Medley' (Melville Gideon with Orchestra)
¶ LUXURY: A blue silk scarf.

25 September 1953
204 Bernard Miles
Actor, producer and director
¶ Mozart, 'Turkish March' (Wanda Landowska *harpsichord*)
¶ Schubert, 'An die Musik' (Lotte Lehmann)
¶ Puccini, 'Si, mi chiamano Mimi' (from *La bohème*) (Claudia Muzio)
¶ Verdi, 'O patria mia' (from *Aida*) (Eva Turner)
¶ Beethoven, 'Komm, O Hoffnung' (from *Fidelio*) (Kirsten Flagstad/Philadelphia Orchestra/Ormandy)

¶ Beethoven, 'Gott, Welch Dunkel hier' (from *Fidelio*) (Helge Roswaenge/Berlin State Opera Orchestra/Seidler-Winkler)
¶ Mozart, 'O Isis und Osiris' (from *The Magic Flute*) (Wilhelm Strienz/Berlin Philharmonic/Beecham)
¶ Handel, 'The Arrival of the Queen of Sheba' (from *Solomon*) (LPO/Beecham)
¶ BOOK: The complete works of Shakespeare.

17 September 1954
205 Mary Ellis
Actress and singer
¶ Dvořák, Symphony No. 8 in G major (New York Philharmonic/Walter)
¶ Bach, Brandenburg Concerto No. 5 in D major (Philharmonia Orchestra/Fischer)
¶ Donizetti, 'Una furtiva lagrima' (from *L'elisir d'amore*) (Enrico Caruso)
¶ Grieg, Piano Concerto in A minor (Benno Moiseiwitsch/Hallé Orchestra/Heward)
¶ R. Strauss, *Der Rosenkavalier* (Act 1 introduction) (Vienna Philharmonic/Heger)
¶ Sibelius, 'The Swan of Tuonela' (Mitchell Miller *cor anglais*/Leopold Stokowski and his Sibelius Orchestra)
¶ Trad. 'Au clair de la lune' (Geraldine Farrar)
¶ Beethoven, Symphony No. 9 in D minor (NBC Symphony/Toscanini)
¶ LUXURY: A keg of eau de Cologne.

24 September 1954
206 Vivian de Gurr St George
Piccadilly shoeblack
¶ 'Stein Song' (Rudy Vallee and his Connecticut Yankees)
¶ Kreisler, 'Caprice Viennois' (Fritz Kreisler *violin*)
¶ 'Goodbye' (Josef Locke)
¶ 'La Golondrina' (Melachrino Strings)
¶ 'A Perfect Day' (Paul Robeson)
¶ 'The Happy Wanderer' (Obernkirchen Children's Choir)

¶ 'Galway Bay' (Bing Crosby)
¶ 'La Paloma' (Celestino Sarobe)
¶ LUXURY: A picture of his South American wife.

1 October 1954
207 Jessie Matthews
Musical comedy actress and film star
¶ Berlin, 'I'll Capture Your Heart' (from film *Holiday Inn*) (Bing Crosby/Fred Astaire)
¶ Falla, 'Ritual Fire Dance' (Artur Rubinstein *piano*)
¶ 'My Very Good Friend, the Milkman' (Fats Waller)
¶ 'Indian Summer' (Glenn Miller and his Orchestra)
¶ 'Sing Me Something Soft and Sentimental' (Johnny Brandon)
¶ Coleridge-Taylor, 'Demande et response' (from *Petite suite de concert*) (LSO/Sargent)
¶ 'Maybe It's Because I'm a Londoner' (Radio Revellers)
¶ Bach/Gounod, 'Ave Maria' (Beniamino Gigli/Berlin State Orchestra/Melichar)
¶ LUXURY: An enormous bottle of perfume.

8 October 1954
208 John Betjeman
Poet and writer
¶ 'My Heart Stood Still' (from *One Damn Thing After Another*) (Hildegarde)
¶ Bach/Hess, 'Jesu, Joy of Man's Desiring' (Myra Hess *piano*)
¶ 'The Meeting of the Waters' (John McCormack/Gerald Moore *piano*)
¶ 'Rock of Ages' (Choir of All Saints' Church, Margaret Street, London)
¶ Recording of Bells of Thaxted Church, Essex
¶ 'Padstow Hobby Horse, May Day Ceremony' (Villagers with drum)
¶ 'When are You Going to Lead Me to the Altar, Walter?' (Randolph Sutton)
¶ Weber, *Der Freischütz* (overture) (Hallé Orchestra/Barbirolli)

¶Country and town railway sound effects (*Extra record allowed for reasons of time.*)
¶LUXURY: The lower half of the west window of Fairford Church, Gloucestershire.

15 October 1954
209 T. E. B. Clarke
Screenwriter
¶'The Trolley Song' (from film *Meet Me in St Louis*) (Judy Garland)
¶'Do not Forsake Me, O my Darling (from film *High Noon*) (Tex Ritter)
¶'Smoke Gets in Your Eyes' (from *Roberta*) (Larry Adler *harmonica*)
¶'The Derby, 17 June 1944' (Commentary by Raymond Glendenning)
¶'Memphis Blues' (Ted Lewis and his Band)
¶Beethoven, Quartet in A minor (opus 132) (Griller String Quartet)
¶'Eton Boating Song' (Eton College Musical Society)
¶Vaughan Williams, 'Sinfonia Antarctica' (Margaret Ritchie/LPO/Boult)
¶BOOK: *Ruff's Guide to the Turf*

22 October 1954
210 Valerie Hobson (2nd appearance)
Actress
¶Butterworth, 'A Shropshire Lad' (Hallé Orchestra/Boult)
¶'Time on My Hands' (Denny Dennis)
¶Rachmaninov, 'Rhapsody on a Theme of Paganini' (Sergei Rachmaninov *piano*/Philadelphia Orchestra/Stokowski)
¶'Melanie's Aria' (from *Conversation Piece*) (Yvonne Printemps)
¶'Holiday for Strings' (David Rose and his Orchestra)
¶Brahms, Symphony No. 4 in E minor (LSO/Krips)
¶'Que reste-il de nos amours' (Charles Trenet)
¶Parry, 'Jerusalem' (Arnold Grier *organ*/Royal Choral Society/Philharmonia Orchestra/Sargent)
¶LUXURY: The Albert Memorial.

29 October 1954
211 Nigel Balchin
Writer
¶Haydn, 'With Verdure Clad' (from *The Creation*) (Isobel Baillie/Hallé Orchestra/Heward)
¶Berlioz, 'Sanctus' (from *Grande messe des morts*) (Georges Jouatte Orchestra/Chorale Emile Passani/Fournet)
¶Sullivan, 'The Lost Chord' (Enrico Caruso)
¶Bach/Bantock, 'Sleepers Wake!' (from Cantata No. 140) (City of Birmingham Orchestra/Weldon)
¶Purcell, 'When I am Laid in Earth' (from *Dido and Aeneas*) (Kirsten Flagstad/Mermaid Theatre Orchestra/Jones)
¶Shakespeare, *Richard II* (excerpt) (Robert Harris)
¶Mozart, Symphony No. 41 in C major (RPO/Beecham)
¶Couperin, 'Les barricades mysterieuses' (Monique Haas *piano*)
¶LUXURY: A figure of an urchin, sculpted by Donatello.

5 November 1954
212 Evelyn Laye
Actress and singer
¶Delius, 'Paris: The Song of a Great City' (LSO/Collins)
¶'Louise' (from film *The Innocents of Paris*) (Maurice Chevalier)
¶Wagner, 'Isolde's *Liebestod*' (from *Tristan und Isolde*) (Kirsten Flagstad/Philharmonia Orchestra/Furtwängler)
¶Ravel, Introduction and Allegro for Harp (John Cockerill *harp*/Jean Pougnet *violin*/David Martin *violin*/Frederick Riddle *viola*/James Whitehead *cello*/Arthur Cleghorn *flute*/Reginald Kell *clarinet*)
¶'The Laughing Trombone' (Chuckle & Jest)
¶Rachmaninov, Piano Concerto No. 1 in F sharp minor (Sergei Rachmaninov/Philadelphia Orchestra/Ormandy)
¶Franck, 'Panis Angelicus' (Beniamino Gigli/Berlin State Opera Orchestra/Seidler-Winkler)

¶Berlin, 'There's No Business Like Show Business' (from film) (Ethel Merman/Mary Martin)
¶LUXURY: Her bed, complete with big French pillows.

12 November 1954
213 Robert Henriques
Novelist
¶Beethoven, Piano Concerto No. 5 in E flat major (opus 73) (Artur Schnabel/Philharmonia Orchestra/Galliera)
¶Bach, Fugue in G minor (Albert Schweitzer *organ*)
¶Bach, Concerto in D minor for Two violins and Orchestra (Arthur Grumiaux/Jean Pougnet/Philharmonia String Orchestra/Susskind)
¶Shakespeare, *The Tempest* (Act 5, Scene 1) (Robert Harris)
¶Bach, 'Sheep May Safely Graze' (from Cantata No. 208) (Elisabeth Schwarzkopf)
¶Vaughan Williams, Sea Symphony (LPO and Choir/Boult)
¶Brahms, Violin Concerto in D major (opus 77) (Ginette Neveu/Philharmonia Orchestra/Dobrowen)
¶'Adon Olom' (Spanish and Portuguese Jewish Congregation, London)
¶LUXURY: Oil paints.

18 November 1954
214 Celia Johnson (2nd appearance)
Actress
¶Bach, 'S!eepers Wake!' (from Cantata No. 140) (Anny Felbermayer/Alfred Uhl/Hans Braun/Bach Guild Choir and Orchestra/Prohaska)
¶'My Resistance is Low' (Hoagy Carmichael)
¶Handel, *Water Music Suite* (LPO/Van Beinum)
¶Offenbach, 'Menelaus' Chorus' (from *La Belle Hélène*, Act 1) (Roger Giraud/Janine Linda/Paris Philharmonic Orchestra and Chorus/Leibowitz)
¶Gluck, 'What is Life?' (from *Orfeo ed Euridice*) (Kathleen Ferrier/LSO/Sargent)
¶'The Twelve Days of Christmas' (The Templars)

¶ O. Straus, *Mariette* (Act 2 finale) (Sacha Guitry/Yvonne Printemps)
¶ Mendelssohn, *A Midsummer Night's Dream* (scherzo) (NBC Symphony/Toscanini)
¶ LUXURY: A rose cutting and some English soil.
¶ BOOK: A book on astronomy.

25 November 1954
215 Captain M. B. B. Banks RM
Arctic explorer
¶ Mozart, 'Madamina' (from *Don Giovanni*) (Paul Schoeffler/Vienna Philharmonic/Böhm)
¶ 'Sunset' (bugle call) (Massed Bands of the Royal Marines)
¶ Mussorgsky, 'The Death of Boris' (from *Boris Godunov*) (Raffaele Arié/LSO/Krips)
¶ Trad. Gaelic 'My Home' (Bowhill Colliery and District Pipe Band)
¶ 'Blues in the Night' (Johnny Mercer/Jo Stafford/Paul Weston and his Orchestra)
¶ Schubert, 'Wanderers Nachtlied' (Ellabelle Davis/Hubert Greenslade *piano*)
¶ 'Life Gets Tee-Jus, Don't It?' (Peter Lind Hayes)
¶ Beethoven, Piano Concerto No. 5 in E flat major (Artur Schnabel/Philharmonia Orchestra/Galliera)
¶ LUXURY: A painting of mushrooms by William Nicholson.

2 December 1954
216 Reginald Dixon
Theatre organist
¶ Luigini, *Ballet Egyptien* (Boston Promenade Orchestra/Fiedler)
¶ 'When Father Papered the Parlour' (Billy Williams)
¶ Grieg, Piano Concerto in A minor (opus 16) (Benno Moiseiwitsch/Philharmonia Orchestra/Ackermann)
¶ 'The Lion and Albert' (Stanley Holloway)
¶ Rimsky-Korsakov, *Scheherazade* (Philharmonia Orchestra/Dobrowen)
¶ Handel, 'O Thou that Tellest Good Tidings' (from *Messiah*) (Kathleen Ferrier/LPO/Boult)

¶ 'Nola' (Les Paul *guitar*)
¶ Bach, Toccata and fugue in D minor (Fernando Germani *organ*)
¶ LUXURY: A harmonium.

9 December 1954
217 Fred Hoyle
Astro-physicist and writer
¶ Clarke/Wood (arr.) 'Trumpet Voluntary' (Amsterdam Concertgebouw/Van Beinum)
¶ Mozart, 'La ci darem la mano' (from *Don Giovanni*) (John Brownlee/Audrey Mildmay/Glyndebourne Festival Opera Orchestra/Busch)
¶ Shakespeare/Walton, 'St Crispin's Day' (from film *Henry V*) Laurence Olivier/Philharmonia Orchestra/Walton)
¶ Purcell, 'Nymphs and Shepherds' (Manchester schoolchildren's choir/Hallé Orchestra/Harty)
¶ Dvořák, Slavonic Dance No. 8 in G minor (Philharmonia Orchestra/Malko)
¶ Schubert, 'Die Junge Nonne' (Kathleen Ferrier/Phyllis Spurr *piano*)
¶ Beethoven, Sonata No. 29 in B flat (scherzo) (Friedrich Gulda *piano*)
¶ Bach, 'Schäfe können sicher wieden' (from Cantata No. 208) (Elisabeth Schwarzkopf)
¶ LUXURY: A large photograph of a lot of people at a race meeting.

16 December 1954
218 Margaret Leighton
Actress
¶ Tchaikovsky, *Eugene Onegin* (Act 2 waltz) (LPO/Beecham)
¶ Vaughan Williams, 'For All the Saints' (Herbert Dawson *organ*/The Templars Octet/Dixon)
¶ Elgar, 'Pomp and Circumstance' March No. 1 in D (Philharmonia Orchestra/Sargent)
¶ Loesser, 'I'll Know' (from *Guys and Dolls*) (Company/Wally Stott and his Orchestra)
¶ Beethoven, Symphony No. 7 in A major (Philharmonia Orchestra/Galliera)

¶ Tchaikovsky, 'Romeo and Juliet Fantasy Overture' (Vienna Philharmonic/von Karajan)
¶ Coward, 'Poor Little Rich Girl' (from *On with the Dance*) (Noël Coward)
¶ Brahms, Symphony No. 3 in F major (NBC Symphony/Toscanini)
¶ LUXURY: A Girl Guide camp bed.

23 December 1954
219 Dorothy Ward
Actress and principal boy
¶ 'Lonely Ballerina' (Mantovani and his Orchestra)
¶ Coward, *Private Lives* (scene) (Gertrude Lawrence/Noël Coward)
¶ Debussy, 'La cathédrale engloutie' (*Preludes*, Book 1, No. 10) (Walter Gieseking *piano*)
¶ 'These Foolish Things' (from *Spread It Abroad*) (Bing Crosby)
¶ Saint-Saëns, 'Valse Caprice' (Yvonne Arnaud *piano*/String Orchestra/Barbirolli)
¶ Gluck, 'What is Life?' (from *Orfeo ed Euridice*) (Kathleen Ferrier/LSO/Sargent)
¶ 'Procession' (Melodi Light Orchestra/Clifford)
¶ 'All the Things You Are' (Allan Jones)
¶ LUXURY: A make-up box.

30 December 1954
220 Bobby Howes
(2nd appearance)
Musical comedy actor
¶ 'Royal Air Force March Past' (Central Band of the Royal Air Force)
¶ Walford Davies, 'God be in My Head' (Choir of St Margaret's, Westminster)
¶ 'I Love Him as He Is' (from *Bet Your Life*) (Sally Ann Howes)
¶ Mussorgsky, 'Song of the Flea' (Feodor Chaliapin)
¶ 'Swing Low, Sweet Chariot' (Ambrose and his Orchestra)
¶ Borodin/Rimsky-Korsakov, *Prince Igor* (Act 2 dances) (LPO/Goossens)
¶ Debussy, 'Clair de lune' (from *Suite bergamasque*) (Harriet Cohen *piano*)

¶ Elgar, 'Pomp and Circumstance' March No. 1 in D major (LSO/Sargent)
¶ LUXURY: Red and white wine.

6 January 1955
221 Dorothy Tutin
Actress
¶ Granados, 'La maja y el ruisenor' (Victoria de los Angeles/Philharmonia Orchestra/Fistoulari)
¶ Gershwin, 'Rhapsody in Blue' (George Gershwin *piano*/Paul Whiteman and his Concert Orchestra)
¶ Mahler, 'Ich Atmet' Einen Linden Duft' (from *Rückert Lieder No. 1*) (Kathleen Ferrier/Vienna Philharmonic/Walter)
¶ Liszt, Hungarian Rhapsody No. 2 (Viennese Seven Singing Sisters)
¶ Brahms, Double Concerto in A minor (opus 102) (Jacques Thibaud *violin*/Pablo Casals *cello*/Pablo Casals Orchestra, Barcelona/Cortot)
¶ 'Bravo Pour le Clown!' (Edith Piaf)
¶ Ravel, Introduction and Allegro for Harp (John Cockerill *harp*/Jean Pougnet *violin*/David Martin *violin*/Frederick Riddle *viola*/James Whitehead *cello*/Arthur Cleghorn *flute*/Reginald Kell *clarinet*)
¶ Bach, 'Truly This was the Son of God' (from *St Matthew Passion*) (Eric Greene/Bach Choir/Jacques Orchestra)
¶ LUXURY: A piano.

13 January 1955
222 Sir Cedric Hardwicke
Actor
¶ Mozart, *Don Giovanni* (overture) (LPO/Beecham)
¶ 'Londonderry Air' (Fritz Kreisler *violin*/Franz Rupp *piano*)
¶ Purcell, 'If Music be the Food of Love' (Keith Falkner/Bernard Richards *cello*/John Ticehurst *harpsichord*)
¶ 'In Other Words' (from *The Bing Boys are Here*) (George Robey)

¶ 'Let's All Go Down the Strand' (Entire company at the Royal Variety Performance, 1952)
¶ Elgar, 'Nimrod' (from *Enigma Variations*, opus 36) (Hallé Orchestra/Barbirolli)
¶ George Bernard Shaw (extract from talk given on his 90th birthday, 24 July 1946)
¶ Bach, Suite No. 2 in B minor (Marcel Moyse *flute*/Adolf Busch Chamber Players)
¶ LUXURY: A newspaper.

20 January 1955
223 Harriet Cohen
Pianist
¶ Sibelius, 'Tapiola' (symphonic poem, opus 112) (LSO/Kajanus)
¶ Bach, Suite No. 5 in C minor (Pablo Casals *cello*)
¶ 'Three Coins in the Fountain' (from film) (Frank Sinatra)
¶ Debussy, Image No. 2: 'Iberia' (Orchestra of the Société des Concerts/Coppola)
¶ Byrd, *Mass for Five Voices* (Fleet Street Choir)
¶ Dvořák, Symphony No. 7 in D minor (opus 70) (Philharmonia Orchestra/Kubelik)
¶ Bax, 'The Garden of Fand' (RPO/Beecham)
¶ Verdi, *Falstaff* (Act 1, Part 2) (Sextet/Italian Radio Orchestra/Rossi)
¶ LUXURY: A box of make-up.

27 January 1955
224 Eric Ambler
Novelist
¶ Dohnanyi, 'Variations on a Nursery Theme' (Cyril Smith *piano*/Royal Liverpool Philharmonic/Sargent)
¶ Stravinsky, 'Danse Russe' (from *Petrushka*) (LPO/Ansermet)
¶ 'Ain't Misbehavin'' (Fats Waller)
¶ Ravel, Introduction and Allegro for Harp (John Cockerill *harp*/Jean Pougnet *violin*/David Martin *violin*/Frederick Riddle *viola*/James Whitehead *cello*/Arthur Cleghorn *flute*/Reginald Kell *clarinet*)

¶ 'Monsieur Ernest a reussi' (Edith Piaf)
¶ 'Runnin' Wild' (Benny Goodman Quartet)
¶ Gershwin, 'Bess, You is My Woman Now' (from *Porgy and Bess*) (Lawrence Winters/Camilla Williams)
¶ Sibelius, Symphony No. 5 in E flat major (Boston Symphony/Koussevitzky)
¶ LUXURY: A globe of the world.

10 February 1955
225 Robert Harris
Actor
¶ Chopin, Nocturne in E flat major (Ignace Jan Paderewski *piano*)
¶ Quilter/Shakespeare, 'O Mistress Mine' (Gervase Elwes)
¶ Bach, Brandenburg Concerto No. 2 in F major (Danish Broadcasting Chamber Orchestra/Woldike)
¶ Hahn/Guitry, 'Air de la lettre' (from *Mozart*) (Yvonne Printemps)
¶ Schubert, 'Ständchen' (Sam Swaap *violin*)
¶ Mussorgsky, 'Song of the Flea' (Feodor Chaliapin)
¶ Vaughan Williams, Pastoral Symphony (LPO/Boult)
¶ 'Blow the Wind Southerly' (Kathleen Ferrier)
¶ LUXURY: A tuning fork.

17 February 1955
226 Osbert Lancaster
Cartoonist, writer and designer
¶ 'Papa peint dans les bois' (Les Frères Jacques)
¶ Donizetti, *Don Pasquale* (Act 2 quintet) (Alda Noni/Cesare Valleti/Mario Borriello/Sesto Bruscantini/Armando Benzi)
¶ 'Any Old Iron' (Harry Champion)
¶ Mozart, 'Il mio tesoro' (from *Don Giovanni*) (Richard Tauber)
¶ 'Drum, Drum' (Danae & T. Maroudas)
¶ Mozart, Piano Concerto in B flat major (K. 595) (Artur Schnabel/LSO/Barbirolli)
¶ 'Bridge Game' (from revue *Nine Sharp*) (Little Theatre Company)

¶ Stravinsky, *Apollon Musagète* (Boston Symphony/ Koussevitzky)
¶ LUXURY: The *Venus de Milo*.

24 February 1955
227 Chris Chataway
Athlete
¶ 'Life Gets Tee-Jus, Don't It' (Peter Lind Hayes)
¶ Leoncavallo, 'Vesti la giubba' (from *Pagliacci*) (Enrico Caruso)
¶ 'Sh-Boom' (The Crew-Cuts/ David Carroll and his Orchestra)
¶ Sibelius, Symphony No. 1 in E minor (opus 39) (RPO/ Beecham)
¶ Berlin, 'You Can't Get a Man with a Gun' (from *Annie Get Your Gun*) (Dolores Gray)
¶ Schubert, 'Der Erlkönig' (opus 1) (Dietrich Fischer-Dieskau/Gerald Moore *piano*)
¶ Beethoven, Symphony No. 9 in D minor (opus 125) (Hilde Gueden/Sieglinde Wagner/ Anton Dermota/Ludwig Weber/Vienna Philharmonic/ Kleiber)
¶ LUXURY: Underwater breathing apparatus.

3 March 1955
228 Pat Smythe
Showjumper
¶ Bach, Suite No. 3 in D major (Stuttgart Chamber Orchestra/ Munchinger)
¶ 'Fait trotter ta mule' (from *Doce Gascabeles*) (Manolo Leira y sus flamencos)
¶ 'Phonetic Punctuation' (Victor Borge)
¶ Puccini, 'Nessun dorma!' (from *Turandot*) (Beniamino Gigli/Philharmonia Orchestra/ Robinson)
¶ 'Mountain Home Yodel' (Harry Torrani)
¶ Borodin, *Prince Igor* (overture) (Philharmonia Orchestra/Dobrowen)
¶ 'Io vendo unos ojos negros' (Elba Atamirano *guitar*)
¶ Vittoria, 'Kyrie' (La Maîtrise de la Cathedrale de Dijon)
¶ LUXURY: Her guitar.

10 March 1955
229 Pat Kirkwood
(2nd appearance)
Actress and singer
¶ 'The London Saga' (Ray Martin and his Concert Orchestra)
¶ Gershwin, 'Summertime' (from *Porgy and Bess*) (Camilla Williams)
¶ 'It's in the Book' (Johnny Standley/Horace Heidt and his Musical Knights)
¶ Massenet, 'Elegie' (Mantovani and his Orchestra)
¶ 'Experiment' (from *Nymph Errant*) (Gertrude Lawrence)
¶ 'Ae Fond Kiss' (Matthew Dickie/Jeanette Lamb *piano*)
¶ Grieg, Piano Concerto in A minor (opus 16) (Dinu Lipatti/ Philharmonia Orchestra/ Galliera)
¶ 'Born in a Trunk' (from film *A Star is Born*) (Judy Garland)
¶ LUXURY: A gardenia bush.

17 March 1955
230 Sir Alan (A. P.) Herbert
Writer, humourist and politician
¶ Handel, 'Largo' (G. Thalben-Ball *organ*)
¶ Offenbach, *La Belle Hélène* (selection) (Columbia Light Opera Company with Orchestra)
¶ Tchaikovsky, Symphony No. 6 in B minor (opus 74) (Philharmonia Orchestra/ Cantelli)
¶ A. P. Herbert/Elgar, 'Song of Liberty' (Denis Noble/Chorus and Band of HM Coldstream Guards)
¶ Bach, 'Wachet Auf' (from Cantata No. 140) (Choir and Orchestra of the Bach Guild/ Prohaska)
¶ Puccini, 'Quando me'n vo'' (from *La bohème*) (Ljuba Welitsch/Vienna State Opera Orchestra)
¶ *Big Ben* (selection) (Lizbeth Webb/Noel Gordon/Trefor Jones/Eric Palmer)
¶ 'Rule Britannia' (Royal Choral Society/Philharmonia Orchestra/Sargent)
¶ LUXURY: Field glasses.

24 March 1955
231 Tod Slaughter
Actor-manager
¶ 'Cornish Rhapsody' (from film *Love Story*) (Harriet Cohen *piano*/LSO/Bath)
¶ 'The Police Station' (Robb Wilton)
¶ 'Song of the Volga Boatmen' (Paul Robeson)
¶ 'Spanish Serenade' (Albert Sandler *violin*)
¶ 'Mister Sandman' (Max Bygraves)
¶ 'Home Sweet Home' (Clara Butt)
¶ 'Post Horn Galop' (Band of HM Royal Marines, Plymouth Division)
¶ 'Alone with My Dreams' (Hutch)
¶ LUXURY: A harmonica.

21 April 1955
232 Arthur Askey
(2nd appearance)
Comedian
¶ Rachmaninov, Piano Concerto No. 2 in C minor (opus 18) (Cyril Smith/Royal Liverpool Philharmonic/ Sargent)
¶ 'Cry' (Johnny Ray)
¶ J. Strauss, 'The Blue Danube Waltz' (opus 314) (Vienna Philharmonic/von Karajan)
¶ 'Once There Lived a Lady Fair' (from film *Blossom Time*) (Richard Tauber)
¶ Tchaikovsky, 'Romeo and Juliet Fantasy Overture' (Vienna Philharmonic/von Karajan)
¶ 'The Inchworm' (from film *Hans Christian Andersen*) (Danny Kaye)
¶ Grieg, 'Wedding Day at Troldhaugen' (opus 65, no. 6) (Walter Gieseking *piano*)
¶ Borodin, 'Polovtsian Dances' (from *Prince Igor*) (LPO and Choir/Van Beinum)
¶ LUXURY: A piano.

28 April 1955
233 Sir Malcolm Sargent
Conductor and broadcaster
¶ Handel, 'Surely He Hath Borne Our Griefs' (from *Messiah*) (Huddersfield Choral Society/Ernest Cooper *organ*/Royal Liverpool Philharmonic/Sargent)
¶ Elgar, 'Sanctus Fortis, Sanctus Deus' (from *The Dream of Gerontius*) (Richard Lewis/Ernest Cooper *organ*/Royal Liverpool Philharmonic/Sargent)
¶ Bach, 'Sanctus' (from *Mass in B minor*) (Chorus and Orchestra of the Society of the Friends of Music/von Karajan)
¶ Beethoven, Symphony No. 9 in D minor (Vienna Philharmonic/von Karajan)
¶ Kreisler, 'Caprice viennois' (Fritz Kreisler *violin*/Franz Rupp *piano*)
¶ Dohnanyi, Suite for Orchestra in F sharp minor (opus 19) (LSO/Sargent)
Also chosen, but not played:
¶ Elgar, Violin Concerto in B minor (opus 61) (Jascha Heifitz *violin*/LSO/Sargent)
¶ Beethoven: one of the concertos Sir Malcolm Sargent recorded with Artur Schnabel
¶ LUXURY: A dog.

5 May 1955
234 Anthony Asquith
Film director
¶ Verdi, 'Salce, salce' (from *Otello*) (Nellie Melba)
¶ Beethoven, Sonata in C minor (opus 13) (Wilhelm Kempff *piano*)
¶ 'If You Were the Only Boy in the World' (from *The Bing Boys are Here*) (Violet Loraine/George Robey)
¶ Monteverdi, 'Amor (Lamento della ninfa)' (Marie-Blanche de Polignac/Paul Derenne/Hugues Cuénod/Doda Conrad/Nadia Boulanger *piano*)
¶ Bach, 'Sanctus' (from *Mass in B minor*) (Chorus and Orchestra of the Society of the Friends of Music/von Karajan)

¶ J. Strauss, 'Brüderlein und Schwesterlein' (from *Die Fledermaus*) (Julius Patzak/Hilde Gueden/Siegelinde Wagner/Wilma Lipp/Kurt Preger/Alfred Poell/Vienna State Opera Chorus/Vienna Philharmonic/Krauss)
¶ 'Knock'd 'Em in the Old Kent Road' (Reg Grant)
¶ Schubert, Quintet in C major (opus 163) (William Pleeth *cello*/Amadeus String Quartet)
¶ LUXURY: A seaside pier, equipped with penny-in-the-slot machines, etc.

12 May 1955
235 Tommy Farr
Heavyweight boxer
¶ 'Sing a Song of Sunbeams' (from film *East Side of Heaven*) (Bing Crosby)
¶ 'My Yiddishe Momme' (Sophie Tucker)
¶ Monti, 'Czardas' (V. Marzorati *violin*/Ferruzzi Orchestra)
¶ 'I Saw Mommy Kissing Santa Claus' (Jimmy Boyd)
¶ Tauber, 'My Heart and I' (from *Old Chelsea*) (Luton Girls' Choir/Melachrino Orchestra)
¶ 'Charmaine' (Mantovani and his Orchestra)
¶ Puccini, 'E lucevan le stelle' (from *Tosca*) (Beniamino Gigli/La Scala Orchestra/Ghione)
¶ 'Land of My Fathers' (Crowd at Wales *v* Ireland rugby match, Swansea, 12 March 1949)
¶ LUXURY: The longest bar of soap in the world.

19 May 1955
236 Barbara Kelly
Actress and broadcaster
¶ 'Gone Fishin'' (Bing Crosby/Louis Armstrong)
¶ Coward, 'Uncle Harry' (from *Pacific 1860*) (Noël Coward)
¶ Bartók, *44 Duets for Two Violins* (no. 20) (Victor Aitay/Michael Kuttner)
¶ 'I Wonder as I Wander' (Jo Stafford)
¶ 'Over the Sea to Skye' (Scottish Junior Singers)
¶ 'Narcissus' (Joyce Grenfell/Norman Wisdom)

¶ Tchaikovsky, 'Pilgrim's Song' (opus 47, no. 5) (Lawrence Tibbett)
¶ 'Blues in Burlesque' (Stan Kenton and his Orchestra)
¶ LUXURY: A big coloured beach ball.

7 June 1955
237 Emlyn Williams (2nd appearance)
Actor and playwright
¶ 'David of the White Rock' (David Lloyd/Band of HM Welsh Guards)
¶ Holst, *The Perfect Fool* (ballet suite, opus 39) (LPO/Boult)
¶ 'Experiment' (from *Nymph Errant*) (Gertrude Lawrence)
¶ Dylan Thomas, *Under Milk Wood* (opening speech) (Richard Burton)
¶ 'Three Green Bonnets' (Gracie Fields)
¶ Shakespeare, 'What a Rogue and Peasant Slave am I' (from *Hamlet*, Act 2) (John Barrymore)
¶ Shakespeare, 'What a Rogue and Peasant Slave am I' (from *Hamlet*, Act 2) (John Gielgud)
¶ 'Noah Found Grace in the Eyes of the Lord' (Burl Ives)
¶ 'I'll Follow My Secret Heart' (from *Conversation Piece*) (Noël Coward/Yvonne Printemps)
(Mr Williams was unable to make up his mind which version of the Hamlet *speech he would take.)*
¶ LUXURY: The biggest and best encyclopaedia.

14 June 1955
238 Tony Mottram
Tennis player
¶ 'Frenesi' (Artie Shaw and his New Orchestra)
¶ Tchaikovsky, 'Swan Theme' (from *Swan Lake*, opus 20) (Hallé Orchestra/Barbirolli)
¶ 'The Road to the Isles' (from *Songs of the Hebrides*) (Polish Army Choir)
¶ Puccini, 'Addio fiorito asil' (from *Madam Butterfly*) (Beniamino Gigli/Mario Basiola/Rome Opera House Orchestra/de Fabritiis)
¶ 'Alligator Crawl' (Fats Waller)

¶ Grieg, Piano Concerto in A minor (opus 16) (Dinu Lipatti/Philharmonia Orchestra/Galliera)
¶ 'La vie en rose' (Jacqueline François)
¶ Rodgers & Hammerstein, *South Pacific* (selection) (Drury Lane Theatre/Burston)
¶ LUXURY: Writing paper and pencils.

21 June 1955
239 Nicholas Monsarrat
Novelist
¶ Handel, 'Art Thou Troubled?' (from *Rodelinda*) (Kathleen Ferrier/LSO/Sargent)
¶ 'Rockin' Chair' (Louis Armstrong and his All Stars)
¶ J. Strauss, 'The Blue Danube' (LPO/Dorati)
¶ Mozart, 'Hm! Hm! Hm!' (from *The Magic Flute*, Act I) (Gerhard Husch/Helge Roswaenge/Hilde Scheppan/Elfride Marherr/Rut Berglund/Berlin Philharmonic/Beecham)
¶ Bach/Hess, 'Jesu, Joy of Man's Desiring' (Myra Hess *piano*)
¶ Mozart, Quintet for Clarinet and Strings in A major (Reginald Kell *clarinet*/Philharmonia String Quartet)
¶ 'The Girl on the Rock' (from *Seven Dreams*) (Laurie Carroll/Bill Lee/Ralph Brewster Singers/Gordon Jenkins and his Orchestra)
(Mr Monsarrat also chose the Rodgers & Hammerstein song, 'If I Loved You', from Carousel, *but this was not played.)*
¶ LUXURY: A collection of autograph letters of Lord Nelson.

28 June 1955
240 Michael Redgrave (2nd appearance)
Actor
¶ Loesser, 'Sit Down, You're Rocking the Boat' (from *Guys and Dolls*) (Stubby Kaye)
¶ Schubert, Quartet for Flute, Guitar, Viola and Cello in G major (Karl Friedrich Mess *flute*/Siegfried Barchet *cello*/Heinz Kirchner *viola*/Arthur Faiss *guitar*)

¶ Britten, 'O What a Lovely Day' (from *The Rape of Lucretia*) (Margaret Ritchie/Flora Neilson/Chamber Orchestra/Goodall)
¶ 'A Nature Walk' (Arthur Marshall)
¶ R. Strauss, *Der Rosenkavalier* (Act 3 trio) (Lotte Lehmann/Elisabeth Schumann/Maria Olszewska/Vienna Philharmonic/Heger)
¶ 'Water Boy' (Paul Robeson)
¶ Shakespeare, *As You Like It* (scenes) (Edith Evans)
¶ J. Strauss, *Die Fledermaus* (overture) (Vienna Philharmonic/Krauss)
¶ LUXURY: Pipes and tobacco.

5 July 1955
241 Yehudi Menuhin
Violinist
¶ Bach, 'Have Mercy, Lord, on Me' (from *St Matthew Passion*) (Kathleen Ferrier/Jacques Orchestra)
¶ Wagner, 'Brünnhilde's Immolation' (from *Götterdämmerung*) (Kirsten Flagstad/Philharmonia Orchestra/Furtwängler)
¶ 'Schreechenrauf' (from *For the Dramatic Soprano*) (Anna Russell)
¶ Bizet, 'Flower Song' (from *Carmen*) (Georges Thill)
¶ Schubert, 'Heidenröslein' (Irmgard Seefried/Hermann von Nordberg *piano*)
¶ Dylan Thomas, 'And Death Shall Have No Dominion' (Dylan Thomas)
¶ Bartók, Quartet No. 2 in A minor (opus 17) (Budapest String Quartet)
¶ Beethoven, Symphony No. 7 in A major (opus 92) (Vienna Philharmonic/Furtwängler)
¶ LUXURY: A violin, with spare strings.

12 July 1955
242 Lionel Gamlin
Broadcaster
¶ Vaughan Williams, *The Wasps* (Hallé Orchestra/Sargent)
¶ 'Les enfants s'ennuient le dimanche' (Charles Trenet)
¶ 'Sid Field Plays Golf' (Sid Field/Company)

¶ Schumann, Piano Concerto in A minor (opus 54) (Myra Hess/Orchestra/Goehr)
¶ 'The Lord is My Shepherd' (Dr Osborne Peasgood *organ*/Choirs of Westminster Abbey and HM Chapels Royal/McKie)
¶ Meyerbeer, 'O Paradiso' (from *L'africaine*) (Jussi Björling/RCA Victor Orchestra/Cellini)
¶ Berlin, 'You're Just in Love' (from *Call Me Madam*) (Ethel Merman/Dick Haymes)
¶ Sibelius, Symphony No. 2 in D major (opus 43) (RPO/Beecham)
¶ LUXURY: A set of back numbers of *The New Yorker*.

19 July 1955
243 Ursula Jeans
Actress
¶ 'K'Arawi' (Yma Sumac)
¶ Chopin, Nocturne in E flat (opus 9, no. 2) (Solomon *piano*)
¶ Massenet, 'O dolce incanto' (from *Manon*) (Beniamino Gigli/Orchestra/Barbirolli)
¶ Verdi, 'Della vittoria' (from *Aida*) (Stage Band, Orchestra and Chorus of the Rome Opera House/Serafin)
¶ Grieg, 'Fra Monte Pincio' (opus 39, no. 1) (Kirsten Flagstad/Philharmonia Orchestra/Braithwaite)
¶ 'Core n'grato' (Beniamino Gigli/Royal Opera House Orchestra, Covent Garden/Zamboni)
¶ 'Young at Heart' (Frank Sinatra)
¶ Grieg, 'Schlaf' du teuerster knabe mein' (from *Peer Gynt*) (Margarete Teschemacher/Berlin State Opera Orchestra/Zweig)
¶ LUXURY: Sunburn lotion.

26 July 1955
244 Edward Allcard
Yachtsman
¶ Spanish Hugophone language records
¶ 'Lady of Spain' (Eddie Fisher)
¶ J. Strauss, 'The Blue Danube Waltz' (Vienna Philharmonic/von Karajan)
¶ 'Old Shoes' (Frankie Laine)

¶ 'The Donkey Serenade' (from film The *Firefly*) (Hal McIntyre and his Orchestra)
¶ Porter 'I Love Paris' (from film *Can-Can*) (Charlie Applewhite)
¶ 'Conga de la Havane' (Lecuona Cuban Boys)
¶ Part of a private recording made by Mr Allcard in America with his cousin, Barbara Masters
¶ LUXURY: A five-ton block of lead (to bring home as a keel for his new schooner).

2 August 1955
245 Isobel Baillie
Soprano
¶ Harty, An Irish Symphony (Hallé Orchestra/Harty)
¶ Rachmaninov, Piano Concerto No. 3 in D minor (opus 30) (Sergei Rachmaninov/ Philadelphia Orchestra/ Ormandy)
¶ Vaughan Williams, 'Serenade to Music' (16 soloists/BBC Orchestra/Wood)
¶ Elgar, *The Dream of Gerontius* (Richard Lewis/John Cameron/ Huddersfield Choral Society/ Royal Liverpool Philharmonic/ Sargent)
¶ R. Strauss, *Rosenkavalier Suite* (Hallé Orchestra/ Barbirolli)
¶ Rodgers & Hammerstein, 'Happy Talk' (from *South Pacific*) (Muriel Smith)
¶ 'I'll Follow My Secret Heart' (from *Conversation Piece*) (Noël Coward/Yvonne Printemps)
¶ 'Trains' (Reginald Gardiner)
¶ LUXURY: A supply of Darjeeling tea.

9 August 1955
246 Michael Ayrton
Artist and writer
¶ Berlioz, 'Dido's Garden by the Sea' (from *Les Troyens à Carthage*) (Arda Mandikian/ Jean Giraudeau/Janine Collard/ Xavier Depraz/Micheline Rolle/ André Dran/Gerard Abdoun/Bernard Gallet/ Ensemble Vocal de Paris/Paris Conservatoire Orchestra/ Scherchen)

¶ Gabrieli, 'Sonata: Pian'e forte' (New York Brass Ensemble/ Baron)
¶ Mozart, 'Dala sua pace' (from *Don Giovanni*) (Koloman van Pataky/Glyndebourne Festival Opera Company/Busch)
¶ Gluck, 'Dance of the Blessed Spirits' (from *Orfeo ed Euridice*) (NBC Symphony/Toscanini)
¶ Berlioz, 'Requiem' (from *Grande messe des morts*) (Orchestre et la Chorale Emile Passani/Fournet)
¶ Bellini, 'Casta diva' (from *Norma*) (Rosa Ponselle/ Metropolitan Opera House Chorus and Orchestra/Setti)
¶ Purcell, 'Hail, Great Parent' (from *The Faerie Queen*) (Cambridge Festival Chorus and Orchestra/Pinkham)
¶ LUXURY: *The Moscopherus*, a piece of ancient Greek sculpture.

16 August 1955
247 Claire Bloom
Actress
¶ Duparc/Baudelaire, 'L'invitation au voyage' (Gerard Souzay/Jacqueline Bonneau *piano*)
¶ Bach, Brandenburg Concerto No. 5 in D major (Stuttgart Chamber Orchestra/ Munchinger)
¶ Verdi, 'Addio del passato' (from *La traviata*) (Margherita Carosio/Royal Opera House Orchestra, Covent Garden/ Patane)
¶ Vivaldi, Concerto in D major for Violin and Strings (Montserrat Cervera/I Musici, Rome)
¶ Gershwin, 'A Foggy Day' (from film *Damsel in Distress*) (Frank Sinatra)
¶ Albéniz, 'Sevilla' (from *Suite Espagnole*, no. 3) (Andrés Segovia *guitar*)
¶ Brahms, Piano Concerto No. 2 in B flat major (opus 83) (Vladimir Horowitz/NBC Symphony/Toscanini)
¶ Gretchaninov, 'The Creed' (Feodor Chaliapin/Choir of the Russian Church of the Metropolitan of Paris/Afonsky)

23 August 1955
248 R. C. Sherriff
Playwright and writer
¶ Shostakovitch, Prelude in A flat (Philadelphia Orchestra/ Stokowski)
¶ 'It Happened in Monterey' (from film *King of Jazz*) (John Boles)
¶ Verdi, *La traviata* (prelude) (Philharmonic Orchestra/ Galliera)
¶ 'Eton Boating Song' (Eton College Musical Society)
¶ Granados, *Goyescas* (intermezzo) (Boston Promenade Orchestra/Fiedler)
¶ Verdi, 'Miserere' (from *Il trovatore*) (Joan Cross/Webster Booth/Sadler's Wells Chorus and Orchestra/Collingwood)
¶ Jaubert, 'Valse grise' (from *Le carnet du bal*) (Orchestre Symphonique de Paris)
¶ Wagner, 'Magic Fire Music' (from *Die Walküre*, Act 3) (Herbert Janssen/New York Philharmonic/Rodzinski)
¶ LUXURY: A bottle of Scotch whisky.

30 August 1955
249 Herbert Wilcox
Film producer and director
¶ Tchaikovsky, Symphony No. 6 in B minor (Vienna Philharmonic/von Karajan)
¶ 'The Road to the Isles' (from *Songs of the Hebrides*) (Stuart Robertson)
¶ Handel, 'Hallelujah Chorus' (from *Messiah*) (Huddersfield Choral Society/Ernest Cooper *organ*/Royal Liverpool Philharmonic/Sargent)
¶ 'Blow the Wind Southerly' (Kathleen Ferrier)
¶ Ravel, 'Bolero' (Boston Symphony/Koussevitzky)
¶ Puccini, 'O soave fanciulla' (from *La bohème*) (Enrico Caruso/Nellie Melba)
¶ Elgar, 'Pomp and Circumstance' March No. 4 in G major (BBC Symphony/ Elgar)
¶ Novello, 'Some Day My Heart will Awake' (from *King's Rhapsody*) (Vanessa Lee)
¶ LUXURY: Toothbrush and toothpaste.

6 September 1955
250 Eileen Joyce (2nd appearance)
Concert pianist
¶ Brahms, Symphony No. 3 in F major (Vienna Philharmonic/Walter)
¶ Mendelssohn, 'Hear Ye! Israel' (from *Elijah*) (Isobel Baillie)
¶ Debussy, *Prélude à l'après-midi d'un faune* (LPO/Beecham)
¶ Puccini, 'O mio babbino caro' (from *Gianni Schicchi*) (Joan Hammond)
¶ T. S. Eliot, *Murder in the Cathedral* (excerpt) (Robert Donat)
¶ 'The Happy Wanderer' (Obernkirchen Children's Choir)
¶ C. P. E. Bach, Double Concerto for Harpsichord and Fortepiano in E flat (George Malcolm *harpsichord*/Charles Spinks *piano*/London Baroque Orchestra/Haas)
¶ Elgar, 'Pomp and Circumstance' March No. 1 in D major (Royal Festival Orchestra and Choir/Sargent)
¶ LUXURY: A big encyclopaedia.

13 September 1955
251 Philip Harben
Radio and television cook
¶ Puccini, 'Shepherd Boy's Song' (from *Tosca*) (Alvaro Dordova/La Scala Orchestra, Milan/de Sabata)
¶ Schumann, 'Carnaval' (opus 9) (Nikita Magaloff *piano*)
¶ 'It's in the Book (Grandma's Lye Soap)' (Johnny Standley/Horace Heidt and his Musical Knights)
¶ 'How to Make an Omelette Part 2: Practice' (Xavier Marcel Boulestin)
¶ Menotti, 'The Three Kings' (from *Amahl and the Night Visitors*) (Andrew McKinley/David Aiken/Leon Lishner/Orchestra/Schippers)
¶ Chopin, Étude No. 19 in C sharp minor (opus 25, no. 7) (Wilhelm Backhaus *piano*)
¶ 'Ordering a Meal' (from Linguaphone French lessons) (Jacques Brunius/Charles Bassompierre/Maya Noël)

¶ Beethoven, Symphony No. 9 in D minor (opus 125) (Eileen Farrell/Nan Merriman/Jan Peerce/Norman Scott/Robert Shaw Chorale/NBC Symphony/Toscanini)
¶ LUXURY: A pair of field glasses.

26 September 1955
252 Leslie Welch
'The Memory Man'
¶ 'Colonel Bogey March' (Band of HM Royal Marines, Plymouth Division)
¶ 'Blue Skies' (Mantovani and his Orchestra)
¶ Rimsky-Korsakov, *Scheherazade* (Philharmonia Orchestra/Dobrowen)
¶ Puccini, 'They Call Me Mimi' (from *La bohème*) (Joan Hammond)
¶ Khachaturian, *Masquerade Suite* (waltz) (Boston Promenade Orchestra/Fiedler)
¶ Borodin, 'Polovtsian Dances' (from *Prince Igor*) (LPO and Choir/Van Beinum)
¶ 'Brazil' (Boston Promenade Orchestra/Fiedler)
¶ 'Happy Days are Here Again' (from *Chasing Rainbows*) (Layton & Johnstone)
¶ LUXURY: A bed, with an inner-spring mattress.

3 October 1955
253 John Gregson
Actor
¶ 'Cool Water' (Sons of the Pioneers)
¶ 'Barbara Allen' (Burl Ives)
¶ 'At Sundown' (Muggsy Spanier and his Ragtime Band)
¶ Puccini, 'O mio babbino caro' (from *Gianni Schicchi*) (Joan Hammond/Hallé Orchestra/Heward)
¶ Mascagni, *Cavalleria rusticana* (intermezzo) (Anton Heiller *organ*/Vienna Philharmonic/von Karajan)
¶ Foster, 'Jeannie with the Light Brown Hair' (Sydney MacEwen)
¶ 'Canzone Ballabile' (from *Vola Colomba*) (Marisa Fiordaliso/Gian Mario Guarino and his Orchestra)
¶ 'I'll be Seeing You' (Bing Crosby)
¶ LUXURY: A guitar.

10 October 1955
254 Max Bygraves
Comedian and vocalist
¶ Smetana, 'Dance of the Comedians' (from *The Bartered Bride*) (RPO/Beecham)
¶ 'The Birth of the Blues' (Frank Sinatra)
¶ 'Misirlou' (Jan August *piano*)
¶ 'Dummy Song' (Hoosier Hot Shots)
¶ Chaplin, 'Theme from *Limelight*' (from film) (Melachrino Strings)
¶ 'You're a Pink Toothbrush' (Max Bygraves/Children's Chorus and Orchestra)
¶ Rodgers & Hammerstein, 'You'll Never Walk Alone' (from *Carousel*) (Judy Garland)
¶ 'Do, Do, Do, Do, Do, Do, Do It Again' (The Coronets)
¶ LUXURY: Golf clubs and balls.

17 October 1955
255 James Robertson Justice
Actor
¶ Monteverdi, 'Vespro della Beata Vergine' (Swabian Choral Singers/Stuttgart Bach Orchestra/Grischkat)
¶ Bach, Unaccompanied Partita No. 2 in D minor (Yehudi Menuhin *violin*)
¶ Beethoven, Quartet in A minor (opus 132, beginning of 2nd movement) (Busch Quartet)
¶ Beethoven, Quartet in A minor (opus 132, beginning of 3rd movement) (Busch Quartet)
¶ Beethoven, Quartet in A minor (opus 132, another part of 3rd movement) (Busch Quartet)
¶ Bartók, Piano Concerto No. 2 (Edith Farnadi/Vienna State Opera Orchestra/Scherchen)
¶ Recording of the call of a flock of pink-footed geese
¶ 'The Flowers of the Forest' (lament) (John Burgess/*Scottish Highland Bagpipes*)
¶ LUXURY: A packet of mixed seeds of the flowers one grows at home.

24 October 1955
256 Sidonie Goossens
Harpist
¶ 'Solitude' (Duke Ellington and his Famous Orchestra)
¶ 'Les trois gendarmes' (from *Un mois de vacances*) (Mireille)
¶ 'The Peanut Vendor' (Louis Armstrong and his Orchestra)
¶ 'The Herdmaiden's Song' (Glasgow Orpheus Choir/ Roberton)
¶ Smetana, *The Bartered Bride* (polka) (RPO/Beecham)
¶ 'Couchés dans le foin' (Jacques Pills/Georges Tabet)
¶ 'Shadrack' (Louis Armstrong/ Lyn Murray Chorus)
¶ Warlock, 'Corpus Christi' (Ann Wood/Peter Pears/BBC Chorus/Woodgate)
¶ LUXURY: Handbag with usual contents, including lipstick, mirror, diary, pencil, etc.

31 October 1955
257 Frances Day
Actress
¶ 'We'll be Together Again' (The Four Freshmen)
¶ Recording of the bark of a Rhodesian lion dog
¶ 'My Funny Valentine' (Frank Sinatra)
¶ '28 Rational Exercises for Women' (Madame Bertram)
¶ 'The Wheels of Love' (Frances Day and her Knights)
¶ Tchaikovsky, 'Romeo and Juliet Fantasy Overture' (Vienna Philharmonic/von Karajan)
¶ 'Four Months, Three Weeks, Two Days, One Hour Blues' (June Christy/Stan Kenton and his Orchestra)
¶ Porter, 'It's De-Lovely' (from film *Born to Dance*) (Ray Anthony and his Orchestra)
¶ LUXURY: A piano.

7 November 1955
258 Valentine Dyall
Actor
¶ Puccini, 'Que cette main est froide' (from *La bohème*) (Georges Thill/Orchestra/ Bigot)
¶ Weber, 'Invitation to the Dance' (NBC Symphony/ Toscanini)

¶ Gomez, 'Granada Arabe' (Vicente Gomez *guitar*)
¶ Mussorgsky, 'Death of Boris' (from *Boris Godunov*) (Feodor Chaliapin)
¶ 'La dernière bergère' (Django Reinhardt *guitar*/Alex Siniavine *piano*)
¶ 'Running Ragged' (Joe Venuti Blue Four)
¶ Abeniz, 'Sevillanas' (Nino Ricardo *guitar*)
¶ Haydn, Concerto for Trumpet and Orchestra in E flat (Georges Eskdale/Orchestra/Goehr)
¶ LUXURY: A trumpet.

14 November 1955
259 Vic Oliver (2nd appearance)
Comedian, actor and musician
¶ Kabalevsky, *Colas Breugnon* (overture) (Philharmonia Orchestra/Schuchter)
¶ 'Love is a Dancing Thing' (from *Follow the Sun*) (Maurice Winnick and his Orchestra)
¶ Tchaikovsky, 'Francesca da Rimini' (opus 32) (LPO/ Beecham)
¶ Verdi, *La traviata* (Act 3 prelude) (NBC Symphony/ Toscanini)
¶ 'Comes A-Long A-Love' (Kay Starr)
¶ Delius, 'A Walk to the Paradise Garden' (from *A Village Romeo and Juliet*) (RPO/ Beecham)
¶ Wagner, 'Ride of the Valkyries' (from *Die Walküre*) (Vienna Philharmonic/ Furtwängler)
¶ 'Prelude to the Stars' (Mantovani and his Orchestra)
¶ LUXURY: Music manuscript paper and pencils.

21 November 1955
260 Beverley Nichols
Novelist, playwright and journalist
¶ Franck, 'Fantaisie in A' (from *Trois pièces pour grand orgue 1878*) (Jeanne Demessieux *organ*)
¶ Charpentier, 'Depuis le jour que je me suis donnée' (from *Louise*) (Nellie Melba)

¶ Mozart, 'Der Höhe Rache' (from *The Magic Flute*) (Florence Foster Jenkins/ Cosmo McMoon *piano*)
¶ Couperin, 'Les Ondes' (from *Cinquième ordre III*) (Ruggero Gerlin *harpsichord*)
¶ Elgar, Violin Concerto in B minor (opus 61) (Yehudi Menuhin/LSO/Elgar)
¶ Chopin, Scherzo No. 3 in C sharp minor (opus 39) (Artur Rubinstein *piano*)
¶ Delius, 'A Walk to the Paradise Garden' (from *A Village Romeo and Juliet*) (RPO/ Beecham)
¶ Rachmaninov, 'Rhapsody on a Theme of Paganini' (Sergei Rachmaninov *piano*/ Philadelphia Orchestra/ Stokowski)
¶ LUXURY: An easel and oil-painting equipment.

28 November 1955
261 Jack Train
Comedian and broadcaster
¶ 'My Resistance is Low' (Hoagy Carmichael)
¶ 'Banjo and Fiddle' (Jascha Heifetz *violin*/Emanuel Bay *piano*)
¶ 'Make Yourself Comfortable' (Andy Griffiths)
¶ Puccini, 'Nessun dorma' (from *Turandot*) (Jussi Björling)
¶ Weber, Concertstück in F minor for Piano and Orchestra (Robert Casadesus/Orchestre Symphonique de Paris/Bigot)
¶ 'Mr Froggie Went A-Courtin'' (Burl Ives)
¶ 'Twelfth Street Rag' (Liberace *piano*/George Liberace and his Orchestra)
¶ Rezniček, *Donna Diana* (overture) (Vienna Philharmonic/von Karajan)
¶ LUXURY: A rose bush.
¶ BOOK: The Bible.

5 December 1955
262 Bernard Braden
Actor, comedian and broadcaster
¶ 'On the Sunny Side of the Street' (Tommy Dorsey and his Orchestra)
¶ Coward, 'Matelot' (from *Sigh No More*) (Noël Coward)

¶Lehmann, 'Myself When Young' (from *In a Persian Garden*) (Lawrence Tibbett)
¶Gershwin, 'The Man that Got Away' (from film *A Star is Born*) (Judy Garland)
¶Debussy, 'Clair de lune' (from *Suite bergamasque*) (Harriet Cohen *piano*)
¶'Laura' (from film) (Dick Haymes)
¶Grofé, 'On the Trail' (from *The Grand Canyon Suite*) (NBC Symphony/Toscanini)
¶Carmichael, 'In the Cool, Cool, Cool of the Evening' (from *Here Comes the Groom*) (Bing Crosby/Jane Wyman)
¶LUXURY: A pair of good earrings belonging to his wife, Barbara Kelly.

12 December 1955
263 Bob Monkhouse and Dennis Goodwin
Comedians and comedy writers
¶Bizet/Hammerstein, 'Dere's a Café on de Corner' (from *Carmen Jones*) (Marilyn Horne)
¶'Living the Life I Love' (from *The Jazz Singer*) (Danny Thomas)
¶Prokofiev, Symphony No. 1 in D major (opus 25) (Paris Conservatoire Orchestra/Ansermet)
¶'I Keep Her Picture Hanging Upside Down' (Jerry Lewis)
¶Borodin/Wright & Forrest (arr.), 'And This is My Beloved' (from *Kismet*) (Doretta Merrow)
¶Falla, 'Ritual Fire Dance' (from *El amor brujo*) (LPO/Collins)
¶Gershwin, 'Looking for a Boy' (from *Tip-Toes*) (Ella Fitzgerald)
¶'The Girl on the Rock' (from *Seven Dreams*) (Bill Lee/Laurie Carroll/orchestra conducted by Gordon Jenkins)
¶LUXURIES: (Monkhouse) A large coloured picture of Marilyn Monroe; (Goodwin) *Encyclopaedia Britannica*

26 December 1955
264 Anton Dolin
Dancer and choreographer
¶Rodgers & Hammerstein, 'I Whistle a Happy Tune' (from *The King and I*) (Gertrude Lawrence)
¶Franck, Symphony in D minor (Vienna Philharmonic/Furtwängler)
¶Porter, 'I Get a Kick Out of You' (from *Anything Goes*) (Frank Sinatra)
¶'Farewell' (from *The Maid of the Mountains*) (José Collins)
¶Extracts from the speech made by Sir Winston Churchill at his installation as Lord Warden and Admiral of the Cinque Ports, 14 August 1946
¶Puccini, 'In questa reggia' (from *Turandot*) (Maria Callas/Philharmonia Orchestra/Serafin)
¶'Wind Round My Heart' (Beatrice Lillie)
¶Novello, 'Someday My Heart will Awake' (from *King's Rhapsody*) (Vanessa Lee)
¶LUXURY: An album of photographs.

2 January 1956
265 Laurence Harvey
Actor
¶Shostakovich, Symphony No. 7 (Buffalo Philharmonic/Steinberg)
¶'Unchained Melody' (Les Baxter Chorus and Orchestra)
¶'The Yellow Rose of Texas' (Johnny Desmond)
¶Mussorgsky, 'Death of Boris' (from *Boris Godunov*) (Feodor Chaliapin)
¶'Ding Dong, Merrily on High' (King's College Chapel Choir/Ord)
¶Delius, *Hassan* (closing scene) (Royal Opera House Choir, Covent Garden/LPO/Beecham)
¶'Ha' Uyamqala Okanbaba' (Zululand War Dancers)
¶Sibelius, 'The Swan of Tuonela' (Stokowski Symphony Orchestra)
¶LUXURY: A barrel of wine.
¶BOOK: The complete works of Shakespeare.

16 January 1956
266 Sam Costa
Broadcaster
¶J. Strauss, 'Brüderlein und Schwesterlein' (from *Die Fledermaus*) (Julius Patzak/Hilde Gueden/Siegelinde Wagner/Wilma Lipp/Kurt Preger/Alfred Poell/Vienna Philharmonic and Chorus/Krauss)
¶Sarasate, 'Zapateado' (from *Danzas espanolas*) (Ruggiero Ricci *violin*/Louis Persinger *piano*)
¶Bizet/Hammerstein, 'Beat Out Dat Rhythm' (from *Carmen Jones*) (Pearl Bailey)
¶J. Strauss, 'Sweetheart Waltzes' (from *The Gypsy Baron*) (Leonard Pennario *piano*)
¶'California Suite Part 1' (Mel Torme)
¶Albéniz, 'Aragon' (from *Suite espanola*) (Orquesta Lirica Audio Museum, Madrid/Olmedo)
¶Gershwin, 'Bess, You is My Woman Now' (from *Porgy and Bess*) (Lawrence Tibbett/Helen Jepson)
¶Paganini, Violin Concerto No. 1 in E flat major (opus 6) (Michael Rabin/Philharmonia Orchestra/von Matacic)
¶LUXURY: A painting, selected from the National Gallery.

23 January 1956
267 Dora Bryan
Actress
¶'Clarinet à la King' (Benny Goodman and his Orchestra)
¶'He's a Tramp' (from film *Lady and the Tramp*) (Peggy Lee)
¶'Love Me or Leave Me' (Lena Horne)
¶'In the Mood' (Joe Loss and his Orchestra)
¶'I'd Love to Fall Asleep' (Muriel Smith)
¶Porter, 'Just One of Those Things' (from *Jubilee*) (Benny Goodman Sextet)
¶'When I'm Washing Up' (from *The Water Gipsies*) (Pamela Charles)

¶ 'Moonlight Serenade' (Glenn Miller and his Orchestra)
¶ LUXURY: A stereoscope with slides of her family.

6 February 1956
268 David Nixon
Magician and broadcaster
¶ 'Give a Little Whistle' (from film *Pinocchio*)
¶ 'On the Sunny Side of the Street' (from *International Revue*) (Tommy Dorsey and his Orchestra)
¶ Haydn, Symphony No. 103 in E flat major (RPO/Beecham)
¶ 'Stayin' at Home' (Fats Waller and his Rhythm)
¶ 'Life Begins at Forty' (Sophie Tucker)
¶ Leoncavallo, 'On with the Motley' (from *Pagliacci*) (Harry Secombe)
¶ 'The Day that the Circus Left Town' (Eartha Kitt)
¶ 'Mister Meadowlark' (Bing Crosby/Johnny Mercer)
¶ LUXURY: A photograph of his wife and baby son.
¶ BOOK: Lewis Carroll, *Alice in Wonderland*.

13 February 1956
269 Terry-Thomas
Comedian
¶ 'Ciocîrlia' (Grigoras Dinicu and his Orchestra)
¶ Rodgers & Hammerstein, 'Getting to Know You' (from *The King and I*) (Gertrude Lawrence)
¶ 'St Louis Blues' (Paul Robeson)
¶ 'Cloudburst' (Don Lang)
¶ Tchaikovsky, 'Danse des cygnes' (from *Swan Lake*, Act 2) (Philharmonia Orchestra/Irving)
¶ Schubert, 'Heidenröslein' (Richard Tauber)
¶ Granados, Danza Espanola No. 5 in E minor (Andrés Segovia *guitar*)
¶ Herold, *Zampa* (overture) (LPO/Cameron)
¶ LUXURY: A horse saddle.

20 February 1956
270 Ex-Detective Superintendent Robert Fabian of Scotland Yard
¶ 'Keep the Home Fires Burning' (Olive Gilbert)
¶ *Chu Chin Chow* (selection) (Sidney Torch and his Orchestra)
¶ 'Me and My Shadow' (Whispering Jack Smith)
¶ 'Coronation Scot' (Sidney Torch and his Orchestra)
¶ 'When the Lights Go On Again' (Vera Lynn)
¶ 'Shake, Rattle and Roll' (Bill Haley and his Comets)
¶ 'Black and White Rag' (Winifred Atwell)
¶ Coates, 'Knightsbridge March' (from *London Suite*) (Philharmonic Promenade Orchestra/Coates)
¶ LUXURY: An umbrella.

27 February 1956
271 Kenneth More
Actor
¶ Planquette, 'J'ai fait trois fois le tour du monde' (from *Les cloches de Corneville*) (Michel Dens/Lamoureux Orchestra/Gressier)
¶ 'The World is Mine' (theme from *Strategic Air Command*) (Victor Young and his Singing Strings)
¶ 'Hold My Hand' (from film *Susan Slept Here*) (Ronnie Harris)
¶ 'Genevieve' (Percy Faith and his Orchestra)
¶ 'Young at Heart' (Frank Sinatra)
¶ Rimsky-Korsakov, 'Scheherazade' (opus 35) (Philadelphia Orchestra/Ormandy)
¶ 'There's a Rising Moon' (from film *Young at Heart*) (Doris Day)
¶ 'Last Love' (Ronnie Carroll)
¶ LUXURY: An English rock garden.
¶ BOOK: The complete works of Shakespeare.

5 March 1956
272 Nancy Spain
Writer and journalist
¶ 'Tommy Atkins' (Band of HM Coldstream Guards)
¶ 'Play a Simple Melody' (Stanley Black and his Orchestra)
¶ 'Never Gonna Dance' (from film *Swing Time*) (Fred Astaire)
¶ R. Strauss, 'Ständchen' (opus 17, no. 2) (Elisabeth Schumann)
¶ J. Strauss, 'Tales from the Vienna Woods' (Vienna Philharmonic/von Karajan)
¶ 'Le bateau des îles' (Tino Rossi)
¶ 'Maud' (from *Penny Plain*) (Joyce Grenfell)
¶ 'Poor John' (Winifred Atwell)
¶ BOOKS: A small library of four, including *The Fifth Form of St Dominic's* by Talbot Baines Reed, and two racing novels by Nat Gould.

12 March 1956
273 Donald Sinden
Actor
¶ Haydn, Concerto for Trumpet and Orchestra in E flat (Georges Eskdale/Orchestra/Goehr)
¶ 'La vie en rose' (Marlene Dietrich)
¶ Bach, Toccata and Fugue in D minor (Albert Schweitzer *organ*)
¶ Shakespeare, 'How All Occasions Do Inform Against Me' (from *Hamlet*) (John Gielgud)
¶ 'One and Two' (sung by Egyptian film star; no further details available)
¶ 'I'll See You in My Dreams' (Bing Crosby)
¶ Britten, *Seven Sonnets of Michelangelo* (Peter Pears/Benjamin Britten *piano*)
¶ Beethoven, Symphony No. 7 in A major (opus 92) (New York Philharmonic/Toscanini)
¶ LUXURY: A lucky charm of a horseshoe and black cat.
¶ BOOK: The complete works of Shakespeare.

19 March 1956
274 Vanessa Lee
Actress and singer
¶ 'Tenderly' (Philip Green and his Orchestra)
¶ 'Bal, petit bal' (from *New Faces*) (Eartha Kitt)
¶ Chopin, Fantasie-impromptu in C sharp minor (opus 66) (Nikita Magaloff *piano*)
¶ Lehár, 'Vilia' (from *The Merry Widow*) (Elisabeth Schwarzkopf/Philharmonia Orchestra/Ackermann)
¶ 'Mon pays' (Frank Cordell and his Orchestra)
¶ Borodin/Sargent, Nocturne for String Orchestra (Philharmonia String Orchestra/Sargent)
¶ Gounod, 'O Dieu, que de bijoux' (from *Faust*) (Victoria de los Angeles)
¶ Beethoven, Violin Concerto in D major (opus 61) (Yehudi Menuhin/Lucerne Festival Orchestra/Furtwängler)
¶ LUXURY: A clock which tells the date and has a barometer.
¶ BOOK: *Encyclopaedia Britannica*

26 March 1956
275 Cyril Smith
Actor
¶ Paganini/Liszt (arr.) 'La campanella' (Cyril Smith *piano*)
¶ Mendelssohn, *A Midsummer Night's Dream* (overture) (BBC Symphony/Sargent)
¶ 'Got a Date with an Angel' (from *For the Love of Mike*) (Bobby Howes)
¶ 'Kiss Me Again' (from *Mlle Modiste*) (Sidney Torch and his Orchestra)
¶ Recording of Tutankhamun's trumpets
¶ Verdi, *La traviata* (prelude) (BBC Symphony/Toscanini)
¶ Tchaikovsky, 'The Crown of Roses' (Choir of Christ's Hospital, Horsham)
¶ Rachmaninov, 'Rhapsody on a Theme of Paganini' (Benno Moiseiwitsch *piano*/LPO/Cameron)
¶ LUXURY: Two packs of cards.

2 April 1956
276 Bebe Daniels
Film and radio actress
¶ Rodgers & Hammerstein, 'It Might as Well be Spring' (from film *State Fair*) (Paul Fenhoulet and Skyrockets Dance Orchestra)
¶ 'Indian Summer' (Mantovani and his Orchestra)
¶ Falla, 'Ritual Fire Dance' (from *El amor brujo*) (José Iturbi *piano*)
¶ 'Granada' (Bing Crosby)
¶ Grofé, 'On the Trail' (from *The Grand Canyon Suite*) (NBC Symphony/Toscanini)
¶ 'A Nightingale Sang in Berkeley Square' (from *New Faces*) (Geraldo and the Savoy Hotel Orchestra)
¶ 'Stowaway' (Barbara Lyon)
¶ 'Coronation Scot' (Sidney Torch and his Orchestra)
¶ LUXURY: A typewriter and paper.

9 April 1956
277 Stan Kenton
Bandleader
¶ Bartók, Concerto for Orchestra (Amsterdam Concertgebouw/Van Beinum)
¶ 'When It's Sleepy Time Down South' (Louis Armstrong and his All Stars)
¶ 'The House of Strings' (Stan Kenton and his Orchestra)
¶ 'The Blues' (Joya Sherrill/Duke Ellington and his Famous Orchestra)
¶ 'Nancy with the Laughing Face' (Frank Sinatra)
¶ Ibert, 'Rome' (from *Escales*) (New York Philharmonic/Rodzinski)
¶ 'We All Need Love' (Danny Purches)
¶ 'Sixteen Tons' (Tennessee Ernie Ford)
¶ BOOK: H. L. Overstreet, *The Mature Mind*

16 April 1956
278 Marie Burke
Actress and singer
¶ Rachmaninov, 'Rhapsody on a Theme of Paganini' (Sergei Rachmaninov *piano*/Philadelphia Orchestra/Stokowski)

¶ 'I Like You' (from *Up and Doing*) (Pat Burke)
¶ Tchaikovsky, 'Francesca da Rimini' (New York Philharmonic/Stokowski)
¶ 'It's in the Book' (Johnny Standley/Horace Heidt and his Musical Knights)
¶ Delius, 'On Hearing the First Cuckoo in Spring' (RPO/Beecham)
¶ R. Strauss, *Der Rosenkavalier* (waltzes) (André Kostalanetz Orchestra)
¶ Lehár, 'Vilja' (from *The Merry Widow*) (Elisabeth Schwarzkopf/Philharmonia Orchestra/Ackermann)
¶ Albéniz, 'Iberia' (Orchestre des Concerts Lamoureux/de Freitas Branco)
¶ LUXURY: Tea.
¶ BOOK: A large book of short stories.

23 April 1956
279 John Neville
Actor
¶ 'Some of These Days' (Sophie Tucker)
¶ Prokofiev, Symphony No. 1 in D major (opus 25) (NBC Symphony/Toscanini)
¶ Rodgers & Hart, 'The Lady is a Tramp' (from *Babes in Arms*) (Lena Horne)
¶ Sibelius, Violin Concerto in D minor (opus 47) (Ginette Neveu/Philharmonia Orchestra/Susskind)
¶ Verdi, 'O monstruosa colpa!' (from *Otello*) (Jussi Björling/Robert Merrill/RCA Victor Symphony/Cellini)
¶ Mozart, Horn Concerto No. 4 in E flat major (K. 495) (Dennis Brain *horn*/Philharmonia Orchestra/von Karajan)
¶ 'Lovin' Spree' (Eartha Kitt)
¶ Mussorgsky, 'Death of Boris' (from *Boris Godunov*) (Boris Christoff/Philharmonia Orchestra/Dobrowen)
¶ LUXURY: A landscape painting by Ivon Hitchins.

30 April 1956
280 Athene Seyler
Actress

¶ 'Lullay My Liking' (Choir of Temple Church, London)
¶ Elgar, Introduction and Allegro for Strings (opus 47) (National Symphony/Collins)
¶ Mendelssohn, 'Dance of the Clowns' (from *A Midsummer Night's Dream*) (BBC Symphony/Sargent)
¶ Vaughan Williams, 'Sinfonia Antartica' (LPO/Choir/Boult)
¶ Kreisler, 'Caprice viennois' (Fritz Kreisler *violin*/Franz Rupp *piano*)
¶ Walton, 'Popular Song' (from *Façade Suite*) (Philharmonia Orchestra/Lambert)
¶ Tchaikovsky, Symphony No. 5 in E minor (opus 64) (Philharmonia Orchestra/von Karajan)
¶ Stanford, 'Gloria' (recorded at the Coronation Service of HM Queen Elizabeth II)
¶ LUXURY: Six feet of English hedgerow.

7 May 1956
281 Len Harvey
Heavyweight boxer

¶ 'The Floral Dance' (Peter Dawson)
¶ 'The Road to the Isles' (from *Songs of the Hebrides*) (Hall Russell's Male Voice Choir)
¶ Ellis, 'This is My Lovely Day' (from *Bless the Bride*) (Georges Guetary/Lizbeth Webb)
¶ Foster, 'Beautiful Dreamer' (Bing Crosby)
¶ *The Arcadians* (selection) (Light Opera Company)
¶ 'The Kerry Dance' (John McCormack)
¶ Heykens, Serenade No. 1 (Marek Weber and his Orchestra)
¶ Puccini, 'Che gelida manina' (from *La bohème*) (Beniamino Gigli)
¶ LUXURY: A box of books.

14 May 1956
282 Dora Labette
Singer

¶ Ravel, *Daphnis and Chloe: Suite No. 2* (Paris Conservatoire Orchestra/Munch)
¶ Leoncavallo, 'Mattinata' (Jussi Björling)
¶ Mendelssohn, *A Midsummer Night's Dream* (overture) (RPO/Beecham)
¶ Respighi, 'Stornellatrice' (Victoria de los Angeles/Gerald Moore *piano*)
¶ Handel, 'The Arrival of the Queen of Sheba' (from *Solomon*) (LPO/Beecham)
¶ Mendelssohn, Violin Concerto in E minor (opus 64) (Yehudi Menuhin/Orchestre des Concerts Colonne/Enesco)
¶ Wagner, *Lohengrin* (Act 3 prelude) (LPO/Beecham)
¶ 'Once in Royal David's City' (King's College Chapel Choir/Ord)
¶ LUXURY: Writing materials.

21 May 1956
283 David Hughes
Singer

¶ 'Sanctuary of the Heart' (Peter Dawson)
¶ 'One Love Forever' (David Hughes/Jo Stafford)
¶ 'We'll Keep a Welcome' (Lyrian Singers)
¶ Dvořák/Grun (arr.), 'Summer Song' (from *Summer Song*) (Sally Ann Howes)
¶ 'Keep Right on to the End of the Road' (Sir Harry Lauder)
¶ Gounod, 'Salve, dimora casta e pura' (from *Faust*) (Beniamino Gigli)
¶ 'Anna' (from film) (Silvana Mangano)
¶ 'Puppy Love' (David Hughes)
¶ LUXURY: Golf clubs and balls.
¶ BOOK: *Encyclopaedia Britannica*

28 May 1956
284 Robert Atkins
Actor-manager

¶ Grieg, 'Morning' (from *Peer Gynt Suite No. 1*) (Philharmonia Orchestra/Fistoulari)
¶ 'The Cobbler's Song' (from *Chu Chin Chow*) (Bruce Dargavel)

¶ Wagner, 'Love Duet' (from *Tristan und Isolde*) (Kirsten Flagstad/Ludwig Suthaus/Philharmonia Orchestra/Furtwängler)
¶ Mendelssohn, 'Dance of the Clowns' (from *A Midsummer Night's Dream*) (BBC Symphony/Sargent)
¶ 'David of the White Rock' (Marianne Davies)
¶ Verdi, *Falstaff* (finale) (Antonio Madasi/Teresa Stich-Randall/Herva Nelli/Cloe Elmo/Nan Merriman/Giuseppe Valdengo/John Carmen Rossi/Norman Scott/Gabor Garelli/Frank Guerrera/Robert Shaw Chorale/NBC Symphony/Toscanini)
¶ Shakespeare/Arne, 'Blow, Blow, Thou Winter Wind' (John Heddle Nash/Ernest Lush *piano*)
¶ Elgar, 'Pomp and Circumstance' March No. 1 in D major (opus 39) (Royal Festival Orchestra and Choir/Sargent)
¶ LUXURY: A commissioned painting of *A Midsummer Night's Dream* being performed at the Open Air Theatre, Regent's Park.

4 June 1956
285 Stirling Moss
Racing Driver

¶ 'Memories are Made of This' (Dave King)
¶ 'The Charleston' (Joe Daniels' Jazz Group)
¶ 'Unforgettable' (Nat 'King' Cole)
¶ Bizet/Hammerstein, 'You Talk Jus' Like My Man' (from *Carmen Jones*) (Olga James/Harry Belafonte)
¶ 'The Tender Trap' (from film) (Frank Sinatra)
¶ 'Hold My Hand' (from film *Susan Slept Here*) (Lorrae Desmond)
¶ 'A String of Pearls' (Glenn Miller and his Orchestra)
¶ 'Let's Do It' (from *Paris*) (Eartha Kitt)
¶ LUXURY: Some different makes of hair restorer.

11 June 1956
286 Ted Heath
Bandleader and trombonist
¶ 'South Rampart Street Parade' (Billy May and his Orchestra)
¶ 'Too Young to Go Steady' (Nat 'King' Cole)
¶ 'Body and Soul' (Tommy Dorsey *trombone*/Victor Young and his Singing Strings)
¶ 'Love is Just Around the Corner' (The Four Freshmen/five trombones)
¶ 'I Can't Get Started' (Bunny Berigan and his Orchestra)
¶ 'Something Cool' (June Christy)
¶ Rodgers & Hart, 'Slaughter on Tenth Avenue' (from *On Your Toes*) (Les Brown and his Band of Renown)
¶ 'All the Time and Ev'rywhere' (Dickie Valentine)
¶ LUXURY: Racing-form books.

18 June 1956
287 Eartha Kitt
Singer and actress
¶ 'Oba Grelegbuwa' (Irewolede Denge)
¶ 'Into Each Life Some Rain Must Fall' (Ella Fitzgerald)
¶ Gershwin, 'A Foggy Day' (from *Damsel in Distress*) (Frank Sinatra)
¶ Mendelssohn, Symphony No. 3 in A minor (opus 56) (LSO/Solti)
¶ 'You Made Me Love You' (from film *Broadway Melody of 1938*) (Judy Garland)
¶ 'The Woman and the Chivalrous Shark' (Burl Ives)
¶ 'I Cover the Waterfront' (Erroll Garner *piano*)
¶ Respighi, 'Fountains of Rome' (NBC Symphony/Toscanini)
¶ BOOK: Her autobiography.

25 June 1956
288 Eric Maschwitz
Writer and lyricist
¶ 'Belle of the Ball' (Leroy Anderson and his Concert Orchestra)
¶ Bach, 'Bourrée' (from Partita No. 1 in B minor) (Andrés Segovia *guitar*)
¶ Prokofiev, *The Love of Three Oranges* (opus 33a) (LPO/Boult)

¶ Verdi, *La traviata* (prelude) (NBC Symphony/Toscanini)
¶ Dvořák/Grun (arr.) 'Deep Blue Evening' (from *Summer Song*) (Edric Connor Chorus)
¶ *Chu Chin Chow* (selection) (Sidney Torch and his Orchestra)
¶ Liszt, 'Liebestraum No. 3' (José Iturbi *piano*)
¶ 'These Foolish Things' (from *Spread It Abroad*) (André Kostelanetz Orchestra)
¶ LUXURY: Botticelli's *Primavera*.

2 July 1956
289 Leslie Caron
Actress and dancer
¶ Vivaldi, 'Alla Rustica' (Concerto in G major for Strings and Harpsichord) (Virtuosi di Roma/Fasano)
¶ Gershwin, 'Strawberry Woman's Call' (from *Porgy and Bess*) (Helen Dowdy)
¶ Stravinsky, *Petrushka* (Orchestre de la Suisse Romande/Ansermet)
¶ 'Bravo pour le clown!' (Edith Piaf)
¶ 'Les forains' (Orchestre des Concerts Lamoureux/Saugnet)
¶ 'Le loup' (Orchestre du Théâtre des Champs-Elysées/Bonneau)
¶ 'Écoutez bien, messieurs' (*Opening lines of play*) (Sacha Guitry)
¶ Bach, Passacaglia and fugue in C minor (Stokowski Symphony Orchestra)
¶ LUXURY: Artists' materials.

9 July 1956
290 Jim Laker
Cricketer
¶ 'The Cricket Champions' (West Indies *v* MCC, 1954) (Lord Beginner/Caribbean Calypso Band)
¶ Schubert, 'Die Forelle' (opus 32) (Jussi Björling/Frederick Schauwecker *piano*)
¶ 'Lilli Marlene' (Anne Shelton)
¶ Mascagni, 'Mama, quel vino e generoso' (from *Cavalleria Rusticana*) (Beniamino Gigli)
¶ 'Ferryboat Serenade' (Vera Lynn)

¶ 'Goodbye' (from *White Horse Inn*) (Richard Tauber)
¶ Kern & Hammerstein, 'Ol' Man River' (from *Show Boat*) (Paul Robeson)
¶ 'Now is the Hour' (Gracie Fields)
¶ LUXURIES: A cricket ball and a piano.

16 July 1956
291 Eva Turner
(2nd appearance)
Opera singer
¶ Schubert, 'An Die Musik' (opus 88, no. 4) (Kathleen Ferrier/Phyllis Spurr *piano*)
¶ 'O del mio amato ben' (Claudio Muzio)
¶ Wagner, 'Selig, wie die Sonne' (from *Die Meistersinger*) (Elisabeth Schumann/Lauritz Melchior/Friedrich Schorr/Gladys Parr/Ben Williams/LSO/Barbirolli)
¶ Elgar, 'Nimrod' (from *Enigma Variations*) (Queen's Hall Orchestra/Wood)
¶ Verdi, 'Qui Radames verra' (from *Aida*) (Zinka Milanov/RCA Victor Symphony/Cellini)
¶ 'Until (You Find the One You Want)' (Elizabeth Welch)
¶ Puccini, 'Vissi d'arte' (from *Tosca*) (Renata Tebaldi/Orchestre de la Suisse Romande/Erede)
¶ Mozart, Symphony No. 41 in C (K. 551) (RPO/Beecham)
¶ LUXURY: Dresden or Chelsea china figurines.

23 July 1956
292 Tex Ritter
Film actor and singer of Western songs
¶ Foster, 'Beautiful Dreamer' (Roger Wagner Chorale)
¶ 'The Chisholm Trail' (Tex Ritter with String Band)
¶ 'Home on the Range' (Carson Robinson and his Pioneers)
¶ 'Wabash Cannon Ball' (Kay Starr)
¶ 'Rye Whiskey' (Tex Ritter with String Band)
¶ 'Cool Water' (Sons of the Pioneers)

¶ 'Do Not Forsake Me, O my Darling' (from film *High Noon*) (Tex Ritter)
¶ 'Silent Night, Holy Night' (Bing Crosby)
¶ LUXURIES: A pack of cards and his guitar.

30 July 1956
293 Shirley Abicair
Singer
¶ 'When the Saints Go Marching In' (Kid Ory's Creole Jazz Band)
¶ Bach, Prelude and Fugue No. 2 in C minor (Rosalyn Tureck *piano*)
¶ 'I Can't Give You Anything but Love' (from *Blackbirds of 1928*) (Adelaide Hall/Fats Waller *piano*)
¶ Concerto for Clarinet (Artie Shaw and his Orchestra)
¶ 'Big Rock Candy Mountains' (Burl Ives)
¶ Delibes, 'Mazurka' (from *Coppelia Ballet Suite*) (Paris Conservatoire Orchestra/ Desormière)
¶ 'Rockin' Chair' (Louis Armstrong and his All Stars)
¶ Beethoven, Symphony No. 5 in C minor (opus 67) (Philharmonia Orchestra/von Karajan)
¶ LUXURY: A case of avocado pears.

6 August 1956
294 Peter Ustinov (2nd appearance)
Playwright, actor and director
¶ Berlioz, 'Le spectre de la rose' (from *Nuits d'été*) (Eleanor Steber)
¶ 'Le media calandria' (from *Songs of Mexico*) (Trio Aguilillas)
¶ 'Tarantas' (flamenco singer and guitar)
¶ Arne, 'Thomas and Sally' (duet) (Stephen Manton/ Keturah Sorrell)
¶ Mozart, Concerto for Flute, Harp and Orchestra in C major (K. 299) (Camillo Wanausek *flute*/Hubert Jellinek *harp*/Pro Musica Chamber Orchestra of Vienna)

¶ Brecht/Dessau, 'Mother Courage's Song' (from *Mother Courage*) (Germaine Montero)
¶ 'Multos Annos' (Russian Orthodox liturgy) (Choir of the Russian Church of the Metropolitan of Paris)
¶ Janáček, 'Gloria' (from *Glagolitic Mass*) (Moravian Mixed Chorus/Brno Radio Symphony/Bakala)
¶ LUXURY: A tennis racket.
¶ BOOK: An encyclopaedia.

13 August 1956
295 Dennis Brain
French horn player
¶ Moszkowski, 'Guitare' (opus 45, no. 2) (Jascha Heifetz *violin*/ Arpad Sandor *piano*)
¶ Liszt, 'Dance of the Gnomes' (Sergei Rachmaninov *piano*)
¶ 'You Go to My Head' (Frank Sinatra)
¶ R. Strauss, 'Ein Heldenleben' (opus 40) (New York Philharmonic/Mengelberg)
¶ 'Horn Belt Boogie' (Mitch Miller and his Orchestra)
¶ 'The Sally Gardens' (Peter Pears/Benjamin Britten *piano*)
¶ 'Well, Git It!' (Tommy Dorsey and his Orchestra)
¶ Palmgren, 'West-Finnish Dance' (opus 31, no. 5) (Benno Moiseiwitsch *piano*)
¶ LUXURY: A typewriter.
¶ BOOK: Back numbers of motor magazines.

20 August 1956
296 Dennis Price
Actor
¶ Coward, *Cavalcade* (epilogue) (Noël Coward)
¶ Novello, 'Waltz of My Heart' (from *The Dancing Years*) (Mary Ellis/Ivor Novello *piano*)
¶ Gershwin, 'Rhapsody in Blue' (Leonard Pennario *piano*/Paul Whiteman and his Orchestra)
¶ Chopin de Marbot, 'Tristesse' (Etude, opus 10, no. 3) (Tino Rossi)
¶ Mozart, 'Il mio tesoro' (from *Don Giovanni*) (Richard Tauber)

¶ J. Strauss, 'Be My Friend' (from *Oh, Rosalinda*, based on *Der Fledermaus*) (Walter Berry/ Dennis Dowling/Michael Redgrave/Anthony Quayle/Sari Barabas/Wiener Symphoniker Orchestra and Chorus/Melichar)
¶ 'Out of Town' (from film *Charley Moon*) (Max Bygraves)
¶ Albéniz, 'Iberia' (Paris Conservatoire Orchestra/ Argenta)
¶ LUXURY: Painting materials.
¶ BOOK: A volume of Giles cartoons.

27 August 1956
297 Bernard Newman
Writer, traveller and lecturer
¶ Weber, 'Invitation to the Dance' (Royal Opera House Orchestra, Covent Garden/ Rignold)
¶ Beethoven, *Fidelio* (Leonora Overture no. 3) (Vienna Philharmonic/Furtwängler)
¶ Bach, 'Jesu, Joy of Man's Desiring' (Choir of Temple Church, London)
¶ Chopin, Waltz in A flat major (opus 64, no. 3) (Nikita Magaloff *piano*)
¶ Liszt, Hungarian Rhapsody No. 1 in F major (Leighton Lucas and his Orchestra)
¶ Wagner, *Tannhäuser* (Act 2, grand march) (Chorus and Orchestra of Munich State Opera/Heger)
¶ Gluck, 'I Have Lost My Euridice' (from *Orfeo ed Euridice*) (Hilary Newman)
¶ Gounod, *Faust* (final trio) (Victoria de los Angeles/Boris Christoff/Nicolai Gedda/Paris Opera Orchestra/Cluytens)
¶ LUXURIES: An atlas and a continental railway timetable.

3 September 1956
298 Humphrey Lyttelton
Jazz trumpeter and bandleader
¶ 'Café Society Blues' (Count Basie and his All-American Rhythm Section)
¶ 'African Queen' (Sandy Brown's Jazz Band)
¶ 'Basin Street Blues' (Louis Armstrong and his Orchestra)

¶Waller, 'Ain't Misbehavin''
(Louis Armstrong and his All
Stars)
¶'Gone Away Blues' (Mezzrow-
Bechet Quintet)
¶'Rock Island Line' (Stan
Freberg and his Sniffle Group)
¶'Louisiana Blues' (Muddy
Waters/Little Walter *harmonica*)
¶'Panama' (Luis Russell and
his Orchestra)
¶LUXURIES: A trumpet and a
harmonium.

10 September 1956
299 Harry Secombe
Comedian and singer
¶Vaughan Williams, 'Fantasia
on Greensleeves' (Hallé
Orchestra/Barbirolli)
¶'Sospan Fach' (Royal Welsh
Male Choir)
¶'Casarella' (Beniamino Gigli)
¶Mendelssohn, 'Oh, for the
Wings of a Dove' (Ernest
Lough/G. Thalben-Ball *organ*/
Choir of Temple Church,
London)
¶Puccini, 'E lucevan le stelle'
(from *Tosca*) (Giuseppe di
Stefano)
¶Dylan Thomas, 'Polly Garter's
Song' (from *Under Milk Wood*)
(Diana Maddox)
¶'Underneath the Arches'
(Flanagan & Allen)
¶'September Song' (from
Knickerbocker Holiday) (Walter
Huston)
¶LUXURY: A collapsible concrete
model of Broadcasting House,
with small plastic announcers
and a cast-iron commissionaire.

17 September 1956
300 Valentine Britten
BBC gramophone librarian
¶Schubert, Symphony No. 8 in
B minor (Vienna Philharmonic/
Walter)
¶'The Snare' (from *Songs of the
Clay*) (James Stephens)
¶'Stop and Shop at the Co-op
Shop' (Gracie Fields)
¶Elgar, Symphony No. 1 in A
flat major (opus 55) (LPO/
Boult)
¶'O Vox Omnes' (Schola
Cantorum de la Universidad
Pontificia de Comillas)

¶'The Green Autumn Stubble'
(Kitty Gallagher)
¶Mozart, 'Non so più' (from
The Marriage of Figaro) (Sena
Jurinac/Vienna Philharmonic/
von Karajan)
¶'Salve Regina' (Gregorian
chant) (Monks' Choir of St
Pierre de Solesmes Abbey)
¶LUXURY: A photograph of
Battersea Power Station and
dress-making materials.

24 September 1956
301 Turner Layton
Singer at the piano
¶Coleridge-Taylor, 'The Death
of Minnehaha' (from *Hiawatha*)
(Elsie Suddaby/Royal Choral
Society/Sargent)
¶Tchaikovsky, Symphony No.
6 in B minor (opus 74)
(Philharmonia Orchestra/
Malko)
¶Duparc, 'L'invitation au
voyage' (Charles Panzera)
¶Debussy, *Prélude à l'après-
midi d'un faune* (Philharmonia
Orchestra/Cantelli)
¶'Caroline' (Turner Layton)
¶'Rockin' Chair' (Mills
Brothers)
¶'Ring Dem Bells' (Duke
Ellington and his Orchestra)
¶'Let's Do It' (from *Paris*)
(Hutch)
¶LUXURY: A piano.

1 October 1956
302 Kenneth Tynan
Theatre critic and writer
¶'The Mooche' (Duke
Ellington and his Orchestra)
¶'Le rififi' (from film *Du rififi
chez les hommes*) (Lucienne
Delyle)
¶'Show Me a Rose' (Groucho
Marx)
¶'Ostrich Walk' (Frankie
Trumbauer and his Orchestra)
¶Brecht/Dessau, 'Mother
Courage's Song' (from *Mother
Courage*) (Germaine Montero)
¶'Twisted' (Annie Ross)
¶Brecht/Weill, 'Surabaya
Johnny' (from *Happy End*)
(Lotte Lenya)
¶Scarlatti, Piano Sonata in G
major (Charles Rosen)
¶LUXURY: The pleasure gardens
of Barcelona.

8 October 1956
303 Ada Cherry Kearton
Singer and traveller
¶J. Strauss, 'Mein Herr
Marquis' (from *Die Fledermaus*)
(Elisabeth Schumann)
¶'I'll Walk Beside You' (John
McCormack)
¶Mozart, Symphony No. 35 in
D major (K. 385) (RPO/
Beecham)
¶Puccini, 'O soave fanciulla'
(from *La bohème*) (Nellie
Melba/Enrico Caruso)
¶Rossini, *William Tell*
(overture) (NBC Symphony/
Toscanini)
¶Wagner, 'Isolde's *Liebestod*'
(from *Tristan und Isolde*)
(Kirsten Flagstad)
¶Mendelssohn, 'Oh, for the
Wings of a Dove' (Ernest
Lough/G. Thalben-Ball *organ*/
Choir of Temple Church,
London)
¶'Down in the Forest' (Jennie
Tourel)
¶LUXURY: Playing cards.

15 October 1956
304 Peter Katin
Concert pianist
¶Mozart, 'Das Kinderspiel' (K.
598) (Elisabeth Schwarzkopf/
Walter Gieseking *piano*)
¶'Mambo' (from *Lanigro*)
(Kirchin Band)
¶Chopin, 'Berceuse' (opus 57)
(Solomon *piano*)
¶'The Valley' (Mazowsze
Choral Ensemble)
¶'Wind Round My Heart'
(Beatrice Lillie)
¶Vaughan Williams, 'Fantasia
on a Theme by Thomas Tallis'
(Philharmonic Promenade
Orchestra/Boult)
¶Coward, 'Mrs Worthington'
(Noël Coward)
¶'Blow the Wind Southerly'
(Kathleen Ferrier)
¶LUXURY: Leonardo da Vinci's
The Virgin of the Rocks

22 October 1956
305 Anthony Steel
Actor
¶Berlin, 'Top Hat, White Tie
and Tails' (from film *Top Hat*)
(Fred Astaire)

¶ 'Born in a Trunk' (from film *A Star is Born*) (Judy Garland)
¶ Recording of the sounds of Piccadilly Circus
¶ 'Fools Rush In' (Hutch)
¶ Tchaikovsky, Symphony No. 5 in E minor (opus 64) (Philharmonia Orchestra/von Karajan)
¶ 'Scalinatella' (from *The Companion-way*) (Tino Christidi and his Neapolitan Serenaders)
¶ 'One Night of Love' (from film) (Grace Moore)
¶ 'Love is a Many-Splendoured Thing' (from film) (The Four Aces)
¶ LUXURY: A commissioned portrait of his wife by Annigoni.

29 October 1956
306 Isobel Barnett
Broadcaster
¶ Beethoven, Sonata No. 23 in F major (opus 57) (Solomon *piano*)
¶ 'The Infant King' (King's College Chapel Choir/Ord)
¶ Chopin, Nocturne No. 8 in D flat major (opus 27, no. 2) (Solomon *piano*)
¶ Coward, 'Mad Dogs and Englishmen' (from *Words and Music*) (Noël Coward)
¶ Schubert, Impromptu in A flat (opus 90, no. 4) (Louis Kentner *piano*)
¶ Brahms, Intermezzo in A minor (opus 116, no. 2) (Artur Schnabel *piano*)
Bach, 'Bist du bei mir' (Elisabeth Schwarzkopf/Gerald Moore *piano*)
¶ Chopin, Waltz in A flat major (opus 34, No. 1) (Dinu Lipatti *piano*)
¶ LUXURY: A hot water bottle.

12 November 1956
307 Donald Campbell
Holder of world's water speed record
¶ 'In the Mood' (Glenn Miller and his Orchestra)
¶ 'Funiculi, Funicula' (Beniamino Gigli)
¶ 'Serenata' (Harry Davidson and his Orchestra)

¶ Verdi, 'Anvil Chorus' (from *Il trovatore*) (Chorus of the Maggio Musicale Fiorentino/Orchestre du Grand Théâtre de Genève/Erede)
¶ 'Cock o' the North' (Pipes and Drums of the HM 1st Battalion Scots Guards)
¶ 'Tea for Two' (from *No, No, Nanette*) (Doris Day)
¶ Rossini, 'Largo al factotum' (from *The Barber of Seville*) (Tito Gobbi)
¶ 'Mon coeur est un violon' (Lucienne Boyer)
¶ LUXURY: Cigarettes.

19 November 1956
308 Dennis Noble
Baritone
¶ 'I Went to Your Wedding' (Spike Jones and his City Slickers)
¶ Verdi, *Aida* (Act 2 finale) (Maria Callas/Richard Tucker/Fedora Barbieri/Tito Gobbi/Orchestra and Chorus of La Scala Opera House/Serafin)
¶ Puccini, 'Love and Music' (from *Tosca*) (Joan Hammond/Philharmonia Orchestra/Curiel)
¶ 'The Long Day Closes' (Tommy Handley Memorial Choir)
¶ Verdi, 'Eri tu che macchiavi quell'anima' (from *Un ballo in maschera*) (Mattia Battistini)
¶ Elgar, 'Praise to the Holiest in the Height' (from *The Dream of Gerontius*) (Huddersfield Choral Society/Sargent)
¶ Verdi, 'From Fair Provence' (from *La traviata*) (Dennis Noble/Hallé Orchestra/Braithwaite)
¶ 'God Save the Queen' (recorded at the Coronation Service of HM Queen Elizabeth II)
¶ LUXURY: A pair of binoculars.

26 November 1956
309 Malcolm Muggeridge
Journalist and broadcaster
¶ Beethoven, Symphony No. 7 in A major (opus 92) (Philharmonia Orchestra/Klemperer)
¶ Bach/Hess, 'Jesu, Joy of Man's Desiring' (Myra Hess *piano*)

¶ Shakespeare/Bridgewater, 'O Mistress Mine' (from *Twelfth Night*) (Murray Dickie/Westminster Light Orchestra/Bridgewater)
¶ Rodgers & Hammerstein, 'Oh, What a Beautiful Morning' (from *Oklahoma*) (Alfred Drake/Joan Roberts)
¶ Howells, 'Magnificat Collegium Regale' (King's College Chapel Choir/Ord)
¶ Mozart, 'Voi che sapete' (from *The Marriage of Figaro*) (Sena Jurinac/Vienna Philharmonic/von Karajan)
¶ Beethoven, Sonata No. 8 in C minor (opus 13) (Solomon *piano*)
¶ Beethoven, 'Benedictus' (from *Missa Solemnis in D major*, opus 123) (Maria Stader/Marianna Radev/Anton Dermota/Josef Greindl/St Hedwig's Cathedral Choir/Berlin Philharmonic/Böhm)
¶ LUXURY: Paper and pencils.

3 December 1956
310 John Watt
Broadcaster and producer
¶ Stravinsky, *Petrushka* (New York Philharmonic/Mitropoulos)
¶ Tchaikovsky, *The Sleeping Beauty* (waltz) (Sadler's Wells Orchestra/Lambert)
¶ 'Rock Around the Clock' (Bill Haley and his Comets)
¶ Kern & Hammerstein, *Show Boat* (selection) (Melachrino Orchestra)
¶ Gershwin, 'Someone to Watch Over Me' (from *Oh, Kay!*) (Gertrude Lawrence)
¶ 'Vienna, City of My Dreams' (Richard Tauber)
¶ Walton, 'Spitfire Prelude' (from film *The First of the Few*) (Hallé Orchestra/Walton)
¶ 'Ça c'est Paris' (Frank Chacksfield and his Orchestra)
¶ LUXURY: A thermos flask.

10 December 1956
311 Spike Milligan
Writer and comedian
¶ Respighi, 'Feste Romane' (NBC Symphony/Toscanini)
¶ Satie, 'Three Gymnopedies' (Concert Arts Orchestra/Golschmann)

¶ Saint-Saëns, 'Danse macabre' (Philharmonia Orchestra/ Markevitch)
¶ 'It Don't Mean a Thing' (Stan Getz/Dizzy Gillespie/Oscar Peterson/Herb Ellis/Ray Brown/Max Roach)
¶ Bax, 'Tintagel' (LPO/Boult)
¶ Handel, 'The Arrival of the Queen of Sheba' (from *Solomon*) (LPO/Beecham)
¶ Ravel, Introduction and Allegro for Harp, Flute, Clarinet and String Quartet (Ann Mason Stockton *harp*/ Arthur Cleghorn *flute*/Mitchell Lurie *clarinet*/Hollywood String Quartet)
¶ Bach/Stokowski, Toccata and Fugue in D minor (Philadelphia Orchestra/Stokowski)
¶ LUXURY: A barometer.

14 December 1956
312 Eight inhabitants of Ascension Island in the South Atlantic
¶ 'A Nightingale Sang in Berkeley Square' (Philip Green and his Orchestra)
¶ Mozart, 'Alleluia' (from *Exsultate Jubilate*, K. 165) (Hilde Gueden/Vienna Philharmonic/Erede)
¶ 'Learnin' the Blues' (Frank Sinatra)
¶ Rodgers & Hart, 'Mountain Greenery' (from film *The Girl Friend*) (Mel Torme)
¶ Vaughan Williams, 'Fantasia on Greensleeves' (Philharmonic Promenade Orchestra/Boult)
¶ 'Cherry Pink and Apple Blossom White' (Eddie Calvert *trumpet*/Norrie Paramor and his Orchestra)
¶ J. Strauss, 'The Blue Danube Waltz' (Vienna Philharmonic/ von Karajan)
¶ Romberg, *The Student Prince* (orchestral introduction) (Callinicos)

17 December 1956
313 Peter Finch
Actor
¶ Bizet/Hammerstein, 'Beat Out Dat Rhythm on a Drum' (from *Carmen Jones*) (Marilyn Horne)

¶ Debussy, 'La cathédrale engloutie' (*Preludes*, Book 1, No. 10) (Walter Gieseking *piano*)
¶ 'King's Cross Climax' (from *Australian Suite*) (Ted Heath and his Music)
¶ Ravel, 'Pavane pour une infante défunte' (Philharmonia Orchestra/Cantelli)
¶ 'All the Things You Are' (from *Very Warm for May*) (Dave Brubeck Quartet)
¶ J. C. Bach, Quartet for Flute and Strings in C major (opus 8, no. 1) (Oxford Ensemble)
¶ 'Hold Me, Thrill Me, Kiss Me' (Muriel Smith)
¶ Massenet, 'The Death of Don Quixote' (from *Don Quixote*) (Feodor Chaliapin)
¶ LUXURY: Painting materials.
¶ BOOK: Cervantes, *Don Quixote*

24 December 1956
314 Janette Scott
Actress
¶ Gershwin, 'Lose That Long Face' (from film *A Star is Born*) (Judy Garland)
¶ *Peter Pan* (incidental music) (London Palladium Orchestra/ Crean)
¶ 'Cock o' the North' (Pipes and Drums of HM 2nd Battalion Scots Guards)
¶ 'I Like Myself' (Gene Kelly)
¶ Tchaikovsky, 'Romeo and Juliet Fantasy Overture' (New York Philharmonic/Stokowski)
¶ Rodgers & Hammerstein, 'The Carousel Waltz' (from *Carousel*)
¶ 'March of the Bob Cats' (Bob Crosby's Bob Cats)
¶ Gershwin, 'Long Ago and Far Away' (from film *Cover Girl*) (Bing Crosby)
¶ LUXURY: A complete glamour outfit.

31 December 1956
315 Tyrone Power
Actor
¶ Chopin, Nocturne in E flat major (opus 9, no. 2) (Arthur Rubinstein *piano*)
¶ Respighi, 'The Triton Fountain at Morn' (from *Fountains of Rome*) (NBC Symphony/Toscanini)

¶ Glière, Symphony No. 3 in B minor (opus 42) (Santa Cecilia Orchestra, Rome/Rachmilovich)
¶ Tchaikovsky, *Swan Lake* (opus 10) (Philharmonia Orchestra/Markevitch)
¶ Rachmaninov, Piano Concerto No. 2 in C minor (opus 18) (Geza Anda/ Philharmonia Orchestra/ Galliera)
¶ Charles Dickens, 'Mr Pickwick's Christmas' (from *Pickwick Papers*) (Charles Laughton)
¶ Offenbach/Rosenthal (arr.), *Gaîté Parisienne* (Royal Opera House Orchestra, Covent Garden/Susskind)
¶ Franck, Symphony in D minor (NBC Symphony/Cantelli)
¶ LUXURY: Leonardo da Vinci's notebooks.

7 January 1957
316 George Cansdale
Television zoo man
¶ Mozart, Quintet in A major for Clarinet and Strings (K. 581) (members of the Vienna Octet)
¶ Bach, Suite No. 2 in B minor (Karl Roznicek *flute*/Vienna State Opera Orchestra/ Prohaska)
¶ Bach, 'Jesu, Joy of Man's Desiring' (Choir and Orchestra of the Bach Cantata Club, London/Kennedy Scott)
¶ Schumann, Piano Concerto in A minor (opus 54) (Dinu Lipatti/Philharmonia Orchestra/von Karajan)
¶ 'Heigh-Ho' and 'With a Smile and a Song' (from film *Snow White and the Seven Dwarfs*) (Charlie Kunz *piano*)
¶ Beethoven, Violin Concerto in D major (opus 61) (Yehudi Menuhin/Philharmonia Orchestra/Furtwängler)
¶ Schubert, Symphony No. 9 in C major (New York Philharmonic Orchestra/ Walter)
¶ Handel, 'I Know that My Redeemer Liveth' (from *Messiah*) (Isobel Baillie/Hallé Orchestra/Heward)
¶ LUXURY: A pair of field glasses.

14 January 1957
317 Gerard Hoffnung
Humorous artist and entertainer
¶ Ravel, 'Cat Duet' (from *L'enfant et les sortilèges*) (Yvon Le Marc'hadour/Marguerite Legouhy/French National Radio Orchestra/Bour)
¶ R. Strauss, *Der Rosenkavalier*(final trio) (Lotte Lehmann/Elisabeth Schumann/Maria Olszewska/Vienna Philharmonic/Heger)
¶ Debussy, Quartet in G minor (opus10) (Quartetto Italiano)
¶ Gershwin, *An American in Paris*(Salvador Camarata and his Orchestra)
¶ Hoffnung Music Festival (excerpts)
¶ Warlock, 'Corpus Christi' (Ann Wood/Peter Pears/BBC Chorus/Woodgate)
¶ Stravinsky, *Le sacre du printemps*(New York Philharmonic/Stravinsky)
¶ Honegger, Symphony No. 3 (Paris Conservatoire Orchestra/Denzler)
LUXURIES: His paintbox and his tuba.

21 January 1957
318 Dilys Powell
Film critic and writer
¶ 'Lord Randall' (Burl Ives)
¶ Chopin, Waltz No. 5 in A flat major (opus 42) (Dinu Lipatti *piano*)
¶ Bach, 'On the first Day of the Festival of Christmas' (from *Christmas Oratorio*) (Soloists of the Akademie Kammerchor/VSO/Grossmann)
¶ Stravinsky, 'Fête populaire de la semaine grasse' (from *Petrouchka*) (Orchestre de la Suisse Romande/Ansermet)
¶ Debussy, *Prélude à l'après-midi d'un faune*(Orchestre de la Suisse Romande/Ansermet)
¶ 'Pass the Football' (from film *Wonderful Town*) (Jordan Bentley)
¶ Falla, 'Nights in the Gardens of Spain' (Clifford Curzon *piano*/National Symphony/Jordan)
¶ Dylan Thomas, 'Fern Hill' (Richard Burton)
¶ LUXURY: Paper and pencils.

28 January 1957
319 Zena Dare
Actress
¶ Rodgers & Hammerstein, 'Oh, What a Beautiful Morning' (from *Oklahoma*) (Gordon Macrae)
¶ 'Tea for Two' (from *No, No, Nanette*) (Victor Silvester and his Ballroom Orchestra)
¶ Ravel, 'Bolero' (RIAS Symphony Orchestra, Berlin/Fricsay)
¶ Franck, 'Panis Angelicus' (Beniamino Gigli/Berlin State Opera Orchestra/Seidler-Winkler)
¶ Novello, 'Mountain Dove' and 'The Gates of Paradise' (from *King's Rhapsody*) (Olive Gilbert/Denis Martin/Vanessa Lee)
¶ 'Time on My Hands' (Carroll Gibbons *piano*)
¶ Porter, 'Begin the Beguine' (from *Jubilee*) (Bing Crosby)
¶ J. Strauss, 'Nun's Chorus' (from *Casanova*) (Anni Frind/Chorus and Orchestra des Grossen Schauspielhauses, Berlin)
¶ LUXURY: A mink coat.

4 February 1957
320 Peter Sellers
Actor and comedian
¶ 'I Want a Big Butter and Egg Man' (Bobby Hackett and his Jazz Band)
¶ Rodgers & Hammerstein, 'I Have Dreamed' (from *The King and I*) (Rita Moreno/Carlos Rivas)
¶ Delius, 'On Hearing the First Cuckoo in Spring' (LSO/Collins)
¶ Berlin, 'Cheek to Cheek' (from film *Top Hat*) (Ella Fitzgerald/Louis Armstrong)
¶ Debussy, 'La fille aux cheveux de lin' (*Preludes*, Book 1, No. 8) (Hans Henkemans *piano*)
¶ Young, 'White' (from *Tone Poems of Colour*) (orchestra conducted by Frank Sinatra)
¶ 'Laura' (from film) (Erroll Garner *piano*)
¶ 'I Like to Recognize the Tune' (Mel Torme)
¶ LUXURY: A snorkel outfit.
¶ BOOK: Charles Dickens, *Pickwick Papers*

11 February 1957
321 Peggy Ashcroft
Actress
¶ Beethoven, Violin Concerto in D major (opus 61) (Yehudi Menuhin/Philharmonia Orchestra/Furtwängler)
¶ Dylan Thomas, *Under Milk Wood*(excerpt) (Richard Burton/Diana Maddox/Mary Jones)
¶ 'Stop Your Tickling, Jock' (Sir Harry Lauder)
¶ Mozart, Symphony No. 39 in E flat major (K. 543) (RPO/Beecham)
¶ Oscar Wilde, *The Importance of Being Earnest*(Act 1) (Edith Evans/John Gielgud)
¶ Bach, Brandenburg Concerto No. 5 in D minor (beginning of 1st movement) (Stuttgart Chamber Orchestra/Münchinger)
¶ Bach, Brandenburg Concerto No. 5 in D minor (conclusion of 2nd movement) (Stuttgart Chamber Orchestra/Münchinger)
¶ Bach, Brandenburg Concerto No. 5 in D minor (beginning of 3rd movement) (Stuttgart Chamber Orchestra/Münchinger)
¶ LUXURY: A frogwoman's outfit.

18 February 1957
322 Jack Solomons
Boxing promoter
¶ J. Strauss, 'Perpetuum Mobile' (Vienna Philharmonic/Krauss)
¶ 'My Mammy' (from film *The Jazz Singer*) (Al Jolson)
¶ 'Down Every Street' (Flanagan & Allen)
¶ 'Take Care of Yourself' (Petula Clark)
¶ Loesser, 'A Woman in Love' (from film *Guys and Dolls*) (Frankie Laine)
¶ 'Half as Much' (Rosemary Clooney)
¶ 'Whiffenpoof Song' (Bing Crosby)
¶ 'Keep Right on to the End of the Road' (Sir Harry Lauder)
¶ LUXURY: A punchbag.

25 February 1957
323 Edgar Lustgarten
Writer and broadcaster
¶ 'La vie en rose' (Edith Piaf)
¶ 'Fred Fannakapan' (Gracie
Fields)
¶ Coward, 'Mrs Worthington'
(Noël Coward)
¶ 'Ciribiribin' (Bing Crosby/
The Andrews Sisters)
¶ 'I was Leaning on a Lamp Post
at the Corner of the Street'
(George Formby Snr)
¶ 'Happy Days are Here Again'
(Layton & Johnstone)
¶ 'Man not a Mouse' (from *Grab
Me a Gondola*) (Joan Heal)
¶ 'Morning Light' (Paul
Franklin and his Orchestra)
¶ LUXURY: A woman's evening
gown to gaze at.

4 March 1957
324 Anthony Quayle
Actor and director
¶ Beethoven, Symphony No. 3
in E flat major (opus 55)
(Philharmonia Orchestra/
Klemperer)
¶ 'Y'a tant d'amour' (Maurice
Chevalier)
¶ Franck, 'Symphonic
Variations' (Robert Casadesus
piano/Philharmonia Orchestra/
Weldon)
¶ 'I Gave My Love a Cherry'
(Eddie Arnold)
¶ Dylan Thomas, 'Polly Garter's
Song' (from *Under Milk Wood*)
(Diana Maddox)
¶ Sibelius, Symphony No. 2 in
D major (opus 43) (LSO/
Collins)
¶ 'Look for the Silver Lining'
(from *Sally*) (Dorothy Dickson)
¶ Beethoven, Symphony No. 6
in F major (opus 68) (VSO/
Klemperer)
¶ LUXURY: Writing materials.

11 March 1957
325 Elizabeth Bowen
Novelist
¶ 'St Louis Blues' (Paul
Robeson)
¶ 'Hallelujah' (from *Hit the
Deck*) (André Kostelanetz
Orchestra)
¶ Beethoven, Sonata in C sharp
minor (opus 27, no. 2) (Artur
Schnabel *piano*)

¶ Schubert, Symphony No. 8 in
B minor (Boston Symphony/
Munch)
¶ Mozart, Concerto in D minor
(K. 466) (Bruno Walter *piano
and conducting*/Vienna
Philharmonic)
¶ R. Strauss, 'Ohne mich' (from
Der Rosenkavalier) (Richard
Mayr/Vienna Philharmonic/
Heger)
¶ Bach/Walton, 'Sheep May
Safely Graze' (from *The Wise
Virgins Ballet Suite*) (Sadler's
Wells Orchestra/Walton)
¶ Clarke, 'Trumpet Voluntary'
(George Eskdale *trumpet*/LSO/
Mackerras)
¶ LUXURY: A kaleidoscope.
¶ BOOK: Jane Austen, *Emma*

18 March 1957
326 Alan Melville
Playwright and actor
¶ Rossini, *The Barber of Seville*
(overture) (NBC Symphony/
Toscanini)
¶ 'On Such a Night as This'
(from *Gay's the Word*) (Vanessa
Lee)
¶ Lalo, Symphonie Espagnole
(opus 21) (Jascha Heifetz *violin*/
RCA Victor Symphony/
Steinberg)
¶ Gershwin, 'My One and Only
Highland Fling' (from film *The
Barkleys of Broadway*) (Jo
Stafford/Gordon Macrae)
¶ *Comedy in Music* (volume 1)
(Victor Borge)
¶ Puccini, 'Che gelida manina'
(from *La bohème*) (Jussi
Björling)
¶ 'All on Account of a Guy'
(from *Bet Your Life*) (Muriel
Smith)
¶ Bach/Gounod, 'Ave Maria'
(Joan Hammond)
¶ LUXURY: A practice wall for
tennis, with two rackets and a
gross of balls.

25 March 1957
327 Bud Flanagan
Comedian
¶ 'Theatreland March' (Harry
Fryer and his Orchestra)
¶ 'I'll Get By' (Val Merrall/Fred
Hartley and his Music)
¶ 'When Irish Eyes are Smiling'
(John McCormack)

¶ 'Kiss Me Again' (from *Mlle
Modiste*) (Mantovani and his
Orchestra)
¶ 'Soldiers in the Park' (BBC
Wireless Military Band)
¶ 'Just a Gigolo' (Bing Crosby)
¶ 'Peg o' My Heart' (Glenn
Miller and his Orchestra)
¶ 'Wish You were Here' (from
Wish You were Here) (Eddie
Fisher)
¶ LUXURY: Premium bonds.

1 April 1957
328 Chris Brasher
Athlete
¶ Sibelius, Symphony No. 5 in
E flat major (opus 82)
(Philharmonia Orchestra/von
Karajan)
¶ Kern & Hammerstein, 'I
Can't Help Lovin' Dat Man'
(from *Show Boat*) (Ava
Gardner)
¶ Beethoven, Piano Concerto
No. 5 in E flat major (opus 73)
(Denis Matthews/Philharmonia
Orchestra/Susskind)
¶ Prokofiev, *Romeo and Juliet*
(Suite No. 2) (Leningrad State
Philharmonic/Mravinsky)
¶ 'Sh-boom' (Stan Freberg/The
Toads)
¶ Rodgers & Hammerstein,
'Younger than Springtime'
(from *South Pacific*) (William
Tabbert)
¶ 'Je cherche un homme'
(Eartha Kitt)
¶ Beethoven, Symphony No. 9
in D minor (opus 125)
(Elisabeth Schwarzkopf/
Elisabeth Höngen/Hans Hopf/
Otto Edelmann/Bayreuth
Festival Chorus and Orchestra/
Furtwängler)
¶ LUXURY: A sailing dinghy, not
to be used for escaping.

8 April 1957
329 Cicely Courtneidge
(2nd appearance)
Actress and comedienne
¶ Coates, 'Elizabeth Tudor'
(from *The Three Elizabeths
Suite*) (New Symphony
Orchestra/Coates)
¶ Puccini, 'One Fine Day' (from
Madam Butterfly) (Joan
Hammond/Philharmonia
Orchestra/Curiel)

¶ Mendelssohn, *A Midsummer Night's Dream* (scherzo) (BBC Symphony/Sargent)
¶ 'My Hat's on the Side of My Head' (from film *Jack Ahoy*) (Jack Hulbert)
¶ 'Anthem and Greeting' (from *Vivat Regina Elizabetha*, performed at the Coronation Service of HM Queen Elizabeth II)
¶ Tchaikovsky, *The Sleeping Beauty Suite* (waltz) (Philharmonia Orchestra/von Karajan)
¶ Rodgers & Hammerstein, 'A Wonderful Guy' (from *South Pacific*) (Mary Martin)
¶ Elgar, 'Pomp and Circumstance' March No. 1 in D major (opus 39) (LSO/Sargent)
¶ LUXURY: The family photograph album.

15 April 1957
330 Ralph Wightman
Countryman and broadcaster
¶ Vaughan Williams, 'Linden Lea' (George Hancock/Gerald Moore *piano*)
¶ Mendelssohn, 'Oh, for the Wings of a Dove' (Ernest Lough/G. Thalben-Ball *organ*/Choir of Temple Church, London)
¶ 'Don't Knock the Rock' (Bill Haley and his Comets)
¶ J. Strauss, 'The Blue Danube Waltz' (Vienna Philharmonic/Krauss)
¶ 'The One-Eyed Riley' (Robert Irwin and chorus)
¶ Elgar, 'Pomp and Circumstance' March No. 1 in D major (opus 39) (LSO/Sargent)
¶ Kern & Hammerstein, 'Ol' Man River' (from *Show Boat*) (Paul Robeson)
¶ Parry, 'Jerusalem' (Ilford Girls' Choir)
¶ LUXURY: Pipecleaners.

22 April 1957
331 Tommy Steele
Rock 'n' roll performer
¶ 'Caravan' (Ralph Marterie and his Orchestra)
¶ 'Gotta Have Me Go with You' (from film *A Star is Born*) (Judy Garland)

¶ 'London Fantasia' (Columbia Light Symphony/Williams)
¶ 'What a Mouth, What a Mouth' (Two Bills from Bermondsey)
¶ 'Banana Boat Song' (Stan Freberg/Billy May's Music)
¶ Tchaikovsky, Piano Concerto No. 1 in B flat minor (opus 23) (Solomon/Philharmonia Orchestra/Dobrowen)
¶ 'Cannibal Pot' (Tommy Steele and the Steelmen)
¶ 'Rudy's Rock' (Bill Haley and his Comets)
¶ BOOK: A do-it-yourself book.

29 April 1957
332 Gwen Catley
Soprano
¶ Mendelssohn, *A Midsummer Night's Dream* (overture) (RPO/Beecham)
¶ Tchaikovsky, 'Variations on a Rococo Theme' (opus 33) (Pierre Fournier *cello*/Philharmonia Orchestra/Sargent)
¶ Verdi, 'Tutte le feste al tempio' (from *Rigoletto*) (Maria Callas/Tito Gobbi/Orchestra of La Scala Opera House/Serafin)
¶ Bizet, 'Serenade' (from *The Fair Maid of Perth*) (John Heddle Nash)
¶ 'Ding Dong, Merrily on High' (Royal Choral Society/Sargent)
¶ Chopin, Étude No. 13 in A flat major (opus 25, no. 1) (Shura Cherkassky *piano*)
¶ *A Mozart Opera by Borge* (Victor Borge)
¶ 'Anthem and Greeting' (from *Vivat Regina Elizabetha*, performed at the Coronation Service of HM Queen Elizabeth II)
¶ LUXURY: A painting of London to be commissioned from Graham Sutherland.

6 May 1957
333 David Attenborough
Zoologist
¶ 'Trouble in Mind' (Ottilie Patterson/Chris Barber's Jazz Band)
¶ Bach/Mangiagelli (arr.), Violin Sonata No. 6: Prelude in E major (Boston Symphony/Koussevitzky)

¶ Sousa, 'Stars and Stripes Forever' (Boston Promenade Orchestra/Fiedler)
¶ Schubert, Quintet in C major (opus 163) (Kurt Reher *cello*/Hollywood String Quartet)
¶ 'Maladie d'amour' (Henri Salvador)
¶ Handel, 'Haste Thee Nymph' (Glasgow Orpheus Choir/Roberton)
¶ Sibelius, 'Tapiola' (opus 112) (Amsterdam Concertgebouw/Van Beinum)
¶ Vaughan Williams (arr.), 'All People that on Earth Do Dwell' (from Coronation Service of HM Queen Elizabeth II)
¶ LUXURY: A piano.

13 May 1957
334 Rawicz & Landauer
Piano duettists
¶ Respighi, 'Feste Romane' (Minneapolis Symphony/Dorati)
¶ Elgar, 'Nimrod' (from *Enigma Variations*, opus 36) (NBC Symphony/Toscanini)
¶ Rodgers & Hammerstein, 'I Have Dreamed' (from *The King and I*) (Doreen Duke/Jan Mazurus)
¶ Fauré, 'Pavane' (opus 50) (Detroit Symphony/Paray)
¶ Rachmaninov, Symphony No. 3 in A minor (opus 44) (BBC Symphony/Sargent)
¶ Chopin, Étude in F minor (opus 25, no. 2) (Claudio Arrau *piano*)
¶ Ravel, 'Rhapsodie espagnole' (Orchestre de la Suisse Romande/Ansermet)
¶ 'The Heart of Budapest' (Mantovani and his Orchestra)
¶ LUXURY: (Rawicz) soap; (Landauer) biographies of composers.

20 May 1957
335 Dick Bentley
Comedian and broadcaster
¶ Paganini, Violin Concerto No. 2 in B minor (opus 7) (Yehudi Menuhin/Philharmonia Orchestra/Fistoulari)
¶ 'Waltzing Matilda' (Horrie Dargie and his Rocking Reeds)
¶ 'My Love for You' (Frank Sinatra)

¶ Borodin/Wright & Forrest (arr.), 'And This is My Beloved' (from *Kismet*) (Doretta Morrow)
¶ 'The Ying Tong Song' (The Goons)
¶ Arlen & Harburg, 'Over the Rainbow' (from film *The Wizard of Oz*) (Judy Garland)
¶ 'Romance' (Mantovani and his Orchestra)
¶ 'Mr Wonderful' (Peggy Lee)
¶ LUXURY: A do-it-yourself champagne-making kit.

27 May 1957
336 Victor Borge
Entertainer
¶ Mozart, Symphony No. 40 in G minor (K. 550) (RPO/Beecham)
¶ Beethoven, Violin Concerto in D major (opus 61) (Jascha Heifetz/NBC Symphony/Toscanini)
¶ Mendelssohn, *A Midsummer Night's Dream* (scherzo) (Benno Moiseiwitsch *piano*)
¶ R. Strauss, 'Ein Heldenleben' (opus 40) (Vienna Philharmonic/Krauss)
¶ Rachmaninov, 'Rhapsody on a Theme of Paganini' (Sergei Rachmaninov *piano*/Philadelphia Orchestra/Stokowski)
¶ Bartók, Sonata for Solo Violin (Ivry Gitlis)
¶ 'The War of the Unknown Warriors' (broadcast speech, 14 July 1940) (Sir Winston Churchill)
¶ Ravel, 'La valse' (Boston Symphony/Munch)
¶ LUXURY: The thought that he is paying no tax or insurance.

3 June 1957
337 Alec Robertson
Music critic and broadcaster
¶ Gluck, 'Dance of the Blessed Spirits' (from *Orfeo ed Euridice*) (NBC Symphony/Toscanini)
¶ Palestrina, 'Kyrie Eleison' (from *Missa Papae Marcelli*) (Netherlands Chamber Choir/de Nobel)
¶ Schubert, 'Das Lied Inn Grünen' (Elisabeth Schumann/Edwin Fischer *piano*)

¶ Elgar, Introduction and Allegro for Strings (opus 47) (Hallé Orchestra/Barbirolli)
¶ Handel/Beecham, *The Faithful Shepherd Suite* (RPO/Beecham)
¶ Mozart, 'Deh! Vieni, non tardar' (from *The Marriage of Figaro*) (Irmgard Seefried)
¶ Mozart, Symphony No. 41 in C major (K. 551) (RIAS Radio Symphony, Berlin/Fricsay)
¶ Bach, Double Violin Concerto in D minor (Yehudi Menuhin/Georges Enesco/Orchestra/Monteux)
¶ LUXURY: A large china cat.
¶ BOOK: An anthology of poetry.

10 June 1957
338 Count Basie
Bandleader
¶ 'I've Got My Love to Keep Me Warm' (Les Brown and his Band of Renown)
¶ 'Hard-Hearted Hannah, the Vamp of Savannah' (Ella Fitzgerald)
¶ 'Honeysuckle Rose' (Fats Waller and his Rhythm)
¶ 'I'm Gettin' Sentimental Over You' (Tommy Dorsey and his Orchestra)
¶ 'Good-bye' (Billy Eckstine/Jack Miller and his Orchestra)
¶ 'Confessin'' (Louis Armstrong and his Orchestra)
¶ 'How High the Moon' (Sarah Vaughan)
¶ 'Warm Valley' (Duke Ellington and his Famous Orchestra)
¶ LUXURY: A picture of his family with a New York background.

17 June 1957
339 Percy Edwards
Bird and animal imitator
¶ 'At Dawning' (Paul Robeson)
¶ Mascagni, *Cavalleria rusticana* (intermezzo) (Philharmonia Orchestra/von Karajan)
¶ Saint-Saëns, 'Softly Awakes My Heart' (from *Samson and Delilah*) (Marion Anderson)
¶ Delius, 'On Hearing the first Cuckoo in Spring' (RPO/Beecham)
¶ 'Song of a Woodlark' (from *Songs of British Birds No. 3: Fields and Hedgerows*)

¶ Gluck, 'Che faro?' (from *Orfeo ed Euridice*) (Kathleen Ferrier/LSO/Sargent)
¶ Vaughan Williams, 'Fantasia on Greensleeves' (Philharmonic Promenade Orchestra/Boult)
¶ 'I Travel the Road' (Denis Noble/Gerald Moore *piano*)
¶ LUXURY: Constable's painting of Willy Lott's cottage.

24 June 1957
340 Mantovani
Orchestra leader
¶ Wieniawski, Violin Concerto No. 2 in D minor (opus 22) (Jascha Heifetz/LPO/Barbirolli)
¶ Coward, 'My Horse Has Cast a Shoe' (from *Pacific 1860*) (Mary Martin/Graham Payn/Mantovani and his Theatre Orchestra)
¶ Verdi, 'O terra addio' (from *Aida*) (Renata Tebaldi/Mario del Monaco/Ebe Stignani/Santa Cecilia Chorus and Orchestra, Rome/Erede)
¶ 'Serenata d'amore' (Rawicz & Landauer *pianos*/Mantovani and his Orchestra)
¶ Beethoven, Symphony No. 5 in C minor (opus 67) (Amsterdam Concertgebouw/Kleiber)
¶ Berlin, 'White Christmas' (from film *Holiday Inn*) (Bing Crosby)
¶ Bach/Mangiagelli, Violin Sonata No. 6: Prelude in E major (Boston Symphony/Koussevitzky)
¶ 'Mary Had a Little Lamb' (André Kostelanetz Orchestra)
¶ LUXURIES: Music manuscript paper, pencils and a rubber – and some indigestion tablets.

1 July 1957
341 Harold Hobson
Theatre critic
¶ Handel, 'Ombra mai fu' (from *Xerxes*) (Enrico Caruso)
¶ T. S. Eliot, *The Cocktail Party* (Act 2, Scene 1) (Irene Worth/Alec Guinness)
¶ 'Fancy Our Meeting' (from *That's a Good Girl*) (Jack Buchanan/Elsie Randolph)
¶ Dumas, *La Dame aux Camelias* (excerpt) (Edwige Feuillère/Louis Seigner)

¶ Beethoven, Sonata No. 29 in B flat (opus 106) (Kurt Appelbaum *piano*)
¶ Rodgers & Hammerstein, 'Oh, What a Beautiful Morning' (from *Oklahoma*) (Howard Keel)
¶ Beethoven, Symphony No. 9 in D minor (opus 125) (Eileen Farrell/Nan Merriman/Jan Peerce/Norman Scott/Robert Shaw Chorale/BBC Symphony/Toscanini)
¶ Mozart, Clarinet Concerto in A (K. 622) (Louis Cahuzac/Danish State Radio Chamber Orchestra/Woldike)
¶ LUXURY: A cricket bat.

8 July 1957
342 Tamara Karsavina
Prima ballerina
¶ Mozart, Serenade in G major (from *Eine Kleine Nachtmusik*, K. 525) (Philharmonia Orchestra/Klemperer)
¶ Berlioz, 'Le spectre de la rose' (from *Nuits d'été*) (Victoria de los Angeles/Boston Symphony/Munch)
¶ Schubert, Quintet in A major (opus 114) (Vienna Konzerthaus Quintet)
¶ Gershwin, 'I Got Plenty of Nuttin'' (from *Porgy and Bess*) (Lawrence Winters)
¶ Stravinsky, 'The Shrovetide Fair' (from *Petrushka*) (Orchestre de la Suisse Romande/Ansermet)
¶ Gluck, 'Che faro senza Euridice' (from *Orfeo ed Euridice*) (Tito Schipa)
¶ Holst, 'Jupiter' (from *The Planets*) (Philharmonic Promenade Orchestra/Boult)
¶ 'Along the St Petersburg Road' (M. Konstantinoff/Don Cossack Choir)
¶ LUXURY: Carved wooden statue of St Florian.

15 July 1957
343 Fred Streeter
Broadcaster on gardening
¶ 'The Holy City' (Walter Midgley/LSO/Weldon)
¶ Bishop, 'Home, Sweet Home' (Adelina Patti)
¶ Ketelbey, 'In a Monastery Garden' (National Symphony/Robinson)

¶ 'Roses of Picardy' (John McCormack)
¶ 'The Broken Melody' (Auguste Van Biene *cello*)
¶ 'Carry Me Back to Green Pastures' (Kentucky Minstrels)
¶ Novello, 'We'll Gather Lilacs' (from *Perchance to Dream*) (Richard Tauber)
¶ 'Sussex by the Sea' (march) (Band of HM Royal Air Force)
¶ LUXURY: A greenhouse for growing orchids.
¶ BOOK: A gardening dictionary.

22 July 1957
344 Blanche Thebom
Operatic mezzo-soprano
¶ Sibelius, 'The Swan of Tuonela' (opus 22, no. 3) (Danish State Radio Symphony/Jensen)
¶ Shakespeare/Walton, 'St Crispin's Day' (from film *Henry V*) (Sir Laurence Olivier/Philharmonia Orchestra/Walton)
¶ Bach, Toccata and Fugue in D minor (Philadelphia Orchestra/Ormandy)
¶ Wagner, *Tristan und Isolde* (Act 1) (Kirsten Flagstad/Philharmonia Orchestra/Furtwängler)
¶ Mozart, 'Prendero quel brunettino' (from *Cosi fan tutte*) (Sena Jurinac/Blanche Thebom/Glyndebourne Festival Orchestra/Busch)
¶ Verdi, 'Nel giardin del bello saracin' (from *Don Carlos*) (Blanche Thebom/LSO/Braithwaite)
¶ Grofé, 'On the Trail' (from *The Grand Canyon Suite*) (André Kostelanetz Orchestra)
¶ J. Strauss, 'Adele's Laughing Song' (from *Die Fledermaus*) (Florence Foster Jenkins/Cosmo McMoon *piano*)
¶ LUXURY: The jewelled gold statuette of St George and the Dragon, in the Schutzkammar, Munich.

29 July 1957
345 Audrey Russell
BBC commentator
¶ Call of a blackbird (recorded on Bucklebury Common, Berkshire)

¶ 'The Ugly Duckling' (from film *Hans Christian Andersen*) (Danny Kaye)
¶ Vaughan Williams, 'Romance for Harmonica' (Larry Adler/strings/piano/Sargent)
¶ Dylan Thomas, 'Poem in October' (Richard Burton)
¶ Coward, 'Mad Dogs and Englishmen' (from *Words and Music*) (Noël Coward)
¶ Britten, 'Dawn' (from 'Four Sea Interludes', *Peter Grimes*) (Amsterdam Concertgebouw/Van Beinum)
¶ Shakespeare, *Hamlet* (Act 3, Scene 2) (Laurence Olivier/Harcourt Williams)
¶ Chopin, Nocturne No. 8 in D flat major (opus 27, no. 2) (Solomon *piano*)
¶ LUXURY: An astronomical telescope.

5 August 1957
346 Tony Hancock
Comedian
¶ Rossini, *The Thieving Magpie* (overture) (NBC Symphony/Toscanini)
¶ Franck, 'Symphonic Variations' (Walter Gieseking *piano*/LPO/Wood)
¶ Gershwin, 'The Man that Got Away' (from film *A Star is Born*) (Judy Garland)
¶ Sibelius, 'The Swan of Tuonela' (opus 22, no. 3) (Danish State Radio Symphony/Jensen)
¶ 'Migraine Melody' (David Rose and his Orchestra)
¶ 'Gloomy Sunday' (Artie Shaw and his New Orchestra)
¶ 'Soleares' (Pepe de Alzeria *guitar*)
¶ 'Un jour tu verras' (from film *Secrets d'alcove*) (Mouloudji)
¶ LUXURY: A television set.

12 August 1957
347 Owen Berry
Actor and pioneer in the Boy Scout movement
¶ Mendelssohn, 'Hear My Prayer' (Ernest Lough/G. Thalben-Ball *organ*/Choir of Temple Church, London)
¶ 'The Hampshire Regimental March' (National Military Band)

¶ Shakespeare/Arne, 'Where the Bee Sucks' (John Heddle Nash/Ernest Lush *piano*)
¶ 'Alâpana' (from an anthology of Indian classical music) (Mode Kambodhi)
¶ Sibelius, 'Finlandia' (opus 26) (Danish State Radio Symphony/Tuxen)
¶ Chaminade, 'The Little Silver Ring' (Clara Butt)
¶ Vaughan Williams, 'Linden Lea' (Robert Irwin)
¶ 'Boy Scout Pageant' (performed at the Royal Albert Hall)
¶ LUXURY: A photograph of Granny Grove (a character in a television serial).

19 August 1957
348 Leopold Stokowski
Conductor
¶ Bach/Stokowski, 'Nun kommt der Heiden Heiland' (choral prelude) (Philadelphia Orchestra/Stokowski)
¶ Mozart, 'Rex Tremendae' (from *Requiem*, K. 626) (Choir of the Vienna State Opera/Vienna Philharmonic/Jochum)
¶ Beethoven, Symphony No. 7 in A major (opus 92) (Philadelphia Orchestra/Stokowski)
¶ Brahms, Symphony No. 3 in F major (opus 90) (Vienna Philharmonic/Walter)
¶ Debussy, 'Sirènes' (*Nocturne No. 3*) (Philadelphia Orchestra/Stokowski)
¶ Tchaikovsky, 'Solitude' (Philadelphia Orchestra/Stokowski)
¶ 'Are You From Dixie?' (Wilbur de Paris and his New Orleans Jazz)
¶ 'Al compas del corazon' (Miguel Calo y su Orquesta Tipica)
¶ LUXURY: A tape recorder.

26 August 1957
349 David Farrar
Actor
¶ Vaughan Williams, *The Wasps* (overture) (LPO/Boult)
¶ Tchaikovsky, Symphony No. 5 in E minor (Leningrad Philharmonic/Mravinsky)

¶ Dvořák, Symphony No. 8 in G major (New York Philharmonic/Walter)
¶ Rachmaninov, Piano Concerto No. 2 in C minor (opus 18) (Benno Moiseiwitsch/Philharmonia Orchestra/Rignold)
¶ Ravel, 'Le jardin féerique' (from *Ma mère l'oye*) (Orchestre de la Suisse Romande/Ansermet)
¶ Puccini, 'Nessun dorma!' (from *Turandot*) (Beniamino Gigli/Philharmonia Orchestra/Robinson)
¶ Puccini, 'Vissi d'arte' (from *Tosca*) (Joan Hammond/Philharmonia Orchestra/Curiel)
¶ Chaplin, 'Terry's Theme' (from film *Limelight*) (Frank Chacksfield and his Orchestra)
¶ LUXURY: Golf clubs and balls.

2 September 1957
350 Alma Cogan
Vocalist
¶ Coward, 'Mad Dogs and Englishmen' (from *Words and Music*) (Noël Coward)
¶ 'It's Easy to Remember' (from film *Mississippi*) (Frank Sinatra)
¶ Gershwin, 'They Can't Take that Away from Me' (from film *Shall We Dance?*) (Ella Fitzgerald/Louis Armstrong)
¶ Debussy, 'Clair de lune' (from *Suite bergamasque*) (Walter Gieseking *piano*)
¶ 'You, Me and Us' (Alma Cogan)
¶ 'Moonglow' (from film *Picnic*) (Columbia Pictures Orchestra)
¶ Porter, 'Well, Did You Evah?' (from film *High Society*) (Frank Sinatra/Bing Crosby)
¶ Coward, 'Mad About the Boy' (from *Words and Music*) (Mary Kaye Trio)
¶ LUXURIES: Paper, pencils and paints.

9 September 1957
351 Eric Barker
Comedian
¶ Delius, 'On Hearing the First Cuckoo in Spring' (RPO/Beecham)
¶ Philips/Terry, 'Ascendit Deus' (Canterbury Cathedral Choir)

¶ Beethoven, Symphony No. 5 in C minor (opus 67) (Philharmonia Orchestra/Klemperer)
¶ Rodgers & Hart, 'Mountain Greenery' (from film *Words and Music*) (Bing Crosby)
¶ Tchaikovsky, *Swan Lake Ballet Suite* (opus 20) (LPO/Barbirolli)
¶ Rachmaninov, Piano Concerto No. 2 in C minor (opus 18) (Benno Moiseiwitsch/Philharmonia Orchestra/Rignold)
¶ Rodgers & Hammerstein, 'There is Nothin' Like a Dame' (from *South Pacific*) (Danny Kaye)
¶ 'Sunset' (from *Beating Retreat*) (Massed Bands of HM Royal Marines/Memorial Silver Trumpets of the Royal Marines School of Music)
¶ LUXURY: A cricket-bowling machine.

16 September 1957
352 C. A. Lejeune (2nd appearance)
Film critic
¶ Verdi, 'Love Duet' (from *Otello*) (Renata Tebaldi/Mario del Monaco/Santa Cecilia Orchestra, Rome/Erede)
¶ Wagner, *Die Meistersinger* (overture) (Württemberg State Orchestra, Stuttgart/Leitner)
¶ 'Dawn Chorus' (recording on Bucklebury Common, Berkshire)
¶ 'Immer Oder Nimmer' (Dol Dauber Salon-Orchester)
¶ Puccini, *La bohème* (Act 3 quartet) (Victoria de los Angeles/Jussi Björling/Lucine Amara/Robert Merrill/RCA Victor Symphony/Beecham)
¶ 'The Three Kings' (Choir of King's College Chapel, Cambridge/Ord)
¶ Leoncavallo, 'Mattinata' (Beniamino Gigli)
¶ 'Over the Sea to Skye' (Scottish Junior Singers)
¶ LUXURY: Garden soil and rose bushes.

56

23 September 1957
353 Christopher Stone (2nd appearance)
Record presenter
¶ 'Rose, Rose, I Love You' (sung in Chinese) (Miss Hue Lee)
¶ Schumann/Jacob, *Carnaval* (opus 9) (Philharmonia Orchestra/Irving)
¶ Delius, 'La calinda' (from *Koanga*) (LPO/Beecham)
¶ Mozart, Divertimento No. 15 in B flat major (K. 287) (members of the Vienna Octet)
¶ 'Why Must We Keep on Working?' (The Two Leslies)
¶ Auber, *The Bronze Horse* (overture) (Paris Conservatoire Orchestra/Wolff)
¶ 'April in Paris' (from *Walk a Little Faster*) (Glenn Miller and his Orchestra)
¶ 'When Everyone Else Has Passed You By' (Scovell & Wheldon)
¶ LUXURIES: Paper and a fountain pen.

30 September 1957
354 Marius Goring
Actor
¶ Bach, 'Bist du bei mir' (Elisabeth Schumann)
¶ Debussy, 'La Mer' (NBC Symphony/Toscanini)
¶ 'Pack' Die Badehose Ein!' (Die Kleine Cornelia)
¶ 'De l'autre côté de la rue' (Edith Piaf)
¶ Purcell, 'Nymphs and Shepherds' (Manchester schoolchildren's choir/Hallé Orchestra/Harty)
¶ Chopin, 'Barcarolle' (opus 60) (Dinu Lipatti *piano*)
¶ 'I am Wax in Your Hands' (from *Nina*) (Lucie Mannheim)
¶ Handel, 'The Arrival of the Queen of Sheba' (from *Solomon*) (LPO/Beecham)
¶ LUXURY: A piano.

7 October 1957
355 Moura Lympany
Concert pianist
¶ Beethoven, Piano Concerto No. 4 in G major (opus 58) (Artur Schnabel/Philharmonia Orchestra/Dobrowen)

¶ Ravel, *Daphnis and Chloe Suite No. 2* (Boston Symphony/Koussevitzky)
¶ Rachmaninov, 'Rhapsody on a Theme of Paganini' (Sergei Rachmaninov *piano*/Philadelphia Orchestra/Stokowski)
¶ Debussy, 'Voiles' (*Preludes*, Book 1, No. 2) (Walter Gieseking *piano*)
¶ 'La vie en rose' (Jacqueline François)
¶ 'Deep Purple' (Bing Crosby)
¶ Bach/Gounod, 'Ave Maria' (John McCormack)
¶ Coward, 'I'll See You Again' (from *Bitter Sweet*) (Noël Coward)
¶ LUXURY: Flower seeds.
¶ BOOK: Marcel Proust, *À la recherche du temps perdu*

14 October 1957
356 Johnny Dankworth
Composer and bandleader
¶ 'Sepia Panorama' (Duke Ellington and his Famous Orchestra)
¶ 'You Make Me Feel So Young' (Frank Sinatra)
¶ 'Caprice en forme de valse' (Marcel Mule *saxophone*/Marthe Lenom *piano*)
¶ Ravel, 'La valse' (Paris Conservatoire Orchestra/Ansermet)
¶ 'Just Friends' (Charlie Parker)
¶ 'Banbala Dance' (drums, rattles, mixed voices: recorded in the Belgian Congo)
¶ Reizenstein, 'Concerto Popolare' (from Hoffnung Music Festival Concert, 1956) (Yvonne Arnaud *piano*/Morley College Symphony/del Mar)
¶ 'Clarinet à la King' (Benny Goodman and his Orchestra)
¶ LUXURY: A saxophone.
¶ BOOK: Cricket annuals from 1920 onwards.

21 October 1957
357 Commander Ibbett RN
Broadcaster
¶ Mendelssohn, 'The Hebrides Overture' (Philharmonia Orchestra/Malko)
¶ 'Only a Rose' (from *The Vagabond King*) (Bebe Daniels/Sam Browne)

¶ J. Strauss, 'Nun's Chorus' (from *Casanova*) (Luton Girls' Choir)
¶ 'O sole mio' (Beniamino Gigli)
¶ Mascagni, 'Inneggiamo, il signor non e morto!' (from *Cavalleria rusticana*) Zinka Milanov/Robert Shaw Chorale/RCA Victor Symphony/Cellini)
¶ 'Hen Wlad Fy Nhadau' (Rhos Male Voice Choir)
¶ 'Blow the Wind Southerly' (Kathleen Ferrier)
¶ Puccini, 'Humming Chorus' (from *Madam Butterfly*) (Santa Cecilia Chorus and Orchestra, Rome/Erede)
¶ LUXURY: A barrel of beer.

28 October 1957
358 Belinda Lee
Actress
¶ Rodgers & Hammerstein, 'Bali Ha'i' (from *South Pacific*) (Bing Crosby)
¶ Rodgers, 'The Song of the High Seas' (from *Victory at Sea*) (NBC Symphony/Bennett)
¶ Gershwin, 'The Man that Got Away' (from film *A Star is Born*) (Judy Garland)
¶ Rachmaninov, Piano Concerto No. 2 in C minor (opus 18) (Benno Moiseiwitsch/Philharmonia Orchestra/Rignold)
¶ 'Guaglione' (Roberto Murolo *guitar*)
¶ Puccini, 'Un bel di, vedremo' (from *Madam Butterfly*) (Maria Callas/Philharmonia Orchestra/Serafin)
¶ Rachmaninov, 'Rhapsody on a Theme of Paganini' (Sergei Rachmaninov *piano*/Philadelphia Orchestra/Stokowski)
¶ 'Banana Boat Song (Day-o)' (Harry Belafonte)
¶ LUXURY: Language teaching records, for all languages available.

4 November 1957
359 Bransby Williams
Actor and variety star
¶ 'Carry Me Back to Green Pastures' (Kentucky Minstrels)
¶ Liszt, Hungarian Rhapsody No. 2 in C sharp minor (Louis Kentner *piano*)

¶Mussorgsky, 'Song of the Flea' (Feodor Chaliapin)
¶Tchaikovsky, Piano Concerto No. 1 in B flat minor (Solomon/Philharmonia Orchestra/Dobrowen)
¶Mascagni, *Cavallaria rusticana* (intermezzo) (Philharmonia Orchestra/von Karajan)
¶Elgar, 'Pomp and Circumstance' March No. 1 in D major (opus 39) (LPO/Boult)
¶Handel, 'Largo' (from *Xerxes*) (Gladys Ripley)
¶Wagner, 'Ride of the Valkyries' (from *Die Walküre*) (NBC Symphony/Toscanini)
¶LUXURY: Paper and pencils.

11 November 1957
360 Jack Teagarden
Jazz trombonist and vocalist
¶'Basin Street Blues' (Charleston Chasers)
¶'You Rascal, You' (Fats Waller *piano*/Jack Teagarden and his Orchestra)
¶'Georgia on My Mind' (Hoagy Carmichael and his Orchestra)
¶'She's a Great, Great Girl' (Roger Wolfe Kahn and his Orchestra)
¶'Knockin' a Jug' (Louis Armstrong and his Orchestra)
¶'Junk Man' (Jack Teagarden and his Orchestra)
¶'Rockin' Chair' (Louis Armstrong and his All Stars)
¶'The Waiter and the Porter and the Upstairs Maid' (from film *The Birth of the Blues*) (Bing Crosby/Mary Martin/Jack Teagarden and his Orchestra)
¶LUXURIES: A trombone, and materials for making a crystal radio set.

18 November 1957
361 Joan Cross
Operatic soprano
¶Falla, *La vida breve* (Act 2 chorus) (Capilla Clásica Polifónica/Barcelona Opera Orchestra/Halffter)
¶Verdi, *Otello* (Act 1) (NBC Symphony and Chorus/Toscanini)
¶Spontini, 'Tu che invoco' (from *La Vestale*) (Rosa Ponselle)

¶Oscar Wilde, *The Importance of Being Earnest* (Act 1) (John Gielgud/Edith Evans)
¶'All the Things You Are' (from *Very Warm for May*) (Richard Tauber)
¶'No me tires indire' (Amalia Rodriquez/Jaime Santos and Santos Moreira *guitars*)
¶'Mood Indigo' (Duke Ellington and his Orchestra)
¶Britten (arr.), 'The Foggy, Foggy Dew' (Peter Pears/Benjamin Britten *piano*)
¶LUXURY: Playing cards.

25 November 1957
362 James Fisher
Naturalist
¶Granados, 'La maja y el ruisenor' (from *Goyescas*) (Victoria de los Angeles/Philharmonia Orchestra/Fistoulari)
¶Handel, 'O Ruddier than the Cherry' (from *Acis and Galatea*) (Norman Walker)
¶'St Louis Blues' (Louis Armstrong and his Orchestra)
¶Britten, 'Sammy's Bath' (from *The Little Sweep*) (Choir of Alleyn's School/English Opera Group Orchestra/Britten)
¶'Alligator Crawl' (Fats Waller)
¶Prokofiev, Violin Concerto No. 2 in G minor (Leonid Kogan/LSO/Cameron)
¶Beethoven, Quartet No. 13 in B flat major (Hungarian String Quartet)
¶Bach, 'Sanctus' (from *Mass in B minor*) (Vienna Singverein/Berlin Philharmonic/von Karajan)
¶LUXURIES: A pair of field glasses, and modern plumbing.

2 December 1957
363 Moira Shearer
Dancer and actress
¶R. Strauss, 'Don Juan' (Symphonic poem, opus 20) (NBC Symphony/Toscanini)
¶Bach, Brandenburg Concerto No. 5 in D major (Marcel Moyse *flute*/Adolf Busch *violin*/Rudolf Serkin *piano*/Busch Chamber Orchestra)

¶Turina, 'Poema en forma de canciones' (from *Cantares*) (Victoria de los Angeles/Philharmonia Orchestra/Susskind)
¶Stravinsky, *The Firebird Suite* (Orchestre de la Suisse Romande/Ansermet)
¶'Le fiacre' (Jean Sablon)
¶Ravel, *Daphnis and Chloe Suite No. 2* (Philharmonia Orchestra/Cantelli)
¶Beethoven, Symphony No. 8 in F major (NBC Symphony/Toscanini)
¶'The World is Waiting for the Sunrise' (Chris Barber's Jazz Band)
¶LUXURY: Champagne.

9 December 1957
364 Eric Sykes
Comedian and scriptwriter
¶'Bluebell Polka' (Jimmy Shand and his Band)
¶Debussy, 'Clair de lune' (from *Suite bergamasque*) (Walter Gieseking *piano*)
¶Suppé, *Light Cavalry* (overture) (Philharmonia Orchestra/von Karajan)
¶Foster, 'Beautiful Dreamer' (Bing Crosby)
¶'Scotland the Brave' (Pipes and drums of the Dagenham Girl Pipers)
¶Bach, Prelude and Fugue No. 34 in E minor (Rosalyn Tureck *piano*)
¶'Cowpuncher's Cantata' (Max Bygraves)
¶Mussorgsky/Rimsky-Korsakov, 'Night on the Bare Mountain' (Paris Conservatoire Orchestra/Ansermet)
¶LUXURY: A typewriter and paper.

16 December 1957
365 Earl Hines
Jazz pianist
¶'Cherry' (Bobby Hackett *trumpet*/Jackie Gleason and his Orchestra)
¶'Makin' Whoopee' (from *Whoopee*) (Nat 'King' Cole)
¶'You've Changed' (Connie Russell)
¶'April in Paris' (from *Walk a Little Faster*) (Count Basie and his Orchestra)

¶'I Hadn't Anyone Till You' (Bob Manning)
¶'It's All Right with Me' (Lena Horne)
¶'Somehow' (Billy Eckstine/ Earl Hines and his Orchestra)
¶'Love is Just Around the Corner' (Les Elgart and his Orchestra)
¶LUXURY: A piano.

23 December 1957
366 Sir Thomas Beecham, Bart.
Conductor
¶Puccini, 'Sono andati' (from *La Bohème*) (Victoria de los Angeles/Jussi Björling/RCA Victor Symphony/Beecham)
¶Handel/Beecham, 'Hornpipe' (from *The Great Elopement*) (RPO/Beecham)
¶Mozart, 'Dies Bildnis' (from *The Magic Flute*) (Richard Tauber)
¶'À la manière de Wagner' and 'À la manière de Rossini' (from *Pastiches musicaux*) (Bétove)
¶J. Strauss, 'Adele's Laughing Song' (from *Die Fledermaus*) (Florence Foster Jenkins/ Cosmo McMoon *piano*)
¶Balakirev, Symphony No. 1 in C major (RPO/Beecham)
¶'I Love a Lassie' (Sir Harry Lauder)
¶Delius, *A Mass of Life* (Part 1) (London Philharmonic Choir/ RPO/Beecham)
¶LUXURY: Havana cigars.

30 December 1957
367 Lupino Lane
Comedian and actor
¶J. Strauss, 'The Emperor Waltz' (opus 437) (Philharmonia Orchestra/von Karajan)
¶'Love's Old Sweet Song' (Melachrino Strings)
¶'Lambeth Walk' (from *Me and My Girl*) (in Chinese)
¶'The Windsor Melody' (Mantovani and his Concert Orchestra)
¶Schumann/Titherage, 'An Elephant Never Forgets' (from *The Golden Toy*) (Lupino Lane)
¶Elgar 'Pomp and Circumstance' March No. 1 in D major (RPO/Sargent)

¶'Time on My Hands' (from *Smiles*) (André Kostelanetz Orchestra)
¶*Me and My Girl* (selection) (Teddie St Denis/Lupino Lane)
¶LUXURY: A camera.

6 January 1958
368 Wendy Toye
Dancer, actress, choreographer and director
¶'This is My Lucky Day' (from *George White's Scandals of 1925*) (Judy Garland)
¶Bach/Hess, 'Jesu, Joy of Man's Desiring' (Myra Hess *piano*)
¶'I've Got to Fall in Love Again' (Bing Crosby)
¶Beethoven, Symphony No. 7 in A major (opus 92) (NBC Symphony/Toscanini)
¶'Honeysuckle Rose' (Lena Horne)
¶Mahler, 'Abschied' (from *Das Lied von der Erde*) (Kathleen Ferrier/Vienna Philharmonic/ Walter)
¶'Solfeggio (The Do-Re-Mi Song)' (Frank Cordell and his Orchestra)
¶'Makin' Whoopee' (from *Whoopee*) (Frank Sinatra)
¶LUXURY: Framed Ronald Searle drawings.

13 January 1958
369 Lionel Hale
Critic, playwright and broadcaster
¶Vivaldi, 'Summer' (from *The Four Seasons*) (Felix Ayo *violin*/ I Musici)
¶Brahms, 'Botschaft' (opus 47, no. 1) (Kathleen Ferrier/Phyllis Spur *piano*)
¶'She's Funny that Way' (Ted Lewis and his Band)
¶Beethoven, Sonata No. 7 in C minor (opus 30, no. 2) (Yehudi Menuhin *violin*/Louis Kentner *piano*)
¶Berlioz, 'Dies Irae' (from *Grande messe des morts*) (Rochester Oratorio Society/ Hollenbach)
¶Villa-Lobos, Bachianas Brasileiras No. 5 (Bidu Sayao/ eight cellos)

¶Mozart, *Don Giovanni* (Act 2, Scene 5) (Cesare Siepi/ Fernando Corena/Kurt Böhme/ Lisa della Casa/Vienna Philharmonic/Krips)
¶Gilbert & Sullivan, *The Pirates of Penzance* (overture) (Boston Promenade Orchestra/Fiedler)
¶LUXURY: A model theatre.

20 January 1958
370 Max Jaffa
Violinist
¶R. Strauss, 'Don Juan' (symphonic poem, opus 20) (NBC Symphony/Toscanini)
¶Sousa/Horowitz (arr.), *Stars and Stripes Forever* (Vladimir Horowitz *piano*)
¶R. Strauss, 'Frühling' (from *Four Last Songs*) (Lisa della Casa/Vienna Philharmonic/ Böhm)
¶Recording of a rehearsal of Mozart's Symphony No. 36 in C (Columbia Symphony/ Walter)
¶'Paganiniana' (Nathan Milstein *violin*)
¶Gretchaninov, 'Glory to Thee, O Lord' (from *Two-fold Litany*) (Feodor Chaliapin/Choir of the Russian Church of the Metropolitan of Paris/Afonsky)
¶Foster, 'Jeannie with the Light Brown Hair' (Max Jaffa *violin*/ Jack Byfield *piano*/Reginald Kilbey *cello*)
¶Brahms, Violin Concerto in D major (opus 77) (Jascha Heifetz/ CSO/Reiner)
¶LUXURIES: A violin and champagne.

27 January 1958
371 Victor Silvester
Orchestra leader and dance instructor
¶'When I Fall in Love' (Nat 'King' Cole)
¶'At the Woodchopper's Ball' (Woody Herman and his Orchestra)
¶'Because You're Mine' (Mario Lanza)
¶'Moonlight Serenade' (Glenn Miller Orchestra)
¶'You Do Something to Me' (from *Fifty Million Frenchmen*) (Ella Fitzgerald)

¶ Debussy/Stokowski, 'Clair de lune' (from *Suite bergamasque*) (Stokowski Symphony Orchestra)
¶ 'Nancy with the Laughing Face' (Frank Sinatra)
¶ 'They Didn't Believe Me' (from *The Girl from Utah*) (Victor Silvester and his Silver Strings)
¶ LUXURY: A piano.

3 February 1958
372 Anton Walbrook
Actor
¶ Verdi, *La traviata* (prelude) (NBC Symphony/Toscanini)
¶ Villa-Lobos, 'Prelude No. 1 in E minor' (Andrés Segovia *guitar*)
¶ 'Z' Lauterbach hab' mein Strumpf Verlorn' (Maria Ivogün)
¶ Wolf, Italian Serenade in G major (Budapest String Quartet)
¶ Bach, Brandenburg Concerto No. 5 in D major (Rudolf Serkin *piano*/Busch Chamber Orchestra)
¶ Brahms, Violin Concerto in D major (Yehudi Menuhin/ Lucerne Festival Orchestra/ Furtwängler)
¶ Schubert, 'Gute Nacht' (from *Winterreise*) (Heinrich Schlusnus/Sebastian Peschko *piano*)
¶ 'Le fiacre' (Yvette Guilbert)
¶ LUXURIES: An Indo-Chinese Buddha, and some music.

10 February 1958
373 Rex Palmer
Veteran broadcaster
¶ Lehár, *The Count of Luxembourg* (waltz) (Marek Weber and his Orchestra)
¶ Elgar, Violin Concerto in B minor (opus 61) (Yehudi Menuhin/LSO/Elgar)
¶ 'The Garden Where the Praties Grow' (John McCormack)
¶ R. Strauss, *Der Rosenkavalier* (final trio) (Lotte Lehmann/ Elisabeth Schumann/Maria Olszewska/Vienna Philharmonic/Heger)
¶ Beethoven, *Coriolan* (overture, opus 62) (NBC Symphony/Toscanini)

¶ Porter, 'Night and Day' (from *The Gay Divorce*) (Comedy Harmonists)
¶ Puccini, 'E lucevan le stelle' (from *Tosca*) (Jussi Björling)
¶ Adam, *Giselle* (Act 1) (LSO/ Fistoulari)
¶ LUXURY: Alcohol.

17 February 1958
374 Ben Lyon
Comedian
¶ 'Beyond the Blue Horizon' (from film *The Love Parade*) (Melachrino Strings)
¶ 'As Round and Round We Go' (from *Haw Haw*) (Bebe Daniels)
¶ 'Armen's Theme' (Ken Jones and his Music/The Tonettes)
¶ 'Stowaway' (Barbara Lyon)
¶ 'Coronation Scot' (Sidney Torch and his Orchestra)
¶ 'As Time Goes By' (from film *Casablanca*) (Vera Lynn)
¶ 'Fiddle Faddle' (Kingsway Symphony/Camarata)
¶ 'The London I Love' (Maxine Daniels)
¶ LUXURY: A film projector and films of his family.

24 February 1958
375 Margaret Rawlings
Actress
¶ Chopin, Waltz in G flat major (opus 70, no. 1) (Dinu Lipatti *piano*)
¶ Dylan Thomas, *Under Milk Wood* (excerpt) (Richard Burton/Mary Jones/Rachel Thomas)
¶ Handel, Concerto Grosso in G major (opus 6, no. 1) (Boyd Neel String Orchestra)
¶ 'Plaisir d'amour' (Yvonne Printemps)
¶ Coward, 'Mad Dogs and Englishmen' (from *Words and Music*) (Noël Coward)
¶ Beethoven, Symphony No. 7 in A major (opus 92) (Philharmonia Orchestra/ Klemperer)
¶ 'When My Blue Moon Turns to Gold Again' (Elvis Presley)
¶ Stanford, 'Magnificat in G' and 'Second Lesson: St Luke 4:16–32' (King's College Chapel Choir, Cambridge/Ord)
¶ LUXURY: Tapestry-making materials.

3 March 1958
376 Michael Flanders & Donald Swann
Entertainers
¶ (Flanders) 'Frenesi' (Artie Shaw and his New Orchestra)
¶ (Swann) 'Arvanitovlacha' (Greek Folk Dances and Songs Society)
¶ (F) Mussorgsky, 'In the Town of Kazan' (from *Boris Godunov*) (Feodor Chaliapin)
¶ (S) 'Run, Come See Jerusalem' (Gateway Singers)
¶ (F) Howells, 'Puck's Minuet' (Symphony Orchestra/Clifford)
¶ (S) 'Alleluia' and 'Dominus Dixit Ad Me' (from *Midnight Mass*, Mode VIII) (Monks of the Abbey of St Pierre de Solesmes)
¶ (F) 'Singin' in the Rain' (from film) (Gene Kelly)
¶ (S) Scarlatti, Sonata in G major (Longo 487) (George Malcolm *harpsichord*)
¶ LUXURIES: Two pianos.

10 March 1958
377 Beryl Grey
Prima ballerina
¶ Chopin, Étude in C minor (opus 10, no. 12) (Malcuzynski *piano*)
¶ Dvořák, 'O Silver Moon' (from *Rusalka*) (Joan Hammond/Philharmonia Orchestra/Tausky)
¶ Tchaikovsky, *Swan Lake* (Act 2 overture) (Philharmonia Orchestra/Markevich)
¶ Wagner, 'Ein Schwert Verhiess Mir Der Vater' (from *Die Walküre*) (Set Svanholm/ RCA Victor Symphony/ Weissman)
¶ Beethoven, Cello Sonata No. 5 in D major (opus 102, no. 2) (Gregor Piatigorsky/Solomon *piano*)
¶ Rodgers & Hammerstein, 'Some Enchanted Evening' (from *South Pacific*) (Ezio Pinza)
¶ Vivaldi, Concerto in D major for Violin and Strings (Montserrat Cervera/I Musici)

¶ Beethoven, Symphony No. 9 in D minor (Elisabeth Schwarzkopf/Elisabeth Höngen/Hans Hopf/Otto Edelmann/Bayreuth Festival Chorus and Orchestra/Furtwängler)
¶ LUXURIES: A little Swedish wooden horse, and watercolour painting materials.

17 March 1958
378 Frankie Vaughan
Variety singer
¶ 'Narcissus' (Joyce Grenfell/Norman Wisdom)
¶ 'Bells in My Heart' (Joyce Shock)
¶ 'Balmoral Melody' (Murray Campbell *trumpet*/Wally Stott and his Orchestra)
¶ 'Mama' (Beniamino Gigli)
¶ 'Red River Rose' (Wally Stott and his Orchestra)
¶ 'Malaguena' (Los Paraguayos)
¶ 'So Tired' (Russ Morgan and his Orchestra)
¶ 'We are Not Alone' (Frankie Vaughan)
¶ LUXURY: Painting equipment.

24 March 1958
379 Flora Robson
Actress
¶ 'Over the Sea to Skye' (Scottish Junior Singers)
¶ Grieg, 'Homage March' (from *Sigurd Jorsalfar Suite*) (Royal Opera House Orchestra, Covent Garden/Hollingsworth)
¶ Lehár, 'Vilja' (from *The Merry Widow*) (Elisabeth Schwarzkopf/Philharmonia Orchestra and Chorus/Ackermann)
¶ 'Over the Fields' (Soviet Army Ensemble)
¶ 'La Mer' (Charles Trenet)
¶ 'Why Do Fools Fall in Love?' (Frankie Lymon and the Teenagers)
¶ Puccini, 'O mio babbino caro' (from *Gianni Schicchi*) (Joan Hammond/Philharmonia Orchestra/Curiel)
¶ 'Greeting' (from *Vivat Regina Elizabetha*, performed at the Coronation Service of HM Queen Elizabeth II) (Scholars of Westminster School)
¶ LUXURY: Sun-bathing oil.

31 March 1958
380 Geraldo
Bandleader
¶ Beethoven, Symphony No. 9 in D minor (Eileen Farrell/Nan Merriman/Jan Peerce/Norman Scott/Robert Shaw Chorale/NBC Symphony/Toscanini)
¶ 'The Meanderings of Monty' (Part 1) (Milton Hayes)
¶ 'She's Funny that Way' (Ted Lewis and his Band)
¶ 'Oh Gee! Oh Gosh!' (from *Stop Flirting*) (Fred and Adele Astaire)
¶ Kahn, 'Ave Maria' (Enrico Caruso)
¶ 'The Birth of the Blues' (Paul Whiteman and his Orchestra)
¶ 'Poor Papa (He's Got Nothin' at All)' (Whispering Jack Smith)
¶ Mozart, Violin Concerto No. 4 in D major (Fritz Kreisler/LPO/Sargent)
¶ LUXURY: A piano.

7 April 1958
381 Ian Carmichael
Actor
¶ 'Les Girls' (from film) (Gene Kelly)
¶ 'Prisoner of Love' (Bing Crosby)
¶ Gershwin, 'Let's Kiss and Make Up' (from film *Funny Face*) (Fred Astaire)
¶ *The Lilac Domino* (selection) (London Palladium Orchestra/Frere)
¶ 'Moonlight Serenade' (Glenn Miller Orchestra)
¶ 'How Deep is the Ocean' (Kay Thompson)
¶ Tchaikovsky, *Swan Lake* (Act 1 waltz) (Philharmonia Orchestra/von Karajan)
¶ 'I've Got the World on a String' (Frank Sinatra)
¶ LUXURIES: Writing materials and beer.

14 April 1958
382 Cleo Laine
Vocalist
¶ 'A Fine Romance' (from film *Swing Time*) (Ella Fitzgerald/Louis Armstrong/Oscar Peterson Trio)
¶ 'Trick or Treat' (Ray Copeland and Company)

¶ 'Autumn in New York' (from *Thumbs Up*) (Billie Holiday)
¶ 'Sonnet for Hank Cinq' (Duke Ellington and his Orchestra)
¶ Ravel, 'La valse' (Boston Symphony/Munch)
¶ 'I Won't Dance' (from *Roberta*) (Frank Sinatra)
¶ 'Shiny Stockings' (Count Basie and his Orchestra)
¶ Coward, *Private Lives* (Act 1 love scene) (Gertrude Lawrence/Noël Coward)
¶ LUXURY: Perfume.

21 April 1958
383 Billy Mayerl
Pianist and composer of light music
¶ Ravel, *Mother Goose Suite* (Philharmonia Orchestra/Giulini)
¶ 'Vanity Fair' (London Promenade Orchestra/Collins)
¶ Stravinsky, 'Le chant du rossignol' (Cincinnati Symphony/Goossens)
¶ Quilter, 'A Children's Overture' (LPO/Wood)
¶ Ireland, 'Sea Fever' (Frederick Harvey)
¶ 'State Occasion' (Queen's Hall Light Orchestra/Farnon)
¶ Milhaud, 'Sumare' (Jascha Heifetz *violin*/Arpad Sandor *piano*)
¶ J. Strauss, 'Mein Herr Marquis' (from *Die Fledermaus*) (Sari Barabas/Chorus of the Landestheater, Hanover/Hamburg Radio Philharmonic/Schüchter)
¶ LUXURY: A well-stocked bar.

28 April 1958
384 Ruby Miller
Actress
¶ Tchaikovsky, Violin Concerto in D major (Ruggiero Ricci/National Symphony/Sargent)
¶ Debussy, 'Clair de lune' (from *Suite bergamasque*) (Semprini *piano*)
¶ 'Joseph' (from *Madame Pompadour*) (Evelyn Laye/Huntley Wright)
¶ Chaminade, 'Pierrette' (Max Darewski *piano*)

¶Novello, 'The Violin Began to Play' (from *King's Rhapsody*) (Vanessa Lee)
¶Grieg, Piano Concerto in A minor (Winifred Atwell/LPO/Robinson)
¶'A Handful of Stars' (The Continental)
¶*Our Miss Gibbs* (selection) (London Coliseum Orchestra/Burston)
¶LUXURY: Perfume.
¶BOOK: A novel by Somerset Maugham.

5 May 1958
385 Oliver Messel
Stage designer
¶Recording of Noël Coward introducing Marlene Dietrich at the Café de Paris
¶Tchaikovsky, 'Rose Adagio' (from *Sleeping Beauty*) (Minneapolis Symphony/Dorati)
¶'I am in Love' (Ella Fitzgerald)
¶Mozart, 'Zeffiretti lusinghieri' (from *Idomeneo*) (Sena Jurinac/Glyndebourne Festival Chorus and Orchestra/Pritchard)
¶Mozart, 'O voto tremendo' (from *Idomeneo*) (Glyndebourne Festival Chorus and Orchestra/Pritchard)
¶Mozart, 'Porgi amor' (from *The Marriage of Figaro*) (Elisabeth Schwarzkopf/Vienna Philharmonic/von Karajan)
¶Mozart, *The Marriage of Figaro* (finale) (Sena Jurinac/Elisabeth Schwarzkopf/George London/Irmgaard Seefried/Erich Kunz/Vienna Philharmonic/von Karajan)
¶'Bamboo Cage' (from *House of Flowers*) (Dolores Harper/Ada Moore/Enid Mosier)
¶LUXURY: Painting materials.

12 May 1958
386 Roy Plomley (2nd appearance) interviewed by Eamonn Andrews
¶Porter, 'Another Op'nin', Another Show' (from *Kiss Me Kate*) (Annabelle Hill)
¶'Harmonizing' (Fred Elizalde *piano*)

¶J. Strauss, 'Oh, What a Feast, What a Wondrous Night' (from *Die Fledermaus*) (Covent Garden Opera Company/LSO/Barbirolli)
¶'Chou Ying-Tai au tombeau de Liang Chan-Po' (from *Les amours de Liang Chan-Po et Chou Ying-Tai*) (Tou Tsin-Fan/Peking Opera Orchestra)
¶'Thanks for the Memory' (from the film) (Shirley Ross/Bob Hope)
¶Archangelsky, 'Eucharist Canon' (Choir of the Russian Church of the Metropolitan of Paris/Spassky)
¶O. Strauss, *Mariette* (Act 2 finale) (Yvonne Printemps/Sacha Guitry)
¶Beethoven, Piano Concerto No. 5 in E flat major (Rudolf Serkin/Philadelphia Orchestra/Ormandy)
¶LUXURY: A desk with a typewriter and paper.
¶BOOK: *Who's Who in the Theatre*

19 May 1958
387 Agnes Nicholls
Singer
¶Mozart, *The Marriage of Figaro* (overture) (Philharmonia Orchestra/Kubelik)
¶Tchaikovsky, 'Danse des cygnes' (from *Swan Lake*) (LSO/Fistoulari)
¶Puccini, 'Addio di Mimi' (from *La bohème*) (Nellie Melba)
¶Harty, An Irish Symphony (Hallé Orchestra/Harty)
¶Elgar, 'Nimrod' (from *Enigma Variations*) (RPO/Beecham)
¶Wagner, 'Winter Storms Have Waned' (from *Die Walküre*) (Walter Hyde)
¶Wagner, 'Siegfried's Funeral March' (from *Götterdämmerung*) (RPO/Beecham)
¶Handel, 'Hallelujah Chorus' (from *Messiah*) (Huddersfield Choral Society/Royal Liverpool Philharmonic/Sargent)
¶LUXURY: Perfume.
¶BOOK: An illustrated dictionary.

26 May 1958
388 Kay Smart
Circus performer
¶'Ebb Tide' (Frank Chacksfield and his Orchestra)
¶'House of Singing Bamboo' (from film *Pagan Love Song*) (Howard Keel)
¶'Entry of the Gladiators' (Ringling Bros./Barnum & Bailey Circus Band)
¶'Memories are Made of This' (Dave King)
¶'Jailhouse Rock' (Elvis Presley)
¶'Smiley' (from film) (Shirley Abicair)
¶'French Heels' (Debbie Reynolds)
¶'Once-a-Year-Day' (from *The Pajama Game*) (Doris Day/John Raitt)
¶LUXURY: Champagne.

2 June 1958
389 Eric Robinson
Conductor
¶R. Strauss, *Der Rosenkavalier* (Act 3 conclusion) (Sena Jurinac/Hilde Gueden/Vienna Philharmonic/Kleiber)
¶'O sole mio' (Giuseppe di Stefano)
¶Lehar, 'The Merry Widow Waltz' (Eric Robinson and his Music for You Orchestra)
¶Puccini, 'In questa reggia' (from *Turandot*) (Joan Hammond/Philharmonia Orchestra/Robinson)
¶Chopin, Waltz No. 6 in D flat major (opus 64, no. 1) (Malcuzynski *piano*)
¶'Minute Waltz' (Victor Borge)
¶'It Had to be You' (Bing Crosby)
¶Elgar, 'Nimrod' (from *Enigma Variations*) (Royal Albert Hall Orchestra/Elgar)
¶LUXURY: £1 million in pound notes.

9 June 1958
390 Naomi Jacob
Novelist, biographer and actress
¶Verdi, *La traviata* (prelude) (NBC Symphony/Toscanini)
¶Chopin, Prelude in C (opus 28, no. 1) (Alfred Cortot *piano*)

¶ Ponchielli, 'Suicidio' (from *La Gioconda*) (Gina Cigna)
¶ Dvořák, 'Songs My Mother Taught Me' (Fritz Kreisler *violin*/Carl Lamson *piano*)
¶ Puccini, 'Vissi d'arte' (from *Tosca*) (Renata Tebaldi/Santa Cecilia Orchestra, Rome/Erede)
¶ 'Now is the Hour' (Gracie Fields)
¶ Puccini, 'Nessun dorma' (from *Turandot*) (Jussi Björling)
¶ Novello, 'We'll Gather Lilacs' (from *Perchance to Dream*) (Harry Acres and his Orchestra)
¶ LUXURY: An unlimited quantity of very good soap.

16 June 1958
391 Jean Sablon
French romantic singer
¶ 'La rue s'allume' (Michele Arnaud)
¶ 'The Biggest Aspidistra in the World' (Gracie Fields)
¶ Mozart, Sinfonia Concertante in E flat major (K. 297B) (Philharmonia Orchestra/von Karajan)
¶ 'La chanson du chevrier' (from *Fête des vignerons, 1927*) (Mixed Choir of Lutry)
¶ 'Nao tem volucao' (Dorival Caymmi/Orchestra Coro e Arranjos de Luiz Arruda Paes)
¶ Offenbach, *Orpheus in the Underworld* (selection) (Rawicz & Landauer *pianos*)
¶ 'Tamure' (Royal Polynesians)
¶ 'Reine de musette' (Maurice Lagrange *accordion*)
¶ LUXURY: The menu from Maxim's restaurant, Paris.

23 June 1958
392 Derek McCulloch
'Uncle Mac' of *Children's Hour*
¶ Delius, Irmelin (intermezzo) (LPO/Beecham)
¶ Adam, 'Variations on a Nursery Theme' (Gwen Catley)
¶ Cimarosa/Benjamin, Concerto for Oboe and Strings (Leon Goossens/Royal Liverpool Philharmonic/Sargent)
¶ Mendelssohn, 'Oh, for the Wings of a Dove' (Isobel Baillie)

¶ 'Cuckoo Cries' (Obernkirchen Children's Choir)
¶ 'Lovely like the Dawn of Spring' (from film *The Blonde Carmen*) (Marta Eggerth)
¶ Massenet, 'Dream Song' (from *Manon*) (Nicolai Gedda/Philharmonia Orchestra/Galliera)
¶ 'Cornish Rhapsody' (from film *Love Story*) (Harriet Cohen *piano*/LSO/Bath)
¶ LUXURY: An inflatable rubber pillow.
¶ BOOK: An encyclopaedia.

30 June 1958
393 Sarah Vaughan
Vocalist
¶ 'Jumpin' at the Woodside' (Count Basie and his orchestra)
¶ 'Misty' (Erroll Garner Trio)
¶ 'My Personal Possession' (Nat 'King' Cole and the Four Knights)
¶ 'The Champ' (Ted Heath and his Music)
¶ 'I Apologize' (Billy Eckstine)
¶ 'Tonight I Shall Sleep' (Tommy Dorsey/Duke Ellington and his Famous Orchestra)
¶ 'No More' (Billie Holiday)
¶ 'April in Paris' (from *Walk a Little Faster*) (Robert Farnon and his Orchestra)
¶ LUXURY: Golf clubs and balls.

7 July 1958
394 Tito Gobbi
Operatic baritone
¶ Chopin, Polonaise No. 3 in A (opus 40, no. 1) (Stefan Askenase *piano*)
¶ Leoncavallo, 'Testa adorata' (from *La bohème*) (Enrico Caruso)
¶ Verdi, *Otello* (Act 1 introduction) (NBC Symphony/Toscanini)
¶ 'The River of No Return' (from film) (Marilyn Monroe)
¶ 'Stormy Weather' (from *Cotton Club Parade of 1933*) (André Kostelanetz Orchestra)
¶ Verdi, 'Hymn of the Nations' (Italian section) (Jan Peerce/NBC Symphony/Westminster Choir/Toscanini)

¶ Drigo, 'Notturno d'amore' (Beniamino Gigli)
¶ Verdi, 'Tutto nel mondo è bura' (from *Falstaff*) (Tito Gobbi/Luigi Alva/Rolando Panerai/Elisabeth Schwarzkopf/Anna Moffo/Nan Merriman/Fedora Barbieri/Philharmonia Orchestra and Chorus/von Karajan)
¶ LUXURY: A very expensive ivory back-scratcher.

14 July 1958
395 Wilfred Hyde-White
Actor
¶ 'Rock-a-Bye Your Baby' (from film *Jolson Sings Again*) (Judy Garland)
¶ 'And the Angels Sing' (Bing Crosby)
¶ Bizet/Hammerstein, 'You Talk Jus' Like My Man' (from film *Carmen Jones*) (Olga James/LeVern Hutcherson)
¶ 'My Very Good Friend the Milkman' (Fats Waller)
¶ Berlin, 'They Say It's Wonderful' (from *Annie Get Your Gun*) (Ethel Merman/Ray Middleton)
¶ Recording of the finish of the 1949 Derby (commentary by Raymond Glendenning)
¶ 'Shake, Rattle and Roll' (Elvis Presley)
¶ 'Sally' (from film *Sally in Our Alley*) (Gracie Fields)
¶ LUXURIES: A photograph of Charlie Chaplin, and a scale model of a Rolls Royce of the best vintage year.

21 July 1958
396 Jean Pougnet
Violinist
¶ Beethoven, Quartet No. 14 in C sharp minor (opus 131) (Budapest String Quartet)
¶ Beethoven, Violin Concerto in D major (Fritz Kreisler/LPO/Barbirolli)
¶ Sibelius, 'Tapiola' (Symphonic poem) (RPO/Beecham)
¶ Walton, Violin Concerto (Jascha Heifetz/Philharmonia Orchestra/Walton)
¶ Debussy, 'Fêtes' (*Nocturne, No. 2*) (Orchestre de la Suisse Romande/Ansermet)

¶ Mozart, Divertimento in E flat major for string trio (K. 563) (Jean Pougnet *violin*/Frederic Riddle *viola*/Anthony Pini *cello*)
¶ Delius, 'Brigg Fair' (RPO/Beecham)
¶ Brahms, Symphony No. 1 in C minor (Philharmonia Orchestra/Cantelli)
¶ LUXURY: A cask of brandy.
¶ BOOK: Leo Tolstoy, *War and Peace*

28 July 1958
397 Elisabeth Schwarzkopf
Soprano
¶ Brahms, 'Ye Who Now Sorrow' (from *Requiem*) (Elisabeth Schwarzkopf/Singverein der Gesellschaft der Musikfreunde in Wien/Vienna Philharmonic/von Karajan)
¶ J. Strauss, 'Wiener Blut Waltz' (Elisabeth Schwarzkopf/Nicolai Gedda/Philharmonia Orchestra/Ackermann)
¶ Wagner, 'Selig, wie die Sonne' (from *Die Meistersinger*) (Elisabeth Schwarzkopf/Otto Edelmann/Hans Hopf/Gerard Unger/Ira Malaniuk/Bayreuth Festival Orchestra/von Karajan)
¶ Mozart, 'An Chloë' (K. 524) (Elisabeth Schwarzkopf/Walter Gieseking *piano*)
¶ Wolf, 'Elfenlied' (Elisabeth Schwarzkopf/Gerald Moore *piano*)
¶ Verdi, 'Tutto nel mundo è bura' (from *Falstaff*) (Elisabeth Schwarzkopf/Fedora Barbieri/Nan Merriman/Anna Moffo/Tito Gobbi/Rolando Panerai/Luigi Alva/Philharmonia Orchestra and Chorus/von Karajan)
¶ Humperdinck, *Hansel und Gretel* (Act 2, Scene 1) (Elisabeth Schwarzkopf/Elisabeth Grümmer/Philharmonia Orchestra/von Karajan)
¶ R. Strauss, *Der Rosenkavalier* (prelude) (Philharmonia Orchestra/von Karajan)
¶ LUXURY: Sun-tan oil
¶ BOOK: A French cookery book.

4 August 1958
398 Eamonn Andrews
Broadcaster
¶ 'A Foggy Day in London Town' (from film *A Damsel in Distress*) (Ella Fitzgerald)
¶ 'I'm A-Rollin'' (Jackie Miles)
¶ Ibert, 'Valse' (from *Divertissement*) (Hallé Orchestra/Barbirolli)
¶ 'Goodnight Vienna' (from film) (Jack Buchanan)
¶ 'Intermezzo' (from film *Escape to Happiness*) (Albert Sandler Trio)
¶ Puccini, 'One Fine Day' (from *Madam Butterfly*) (Joan Hammond/Philharmonia Orchestra/Curiel)
¶ 'Ebb Tide' (Frank Chacksfield and his Orchestra)
¶ Franck, 'Panis Angelicus' (John McCormack)
¶ LUXURY: A pair of field glasses.
¶ BOOK: The collected short stories of Somerset Maugham.

11 August 1958
399 Elsie & Doris Waters
Entertainers
¶ 'A Gal in Calico' (Bing Crosby)
¶ Schubert, Symphony No. 8 in B minor (NBC Symphony/Toscanini)
¶ Rossini, 'Venez, amis' (from *Le Comte Ory*) (Juan Oncina/Cora Canne-Meijer/Sari Barabas/Monica Sinclair/Glyndebourne Festival Orchestra and Chorus/Gui)
¶ 'Time on My Hands' (Ronnie Hilton)
¶ 'RAF March Past' (Band of HM Grenadier Guards)
¶ Stanford, 'Magnificat in G' (from *Evensong*) (Choir of King's College Chapel, Cambridge/Ord)
¶ Debussy, 'La fille aux cheveux de lin' (*Prelude*, Book 1, No. 8) (Fritz Kreisler *violin*/Carl Lamson *piano*)
¶ Lerner & Loewe, 'With a Little Bit of Luck' (from *My Fair Lady*) (Stanley Holloway)

¶ LUXURIES: (Elsie) a decorative sunshade; (Doris) a garbage disposal unit.
¶ BOOKS: (Elsie) Kenneth Grahame, *Wind in the Willows* or Charlotte Brontë, *Jane Eyre*; (Doris) George and Weedon Grossmith, *Diary of a Nobody*

18 August 1958
400 Dr Ludwig Koch
Ornithologist
¶ Berlioz, 'Hungarian March' (from *The Damnation of Faust*) (Budapest Philharmonic/Dohnanyi)
¶ 'Carnevale di Venezia' (Luisa Tetrazzini)
¶ Bellini, 'A te o cara' (Alessandro Bonci)
¶ Weber, 'Invitation to the Waltz' (Basle Symphony/Weingartner)
¶ Haydn, Minuet No. 6 (from *The Quail*) (Haydn's flute clock)
¶ Kreisler, 'Schön Rosmarin' (Fritz Kreisler *violin*/RCA Victor Symphony/O'Connell)
¶ 'Les rameaux' (Enrico Caruso)
¶ Beethoven, 'Creation Hymn' (Chorus and Orchestra of Berlin State Opera/Schmalstich)
¶ LUXURY: The mechanical singing bird in a cage which once belonged to Hans Christian Andersen.

25 August 1958
401 Hephzibah Menuhin
Concert pianist
¶ Bach, Prelude and Fugue No. 24 in B minor (Rosalyn Tureck *piano*)
¶ Schubert, 'Nacht und Träume' (opus 43, no. 2) (Irmgaard Seefried/Gerald Moore *piano*)
¶ Bloch, Quintet for Piano and Strings (Quintetto Chigiano)
¶ Beethoven, Trio No. 6 in B flat major (opus 97) (Artur Rubinstein *piano*/Jascha Heifetz *violin*/Emanuel Feuermann *cello*)
¶ Mozart, 'Ave, Verum Corpus' (K. 618) (Robert Shaw Chorale)
¶ Brahms, Symphony No. 1 in C minor (opus 68) (Philharmonia Orchestra/Klemperer)

¶ Vivaldi, 'Serenata a tre' (from *La ninfa e il pastore*) (Amilcare Blaffard/Orchestra da Camera di Milano/Loehter)
¶ Bartók, Sonata for Violin Solo (Yehudi Menuhin)
¶ LUXURY: A Chinese language course.

1 September 1958
402 Jack Payne
Bandleader
¶ 'Tangerine' (Les Brown and his Band of Renown)
¶ Rachmaninov, Piano Concerto No. 2 in C minor (opus 18) (Benno Moiseiwitsch/Philharmonia Orchestra/Rignold)
¶ 'You're Blasé (from *Bow Bells*) (Peggy Lee)
¶ 'A Garden in the Rain' (Perry Como)
¶ Tchaikovsky, Symphony No. 4 in F minor (Boston Symphony/Munch)
¶ 'El Alamein Concerto' (Peggy Cochrane *piano*/Jack Payne and his Orchestra)
¶ Ravel, 'Bolero' (Jack Payne and his BBC Dance Orchestra)
¶ Porter, 'Begin the Beguine' (from *Jubilee*) (Artie Shaw and his Orchestra)
¶ LUXURY: A piano.

8 September 1958
403 Percy Kahn
Composer and accompanist
¶ Rachmaninov, Piano Concerto No. 2 in C minor (opus 18) (Sergei Rachmaninov/Philadelphia Orchestra/Stokowski)
¶ Delibes, 'Bell Song' (from *Lakmé*) (Luisa Tetrazzini)
¶ Pente, 'Les farfadets' (Mischa Elman *violin*/Percy Kahn *piano*)
¶ Kahn, 'Ave Maria' (Enrico Caruso/Mischa Elman *violin*/Percy Kahn *piano*)
¶ Mussorgsky, 'Parassia's Aria' (from *Sorochintsy Fair*) (Oda Slobodskaya/Percy Kahn *piano*)
¶ Liszt, 'Gnomenreigen' (Simon Barer *piano*)
¶ R. Strauss, 'Ich trage meine Minne' (opus 32, no. 1) (Richard Tauber/Percy Kahn *piano*)

¶ Rimsky-Korsakov, 'The Nightingale and the Rose' (opus 2 no. 2) (Rosa Ponselle)
¶ LUXURY: A tape recorder.

15 September 1958
404 Dickie Valentine
Vocalist
¶ 'Laura' (from film) (Pete Rugolo and his Orchestra)
¶ 'Pennies from Heaven' (from film) (Guy Mitchell/Glenn Osser and his Orchestra)
¶ Rodgers, 'The Pacific Boils Over' (from *Victory at Sea*) (NBC Symphony/Bennett)
¶ 'Get Happy' (Frank Sinatra)
¶ Holst, 'Mars, the Bringer of War' (from *The Planets*) (Philharmonic Promenade Orchestra/Boult)
¶ 'Lonesome Polecat' (from film *Seven Brides for Seven Brothers*) (Bill Lee and Brothers)
¶ 'I've Got Five Dollars' (from *America's Sweetheart*) (Bing Crosby)
¶ 'King's Cross Climax' (from *Australian Suite*) (Ted Heath and his Music)
¶ LUXURY: A ciné projector and films.

22 September 1958
405 Alicia Markova
Prima ballerina
¶ Lehár, *The Merry Widow* (overture) (Tonhalle Orchestra of Zurich/Lehár)
¶ 'Minha cançao e saudade' (Amalia Rodrigues)
¶ Tchaikovsky, *The Sleeping Beauty Ballet Suite* (Act 2) (Philharmonia Orchestra/von Karajan)
¶ Saint-Saëns, 'Softly Awakes My Heart' (from *Samson and Delilah*) (Marian Anderson)
¶ 'Cherry Pink and Apple Blossom White' (Perez 'Prez' Prado and his Orchestra)
¶ Verdi, 'Ritorna vincitor' (from *Aida*) (Renata Tebaldi, Orchestre de la Suisse Romande/Erede)
¶ Gluck, 'Dance of the Blessed Spirits' (from *Orfeo ed Euridice*) (NBC Symphony/Toscanini)
¶ 'Bo Dodi' (Shoshana Damari)
¶ LUXURY: Perfume.

29 September 1958
406 Hardy Amies
Fashion designer
¶ Wagner, *Die Meistersinger* (overture) (Berlin Philharmonic/von Karajan)
¶ Debussy, 'Letter Song' (from *Pelléas et Mélisande*) (Clare Croiza)
¶ Beethoven, Trio in B flat (opus 97) (Alfred Cortot *piano*/Jacques Thibaud *violin*/Pablo Casals *cello*)
¶ Mozart, 'Il mio tesoro' (from *Don Giovanni*) (Richard Tauber)
¶ Puccini, 'Humming Chorus' (from *Madam Butterfly*) (Santa Cecilia Chorus and Orchestra, Rome/Erede)
¶ Bach, Brandenburg Concerto No. 3 in D major (Boyd Neel Orchestra)
¶ Verdi, 'Ella giammai m'amo' (from *Don Carlos*) (Boris Christoff/Rome Opera House Orchestra/Santini)
¶ R. Strauss, *Der Rosenkavalier* (finale) (Elisabeth Schumann/Maria Olszewska/Vienna Philharmonic/Heger)
¶ LUXURY: A dressing case.

6 October 1958
407 Harry Belafonte
Actor and singer
¶ 'Baby, Won't You Please Come Home?' (Lena Horne)
¶ 'You Forgot Your Gloves' (Jeri Southern)
¶ 'Bluesology' (from *Suite: Fontessa*) (Modern Jazz Quartet)
¶ 'Didn't It Rain?' (Mahalia Jackson)
¶ 'Flamenco' (from *Sevillanas*) (Carmen Amaya and company)
¶ Brahms, Violin Concerto in D major (Jascha Heifetz/LSO/Reiner)
¶ 'Smack Dab in the Middle' (Joe Williams/Count Basie and his Orchestra)
¶ 'Scarlet Ribbons' (Harry Belafonte)
¶ LUXURY: Michelangelo's statue, *David*.

13 October 1958
408 Richard Dimbleby
Radio and television commentator

¶ Wagner, 'Ride of the Valkyries' (from *Die Walküre*) (NBC Symphony/Toscanini)

¶ Bach, Toccata and Fugue in D minor (Albert Schweitzer *organ*)

¶ 'The Little Irish Girl' (Brendan O'Dowda)

¶ Saint-Saëns, 'Le cygne' (from *Carnaval des Animaux*) (Pablo Casals *cello*/Nikolai Mednikoff *piano*)

¶ 'All People that on Earth Do Dwell (The Old Hundredth)' (from Coronation Service HM Queen Elizabeth II)

¶ 'Woodman, Spare that Tree' (Phil Harris and his Orchestra)

¶ Vaughan Williams, 'Galliard of the Sons of the Morning' (from *Job: A Masque for Dancing*) (LPO/Boult)

¶ Walton, 'Crown Imperial: Coronation March 1937' (Philharmonia Orchestra/Walton)

¶ LUXURY: A piano.

20 October 1958
409 Elizabeth Seal
Actress and singer

¶ Porter, 'Just One of Those Things' (from *Jubilee*) (Frank Sinatra)

¶ 'Capricciatiello' (from film *Wild is the Wind*) (Anna Magnani)

¶ Tchaikovsky, *The Sleeping Beauty* (prologue) (Minneapolis Symphony/Dorati)

¶ 'Alegrias' (Carmen Amaya and company)

¶ Dis-donc, dis-donc' (from *Irma La Douce*) (Elizabeth Seal)

¶ 'Bumblebee' (from *Music from Bali*) (Gamelan Orchestra from Pliatan, Indonesia)

¶ Gershwin, 'One Life to Live' (from *Lady in the Dark*) (Gertrude Lawrence)

¶ 'Come Runnin'' (Lena Horne)

¶ LUXURY: Tea.

27 October 1958
410 Benno Moiseiwitsch
Concert pianist

¶ 'This was their finest hour' (speech, 18 June 1940) (Sir Winston Churchill)

¶ Verdi, *Otello* (recording of rehearsal led by Toscanini)

¶ Villa-Lobos, Bachianas Brasileiras No. 5 (Bidu Sayao)

¶ Sousa/Horowitz (arr.), 'Stars and Stripes Forever' (Vladimir Horowitz *piano*)

¶ Chopin, 'Minute Waltz' (from *Caught in the Act*) (Victor Borge)

¶ Mussorgsky, 'Death of Boris' (from *Boris Godunov*) (Feodor Chaliapin)

¶ Rachmaninov, 'Rhapsody on a Theme of Paganini' (Sergei Rachmaninov *piano*/Philadelphia Orchestra/Stokowski)

¶ Mendelssohn, A Midsummer Night's Dream (scherzo) (Benno Moiseiwitsch *piano*)

¶ LUXURY: A roulette table.

3 November 1958
411 Edmundo Ros
Leader of Latin-American band

¶ 'Runnin' Wild' (Benny Goodman Quartet)

¶ 'Without a Word of Warning' (Bing Crosby/Dorsey Brothers Orchestra)

¶ Debussy, 'Clair de lune' (from *Suite bergamasque*) (Columbia Symphony/Rodzinski)

¶ 'Could It Be?' (Edmundo Ros and his Orchestra)

¶ 'Cae, cae' (Carmen Miranda)

¶ 'London Fantasia' (Columbia Light Orchestra/Williams)

¶ 'A Lovely Way to Spend an Evening' (from film *Higher and Higher*) (Frank Sinatra)

¶ 'Cancion Cubana' (from film *Cuban Love Song*) (Edmundo Ros and his Rumba Band)

¶ LUXURY: A film projector and films.

10 November 1958
412 Elena Gerhardt
Lieder singer

¶ Schumann, 'Träumerei' (from *Kinderscenen*, opus 15) (Pablo Casals *cello*/Otto Schulhof *piano*)

¶ 'Clavelitos' (Victoria de los Angeles/Gerald Moore *piano*)

¶ Bach/Hess, 'Jesu, Joy of Man's Desiring' (Myra Hess *piano*)

¶ Verdi, 'Pace, pace mio dio!' (from *La forza del destino*) (Rosa Ponselle)

¶ Beethoven, Violin Concerto in D major (Yehudi Menuhin/Philharmonia Orchestra/Furtwängler)

¶ R. Strauss, 'Mir ist die Ehre Widerfahren' (from *Der Rosenkavalier*) (Elisabeth Schumann/Maria Olszewska/Vienna Philharmonic/Heger)

¶ Meyerbeer, 'O paradiso' (from *L'africaine*) (Enrico Caruso)

¶ Schubert, 'Abschied' (Elena Gerhardt)

¶ LUXURY: Materials for tapestry-making.

¶ BOOK: A philosophical work by Goethe.

17 November 1958
413 June Paul
Athlete

¶ 'Autumn Leaves' (Yves Montand)

¶ 'Cyril's Blues' (Cyril Blake and his Jigs Club Band)

¶ O. Straus, 'La ronde de l'amour' (from film *La ronde*) (Marcel Pagnoul and his Viennese Waltz Orchestra)

¶ Puccini, 'Humming Chorus' (from *Madam Butterfly*) (Santa Cecilia Orchestra and Chorus, Rome/Erede)

¶ 'Pasodoble: Te Quiero (Flamenco)' (Carbonerillo di Jerez/Andres Conde)

¶ Wagner, 'The Ride of the Valkyries' (from *Die Walküre*) (Vienna Philharmonic/Furtwängler)

¶ 'Phoney Folklore' (Peter Ustinov)

¶ 'Stille Nacht, Heilige Nacht' (Elisabeth Schwarzkopf)

¶ LUXURY: A painting by Gauguin.

24 November 1958
414 G. H. Elliott
The 'Chocolate-Coloured
Coon' of the music halls
¶ 'My Heart and I' (from *Old Chelsea*) (Harry Secombe)
¶ 'I've Got a Lovely Bunch of Coconuts' (Billy Cotton and his Band)
¶ Berlin, 'White Christmas' (from film *Holiday Inn*) (Bing Crosby)
¶ 'Silver Bell' (Gertie Gitana)
¶ 'I Belong to Glasgow' (Will Fyffe)
¶ Porter, 'Begin the Beguine' (from *Jubilee*) (Mantovani and his Orchestra)
¶ 'Yours' (Vera Lynn)
¶ 'Keep Right on to the End of the Road' (Sir Harry Lauder)
¶ LUXURIES: The waistcoat that has been his mascot since 1903, and a barrel of beer.

1 December 1958
415 Paul Robeson
Actor and singer
¶ 'Steal Away' (Paul Robeson)
¶ 'After You've Gone' (Bessie Smith)
¶ Bach, 'Liebster Jesu, mein Verlangen' (*Cantata No. 32*) (Magda Laszlo/Vienna State Opera Orchestra/Scherchen)
¶ 'Eriskay Love Lilt' (Father Sydney MacEwan)
¶ 'Tso Fang Tsao' (Modern Drama from China)
¶ Vaughan Williams, 'Fantasia on a Theme by Thomas Tallis' (Boyd Neel Orchestra)
¶ Bartók, 'Mikrokosmos No. 86' (Two major pentachords) (Ivan Engel *piano*)
¶ Mussorgsky, 'I Have Attained the Highest Power' (from *Boris Godunov*) (Feodor Chaliapin)
¶ LUXURY: A carved Benin head.

8 December 1958
416 Stanley Black
Pianist, composer and
orchestra leader
¶ Beethoven, Symphony No. 7 in A major (opus 92) (Philharmonia Orchestra/Klemperer)
¶ Shakespeare/Walton, 'St Crispin's Day Speech' (from film *Henry V*) (Sir Laurence Olivier/Philharmonia Orchestra/Walton)
¶ Bloch, 'Sacred Service' (Marko Rothmuller/LPO/Bloch)
¶ Tchaikovsky, Piano Concerto No. 1 in B flat minor (Vladimir Horowitz/NBC Symphony/Toscanini)
¶ 'Conga Brava' (Duke Ellington and his Famous Orchestra)
¶ Bach, 'Sanctus' (from *Mass in B minor*) (Swabian Choral Society/Pro Musica Orchestra, Stuttgart/Grischkat)
¶ Gershwin, 'A Foggy Day' (from film *A Damsel in Distress*) (Frank Sinatra)
¶ 'Tropical' (Stanley Black *piano*)
¶ LUXURY: A piano.

15 December 1958
417 Aaron Copland
Composer
*¶ Bach, 'Liebster Jesu, wir sind hier' (from Choral Prelude No. 35, BWV 633) (Helmut Walcha *organ*)
¶ Purcell, 'When I am Laid in Earth' (from *Dido and Aeneas*) (Kirsten Flagstad/Mermaid Orchestra/Jones)
¶ Debussy, 'Les collines d'Anacapri' (*Prelude*, Book 1, No. 5) (Walter Gieseking *piano*)
¶ Beethoven, *33 Variations on a Waltz by Diabelli* (no. 24) (Artur Schnabel *piano*)
¶ Berlioz, 'Flight into Egypt' (from *L'enfance du Christ*) (Giorgio Tozzi/Boston Symphony/Munch)
¶ Stravinsky, 'Alleluia' (from *Symphony of Psalms*) (LPO and Choir/Ansermet)
¶ Schönberg, *Five Pieces for Orchestra* (no. 4) (CSO/Kubelik)

¶ Copland, Symphony No. 3 (Minneapolis Symphony/Dorati)
¶ LUXURY: A chess set.

22 December 1958
418 Charlie Drake
Comedian
¶ Chopin/Gretchaninov, 'Grande Valse Brillante' (from *Les Sylphides*) (Philadelphia Orchestra/Ormandy)
¶ 'Let's Do It' (from *Paris*) (Louis Armstrong/Oscar Peterson Trio)
¶ 'Shame! Shame!' (Fats Waller)
¶ 'Tom Thumb's Tune' (from film *Tom Thumb*) (Charlie Drake)
¶ 'Cockney spirit during the Blitz, as expressed by cab-driver Harry Anderson' (from film *The Lion Has Wings*)
¶ 'Sweet Georgia Brown' (Firehouse Five Plus Two)
¶ Berlin, 'White Christmas' (from film *Holiday Inn*) (Bing Crosby)
¶ Wagner, 'Ride of the Valkyries' (from *Die Walküre*) (Vienna Philharmonic/Solti)
¶ LUXURY: A Regency candelabra.
¶ BOOK: An encyclopaedia.

29 December 1958
419 Sandy Macpherson
Theatre organist
*¶ Tchaikovsky, Symphony No. 4 in F minor (Philharmonia Orchestra/von Karajan)
¶ Berlin, 'White Christmas' (from film *Holiday Inn*) (Bing Crosby)
¶ 'The Wedding of the Painted Doll' (From film *Broadway Melody*) (Frank Chacksfield and his Orchestra)
¶ Mendelssohn, *A Midsummer Night's Dream* (scherzo) (Philharmonia Orchestra/Kubelik)
¶ 'Brazil' (George Wright *Wurlitzer organ*)
¶ Archangelsky, 'The Creed' (Feodor Chaliapin/Choir of the Rusian Church of the Metropolitan of Paris/Afonsky)

¶Recording of Sparkie Williams, 1958 champion talking budgerigar
¶Lerner & Loewe, 'Wouldn't It be Loverly' (from *My Fair Lady*) (Julie Andrews)
¶LUXURY: A radio set.

5 January 1959
420 Ronnie Boyer & Jeanne Ravel
Dancers
¶Porter, 'Night and Day' (from *The Gay Divorce*) (Stanley Black and his Orchestra)
¶Bach, Brandenburg Concerto No. 3 in G major (Chamber Ensemble of Schola Cantorum Basiliensis/Wenzinger)
¶Carmichael, 'Stardust' (Larry Adler *harmonica*)
¶Chopin, Piano Concerto No. 2 in F minor (Alfred Cortot/Orchestra/Barbirolli)
¶Glazunov, Violin Concerto in A minor (Jascha Heifetz/LPO/Barbirolli)
¶'Mambo No. 5' (Perez 'Prez' Prado and his Orchestra)
¶'Bubble, Bubble, Bubble (Pink Champagne)' (Frank Cordell and his Orchestra and Chorus)
¶Stravinsky, 'Shrovetide Fair' (from *Petrushka*) (Orchestre de la Suisse Romande/Ansermet)
¶LUXURIES: (Ravel) soap; (Boyer) top hat, white tie and tails.
¶BOOKS: (Ravel) Evelyn Underhill, *Mysticism*; (Boyer) encyclopaedia.

12 January 1959
421 Ronald Searle
Artist, illustrator and creator of St Trinian's school
*¶'It's All Right with Me' (Lena Horne)
¶'De l'autre côté de la rue' (Edith Piaf)
¶Grieg, Piano Concerto in A minor (Artur Rubinstein/RCA Victor Symphony/Wallenstein)
¶'Ding, Dong, Ding' (King's College Chapel Choir/Ord)
¶'Half the Fun' (from *Such Sweet Thunder*) (Duke Ellington and his Orchestra)

¶Gershwin, 'Bess, You is My Woman Now' (from *Porgy and Bess*) (Todd Duncan/Anne Brown)
¶Respighi, *The Fountains of Rome* (NBC Symphony/Toscanini)
¶'On the Sunny Side of the Street' (from *International Revue*) (Louis Armstrong and his All Stars)
¶LUXURY: A car fitted with a telescope.
¶BOOK: Reproductions of Gillray.

19 January 1959
422 John Osborne
Actor and playwright
¶'Tank Town Bump' (Jelly Roll Morton and his Red Hot Peppers)
¶Vaughan Williams, 'The Lark Ascending' (Jean Pougnet *violin*/LPO/Boult)
¶'Crinoline Gown' (from *The Co-optimists*) (Melville Gideon)
¶Mozart, Symphony No. 41 in C (RPO/Beecham)
¶'My Heart is a Violin' (Vicky Autier)
¶Rodgers & Hart, 'My Funny Valentine' (from *Babes in Arms*) (Ella Fitzgerald)
¶Gay, 'If the Heart of a Man' (from *The Beggar's Opera*) (Michael Redgrave)
¶Vaughan Williams, Symphony No. 6 in E minor (LPO/Boult)
¶LUXURY: Perfume.

26 January 1959
423 Frederick Ashton
Choreographer and joint artistic director of the Royal Ballet
¶Tchaikovsky, *The Sleeping Beauty* (Panorama) (Royal Opera House Orchestra, Covent Garden/Lambert)
¶Archangelsky, 'The Creed' (Choir of the Russian Church of the Metropolitan of Paris/Afonsky)
¶Hahn/Guitry, 'Air de la lettre' (from *Mozart*) (Yvonne Printemps)
¶Poulenc, *Les Biches Ballet Suite* (Paris Conservatoire Orchestra/Desormière)

¶'I Can't Give You Anything but Love' (from *Blackbirds of 1928*) (Ethel Waters/Duke Ellington and his Orchestra)
¶Franck, 'Symphonic Variations' (Walter Gieseking *piano*/Philharmonia Orchestra/von Karajan)
¶Prokofiev, *Romeo and Juliet: 2nd Ballet Suite* (Leningrad State Philharmonic/Mravinsky)
¶Ravel, 'La Valse' (Paris Conservatoire Orchestra/Ansermet)
¶LUXURIES: Happy pills and painting materials.

2 February 1959
424 June Thorburn
Actress
¶'Young at Heart' (Frank Sinatra)
¶Rodgers & Hart, 'Slaughter on Tenth Avenue' (from *On Your Toes*) (soundtrack)
¶'Danny Boy' (Harry Belafonte)
¶'I Know Why' (Mel Torme)
¶'It's a Blue World' (from film *Picnic*) (soundtrack)
¶'Try a Little Tenderness' (Frank Sinatra)
¶'A Smile and a Ribbon' (Prudence)
¶'Ev'ry Time We Say Goodbye' (from *Seven Lively Arts*) (Ella Fitzgerald)
¶LUXURY: A mink stole.

9 February 1959
425 Chris Barber
Jazz bandleader
¶'Market Street Stomp' (Missourians)
¶'Right On, Your Time Ain't Long' (Biddleville Quintette)
¶'Hotter than That' (Louis Armstrong and his Hot Five)
¶'Versailles' (from *Suite: Fontessa*) (Modern Jazz Quartet)
¶'Heavenly Sunshine' (Laura Henton)
¶'Chicago Breakdown' (Big Maceo *piano*/Hudson Whittaker *guitar*/Charles R. Sanders *drums*)
¶'Automobile' (Lightnin' Hopkins)

¶'Saratoga Shout' (Luis Russell and his Orchestra)
¶LUXURIES: His sports car and petrol.

16 February 1959
426 John Morris
Writer, journalist, mountaineer and ex-Controller, BBC Third Programme
¶Donizetti, 'Mad Scene' (from *Lucia di Lammermoor*) (Toti dal Monte)
*¶Chopin, Sonata in B flat minor (opus 35) (Sergei Rachmaninov *piano*)
¶Poulenc, *The Carmelites* (Act 1, Scene 3) (Liliane Berton/Paris Opera Orchestra/Devaux)
¶Stravinsky, 'Russian Dance' (from *Petrushka*) (Orchestre de la Suisse Romande/Ansermet)
¶R. Strauss, 'Morgen' (Elisabeth Schumann)
¶Berg, Concerto for Violin and Orchestra (André Gertler/Philharmonia Orchestra/Kletzki)
¶R. Strauss, 'Zerbinetta's Aria' (from *Ariadne auf Naxos*) (Maria Ivogün/Berlin State Opera Orchestra/Blech)
¶Mozart, Serenade No. 11 in E flat major for Wind Instruments (K. 375) (Vienna Philharmonic Wind Group)
¶LUXURIES: Soap and a piano.
¶BOOK: Dostoevsky, *The Brothers Karamazov*

23 February 1959
427 Peter Cushing
Actor
¶Rezniček, *Donna Diana* (overture) (RPO/Mackerras)
¶J. Strauss, 'Im Feuerstrom der Reben' (from *Die Fledermaus*) (Soloists/Vienna Philharmonic/Krauss)
*¶Sibelius, Symphony No. 1 in E minor (RPO/Beecham)
¶'I'm a Vulture for Horticulture' (Jimmy Durante)
¶R. Strauss, *Der Rosenkavalier* (excerpt from Act 2) (Otto Edelmann/Philharmonia Orchestra/von Karajan)
¶'El Limpiabotas' (Cuates Castilla)

¶'I'll Follow My Secret Heart' (from *Conversation Piece*) (Yvonne Printemps/Noël Coward)
¶Berlioz, 'Royal Hunt' and 'Storm' (from *The Trojans*) (RPO/Chorus/Beecham)
¶LUXURIES: Painting materials, and his collection of model soldiers.

2 March 1959
428 Cyril Fletcher
Comedian
¶Clarke, 'Trumpet Voluntary' (Harold Jackson/RPO/Kletzki)
¶Rodgers & Hammerstein, 'Oh, What a Beautiful Morning' (from *Oklahoma*) (Gordon Macrae)
¶Shakespeare, 'When in Disgrace with Fortune' (sonnet) (John Gielgud)
¶Tchaikovsky, 'Romeo and Juliet Fantasy Overture' (Philharmonia Orchestra/Cantelli)
¶'Entry of the Gladiators' (Pietro Tedosco's Circus Orchestra)
¶Beethoven, Sonata in C sharp minor (opus 27, no. 2) (Benno Moiseiwitsch *piano*)
¶'The Chipmunk Song' (David Seville and the Chipmunks)
¶Rachmaninov, 'Rhapsody on a Theme of Paganini' (Rawicz & Landauer *pianos*)
¶LUXURY: A tape recorder.

9 March 1959
429 Judy Grinham
Swimmer, Olympic gold medallist and world record holder
¶'Warsaw Concerto' (from film *Dangerous Moonlight*) (LSO/Mathieson)
¶Rodgers & Hammerstein, 'This Nearly was Mine' (from *South Pacific*) (Giorgio Tozzi)
¶'Just an Old-Fashioned Girl' (Eartha Kitt)
¶Rodgers & Hammerstein, 'You'll Never Walk Alone' (from *Carousel*) (Shirley Jones)
¶'Big Man' (The Four Preps)
¶Puccini, 'O My Beloved Father' (from *Gianni Schicchi*) (Joan Hammond/Philharmonia Orchestra/Curiel)

¶'J'attendrai' (Tino Rossi)
*¶'Ev'ry Time We Say Goodbye' (from *Seven Lively Arts*) (Ella Fitzgerald)
¶LUXURY: A typewriter and paper.
¶BOOK: Leo Tolstoy, *War and Peace*

16 March 1959
430 Ernest Thesiger
Actor
¶Schumann, Piano Quintet in E flat (opus 44) (Isaac Stern *violin*/Alexander Schneider *violin*/Milton Thomas *viola*/Paul Tortelier *cello*/Myra Hess *piano*)
*¶Wagner, 'Selig, wie die Sonne' (from *Die Meistersinger*) (Elisabeth Schumann/Lauritz Melchior/Frederick Schorr/Gladys Parr/Ben Williams/LSO/Barbirolli)
¶Prokofiev, *Romeo and Juliet* (Boston Symphony/Munch)
¶Duparc, 'L'invitation au voyage' (Gérard Souzay/Jacqueline Bonneau *piano*)
¶Elgar, *The Dream of Gerontius* (prelude) (Royal Liverpool Philharmonic/Sargent)
¶Puccini, *Tosca* (Act 3 prelude) (Santa Cecilia Orchestra, Rome/Erede)
¶Puccini, 'O principi, che a lunghe carovane' (from *Turandot*) (Eva Turner)
¶Coates, 'Westminster' (from London Suite) (Philharmonic Promenade Orchestra/Coates)
¶LUXURY: Painting materials.

23 March 1959
431 Malcolm Arnold
Composer
¶'Fight Fiercely, Harvard' (Tom Lehrer)
¶Stravinsky, 'Alleluia' (from *Symphony of Psalms*) (LPO and Choir/Ansermet)
¶'Dippermouth Blues' (Muggsy Spanier and his Ragtime Band)
¶Berlioz, Symphonie Fantastique (Amsterdam Concertgebouw/Van Beinum)
¶Holst, 'This Have I Done for My True Love' (BBC Chorus/Woodgate)

¶Sibelius, Symphony No. 4 in A minor (LPO/Beecham)
¶Purcell, 'Fantasia upon One Note' (Zorian String Quartet, Benjamin Britten *viola*)
¶Elgar, Introduction and Allegro for Strings (Hallé Orchestra/Barbirolli)
¶LUXURY: Green Havana cigars.
¶BOOK: *The Oxford Book of English Verse*

30 March 1959
432 Laurens van der Post
Writer and traveller
¶Handel, *Water Music Suite* (Philharmonic Promenade Orchestra/Boult)
¶'Sarie Marais' (Burger & Van Dyl)
¶Chopin, Nocturne No. 5 in F minor (Peter Katin *piano*)
¶'Sous les toits de Paris' (from film) (Orchestre de Danse Alexander)
¶Britten, 'Storm' (from Four Sea Interludes, *Peter Grimes*) (Amsterdam Concertgebouw/ Van Beinum)
¶Ravel, 'La valse' (Orchestre de la Suisse Romande/Ansermet)
¶Beethoven, Piano Concerto No. 5 in E flat major (opus 73) (Emil Gilels/Philharmonia Orchestra/Ludwig)
¶'The First Nowell' (in Swahili) (St Andrew's College Choir, East Africa)
¶LUXURY: A piano.
¶BOOK: Homer's *Odyssey*

6 April 1959
433 Sylvia Sims
Actress
¶Bach, Italian Concerto in F major (BWV 971) (George Malcolm *harpsichord*)
¶Verdi, 'Si, pel ciel marmoreo giuro' (from *Otello*) (Jussi Björling/Robert Merrill/RCA Victor Symphony/Cellini)
¶Ben Jonson, 'The Triumph' (John Gielgud)
¶'And Her Mother Came Too' (from *A to Z*) (Jack Buchanan)
¶Sibelius, *Karelia Suite* (intermezzo, opus 11) (Danish State Radio Symphony/Jensen)
¶Gershwin, 'Love is Here to Stay' (from film *An American in Paris*) (Gene Kelly)

¶Berlioz, Symphonie Fantastique (French National Radio Orchestra/Beecham)
¶Lalo, 'Vainement, ma bien aimée' (from *Le roi d'Ys*) (Beniamino Gigli)
¶LUXURY: Tapestry-making materials.
¶BOOK: Her husband's handwritten collection of limericks.

14 April 1959
434 Edric Connor
Actor and singer
¶Bizet, 'Au fond du temple saint' (from *Les pêcheurs de perles*) (Jussi Björling/Robert Merrill/RCA Victor Symphony/Cellini)
¶Tchaikovsky, 'Danse des Cygnes' (from *Swan Lake*) (Orchestre de la Suisse Romande/Ansermet)
¶'The Drums of Trinidad' (Trinidad Calypso Singers and Players)
¶Archangelsky, 'The Creed' (Choir of the Russian Church of the Metropolitan of Paris/ Afonsky)
¶Oscar Wilde, *The Importance of Being Earnest* (Act 1) (Edith Evans/John Gielgud)
¶'The Lord is My Shepherd' (Glasgow Orpheus Choir/ Roberton)
¶Dvořák, 'Deep Blue Evening' (from *Summer Song*) (Edric Connor)
¶Handel, *Zadok the Priest* (anthem) (performed at the Coronation Service of HM Queen Elizabeth II)
¶LUXURY: A toothbrush.
¶BOOK: Alan Paton, *Cry, the Beloved Country*

20 April 1959
435 Tyrone Guthrie
Director
¶Bach, Fantasia in C minor (Wanda Landowska *harpsichord*)
¶Dylan Thomas, 'Fern Hill' (Dylan Thomas)
¶'Stop Yer Tickling, Jock' (Sir Harry Lauder)

¶Mozart, 'I Remember' (from *The Marriage of Figaro*) (Joan Cross/Sadler's Wells Orchestra/ Collingwood)
¶Bizet, 'Flower Song' (from *Carmen*) (James Johnston/Royal Opera House Orchestra, Covent Garden/Mudie)
¶James Joyce, 'Anna Livia Plurabelle' (from *Finnegans Wake*) (James Joyce))
¶'The Kiddies Go Carolling' (Harry Hemsley)
*¶Bach, Double Concerto in D minor (Yehudi Menuhin and Gioconda de Vito *violins*/ Philharmonia Orchestra/ Bernard)
¶LUXURY: A cask of rum.
¶BOOK: An anthology of poetry, to include some in French and German.

27 April 1959
436 Marjorie Westbury
Radio actress and singer
¶Ravel, *Daphnis and Chloe Suite No. 2* (NBC Symphony/ Toscanini)
*¶Mozart, *Cosi fan tutte* (Act 1 trio) (Elisabeth Schwarzkopf/ Nan Merriman/Sesto Bruscantini/Philharmonia Orchestra/von Karajan)
¶'Grands boulevards' (Yves Montand)
¶Gershwin, *An American in Paris* (Minneapolis Symphony/ Dorati)
¶Granados, 'La maja dolorosa' (from *Tonadillas*) (Victoria de los Angeles/Gerald Moore *piano*)
¶Fauré, 'Mandoline' (opus 58, no. 1) (Gérard Souzay/ Jacqueline Bonneau *piano*)
¶Schumann, 'Im wunderschönen Monat Mai' (from *Dichterliebe*, opus 48) (Dietrich Fischer-Dieskau/Jörg Demus *piano*)
¶Bach, Double Concerto in D minor (Yehudi Menuhin and Gioconda de Vito *violins*/ Philharmonia Orchestra/ Bernard)
¶LUXURY: A blue-green silk robe, with packets of flower seeds in the pockets.
¶BOOK: Sir J. G. Frazer, *The Golden Bough*

4 May 1959
437 Lord Brabazon of Tara
Pioneer in aviation and motor-racing

¶ Tchaikovsky, *The Nutcracker Suite* (Orchestre de la Suisse Romande/Ansermet)
¶ Chaplin, 'Theme from *Limelight*' (from film) (Melachrino Strings)
¶ 'The Banjo Song' (Paul Robeson)
¶ Puccini, 'Mimi e una civetta' (from *La bohème*) (Jussi Björling/Robert Merrill/Victoria de los Angeles/RCA Victor Symphony/Beecham)
¶ Lehár, 'You are My Heart's Delight' (from *The Land of Smiles*) (Richard Tauber)
*¶ Tchaikovsky, Symphony No. 6 in B minor (Leningrad Philharmonic/Mravinski)
¶ 'Kentucky Babe' (Bing Crosby)
¶ 'Auf Wiederseh'n Sweetheart' (Vera Lynn with soldiers and airmen)
¶ LUXURY: A hot water bottle.
¶ BOOK: MacNeill Dixon, *The Human Situation*

11 May 1959
438 Ray Ellington
Entertainer and jazz musician

¶ 'Fiesta de Jerez' (Carmen Amaya and Company)
¶ 'That's My Girl' (Nat 'King' Cole)
¶ Stravinsky, *Petrushka* (Orchestre de la Suisse Romande/Ansermet)
¶ 'The Banana Boat Song' (Stan Freberg)
¶ Rodgers & Hart, 'Where or When?' (from *Babes in Arms*) (Erroll Garner *piano*)
¶ 'When Your Lover Has Gone' (Jackie Gleason and his Orchestra)
¶ Berlioz, Symphonie Fantastique (Amsterdam Concertgebouw/Van Beinum)
¶ 'From This Moment On' (Ray Ellington Quartet)
¶ LUXURY: A bed with a mosquito net.
¶ BOOK: Charles Dickens, *David Copperfield*

18 May 1959
439 Dame Rebecca West
Writer and journalist

¶ Schumann, *Carnaval* (opus 9) (Myra Hess *piano*)
¶ Schubert, 'The Shepherd on the Rock' (opus 129) (Elisabeth Schumann/Reginald Kell *clarinet*/George Reeves *piano*)
¶ Mozart, Piano Concerto No. 24 in C minor (K. 491) (Clifford Curzon/LSO/Kripps)
¶ Bach, Prelude and Fugue No. 8 in E flat minor (Harriet Cohen *piano*)
¶ Mozart, 'Deh vieni, non tardar' (from *The Marriage of Figaro*) (Audrey Mildmay/Glyndebourne Festival Orchestra/Busch)
¶ 'The Day the Circus Left Town' (Eartha Kitt)
¶ Poulenc, *Les Dialogues des Carmelites* (excerpt) (Liliane Berton/Denise Duval/Paris Opera Orchestra/Dervaux)
¶ Bartók, *Bluebeard's Castle* (excerpt) (Judith Hellwigh/Endre Koreh/National Symphony/Susskind)
¶ LUXURY: The carved stone head of a Chinese philosopher, c. 1300.
¶ BOOK: The plays of Racine.

25 May 1959
440 Alfred Marks
Actor and comedian

¶ 'Maybe It's Because I'm a Londoner' (Bud Flanagan)
¶ Coward, 'Mad Dogs and Englishmen' (from *Words and Music*) (Noël Coward)
*¶ 'La via en rose' (Edith Piaf)
¶ Mendelssohn, 'On Wings of Song' (Isobel Baillie)
¶ 'The Pansy' (Gegè di Giacomo)
¶ Mozart, 'O Isis und Osiris' (from *The Magic Flute*) (Owen Brannigan/RPO/Susskind)
¶ Gershwin, 'Bess, You is My Woman Now' (from *Porgy and Bess*) (Camilla Williams/Lawrence Winters)
¶ Tchaikovsky, *Swan Lake* (opus 20) (Orchestre de la Suisse Romande/Ansermet)
¶ LUXURY: A telephone that does not work.
¶ BOOK: Lewis Carroll, *Alice in Wonderland*

1 June 1959
441 Robert Farnon
Composer, conductor and arranger

¶ Rodgers & Hammerstein, 'Soliloquy' (from *Carousel*) (John Raitt)
¶ 'The Kid from Red Bank' (Count Basie and his Orchestra)
¶ Bartók, Music for Strings, Percussion and Celesta (LPO/Solti)
¶ Ravel, *Daphnis and Chloe Suite No. 2* (French National Radio Orchestra/Cluytens)
¶ Gershwin, 'My Man's Gone Now' (from *Porgy and Bess*) (Anne Brown)
¶ Debussy, 'Iberia' (*Images*, no. 2) (Paris Conservatoire Orchestra/Munch)
¶ Lerner & Loewe, 'Thank Heaven for Little Girls' (from film *Gigi*) (André Previn and his Pals)
¶ Elgar, 'Nimrod' (from *Enigma Variations*) (LPO/Boult)
¶ LUXURY: An astronomical telescope.
¶ BOOK: Isaac Newton, *Optics*

8 June 1959
442 Brian Vesey-Fitzgerald
Naturalist

¶ 'Wi' a Hundred Pipers' (Pipes and Drums of HM 2nd Battalion Scots Guards)
¶ Dawn chorus, recorded at Bucklebury Common, Berkshire
¶ 'Land of My Fathers' (Rhos Male Voice Choir)
¶ 'Leanin'' (Owen Brannigan/Gerald Moore *piano*)
¶ 'Betty Co-ed' (march) (Marenghi Fairground organ)
¶ 'The Foggy, Foggy Dew' (Chief Petty Officer Bill McDermaid)
¶ Shakespeare/Walton, 'St Crispin's Day Speech' (from film *Henry V*) (Sir Laurence Olivier/Philharmonia Orchestra/Walton)
¶ 'O Come, All Ye Faithful' (King's College Chapel Choir/Ord)

¶LUXURY: Tobacco.
¶BOOK: The works of Jane Austen, or Gibbon's *Decline and Fall of the Roman Empire*.

15 June 1959
443 Henry Sherek
Theatrical manager
¶Verdi, 'Bella figlia dell'amore' (from *Rigoletto*) (Enrico Caruso/ Amelita Galli-Curci/Flora Perini/Giuseppe de Luca)
¶Dylan Thomas, *Under Milk Wood* (excerpt) (Richard Burton)
*¶Dylan Thomas, 'Polly Garter's Song' (from *Under Milk Wood*) Diana Maddox/Richard Burton)
¶Bach, Violin Concerto in A minor (Isaac Stern/Philadelphia Orchestra/Ormandy)
¶T.S. Eliot, *The Cocktail Party* (Act 2, Scene 1) (Irene Worth/ Alec Guinness)
¶Rossini, 'Una voce poco fa' (from *The Barber of Seville*) (Lily Pons)
¶'The Ballad of Bethnal Green' (Paddy Roberts)
¶R. Strauss, *Der Rosenkavalier* (Act 2 waltz) (Gustav Neidlinger/ Sieglinde Wagner/Berlin Philharmonic/Schüchter)
¶LUXURY: An Epstein statue that he owns.
¶BOOKS: *Not in Front of the Children* by himself, and Charles Dickens, *Nicholas Nickleby*

22 June 1959
444 Lotte Lehmann
Singer
¶Wagner, *Die Meistersinger* (Act 1 prelude) (NBC Symphony/Toscanini)
¶Mahler, 'Um Mitternacht' (Kathleen Ferrier/Vienna Philharmonic/Walter)
¶R. Strauss, 'Freundliche Vision' (opus 48, no. 1) (Elisabeth Schumann/Ivor Newton *piano*)
¶Wolf, 'Sterb Ich, So Hüllt In Blumen Meine Glieder' (Dietrich Fischer-Dieskau/ Hertha Klust *piano*)
¶Duparc, 'Serenade Florentine' (Gérard Souzay/Jacqueline Bonneau *piano*)
¶Beethoven, Symphony No. 5 in C minor (opus 67) (Vienna Philharmonic/Schalk)

¶Sienczynsky, 'Wien, Du Stadt Meinen Träume' (Lotte Lehmann/Paul Ulanowsky *piano*)
¶R. Strauss, *Der Rosenkavalier* (final trio) (Lotte Lehmann/ Elisabeth Schumann/Maria Olszewska/Vienna Philharmonic/Heger)
¶LUXURY: Painting materials.
¶BOOK: Goethe's *Faust*

29 June 1959
445 Uffa Fox
Yachtsman
¶Handel, 'Hornpipe' (from *Water Music*) (Boyd Neel Orchestra)
*¶Schubert, 'To Music' (Isobel Baillie/Gerald Moore *piano*)
¶Mendelssohn, 'Oh, for the Wings of a Dove' (Ernest Lough/ G. Thalben-Ball *organ*/Choir of Temple Church, London)
¶Massenet, 'Meditation' (from *Thais*) (Philharmonia Orchestra/von Karajan)
¶'Leanin'' (Roy Henderson)
¶Beethoven, Sonata in C minor (opus 13) (Solomon *piano*)
¶'The Last Rose of Summer' (Ada Alsop)
¶Clifford, 'Royal Visitor' (from *The Cowes Suite*) (Royal Marine School of Music)
¶LUXURY: Painting materials.
¶BOOK: An anthology of world poetry.

6 July 1959
446 Hermione Baddeley
Actress
*¶Mozart, *The Marriage of Figaro* (overture) (LPO/Beecham)
¶'June in January' (from *Here is My Heart*) (Bing Crosby)
¶Brahms/Lovett-Smith, 'Cradle Song' (opus 49, no. 4) (Boston Promenade Orchestra/Fiedler)
¶Porter, 'I Get a Kick Out of You' (from *Anything Goes*) (Ella Fitzgerald)
¶Gershwin, 'Rhapsody in Blue' (Leonard Pennario *piano*/ Hollywood Bowl Symphony/ Slatkin)
¶Tchaikovsky, *Swan Lake* (opus 20) (Orchestre de la Suisse Romande/Ansermet)
¶'The Four Winds and the Seven Seas' (Mel Torme)

¶Mozart, Piano Concerto No. 24 in C minor (K. 491) (Walter Gieseking/Philharmonia Orchestra/von Karajan)
¶LUXURY: A painting by Renoir.
¶BOOK: Kenneth Grahame, *The Wind in the Willows*

13 July 1959
447 Harold Abrahams
Athlete
*¶Gilbert & Sullivan, *The Yeomen of the Guard* (overture) (Pro Arte Orchestra/Robinson)
¶Sibelius, 'The Swan of Tuonela' (Philharmonic Promenade Orchestra/Boult)
¶'It's Raining Sunbeams' (from film *100 Men and a Girl*) (Deanna Durbin)
¶Shakespeare, *Hamlet* (Act 3, Scene 4) (John Gielgud, Coral Browne)
¶'An Eriskay Love Lilt' (Lois Marshall)
¶Humperdinck, 'Evening Prayer' (from *Hansel und Gretel*) (Elisabeth Schumann)
¶Dvořák, Symphony No. 9 in E minor (Philadelphia Orchestra/ Stokowski)
¶Lerner & Loewe, 'With a Little Bit of Luck' (from *My Fair Lady*) (Stanley Holloway)
¶LUXURY: A microfilm of *Bell's Life*, a sporting paper published at the beginning of the 18th century.
¶BOOK: Stevenson's book of quotations.

20 July 1959
448 George Melachrino
Conductor, composer and arranger
*¶Delius, 'On Hearing the First Cuckoo in Spring' (RPO/ Beecham)
¶Poulenc/Heifitz, 'Mouvement perpetuel' (from *Cinq pièces*) (Jascha Heifetz *violin*/ Emmanuel Bay *piano*)
¶'Hobo, You Can't Ride This Train' (Louis Armstrong and his Orchestra)
¶Tauber, 'My Heart and I' (from *Old Chelsea*) (Richard Tauber)
¶Beethoven, Symphony No. 7 in A major (NBC Symphony/ Toscanini)

72

¶'Down by the River' (from *Mississippi*) (Bing Crosby)
¶'Molly Brannigan' (John McCormack)
¶Debussy, *Prélude à l'après-midi d'un faune* (Orchestre de la Suisse Romande/Ansermet)
¶LUXURY: Turkish delight.
¶BOOK: Plato.

27 July 1959
449 Ivor Newton
Accompanist
¶Wagner, 'Du Bist Der Lenz' (from *Die Walküre*) (Kirsten Flagstad/Vienna Philharmonic/Knappertsbusch)
¶'Down the Petersky' (Feodor Chaliapin)
¶Mendelssohn, Trio No. 1 in D minor (opus 49) (Artur Rubinstein *piano*/Jascha Heifetz *violin*/Gregor Piatigorsky *cello*)
¶Granados, 'El maja discreto' (from *Tonadillas*) (Conchita Supervia)
*¶Shakespeare, 'The Seven Ages of Man' (from *As You Like It*, Act 2 (John Gielgud)
¶Elgar, Violin Concerto in B minor (opus 61) (Yehudi Menuhin/LSO/Elgar)
¶R. Strauss, 'Da geht er hin' (from *Der Rosenkavalier*) (Lotte Lehmann/Vienna Philharmonic/Heger)
¶Puccini, 'Mimi's Farewell' (from *La bohème*) (Joan Hammond/Hallé Orchestra/Heward)
¶LUXURY: Champagne.
¶BOOK: The London telephone directory.

3 August 1959
450 B. C. Hilliam ('Flotsam')
Entertainer at the piano
¶O'Neill, incidental music to *Mary Rose* (New Light Symphony/O'Neill)
¶'The Typewriter' (Leroy Anderson)
¶Rachmaninov, 'To the Children' (opus 26, no. 7) (John McCormack)
¶'The Headless Horsemen' (Ron Goodwin and his Concert Orchestra)

¶Tchaikovsky, 'None but the Lonely Heart' (opus 6, no. 6) (Lawrence Tibbett)
¶Weber, 'Perpetuum Mobile' (Benno Moiseiwitsch *piano*)
¶'Serenade to a Beautiful Day' (Gladys Ripley)
¶'Changing of the Guard' (Malcolm McEachern)
¶LUXURY: Whisky.
¶BOOK: Leslie Bailey's book on Gilbert and Sullivan.

10 August 1959
451 Norman Fisher
Chairman of *The Brains Trust*
¶Bach, 'Have Mercy, Lord, on Me' (from *St Matthew Passion*) (Kathleen Ferrier/Bach Choir/Jacques Orchestra)
¶Handel, 'Worthy is the Lamb' (from *Messiah*) (LPO/Choir/Boult)
¶Mozart, Clarinet Quintet in A major (Simeon Bellison/Roth String Quartet)
*¶Brahms, Symphony No. 4 in E minor (Philharmonia Orchestra/Klemperer)
¶Chopin, Waltz No. 7 in C sharp minor (opus 64, no. 2) (Dinu Lipatti *piano*)
¶Beethoven, Quartet No. 13 in B flat major (opus 130) (Hungarian String Quartet)
¶J. Strauss, 'Klange der Heimat' (from *Die Fledermaus*) (Elisabeth Schwarzkopf/Philharmonia Orchestra/von Karajan)
¶Bach, Double Concerto in D minor (Yehudi Menuhin and Gioconda de Vito *violins*/Philharmonia Orchestra/Bernard)
¶LUXURIES: Writing materials and a microscope.
¶BOOK: *The Dialogues of Plato*.

17 August 1959
452 Bessie Love
Actress
¶'St Louis Blues' (Bessie Smith)
¶'Cotton Club Stomp' (Duke Ellington and his Orchestra)
¶Shakespeare, 'Wilt Thou be Gone' (from *Romeo and Juliet*, Act 3) (John Gielgud/Pamela Brown)

¶'Tight Like This' (Louis Armstrong and his Orchestra)
¶Delibes, 'Bell Song' (from *Lakmé*) (Amelita Galli-Curci)
¶'Mississippi Mud' (Paul Whiteman's Rhythm Boys)
¶'The Things We Did Last Summer' (Frank Sinatra)
¶Porter, 'Now You Has Jazz' (from film *High Society*) (Bing Crosby/Louis Armstrong)
¶LUXURY: Eau de Cologne.
¶BOOK: Drawings by Fougasse.

24 August 1959
453 Charles Mackerras
Conductor
¶Mozart, *The Marriage of Figaro* (Act 3 sextet) (Soloists/Glyndebourne Festival Orchestra/Gui)
¶Verdi, 'Va pensiero sull'ali dorate' (from *Nabucco*) (Westminster Choir/NBC Symphony/Toscanini)
¶Mozart, Clarinet Concerto in A (K. 622) (Vladimir Riha/Czech Philharmonic/Talich)
¶Bellini, 'Mira O Norma' (from *Norma*) (Maria Callas/Ebe Stignani/La Scala Orchestra/Serafin)
¶Handel, *Music for the Royal Fireworks* (overture) (Wind Ensemble/Mackerras)
¶Luther (attr.), 'Von Himmel Hoch' (Elisabeth Schwarzkopf)
¶Mahler, 'Abschied' (from *Das Lied von der Erde*) (Kathleen Ferrier/Vienna Philharmonic/Walter)
¶Janáček, 'Sinfonietta' (Vienna Philharmonic/Kubelik)
¶LUXURY: Wine.
¶BOOK: A foreign translation of a long English novel.

31 August 1959
454 John Snagge
BBC chief announcer
¶Bach, Suite No. 3 in D (Philharmonia Orchestra/Klemperer)
¶Sousa, 'High School Cadets' (Band of HM Grenadier Guards)
¶'Water Boy' (Paul Robeson)
¶'The Eton Boating Song' (Eton College Musical Society)

¶ Handel, *Zadok the Priest* (anthem) (performed at the Coronation Service of HM Queen Elizabeth II)
¶ Elgar, 'Nimrod' (from *Enigma Variations*) (Royal Albert Hall Orchestra/Elgar)
¶ Rimsky-Korsakov, 'Marriage Feast' (From *Le coq d'or*) (RPO/Beecham)
¶ *ITMA* (excerpt) (Tommy Handley and company)
¶ LUXURY: A painting by Rembrandt.
¶ BOOK: Giovanni Guareschi, *The Little World of Don Camillo*

7 September 1959
455 Sir Leonard Hutton
Captain of the England Cricket team
¶ Gilbert & Sullivan selection (New Mayfair Orchestra)
¶ 'What is a Boy?' (Jan Peerce)
¶ 'Charlie Kunz Piano Medley' (including Rodgers' & Hart's 'Where or When?' from *Babes in Arms* and 'There's a Small Hotel' from *On Your Toes*) (Charlie Kunz)
¶ 'Island in the Sun' (Harry Belafonte)
¶ 'Sarie Marais' (Eve Boswell)
¶ 'Waltzing Matilda' (Peter Dawson)
¶ 'The London I Love' (Maxine Daniels)
¶ 'On Ilkla' Moor 'Baht 'At' (Yorkshire Vocal Quartette)
¶ LUXURY: Golf clubs.
¶ BOOK: A history of cricket.

14 September 1959
456 Douglas Byng
Revue and cabaret artist
¶ Debussy, *Prélude à l'après-midi d'un faune* (Boston Symphony/Munch)
¶ 'What Do I Want with Love' (from *Valmouth*) (Peter Gilmore)
¶ Gershwin, 'Who Cares?' (from *Of Thee I Sing*) (Frank Luther)
¶ 'C. B. Cochran Medley' (Elizabeth Welch/Edward Cooper/Ray Noble and his Orchestra)
¶ 'Memories Part 2' (Alice Delysia)

¶ 'Between the Devil and the Deep Blue Sea' (Cab Calloway and his Orchestra/Chorus)
¶ 'As I Sit Here' (Leslie Hutchinson)
¶ 'God Save the Queen' (*not played*)
¶ LUXURY: Photographs.
¶ BOOK: *The Rubáiyát of Omar Khayyám*

21 September 1959
457 Peggy Cochrane
Pianist, violinist, composer and cabaret artist
¶ 'Have You Met Miss Jones?' (from *I'd Rather be Right*) (Bing Crosby)
¶ Ravel, Piano Concerto in G major (Monique Haas/Hamburg Radio Symphony/Schmidt-Isserstedt)
¶ Ellington, 'Things Ain't What They Used to Be' (Ray Ellington Quartet)
¶ 'Lazy Day' (Patrick Waddington/Peggy Cochrane *piano*)
¶ Rodgers & Hart, 'There's a Small Hotel' (from *On Your Toes*) (Jack Payne and his Orchestra)
*¶ Ravel, 'Daybreak' (from *Daphnis and Chloe Suite No. 2*) (Philadelphia Orchestra/Ormandy)
¶ 'Westminster Waltz' (Wally Stott and his Orchestra)
¶ Rachmaninov, Symphony No. 3 in A minor (Philadelphia Orchestra/Rachmaninov)
¶ LUXURY: A piano.
¶ BOOK: *The Week-end Book*

28 September 1959
458 Frankie Howerd
Comedian
¶ Parry, 'Jerusalem' (Royal Festival Choir/South Australian Symphony/Chinner)
¶ Kalman, 'Love's Sweet Song' (from *The Gypsy Princess*) (Hilde Guede/VSO/Chorus/Loibner)
¶ 'Lilliburlero' (RAF Central Band)
¶ O. Straus, 'Waltz Dream' (André Kostelanetz Orchestra)
¶ 'My Very Good Friend the Milkman' (Fats Waller)

¶ 'Torna a Surriento' (Beniamino Gigli)
¶ 'Song and Dance Man' (Frankie Howerd)
¶ 'Abide with Me' (Bach Choir)
¶ LUXURY: Photographs.
¶ BOOK: Leo Tolstoy, *War and Peace*

5 October 1959
459 Robertson Hare (2nd appearance)
Character actor
¶ Lerner & Loewe, 'I Could Have Danced All Night' (from *My Fair Lady*) (Julie Andrews)
¶ Wagner, 'Ride of the Valkyries' (from *Die Walküre*) (LPO/Rodzinski)
¶ Shakespeare, 'To Be or Not to Be' (from *Hamlet*, Act 3) (Henry Ainley)
¶ 'Lady on the Riviera' (Ted Heath and his Music)
¶ Coward, 'Mad Dogs and Englishmen' (from *Words and Music*) (Noël Coward)
¶ 'Sunset' (Royal Marines Massed Bands)
¶ 'Transatlantic Lullaby' (from *The Gate Revue*) (Turner Layton *piano*)
¶ Elgar, 'Pomp and Circumstance' March No. 1 in D major (LSO/Sargent)
¶ LUXURY: A telescope.
¶ BOOK: His own autobiography, *Yours Indubitably*

12 October 1959
460 Dave Brubeck
Jazz pianist
¶ Bach, Brandenburg Concerto No. 2 in F major (Stuttgart Chamber Orchestra/Munchinger)
¶ 'Cotton Tail' (Duke Ellington and his Famous Orchestra)
¶ 'Tiger Rag' (Art Tatum *piano*)
¶ Debussy, String Quartet in G minor (Loewenguth Quartet)
¶ Milhaud, *La création du monde* (Chamber Orchestra/Bernstein)
¶ 'Didn't It Rain?' (Mahalia Jackson)
¶ Shostakovich, Symphony No. 5 (LPO/Rodzinski)

¶Beethoven, Symphony No. 9 in D minor (Elisabeth Schwarzkopf/Marga Höffgen/Ernst Haefliger/Otto Edelmann/Philharmonia Orchestra and Chorus/von Karajan)
¶LUXURY: A piano.
¶BOOK: An encyclopaedia.

19 October 1959
461 Alfred Hitchcock
Film director
¶Roussel, Symphony No. 3 in G minor (Orchestre de la Suisse Romande/Ansermet)
¶'A Sister to Assist 'Er' (Fred Emney/Sydney Fairbrother)
¶Elgar, 'Cockaigne: Concert Overture' (Hallé Orchestra/Barbirolli)
*¶Wagner, 'Siegfried's Horn Call' (from *Siegfried*) (Lucien Thévet *French horn*)
¶'The Fact Is' (from *The Bing Boys on Broadway*) (George Robey)
¶Dohnanyi, 'Variations on a Nursery Theme' (Cyril Smith *piano*/Philharmonia Orchestra/Sargent)
¶Schumann, 'Préambule' (from *Carnaval*) (Artur Rubinstein *piano*)
¶Gounod, 'Funeral March of a Marionette' (Boston Symphony/Fiedler)
¶LUXURY: A continental railway timetable.
¶BOOK: Mrs Beeton's *Household Management*

26 October 1959
462 George Thalben-Ball
Organist
¶Rachmaninov, Piano Concerto No. 3 in D minor (Cyril Smith/City of Birmingham Orchestra/Weldon)
¶Bach, Double Concerto in D minor (David & Igor Oistrakh *violins*/Gewandhaus Orchestra, Leipzig/Konwitschny)
¶Mendelssohn, 'I Waited for the Lord' (Choir of Temple Church, London)
¶Elgar, Cello Concerto in E minor (Paul Tortelier/BBC Symphony/Sargent)

¶'Piece for Two Tromboniums' (J. Johnson/Kai Winding/trombone octet)
¶Schubert, Piano Quintet in A major (opus 114) (Clifford Curzon/members of the Vienna Octet)
¶'A Mozart Opera' (from *Caught in the Act*) (Victor Borge)
*¶Vaughan Williams, Sea Symphony (LPO/Choir/Boult)
¶LUXURY: A white rug.
¶BOOK: Jerome K. Jerome, *Three Men in a Boat*

2 November 1959
463 Steve Race
Pianist, composer, journalist and broadcaster
¶Massenet, 'Elegie' (Art Tatum *piano*)
¶Elgar, 'Cockaigne Overture' (Hallé Orchestra/Barbirolli)
¶Gershwin, 'But Not for Me' (from *Girl Crazy*) (Ella Fitzgerald)
¶Falla, 'El amor brujo' (Paris Conservatoire Orchestra/Argenta)
¶'California Suite Part 1' (Mel Torme)
¶Wagner, *Die Meistersinger* (overture) (Berlin Philharmonic/von Karajan)
¶'Sky Symphony' (from film *Around the World in Eighty Days*) (Victor Young Orchestra)
¶'The Twenty-Third Psalm' (Westminster Cathedral Choir)
¶LUXURY: A chess set.
¶BOOK: A. A. Milne, *The House at Pooh Corner*

9 November 1959
464 Sir Arthur Bliss
Composer
¶Bach, 'Credo' (from *Mass in B minor*) (LPO/Coates)
*¶Mozart, 'Ach, ich fuhl's' (from *The Magic Flute*) (Irmgaard Seefried/Vienna Philharmonic/von Karajan)
¶Ravel, 'Pavane pour une infante défunte' (Robert Casadesus *piano*)
¶Stravinsky, 'Dance of the Coachmen' (from *Petrushka*) (Philadelphia Orchestra/Stokowski)

¶Beethoven, String Quartet No. 9 in C major (opus 59, no. 3) (Koeckert Quartet)
¶Dawn chorus, recorded on Bucklebury Common, Berkshire
¶Bliss, Violin Concerto (Alfredo Campoli/LPO/Bliss)
¶Schönberg, Variations for Orchestra (opus 31) (Columbia Symphony/Craft)
¶LUXURY: A telescope.
¶BOOK: A work on astronomy.

16 November 1959
465 Benny Hill
Comedian
¶'Viens danser' (Gilbert Bécaud)
¶'Sur la plage' (Gérard Calvi and his Orchestra)
¶'Aurora' (The Andrews Sisters)
¶'With Every Breath I Take' (Bing Crosby)
*¶'Le gamin d'Paris' (Yves Montand)
¶'Lullaby of the Leaves' (BBC Dance Orchestra/Hall)
¶'Would You?' (Frank Chacksfield and his Orchestra)
¶Vaughan Williams, 'Fantasia on Greensleeves' (Philharmonic Promenade Orchestra/Boult)
¶LUXURY: A film camera.
¶BOOK: A collection of language courses.

23 November 1959
466 Joan Sutherland
Operatic soprano
¶Ponchielli, 'L'amo come il fulgor del creato' (from *La Gioconda*) (Gina Cigna/Cloe Elmo/EIAR Symphony, Turin/Tansini)
¶Bellini, 'Come per me sereno' (from *La Sonnambula*) (Amelita Galli-Curci)
¶Gounod, 'O, d'amor messaggera' (from *Mireille*) (Luisa Tetrazzini)
*¶Bellini, 'Mira, O Norma' (from *Norma*) (Rosa Ponselle/Marion Telva/Metropolitan Opera House Orchestra/Setti)
¶Puccini, 'In questa reggia' (from *Turandot*) (Eva Turner)

¶ Donizetti, 'Mad Scene' (from *Lucia de Lammermoor*) (Joan Sutherland/Paris Conservatoire Orchestra/Santi)
¶ Chapi, 'Carceleras' (from *Las Hijas de Zebedeo*) (Elvira de Hidalgo)
¶ Puccini, 'Mimi's Farewell' (from *La bohème*) (Claudia Muzio)
¶ LUXURY: A bed.
¶ BOOK: *Memoirs of Jenny Lind*, collected by Otto Goldschmidt

30 November 1959
467 Billy Cotton
Bandleader
¶ Coates, 'Dam Busters March' (from film *The Dam Busters*) (Billy Cotton and his Band)
¶ 'Underneath the Arches' (Flanagan & Allen)
¶ 'Snow Coach' (Russ Conway *piano*)
¶ 'Tammy' (Kathie Kay)
¶ Handel, 'Hallelujah Chorus' (from *Messiah*) (Percy Faith and his Orchestra)
¶ 'Who Made the Morning?' (Max Bygraves)
¶ 'I've Got a Lovely Bunch of Coconuts' (Billy Cotton and his Band)
¶ 'In the Wee Small Hours of the Morning' (Frank Sinatra)
¶ LUXURY: A ticket home.
¶ BOOK: Two historical novels bound together.

7 December 1959
468 John Paddy Carstairs
Novelist, painter and film director
¶ Vaughan Williams, 'Fantasia on Greensleeves' (Hallé Orchestra/Barbirolli)
¶ 'La mer' (Charles Trenet)
¶ Grieg, 'Solveig's Song' (from *Peer Gynt*) (LSO/Fjeldstad)
¶ 'One Sweet Letter from You' (Humphrey Lyttelton and his Band)
*¶ Tchaikovsky, *Swan Lake* (Act 2) (Orchestre de la Suisse Romande/Ansermet)
¶ 'I'm Old-Fashioned' (from *You Were Never Lovelier*) (Fred Astaire)

¶ Mendelssohn, *A Midsummer Night's Dream* (scherzo, opus 61, no. 1) (Philharmonia Orchestra/Kubelik)
¶ 'Silent Night, Holy Night' (Hollywood Bowl Symphony/Dragon)
¶ LUXURY: A piano.
¶ BOOK: *Roget's Thesaurus*

14 December 1959
469 Andor Foldes
Concert pianist
¶ Beethoven, Symphony No. 7 in A major (Philharmonia Orchestra/Klemperer)
¶ Mozart, 'Non so piu' (from *The Marriage of Figaro*) (Louise Helletsgruber/Glyndebourne Festival Opera/Busch)
¶ Schubert, Quartet No. 13 in A minor (opus 29) (Budapest String Quartet)
¶ Tchaikovsky, Symphony No. 4 in F minor (Leningrad Philharmonic/Sanderling)
¶ Britten, *Peter Grimes* (prologue) (Owen Brannigan/Peter Pears/Chorus and Orchestra of the Royal Opera House, Covent Garden/Britten)
¶ Bach, 'Erbarme dich' (from *St Matthew Passion*) (Herta Töpper/Bach Orchestra, Munich/Richter)
¶ Bartók, *Bluebeard's Castle* (opening) (Mihály Székely/Klara Palánkay/Budapest Philharmonic/Ferencsik)
¶ Brahms, Symphony No. 1 in C minor (NBC Symphony/Toscanini)
¶ LUXURY: The Dürer engraving, *The Angel Appears to Joachim*.
¶ BOOK: The anthology of English verse, collected by Edith Sitwell.

21 December 1959
470 Eve Boswell
Vocalist
¶ 'Life is Just a Bowl of Cherries' (from *George White's Scandals of 1931*) (The Hi-Lo's)
¶ Gershwin, 'They Can't Take That Away from Me' (from film *Shall We Dance?*) (Frank Sinatra)

¶ Rachmaninov, Piano Concerto No. 2 in C minor (Artur Rubinstein/CSO/Reiner)
¶ 'Cherry Ripe' (Geraldo and the Tip Top Tunes Orchestra)
¶ 'Gone Fishin'' (Bing Crosby/Louis Armstrong)
¶ Tchaikovsky, 'Romeo and Juliet Fantasy Overture' (Philadelphia Orchestra/Ormandy)
¶ 'Moonlight Serenade' (Glenn Miller Orchestra)
¶ Berlin, 'There's No Business Like Show Business' (from film) (Ethel Merman)
¶ LUXURY: A piano.
¶ BOOK: A book on one of the world's philosophies.

28 December 1959
471 Edward Moult
Farmer and broadcaster
¶ Brahms, Symphony No. 2 in D major (Philharmonia Orchestra/Klemperer)
¶ 'Just an Old-Fashioned Girl' (Eartha Kitt)
¶ Mendelssohn, Violin Concerto in E minor (Ruggiero Ricci/LSO/Gamba)
¶ Handel, 'The Trumpet Shall Sound' (from *Messiah*) (James Milligan/Alan Stringer *trumpet*/Royal Liverpool Philharmonic/Sargent)
¶ Sibelius, *Karelia Suite* (march) (Danish State Radio Symphony/Jensen)
¶ 'The Dashing White Sergeant' (Jimmy Shand and his Band)
*¶ Beethoven, Symphony No. 6 in F major (opus 68) (Philharmonia Orchestra/Klemperer)
¶ Vaughan Williams, 'The Lark Ascending' (Jean Pougnet *violin*/LPO/Boult)
¶ LUXURY: Drawing equipment.
¶ BOOK: Charles Dickens, *The Pickwick Papers*

4 January 1960
472 S. P. B. Mais
Writer and journalist
¶ 'Glorious Devon' (Harold Williams and Male Chorus)
¶ 'On Ilkla' Moor 'Baht 'At' (Leslie Sarony)

¶ 'Skye Boat Song' (John McHugh)

¶ 'Sussex by the Sea' (march) (HM RAF Band)

¶ 'D'ye Ken John Peel' (Stuart Robertson)

¶ 'Sea Fever' (Frederick Harvey)

¶ 'Smoke Gets in Your Eyes' (from *Roberta*) (Eartha Kitt)

¶ 'Who Would True Valour See' (Sutton High School Choir)

¶ LUXURY: Writing materials.

¶ BOOK: Homer in the original Greek.

11 January 1960
473 Semprini
Pianist

¶ 'Bugle Call Rag' (Red Nichols and his Five Pennies)

*¶ Schubert, Symphony No. 8 in B minor (Vienna Philharmonic/ Böhm)

¶ 'When I Go to Chile' (Carmen Amaya and Sabicas)

¶ Bach, Passacaglia and Fugue in C minor (Geraint Jones *organ*)

¶ Granados, 'The Maiden and the Nightingale' (Artur Rubinstein *piano*)

¶ 'Yesterdays' (Jo Stafford/Paul Weston and his Orchestra)

¶ Chopin, Sonata No. 3 in B minor (opus 58) (Dinu Lipatti *piano*)

¶ Ravel, *Daphnis and Chloe* (Orchestre de la Suisse Romande/Ansermet)

¶ LUXURY: An astronomical telescope.

¶ BOOK: Sir Arthur Eddington, *The Nature of the Physical World*

18 January 1960
474 Joan Heal
Actress and comedienne

¶ 'Don't Explain' (Billie Holiday)

¶ 'Violins' (Kay Thompson)

¶ Tarrega, 'Tremolo Study' (Andrés Segovia *guitar*)

¶ 'L'accordéoniste' (Edith Piaf)

¶ Porter, 'Begin the Beguine' (from *Jubilee*) (Eddie Heywood and his Orchestra)

¶ Vaughan Williams, 'Fantasia on Greensleeves' (LSO/Sargent)

¶ 'Early Morning' (Negro work song) (Inmates of Mississippi State Penitentiary)

*¶ Ravel, 'Pavane pour une infante défunte' (Philharmonia Orchestra/Cantelli)

¶ LUXURY: Insecticide.

¶ BOOK: The complete works of Oscar Wilde.

25 January 1960
475 Antonia Ridge
Writer and broadcaster

¶ 'Bourrasque' (Dutch barrel organ)

¶ Gounod, 'Jewel Song' (from *Faust*) (Victoria de los Angeles/ Paris Opera Orchestra/ Cluytens)

¶ Vaughan Williams, 'Fantasia on Greensleeves' (Hallé Orchestra/Barbirolli)

¶ 'Ma Normandie' (Reda Caire)

¶ Massenet, 'Elégie' (Hollywood Bowl Symphony/ Dragon)

¶ 'The Happy Wanderer' (Obernkirchen Children's Choir)

¶ Rimsky-Korsakov, 'The Flight of the Bumble Bee' (Hallé Orchestra/Weldon)

*¶ Franck, 'Panis Angelicus' (Brychan Powell)

¶ LUXURY: A spare pair of unbreakable spectacles.

¶ BOOK: Chaucer's *Canterbury Tales*

1 February 1960
476 Barrington Dalby
(2nd appearance)
Sports commentator

¶ Elgar, 'Pomp and Circumstance' March No. 1 in D major (opus 39) (LPO/Boult)

¶ Coward, 'Mad Dogs and Englishmen' (from *Words and Music*) (Noël Coward)

¶ Gounod, 'Serenade (Quand tu chantes)' (Pierre Bernac/ Francis Poulenc *piano*)

¶ Verdi, 'Bella figlia dell'amore' (from *Rigoletto*) (Enrico Caruso/ Amelita Galli-Curci/Flora Perini/Giuseppe da Luca)

¶ Entry into Westminster Abbey and Greeting ('Vivat, Vivat Regina') from Coronation Service of HM Queen Elizabeth II

¶ Saint-Saëns, Piano Concerto No. 2 in G minor (Artur Rubinstein/Symphony of the Air/Wallenstein)

¶ 'The Dashing White Sergeant' (Glasgow Orpheus Choir/ Roberton)

¶ 'New-Fangled Tango' (Lena Horne)

¶ LUXURY: A pair of binoculars.

¶ BOOK: One on tropical birds.

8 February 1960
477 Herbert Lom
Actor

¶ Dvořák, Symphony No. 7 in D minor (Vienna Philharmonic/ Kubelik)

¶ 'A Pretty Girl is Like a Melody' (from *The Great Ziegfeld*) (Tony Martin)

*¶ Shakespeare, 'To Be or Not to Be' (from *Hamlet*, Act 3) (Laurence Olivier)

¶ Shostakovich, Symphony No. 7 (opus 60) (Berlin Philharmonic/Celibidache)

¶ Rodgers & Hammerstein, 'People Will Say We're in Love' (from *Oklahoma*) (Betty Jane Watson)

¶ Rodgers & Hammerstein, 'Something Wonderful' (from *The King and I*) (Muriel Smith)

¶ Stravinsky, 'The Shrovetide Fair' (from *Petrushka*) (Orchestre de la Suisse Romande/Ansermet)

¶ Applause (sound-effects disc)

¶ LUXURY: Modelling clay.

¶ BOOK: Edward Lear's nonsense rhymes.

15 February 1960
478 Léon Goossens
Oboist

¶ Puccini, 'Dawn: Church Bells' (from *Tosca*, Act 3) (La Scala Orchestra/Sabata)

¶ Torroba, 'Nocturno' (Andrés Segovia *guitar*)

*¶ Bach, 'I Call on Thee, O Lord' (choral prelude) (Helmut Walcha *organ*)

¶ Mozart, Oboe Quartet in F major (K. 370) (Léon Goossens/ J. Léner *violin*/S. Roth *viola*/J. Hartman *cello*)

¶ 'Misalliance' (from *At the Drop of a Hat*) (Michael Flanders/ Donald Swann)

¶ Wagner, 'Magic Fire Music' (from *Die Walküre*) (Otto Edelmann/Vienna Philharmonic/Solti)
¶ 'The Crowning' from the Coronation Service of HM Queen Elizabeth II
¶ Handel, 'The Arrival of the Queen of Sheba' (from *Solomon*) (LPO/Beecham)
¶ LUXURY: A camp bed.
¶ BOOK: A nautical almanac.

22 February 1960
479 Sir Arthur Bryant
Historian
¶ Scarlatti, 'Gia il sole dal Gange' (Magda Laszlo/Franz Holetschek *piano*)
¶ Gay, 'O What Pain It is to Part' (from *The Beggar's Opera*) (Audrey Mildmay/Michael Redgrave)
¶ Grainger, 'Mock Morris' (Boyd Neel String Orchestra)
¶ Mozart, 'Crudel, perche finora' (from *The Marriage of Figaro*) (Felicie Hüni-Mihacsek/Willi Domgraf-Fassbänder)
¶ Bach, Brandenburg Concerto No. 6 in B flat major (Hamburger Kammerorchester/Newstone)
¶ 'Pat-a-Cake' (The Singing Dogs)
¶ Elgar, Cello Concerto in E minor (Paul Tortelier/BBC Symphony/Sargent)
*¶ 'Sweet Nightingale' (Alfred Deller/Desmond Dupré *piano*)
¶ LUXURY: A painting by Kneller of a girl in a golden gown.
¶ BOOK: Boswell's *Life of Johnson*

29 February 1960
480 Jack Jackson
Broadcaster
¶ 'He's a Tramp' (from film *Lady and the Tramp*) (Peggy Lee)
¶ 'So Little Time' (Peter Sellers)
*¶ 'In a Mist' (Bix Beiderbecke *piano*)
¶ Delius, 'On Hearing the First Cuckoo in Spring' (RPO/Beecham)
¶ 'Yesterdays' (George Shearing)

¶ Mussorgsky, 'The Gnome' (from *Pictures at an Exhibition*) (NBC Symphony/Toscanini)
¶ 'Tenderly' (Maynard Ferguson and his Orchestra)
¶ Haydn, Symphony No. 94 (from Hoffnung Music Festival concert) (Morley College Symphony/Leonard)
¶ LUXURY: A television set.
¶ BOOK: A book on do-it-yourself boat building.

5 March 1960
481 Marty Wilde
Pop singer
¶ Tchaikovsky, '1812 Overture' (Minneapolis Symphony/Dorati)
¶ 'La Cumparsita' (André Kostelanetz Orchestra)
¶ 'Don't be Cruel' (Elvis Presley)
¶ Tchaikovsky, *Swan Lake* (Act 2) (Orchestre de la Suisse Romande/Ansermet)
¶ 'That's All Right' (Elvis Presley)
¶ 'It's All Right with Me' (Sammy Davis Jnr)
¶ 'La Bamba' (Ritchie Valens)
*¶ 'Let It Be Me' (The Everly Brothers)
¶ LUXURY: A guitar.
¶ BOOK: *Jane's All the World's Aircraft*

7 March 1960
482 HRH Prince Chula-Chakrabongse of Thailand
*¶ Brahms, Symphony No. 4 in E minor (New York Philharmonic/Walter)
¶ Mozart, Quartet in G major (K. 387) (Amadeus String Quartet)
¶ 'And Her Mother Came Too' (from *A to Z*) (Jack Buchanan)
¶ Coward, *Private Lives* (Act 1 love scene) (Gertrude Lawrence/Noël Coward)
¶ Porter, 'Night and Day' (from *The Gay Divorce*) (André Kostelanetz Orchestra)
¶ Rodgers & Hammerstein, 'Some Enchanted Evening' (from *South Pacific*) (Wilbur Evans)

¶ Lehár, 'Vilja' (from *The Merry Widow*) (June Bronhill/Sadler's Wells Opera Orchestra/Reid)
¶ 'A Thai Wedding Overture' (private disc)
¶ LUXURY: An album of family photographs.
¶ BOOK: *Who's Who*

14 March 1960
483 Russ Conway
Light music composer and pianist
¶ 'Song of the Clyde' (Kenneth McKellar)
¶ 'Far Away' (Gracie Fields)
¶ Khachaturian, 'Sabre Dance' (from *Gayaneh*) (Geoff Love and his Orchestra)
¶ 'Fings Ain't Wot They Used Ter Be' (from show) (Billy Cotton/Rita Williams Singers/Geoff Love and his Orchestra)
¶ Gershwin, 'Summertime' (from *Porgy and Bess*) (Humphrey Lyttelton *trumpet* and his band)
¶ 'Every Street's a Boulevard in Old New York' (from film *Living It Up*) (Dean Martin/Jerry Lewis)
¶ 'The Young Have No Time to Lose' (Eddie Falcon)
¶ Elgar, 'Land of Hope and Glory' (Gracie Fields)
¶ LUXURY: A typewriter and paper.
¶ BOOK: An omnibus edition of C. S. Forrester's *Hornblower* stories.

21 March 1960
484 Michael Somes
Dancer
¶ Berlioz, Symphonie Fantastique (French National Radio Orchestra/Beecham)
¶ Tchaikovsky, 'Pas de deux' (from *The Nutcracker Suite*) (Orchestre de la Suise Romande/Ansermet)
¶ Lambert, 'Bacchanale' (from *Horoscope*) (Philharmonia Orchestra/Lambert)
¶ 'Love Me a Little Today' (from *Home and Beauty*) (Binnie Hale)
¶ Delius, 'Paris' (RPO/Beecham)
¶ Glazunov/Irving, *Birthday Offering* (RPO/Irving)

*¶R. Strauss, 'Beim Schlafengehen' (from *Four Last Songs*) (Lisa della Casa/Vienna Philharmonic/Böhm)
¶Stravinsky, *The Fire Bird* (Orchestre de la Suisse Romande/Ansermet)
¶LUXURY: An astronomical telescope.
¶BOOK: Tamara Karsavina, *Theatre Street*

28 March 1960
485 Sir Adrian Boult
Conductor
*¶Mozart, Symphony No. 36 in C major (recording of a rehearsal) (LSO/Walter)
¶Mozart, Horn Concerto in E flat (K. 447) (Aubrey Brain/BBC Symphony/Boult)
¶Weber, *Der Freischütz* (overture) (LSO/Nikisch)
¶Brahms, 'Der Schmied' (opus 19, no. 4) (Elena Gerhardt/Arthur Nikisch *piano*)
¶Silver Jubilee message to the Empire by HM King George V, 6 May 1935
¶Vaughan Williams, 'O Taste and See' (anthem performed at Coronation Service of HM Queen Elizabeth II
¶Rossini, *La scala di seta* (overture) (BBC Symphony/Toscanini)
¶Vaughan Williams, 'Galliard for the Sons of the Morning' (from *Job: A Masque for Dancing*) (LPO/Boult)
¶LUXURY: A blanket.
¶BOOK: John Bunyan, *Pilgrim's Progress*

4 April 1960
486 Sidney James
Actor
*¶Rossini/Respighi, 'Can-Can' (from *La boutique fantasque*) (Philharmonia Orchestra/Irving)
¶Gershwin, 'I Got Plenty of Nuttin'' (from *Porgy and Bess*) (Sammy Davis Jnr)
¶'Malaguena' (Ted Heath and his Orchestra)
¶Borodin, "Polovtsian Dances' (from *Prince Igor*) (Philharmonia Orchestra/Matacic)

¶Rodgers & Hammerstein, 'The Surrey with the Fringe on Top' (from *Oklahoma*) (Lena Horne)
¶Rimsky-Korsakov, 'The Story of the Kalender Prince' (from *Scheherazade*) (RPO/Beecham)
¶Rodgers & Hammerstein, 'I Enjoy Being a Girl' (from *Flower Drum Song*) (Pat Suzuki)
¶'Sunday Afternoon at Home' (from series *Hancock's Half Hour*) (Tony Hancock/Sidney James/Bill Kerr)
¶LUXURY: A double bed.
¶BOOK: *Encyclopaedia Britannica*

11 April 1960
487 John Freeman
Television interviewer
¶Brahms, Violin Concerto in D major (Nathan Milstein/Pittsburgh Symphony/Steinberg)
¶Gluck, 'What is Life?' (from *Orfeo ed Euridice*) (Kathleen Ferrier/LSO/Sargent)
¶'Brother, Can You Spare a Dime?' (Bing Crosby)
¶Berlioz, *Les francs juges* (overture) (RPO/Beecham)
¶Dylan Thomas, 'And Death Shall Have No Dominion' (Dylan Thomas)
¶Beethoven, Piano Concerto No. 5 in E flat (Wilhelm Kempff/Berlin Philharmonic/van Kempen)
¶'Strange Fruit' (Billie Holiday)
*¶Verdi, 'Agnus Dei' (from *Requiem Mass*) (Herva Nelli/Fedora Barbieri/Robert Shaw Chorale/NBC Symphony/Toscanini)
¶LUXURY: A typewriter.
¶BOOK: *Oxford English Dictionary*

18 April 1960
488 Anne Heywood
Actress
¶Glazunov, 'Summer' (from *The Seasons*) (Paris Conservatoire Orchestra/Wolff)
¶Ravel, 'Daybreak' (from *Daphnis and Chloe*) (Philharmonia Orchestra/Galliera)

¶Sibelius, Violin Concerto in D minor (David Oistrakh/Stockholm Festival Orchestra/Ehrling)
¶Sibelius, Symphony No. 2 in D major (BBC Symphony/Sargent)
¶Delius, 'A Walk to the Paradise Garden' (from *A Village Romeo and Juliet*) (RPO/Beecham)
¶'The Lark in the Clear Air' (Melodi Light Orchestra/Jensen)
*¶'Carina' (Natalino Otto)
¶Vaughan Williams, 'The Lark Ascending' (Jean Pougnet *violin*/LPO/Boult)
¶LUXURY: Painting equipment.
¶BOOK: Leo Tolstoy, *What Then Must We Do?*

25 April 1960
489 Anthony Newley
Actor and singer
¶'Sevillanas' (Carmen Amaya/Alvarado)
¶'Reaping, Reaping was the Little Girl' (E. Osipova)
¶'À la claire fontaine' (Mixed Choir)
¶Rimsky-Korsakov, *Scheherazade* (Vienna State Opera Orchestra/Rossi)
¶'Misionera' (Los Paraguayos)
¶Orff, 'Fortune, Empress of the World' (from *Carmina Burana*) (West German Radio Chorus/Cologne Radio Symphony/Sawallisch)
¶Vaughan Williams, 'Fantasia on a Theme by Thomas Tallis' (Philharmonia Orchestra/Sargent)
¶Tchaikovsky, '1812 Overture' (Philharmonia Orchestra/von Karajan)
¶LUXURY: Writing materials.
¶BOOK: A volume of short stories.

2 May 1960
490 David Langdon
Cartoonist
*¶Puccini, 'Recondita armonia' (from *Tosca*) (Giuseppe di Stefano/Melchiorre Luise/La Scala Orchestra/Sabata)
¶'My Very Good Friend the Milkman' (Fats Waller)

¶ Mozart, 'Bei Männern' (from *The Magic Flute*) (Irmgaard Seefried/Erich Kunz/Vienna Philharmonic/von Karajan)
¶ 'The Way You Look Tonight' (from film *Swing Time*) (Eddie Condon and his Orchestra)
¶ Sibelius, Symphony No. 1 in E minor (RPO/Beecham)
¶ 'Sov'vuni' (Israel Itzhaki)
¶ Bartók, Violin Concerto No. 2 (Yehudi Menuhin/Philharmonia Orchestra/Furtwängler)
¶ Bernstein/Sondheim, 'I Feel Pretty' (from *West Side Story*) (Carol Lawrence/Marilyn Cooper/Carmen Guiterrez/Elizabeth Taylor)
¶ LUXURY: A piano.
¶ BOOK: Charles Dickens' novels.

9 May 1960
491 Shirley Bassey
Singer
¶ 'Charmaine' (Mantovani and his Orchestra)
¶ 'Because of You' (Sammy Davis Jnr)
¶ 'The Chipmunk Song' (David Seville and the Chipmunks)
*¶ 'Lonely Town' (Frank Sinatra)
¶ Debussy, 'Clair de lune' (from *Suite bergamasque*) (Liberace)
¶ 'Life is Just a Bowl of Cherries' (from *George White's Scandals of 1931*) (Judy Garland)
¶ 'We'll Keep a Welcome' (Harry Secombe)
¶ Gershwin, 'A Foggy Day' (from film *Damsel in Distress*) (Shirley Bassey)
¶ LUXURY: Lipstick.
¶ BOOK: Daniel Defoe, *Robinson Crusoe*

16 May 1960
492 Brian Rix
Actor-manager
¶ 'The Whistler and his Dog' (Band of HM Coldstream Guards)
¶ Tchaikovsky/Schmid, 'Andante Cantabile' (from Quartet No. 1 in D major, opus 11) (BBC Symphony/Sargent)
¶ 'Sugar Mixture' (Tommy Watt and his Orchestra)

*¶ Borodin/Wright & Forrest (arr.), 'Baubles, Bangles and Beads' (from *Kismet*) (Frank Sinatra)
¶ 'On a Slow Boat to China' (Sammy Davis Jnr)
¶ 'April in Paris' (from *Walk a Little Faster*) (Count Basie and his Orchestra)
¶ 'Let's Put Out the Lights and Go to Sleep' (Billy May and his Orchestra)
¶ 'The Party's Over' (from *The Bells are Ringing*) (Nat 'King' Cole)
¶ LUXURY: A tape-recorder.
¶ BOOK: The plays of George Bernard Shaw.

23 May 1960
493 Liberace
Pianist
*¶ Rachmaninov, 'Rhapsody on a Theme of Paganini' (Sergei Rachmaninov *piano*/Philadelphia Orchestra/Stokowski)
¶ Tchaikovsky, Violin Concerto in D (Jascha Heifetz/LSO/Reiner)
¶ Rimsky-Korsakov, *Scheherazade* (RPO/Beecham)
¶ 'Hallelujah' (from *Hit the Deck*) (Glenn Miller Orchestra)
¶ Weill, 'September Song' (from *Knickerbocker Holiday*) (Mantovani and his Orchestra)
¶ R. Strauss, 'Death and Transfiguration' (New York Philharmonic/Walter)
¶ Puccini, *La bohème* (Act 4 duet) (Renata Tebaldi/Carlo Bergonzi/Santa Cecilia Orchestra, Rome/Serafin)
¶ 'Lost in the Stars' (from *Lost in the Stars*) (Frank Sinatra)
¶ LUXURY: A piano.
¶ BOOK: Claude Bristol, *The Magic of Believing*

30 May 1960
494 Madame Marie Rambert
Leading figure in ballet
¶ 'The Little Quail' (Mazowsze Choral Ensemble)
¶ Mussorgsky, 'I Have Attained the Highest Power' (from *Boris Godunov*) (Feodor Chaliapin)

¶ Warlock, 'Pavane' (from *Capriol Suite*) (Constant Lambert String Orchestra)
¶ Chausson, 'Poème' (Yehudi Menuhin *violin*/LPO/Boult)
¶ Gluck, 'Che farò' (from *Orfeo ed Euridice*) (Kathleen Ferrier/Southern Philharmonic/Stiedry)
¶ 'Ça c'est Paris' (Mistinguett)
¶ Shakespeare, 'To Be or Not to Be' (from *Hamlet*, Act 3) (Henry Ainley)
*¶ Bach, 'Sanctus' (from *Mass in B minor*) (Chorus and Orchestra of Vienna Singverein/von Karajan)
¶ LUXURY: Writing materials.
¶ BOOK: John Milton's *Paradise Lost*

6 June 1960
495 Dickie Henderson
Comedian
¶ 'Moonlight Serenade' (Glenn Miller Orchestra)
¶ 'The Last Dance' (Frank Sinatra)
¶ 'I Went to Your Wedding' (Spike Jones and his City Slickers)
¶ Rodgers & Hammerstein, 'The Surrey with the Fringe on Top' (from *Oklahoma*) (Howard Keel)
*¶ 'Laura' (from film) (Erroll Garner)
¶ Rodgers & Hammerstein, 'Shall We Dance?' (from *The King and I*) (Deborah Kerr/Yul Brynner)
¶ Lerner & Loewe, 'I'm Glad I'm Not Young Anymore' (from film *Gigi*) (Maurice Chevalier)
¶ Berlin, 'There's No Business Like Show Business' (from film) (Ethel Merman)
¶ LUXURY: Golf clubs and balls.
¶ BOOK: *How to Play Your Best Golf All the Time*

13 June 1960
496 Professor A. C. B. Lovell
Scientist and Director of the Jodrell Bank Experimental Station
¶ Beethoven, Sonata in E major (opus 109) (Artur Schnabel *piano*)
¶ Brahms, Sonata in F minor (opus 5) (Solomon *piano*)

¶ Bach, Toccata and Fugue in D minor (Fernando Germani *organ*)

¶ Brahms, Symphony No. 3 in F (New York Philharmonic/Walter)

¶ Sibelius, Symphony No. 2 in D major (Hallé Orchestra/Barbirolli)

¶ Elgar, 'Sanctus Fortis' (from *The Dream of Gerontius*) (Richard Lewis/Royal Liverpool Philharmonic/Sargent)

¶ Beethoven, Grosse Fugue in B flat (opus 133) (Koeckert Quartet)

¶ Bach, 'Et Incarnatus Est' (from *Mass in B minor*) (Chorus and Orchestra of Vienna Singverein/von Karajan)

¶ LUXURY: A piano that can be converted into an organ.

¶ BOOK: One on musical theory and composition.

20 June 1960
497 Julian Slade
Theatre composer

¶ Rodgers & Hammerstein, 'Oklahoma!' (from *Oklahoma*) (Alfred Drake/New York cast)

¶ Rossini/Respighi, 'Can-Can' (from *La boutique fantasque*) (RPO/Goossens)

¶ 'The Time of My Life' (from *Salad Days*) (Eleanor Drew)

¶ Beethoven, String Quartet No. 15 in A minor (Griller String Quartet)

¶ Mozart, 'Der Vogelfänger bin ich Ja' (from *The Magic Flute*) (Dietrich Fischer-Dieskau/Berlin Radio Symphony/Fricsay)

¶ Wagner, 'Liebestod' (from *Tristan und Isolde*) (Berlin Philharmonic/Furtwängler)

*¶ Handel, 'Art Thou Troubled?' (from *Rodelinda*) (Kathleen Ferrier/LSO/Sargent)

¶ Shakespeare, 'Prospero's Speech' (from *The Tempest*, Act 4) (John Gielgud)

¶ LUXURY: A violin.

¶ BOOK: Leo Tolstoy, *War and Peace*

27 June 1960
498 Sir Alec Guinness
Actor

¶ 'Three Compline Hymns' (Gregorian chants) (Choir of the Monks of St Pierre de Solesmes)

¶ Fauré, Sonata No. 2 in G minor for Cello and Piano (Monique Fallot *piano*/Guy Fallot *cello*)

¶ Schumann, Piano Concerto in A minor (Dinu Lipatti/Philharmonia Orchestra/von Karajan)

¶ 'Barney's Bugle' (Buddy Rich *drums*/Harry 'Sweets' Edison *trumpet*)

¶ Haydn, Symphony No. 94 in G major (Berlin Philharmonic/Lehmann)

¶ 'Capricho arabe' (Laurindo Almeida *guitar*)

*¶ Verdi, 'Agnus Dei' (from *Requiem Mass*) (Elisabeth Schwarzkopf/Oralia Dominguez/La Scala Orchestra/Sabata)

¶ 'It's the Talk of the Town' (Ray Conniff Singers)

¶ LUXURY: Apricot brandy.

¶ BOOK: John Milton's *Paradise Lost*

7 July 1960
499 Claudio Arrau
Concert pianist

*¶ Schubert, Symphony No. 9 in C major (Berlin Philharmonic/Furtwängler)

¶ Ravel, 'La flûte enchantée' (from *Scheherazade*) (Jennie Tourel/Columbia Symphony/Bernstein)

¶ Granados, 'Los requiebros' (Alicia de Larrocha *piano*)

¶ Saint-Saëns, Piano Concerto No. 2 in G minor (Emils Gilels/Paris Conservatoire Orchestra/Cluytens)

¶ Schubert, 'Die Junge Nonne' (opus 43, no. 1) (Elisabeth Schwarzkopf/Edwin Fischer *piano*)

¶ Schubert, Piano Sonata No. 20 in A major (Artur Schnabel)

¶ Beethoven, String Quartet No. 15 in A minor (opus 132) (Koeckert Quartet)

¶ LUXURY: An early Chinese statuette that he owns.

¶ BOOK: The works of Goethe.

11 July 1960
500 Eddie Calvert
Trumpeter

*¶ 'Enchanted April' (Norrie Paramor and his Concert Orchestra)

¶ 'Je sais comment' (Edith Piaf)

¶ Code, 'Zelda (Caprice)' (Foden's Motor Works Band/Mortimer)

¶ 'The Day that the Circus Left Town' (Eartha Kitt)

¶ Rodgers & Hart, 'I Could Write a Book' (from *Pal Joey*) (Harold Lang)

¶ 'Just A-Wearyin' for You' (Eddie Calvert *trumpet*)

¶ Borodin/Wright & Forrest (arr.), 'And This is My Beloved' (from *Kismet*) (Doretta Morrow)

¶ 'Forget-Me-Not' (Vera Lynn)

¶ LUXURY: A piano.

¶ BOOK: A piano tutor.

18 July 1960
501 C. Day Lewis
Poet

¶ Bach, Brandenburg Concerto No. 6 in B flat major (Stuttgart Chamber Orchestra/Munchinger)

¶ Chopin, 'Grande valse brillante' (opus 18) (Dinu Lipatti *piano*)

*¶ Verdi, 'Offertorio' (from *Requiem Mass*) (Maria Caniglia/Ebe Stignani/Beniamino Gigli/Ezio Pinza/Rome Opera Orchestra/Serafin)

¶ Beethoven, Quartet No. 15 in A minor (opus 132) (Budapest String Quartet)

¶ Mozart, Piano Concerto No. 23 in A major (K. 488) (Clifford Curzon/LSO/Krips)

¶ Elgar, Cello Concerto in E minor (André Navarra/Hallé Orchestra/Barbirolli)

¶ Handel, 'Come My Beloved' (from *Atalanta*) (John McCormack)

¶ 'The Wife of Usher's Well' (John Laurie)

¶ LUXURY: Wine.

¶ BOOK: The novels of Jane Austen.

25 July 1960
502 Antal Dorati
Conductor

¶ Bach, 'Ich will den Kreuzstab gerne tragen' (from *Cantata No. 56*) (Gérard Souzay/Geraint Jones Orchestra)

¶ Schubert, Quartet No. 13 in A minor (D. 804) (Budapest String Quartet)

¶ Kodály, *Háry János* (excerpt) (Izabella Nagy/Imre Pallo)

¶ Bartók, Divertimento for String Orchestra (Philharmonia Hungarica/Dorati)

¶ Brahms, Symphony No. 2 in D major (Minneapolis Symphony/Dorati)

¶ Mozart, 'Bei Männern' (from *The Magic Flute*) (Tiana Lemnitz/Gerhard Hüsch/Berlin Philharmonic/Beecham)

¶ Verdi, *Otello* (Act 1, closing passage) (Ramon Vinay/Herva Nelli/NBC Symphony/ Toscanini)

*¶ Beethoven, 'O namenlose Freude' (from *Fidelio*) (Martha Mödl/Wolfgang Windgassen/ Vienna Philharmonic/ Furtwängler)

¶ LUXURY: A painting of a sleeping girl by Dominico Feti.

¶ BOOK: A personally compiled anthology.

1 August 1960
503 Johnny Morris
Broadcaster and traveller

¶ Keler-Béla, *Lustspiel* (overture) (Berlin State Opera Orchestra/Schmalstich)

*¶ J. Strauss, 'Spiel ich die Unschuld' (from *Die Fledermaus*) (Wilma Lipp/ Vienna State Opera Chorus/ Vienna Philharmonic/Krauss)

¶ 'Zapateado' (Antonio and his Spanish Dancers)

¶ Rossini, *The Thieving Magpie* (overture) (NBC Symphony/ Toscanini)

¶ Bizet, *The Fair Maid of Perth* (serenade) (Heddle Nash)

¶ Haydn, Symphony No. 101 in D major (RPO/Beecham)

¶ 'I'm Gonna Sit Right Down and Write Myself a Letter' (Fats Waller and his Rhythm)

¶ Rossini, 'Una voce poco fa' (from *The Barber of Seville*) (Teresa Berganza/LSO/Gibson)

¶ LUXURY: Yeast.

¶ BOOK: James Joyce, *Finnegans Wake*

8 August 1960
504 Lord Boothby
Politician and journalist

¶ Rachmaninov, Piano Concerto No. 2 in C minor (Benno Moiseiwitsch/ Philharmonia Orchestra/ Rignold)

¶ Wagner, *Die Meistersinger* (Act 2 duet of Eva and Sachs) (Elisabeth Grummer/Ferdinand Frantz/Berlin Philharmonic/ Kempe)

¶ Delius, 'The Walk to the Paradise Garden' (from *A Village Romeo and Juliet*) (RPO/ Beecham)

*¶ Debussy, *La Mer* (NBC Symphony/Toscanini)

¶ Wagner, *Tristan und Isolde* (Act 1 conclusion) (Kirsten Flagstad/Ludwig Suthaus/ Philharmonia Orchestra/ Furtwängler)

¶ Wagner, 'Love Duet' (from *Tristan und Isolde*) (Kirsten Flagstad/Ludwig Suthaus/ Philharmonia Orchestra/ Furtwängler)

¶ Brahms, Piano Concerto No. 1 in D minor (Solomon/ Philharmonia Orchestra/ Kubelik)

¶ Sibelius, Symphony No. 5 in E flat (Hallé Orchestra/ Barbirolli)

¶ LUXURY: Golf clubs and balls.

¶ BOOK: Somerset Maugham's short stories.

15 August 1960
505 Danny Blanchflower
Footballer

¶ 'April Showers' (Al Jolson)

*¶ 'The Breeze and I' (Caterina Valente)

¶ 'Sleepy Time Gal' (Guy Lombardo and his Royal Canadians)

¶ 'A Drop of the Hard Stuff' (Peter Sellers)

¶ Rubinstein, Romance in E flat (Capitol Symphony/Dragon)

¶ Carmichael, 'Stardust' (Artie Shaw and his Orchestra)

¶ 'Dearly Beloved' (from film *You Were Never Lovelier*) (Max Jaffa *violin and conducting*)

¶ Arlen & Harburg, 'Over the Rainbow' (from film *The Wizard of Oz*) (Judy Garland)

¶ LUXURY: Golf clubs and balls.

¶ BOOK: Lawrence Durrell, *The Alexandria Quartet*

22 August 1960
506 Pat Suzuki
Actress and singer

¶ Gershwin, 'I was Doing All Right' (Buddy De Franco *clarinet*/Oscar Peterson *piano*)

¶ Sibelius, Symphony No. 1 in E minor (Hallé Orchestra/ Barbirolli)

¶ 'Blue in Green' (Miles Davis *trumpet*)

¶ Bernstein, *West Side Story* (overture) (Orchestra/ Goberman)

¶ 'No Moon at All' (Jeri Southern)

¶ Rachmaninov, Piano Concerto No. 2 in C minor (Sergei Rachmaninov/ Philadelphia Orchestra/ Stokowski)

*¶ Haydn, Quartet in G major (opus 77, No. 1) (Amadeus String Quartet)

¶ ''Tain't What You Do' (Jimmie Lunceford and his Orchestra)

¶ LUXURY: Cosmetics.

¶ BOOK: *Encyclopaedia Britannica*

29 August 1960
507 Godfrey Talbot
Senior reporter of the BBC

¶ Puccini, *Tosca* (Act 1 excerpt) (Melchiorre Luise/La Scala Orchestra/Sabata)

¶ R. Strauss, 'Ohne Mich' (from *Der Rosenkavalier*) (Hollywood Bowl Orchestra/Slatkin)

¶ 'The Lord is My Shepherd' (23rd Psalm) (Glasgow Orpheus Choir/Roberton)

¶ 'Lilli Marlene' (Lale Andersen)

¶ Porter, 'Why Can't You Behave?' (from *Kiss Me Kate*) (Lisa Kirk)

¶ 'Dearly Beloved' and 'As Time Goes By' (Charlie Kunz *piano*)
¶ 'The Scoutmaster' (John Tilley)
*¶ Rachmaninov, Piano Concerto No. 2 in C minor (Eileen Joyce/LPO/Leinsdorf)
¶ LUXURY: Writing materials.
¶ BOOK: Thomas Macaulay, *Critical and Historical Essays*

5 September 1960
508 Paul Beard
Leader of the BBC Symphony Orchestra
¶ J. Strauss, *Die Fledermaus* (overture) (Philharmonia Orchestra/von Karajan)
¶ Beethoven, Violin Concerto in D major (Fritz Kreisler/LPO/ Barbirolli)
¶ R. Strauss, 'Ein Heldenleben' (RPO/Beecham)
¶ Dvořák, Cello Concerto in B minor (Pablo Casals/Czech Philharmonic/Szell)
*¶ Bizet, 'Habanera' (from *Carmen*) (Conchita Supervia)
¶ Berlioz, 'Queen Mab Scherzo' (from *Romeo and Juliet*) (NBC Symphony/Toscanini)
¶ Brahms, Violin Concerto in D major (Ginette Neveu/ Philharmonia Orchestra/ Dobrowen)
¶ Berlioz, Symphonie Fantastique (French National Radio Orchestra/Beecham)
¶ LUXURY: Golf clubs and balls.
¶ BOOK: Balzac's *Droll Stories*

12 September 1960
509 Gladys Young
Radio actress
*¶ Grieg, 'Morning' (from *Peer Gynt*) (RPO/Beecham)
¶ Shakespeare, 'Now is the Winter of Our Discontent' (from *Richard III*) (Laurence Olivier)
¶ Tchaikovsky, 'Dance of the Little Swans' (from *Swan Lake*, Act 2) (Orchestre de la Suisse Romande/Ansermet)
¶ 'This was Their Finest Hour' (speech by Sir Winston Churchill, 18 June 1940)
¶ 'Sigh No More Ladies' (Gervase Elwes)

¶ Shakespeare, *Hamlet* (Act 3, closet scene) (John Gielgud/ Coral Browne)
¶ 'The Lion and Albert' (Stanley Holloway)
¶ Schumann, 'Träumerei' (from *Kinderszenen*, opus 15) (Clifford Curzon *piano*)
¶ LUXURY: A supply of pairs of spectacles.
¶ BOOK: Norman Collins, *London Belongs to Me*

19 September 1960
510 Michaela & Armand Denis
Explorers and big-game photographers
¶ Rachmaninov, 'Rhapsody on a Theme of Paganini' (Benno Moiseiwitsch *piano*/ Philharmonia Orchestra/ Rignold)
¶ Dukas, 'The Sorcerer's Apprentice' (Boston Symphony/Munch)
¶ Gershwin, Piano Concerto in F (Eugene List/Eastman-Rochester Symphony/Hanson)
¶ 'The Harry Lime Theme' (from film *The Third Man*) (Anton Karas *zither*)
¶ 'Pembe' (Orchestre Devereux)
¶ 'Gao Tarane Manke' (from film *Aan*) (Shamshad/Lata/ Rafi/Chorus)
¶ 'Misionera' (Trio Los Paraguayos)
¶ Salute to a chief by the Yoruba, recorded in Nigeria
¶ LUXURY: (Michaela) a diamond ring; (Armand) a loud-hailer.
¶ BOOK: (Michaela) *Encyclopaedia Britannica*; (Armand) a treatise on mathematics.

26 September 1960
511 Lionel Bart
Composer and writer
¶ Arlen & Harburg, 'Over the Rainbow' (from film *The Wizard of Oz*) (Judy Garland)
¶ R. Strauss, 'Don Juan' (Vienna Philharmonic/ Furtwängler)
¶ 'Water, Water' (from film *The Tommy Steele Story*) (Tommy Steele and the Steelmen)

¶ Bart, 'As Long as He Needs Me' (from *Oliver!*) (Shirley Bassey)
¶ 'Any Old Iron' (Peter Sellers/ Mate's Spoffle Group)
*¶ Rodgers & Hammerstein, 'Soliloquy' (from *Carousel*) (Gordon Macrae)
¶ Gershwin, 'There's a Boat Dat's Leavin' Soon for New York' (from *Porgy and Bess*) (Sammy Davis Jnr)
¶ Gershwin, 'Oh Lawd, I'm on My Way' (from *Porgy and Bess*) (Robert McFerrin)
¶ LUXURY: Nelson's Column.
¶ BOOK: Dylan Thomas, *Under Milk Wood*

3 October 1960
512 Diane Cilento
Actress
¶ Arlen, *House of Flowers* (overture) (Orchestra/Arlen)
¶ 'Lazzarella' (Domenico Modugno *guitar*)
¶ 'Taking a Chance on Love' (Eydie Gormé)
¶ 'Les enfants qui s'aiment' (Yves Montand)
*¶ 'Ode to a Cowboy' (Dave Brubeck Quartet)
¶ Mozart, Andante for Flute and Orchestra in C major (K. 315) (Camillo Wanausek/ Vienna Pro Musica Chamber Orchestra)
¶ 'Roll 'Em, Pete' (Joe Williams/Count Basie and his Orchestra)
¶ Brecht/Weill, 'Alabama Song' (from *The Rise and Fall of the City of Mahagonny*) (Lotte Lenya)
¶ LUXURY: Painting materials.
¶ BOOK: J. D. Salinger, *The Catcher in the Rye*

10 October 1960
513 Alec Bedser
Cricketer
¶ Lerner & Loewe, 'I Could Have Danced All Night' (from *My Fair Lady*) (Mantovani and his Orchestra)
¶ 'Hey Neighbour' (from *Nights of Madness*) (Flanagan & Allen)

*¶Mendelssohn, 'Oh, for the Wings of a Dove' (Ernest Lough/G. Thalben-Ball *organ*/ Temple Church Choir, London)
¶'Alec Bedser Calypso' (Lord Kitchener/St Vincent St Six)
¶'Waltzing Matilda' (Hollywood Studio Symphony)
¶'Ye Banks and Braes' (Kathleen Ferrier)
¶'Come Back to Sorrento' (Harry Secombe)
¶'Scotland the Brave' (Massed Bands)
¶LUXURY: A razor.
¶BOOK: A set of Wisden.

17 October 1960
514 Sidney Torch
Light music composer and conductor
¶Offenbach/Rosenthal (arr.) *Gaîté Parisienne* (overture) (Philharmonia Orchestra/von Karajan)
*¶'Narcissus' (Joyce Grenfell/ Norman Wisdom)
¶Rodgers & Hammerstein, 'There's Nothing Like a Dame' (from *South Pacific*) (Chorus and orchestra/Dell 'Isola)
¶Tchaikovsky, Serenade for Strings (waltz) (Boston Symphony/Koussevitzky)
¶'I'm the Guy who Found the Lost Chord' (Jimmy Durante)
¶'Green Hills o' Somerset' (Joan Hammond)
¶'Singin' in the Rain' (from film) (Gene Kelly)
¶'More Comic Cuts' (Queen's Hall Light Orchestra/Farnon)
¶LUXURY: Golf clubs and balls.
¶BOOK: Jerome K. Jerome, *Three Men in a Boat*

24 October 1960
515 Ernest Lough
Ex-soloist of the Choir of Temple Church, London
¶Tchaikovsky, 'Romeo and Juliet Fantasy Overture' (NBC Symphony/Toscanini)
¶Bach/Howe, 'Sheep May Safely Graze' (Phyllis Sellick/ Cyril Smith *piano*)
¶Mendelssohn, 'Hear Ye, Israel' (from *Elijah*) (Ernest Lough/Temple Church Choir)

¶Grieg, Piano Concerto in A minor (Dinu Lipatti/ Philharmonia Orchestra/ Galliera)
¶'The Holly and the Ivy' (Temple Church Choir)
¶Tchaikovsky, 'Dance of the Mirlitons' (from *The Nutcracker Suite*) (Paris Conservatoire Orchestra/Fistoulari)
¶Fauré, 'Pié Jesu' (from *Requiem*) (Suzanne Danco/ Orchestre de la Suisse Romande/Ansermet)
¶Parry, 'I was Glad' (from Coronation Service of HM Queen Elizabeth II)
¶LUXURY: A radio receiver.
¶BOOK: A manual of astronomy.

31 October 1960
516 Cliff Richard
Pop singer and film actor
¶Bizet/Hammerstein, 'Beat Out Dat Rhythm on a Drum' (from film *Carmen Jones*) (Marilyn Horne)
¶'Tammy' (Debbie Reynolds)
¶'Heartbreak Hotel' (Elvis Presley)
¶'My Funny Valentine' (Dakota Staton)
¶'How You Say It' (Lena Horne)
¶'That's My Desire' (Dion and the Belmonts)
*¶'Rock Around the Clock' (Bill Haley and his Comets)
¶'Am I Blue?' (Ray Charles)
¶LUXURY: A guitar.
¶BOOK: Johann David Wyss, *The Swiss Family Robinson*

7 November 1960
517 Freddy Grisewood (2nd appearance)
Broadcaster
¶Tchaikovsky, Piano Concerto No. 1 in B flat minor (Vladimir Horowitz/NBC Symphony/ Toscanini)
¶R. Strauss, 'Morgen' (Elisabeth Schumann)
*¶Byron, 'So We'll Go No More A-Roving' (Gervase Elwes)
¶Chopin, Fantaisie Impromptu in C sharp minor (opus 66) (Benno Moiseiwitsch *piano*)
¶Delius, 'On Hearing the First Cuckoo in Spring' (RPO/ Beecham)

¶'The Old Sow' (Albert Richardson)
¶Schubert, 'Das Wandern' (Sir George Henschel)
¶Dvořák/Wagner, 'Goin' Home' (Capitol Symphony/ Chorale/Wagner)
¶LUXURY: A compendium of parlour games.
¶BOOK: George MacDonald, *Phantastes*

14 November 1960
518 Ursula Bloom
Novelist and journalist
*¶'A Message to the Empire' (HM King George VI, 25 December 1939)
¶Wagner, *Tannhäuser* (overture) (Philharmonia Orchestra/Klemperer)
¶'Homing' (Webster Booth)
¶Charles Dickens, *Dombey and Son* (excerpt) (Emlyn Williams)
¶Coward, 'Mad Dogs and Englishmen' (from *Words and Music*) (Noël Coward)
¶'Land of My Fathers' (Morriston Orpheus Male Choir)
¶'Abide with Me' (Clara Butt)
¶Recording of the bells of St Mary's, Puddletown, Dorset (Victory Day, 8 May 1945)
¶LUXURY: Writing materials.
¶BOOK: *The Book of Common Prayer*

21 November 1960
519 Edmund Hockridge
Actor and singer
¶'Zip-a-Dee-Doo-Dah' (from film *Song of the South*) (Ray Conniff Singers and Orchestra)
¶Tchaikovsky, Symphony No. 6 in B minor (CSO/Kubelík)
¶Lerner & Loewe, 'Gigi' (from film) André Previn *piano* and others)
*¶Rodgers & Hammerstein, 'Carousel Waltz' (from *Carousel*) (Orchestra/Newman)
¶'Suddenly It's Folk Song' (Peter Sellers)
¶Rachmaninov, Piano Concerto No. 2 in C minor (Julius Katchen/New Symphony Orchestra/ Fistoulari)

¶Puccini, 'O Mimi, tu più non torni' (from *La Bohème*) (Jussi Björling/Robert Merrill/RCA Victor Symphony/Beecham)
¶'It's Nice to Go Trav'ling' (Frank Sinatra)
¶LUXURY: Painting equipment.
¶BOOK: *Encyclopaedia Britannica*

28 November 1960
520 Frank Muir & Denis Norden
Comedy scriptwriters
¶(Muir) 'Don't Bring Lulu' (Bobby Short and his Orchestra)
¶(Norden) 'Manhattan' (Ella Fitzgerald)
¶(M) 'Yes, My Darling Daughter' (Glenn Miller and his Orchestra)
¶(N) 'How Long Has This Been Going On?' (Julie London)
¶(M) 'La Vie en rose' (Edith Piaf)
¶(N) Dylan Thomas, *A Few Words of a Kind* (excerpt) (Dylan Thomas)
¶(M) 'You Make Me Feel So Young' (Frank Sinatra)
¶(N) 'Rose Room' (Jonah Jones and his Quartet)
¶LUXURIES: (M) a Stradivarius violin; (N) 4-foot-high model of the Tower of London.
¶BOOK: (M) a cookery book; (N) *The Treasury of Ribaldry*.

5 December 1960
521 Oda Slobodskaya
Singer
¶Rimsky-Korsakov, 'The Battle of Kershenetz' (Boston Symphony/Koussevitzky)
¶Stravinsky, 'Russian Maiden's Song' (Nathan Milstein *violin*/Leon Pommers *piano*)
¶Wagner, *Tannhäuser* (overture) (LPO/Beecham)
¶Britten, 'Fanfare' (from *Les Illuminations*) (Peter Pears/New Symphony Orchestra/Goossens)
¶Tchaikovsky, 'The Golden Cornfields' (Oda Slobodskaya/Ivor Newton *piano*)
¶Rachmaninov, 'Vocalise' (Maria Kurenko)

¶Dargomizhsky, 'The Miller's Aria' (from *The Rusalka*) (Feodor Chaliapin)
*¶Rachmaninov (arr.) 'Powder and Paint' (Nadezha Plevitskaya/Sergei Rachmaninov *piano*)
¶LUXURY: A radio receiver.
¶BOOK: The plays of Sheridan.

12 December 1960
522 Don Thompson
Athlete
¶'Westering Home' (Kenneth McKellar)
¶Vaughan Williams, *The Wasps* (overture) (LPO/Boult)
¶Scarlatti, Sonata in D minor (L. 413) (Peter Katin *piano*)
¶Bach, Brandenburg Concerto No. 2 in F major (Chamber Orchestra of Schola Cantorum Basiliensis/Wenzinger)
¶Rodgers & Hammerstein, 'Oh, What a Beautiful Morning' (from *Oklahoma*) (Alfred Drake)
¶Bach, Suite No. 3 in D major (Philharmonia Orchestra/Klemperer)
¶Haydn, Symphony No. 88 in G major (Vienna Philharmonic/Münchinger)
*¶Bach, 'Gavotte' (Andrés Segovia *guitar*)
¶LUXURY: A clarinet.
¶BOOK: G. M. Trevelyan, *English Social History*

19 December 1960
523 Harry Mortimer
Trumpeter and brass band conductor
*¶Bliss, *Kenilworth Suite* (Foden's Motor Works Band/Fred Mortimer)
¶Berlioz, *Le Carnaval Romain* (overture) (Hallé Orchestra/Harty)
¶Handel, 'The Trumpet Shall Sound' (from *Messiah*) (Norman Walker/Harry Mortimer *trumpet*/Royal Liverpool Philharmonic/Sargent)
¶Rossini, *The Silken Ladder* (overture) (LPO/Beecham)
¶R. Strauss, Horn Concerto No. 1 in E flat (opus 11) (Dennis Brain/Philharmonia Orchestra/Sawallisch)

¶'Alpine Echoes' (Harry Mortimer *cornet*/Foden's Motor Works Band/Fred Mortimer)
¶Bliss, 'Fanfares for a Dignified and for a Festive Occasion' (Trumpeters of Royal Military School of Music)
¶Tchaikovsky, '1812 Overture' (Massed Brass Bands of Foden's Motor Works, Fairey Aviation and Morris Motors/Harry Mortimer)
¶LUXURY: A ciné camera.
¶BOOK: Leslie Charteris, *The Saint* (omnibus edition)

26 December 1960
524 Dave King
Comedian
¶Porter, 'Night and Day' (from *The Gay Divorce*) (Esquivel and his Orchestra)
*¶'Tone Poems of Colour: White' (Orchestra/Sinatra)
¶'Tequila' (Ted Heath and his Music)
¶'You Go to My Head' (Eve Boswell)
¶'How Do You Do?' (Mike & Bernie Winters)
¶'Chinese Lullaby' (Anita Darian)
¶'Blue Tango' (Ray Martin and his Concert Orchestra)
¶'Jubilation T. Cornpone' (from film *L'il Abner*) (Stubby Kaye and the Dogpatchers)
¶LUXURY: A football.
¶BOOK: An English dictionary.

2 January 1961
525 Victor Gollancz
Publisher
¶Stravinsky, *The Firebird* (finale) (Orchestre de la Suisse Romande/Ansermet)
¶Berlioz, 'Voici des roses' (from *The Damnation of Faust*) (Charles Panzéra)
¶Mozart, 'Contessa Perdono' (from *The Marriage of Figaro*) (Sena Jurinac/Franco Calabrese/Glyndebourne Festival Ochestra/Gui)
¶Beethoven, 'Governor's Aria' (from *Fidelio*, Act 2) (Alfred Poell/Vienna State Opera Chorus/Vienna Philharmonic/Furtwängler)

¶Verdi, 'Libiamo, libiamo' (from *La traviata*) (Enrico Caruso/Alma Gluck)
¶Schubert, Symphony No. 9 in C (Berlin Philharmonic/ Furtwängler)
¶Bach, Violin Concerto in E major (Yehudi Menuhin/ Robert Masters Chamber Orchestra)
*¶Beethoven, Symphony No. 3 in E flat major (Philharmonia Orchestra/Klemperer)
¶LUXURY: A Meerschaum pipe.
¶BOOK: *The Year of Grace*, an anthology compiled by Victor Gollancz.

16 January 1961
527 The Beverley Sisters
Close-harmony singers
¶Sibelius, *Karelia Suite* (intermezzo) (Danish State Radio Symphony/Jensen)
¶Bart, 'You've Got to Pick a Pocket or Two' (from *Oliver!*) (Ron Moody)

9 January 1961
526 Kenneth Horne (2nd appearance)
Radio and television comedian
¶Borodin, 'Vladimir's Cavatina' (from *Prince Igor*, Act 2) (Jussi Björling)
¶Debussy, 'Clair de lune' (from *Suite bergamasque*) (Walter Gieseking *piano*)
¶Brahms, Quartet in B flat major (opus 67) (Amadeus String Quartet)
¶'Body and Soul' (Coleman Hawkins and his All Stars Orchestra)
¶Rodgers & Hammerstein, 'Something Wonderful' (from *The King and I*) (Terry Saunders)
¶Tchaikovsky, '1812 Overture' (Philharmonia Orchestra/von Karajan)
¶Berlin, 'White Christmas' (from film *Holiday Inn*) (Bing Crosby)
*¶Puccini, 'Si, mi chiamano Mimi' (from *La Bohème*) (Renata Tebaldi/Santa Cecilia Orchestra, Rome/Serafin)
¶LUXURY: A piece of crystal.
¶BOOK: An anthology of English verse.

¶Beethoven, Symphony No. 6 in F major (LPO/Kleiber)
¶'Mr Custer' (Charlie Drake)
¶'Cottage for Sale' (The Beverley Sisters)
¶'Nobody's Using It Now' (from film *The Love Parade*) (Maurice Chevalier)
¶'Green Leaves of Summer' (from film *The Alamo*) (The Brothers Four)
*¶Elgar, 'Pomp and Circumstance' March No. 1 in D major (Royal Festival Orchestra and Choir/Sargent)
¶LUXURIES: (Joy) a Rolls-Royce; (Teddy) water skis; (Babs) a piano.
¶BOOKS: (Joy) Billy Wright's *Book of Soccer*; (Teddy) Van Loon, *History of Mankind*; (Babs) Julian Huxley, H.G. Wells & G.P. Wells, *The Science of Life*.

23 January 1961
528 Ted Williams
Horseman
¶'South of the Border' (Gene Autry)
¶'High Hopes' (from film *A Hole in the Head*) (Frank Sinatra)
¶Weill, 'September Song' (from *Knickerbocker Holiday*) (Walter Huston)
¶'When the Saints Come Marching In' and 'Charleston' (US Third Air Force Band)
*¶'Around the World' (from film *Around the World in Eighty Days*) (Bing Crosby)
¶'Little Town in the Ould County Down' (Cavan O'Connor)
¶'In a Shady Nook by a Babbling Brook' (Donald Peers)
¶'Arrivederci Darling' (Anne Shelton)
¶LUXURY: Cigarettes.
¶BOOK: A bound volume of *Horse and Hound*.

30 January 1961
529 Cyril Mills
Circus director
¶'J'attendrai' (Jean Sablon)
¶'Warsaw Concerto' (from film *Dangerous Moonlight*) (LSO/ Mathieson)

¶Puccini, 'Un bel di vedremo' (from *Madam Butterfly*) (Victoria de los Angeles/Rome Opera Orchestra/Gavazzeni)
¶Berlin, 'White Christmas' (from film *Holiday Inn*) (Bing Crosby)
¶'Every Man to His Post' (Sir Winston Churchill, speech, 11 September 1940)
¶Verdi, 'Celeste Aida' (from *Aida*) (Jussi Björling)
¶Lerner & Loewe, 'Thank Heaven for Little Girls' (from film *Gigi*) (Maurice Chevalier)
*¶Rodgers & Hammerstein, 'People Will Say We're in Love' (from *Oklahoma*) (Alfred Drake/Joan Roberts)
¶LUXURY: A bed.
¶BOOK: Victor Hugo, *Les Misérables*

6 February 1961
530 Mary Ure
Actress
¶'The Reel of the 51st Division' (Jimmy Shand and his Band)
¶'Louisiana' (Eddie Condon and his All Stars)
¶Dylan Thomas, 'In My Craft or Sullen Art' (Richard Burton)
¶'Old-Fashioned Love' (Bob Wilber's Wildcats)
¶'Mah Lindy Lou' (Paul Robeson)
*¶Mozart, Piano Concerto No. 23 in A (Solomon/Philharmonia Orchestra/Menges)
¶Brecht/Weill, 'Alabama Song' (from *The Rise and Fall of the City of Mahagonny*) (Lotte Lenya)
¶Mendelssohn, 'The Hebrides Overture' (RPO/Beecham)
¶LUXURY: A painting by Rembrandt in the National Gallery.
¶BOOK: The collected plays of John Osborne.

13 February 1961
531 Antonio
Dancer
¶Holst, 'Neptune' (from *The Planets*) (BBC Symphony/ Sargent)
¶'The Clock' (Don Marino Barreto Jnr)

¶ Gershwin, 'Rhapsody in Blue' (Leonard Bernstein *piano*/Columbia Symphony)

¶ Falla, 'Nights in the Gardens of Spain' (Artur Rubinstein *piano*/San Francisco Symphony/Jorda)

¶ 'Doucement, doucement' (Henry Salvador and his Orchestra)

¶ 'All Too Soon' (Peggy Lee/George Shearing Quintet)

*¶ 'El luto que llevo en mi corazon' (from *Seguiriyas*) (Antonio Mairena *guitar*)

¶ 'Granada' (Mario Lanza)

¶ LUXURIES: The crucifix he wears around his neck, and the family photograph album.

¶ BOOK: Cervantes, *Don Quixote*

20 February 1961
532 Jimmy Edwards
(2nd appearance)
Comedian

¶ R. Strauss, 'Don Juan' (Vienna Philharmonic/Krauss)

*¶ 'Believe Me if All Those Endearing Young Charms' (Bert Sullivan *euphonium*/Munn & Felton's Footwear Band)

¶ R. Strauss, Horn Concerto No. 1 in E flat (opus 11) (Dennis Brain/Philharmonia Orchestra/Sawallisch)

¶ Holst, 'Mars' (from *The Planets*) (BBC Symphony/Sargent)

¶ Tchaikovsky, Symphony No. 4 in F minor (Berlin Philharmonic/von Karajan)

¶ 'Solving the Riddle' (Billy May's Big Fat Brass)

¶ 'Jet Plane' (from *USAF: A Portrait in Sound*)

¶ 'I've Never Seen a Straight Banana' (Jimmy Edwards)

¶ LUXURY: A euphonium.

¶ BOOK: D. H. Lawrence, *Lady Chatterley's Lover*

27 February 1961
533 June Bronhill
Singer

¶ 'La vie en rose' (Mantovani and his Orchestra)

¶ Rodgers & Hammerstein, 'Bali Ha'i' (from *South Pacific*) (Juanita Hall)

¶ Donizetti, 'O luce di quest'anima' (from *Linda di Chamounix*) (Joan Sutherland/Paris Conservatoire Orchestra/Santi)

¶ 'My Lovely Celia' (Dino Borgioli)

¶ 'Goodness Gracious Me' (Peter Sellers/Sophia Loren)

¶ Tchaikovsky, 'Romeo and Juliet Fantasy Overture' (Michael Collins and his Strings for Romance)

¶ Cilèa, 'Poveri fiori' (from *Adriana Lecouvreur*) (Renata Tebaldi/Santa Cecilia Orchestra, Rome/Erede)

¶ 'La luna y el sol' (Carbonerillo de Jerez)

¶ LUXURY: Sun-tan oil.

¶ BOOK: Ogden Nash poems.

6 March 1961
534 James Mason
Actor

¶ 'Weary Blues' (Duke Ellington/Johnny Hodges/Ensemble)

¶ 'The Kid from Red Bank' (Count Basie and his Orchestra)

¶ Villa Lobos, Prelude No. 3 in A minor (Julian Bream *guitar*)

¶ Grieg, Piano Concerto in A minor (Wilhelm Backhaus/New Symphony Orchestra/Barbirolli)

¶ Bartók, *The Miraculous Mandarin Suite* (Minneapolis Symphony/Dorati)

*¶ 'My Man' (Billie Holiday)

¶ Cimarosa/Benjamin, Concerto for Oboe and Strings (Léon Goossens/Royal Liverpool Philharmonic/Sargent)

¶ 'Scotland the Brave' (Black Watch Pipes, Drums and Regimental Band)

¶ LUXURY: Bagpipes.

¶ BOOK: James Joyce, *Finnegans Wake*

13 March 1961
535 Carmen Dragon
Conductor

¶ Gershwin, 'Summertime' (from *Porgy and Bess*) (Ella Fitzgerald)

¶ Bach/Stokowski, Toccata and Fugue in D minor (Philadelphia Orchestra/Stokowski)

¶ 'Mood Indigo' (Duke Ellington and his Orchestra)

¶ Rodgers & Hammerstein, 'Oklahoma' (from *Oklahoma*) (Gordon Macrae)

¶ Tchaikovsky, 'Dance of the Sugar Plum Fairy' (from *The Nutcracker Suite*) (RPO/Beecham)

¶ Bizet, 'Les tringles des sistres' (from *Carmen*) (Victoria de los Angeles/Marcelle Croisier/Denise Monteil/French National Radio Chorus and Orchestra/Beecham)

¶ Debussy, 'Rêverie' (Hollywood Bowl Symphony/Dragon)

*¶ Beethoven, Symphony No. 9 in D minor (opus 125) (Elisabeth Schwarzkopf/Elisabeth Höngen/Hans Hopf/Otto Edelmann/1951 Bayreuth Festival Chorus and Orchestra/Furtwängler)

¶ LUXURY: An astronomical telescope.

¶ BOOK: A book on astronomy.

20 March 1961
536 Michael Wilding
Actor

¶ Ellis, 'I'm a One-Man Girl' (from *Mr Cinders*) (Bobby Howes/Binnie Hale)

¶ 'These Foolish Things' (from *Spread It Abroad*) (Frank Sinatra)

*¶ 'Piccadilly Incident' (from film) (Louis Levy Orchestra)

¶ Puccini, 'Love and Music' (from *Tosca*) (Joan Hammond/Philharmonia/Curiel)

¶ Wagner, 'Liebestod' (from *Tristan und Isolde*) (Vienna Philharmonic/Kempe)

¶ Arlen & Harburg, 'Over the Rainbow' (from film *The Wizard of Oz*) (Judy Garland)

¶ Porter, 'True Love' (from film *High Society*) (Bing Crosby/Grace Kelly)

¶ 'Let Me Love You' (Lena Horne)

¶ LUXURY: Golf clubs and balls

¶ BOOK: *Encyclopaedia Britannica*

27 March 1961
537 Kenneth McKellar
Singer
¶ 'The Dashing White Sergeant' (Jimmy Shand and his Band)
*¶ Bach, 'Sanctus' (from *Mass in B minor*) (Chorus and Orchestra of the Vienna Singverein/von Karajan)
¶ Puccini, 'O Mimi, tu più non torni' (from *La bohème*) (Beniamino Gigli/Giuseppe de Luca/Metropolitan Opera Orchestra/Setti)
¶ Vaughan Williams, 'The Lark Ascending' (Jean Pougnet *violin*/LPO/Boult)
¶ Lehár, 'Waltz Song' (from *The Merry Widow*) (Richard Tauber)
¶ Fauré, 'Clair de lune' (opus 46, no. 2) (Mattiwilda Dobbs/Gerald Moore *piano*)
¶ 'Arrivederci Roma' (Rino Salviati)
¶ 'The Flowers of the Forest' (Kenneth McKellar)
¶ LUXURY: A tuning fork.
¶ BOOK: *Encyclopaedia Britannica*

3 April 1961
538 Peter Scott (2nd appearance)
Naturalist, painter and sailor
*¶ Beethoven, Symphony No. 9 in D minor (opus 125) (NBC Symphony/Toscanini)
¶ Brahms, Violin Concerto in D major (Isaac Stern/RPO/Beecham)
¶ Verdi, 'E l'amor mio' (from *Aida*) (Maria Callas/La Scala Orchestra/Serafin)
¶ Sibelius, Symphony No. 1 in E minor (LSO/Collins)
¶ 'Isa Lei' (Fijian girls)
¶ Schubert, Quintet in C major (William Pleeth *cello*/Amadeus String Quartet)
¶ Mahler, Symphony No. 9 in D minor (Vienna Symphony/Horenstein)
¶ R. Strauss, *Der Rosenkavalier* (finale) (Sena Jurinac/Hilde Gueden/Vienna Philharmonic/Kleiber)
¶ LUXURY: An underwater mask.
¶ BOOK: The drawings of Leonardo da Vinci.

10 April 1961
539 Barbara Jefford
Actress
¶ Khachaturian, Violin Concerto (David Oistrakh/Philharmonia Orchestra/Khachaturian)
¶ Fauré, 'Libera Me' (from *Requiem*) (Gérard Souzay/Orchestre de la Suisse Romande/Ansermet)
¶ Coward, 'Sigh No More' (from *Sigh No More*) (George Shearing *piano*)
¶ Prokofiev, 'Dance of the Knights' (from *Romeo and Juliet*) (Boston Symphony/Munch)
¶ Albinoni/Giazotto, Adagio for Strings and Organ (Denyse Gouarne *organ*/Ensemble Instrumental Sinfonia/Witold)
¶ 'The Edge of Shelley Berman' (Shelley Berman)
¶ Granados, 'El mirar de la maja' (from *Tonadillas*) (Victoria de los Angeles/Gerald Moore *piano*)
*¶ Mozart, Symphony No. 40 in G minor (RPO/Beecham)
¶ LUXURY: A piano.
¶ BOOK: Sir Winston Churchill, *History of the English-speaking Peoples*

17 April 1961
540 Brian Reece (2nd appearance)
Actor
¶ 'Vitality' (from *Gay's the Word*) (Cicely Courtneidge)
¶ Mascagni, *Cavalleria rusticana* (prelude) (Santa Cecilia Orchestra, Rome/Serafin)
¶ Ellis, 'This is My Lovely Day' (from *Bless the Bride*) (Georges Guetary/Lizbeth Webb)
¶ 'Eat, Drink and be Merry' (from *Bet Your Life*) (Arthur Askey/Julie Wilson)
¶ Rodgers & Hammerstein, 'Soliloquy' (from *Carousel*) (Edmund Hockridge)
*¶ Puccini, 'Love and Music' (from *Tosca*) (Joan Hammond/Philharmonia Orchestra/Curiel)
¶ 'I Went to Your Wedding' (Spike Jones and his City Slickers)

¶ 'Silent Night, Holy Night' (Bach Choir/Jacques)
¶ LUXURY: A still.
¶ BOOK: A navigational manual.

24 April 1961
541 Adam Faith
Pop singer
¶ Tchaikovsky, 'Capriccio Italien' (Paris Conservatoire Orchestra/Schuricht)
¶ 'Because of You' (Sammy Davis Jnr)
¶ 'Lost John' (Lonnie Donegan)
¶ 'What Do You Want?' (Adam Faith)
¶ Dvořák, Slavonic Dance No. 2 in E minor (Vienna Symphony/Ancerl)
¶ 'What'd I Say?' (Ray Charles)
¶ 'What'll I Do' (Johnny Mathis)
¶ Sibelius, Symphony No. 2 in D major (BBC Symphony/Sargent)
¶ LUXURIES: A cold cure, a pack of cards and writing materials.
¶ BOOK: Aldous Huxley, *Brave New World*

1 May 1961
542 Finlay Currie
Actor
¶ 'My Ain Folk' (Janet Howe)
¶ Franck, Chorale No. 3 in A minor (Marcel Dupré *organ*)
*¶ Handel, 'He was Despised' (from *Messiah*) (Kathleen Ferrier/LPO/Boult)
¶ 'The Mountains of Mourne' (Peter Dawson)
¶ Brahms, 'Academic Festival Overture' (RPO/Beecham)
¶ 'Eightsome Reel' (Jimmy Shand and his Band)
¶ Dvořák, Symphony No. 9 in E minor (Columbia Symphony/Walter)
¶ Elgar, 'Pomp and Circumstance' March No. 1 in D major (BBC Symphony/Sargent)
¶ LUXURY: 17th-century miniature by Peter Oliver.
¶ BOOK: *The Dictionary of National Biography*

8 May 1961
543 Ralph Reader
(2nd appearance)
Director of musicals, song writer and Boy Scout leader
¶ Berlin, 'There's No Business Like Show Business' (from film) (Ethel Merman)
¶ 'Sittin' on the Bridge Below the Town' (Eileen Donaghy)
¶ Novello, 'Waltz of My Heart' (from *The Dancing Years*) (Norrie Paramor and his Orchestra)
*¶ 'These are the Times' (from *The Gang Show*)
¶ 'RAF March' (HM RAF Band/O'Donnell)
¶ Rodgers & Hammerstein, 'You'll Never Walk Alone' (from *Carousel*) (Shirley Jones)
¶ 'Any Old Iron' (Peter Sellers)
¶ Handel, 'Hallelujah Chorus' (from *Messiah*) (Huddersfield Choral Society/Royal Liverpool Philharmonic/Sargent)
¶ LUXURY: Typewriter and paper.
¶ BOOK: James Hilton, *Goodbye Mr Chips*

15 May 1961
544 Pietro Annigoni
Artist
¶ Beethoven, Symphony No. 6 in F major (opus 68) (Philadelphia Orchestra/Walter)
¶ Corelli, 'Sonata' (opus 5, no. 12) (Arthur Grumiaux *violin*/Riccardo Castagnone *piano*)
*¶ Mozart, Piano, Concerto No. 20 in D minor (K. 466) (Sviatoslav Richter/National Philharmonic Symphony, Warsaw/Wislocki)
¶ Vitali, 'Chaconne' (Arthur Grumiaux *violin*/Riccardo Castagnone *piano*)
¶ Verdi, *La traviata* (Act 3 prelude) (NBC Symphony/Toscanini)
¶ 'Les feuilles mortes' (Yves Montand)
¶ Beethoven, Symphony No. 7 in A major (opus 92) (Columbia Symphony/Walter)
¶ 'La porti un bacione a Firenze' (Odoardo Spadaro)

¶ LUXURIES: Drawing materials and a pillow.
¶ BOOK: An international timetable of ships and trains.

22 May 1961
545 Kenneth Williams
Comedian
¶ Ovalle, 'Azuálaò' (Gérard Souzay)
¶ Beethoven, Sonata No. 26 in E flat (opus 81a) (Guiomar Novaes *piano*)
¶ Buxtehude, Prelude and Fugue in G minor (Finn Videro *organ*)
¶ 'My Love is Like a Red, Red Rose' (Kenneth McKellar)
*¶ Bach, Brandenburg Concerto No. 6 in B flat major (Yehudi Menuhin *violin*/Bath Festival Chamber Orchestra)
¶ Schumann, 'Chiarina' (from *Carnaval*, opus 9) (Geza Anda *piano*)
¶ Brahms, 'O How Amiable are Thy Dwellings' (from *A German Requiem*) (St Hedwig's Cathedral Choir, Berlin/Berlin Philharmonic/Kempe)
¶ 'Clear Bright Morning' (from *After the Ball*) (Vanessa Lee)
¶ LUXURY: Michelangelo's *Apollo*
¶ BOOK: The collected works of George Bernard Shaw.

29 May 1961
546 Kingsley Amis
Novelist and poet
¶ 'Moonlight Kisses' (Troise and his Mandoliers)
*¶ 'Shim-Me-Sha-Wabble' (Bud Freeman and his Famous Chicagoans)
¶ Lambert/Sitwell, 'Such a Space of Silence in the Town' (from *The Rio Grande*) (Philharmonia Orchestra and Chorus/Lambert)
¶ 'Sempre que Lisboa canta' (Carlos Ramos)
¶ 'Jolly Bob' (Karin Juel)
¶ 'Django' (Modern Jazz Quartet)
¶ 'Many Tears Ago' (Connie Francis)

¶ Mozart, Piano Concerto No. 22 in E flat (K. 482) (Annie Fischer/Philharmonia Orchestra/Sawallisch)
¶ LUXURY: American whiskey.
¶ BOOK: The collected poetry of Robert Graves.

5 June 1961
547 Julian Bream
Guitarist
*¶ Schubert, Quintet in C major (opus 163) (Kurt Reher *cello*/Hollywood String Quartet)
¶ Purcell, 'When I am Laid in Earth' (from *Dido and Aeneas*) (Kirsten Flagstad/Mermaid Orchestra/Jones)
¶ Tarrega, 'Tremolo Study' (Andrés Segovia *guitar*)
¶ 'Billets doux' (Stephane Grappelli *violin*/Django Reinhardt *guitar*/Quintet of the Hot Club of France)
¶ Morley, 'It was a Lover and his Lass' (Peter Pears/Julian Bream *lute*)
¶ Villa-Lobos, Bachianas Brasileiras No. 5 (Bidu Sayao/Leonard Rose *cello*/Villa-Lobos)
¶ Vivaldi/Bach, Concerto for Four Harpsichords in A minor (Eileen Joyce/Thurston Dart/George Malcolm/Denis Vaughan/Pro Arte Orchestra/Ord)
¶ Mozart, Quintet in G minor (K. 516) Cecil Aronowitz *viola*/Amadeus String Quartet)
¶ LUXURIES: A guitar, music manuscript paper and pens.
¶ BOOK: A collection of 16th- and 17th-century English poetry.

12 June 1961
548 Richard Murdoch
(2nd appearance)
Entertainer
¶ 'Now, Baby, Now' (Julie London)
¶ 'Tough' (Dave Barbour and his Orchestra)
¶ Liszt, Fantasia on Hungarian Folk Tunes in E minor for Piano and Orchestra (Gyrgy Cziffra/Paris Conservatoire Orchestra/Dervaux)
¶ 'You Make Me Feel So Young' (Frank Sinatra)

¶ Schumann, Symphony No. 1 in B flat major (Orchestre de la Suisse Romande/Ansermet)
¶ 'You Deserve' (Peggy Lee)
¶ 'Whirly-Bird' (Count Basie and his Orchestra)
¶ R. Strauss, 'Beim Schlafengehen' (from the *Four Last Songs*) (Elisabeth Schwarzkopf/Philharmonia Orchestra/Ackermann)
¶ LUXURY: Golf clubs and balls.
¶ BOOK: A history of the world.

19 June 1961
549 Dr W. Grey Walter
Scientist
¶ Enkoito Drum Rhythms from East Africa
¶ 'First Delphic Hymn' (Arda Mandikian)
¶ 'Tailgate Ramble' (Wingy Manone's Dixieland Band)
¶ Beethoven, String Quartet No. 15 in A minor (opus 132) (Koeckert Quartet)
¶ 'Fugue on Bop Themes' (Fabulous Dave Brubeck Octet)
¶ Schoenberg, 'March' (from *Serenade*, opus 24) (Gervase de Peyer *clarinet*/Wilfred Hambleton *bass clarinet*/Hugo d'Alton *mandolin*/Freddie Phillips *guitar*/Eli Goren *violin*/Cecil Aronowitz *viola*/Terence Weil *cello*/Seiber)
¶ Krenek, 'Spiritus Intelligentiae Sanctus' (Kathe Möller-Siepermann/Martin Häusler/Ernst Krenek)
¶ Wirén, 'Serenade for Strings' (Stockholm Radio Orchestra/Westerberg)
¶ LUXURY: A computer.
¶ BOOK: E. C. Large, *Everybody's Handbook for Survival on a Desert Island*

26 June 1961
550 Ann Haydon
Tennis player
¶ 'Brazil' (Ray Conniff Orchestra and Chorus)
¶ Gershwin, 'Oh, I Got Plenty o' Nuttin'' (from *Porgy and Bess*) (Frank Sinatra)
¶ 'Tout le long des rues' (Tino Rossi)
¶ Holst, 'Mars' (from *The Planets*) (BBC Symphony/Sargent)

¶ 'Yo vendo unos ojos negros' (Nat 'King' Cole)
¶ Rodgers & Hammerstein, 'Sixteen Going on Seventeen' (from *The Sound of Music*) (Lori Peters/Brian Davies)
¶ 'Arrivederci Roma' (Rino Salviati)
*¶ Debussy, 'Clair de lune' (from *Suite bergamasque*) (Stokowski Symphony)
¶ LUXURY: Insect repellent.
¶ BOOK: The plays of Goethe.

3 July 1961
551 Roy Hay
Gardening expert
¶ 'Paris, tu n'as pas changé' (Jean Sablon)
¶ Chopin, Étude No. 2 in A minor (opus 10) and Étude No. 3 in E major (opus 10) (Alfred Cortot *piano*)
¶ 'Oh How I Weary, Deary' (Sir Harry Lauder)
¶ 'I Hear You Calling Me' (John McCormack)
*¶ Beethoven, Symphony No. 6 in F major (opus 68) (BBC Symphony/Toscanini)
¶ J. Strauss, 'Emperor Waltz' (Vienna Philharmonic/Krips)
¶ 'Bras dessus, bras dessous' (Les Compagnons de la Chanson)
¶ Bizet, 'Farandole' (from *L'arlésienne*) (RPO/Beecham)
¶ LUXURY: Asparagus seed.
¶ BOOK: Voltaire, *Candide*

10 July 1961
552 Anna Massey
Actress
*¶ Beethoven, Symphony No. 7 in A major (opus 92) (RPO/Beecham)
¶ Tchaikovsky, 'Romeo and Juliet Fantasy Overture' (Vienna Philharmonic/von Karajan)
¶ 'My Very Good Friend the Milkman' (Fats Waller)
¶ Tchaikovsky, *Swan Lake* (Minneapolis Symphony/Dorati)
¶ 'Day In, Day Out' (Lena Horne)
¶ 'Natasha's Waltz' (from film *War and Peace*) (Orchestra/Ferrara)

¶ Grieg, Piano Concerto in A minor (Artur Rubinstein/RCA Victor Symphony/Wallenstein)
¶ 'You're Getting to be a Habit with Me' (Frank Sinatra)
¶ LUXURIES: Family photographs and a tape recorder.
¶ BOOK: A book on mathematics.

17 July 1961
553 Joe Davis
Billiards and snooker champion
¶ 'Dolores' and 'Dearly Beloved' (Charlie Kunz *piano*)
¶ Lerner & Loewe, 'Get Me to the Church on Time' (from *My Fair Lady*) (Stanley Holloway)
¶ 'When I Fall in Love' (Nat 'King' Cole)
¶ 'Yours' (Vera Lynn)
¶ Mendelssohn, Violin Concerto in E minor (Campoli/LPO/Van Beinum)
¶ 'It's Easy to Remember' (from film *Mississippi*) (Perry Como)
¶ Porter, 'Who Wants to be a Millionaire?' (from film *High Society*) (Frank Sinatra and Celeste Holm)
*¶ Beethoven, Piano Concerto No. 5 in E flat major (Emils Gilels/Philharmonia Orchestra/Ludwig)
¶ LUXURY: Golf clubs and balls.
¶ BOOK: *Whitaker's Almanack*

24 July 1961
554 Nelson Riddle
Orchestra leader, arranger and composer
*¶ 'Frenesi' (Artie Shaw *clarinet* and his Orchestra)
¶ Kern & Hammerstein, 'Lonesome Road' (from film *Show Boat*) (Tommy Dorsey and his Orchestra)
¶ 'Sunny Side of the Street' (from *International Revue*) (Tommy Dorsey and his Orchestra)
¶ Carmichael, 'Stardust' (Artie Shaw and his Orchestra)
¶ 'Li'l Darlin' (Count Basie and his Orchestra)
¶ Delibes/Evans, 'Maid of Cadiz' (Miles Davis *trumpet*)
¶ 'Benny Rides Again' (Benny Goodman and his Orchestra)
¶ LUXURY: A piano.
¶ BOOK: The collected poetry of Robert Frost.

31 July 1961
555 Yvonne Mitchell
Actress

*¶Purcell, 'Trumpet Sonata' (Dennis Egan/Philomusica of London/Lewis)
¶'Sweet and Lovely' (Thelonius Monk *piano*)
¶Bach, Goldberg Variations (Gustav Leonhardt *harpsichord*)
¶'Do You Mind?' (Anthony Newley)
¶Mozart, Variations on 'Ah, vous dirai-je, maman' (Clara Haskil *piano*)
¶Purcell, 'Sound the Trumpet' (from *Come Ye Sons of Art*) (Alfred Deller/John Whitworth)
¶Corelli/Barbirolli, Concerto for Oboe and Strings (Evelyn Rothwell/Hallé Orchestra/Barbirolli)
¶Bach, Brandenburg Concerto No. 2 in F major (Denis Clift *trumpet*/Bach Festival Chamber Orchestra/Menuhin)
¶LUXURY: Writing materials.
¶BOOK: A compilation of works of philosophy.

7 August 1961
556 Gerald Durrell
Zoologist and writer

¶Lerner & Loewe, 'A Hymn to Him' (from *My Fair Lady*) (Rex Harrison)
¶'Guabi Guabi' (Zulu music)
¶'The Almond Tree' (Chorus with mandolin and orchestra)
¶'Tikiminiki' (Los Incas)
¶'A Gnu' (Michael Flanders/Donald Swann)
¶'Just an Old-Fashioned Girl' (Eartha Kitt)
*¶Beethoven, Symphony No. 8 in F major (opus 93) (Philharmonia Orchestra/Klemperer)
¶Mozart, 'Der Hohe Rache' (from *The Magic Flute*) (Florence Foster Jenkins/Cosme McMoon *piano*)
¶LUXURY: Writing materials.
¶BOOK: *Encyclopaedia Britannica*

14 August 1961
557 Jack Fingleton
Cricketer, writer and broadcaster

¶Chopin, Prelude No. 7 in A major (opus 28) (Arthur Rubinstein *piano*)
¶'Catch a Falling Star' (Perry Como)
¶Lerner & Loewe, 'Thank Heaven for Little Girls' (from film *Gigi*) (Maurice Chevalier)
¶Porter, 'True Love' (from film *High Society*) (Bing Crosby/Grace Kelly)
¶Chopin/Douglas, *Les Sylphides* (Philharmonia Orchestra/Irving)
¶'Whatever Will Be, Will Be' (from film *The Man Who Knew Too Much*) (Doris Day)
*¶Bach/Gounod, 'Ave Maria' (Joan Hammond)
¶'Waltzing Matilda' (Peter Dawson)
¶LUXURY: Golf clubs and balls.
¶BOOK: Thomas à Kempis, *Imitation of Christ*

21 August 1961
558 Diana Dors
Actress

¶Rimsky-Korsakov, *Scheherazade* (Orchestre de la Suisse Romande/Ansermet)
¶Arlen & Harburg, 'Over the Rainbow' (from film *The Wizard of Oz*) (Judy Garland)
¶Sibelius, 'Valse triste' (opus 44) (RPO/Beecham)
¶'That Old Black Magic' (from film *Star-Spangled Rhythm*) (Sammy Davis Jnr)
¶Rodgers & Hammerstein, 'Soliloquy' (from *Carousel*) (Frank Sinatra)
¶'Pennies from Heaven' (from film) (Al Hibbler)
*¶Ravel, 'Pavane pour une infante défunte' (Philharmonia Orchestra/Cantelli)
¶Berlin, 'Let Yourself Go' (from film *Follow the Fleet*) (Nelson Riddle and his Orchestra)
¶LUXURY: Writing materials.
¶BOOK: An anthology of poetry.

28 August 1961
559 Edward Ward
Radio foreign correspondent

¶'The Hawk' (Los Torrealberos)
¶'La montanara' (Societa Alpinisti Tridentini)
¶Verdi, 'Brindisi, libiamo, libiamo' (from *La traviata*) (Victoria de los Angeles/Carlo del Monte/Rome Opera Chorus and Orchestra/Serafin)
¶'Song of the Plains' (Alexandrov Song & Dance Ensemble)
¶'That's All Right' (Alan Lomax)
¶'I Loved You' (Alexandrov Song & Dance Ensemble)
¶'On Top of Old Smoky' (Josh White)
*¶Mozart, Symphony No. 35 in D (RPO/Beecham)
¶LUXURY: Carving Tools.
¶BOOK: *Encyclopaedia Britannica*

4 September 1961
560 John Slater
Actor

¶Gilbert & Sullivan, *The Gondoliers* (overture) (D'Oyly Carte Opera Orchestra/Godfrey)
*¶Purcell, 'An Evening Hymn' (Alfred Deller/Geraint Jones *organ*)
¶Outside Shelley Berman (Shelley Berman)
¶Mendelssohn, 'Wedding March' (from *A Midsummer Night's Dream*) (BBC Symphony/Sargent)
¶'The Kid's Last Fight' (Frankie Laine)
¶'See the Conquering Hero Comes' and 'Old Comrades' (Massed Bands, Drums and Fifes at British Legion Festival of Empire and Remembrance, 1933)
¶Rodgers & Hart, 'My Funny Valentine' (from *Babes in Arms*) (Shirley Bassey)
¶Beethoven, Trio in B flat (opus 97) (Alfred Cortot *piano*/Jacques Thibaud *violin*/Pablo Casals *cello*)
¶LUXURY: A still.
¶BOOK: *Plays* and *Prefaces* by George Bernard Shaw.

11 September 1961
561 Coral Browne
Actress
*¶ 'Waltzing Matilda' (Burl Ives)
¶ Tchaikovsky, *The Sleeping Beauty* (Act 1 waltz) (Philharmonia Orchestra/ Kurtz)
¶ Borodin/Wright & Forrest (arr.), 'Stranger in Paradise' (from *Kismet*) (Johnny Mathis)
¶ 'Fancy Our Meeting' (from *That's a Good Girl*) and 'Who?' (from *Sunny*) (Jack Buchanan/ Elsie Randolph)
¶ Shakespeare, Sonnets 18 and 16 (John Gielgud)
¶ Brahms, Piano Concerto No. 2 in B flat (Sviatoslav Richter/ LSO/Leinsdorf)
¶ Meyerbeer, 'Shadow Song' (from *Dinorah*) (Maria Callas/ Philharmonia Orchestra/ Serafin)
¶ 'Mademoiselle de Paris' (Frank Bernardi/Armand Migiani Orchestra)
¶ LUXURY: A sable coat.
¶ BOOK: Oscar Wilde, *The Happy Prince and Other Tales*

18 September 1961
562 Commander Sir Stephen King-Hall
Sailor, playwright, novelist, farmer and newsletter editor
¶ Wagner, *Götterdämmerung* (Act 3) (Set Svanholm/Oslo Philharmonic/Norwegian State Radio Orchestra/Fjeldstad)
*¶ Elgar, 'Jesu Maria' (from *The Dream of Gerontius*) (Heddle Nash/Royal Liverpool Philharmonic/Sargent)
¶ Debussy, 'La cathédrale engloutie' (from *Preludes*, Book 1, No. 10) (Walter Gieseking *piano*)
¶ Bach, Passacaglia and Fugue in C minor (Karl Richter *organ*)
¶ Beethoven, Symphony No. 7 in A major (opus 92) (NBC Symphony/Toscanini)
¶ Chopin, Nocturne in C sharp minor (Vladimir Horowitz *piano*)
¶ Schubert, 'Die Forelle' (Walther Ludwig/Walter Bohle *piano*)

¶ 'If You were the Only Girl in the World' (from *The Bing Boys are Here*) (Violet Loraine/ George Robey)
¶ LUXURY: Goya's portrait of the Duke of Wellington.
¶ BOOK: Erskine-May's manual of procedure in the House of Commons.

13 September 1961
563 E. Arnot Robertson
(This was not broadcast, as Miss Robertson died before the transmission date.)
¶ 'Sous les toits de Paris'
¶ Chopin, Impromptu No. 4 in C sharp minor (Alfred Cortot *piano*)
¶ 'Sometimes I Feel like an Eagle on the Heights' or 'The Old Ark's A-Movering' (Paul Robeson)
¶ Bach, Suite No. 3 in D
¶ West Indian folk song
¶ Wordsworth, 'Upon Westminster Bridge', or Kipling, 'The Way Through the Woods' (Robert Donat)
¶ Delius, *Hassan* (prelude) (BBC chorus/RPO/Beecham)
¶ Beethoven, Symphony No. 5 in C minor (opus 67)
No further information is available.

2 October 1961
564 Tommy Reilly
Harmonica Player
¶ Mendelssohn, Symphony No. 4 in A major (Philharmonia Orchestra/Cantelli)
¶ 'Soirée romantique' (Maurice Larcange *accordion*)
¶ Kreisler, 'Schön Rosmarin' (Fritz Kreisler *violin*)
*¶ 'A Tree in the Meadow' (Dorothy Squires)
¶ 'The Wedding Dance' (Micky Katz and his Orchestra)
¶ 'You'll Never Know' (Shirley Bassey)
¶ 'Banjo and Fiddle' (Jascha Heifetz *violin*/Emanuel Bay *piano*)
¶ R. Strauss, *Der Rosenkavalier* (closing duet) (Elisabeth Schumann/Maria Olszewska/ Vienna Philharmonic/Heger)

¶ LUXURY: A harmonica.
¶ BOOK: Pictures of the English countryside.

9 October 1961
565 Canon Noel Duckworth
Ex-university boat-race cox, and Chaplain of Churchill College, Cambridge
*¶ Handel, 'I Know that My Redeemer Liveth' (from *Messiah*) (Ernest Lough/G. Thalben-Ball *organ*)
¶ Weber, 'Invitation to the Dance' (opus 65) (Stokowski Symphony)
¶ Handel, 'Hallelujah Chorus' (from *Messiah*) (Huddersfield Choral Society/Royal Liverpool Philharmonic/Sargent)
¶ Walford Davies 'Solemn Melody' (Philharmonia Orchestra/Weldon)
¶ 'Saturday Night' (E. C. Arinze and his Music)
¶ Haydn, 'The Heavens are Telling' (from *The Creation*) (Royal Choral Society/Royal Liverpool Philharmonic/ Sargent)
¶ 'The Haunted Ballroom' (Richard Crean and his Orchestra)
¶ Brahms, 'Academic Festival Overture' (opus 80) (RPO/ Beecham)
¶ LUXURY: A radio receiver.
¶ BOOK: Thomas à Kempis, *Imitation of Christ*

16 October 1961
566 Hattie Jacques
Comedienne and actress
¶ Beethoven, Symphony No. 9 in D minor (opus 125) (Robert Shaw Chorale/NBC Symphony/ Toscanini)
¶ 'Hello Little Girl' (Duke Ellington and his Orchestra)
¶ Handel, 'Let the Bright Seraphim' (from *Samson*) (Joan Sutherland/Royal Opera House Orchestra, Covent Garden/ Molinari-Pradelli)
*¶ Bach/Münchinger, Fugue in A minor (Stuttgart Chamber Orchestra/Münchinger)
¶ 'On the Sunny Side of the Street' (Tommy Dorsey and his Orchestra)

¶ 'God Rest Ye, Merry Gentlemen' (Modern Jazz Quartet)
¶ 'Lord Badminton's Memoirs' (Peter Sellers)
¶ 'The Red Balloon' (from *The Letter*) (Judy Garland/Gordon Jenkins Orchestra)
¶ LUXURIES: A photograph and recording of her family.
¶ BOOK: *The Oxford Dictionary of Quotations*

23 October 1961
567 Francis Chichester
Writer, aviator and yachtsman
¶ J. Strauss, 'The Blue Danube' (Vienna Philharmonic/Krips)
¶ Rogers, Hart, 'Blue Room' (from *The Girl Friend*) (Bruce Trent)
¶ 'Singin' in the Rain' (from film *The Hollywood Revue*) (Ukelele Ike/Cliff Edwards)
¶ 'Dojoji' (Azuma Kabuki Musicians)
¶ Offenbach, *Orpheus in the Underworld* (overture) (RPO/Gamley)
¶ Tchaikovsky, *Swan Lake* (Act 2) (Orchestre de la Suisse Romande/Ansermet)
¶ Rodgers & Hammerstein, 'Some Enchanted Evening' (from *South Pacific*) (Ezio Pinza)
¶ Beethoven, Piano Concerto No. 5 in E flat major (Emil Gilels/Philharmonia Orchestra/Ludwig)

30 October 1961
568 Sir Gerald Beadle
BBC administrator
¶ Sibelius, Symphony No. 2 in D major (BBC Symphony/Sargent)
¶ Puccini, 'One Fine Day' (from *Madam Butterfly*) (Elisabeth Schwarzkopf/Philharmonia Orchestra/Galliera)
¶ Vaughan Williams, 'Fantasia on a Theme by Thomas Tallis' (Philharmonia Orchestra/Sargent)
¶ Prokofiev, Sonata No. 7 in B flat major (Sviatoslav Richter *piano*)

*¶ Beethoven, Piano Concerto No. 5 in E flat major (Emil Gilels/Philharmonia Orchestra/Ludwig)
¶ Mussorgsky, 'Varlaam's Song' (from *Boris Godunov*) (Boris Christoff/Philharmonia Orchestra/Dobrowen)
¶ Mussorgsky, *Pictures from an Exhibition* (Sviatoslav Richter *piano*)
¶ Bach/Stokowski, Toccata and Fugue in D minor (Stokowski Symphony)
¶ LUXURY: Claret.
¶ BOOK: Boswell's *Life of Samuel Johnson*

6 November 1961
569 Wee Georgie Wood
Music-hall artist
¶ 'Abide with Me' (Clara Butt)
¶ 'Keep Smiling at Trouble' (Al Jolson)
¶ 'Leanin'' (Owen Brannigan)
¶ 'Keep Right On to the End of the Road' (Sir Harry Lauder)
*¶ Coward, *Private Lives* (Act 1 love scene) (Noël Coward/Gertrude Lawrence)
¶ Schubert, Symphony No. 8 in B minor (RPO/Beecham)
¶ Shakespeare, 'All the World's a Stage' (from *As You Like It*, Act 2) (John Gielgud)
¶ Raff, 'Cavatina' (Mischa Elman *violin*/Josef Bonime *piano*)
¶ LUXURY: Writing materials.
¶ BOOK: Walter De la Mare, *Memoirs of a Midget*

13 November 1961
570 Rupert Davies
Actor
¶ Rimsky-Korsakov, *Scheherazade* (Orchestre de la Suisse Romande/Ansermet)
¶ 'I'm in a Dancing Mood' (from *This'll Make You Whistle*) (Dave Brubeck Quartet)
¶ Franck, Symphony in D minor (French National Radio Orchestra/Beecham)
¶ Bach, Partita No. 1 in B minor (sarabande) (Yehudi Menuhin *violin*)
¶ 'Arlette' (theme from TV series *Inspector Maigret*) (Ron Grainer and his Music)

*¶ Massenet, 'Elégie' (Feodor Chaliapin/Ivor Newton *piano*/Cedric Sharpe *cello obligato*)
¶ Templeton, 'Bach Goes to Town' (Benny Goodman and his Orchestra)
¶ Tchaikovsky, Symphony No. 5 in E minor (Leningrad Philharmonic/Mravinsky)
¶ LUXURY: A lump of jade.
¶ BOOK: Voltaire, *Candide*

20 November 1961
571 Virgil Thomson
Composer and critic
¶ Bach, Goldberg Variations No. 29 (Wanda Landowska *harpsichord*)
*¶ Mozart, 'Proteggia il giusto cielo' (from *Don Giovanni*) (Joan Sutherland/Elisabeth Schwarzkopf/Luigi Alva/Philharmonia Orchestra/Giulini)
¶ Satie, 'Le Banquet' (from *Socrate*) (Violette Journeaux/Paris Philharmonic/Leibowitz)
¶ Debussy, 'Pour les accords' (from Étude No. 12) (Walter Gieseking *piano*)
¶ 'Dance of the Great Peace' (from *Gagaku*, Japanese court music) (Instrumental ensemble)
¶ Schubert, 'Meeres stille' (Dietrich Fischer-Dieskau/Jörg Demus *piano*)
¶ Varese, 'Intégrales' (New York Wind Ensemble/Juilliard Percussion Orchestra/Waldman)
¶ 'Barnyard Blues' (Original Dixieland Five)
¶ LUXURIES: Music manuscript paper, pencils and rubber.
¶ BOOK: *Encyclopaedia Britannica*

27 November 1961
572 Joan Collins
Actress
¶ 'Come Fly with Me' (Frank Sinatra)
¶ 'Lover' (from film *Love Me Tonight*) (Peggy Lee)
¶ 'Hava Nagila' (Harry Belafonte)
¶ 'Serenata' (Sarah Vaughan)
¶ Ellis, 'I was Never Kissed Before' (from *Bless the Bride*) (Anthony Newley)

¶ 'Mambo Inn' (Rene Touzet and his Orchestra)
*¶ Gershwin, 'My Ship' (from *Lady in the Dark*) (Toni Harper)
¶ 'Milord' (Edith Piaf)
¶ LUXURY: A television set.
¶ BOOK: A teach-yourself manual of the principal foreign languages.

4 December 1961
573 Paul Gallico
Novelist, journalist and short-story writer
¶ Mozart, Symphony No. 6 in F major (K. 43) (Philharmonic Symphony, London/Leinsdorf)
¶ Beethoven, Piano Concerto No. 1 in C major (Artur Schnabel/LSO/Sargent)
¶ Rodgers & Hart, 'Where or When?' (from *Babes in Arms*) (Frank Sinatra)
¶ Prokofiev, Violin Concerto No. 2 in G minor (Jascha Heifetz/Boston Symphony/Münch)
¶ 'The British Grenadiers' (Pride of the '48 Band)
¶ R. Strauss, *Der Rosenkavalier* (Act 3 trio) (Lotte Lehmann/Elisabeth Schumann/Maria Olszewska/Vienna Philharmonic/Heger)
¶ 'Come to Me, Bend to Me' (from *Brigadoon*) (Jan Peerce)
*¶ Bach/Stokowski, Passacaglia and Fugue in C minor (Stokowski Symphony)
¶ LUXURY: Writing materials.
¶ BOOK: Lewis Carroll, *Alice in Wonderland*

11 December 1961
574 Sir Michael Balcon
Film producer
¶ Donizetti, 'Mad Scene' (from *Lucia di Lammermoor*) (Joan Sutherland/Paris Conservatoire Orchestra/Santi)
¶ Ravel, 'Lever du jour' (from *Daphnis and Chloe*) (Chorus of the Royal Opera House, Covent Garden/LSO/Monteux)
¶ Chopin, Waltz No. 10 in B minor (opus 69, no. 2) (Dinu Lipatti *piano*)
¶ Vaughan Williams, Sinfonia Antarctica (LPO/Boult)

¶ R. Strauss, 'Ohne Mich' (from *Der Rosenkavalier*) (Kerstin Meyer/Otto Edelmann/Philharmonia Orchestra/von Karajan)
¶ Shakespeare, 'Shall I Compare Thee to a Summer's Day?' (Sonnet 18) (John Gielgud)
¶ Puccini, 'In quelle trine morbide' (from *Manon Lescaut*) (Renata Tebaldi/Santa Cecilia Orchestra, Rome/Erede)
*¶ Brahms, Symphony No. 1 in C minor (Philharmonia Orchestra/Klemperer)
¶ LUXURY: Wine.
¶ BOOK: *Oxford English Dictionary*

18 December 1961
575 Bob Hope
Actor and comedian
¶ Arlen & Harburg, 'Over the Rainbow' (from film *The Wizard of Oz*) (Judy Garland)
¶ 'Jailhouse Rock' (Elvis Presley)
*¶ 'It's Only a Paper Moon' (Ella Fitzgerald)
¶ 'Smoke Gets in Your Eyes' (from *Roberta*) (André Kostelanetz Orchestra)
¶ Lerner & Loewe, 'Thank Heaven for Little Girls' (from film *Gigi*) (Maurice Chevalier)
¶ Berlin, 'White Christmas' (from film *Holiday Inn*) (Bing Crosby)
¶ Debussy, 'Clair de lune' (from *Suite bergamasque*) (Stokowski Symphony)
¶ 'Thanks for the Memory' (from film) (Shirley Ross/Bob Hope)
¶ LUXURY: A little money.
¶ BOOK: Margaret Mitchell, *Gone with the Wind*

25 December 1961
576 Gracie Fields
(2nd appearance)
Actress, singer and comedienne
¶ 'The Little Drummer Boy' (Harry Simeone Chorale)
¶ Lerner & Loewe, 'I Remember It Well' (from film *Gigi*) (Maurice Chevalier/Hermione Gingold)

*¶ Rachmaninov, Piano Concerto No. 2 in C minor (Sergei Rachmaninov/Philadelphia Orchestra/Stokowski)
¶ Rodgers & Hammerstein, 'Twin Soliloquies' (from *South Pacific*) (Mary Martin/Ezio Pinza)
¶ Vaughan Williams, 'Fantasia on Greensleeves' (Hallé Orchestra/Barbirolli)
¶ Gold, 'Theme from *Exodus*' (Sinfonia of London/Gold)
¶ 'The Holy City' (Gracie Fields)
¶ 'Charmaine' (Mantovani and his Orchestra)
¶ LUXURY: A reproduction of Renoir's *The Picnic*.
¶ BOOK: John Galsworthy, *The Forsyte Saga*

1 January 1962
577 James Gunn RA
Portrait painter
*¶ Beethoven, Violin Concerto in D (Jascha Heifetz/Boston Symphony/Münch)
¶ 'An Eriskay Love Lilt' (Kenneth McKellar)
¶ 'La vie en rose' (Edith Piaf)
¶ Bach/Wilhelmj, Suite No. 3 in D major (Mischa Elman *violin*)
¶ Tchaikovsky, *Swan Lake* (Act 2 pas de deux) (Minneapolis Symphony/Dorati)
¶ Beethoven, Trio in B flat (opus 97) (Alfred Cortot *piano*/Jacques Thibaud *violin*/Pablo Casals *cello*)
¶ Mendelssohn, *A Midsummer Night's Dream* (scherzo) (Benno Moiseiwitsch *piano*)
¶ Schubert, 'Ave Maria' (opus 52, no. 6) (Kirsten Flagstad)
¶ LUXURY: Painting materials.
¶ BOOK: A large anthology of poetry.

8 January 1962
578 Hughie Green
Entertainer, and talent show host
¶ 'I've Got the World on a String' (Frank Sinatra)
¶ 'The High and the Mighty' (from film) (Les Baxter Orchestra)
*¶ 'That's What a Rainy Day is For' (Connie Russell)

¶ 'Song and Dance Man'
(Sammy Davis Jnr)
¶ 'Ponce' (Elliot Lawrence and
his Band)
¶ Chopin/Douglas, *Les sylphides*
(Philharmonia Orchestra/
Irving)
¶ 'Lover' (from film *Love Me
Tonight*) (Gene Krupa
Orchestra)
¶ 'Autumn Nocturne' (Ray
Charles Singers)
¶ LUXURY: A looking glass.
¶ BOOK: Theodore Dreiser, *An
American Tragedy*

15 January 1962
579 Stuart Hibberd
Veteran BBC announcer
*¶ Massenet, 'Navarraise' (from
Le Cid, Act 2) (Royal Opera
House Orchestra, Covent
Garden/Braithwaite)
¶ 'Jamaican Rumba' (Rawicz &
Landauer *pianos*)
¶ 'Deep River' (Paul Robeson)
¶ Dohnanyi, Cappriccio in F
minor (opus 28, no. 6)
(Vladimir Horowitz *piano*)
¶ Bizet, *The Fair Maid of Perth*
(serenade) (Heddle Nash)
¶ 'Pick Up Tha' Musket'
(Stanley Holloway)
¶ 'The Infant Sing (Sing
Lullaby)' (King's College
Chapel Choir/Ord)
¶ 'Carry Me Back to Green,
Green Pastures' (Kentucky
Minstrels)
¶ LUXURY: A recorder.
¶ BOOK: Victoria Sackville-West
& Harold Nicolson, *Another
World than This*

22 January 1962
580 Ken Sykora
Broadcaster and guitarist
¶ 'Theme de Nuayno' (Los
Incas)
¶ 'Dusk' (Duke Ellington and
his Famous Orchestra)
¶ 'It's Easy to Remember' (from
film *Mississippi*) (Bing Crosby)
¶ Bach, 'Gavotte' (transcribed
from Suite No. 1 in D major for
solo cello) (Andrés Segovia
guitar)
¶ 'Things are Swinging' (Peggy
Lee)

¶ Bruch, Violin Concerto No. 1
in G minor (David Oistrakh/
LSO/von Matacic)
¶ 'Una aventura mas' (Trio Los
Panchos)
*¶ 'Nuages' (Django Reinhardt
guitar)
¶ LUXURY: A guitar.
¶ BOOK: *Science for the Citizen*

29 January 1962
581 Sir John Gielgud
Actor
*¶ Bach, Double Concerto in D
minor (Yehudi Menuhin &
Christian Ferras *violins*/Festival
Chamber Orchestra/Menuhin)
¶ Mozart, Rondo in D major for
piano and orchestra (K. 382)
(Annie Fischer/Bayerisches
Staatsorchester/Fricsay)
¶ Mozart, Clarinet Concerto in
A major (K. 622) (Heinrich
Geuser/Berlin Radio
Symphony/Fricsay)
¶ Schubert, 'Wohin?' (from *Die
Schöne Müllerin*) (Peter Pears/
Benjamin Britten *piano*)
¶ Mozart, Piano Concerto No.
20 in D minor (K. 466)
(Sviatoslav Richter/National
Philharmonic Symphony/
Wislocki)
¶ Dvořák, 'Die Bescheidene'
(from *Moravian Duet* Op. 32,
No. 3) (Elisabeth Schwarzkopf/
Irmgaard Seefried/Gerald
Moore *piano*)
¶ Brahms, Symphony No. 3 in
F major (Philharmonia
Orchestra/Klemperer)
¶ Purcell, Tune and Air in D for
Trumpet and Orchestra (Roger
Voisin *trumpet*/Daniel Pickham
organ/Unicorn Concerto
Orchestra/Dickson)
¶ LUXURY: A water-colour of
Versailles by Raoul Dufy.
¶ BOOK: *The Oxford Dictionary of
Quotations*

5 February 1962
582 Kay Cavendish
Pianist and vocalist
*¶ Bach, Double Concerto in D
minor (Gioconda de Vito &
Yehudi Menuhin *violins*/
Philharmonia Orchestra/
Bernard)
¶ 'Holiday for Strings' (Stanley
Black and his Orchestra)

¶ 'Ezekiel' (Harry Belafonte)
¶ 'Do I Love You?' (from film
Dubarry was a Lady) (Peggy
Lee/George Shearing Quintet)
¶ Franck, Symphonic
Variations (Moura Lympany
piano/RPO/Silvestri)
¶ 'What is This Thing Called
Love?' (from *Wake Up and
Dream*) (Clebanoff Strings and
Percussion)
¶ Speech at the Oxford Union
(Gerard Hoffnung)
¶ 'O Come All Ye Faithful'
(Elisabeth Schwarzkopf)
¶ LUXURIES: Flower seeds and an
armchair.
¶ BOOK: *Encyclopaedia
Britannica*

12 February 1962
583 Stanley Holloway
(2nd appearance)
Comedy star
¶ 'Railroad Rhythm' (Billy
Mayerl *piano*)
¶ 'Blow the Wind Southerly'
(Kathleen Ferrier)
¶ 'Down Love Lane' (from *The
Co-optimists*) (Elsa MacFarlane/
Stanley Holloway)
¶ Gershwin, 'A Few Drinks'
(from *Funny Face*) (Sydney
Howard/Leslie Hanson)
¶ Templeton, 'Bach Goes to
Town' (George Malcolm
harpsichord)
¶ 'Three Green Bonnets' (Gracie
Fields)
¶ Lerner & Loewe, 'Wouldn't It
be Loverly' (from *My Fair
Lady*) (Peter Sellers)
*¶ Elgar, 'Chanson du matin'
(opus 15, no. 2) (LPO/Boult)
¶ LUXURY: A parking meter and
plenty of change.
¶ BOOK: *Mrs Beeton's Household
Management*

19 February 1962
584 Frank Chacksfield
Light music conductor
¶ Bach, Toccata and Fugue in D
minor (Albert Schweitzer *organ*)
¶ 'The Things We Did Last
Summer' (Frank Sinatra)
*¶ Debussy, 'Clair de lune' (from
Suite bergamasque) (André
Kostelanetz Orchestra)
¶ 'I Raised My Hat' (Ben Fields
and his Band)

¶ Mozart, 'Papageno's Bell Song' (from *The Magic Flute*) (Walter Berry/Vienna Philharmonic Orchestra and Chorus/Böhm)
¶ 'I'm Gonna Sit Right Down and Write Myself a Letter' (Fats Waller and his Rhythm)
¶ 'Sous les toits de Paris' (from film) (Orchestre de Danse Alexander)
¶ 'Ebb Tide' (Frank Chacksfield and his Orchestra)
¶ LUXURY: A ciné camera.
¶ BOOK: Charles Dickens, *The Pickwick Papers*

26 February 1962
585 H. E. Bates
Novelist and short-story writer
*¶ 'Tupu Te Ruki' (Eddie Lund and his Tahitians)
¶ Gilbert & Sullivan, *HMS Pinafore* (opening chorus) (Pro Arte Orchestra/Glyndebourne Festival Chorus/Sargent)
¶ Mozart, Piano Concerto No. 24 in C minor (Ingrid Haebler/Pro Musica Orchestra, Vienna/Walter)
¶ Butterworth, 'Rhapsody' (A Shropshire Lad) (LPO/Boult)
¶ Mozart, 'Prendero quel brunettino' (from *Così fan tutte*) (Sena Jurinac/Blanche Thebom/Glyndebourne Festival Orchestra/Busch)
¶ Schubert, 'Wonne der Wehmut' (Ernst Häfliger/Hertha Klust *piano*)
¶ Sibelius, Symphony No. 2 in D major (BBC Symphony/Sargent)
¶ Schumann, 'Der Nussbaum' (Elisabeth Schwarzkopf/Gerald Moore *piano*)
¶ LUXURY: A banjo.
¶ BOOK: English lyrics.

5 March 1962
586 Irene Handl
Actress
¶ 'Boum' (Charles Trenet)
¶ 'La mer' (Charles Trenet)
¶ 'Le carilloneur' (Charles Aznavour)
¶ 'Il faut savoir' (Charles Aznavour)
¶ 'Tower of Strength' (Frankie Vaughan)

¶ 'Heartbreak Hotel' (Elvis Presley)
¶ Wagner, 'The Ride of the Valkyries' (from *Die Walküre*) (Vienna Philharmonic/Furtwängler)
*¶ Schubert, 'Ave Maria' (Yehudi Menuhin *violin*/Gerald Moore *piano*)
¶ LUXURY: Pencils and paper.
¶ BOOK: A portfolio of reproductions of her favourite pictures.

12 March 1962
587 Colonel A. D. Wintle
MC
Soldier, writer and individualist
¶ 'Cavalry Reveille' (Massed Cavalry Trumpets)
¶ 'Light of Foot' (Band of HM Coldstream Guards)
*¶ Mozart, *The Magic Flute* (overture) (Berlin Philharmonic/Beecham)
¶ Schubert, 'Serenade' (Hollywood Bowl Symphony/Dragon)
¶ Suppé, *Light Cavalry* (overture) (Philharmonia Orchestra/von Karajan)
¶ Gounod, *Faust* (excerpt from garden scene, Act 3) (Victoria de los Angeles/French National Opera Theatre Orchestra/Cluytens)
¶ J. Strauss, 'Wiener Blut Waltz' (Vienna Philharmonic/Boskovsky)
¶ 'For All the Saints' (Cloister Choir)
¶ LUXURY: A dog whip.
¶ BOOK: A large blank book for writing in.

19 March 1962
588 Louis Kentner
Concert pianist
¶ Tosti, 'Serenata' (Amelita Galli-Curci/Homer Samuels *piano*)
¶ Mozart, Oboe Quartet in F major (K. 370) (Léon Goossens/J. Léner *violin*/S. Roth *viola*/J. Hartman *cello*)
*¶ Liszt, A Faust Symphony (RPO/Beecham)
¶ Bizet, *Carmen* (Act 3 entr'acte) (French National Radio Orchestra/Beecham)

¶ Scriabin, 'Prometheus' (Philadelphia Orchestra/Stokowski)
¶ Debussy, *Prélude à l'après-midi d'un faune* (RPO/Beecham)
¶ 'Brezairola' (from *Chants de l'Auvergne*) (Madeline Grey)
¶ 'Japanese Sandman' (Paul Whiteman's Swinging Strings)
¶ LUXURY: A piano.
¶ BOOK: Goncharov, *Oblomov*

26 March 1962
589 Raymond Glendenning
Sports commentator
¶ Donizetti, 'Chi mi frena' (from *Lucia di Lammermoor*) (Amelita Galli-Curci/Enrico Caruso/Minnie Egener/Giuseppe de Luca/Marcel Journet/Angelo Bada)
¶ 'I'll Take You Home Again, Kathleen' (Cavan O'Connor)
¶ Gilbert & Sullivan, 'Love Unrequited Robs Me of My Rest' (from *Iolanthe*) (George Baker)
¶ 'The Spanish Lady' (Stuart Robertson)
¶ 'The 23rd Psalm' (Crimond) (Glasgow Orpheus Choir)
¶ 'There's a Hole in my Bucket' (Harry Belafonte)
¶ Novello, 'Wings of Sleep' (from *The Dancing Years*) (Mary Ellis/Olive Gilbert/Ivor Novello *piano*)
*¶ Bach/Stokowski, Toccata and Fugue in D minor (Stokowski Symphony)
¶ LUXURY: Water-colour paints.
¶ BOOK: *Pears Cyclopaedia*

2 April 1962
590 Frank Launder & Sidney Gilliat
Film producers, writers and directors
¶ (Launder) 'C'est l'amour' (Edith Piaf)
¶ (Gilliat) Mozart, 'Finch'han del vino' (from *Don Giovanni*) (Ezio Pinza)
¶ (L) 'I'll Walk Beside You' (John McCormack)
¶ (G) Bizet, 'Je crois entendre encore' (from *Les pêcheurs de perles*) (John McCormack)

¶(L) Bizet/Hammerstein, 'Dat's Love' (from *Carmen Jones*) (Marilyn Horne)

¶(G)Brahms, Piano Concerto No. 1 in D minor (Julius Katchen/LSO/Monteux)

¶(L) Porter, 'Night and Day' (from *The Gay Divorce*) (Frank Sinatra)

¶(G) Rachmaninov, 'Rhapsody on a Theme of Paganini' (Leonard Pennario *piano*/Los Angeles Philharmonic/ Leinsdorf)

¶LUXURIES: (L) writing materials; (G) a reclining chair.

¶BOOKS:(L) O. Henry, *Short Stories*; (G) 'A Child's Guide to Boatbuilding'.

9 April 1962
591 Leslie Phillips
Actor

¶Chopin, Nocturne in E flat (opus 9, no. 2) (Benno Moiseiwitsch *piano*)

¶Puccini, 'In questa reggia' (from *Turandot*) (Eva Turner)

¶Oscar Wilde, *The Importance of Being Earnest* (excerpt from Act 1) (Edith Evans/John Gielgud)

¶Bizet/Hammerstein, 'Dat's Love' (from *Carmen Jones*) (Marilyn Horne)

*¶'You Make Me Feel So Young' (Frank Sinatra)

¶'Mama's Doin' the Twist' (The Viscounts)

¶'Mambo No. 8' (Xavier Cugat and his Orchestra)

¶Gilbert & Sullivan, 'Love Unrequited Robs Me of My Rest' (from *Iolanthe*) (Martyn Green/New Symphony Orchestra/Godfrey)

¶LUXURY: Chess board with a set of jade pieces.

¶BOOK: The rudiments of several useful languages.

16 April 1962
592 Billy Butlin
Showman and holiday-camp owner

*¶J. Strauss, 'Wiener Blut Waltz' (Carousel Becquart fairground organ)

¶'Brother, Can You Spare a Dime?' (Bing Crosby)

¶'Elephant Tango' (Cyril Stapleton and his Orchestra)

¶'The March of the Herald' (Foden's Motor Works Band)

¶'Ramona' (from film) (Mantovani and his Orchestra)

¶'Stage Coach' (Eric Winstone and his Orchestra)

¶'Wish You Were Here' (from *Wish You Were Here*) (Bruce Trent)

¶'Goodnight, Sweetheart' (Melachrino Strings)

¶LUXURY: A drawing board, paper and pencils.

¶BOOK: O. Henry, *Short Stories*

23 April 1962
593 Robert Morley
Actor and playwright

¶Leoncavallo, 'On with the Motley' (from *Pagliacci*) (Enrico Caruso)

¶'My Heart Stood Still' (from *One Damn Thing After Another*) (Edythe Baker *piano*)

¶'Miss Otis Regrets' (Douglas Byng)

¶Stravinsky, 'Infernal Dance of King Kastchei' (from *The Firebird Suite*) (Paris Conservatoire Orchestra/ Monteux)

¶Puccini, 'Un bel di vedremo' (from *Madam Butterfly*) (Victoria de los Angeles/Rome Opera House Orchestra/ Santini)

¶'Abe Lincoln *v* Madison Avenue' (Bob Newhart)

¶'Man dole mera tan dole' (Lata Mangeshkar)

¶Tippett, 'Ritual Dances' (from *The Midsummer Marriage*) (Royal Opera House Orchestra, Covent Garden/Pritchard)

¶LUXURY: Two packs of cards with photographs of his family on the backs.

¶BOOK: The rules of patience.

30 April 1962
594 Christina Foyle
Bookseller

¶'Among My Souvenirs' (Bing Crosby)

¶'Side by Side' (Savoy Havana Band)

¶Gershwin, 'S'Wonderful' (from *Funny Face*) (Fred Astaire)

¶'The Man Who Broke the Bank at Monte Carlo' (Charles Coburn)

¶'Bill Bailey, Won't You Please Come Home?' (Jimmy Durante)

¶Kern & Hammerstein, 'Lonesome Road' (from *Show Boat*) (Paul Robeson)

¶'The Road to Morocco' (from film) (Bing Crosby/Bob Hope)

*¶Chopin/Douglas, *Les sylphides* (Royal Opera House Orchestra, Covent Garden/Irving)

¶LUXURY: Her commonplace book.

¶BOOK: George & Weedon Grossmith, *The Diary of a Nobody*

7 May 1962
595 Leslie Crowther
Comedian

¶Beethoven, Piano Concerto No. 5 in E flat major (Emperor) (Claudio Arrau/Philharmonia Orchestra/Galliera)

¶'My Mother's Eyes' (from film *Lucky Boy*) (George Chisholm and the Tradsters)

¶Bellini, 'Casta diva' (from *Norma*) (Maria Callas/La Scala Orchestra/Serafin)

¶'Swing Low, Sweet Chariot' (Louis Armstrong)

*¶Mendelssohn, *A Midsummer Night's Dream* (scherzo) (BBC Symphony/Sargent)

¶'Ev'ry Time We Say Goodbye' (from *Seven Lively Arts*) (Ella Fitzgerald)

¶Bizet, 'Au fond du temple saint' (from *Les pêcheurs de perles*) (Jussi Björling/Robert Merrill/RCA Victor Symphony/Cellini)

¶'When I Love I Love' and 'The Bandit' (Black and White Minstrels/Mitchell)

¶LUXURY: A sport suit.

¶BOOK: Sir Winston Churchill, *The Second World War*

14 May 1962
596 Sir Fitzroy Maclean
MP
Writer, traveller and politician

*¶Mozart, Symphony No. 41 in C (RPO/Beecham)

¶Offenbach, *Orpheus in the Underworld* (overture) (Sadler's Wells Orchestra/Faris)

¶'The Barren Rocks of Aden' (Black Watch Pipes and Drums)
¶'Lilli Marlene' (Lale Andersen)
¶Tchaikovsky, *Swan Lake* (Act 1, waltz no. 2) (Orchestra de la Suisse Romande/Ansermet)
¶'Volare' (Domenico Modugno)
¶Berlin, 'Alexander's Ragtime Band' (Temperance Seven Plus One)
¶Mozart, 'Voi che sapete' (from *The Marriage of Figaro*) (Sena Jurinac/Vienna Philharmonic/ von Karajan)
¶LUXURY: A still.
¶BOOK: As many works by Robert Louis Stevenson as can be packed into one binding.

21 May 1962
597 Sidney Nolan
Artist
¶Dylan Thomas, 'Poem on His Birthday' (Dylan Thomas)
¶Aboriginal tribal music (recorded in Arnhem Land by Professor A. P. Elkin)
¶Beethoven, Quartet No. 13 in B flat major (opus 130) (Hungarian String Quartet)
¶'Janani Mamara' (traditional classical Indian music)
¶Coleridge, *The Ancient Mariner* (excerpt) (Ralph Richardson)
*¶Britten, *Les Illuminations* (Peter Pears/New Symphony Orchestra/Goossens)
¶Stravinsky, *The Rite of Spring* (Columbia Symphony/ Stravinsky)
¶'Somebody Stole My Gal' (Bix Beiderbecke *cornet*)
¶LUXURY: A snorkel mask.
¶BOOK: A Chinese language course.

28 May 1962
598 Sir Alan Cobham
Pioneer in long-distance aviation
¶Sibelius, 'Finlandia' (New Symphony Orchestra/ Mackerras)
¶Debussy, 'Rêverie' (Walter Gieseking *piano*)
¶Holst, 'Mars' (from *The Planets*) (BBC Symphony/ Sargent)

¶Lerner & Loewe, 'Gigi (Gaston's Soliloquy)' (from film) (Louis Jourdan)
¶Delius, 'A Walk to the Paradise Gardens' (from *A Village Romeo and Juliet*) (LSO/ Collins)
¶Enesco, Rumanian Rhapsody No. 1 (opus 1) (Vienna Philharmonic/Silvestri)
¶Puccini, 'O soave fanciulla' (from *La Bohème*) (Renata Tebaldi/Giacinto Prandelli/ Santa Cecilia Orchestra, Rome/ Erede)
*¶Tchaikovsky, Symphony No. 4 in F minor (Philharmonia Orchestra/Silvestri)
¶LUXURY: Jamaican cigars.
¶BOOK: Sir Winston Churchill, *History of the English-speaking Peoples*

4 June 1962
599 Eric Hosking
Ornithologist and bird photographer
¶Beethoven, Symphony No. 6 in F major (opus 68) (Philharmonia Orchestra/ Klemperer)
¶Handel, 'For Unto Us a Child is Born' (from *Messiah*) (LSO and Chorus/Boult)
¶Rachmaninov, Piano Concerto No. 2 in C minor (Sergei Rachmaninov/ Philadelphia Orchestra/ Stokowski)
¶Bach/Hess, 'Jesu, Joy of Man's Desiring' (Myra Hess *piano*)
¶Birdsong: blackbird, robin (spring song), nightingale (spring song/alarm call)
¶Brahms, Piano Concerto No. 2 in B flat (orchestral introduction) (LSO/Reiner)
¶Grieg, Piano Concerto in A minor (Dinu Lipatti/ Philharmonia Orchestra/ Galliera)
*¶Elgar, 'Nimrod' (from *Enigma Variations*) (RPO/Beecham)
¶LUXURY: A camera and film.
¶BOOK: A field guide to the island's birds.

11 June 1962
600 Alistair Cooke
Journalist and broadcaster
¶Mozart, 'Within These Sacred Halls' (from *The Magic Flute*) (Ezio Pinza/RCA Victor Symphony/Wallenstein)
¶'Dallas Blues' (Ted Lewis and his Band/Fats Waller)
¶'Clarinet Lament' (Duke Ellington and his Orchestra)
¶'Blues of Israel' (Gene Krupa and his Chicagoans)
¶'Basin Street Blues' (Charleston Chasers)
*¶'I Can't Give You Anything but Love' (from *Blackbirds of 1928*) (Earl Hines *piano*)
¶Purcell, *Abdelazer* (rondo) (LSO Strings/Sargent)
¶'A Closer Walk' (Pete Fountain *clarinet*)
¶LUXURY: A tape recorder.
¶BOOK: H. L. Mencken, *Chrestomathy*

18 June 1962
601 Giovanni Martinelli
Operatic tenor
¶Mozart, 'Il mio tesoro intanto' (from *Don Giovanni*) (John McCormack)
¶Thomas, 'Brindisi' (from *Hamlet*) (Titta Ruffo)
¶Verdi, 'Addio del passato' (from *La traviata*) (Claudio Muzio)
¶Bizet, 'Mi par d'udir ancora' (from *Les pêcheurs de perles*) (Beniamino Gigli)
¶Meyerbeer, 'Shadow Song' (from *Dinorah*) (Amelita Galli-Curci)
¶Cilèa, 'E la solita storia' (from *L'arlésienne*) (Tito Schipa)
*¶'Tu, ca nun chaigne' (Enrico Caruso)
¶Verdi, 'Ernani involami' (from *Ernani*) (Rosa Ponselle)
¶LUXURY: A bronze statuette of David by Verrocchio.
¶BOOK: Dante's *Inferno*

25 June 1962
602 John Allegro
Authority on the Dead Sea Scrolls

*¶ Handel, 'O Thou That Tellest Good Tidings' (from *Messiah*) (Kathleen Ferrier/LPO/Boult)
¶ Dvořák, Symphony No. 9 in E minor (Vienna Philharmonic/Kubelik)
¶ Fauré, 'Piè Jesu' (from *Requiem*) (Pierrete Alarie/Lamoureux Concert Orchestra/Fournet)
¶ Gilbert & Sullivan, 'As Some Day It May Happen' (from *The Mikado*) (Peter Pratt/New Symphony Orchestra/Godfrey)
¶ Tchaikovsky, Symphony No. 6 in B minor (Leningrad Philharmonic/Mravinsky)
¶ Mozart, Symphony No. 33 in B flat major (Amsterdam Concertgebouw/Van Beinum)
¶ Brahms, Violin Concerto in D (Yehudi Menuhin/Berlin Philharmonic/Kempe)
¶ 'Blow the Wind Southerly' (Kathleen Ferrier)
¶ LUXURY: A Rolls-Royce engine.
¶ BOOK: Some P. G. Wodehouse novels bound together.

2 July 1962
603 Franklin Engelmann
Broadcaster

*¶ Bach, *St Matthew Passion* (final chorus) (St Hedwig's Cathedral Choir, Berlin/Berlin Philharmonic/Forster)
¶ 'You Make Me Feel So Young' (Frank Sinatra)
¶ 'National Emblem' Mauch (Massed Bands)
¶ 'Moonlight Serenade' (Glenn Miller and his Orchestra)
¶ Chopin, Nocturne No. 7 in C sharp minor (opus 27, no. 1) (Moura Lympany *piano*)
¶ 'Maria Dolores' (Luis Alberto del Parana/Trio Los Paraguayos)
¶ 'Bachwinkel Ländler' (Die Lustigen Salzburger)
¶ Bach, Brandenburg Concerto No. 2 in F major (Stuttgart Chamber Orchestra/Münchinger)
¶ LUXURY: Painting materials.
¶ BOOK: An English dictionary.

9 July 1962
604 Stephen Spender
Poet

¶ Mozart, 'Lo sdegno calmate' (from *The Marriage of Figaro*) (Hilde Gueden/Alfred Poell/Cesare Siepi/Anny Felbermayer/Hilde Rössl-Majdan/Fernando Corena/Hugo Meyer-Welfing/Vienna Philharmonic/Kleiber)
¶ 'The Critics' (Peter Sellers/Irene Handl)
*¶ Beethoven, Quartet No. 15 in A minor (opus 132) (Budapest String Quartet)
¶ W. H. Auden, 'Musée des Beaux Arts' (W. H. Auden)
¶ 'St James' Infirmary' (Louis Armstrong and his Orchestra)
¶ Stravinsky, *Oedipus Rex* (Act 2) (Ernst Häfliger/Société Chorale du Brassus/Orchestre de la Suisse Romande/Ansermet)
¶ 'What More Can I Do with My Life?' (Greek vocalist and instrumentalists)
¶ Wagner, 'Eilig zur Warte' (from *Tristan und Isolde*) (Ludwig Suthaus/Dietrich Fischer-Dieskau/Philharmonia Orchestra/Furtwängler)
¶ LUXURY: Painting materials.
¶ BOOK: Burckhardt's *History of the Renaissance*

16 July 1962
605 Bruce Forsyth
Comedian

¶ 'I'm Lost' (Nat King Cole Trio)
¶ 'A Square at the Round Table' (Count Basie Orchestra)
¶ Newley, 'Once in a Lifetime' (from *Stop the World, I Want to Get Off*) (Anthony Newley)
¶ Rimsky-Korsakov, *Scheherazade* (RPO/Beecham)
¶ Newley, 'Someone Nice Like You' (from *Stop the World, I Want to Get Off*) (Sammy Davis, Jnr)
¶ 'Carriage and Pair' (Mantovani and his Orchestra)
¶ 'Day In, Day Out' (Frank Sinatra)
*¶ 'Sparks' (Penny)
¶ LUXURY: Golf clubs and balls.
¶ BOOK: Omar Khayyám, *The Rubáiyát*

23 July 1962
606 Paul Rogers
Actor

¶ Elgar, Cello Concerto in E minor (Paul Tortelier/BBC Symphony/Sargent)
¶ Handel, 'And the Glory of the Lord' (from *Messiah*) (Huddersfield Choral Society/Royal Liverpool Philharmonic/Sargent)
¶ Stravinsky, *Petrushka* (Columbia Symphony/Stravinsky)
¶ Sibelius, 'The Swan of Tuonela' (RPO/Collins)
¶ Mozart, Symphony No. 41 in C (RPO/Beecham)
*¶ Bach, Brandenburg Concerto No. 4 in G major (Yehudi Menuhin *violin*/Bath Festival Chamber Orchestra/Menuhin)
¶ Beethoven, Quartet No. 13 in B flat (opus 130) (Hollywood String Quartet)
¶ Brahms, Waltz No. 15 in A flat (Carl Seemann *piano*)
¶ LUXURY: A penny whistle.
¶ BOOK: *Chambers' Encyclopaedia*

30 July 1962
607 Merfyn Turner
Pioneer social worker in prisons

¶ Handel, 'Glory to God' (from *Messiah*) (LSO and Chorus/Boult)
¶ 'Rosie' (work song recorded at the Mississippi State Penitentiary)
¶ 'Tell Laura I Love Her' (Richie Valens)
¶ 'The Riddle Song' (Paul Robeson)
¶ 'Were You There?' (Harry Belafonte)
¶ 'This Old Man (Nick Nack Paddy Wack)' (from film *Inn of the Sixth Happiness*) (Dr Barnardo's Children)
*¶ 'The Lord is My Shepherd' (Glasgow Orpheus Choir/Roberton)
¶ 'God be in My Head' (Temple Church Choir/Thalben-Ball)
¶ LUXURY: Piccasso's *The Child and the Dove*
¶ BOOK: A history of Wales.

8 August 1962
608 Charlie Chester
Comedian
*¶Humperdinck, 'Dance Duet' (from *Hansel und Gretel*) (Manchester schoolchildren's choir/Hallé Orchestra/Harty)
¶'The Birth of the Blues' (Pearl Bailey)
¶'Down Forget-Me-Not Lane' (Flanagan & Allen)
¶Verdi, *La traviata* (prelude) (Philharmonia Orchestra/ Giulini)
¶'Good Luck, Good Health, God Bless You' (Steve Conway)
*¶*Meet the Minstrels* (selection) (George Mitchell Minstrels)
¶Foster, 'Beautiful Dreamer' (Bing Crosby)
¶'Side by Side' (Kay Starr)
¶LUXURY: A typewriter and paper.
¶BOOK: John Galsworthy, *The Forsyte Saga*

13 August 1962
609 Lionel Tertis
Violist
¶Smetana, *The Bartered Bride* (overture) (New York Philharmonic/Barbirolli)
¶Beethoven, Piano Concerto No. 3 in C minor (Solomon/ Philharmonia Orchestra/ Menges)
¶Haydn (attrib.), Concerto in C major for Oboe and Orchestra (Evelyn Rothwell/Hallé Orchestra/Barbirolli)
¶Chopin, Valse brillante No. 2 in A flat (opus 34, no. 1) (Artur Rubinstein *piano*)
¶Boccherini, String Quartet in A major (Carmirelli Quartet)
¶'Folies musicales' (imitations of national song styles) (Bétove)
¶'Cherry Ripe' (Lionel Tertis)
*¶Kreisler, 'Tambourin chinois' (Fritz Kreisler *violin*/Franz Rupp *piano*)
¶LUXURY: A portrait of his wife.
¶BOOK: Books by H. Rider Haggard, Sir Arthur Conan Doyle and Jules Verne bound together.

20 August 1962
610 Edith Day
Musical comedy star
¶Khachaturian, 'Sabre Dance' (from *Gayaneh*) (LSO/Dorati)
¶Kreisler, 'Caprice viennois' (opus 2) (Fritz Kreisler *violin*)
¶'Holiday for Strings' (David Rose and his Orchestra)
¶'One Alone' (from *The Desert Song*) (Harry Welchmann)
*¶'Singin' in the Rain' (from film) (Gene Kelly)
¶Gershwin, 'Rhapsody in Blue' (George Gershwin *piano*/Paul Whiteman and his Concert Orchestra)
¶Coward, 'I'll See You Again' (from *Bitter Sweet*) (Noël Coward)
¶Ravel, 'Bolero' (Boston Symphony/Münch)
¶LUXURY: A radio receiver.
¶BOOK: Ralph Waldo Emerson, *Essays*

27 August 1962
611 Mario del Monaco
Operatic tenor
¶Wagner, 'Mit Waffen wehrt sich der Mann' (from *Die Walküre*) (Lauritz Melchior/ Vienna Philharmonic/Walter)
¶Verdi, 'Bella figlia dell'amore' (from *Rigoletto*) (Mario del Monaco/Aldo Protti/Hilde Gueden/Cesare Siepi/Santa Cecilia Orchestra, Rome/ Erede)
*¶Beethoven, Symphony No. 6 in F major (opus 68) (NBC Symphony/Toscanini)
¶Rossini, 'Mi par d'esser' (from *The Barber of Seville*) (Giulietta Simionato/Rina Cavallari/ Alvinia Misciano/Ettore Bastianini/Fernando Corena/ Cesare Siepi/Orchestra of Maggio Musicale Fiorentino/ Erede)
¶Mendelssohn, Violin Concerto in E minor (Zino Francescatti/ New York Philharmonic/ Mitropoulos)
¶Handel, 'Ombra mai fu' (from *Xerxes*) (Enrico Caruso)
¶Verdi, 'Vuoco di gioia' (from *Otello*) (Vienna State Opera Chorus/Vienna Philharmonic/ von Karajan)

¶Mussorgsky, 'Death of Boris' (from *Boris Godunov*) (Feodor Chaliapin)
¶LUXURY: Raphael's *The Marriage of Maria*
¶BOOK: An English grammar.

3 September 1962
612 R. F. Delderfield
Playwright, novelist and scriptwriter
¶'Missouri Waltz' (Cyril Stapleton and his Orchestra)
¶'Tara's Theme' (from film *Gone with the Wind*) (Sinfonia of London/Mathieson)
¶*The Student Prince* (selection) (Marek Weber and his Orchestra)
¶'La Marseillaise' (Musique de la Garde Républicaine)
¶Schumann, 'The Merry Peasant' (Maureen Tomlin *piano*)
¶'Forty Years On' (Harrow School song) (Harrow School Boys)
*¶J. Strauss, 'Tales from the Vienna Woods' (Vienna Philharmonic/von Karajan)
¶Wagner, 'The Ride of the Valkyries' (from *Die Walküre*) (Vienna Philharmonic/ Furtwängler)
¶LUXURY: A typewriter and paper.
¶BOOK: Thomas Carlyle, *The French Revolution*

10 September 1962
613 Stanley Unwin
Inventor and speaker of his own nonsense language
¶Beethoven, Symphony No. 6 in A major (opus 68) (Columbia Symphony/Walter)
¶Franck, Violin Sonata in A major (Yehudi Menuhin/Louis Kentner *piano*)
¶'The Floral Dance' (Peter Dawson)
*¶Bach, Toccata and Fugue in D minor (Albert Schweitzer *organ*)
¶Gershwin, 'That Certain Feeling' (from *Tip-Toes*) (Ella Fitzgerald)
¶Bach/Segovia, Suite No. 3 in C major for Solo Cello (Andrés Segovia *guitar*)
¶'David of the White Rock' (Swansea Imperial Singers)

¶ Liszt, Valse oubliée No. 1
(Alexander Brailowsky *piano*)
¶ LUXURY: Painting materials.
¶ BOOK: *Grove's Dictionary of
Music and Musicians*

17 September 1962
614 L. Hugh Newman
**Butterfly farmer and
broadcaster**
¶ 'Lazy' (Layton & Johnstone)
¶ 'Eileen Oge' (Barbara Mullen)
¶ Schumann, 'Du bist wie eine
Blume' (Eric Marshall)
*¶ Beethoven, Piano Sonata No.
8 in C minor (Walter Gieseking)
¶ Gounod, 'Lend Me Your Aid'
(from *Queen of Sheba*) (Walter
Widdop)
¶ 'East Side of Heaven' (Bing
Crosby)
¶ Ellis, 'This is My Lovely Day'
(from *Bless the Bride*) (Georges
Guetary/Lisbeth Webb)
¶ 'Stranger on the Shore' (Acker
Bilk *clarinet*)
¶ LUXURY: A bed.
¶ BOOK: George Bernard Shaw's
Plays and Prefaces

24 September 1962
615 Peter Jones
Actor and comedian
¶ 'Mammy' (Paul Robeson)
¶ 'This Year's Kisses' (from film
On the Avenue) (Billie Holiday)
¶ J. Strauss, 'Tales from the
Vienna Woods' (Vienna
Philharmonic/von Karajan)
¶ Community singing at the
Metropolitan Music Hall,
London
¶ Verdi, 'Grand March' (from
Aida) (St Hilda's Professional
Band/Oliver)
¶ 'Manhattan' (from *The
Garrick Gaieties*) (Ella
Fitzgerald)
¶ 'Paris, Stay the Same' (From
The Love Parade) (Maurice
Chevalier)
*¶ Beethoven, Violin Concerto in
D major (opus 61) (Yehudi
Menuhin/Vienna
Philharmonic/Silvestri)
¶ LUXURY: An astronomical
telescope.
¶ BOOK: A book on astronomy.

1 October 1962
616 Antony Hopkins
**Composer, conductor, pianist
and broadcaster**
¶ Ravel, *Valses nobles et
sentimentales* (no. 3) (Vlado
Perlemuter *piano*)
¶ Rachmaninov, Piano
Concerto No. 3 in D minor
(Cyril Smith/City of
Birmingham Orchestra/
Weldon)
¶ Tippett, Concerto for Double
String Orchestra (Philharmonia
Orchestra/Goehr)
¶ Mozart, 'Letter Duet' (from
The Marriage of Figaro)
(Irmgaard Seefried/Maria
Stader/Berlin Radio
Symphony/Fricsay)
*¶ Schubert, Quintet in C major
(opus 163) (Quintetto
Boccherini)
¶ Brahms, Piano Concerto No.
2 in B flat major (Artur
Rubinstein/Boston Symphony/
Münch)
¶ Elgar, Violin Concerto in B
minor (Yehudi Menuhin/LSO/
Elgar)
¶ 'Vingt-quatre heures du Mans
1957' (commentary by Nevil
Lloyd)
¶ LUXURY: A piano.
¶ BOOK: The Beethoven piano
sonatas.

8 October 1962
**617 Gwen Ffrangcon-
Davies**
Actress
¶ Bach, Double Concerto in D
minor (David & Igor Oistrakh
violins/RPO/Goossens)
¶ Delius, 'On Hearing the First
Cuckoo in Spring' (RPO/
Beecham)
¶ Mozart, Clarinet Concerto in
A (K. 622) (Gervase de Peyer/
LSO/Maag)
¶ Wagner, 'Brunnhilde's
Immolation' (from
Götterdämmerung) (Kirsten
Flagstad/Philharmonia
Orchestra/Furtwängler)
¶ Beethoven, Symphony No. 6
in F major (opus 68) (NBC
Symphony/Toscanini)

¶ R. Strauss, *Der Rosenkavalier*
(final trio) (Lotte Lehmann/
Elisabeth Schumann/Maria
Olszewska/Vienna
Philharmonic/Heger)
¶ Mahler, 'Die zwei blauen
Augen' (from *Lieder Eines
fahrenden Gesellen*) (Dietrich
Fischer-Dieskau/Philharmonia
Orchestra/Furtwängler)
*¶ Bach/Hess, 'Jesu, Joy of
Man's Desiring' (Myra Hess
piano)
¶ LUXURY: Skin food.
¶ BOOK: Johann David Wyss,
The Swiss Family Robinson

15 October 1962
**618 Fanny & Johnnie
Cradock**
Food and wine experts
*¶ (Johnnie) Chopin/Douglas,
Les sylphides (Paris
Conservatoire Orchestra/Maag)
¶ (Fanny) Franck, String
Quartet in D (Prague City
Quartet)
¶ (J) Dvořák, Slavonic Dance in
C major (opus 46, no. 1)
(Bamberg Symphony/
Keilberth)
*¶ (F) Beethoven, Symphony
No. 5 in C minor (opus 67)
(NBC Symphony/Toscanini)
¶ (J) Debussy, 'Clair de lune'
(from *Suite bergamasque*)
(Walter Gieseking *piano*)
¶ (F) Mozart, Oboe Concerto in
C major (K. 314) (Léon
Goossens/Sinfonia of London/
Davis)
¶ (J) Rimsky-Korsakov,
Scheherazade (RPO/Beecham)
¶ (F) Tchaikovsky, 'None but
the lonely heart' (New York
Philharmonic/Kostelanetz)
¶ LUXURIES: (F) a typewriter and
paper; (J) golf clubs and balls.
¶ BOOKS: (F) Smith's *Dictionary
of Greek and Roman Biography
and Mythology*: (J) Sir Winston
Churchill, *History of the English-
speaking Peoples*.

22 October 1962
619 Norman Tucker
Director of Opera, Sadler's Wells Theatre

¶ Mozart, Quintet in A major for Clarinet and Strings (K. 581) (Reginald Kell *clarinet*/ Fine Arts Quartet)
¶ Beethoven, Violin Concerto in D major (opus 61) (Yehudi Menuhin/Vienna Philharmonic/Silvestri)
¶ Brahms, Piano Concerto No. 2 in B flat (Sviatoslav Richter/ LSO/Leinsdorf)
¶ Verdi, 'O terra addio' (from *Aida*) (Rosa Ponselle/Giovanni Martinelli)
¶ Offenbach, 'King of the Beoetians' (from *Orpheus in the Underworld*) (Alan Crofoot/ Sadler's Wells Theatre Orchestra/Faris)
*¶ Beethoven, Quartet No. 13 in B flat major (Budapest String Quartet)
¶ Handel, 'I Know that My Redeemer Liveth' (from *Messiah*) (Elsie Morison/Royal Liverpool Philharmonic/ Sargent)
¶ R. Strauss, *Don Quixote* (epilogue) (Gregor Piatigorsky *cello*/Boston Symphony/ Münch)
¶ LUXURY: A piano.
¶ BOOK: The works of Sophocles, in Greek.

29 October 1962
620 Pamela Hansford-Johnson
Novelist and broadcaster

¶ D'Indy, Symphony No. 1 in G for Piano and Orchestra (Jean Doyen/Lamoureux Orchestra/ Fournet)
¶ 'Compagnons des mauvais jours' (Yves Montand)
¶ Debussy, 'L'île joyeuse' (Sviatoslav Richter *piano*)
¶ Shakespeare/Young, 'O Mistress Mine' (Cleo Laine)
¶ Bach, P Fugue No. 1 in C major (Rosalyn Tureck *piano*)
¶ Thomas Hardy, 'Weathers' (Richard Burton)

*¶ Bach, Brandenburg Concerto No. 4 in G major (Hugh Bean *violin*/Gareth Morris and Arthur Ackroyd *flutes*/George Malcolm *harpsichord*/ Philharmonia Orchestra/ Klemperer)
¶ Bach/Luther, 'A Mighty Fortress is Our God' (Paul Robeson/Alan Booth *piano*)
¶ LUXURY: Van Eyck's *Adoration of the Immaculate Lamb*
¶ BOOK: Marcel Proust, *À la recherche du temps perdu*

5 November 1962
621 George Shearing
Jazz pianist

¶ 'T'ain't What You Do' (Jimmie Lunceford and his Orchestra)
¶ Debussy, 'La cathédrale engloutie' (*Prelude*, Book 1, No. 10) (Walter Gieseking *piano*)
¶ Dvořák, 'Humoresque' in G flat (Art Tatum *piano*)
¶ Rachmaninov, Piano Concerto No. 2 in C minor (Sergei Rachmaninov/ Philadelphia Orchestra/ Stokowski)
¶ 'Lullaby of Birdland' (Erroll Garner *piano*)
¶ 'Don't Blame Me' (Teddy Wilson *piano*)
*¶ Bach, 'Widerstehe Doch der Sünde' (Cantata No. 54) (Alfred Deller/Leonhardt Baroque Ensemble)
¶ Delius, 'On Hearing the First Cuckoo in Spring' (RPO/ Beecham)
¶ LUXURY: A metal construction set.
¶ BOOK: Captain Frederick Marryat, *Masterman Ready*

10 November 1962
622 Val Gielgud
Playwright, novelist and Head of BBC radio drama

¶ J. Strauss/Désormière, *Le beau Danube* (ballet) (LPO/ Martinon)
¶ Elgar, Serenade in E minor for Strings (RPO/Beecham)
¶ Schumann, Piano Concerto in A minor (Alfred Cortot/LSO/ Ronald)

¶ Delius, 'Serenade' (from *Hassan*) (Arthur Leavins *violin*/ RPO/Beecham)
*¶ Chopin, Ballade No. 3 in A flat major (opus 47) (Claudio Arrau *piano*)
¶ Franck, Violin Sonata in A major (Yehudi Menuhin/Louis Kentner *piano*)
¶ Shakespeare, 'Our Revels Now are Ended' (from *The Tempest*, Act 4, Scene 1) (John Gielgud)
¶ Tchaikovsky, Symphony No. 6 in B minor (Vienna Philharmonic/Kubelik)
¶ LUXURY: Cigars.
¶ BOOK: Naomi Mitchison, *The Corn King and the Spring Queen*

12 November 1962
623 Dr Robert Stopford
The Bishop of London

¶ Slade, 'We Said We Wouldn't Look Back' (from *Salad Days*) (Eleanor Drew/John Warner)
*¶ Bach, 'Credo' (from *Mass in B minor*) (Munich Bach Choir and Orchestra/Richter)
¶ Bach, Toccata and Fugue in D minor (Albert Schweitzer *organ*)
¶ Clarke, 'Trumpet Voluntary' (George Thalben-Ball *organ*)
¶ Chopin, Mazurka No. 5 in B flat major (opus 7, no. 1) (Nikita Magaloff *piano*)
¶ Handel, *Water Music Suite* (LSO/Dorati)
¶ Gilbert & Sullivan, 'Never Mind the Why and Wherefore' (from *HMS Pinafore*) (John Cameron/Elsie Morison/George Baker/Glyndebourne Festival Chorus/Pro Arte Orchestra/ Sargent)
¶ Elgar, 'Nimrod' (from *Enigma Variations*) (LPO/Boult)
¶ LUXURY: Painting materials.
¶ BOOK: *The Oxford Book of English Verse*

19 November 1962
624 Jack Warner
(2nd appearance)
Actor and comedian

¶ 'I'm Looking over a Four-Leaf Clover' (Eddie Peabody *banjo*)
¶ 'Right, Said Fred' (Bernard Cribbins)

¶ 'La madelon' (Musique de la Garde Républicaine)
¶ 'You Can't Keep a Good Dreamer Down' (from film *London Town*) (Sid Field)
¶ 'Old Father Thames' (Peter Dawson)
*¶ Rodgers & Hammerstein, 'The Carousel Waltz' (from *Carousel*)
¶ 'Lords of the Air' (Billy Cotton and his Band)
¶ 'Bless This House' (Walter Midgley/Gladys Vernon *piano*)
¶ LUXURY: Soap.
¶ BOOK: Charles Dickens, *A Tale of Two Cities*, in both English and French.

26 November 1962
625 Peter Saunders
Theatre impresario
¶ Ravel, Introduction and Allegro for Harp, Flute, Clarinet and String Quartet (Osian Ellis *harp*/Melos Ensemble)
¶ 'Sophisticated Lady' (Art Tatum *piano*)
¶ Gershwin, 'Someone to Watch Over Me' (from *Oh, Kay!*) (Percy Faith and his Orchestra)
¶ Tchaikovsky, 'Romeo and Juliet Fantasy Overture' (Berlin Philharmonic/Maazel)
¶ *The Water Gipsies* (overture) (Jack Coles and his Orchestra)
¶ Puccini, 'Si, mi chiamano Mimi' (from *La Bohème*) (Maria Callas/Philharmonia Orchestra, Serafin)
¶ Debussy, 'La fille aux cheveux de lin' (*Prelude*, Book 1, No. 8) (Yehudi Menuhin *violin*/Marcel Gazelle *piano*)
*¶ 'Chicago' (Judy Garland)
¶ LUXURY: An electric blanket.
¶ BOOK: *Who's Who in the Theatre*

3 December 1962
626 Anna Russell
International entertainer
*¶ Bach, Brandenburg Concerto No. 1 in F major (Philharmonia Orchestra/Klemperer)
¶ Tchaikovsky, Symphony No.5 in E minor (Leningrad Philharmonic/Mravinsky)

¶ Handel, *Water Music Suite* (RPO/Sargent)
¶ Wagner, 'Siegfried's Rhine Journey' (from *Götterdämmerung*) (Vienna Philharmonic/Furtwängler)
¶ 'A Visit to America' (lecture) (Dylan Thomas)
¶ Rossini, *The Thieving Magpie* (overture) (RPO/Beecham)
¶ Berg, *Wozzeck* (Act 3, orchestral interlude) (New York Philharmonic/Mitropoulos)
¶ 'Minnie the Moocher' (Danny Kaye)
¶ LUXURY: A mobile from the Museum of Modern Art.
¶ BOOK: *Encyclopaedia Britannica*

10 December 1962
627 Acker Bilk
Bandleader and jazz clarinettist
¶ 'Burgundy Street Blues' (George Lewis' Ragtime Band)
¶ 'Diminuendo and Crescendo in Blue' (Duke Ellington and his Orchestra)
¶ 'Doctor Jazz Stomp' (Jelly Roll Morton and his Red Hot Peppers)
*¶ 'Papa Dip' (New Orleans Wanderers)
¶ 'You Made Me Love You' (from film *Broadway Melody of 1938*) (Edmond Hall *clarinet*/Lopez Furst *piano*)
¶ 'Singin' the Blues' (Bix Beiderbecke *cornet*)
¶ 'I Know It was the Lord' (Famous Ward Singers)
¶ 'Stompin' at the Savoy' (Ella Fitzgerald/Louis Armstrong)
¶ LUXURY: Apple seeds.
¶ BOOK: Kenneth Grahame, *The Wind in the Willows*

17 December 1962
628 A. G. Street
Writer, farmer and broadcaster
¶ Dawn chorus
¶ John Milton, 'Lycidas' (Stephen Murray)
¶ 'Drinking' (Malcolm McEachern)
¶ Rubinstein, 'Melody in F' (Pablo Casals *cello*/Nikolai Mednikoff *piano*)
*¶ Hounds in full cry (The Hunt) (recorded by Michael Berry)

¶ Shakespeare/Quilter, 'Hey Ho! The Wind and the Rain' (John Heddle Nash/Ernest Lush *piano*)
¶ Beethoven, Sonata in C sharp minor (opus 27, no. 2) (Benno Moiseiwitsch *piano*)
¶ 'Nights of Gladness' (Blue Hungarian Band)
¶ LUXURY: A painting of the South Wiltshire countryside.
¶ BOOK: Ford Madox Ford, *Ladies Whose Bright Eyes*

22 December 1962
629 Lord George Sanger
Circus proprietor
¶ 'Quand madelon' (Vienna Symphony/Stolz)
¶ 'Over the Sticks' (CWS [Manchester] Band)
¶ 'The Voice of the Guns' (Band of HM Royal Marines)
¶ 'The Whistling Waltz' (Muller-Lampertz and his Orchestra)
¶ 'Soldiers of the Queen' (Devereaux Orchestra)
¶ 'Canadian Capers' (Jack Fina and his Orchestra)
¶ 'Yip I Addy I Ay' (Prima Scala and his Accordion Band)
*¶ Coward, 'I'll See You Again' (from *Bitter Sweet*) (Anne Ziegler/Webster Booth)
¶ LUXURY: Tea.
¶ BOOK: His autobiography, *Seventy Years a Showman*

24 December 1962
630 Clarkson Rose
Actor, concert party proprietor and pantomime dame
¶ Coates, 'The Dambusters March' (from film *The Dambusters*) (Central Band of RAF)
¶ 'Some of These Days' (Sophie Tucker)
*¶ 'The Floral Dance' (Peter Dawson)
¶ 'More than Anybody' (Clarkson Rose)
¶ German, 'Love is Meant to Make Us Glad' (from *Merrie England*) (June Bronhill)
¶ Grainger, 'Handel in the Strand' (Eastman-Rochester 'Pops' Orchestra)

¶'Mr Gallagher and Mr Sheen' (Bing Crosby/Johnny Mercer)
¶Gilbert & Sullivan, 'For He is an Englishman' (from *HMS Pinafore*) (George Baker/John Cameron/Richard Lewis/Owen Brannigan/Glyndebourne Festival Chorus/Pro Arte Orchestra/Sargent)
¶LUXURY: Writing materials.
¶BOOK: Sir Winston Churchill, *History of the English-speaking Peoples*

31 December 1962
631 George Mitchell
Choirmaster and arranger
¶Ravel, 'Lever du jour' (from *Daphnis and Chloe Suite No. 2*) (Philharmonia Orchestra/Giulini)
¶R. Strauss, 'Don Juan' (NBC Symphony/Toscanini)
¶'Wimoweh' (George Mitchell Choir)
¶Chopin, Scherzo in C sharp minor (opus 39) (Vladimir Horowitz *piano*)
¶Schumann, 'Wanderlied' (from *Twelve Poems*, opus 35) (Dietrich Fischer-Dieskau)
¶Bach/Stokowski, Fugue in G minor (Stokowski Symphony)
¶'Side by Side' (George Mitchell Minstrells)
*¶Wagner, *Götterdämmerung* (closing scene) (Cleveland Orchestra/Szell)
¶LUXURY: Music manuscript paper and pencils.
¶BOOK: The score of *The Ring* cycle.

7 January 1963
632 Dorothy Squires
Singer
¶Debussy, 'Clair de lune' (from *Suite bergamasque*) (André Kostelanetz Orchestra)
¶'The Secrets of the Seine' (Tony Osborne *piano* and his Orchestra)
¶'Roses of Picardy' (Dorothy Squires/Russ Conway *piano*)
¶'Tammy Tell Me True' (from film) (Percy Faith and his Orchestra)
¶'Esther' (Eddie Calvert *trumpet*)

¶Rodgers & Hammerstein, 'Climb Every Mountain' (from *The Sound of Music*) (Edmundo Ros and his Orchestra)
*¶'Concerto for Dreamers' (Russ Conway *piano*)
¶''Til Tomorrow' (from *Fiorello*) (Kathie Kay)
¶LUXURY: A piano.
¶BOOK: *Vaughan Haddock's Book of Modern Music*

14 January 1963
633 Basil Boothroyd
Humorous writer and broadcaster
¶Palestrina, 'Super Flumina Babylonis' (Westminster Abbey Choir)
¶Moszkowski, 'Etincelles' (Vladimir Horowitz *piano*)
¶'Devotion' (Coleman Hawkins/Freddy Johnson)
¶Tchaikovsky, 'Don Juan's Serenade' (opus 38, no. 1) (Boris Christoff/Alexandre Labinsky *piano*)
*¶Mozart, Piano Concerto No. 23 in A major (K. 488) (orchestral opening) (LSO/Krips)
¶'Georgia on My Mind' (Dave Brubeck Quartet)
¶Shakespeare, 'To Be or Not to Be' (from *Hamlet*, Act 2) (John Gielgud)
¶'Verily' (Bernard Cribbins)
¶LUXURY: A copy of a current popular newspaper.
¶BOOK: *The Oxford Dictionary of Quotations*

19 January 1963
634 Gerry Lee
Animal impersonator
*¶Schubert, 'The Flower' (from *Lilac Time*) (Anne Ziegler/Webster Booth)
¶'Lavender Blue' (Donald Peers)
¶'Oh Johnny' (Pat Kirkwood)
¶'Fascination Waltz' (Melachrino Strings)
¶'Ma, I Miss Your Apple Pie' (Ambrose and his Orchestra)
¶'Warsaw Concerto' (From film *Dangerous Moonlight*) (Rawicz & Landauer *pianos*/Mantovani and his Orchestra)
¶'Bachelor Boy' (Cliff Richard)

¶Gilbert & Sullivan, 'The Sun, Whose Rays are All Ablaze' (from *The Mikado*) (Marion Studholme/Sadler's Wells Orchestra/Faris)
¶LUXURY: A theatrical skip full of his animal skins.
¶BOOK: Horace Vachell, *Quinneys*

21 January 1963
635 Richard Lewis
Tenor
¶Mendelssohn, 'Hear My Prayer' (Ernest Lough/G. Thalben-Ball *organ*/Temple Church Choir, London)
¶Mozart, 'Dalla sua pace' (from *Don Giovanni*) (Richard Tauber)
¶Mozart, 'Andro ramingo e solo' (from *Idomeneo*) (Glyndebourne cast and orchestra/Pritchard)
¶Walton, *Troilus and Cressida* (Act 2, interlude) (Philharmonia Orchestra/Walton)
¶Shakespeare/Walton, 'Once More unto the Breach', Lawrence Olivier (from film *Henry V*) (Philharmonia Orchestra/Walton)
¶Brahms, Symphony No. 2 in D major (Columbia Symphony/Walter)
¶'Autumn Leaves' (George Shearing *piano*)
*¶Elgar, 'Sanctus Fortis' (from *The Dream of Gerontius*) (Richard Lewis/Royal Liverpool Philharmonic/Sargent)
¶LUXURY: A film projector.
¶BOOK: Professor A. W. & Dora Jane Janson, *History of Art*

28 January 1963
636 Noël Coward
Playwright, composer and actor
¶Rachmaninov, Piano Concerto No. 2 in C minor (Sergei Rachmaninov/Philadelphia Orchestra/Stokowski)
¶'All the Way' (Frank Sinatra)
¶Coward, *Private Lives* (love scene) (Gertrude Lawrence/Noël Coward)

¶ Bellini, 'Casta diva' (from *Norma*) (Maria Callas/La Scala Orchestra/Serafin)
¶ Shakespeare, 'Shall I Compare Thee to a Summer's Day?' (sonnet) (Edith Evans)
¶ The Critics' (Peter Sellers/Irene Handl)
*¶ The Hole in the Ground' (Bernard Cribbins)
¶ Verdi, 'Dies Irae' (from *Requiem*) (La Scala Orchestra and Chorus/de Sabata)
¶ LUXURY: Painting materials.
¶ BOOK: McNeill Dixon, *The Human Situation*

4 February 1963
637 Sir Learie Constantine
Cricketer
¶ 'Graf Zeppelin' (Raymond Quevedo)
¶ Kern & Hammerstein, 'Ol' Man River' (from *Show Boat*) (Paul Robeson)
¶ Massenet, 'Meditation' (from *Thaïs*) (Zino Francescatti *violin*)
¶ Beethoven, Piano Concerto in E flat No. 5 (Rudolf Serkin/Philadelphia Orchestra/Ormandy)
¶ Saint-Saëns, 'Softly Awakes My Heart' (from *Samson and Delilah*) (Marian Anderson)
¶ 'Australia *v* West Indies Calypso' (Lord Beginner)
*¶ 'De L'il Piccaninny's Gone to Sleep' (Paul Robeson)
¶ Bishop, 'Lo! Hear the Gentle Lark' (Amelita Galli-Curci)
¶ LUXURY: A cricket ball.
¶ BOOK: Charles Dickens, *The Old Curiosity Shop* and *David Copperfield*

11 February 1963
638 Michael Bentine
Writer and comedian
*¶ 'Temas en farruca' (Carlos Montoya *guitar*)
¶ Villa-Lobos, 'Uirapurú' (symphonic poem) (New York Philharmonic/Kurtz)
¶ Liszt, 'Mephisto Waltz' No. 1 (Alexander Brailowsky *piano*)
¶ Ravel, 'Lever du jour' (from *Daphnis and Chloe Suite No. 2*) (Detroit Symphony/Paray)

¶ Beethoven, Symphony No. 6 in F major (opus 68) (Philharmonia Orchestra/Klemperer)
¶ Stravinsky, 'The Sacrifice' (from *The Rite of Spring*) (Columbia Symphony/Stravinsky)
¶ Rimsky-Korsakov, 'Capriccio espagñol' (Vienna Philharmonic/Silvestri)
¶ 'Les trois cloches' (Edith Piaf/Les Compagnons de la Chanson)
¶ LUXURY: *Encyclopaedia Britannica*

18 February 1963
639 Quentin Reynolds
Writer, journalist and ex-war correspondent
¶ Beethoven, Symphony No. 5 in C minor (opus 67) (Orchestre de la Suisse Romande/Ansermet)
*¶ Rodgers & Hart, 'There's a Small Hotel' (from *On Your Toes*) (Ella Fitzgerald)
¶ Wagner, 'Liebestod' (from *Tristan und Isolde*) (RPO/Walter)
¶ 'Underneath the Arches' (Flanagan & Allen)
¶ Lerner & Loewe, 'The Rain in Spain' (from *My Fair Lady*) (Rex Harrison/Julie Andrews)
¶ 'The Malayan Ambassador' (Vaughan Meader)
¶ 'A Nightingale Sang in Berkeley Square' (from *New Faces*) (Frank Sinatra)
¶ Sir Winston Churchill, 'This was Their Finest Hour' (speech, 18 June 1940)
¶ LUXURY: A typewriter and paper.
¶ BOOK: Edward Gibbon, *The History of the Decline and Fall of the Roman Empire*

25 February 1963
640 Cyril Ornadel
Light music composer and conductor
¶ Vaughan Williams, *The Wasps* (overture) (Hallé Orchestra/Barbirolli)
¶ Rachmaninov, Piano Concerto No. 2 in C minor (Sergei Rachmaninov/Philadelphia Orchestra/Stokowski)

¶ Mozart, 'O Isis und Osiris' (from *The Magic Flute*) (Kurt Böhme/Vienna Philharmonic/Böhm)
*¶ Bruch, Violin Concerto No. 1 in G minor (David Oistrakh/LSO/von Matacic)
¶ 'Nancy with the Laughing Face' (Frank Sinatra)
¶ Longfellow/Coleridge-Taylor, *Hiawatha's Wedding Feast* (finale) (Royal Choral Society/Philharmonia Orchestra/Sargent)
¶ Gilbert & Sullivan, 'I am So Proud' (from *The Mikado*) (Peter Pratt/Alan Styler/Kenneth Sandford/New Symphony Orchestra/Godfrey)
¶ Borodin/Wright & Forrest (arr.), 'And This is My Beloved' (from *Kismet*) (Doretta Morrow)
¶ LUXURY: A piano.
¶ BOOK: The Talmud.

4 March 1963
641 Percy Thrower
Gardener and broadcaster
¶ 'Moulin Rouge' (from film) (Mantovani and his Orchestra)
*¶ Waldteufel, 'Skaters' Waltz' (Eric Robinson and his Orchestra)
¶ Grainger, 'Country Gardens' (Eastman-Rochester 'Pops' Orchestra/Fennell)
¶ J. Strauss, 'The Blue Danube Waltz' (Vienna Philharmonic/Krips)
¶ 'Bobby's Girl' (Susan Maugham)
¶ 'Sally' (from film *Sally in Our Alley*) (Gracie Fields)
¶ 'The Happy Wanderer' (The Beverley Sisters)
¶ 'The Shrewsbury Lasses' (Folk Dance Orchestra)
¶ LUXURY: Flower seeds.
¶ BOOK: A gardening encyclopaedia.

11 March 1963
642 Arthur Haynes
Comedian
¶ Rodgers & Hammerstein, 'The Carousel Waltz' (from *Carousel*) (Orchestra/Newman)
¶ 'Arlette' (theme from series *Maigret*) (Joe Loss and his Orchestra)

¶ 'The Irish are Havin' a Great Time Tonight' (Frederick Fennell and Orchestra)
¶ 'The Melba Waltz' (from film *Melba*) (Mantovani and his Orchestra)
¶ 'Shadoogie' (The Shadows)
¶ 'Kiss Me Again' (Frank Chacksfield and his Orchestra)
*¶ Prokofiev, *Love for Three Oranges* (march) (Philharmonia Orchestra/Kurtz)
¶ 'Faraway Music' (Steve Race and his Orchestra)
¶ LUXURY: A ukelele.
¶ BOOK: A French language course.

18 March 1963
643 Dudley Perkins
'Can I Help You?' broadcaster
¶ Bach, Brandenburg Concerto No. 2 in F major (Schola Cantorum Basiliensis/ Wenzinger)
¶ Delius, 'Brigg Fair' (RPO/ Beecham)
¶ 'Sussex Carol' (King's College Chapel Choir/Willcocks)
¶ Mozart, Quintet in A major for Clarinet and Strings (K. 581) (Reginald Kell/Fine Arts Quartet)
*¶ Beethoven, Symphony No. 9 in D minor (opus 125) (Eileen Farrell/Nan Merriman/Jan Peerce/Norman Scott/NBC Symphony/Toscanini)
¶ Brahms, Symphony No. 3 in F major (Vienna Philharmonic/ Böhm)
¶ Verdi, 'Dies Irae' (from *Requiem*) (RIAS Symphony and Choir, Berlin/Fricsay)
¶ Beethoven, Piano Concerto No. 4 in G major (Artur Rubinstein/Symphony of the Air/Krips)
¶ LUXURY: A piano.
¶ BOOK: The complete works of John Milton.

25 March 1963
644 L. G. Illingworth
Political cartoonist
¶ 'Nasareth' (Froncysyllte Male Voice Choir)
*¶ Beethoven, Symphony No. 6 in F major (opus 68) (Amsterdam Concertgebouw/ Kleiber)

¶ Dylan Thomas, 'Polly Garter's Song' (from *Under Milk Wood*) (Diana Maddox)
¶ 'Kansas City Man Blues' (Wally Fawkes and his Troglodytes)
¶ Segovia, 'Study' (Andrés Segovia *guitar*)
¶ Smetana, 'Vltava' (from *Má Vlast*) (Vienna Philharmonic/ Kubelik)
¶ 'Oh You Steppe So Wide' (Sveshnikov Chorus)
¶ 'The Three Scourges' (Peking Opera Ensemble)
¶ LUXURY: Painting materials.
¶ BOOK: Instructions for making a still.

1 April 1963
645 Sir Harry Whitlohn (alias Henry Sherek)
*¶ Brahms, Symphony No. 3 in F (Vienna Philharmonic/ Walter)
¶ Nono, 'Incontri' (ensemble/ Boulez)
¶ Lamaist chanting (from *The History of Music in Sound: Tibet*)
¶ William McGonagall, 'The Death of Lord and Lady Dalhousie' (Alec Guinness)
¶ Rodgers & Hammerstein, 'Climb Every Mountain' (from *The Sound of Music*) (David Whitfield)
¶ 'Just a Little While to Stay Here' (Young Tuxedo Brass Band)
¶ Shakespeare, 'Closet Scene' (from *Hamlet*) (Gerald Lawrence)
¶ Montage of Lichtenstein street sounds (BBC Library effects disc)
¶ LUXURY: A mountain.
¶ BOOK: The telephone directory.
(This was an April Fool's Day programme.)

8 April 1963
646 Ted Willis
Writer
¶ Blake/Parry, 'Jerusalem' (Royal Choral Society/ Philharmonia Orchestra/ Sargent)
¶ Dvořák, 'Songs My Mother Taught Me' (Paul Robeson)
¶ 'Don't Have Any More, Mrs Moore' (David Kossoff)

¶ 'An Ordinary Copper' (from TV series *Dixon of Dock Green*) (Jack Warner)
¶ Tchaikovsky, Symphony No. 6 in B minor (Leningrad Philharmonic/Mravinsky)
¶ 'Click Go the Shears' (Lionel Long)
¶ 'Come Outside' (Mike Sarne)
*¶ Sibelius, Symphony No. 2 in D major (BBC Symphony/ Beecham)
¶ LUXURY: A concertina.
¶ BOOK: Leo Tolstoy, *War and Peace*

15 April 1963
647 David Frost
Broadcaster
¶ 'The Old Rugged Cross' (Ballarat City Choir)
¶ 'Charlie' (from film *Shoot the Pianist*) (Georges Delerue)
¶ 'Aftermyth of War' (from *Beyond the Fringe*) (Alan Bennett)
¶ *That Was the Week that Was* (opening number) (Millicent Martin and others)
¶ 'Just in Time' (Oscar Peterson Trio)
¶ 'St Louis Blues' (Helen Shapiro)
¶ 'Everything I've Got' (Joanie Sommers)
*¶ 'Non, je ne regrette rien' (Edith Piaf)
¶ LUXURY: Potato crisps.
¶ BOOK: The works of Chaucer.

22 April 1963
648 Marjorie Proops
Newspaper columnist
¶ 'Take the "A" Train' (Dave Brubeck Quartet)
¶ Donizetti, 'Una furtiva lacrima' (from *L'elisir d'amore*) (Giuseppe di Stefano)
¶ 'Ev'ry Time We Say Goodbye' (from *Seven Lively Arts*) (Ella Fitzgerald)
¶ 'Tau Mafatu' (Eddie Lund and his Tahitians)
¶ Prokofiev, Violin Concerto No. 1 in D (Isaac Stern/New York Philharmonic/ Mitropoulos)
¶ 'My Kind of Girl' (Frank Sinatra)

¶ Bernstein/Sondheim, 'Somewhere' (from *West Side Story*) (Reri Grist)
*¶ Beethoven, Piano Concerto No. 5 in E flat major (Solomon/ Philharmonia Orchestra/ Menges)
¶ LUXURY: A looking glass.
¶ BOOK: The Larousse cookery book.

27 April 1963
649 Vivienne Chatterton
Broadcaster
¶ Chabrier, 'España' (RPO/ Beecham)
¶ Bruch, 'Ave Maria' (Joan Hammond/PO/Susskind)
¶ Wagner, 'Love Duet' (from *Tristan und Isolde*) (Frida Leider/Lauritz Melchior)
¶ Debussy, *Prélude à l'après-midi d'un faune* (RPO/Beecham)
¶ Beethoven, Violin Concerto in D major (Yehudi Menuhin/ Philharmonia Orchestra/ Furtwängler)
¶ Gerard Hoffnung at the Oxford Union
¶ Wagner, 'Brünnhilde's Immolation' (from *Götterdämmerung*) (Kirsten Flagstad/Philharmonia Orchestra/Furtwängler)
¶ Humperdinck, *Hansel und Gretel* (overture) (Philharmonia Orchestra/Klemperer)
(*For reasons of time, the last two records were not played.*)
¶ LUXURY: Insect repellent.
¶ BOOK: Harold Barlow and Sam Morgenstern, *Dictionary of Musical Themes*

29 April 1963
650 George Chisholm
Jazz trombonist
¶ 'The Boy Next Door' (Bobby Hackett *trumpet*)
¶ Debussy, 'Première arabesque' (Leonard Pennario *piano*)
¶ 'Thanks a Million' (Louis Armstrong and his Orchestra)
¶ Mozart, Horn Concerto No. 4 in E flat major (K. 495) (Dennis Brain/Philharmonia Orchestra/ von Karajan)
¶ 'The Sewers of the Strand' (Spike Milligan)

¶ Gershwin, 'I Got Rhythm' (from *Girl Crazy*) (Ella Fitzgerald)
*¶ 'Don't Tell a Man about His Woman' (Jack Teagarden)
¶ Dvořák, 'Humoresque' in G flat (Art Tatum *piano*)
¶ LUXURIES: A trombone and hair restorer.
¶ BOOK: An anthology of humour.

6 May 1963
651 Professor L. Dudley Stamp
Geographer and traveller
¶ 'The Wedding of Sandy McNab' (Sir Harry Lauder)
¶ 'Il bacio' (Erna Sack)
¶ J. Strauss, 'The Blue Danube Waltz' (Vienna Philharmonic/ Boskovsky)
¶ Chopin, Waltz No. 1 in E flat (opus 18) (Alexander Uninsky *piano*)
¶ Grieg, 'Morning' (from *Peer Gynt*, Act 4) (RPO/Beecham)
¶ Rodgers & Hammerstein, 'Bali Ha'i' (from *South Pacific*) (Muriel Smith)
¶ Vaughan Williams, 'Fantasia on Greensleeves' (Boyd Neel Orchestra)
*¶ Handel, 'Hallelujah Chorus' (from *Messiah*) (Huddersfield Choral Society/Royal Liverpool Philharmonic/Sargent)
¶ LUXURY: Wine.
¶ BOOK: *Everyman's Encyclopaedia*

13 May 1963
652 Frank Worrell
Cricketer
¶ 'Manhattan' (from *Garrick Gaieties*) (Victor Silvester and his Silver Strings)
¶ 'Federation' (Mighty Sparrow)
*¶ 'Skylark' (Bing Crosby)
¶ 'The White Cliffs of Dover' (Vera Lynn)
¶ 'April in Portugal' (Mantovani and his Orchestra)
¶ 'Waltzing Matilda' (Peter Dawson)
¶ 'It Happened in Monterey' (from film *The King of Jazz*) (Frank Sinatra)
¶ 'Londonderry Air' (Reg Owen and his Orchestra)

¶ LUXURY: A film projector and cricket films.
¶ BOOK: A work on anthropology by Professor Gluckman.

20 May 1963
653 Rowland Emett
Humorous artist
¶ Mozart, Oboe Concerto in C major (Léon Goossens/Sinfonia of London/Davis)
¶ Schubert, 'Die Forelle' (Gérard Souzay)
¶ Brahms, Symphony No. 2 in D major (Philharmonia Orchestra/Klemperer)
¶ Rachmaninov, Piano Concerto No. 2 in C minor (Benno Moiseiwitsch/ Philharmonia Orchestra/ Rignold)
¶ Bach, Brandenburg Concerto No. 5 in D major (Yehudi Menuhin *violin*/Elaine Shaffer *flute*/George Malcolm *harpsichord*/Bath Festival Chamber Orchestra/Menuhin)
*¶ Beethoven, Quartet No. 8 in E minor (opus 59, no. 2) (Budapest String Quartet)
¶ 'The Owl and the Pussycat' (Elton Hayes)
¶ Handel, 'The Arrival of the Queen of Sheba' (from *Solomon*) (RPO/Beecham)
¶ LUXURY: His daughter's teddy bear.
¶ BOOK: Robert Burton, *The Anatomy of Melancholy*

27 May 1963
654 Birgit Nilsson
Dramatic soprano
¶ Weber, 'Leise, leise, fromme Weise!' (from *Der Freischütz*) (Birgit Nilsson/Philharmonia Orchestra/Wallberg)
¶ Schubert, 'Die Forelle' (Elisabeth Schumann)
¶ Lerner & Loewe, 'I Could Have Danced All Night' (from *My Fair Lady*) (Birgit Nilsson/ Vienna Philharmonic/von Karajan)
¶ Puccini, 'Nessun dorma' (from *Turandot*) (Jussi Björling/ Rome Opera House Orchestra/ Leinsdorf)
¶ Grieg, 'I Love Thee' (Birgit Nilsson)

¶ Wagner, *Siegfried* (final duet) (Birgit Nilsson/Wolfgang Windgassen/Vienna Philharmonic/Solti)

¶ R. Strauss, *Salome* (excerpt) (Birgit Nilsson/Vienna Philharmonic/Solti)

*¶ Wagner, 'Isolde's Liebestod' (from *Tristan und Isolde*) (Birgit Nilsson/Vienna Philharmonic/Solti)

(For reasons of time, the last two discs were not played.)

¶ LUXURY: Swedish crossword puzzles.

¶ BOOK: Sir Winston Churchill, *The Second World War*

3 June 1963
655 Barry Bucknell
Do-it-yourself expert

¶ 'Waiting for Johnny to Come Home' (Cleo Laine)

¶ Bach, Toccata and Fugue in D minor (Fernando Germani *organ*)

¶ 'Mah Lindy Lou' (Paul Robeson)

¶ Ravel, Introduction and Allegro (Osian Ellis *harp*/Melos Ensemble)

¶ 'Nightingale, Don't Wake the Soldiers' (Red Banner Song and Dance Ensemble)

¶ Purcell/A. Coates, 'Rondeau' (LSO Strings/Sargent)

¶ Russo, Suite No. 2 (opus 8) (Bill's Blues/London Jazz Orchestra/Russo)

*¶ Beethoven, Violin Concerto in D major (Zino Francescatti/Columbia Symphony/Walter)

¶ LUXURY: A toilet set.

¶ BOOK: An anthology of poetry.

10 June 1963
656 Eva Bartok
Actress

¶ Liszt, Hungarian Rhapsody No. 2 (RIAS Radio Symphony, Berlin/Fricsay)

¶ Beethoven, Symphony No. 9 in D minor (opus 125) (Eileen Farrell/Nan Merriman/Jan Peerce/Norman Scott/NBC Symphony/Toscanini)

¶ 'Hungarian Airs' (Magyari Imre and his Hungarian Gypsy Orchestra)

¶ 'Sevillianas de triana' (Los Macarenos)

¶ Gershwin, 'Summertime' (from *Porgy and Bess*) (New York Philharmonic/Kostelanetz)

¶ Bach, Brandenburg Concerto No. 3 in G major (Philharmonia Orchestra/Klemperer)

¶ Beethoven, Symphony No. 7 in A major (opus 92) (NBC Symphony/Toscanini)

*¶ 'I Believe' (Frankie Laine)

¶ LUXURY: Painting materials.

¶ BOOK: Antoine de St-Exupéry, *The Little Prince*

17 June 1963
657 Joe Loss
Bandleader

¶ 'Moonlight Serenade' (Glenn Miller and his Orchestra)

¶ Porter, 'Now You Has Jazz' (from film *High Society*) (Bing Crosby/Louis Armstrong)

¶ Debussy, 'Clair de lune' (from *Suite bergamasque*) (David Oistrakh *violin*/Vladimir Yampolsky *piano*)

¶ Porter, 'Begin the Beguine' (from *Jubilee*) (Joe Loss and his Band)

*¶ 'Kol Nidrei' (Jan Peerce)

¶ 'Let's Twist Again' (Chubby Checker)

¶ Leoncavallo, 'Vesti la giubba' (from *Pagliacci*) (Jussi Björling)

¶ 'In the Mood' (Joe Loss and his Orchestra)

¶ LUXURY: A radio receiver.

¶ BOOK: A bound selection of letters that he has received.

24 June 1963
658 Beryl Reid
Comedienne

¶ 'Ev'ry Time We Say Goodbye' (from *Seven Lively Arts*) (Ella Fitzgerald)

¶ Handel, 'I Know that My Redeemer Liveth' (from *Messiah*) (Isobel Baillie/Hallé Orchestra/Heward)

¶ 'Shadows on the Grass' (Irene Handl/Peter Sellers)

¶ 'Kiss Me Again' (Frank Sinatra)

*¶ Delius, 'Summer Night on the River' (RPO/Beecham)

¶ 'I'm the Guy Who Found the Lost Chord' (Jimmy Durante)

¶ Puccini, 'None Shall Sleep' (from *Turandot*) (Harry Secombe)

¶ Bach, Suite No. 3 in D major (Yehudi Menuhin *violin*)

¶ LUXURY: Lipsticks.

¶ BOOK: *The World Encyclopaedia of Cookery*

1 July 1963
659 Boyd Neel
(2nd appearance)
Conductor

¶ Wagner, *Die Meistersinger* (Act 3 prelude) (NBC Symphony/Toscanini)

¶ Schubert, Sonata in B flat (D. 960) (Artur Schnabel *piano*)

¶ Mozart, Sinfonia Concertante in E flat major (K. 364) (Norbert Brainin *violin*/Peter Schidlof *viola*/London Mozart Players/Blech)

¶ Britten, 'Variations on a Theme of Frank Bridge' (Boyd Neel String Orchestra)

¶ Beethoven, Quartet No. 16 in F (opus 135) (Budapest String Quartet)

¶ R. Strauss, *Der Rosenkavalier* (final trio) (Lotte Lehmann/Elisabeth Schumann/Maria Olszewska/Vienna Philharmonic/Heger)

¶ 'The Irish Washerwoman' (Eastman-Rochester 'Pops' Orchestra/Fennell)

*¶ Grieg, 'Spring' (from *Two Elegiac Melodies*) (Boyd Neel String Orchestra)

¶ LUXURY: Whisky.

¶ BOOK: Lewis Carroll, *Alice in Wonderland*

8 July 1963
660 Juliette Greco
Cabaret singer and actress

*¶ Mozart, *Eine Kleine Nachtmusik* (Bath Festival Chamber Orchestra/Menuhin)

¶ 'I Wanna be Around' (Tony Bennett)

¶ Mozart, Piano Concerto No. 23 in A major (K. 488) (Clara Haskil/Vienna Symphony/Sacher)

¶ 'You've Changed' (Billie Holiday)

¶ Falla/Evans, 'Will o' the Wisp' (from *El amor brujo*) (Miles Davis *trumpet*)

¶ 'Oh, Susannah' (Dave Brubeck Quartet)
¶ Bach/Hess, 'Jesu, Joy of Man's Desiring' (Myra Hess *piano*)
¶ Beethoven, Symphony No. 7 in A major (opus 92) (Philharmonia Orchestra/ Cantelli)
¶ LUXURY: Writing materials.
¶ BOOK: An atlas.

13 July 1963
661 Ken Dodd
Comedian
¶ 'The Folks Who Live on the Hill' (Peggy Lee)
¶ 'How Do You Do It?' (Gerry and the Pacemakers)
*¶ 'The Floral Dance' (Peter Dawson)
¶ Chopin, Fantaisie-Impromptu (opus 66) (Raymond Lewenthal *piano*)
¶ 'Mammy' (Al Jolson)
¶ Heuberger, 'Im chambre séparée' (from *Der Opernball*) (Elisabeth Schwarzkopf/ Philharmonia Orchestra/ Ackermann)
¶ Gershwin, 'Our Love is Here to Stay' (from film *Goldwyn Follies*) (Frank Sinatra)
¶ 'O sole mio' (Beniamino Gigli)
¶ LUXURY: Tea.
¶ BOOK: A dictionary.

15 July 1963
662 Geraint Evans
Operatic baritone
¶ Wagner, *Die Meistersinger* (overture) (Philharmonia Orchestra/Klemperer)
¶ Dylan Thomas, *Under Milk Wood* (excerpt) (Richard Burton/Dafydd Havard/Sybil Williams)
¶ R. Strauss, *Der Rosenkavalier* (final trio) (Maria Reining/Sena Jurinac/Hilde Gueden/Vienna Philharmonic/Kleiber)
¶ Ellis, 'Ma belle Marguerite' (from *Bless the Bride*) (Georges Guetary)
¶ Verdi, *La traviata* (prelude) (Hallé Orchestra/Barbirolli)
¶ 'Little White Bull' (Tommy Steele)
*¶ 'Aberystwyth' (Massed Welsh Choirs)

¶ Mozart, *The Marriage of Figaro* (overture) (Glyndebourne Festival Orchestra/Gui)
¶ LUXURY: A mouth organ.
¶ BOOK: An anthology of 20th-century verse.

22 July 1963
663 Vivienne
Photographer
*¶ Massenet, 'Meditation' (from *Thaïs*) (Michael Rabin *violin*/ Hollywood Bowl Symphony/ Slatkin)
¶ Puccini, 'In questa reggia' (from *Turandot*) (Eva Turner)
¶ Royal entrance into Westminster Abbey and Greeting 'Vivat, Vivat': Coronation Service of HM Queen Elizabeth II
¶ Delius, 'The Walk to the Paradise Garden' (from *A Village Romeo and Juliet*) (RPO/ Beecham)
¶ Puccini, 'Vissi d'arte' (from *Tosca*) (Maria Callas/La Scala Orchestra/de Sabata)
¶ 'These Foolish Things' (from *Spread It Abroad*) (Hutch)
¶ Beethoven, Violin Concerto in D minor (opus 61) (Yehudi Menuhin/Vienna Philharmonic/Silvestri)
¶ Liszt, Liebestraum No. 3 (Gyorgy Cziffra *piano*)
¶ LUXURY: Painting materials.
¶ BOOK: Lewis Carroll, *Alice in Wonderland*

27 July 1963
664 Carleton Hobbs
Actor
¶ 'The Royal Artillery Slow March' (HM Royal Artillery Band)
¶ 'If You were the Only Girl in the World' (from *The Bing Boys are Here*) (Violet Loraine/ George Robey)
¶ 'Londonderry Air' (Fritz Kreisler *violin*)
¶ Mussorgsky, 'I Have Attained the Highest Power' (from *Boris Godunov*) (Feodor Chaliapin)
*¶ O. Straus, 'C'est le destin peut-être' (from *Les trois valses*) (Yvonne Printemps)
¶ Porter, 'Begin the Beguine' (from *Jubilee*) (Hutch)

¶ O. Straus, 'Jede Frau hat irgendeine Sehnsucht' (Fritzi Massary)
¶ Gilbert & Sullivan, 'When the Wooer Goes A-Wooing' (from *Yeomen of the Guard*) (Glyndebourne Festival Chorus/Sargent)
¶ LUXURY: A radio receiver.
¶ BOOK: John Galsworthy, *The Forsyte Saga*

5 August 1963
665 Ian Fleming
Writer of thrillers
¶ 'Cecilia' (Whispering Jack Smith)
¶ 'Dinah' (The Revellers)
¶ 'La vie en rose' (Edith Piaf)
¶ 'If I Didn't Care' (The Inkspots)
¶ 'This Ole House' (Rosemary Clooney)
¶ 'Theme from *A Summer Place*' (Billy Vaughan)
¶ 'The Harry Lime Theme' (From film *The Third Man*) (Anton Karas *zither*)
*¶ 'The Darktown Strutters Ball' (Joe 'Fingers' Carr)
¶ LUXURY: A typewriter and paper.
¶ BOOK: Leo Tolstoy, *War and Peace*, in German.

12 August 1963
666 Sir Charles Maclean
Chief Scout of the Commonwealth
¶ 'Underneath the Arches' (Flanagan & Allen)
¶ 'Hark the Herald Angels Sing' (King's College Chapel Choir/ Willcocks)
¶ Mendelssohn, 'Hebrides Overture' (opus 26) (BBC Symphony/Boult)
¶ 'The Fiddler's Joy' and 'Johnny Macdonald' (Massed Pipers of the Scots Guards)
¶ 'Sail Your Dreamboat' (The Gang)
*¶ Widor, Symphony No. 5 in F minor (toccata) (Marcel Dupré *organ*)
¶ 'Anywhere I Wander' (Danny Kaye)

¶'National Anthem' (from Coronation Service of HM Queen Elizabeth II)
¶LUXURY: A piano.
¶BOOK: A set of bound volumes of *The Illustrated London News*.

19 August 1963
667 Graham Hill
Racing driver
*¶Arlen & Harburg, 'Over the Rainbow' (from film *The Wizard of Oz*) (Judy Garland)
¶'When the Saints Go Marching In' (Chris Barber's Jazz Band)
¶Lerner & Loewe, 'Wouldn't It be Lovely?' (from *My Fair Lady*) (Julie Andrews)
¶Sibelius, 'Finlandia' (Danish State Radio Symphony/Tuxen)
¶'Let There be Love' (Nat 'King' Cole)
¶Chopin, Nocturne No. 2 in E flat major (opus 9, no. 2) (Stefan Askenase *piano*)
¶'Eton Boating Song' (Eton College Musical Society)
¶'The Blood Donor' (Tony Hancock and company)
¶LUXURY: An armchair.
¶BOOK: A volume of short stories by Ernest Hemingway.

24 August 1963
668 Scobie Breasley
Jockey
¶'It Had to be You' (Count Basie and his Orchestra)
¶'Tie Me Kangaroo Down, Sport' (Leslie Ross Singers)
¶'Did You Ever See a Dream Walking?' (Maurice Chevalier)
*¶Porter, 'Don't Fence Me In' (from film *Hollywood Canteen*) (Bing Crosby/The Andrews Sisters)
¶'In Heimatstil' (Erika Feldman/Heidi Benz)
¶'Too Young' (Joni James)
¶Commentary of the finish of the 1949 Derby (Raymond Glendenning)
¶'Aloha Oe' (Hawaiian Islanders)
¶LUXURY: Golf clubs and balls.
¶BOOK: An encyclopaedia.

26 August 1963
669 Dr Reginald Jacques
Conductor and lecturer
¶Bach, Cantata No. 82: 'Ich habe genug' (Dietrich Fischer-Dieskau/Karl Ristenpart Chamber Orchestra)
¶Mozart, Symphony No. 41 in C (RPO/Beecham)
¶Elgar, 'Cockaigne Overture' (RPO/Beecham)
*¶Bach, 'Oh Man, Thy Grievous Sin Bemoan' (from *St Matthew Passion*) (Bach Choir/Jacques Orchestra)
¶Bach, 'Have Mercy, Lord, on Me' (from *St Matthew Passion*) (Kathleen Ferrier/Jacques Orchestra)
¶Delius, 'On Hearing the First Cuckoo in Spring' (RPO/Beecham)
¶Gilbert & Sullivan, 'A More Humane Mikado' (from *The Mikado*) (Darrell Fancourt/D'Oyly Carte Opera Company)
¶Vaughan Williams, A Sea Symphony (LPO/Boult)
¶LUXURY: Music manuscript paper and pencils.
¶BOOKS: Dorothy L. Sayers, *The Nine Tailors* and *Busman's Honeymoon*

2 September 1963
670 Sophie Tucker
Entertainer
¶'Blame It on the Bossa Nova' (Eydie Gormé)
¶Rodgers & Hammerstein, 'The Surrey with the Fringe on Top' (from *Oklahoma*) (Lena Horne)
¶Bart, 'As Long as He Needs Me' (from *Oliver!*) (Shirley Bassey)
¶'The Second Time Around' (Frank Sinatra)
*¶'The Garden of Eden' (Frankie Vaughan)
¶'Bachelor Boy' (Cliff Richard)
¶'Cannibal Pot' (Tommy Steele)
¶'Some of These Days' (Sophie Tucker)
¶LUXURY: Make-up.
¶BOOK: Herbert Tarr, *The Conversion of Charlie Cohen*

9 September 1963
671 Raymond Baxter
Radio commentator
¶'Some Day My Prince will Come' (from film *Snow White and the Seven Dwarfs*) (Dave Brubeck Quartet)
¶Elgar, *Enigma Variations* (Philharmonia Orchestra/Sargent)
¶'The Darktown Strutters Ball' (Mugsy Spanier's Ragtimers)
¶Parry, 'I was Glad' (from Coronation Service of HM Queen Elizabeth II)
¶Sibelius, Symphony No. 5 in E flat major (Danish State Radio Symphony/Tuxen)
¶'Tales of Men's Shirts' (from *The Best of the Goon Shows*)
¶Rachmaninov, Piano Concerto No. 2 in C minor (Andor Foldes/Berlin Philharmonic/Ludwig)
*¶Bruch, Violin Concerto No. 1 in G minor (Yehudi Menuhin/Philharmonia Orchestra/Susskind)
¶LUXURY: The statue, *Danae*, by Rodin.
¶BOOK: *Encyclopaedia Britannica*

16 September 1963
672 Norman del Mar
Conductor
¶Bach, 'Et In Unum' (from *Mass in B minor*) (Elisabeth Schumann/Margaret Balfour/LSO/Coates)
¶Wagner, *Die Walküre* (excerpt from Act 3) (Frida Leider/Friedrich Schorr/Berlin State Opera Orchestra/Blech)
*¶Beethoven, Symphony No. 9 in D minor (opus 125) (Richard Mayr/Vienna Philharmonic/Chorus/Weingartner)
¶R. Strauss, 'Wer bist denn du?' (from *Elektra*) (Erna Schluter/RPO/Beecham)
¶Bartók, Quartet No. 3 (Juilliard String Quartet)
¶Verdi, 'Quel viso santo' (from *Otello*) (Nicola Fusati/La Scala Orchestra and Chorus/Sabajno)
¶Boulez, 'Le marteau sans maître' (Marie-Thérèse Cahn/soloists/Boulez)

¶ 'A Transport of Delight' (from *At the Drop of a Hat*) (Michael Flanders/Donald Swann)
¶ LUXURY: A piano.
¶ BOOK: *Le Petit Larousse Illustré*

30 September 1963
673 Group Captain Leonard Cheshire VC
Founder of the Cheshire Homes for the Sick
¶ 'Red Sails in the Sunset' (Bing Crosby)
¶ Debussy, 'Clair de lune' (from *Suite bergamasque*) (Walter Gieseking *piano*)
¶ 'Waltzing Matilda' (Leslie Ross Singers)
¶ 'Silent Night, Holy Night' (Royal Choral Society/Sargent)
¶ 'Rapuk Tal' (Ravi Shankar *sitar*)
¶ 'Elizabethan Serenade' (Ron Goodwin and his Orchestra)
*¶ 'Christus Factus Est' (Choir of the Carmelite Priory, London)
¶ 'Salve Regina' (from *Antiphon*) (Choir of the Institute of St Gregory, Lyon)
¶ LUXURY: A photograph of the face on the Holy Shroud at Turin.
¶ BOOK: A breviary.

7 October 1963
674 Bernard Cribbins
Actor
¶ 'My Very Good Friend, The Milkman' (Fats Waller)
¶ 'The Flogging Reel' (Frank Lee's Tara Ceilidh Orchestra)
*¶ Ravel, 'Lever du jour' (from *Daphnis and Chloe Suite No. 2*) (Philharmonia Orchestra/Giulini)
¶ 'Come Rain or Come Shine' (Judy Garland)
¶ 'Skylark' (Hoagy Carmichael)
¶ 'Saro Jane' (Odetta)
¶ Bach/Segovia, 'Gavotte' (from Partita in E major for Unaccompanied Violin) (Andrés Segovia *guitar*)
¶ 'Dishonoured' (from *The Best of the Goon Shows*)
¶ LUXURY: Michelangelo's *Pietà*
¶ BOOK: Henry Williamson, *Tarka the Otter*

14 October 1963
675 Pat Moss
Showjumper and rally driver
*¶ 'Pepito' (Los Machucambos)
¶ 'These Foolish Things' (from *Spread It Abroad*) (Nat 'King' Cole)
¶ 'There will Never be Another You' (Keely Smith)
¶ Bach/Gounod, 'Ave Maria' (Mario Lanza)
¶ Porter, 'Easy to Love' (from film *Born to Dance*) (Ray Coniff and his Orchestra)
¶ 'Misty' (Johnny Mathis)
¶ 'Quando, quando, quando' (Marino Marini Quartet)
¶ LUXURY: A bed.
¶ BOOK: Ian Fleming's James Bond novels.

19 October 1963
676 Norman Shelley
Actor
¶ Debussy, 'Syrinx' (Aurèle Nicolet *flute*)
¶ Nicolai, *The Merry Wives of Windsor* (overture) (Vienna Philharmonic/Kempe)
¶ 'Steal Away' (Paul Robeson)
¶ Beethoven, Symphony No. 3 in E flat major (opus 55) (Philharmonia Orchestra/Klemperer)
¶ Fraser-Simson, 'Three Cheers for Pooh' (Norman Shelley/David Davis)
¶ Mendelssohn, *A Midsummer Night's Dream* (nocturne) (Vienna Philharmonic/Monteux)
¶ Gay, 'Would I Might be Hanged' (from *The Beggar's Opera*) (Dennis Noble/Carmen Prietto/Martha Lipton)
*¶ Bach, 'Jesu, Joy of Man's Desiring' (Temple Church Choir, London)
¶ LUXURY: Painting materials.
¶ BOOK: Kenneth Grahame, *The Wind in the Willows*

21 October 1963
677 Admiral Sir Michael Maynard Denny
Sailor and broadcaster
*¶ Royal entrance into Westminster Abbey and Greeting (Vivat, Vivat) from Coronation Service of HM Queen Elizabeth II

¶ Dvořák, Symphony No. 9 in E minor (NBC Symphony/Toscanini)
¶ Ponchielli, 'Dance of the Hours' (from *La Gioconda*) (Philharmonia Orchestra/von Karajan)
¶ Tchaikovsky, 'Pas de deux' (from *The Nutcracker Suite*) (CSO/Reiner)
¶ Mahler, 'Um Mitternacht' (from *Ruckert Songs*, no. 5) (Kathleen Ferrier/Vienna Philharmonic/Walter)
¶ Gounod, 'Le sommeil de Juliette' (from *Romeo et Juliette*) (RPO/Beecham)
¶ Saint-Saëns, Symphony No. 3 in C minor (Boston Symphony/Münch)
¶ Elgar, 'Nimrod' (from *Enigma Variations*) (NBC Symphony/Toscanini)
¶ LUXURY: A pair of binoculars.
¶ BOOK: Limberg, *The Ship*

28 October 1963
678 Patrick Moore
Astronomer and broadcaster
¶ Sibelius, 'At the Castle Gate' (from *Pelléas et Mélisande*) (Frank Chacksfield and his Orchestra)
¶ Grieg, Piano Concerto in A minor (Clifford Curzon/LSO/Fjeldstad)
¶ Gilbert & Sullivan, *Princess Ida* (overture) (New Symphony Orchestra/Godfrey)
¶ Josef Strauss, 'Dynamiden Waltz' (Vienna Philharmonic/Kempe)
¶ Chopin, Étude in C minor (opus 10, no. 2) (Malcuzynski *piano*)
¶ Grieg, 'Homage March' (from *Sigurd Jorsalfar*) (LSO/Fjeldstad)
*¶ Komzák, 'Bad'ner Mad'ln Waltz' (Vienna Philharmonic/Knappertsbusch)
¶ Tchaikovsky/Bogatyryev, Symphony No. 7 in E flat major (Philadelphia Orchestra/Ormandy)
¶ LUXURY: An astronomical telescope.
¶ BOOK: *The Norton Star Atlas*

4 November 1963
679 Joan Bennett
Actress

¶ Porter, 'You're the Top' (from *Anything Goes*) (Bing Crosby)

*¶ Puccini, 'Chi il bel sogno di doretta' (from *La rondine*) (Leontyne Price/Rome Opera House Orchestra/de Fabritiis)

¶ 'The Banana Boat Song' (Harry Belafonte)

¶ 'The Road to Morocco' (from film) (Bing Crosby/Bob Hope)

¶ Newley, 'Gonna Build a Mountain' (from *Stop the World, I Want to Get Off*) (Anthony Newley)

¶ 'My Romance' (from film *Jumbo*) (Dinah Shore/Frank Sinatra)

¶ 'Thou Swell' (from film *A Connecticut Yankee in King Arthur's Court*) (Sammy Davis Jnr)

¶ Rodgers & Hammerstein, 'If I Loved You' (from *Carousel*) (John Raitt)

¶ LUXURY: Suntan lotion.

¶ BOOK: Gerald Durrell, *My Family and Other Animals*

11 November 1963
680 Stephen Potter
Writer and inventor of One-Upmanship

¶ Elgar, *The Wand of Youth* Suite No. 2 (march) (LPO/Van Beinum)

¶ Gilbert & Sullivan, 'A British Tar is a Soaring Soul' (from *HMS Pinafore*) (Thomas Round/George Cook/Eric Wilson-Hyde/D'Oyly Carte Opera Chorus and Orchestra/Godfrey)

*¶ Beethoven, String Quartet in C minor (opus 18, no. 4) (Amadeus Quartet)

¶ Stravinsky, 'The Shrovetide Fair' (from *Petrushka*) (Columbia Symphony/Stravinsky)

¶ Bach, Double Concerto in D minor (Yehudi Menuhin and Christian Ferras *violins*/Festival Chamber Orchestra)

¶ Berlin, 'Top Hat, White Tie and Tails' (from film *Top Hat*) (Fred Astaire)

¶ Bach, Toccata, Adagio and Fugue in C major (Egon Petri *piano*)

¶ Poulenc, *Les Biches* (finale) (Paris Conservatoire Orchestra/Désormière)

¶ LUXURY: A pair of field glasses.

¶ BOOK: A book about sea birds and waders.

18 November 1963
681 Gordon Pirie
Athlete

*¶ 'The Very Thought of You' (Norrie Paramor and his Orchestra)

¶ Elgar, 'Pomp and Circumstance' March No. 1 in D major (LSO/Sargent)

¶ 'Bei mir bist du Schön' (Nina & Frederick)

¶ 'El Cumbanchero' (Caterina Valente)

¶ Offenbach, 'Barcarolle' (from *The Tales of Hoffmann*) (Royal Opera House Orchestra, Covent Garden/Solti)

¶ 'Non, je ne regrette rien' (Edith Piaf)

¶ 'Chariot' (Petula Clark)

¶ Debussy/Stokowski, 'Clair de lune' (from *Suite bergamasque*) (Stokowski Symphony)

¶ LUXURY: A motor car.

¶ BOOK: *Gray's Anatomy*

25 November 1963
682 Ron Grainer
Composer

¶ *The Play of Daniel* (overture) (New York Pro Musica/Greenberg)

¶ Bach, Brandenburg Concerto No. 4 in G major (Stuttgart Chamber Orchestra/Münchinger)

¶ Brahms, Piano Quintet in F minor (Sviatoslav Richter/Borodin Quartet)

¶ Debussy/Verlaine, 'Green' (Maggie Teyte/Gerald Moore *piano*)

¶ Ravel, 'La flûte enchantée' (from *Scheherazade*) (Suzanne Danco/Orchestre de la Suisse Romande/Ansermet)

¶ Stravinsky, Symphonies of Wind Instruments (Eastman Symphonic Wind Ensemble/Fennell)

*¶ 'Spring Season' (Ravi Shankar *sitar*)

¶ 'Flamenco Sketches' (Miles Davis *trumpet*)

¶ LUXURY: A flame opal.

¶ BOOK: Louis Mumford, *Techniques and Civilization*

2 December 1963
683 T. R. Robinson
Expert on clocks

¶ Respighi, 'Gagliarda' (from *Ancient Airs and Dances for the Lute, Suite No. 1*) (Philharmonia Orchestra/Dorati)

*¶ Haydn, 'Trumpet Concerto in E flat (Harry Mortimer/Philharmonia Orchestra/Weldon)

¶ Dvořák, Symphony No. 9 in E minor (LPO/Rignold)

¶ Schubert, 'Ave Maria' (Clifford E. Ball *carillon*, recorded at the Croydon Bell Foundry)

¶ Handel/Beecham, 'Hornpipe' (from *The Gods Go A'Begging*) (RPO/Beecham)

¶ 'Jack's Maggot' (Country Dance Players)

¶ 'The Infant King' (King's College Chapel Choir/Ord)

¶ 'The Old Clockmaker' (Queen's Hall Light Orchestra/Williams)

¶ LUXURY: A marine chronometer.

¶ BOOK: A volume of illustrations of the English countryside.

9 December 1963
684 Millicent Martin
Actress and singer

¶ 'It Can Happen to You' (Herb Ellis *guitar* and accompaniment)

¶ Elgar, 'Pomp and Circumstance' March No. 4 in G major (Philharmonia Orchestra/Barbirolli)

¶ Mussorgsky, 'Simpleton's Aria' (from *Boris Godunov*, Act 4) (Kiril Dulguerov/Paris Conservatoire Orchestra and Chorus/Cluytens)

¶ 'Southside' (Wardell Gray *tenor saxophone* and accompaniment)

¶ Puccini, 'In questa reggia' (from *Turandot*) (Amy Shuard/Royal Opera House Orchestra, Covent Garden/Downes)

¶Dylan Thomas, *Under Milk Wood* (opening) (Richard Burton)
*¶'I Am' (Ronnie Carroll)
¶Bach, Fugue in D minor (Swingle Singers)
¶LUXURY: A four-poster bed.
¶BOOK: Lao-tzu, *A Way of Life*

16 December 1963
685 Hartford Montgomery Hyde
Writer
¶Handel, 'Where'er You Walk' (from *Semele*) (John McCormack)
¶Mozart, Divertimento in E flat for Violin, Viola and Cello (K. 563) (Kehr Trio)
¶Mozart, 'Ruhe Sanft' (from *Zaide*) (Rita Streich/Radio Symphony, Berlin/Rother)
¶Mozart, Sinfonia Concertante in E flat (K. 364) (London Mozart Players/Blech)
¶Mozart, 'Dies Bildnis' (from *The Magic Flute*) (Richard Tauber)
*¶Beethoven, Piano Concerto No. 5 in E flat major (Wilhelm Kempff/Berlin Philharmonic/Leitner)
¶Tchaikovsky, *Eugene Onegin* (Act 2 waltz) (RPO/Beecham)
¶'The Lark in the Clear Air' (Kenneth McKellar)
¶LUXURY: Brandy.
¶BOOK: James Boswell's *Life of Johnson*

23 December 1963
686 Nicolai Poliakoff (Coco the Clown)
Circus performer
¶'Entry of the Gladiators' (Ringling Brothers Barnum & Bailey Circus Band)
¶'Kalinka' (Red Army Ensemble)
¶Tchaikovsky, *Swan Lake* (Orchestre de la Suisse Romande/Ansermet)
¶'The Anniversary Waltz' (Joe Loss and his Orchestra)
¶Puccini, *Madam Butterfly* (Act 2 finale) (Renata Tebaldi/St Cecilia Orchestra, Rome/Serafin)
¶'Ich Glaub' Nie Mehr An Eine Frau' (Richard Tauber)

*¶'Black Eyes' (Balalaika Orchestra)
¶'The Story of Charlie' (Coco the Clown)
¶LUXURY: Writing materials to write children's stories, and empty bottles to send them to be published.
¶BOOK: An English dictionary.

30 December 1963
687 Cyril Smith & Phyllis Sellick
Piano duettists
¶(CS) Schumann, 'Reconnaissance' (from *Carnaval*) (Sergei Rachmaninov *piano*)
¶(PS) Vaughan Williams/Shakespeare, 'Serenade to Music' (Isobel Baillie/BBC Symphony/Wood)
*¶(CS) Brahms, Piano concerto No. 2 in B flat (Solomon *piano*/Philharmonia Orchestra/Dobrowen)
¶(PS) Schubert, Trio in B flat major (opus 99) (Alfred Cortot *piano*/Jacques Thibaud *violin*/Pablo Casals *cello*)
¶(CS) Bizet, 'Galop' (from *Jeux d'enfants*) (Cyril Smith and Phyllis Sellick *pianos*)
¶(PS) Bach, Double Concerto in D minor (Yehudi Menuhin and Georges Enesco *violins*/Paris Symphony/Monteux)
¶(CS) Sibelius, Symphony No. 5 in E flat (Hallé Orchestra/Barbirolli)
*¶(PS) Rachmaninov, 'Rhapsody on a Theme of Paganini' (Cyril Smith *piano*/Philharmonia Orchestra/Sargent)
¶LUXURIES: (PS) a coloured picture of their children; (CS) a microphone and amplifier for hearing birdsong.
¶BOOKS: (PS) *The Oxford Book of English Verse*; (CS) *Encyclopaedia Britannica*.

4 January 1964
688 Dorita & Pepe
Singers of Latin-American folk songs
¶(Dorita) Torroba, 'Sonatina' (John Williams *guitar*)
¶(Pepe) 'I Saw Stars' (Quintet of the Hot Club of France)

¶(D) Bach/Stokowski, Toccata and Fugue in D minor (Stokowski Symphony)
¶(P) 'Huapango' (Mexico Symphony/Chavez)
*¶(D) 'Mborayjhu Mombyry' (Trio Los Paraguayos)
¶(P) 'Historia de un amor' (Trio Los Panchos)
¶(D) Dankworth, 'Ghosts' (from *What the Dickens*) (Johnny Dankworth and his Orchestra)
*¶(P) 'Memorias mias' (Los Tres Reyes)
¶LUXURIES: (P) a guitar; (D) a cine projector and films of Sylvester, the cartoon cat.
¶BOOKS: (P) J. R. R. Tolkien, *The Lord of the Rings*; (D) fashion magazines.

6 January 1964
689 Ethel Revnell
Comedienne
¶'Half a Sixpence' (from *Half a Sixpence*) (Tommy Steele/Marti Webb)
¶Lerner & Loewe, 'I Remember It Well' (from film *Gigi*) (Hermione Gingold/Maurice Chevalier)
¶'The London I Love' (Vera Lynn)
¶Tchaikovsky, Piano Concerto No. 1 in B flat minor (Artur Rubinstein/Boston Symphony/Leinsdorf)
¶'April Showers' (from film) (Judy Garland)
*¶'British Institutions: The Police' (explained by Tony Fayne)
¶'Soldiers of the Queen' (Billy Cotton and his Band)
¶'Looking after the Baby' (Ethel Revnell/Gracie West)
¶LUXURY: Writing materials.
¶BOOK: A biography of Bette Davis.

13 January 1964
690 Leslie Baily
Writer and journalist
¶Tchaikovsky, 'Pas de deux' (from *The Sleeping Beauty*, Act 3) (Philharmonia Orchestra/Kurtz)
¶'Early One Morning' (Peter Pears/Benjamin Britten *piano*)

¶ Lewis Carroll, 'The Lobster Quadrille' (from *Alice in Wonderland*) (Jane Asher/Norman Shelley/Ian Wallace)
¶ 'Last Night on the Back Porch' (The Andrews Sisters)
¶ Handel, 'And the Glory of the Lord' (from *Messiah*) (Huddersfield Choral Society/Royal Liverpool Philharmonic/Sargent)
¶ Sullivan/Mackerras (arr.), *Pineapple Poll* (RPO/Mackerras)
¶ Elgar, Violin Concerto in B minor (Yehudi Menuhin/LSO/Elgar)
*¶ Rachmaninov, Piano Concerto No. 2 in C minor (Benno Moiseiwitsch/Philharmonia Orchestra/Rignold)
¶ LUXURY: Woodworker's tools.
¶ BOOK: *Come Hither*, an anthology of poetry compiled by Walter de la Mare.

20 January 1964
691 Richard Attenborough (2nd appearance)
Actor and film producer
¶ Handel, 'Hallelujah Chorus' (from *Messiah*) (Huddersfield Choral Society/Royal Liverpool Philharmonic/Sargent)
¶ Elgar, Symphony No. 1 in A flat (Philharmonia Orchestra/Barbirolli)
¶ Tchaikovsky, *The Nutcracker Suite* (RPO/Irving)
¶ Handel/Beecham, 'Hornpipe' (from *Love in Bath*) (RPO/Beecham)
¶ 'Azualao' (Gérard Souzay/Dalton Baldwin *piano*)
¶ Gershwin, 'Swanee' (from *Sinbad*) (Judy Garland)
¶ 'Were You There?' (Ellabelle Davis)
*¶ Beethoven, Symphony No. 9 in D minor (opus 125) (Eileen Farrell/Nan Merriman/Jan Peerce/Norman Scott/Robert Shaw Chorale/NBC Symphony/Toscanini)
¶ LUXURIES: A piano and a conductor's baton.
¶ BOOK: A biography of Mahatma Gandhi.

27 January 1964
692 Regina Resnik
Opera singer
¶ Verdi, 'Dies Irae' (from *Requiem*) (Robert Shaw Chorale/NBC Symphony/Shaw)
¶ Brahms, Violin Concerto in D major (Jascha Heifetz/LSO/Reiner)
¶ Spontini, 'O nume tutelar' (from *La vestale*) (Rosa Ponselle)
¶ Villa-Lobos, Bachianas Brasileiras No. 5 (Bidu Sayao/Leonard Rose *cello ensemble*/Villa-Lobos)
¶ Beethoven, Symphony No. 7 in A major (opus 92) (New York Philharmonic/Walter)
¶ Halévy, 'Rachel! Quand de seigneur la grace tutélaire' (from *La Juive*) (Enrico Caruso)
¶ 'Mock Mozart' (Peter Ustinov/Antony Hopkins *harpsichord*)
*¶ Tchaikovsky, Piano Sonata in G major (opus 37) (Sviatoslav Richter)
¶ LUXURY: A toothbrush.
¶ BOOK: A book with blank pages, and a pen.

3 February 1964
693 Julie Andrews
Actress and singer
¶ 'A Portrait of Bert Williams' (André Previn *piano*)
¶ Puccini, 'Nessun dorma' (from *Turandot*) (Jussi Björling)
¶ 'Wait Till the Sun Shines, Nellie' (from film *The Birth of the Blues*) (Mary Martin/Bing Crosby)
*¶ Brahms, Piano Concerto No. 2 in B flat (Sviatoslav Richter/Leinsdorf)
¶ 'Small World' (from *Gypsy*) (Ethel Merman)
¶ Bellini, 'Casta diva' (from *Norma*) (Royal Opera House Orchestra, Covent Garden, Molinari-Pradelli)
¶ 'The Stripper' (David Rose and his Orchestra)
¶ Ravel, *Daphnis and Chloe* (Motet Choir of Geneva/Orchestre de la Suisse Romande/Ansermet)
¶ LUXURY: A piano.
¶ BOOK: T. H. White, *The Once and Future King*

8 February 1964
694 Wilson Whineray
Captain of the All Blacks rugby team
¶ Lerner & Loewe, 'I Talk to the Trees' (from *Paint Your Wagon*) (Robert Goulet)
¶ 'Oh, Didn't He Ramble' (Kid Ory and his Creole Jazz Band)
¶ Verdi, 'Va pensiero sull'ali dorate' (from *Nabucco*) (La Scala Chorus/Serafin)
¶ 'One More Dance' (Miriam Makeba)
¶ Rodgers & Hart, 'Isn't It Romantic?' (from film *Love Me Tonight*) (Ella Fitzgerald)
¶ 'Kara karu' (Maori fishing chant) (Deane Waretini/Arawa Concert Party)
¶ 'Listen to the Ocean' (Nina & Frederick)
*¶ Handel, 'Largo' (from *Xerxes*) (LSO/Szell)
¶ LUXURY: A guitar.
¶ BOOK: Sir Winston Churchill, *History of the English-speaking Peoples*

30 March 1964
695 Wilfred Brambell
Actor
¶ Beethoven, Symphony No. 7 in A major (opus 92) (Philharmonia Orchestra/Klemperer)
¶ 'Louise' (from film *Innocents of Paris*) (Maurice Chevalier)
¶ 'Plaisir d'amour' (Maggie Teyte/Gerald Moore *piano*)
*¶ Bach/Hess, 'Jesu, Joy of Man's Desiring' (Myra Hess *piano*)
¶ Bizet, 'Serenade' (from *The Fair Maid of Perth*) (John Heddle Nash)
¶ Mozart, 'Der Holle Rache' (from *The Magic Flute*, Act 2) (Rita Streich/RIAS Radio Symphony, Berlin/Fricsay)
¶ 'These Foolish Things' (from *Spread It Abroad*) (Frank Sinatra)
¶ Mozart, 'La ci darem la mano' (from *Don Giovanni*) (Irmgaard Seefried/Dietrich Fischer-Dieskau/RIAS Radio Symphony/Fricsay) (*This was not played for reasons of time.*)
¶ LUXURY: Scotch whisky and lager.
¶ BOOK: An English dictionary.

6 April 1964
696 Sir Miles Thomas
Industrialist
¶ 'March of the Men of Harlech' (David Lloyd/Chorus/HM Welsh Guards Band)
¶ 'Swing Me Higher, Obadiah' (Florrie Forde)
¶ 'Chinatown, My Chinatown' (Jack Teagarden and his Orchestra)
¶ 'Parlez-moi d'amour' (Lucienne Boyer)
¶ 'Sizilietta' (The Bohemians)
¶ 'Hors d'oeuvres' (Sid Phillips and his Band)
*¶ 'Noël Coward Fantasy' (Melachrino Orchestra)
¶ 'Don't Blame Me' (Frank Ifield)
¶ LUXURY: Toothpaste.
¶ BOOK: Sir Winston Churchill, *The Second World War*

13 April 1964
697 Stan Barstow
Novelist
¶ 'The Big Country' (from film) (soundtrack/Morross)
¶ 'Clarinet à la King' (Benny Goodman and his Orchestra)
¶ R. Strauss, *Don Quixote* (excerpt) (Frank Miller *cello*/NBC Symphony/Toscanini)
*¶ Elgar, Symphony No. 2 in E flat (Hallé Orchestra/Barbirolli)
¶ Brahms, Symphony No. 2 in D major (Philharmonia Orchestra/von Karajan)
¶ 'Moonglow' (Artie Shaw and his Orchestra)
¶ Sibelius, Symphony No. 5 in E flat (Philharmonia Orchestra/von Karajan)
¶ 'Moose March' (Bob Wallis and his Storyville Jazzmen) (*This was not played for reasons of time.*)
¶ LUXURY: Writing materials.
¶ BOOK: H. E. Bates, *The Modern Short Story*

20 April 1964
698 Ian Wallace
Singer and entertainer
¶ 'Music Hall Burlesque' (Wally Stott and his Orchestra)
¶ Poulenc, 'L'embarquement pour Cythère' (Vitya Vronsky and Victor Babin *pianos*)

¶ 'Welcome Home' (from *Fanny*) (Ezio Pinza)
¶ 'A Gnu' (from *At the Drop of a Hat*) (Michael Flanders/Donald Swann)
¶ 'Scotland the Brave' (Kenneth McKellar)
*¶ 'I Wonder as I Wander' (Salli Terri)
¶ Rossini, 'Un segreto d'importanza' (from *La cenerentola*) (Ian Wallace/Sesto Bruscantini/Glyndebourne Festival Orchestra/Gui)
¶ Beethoven, Symphony No. 9 in D minor (opus 125) (Philharmonia Orchestra/Klemperer) (*This was not played for reasons of time.*)
¶ LUXURY: A guitar.
¶ BOOK: The short stories of Somerset Maugham.

27 April 1964
699 Rex Alston
BBC sports commentator
¶ Brahms, 'Rede, Mädchen, allzu Liebes' (from *Liebeslieder Wälzer No. 1*) (Elsie Morison/Marjorie Thomas/Richard Lewis/Donald Bell/Vitya Vronsky and Victor Babin *pianos*)
¶ Berlin, 'Cheek to Cheek' (from film *Top Hat*) (Fred Astaire)
*¶ 'Abide with Me' (King's College Chapel Choir/Willcocks)
¶ 'The Old Grey Mare' (Humphrey Lyttelton and his Band)
¶ 'The Denis Compton Calypso' (Lord Kitchener/Freddy Grant's Caribbean Rhythm)
¶ 'Waltzing Matilda' (Band and Chorus/Sharples)
¶ 'When I Grow Too Old to Dream' (from film *The Night is Young*) (John Boulter/George Mitchell Minstrels)
¶ Handel, 'Where'er You Walk' (from *Semele*) (John McCormack)
¶ LUXURY: A bed.
¶ BOOK: A set of *Wisden*.

4 May 1964
700 Jim Clark
Racing driver
¶ 'By Cool Siloam's Shady Rill' (Glasgow Orpheus Choir/Roberton)
¶ 'Whistlin' Rufus' (Chris Barber and his Band)
¶ 'The Double Foursome' (Jimmy Shand and his Band)
¶ 'Little Children' (Billy J. Kramer and the Dakotas)
¶ Speech at the Oxford Union (Gerard Hoffnung)
¶ Bach/Walton, 'Sheep May Safely Graze' (from *The Wise Virgins Suite*) (Concert Arts Orchestra/Irving)
¶ 'The Muckin' o' Geordie's Byre' (Andy Stewart)
*¶ 'The Party's Over' (from *Bells are Ringing*) (Peggy Lee)
¶ LUXURY: A radio receiver.
¶ BOOK: Jim Clark, *At the Wheel*

11 May 1964
701 David Kossoff
Actor and story-teller
¶ Puccini, 'Si, mi chiamano Mimi' (from *La bohème*) (Victoria de los Angeles/RCA Victor Symphony/Beecham)
¶ Bernstein/Sondheim, 'America' (from *West Side Story*) (Chita Rivera)
¶ 'Non, je ne regrette rien' (Edith Piaf)
*¶ 'Hava Nagila' (Harry Belafonte)
¶ 'Doce cascabeles' (Amalia Rodrigues)
¶ Khachaturian, Violin Concerto (Igor Oistrakh/Philharmonia Orchestra/Goossens)
¶ Beethoven, Symphony No. 7 in A major (opus 92) (NBC Symphony/Toscanini)
¶ (*Mr Kossoff's eighth choice would have been a pop disc, to be chosen at the last minute. It was not chosen or played for reasons of time.*)
¶ LUXURY: Michelangelo's *David*
¶ BOOK: The story of the Marx Brothers.

18 May 1964
702 Dame Edith Evans
Actress

¶ Brahms, Rhapsody for Contralto, Male Chorus and Orchestra (Kathleen Ferrier/LPO and Choir/Krauss)

¶ Shakespeare, 'Shall I Compare Thee to a Summer's Day?' (Sonnet 18) (John Gielgud)

¶ 'The Grand Prix of Gibraltar' (Peter Ustinov)

*¶ Bellini, 'Casta diva' (from *Norma*) (Joan Sutherland/Royal Opera House Orchestra, Covent Garden/Molinari-Pradelli)

¶ Coward, 'Mad Dogs and Englishmen' (from *Words and Music*) (Noël Coward)

¶ 'Kalinka' (Red Army Ensemble)

¶ 'Rawhide' (Frankie Laine)

¶ Rodgers & Hammerstein, 'Some Enchanted Evening' (from *South Pacific*) (Ezio Pinza) (*This was not played for reasons of time.*)

¶ LUXURY: Personal photographs.

¶ BOOK: Mary Baker Eddy, *Science and Health, with a Key to the Scriptures*

25 May 1964
703 David Jacobs
Broadcaster

¶ 'Satin Doll' (Duke Ellington and his Famous Orchestra)

¶ 'The Trolley Song' (from film *Meet Me in St Louis*) (Judy Garland)

¶ Tchaikovsky, 'Romeo and Juliet Fantasy Overture' (Vienna Philharmonic/von Karajan)

¶ 'She Loves You' (The Beatles)

*¶ 'God be in My Head' (Temple Church Choir/Thalben-Ball)

¶ 'Manhattan' (from *Garrick Gaieties*) (Ella Fitzgerald)

¶ 'It's the Talk of the Town' (Erroll Garner *piano*)

¶ Porter, 'I Love You, Samantha' (from film *High Society*) (Bing Crosby)

¶ LUXURIES: A piano, and family photographs.

¶ BOOK: *A Hundred-and-One Things a Girl Can Do*

1 June 1964
704 Richard Wattis
Actor

¶ Porter, 'I Love You, Samantha' (from film *High Society*) (Kenny Ball and his Jazzmen)

*¶ Mozart, Piano Concerto No. 20 in D minor (Sviatoslav Richter/National Philharmonic, Warsaw/Wislocki)

¶ Gershwin, 'Dear Little Girl' (from *Oh, Kay!*) (Jack Cassidy)

¶ 'Ventu d'estati' (Domenico Modugno and his Quintet)

¶ Seeger, 'Where Have All the Flowers Gone?' (Marlene Dietrich)

¶ Rachmaninov, Prelude in B minor (opus, 32, no. 10) (Cor de Groot *piano*)

¶ 'Adieu tristesse' (from *Black Orpheus*) (Gérard La Viny)

¶ Sibelius, Symphony No. 2 in D major (BBC Symphony/Beecham) (*This was not played for reasons of time.*)

¶ LUXURY: A bed.

¶ BOOK: André Maurois, *The Life of Disraeli*

8 June 1964
705 Harry Wheatcroft
Rose grower and writer

*¶ Debussy, 'Clair de lune' (from *Suite bergamasque*) (David Oistrakh *violin*/Vladimir Yampolsky *piano*)

¶ Gilbert & Sullivan, 'When All Night Long' (from *Iolanthe*) (Sydney Granville)

¶ Tchaikovsky, *Swan Lake* (Bolshoi Theatre Orchestra/Faier)

¶ Bizet, 'Votre toast' (from *Carmen*) (Tom Krause/Orchestre de la Suisse Romande/Schippers)

¶ Rimsky-Korsakov, 'The Flight of the Bumble Bee' (from *The Legend of Tsar Saltan*) (Pablo Casals *cello*/Blas Net *piano*)

¶ Rachmaninov, Prelude No. 1 in C sharp minor (opus 3, no. 2) (Moura Lympany *piano*)

¶ German, 'The English Rose' (from *Merrie England*) (Frank Titterton)

¶ Gilbert & Sullivan, *The Gondoliers* (overture) (*This was not played for reasons of time.*)

¶ LUXURY: Rose trees.

¶ BOOK: Plutarch's *Lives*

15 June 1964
706 Paul Tortelier
Cellist

¶ Ravel, 'Lever du jour' (from *Daphnis and Chloe*) (Champs-Élysées Theatre Orchestra/Inghelbrecht)

¶ Fauré, *Pénélope* (prelude) (Orchestre de la Suisse Romande/Ansermet)

*¶ Schumann, 'Er, der Herrlichste von allen' (from *Frauenliebe und Leben*) (Kathleen Ferrier/John Newmark *piano*)

¶ Schubert, String Quintet in C (D. 956) (Isaac Stern and Alexander Schneider *violins*/Milton Katims *viola*/Pablo Casals and Paul Tortelier *cellos*)

¶ 'How High the Moon' (Ella Fitzgerald)

¶ Mozart, Sinfonia Concertante in E flat (K. 364) (Isaac Stern *violin*/William Primrose *viola*/Pablo Casals *cello and conducting*/Perpignan Festival Orchestra)

¶ Bach, *Christmas Oratorio* (first chorus) (Berlin Motettenchor/Berlin Philharmonic/Lehmann)

¶ Bach, Brandenburg Concerto No. 1 in F major (Bath Festival Chamber Orchestra/Menuhin) (*This was not played for reasons of time.*)

¶ LUXURIES: A bicycle and a bottle of cider.

¶ BOOK: *La chronique de Magdalena Bach*

22 June 1964
707 Kenneth Connor
Actor

¶ Porter, 'I Love You, Samantha' (from film *High Society*) (Bing Crosby)

¶ 'Quandos os sinos dobram' (Augusto Camacho)

*¶ 'Little Bit This, Little Bit That' (Jimmy Durante)

¶ 'Down South' (The Banjo Kings)

¶ 'East of the Sun' (Frank Sinatra)

¶ Beethoven, Sonata No. 14 in C sharp minor (opus 27, no. 2) (Benno Moiseiwitsch *piano*)
¶ Chopin/Desormière, 'Nocturne' (from *Les sylphides*) (Paris Conservatoire Orchestra/Désormière)
¶ 'A Life on the Ocean Wave' (Royal Yacht Band)
¶ LUXURY: A guitar.
¶ BOOK: J. B. Priestley, *Margin Released*

29 June 1964
708 Glen Byam Shaw
Actor, director and theatre administrator
¶ Mozart, *Cosi fan tutte* (overture) (RPO/Davis)
¶ 'Kate in the Call Box' (Angela Baddeley)
¶ Beethoven, Symphony No. 9 in D minor (opus 125) (Eileen Farrell/Nan Merriman/Jan Peerce/Norman Scott/Robert Shaw Chorale/NBC Symphony/Toscanini)
¶ Stravinsky, 'Anne Truelove's Aria' (from *The Rake's Progress*, Act 1) (Hilde Gueden/Metropolian Opera Chorus and Orchestra/Stravinsky)
¶ Porter, 'Now You Has Jazz' (from film *High Society*) (Bing Crosby/Louis Armstrong and his Orchestra)
¶ 'When the Saints Go Marching In' (Louis Armstrong and his Orchestra)
¶ Mozart, 'Andro ramingo e solo' (from *Idomeneo*) (Richard Lewis/Leopold Simoneau/Sena Jurinac/Lucille Udovick/Glyndebourne Festival Orchestra/Pritchard)
*¶ 'The Last Post' (from the Remembrance Festival at the Royal Albert Hall, 1928)
¶ LUXURY: A first-aid kit.
¶ BOOK: Leo Tolstoy, *War and Peace*

6 July 1964
709 Dorian Williams
Showjumping commentator
¶ Rachmaninov, Piano Concerto No. 2 in C minor (Sergei Rachmaninov/Philadelphia Orchestra/Stokowski)
¶ 'La mer' (Charles Trenet)

¶ Tchaikovsky, 'Romeo and Juliet Fantasy Overture' (NBC Symphony/Toscanini)
¶ Sibelius, Symphony No. 2 in D major (BBC Symphony/Beecham)
¶ Puccini, 'O soave fanciulla' (from *La Bohème*) (Joan Hammond/David Lloyd/City of Birmingham Orchestra/Leslie Heward)
*¶ Elgar, 'Praise to the Holiest in the Height' (from *The Dream of Gerontius*) (Huddersfield Choral Society/Royal Liverpool Philharmonic/Sargent)
¶ Coward, *Private Lives* (Act 1 love scene) (Gertrude Lawrence/Noël Coward)
¶ 'Sunset' and 'Salute for Heroes' (Royal Marines Massed Bands)
¶ LUXURY: Writing materials.
¶ BOOK: An omnibus edition of Surtees.

13 July 1964
710 Vanessa Redgrave
Actress
*¶ 'Voice of the Stars' (excerpts from film soundtracks) (Shirley Temple/Will Hay/Grace Moore)
¶ Couperin, 'La Steinquerque' (Isabelle Nef and Ruggero Gerlin *harpsichords*)
¶ Britten, 'Kyrie Eleison' (from Missa Brevis in D) (Boys of Westminster Cathedral Choir/George Malcolm *organ*)
¶ Delerue, 'Le tourbillon' (from film *Jules et Jim*) (Jeanne Moreau)
¶ Bach/Loussier, Prelude and Fugue No. 1 (Jacques Loussier Trio)
¶ 'Samba de Orfeu' (from film *Black Orpheus*) (soundtrack)
¶ Mozart, Concerto for Flute, Harp and Orchestra (K. 299) (Karlheinz Zöller *flute*/Nicanor Zabaleta *harp*/Berlin Philharmonic/Märzandorfer)
¶ Delerue, 'Generique' (from film *Jules et Jim*) (Georges Delerue and his Orchestra)
¶ LUXURY: Tins of coffee and condensed milk.
¶ BOOK: Leo Tolstoy, *Anna Karenina*

20 July 1964
711 David Wynne
Sculptor
¶ Mozart, Clarinet Concerto in A (K. 622) (Gervase de Peyer/LSO/Maag)
¶ Beethoven, Violin Concerto in D (Yehudi Menuhin/Philharmonia Orchestra/Furtwängler)
¶ 'Home Sweet Home' (Amelita Galli-Curci)
¶ 'I Saw Her Standing There' (The Beatles)
¶ Schutz, *The Resurrection* (excerpt) (Soloists/instrumental ensemble/chorus/Salzburg Mozarteum/Hinreiner)
¶ 'Once in Royal David's City' (King's College Chapel Choir/Willcocks)
*¶ Bach, Goldberg Variations 13–15 (Wanda Landowska *harpsichord*)
¶ Mozart, Symphony No. 41 in C (RPO/Beecham)
¶ LUXURY: Cocoa.
¶ BOOK: Dante in the original Italian and in English translation.

27 July 1964
712 Roy MacGregor-Hastie
Historian and political journalist
¶ Cardillo, 'Core 'ngrato' (Beniamino Gigli/Royal Opera House Orchestra, Covent Garden/Zamboni)
*¶ Vivaldi, 'Spring' (from *The Four Seasons*) (Virtuosi di Roma/Fasano)
¶ 'Careless Love Blues' (Humphrey Lyttelton and his Band)
¶ 'Tipperary' (Red Army Ensemble)
¶ Delibes, *Coppelia* (Act 1 waltz) (Orchestre de la Suisse Romande/Ansermet)
¶ 'Hura' (Romanian folk song) (Barbu Lautaru Popular Ensemble)
¶ 'Solo de seron' (Mamadi Dioubaté *harp-lute*)

¶ Sibelius, *Karelia Suite* (intermezzo) (Danish State Radio Symphony/Jensen)
¶ LUXURY: Cigarettes.
¶ BOOK: Roy MacGregor-Hastie, *The Day of the Lion*

3 August 1964
713 Dick Chipperfield
Animal trainer and circus proprietor
*¶ 'Rose of England' (from *The Crest of a Wave*) (Ivor Emmanuel)
¶ 'Keep Right on to the End of the Road' (Kenneth McKellar)
¶ 'We'll Keep a Welcome' (Harry Secombe)
¶ 'Forty Shades of Green' (Eileen Donaghy)
¶ 'Father O'Callaghan' (Brendan O'Dowda)
¶ 'Granada' (Frankie Laine)
¶ 'Ça c'est Paris' (Colette Renard)
¶ 'Sarie Marais' (Eve Boswell)
¶ LUXURY: A ciné projector and circus films.
¶ BOOK: *Black's Veterinary Dictionary*

10 August 1964
714 Stephen Grenfell
Writer and broadcaster
¶ 'Sarie Marais' (Eve Boswell)
¶ 'Ramona' (Mantovani and his Orchestra)
*¶ 'The Last Post' (Sikh Regiment 2nd Battalion Buglers)
¶ Gershwin, 'Rhapsody in Blue' (Columbia Symphony/Bernstein)
¶ Foster, 'I Dream of Jeannie with the Light Brown Hair' (Bing Crosby)
¶ Shakespeare, 'Shall I Compare Thee to a Summer's Day?' (Sonnet 18) (Peggy Ashcroft)
¶ 'The Legend of the Glass Mountain' (from film *The Glass Mountain*) (Melachrino Orchestra)
¶ 'Abide with Me' (King's College Chapel Choir/Willcocks)
¶ LUXURY: Writing materials.
¶ BOOK: Palgrave's *Golden Treasury*

17 August 1964
715 Percy Merriman
Roosters Concert Party performer
*¶ 'Route March' (from *Army Reminiscences*) (Roosters Concert Party/Military Band)
¶ German, 'Henry VIII Dances' (Pro Arte Orchestra/Sargent)
¶ 'Roses of Picardy' (Webster Booth)
¶ 'Old Comrades Reunion' (Roosters Concert Party)
¶ 'Autumn Concerto' (Frank Chacksfield and his Orchestra)
¶ 'A Village Concert' (Roosters Concert Party)
¶ *Bric-à-Brac* (selection) (Palace Theatre Orchestra/Finck)
¶ 'Lights Out' (Roosters Concert Party)
¶ LUXURY: A pair of field glasses.
¶ BOOK: *Dictionary of National Biography*

24 August 1964
716 Cilla Black
Singer
¶ 'My Yiddishe Momme' (Sophie Tucker)
¶ Bernstein/Sondheim, 'America' (from *West Side Story*) (Rita Moreno/George Chakiris)
¶ 'Love Me Do' (The Beatles)
*¶ 'Anyone Who Had a Heart' (Cilla Black)
¶ Mancini, 'Moon River' (from film *Breakfast at Tiffany's*) (Henry Mancini Orchestra and Chorus)
¶ 'Priscilla' (Frankie Vaughan)
¶ Bach, Fugue in D minor (Swingle Singers)
¶ 'September in the Rain' (Dinah Washington)
¶ LUXURY: Leonardo da Vinci's *Mona Lisa*
¶ BOOK: Lewis Carroll, *Alice in Wonderland*

31 August 1964
717 Lord Thomson of Fleet
Newspaper proprietor
¶ 'Wishing' (Vera Lynn)
¶ 'Cruising Down the River' (Sing-It-Again Ensemble/Steve Race Four)

¶ 'Everywhere You Go' (Guy Lombardo and his Royal Canadians)
¶ 'A Pretty Girl is Like a Melody' (from *Ziegfeld Follies of 1919*) (Rikki Henderson)
¶ 'The Band Played On' (Guy Lombardo and his Royal Canadians)
¶ 'If You Were the Only Girl in the World' (from *The Bing Boys are Here*) (Ray Charles Singers)
¶ 'Underneath the Arches' (Flanagan & Allen)
*¶ J. Strauss, 'The Blue Danube Waltz' (Vienna Light Opera Orchestra/Marek)
¶ LUXURY: A radio receiver.
¶ BOOK: *Encyclopaedia Britannica*

7 September 1964
718 Stratford Johns
Actor
¶ Sibelius, Symphony No. 1 in E minor (RPO/Beecham)
¶ 'Noises of London' and 'I Want to be Happy' (from *No, No, Nanette*) (Stanelli and his 'Hornchestra')
¶ 'At the Woodchoppers' Ball' (Woody Herman and his Orchestra)
*¶ 'Tea for Two' (from *No, No, Nanette*) (Binnie Hale/Seymour Beard)
¶ Stravinsky, *The Rite of Spring* (Columbia Symphony/Stravinsky)
¶ 'Hold On' (Shelley Berman)
¶ Beethoven, Piano Sonata No. 8 in C minor (Wilhelm Kempff)
¶ Kern & Hammerstein, 'Ol' Man River' (from *Show Boat*) (Frank Sinatra)
¶ LUXURY: A painting by Goya.
¶ BOOK: *Encyclopaedia Britannica*

14 September 1964
719 Russell Brockbank
Cartoonist and illustrator
¶ Gershwin, 'Summertime' (from *Porgy and Bess*) (Miles Davis *trumpet*)
¶ Widor, Organ Symphony No. 5 (toccata) (Simon Preston)
¶ Sibelius, 'Finlandia' (New Symphony Orchestra/Mackerras)

¶ Villa-Lobos, 'Prelude' (Andrés Segovia *guitar*)
¶ BRM V16 racing car in circuit at Silverstone
¶ 'Past Three o'clock' (King's College Chapel Choir/Willcocks)
¶ 'Tenderly' (Oscar Peterson Trio)
*¶ Brahms, Violin Concerto in D (Jascha Heifetz/CSO/Reiner)
¶ LUXURY: Drawing materials.
¶ BOOK: A navigation manual.

21 September 1964
720 Robbie Brightwell
Athlete
¶ Beethoven, Symphony No. 6 in F major (opus 68) (Philharmonia Orchestra/Klemperer)
¶ *Tales of Old Dartmoor* (excerpt) (The Goons)
¶ Wagner, 'Pilgrims' Chorus' (from *Tannhäuser*) (Bavarian Radio Chorus and Symphony/Lehmann)
*¶ 'When I Fall in Love' (Nat 'King' Cole)
¶ Lerner & Loewe, 'Wouldn't It be Loverly?' (from *My Fair Lady*) (Peter Sellers)
¶ 'O Come, All Ye Faithful' (Royal Choral Society/Sargent)
¶ 'This was Their Finest Hour' (Sir Winston Churchill, speech, 18 June 1940)
¶ 'The Call of the Faraway Hills' (from film *Shane*) (Geoff Love and his Orchestra)
¶ LUXURY: A safety razor.
¶ BOOK: W. MacNeill Dixon, *The Human Situation*

28 September 1964
721 Dirk Bogarde
Actor
¶ Liszt, Consolation in D flat (Jorge Bolet *piano*)
¶ O. Straus, 'C'est la saison d'amour' (from *Les trois valses*) (Yvonne Printemps)
¶ Liszt, Piano Concerto No. 1 in E flat and 'Hungarian Fantasy' (Jorge Bolet/Los Angeles Philharmonic/Stoloff)
¶ 'The Worst Kind of Man' (from *The Letter*) (Judy Garland/Gordon Jenkins Orchestra)

¶ Lehár, 'Vilja' (from *The Merry Widow*) (Elisabeth Schwarzkopf/Philharmonia Orchestra/Chorus/Matacic)
*¶ Beethoven, Symphony No. 5 in C minor (opus 67) (Columbia Symphony/Walter)
¶ 'Hello Dolly' (from *Hello Dolly*) (Carol Channing)
¶ Lerner & Loewe, 'I've Grown Accustomed to Her Face' (from *My Fair Lady* (Rex Harrison) (*This was not played for reasons of time.*)
¶ LUXURY: John Singer Sargent's painting of the Sitwells, *Conversation Piece.*
¶ BOOK: Johann David Wyss, *The Swiss Family Robinson*

5 October 1964
722 John Bratby
Painter
¶ 'Carry Me Back to Old Virginny' (Alma Gluck)
¶ 'Glendora' (Perry Como/Ray Charles Singers)
¶ 'Tangerine' (Anne Shelton)
¶ 'Morse Code Melody' (The Alberts)
¶ 'Heartbreak Hotel' (Elvis Presley)
¶ 'Animal Crackers in My Soup' (from film *Curly Top*) (Shirley Temple)
¶ 'Pasadena' (Temperance Seven)
*¶ 'Empty Bed Blues' (Bessie Smith)
¶ LUXURY: A typewriter and paper.
¶ BOOK: John Bratby, *Breakdown*

12 October 1964
723 Jon Pertwee
Actor and entertainer
*¶ 'Georgia on My Mind' (Ray Charles)
¶ Mozart, 'Venite inginocchiatevi' (from *The Marriage of Figaro*) (Elisabeth Schumann)
¶ 'Multos Annos' (Choir of the Russian Church of the Metropolitan of Paris/Spassky)
¶ 'Love is Strange' (Lonnie Donegan)
¶ 'Cuatro Saetas' (Rafael Romero/R. Montoya Jarrito)
¶ 'Dimples' (John Lee Hooker)

¶ Mozart, 'Der Hohe Rache' (from *The Magic Flute*) (Florence Foster Jenkins/Cosme McMoon *piano*)
¶ 'Suliram' (Indonesian lullaby) (Miriam Makeba)
¶ LUXURY: A guitar.
¶ BOOK: F. A. Hornibrook, *The Culture of the Abdomen: A Cure of Obesity and Constipation*

19 October 1964
724 The Reverend W. Awdry
Writer of children's books and railway enthusiast
¶ Train sound effects (West Highland Line near Tyndrum)
*¶ Mendelssohn, 'Baal, We Cry to Thee' (from *Elijah*) (Huddersfield Choral Society/Royal Liverpool Philharmonic/Sargent)
¶ 'The Bugginses Prepare for a Party' (Mabel Constanduros/Michael Hogan)
¶ Bach, 'Jesu, Joy of Man's Desiring' (D. J. Rees *organ*)
¶ Gilbert & Sullivan, 'When I was a Lad' (from *HMS Pinafore*) (Henry Lytton/Symphony Orchestra/Sargent)
¶ Train sound effects (trains in the hills)
¶ Awdry, 'Edward and Gordon' (Johnny Morris)
¶ 'The Old Lady Drives to Dolgoch' (sound picture of Talyllyn Railway)
¶ LUXURY: Writing materials.
¶ BOOK: Daniel Defoe, *Robinson Crusoe*

26 October 1964
725 William Douglas Home
Playwright
¶ Handel, 'Largo' (from *Xerxes*) (LSO/Szell)
¶ 'Flowers o' the Forest' (2nd Battalion Scots Guards Pipes and Drums)
¶ 'Two Bouquets' (from film *Kicking the Moon Around*) (Hutch)
*¶ 'Galway Bay' (Brendan O'Dowda)
¶ 'O Love that Wilt Not Let Me Go' (London Crusader Choir)

¶Verdi, 'Di provenza il mar' (from *La traviata*) (Ugo Savarese/GIAR Radio Symphony, Turin/Santini)
¶*Lord Badminton's Memoirs* (excerpt) (Peter Sellers)
¶Britten (arr.), 'The Foggy, Foggy Dew' (Peter Pears/Benjamin Britten *piano*)
¶LUXURY: Two teddy bears, Norman and George, belonging to his young daughters.
¶BOOK: The collected plays of William Douglas Home.

2 November 1964
726 Sir Harry Brittain KBE
Writer, politician, barrister and traveller
*¶'Silent Night, Holy Night' (Massed miners' choirs)
¶Gilbert & Sullivan, 'A More Humane Mikado' (from *The Mikado*) (Darrell Fancourt)
¶'He Who Would True Valour See' (St Mark's Church Choir, North Audley Street, London)
¶Gretchaninov, 'Glory to Thee, O Lord' (from *Twofold Litany*) (Feodor Chaliapin/Choir of the Russian Church of the Metropolitan of Paris/Alfonsky)
¶'Goodbye' (from *White Horse Inn*) (Richard Tauber)
¶'D'ye Ken John Peel?' (Peter Dawson)
¶'Eternal Father, Strong to Save' (Massed chorus of 200 voices)
¶Britten, Spring Symphony (Jennifer Vyvyan/Norma Procter/Peter Pears/Boys from Emanuel School, Wandsworth/Royal Opera House Orchestra and Chorus, Covent Garden/Britten)
¶LUXURY: Wine.
¶BOOK: Gilbert White, *The Natural History of Selborne*

9 November 1964
727 Hardie Ratcliffe
Trade union official
¶J. Strauss, 'Thunder and Lightning' (polka) (Philharmonia Orchestra/von Karajan)
¶Wolf-Ferrari, *The Jewels of the Madonna* (Act 3 intermezzo) (Philharmonia Orchestra/Mackerras)

¶Larsson, Concerto for Saxophone (Sigurd Rascher/Stockholm Radio Orchestra/Tonsattaren)
¶'Charleston' (Harry Gold and his Band)
*¶Rimsky-Korsakov, *Scheherazade* (RPO/Beecham)
¶'South Rampart Street Parade' (Ted Heath and his Music)
¶R. Strauss, 'Till Eulenspiegel' (Philharmonia Orchestra/Maazel)
¶Bellini, *La Sonnambula* (Act 2) (Maria Callas/La Scala Orchestra and Chorus/Votto)
¶LUXURY: A guitar.
¶BOOK: A Russian grammar.

16 November 1964
728 Honor Blackman
Actress
¶'Manha de carnaval' (Joan Baez)
¶Telemann, Suite in A minor for Recorder and Strings (Bernard Krainis/Krainis Baroque Ensemble)
¶'The Second Time Around' (Frank Sinatra)
¶'Alorno y verdial' (Carlos Montoya *guitar*)
¶'Today I Love Everybody' (Lena Horne)
*¶Willson, 'Ya Got Trouble' (from *The Music Man*) (Robert Preston/ensemble)
¶'*Avengers* Theme' (Johnny Dankworth and his Orchestra)
¶'Teach Me Tonight' (Erroll Garner *piano*)
¶LUXURY: Michelangelo's *David*
¶BOOK: A personal anthology of poetry.

23 November 1964
729 Frank Phillips
BBC announcer and newsreader
¶Brahms, Symphony No. 3 in F major (Hallé Orchestra/Barbirolli)
¶Puccini, 'In questa reggia' (from *Turandot*) (Eva Turner)
*¶Chopin, Étude No. 13 in A flat major (opus 25, no. 1) (Shura Cherkassky *piano*)
¶'Vous qui passez sans me voir' (Jean Sablon/Wal Berg and his Orchestra)

¶Gershwin, 'Bess, You is My Woman Now' (from *Porgy and Bess*) (Robert McFerrin/Adele Addison)
¶'She Moved Through the Fair' (Kenneth McKellar)
¶'In the Mood' (Joe Loss and his Band)
¶Elgar, 'The Dream Interlude' (from *Falstaff*) (LSO/Elgar)
¶LUXURY: An armchair.
¶BOOK: Eric Partridge, *A Dictionary of Origins*

30 November 1964
730 Brian Epstein
Manager of The Beatles
¶Lennon & McCartney, 'All My Loving' (George Martin Orchestra)
¶Bach, Brandenburg Concerto No. 5 in D major (Stuttgart Chamber Orchestra/Münchinger)
*¶'Kilimanjaro' (Quartette Très Bien)
¶Lennon & McCartney, 'She's a Woman' (The Beatles)
¶Sibelius, Symphony No. 2 in D (Orchestre de la Suisse Romande/Ansermet)
¶'Odun De! Odun De! (Happy New Year)' (Michael Olatunji/ensemble)
¶Bruch, Violin Concerto No. 1 in G minor (Isaac Stern/Philadelphia Orchestra/Ormandy)
¶'Fiesta de Jerez' (Carmen Amaya/company)
¶LUXURY: Painting equipment.
¶BOOK: Thomas Merton, *Elected Silence*

7 December 1964
731 George Malcolm
Harpsichordist, organist and conductor
¶'The Trumpet Volunteer' (Peter Sellers)
¶Bellini, 'Ah! Non credea mirarti' (from *La Sonnambula*) (Luisa Tetrazzini)
¶Mozart, 'Non ti fidar, O misera' (from *Don Giovanni*) (Ina Souez/Luise Helletsgruber/Koloman von Pataky/John Brownlee/Glyndebourne Festival Orchestra and Chorus/Busch)

*¶Victoria, 'Recessit Pastor Noster' (Responsories for Tenebrae – Holy Saturday) (Westminster Cathedral Choir/Malcolm)

¶Wagner, 'Abendlich Strahlt' (from *Das Rheingold*) (Friedrich Schorr/Berlin State Opera Chorus and Orchestra/Blech)

¶Britten, 'A New Year Carol' (from *Friday Afternoons*) (John Hahessy/Benjamin Britten *piano*)

¶Elgar, Violin Concerto in B minor (Yehudi Menuhin/LSO/Elgar)

¶Britten, 'Gloria' (from *Missa Brevis*) (Westminster Cathedral Boys' Choir/George Malcolm *organ*)

¶LUXURY: A clavichord.

¶BOOK: An Evelyn Waugh omnibus.

14 December 1964
732 Tallulah Bankhead
Actress

¶ 'On the Sunny Side of the Street' (Louis Armstrong and his All Stars)

¶Leoncavallo, 'Vesti la giubba' (from *Pagliacci*) (Enrico Caruso)

¶Rodgers & Hart, 'My Funny Valentine' (From *Babes in Arms*) (Frank Sinatra)

¶Weill, 'September Song' (from *Knickerbocker Holiday*) (Walter Huston)

¶ 'Strange Fruit' (Billie Holiday)

¶ 'Love for Sale' (from *The New Yorkers*) (Ella Fitzgerald)

¶Wagner, 'Liebestod' (from *Tristan und Isolde*) (Kirsten Flagstad/Philharmonia Orchestra/Furtwängler)

¶Malotte, 'The Lord's Prayer' (Perry Como)

¶LUXURY: The portrait of her by Augustus John.

¶BOOK: W. MacNeill Dixon, *The Human Situation*

21 December 1964
733 Lavinia Young
Matron of London's Westminster Hospital

¶Vaughan Williams, 'Somerset' (from *English Folk Song Suite*) (Eastman Symphonic Wind Ensemble/Fennell)

¶ 'Whence is That Goodly Fragrance' (Westminster Abbey Choir/McKie)

¶Rodgers & Hammerstein, 'Do-re-mi' (from *The Sound of Music*) (Mary Martin)

¶Grieg, Piano Concerto in A minor (Eileen Joyce/Royal Danish Orchestra/Frandsen)

¶ 'Abide with Me' (Clara Butt)

¶Lennon & McCartney, 'She Loves You' (The Beatles)

¶Elgar, 'Nimrod' (from *Enigma Variations*) (RPO/Beecham)

*¶Handel, 'Hallelujah Chorus' (from *Messiah*) (Huddersfield Choral Society/Royal Liverpool Philharmonic/Sargent)

¶LUXURY: A telescope.

¶BOOK: A manual of astronomy, plus a bookmark with a photograph of Michelangelo's *Pietà*.

26 December 1964
734 Jack De Manio
Broadcaster

*¶ 'The Faithful Hussar' (Louis Armstrong and his All Stars)

¶Mozart, *Eine Kleine Nachtmusik* (K. 525) (Bath Festival Chamber Orchestra/Menuhin)

¶ 'I'm Crazy About My Baby' (Fats Waller)

¶Harold Pinter, 'The Last to Go' (from *Pieces of Eight*) (Kenneth Williams/Peter Reeves)

¶ 'Call Me Irresponsible' (Frank Sinatra)

¶Lerner & Loewe, 'I Could Have Danced All Night' (from *My Fair Lady*) (Julie Andrews)

¶ 'Where Did Our Love Go?' (The Supremes)

¶Rachmaninov, 'Rhapsody on a Theme of Paganini' (Julius Katchen *piano*/LPO/Boult)

¶LUXURY: Scented soap.

¶BOOK: Leo Tolstoy, *War and Peace*

28 December 1964
735 John Clements
(2nd appearance)
Actor-manager

¶Mozart, *Don Giovanni* (overture) (Glyndebourne Festival Orchestra/Busch)

¶ 'Giorgio' (Nella Colombo)

¶Chopin, Étude No. 13 in A flat major (opus 25, no. 1) (Shura Cherkassky *piano*)

¶Puccini, 'E lucevan le stelle' (from *Tosca*) (Ferruccio Tagliavini/RCA Victor Symphony/Morel)

¶Lerner & Loewe, 'The Night They Invented Champagne' (from film *Gigi*) (Leslie Caron/Louis Jourdan/Hermione Gingold)

¶Shakespeare, *Richard II* (Act 4, Scene 1) (John Gielgud)

¶Coward, 'Mad Dogs and Englishmen' (from *Words and Music*) (Noël Coward)

*¶Beethoven, Violin Concerto in D major (Yehudi Menuhin/Vienna Philharmonic/Silvestri)

¶LUXURY: Champagne.

¶BOOK: The collected works of George Bernard Shaw.

4 January 1965
736 Marlene Dietrich
Actress

*¶Stravinsky, *The Rite of Spring* (New York Philharmonic/Stravinsky)

¶ 'Always Something There to Remind Me' (Sandie Shaw)

¶Beethoven, Sonata No. 23 in F minor (Sviatoslav Richter *piano*)

¶Beethoven, Symphony No. 3 in E flat major (opus 55) (NBC Symphony/Toscanini)

¶ 'A Message to Martha' (Adam Faith)

¶ 'Reach Out for Me' (Dionne Warwick)

¶Ravel, 'La valse' (New York Philharmonic/Bernstein)

¶Ravel, 'Cat Duet' (from *L'enfant et les sortilèges*) (Camille Maurane/Jeanne Berbié/French National Radio Orchestra/Maazel)

¶LUXURY: A box containing mementoes, and more records by Sviatoslav Richter.
¶BOOK: Constantine Paustovsky, *A Story of a Life*, plus a short story, 'The Telegram', by the same author.

11 January 1965
737 Dawn Addams
Actress
¶Mozart, Serenade No. 1 in D major (K. 100) (Camerata Academica des Mozarteums, Salzburg/Baumgartner)
¶'My Kind of Girl' (Frank Sinatra/Count Basie Orchestra)
¶Bach, Double Concerto in D (David & Igor Oistrakh *violins*/RPO/Goossens)
¶'Resta cu'mme' (Domenico Modugno)
¶Beethoven, Quartet No. 16 in F major (opus 135) (Hungarian String Quartet)
¶Bruch, Violin Concerto No. 1 in G minor (Yehudi Menuhin/Philharmonia Orchestra/Susskind)
*¶Britten, 'Dies Irae' (from *War Requiem*) (Bach Choir/Highgate School Choir/Melos Ensemble/LSO and Chorus/Britten)
¶Tchaikovsky, 'Lenski's Aria' (from *Eugene Onegin*) (Sergei Lemeshev/Bolshoi Theatre Orchestra/Khaikin)
¶LUXURY: Writing materials.
¶BOOK: An anthology of poetry.

18 January 1965
738 Frank Ifield
Singer
¶'Why Try to Change Me Now?' (Brook Benton)
*¶Tchaikovsky, 'Dance of the Reed Flutes' (from *The Nutcracker Suite*) (Stokowski Symphony)
¶'Do Not Forsake Me, O My Darling' (from film *High Noon*) (Tex Ritter)
¶'Living Doll' (Cliff Richard)
¶Bernstein/Sondheim, 'Somewhere' (from *West Side Story*) (Matt Monro)
¶'The Whistler and His Dog' (London Palladium Orchestra)
¶'I'm a Woman' (Peggy Lee)

¶'Theme from *A Summer Place*' (Percy Faith and his Orchestra)
¶LUXURY: A family photograph album.
¶BOOK: A blank book with a pencil.

1 February 1965
739 Sir Basil Spence
Architect of Coventry Cathedral
¶'Janani Mamava' (K. S. Narayanaswami and Narayana Menon *veenas*/Palghat Raghu *mridangam*)
¶'Under the Bridges of Paris' (Eartha Kitt)
¶Bach, Brandenburg Concerto No. 3 in G major (Mainz Chamber Orchestra/Kehr)
¶Beethoven, Piano Concerto No. 5 in E flat major (Wilhelm Backhaus/Vienna Philharmonic/Krauss)
¶'The Very Thought of You' (Nat 'King' Cole)
*¶Britten, *War Requiem* (opening) (Bach Choir/Highgate School Choir/Melos Ensemble/LSO and Chorus/Britten)
¶Bach, Partita No. 2 (Yehudi Menuhin *violin*)
¶Puccini, 'E lucevan le stelle' and following scene (from *Tosca*) (Giuseppe di Stefano/Maria Callas/La Scala Orchestra/Sabata)
¶LUXURY: Spaghetti.
¶BOOK: Sir Bannister Fletcher, *History of Architecture on the Comparative Method*

8 February 1965
740 Owen Brannigan
Bass singer
¶Mozart, *Don Giovanni* (overture and 'Notte e giorno faticar') (Salvatore Baccaloni/Glyndebourne Festival Orchestra/Busch)
¶'Drinking' (Alec Mortimer *euphonium*/Foden's Motor Works Band/Fred Mortimer)
¶Gilbert & Sullivan, 'My Boy, You May Take It from Me' (from *Ruddigore*) (George Baker/Richard Lewis/Pro Arte Orchestra/Sargent)

¶Vaughan Williams, 'Serenade to Music' (16 soloists/BBC Symphony/Wood)
¶'Blaydon Races' (Consett Citizens' Choir)
¶Elgar, 'And I Hold in Veneration' (from *The Dream of Gerontius*) (John Heddle Nash/Royal Liverpool Philharmonic/Sargent)
¶Beethoven, Symphony No. 9 in D minor (opus 125) (Arnold van Mill/Orchestre de la Suisse Romande/Ansermet)
*¶Britten, *Noye's Fludde* (closing passage) (Trevor Anthony/English Chamber Orchestra/del Mar)
¶LUXURY: A trombone.
¶BOOK: The collected works of G. K. Chesterton.

15 February 1965
741 Gale Pedrick
Author, journalist and scriptwriter
¶Saint-Saëns, 'The Fossils' (from *Carnival of the Animals*) (Noël Coward/André Kostelanetz Orchestra)
¶Chopin, Waltz No. 2 in A flat major (Opus 34, no. 1) (Moura Lympany *piano*)
*¶'Flowers' (Hermione Gingold)
¶Tosti, ''A vucchella' (Tito Gobbi/Gerald Moore *piano*)
¶'Steptoe and Son at Buckingham Palace' (Wilfred Brambell/Harry H. Corbett)
¶Offenbach, 'King of the Boeotians' (from *Orpheus in the Underworld*) (Alan Crofoot/Sadler's Wells Orchestra/Faris)
¶Harty, An Irish Symphony (Hallé Orchestra/Harty)
¶Gilbert & Sullivan, 'A Magnet Hung in a Hardware Shop' (from *Patience*) (Kenneth Sandford/D'Oyly Carte Opera Chorus/New Symphony Orchestra/Godfrey)
¶LUXURY: Writing materials.
¶BOOK: *Who's Who*

22 February 1965
742 Sir Paul Dukes
Musician, writer and ex-secret agent
¶ Gretchaninov, 'Glory to Thee, O Lord' (from *Twofold Litany*) (Feodor Chaliapin/Choir of the Russian Church of the Metropolitan of Paris/Afonsky)
¶ Elgar, 'Organ Grinder's Song No. 1' (from *The Starlight Express*) (Frederick Harvey/RPO/Collingwood)
¶ Wagner, *Die Meistersinger* (overture) (Symphony Orchestra/Coates)
¶ Rachmaninov, Piano Concerto No. 2 in C minor (Sergei Rachmaninov/Philadelphia Orchestra/Stokowski)
¶ Rimsky-Korsakov, 'Song of the Indian Guest' (from *Sadko*) (Ivan Kozlovsky/Bolshoi Theatre Orchestra/Golovanov)
¶ Massenet, 'Meditation' (from *Thaïs*) (Fritz Kreisler *violin*/Carl Lamson *piano*)
¶ Gershwin, 'Rhapsody in Blue' (George Gershwin *piano*/Paul Whiteman and his Concert Orchestra)
*¶ 'Rhythmic Headstand' (from *Keep Young and Healthy*) (Sir Paul Dukes)
¶ LUXURY: Soap.
¶ BOOK: Omar Khayyám, *The Rubáiyát*

1 March 1965
743 Arthur Fiedler
Conductor
¶ Bach, Prelude and Fugue No. 3 in C sharp (Wanda Landowska *harpsichord*)
¶ Berlioz, 'Queen Mab Scherzo' (from *Romeo et Juliette*) (NBC Symphony/Toscanini)
¶ Beethoven, Symphony No. 9 in D minor (opus 125) (Philharmonia Orchestra/Klemperer)
¶ Mendelssohn, *A Midsummer Night's Dream* (scherzo) (Sergei Rachmaninov *piano*)
¶ Offenbach/Rosenthal (arr.), *Gaîté Parisienne* (Boston Promenade Orchestra/Fiedler)
¶ J. Strauss, *Die Fledermaus* (overture) (Vienna Philharmonic/von Karajan)

¶ Verdi, 'Dies Irae' (from *Requiem*) (Robert Shaw Chorale/NBC Symphony/Toscanini)
¶ Stravinsky, *The Rite of Spring* (Paris Conservatoire Orchestra/Monteux)
¶ LUXURY: A pair of binoculars.
¶ BOOK: *Encyclopaedia Britannica*

8 March 1965
744 Dick Richards
Entertainment journalist
¶ Vaughan Williams, 'Fantasia on Greensleeves' (Philadelphia Orchestra/Ormandy)
¶ Weill, 'September Song' (from *Knickerbocker Holiday*) (Bing Crosby)
¶ Rodgers & Hammerstein, 'You'll Never Walk Alone' (from *Carousel*) (Judy Garland)
¶ 'Manic Depressive Presents' (from film *Up in Arms*) (Danny Kaye)
¶ Beethoven, Symphony No. 3 in E flat major (opus 55) (NBC Symphony/Toscanini)
¶ 'Silent Night, Holy Night' (Beniamino Gigli)
¶ 'Falling in Love Again' (from film *The Blue Angel*) (Marlene Dietrich)
*¶ Gershwin, 'An American in Paris' (from film) (MGM Studio Orchestra/Green)
¶ LUXURY: A travel itinerary.
¶ BOOK: An encyclopaedia.

15 March 1965
745 Sir Richard Woolley
Astronomer Royal
¶ Rimsky-Korsakov, *Scheherazade* (RPO/Beecham)
¶ Schumann, Piano Concerto in A minor (Sviatoslav Richter/National Philharmonic, Warsaw/Rowicki)
¶ Bach, Prelude and Fugue No. 30 in D minor (Rosalyn Tureck *piano*)
¶ Bach, Piano Concerto No. 1 in D minor (Vasso Devetzi/Moscow Chamber Orchestra/Barshai)
¶ Bach, Fantasia and Fugue in G minor (Helmut Walcha *organ*)
¶ Bach/Isaacs, 'Contrapuntus 7' (from *The Art of Fugue*) (Philomusica of London/Malcolm)

¶ Bach, Goldberg Variations No. 30 (George Malcolm *harpsichord*)
¶ Beethoven, Variations on a Waltz by Diabelli (Wilhelm Backhaus *piano*)
¶ LUXURY: Soap.
¶ BOOK: Edward Gibbon, *The History of the Decline and Fall of the Roman Empire*

22 March 1965
746 Bert Weeden
Guitarist
¶ 'I Wonder Where My Baby is Tonight' (Quintet of Hot Club of France)
¶ 'Travelling Alone' (John Slater)
*¶ Tarrega, 'Recuerdos de la Alhambra' (Laurindo Almeida *guitar*/Capitol Symphony/Dragon)
¶ Gershwin, 'A Foggy Day' (from film *Damsel in Distress*) (Frank Sinatra)
¶ Bach/Segovia, 'Gavotte' (Andrés Segovia *guitar*)
¶ 'What is a Boy?' (Jackie Gleason)
¶ 'Whirly Bird' (Count Basie and his Orchestra)
¶ 'Narcissus' (Joyce Grenfell/Norman Wisdom)
¶ LUXURY: A guitar.
¶ BOOK: Rabindranath Tagore, *Gitanjali*

29 March 1965
747 Anatole Grunwald
Film producer
¶ 'The Songs of the Black Hussars' (Chauve Souris Company)
¶ 'Bye-Bye Blackbird' (Layton & Johnstone)
¶ Chopin, Étude in C minor (opus 10, no. 12) (Ignace Jan Paderewski *piano*)
¶ 'Don't Say Goodbye' (from *Wild Violets*) (Barbara Leigh)
*¶ 'The Way to the Stars' (from film) (Two Cities Symphony/Williams)
¶ 'Hello Dolly' (from *Hello Dolly*) (Louis Armstrong)
¶ Puccini, *Tosca* (excerpt from last act) (Maria Callas/Giuseppe di Stefano/La Scala Orchestra and Chorus/de Sabata)

¶ 'Forget Domani' (Connie Francis)
¶ LUXURY: Caviar.
¶ BOOK: P. G. Wodehouse's golfing stories.

5 April 1965
748 George Baker
Singer

¶ Bach, Prelude and Fugue in C major (Harold Samuel *piano*)
*¶ Elgar, 'Praise to the Holiest in the Height' (from *The Dream of Gerontius*) (John Heddle Nash/Gladys Ripley/Huddersfield Choral Society/Royal Liverpool Philharmonic/Sargent)
¶ Debussy, *Prélude à l'après-midi d'un faune* (LSO/Monteux)
¶ Messager, 'Petite Dinde, ah quel outrage' (from *Véronique*) (Maggie Teyte)
¶ Schumann, 'Ich grolle nicht' (from *Dichterliebe*) (Dietrich Fischer-Dieskau/Jörg Demus *piano*)
¶ Wagner, *Die Meistersinger* (overture) (Hallé Orchestra/Barbirolli)
¶ Lehmann, 'Oh Tell Me, Nightingale' (Olive Groves/Gerald Moore *piano*)
¶ Bizet, 'Gypsy Air and Dance' (from *Carmen*, Act 2) (Victoria de los Angeles/Marcel Croisier/Denise Montell/French National Radio Orchestra and Chorus/Beecham)
¶ LUXURY: Writing materials.
¶ BOOK: His favourite works of Charles Dickens.

10 April 1965
749 Dr W. E. Shewell-Cooper
Horticulturist

¶ Edward Purcell, 'Passing By' (Webster Booth/Gerald Moore *piano*)
¶ Beethoven, Piano Sonata in C sharp minor (opus 27, no. 2) (Mark Hambourg)
¶ 'Vat Jou Coed En Trek' (Vier Vrolike Kêrels)
¶ Arne, 'The Lass with the Delicate Air' (Gwen Catley/Gerald Moore *piano*)
¶ Handel, Concerto Grosso in G major (opus 6 no. 1) (Bath Festival Orchestra/Menuhin)

*¶ 'He's Got the Whole World in His Hands' (George Beverly Shea)
¶ 'Misalliance' (from *At the Drop of a Hat*) (Michael Flanders/Donald Swann)
¶ 'If We Never Meet Again' (Donna Parschauer, age 7)
¶ LUXURY: Seeds.
¶ BOOK: Matthew Henry's Bible commentary.

12 April 1965
750 Dame Margot Fonteyn
Ballerina

¶ Ravel, 'Lever du jour' (from *Daphnis and Chloe*) (Motet Choir of Geneva/Orchestre de la Suisse Romande/Ansermet)
¶ Mozart, Sinfonia Concertante in E flat major (K. 364) (Yehudi Menuhin *violin and conducting*/Rudolf Barshai *viola*/Bath Festival Orchestra)
*¶ Bach, Passacaglia and Fugue in C minor (Helmut Walcha *organ*)
¶ 'Mañanita de San Juan' (Teresa Berganza/Felix Lavilla *piano*)
¶ Berlioz, 'Dies Irae' (from *Requiem*) (New England Conservatory Chorus/Boston Symphony/Münch)
¶ Chopin, Étude in E major (opus 10, no. 3) (Sviatoslav Richter *piano*)
¶ 'Honeysuckle Rose' (Lena Horne)
¶ Puccini, 'Invocation to the Moon' (from *Turandot*) (La Scala Orchestra and Chorus/Serafin)
¶ LUXURY: A skin-diver's mask.
¶ BOOK: Marguerite Yourcenar, *Hadrian's Memoirs*

19 April 1965
751 Al Read
Comedian

*¶ 'Waltzing Matilda' (Frank Ifield)
¶ Tchaikovsky, 'Romeo and Juliet Fantasy Overture' (Philharmonia Orchestra/Giulini)
¶ Shakespeare/Walton, 'Once More unto the Breach' (from film *Henry V*) (Laurence Olivier/Philharmonia Orchestra/Walton)

¶ 'Charmaine' (Mantovani and his Orchestra)
¶ 'Forest Meeting' (from film *Spartacus*) (soundtrack/North)
¶ 'Governor's Speech' (from *The Grand Prix of Gibraltar*) (Peter Ustinov)
¶ Malotte, 'The Lord's Prayer' (Mormon Tabernacle Choir/Philadelphia Orchestra/Ormandy)
¶ 'Serenade in Blue' (Glenn Miller and his Orchestra)
¶ LUXURY: An album of family photographs.
¶ BOOK: 'Think and Grow Rich' or 'I'll Teach You Personality'.

26 April 1965
752 Bill Shankly
Football manager

*¶ 'My Love is Like a Red, Red Rose' (Kenneth McKellar)
¶ 'When the Saints Go Marching In' (from film *The Five Pennies*) (Danny Kaye/Louis Armstrong)
¶ 'The Last Rose of Summer' (Sydney MacEwan/Robinson Cleaver *organ*)
¶ 'Danny Boy' (Jim Reeves)
¶ Chopin, Étude No. 3 in E major (Claudio Arrau *piano*)
¶ 'Because' (Mario Lanza)
¶ German, 'The English Rose' (from *Merrie England*) (Webster Booth)
¶ Rodgers & Hammerstein, 'You'll Never Walk Alone' (from *Carousel*) (Gerry and the Pacemakers)
¶ LUXURY: A football.
¶ BOOK: James Back, *The Life of Robert Burns*

3 May 1965
753 Sheila Hancock
Actress

¶ Prokofiev, *Romeo and Juliet* (Act 1) (Berlin Philharmonic/Maazel)
¶ *Pardon My Blooper!* (broadcast disasters collected by Kermit Schafer)
¶ 'I Stayed Too Long at the Fair' (Barbra Streisand)
¶ 'A Sunday Afternoon at Home' (from radio series *Hancock's Half Hour*) (Tony Hancock/Kenneth Williams)

*¶ Verdi, 'Ah, fors' e lui' (from *La traviata*) (Joan Sutherland/ Chorus and Orchestra of Maggio Musicale Fiorentino/ Pritchard)
¶ 'Three Little Fishes' (Frankie Howerd)
¶ Dylan, 'Blowin' in the Wind' (Lena Horne)
¶ Rodrigo, Guitar Concerto (Narciso Yepes/National Orchestra of Spain/Argenta)
¶ LUXURY: Cat food.
¶ BOOK: *The Girl Guides' Handbook*

10 May 1965
754 Hayley Mills
Actress
¶ 'Theme from *A Summer Place*' (Percy Faith and his Orchestra)
¶ 'La Mamma' (Georges Jouvin *trumpet*/chorus/orchestra)
¶ 'I'm on a See-Saw' (from *Jill Darling*) (John Mills/Louise Brown)
¶ Tchaikovsky, 'Romeo and Juliet Fantasy Overture' (Philharmonia Orchestra/ Giulini)
¶ 'Beer Barrel Polka' (Mrs Mills *piano*)
¶ Rodgers & Hammerstein, 'If I Loved You' (from *Carousel*) (Richard Anthony)
¶ Rachmaninov, Piano Concerto No. 2 in C minor (Philippe Entremont/New York Philharmonic/Bernstein)
*¶ 'Kalinka' (Red Army Ensemble)
¶ LUXURY: Writing materials.
¶ BOOK: *Roget's Thesaurus*

17 May 1965
755 Julian Herbage
Writer and broadcaster
¶ Gilbert & Sullivan, *Iolanthe* (overture) (Pro Arte Orchestra/ Sargent)
¶ Debussy, Quartet in G minor (Curtis String Quartet)
¶ J. Strauss, *Die Fledermaus* (overture) (Columbia Symphony/Walter)
*¶ Ireland, Piano Concerto in E flat major (Colin Horsley/RPO/ Cameron)
¶ Beethoven, Symphony No. 6 in F major (opus 68) (BBC Symphony/Toscanini)

¶ Elgar, Cello Concerto in E minor (Pablo Casals/BBC Symphony/Boult)
¶ Shakespeare/Arne, 'Where the Bee Sucks' (Elisabeth Schumann)
¶ Chabrier, 'España' (RPO/ Beecham)
¶ LUXURY: Aladdin's lamp.
¶ BOOK: An encyclopaedia.

24 May 1965
756 Robert Marx
Underwater archaeologist
¶ 'Ebb Tide' (Frank Chacksfield and his Orchestra)
¶ 'Virgin of the Sun God' (Yma Sumac)
¶ 'Cherry Pink and Apple Blossom White' (Perez 'Prez' Prado and his Orchestra)
¶ Borodin/Wright & Forrest (arr.), 'Stranger in Paradise' (from *Kismet*) (Tony Martin)
¶ Rodgers, 'The Song of the High Seas' (from film *Victory at Sea*) (RCA Victor Symphony/ Bennett)
*¶ Bach/Gounod, 'Ave Maria' (Sistine Choir)
¶ 'Off Shore' (Earl Bostic and his Orchestra)
¶ 'Love is a Many-Splendoured Thing' (from film) (Frank Sinatra)
¶ LUXURY: A pair of binoculars.
¶ BOOK: *Webster's Dictionary*

31 May 1965
757 Joseph Szigeti
Violinist
¶ Mozart, String Quintet in G minor (K. 516) (Walter Trampler *viola*/Budapest String Quartet)
¶ J. Strauss, 'Czárdás' (from *Die Fledermaus*) (Maria Ivogün/ Berlin State Opera Orchestra/ Blech)
¶ Bizet, Symphony in C (French National Radio Orchestra/ Beecham)
¶ Schubert, Trio No. 2 in E flat major (opus 100) (Adolf Busch *violin*/Hermann Busch *cello*/ Rudolf Serkin *piano*)
¶ Mendelssohn, Violin Concerto in E minor (Joseph Szigeti/ LPO/Beecham)
¶ Bach, Suite No. 5 in C minor for Solo Cello (Pablo Casals)

¶ Beethoven, Symphony No. 4 in B flat major (opus 60) (Philharmonia Orchestra/ Klemperer)
¶ Bartók, Rhapsody No. 1 (Joseph Szigeti *violin*/Bela Bartók *piano*)
¶ LUXURY: Reproductions of his favourite pictures.
¶ BOOK: Lady Muraski, *The Tale of Gengi*, translated by Arthur Waley.

5 June 1965
758 Maurice Denham
Actor
¶ Mendelssohn, *Ruy Blas* (overture) (Wireless Symphony/ Pitt)
¶ Gilbert & Sullivan, 'Brightly Dawns Our Wedding Day' (from *The Mikado*) (Thomas Round/Jean Hindmarsh/Beryl Dixon/Owen Grundy/New Symphony Orchestra/Godfrey)
¶ Gershwin, 'Rhapsody in Blue' (George Gershwin *piano*/Paul Whiteman and his Concert Orchestra)
¶ Dvořák, Symphony No. 9 in E minor (Philharmonia Orchestra/Giulini)
¶ 'Red Sails in the Sunset' (Al Bowlly)
*¶ Mozart, Symphony No. 36 in C major (rehearsal) (Columbia Symphony/Walter)
¶ Grieg, Piano Concerto in A minor (Clifford Curzon/LSO/ Fjeldstad)
¶ Sibelius, Symphony No. 2 in D major (LSO/Collins)
¶ LUXURY: Morning glory seeds.
¶ BOOK: His favourite novels by Charles Dickens.

7 June 1965
759 Hugh Lloyd
Actor, entertainer and comedian
¶ 'Teach Me Tonight' (Erroll Garner *piano*)
¶ 'He Who Would Valiant Be' (Templars Octet)
¶ 'Blaze Away' (Combined Bands of Fairey's, Foden's and BMC Motor Works)
¶ 'The Blood Donor' (from radio series *Hancock's Half Hour*) (Tony Hancock/June Whitfield)

125

¶'Lollipops and Roses' (Jack Jones)
¶Malotte, 'The Lord's Prayer' (Mormon Tabernacle Choir/Philadelphia Orchestra/Ormandy)
¶'Let Me Entertain You' (from *Gypsy*) (Sandra Church)
*¶Tchaikovsky, 'Romeo and Juliet Fantasy Overture' (Hallé Orchestra/Barbirolli)
¶LUXURY: Writing materials.
¶BOOK: A Charles Dickens anthology.

14 June 1965
760 Harold Pinter
Playwright
¶Bach, Brandenburg Concerto No. 4 in G major (Schola Cantorum Basiliensis/Wenzinger)
¶Bach, Suite No. 3 in D major (Janos Starker *cello*)
¶'Funky Blues' (Charlie Parker)
¶'Pyramid' (Modern Jazz Quartet)
¶''Round Midnight' (Thelonius Monk *piano*/Gerry Mulligan *saxophone*)
¶'Flamenco Sketches' (Miles Davis *trumpet*)
¶Bach, Brandenburg Concerto No. 6 in B flat major (Schola Cantorum Basiliensis/Wenzinger)
*¶Beethoven, Quartet No. 15 in A minor (opus 132) (Budapest String Quartet)
¶LUXURY: Writing materials.
¶BOOK: An anthology of 16th-, 17th- and 18th-century English poetry.

21 June 1965
761 Ginette Spanier
Director of a Paris fashion house
¶Coward, *Private Lives* (Act 1 love scene) (Gertrude Lawrence/Noël Coward)
*¶Porter, 'You're Sensational' (from film *High Society*) (Frank Sinatra)
¶'Now!' (Lena Horne)
¶'On the Death of King George VI' (written and read by Sir Laurence Olivier)

¶Dylan, 'Go Away from My Window' (Marlene Dietrich)
¶Bach, Piano Concerto No. 1 in D minor (Sviatoslav Richter/Czech Philharmonic/Talich)
¶Bach, Brandenburg Concerto No. 1 in F major (Yehudi Menuhin/Bath Festival Chamber Orchestra)
¶'London is a Little Bit of All Right' (from *The Girl Who Came to Supper*) (Tessie O'Shea)
¶LUXURY: A silver box.
¶BOOK: A notebook and pencil.

28 June 1965
762 Maxwell Knight
Naturalist
¶'March of the Men of Harlech' (Morriston Orpheus Choir)
¶'King Porter Stomp' (Jelly Roll Morton *piano*)
*¶'The Waiter and the Porter and the Upstairs Maid' (from film *The Birth of the Blues*) (Bing Crosby/Mary Martin)
¶Saint-Saëns, 'Softly Awakes My Heart' (from *Samson and Delilah*) (Marian Anderson)
¶'I've Lost My Heart to Dixieland' (Original Dixieland Jazz Band)
¶'Preachin' Blues' (Sidney Bechet and his New Orleans Feetwarmers)
¶'Downhearted Blues' (Mildred Bailey and her Alley Cats)
¶'Junk Man' (Jack Teagarden and his Orchestra)
¶LUXURY: A microscope.
¶BOOK: *The Cambridge Natural History*

5 July 1965
763 Mary Stocks
Teacher, social worker and broadcaster
¶'Soldiers of the Queen' (Josef Locke)
¶Mascagni, *Cavalleria Rusticana* (intermezzo) (Santa Cecilia Orchestra, Rome/Serafin)
¶Wagner, 'Liebestod' (from *Tristan und Isolde*) (Frida Leider/Orchestra)
¶Schumann, 'Valse allemande' (from *Carnival Suite No. 16*) (Myra Hess *piano*)

¶'The Little Puddin' Basin' (Gracie Fields)
¶'Love Song' (from film *Sanders of the River*) (Paul Robeson)
¶'Transatlantic Lullaby' (from *The Gate Revue*) (Turner Layton)
*¶Bach, 'In Tears of Grief' (from *St Matthew Passion*, final chorus) (Bach Choir/Jacques Orchestra)
¶LUXURY: A radio receiver.
¶BOOK: The collected novels of Jane Austen.

12 July 1965
764 Sir Lewis Casson
Actor and director
*¶Bach, Toccata and Fugue in D minor (Jeanne Demessieux *organ*)
¶Mendelssohn, 'War March of the Priest' (from *Athalie*) (Boston Pops Orchestra/Fiedler)
¶Mozart, 'Ave Verum Corpus (K. 618) (Royal Choral Society/Sargent)
¶Schumann, 'Warum?' (from *Fantasiestücke*) (Artur Rubinstein *piano*)
¶Schubert, Symphony No. 8 in B minor (New York Philharmonic/Walter)
¶Stravinsky, *The Rite of Spring* (Columbia Symphony/Stravinsky)
¶Warlock, 'Sleep' (Kathleen Ferrier/Frederick Stone *piano*)
¶'Now Thank We All Our God' (Temple Church Choir/Thalben-Ball)
¶LUXURIES: A recorder, and the portrait of Dame Sybil Thorndike painted in 1912.

19 July 1965
765 Sir William Walton
Composer
¶Stravinsky, *Pulcinella* (Cleveland Orchestra/Stravinsky)
¶Mozart, Piano Concerto No. 19 in F major (K. 459) (Rudolf Serkin/Columbia Symphony/Szell)
¶Beethoven, Piano Sonata No. 29 in B flat major (Louis Kentner)

¶ Henze, *Five Neapolitan Songs* (no. 2) (Dietrich Fischer-Dieskau/Berlin Philharmonic/Kraus)
¶ Bellini, 'Come per me sereno' (from *La Sonnambula*) (Joan Sutherland/Royal Opera House Orchestra, Covent Garden/Molinari-Pradelli)
¶ Debussy, *Six epigraphes antiques* (no. 1) (Orchestre de la Suisse Romande/Ansermet)
*¶ Schoenberg, Variations for Orchestra (CBC Symphony/Craft)
¶ Walton, Symphony No. 2 (Cleveland Orchestra/Szell)
¶ LUXURY: A small piece of sculpture.
¶ BOOK: Sir James Frazer, *The Golden Bough*

26 July 1965
766 Annie Ross
Jazz singer and actress
¶ 'Teddy the Road' (Count Basie and his Orchestra)
¶ 'Just Friends' (Charlie Parker *saxophone*)
¶ Villa-Lobos, Bachianas Brasileiras No. 5 (Bidu Sayao/8 cellos/Villa-Lobos)
¶ 'Chelsea Bridge' (Duke Ellington and his Orchestra)
¶ 'Last Night When We Were Young' (Judy Garland)
¶ Weill, 'Surabaya Johnny' (from *Happy End*) (Georgia Brown)
¶ J. Strauss, 'Adele's Laughing Song' (from *Die Fledermaus*) (Florence Foster Jenkins/Cosmo McMoon *piano*)
*¶ 'Good Morning, Heartache' (Billie Holiday)
¶ LUXURY: False eyelashes.
¶ BOOK: Marguerite Steen, *The Sun is My Undoing*

2 August 1965
767 Ambrose
Bandleader
¶ 'Copenhagen' (Ambrose and his Orchestra)
¶ Kreisler, 'Caprice Viennois' (Fritz Kreisler *violin*)
¶ Gershwin, 'Rhapsody in Blue' (George Gershwin *piano*/Paul Whiteman and his Concert Orchestra)

*¶ 'The Moon was Yellow' (Ambrose and his Orchestra)
¶ J. Strauss, 'The Blue Danube Waltz' (Vienna Philharmonic/Krips)
¶ 'Secret Love' (Kathie Kirby)
¶ 'When Gimble Hits the Cymbal' (Ambrose and his Orchestra)
¶ 'When Day is Done' (Ambrose and his Orchestra)
¶ LUXURY: Tea bags.
¶ BOOK: Harold Robbins, *The Carpetbaggers*, and Irwin Shaw, *The Young Lions*.

9 August 1965
768 Harry Corbett
Children's entertainer
*¶ 'There will Never be Another You' (André Previn *piano* and rhythm group)
¶ Beethoven, Symphony No. 5 in C minor (opus 67) (Hallé Orchestra/Barbirolli)
¶ Purcell, 'Nymphs and Shepherds' (Manchester schoolchildren's choir/Hallé Orchestra/Harty)
¶ Rachmaninov, Piano Concerto No. 2 in C minor (Benno Moiseiwitsch/Philharmonia Orchestra/Rignold)
¶ Lear, 'The Pobble Who Had No Toes' (Stanley Holloway)
¶ Sullivan, 'The Lost Chord' (Cwmbach United Male Choir)
¶ Rodgers & Hammerstein, 'My Favourite Things' (from *The Sound of Music*) (Julie Andrews)
¶ 'Londonderry Air' (Mantovani and his Orchestra)
¶ LUXURY: A trumpet.
¶ BOOK: *The Best of Beachcomber*

16 August 1965
769 Macdonald Hastings
Journalist, novelist and television commentator
¶ Eckert, 'Echo Song' (Amelita Galli-Curci)
¶ Gilbert & Sullivan, *The Mikado* (selection) (Harry Davidson and his Orchestra)
¶ Mussorgsky, 'Song of the Flea' (Feodor Chaliapin)
¶ 'Song of the Vagabonds' (from *The Vagabond King*) (Alfred Drake)
¶ 'La vie en rose' (Edith Piaf)

¶ 'A Bachelor Gay' (from *The Maid of the Mountains*) (John Hanson)
¶ 'La Mer' (Charles Trenet)
¶ Bach, 'Gloria In Excelsis Deo' (from *Mass in B minor*) (Bavarian Radio Chorus and Orchestra/Jochum)
¶ LUXURY: Handkerchiefs.
¶ BOOK: A field guide to the flora and fauna of the island.

23 August 1965
770 William Hartnell
Actor, television's first 'Dr Who'
¶ 'Trees' (Paul Robeson)
¶ Borodin, 'Polovtsian Dances' (from *Prince Igor*) (LSO and Chorus/Dorati)
¶ Beethoven, Sonata No. 9 in A (opus 47) (Yehudi & Hephzibah Menuhin *violin and piano*)
¶ Arlen, El Alamein Concerto (Peggy Cochrane *piano*/Jack Payne and his Orchestra)
¶ 'Lawd, You Made the Night Too Long' (Louis Armstrong)
¶ Rachmaninov, Piano Concerto No. 2 in C minor (Benno Moiseiwitsch/Philharmonia Orchestra/Rignold)
¶ 'Underneath the Arches' (Flanagan & Allen)
*¶ Chaplin, 'The Spring Song' (from film *A King in New York*) (soundtrack/Charlie Chaplin)
¶ LUXURY: Cigarettes.
¶ BOOK: G. M. Trevelyan, *English Social History*

30 August 1965
771 William Connor ('Cassandra')
Newspaper columnist
¶ MacDowell, 'To a Wild Rose' (from *Woodland Sketches*, opus 51) (Marjorie Mitchell *piano*)
¶ Litolff, Concerto symphonique No. 4 (scherzo) (Leonard Pennario *piano*/Boston Pops Orchestra/Fiedler)
¶ Carmichael, 'Stardust' (Glenn Miller and the Army Air Force Band)
¶ Scarlatti, Harpsichord Sonata in D minor (L. 413) (Fernando Valenti)

¶Gilbert & Sullivan, 'Is Life a Boon?' (from *The Yeomen of the Guard*) (Leonard Osborn/ D'Oyly Carte Opera Company Orchestra/Godfrey)
¶'Honeysuckle Rose' (Fats Waller)
¶Rossini, *The Italian Girl in Algiers* (overture) (Orchestra of Maggio Musicale Fiorentino/ Varviso)
*¶Wolf-Ferrari, *I quatro rusteghi* (Act 2 intermezzo) (Philharmonia Orchestra/ Mackerras)
¶LUXURIES: A pair of braces, and a hot water system.
¶BOOK: Kenneth Grahame, *The Wind in the Willows*

6 September 1965
772 Rae Jenkins
Conductor
¶Bach/Wood, Partita in E (New Queen's Hall Orchestra/ Wood)
¶'When Evening's Twilight Falls' (massed choirs)
¶'Morning Bird' (Fanica Luca *pan pipes*/Barbu Lautaru Orchestra of Bucharest/ Budisteanu)
*¶'All the Things You Are' (from *Very Warm for May*) (André Kostelanetz Orchestra)
¶J. Strauss, 'Czárdás' (from *Die Fledermaus*) (Sari Barabas/ Philharmonia Orchestra/ Schüchter)
¶Ravel, 'Alborada del gracioso' (from *Miroirs*, no. 4) (French National Radio Orchestra/ Cluytens)
¶Mozart, Horn Concerto No. 4 in E flat (K. 495) (Dennis Brain/ Philharmonia Orchestra/von Karajan)
¶Verdi, 'Dies Irae' (from *Requiem*) (Robert Shaw Chorale/NBC Symphony/ Toscanini)
¶LUXURY: Fly-tying materials.
¶BOOK: Skues, *The Way of a Trout with a Fly*

13 September 1965
773 Ian Hunter
Impresario
¶Gluck, 'What is Life?' (from *Orfeo ed Euridice*) (Kathleen Ferrier/LSO/Sargent)
¶R. Strauss, *Der Rosenkavalier Suite* (Philadelphia Orchestra/ Ormandy)
¶Shakespeare, 'John of Gaunt speech' (from *Richard II*) (John Gielgud)
¶Gilbert & Sullivan, *The Yeomen of the Guard* (overture) (Pro Arte Orchestra/Sargent)
¶'A World of Our Own' (The Seekers)
¶Grétry Beecham, *Zémire et Azor* (RPO/Beecham)
¶Britten, 'Sanctus' (from *War Requiem*) (Galina Vishnevskaya/ LSO/Britten)
*¶Bach, Partita No. 2 in D minor for Solo Violin (Yehudi Menuhin)
¶LUXURY: Cigars.
¶BOOK: The collected works of T. S. Eliot.

20 September 1965
774 Rita Tushingham
Actress
¶Brahms, Double Concerto in A minor (David Oistrakh *violin*/ Pierre Fournier *cello*/ Philharmonia Orchestra/ Galliera)
¶'I Don't Want to Play in Your Yard' (Peggy Lee)
¶'Cortège' (Modern Jazz Quartet)
¶Shakespeare/Morley, 'O Mistress Mine' (Alfred Deller/ Desmond Dupré *lute*)
¶Brahms, String Sextet No. 1 in B flat (Isaac Stern and Alexander Schneider *violins*/ Milton Katims and Milton Thomas *violas*/Pablo Casals and Madeline Foley *cellos*)
¶'His Eye is on the Sparrow' (Della Reese)
*¶Sibelius, Symphony No. 4 in A minor (Philadelphia Orchestra/Ormandy)
¶Lennon & McCartney, 'Help!' (from film) (The Beatles)
¶LUXURY: The Albert Memorial.
¶BOOK: *Plays* and *Prefaces* by George Bernard Shaw.

27 September 1965
775 The Reverend David Sheppard
Parson and captain of the England Test team
¶Schubert, 'Who is Sylvia?' (Ernest Lough)
¶Mozart, Piano Concerto No. 20 in D minor (K. 466) (Edwin Fischer/Philharmonia Orchestra/Edwin Fischer)
¶'Cricket, Lovely Cricket' (Lord Beginner/Calypso Rhythm Kings)
*¶Bach, 'Make Thee Clean, My Heart' (from *St Matthew Passion*) (William Parsons/ Jacques Orchestra)
¶Rodgers & Hammerstein, 'Some Enchanted Evening' (from *South Pacific*) (Giorgio Tozzi)
¶'I'm Forever Blowing Bubbles' (Pat Dodd)
¶'I'm into Something Good' (Herman's Hermits)
¶'Gentle Christ' (from *A Man Dies*) (Valerie Mountain)
¶LUXURY: Writing materials.
¶BOOK: A volume of reproductions of works by Dutch painters.

4 October 1965
776 Robert Carrier
Authority on food and cooking
¶'Rock-a-Bye Your Baby' (from film *Jolson Sings Again*) (Judy Garland)
¶'Paper Moon' (Ethel Waters)
*¶'Emporte-moi' (Edith Piaf)
¶'When I Fall in Love' (Nat 'King' Cole)
¶Sauguet, *Les forains* (Lamoureux Concert Orchestra/ Sauguet)
¶'Doctor Blues' (Jimmy Rushing)
¶Theodorakis, 'Zorba's Dance' (from film *Zorba the Greek*) (soundtrack/Theodorakis)
¶Lennon & McCartney, 'Help!' (from film) (The Beatles)
¶LUXURY: Burgundy.
¶BOOK: Curnonsky, *Cuisine et vins de France*

11 October 1965
777 Adèle Leigh
Singer

¶ Ravel, 'Lever du jour' (from *Daphnis and Chloe*) (Royal Opera House Chorus, Covent Garden/LSO/Monteux)
¶ Schubert, Impromptu in G flat major (opus 90, no. 3) (Dinu Lipatti *piano*)
¶ Mozart, 'Ach, ich fühl's' (from *The Magic Flute*) (Tiana Lemnitz/Berlin Philharmonic/Beecham)
¶ Puccini, 'Nessun dorma' (from *Turandot*) (Harry Secombe)
¶ J. Strauss, 'Watch Duet' (from *Die Fledermaus*) (Adèle Leigh/Eberhard Wächter/Vienna State Opera Orchestra/Danon)
*¶ 'Ev'ry Time We Say Goodbye' (from *Seven Lively Arts*) (Ella Fitzgerald)
¶ Paganini/Kreisler, 'La Campanella' (opus 7) (Yehudi Menuhin *violin*/Hubert Giesen *piano*)
¶ Lennon & McCartney, 'Help!' (The Beatles)
¶ LUXURY: A fully equipped make-up table.
¶ BOOK: Sir Winston Churchill, *The Second World War*

18 October 1965
778 Nadia Nerina
Prima ballerina

¶ Weill, 'The Hills of Ixopo' (from *Lost in the Stars*) (Frank Roane)
*¶ Britten, *Seven Sonnets of Michelangelo* (no. 30) (Peter Pears/Benjamin Britten *piano*)
¶ Vaughan Williams, 'Elihu's Dance of Youth' (from *Job*) (LPO/Boult)
¶ Farrant, 'Hide Not Thou Thy Face from Us' (King's College Chapel Choir/Willcocks)
¶ Shostakovich, Symphony No. 7 (Czech Philharmonic/Ancerl)
¶ Bach/Loussier, Prelude No. 6 (Jacques Loussier Trio)
¶ Walton, 'Four in the Morning' (from *Façade*) (Russell Oberlin)
¶ Albinoni/Giazotto, Adagio for Strings and Organ (Sinfonia Instrumental Ensemble/Witold)
¶ LUXURY: A piece of sculpture.
¶ BOOK: An illustrated book on Greek mythology.

25 October 1965
779 Peter Hall
Theatre director and producer

¶ Bach, English Suite No. 1 in A major (Ralph Kirkpatrick *harpsichord*)
¶ Ellington, 'Madness in Great Ones' (from *Such Sweet Thunder*) (Duke Ellington and his Orchestra)
¶ R. Strauss, 'September' (from *Four Last Songs*) (Lisa della Casa/Vienna Philharmonic/Böhm)
¶ Speech at the Oxford Union (Gerard Hoffnung)
¶ 'Buddy Bolden's Blues' (Jelly Roll Morton *piano*)
¶ Schoenberg, *Moses and Aaron* (Act 1, Scene 2 prelude) (North German Radio Orchestra/Rosbaud)
¶ Mozart, 'Bei Männern' (from *The Magic Flute*) (Walter Berry/Gundula Janowitz/Philharmonia Orchestra/Klemperer)
*¶ Bach, *St Matthew Passion* (no. 71) (Peter Pears/Hermann Prey/Stuttgart Chamber Orchestra/Münchinger)
¶ LUXURY: A two-manual harpsichord.
¶ BOOK: The letters of John Keats.

1 November 1965
780 Sir John Rothenstein
Art historian

¶ 'A Bird in a Gilded Cage' (The Naughty Nineties Singers)
¶ 'Nottamun Town' (John Langstaff)
¶ Victoria, 'Tenebrae Factae Sunt' (Responsories for Tenebrae – Good Friday) (Westminster Cathedral Choir/Malcolm)
¶ 'Honky Tonk Train Blues' (Meade Lux Lewis *piano*)
¶ Archangelsky, 'The Creed' (Choir of the Russian Church of the Metropolitan of Paris/Afonsky)
*¶ Beethoven, Symphony No. 6 in F major (NBC Symphony/Toscanini)
¶ 'Flowers o' the Forest' (2nd Battalion Scots Guards Pipes and Drums)
¶ Tchaikovsky, *Swan Lake* (Orchestre de la Suisse Romande/Ansermet)
¶ LUXURY: A hot water system.
¶ BOOK: The works of Dante.

8 November 1965
781 Constance Shacklock
Opera singer

¶ Wagner, 'The Ride of the Valkyries' (from *Die Walküre*) (NBC Symphony/Toscanini)
¶ Puccini, 'Un bel di, vedremo' (from *Madam Butterfly*) (Victoria de los Angeles/Rome Opera House Orchestra/Santini)
¶ Delius, 'The Walk to the Paradise Garden' (from *A Village Romeo and Juliet*) (RPO/Beecham)
¶ 'Tubby the Tuba' (Danny Kaye)
*¶ R. Strauss, *Der Rosenkavalier* (final trio) (Maria Reining/Sena Jurinac/Hilde Gueden/Vienna Philharmonic/Kleiber)
¶ Rodgers & Hammerstein, *The Sound of Music* (preludium) (London company/Lowe)
¶ Wagner, 'Liebestod' (from *Tristan und Isolde*) (Kirsten Flagstad/Philharmonia Orchestra/Furtwängler)
¶ Widor, Symphony No. 5 in F minor (Marcel Dupré *organ*)
¶ LUXURY: A bed.
¶ BOOK: *Letters of the Scattered Brotherhood*, edited by Mary Strong.

15 November 1965
782 Sir Robert Mayer
Patron of music

¶ Beethoven, Sonata in F major (Adolf Busch *violin*/Rudolf Serkin *piano*)
¶ Wagner, 'Selig, wie die Sonne' (from *Die Meistersinger*) (Elisabeth Schumann/Gladys Parr/Lauritz Melchior/Ben Williams/Friedrich Schorr/LSO/Barbirolli)
¶ Lehár, 'Vilja' (from *The Merry Widow*) (Elisabeth Schwarzkopf/Philharmonia Orchestra and Chorus/Matacic)
¶ Mozart, Sinfonia Concertante in E flat (K. 364) (Jascha Heifetz *violin*/William Primrose *viola*/orchestra/Solomon)

¶Schubert, Sonata in B flat (D. 960) (Artur Schnabel *piano*)
¶Bartok, Sonata for Two Pianos and Percussion (Robert & Gaby Casadesus *pianos*/Jean-Claude Casadesus and Jean-Paul Drouet *percussion*)
*¶Schubert, 'An die Musik' (Elena Gerhardt/Arthur Nikisch *piano*)
¶Mozart, 'Di scrivermi ogni giorno' (from *Cosi fan tutte*) (Ina Souez/Luise Helletsgruber/John Heddle Nash/Willy Domgraf-Fassbänder/John Brownlee/Glyndebourne Festival Orchestra/Busch)
¶LUXURY: A piano.
¶BOOK: A blank book and a pencil.

22 November 1965
783 Hildegarde
Cabaret singer
¶Tchaikovsky, Piano Concerto No. 1 in B flat minor (Artur Rubinstein/Boston Symphony/Leinsdorf)
¶Debussy, 'La plus que lente' (waltz) (Jascha Heifetz *violin*/Isidor Achron *piano*)
¶Mancini, 'Moon River' (Andy Williams)
¶Coward 'Has Anybody Seen Our Ship?' (from *Red Peppers*) (Gertrude Lawrence/Noël Coward)
¶Bach, 'Wir glauben all' an einen Gott' (choral prelude) (Stokowski Symphony)
¶'People' (from *Funny Girl*) (Barbra Streisand)
¶Rimsky-Korsakov, 'King Dodon in His Palace' (from *Le coq d'or*) (RPO/Beecham)
*¶Beethoven, Piano Concerto No. 3 in C minor (Artur Schnabel/Philharmonia Orchestra/Dobrowen)
¶LUXURY: Face and hand creams.
¶BOOK: Pope John XXIII, *The Drill of a Soul*

29 November 1965
784 Lord Robens
Chairman of the National Coal Board
*¶Kreisler, 'Caprice viennois' (Fritz Kreisler *violin*)
¶Offenbach, 'Barcarolle' (from *The Tales of Hoffmann*) (Royal Opera House Orchestra, Covent Garden/Solti)
¶Parry/Blake, 'Jerusalem' (Royal Choral Society/Philharmonia Orchestra/Sargent)
¶'Leanin'' (Owen Brannigan/Ernest Lush *piano*)
¶Tchaikovsky, Piano Concerto No. 1 in B flat minor (Sviatoslav Richter/Vienna Symphony/von Karajan)
¶Holst, 'Venus' (from *The Planets*) (BBC Symphony/Sargent)
¶Gershwin, 'Rhapsody in Blue' (Leonard Bernstein *piano and conducting*/Columbia Symphony)
¶Rodgers & Hammerstein, 'Climb Every Mountain' (from *The Sound of Music*) (soundtrack/Kostal)
¶LUXURY: An electric razor with batteries.
¶BOOK: Edward Gibbon, *The History of the Decline and Fall of the Roman Empire*

6 December 1965
785 John Hanson
Singer and actor
¶Mendelssohn, 'Oh, for the Wings of a Dove' (Ernest Lough/G. Thalben-Ball *organ*/Temple Church Choir, London)
¶Gilbert & Sullivan, *Iolanthe* (overture) (Pro Arte Orchestra/Sargent)
¶Verdi, 'Celeste Aida' (from *Aida*) (Jussi Björling)
¶'They Didn't Believe Me' (from *The Girl from Utah*) (Dinah Shore)
¶'Mighty Lak a Rose' (Paul Robeson)
¶'September in the Rain' (Mantovani and his Orchestra)
¶Romberg, 'One Alone' (from *The Desert Song*) (Giorgio Tozzi)
*¶'Come Back to Sorrento' (Roger Wagner Chorale)

¶LUXURY: A piano, with music manuscript paper and a pencil.
¶BOOK: A manual of orchestration.

13 December 1965
786 General Frederick Coutts
International leader of the Salvation Army
¶'Minneapolis IV' (march) (Salvation Army Brisbane Temple Band)
¶'I'm Going to Sing' (National Songsters)
¶'By Cool Siloam's Shady Rill' (Glasgow Orpheus Choir/Roberton)
¶Berlioz, *Le Carnaval romain* (overture) (RPO/Sargent)
¶'The Only One' (Joy Strings)
¶'Joshua Fit de Battle of Jericho' (New York Staff Band/Salvation Army Male Chorus)
¶'The Holy War' (tone poem) (International Staff Band)
*¶'O Boundless Salvation' (from Salvation Army Meeting of Thanksgiving, Westminster Abbey, 2 July 1965)
¶LUXURY: A Salvation Army crest.
¶BOOK: *The Oxford Dictionary of Quotations*

20 December 1965
787 Sir William Coldstream
Painter and head of the Slade School of Fine Art
¶Debussy, *Prélude à l'après-midi d'un faune* (LSO/Monteux)
¶'Bye-Bye Blackbird' (Layton & Johnstone)
¶Stravinsky, 'Ragtime' (from *The Soldier's Tale*) (instrumental ensemble/Stravinsky)
*¶Mozart, Quintet in A major for Clarinet and Strings (K. 581) (Gervase de Peyer *clarinet*/Melos Ensemble)
¶Porter, 'You're the Top' (from *Anything Goes*) (Ethel Merman)
¶Verdi, 'Io vengo a domandar' (from *Don Carlos*) (Eileen Farrell/Richard Tucker/Columbia Symphony/Cleva)
¶Mozart, 'La ci darem la mano' (from *Don Giovanni*) (Hilde Gueden/Cesare Siepi/Vienna Philharmonic/Krips)

¶Chopin/Douglas, *Les Sylphides* (Paris Conservatoire Orchestra/Maag)
¶LUXURY: Paper and pencils.
¶BOOK: An encyclopaedia.

25 December 1965
788 The Earl of Harewood
Writer and music administrator
¶Purcell, 'When I am Laid in Earth' (from *Dido and Aeneas*) (Janet Baker/English Chamber Orchestra/Lewis)
¶Mozart, Serenade No. 10 in B flat (K. 361) (Vienna Philharmonic/Furtwängler)
¶Verdi, 'Ella giammai m'amo' (from *Don Carlos*) (Boris Christoff/Philharmonia Orchestra/Semkov)
*¶Schubert, Quintet in C major (opus 163, D. 956) (Isaac Stern and Alexander Schneider *violins*/Milton Katims *viola*/Pablo Casals and Paul Tortelier *cellos*)
¶Janáček, *The Cunning Little Vixen* (orchestral suite) (Czech Philharmonic/Talich)
¶Stravinsky, Symphony in Three Movements (Columbia Symphony/Stravinsky)
¶Schoenberg, 'Nun sag' ich dir zum Ersten Mai' (from *Gurrelieder*) (Inge Borkh/Bavarian Radio Symphony and Chorus/Kubelik)
¶Britten, Serenade for Tenor, Horn and Strings (Peter Pears/Barry Tuckwell *horn*/LSO/Britten)
¶LUXURY: A typewriter, ribbons and paper.
¶BOOK: An encyclopaedia.

27 December 1965
789 Michael Flanders (2nd appearance)
Entertainer
¶Britten, 'Tarantella' (from *Soirées musicales*) (Philharmonia Orchestra/Irving)
¶Brahms, Sonata No. 1 in G (opus 78) (Igor Oistrakh *violin*/Anton Ginsburg *piano*)
¶Bach, Fugue in D minor (Swingle Singers)
¶Lerner & Loewe, 'Camelot' (from *Camelot*) (Richard Burton)

¶'I've Been Wrong Before' (Cilla Black)
*¶Ramirez, 'Sanctus' and 'Agnus Dei' (from *Missa Criolla*) (Cantoria de la Basilica del Soccorro)
¶'Chemirocha' (Kipsigis tribe with chepkong lyre)
¶Mozart, Horn Concerto No. 4 in E flat (K. 495) (Dennis Brain/Philharmonia Orchestra/von Karajan)
¶LUXURY: A horn.
¶BOOK: A book with blank pages, and pencils.

1 January 1966
790 Jimmy Shand
Scottish dance band leader and accordionist
¶'Old Comrades' (march) (Eastman Wind Ensemble)
¶'Bonnie Strathyre' (Robert Wilson)
¶'Miss Elspeth Campbell' (pipe march) (Edinburgh City Police Pipe Band)
*¶'Welcome Christmas Morning' (Jimmy Shand and his Band)
¶'The Lark in the Clear Air' (Kenneth McKellar)
¶Schubert, 'Marche militaire' (D. 733, no. 1) (Philharmonia Orchestra/Kurtz)
¶'The Duke of Atholl's Reel' (Jimmy Shand Jnr and his Band)
¶Foster, 'Swanee River' (Paul Robeson)
¶LUXURY: A tin whistle.
¶BOOK: Sir Winston Churchill, *The Second World War*

3 January 1966
791 Professor W E. Swinton
Scientist, naturalist and authority on prehistoric animals
*¶Tchaikovsky, Piano Concerto No. 1 in B flat minor (Sviatoslav Richter/Vienna Symphony/von Karajan)
¶'Underneath the Arches' (Flanagan & Allen)
¶'Eton Boating Song' (Eton College Musical Society)
¶'Clémentine' (Yves Montand)

¶Chopin/Semprini, *Les sylphides* (Semprini *piano*/New Abbey Light Symphony/Semprini)
¶Dylan Thomas, 'A Child's Christmas in Wales' (Dylan Thomas)
¶Lerner & Loewe, 'I've Grown Accustomed to Her Face' (from *My Fair Lady*) (Rex Harrison)
¶'Loch Lomond' (Jimmy Shand and his Band)
¶LUXURY: A library.
¶BOOK: *Whitaker's Almanack*

10 January 1966
792 Patience Strong
Writer of verse
¶Archangelsky, 'The Creed' (Choir of the Russian Church of the Metropolitan of Paris/Afonsky)
¶Excerpts from Coronation Service of HM Elizabeth II
¶'Once in Royal David's City' (King's College Chapel Choir/Ord)
¶Debussy, 'Jardins sous la pluie' (Walter Gieseking *piano*)
¶'Wonderful One' (David Whitfield)
*¶Mendelssohn, *A Midsummer Night's Dream* (scherzo) (Amsterdam Concertgebouw/Van Beinum)
¶Stanford, 'Magnificat in G' (King's College Chapel Choir/Ord)
¶'Somewhere Over the Hill' (Richard Tauber)
¶LUXURY: An Indian painting in her possession, showing John leading Mary away from the scene of the Crucifixion.
¶BOOK: The complete works of Wordsworth.

24 January 1966
793 Charlton Heston
Film actor
*¶Brahms, Symphony No. 2 in D (Columbia Symphony/Walter)
¶'As Time Goes By' (from film *Casablanca*) (Frank Sinatra)
¶Sibelius, Symphony No. 5 in E flat (Berlin Philharmonic/von Karajan)
¶Walton, *Henry V Suite* (from film) (Philharmonia Orchestra/Walton)

¶ 'Laura Lee' (from film *Major Dundee*) (Wayne Newton)
¶ 'Shenandoah' (Roger Wagner Chorale)
¶ Mozart, Symphony No. 40 in G minor (RPO/Beecham)
¶ Porter, 'Night and Day' (from *The Gay Divorce*) (Lena Horne)
¶ LUXURY: Tennis practice equipment.
¶ BOOK: *Encyclopaedia Britannica*

31 January 1966
794 Tommy Simpson
World champion cyclist
¶ Lennon & McCartney, 'Yesterday' (Matt Munro)
¶ 'Banana Carrier' (Alain Mottet and his Tahitian Band)
¶ Vaughan Williams, 'Fantasia on Greensleeves' (Boyd Neel Orchestra)
¶ 'Downtown' (Petula Clark)
¶ Beethoven, Symphony No. 6 in F major (RPO/Beecham)
¶ Lerner & Loewe, 'I Remember It Well' (from film *Gigi*) (Maurice Chevalier/Hermione Gingold)
¶ 'Lord Badminton's Memoirs' (Peter Sellers)
*¶ 'Ari's Theme' (from film *Exodus*) (London Festival Orchestra/Black)
¶ LUXURY: Golfing equipment.
¶ BOOK: Charles Dickens, *The Pickwick Papers*

7 February 1966
795 Christopher Hopper
Manager and Secretary of the Royal Albert Hall
¶ Wagner, *The Flying Dutchman* (overture) (Philharmonia Orchestra/Klemperer)
¶ Bach, Toccata and Fugue in D minor (George Thalben-Ball *organ*)
*¶ Holst, 'Jupiter' (from *The Planets*) (BBC Symphony/Sargent)
¶ Elgar, 'Nimrod' (from *Enigma Variations*) (Royal Albert Hall Orchestra/Elgar)
¶ Verdi, 'Ingemisco Tanquam Reus' (from *Requiem*) (Beniamino Gigli/Rome Opera House Orchestra/Serafin)

¶ Vivaldi, Concerto in D minor for Two Violins, Strings and Continuo (P. 281) (Isaac Stern/David Oistrakh/Philadelphia Orchestra/Ormandy)
¶ 'The Birth of the Blues' (from film) (Bing Crosby)
¶ 'Sunset' (Royal Marines Massed Bands)
¶ LUXURY: A landscape by Constable.
¶ BOOK: A history of England.

14 February 1966
796 Andrew Cruickshank
Actor
¶ Elgar, Cello Concerto in E minor (Jacqueline du Pré/LSO/Barbirolli)
¶ Gershwin, 'Summertime' (from *Porgy and Bess*) (Leontyne Price/RCA Victor Symphony/Henderson)
¶ Wagner, *Die Meistersinger* (Act 4 quintet) (Ferdinand Frantz/Rudolf Schock/Elisabeth Grümmer/Gerhard Unger/Marga Höffgen/Berlin Philharmonic/Kempe)
¶ Falla, 'Nights in the Gardens of Spain' (Artur Rubinstein *piano*/San Francisco Symphony/Jorda)
¶ Beethoven, String Quartet in B flat (opus 130) (Amadeus Quartet)
¶ Stravinsky, *The Rite of Spring* (Paris Conservatoire Orchestra/Monteux)
¶ New English Bible: Letters of Paul to the Colossians (extract) (Andrew Cruickshank)
*¶ Crimond, 'The Twenty-Third Psalm' (Glasgow Orpheus Choir/Roberton)
¶ LUXURY: Renoir's *The Bar at the Folies Bergère*
¶ BOOK: Søren Kierkegaard, *Journal*

21 February 1966
797 Marie Collier
Opera singer
*¶ Ravel, *Shéhérazade* (Victoria de los Angeles/Paris Conservatoire Orchestra/Prêtre)
¶ 'Les feuilles mortes' (Yves Montand)
¶ 'Rondine al nido' (Ferruccio Tagliavini)

¶ Debussy, 'La cathédrale engloutie' (*Prélude*, Book 1, no. 10) (Walter Gieseking *piano*)
¶ Verdi, 'Come in quest'ora bruna' (from *Simon Boccanegra*) (Victoria de los Angeles/Rome Opera House Orchestra/Santini)
¶ 'Non, je ne regrette rien' (Edith Piaf)
¶ Rodrigo, Guitar Concerto (Narciso Yepes/National Orchestra of Spain/Argenta)
¶ Lerner & Loewe, 'They Call the Wind Maria' (from *Paint Your Wagon*) (John Raitt)
¶ LUXURY: An Etruscan frieze of horses.
¶ BOOK: Marguerite Young, *Mrs Mackintosh, My Darling*

28 February 1966
798 Cyril Connolly
Writer and critic
¶ 'Akinek A Könnye Pereg' (Varsányi Rudolf)
¶ 'Malagueña' (La Nina de los Peines)
¶ Scarlatti, Harpsichord Sonata in C major (L. 205) (Fernando Valenti)
¶ Debussy, *Pelléas et Mélisande* (Act 3, Scene 1) (Erna Spoorenberg/Camille Maurane/George London/Orchestre de la Suisse Romande/Ansermet)
¶ Mozart, *The Marriage of Figaro* (Act 2, Scene 9) (Dietrich Fischer-Dieskau/Maria Stader/Irmgaard Seefried/Berlin Radio Symphony/Fricsay)
*¶ Beethoven, Quartet No. 15 in A minor (opus 132) (Budapest String Quartet)
¶ Stravinsky, *The Rake's Progress* (Act 3, Scene 3) (Hilde Gueden/Chorus and Orchestra of Metropolitan Opera Association/Stravinsky)
¶ De Monte, 'Agnus Dei' (from *Mass*) (Brompton Oratory Choir/Washington)
¶ LUXURY: A foam rubber sleeping bag.
¶ BOOK: Marcel Proust, *À la recherche du temps perdu*

7 March 1966
799 Bill Fraser
Actor
¶ Dvořák, 'Humoresque' (opus 101, no. 7) (Leonard Pennario *piano*)
¶ *White Horse Inn* (overture) (Tony Osborne and his Orchestra)
¶ Wagner, 'Liebestod' (from *Tristan und Isolde*) (Philharmonia Orchestra/ Klemperer)
¶ Beethoven, Sonata No. 14 in C sharp minor (opus 27, no. 2) (Benno Moiseiwitsch *piano*)
¶ 'My Yiddishe Momme' (Issy Bonn)
¶ Bernstein/Sondheim, *West Side Story* (prologue) (soloists and orchestra/Goberman)
¶ 'Lead, Kindly Light' (massed bands)
*¶ Tchaikovsky, *Swan Lake* (Act 1 waltz) (LSO/Monteux)
¶ LUXURY: Writing materials.
¶ BOOK: An Italian language course.

14 March 1966
800 Sir Frank Francis
Director and Principal Librarian of the British Museum
¶ Beethoven, Symphony No. 3 in E flat major (opus 55) (Philharmonia Orchestra/ Klemperer)
¶ Handel, 'He Shall Feed His Flock' (from *Messiah*) (Grace Bumbry/LSP/Boult)
¶ Mozart, Horn Concerto No. 3 in E flat major (K. 447) (Dennis Brain/Philharmonia Orchestra/ von Karajan)
¶ Lerner & Loewe, 'Why Can't the English?' (from *My Fair Lady*) (Rex Harrison)
¶ Bernstein/Sondheim, *West Side Story* (overture) (soundtrack/Goberman)
¶ Bach, 'Wiessage uns, Christe, wer ist's, der dich Schlug' (from *St Matthew Passion*) (Philharmonia Choir and Orchestra/Klemperer)

¶ Gilbert & Sullivan, 'In a Contemplative Fashion' (from *The Gondoliers*) (Richard Lewis/ John Cameron/Elsie Morison/ Marjorie Thomas/Pro Arte Orchestra/Sargent)
*¶ Beethoven, Symphony No. 5 in C minor (opus 67) (NBC Symphony/Toscanini)
¶ LUXURY: Golf clubs and balls.
¶ BOOK: *The Oxford English Dictionary*, and Anthony Trollope, *The Duke's Children*.

21 March 1966
801 G. O. Nickalls
Oarsman
*¶ Bach, 'Jesu, Joy of Man's Desiring' (Guildford Cathedral Choir/Rose)
¶ Mozart, 'Dove sono' (from *The Marriage of Figaro*) (Sena Jurinac/Glyndebourne Festival Orchestra/Gui)
¶ 'Ich weiss auf den Wieden ein kleines Hotel' (Helga Mott)
¶ Gilbert & Sullivan, 'Strange Adventure' (from *The Yeomen of the Guard*) (Philip Potter/Gillian Knight/John Reed/Kenneth Sandford/RPO/Sargent)
¶ Rodgers & Hammerstein, 'Younger than Springtime' (from *South Pacific*) (John Kerr)
¶ Wilson, 'Cry of the Peacock' (from *Valmouth*) (Cleo Laine)
¶ Lennon & McCartney, 'All My Loving' (The Beatles)
¶ Spofforth, 'The Bee and the Snake' (Deller Consort)
¶ LUXURY: Rembrandt's *Titus*
¶ BOOK: *Pear's Cyclopaedia*

28 March 1966
802 Sara Leighton
Painter
¶ Tchaikovsky, Violin Concerto in D (Henryk Szeryng/Boston Symphony/Münch)
¶ 'I'll Tell the Man in the Street' (from *I Married an Angel*) (Barbra Streisand)
¶ Stravinsky, *The Firebird* (New York Philharmonic/Stravinsky)
¶ 'Ribbons Down My Back' (from *Hello Dolly*) (Marilynn Lovell)
¶ Brahms, Symphony No. 1 in C minor (Philharmonia Orchestra/Klemperer)

*¶ 'Out of This World' (from film) (Sammy Davis Jnr)
¶ Fauré, 'Pavane' (opus 50) (London Chamber Orchestra/ Bernard)
¶ Sibelius, Symphony No. 2 in D major (BBC Symphony/ Beecham)
¶ LUXURY: Michelangelo's *Pietà*
¶ BOOK: The poetry of T. S. Eliot.

4 April 1966
803 Hubert Gregg
Actor, playwright and songwriter
¶ 'Excuse Me, Lady' (Layton & Johnstone)
¶ 'Church Parade' (Ellaline Terriss/Seymour Hicks)
¶ Debussy, 'La fille aux cheveux de lin' (from *Préludes*, Book 1, no. 8) (Jascha Heifetz *violin*/ Emanuel Bay *piano*)
¶ Thomas Gray, *Elegy Written in a Country Churchyard* (Ion Swinley)
¶ 'Truckin'' (Fats Waller and his Rhythm)
¶ 'I'm Going to Get Lit Up' (Carroll Gibbons/Savoy Hotel Orpheans)
*¶ 'Love is a Game' (from *Chrysanthemum*) (Pat Kirkwood/Hubert Gregg)
¶ 'Time Was' (Nelson Riddle and his Orchestra)
¶ LUXURY: Pink champagne
¶ BOOKS: Sir Winston Churchill, *History of the English-speaking Peoples*, and Charles Dickens, *David Copperfield*.

11 April 1966
804 Terry Scott
Comedian and actor
*¶ Tchaikovsky, *The Sleeping Beauty* (RPO/Irving)
¶ 'Improvisations to Music (Rachmaninov's Piano Concerto No. 2)' (Mike Nichols/Elaine May)
¶ Harty, *A John Field Suite No. 1* (polka) (Royal Liverpool Philharmonic/Sargent)
¶ 'I Go to Sleep' (Peggy Lee)
¶ Bach, Toccata and Fugue in D minor (Helmut Walcha *organ*)
¶ 'Do You Love Me?' (from *Fiddler on the Roof*) (Zero Mostel/Maria Karnilova)

¶Mozart, 'Der Hohe Rache' (from *The Magic Flute*) (Florence Foster Jenkins/Cosmo McMoon *piano*)

¶Berlioz, *Symphonie fantastique* (Boston Symphony/Münch)

¶LUXURY: Eau de Cologne.

¶BOOK: A French language course.

18 April 1966
805 Alan Bullock
Historian and Master of St Catherine's College, Oxford

¶Vivaldi, 'Autumn' (from *The Four Seasons*) (John Corigliano *violin*/New York Philharmonic/Cantelli)

¶Mozart, Piano Quartet No. 1 in G minor (K. 478) (Clifford Curzon/members of Amadeus Quartet)

¶Mozart, 'Dove sono' (from *The Marriage of Figaro*) (Lisa della Casa/Vienna Philharmonic/Leinsdorf)

¶Bach/Segovia, Suite No. 3 in C for Solo Cello (Andrés Segovia *guitar*)

¶Mozart, Clarinet Concerto in A major (K. 622) (Jack Brymer/RPO/Beecham)

*¶Beethoven, Thirty-three Variations on a Waltz by Diabelli (opus 120) (Hans Richter-Haaser *piano*)

¶Haydn, 'And God Created Whales' (from *The Creation*, no. 16) (Kim Borg/Berlin Philharmonic/Markevitch)

¶Wagner, 'Brünnhilde's Immolation' (from *Götterdämmerung*) (Birgit Nilsson/Vienna Philharmonic/Solti)

¶LUXURY: Writing materials.

¶BOOK: Leo Tolstoy, *War and Peace*

25 April 1966
806 Bob & Alf Pearson
Duettists

¶(B) J. F. Wagner, 'Under the Double Eagle' (Munn & Felton's Footwear Band)

¶(A) 'Straight Down the Middle' (Bing Crosby)

¶(B) Schubert, 'Hark, Hark, the Lark' (William Murdoch *piano*)

¶(A) 'My Love is Like a Red, Red Rose' (Robert Wilson)

¶(B) Stainer, 'Fling Wide the Gates' (from *The Crucifixion*) (Leeds Philharmonic Choir/Bardgett)

*¶(A) 'Tiger Rag' (André Kostelanetz Orchestra)

*¶(B) 'These Precious Things' (Julie Andrews)

¶(A) Berlin, 'There's No Business Like Show Business' (from film) (Ethel Merman/Donald O'Connor/Dan Dailey)

¶LUXURIES: (B) seeds; (A) a piano.

¶BOOKS: (B) Sir Winston Churchill, *History of the English-speaking Peoples*; (A) *ABC Railway Timetable*.

2 May 1966
807 Lord Soper
Methodist minister

¶Järnefelt, 'Praeludium' (Pro Arte Orchestra/Vinter)

¶*Multos Annos* (Russian Orthodox liturgy) (Choir of the Russian Church of the Metropolitan of Paris/Spassky)

¶'Spring Cleaning' (Fats Waller and his Rhythm)

¶Britten, 'Storm Scene' (from *Noye's Fludde*) (English Chamber Orchestra and Chorus/del Mar)

¶'I'll Sing Thee Songs of Araby' (Thomas L. Thomas)

*¶Bach, Brandenburg Concerto No. 2 in F major (Stuttgart Chamber Orchestra/Münchinger)

¶Gilbert & Sullivan, *The Pirates of Penzance* (overture) (New Symphony Orchestra/Godfrey)

¶Handel/Wesley, 'Rejoice, the Lord is King' (Cantata Choir of St Martin-in-the-Fields/Churchill)

¶LUXURY: A trombone.

¶BOOK: Jerome K. Jerome, *Three Men in a Boat*

9 May 1966
808 Inia Te Wiata
Singer

¶'O sole mio' (Enrico Caruso)

¶'La paloma' (50 Guitars of Tommy Garrett)

¶Lehár/Grey, 'The White Dove' (from film *Rogue Song*) (Lawrence Tibbett)

*¶Mozart, *Il seraglio* (overture) (Philharmonia Orchestra/Klemperer)

¶Gershwin, 'Summertime' (from *Porgy and Bess*) (June McMechen/Lehman Engel Orchestra)

¶Wagner, 'Procession of the Masters' (from *Die Meistersinger*, Act 3) (RPO/Beecham)

¶'The Most Happy Fella' (from *The Most Happy Fella*) (Inia Te Wiata)

¶Handel, 'Hallelujah Chorus' (from *Messiah*) (RPO and Chorus/Beecham)

¶LUXURY: A painting by Michelangelo.

¶BOOK: Hamilton's *Arts and Crafts of the Maori People*

16 May 1966
809 Henry Cooper
Heavyweight boxer

¶Lerner & Loewe, 'Thank Heaven for Little Girls' (from film *Gigi*) (Maurice Chevalier)

¶Lennon & McCartney, 'Help!' (from film) (The Beatles)

¶'It's a Sin to Tell a Lie' (Arthur Tracy)

¶'I Left My Heart in San Francisco' (Andy Williams)

¶'Believe Me, if All Those Endearing Young Charms' (John McCormack)

¶'Una lacrima sul viso' (Bobby Solo)

¶Rodgers & Hart, 'The Lady is a Tramp' (from film *Words and Music*) (Ella Fitzgerald)

*¶Schubert, 'Ave Maria' (Mario Lanza)

¶LUXURY: Training gear.

¶BOOK: A do-it-yourself manual.

23 May 1966
810 Emily MacManus
Retired Sector Matron of the Guy's Hospital Group

¶Lehár, *The Merry Widow* (selection) (Melachrino Orchestra)

¶'Mah Lindy Lou' (Paul Robeson)

¶Elgar, 'The Sweepers' (from *Fringes of the Fleet*, no. 4) (Keith Falkner)

¶ Mozart, *Don Giovanni* (overture) (Vienna Philharmonic/Leinsdorf)

*¶ 'The Lark in the Clear Air' (Kenneth McKellar)

¶ Handel, 'O, Thou that Tellest Good Tidings' (from *Messiah*) (Kathleen Ferrier/LPO/Boult)

¶ Peel, 'In Summertime on Bredon' (Robert Irwin/Gerald Moore *piano*)

¶ Tchaikovsky, '1812 Overture' (University of Minnesota Brass Band/Minneapolis Symphony/Dorati)

¶ LUXURY: Foam rubber mattress and mosquito net.

¶ BOOK: Rudyard Kipling, *Kim*

30 May 1966
811 Bill Simpson
Actor

¶ 'At the Woodchoppers' Ball' (Woody Herman and his Orchestra)

¶ 'Le bateau des îles' (Tino Rossi)

¶ 'De'il Amang the Tailors' (from *Eightsome Reel*) (Jimmy Shand and his Band)

¶ Borodin, String Quartet No. 2 in D (Borodin Quartet)

¶ 'Never on Sunday' (from film) (soundtrack/Hadjidakis)

*¶ Beethoven, Symphony No. 5 in C minor (opus 67) (Philharmonia Orchestra/Klemperer)

¶ J. Strauss, 'Roses from the South: Waltz' (Vienna Philharmonic/Krips)

¶ 'Mingulay Boat Song' (The Galliards)

¶ LUXURY: Sports equipment.

¶ BOOK: Songs and poems by Robert Burns.

6 June 1966
812 Charles Craig
Operatic tenor

¶ Leoncavallo, 'Vesti la giubba' (from *Pagliacci*) (Enrico Caruso)

¶ 'Last Rose of Summer' (Amelita Galli-Curci/Homer Samuels *piano*)

¶ Mozart, *Eine Kleine Nachtmusik* (K. 525) (Vienna Philharmonic/Kertesz)

¶ Beethoven, Symphony No. 6 in F major (RPO/Beecham)

¶ Sarasate, 'Gypsy Airs' (Jascha Heifetz *violin*/RCA Victor Symphony/Steinberg)

¶ Beethoven, Violin Concerto in D (Jascha Heifetz/Boston Symphony/Münch)

¶ Giordani, 'Caro mio ben' (Charles Craig)

¶ Wagner, 'Ride of the Valkyries' (from *Die Walküre*) (New Symphony Orchestra/Gibson)

¶ LUXURY: A bed.

¶ BOOK: *Who's Who*

13 June 1966
813 Nina & Frederick
Singing duettists

¶ (N) Vivaldi, 'Spring' (from *The Four Seasons*) (Wolfgang Schneiderhan *violin*/Festival Strings, Lucerne/Baumgartner)

¶ (F) Gershwin, 'Summertime' (from *Porgy and Bess*) (Ella Fitzgerald/Louis Armstrong)

*¶ (N) Bellini, 'Qual cor, qual cor tradisti' (from *Norma*) (Maria Callas/Franco Corelli/La Scala Orchestra/Serafin)

¶ (F) 'Teach Me Tonight' (Erroll Garner *piano*)

¶ (N) Mendelssohn, Violin Concerto in E minor (David Oistrakh/Philadelphia Orchestra/Ormandy)

*¶ (F) 'Madhyamam' (from *Raga Simhendra*) (Ravi Shankar *sitar*)

¶ (N) Rodrigo, Concierto de Aranjuez (Julian Bream *guitar*/Melos Ensemble/Davis)

¶ (F) Bruckner, Symphony No. 8 in C minor (Berlin Philharmonic/Jochum)

¶ LUXURIES: (N) a harp; (F) a flute.

¶ BOOKS: (N) Edward Gibbon, *The History of the Decline and Fall of the Roman Empire*; (F) *I Ching*.

20 June 1966
814 Lilli Palmer
Actress

¶ Schumann, 'Im wunderschönen Monat Mai' (from *Dichterliebe*) (Richard Tauber/Percy Kahn *piano*)

¶ Mozart, 'Protegga il giusto ciel' (from *Don Giovanni*) (Joan Sutherland/Elisabeth Schwarzkopf/Luigi Alva/Philharmonia Orchestra/Giulini)

¶ R. Strauss, *Der Rosenkavalier* (final trio) (Lotte Lehmann/Elisabeth Schumann/Maria Olszewska/Vienna Philharmonic/Heger)

*¶ Bach/Stokowski, Toccata and Fugue in D minor (Philadelphia Orchestra/Stokowski)

¶ Schumann, 'Des Abends' (from *Fantasiestücke*, opus 12) (Sviatoslav Richter *piano*)

¶ 'Malagueña' (Luis Alberto del Parana and his Trio los Paraguayos)

¶ Beethoven, Piano Sonata No. 30 in E major (opus 109) (Artur Schnabel)

¶ Mahler, 'Ich bin der Welt abhanden gekommen' (from *Four Rückert Songs*, no. 4) (Dietrich Fischer-Dieskau/Berlin Philharmonic/Böhm)

¶ LUXURY: Painting materials.

¶ BOOK: Goethe's *Faust*

27 June 1966
815 Wilfrid Andrews
Chairman of the Royal Automobile Club, and President of the International Automobile Federation

¶ Clarke, 'Trumpet Voluntary' (Roger Voisin/Unicorn Concert Orchestra/Dickson)

¶ Mendelssohn, Violin Concerto in E minor (Yehudi Menuhin/Philharmonia Orchestra/Kurtz)

¶ 'Old Father Thames' (Peter Dawson)

¶ Handel, *Berenice* (minuet) (LSO/Mackerras)

¶ Schumann, Piano Concerto in A minor (Solomon/Philharmonia Orchestra/Menges)

¶ Elgar, 'Nimrod' (from *Enigma Variations*) (Philharmonia Orchestra/Sargent)

¶German, 'The Yeomen of England' (from *Merrie England*) (Peter Glossop)

*¶Vaughan Williams, 'All People that on Earth Do Dwell' (from Coronation Service of HM Queen Elizabeth II)

¶LUXURY: Painting materials.

¶BOOK: His press-cutting albums.

4 July 1966
816 Dame Ninette de Valois
Leading figure in British ballet
*¶Britten, 'Dawn' (from 'Four Sea Interludes', *Peter Grimes*) (Royal Opera House Orchestra, Covent Garden/Britten)

¶Britten, 'Their Spinning Wheel Unwinds' (from *The Rape of Lucretia*, Act 1) (Peter Pears/Joan Cross/chamber orchestra/Goodall)

¶Hadjidakis, 'Evening Stroll' (from *15 Hesperini*) (instrumental ensemble)

¶Mahler, 'Der Einsame im Herbst' (from *Das Lied von der Erde*) (Kathleen Ferrier/Vienna Philharmonic/Walter)

¶Bach/Hess, 'Jesu, Joy of Man's Desiring' (Dinu Lipatti *piano*)

¶Mozart, Piano Concerto No. 20 in D minor (K. 466) (Géza Anda *piano and conducting*/Saltzburg Mozarteum Camerata Academica)

¶Archangelsky, 'The Creed' (Feodor Chaliapin/Choir of the Russian Church of the Metropolitan of Paris/Afonsky)

¶Rimsky-Korsakov, *The Snow Maiden* (final chorus) (Chorus and Orchestra of National Opera, Belgrade/Baranovich)

¶LUXURY: Writing materials.

¶BOOK: The poetry of W. B. Yeats.

11 July 1966
817 Sir Stanley Rous
Football administrator
¶Rodgers & Hammerstein, 'Bali Ha'i' (from *South Pacific*) (Juanita Hall)

¶Silcher, 'Ich weiss Nicht, was Solles Bedeuten' (from *Die Lorelei*) (Richard Tauber/Percy Kahn *piano*)

¶'Waltzing Matilda' (Peter Dawson)

¶Tchaikovsky, 'Dance of the Swans' (from *Swan Lake*, Act 2) (LSO/Monteux)

¶'Cielito lindo' (Ballet Folklorico de Mexico)

¶Lerner & Loewe, 'With a Little Bit of Luck' (From *My Fair Lady*) (Stanley Holloway)

¶Verdi, 'Triumphal March' (from *Aida*, Act 2) (Rome Opera House Orchestra and Chorus/Solti)

*¶'Abide with Me' (King's College Chapel Choir/Willcocks)

¶LUXURY: A pair of field glasses.

¶BOOK: Robert Louis Stevenson, *Virginibus Puerisque*

18 July 1966
818 Jennifer Vyvyan
Singer
¶R. Strauss, 'Beim Schlafengehen' (from *Four Last Songs*) (Lisa della Casa/Vienna Philharmonic/Böhm)

¶Congreve, *The Way of the World* (excerpt from Act 4) (Edith Evans/John Gielgud)

¶Britten, *Peter Grimes* (Act 2, Scene 2) (Peter Pears/Royal Opera House Orchestra, Covent Garden/Britten)

¶Rimsky-Korsakov, 'Flight of the Bumble Bee' (from *The Legend of Tsar Saltan*) (George Malcolm *harpsichord*)

¶Shostakovich, Violin Concerto (David Oistrakh/New York Philharmonic/Mitropoulos)

¶Schumann, *Liederkreis No. 2* (intermezzo) (Dietrich Fischer-Dieskau/Gerald Moore *piano*)

¶'Suddenly It's Folk Song' (Peter Sellers)

*¶Mozart, 'Soave sia il vento' (from *Cosi fan tutte*) (Elisabeth Schwarzkopf/Nan Merriman/Sesto Bruscantini/Philharmonia Orchestra/von Karajan)

¶LUXURY: Painting equipment.

¶BOOK: Her favourite novels by Charles Dickens.

25 July 1966
819 Virginia McKenna
Actress
¶Paganini, Violin Concerto No. 4 in D minor (Arthur Grumiaux/Lamoureux Orchestra/Gallini)

¶Shakespeare, *Richard II* (speech) (John Gielgud)

¶Brahms, Symphony No. 4 in E minor (opus 98) (Bavarian Radio Symphony/Schuricht)

¶Delibes, 'Bell Song' (from *Lakmé*) (Mado Robin/New Symphony Orchestra/Blareau)

¶'Greensleeves' (Julian Bream *lute*)

¶Beethoven, Piano Concerto No. 4 in G major (opus 58) (Lili Kraus/Vienna State Opera Orchestra/Desarzens)

¶Dylan Thomas, 'Do Not Go Gentle into That Good Night' (Dylan Thomas)

*¶Albinoni/Giazotto, Adagio in G minor for Strings and Orchestra (Orchestre de Chambre de la Radiodiffusion Sarroise/Ristenpart)

¶LUXURY: Writing materials.

¶BOOK: Bill Travers, *On Playing with Lions*

1 August 1966
820 Nat Gonella
Bandleader and jazz trumpeter
¶'Basin Street Blues' (Louis Armstrong/Earl Hines *piano*)

¶Handel, 'Hallelujah Chorus' (from *Messiah*) (Huddersfield Choral Society/Royal Liverpool Philharmonic/Sargent)

*¶'Wild Man Blues' (Louis Armstrong)

¶'Whispering' (Roy Fox and his Band)

¶'Georgia on My Mind' (Louis Armstrong and his All Stars)

¶'I'm Coming, Virginia' (Benny Goodman and his Orchestra)

¶Verdi, 'O don fatale' (from *Don Carlos*) (Maria Callas/Paris Conservatoire Orchestra/Rescigno)

¶'Trumpet Blues' (Harry James and His Orchestra)

¶LUXURY: Golf clubs and balls.

¶BOOK: The collected short stories of Damon Runyon.

8 August 1966
821 Michael Craig
Actor

¶ Porter, 'Well, Did You Evah?' (from film *High Society*) (Bing Crosby/Frank Sinatra)
¶ Mozart, Clarinet Quintet in A major (K. 581) (Benny Goodman/Boston Symphony String Quartet)
¶ 'La vie en rose' (Edith Piaf)
¶ Delibes, *Coppélia* (waltz) (Orchestre de la Suisse Romande/Ansermet)
¶ Mahler, 'Der Abschied' (from *Das Lied von der Erde*) (Kathleen Ferrier/Vienna Philharmonic/Walter)
*¶ Sibelius, 'The Swan of Tuonela' (Stokowski Symphony)
¶ 'We Shall Overcome' (Joan Baez)
¶ Vaughan Williams, 'Fantasia on Greensleeves' (Sinfonia of London/Barbirolli)
¶ LUXURY: A musical instrument.
¶ BOOK: Kenneth Grahame, *The Wind in the Willows*

15 August 1966
822 Peter Diamand
Director of Edinburgh International Festival

*¶ Schubert, String Quintet in C major (William Pleeth *cello*/Amadeus String Quartet)
¶ Bach, Brandenburg Concerto No. 6 in B flat major (Netherlands Chamber Orchestra/Goldberg)
¶ Beethoven, Piano Sonata No. 32 in C minor (opus 111) (Artur Schnabel)
¶ Verdi, 'Una macchia e qui tuttora!' (from *Macbeth*) (Maria Callas/Philharmonia Orchestra/Rescigno)
¶ Stravinsky, *Petrushka* (Paris Conservatoire Orchestra/Monteux)
¶ Britten, 'Queen and Huntress' (from Serenade for Tenor Solo, Horn and Strings) (Peter Pears/Barry Tuckwell *horn*/LSO/Britten)
¶ Mozart, String Quintet in G minor (K. 516) (Cecil Aronowitz *viola*/Amadeus String Quartet)

¶ Mahler, 'Der Abschied' (from *Das Lied von der Erde*) (Kathleen Ferrier/Vienna Philharmonic/Walter)
¶ LUXURY: The head of Nefertiti, from the Berlin Museum.
¶ BOOK: *Encyclopaedia Britannica*

22 August 1966
823 Bryan Forbes
Film producer, director, writer and actor

¶ 'Les jeux interdits' (from film) (Manuel Diaz Cano *guitar*)
¶ Brahms, Piano Concerto No. 1 in D minor (Rudolf Serkin/Philadelphia Orchestra/Ormandy)
¶ 'Tale of Men's Shirts' (from radio series *The Goon Show*) (The Goons)
¶ 'Theme from *King Rat*' (John Barry and his Orchestra)
¶ Puccini, 'O soave fanciulla' (from *La Bohème*) (Victoria de los Angeles/Jussi Björling/RCA Victor Symphony/Beecham)
¶ Bart, 'Where is Love?' (from *Oliver!*) (Keith Hamshere)
*¶ Orff, *Carmina Burana* (Rutgers University Choir/Philadelphia Orchestra/Ormandy)
¶ 'When I Fall in Love' (Nat 'King' Cole)
¶ LUXURY: A roulette wheel.
¶ BOOK: Edmond Rostand, *Cyrano de Bergerac*

29 August 1966
824 Morecambe & Wise
Comedians

¶ (M) 'The Kid from Red Bank' (Count Basie and his Orchestra)
¶ (W) 'Summer Song' (Dave Brubeck Quartet)
¶ (M) 'My Future Just Passed' (Carmen McRae)
¶ (W) Porter, 'Begin the Beguine' (from *Jubilee*) (Artie Shaw and his Orchestra)
¶ (M) Lennon & McCartney, 'Yesterday' (The Beatles)
*¶ (W) 'Pennsylvania Six-Five-Thousand' (Glen Miller and his Orchestra)
*¶ (M) 'I Wish You Love' (Jack Jones)

¶ (W) Rodgers & Hammerstein, 'Mister Snow' (from *Carousel*) (Barbara Ruick)
¶ LUXURIES: (M) a deckchair; (W) a deckchair ticket machine.
¶ BOOKS: (M) *Encyclopaedia Britannica*; (W) Sir Winston Churchill, *History of the English-speaking Peoples*.

5 September 1966
825 David Hicks
Interior decorator and designer

¶ 'I'm Gonna Get Lit Up' and 'Maybe It's Because I'm a Londoner' (Vanessa Less/Michael Sammes Singers)
¶ Sibelius, Symphony No. 2 in D (LSO/Monteux)
¶ Lennon & McCartney, 'A Hard Day's Night' (from film) (Keely Smith)
¶ 'I Wish You Love' (Pat Thomas)
¶ 'People' (from *Funny Girl*) (Barbra Streisand)
¶ Britten, 'Festival Te Deum' (St John's College Choir, Cambridge/Guest)
¶ Prokofiev, 'Dance of the Malachites' (from *The Stone Flower*) (Orchestre de la Suisse Romande/Varviso)
*¶ Wagner, 'Ride of the Valkyries' (from *Die Walküre*) (Philharmonia Orchestra/Klemperer)
¶ LUXURY: A Mexican crystal skull from the British Museum.
¶ BOOK: Marcel Proust, *À la recherche du temps perdu*

12 September 1966
826 Derek Oldham
Musical comedy star

¶ 'The Blue Bird' (Glasgow Orpheus Choir/Roberton)
¶ Giordano, 'Un di, all'azzurro spazio' (from *André Chénier*) (Aureliano Pertile/New Symphony Orchestra/Barbirolli)
¶ 'Love is a Dancing Thing' (from *At Home Abroad*) (Ramona and her Grand Piano)
¶ Gilbert & Sullivan, 'When the Buds are Blossoming' (from *Ruddigore*) (Muriel Dickson/Dorothy Gill/Derek Oldham/Stuart Robertson)

¶ Saint-Saëns, 'Song of the Nightingale' (Evelyn Scotney)
*¶ Wagner, 'Siegfried Idyll' (Columbia Symphony/Walter)
¶ 'Nobody Knows the Trouble I've Seen' (Louis Armstrong/Lyn Murray Chorus)
¶ Franck, Symphonic Variations for Piano and Orchestra (Peter Katin/LSO/Goossens)
¶ LUXURY: Insect repellent.
¶ BOOK: Encyclopaedia Britannica

19 September 1966
827 June Ritchie
Actress
¶ Beethoven, 'Für Elise' (Wilhelm Kempff piano)
¶ 'Non, je ne regrette rien' (Edith Piaf)
*¶ Puccini, 'Musetta's Waltz Song' (from La Bohème) (Lucine Amara/RCA Victor Symphony/Beecham)
¶ Rachmaninov, 'Rhapsody on a Theme of Paganini' (Sergei Rachmaninov piano/Philadelphia Orchestra/Stokowski)
¶ 'I, Who Have Nothing' (Shirley Bassey)
¶ Puccini, 'Humming Chorus' (from Madam Butterfly) (La Scala Orchestra and Chorus/von Karajan)
¶ Rodgers & Hammerstein, 'Something Wonderful' (from The King and I) (Terry Saunders)
¶ 'Triplets' (from Between the Devil—) (Danny Kaye)
¶ LUXURY: Onion plants
¶ BOOK: Paul Gallico, The Snow Goose

26 September 1966
828 Peter Wilson
Auctioneer
¶ Ravel, Introduction and Allegro for Harp, Flute, Clarinet and String Quartet (Osian Ellis harp/Melos Ensemble)
¶ Schumann, Piano Concerto in A minor (Annie Fischer/Philharmonia Orchestra/Klemperer)

¶ Gershwin, 'Rhapsody in Blue' (Leonard Bernstein piano and conducting/Columbia Symphony)
¶ 'Non, je ne regrette rien' (Edith Piaf)
*¶ Beethoven, Piano Concerto No. 5 in E flat major (Artur Rubinstein/Boston Symphony/Leinsdorf)
¶ Mahler, Symphony No. 1 in D major (LSO/Solti)
¶ Beethoven, 'Mir ist so wunderbar' (from Fidelio) (Ingeborg Hallstein/Christa Ludwig/Gottlob Frick/Gerhard Unger/Philharmonia Orchestra/Klemperer)
¶ Rossini/Respighi, La boutique fantasque (Boston Pops Orchestra/Fiedler)
¶ LUXURY: Bertholdo's Apollo, in the Louvre.
¶ BOOK: His favourite novels by E. M. Forster.

3 October 1966
829 Talbot Duckmanton
Australian Radio administrator
¶ Borodin, String Quartet No. 2 in D (Borodin Quartet)
¶ Schumann, 'Der Nussbaum' (Lotte Lehmann/Paul Ulanowsky piano)
¶ 'Twilight Time' (Bert Kaempfert and his Orchestra)
¶ Bach, 'Jesu, Joy of Man's Desiring' (Temple Church Choir/Léon Goossens oboe/Thalben-Ball)
*¶ Schubert, Symphony No. 8 (Berlin Philharmonic/von Karajan)
¶ Lerner & Loewe, 'If Ever I Would Leave You' (from Camelot) (Robert Goulet)
¶ Rodgers & Hart, 'Mimi' (from film Love Me Tonight) (Maurice Chevalier)
¶ Lerner & Loewe, 'Camelot' (from Camelot) (Richard Burton)
¶ LUXURY: Soap.
¶ BOOK: Samuel Pepys' Diary.

10 October 1966
830 Katharine Whitehorn
Newspaper columnist
*¶ Mozart, Horn Concerto No. 3 in E flat major (K. 447) (Dennis Brain/Philharmonia Orchestra/von Karajan)
¶ 'Je tire ma révérence' (Jean Sablon/Wal Berg and his Orchestra)
¶ Bach, Violin Concerto in E major (BWV 1042) (Yehudi Menuhin violin and conducting/Robert Masters Chamber Orchestra)
¶ 'I'm Just a Country Boy' (Harry Belafonte)
¶ Mozart, Piano Concerto No. 21 in C major (K. 467) (Annie Fischer/Philharmonia Orchestra/Sawallisch)
¶ Beethoven, Symphony No. 7 in A major (opus 92) (Berlin Philharmonic/von Karajan)
¶ 'One Never Knows' (Modern Jazz Quartet)
¶ Bach, Double Concerto in D minor (BWV 1043) (Yehudi Menuhin and Christian Ferras violins/Festival Chamber Orchestra/Menuhin)
¶ LUXURY: A négligée.
¶ BOOK: Her favourite works by William Faulkner.

17 October 1966
831 Jacques Brunius
Writer, director and critic
¶ 'Two Little Babes in the Wood' (from Paris) (Cole Porter vocal and piano)
¶ Satie/Debussy, Gymnopédie No. 3 (Concert Arts Orchestra/Golschmann)
¶ 'You Done Played Out Blues' (Billie Young/Jelly Roll Morton)
¶ Weill/Brecht, The Threepenny Opera (selection) (Berlin cast/Lewis-Ruth Band)
*¶ 'West End Blues' (Louis Armstrong's Hot Seven)
¶ 'Blackstrap Molasses' (Danny Kaye/Jimmy Durante/Groucho Marx/Jane Wyman/Four Hits and a Miss/Orchestra/Burke)
¶ Monteverdi, 'Si ch'io vorrei morire' (madrigal) (Cambridge University Madrigal Society/Leppard)

¶ Wagner, *Tristan und Isolde* (prelude) (NBC Symphony/Toscanini)
¶ LUXURY: A broken and unplayable record by a pop group.
¶ BOOK: The complete works of Lewis Carroll.

24 October 1966
832 Danny La Rue
Stage and cabaret comedian
¶ 'Glorious Devon' (Peter Dawson)
¶ 'A House is Not a Home' (from film) (Dionne Warwick)
¶ Arlen & Harburg, 'Over the Rainbow' (from film *The Wizard of Oz*) (Judy Garland)
¶ Prokofiev, 'Montagues and Capulets' (from *Romeo and Juliet*) (Boston Symphony/Münch)
¶ Coward, 'Mrs Worthington' (Noël Coward)
¶ Bart, 'As Long as He Needs Me' (from *Oliver!*) (Shirley Bassey)
*¶ Rachmaninov, Piano Concerto No. 2 in C minor (opus 18) (John Ogdon/Philharmonia Orchestra/Pritchard)
¶ Malotte, 'The Lord's Prayer' (Gracie Fields)
¶ LUXURY: A refrigerator.
¶ BOOK: An encyclopaedia.

31 October 1966
833 Mitch Miller
Oboist, orchestra leader and arranger
¶ Beethoven, Symphony No. 3 in E flat major (opus 55) (NBC Symphony/Toscanini)
*¶ Bach, Suite No. 3 in C major for Solo Cello (BWV 1009) (Pablo Casals)
¶ Mahler, 'Nun will die Sonn' so hell aufgeh'n' (from *Kindertotenleider*) (Kathleen Ferrier/Vienna Philharmonic/Walter)
¶ Mozart, Quartet in F major (K. 370) (Léon Goossens *oboe*/Léner Quartet)
¶ Bach, Brandenburg Concerto No. 1 in F major (BWV 1046) (Adolf Busch Chamber Orchestra)

¶ Mozart, 'Queen of the Night Aria' (from *The Magic Flute*) (Erna Berger/Berlin Philharmonic/Beecham)
¶ Stravinsky, *The Rite of Spring* (Orchestre de la Suisse Romande /Ansermet)
¶ Schubert, Symphony No. 9 in C major (Philadelphia Orchestra/Toscanini)
¶ LUXURY: An oboe.
¶ BOOK: An anthology of poetry.

7 November 1966
834 Arnold Wesker
Playwright
*¶ Mahler, *Das Lied von der Erde* (Kathleen Ferrier/Vienna Philharmonic/Walter)
¶ 'Di elegive fun fastrigosso' (Bursteins)
¶ Coperario, 'Fantasia à cinque' (New York Pro Musica/Greenberg)
¶ Beethoven, Quartet No. 7 in F major (opus 59, no. 1) (Budapest String Quartet)
¶ Lennon & McCartney, 'Eleanor Rigby' (The Beatles)
¶ Weill, 'Surabaya Johnny' (from *Happy End*) (Lotte Lenya)
¶ Berg, Concerto for Violin and Orchestra (Isaac Stern/New York Philharmonic/Bernstein)
¶ Mahler, Symphony No. 3 in D minor (New York Philharmonic/Bernstein)
¶ LUXURY: A selection of pictures.

14 November 1966
835 Stephen Bishop
Pianist
¶ Mozart, Symphony No. 41 in C major (K. 551) (Philharmonia Orchestra/Klemperer)
¶ Bartók, *The Miraculous Mandarin Suite* (opus 19) (LSO/Solti)
¶ Berlioz, 'Royal Hunt and Storm' (from *The Trojans*) (Boston Symphony/Münch)
*¶ Bellini, 'Vien diletto e in ciel la luna' (from *I puritani*) (Maria Callas/EIAR Radio Symphony, Turin/Santini)

¶ Bach, Brandenburg Concerto No. 6 in B flat major (Stuttgart Chamber Orchestra/Münchinger)
¶ Rachmaninov, Piano Concerto No. 3 in D minor (opus 30) (Sergei Rachmaninov/Philadelphia Orchestra/Ormandy)
¶ Beethoven, String Quartet in C sharp minor (opus 131) (Amadeus String Quartet)
¶ 'Les amis de la musique' (Brigitte Bardot)
¶ LUXURY: A piano.
¶ BOOK: Dostoevski, *The Idiot*

21 November 1966
836 Sarah Churchill
Actress
*¶ Brahms, Symphony No. 1 in C minor (opus 68) (LPO/Boult)
¶ Chopin, Ballade No. 3 in A flat major (opus 47) (Benno Moiseiwitsch *piano*)
¶ 'The Physician' (from *Nymph Errant*) (Gertrude Lawrence)
¶ 'Patron of the Arts' (Jimmy Durante)
¶ Shakespeare, *The Tempest* (Act 4, Scene 1) (John Gielgud)
¶ Wagner, 'Selig, Wie Die Sonne' (from *Die Meistersinger*) (Elisabeth Schumann/Gladys Parr/Lauritz Melchior/Ben Williams/Friedrich Schorr/LSO/Barbirolli)
¶ Debussy, *Prélude à l'après-midi d'un faune* (Orchestre de la Suisse Romande/Ansermet)
¶ 'Mood Indigo' (Duke Ellington/Ella Fitzgerald)
¶ LUXURY: A hot water system and a bath.
¶ BOOK: Sir Winston Churchill's reminiscences of his early life.

28 November 1966
837 Anthony Burgess
Writer
¶ Purcell, 'Rejoice in the Lord Alway' (Alfred Deller/Deller Consort/Oriana Concert Orchestra/Deller)
¶ Bach, Goldberg Variations No. 13 (George Malcolm *harpsichord*)
*¶ Elgar, Symphony No. 1 in A flat major (Philharmonia Orchestra/Barbirolli)

¶Wagner, 'Walter's Trial Song' (from *Die Meistersinger*) (Sandor Konya/Berlin Philharmonic/ Kraus)

¶Debussy, 'Fêtes' (Orchestre de la Suisse Romande/ Ansermet)

¶Lambert, 'The Rio Grande' (Philharmonia Orchestra/ Lambert)

¶Walton, Symphony No. 1 in B flat minor (Philharmonia Orchestra/Walton)

¶Vaughan Williams, 'On Wenlock Edge' (Alexander Young/Sebastian String Quartet)

¶LUXURY: Music manuscript paper, pencils and an india-rubber.

¶BOOK: James Joyce, *Finnegans Wake*

5 December 1966
838 Captain John Ridgway & Sergeant Chay Blyth
Transatlantic oarsmen

¶(Chay Blyth) J. Strauss, 'Nun's Chorus' (from *Casanova*) (Anni Frind)

*¶(John Ridgway) Vaughan Williams, 'Sinfonia Antarctica' (John Gielgud/LPO and Choir/ Boult)

*¶(CB) Rodgers & Hammerstein, *The Sound of Music* (overture and preludium) (soundtrack/Kostal)

¶(JR) Wagner, *Tannhäuser* (overture) (Berlin Philharmonic/von Karajan)

¶(CB) 'The Road and the Miles to Dundee' (Andy Stewart)

¶(JR) Dvořák/Grun (arr.), 'Letter Home' (from *Summer Song*) (Lawrence Naismith)

¶(CB) Tchaikovsky, '1812 Overture' (University of Minnesota Brass Band/ Minneapolis Symphony/ Dorati)

¶(JR) Crimond, 'The Twenty-third Psalm' (Glasgow Orpheus Choir/Roberton)

¶LUXURIES: (CB) a shaving kit; (JR) a leather armchair.

¶BOOKS: (CB) a dictionary; (JR) an anthology of poetry.

12 December 1966
839 Leonard Cottrell
Radio and television producer and writer on archaeology

¶Elgar, Symphony No. 2 in E flat (Hallé Orchestra/Barbirolli)

¶'Dinah' (Fats Waller)

¶'O Come, All Ye Faithful' (Philadelphia Orchestra/ Ormandy)

¶'Là ça ira' (from film *Si Versailles m'était conté*) (Edith Piaf)

¶'Behind the Rose Bushes' (Nana Mouskouri)

¶Chopin, Ballade No. 1 in G minor (opus 23) (Vladimir Ashkenazy *piano*)

¶Bach, Brandenburg Concerto No. 6 in B flat major (BWV 1051) (Yehudi Menuhin and Patrick Ireland *violas*/Bath Festival Chamber Orchestra/ Menuhin)

*¶Fauré, 'In Paradisum' (from *Requiem*, opus 48) (Choeurs Elisabeth Brasseur/Paris Conservatoire Orchestra/ Cluytens)

¶LUXURY: A bronze statue of Poseidon in the Athens museum.

¶BOOK: The collected works of Homer.

19 December 1966
840 Jack Brabham
World champion racing driver

¶'Moon of Manakoora' (from film *The Hurricane*) (Royal Hawaiian Guitars/Merry Melody Singers)

¶'Song of the Islands' (Andy Williams)

¶'The Moon was Yellow' (Frank Sinatra)

*¶Gershwin, 'Our Love is Here to Stay' (from film *Goldwyn Follies*) (Nat 'King' Cole)

¶'Arrivederci, Roma' (Nat 'King' Cole)

¶'We Never Talk Much (We Just Sit Around)' (from film *Rich, Young and Pretty*) (Danielle Darrieux/Fernando Lamas)

¶'Don't Blame Me' (Frank Ifield)

¶'My Son, My Son' (Eddie Calvert *trumpet*)

¶LUXURY: None required.

¶BOOK: A textbook on advanced mechanical engineering.

24 December 1966
841 Gwendoline Kirby
Matron of the Great Ormond Street Hospital for Sick Children

¶Vaughan Williams, 'Fantasia on Greensleeves' (Sinfonia of London/Barbirolli)

¶Bach, Brandenburg Concerto No. 5 in D major (Stuttgart Chamber Orchestra/ Münchinger)

*¶'The Lord is My Shepherd (Brother James's Air)' (Orpington Junior Singers)

¶Quilter, 'Children's Overture' (opus 17) (LSO/Weldon)

¶Rodgers & Hammerstein, 'Maria' (from *The Sound of Music*) (Constance Shacklock/ Olive Gilbert/Silvia Beamish/ Lynn Kennington)

¶'King Jesus Hath a Garden' (King's College Chapel Choir/ Willcocks)

¶'Blow the Wind Southerly' (Kathleen Ferrier/Phyllis Spurr *piano*)

¶Ravel, 'Bolero' (Morton Gould and his Orchestra)

¶LUXURIES: A pair of field glasses and an unfinished tapestry.

¶BOOK: J. R. Tolkien, *The Lord of the Rings*

26 December 1966
842 Georg Solti
Conductor and Musical Director of the Royal Opera House, Covent Garden

¶Verdi, 'Dies Irae' (from *Requiem*) (NBC Symphony/ Toscanini)

¶Mozart, String Quintet in G minor (K. 516) (augmented Pro Arte Quartet)

¶'Blood, sweat and tears' (Speech) (Sir Winston Churchill)

¶Wagner, 'Love Duet' (from *Tristan und Isolde*) (Kirsten Flagstad/Ludwig Suthaus/ Philharmonia Orchestra/ Furtwängler)

¶Schumann, Piano Concerto in A minor (opus 54) (Dinu Lipatti/Philharmonia Orchestra/von Karajan)

¶Mahler, Symphony No. 10 (Philadelphia Orchestra/ Ormandy)

¶ Shakespeare, 'When My Love Swears that She is Made of Truth' (Sonnet 138) (John Gielgud)

*¶ Verdi, *Falstaff* (Act 2, Scene 1) (Frank Guarrera/Giuseppe Valdengo/NBC Symphony/Toscanini)

¶ LUXURY: Michelangelo's *The Last Judgement*, in the Sistine Chapel.

¶ BOOK: Goethe's *Faust*

2 January 1967
843 Anne Sharpley
Journalist

*¶ Haydn, Symphony No. 88 in G (Columbia Symphony/Walter)

¶ Berlioz, *Harold in Italy* (opus 16) (NBC Symphony/Toscanini)

¶ Duparc, 'L'invitation au voyage' (Gérard Souzay/Jacqueline Bonneau *piano*)

¶ R. Strauss, *Der Rosenkavalier* (final trio) (Lotte Lehmann/Elisabeth Schumann/Maria Olszewska/Vienna Philharmonic/Heger)

¶ 'Needles and Pins' (The Searchers)

¶ Britten, 'Les Illuminations' (opus 18) (Peter Pears/New Symphony Orchestra/Goossens)

¶ 'Obeah Wedding' (Mighty Sparrow/National Recording Calypso Band)

¶ Bach, *St Matthew Passion* (final chorus) (Philharmonia Choir and Orchestra/Klemperer)

¶ LUXURY: Spices and herbs.

¶ BOOK: Harold Getty, *The Raft Book*

9 January 1967
844 René Cutforth
Broadcaster, reporter and traveller

*¶ Mozart, 'Non so più' (from *The Marriage of Figaro*) (Teresa Berganza/LSO/Pritchard)

¶ 'Leaning on a Lamp Post' (George Formby)

¶ Beethoven, Sonata No. 12 in A flat major (opus 26) (Artur Schnabel *piano*)

¶ 'Stenka Razin' (Red Army Ensemble)

¶ Mozart, Piano Concerto in C minor (K. 491) (Wilhelm Kempff/Bamberg Symphony/Leitner)

¶ 'La vie en rose' (Edith Piaf)

¶ 'Stormy Weather' (Lena Horne)

¶ Bach, Double Concerto in D minor (BWV 1043) (Igor & David Oistrakh *violins*/RPO/Goossens)

¶ LUXURY: Silk vests and pants.

¶ BOOK: Nigel Dennis, *Cards of Identity*

16 January 1967
845 Sheila Scott
Record-breaking pilot

¶ Holst, 'Neptune' (from *The Planets*, opus 32) (BBC Symphony/Sargent)

¶ 'Boogie Woogie' (Tommy Dorsey and his Orchestra)

¶ Mendelssohn, *A Midsummer Night's Dream* (overture) (Bavarian Radio Orchestra/Kubelik)

*¶ Rachmaninov, Piano Concerto No. 3 in D minor (opus 30) (Vladimir Ashkenazy/LSO/Fistoulari)

¶ Rimsky-Korsakov, *Scheherazade* (Orchestre de la Suisse Romande/Ansermet)

¶ 'Twice Times Keyboard' (theme from Tchaikovsky's Piano Concerto No. 1) (arranged and directed by Bill Le Sage)

¶ Wagner, 'Liebestod' (from *Tristan und Isolde*) (Philadelphia Orchestra/Stokowski)

¶ Mancini, 'The Sound of Hatari' (from film *Hatari*) (Henry Mancini and his Orchestra)

¶ LUXURY: Tobacco seeds.

¶ BOOKS: P. D. Ouspensky, *Search for the Miraculous* and *New Model of the Universe*

23 January 1967
846 Richard Goolden
(2nd appearance)
Actor

¶ 'Father's Favourites' (Terance Casey *Wurlitzer organ*)

¶ 'It's a Great Big Shame' (Gus Elen)

¶ *The Pink Lady* (selection) (Jumbo Military Band)

¶ *Toad of Toad Hall* (selection) (New Mayfair Orchestra)

¶ Franck, 'Symphonic Variations' (Artur Rubinstein *piano*/Symphony of the Air/Wallenstein)

¶ 'Le petit cheval' (Georges Brassens)

*¶ Seeger, 'Where Have All the Flowers Gone?' (Marlene Dietrich)

¶ 'Forty Years On' (Harrow School Boys)

¶ LUXURIES: Cigars and a dinner jacket.

¶ BOOK: Charles Lamb, *The Essays of Elia*

30 January 1967
847 Gerald Moore
(2nd appearance)
Accompanist

*¶ Mozart, *The Marriage of Figaro* (Act 3 march) (Glyndebourne Festival Orchestra/Gui)

¶ Wagner, 'Liebestod' (from *Tristan und Isolde*) (Kirsten Flagstad/Philharmonia Orchestra/Furtwängler)

¶ Beethoven, Piano Concerto No. 4 in G major (opus 58) (Solomon/Philharmonia Orchestra/Cluytens)

¶ Schubert, 'Auf der Brück' (Dietrich Fischer-Dieskau/Gerald Moore *piano*)

¶ Elgar, Cello Concerto (Jacqueline du Pré/LSO/Barbirolli)

¶ R. Strauss, 'Frühling' (from *Four Last Songs*) (Elisabeth Schwarzkopf/Berlin Radio Symphony/Szell)

¶ Mozart, Horn Concerto No. 4 in E flat major (K. 495) (Dennis Brain/Philharmonia Orchestra/von Karajan)

¶ 'Adiós Granada' (Victoria de los Angeles)

¶ LUXURY: Wine.

¶ BOOK: *Grove's Dictionary of Music and Musicians*

6 February 1967
848 Renee Houston
Actress and variety artist
¶ 'Road to the Isles' (from *Songs of the Hebrides*) (Kirkintilloch Junior Choir)
¶ 'I, Who Have Nothing' (Shirley Bassey)
¶ Bach/Gounod, 'Ave Maria' (Joan Hammond/Bertram Harrison *organ*/Harry Blech *violin obbligato*)
¶ Debussy, 'Clair de lune' (from *Suite bergamasque*) (Philadelphia Orchestra/Ormandy)
¶ 'Fluter's Holiday' (Bert Kaempfert and his Orchestra)
¶ 'Eili, Eili' (Jan Peerce)
¶ 'Near and Yet So Far' (from film *Princess Charming*) (Evelyn Laye)
*¶ 'Goodbye to Summer' (Renee Houston/Donald Stewart)
¶ LUXURY: Parsley.
¶ BOOK: Gabriel Chevallier, *Clochemerle*

13 February 1967
849 Gerald Harper
Actor
¶ 'Ev'rytime We Say Goodbye' (from *Seven Lively Arts*) (Ray Charles/Betty Carter)
*¶ Verdi, *Otello* (opening) (Mario del Monaco/Santa Cecilia Orchestra, Rome/Erede)
¶ Verdi, *La forza del destina* (Act 3 duet) (Jussi Björling/Robert Merrill/RCA Victor Symphony/Cellini)
¶ Mozart, Symphony No. 41 in C major (K. 551) (RPO/Beecham)
¶ Shakespeare, *Hamlet* (Act 5, Scene 2) (Paul Scofield and cast)
¶ Chopin, Nocturne No. 9 in B major (opus 32, no. 1) (Artur Rubinstein *piano*)
¶ Willson, 'Ya Got Trouble' (from *The Music Man*) (Robert Preston)
¶ Bach, Brandenburg Concerto No. 6 in B flat major (BWV 1051) (Yehudi Menuhin *violin*/Bath Festival Chamber Orchestra)

¶ LUXURY: A videotape or film of the full five-days' play of a Test match.
¶ BOOK: Dale Carnegie, *How to Win Friends and Influence People*

20 February 1967
850 Clement Freud
Gastronome and journalist
¶ 'The Pig Got Up and Slowly Walked Away' (Frank Crumit)
¶ 'Yellow Bird' (Cy Grant)
¶ Rodgers & Hammerstein, *Oklahoma* (selection) (Howard Keel)
¶ 'I Want to be Evil' (Eartha Kitt)
¶ Clarke, 'Trumpet Voluntary' (Roger Voisin/Unicorn Orchestra/Langendoen)
¶ Dvořák, 'Humoresque' (Isaac Stern *violin*/Columbia Symphony/Katims)
¶ Coward, 'Mad Dogs and Englishmen' (from *Words and Music*) (Noël Coward)
*¶ 'Sous les toits de Paris' (from film) (Jacqueline François)
¶ LUXURY: A still.
¶ BOOK: Damon Runyon's short stories.

27 February 1967
851 Arthur Negus
Expert on antiques
¶ 'The Auctioneer' (Chuck Miller/Hugo Peretti and his Orchestra)
¶ Gilbert & Sullivan, 'From the Sunny Spanish Shore' (from *The Gondoliers*) (D'Oyly Carte Opera Company/Godfrey)
¶ 'The Biggest Aspidistra in the World' (Gracie Fields)
¶ Lerner & Loewe, 'The Rain in Spain' (from *My Fair Lady*) (Rex Harrison /Julie Andrews)
¶ Novello, 'We'll Gather Lilacs' (from *Perchance to Dream*) (Olive Gilbert)
¶ 'Les trois cloches' (Les Compagnons de la Chanson/Edith Piaf)
¶ Rodgers & Hammerstein, 'Climb Every Mountain' (from *The Sound of Music*) (Constance Shacklock)
*¶ Handel, 'Hallelujah Chorus' (from *Messiah*) (Huddersfield Choral Society/Royal Liverpool Philharmonic/Sargent)

¶ LUXURY: A Chippendale cabinet.
¶ BOOK: Ralph Edwards, *Dictionary of English Furniture*

6 March 1967
852 Hugh Griffith
Actor
¶ 'David of the White Rock' (David Ffrangcon Thomas *cello*/Osian Ellis *harp*)
¶ Brahms, Violin Concerto in D major (opus 77) (David Oistrakh/French National Radio Orchestra/Klemperer)
¶ Dylan Thomas, *Return Journey* (excerpt) (Hugh Griffith)
¶ 'Basta un poco di musica' (Marino Marini and his Quartet)
¶ 'Nghariad I Lawr Yn Y Berllan' (Amy Parry-Williams/Meredydd Evans/Osian Ellis *harp*)
¶ Bach, Toccata, Adagio and Fugue in C major (Albert Schweitzer *organ*)
¶ Brahms, Symphony No. 4 in E minor (opus 98) (Columbia Symphony/Walter)
*¶ Bach, 'O Haupt voll Blut und Wunden' (from *St Matthew Passion*) (Peter Pears/Otakar Kraus/Elisabeth Schwarzkopf/Christa Ludwig/Philharmonia Choir and Orchestra/Klemperer)
¶ LUXURY: Champagne.
¶ BOOK: Blank paper and pencils.

13 March 1967
853 Barry Briggs
World speedway champion
¶ Ravel, 'Bolero' (Orchestre de la Suisse Romande/Ansermet)
¶ Lennon & McCartney, 'And I Love Him' (Esther Phillips)
*¶ 'You Oughta be in Pictures' (Ray Conniff *trombone*/Billy Butterfield *trumpet*)
¶ 'Manhattan' (from *Garrick Gaieties*) (Ella Fitzgerald)
¶ 'In the Mood' (Glenn Miller Army Air Force Band)
¶ 'Strangers in the Night' (Frank Sinatra)
¶ 'Lara's Theme' (from film *Dr Zhivago*) (MGM Studio Orchestra)

¶ 'Now is the Hour' (Maori farewell song) (Muana Loa Islanders)
¶ LUXURY: A surf board.
¶ BOOK: An encyclopaedia.

20 March 1967
854 Alan Whicker
Television reporter and interviewer
*¶ 'Everything's Coming Up Roses' (from *Gypsy*) (Rosalind Russell)
¶ Lerner & Loewe, 'I've Grown Accustomed to Her Face' (from *My Fair Lady*) (Rex Harrison)
¶ 'Sag Beim Abschied Leise Servus' (Josephine Baker)
¶ 'La première rendez-vous' (George Arlt and his Orchestra)
¶ 'I Stayed Too Long at the Fair' (Barbra Streisand)
¶ 'Call Me Irresponsible' (from film *Papa's Delicate Condition*) (Frank Sinatra)
¶ 'Lara's Theme' (from film *Dr Zhivago*) (MGM Studio Orchestra)
¶ 'The Trend-Setters' (Group-Thirty Orchestra)
¶ LUXURY: A typewriter and paper.
¶ BOOK: An airways timetable.

27 March 1967
855 Dick Francis
Ex-National Hunt jockey, journalist and thriller writer
¶ Rodgers & Hammerstein, 'Oh, What a Beautiful Morning' (from *Oklahoma*) (Alfred Drake)
¶ 'Chattanooga Choo Choo' (Glenn Miller and his Orchestra and Chorus)
¶ Handel, *Water Music Suite* (RPO/Sargent)
¶ 'I've Got Nothing but Time' (Julie Felix)
¶ 'David of the White Rock' (Frederick Harvey/Philharmonia Orchestra/Weldon)
¶ Lennon & McCartney, 'I Wanna Hold Your Hand' (Boston Pops Orchestra/Fiedler)
¶ 'Stranger on the Shore' (Acker Bilk/Leon Young String Chorale)

*¶ 'I Left My Heart in San Francisco' (Tony Bennett)
¶ LUXURY: A mirror.
¶ BOOK: Charles Lindbergh, *The Spirit of St Louis*

3 April 1967
856 Rolf Harris
Entertainer
¶ 'Malagueñas flamencas' (Manitas de Plata)
¶ 'Trains' (Reginald Gardiner)
¶ 'The Day that the Circus Left Town' (Eartha Kitt)
¶ 'Kalinka' (Red Army Ensemble)
¶ 'Ai Mere Dile Nadan' (Lata Mangeshkar)
¶ Mozart, Horn Concerto No. 4 in E flat major (K. 495) (Dennis Brain/Philharmonia Orchestra/von Karajan)
¶ 'The Click Song' (Miriam Makeba)
*¶ 'Matila' (Yves Montand)
¶ LUXURY: Two tape recorders.
¶ BOOK: Frank Dalby Davison, *Dusty*

10 April 1967
857 John Schlesinger
Film director
¶ Rachmaninov, Piano concerto No. 3 in D minor (opus 30) (Vladimir Ashkenazy/LSO/Fistoulari)
¶ Verdi, 'Dies Irae' (from *Requiem*) (Philharmonia Orchestra and Chorus/Giulini)
¶ Mozart, *Così fan tutte* (Act 1 quintet) (Elisabeth Schwarzkopf/Christa Ludwig/Giuseppe Taddei/Walter Berry/Philharmonia Orchestra/Böhm)
¶ Brahms, Clarinet Quintet in B minor (opus 115) (members of the Vienna Octet)
¶ Berlioz, 'Shepherds' Chorus' (from *L'enfance du Christ*, opus 25) (St Anthony Singers/Goldsborough Orchestra/Davis)
¶ Beethoven, Piano Concerto No. 2 (Wilhelm Kempff/Berlin Philharmonic/Leitner)
¶ Wagner, *Götterdämmerung* (finale) (Birgit Nilsson/Vienna Philharmonic/Solti)

*¶ R. Strauss, 'Morgen' (opus 27, no. 4) (Dietrich Fischer-Dieskau/Gerald Moore *piano*)
¶ LUXURY: Insect repellent.
¶ BOOK: Jonathan Swift, *Gulliver's Travels*

17 April 1967
858 Sir Neville Cardus
Music critic and writer on cricket
¶ Schumann, Fantasia in C major (opus 17) (Vladimir Horowitz *piano*)
¶ Wagner, 'Liebestod' (from *Tristan und Isolde*) (Kirsten Flagstad/Philharmonia Orchestra/Furtwängler)
¶ Mozart, Clarinet Concerto in A major (K. 622) (Jack Brymer/RPO/Beecham)
*¶ Beethoven, Symphony No. 4 in B flat major (opus 60) (BBC Symphony/Toscanini)
¶ Mahler, *Das Lied von der Erde* (Kathleen Ferrier/Vienna Philharmonic/Walter)
¶ Schubert, Symphony No. 8 in B minor (D. 759) (New York Philharmonic/Walter)
¶ Prokofiev, Symphony 1, in D major (Classical) (NBC Symphony/Toscanini)
¶ R. Strauss, 'Im Abendrot' (from *Vier Letzte*) (Lisa della Casa/Vienna Philharmonic/Böhm)
¶ LUXURY: Water-colour painting equipment.
¶ BOOK: James Boswell's *Life of Johnson*

24 April 1967
859 Eric Porter
Actor
¶ J. Strauss (Senior), 'Radetzky March' (Vienna Boys' Choir)
¶ Tchaikovsky, '1812 Overture' (New Symphony Orchestra/Gibson)
¶ Borodin, Symphony No. 2 in B minor (Saxon State Orchestra, Dresden/Sanderling)
¶ Shostakovich, *The Golden Age Ballet Suite* (polka) (National Symphony/Mitchell)
¶ 'Vito' (Madrid Bullfight Band)
¶ Bruckner, Symphony No. 7 in E major (Vienna Philharmonic/Solti)

¶ Montage of noises he would be glad to have left behind
*¶ Shostakovich, Symphony No. 5 (opus 47) (New York Philharmonic/Bernstein)
¶ LUXURY: An astronomical telescope, or a microscope.
¶ BOOK: The essays of Montaigne.

1 May 1967
860 The Very Reverend Dr W. R. Matthews
Dean of St Paul's Cathedral
¶ Byrd, 'Ave Verum Corpus' (St Paul's Cathedral Choir)
¶ Bach, *St Matthew Passion* (final chorus) (Bach Choir/ Jacques Orchestra)
¶ Mozart, Violin Concerto No. 4 in D (K. 218) (David Oistrakh/Philadelphia Orchestra/Ormandy)
¶ Gilbert & Sullivan, 'Three Little Girls from School' (from *The Mikado*) (Elsie Morison/ Marjorie Thomas/Jeannette Sinclair/Pro Arte Orchestra/ Sargent)
¶ 'Round Me Falls the Night' (St Paul's Cathedral Choir)
¶ Parry, 'I was Glad' (from Coronation Service of HM Queen Elizabeth II)
¶ 'Give Rest, O Christ' (St Paul's Cathedral Choir)
*¶ Haydn, 'Gloria in Excelsis' (from *Mass in D*) (St Paul's Cathedral Choir)
¶ LUXURY: A beginner's guide to making rafts.
¶ BOOK: Plato's *Republic*

8 May 1967
861 Derek Nimmo
Actor
¶ Handel/Beecham, 'The Pump Room' (from *Love in Bath*) (RPO/Beecham)
¶ Lennon & McCartney, 'Penny Lane' (The Beatles)
¶ 'Go Tell Aunt Rhody' (Robert de Cormier Folk Singers)
¶ 'Gumboot Dance' (from *King Kong*) (original London cast)
¶ 'What Would I Do Without You, Jeeves?' (from *The World of Wooster*) (Ian Carmichael/ Dennis Price)
*¶ 'The Girl from Ipanema' (Stan Getz/João Gilberto)

¶ Seeger, 'Where Have All the Flowers Gone?' (Marlene Dietrich)
¶ Elgar, *Enigma Variations* (Philharmonia Orchestra/ Sargent)
¶ LUXURY: Garlic.
¶ BOOK: Geoffrey Godden, *Illustrated Encyclopaedia of Pottery and Porcelain*

15 May 1967
862 George Woodcock
CBE
General Secretary of the Trades Union Congress
¶ 'Thrills' (Harry Davidson and his Orchestra)
¶ Saint-Saëns, 'Softly Awakes My Heart' (from *Samson and Delilah*) (Marian Anderson)
¶ Handel, 'Ombra mai fu' (from *Xerxes*) (Enrico Caruso)
*¶ Lehár, 'Vilja' (from *The Merry Widow*) (June Bronhill/Sadler's Wells Opera Orchestra and Chorus/Reid)
¶ Bizet, *Carmen* (Act 4 entr'acte) (French National Opera Orchestra/Prêtre)
¶ Yradier, 'La paloma' (Victoria de los Angeles/Sinfonia of London/Frühbeck de Burgos)
¶ Shakespeare, *Richard III* (opening lines) (Laurence Olivier)
¶ 'Three O'clock in the Morning' (Paul Whiteman and his Orchestra)
¶ LUXURY: A cornet.
¶ BOOK: Bartley's philosophic works.

22 May 1967
863 John Barry
Composer and conductor of film music
¶ Prokofiev, Symphony No. 5 (opus 100) (Boston Symphony/ Leinsdorf)
¶ 'It Never Entered My Head' (from *Higher and Higher*) (Frank Sinatra)
¶ 'Fortune of Fools' (Stan Kenton and his Orchestra)
¶ Mahler, Symphony No. 9 (Berlin Philharmonic/ Barbirolli)
¶ Kodály, 'The Gypsy' (Kodály Girls' Choir of Budapest/ Andor)

¶ Shostakovich, Cello Concerto in E flat (opus 107) (Mstislav Rostropovich/Philadelphia Orchestra/Ormandy)
¶ Bartók, Concerto for Orchestra (RPO/Kubelik)
*¶ Prokofiev, 'The Crusaders in Pskov' (from *Alexander Nevsky*, opus 78) (New York Philharmonic/Schippers)
¶ LUXURY: A piano.
¶ BOOK: Thomas à Kempis, *Imitation of Christ*

29 May 1967
864 David Ward
Opera singer
¶ Debussy, 'Clair de lune' (from *Suite bergamasque*) (Walter Gieseking *piano*)
¶ Rossini, *Semiramide* (overture) (New York Philharmonic/Toscanini)
¶ Elgar, *The Dream of Gerontius* (excerpt) (Janet Baker/Richard Lewis/Hallé Orchestra/ Barbirolli)
¶ Wagner, 'Wotan's Farewell' (from *Die Walküre*) (Hans Hotter/Philharmonia Orchestra/Ludwig)
*¶ Verdi, 'Ingemisco' (from *Requiem*) (Beniamino Gigli/ Rome Opera House Orchestra/ Serafin)
¶ Wagner, *Parsifal* (excerpt) (Bayreuth Festival Orchestra/ Knappertsbusch)
¶ Verdi, 'Ella giammai m'amo' (from *Don Carlos*) (Ezio Pinza/ Metropolitan Opera Orchestra/ Cleva)
¶ 'Flowers o' the Forest' (HM 2nd Battalion Scots Guards Pipes and Drums)
¶ LUXURY: Painting materials.
¶ BOOK: The collected works of Robert Burns.

5 June 1967
865 Fenella Fielding
Actress
¶ 'A Taste of Honey' (Morgana King)
¶ 'The Girl from Ipanema' (Stan Getz/João Gilberto)
¶ Coward, 'Countess Mitzi' (from *Operette*) (Fritzi Massary)
¶ Wilson, 'I Will Miss You' (from *Valmouth*) (Cleo Laine/ Doris Hare)

¶Praetorius, 'Dance from Terpsichore' (Collegium Terpsichore)
¶'I'll Follow My Secret Heart' (from *Conversation Piece*) (Noël Coward/Yvonne Printemps)
*¶'Long Long Summer' (Dizzy Gillespie)
¶'I Taught Her Everything' (from *Funny Girl*) (Danny Meehan/Kay Metford)
¶LUXURY: French silk-lined leather gloves.
¶BOOK: Stella Gibbons, *Cold Comfort Farm*

12 June 1967
866 Xenia Field
Gardening editor
¶'Eton Boating Song' (Eton College Musical Society)
¶'Down the Petersky' (Feodor Chaliapin)
¶'Smoke Gets in Your Eyes' (from *Roberta*) (Carroll Gibbons and his Boy Friends)
¶'Any Old Iron' (Harry Champion)
¶Gershwin, 'Summertime' (from *Porgy and Bess*) (June McMechen)
¶Coates, 'The Green Hills o' Somerset' (Joan Hammond/Gerald Moore *piano*)
¶Quilter, 'Now Sleeps the Crimson Petal' (Kathleen Ferrier/Phyllis Spurr *piano*)
*¶Bach, Toccata and Fugue in D minor (Helmut Walcha *organ*)
¶LUXURY: A mattress.
¶BOOK: An encyclopaedia.

19 June 1967
867 Raymond Huntley
Actor
¶'Sid Field Plays Golf' (Sid Field and company)
¶Bach/Hess, 'Jesu, Joy of Man's Desiring' (Myra Hess *piano*)
¶Mendelssohn, Italian Symphony (Orchestre de la Suisse Romande/Ansermet)
¶Wagner, 'The Prize Song' (from *Die Meistersinger*) (Sándor Kónya/Berlin Philharmonic/Kraus)
¶Mozart, Symphony No. 40 (Columbia Symphony/Walter)

¶Coward, *Private Lives* (Act 1 love scene) (Gertrude Lawrence/Noël Coward)
¶Bernstein/Sondheim, 'Somewhere' (from *West Side Story*) (Reri Grist)
*¶Tchaikovsky, Symphony No. 5 in E minor (Boston Symphony/Monteux)
¶LUXURY: Whisky.
¶BOOKS: W. Somerset Maugham, *Cakes and Ale*, *The Razor's Edge* and *The Circle*.

26 June 1967
868 Lord Ritchie-Calder
Science writer, traveller and university professor
¶'Bonnie Dundee' (Argyll and Sutherland Highlanders Pipes and Drums)
¶'Indian Love Call' (from *Rose Marie*) (Edith Day/Derek Oldham)
¶'The Man on the Flying Trapeze' (BBC Dance Orchestra/Hall)
¶Beethoven, Symphony No. 5 in C minor (opus 67) (NBC Symphony/Toscanini)
¶'Deep in the Heart of Texas' (Geraldo and his Orchestra)
*¶'J'attendrai' (Jean Sablon)
¶'Westering Home' (Kenneth McKellar)
¶Gilbert & Sullivan, 'Bow, Bow, Ye Lower Middle Classes' (from *Iolanthe*) (D'Oyly Carte Opera Company/Godfrey)
¶LUXURY: A tape recorder.
¶BOOK: Leo Tolstoy, *War and Peace*

3 July 1967
869 Roy Hudd
Comedian
¶'T'ain't No Sin' (Ottilie Patterson/Chris Barber's Jazz Band)
¶'Afton Water' (Kenneth McKellar)
¶'Your King and Country Want You' (Maggie Teyte)
¶Bernstein/Sondheim, 'Somewhere' (from *West Side Story*) (P. J. Proby)
*¶Handel, 'Sound an Alarm' (from *Judas Maccabaeus*) (John Heddle Nash/Philharmonia Orchestra/Braithwaite)
¶'Rambling Blues' (Jack Elliott)

¶J. Strauss, *Die Fledermaus* (overture) (Vienna Philharmonic/von Karajan)
¶'The Girls I like' (Max Miller)
¶LUXURY: Glass water-filled bowl with snowfall effect.
¶BOOK: Lupino Lane, *How to be a Comedian*

10 July 1967
870 Henry Longhurst
Journalist and authority on golf
¶'She's Funny That Way' (Ted Lewis and his Band)
¶Gershwin, 'Rhapsody in Blue' (George Gershwin *piano*/Paul Whiteman/and his Concert Orchestra)
¶'Colonel Bogey' (Regimental Band of HM Coldstream Guards)
¶Gershwin, 'Bess, You is My Woman Now' (from *Porgy and Bess*) (Robert McFerrin)
¶'Suddenly It's Folk Song' (Peter Sellers)
¶Massenet, 'O souverain! o juge! o père!' (from *Le Cid*) (Enrico Caruso)
*¶Rachmaninov, Piano Concerto No. 2 in C minor (Benno Moiseiwitsch/Philharmonia Orchestra/Rignold)
¶'Show Me the Way to Go Home' (Primo Scala Band)
¶LUXURY: A still.
¶BOOK: Samuel Pepys' *Diary*

17 July 1967
871 Henryk Szeryng
Violinist
¶Leoncavallo, *Pagliacci* (prologue) (Riccardo Stracciari)
¶'For You Alone' (Enrico Caruso)
¶Elgar, 'La capricieuse' (Bronislaw Hüberman *violin*/Siegfried Schultze *piano*)
¶Brahms, Violin Concerto (Fritz Kreisler/Berlin State Opera Orchestra/Blech)
*¶Brahms, Piano Concerto No. 2 in B flat major (opus 83) (Artur Rubinstein/Boston Symphony/Münch)
¶Bernstein/Sondheim, 'Maria' (from *West Side Story*) (Larry Kert)

¶Bach, Prelude and Fugue in A minor (Albert Schweitzer *organ*)
¶Beethoven, Sonata No. 8 in G major for Violin and Piano (Artur Rubinstein *piano*/ Henryk Szeryng *violin*)
¶LUXURY: A painting by Camille Pissarro.
¶BOOK: The essays of Montaigne.

24 July 1967
872 Tom Courtenay
Actor
¶Mendelssohn, Italian Symphony (Philharmonia Orchestra/Klemperer)
¶Schumann, Piano Concerto in A minor (Annie Fischer/ Philharmonia Orchestra/ Klemperer)
¶Bach, Suite No. 1 in G major for Solo Cello (Pablo Casals)
¶Mozart, Piano Concerto No. 19 in F (K. 459) (Ingrid Haebler/LSO/Davis)
¶Schubert, 'Der Jüngling an der Quelle' (Elisabeth Schumann)
¶Beethoven, Symphony No. 3 in E flat major (opus 55) (Philharmonia Orchestra/ Klemperer)
¶Haydn, Trio in G major (opus 73, no. 2) (Alfred Cortot *piano*/ Jacques Thibaud *violin*/Pablo Casals *cello*)
*¶Schubert, String Quintet in C major (D. 956) (Isaac Stern and Alexander Schneider *violins*/ Milton Katims *viola*/Pablo Casals and Paul Tortelier *cellos*)
¶LUXURY: A football.
¶BOOK: Charles Dickens, *Great Expectations*

31 July 1967
873 Heather Jenner
Proprietress of a marriage bureau
¶'The Moon is Low' (Fats Waller)
*¶Beethoven, Sonata No. 18 in E flat major (opus 31, no. 3) (Artur Schnabel *piano*)
¶Bizet, 'Je vais danser en votre honneur' (from *Carmen*) (Conchita Supervia)
¶Chopin, Piano Concerto No. 1 in E minor (Tamás Vásáry/ Berlin Philharmonic/Semkov)

¶Mozart, *The Magic Flute* (Act 1 duet) (Gundula Janowitz/ Walter Berry/Philharmonia Orchestra/Klemperer)
¶Britten, *The Turn of the Screw* (Act 1) (David Hemmings/ Olive Dyer/English Opera Group Orchestra/Britten)
¶'Shadows on the Grass' (Irene Handl/Peter Sellers)
¶Brahms, Piano Concerto No. 2 in B flat (opus 83) (Artur Rubinstein/RCA Victor Symphony/Krips)
¶LUXURY: Golf clubs and balls.
¶BOOK: A bound volume comprising Charles Dickens' *The Pickwick Papers*, *Bleak House* and *Martin Chuzzlewit*.

7 August 1967
874 Miriam Karlin
Actress
¶Leo, Concerto in D major for Cello, Strings and Continuo (Enzo Altobelli *cello*/I Musici)
*¶Mozart, 'Letter Scene' (from *The Marriage of Figaro*) (Sena Jurinac/Graziella Sciutti/ Glyndebourne Festival Orchestra/Gui)
¶Beethoven, Violin Concerto in D (opus 61) (Jascha Heifetz/ Boston Symphony/Münch)
¶Vivaldi, 'Summer' (from *The Four Seasons*) (Felix Ayo *violin*/ I Musici)
¶'Do You Love Me?' (From *Fiddler on the Roof*) (Topol/ Miriam Karlin)
¶Mozart, Clarinet Quintet (K. 581) (members of the Vienna Octet)
¶Bach, Prelude No. 12 in F minor (Swingle Singers)
¶Handel, *Alcina* (aria) Luigi Alva/LSO/Bonynge)
¶LUXURY: Perfume.
¶BOOK: Plato's *Dialogues*

14 August 1967
875 Jeremy Thorpe MP
Leader of the Liberal Party
¶Beethoven, Symphony No. 8 in F major (opus 93) (NBC Symphony/Toscanini)
*¶Bach, Double Concerto in D minor (Yehudi Menuhin and Christian Ferras *violins*/Festival Chamber Orchestra/Menuhin)

¶Rossini, 'Largo al factotum' (from *The Barber of Seville*) (Lawrence Tibbett)
¶Mozart, Horn Concerto No. 4 in E flat major (K. 495) (Dennis Brain/Philharmonia Orchestra/ von Karajan)
¶Rachmaninov, Piano Concerto No. 2 in C minor (opus 18) (Eileen Joyce/LPO/ Leinsdorf)
¶Wagner, 'Liebestod' (from *Tristan und Isolde*) (Kirsten Flagstad/Philharmonia Orchestra/Furtwängler)
¶Elgar, *Enigma Variations* (excerpt) (RPO/Beecham)
¶Paganini, Violin Concerto No. 4 in D minor (Arthur Grumiaux/Lamoureux Concert Orchestra/Gallini)
¶LUXURY: A violin.
¶BOOK: Edward Gibbon, *The History of the Decline and Fall of the Roman Empire*

21 August 1967
876 Richard Briers
Comedy actor
¶Speech on the bombing of London, 11 September 1940 (Sir Winston Churchill)
¶Shakespeare/Walton, 'Fanfare' and 'Music Plays' (from film *Richard III*) (Philharmonia Orchestra/ Walton)
*¶Poulenc, *Les biches* (Paris Conservatoire Orchestra/ Désormière)
¶'St James' Infirmary' (Singleton Palmer and his Dixieland Band)
¶Shakespeare, *The Tempest* (two speeches) (John Gielgud)
¶Lennon & McCartney, 'Within You, Without You' (The Beatles)
¶Chopin, Mazurka No. 41 in C sharp minor (opus 63, no. 3) (Adam Harasiewicz *piano*)
¶'You were There' (from *Shadow Play*) (Gertrude Lawrence/Noël Coward)
¶LUXURY: A piano.
¶BOOK: Samuel Beckett's plays and novels.

26 August 1967
877 Alan Bennett
Playwright and humourist

¶ Walton, Symphony No. 1 in B flat minor (Philharmonia Orchestra/Walton)

¶ R. Strauss, *Der Rosenkavalier* (final trio) (Lotte Lehmann/Elisabeth Schumann/Maria Olszweska/Vienna Philharmonic/Heger)

¶ 'West of Exeter' (railway sounds at a country station)

¶ Berlioz, 'Villanelle' (from *Les nuits d'été*, opus 7) (Eleanor Steber/Columbia Symphony/Mitropoulos)

¶ 'Now Thank We All Our God' (recorded in St Paul's Cathedral during Thanksgiving Service, 13 May 1945)

¶ Brahms, *German Requiem* (opus 45) (Philharmonia Orchestra/Klemperer)

¶ 'Funny How Love Can Be' (The Ivy League)

*¶ Bach, *St Matthew Passion* (last chorus) (Philharmonia Orchestra/Klemperer)

¶ LUXURY: An unending supply of afternoon teas.

¶ BOOK: A complete set of *Horizon*, the wartime literary review edited by Cyril Connolly.

4 September 1967
878 John Ogdon
Concert pianist

¶ 'The Call of the Far-Away Hills' (from film *Shane*) (Victor Young and his Orchestra)

¶ Balakirev, *Tamar* (Orchestre de la Suisse Romande/Ansermet)

*¶ Wagner, 'Selig, wie die Sonne' (from *Die Meistersinger*) (Elisabeth Schumann/Gladys Parr/Lauritz Melchior/Ben Williams/Friedrich Schorr/LSO/Barbirolli)

¶ Elgar, Symphony No. 1 in A flat major (opus 55) (Hallé Orchestra/Barbirolli)

¶ Liszt, 'Orpheus' (symphonic poem) (RPO/Beecham)

¶ Lennon & McCartney, 'Lucy in the Sky with Diamonds' (The Beatles)

¶ 'Ill Wind' (based on Mozart's Concerto for Horn and Orchestra No. 4) (Michael Flanders/Donald Swann)

¶ 'Mock Mozart' (Peter Ustinov/Antony Hopkins *harpsichord*)

¶ LUXURY: A film projector.

¶ BOOK: A collection of the Sherlock Holmes stories.

11 September 1967
879 Michael Hordern
Actor

*¶ Beethoven, Symphony No. 9 in D minor (opus 125) (Philharmonia Orchestra/Klemperer)

¶ Purcell, 'They Shall be Happy' (from *The Fairy Queen*) (St Anthony Singers/Boyd Neel Orchestra/Lewis)

¶ Beethoven, Sonata No. 8 in C minor for Piano (Wilhelm Kempff)

¶ 'Make Me Coffee, Darling' (Predrag Gojković)

¶ Lambert, *The Rio Grande* (Kyla Greenbaum, *piano*/Gladys Ripley/Philharmonia Orchestra and Chorus/Lambert)

¶ Shakespeare, *The Tempest* (Act 5, Scene 1) (Marlowe Society/professional players)

¶ Handel, 'He was Despised' (from *Messiah*) (Janet Baker/English Chamber Orchestra/Mackerras)

¶ Arne, 'Rule Britannia' (from *Alfred*) (Peter Pears/Aldeburgh Festival Choir and Orchestra/Holst)

¶ LUXURY: A piano.

¶ BOOK: An encyclopaedia.

18 September 1967
880 Captain William Warwick
Captain of a new British liner, then known as the Q4 and later as Queen Elizabeth II

*¶ Beethoven, Violin Concerto in D major (opus 61) (Jascha Heifetz/Boston Symphony/Münch)

¶ Leoncavallo, 'Vesti la giubba' (from *Pagliacci*) (Giovanni Martinelli)

¶ Saint-Saëns, Symphony No. 3 in C minor (opus 78) (Maurice Duruflé *organ*/Paris Conservatoire Orchestra/Prêtre)

¶ Mascagni, 'Easter Hymn' (from *Cavalleria rusticana*) (Renata Tebaldi/Chorus and Orchestra of Maggio Musicale Fiorentino/Erede)

¶ Franck, Symphonic Variations (Artur Rubinstein *piano*/Symphony of the Air/Wallenstein)

¶ 'Whatever Lola Wants' (from *Damn Yankees*) (Gwen Verdon)

¶ Beethoven, Symphony No. 6 in F major (opus 68) (Berlin Philharmonic/von Karajan)

¶ Verdi, 'La vergine degl'angeli' (from *La forza del destino*) (Rosa Ponselle/Ezio Pinza/Metropolitan Opera Chorus and Orchestra/Setti)

¶ LUXURIES: A case of whisky, a knife to open it and a private recording made by some of the crew of the *Queen Mary* in 1956.

¶ BOOK: An advanced book on building small boats.

25 September 1967
881 Doris Arnold
BBC broadcaster and ex-producer

¶ Coates, 'The Merrymakers' Overture' (LSO/Mackerras)

¶ *Roberta* (selection) (Doris Arnold and Harry S. Pepper *pianos*)

¶ 'The Better Land' (The Kentucky Minstrels)

¶ Coward, 'Red Peppers' (from *Tonight at 8.30* (Gertrude Lawrence/Noël Coward)

¶ Elgar, 'Nimrod' (from *Enigma Variations*) (Philharmonia Orchestra/Sargent)

¶ Delius, Piano Concerto in C minor (Benno Moiseiwitsch/Philharmonia Orchestra/Lambert)

*¶ Elgar, 'Praise to the Holiest' (from *The Dream of Gerontius*) (Hallé Orchestra and Choir/Barbirolli)

¶Beethoven, Sonata No. 9 in A major (opus 47) (Jascha Heifetz *violin*/Benno Moiseiwitsch *piano*) (*This was not played for reasons of time.*)
¶LUXURY: A mink coat.
¶BOOK: Frances Hodgson Burnett, *The Secret Garden*

30 September 1967
882 Roy Castle
Entertainer
¶'On Ilkla Moor Bah't At' (Grenadier Guards Band)
¶'This is All I Ask' (Perry Como)
¶'Cherokee' (Clifford Brown)
¶'Dancing on the Ceiling' (from *Evergreen*) (George Shearing Quintet)
*¶'Praise My Soul, the King of Heaven' (St John's College Choir, Cambridge/Guest)
¶'Mommy, Gimme a Drinka Water!' (Danny Kaye)
¶'Silent Night, Holy Night' (Wally Stott and his Orchestra and Chorus)
¶'God Save the Queen' (Pride of the '48 Band)
¶LUXURY: A piano.
¶BOOK: Henry Mancini, *Sounds and Scores*

7 October 1967
883 André Previn
Conductor and pianist
¶Mozart, Symphony No. 40 in G minor (K. 550) (NPO/Giulini)
¶Mozart, Quintet in G minor (K. 516) (Cecil Aronowitz *viola*/Amadeus String Quartet)
¶Mozart, Piano Concerto No. 24 in C minor (K. 491) (Solomon/Philharmonia Orchestra/Menges)
¶Beethoven, Symphony No. 5 in C minor (opus 67) (Amsterdam Concertgebouw/Kleiber)
¶Beethoven, Piano Concerto No. 4 in G major (opus 58) (Solomon/Philharmonia Orchestra/Cluytens)
¶Brahms, Symphony No. 4 in E minor (opus 98) (Berlin Philharmonic/von Karajan)
¶Debussy, 'La Mer' (New York Philharmonic/Bernstein)

¶Britten, 'Dies Irae' (from *War Requiem*, opus 66) (Galina Vishnevskaya/Peter Pears/Dietrich Fischer-Dieskau/Bach Choir/LSO and Chorus/Melos Ensemble/Britten)
¶LUXURY: A piano.
¶BOOK: A volume of reproductions of paintings.

14 October 1967
884 Kenneth Wolstenholme
Sports Commentator
*¶'On the Sunny Side of the Street' (Tommy Dorsey and his Orchestra)
¶J. Strauss, 'Nuns' Chorus' (from *Casanova*) (Anni Frind/chorus and orchestra/Hauke)
¶Rossini, *L'Italiana in Algeri* (overture) (La Scala Orchestra/Giulini)
¶'The Girl from Ipanema' (Frank Sinatra)
¶Rodgers & Hammerstein, 'You'll Never Walk Alone' (from *Carousel*) (Judy Garland)
¶Tchaikovsky, 'Romeo and Juliet Fantasy Overture' (Boston Symphony/Münch)
¶'The Lord is My Shepherd' (Temple Church Choir/Thalben-Ball)
¶'On a Wonderful Day Like Today' (Sammy Davis Jnr)
¶LUXURY: Golf clubs and balls.
¶BOOK: Blank pages for writing on.

21 October 1967
885 Professor Sir Denis Brogan
Writer, teacher, broadcaster and journalist
¶'Ye Banks and Braes' (Moira Anderson)
¶Mozart, 'In Diesen Heil'gen Hallen' (from *The Magic Flute*) (Ivar Andresen)
*¶Mozart, 'Voi che sapete' (from *The Marriage of Figaro*) (Sena Jurinac/Vienna Philharmonic/von Karajan)
¶Beethoven, Symphony No. 3 in E flat major (opus 55) (Philharmonia Orchestra/Klemperer)
¶'La Marseillaise' (Paris Police Band)

¶Handel, 'Where'er You Walk' (from *Semele*) (John McCormack)
¶Stravinsky, *The Rite of Spring* (Columbia Symphony/Stravinsky)
¶Porter, 'Night and Day' (from *The Gay Divorce*) (Fred Astaire)
¶LUXURY: Writing materials.
¶BOOK: The works of Dante.

28 October 1967
886 Denis Matthews
Concert pianist
¶Bach, *St Matthew Passion* (last chorus) (Philharmonia Choir and Orchestra/Klemperer)
¶Mozart, *The Marriage of Figaro* (Act 4 excerpt) (Eberhard Wächter/Elisabeth Schwarzkopf/Philharmonia Orchestra/Giulini)
*¶Beethoven, Quartet in C sharp minor (opus 131) (Busch Quartet)
¶Schubert, Sonata in B flat (D. 960) (Artur Schnabel *piano*)
¶Brahms, Symphony No. 4 (NBC Symphony/Toscanini)
¶Wagner, *Die Meistersinger* (Act 2 excerpt) (Ferdinand Frantz/Berlin Philharmonic/Kempe)
¶Verdi, 'Te Deum' (from *Requiem*) (Robert Shaw Chorale/NBC Symphony/Toscanini)
¶Elgar, *Falstaff* (opus 68) (LSO/Elgar)
¶LUXURY: A telescope.
¶BOOK: Frederick Bodnor, *The Loom of Language*

4 November 1967
887 Sir Hugh Casson
Architect and designer
¶Brahms, Piano Concerto No. 2 in B flat (opus 83) (Rudolf Serkin/Philadelphia Orchestra/Ormandy)
¶Bach, Suite No. 2 in B minor (BWV 1067) (Elaine Shaffer *flute*/Bath Festival Chamber Orchestra/Menuhin)
¶'The Shepherds' Cradle Song' (King's College Chapel Choir/Ord)
¶'Mood Indigo' (Duke Ellington and his Orchestra)
¶Elgar, 'Nimrod' (from *Enigma Variations*) (LPO/Boult)

¶ 'Bailero' (from *Songs of the Auvergne*) (Netania Davrath)
*¶ Bach, 'Gloria' (from *Mass in B minor*) (soloists/Munich Bach Choir and Orchestra/Richter)
¶ Monteverdi, 'Love Duet' (from *L'incoronazione di Poppea*) (Magda Laszlo/Richard Lewis/RPO/Pritchard)
¶ LUXURY: Writing materials.
¶ BOOKS: Charles Dickens, *Great Expectations, Nicholas Nickleby* and *Oliver Twist*.

11 November 1967
888 Warren Mitchell
Actor
¶ Mozart, Quintet in A major for Clarinet and Strings (K. 581) (Gervase de Peyer/Melos Ensemble)
¶ Kern, 'Yesterdays' (Stan Getz)
¶ Stockhausen, 'Kontrapunkte' (Orchestra/Boulez)
¶ 'Runnin' Wild' (Benny Goodman Quartet)
¶ Bach, Toccata and Fugue in D minor (BWV 565) (Fernando Germani *organ*)
¶ Wagner, 'Liebestod' (from *Tristan und Isolde*) (Birgit Nilsson/Vienna Philharmonic/Solti)
¶ Weill/Brecht, 'Mack the Knife' (from *The Threepenny Opera*) (Louis Armstrong)
*¶ Sibelius, Symphony No. 2 in D major (opus 43) (Philharmonia Orchestra/von Karajan)
¶ LUXURY: A tenor saxophone.
¶ BOOK: An anthology of verse.

18 November 1967
889 Irene Worth
Actress
¶ Bach, Sonata No. 2 in A major (Yehudi Menuhin *violin*/George Malcolm *harpsichord*/Ambrose Gauntlett *viola da gamba*)
¶ Byrd, 'Mounsiers Almaine' (Julian Bream Consort)
¶ Haydn, 'Fifths' Quartet (opus 76, no. 2) (Hungarian String Quartet)
¶ 'Morning Raga' (Ravi Shankar *sitar*)
*¶ Schoenberg, Five Pieces for Orchestra No. 1 (LSO/Kubelik)
¶ 'Ole Buttermilk Sky' (Hoagy Carmichael)

¶ Mozart, String Quintet in D major (Walter Trampler *viola*/Budapest String Quartet)
¶ Bach, Contrapunctus No. 2 (from *The Art of Fugue*) (Beromünster Radio Orchestra/Scherchen)
¶ LUXURY: 'The Beatles new colour television show.'
¶ BOOK: A textbook on anthropology.

25 November 1967
890 Jacques Loussier
Pianist
¶ Poulenc, Piano Concerto in C sharp minor (Gabriel Tacchino/Paris Conservatoire Orchestra/Prêtre)
¶ Weill, *The Rise and Fall of the City of Mahagonny* (overture) (orchestra/Bruckner-Rüggeberg)
¶ Schumann, 'Scenes of Childhood' (Yves Nat *piano*)
¶ 'Indiana' (Erroll Garner *piano*)
¶ 'Count Me In' (Count Basie Band)
¶ 'Tea for Two' (from *No, No, Nanette*) (Thelonius Monk *piano*)
¶ Ravel, Piano Concerto in G major (Arturo Benedetti Michelangeli/Philharmonia Orchestra/Gracis)
*¶ Bach, 'Come Thou, the World's Redeemer' (choral prelude) (Dinu Lipatti *piano*)
¶ LUXURY: A painting of the Crucifixion by Salvador Dali.
¶ BOOK: Fernand Osendovsky, *Men, Beasts and Gods*

2 December 1967
891 The Reverend Dr P. B. ('Tubby') Clayton
Founder Padre of Toc H
¶ 'Waltzing Matilda' (Peter Dawson)
¶ Gilbert & Sullivan, 'I Have a Song to Sing, O' (from *The Yeomen of the Guard*) (John Reed/Elizabeth Harwood/RPO/Sargent)
¶ 'My Old Dutch' (Peter Sellers)
¶ Bach, Toccata and Fugue in D minor (Albert Schweitzer *organ*)
¶ 'The Biggest Aspidistra in the World' (Gracie Fields)
¶ Smart, Postlude in D major (Gordon Phillips *organ*)

¶ 'He Who Would Valiant Be' (London Recital Group)
*¶ Drink to Me Only with Thine Eyes' (Alvar Lidell/Gerald Moore *piano*)
¶ LUXURIES: Pipes, tobacco and matches, and a compass.
¶ BOOK: Jacques Paul Migne, *Patrologiae Curses Completus* (in 221 volumes!).

9 December 1967
892 The Rt Hon. Sir Edward Boyle MP
Politician
¶ Dvořák, Cello Concerto (Mstislav Rostropovich/RPO/Boult)
*¶ Mozart, Symphony No. 38 in D major (English Chamber Orchestra/Davis)
¶ Haydn, String Quartet in F major (opus 77, no. 2) (Danish Quartet)
¶ Bach, *Vergnügte Ruh* (cantata) (Elisabeth Höngen/Bavarian State Orchestra, Munich/Lehmann)
¶ Beethoven, 'Prisoners' Chorus' (from *Fidelio*) (Philharmonia Chorus and Orchestra/Klemperer)
¶ Schubert, 'Nacht und Träume' (Gérard Souzay/Jacqueline Bonneau *piano*)
¶ Debussy, 'Pour les sonorités opposées' (*Étude*, Book 2, No. 10) (Charles Rosen *piano*)
¶ Wagner, 'Siegfried Idyll' (Philharmonia Orchestra/Cantelli)
¶ LUXURY: A drawing of a lady by Walter Sickert.
¶ BOOK: Marcel Proust, *À la recherche du temps perdu* (in English).

16 December 1967
893 Robert Merrill
Baritone
¶ Leoncavallo, 'Vesti la giubba' (from *Pagliacci*) (Enrico Caruso)
¶ Mascagni, 'Voi lo sapete' (from *Cavalleria rusticana*) (Rosa Ponselle)
¶ Rossini, *The Barber of Seville* (overture) (NBC Symphony/Toscanini)

¶Verdi, 'Di provenza il mar' (from *La traviata*) (Robert Merrill/NBC Symphony/ Toscanini)

¶Mussorgsky, 'Death of Boris' (from *Boris Godunov*) (Feodor Chaliapin)

¶Puccini, 'Nessun dorma' (from *Turandot*) (Jussi Björling/ Rome Opera House Orchestra/ Leinsdorf)

¶'When the Saints Go Marching In' (Louis Armstrong and his Orchestra)

*¶Bloch, *Sacred Service (Avodath Hakodesh)* (Robert Merrill/New York Philharmonic/Bernstein)

¶LUXURY: Michelangelo's *Moses*

¶BOOK: James Michener, *The Source*

23 December 1967
894 Dame Gladys Cooper (2nd appearance)
Actress and manager

*¶Delius, 'On Hearing the First Cuckoo in Spring' (RPO/ Beecham)

¶'Thee I Love' (from film *Friendly Persuasion*) (Pat Boone)

¶Sibelius, 'Finlandia' (Vienna Philharmonic/Sargent)

¶Lerner & Loewe, 'I've Grown Accustomed to Her Face' (from *My Fair Lady*) (Rex Harrison)

¶Coates, 'Elizabeth of Glamis' (from *The Three Elizabeths*) (New Symphony Orchestra/ Coates)

¶Wagner, 'Love Duet' (from *Tristan und Isolde*) (Kirsten Flagstad/Lauritz Melchior/San Francisco Opera Orchestra/ McArthur)

¶Beethoven, Symphony No. 5 in C minor (opus 67) (Berlin Philharmonic/von Karajan)

¶Malotte, 'The Lord's Prayer' (Roger Wagner Chorale)

¶LUXURY: A tape recorder.

¶BOOK: An anthology of poetry.

25 December 1967
895 Colin Davis
Conductor

¶Webern, Six Pieces for Orchestra (opus 6) (South-west Germany Radio Orchestra/ Rosbaud)

¶'Improvisation' (Magid Vafada *violin*)

¶Stravinsky, 'Gloria' (from *Mass*) (St Anthony Singers/ English Chamber Orchestra/ Davis)

¶Beethoven, Sonata in B flat major (opus 106) (Solomon *piano*)

¶Beethoven, 'Sanctus' (from *Missa Solemnis* in D major, opus 123) (Lois Marshall/Nan Merriman/Eugene Conley/ Jerome Hines/Robert Shaw Chorale/NBC Symphony/ Toscanini)

¶Schubert, Quintet in C major (opus 163) (Richard Harand *2nd cello*/Vienna Philharmonic Quartet)

¶Mozart, Quintet in C major (K. 515) (Cecil Aronowitz *viola*/ Amadeus String Quartet)

*¶Beethoven, Quartet No. 16 in F major (opus 135) (Budapest String Quartet)

¶LUXURY: A packing case of books, to include a Persian dictionary.

¶BOOK: One by Hafiz and a Persian dictionary.

30 December 1967
896 Ann Mallalieu
First woman to become President of the Cambridge Union

¶Barber, Adagio for Strings (opus 11) (Boston Symphony/ Münch)

¶'Sunny Afternoon' (The Kinks)

¶Bach, Concerto in C minor for Two Harpsichords (Karl Richter/Hedwig Bilgram/ Munich Bach Orchestra/ Richter)

¶'Do You Want to Dance?' (The Mamas and the Papas)

¶'Moon Dreams' (Miles Davis *trumpet*)

¶'Strangers in the Night' (Frank Sinatra)

¶'Il sirtaki di eftikia' (orchestra/ Nicolai)

*¶'Twist and Shout' (The Beatles)

¶LUXURY: A four-poster bed.

¶BOOK: The works of Jane Austen.

6 January 1968
897 Desmond Morris
Zoologist

*¶'Los peces' (Juerga Flamenca)

¶Lennon & McCartney, 'Yesterday' (The Beatles)

¶Prokofiev, *Scythian Suite* (Orchestre de la Suisse Romande/Ansermet)

¶Dylan, 'Go Away from My Window' (Marlene Dietrich)

¶'Interstellar Overdrive' (Pink Floyd)

¶'O ouranos einai kleetos' (Yiota Lidia)

¶'Raga "Shree"' (Ravi Shankar *sitar*)

¶'It's Not Easy' (The Rolling Stones)

¶LUXURY: A snorkel mask.

¶BOOK: Sir Richard Burton's translation of *The Arabian Nights*.

13 January 1968
898 John Williams
Guitarist

¶Brahms, Violin Concerto in D major (opus 77) (Jascha Heifetz/ LSO/Reiner)

¶Falla, *La vida breve* (Act 2 aria) (Victoria de los Angeles/ National Orchestra of Spain/ Frühbeck de Burgos)

¶Mozart, Piano Concerto No. 23 in A major (K. 488) (Daniel Barenboim *piano and conducting*/English Chamber Orchestra)

¶'It was So Beautiful' (Django Reinhardt *guitar*/Stephane Grappelli and His Hot Four)

¶Gershwin, 'There's a Boat Dat's Leavin' Soon for New York' (from *Porgy and Bess*) (John W. Bubbles/RCA Victor Symphony/Henderson)

¶Dvořák, Symphony No. 7 in D minor (opus 70) (Czech Philharmonic/Kosler)

*¶Bach, *St Matthew Passion* (final chorus) (Philharmonia Choir and Orchestra/ Klemperer)

¶Schubert, Octet in F major (Berlin Philharmonic Octet)

¶LUXURY: A guitar.

¶BOOK: An encyclopaedia.

20 January 1968

899 John Mortimer
Barrister and playwright

*¶ Mozart, 'Voi che sapete' (from *The Marriage of Figaro*) (Sena Jurinac/Vienna Philharmonic/ von Karajan)

¶ Stravinsky, *The Firebird Suite* (Philharmonia Orchestra/ Giulini)

¶ 'Moonlight Serenade' (Glenn Miller and his Orchestra)

¶ Boccherini, Quintet No. 2 in C major for Guitar and Strings (Aliro Diaz *guitar*/Alexander Schneider and Felix Galimar *violins*/Michael Tree *viola*/ David Soyer *cello*/Lynn Harrell *cello*)

¶ Gershwin, 'Summertime' (from *Porgy and Bess*) (Miles Davis *trumpet*/orchestra)

¶ 'Loveless Love' (Louis Armstrong and his All Stars)

¶ Shostakovich, Piano Trio in E minor (Scottish Trio)

¶ Shakespeare, 'Prospero's Farewell' (from *The Tempest*) (John Gielgud)

¶ LUXURY: A marble bath with constant hot water.

¶ BOOK: Marcel Proust, *À la recherche du temps perdu*

27 January 1968

900 John Bird
Writer, director, impersonator and actor

¶ Haydn, Symphony No. 104 in D (Berlin Philharmonic/ Rosbaud)

¶ Boulez, 'Le marteau sans maître' (Marie Thérèse Cahn/ Ensemble/Boulez)

¶ Beethoven, Symphony No. 7 in A major (Philharmonia Orchestra/Klemperer)

¶ Webern, Variations for Orchestra (opus 30) (orchestra/ Craft)

¶ 'So What?' (Miles Davis *trumpet* and his Quintet)

¶ Janáček, *Glagolitic Mass* (Bavarian Radio Orchestra/ Kubelik)

*¶ Beethoven, String Quartet No. 13 in B flat (opus 130) (Amadeus String Quartet)

¶ Bach, Contrapunctus 13b (from *The Art of Fugue*) (Philomusica of London/ Malcolm)

¶ LUXURY: A self-operated nuclear strike force, for defence.

¶ BOOK: Samuel Johnson, *The Lives of the Poets*

3 February 1968

901 Susan Hampshire
Actress

¶ 'Deep Purple' (Carroll Gibbons/Savoy Hotel Orpheans)

¶ Handel, 'Come unto Him' (from *Messiah*) (Elsie Morison/ Royal Liverpool Philharmonic/ Sargent)

¶ 'Saoirse' (Ceol le Sean O Riada)

¶ Puccini, 'Humming Chorus' (from *Madam Butterfly*) (RCA Italiana Opera Orchestra and Chorus/Leinsdorf)

¶ Dumas, *La dame aux camélias* (closing scene) (Edwige Feuillère/cast)

¶ Beethoven, Piano Concerto No. 5 in E flat major (opus 73) (Artur Rubinstein/Boston Symphony/Leinsdorf)

*¶ 'Paris au mois d'Août' (from film) (Charles Aznavour)

¶ Scene from film *Ninotchka* (Greta Garbo/Melvyn Douglas)

¶ LUXURY: A painting, or a 16th-century patch box.

¶ BOOK: Leo Tolstoy, *War and Peace*

10 February 1968

902 Marilyn Horne
Singer

¶ Spontini, 'Tu che invoco con onore' (from *La vestale*) (Rosa Ponselle)

¶ Beethoven, Symphony No. 9 in D minor (opus 125) (1951 Bayreuth Festival Orchestra/ Furtwängler)

¶ Wagner, 'Immolation Scene' (from *Götterdämmerung*) (Helen Traubel/NBC Symphony/ Toscanini)

¶ Arne, 'The Soldier Tir'd' (from *Artaxerxes*) (Joan Sutherland/Royal Opera House Orchestra, Covent Garden/ Molinari-Pradelli)

¶ Meyerbeer, 'O prêtres de Baal' (from *Le prophète*) (Marilyn Horne/Royal Opera House Orchestra, Covent Garden/Lewis)

¶ Rossini, *Semiramide* (Act 2, Scene 3) (Joan Sutherland/ Marilyn Horne/LSO/Bonynge)

¶ Bruckner, Symphony No. 8 in C minor (Amsterdam Concertgebouw/Van Beinum)

*¶ Bach, *St Matthew Passion* (no. 73) (Peter Pears/Philharmonia Orchestra and Chorus/ Klemperer)

¶ LUXURY: Michelangelo's *Pietà*

¶ BOOK: A selection of English poetry.

17 February 1968

903 Bill Boorne
Show business columnist

¶ Verdi, 'Libiamo ne' lieti calici' (from *La traviata*) (Harry Secombe/Adèle Leigh)

*¶ Rachmaninov, Piano Concerto No. 3 in D minor (Vladimir Ashkenazy/LSO/ Fistoulari)

¶ Porter, 'Always True to You, Darling, in My Fashion' (from *Kiss Me Kate*) (Julie Wilson)

¶ Coward, 'I'll See You Again' (from *Bitter Sweet*) (Evelyn Laye)

¶ Shakespeare, 'Now is the Winter of Our Discontent' (from *Richard III*) (Laurence Olivier)

¶ Tchaikovsky, 'Dance of the Little Swans' (from *Swan Lake*) (Vienna Philharmonic/von Karajan)

¶ Britten, 'Jubilate Deo' (St John's College Choir, Cambridge/Guest)

¶ 'I Know Now' (from *Robert and Elizabeth*) (June Bronhill/ Keith Michell)

¶ LUXURY: A snooker table.

¶ BOOK: A. P. Wavell, *Other Men's Flowers*

24 February 1968
904 C. Day Lewis (2nd appearance)
Poet Laureate

¶ Bach, Harpsichord Concerto in D minor (George Malcolm *harpsichord and conducting*/ Stuttgart Chamber Orchestra)
¶ Handel, Oboe Concerto in B flat major (Léon Goossens/Bath Festival Chamber Orchestra/ Menuhin)
¶ Britten, Serenade for Tenor, Horn, and Strings (Peter Pears/ Dennis Brain *horn*/New Symphony Orchestra Strings/ Goossens)
*¶ Mozart, Piano Concerto No. 19 in F major (Clara Haskil/ Berlin Philharmonic/Fricsay)
¶ Verdi, 'Offertorio' (from *Requiem*) (Maria Caniglia/Ebe Stignani/Beniamino Gigli/Ezio Pinza/Rome Opera House Chorus and Orchestra/Serafin)
¶ Franck, Piano Quintet in F minor (Clifford Curzon/Vienna Philharmonic Quartet)
¶ Chopin, Nocturne No. 5 in F sharp major (opus 15, no. 2) (Peter Katin *piano*)
¶ 'The Old House' (John McCormack)
¶ LUXURY: Bourbon whiskey.
¶ BOOK: The short stories of Anton Chekhov.

2 March 1968
905 Rosalinde Fuller
Actress

¶ Bach, Toccata and Fugue in D minor (Stokowski Symphony)
¶ Beethoven, Sonata No. 8 in C minor (Wilhelm Kempff *piano*)
¶ 'The Raggle-Taggle Gypsies' (The Brotherhood)
¶ Prokofiev, 'Romeo at Juliet's Tomb' (from *Romeo and Juliet*) (Minneapolis Symphony/ Skrowaczewski)
¶ Ravel, 'Pavane pour une infante défunte' (Paris Radio Symphony Orchestra/ Leibowitz)
¶ Lennon & McCartney, 'Fool on the Hill' (The Beatles)
¶ Chopin, Piano Concerto No. 1 in E minor (Tamás Vásáry/ Berlin Philharmonic/Semkov)

*¶ 'Non, je ne regrette rien' (Edith Piaf)
¶ LUXURY: A full-length mirror.
¶ BOOK: Blank pages and pencils.

9 March 1968
906 Archie Camden
Bassoonist

¶ Schubert, Impromptu No. 3 in B flat (Wilhelm Kempff *piano*)
¶ Rossini, 'Una voce poco fa' (from *The Barber of Seville*) (Conchita Supervia)
¶ Mozart, 'Queen of the Night Aria' (from *The Magic Flute*) (Florence Foster Jenkins/ Cosmo McMoon *piano*)
¶ Debussy, 'La Mer' (NBC Symphony/Toscanini)
¶ Speech at the Oxford Union (Gerard Hoffnung)
¶ Mozart/Scott, 'An Eighteenth-Century Drawing Room' (Albert Sandler and his Orchestra)
¶ 'Ill Wind' (based on Mozart's Concerto No. 4 for Horn and Orchestra) (Donald Swann/ Michael Flanders)
*¶ Harty, An Irish Symphony (Hallé Orchestra/Harty)
¶ LUXURY: A radio receiver.
¶ BOOKS: Ernest Bramah, *The Wallet of Kai Lung, Kai Lung's Golden Hours* and *Kai Lung Rolls His Mat.*

16 March 1968
907 T. Dan Smith
Newcastle-upon-Tyne City Councillor and Chairman of the Northern Economic Planning Council

¶ 'O sole mio' (Enrico Caruso)
¶ Abse, 'Sunday Evening' (Danny Abse)
¶ Crimond, 'The Twenty-Third Psalm' (Glasgow Orpheus Choir/Roberton)
*¶ Bach, Toccata and Fugue in D minor (Helmut Walcha *organ*)
¶ 'Fairies of Oneiros' (Michael Garrick Trio)
¶ Shakespeare, 'Friends, Romans . . .' (from *Julius Caesar*) (John Gielgud)
¶ 'Meno se kapia geitonia' (Tonis Maroudas)

¶ Parry/Blake, 'Jerusalem' (Kirsten Flagstad/LSO/Boult)
¶ LUXURY: A block of stone.
¶ BOOK: De Wolfe, *Italian Townscape*

23 March 1968
908 Jon Vickers
Tenor

¶ 'Welcome to My Dream' (from film *Road to Utopia*) (Bing Crosby)
¶ Porter, 'True Love' (from film *High Society*) (Mantovani and his Orchestra)
¶ Halévy, 'Rachel! Quand du seigneur la grace tutélaire' (from *La Juive*) (Enrico Caruso)
¶ Crimond, 'The Twenty-Third Psalm' (Glasgow Orpheus Choir/Roberton)
¶ Bach, 'Jesu, Joy of Man's Desiring' (Dinu Lipatti *piano*)
¶ Bach, 'Sheep May Safely Graze' (Phyllis Sellick and Cyril Smith *pianos*)
*¶ Bach, *St Matthew Passion* (final chorus) (Mendelssohn Choir/Toronto Symphony/ Macmillan)
¶ LUXURY: A child's ball.
¶ BOOK: Saki, *Report to Greco*

1 April 1968
909 Alfie Bass
Actor

¶ 'Go to Sleep, My Baby' (Robert Earl)
¶ Handel, 'Where'er You Walk' (from *Semele*) (Jan Peerce/ Vienna State Opera Orchestra/ Schwieger)
¶ Mozart, 'Dies Bildnis' (from *The Magic Flute*) (Richard Tauber)
¶ 'Water Boy' (Paul Robeson)
*¶ Beethoven, Piano Concerto No. 3 in C minor (Benno Moiseiwitsch/Philharmonia Orchestra/Sargent)
¶ 'The Rose in Her Hair' (from film *Broadway Gondolier*) (Pat O'Malley)
¶ Mozart, *Eine Kleine Nachtmusik* (Vienna Philharmonic/Kubelik)
¶ 'Land of Our Fathers' (crowd at Cardiff Arms Park)
¶ LUXURY: None.
¶ BOOK: An encyclopaedia.

8 April 1968
910 Russell Braddon
Writer and broadcaster

¶ Liszt, Hungarian Rhapsody No. 2 (RCA Victor Symphony/ Stokowski)
¶ 'The Holy City' (Charles Craig)
¶ 'Nick Nack Paddy Whack (This Old Man)' (from film *The Inn of the Sixth Happiness*) (Cyril Stapleton and his Orchestra/chorus)
*¶ Bellini, 'Casta diva' (from *Norma*) (Joan Sutherland/LSO/ Bonynge)
¶ 'The Trolley Song' (from film *Meet Me in St Louis*) (Judy Garland)
¶ 'Tie Me Kangaroo Down, Sport' (Rolf Harris)
¶ Schubert, Quintet in A major (Hephzibah Menuhin *piano*/ Amadeus String Quartet)
¶ Donizetti, *Lucia di Lammermoor* (Act 3 sextet) (Joan Sutherland/soloists/Santa Cecilia Orchestra, Rome/ Pritchard)
¶ LUXURY: Red ink.
¶ BOOK: *History of the World*

15 April 1968
911 Dame Maggie Teyte
(2nd appearance)
Singer

¶ Liszt, 'Valse oubliée' (no. 1) (Clifford Curzon *piano*)
¶ Stanford, 'Magnificat in G' (Richard White/King's College Chapel Choir/Ord)
¶ Wagner, 'Immolation Scene' (from *Götterdämmerung*) (Kirsten Flagstad/Philharmonia Orchestra/Furtwängler)
¶ Shakespeare, *The Tempest* (Act 4, Scene 1) (John Gielgud)
¶ Khachaturian, *Masquerade Suite* (waltz) (Philharmonia Orchestra/Khachaturian)
¶ Offenbach, 'Tu n'es pas beau' (from *La périchole*) (Maggie Teyte)
¶ Debussy, 'Clair de lune' (from *Suite bergamasque*) (Jascha Heifetz *violin*/Emanuel Bay *piano*)
¶ Puccini, 'Nessun Dorma' (from *Turandot*) (Harry Secombe)
Book, luxury and favourite record not chosen.

22 April 1968
912 Sir Nicholas Sekers
Industrialist and arts benefactor

¶ Mozart, Symphony No. 40 in G minor (K. 550) (Columbia Symphony/Walter)
¶ Beethoven, Quartet No. 13 in B flat (opus 130) (Budapest String Quartet)
¶ Mozart, Sonata in E minor (Joseph Szigeti *violin*/Nikita de Magaloff *piano*)
¶ Schubert, Quintet in C major (D. 956) (Isaac Stern and Alexander Schneider *violins*/ Milton Katims *viola*/Pablo Casals and Paul Tortelier *cellos*)
¶ Mozart, 'Sacrifice Scene' (from *Idomeneo*) (Sena Jurinac/ Glyndebourne Festival Orchestra and Chorus/ Pritchard)
¶ Mozart, 'Fire and Water Scene' (from *The Magic Flute*) (Helge Roswaenge/Tiana Lemnitz/Berlin Philharmonic Orchestra and Chorus/ Beecham)
¶ Bartok, *Bluebeard's Castle* (conclusion, opus 11) (Mihaly Szekely/Olga Szonyi/LSO/ Dorati)
*¶ Verdi, *Falstaff* (Act 3, Scene 2) (soloists/Robert Shaw Chorale/NBC Symphony/ Toscanini)
¶ LUXURY: A deckchair.
¶ BOOK: Marcel Proust, *À la recherche du temps perdu*

29 April 1968
913 Sir Michael Tippett
Composer

¶ Schubert, Quintet in C major (D. 956) (Isaac Stern and Alexander Schneider *violins*/ Milton Katims *viola*/Pablo Casals and Paul Tortelier *cellos*)
¶ Purcell, 'When I am Laid in Earth' (from *Dido and Aeneas*) (Kirsten Flagstad/Mermaid Orchestra/Jones)
¶ Wagner, 'Dawn' and 'Siegfried's Rhine Journey' (from *Götterdämmerung*) (Vienna Philharmonic/ Furtwängler)
¶ Monteverdi, 'Chiome d'oro' (madrigal) (Nadia Boulanger Ensemble)

*¶ 'St Louis Blues' (Bessie Smith)
¶ Tippett, Symphony No. 2 (LSO/Davis)
¶ Ives, 'The Fourth of July' (New York Philharmonic/ Bernstein)
¶ Stravinsky, Symphonies of Wind Instruments (Orchestre de la Suisse Romande/ Ansermet)
¶ LUXURY: A harmonium.
¶ BOOK: Homer's *Odyssey*

6 May 1968
914 Margaret Drabble
Novelist

¶ Lennon & McCartney, 'A Little Help from My Friends' (The Beatles)
¶ Bach, 'Give, O Give Me Back My Lord' (from *St Matthew Passion*) (William Parsons/ Jacques Orchestra)
¶ Weill/Brecht, 'Seerauber-Jenny' (from *The Threepenny Opera*) (Lotte Lenya)
¶ 'Gloomy Sunday' (Billie Holiday)
¶ Monteverdi, 'Love Duet' (from *L'incoronazione di Poppea*) (Magda Laszlo/ Richard Lewis/RPO/Pritchard)
¶ Dowland, 'Weep You No More, Sad Fountains' (Richard Lewis/Jacqueline Bonneau *piano*)
¶ Bernstein, 'It Must be So' (from *Candide*) (Robert Rounseville)
*¶ Bach, Brandenburg Concerto No. 3 in G major (Bath Festival Chamber Orchestra/Menuhin)
¶ LUXURY: A typewriter and paper.
¶ BOOK: Marcel Proust, *À la recherche du temps perdu*

13 May 1968
915 Leslie Sarony
Vocalist, songwriter, actor and comedian

¶ 'In the Shadows' (New Concert Orchestra/Turner)
¶ 'Somebody' (The Stargazers)
¶ Kern & Hammerstein, 'Ol' Man River' (from *Show Boat*) (Stratford Johns)
¶ Tchaikovsky, 'Waltz of the Flowers' (from *The Nutcracker Suite*) (RPO/Beecham)

¶'When the Guards are on Parade' (HM Grenadier Guards Band)
¶Mendelssohn, 'The Hebrides (Fingal's Cave)' (LSO/Maag)
¶Coates, 'The Three Bears' (Jack Hylton and his Orchestra)
*¶Royal Air Force March Past' (RAF Central Band)
¶LUXURY: A ukelele.
¶BOOK: The works of Sir Winston Churchill.

20 May 1968
916 Trevor Nunn
Artistic Director of the Royal Shakespeare Company
¶Bach, 'Sleepers Awake!' (from Cantata No. 140) (E. Power Biggs *organ*/Columbia Chamber Orchestra/Rozsnyai)
¶Lennon & McCartney, 'Penny Lane' (The Beatles)
¶Beethoven, Symphony No. 7 in A major (opus 92) (Philharmonia Orchestra/Klemperer)
¶Ibert, Divertissement for Chamber Orchestra (Paris Conservatoire Orchestra/Désormière)
¶Brahms, Piano Concerto No. 1 in D minor (opus 15) (Rudolf Firkusny/Pittsburgh Symphony/Steinberg)
*¶Simon, 'The Sound of Silence' (Simon & Garfunkel)
¶Janáček, 'Sinfonietta' (Czech Philharmonic/Ančerl)
¶Dylan, 'Masters of War' (Bob Dylan)
¶LUXURY: One king-size cigarette.
¶BOOK: A manual of yoga.

27 May 1968
917 Janet Baker
Singer
¶Tallis, 'Gaude Gloriosa Dei Mater' (BBC Chorus/Melville)
*¶'Psalm 51' (King's College Chapel Choir/Willcocks)
¶Shakespeare, 'Let Me Not to the Marriage of True Minds' (Sonnet 116) (John Gielgud)
¶Purcell, 'Welcome, Welcome, Glorious Morn' (Ambrosian Singers/English Chamber Orchestra/Leppard)

¶Verdi, 'Stabat Mater' (from *Four Sacred Pieces*) (Philharmonia Chorus and Orchestra/Giulini)
¶Scarlatti, Sonata in G major (L. 487) (George Malcolm *harpsichord*)
¶Bach, 'Meine Seel' erhebt den Herren' (Cantata No. 10) (London Bach Society/English Chamber Orchestra/Steinitz)
¶Elgar, 'Praise to the Holiest in the Height' (from *The Dream of Gerontius*, opus 38) (Sheffield Philharmonic Chorus/Ambrosian Singers/Hallé Choir and Orchestra/Barbirolli)
¶LUXURY: A doll's house.
¶BOOK: J. R. R. Tolkien, *The Lord of the Rings*

3 June 1968
918 Sir Gordon Russell
Designer
¶'The Sweet Primrose' (Philip Tanner)
¶Anon, Allemande and Corrente in G minor (Carl Dolmetsch *recorder*)
¶Byrd, 'Galliard' (Violet Gordon Woodhouse *harpsichord*)
¶Le Bèque, 'Magnificat' (André Isoir *organ*)
¶'Sweet Kate' (Wilfrid Brown/Eileen Poulter/David Channon *lute*)
*¶Handel, *Water Music Suite* (RPO/Sargent)
¶Schubert, 'Die Forelle' (D. 550) (Dietrich Fischer-Dieskau/Gerald Moore *piano*)
¶'A Little of What You Fancy Does You Good' (Marie Lloyd)
¶LUXURY: Claret.
¶BOOK: Gilbert White, *The Natural History of Selborne*

10 June 1968
919 Colin Cowdrey
Cricketer and Captain of the England Test team
¶Rodgers & Hammerstein, 'Do-Re-Mi' (from *The Sound of Music*) (Julie Andrews/children)
¶'We Shall Fight on the Beaches' (speech in the House of Commons, 4 June 1940) (Sir Winston Churchill)

¶Gilbert & Sullivan, 'A Policeman's Lot' (from *The Pirates of Penzance*) (Owen Brannigan/Glyndebourne Festival Chorus/Pro Arte Orchestra)
¶'Jamaica Farewell' (Nina & Frederick)
¶'The Carnival is Over' (The Seekers)
¶'Cowdrey's 100' (highlights of the 1960 Fifth Test Match, England *v* South Africa) (John Arlott/Richie Benaud)
¶'We'll Keep a Welcome' (Harry Secombe)
*¶'Praise My Soul the King of Heaven' (Choirs of Westminster Abbey and HM Chapels Royal)
¶LUXURY: A box of rubber balls.
¶BOOK: The copy of *Wisden* which records his first tour of Australia.

17 June 1968
920 Henry Hall
(2nd appearance)
Bandleader and impresario
*¶'What a Wonderful World' (Louis Armstrong)
¶Chopin, Étude in G flat major (opus 10) (Louis Kentner *piano*)
¶'If I were a Rich Man' (from *Fiddler on the Roof*) (Topol)
¶Jarre, 'Lara's Theme' (from film *Dr Zhivago*) (MGM Studio Orchestra/Jarre)
¶'Dis donc' (from *Irma La Douce*) (Zizi Jeanmaire)
¶Kreisler, 'Caprice viennois' (Fritz Kreisler *violin*/RCA Victor Symphony/O'Connell)
¶'Where are the Shows?' (from *I Do, I Do*) (Anne Rogers/Ian Carmichael)
¶Gershwin, 'Rhapsody in Blue' (Leonard Bernstein *piano and conducting*/Columbia Symphony)
¶LUXURY: A magic lamp.
¶BOOK: Manuals to teach himself foreign languages.

24 June 1968
921 Eleanor Bron
Actress
¶ Chopin Waltz No. 2 in A flat (opus 34, no. 1) (Artur Rubinstein *piano*)
¶ Brahms, Sonata No. 2 in E flat major for Clarinet and Piano (Jacques Lancelot *clarinet*/ Annie D'Arco *piano*)
¶ 'I Don't Know You Anymore' (Dinah Washington)
¶ Bach, Sonata No. 6 in G major (BWV 1019) (Yehudi Menuhin *violin*/George Malcolm *harpsichord*/Ambrose Gauntlett *viola da gamba*)
¶ 'Elsa' (Bill Evans Trio)
¶ 'Ay-Round the Corner' (Jo Stafford)
*¶ Schubert, 'Im Frühling' (D. 882) (Dietrich Fischer-Dieskau/ Gerald Moore *piano*)
¶ Mozart, String Quintet No. 4 in G minor (K. 516) (Heinz-Otto Graf *viola*/Heutling String Quartet)
¶ LUXURY: Sycamore trees.
¶ BOOK: A bi-lingual edition of Homer.

1 July 1968
922 Sir Gilbert Inglefield
Lord Mayor of London
¶ Mozart, Clarinet Quintet in A major (Gervase de Peyer/Melos Ensemble)
¶ Butterworth, 'The Banks of Green Willow' (LPO/Boult)
¶ Beethoven, Piano Concerto No. 5 in E flat major (opus 73) (Artur Rubinstein/Boston Symphony/Leinsdorf)
¶ Bach, 'Truly This was the Son of God' (from *St Matthew Passion*) (Peter Pears/Stuttgart Hymnus Boys' Choir and Chamber Orchestra/ Münchinger)
¶ Verdi, 'Dies Irae' (from *Requiem*) (Philharmonia Orchestra and Chorus/Giulini)
¶ Britten, 'Sunday Morning' (from *Peter Grimes*, Act 2 interlude) (Royal Opera House Orchestra, Covent Garden/ Britten)
¶ Brahms, 'Variations on a Theme of Haydn (St Anthony Chorale)' (LSO/Monteux)

*¶ Handel, 'The Nightingale Chorus' (from *Solomon*) (Beecham Choral Society/RPO/ Beecham)
¶ LUXURY: Botticelli's *Nativity*, from the National Gallery.
¶ BOOK: Bertrand Russell, *A History of Western Philosophy*

8 July 1968
923 Francis Durbridge
Thriller writer
¶ 'Cabaret' (from *Cabaret*) (Jill Haworth/Harold Hastings Orchestra)
¶ Chopin, Nocturne No. 1 in B flat minor (opus 9) (Arthur Rubinstein *piano*)
¶ Sondheim, 'Do I Hear a Waltz?' (from *Do I Hear a Waltz?*) (Sammy Davis Jnr)
*¶ Beethoven, Piano Concerto No. 5 in E flat major (opus 73) (Wilhelm Kempff/Berlin Philharmonic/Leitner)
¶ Rodgers & Hart, 'Manhattan' (from film *Words and Music*) (Mickey Rooney)
¶ Rimsky-Korsakov, *Scheherazade* (RPO/Beecham)
¶ 'Nina' (from *Sigh No More*) (Noël Coward)
¶ 'Ilona' (from *She Loves Me*) (Jack Cassidy)
¶ LUXURY: Henri Matisse, *Still Life with Oriental Rug*.
¶ BOOK: *Plays* and *Prefaces* by George Bernard Shaw.

15 July 1968
924 Thora Hird
Actress
¶ 'Oh, Listen to the Band' (GUS [Footwear] Band)
¶ Massenet, 'Meditation' (from *Thaïs*) (Manoug Parikian *violin*/ Philharmonia Orchestra/von Karajan)
¶ 'Chicken Reel Square Dance' (Guy Lombardo and his Royal Canadians)
¶ 'Keltic Lament' (Jacques Orchestra)
¶ 'Big Noise from Winnetka' (Tommy Kinsman Orchestra)
¶ Schubert, Symphony No. 8 in B minor (Vienna Philharmonic/ Böhm)
¶ 'Comin' Home Baby' (Mel Torme)

*¶ Dvořák, Symphony No. 9 in E minor (Hallé Orchestra/ Barbirolli)
¶ LUXURY: Insect repellent.
¶ BOOK: A history of the world.

22 July 1968
925 Eric Shipton
Explorer and mountaineer
¶ 'Swanee' (Tommy Kinsman and his Orchestra)
¶ Gounod, 'Ballet Music' (from *Faust*) (RPO/Beecham)
¶ 'Room with a View' and 'Dance, Little Lady' (Noël Coward)
¶ 'London Pride' (Noël Coward)
¶ Chopin, Étude in E major (opus 10) (György Cziffra *piano*)
¶ 'These Foolish Things' (from *Spread It Abroad*) (Carroll Gibbons/Savoy Hotel Orpheans)
¶ 'The Glow Worm' (Boston Pops Orchestra/Fiedler)
*¶ 'Londonderry Air' (Hallé Orchestra/Barbirolli)
¶ LUXURY: A snorkel mask.
¶ BOOK: W. McNeill Dixon, *The Human Situation*

29 July 1968
926 Edward Chapman
Actor
¶ Tchaikovsky, Piano Concerto No. 1 in B flat minor (Benno Moiseiwitsch/Philharmonia Orchestra/Weldon)
¶ Porter, 'Now You Has Jazz' (from film *High Society*) (Bing Crosby/Louis Armstrong)
¶ 'On the Road to Mandalay' (Owen Brannigan/Ernest Lush *piano*)
¶ 'I Learned About Women from Her' (Frank Crumit)
*¶ Bach, 'Air on the G String' (Yehudi Menuhin *violin*/Marcel Gazelle *piano*)
¶ 'My Blue Heaven' (Gracie Fields)
¶ Franck, Violin Sonata in A major (Jascha Heifetz/Artur Rubinstein *piano*)
¶ 'I'm Going to See You Today' (Joyce Grenfell)
¶ LUXURIES: Cigarettes and whisky.
¶ BOOK: The novels of Jane Austen.

5 August 1968
927 Louis Armstrong
Jazz trumpeter, bandleader and entertainer
*¶ 'Blueberry Hill' (Louis Armstrong and his All Stars)
¶ Weill/Brecht, 'Mack the Knife' (from *The Threepenny Opera*) (Louis Armstrong)
¶ 'People' (from *Funny Girl*) (Barbra Streisand)
¶ 'Bye Bye Blues' (Guy Lombardo and his Royal Canadians)
¶ 'New Orleans' (Bobby Hackett's Band)
¶ Gershwin, 'Bess, You is My Woman Now' (from *Porgy and Bess*) (Ella Fitzgerald/Louis Armstrong)
¶ 'Stars Fell on Alabama' (Louis Armstrong and his All Stars)
¶ 'What a Wonderful World' (Louis Armstrong Orchestra and Chorus)
¶ LUXURY: A trumpet.
¶ BOOK: His own autobiography.

12 August 1968
928 Sir Francis McLean
BBC Director of Engineering
¶ Rossini, 'Ecco ridente in cielo' (from *The Barber of Seville*) (Luigi Alva/RPO/Gui)
*¶ Dvořák, Symphony No. 9 in E minor (opus 95) (Czech Philharmonic/Ančerl)
¶ Dvořák, 'O Lovely Moon' (from *Rusalka*) (Rita Streich/Berlin Radio Symphony/Gaebel)
¶ 'Czak Egy Kislany Van a Világon' (Kalmár Pál)
¶ Prokofiev, 'Montagues and Capulets' (from *Romeo and Juliet*) (LSO/Abbado)
¶ Mozart, 'La ci darem la mano' (from *Don Giovanni*) (Eberhard Wächter/Graziella Sciutti/Philharmonia Orchestra/Giulini)
¶ Lerner & Loewe, 'Ascot Gavotte' (from *My Fair Lady*) (Chorus/Orchestra/Ornadel)
¶ 'Boum!' (Charles Trenet)
¶ LUXURY: A Dutch flower picture in the Wallace Collection.
¶ BOOK: Edward Gibbons, *The History of the Decline and Fall of the Roman Empire*

19 August 1968
929 Carlo Maria Giulini
Conductor
*¶ Beethoven, String Quartet No. 15 in A minor (opus 132) (Busch Quartet)
¶ Schubert, Impromptu No. 2 in A flat major (Artur Schnabel *piano*)
¶ Mozart, Symphony No. 36 in C major (K. 425) (Columbia Symphony/Walter)
¶ Beethoven, Symphony No. 3 in E flat major (opus 55) (Philharmonia Orchestra/Klemperer)
¶ Brahms, Symphony No. 4 in E minor (Berlin Philharmonic/Furtwängler)
¶ Debussy, 'Fêtes' (from *Three Nocturnes*, no. 2) (Santa Cecilia Orchestra, Rome/de Sabata)
¶ Verdi, *Rigoletto* (Act 3) (Leonard Warren/Zinka Milanov/Jan Peerce/Nan Merriman/Nicola Moscona/NBC Symphony/Toscanini)
¶ Verdi, 'Credo in un dio crudel' (from *Otello*) (Titta Ruffo)
¶ LUXURY: None.
¶ BOOK: St Francis of Assisi, 'The Praise of Created Things' in *The Mirror of Perfection*.

26 August 1968
930 Edwige Feuillère
Actress
*¶ Falla, *El amor brujo* (Philharmonia Orchestra/Giulini)
¶ Grieg, Piano Concerto in A minor (opus 16) (Philippe Entremont/Philadelphia Orchestra/Ormandy)
¶ Monteverdi, *Il combattimento di Tancredi e Clorinda* (excerpt) (Societa Cameristica di Lugano/Loehrer)
¶ Handel, 'Ombra mai fu' (from *Xerxes*) (Kathleen Ferrier/LSO/Sargent)
¶ 'Peripatos' (Manos Hadjidakis)
¶ Weill/Brecht, 'Alabama Song' (from *The Rise and Fall of the City of Mahagonny*) (Lotte Lenya)
¶ Menotti, *The Consul* (Act 2, Scene 2) (Patricia Neway/Gloria Lane)

¶ 'Non, je ne regrette rien' (Edith Piaf)
¶ LUXURY: An ivory ball.
¶ BOOK: An Anglo-French dictionary.

2 September 1968
931 Dame Ngaio Marsh
Crime novelist
¶ Curnow, 'Landfall in Unknown Seas' (Allen Curnow)
¶ Sheridan, *The School for Scandal* (Act 2, Scene 1) (Cecil Parker/Claire Bloom)
¶ Shakespeare, 'When That I was and a Little Tiny Boy' (song from *Twelfth Night*) (Leslie French)
¶ Chekhov, *Uncle Vanya* (Act 3 excerpt) (Laurence Olivier/Rosemary Harris)
¶ Mozart, Quintet in G minor (Max Gilbert *viola*/Griller String Quartet)
¶ Shakespeare, *Henry V* (Act 4 prologue) (Laurence Olivier)
*¶ Bach, Brandenburg Concerto No. 5 in D major (George Malcolm *harpsichord*/Bath Festival Chamber Orchestra/Menuhin)
¶ Lerner & Loewe, 'With a Little Bit of Luck' (from *My Fair Lady*) (Stanley Holloway)
¶ LUXURY: Two Chinese figures of musicians.
¶ BOOK: An anthology of poetry.

9 September 1968
932 Richard Rodney Bennett
Composer
¶ Walton, Viola Concerto (William Primrose/Philharmonic Orchestra/Walton)
¶ 'Jump for Joy' (Sarah Vaughan)
¶ Stravinsky, *The Rite of Spring* (French National Radio Orchestra/Boulez)
¶ 'For All We Know' (Billie Holiday)
¶ 'I'm Gonna Move to the Outskirts of Town' (Lou Rawls)
*¶ Debussy, 'Jeux' (NPO/Boulez)

¶ 'Ten Cents a Dance' (Shirley Horn)
¶ 'I'm Hip' (Blossom Dearie)
¶ LUXURY: A piano.
¶ BOOK: *The Atlantic Book*, compiled by Edith Sitwell.

16 September 1968
933 Dame Anne Godwin
Trade union official
¶ 'Mah Lindy Lou' (Paul Robeson)
*¶ Mozart, Concerto in C major for Flute, Harp and Orchestra (Aurèle Nicolet *flute*/Rose Stein *harp*/Munich Bach Orchestra/Richter)
¶ T. S. Eliot, 'Journey of the Magi' (John Gielgud)
¶ Boughton, *The Immortal Hour* (excerpt) (Arthur Cranmer/Queen's Theatre Orchestra)
¶ Clarke, 'Trumpet Voluntary' (Combined BMC, Fairey and Foden Bands/Mortimer)
¶ 'Valentine' (from film *Innocents of Paris*) (Maurice Chevalier)
¶ Chopin, Fantaisie in F minor (opus 49) (Vlado Perlemuter *piano*)
¶ Grieg, Piano Concerto in A minor (Artur Rubinstein/RCA Victor Symphony/Wallenstein)
¶ LUXURY: Champagne
¶ BOOK: A. P. Wavell's *Other Men's Flowers*

23 September 1968
934 Marty Feldman
Scriptwriter and comedian
¶ 'The Bridge' (Sonny Rollins)
*¶ Albinoni, Concerto in D minor for Oboe, Strings and Continuo (opus 9, no. 2) (Evert Van Tright *oboe*/I Musici)
¶ 'Parker's Mood' (Charlie Parker)
¶ Berlioz, Symphonie Fantastique (LSO/Boulez)
¶ 'God Bless the Child' (Billie Holiday)
¶ 'O Mister Porter' (Mammoth Gavioli Fair Organ)
¶ 'Wednesday Night Prayer Meeting' (Charles Mingus)

¶ Honegger, *Le Roi David* (Janine Micheau/Pierre Mollet/Jean Hervé/Elisabeth Brasseur Choir/French National Radio Orchestra/Honegger)
¶ LUXURY: A piano.
¶ BOOK: Antoine de Saint-Exupéry, *The Little Prince*

30 September 1968
935 Richard Lester
Film director
¶ *The Knack* (opening theme) (film soundtrack)
*¶ Satie, *Three Gymnopédies* (no. 1) (Concert Arts Orchestra/Golschmann)
¶ Ravel, Piano Concerto in G (Leonard Bernstein *piano and conducting*/Columbia Symphony)
¶ Lennon & McCartney, 'Yesterday' (Ray Charles)
¶ Dylan, 'The Times They are A-Changing'' (Bob Dylan)
¶ 'Doina Oltului' (Dubre Constantin *pan pipes*/United Folk Orchestra)
¶ 'Son of Suzy Creamcheese' (The Mothers of Invention)
¶ Copland, Symphony No. 3 (Minneapolis Symphony/Dorati)
¶ LUXURY: A harp.
¶ BOOK: *The Guinness Book of Records*

7 October 1968
936 Billy Russell
Comedian and character actor
¶ Tchaikovsky, 'Dance of the Sugar Plum Fairy' (from *The Nutcracker Suite*, opus 71a) (Vienna Philharmonic/von Karajan)
¶ Rossini, 'Largo al factotum' (from *The Barber of Seville*) (Peter Dawson)
¶ Gounod, 'Ballet Music' (from *Faust*) (Philharmonia Orchestra/von Karajan)
¶ Liszt, Liebestraum No. 3 in A flat (Artur Rubinstein *piano*)
¶ Lerner & Loewe, 'I Could Have Danced All Night' (from *My Fair Lady*) (Julie Andrews/Philippa Bevans)
¶ Handel, 'Largo' (from *Xerxes*) (Reginald Foort *organ*)

¶ Khachaturian, *Masquerade Suite* (waltz) (Prague Radio Symphony/Khachaturian)
*¶ Malotte, 'The Lord's Prayer' (Gracie Fields)
¶ LUXURY: Painting equipment.
¶ BOOK: An encyclopaedia.

14 October 1968
937 Raymond Postgate
Writer, historian and authority on wine and food
¶ Mozart, *Eine Kleine Nachtmusik* (Vienna Philharmonic/Kubelik)
¶ James Joyce, 'Anna Livia Plurabelle' (from *Finnegans Wake*), (James Joyce)
¶ 'If You were the Only Girl in the World' (from *The Bing Boys are Here*) (Violet Loraine/George Robey)
¶ Wilfred Owen, 'Greater Love' (from film *The Days of Wilfred Owen*) (Richard Burton)
¶ 'Moi j' crache dans l'eau' (Lucienne Boyer)
¶ 'Lullaby of Broadway' (from film *Golddiggers of 1935*) (Henry Mancini Orchestra and Chorus)
¶ T. S. Eliot, 'Sweeney among the Nightingales' (T. S. Eliot)
*¶ Parry/Blake, 'Jerusalem' (John McCormack)
¶ LUXURY: Claret.
¶ BOOK: Edward Gibbon, *The History of the Decline and Fall of the Roman Empire*

21 October 1968
938 Barbara Murray
Actress
*¶ Delius, 'The Walk to the Paradise Garden' (from *A Village Romeo and Juliet*) (RPO/Beecham)
¶ Wagner, 'Love Duet' (from *Tristan und Isolde*) (Kirsten Flagstad/Ludwig Suthaus/Philharmonia Orchestra/Furtwängler)
¶ 'Cwm Rhondda' (Treorchy Choir)
¶ Lerner & Loewe, 'Hymn to Him' (from *My Fair Lady*) (Rex Harrison)
¶ 'The Plane Makers March' (New Concert Orchestra)
¶ 'Anyone Who Had a Heart' (Dionne Warwick)

¶ Lennon & McCartney, 'If I Fell' (The Beatles)

¶ Puccini, 'In questa reggia' (from *Turandot*) (Maria Callas/Philharmonia Orchestra/Serafin)

¶ LUXURY: Perfume.

¶ BOOK: *Larousse gastronomique*

28 October 1968
939 Richard Baker
Television newsreader and commentator

¶ Dvořák, Cello Concerto in B minor (Mstislav Rostropovich/Czech Philharmonic/Talich)

¶ Chopin, Nocturne in D flat (opus 27) (Artur Rubinstein *piano*)

¶ Shakespeare, 'Prospero's speech' (from *The Tempest*) (John Gielgud)

¶ Schubert, Quartet in D minor (Amadeus String Quartet)

¶ 'Burlington Bertie from Bow' (Ella Shields)

¶ R. Strauss, 'Presentation of the Silver Rose' (from *Der Rosenkavalier*) (Elisabeth Schumann/Maria Olszewska/Vienna Philharmonic/Heger)

*¶ Mozart, Symphony No. 40 in G minor (K. 550) (NPO/Giulini)

¶ Sullivan/Mackerras, 'Pineapple Poll' (RPO/Mackerras)

¶ LUXURY: A bed.

¶ BOOK: The novels of Jane Austen.

4 November 1968
940 Peggy Mount
Character actress

*¶ Rachmaninov, Piano Concerto No. 2 in C minor (opus 18) (Peter Katin/New Symphony Orchestra/Davis)

¶ 'Lovers Such as I' (The Bachelors)

¶ 'Mirage' (Manuel and the Music of the Mountains)

¶ Prokofiev, *Romeo and Juliet* (Czech Philharmonic/Ančerl)

¶ 'Violets for Your Furs' (Frank Sinatra)

¶ Tchaikovsky, 'Waltz of the Flowers' (from *The Nutcracker Suite*, opus 71a) (LSO/Fistoulari)

¶ 'You Made Me Love You (Dear Mr Gable)' (from film *Broadway Melody of 1938*) (Judy Garland)

¶ Grieg, Piano Concerto in A minor (Clifford Curzon/LSO/Fjeldstad)

¶ LUXURY: An enormous cookery book.

¶ BOOK: The complete works of Oscar Wilde.

11 November 1968
941 Dan Maskell
Tennis player, coach and commentator

¶ 'Up to the Rigi' (Marthi Mumenthaler and Vreni Pfyl *yodellers*/Rigibuebe Ländlerkapelle)

¶ Handel, 'Dead March' (from *Saul*) (Irish Guards Band)

¶ Elgar, Violin Concerto in B minor (Yehudi Menuhin/LSO/Elgar)

¶ 'RAF March Past' (RAF Central Band)

*¶ Lerner & Loewe, 'I Could Have Danced All Night' (from *My Fair Lady*) (Julie Andrews/Philippa Bevans)

¶ 'Warsaw Concerto' (from film *Dangerous Moonlight*) (Leonard Pennario *piano*/Hollywood Bowl Symphony/Dragon)

¶ Rodgers & Hammerstein, 'The Sound of Music' (from *The Sound of Music*) (Julie Andrews)

¶ Ravel, 'Bolero' (Orchestre de la Suisse Romande/Ansermet)

¶ LUXURIES: Tennis balls, golf balls, paper and pencils.

¶ BOOKS: Books by Henry Longhurst.

18 November 1968
942 Lieutenant Colonel C. H. Jaeger
Senior Director of Music in the Brigade of Guards

¶ Mendelssohn, 'Hear My Prayer' (Ernest Lough/Temple Church Choir/Thalben-Ball)

*¶ Bach, Suite No. 3 in D (Munich Bach Orchestra/Richter)

¶ Parry, 'I was Glad' (from Coronation Service of HM Queen Elizabeth II)

¶ Brahms, Symphony No. 3 in F (opus 90) (Vienna Symphony/Sawallisch)

¶ Elgar, 'Nimrod' (from *Enigma Variations*) (Philharmonia Orchestra/Barbirolli)

¶ Prokofiev, Classical Symphony in D major (opus 25) (Orchestre de la Suisse Romande/Ansermet)

¶ 'Jigger's Corn' (Irish Guards Band)

¶ Lennon/McCartney, 'Michelle' (Irish Guards Band)

¶ LUXURY: A chess set.

¶ BOOK: An anthology of modern British poetry.

25 November 1968
943 Sandy Powell
Comedian

¶ 'Tears' (Ken Dodd)

¶ 'The Driving Instructor' (Bob Newhart)

¶ Saint-Saëns, 'The Swan' (from *Carnival of the Animals*) (Raymond Clark *cello*/Abbey Simon and Hephzibah Menuhin *pianos*)

¶ 'Gracie and Sandy's Party' (Gracie Fields/Sandy Powell)

¶ 'Ebb Tide' (Frank Chacksfield and his Orchestra)

¶ 'Me and My Shadow' (Morecambe & Wise)

*¶ 'Silent Night' (Bing Crosby)

¶ Tchaikovsky, '1812 Overture' (Bournemouth Symphony/Silvestri)

¶ LUXURY: A violin.

¶ BOOK: Charlie Chaplin, *My Autobiography*

12 November 1968
944 Sir Paul Gore-Booth
Head of the Diplomatic Service

¶ Bach, 'Sheep May Safely Graze' (Erika Köth/members of the Choir of St Hedwig's Cathedral, Berlin/Berlin Philharmonic/Kempe)

*¶ Mozart, Piano Concerto No. 20 in D minor (K. 466) (Daniel Barenboim *piano and conducting*/English Chamber Orchestra)

¶ Beethoven, Symphony No. 6 in F major (opus 68) (Philharmonia Orchestra/Klemperer)

¶ Verdi, 'Si, pel ciel marmoreo giuro!' (from *Otello*) (Jussi Björling/Robert Merrill/RCA Victor Symphony/Cellini)

¶ Brahms, Violin Concerto in D major (opus 77) (Yehudi Menuhin/Berlin Philharmonic/Kempe)

¶ J. Strauss, *Die Fledermaus* (Act 1 duet) (Anton Dermota/Hilde Gueden/Vienna Philharmonic/Krauss)

¶ 'The Birth of the Blues' (from *One Dam' Thing After Another*) (Edythe Baker *piano*)

¶ Schumann, Piano Concerto in A minor (opus 54) (Sviatoslav Richter/Warsaw National Symphony/Rowicki)

¶ LUXURY: A piano.

¶ BOOKS: Mary Baker Eddy, *Science and Health, with Key to the Scriptures*, and Leo Tolstoy, *War and Peace*

9 December 1968
945 Des Wilson
Director of Shelter, the Campaign for the Homeless

¶ Chopin, Prelude in A major (opus 28) (Vlado Perlemuter *piano*)

¶ 'If I Only Had Time' (John Rowles)

¶ 'My Lodging's in the Cold Ground' (1st Battalion Scots Guards Pipes and Drums)

¶ Inaugural address, 20 January 1961 (John F. Kennedy)

¶ Dylan, 'Blowin' in the Wind' (Bob Dylan)

¶ Shakespeare, 'To Be or Not to Be' (from *Hamlet*) (John Gielgud)

*¶ Brahms, 'Wiegenlied' (opus 49, no. 4) (Alfred Cortot *piano*)

¶ Handel, 'Hallelujah Chorus' (from *Messiah*) (Philharmonia Chorus and Orchestra/Klemperer)

¶ LUXURY: A typewriter and paper.

¶ BOOK: Daniel Defoe, *Robinson Crusoe*

16 December 1968
946 Professor Asa Briggs
Social historian and Vice Chancellor of Sussex University

¶ Walton, *Belshazzar's Feast* (James Milligan/Huddersfield Choral Society/Royal Liverpool Philharmonic/Sargent)

¶ Mozart, 'O Isis und Osiris' (from *The Magic Flute*) (Wilhelm Strienz/Berlin Philharmonic/Beecham)

¶ Scarlatti, Harpsichord Sonata in B flat (L. 500) (Fernando Valenti)

¶ Monteverdi, *L'incoronazione di Poppea* (excerpt) (Magda Laszlo/Richard Lewis/RPO/Pritchard)

¶ Schubert, 'Gute Nacht' (from *Winterreise*) (Dietrich Fischer-Dieskau/Gerald Moore *piano*)

¶ 'Mr Walker' (The Mighty Sparrow)

¶ Shostakovich, Violin Concerto (opus 99) (David Oistrakh/New York Philharmonic/Mitropoulos)

*¶ Beethoven, String Quartet in C sharp minor (opus 131) (Amadeus String Quartet)

¶ LUXURY: The BBC archives from 1945 to 1954.

¶ BOOK: Edward Gibbon, *The History of the Decline and Fall of the Roman Empire*

23 December 1968
947 Arthur Askey
(3rd appearance)
Comedian

¶ Grieg, 'Morning' (from *Peer Gynt Suite No. 1*, opus 46) (Oslo Philharmonic/Grüner-Hegge)

¶ Lerner & Loewe, 'I Could Have Danced All Night' (from *My Fair Lady*) (Julie Andrews/Philippa Bevans)

¶ Borodin, 'Polovtsian Dances' (from *Prince Igor*) (Philharmonia Orchestra/Malko)

¶ 'The Proposal' (from *Band Waggon*) (Arthur Askey/Richard Murdoch)

*¶ Tchaikovsky, 'Romeo and Juliet Fantasy Overture' (Berlin Philharmonic/von Karajan)

¶ Lennon & McCartney, 'All My Loving' (The Beatles)

¶ Rachmaninov, Piano Concerto No. 2 in C minor (Sergei Rachmaninov/Philadelphia Orchestra/Stokowski)

¶ 'If the Whole World Stopped Lovin'' (Val Doonican)

¶ LUXURY: Golf clubs and balls.

¶ BOOK: A golf instruction book.

25 December 1968
948 Rosea Kemp
Radio weather forecaster

¶ 'Jug of Punch' (The Kingston Trio)

¶ Beethoven, Piano Sonata No. 14 in C sharp minor (opus 27, no. 2) (Wilhelm Kempff)

¶ 'Copper Kettle' (Joan Baez)

¶ 'Click Go the Shears' (Burl Ives)

¶ 'How Great Thou Art' (Elaine & Derek)

¶ 'I'm Just an Old-Fashioned Girl' (Eartha Kitt)

*¶ Handel, 'Hallelujah Chorus' (from *Messiah*) (LPO and Chorus/Boult)

¶ Bernstein/Sondheim, 'Something's Coming' (from *West Side Story*) (Richard Beymer)

¶ LUXURY: A four-poster bed.

¶ BOOK: *Enquire Within Upon Everything*

30 December 1968
949 Bob Braithwaite
Olympic clay-pigeon-shooting gold medallist

¶ J. Strauss (sen.), 'Radetzky March' (opus 228) (Vienna Philharmonic/Kempe)

¶ Foster, 'Beautiful Dreamer' (Jim Reeves)

¶ 'Scotland the Brave' (HM Scots Guards Band)

¶ J. Strauss (jun.), 'Dorfschwalben aus Österreich' (Vienna Philharmonic/Boskovsky)

¶ 'Milanollo' (from 'The Coldstream March') (Band of HM Coldstream Guards)

¶ Brahms, 'Wiegenlied' (Rita Streich/Gunther Weissenborn *piano*)

¶ Suppé, *Poet and Peasant* (overture)

*¶ 'Silent Night' (Bing Crosby)
¶ LUXURY: A piano.
¶ BOOK: Sir Winston Churchill, *The Second World War*

6 January 1969
950 Heather Harper
Singer
¶ Tchaikovsky, 'Romeo and Juliet Fantasy Overture' (Vienna Philharmonic/Maazel)
¶ Bach, 'Erbarme Dich, Mein Gott' (from *St Matthew Passion*) (Helen Watts/Philomusica of London/Dart)
¶ R. Strauss, *Der Rosenkavalier* (final trio) (Elisabeth Schwarzkopf/Christa Ludwig/ Teresa Stich-Randall/ Philharmonia Orchestra/von Karajan)
¶ Mahler, Symphony No. 5 in C sharp minor (New York Philharmonic/Bernstein)
¶ Beethoven, 'Praeludium' (from *Missa Solemnis in D major*, opus 123) (NPO/ Klemperer)
*¶ Wagner, 'Brünnhilde, Heilige Braut' (from *Götterdämmerung*) (Wolfgang Windgassen/Vienna Philharmonic/Solti)
¶ Sibelius, 'Valse Triste' (Hallé Orchestra/Barbirolli)
¶ Shakespeare, *As You Like It* (Act 2, Scene 7) (John Gielgud)
¶ LUXURY: Knitting wool and needles.
¶ BOOK: An encyclopaedia.

13 January 1969
951 Alan Pegler
Owner of the Flying Scotsman
¶ 'Stranger on the Shore' (Acker Bilk)
¶ Handel, 'The Arrival of the Queen of Sheba' (from *Solomon*) (Academy of St Martin-in-the-Fields/Marriner)
¶ Gluck, 'What is Life?' (from *Orfeo ed Euridice*) (Kathleen Ferrier/LSO/Sargent)
¶ 'No. 44472 Flying Scotsman' (trackside sounds)
¶ Haydn, Symphony No. 88 in G major (NPO/Klemperer)
*¶ Handel, *Water Music Suite* (Schola Cantorum Basiliensis/ Wenzinger)

¶ Suppé, *Light Cavalry* (overture) (Philharmonia Promenade Orchestra/Krips)
¶ Gilbert & Sullivan, 'When Britain Really Ruled the Waves' (from *Iolanthe*) (Denis Dowling/ Sadler's Wells Orchestra/Faris)
¶ LUXURY: Insect repellent.
¶ BOOK: A. Conan Doyle, *The Complete Sherlock Holmes*

20 January 1969
952 Maurice Jacobson
Adjudicator at music festivals
¶ Bach, 'Magnificat' (Munich Bach Choir and Orchestra)
¶ Ravel, *Daphnis and Chloe Suite No. 2* (Philharmonia Orchestra/Giulini)
¶ Shakespeare/Morley, 'It was a Lover and His Lass' (John Coates/Gerald Moore *piano*)
¶ Stravinsky, *The Rite of Spring* (Paris Conservatoire Orchestra/ Monteux)
¶ Holst, 'Neptune' (from *The Planets*) (members of London Philharmonic Choir/ Philharmonic Promenade Orchestra/Boult)
¶ 'On December 25th' (Orpington Junior Singers)
*¶ Beethoven, Symphony No. 3 in E flat major (opus 55) (RPO/ Beecham)
¶ Stanford, 'The Fairy Lough' (Kathleen Ferrier/Frederick Stone *piano*)
¶ LUXURY: Caviar.
¶ BOOKS: Some paperback detective stories.

27 January 1969
953 Maggie Fitzgibbon
Actress
¶ 'I Won't Dance' (from *Roberta*) (Frank Sinatra/Count Basie Orchestra)
¶ Chopin, Polonaise No. 4 in A (opus 40, no. 1) (Arthur Rubinstein *piano*)
¶ Porter, 'Let's Do It' (from *Paris*) (Noël Coward)
¶ Verdi, 'Ah fors' è lui' (from *La traviata*) (Renata Tebaldi/Santa Cecilia Orchestra, Rome/ Molinari-Pradelli)
¶ Porter, 'Where is the Life that Late I Led?' (from *Kiss Me Kate*) (Alfred Drake)

¶ 'Courtroom Scene' (From *A Man for All Seasons*) (Paul Scofield)
*¶ 'Paddlin' Madelin' Home' (Graham 'Smacka' Fitzgibbon)
¶ Tchaikovsky, 'Romeo and Juliet Fantasy Overture' (Boston Symphony/Münch)
¶ LUXURY: An alabaster cherub.
¶ BOOK: Robert Stroud, *The Birdman of Alcatraz*

3 February 1969
954 Lord David Cecil
Man of letters, biographer, critic and teacher
¶ Schubert, Trio in B flat major (opus 99) (Alfred Cortot *piano*/ Jacques Thibaud *violin*/Pablo Casals *cello*)
¶ Chopin, Sonata No. 3 in B minor (opus 58) (Dinu Lipatti *piano*)
¶ J. Strauss, *Die Fledermaus* (overture) (Vienna Philharmonic/Krauss)
¶ Porter, 'Night and Day' (From *The Gay Divorce*) (Fred Astaire)
¶ Verdi, 'Love Duet' (from *Otello*) (Herva Nelli/Ramon Vinay/NBC Symphony/ Toscanini)
¶ Fauré, 'Clair de lune' (opus 46, no. 2) (Gérard Souzay/ Jacqueline Bonneau *piano*)
¶ Mozart, 'Il mio tesoro' (from *Don Giovanni*) (John McCormack)
*¶ Bach, Brandenburg Concerto No. 5 in D major (BWV 1050) (Yehudi Menuhin *violin*/Bath Festival Chamber Orchestra)
¶ LUXURY: Donatello's great altar in St Anthony's Church, Padua.
¶ BOOK: Leo Tolstoy, *War and Peace*

12 February 1969
955 Hylda Baker
Actress and variety artist
¶ 'Look to the Rainbow' (from film *Finian's Rainbow*) (Petula Clark/Don Francis/Fred Astaire)
*¶ 'Be My Love' (Mario Lanza)
¶ 'All's Going Well, My Lady Montmorency' (Margaret Rutherford/Frankie Howerd)

¶Puccini, 'One Fine Day' (from *Madam Butterfly*) (Maria Callas/Philharmonia Orchestra/Serafin)
¶'Supercalifragilisticexpialidocius' (from film *Mary Poppins*) (Julie Andrews/Dick van Dyke)
¶Jarre, 'Lara's Theme' (from film *Dr Zhivago*) (Los Paraguayos)
¶'This is My Life' (Shirley Bassey)
¶'Give Us a Kiss' (from *Mr and Mrs*) (Hylda Baker)
¶LUXURY: A family photograph album.
¶BOOK: Margaret Mitchell, *Gone with the Wind*

17 February 1969
956 Edward Downes
Opera conductor
¶Gershwin, 'Summertime' (from *Porgy and Bess*) (Leontyne Price/RCA Victor Symphony/Henderson)
¶Bruckner, Symphony No. 7 in E major (Vienna Philharmonic/Solti)
¶Borodin, Symphony No. 2 in B minor (Vienna Philharmonic/Kubelik)
¶Mussorgsky, *Khovanshchina* (prelude) (Cleveland Orchestra/Szell)
¶Debussy, 'La mer' (NPO/Boulez)
*¶'Bailero' (from *Songs of the Auvergne*) (Madeleine Grey)
¶W. B. Yeats, 'The Lake Isle of Innisfree' (W. B. Yeats)
¶Wagner, *Tristan und Isolde* (Act 3 excerpt) (Ludwig Suthaus/Philharmonia Orchestra/Furtwängler)
¶LUXURY: A Chinese language course.
¶BOOK: An encyclopaedia.

24 February 1969
957 Angus Wilson
Novelist and short-story writer
¶'The Blasted Oak' (Nellie Wallace)
¶'My Very Good Friend, the Milkman' (Fats Waller)
¶'Rose of Washington Square' (from film) (Alice Faye)

¶Britten, *The Turn of the Screw* (Act 1 excerpt) (Jennifer Vyvyan/English Opera Group Orchestra/Britten)
¶Weber, *Oberon* (excerpt) (Philharmonia Orchestra/Sawallisch)
*¶Mendelssohn, Symphony No. 4 in A (opus 90) (Boston Symphony/Münch)
¶Handel, 'Why Do the Nations' (from *Messiah*) (John Shirley-Quirk/LSO and Choir/Davis)
¶Mozart, 'Ah, chi mi dice mai' (from *Don Giovanni*) (Elisabeth Schwarzkopf/Philharmonia Orchestra/Giulini)
¶LUXURY: Champagne.
¶BOOK: A volume on mathematical logic.

3 March 1969
958 Zena Skinner
Cookery expert
¶Prokofiev, *Peter and the Wolf* (Peter Ustinov *narrator*/Philharmonia Orchestra/von Karajan)
¶Bath, 'Cornish Rhapsody' (from film *Love Story*) (Harriet Cohen *piano*/LSO/Bath)
¶Ellis, 'This is My Lovely Day' (from *Bless the Bride*) (Georges Guetary/Lizbeth Webb)
¶'April in Portugal' (Mantovani and his Orchestra)
¶Parry/Blake, 'Jerusalem' (Royal Choral Society/Philharmonia Orchestra/Sargent)
¶Novello, 'Coronation Scene and Finale' (from *King's Rhapsody*) (Vanessa Lee/Olive Gilbert)
¶'A Walk in the Black Forest' (Herb Alpert and the Tijuana Brass)
*¶Rodgers & Hammerstein, 'Climb Every Mountain' (from *The Sound of Music*) (Peggy Wood)
¶LUXURY: A tape recorder.
¶BOOK: Sir Winston Churchill, *The Second World War*

10 March 1969
959 Mary Wilson
Wife of the Prime Minister and poet
¶Faber, 'Hark, Hark My Soul' (Wilfrid Brown/Hervey Alan)
¶'Sellenger's Round' (Country Dance Players)
¶Coward, 'I'll See You Again' (from *Bitter Sweet*) (Peggy Wood/George Metaxa)
¶Grétry, 'Air de ballet' (from *Zémire et Azor*) (RPO/Beecham)
¶Purcell, *Te Deum* (James Bowman/King's College Chapel Choir/English Chamber Orchestra/Willcocks)
¶Sibelius, 'The Swan of Tuonela' (Berlin Philharmonic/von Karajan)
¶Shakespeare, *Othello* (Act 1, Scene 3) (Laurence Olivier)
*¶Gounod, *Faust* (final chorus) (Paris Opera Chorus and Orchestra/Cluytens)
¶LUXURY: A make-up set, mirror and comb.
¶BOOK: Emily Brontë, *Wuthering Heights*

17 March 1969
960 L. Marsland Gander
Journalist and radio and television correspondent
¶Robert Johnson, 'Where the Bee Sucks' (from Shakespeare, *The Tempest*) (Leslie French)
¶'Dinah' (Savoy Hotel Orpheans)
¶Chopin, Waltz No. 5 in A flat major (opus 42) (Artur Rubinstein *piano*)
¶Gilbert & Sullivan, 'For the Merriest Fellows are We' (from *The Gondoliers*) (D'Oyly Carte Opera Company/Godfrey)
¶Wagner, 'The Ride of the Valkyries' (from *Die Walküre*) (Philharmonia Orchestra/Sargent)
*¶'English Country Garden' (Jimmie Rodgers)
¶Coward, 'Why Must the Show Go On?' (Noël Coward)
¶Wood (arr.), 'Fantasia on British Sea Songs' (LSO/Wood)
¶LUXURY: An astronomical telescope.
¶BOOK: An encyclopaedia.

24 March 1969
961 Lady Diana Cooper
Writer, actress and leading
figure in Society
¶ 'Au clair de lune' (Yvonne
Printemps)
¶ Beethoven, Symphony No. 5
in C minor (opus 67) (NBC
Symphony/Toscanini)
*¶ Beethoven, 'Wotan Puts
Brünnhilde to Sleep' (from *Die
Walküre*) (Hans Hotter/Vienna
Philharmonic/Solti)
¶ Humperdinck, *The Miracle*
(excerpt) (LSO/Nilson)
¶ Schumann, 'The Two
Grenadiers' (Feodor Chaliapin)
¶ Chopin, *Les Sylphides* (Royal
Opera House Orchestra, Covent
Garden/Sargent)
¶ Granados, 'Andaluza' (*Danzas
espanole*, no. 5) (Artur
Rubinstein *piano*)
¶ Coward, 'Mad Dogs and
Englishmen' (from *Words and
Music*) (Noël Coward)
¶ LUXURY: A bag of pillows, in
which she will attempt to
smuggle her small dog ashore.
¶ BOOKS: Her volumes of
autobiography: *The Rainbow
Comes and Goes, The Light of
Common Day* and *Trumpets from
the Steep*.

31 March 1969
962 Jill Bennett
Actress
¶ Mozart, 'Champagne Aria'
(from *Don Giovanni*) (Eberhard
Wächter/Philharmonia
Orchestra/Giulini)
¶ 'I Left My Heart in San
Francisco' (Tony Bennett)
¶ 'Countdown' (Dave Brubeck
Quartet)
¶ 'Baby Love' (Diana Ross and
the Supremes)
*¶ R. Strauss, *Der Rosenkavalier*
(closing duet) (Christa Ludwig/
Teresa Stich-Randall/
Philharmonia Orchestra/von
Karajan)
¶ 'I'm Going to Sit Right Down
and Write Myself a Letter' (Fats
Waller)
¶ 'Mary from the Dairy' (Max
Miller)

¶ Handel, 'But Oh! What Art
Can Teach' (from *Ode for St
Cecilia's Day*) (Teresa Stich-
Randall/London Chamber
Orchestra/Bernard)
¶ LUXURY: Scent.
¶ BOOK: Anton Chekhov, *The
Three Sisters*

7 April 1969
963 Sir Alec Rose
Round-the-world sailor
¶ German, 'O Peaceful England'
(from *Merrie England*) (Monica
Sinclair)
¶ Tchaikovsky, '1812 Overture'
(Band of HM Coldstream
Guards/LSO/Boult)
¶ Ellis, 'This is My Lovely Day'
(from *Bless the Bride*) (Georges
Guetary/Lizbeth Webb)
¶ 'Greensleeves' (Melachrino
Strings)
¶ 'What a Wonderful World'
(Louis Armstrong)
¶ Parry/Blake, 'Jerusalem'
(Elizabeth Bainbridge/Royal
Choral Society/NPO/Bliss)
¶ Beethoven, Symphony No. 6
in F major (Philharmonia
Orchestra/Klemperer)
*¶ Malotte, 'The Lord's Prayer'
(Eric Rogers Chorale and
Orchestra)
¶ LUXURY: A radio receiver.
¶ BOOK: A history of England.

14 April 1969
964 Hetty King
Music-hall male impersonator
¶ 'Three Coins in the Fountain'
(from film) (Frank Sinatra)
¶ 'The Donkey Serenade' (from
film *Firefly*) (Tony Martin)
¶ 'Love will Find a Way' (from
The Maid of the Mountains)
(José Collins)
¶ Kern & Hammerstein, 'Ol'
Man River' (from *Show Boat*)
(Paul Robeson)
¶ 'That's Life' (Al Read)
¶ Porter, 'Night and Day' (from
The Gay Divorce) (Bing Crosby)
¶ 'All Through the Night'
(Harry Secombe)
¶ 'Give Me the Moonlight'
(Frankie Vaughan)
¶ LUXURY: A talking parrot.
¶ BOOK: A history of the world.

21 April 1969
965 Mary Stewart
Novelist
¶ Bach, 'Sheep May Safely
Graze' (Cyril Smith and Phyllis
Sellick *pianos*)
¶ Mozart, Clarinet Concerto
No. 1 in A major (Gervase de
Peyer/LSO/Maag)
¶ Shakespeare, 'Shall I Compare
Thee to a Summer's Day?'
(Sonnet 18) (John Gielgud)
¶ Tartini, Trio in F major
(David & Igor Oistrakh *violins*/
Hans Pischner *harpsichord*)
¶ 'Blow the Wind Southerly'
(Kathleen Ferrier/Phyllis Spurr
piano)
¶ Brahms, Intermezzo in E flat
major (Clifford Curzon *piano*)
¶ Beethoven, Quartet in B flat
(opus 130) (Amadeus String
Quartet)
*¶ Bach, *St Matthew Passion*
(excerpt) (Ernst Haefliger/
Munich Bach Orchestra/
Richter)
¶ LUXURY: Paper and pencils.
¶ BOOK: An encyclopaedia.

28 April 1969
966 Dr Elsie Hall
Pianist
¶ Scarlatti, Sonata in A major
(L. 391) (Vladimir Horowitz
piano)
¶ Fauré, 'Claire de lune' (opus
46, no. 2) (Gerard Souzay/
Jacqueline Bonneau *piano*)
¶ Beethoven, Violin Concerto in
D (opus 61) (Arthur Grumiaux/
NPO/Galliera)
¶ Brahms, 'Vergebliches
Ständchen' (opus 84, no. 4)
(Elisabeth Schumann/George
Reeves *piano*)
¶ R. Strauss, *Der Rosenkavalier*
(closing duet) (Elisabeth
Schumann/Maria Olszewska/
Vienna Philharmonic/Heger)
¶ Coward, 'I'll See You Again'
(from *Bitter Sweet*) (Noël
Coward)
¶ R. Strauss, 'Ständchen'
(Dietrich Fischer-Dieskau/
Gerald Moore *piano*)
*¶ Brahms, Symphony No. 1 in
C minor (Berlin Philharmonic/
von Karajan)

¶LUXURY: A billiard table, cue and balls.
¶BOOK: Leo Tolstoy, *War and Peace*

5 May 1969
967 Alvar Lidell (2nd appearance)
BBC announcer and newsreader
¶Reznicek, *Donna Diana* (overture) (Vienna Philharmonic/Boskovsky)
¶Chopin, Barcarolle in F sharp minor (opus 60) (Dinu Lipatti *piano*)
¶Beethoven, Symphony No. 3 in E flat major (opus 55) (NBC Symphony/Toscanini)
¶Grieg, 'Jeg Elsker Dig' (opus 5, no. 3) (Kirsten Flagstad/ Edwain McArthur *piano*)
¶Elgar, Cello Concerto in E minor (opus 85) (Jacqueline du Pré/LSO/Barbirolli)
¶Fauré, 'Après un rêve' (Maggie Teyte/George Reeves *piano*)
*¶Schubert, String Quintet in C major (D. 956) (William Pleeth *cello*/Amadeus String Quartet)
¶Brahms, 'Academic Festival Overture' (LPO/Boult)
¶LUXURY: Two packs of playing cards.
¶BOOK: *The Oxford English Dictionary*

12 May 1969
968 Nicolai Gedda
Tenor
¶'First Psalm of David' (Don Cossacks Choir)
¶Verdi, 'Sailors' Song' (from *Un ballo in maschera*) (Beniamino Gigli/Rome Opera House Orchestra/Serafin)
¶Daza, 'Enfermo Estaba Antioco' (Victoria de los Angeles)
¶Puccini, *Turandot* (Act 3 duet) (Birgit Nilsson/Franco Corelli/ Rome Opera House Orchestra/ Molinari-Pradelli)
¶Lehár, *The Merry Widow* (introduction) Philharmonia Orchestra/Matacic)
*¶'A Song to My Son' (Vladimir Troshin)
¶Theodorakis, 'Theme from *Zorba the Greek*' (from film) (soundtrack/Theodorakis)

¶Lennon & McCartney, 'Sergeant Pepper's Lonely Hearts Club Band' (The Beatles)
¶LUXURY: A rubber mattress.
¶BOOK: Fyodor Dostoevsky, *The Brothers Karamazov* and *The Idiot*.

19 May 1969
969 Virginia Wade
Tennis champion
¶Rachmaninov, Piano Concerto No. 2 in C minor (opus 18) (Vladimir Ashkenazy/ Moscow Philharmonic/ Kondrashin)
¶Dylan Thomas, *Under Milk Wood* (extract) (Richard Burton)
¶Bach, Brandenburg Concerto No. 3 in G major (Yehudi Menuhin *violin*/Bath Festival Chamber Orchestra)
¶Brahms, Violin Concerto in D major (opus 77) (Christian Ferras/Berlin Philharmonic/ von Karajan)
¶Berlin, 'Cheek to Cheek' (from film *Top Hat*) (Ella Fitzgerald/Louis Armstrong)
¶Shostakovich, Symphony No. 5 in D minor (opus 47) (LSO/ Previn)
¶'There but for Fortune' (Joan Baez)
*¶Beethoven, Sonata No. 5 in F major (opus 24) (Hephzibah & Yehudi Menuhin *piano and violin*)
¶LUXURY: Writing and sketching materials.
¶BOOK: *Mrs Beeton's Household Management*

26 May 1969
970 Ginger Rogers
Film actress
¶'Tangerine' (Harry James Orchestra)
¶Elgar, 'Salut d'amour' (RPO/ Collingwood)
*¶Tchaikovsky, 'Romeo and Juliet Fantasy Overture' (Boston Symphony/Münch)
¶Gershwin, 'My One and Only Highland Fling' (from film *The Barkleys of Broadway*) (Fred Astaire/Ginger Rogers)
¶Dohnányi, Rhapsody in C major (Eileen Joyce *piano*)

¶Enesco, Rumanian Rhapsody No. 1 (Hollywood Bowl Symphony/Rozsa)
¶Lalo, *Symphonie espagnole* (Yehudi Menuhin *violin*/ Philharmonia Orchestra/ Goossens)
¶'He's Got the Whole World in His Hands' (McHenry Boatwright)
¶LUXURY: Painting equipment.
¶BOOK: Mary Baker Eddy, *Science and Health, with Key to the Scriptures*

2 June 1969
971 Lady Antonia Fraser
Writer
¶Verdi, 'Triumphal March' (from *Aïda*) (Günther Brausinger *organ*)
¶Rossini, 'Serbami ognor si fido' (from *Semiramide*) (Joan Sutherland/Marilyn Horne/ LSO/Bonynge)
¶'La mer' (Charles Trenet)
¶Verdi, 'E lui! Desso!' (from *Don Carlos*) (Tito Gobbi/Mario Filippeschi/Rome Opera House Orchestra/Santini)
¶'A Scottish Soldier' (Andy Stewart)
¶Wagner, 'Immolation Scene' (from *Götterdämmerung*) (Birgit Nilsson/Vienna Philharmonic/ Solti)
¶Brahms, Sonata in F minor (opus 120, no.1) (Gervase de Peyer *clarinet*/Daniel Barenboim *piano*)
*¶Beethoven, Symphony No. 9 in D minor (opus 125) (soloists/ Philharmonia Chorus and Orchestra/Klemperer)
¶LUXURY: A typewriter and paper.
¶BOOK: Virgil's *Aeneid*, in Latin.

9 June 1969
972 Stanford Robinson
Conductor
¶'These Foolish Things' (from *Spread It Abroad*) (Hutch)
¶Rimsky-Korsakov, 'Flight of the Bumble Bee' (from *The Legend of Tsar Saltan*) (orchestra/Eric Robinson)
¶Delius, *A Village Romeo and Juliet* (excerpt) (Lorely Dyer/ RPO/Beecham)

¶Porter, 'Let's Do It' (from *Paris*) (Noël Coward)

¶Shakespeare, *As You Like It* (excerpt) (Vanessa Redgrave/ Keith Michell)

*¶Ravel, *Daphnis and Chloe* (Orchestre de la Suisse Romande/Ansermet)

¶'If Only' (from *Pieces of Eight*) (Kenneth Williams/Fenella Fielding)

¶Massenet, *Manon* (Act 3 duet) (Victoria de los Angeles/Henri Legay/Opéra Comique Chorus and Orchestra, Paris/Monteux)

¶LUXURY: A radio receiver.

¶BOOK: *Grove's Dictionary of Music and Musicians*

16 June 1969
973 John Trevelyan
Film censor

¶Bach, Double Concerto in D minor (BWV 1043) (David & Igor Oistrakh *violins*/RPO/ Goossens)

¶'O Waly Waly' (Kathleen Ferrier/Phyllis Spurr *piano*)

¶Beethoven, String Quartet in C minor (opus 18, no. 4) (Amadeus String Quartet)

¶Handel, 'For unto Us a Child is Born' (from *Messiah*) (Marjorie Thomas/James Milligan/Huddersfield Choral Society/Royal Liverpool Philharmonic/Sargent)

¶'Georgia on My Mind' (Oscar Peterson Trio)

¶Schubert, Quintet in C major (opus 163) (William Pleeth *cello*/ Amadeus String Quartet)

¶'Once in Royal David's City' (King's College Chapel Choir/ Ord)

*¶Brahms, Symphony No. 1 in C minor (opus 68) (Orchestre de la Suisse Romande/Ansermet)

¶LUXURY: A piano.

¶BOOK: An airways timetable.

23 June 1969
974 Evelyn Laye
(2nd appearance)
Actress and singer

¶Delius, 'The Walk to the Paradise Garden' (from *A Village Romeo and Juliet*) (LSO/ Barbirolli)

¶Debussy, 'Clair de lune' (from *Suite bergamasque*) (Benno Moiseiwitsch *piano*)

*¶Coward, 'There are Bad Times Just Around the Corner' (Noël Coward)

¶Mozart, 'Il mio tesoro' (from *Don Giovanni*) (Richard Tauber)

¶Gershwin, Piano Concerto in F (Leonard Pennario/ Pittsburgh Symphony/ Steinberg)

¶'We Shall Fight on the Beaches' (speech in the House of Commons, 4 June 1940) (Sir Winston Churchill)

¶Bach, 'Jesu, Joy of Man's Desiring' (Temple Church Choir/Thalben-Ball)

¶Tchaikovsky, *Swan Lake* (finale) (Vienna Philharmonic/ von Karajan)

¶LUXURY: Cosmetics.

¶BOOK: Alice Bailey, *White Magic*

30 June 1969
975 Kenneth More
(2nd appearance)
Actor

¶J. Strauss, 'Thunder and Lightning Polka' (Vienna Philharmonic/Boskovsky)

¶Lennon & McCartney, 'And I Love Him' (Esther Phillips)

¶Rachmaninov, Piano Concerto No. 2 in C minor (opus 18) (Vladimir Ashkenazy/ Moscow Philharmonic/ Kondrashin)

¶'Passing the Time Away' (from *Max at the Met*) (Max Miller)

¶'I Wish You Love' (Keely Smith)

¶Mendelssohn, *A Midsummer Night's Dream* (opus 21) (RPO/ Kempe)

*¶'All the Way' (Frank Sinatra)

¶Dvořák, Symphony No. 9 in E minor (LSO/Kertesz)

¶LUXURY: A comfortable mattress.

¶BOOK: Edward Gibbon, *The History of the Decline and Fall of the Roman Empire*

7 July 1969
976 Leonard Henry
Comedian

¶Handel, 'Amen Chorus' (from *Messiah*) (RPO and Choir/ Sargent)

¶'The Spinning Wheel' (Rawicz & Landauer *pianos*)

¶'Poor Little Rich Girl' (Judy Garland)

¶'Any Old Iron' (Peter Sellers)

¶Kreisler, 'Polichinelle Serenade' (Fritz Kreisler *violin*)

¶Rimsky-Korsakov, *Scheherazade* (Erich Gruenberg *violin*/LSO/Markevitch)

*¶Delius, 'On Hearing the First Cuckoo in Spring' (RPO/ Beecham)

¶'Look for the Silver Lining' (from *Sally*) (Mario Lanza)

¶LUXURY: A piano.

¶BOOK: A thesaurus.

14 July 1969
977 Vincent Price
Actor

¶Debussy, 'L'île joyeuse' (Walter Gieseking *piano*)

¶Schumann, 'Frauenliebe und Leben' (Kathleen Ferrier/John Newmark *piano*)

¶Beethoven, 'Ich Liebe Dich' (Kirsten Flagstad/Edwin MacArthur *piano*)

¶'Human Rights' (speech) (Franklin D. Roosevelt)

¶Shakespeare, 'Fear No More the Heat o' the Sun' (from *Cymbeline*) (John Gielgud)

*¶'America the Beautiful' (Vincent Price)

¶'Nature Boy' (Nat 'King' Cole)

¶T. S. Eliot, *The Cocktail Party* (excerpt) (Alec Guinness)

¶LUXURY: A double bed.

¶BOOK: Walt Whitman, *Leaves of Grass*

21 July 1969
978 Peter Pears
Tenor

¶Delius, 'Brigg Fair' (LSO/ Toye)

¶Dowland, 'Captain Piper's Galliard' (Julian Bream *lute*)

¶Bach, 'Et In Unum' (from *Mass in B minor*) (Elisabeth Schumann/Margaret Balfour/ LSO/Coates)

¶ Britten, 'Moonlight' (from *Peter Grimes*) (Royal Opera House Orchestra, Covent Garden/Britten)
¶ Schubert, 'Im Dorfe' (from *Winterreise*, D. 911) (Peter Pears/Benjamin Britten *piano*)
¶ Shakespeare, 'Fear No More the Heat o' the Sun' (from *Cymbeline*) (John Gielgud)
¶ Scarlatti, Sonata in E major (L. 23) (George Malcolm *harpsichord*)
¶ 'Solo for Shehnai' (Bismillah Khan *shehnai*)
¶ LUXURY: A bed.
¶ BOOK: Brugermann, *Tropical Plants and Their Cultivation*

28 July 1969
979 Rachael Heyhoe
Captain of women's Test cricket team
¶ Purcell, 'Harm's Our Delight' (from *Dido and Aeneas*) (Patricia Johnson/Ambrosian Singers/English Chamber Orchestra/Barbirolli)
¶ Lennon & McCartney, 'Hey Jude' (The Beatles)
*¶ 'Nursery School' (Joyce Grenfell)
¶ 'Ten Guitars' (Engelbert Humperdinck)
¶ 'Pokarekare Ana' (St Joseph's Maori Girls' Choir, New Zealand)
¶ 'Love is a Many-Splendoured Thing' (from film) (Ray Conniff Orchestra and Chorus)
¶ Dvořák, Symphony No. 9 in E minor (opus 95) (Vienna Symphony/Horenstein)
¶ 'Georgy Girl' (The Seekers)
¶ LUXURY: A ukelele.
¶ BOOK: A book on desert island cookery.

4 August 1969
980 Cyril Harmer
Stamp collector and auctioneer
¶ Lehár, 'Girls were Made to Love and Kiss' (from *Paganini*) (Richard Tauber)
¶ 'Sussex by the Sea' (PC Alexander Morgan/Metropolitan Police Band)
¶ 'Abdul Abulbul Amir' (Frank Crumit)

¶ 'Those Magnificent Men in Their Flying Machines' (from film) (soundtrack/Goodwin)
¶ 'The Auctioneer Song' (Leroy van Dyke)
¶ 'The Lift Girls' Lament' (from *Wait a Minim!*) (Andrew Tracey/Jeremy Taylor/Paul Tracey/Jeanette James)
¶ 'Squid Jiggin' Ground' (Omar Blondahl)
*¶ Tchaikovsky, 'Waltz of the Flowers' (from *The Nutcracker Suite*) (Royal Opera House Orchestra, Covent Garden/Ansermet)
¶ LUXURY: A centrally heated sleeping bag.
¶ BOOK: Sir Winston Churchill, *The Second World War*

11 August 1969
981 Stanley Rubinstein
Lawyer
¶ 'Skye Boat Song' (Shirley Abicair)
¶ Gilbert & Sullivan, 'The Ruler of the Queen's Navy' (from *HMS Pinafore*) (George Baker/Pro Arte Orchestra/Sargent)
¶ Litolff, Piano Concerto (Irene Scharrer/LSO/Wood)
¶ Elgar, Violin Concerto (Albert Sammons/New Queen's Hall Orchestra/Wood)
¶ Mendelssohn, 'Spring Song' (Mark Hamourg *piano*)
¶ Rachmaninov, 'Rhapsody on a Theme of Paganini' (Benno Moiseiwitsch *piano*/Philharmonia Orchestra/Rignold)
¶ Handel, 'Why Do the Nations' (from *Messiah*) (Owen Brannigan/LPO/Boult)
*¶ Wagner, 'Selig, wie die Sonne' (from *Die Meistersinger*) (soloists/Berlin Philharmonic/Kempe)
¶ LUXURY: An album of family photographs.
¶ BOOK: John Skow's *Survey of London* (1598)

18 August 1969
982 Hermione Gingold (2nd appearance)
Actress
¶ R. Strauss, 'Also Sprach Zarathustra' (Berlin Philharmonic/Böhm)
¶ 'What the World Needs Now is Love' (Dionne Warwick)
¶ Britten, 'Young Person's Guide to the Orchestra' (LSO/Britten)
¶ Bach/Hess, 'Jesu, Joy of Man's Desiring' (Myra Hess *piano*)
¶ Lennon & McCartney, 'Eleanor Rigby' (The Beatles)
¶ Prokofiev, Classical Symphony (New York Philharmonic/Bernstein)
¶ Elgar, *Enigma Variations* (no. 7) (Philharmonia Orchestra/Barbirolli)
*¶ Mancini, 'Moon River' (Kate Smith)
¶ LUXURY: A barrel of lipstick.
¶ BOOK: *Mrs Beeton's Household Management*

25 August 1969
983 Olivia Manning
Novelist
¶ 'Romany Violin' (Laszlo Tabor and his Orchestra)
¶ 'She Moved Through the Fair' (John McCormack)
*¶ Sibelius, 'The Swan of Tuonela' (opus 22, no. 2) (Berlin Philharmonic/von Karajan)
¶ Mozart, Clarinet Quintet in A (K. 581) (Thea King/Aeolian String Quartet)
¶ Lennon & McCartney, 'Penny Lane' (The Beatles)
¶ 'Allegro Bouzouki' (George Zambetas)
¶ Gluck, 'Dance of the Blessed Spirits' (from *Orfeo ed Euridice*) (Rome Opera House Orchestra/Monteux)
¶ 'Song of the Plains' (Alexandrov Song and Dance Ensemble)
¶ LUXURY: A clue to buried treasure.
¶ BOOK: D'Arcy Thompson, *Growth and Form*

1 September 1969
984 Des O'Connor
Entertainer
¶'Up, Up and Away' (Mike Sammes Singers)
¶'I Left My Heart in San Francisco' (Tony Bennett)
¶Rodgers & Hammerstein, 'The Sound of Music' (from *The Sound of Music*) (Julie Andrews)
*¶'Caught in the Act' (Victor Borge)
¶'The Man with the Golden Arm' (from film) (Henry Mancini and his Orchestra)
¶'V-E Day Speech' (Sir Winston Churchill)
¶Offenbach, 'Barcarolle' (from *The Tales of Hoffmann*) (Royal Opera House Orchestra, Covent Garden/Solti)
¶'My Way' (Frank Sinatra)
¶LUXURY: Having *The Sporting Life* delivered daily.
¶BOOK: An encyclopaedia.

8 September 1969
985 Robin Day
Television reporter and interviewer
¶'When the Saints Go Marching In' (from film *The Five Pennies*) (Danny Kaye/ Louis Armstrong)
¶Inaugural Address, 20 January 1961 (John F. Kennedy)
¶'Underneath the Arches' (Flanagan & Allen)
¶Rachmaninov, Symphony No. 1 in D minor (opus 13) (Philadelphia Orchestra/ Ormandy)
¶'This was Their Finest Hour' (speech, 18 June 1940) (Sir Winston Churchill)
¶'Hawaiian Wedding Song' (Hawaii Calls Orchestra)
*¶Shakespeare, 'John of Gaunt's Speech' (from *Richard II*) (John Gielgud)
¶'You Made Me Love You' (from film *Broadway Melody of 1938*) (Al Jolson)
¶LUXURY: Champagne.
¶BOOK: *The Oxford Dictionary of Quotations*

13 September 1969
986 Donald Zec
Newspaper columnist
¶Mozart, *Mass in C minor* (K. 317) (Sarrebrück Conservatory Chorus and Orchestra/ Ristenpart)
¶Paganini, Caprice No. 24 (John Williams *guitar*)
¶Mozart, 'Vesperae Solemnes De Confessore' (from *Laudate Dominum*, K. 339) (Maria Stader/RIA Chamber Choir/ Berlin Radio Symphony/ König)
¶Debussy, 'Clair de lune' (from *Suite bergamasque*) (John Ogdon *piano*)
¶Mozart, Divertimento in D major (K. 136) (Vienna Octet)
¶Beethoven, Violin Concerto in D major (opus 61) (Alan Loveday/Royal Danish Orchestra/Hurst)
¶'Misty' (Erroll Garner *piano*)
*¶Brahms, Symphony No. 1 in C minor (opus 68) (Cleveland Orchestra/Szell)
¶LUXURY: An ice-cream machine.
¶BOOK: Ernest Bramah, *The Wallet of Kai Lung*

20 September 1969
987 Sir John Wolfenden
Director and Principal Librarian of the British Museum
*¶Handel, *Water Music Suite No. 1 in F major* (Bath Festival Orchestra/Menuhin)
¶Vivaldi, 'Spring' (from *The Four Seasons*) (Philharmonia Orchestra/Giulini)
¶Wagner, 'The Ride of the Valkyries' (from *Die Walküre*) (Vienna Philharmonic/Solti)
¶Beethoven, Symphony No. 5 in C minor (opus 67) (Vienna Philharmonic/Schmidt-Isserstedt)
¶Schubert, String Quartet in D minor (Amadeus String Quartet)
¶Handel, 'Hallelujah Chorus' (from *Messiah*) (Huddersfield Choral Society/Royal Liverpool Philharmonic/Sargent)
¶Elgar, 'Nimrod' (from *Enigma Variations*) (Philharmonia Orchestra/Sargent)

¶'The Old Hundredth' (from Coronation Service of HM Queen Elizabeth II)
¶LUXURY: A tape recorder.
¶BOOK: Leo Tolstoy, *War and Peace*

27 September 1969
988 Cliff Morgan
Rugby player and broadcaster
¶'Big Spender' (from *Sweet Charity*) (Shirley Bassey)
¶'Si Lwli, Lwli' (Meredydd Evans/Maria Korchinska *harp*)
*¶'Westminster' (narration with sound effects) (Hywel Davies)
¶Mendelssohn, 'Is Not His Word Like a Fire?' (from *Elijah*) (Geraint Evans/BBC Welsh Orchestra/Thomas)
¶Sibelius, *Karelia Suite* (opus 11) (Danish State Radio Symphony/Jensen)
¶'Autumn Leaves' (Erroll Garner *piano*)
¶'These Foolish Things' (from *Spread It Abroad*) (Nat 'King' Cole)
¶'A Nation Sings' (6500 Welsh voices in the Royal Albert Hall)
¶LUXURY: A piano.
¶BOOK: A teach-yourself encyclopaedia.

4 October 1969
989 Thea Holme
Actress and writer
¶Gay, 'Were I Laid on Greenland's Coast' (from *The Beggar's Opera*) (Sylvia Nelis/ Frederick Ranalow)
¶Scarlatti, Sonata in D major (Rudolph Dolmetsch *harpsichord*)
¶Delius, 'Serenade' (from *Hassan*) (RPO/Beecham)
¶Handel, 'I Know that My Redeemer Liveth' (from *Messiah*) (Jennifer Vyvyan/ RPO/Beecham)
*¶Mozart, Quintet in A major for Clarinet and Strings (K. 581) (Gervase de Peyer/ Melos Ensemble)
¶Debussy, 'La fille aux cheveux de lin' (*Prélude*, Book 1, No. 8) (Walter Gieseking *piano*)
¶George Bernard Shaw, *Saint Joan* (excerpt) (Barbara Jefford/ Alec McCowen)

¶Handel, 'Bourrée' and 'Hornpipe' (from *Water Music Suite*) (Boyd Neel Orchestra)
¶LUXURY: Writing and painting materials.
¶BOOK: The works of Beatrix Potter.

11 October 1969
990 Henry Williamson
Writer
¶Delius, 'Cynara' (John Shirley-Quirk/Royal Liverpool Philharmonic/Groves)
¶Vaughan Williams, 'Fantasia on a Theme by Thomas Tallis' (Sinfonia of London/Barbirolli)
¶Debussy, 'La mer' (Orchestre de la Suisse Romande/Ansermet)
¶Ravel, *Daphnis and Chloe* (RPO/Prêtre)
¶Holst, 'Mars' (from *The Planets*) (NPO/Boult)
¶Stravinsky, 'Le rossignol' (French National Radio Orchestra/Cluytens)
¶Rachmaninov, 'Rhapsody on a Theme of Paganini' (Sergei Rachmaninov *piano*/Philadelphia Orchestra/Ormandy)
*¶Wagner, *Tristan und Isolde* (excerpt from Act 3) (Vienna Philharmonic/Solti)
¶LUXURY: A cor anglais.
¶BOOK: Richard Jefferies, *The Story of My Heart*

18 October 1969
991 Max Adrian
Actor
¶Bach, Brandenburg Concerto No. 5 in D major (BWV 1050) (Munich Bach Orchestra/Richter)
¶Dohnányi, 'Variations on a Nursery Theme' (opus 25) (Julius Katchen *piano*/LPO/Boult)
¶Schubert, Piano Quintet in A major (Clifford Curzon/members of Vienna Octet)
¶Handel, 'O Thou That Tellest Good Tidings to Zion' (from *Messiah*) (Kathleen Ferrier/LPO/Boult)
¶Handel, 'Silent Worship' (from *Ptolemy*) (John Heddle Nash/Gerald Moore *piano*)

*¶Mozart, *Eine Kleine Nachtmusik* (K. 525) (Vienna Philharmonic/Kertesz)
¶Rachmaninov, 'To the Children' (John McCormack/Edwin Schneider *piano*)
¶Delius, 'The Walk to the Paradise Garden' (from *A Village Romeo and Juliet*) (LSO/Barbirolli)
¶LUXURY: Tapestry-making materials.
¶BOOK: Blank pages, and pencils.

25 October 1969
992 Raymond Mays
Ex-racing driver and builder of racing cars
¶'Roses of Picardy' (Fred Emney)
*¶'Love Will Find a Way' (from *The Maid of the Mountains*) (José Collins)
¶'I Love the Moon' (Russ Conway)
¶Arlen & Harburg, 'Over the Rainbow' (from film *The Wizard of Oz*) (Judy Garland)
¶Novello, 'I Can Give You the Starlight' (from *The Dancing Years*) (Mary Ellis)
¶Borodin/Wright & Forrest (arr.), 'Stranger in Paradise' (from *Kismet*) (Doretta Morrow/Richard Kiley)
¶'Tea for Two' (from *No, No, Nanette*) (Binnie Hale)
¶Lehár, *The Merry Widow* (duet) (June Bronhill/Thomas Round/Sadler's Wells Opera Company and Orchestra/Reid)
¶LUXURY: An umbrella.
¶BOOK: W. MacQueen Pope, *Gaiety, Theatre of Enchantment*

1 November 1969
993 Anthony Grey
Foreign correspondent
¶'Exodus' (Edith Piaf)
¶Tchaikovsky, Piano Concerto No. 1 in B flat minor (Sviatoslav Richter/Leningrad Philharmonic/Mravinsky)
¶Lennon & McCartney, 'She's Leaving Home' (The Beatles)
¶'The East is Red' (brass band)
¶'The Art Gallery' (Peter Cook/Dudley Moore)

¶Elgar, 'Nimrod' (from *Enigma Variations*) (Philharmonia Orchestra/Barbirolli)
*¶Handel, Concerto Grosso in C major (Philomusica of London/Jones)
¶'My Way' (Frank Sinatra)
¶LUXURY: The book stall in Victoria Station.
¶BOOK: A dictionary.

8 November 1969
994 Evelyn Rothwell
Oboist
*¶Schubert, Trio No. 1 in B flat (opus 99) (Alfred Cortot *piano*/Jacques Thibaud *violin*/Pablo Casals *cello*)
¶Lehár, 'You are My Heart's Delight' (from *The Land of Smiles*) (Richard Tauber)
¶Mozart, *Così fan tutte* (overture) (Glyndebourne Festival Opera Orchestra/Busch)
¶Bach, Brandenburg Concerto No. 1 in F major (BWV 1046) (Adolf Busch Chamber Orchestra)
¶Kreisler, 'Liebeslied' (Fritz Kreisler *violin*/Franz Rupp *piano*)
¶Vaughan Williams, 'Fantasia on a Theme by Thomas Tallis' (Sinfonia of London/Barbirolli)
¶Brahms, Symphony No. 3 in F major (opus 90) (Vienna Philharmonic/Barbirolli)
¶Verdi, *Otello* (closing passage) (James McCracken/NPO/Barbirolli)
¶LUXURY: Writing materials.
¶BOOK: An encyclopaedia.

15 November 1969
995 Dudley Moore
Comedian, composer, pianist and actor
¶Bach, *Mass in B minor* (BWV 232) (Maria Stader/Hertha Töpper/Munich Bach Orchestra/Richter)
¶'Spinning Wheel' (Blood, Sweat and Tears)
¶Mahler, 'Nun seh' ich wohl warum so dunkle Flammen' (from *Kindertotenlieder*) (Kathleen Ferrier/Vienna Philharmonic/Walter)

¶ 'Little Miss Britten' (from *Beyond the Fringe*) (Dudley Moore)

¶ 'Diminuendo and Crescendo in Blue' (Duke Ellington and his Orchestra)

¶ Webern, Bagatelles for String Quartet (Pro Arte Quartet)

¶ 'Lilian Lust' (from *Bedazzled*) (Dudley Moore)

*¶ Beethoven, Symphony No. 3 in E flat major (opus 55) (Philharmonia Orchestra/Klemperer)

¶ LUXURY: A piano.

¶ BOOK: A study of psychology.

22 November 1969
996 Irmgard Seefried
Soprano

¶ Beethoven, Piano Concerto No. 5 in E flat major (opus 73) (Edwin Fischer/Philharmonia Orchestra/Furtwängler)

¶ Chopin, Waltz No. 11 in G flat major (opus 70, no. 1) (Artur Rubinstein *piano*)

¶ Mozart, 'The Letter Duet' (from *The Marriage of Figaro*) (Elisabeth Schwarzkopf/Irmgard Seefried/Vienna Philharmonic/von Karajan)

¶ Bruckner, Symphony No. 4 (Philharmonia Orchestra/Klemperer)

*¶ Beethoven, Violin Concerto in D major (opus 61) (Wolfgang Schneiderhan/Berlin Philharmonic/van Kempen)

¶ R. Strauss, 'The Presentation of the Silver Rose' (from *Der Rosenkavalier*) (Rita Streich/Irmgard Seefried/Saxon State Orchestra/Böhm)

¶ Schumann, 'Tragödie III' (with text by Heine spoken simultaneously) (Irmgard Seefried/Oskar Werner *narrator*/Erik Werba *piano*)

¶ R. Strauss, *Ariadne auf Naxos* (excerpt) (Vienna State Opera/Böhm)

¶ LUXURY: A string of pearls.

¶ BOOK: *Herr, Hier Bin Ich (Prayers of Life)*

29 November 1969
997 Lilian Board
Athlete

*¶ Theodorakis, 'Theme from *Zorba the Greek*' (from film) (soundtrack/Theodorakis)

¶ Simon, 'A Poem on the Underground Wall' (Simon & Garfunkel)

¶ 'When I Fall in Love' (Nat 'King' Cole)

¶ 'Guantanamera' (The Sandpipers)

¶ Paxton, 'The Last Thing on My Mind' (Tom Paxton)

¶ Williams, 'Classical Gas' (Mason Williams)

¶ 'Without Her' (Jack Jones)

¶ Mitchell, 'Both Sides Now' (Judy Collins)

¶ LUXURY: A bed.

¶ BOOK: A family photograph album.

6 December 1969
998 Godfrey Baseley
Countryman

¶ 'Jesu, Lover of My Soul' (Treorchy Male Choir)

¶ Wagner, 'The Ride of the Valkyries' (from *Die Walküre*) (Philharmonia Orchestra/Klemperer)

¶ 'Close Your Eyes' (Al Bowlly/Lew Stone and his Band)

¶ Clarke, 'Trumpet Voluntary' (Harry Mortimer/Reginald Foort *organ*/London Brass Players/Weldon)

¶ Debussy, 'Clair de lune' (from *Suite bergamasque*) (Walter Gieseking *piano*)

¶ Gilbert & Sullivan, *The Pirates of Penzance* (excerpt) (Owen Brannigan/Glyndebourne Festival Chorus/Pro Arte Orchestra/Sargent)

¶ 'Georgy Girl' (The Seekers)

*¶ 'Barwick Green' (signature tune of *The Archers*) (Sidney Torch and his Orchestra)

¶ LUXURY: A bed.

¶ BOOK: *Royal Horticultural Society Dictionary*

13 December 1969
999 Moira Anderson
Singer

¶ Wagner, *Lohengrin* (Act 3 prelude) (Philharmonia Orchestra/Klemperer)

¶ 'By Cool Siloam's Shady Rill' (Kirkintilloch Junior Choir)

¶ Mozart, Piano Concerto No. 23 in A major (K. 488) (Annie Fischer/Philharmonia Orchestra/Boult)

¶ 'Cambeltown Loch' (Andy Stewart)

*¶ 'Dr Macleod's Fancy' (John Ellis/Highland Country Dance Band)

¶ Mozart, 'Ave Verum Corpus' (K. 618) (Vienna Boys' Choir/Vienna Chorus/Vienna Cathedral Orchestra/Ferdinand Grossman)

¶ Zeller, 'Rosenlied' (from *Der Volgelhändler*) (Elisabeth Schwarzkopf)

¶ Elgar, Introduction and Allegro for String Orchestra (opus 47) (LPO/Boult)

¶ LUXURY: A bathroom suite.

¶ BOOK: Robert Baden-Powell, *Scouting for Boys*

20 December 1969
1000 Viscount Montgomery of Alamein
Field Marshal

¶ Howe, 'Battle Hymn of the Republic' (Mormon Tabernacle Choir/Philadelphia Orchestra/Ormandy)

¶ 'My Love is Like a Red, Red Rose' (Kenneth McKellar)

¶ Lehár, 'You are My Heart's Delight' (from *The Land of Smiles*) (Richard Tauber)

¶ Weber, 'Invitation to the Dance' (opus 65) (Vienna Philharmonic/Boskovsky)

*¶ Zeller, 'Sei Nicht Bös' (from *Der Obersteiger*) (Elisabeth Schwarzkopf)

¶ 'All Through the Night' (Treorchy Male Choir)

¶ 'Cockles and Mussels' (William Clauson)

¶ Mendelssohn, 'Oh, for the Wings of a Dove' (Alastair Roberts/St John's College Choir, Cambridge/Guest)
¶ LUXURY: A piano.
¶ BOOK: His own book, *The History of Warfare*.

27 December 1969
1001 Tommy Steele (2nd appearance)
Actor and singer
¶ 'London Fantasia' (Clive Richardson *piano*/Columbia Light Symphony/Williams)
¶ 'The Cat from Coos Bay' (Big Dave and his Orchestra)
¶ 'Foggy Mountain Breakdown' (Lester Flatt/Earl Scruggs)
*¶ 'World Cup Final 1966' (summing-up by Peter Lloyd/ 'Geevers' Wynne Jones/Jeff Ewer)
¶ Tchaikovsky, '1812 Overture' (opus 49) (LSO/HM Grenadier Guards Band/Alwyn)
¶ 'A Guy is a Guy' (Doris Day/ Paul Weston's Chorus and Orchestra)
¶ R. Strauss, 'Also Sprach Zarathustra' (Berlin Philharmonic/Böhm)
¶ 'River Deep, Mountain High' (Ike & Tina Turner)
¶ LUXURY: A sports car.
¶ BOOK: *Dictionary of Word and Phrase*

3 January 1970
1002 Fyfe Robertson
Writer and television reporter
¶ Handel, 'Since by Man Came Death' (from *Messiah*) (Huddersfield Choral Society/ Royal Liverpool Philharmonic/ Sargent)
¶ Bach, Suite No. 3 in D major (BWV 1068) (Marlboro Festival Orchestra/Casals)
¶ Borodin, 'Polovtsian Dances' (from *Prince Igor*) (Leeds Festival Choir/LPO/Beecham)
¶ Dvořák, Cello Concerto in B minor (opus 104) (Mstislav Rostropovich/Berlin Philharmonic/von Karajan)
¶ Lennon & McCartney, 'Come Together' (The Beatles)
*¶ Handel, 'Sound an Alarm' (from *Judas Maccabaeus*) (Richard Lewis/LSO/Sargent)

¶ Mozart, *The Magic Flute* (overture) (Philharmonia Orchestra/Klemperer)
¶ Monteverdi, 'Seneca's Death' (from *L'incoronazione di Poppea*) (Carlo Cava/RPO/ Pritchard)
¶ LUXURY: A cello.
¶ BOOK: Korzibsky's *General Semantics*

10 January 1970
1003 Leonard Sachs
Actor
¶ Mozart, Piano Quartet in E flat major (K. 493) (Yehudi Menuhin *violin*/Walter Gerhardt *viola*/Gaspar Cassado *cello*/Fou Ts'ong *piano*)
¶ Debussy, 'The Little Shepherd' (from *Children's Corner*) (Peter Frankl *piano*)
¶ Schubert, 'Gretchen am Spinnrade' (opus 2) (Kathleen Ferrier/Phyllis Spurr *piano*)
¶ 'Go Down Moses' (Paul Robeson)
¶ Porter, 'Begin the Beguine' (from *Jubilee*) (Grand Popular Orchestra of the Americas)
*¶ 'What More is There to Say?' (from *The Golden Gate*) (Eleanor Summerfield)
¶ 'Boum!' (Charles Trenet)
¶ Arlen & Harburg, 'The Yellow Brick Road' (from film *The Wizard of Oz*) (Judy Garland)
¶ LUXURY: A radio receiver.
¶ BOOK: Charles Dickens, *David Copperfield*

17 January 1970
1004 Val Doonican
Singer and entertainer
¶ Bach, 'Bourrée II' (from *English Suite No. 2*) (Swingle Singers)
¶ Vaughan Williams, 'Fantasia on a Theme by Thomas Tallis' (Sinfonia of London/Barbirolli)
¶ 'Four-o-Thirty-Three' (George Jones)
¶ Castelnuovo-Tedesco, Concerto in D for Guitar and Orchestra (opus 99) (John Williams/Philadelphia Orchestra/Ormandy)

¶ Rodgers & Hammerstein, 'People Will Say We're in Love' (from *Oklahoma*) (Erroll Garner *piano*)
¶ Dvořák, Symphony No. 8 in G major (opus 88) (Vienna Philharmonic/von Karajan)
*¶ 'Scarborough Fair' (Simon & Garfunkel)
¶ 'As Praias Desertas' (Charlie Byrd *guitar* with Strings, Brass and Woodwinds)
¶ LUXURIES: A guitar, with music manuscript paper and pencils.
¶ BOOK: A big anthology.

24 January 1970
1005 Professor A. S. C. Ross
Professor of linguistics
¶ Bach, Prelude No. 24 in B minor (Rosalyn Tureck *piano*)
¶ Schumann, Symphony No. 4 in D minor (opus 120) (Vienna Philharmonic/Solti)
*¶ Brahms, Variations on a Theme by Haydn (opus 56a) (St. Antoni Chorale) (Philharmonia Orchestra/ Klemperer)
¶ 'A Walk in the Black Forest' (Horst Jankowski *piano* and his Orchestra)
¶ D. Scarlatti, Sonata in G minor (K. 30) (The Cat's Fugue) (Varda Nishry *piano*)
¶ Sibelius, 'The Fool's Song' (from Incidental Music to King Christian II) (Waino Sola/ Orchestra)
¶ Wagner, 'The Prize Song' (from *Die Meistersinger*) (Sándor Kónya/Berlin Philharmonic/ Krauss)
¶ Chopin, Sonata No. 3 in B minor (opus 58) (Dinu Lipatti *piano*)
¶ LUXURY: A television.
¶ BOOK: Whitaker & Watson, *A Course of Modern Analysis*

31 January 1970
1006 Stanley Baxter
Actor and comedian
¶ Delius, 'La calinda' (from *Koanga*) (Hallé Orchestra/ Lambert)
¶ 'Serenata' (Sarah Vaughan)
¶ 'How About You?' (Frank Sinatra)

¶ 'Sweet Georgie Fame' (Blossom Dearie)
¶ 'Where is She?' (from *Phil the Fluter*) (Mark Wynter)
¶ Borodin, 'Polovtsian Dances' (from *Prince Igor*) (Philharmonia Orchestra/von Karajan)
*¶ 'San Francisco' (from film) (Judy Garland)
¶ 'Belle of the Ball' (Mantovani and his Orchestra)
¶ LUXURY: The Koh-i-noor diamond.
¶ BOOK: Louis de Rouvroy, Duc de Saint-Simon, *Memoirs*

7 February 1970
1007 Isidore Godfrey
Conductor
*¶ Franck, Symphony in D minor (Philadelphia Orchestra/ Ormandy)
¶ Scriabin, Poème de l'extase (USSR Symphony/Svetlanov)
¶ Grieg, Piano Concerto in A minor (Arthur de Greef/Royal Albert Hall Orchestra/Ronald)
¶ Gilbert & Sullivan, 'When a Wooer Goes A-Wooing' (from *The Yeomen of the Guard*) (D'Oyly Carte Opera Company/ Godfrey)
¶ Elgar, Violin Concerto in B minor (opus 61) (Yehudi Menuhin/LSO/Elgar)
¶ Gilbert & Sullivan, 'Sir Roderick's Song' (from *Ruddigore*) (Donald Adams/ Royal Opera House Orchestra, Covent Garden/Godfrey)
¶ Schubert, Symphony No. 9 in C (Great) (Hallé Orchestra/ Barbirolli)
¶ Gilbert & Sullivan, 'Hail, Poetry' (from *The Pirates of Penzance*) (D'Oyly Carte Opera Chorus/RPO/Godfrey)
¶ LUXURY: A piano.
¶ BOOK: The scores of the Tchaikovsky symphonies.

14 February 1970
1008 Frank Gillard
BBC war correspondent and administrator
¶ 'Michael Row the Boat Ashore' (George Mitchell Minstrels)
¶ Templeton, 'Bach Goes to Town' (George Malcolm *harpsichord*)
¶ Ravel, String Quartet in F major (Drolc Quartet)
¶ Gay, 'Let Us Take the Road' (from *The Beggar's Opera*) (William McAlpine/Argo Chamber Ensemble/Austin)
*¶ Gerhard, Concerto for Orchestra (BBC Symphony/del Mar)
¶ Vaughan Williams, 'Fantasia on a Theme by Thomas Tallis' (Sinfonia of London/Barbirolli)
¶ Berlioz, Symphonie fantastique (Paris Orchestra/ Münch)
¶ Arne, 'Rule Britannia' (from *Alfred*) (Royal Choral Society/ Philharmonia Orchestra/ Sargent)
¶ LUXURY: A set of lenses.
¶ BOOK: A naturalist's guide.

21 February 1970
1009 Richard Church
Poet, novelist and essayist
¶ Monteverdi, *Mass for Four Voices* (1640) (St John's College Choir, Cambridge/Guest)
*¶ Bach, Prelude No. 1 in C major (from *The Well-Tempered Clavier, Book 1*) (Martin Galling *harpsichord*)
¶ Gluck, 'Che faro' (from *Orfeo ed Euridice*) (Kathleen Ferrier/ Southern Philharmonic/ Stiedry)
¶ Berlioz, 'Harold in the Mountains' (from *Harold in Italy*) (Walter Trampler *viola*/ LSO/Prêtre)
¶ Chopin, Barcarolle in F sharp (opus 60) (Vladimir Ashkenazy *piano*)
¶ Dvořák, 'O Lovely Moon' (from *Rusalka*) (Joan Hammond/Philharmonia Orchestra/Tausky)
¶ Vaughan Williams, 'The Lark Ascending' (Hugh Bean *violin*/ NPO/Boult)

¶ Britten, *Peter Grimes* (interlude before Act 3) (Royal Opera House Orchestra, Covent Garden/Britten)
¶ LUXURY: Writing materials.
¶ BOOK: *The Oxford English Dictionary*

28 February 1970
1010 Isobel Baillie (2nd appearance)
Singer
¶ Chopin, Piano Concerto No. 2 in F minor (André Watts/New York Philharmonic/Schippers)
¶ Brahms, Symphony No. 4 in E minor (opus 98) (Philharmonic Promenade Orchestra/Boult)
¶ Shakespeare, 'St Crispin's Day Speech' (from *Henry V*) (Laurence Olivier)
*¶ Handel, 'Worthy is the Lamb' (from *Messiah*) (Huddersfield Choral Society/Royal Liverpool Philharmonic/Sargent)
¶ Purcell, The Blessed Virgin's Expostulation (Tell me, some pitying Angel) (Isobel Baillie/ Arnold Goldsbrough *organ*)
¶ Vautor, 'Sweet Suffolk Owl' (madrigal) (Isobel Baillie/ Margaret Field-Hyde/Gladys Winmill/René Soames/Keith Falkner/Ord)
¶ Elgar, 'Take Me Away' (from *The Dream of Gerontius*) (John Heddle Nash)
¶ Hedgcock, 'Sleep My Saviour, Sleep' (Isobel Baillie/Muriel Brunskill/John Heddle Nash/ Norman Allin/String Orchestra)
¶ LUXURY: A guitar.
¶ BOOK: Cornelia Otis Skinner, *Our Hearts were Young and Gay*

7 March 1970
1011 Dr Roy Strong
Director of the National Portrait Gallery
¶ Novello, 'Rose of England' (from *Crest of the Wave*) (Edgar Elmes/Drury Lane Theatre Chorus and Orchestra/Prentice)
¶ Tchaikovsky, *The Sleeping Beauty* (Orchestre de la Suisse Romande/Ansermet)
¶ 'The Laziest Girl in Town' (from film *Stage Fright*) (Marlene Dietrich)

¶Bull, 'Queen Elizabeth's Pavane' (Thurston Dart *harpsichord*)

*¶Ellen Terry, recalled by Sybil Thorndike

¶Purcell, 'How Blest are Shepherds' (from *King Arthur*) (St Anthony Singers/Lewis)

¶Verdi, 'Ascolta! Le porte dell'asil' (from *Don Carlos*) (Carlo Bergonzi/Dietrich Fischer-Dieskau/Royal Opera House Orchestra, Covent Garden/Solti)

¶'For All the Saints' (Rodney Christian Fellowship Festival Choir)

¶LUXURY: Vermeer's *View of Delft*

¶BOOK: *Larousse gastronomique*

14 March 1970
1012 Richard Chamberlain
Actor

*¶Vivaldi, 'Winter' (from *The Four Seasons*) (Virtuosi di Roma/Fasano)

¶'A Call from Long Island' (from *You Don't Have to be Jewish*) (Betty Walker/Arlene Golonka)

¶Mitchell, 'Both Sides Now' (Joni Mitchell)

¶Mozart, Symphony No. 40 in G minor (K. 550) (Berlin Radio Symphony/Maazel)

¶'Ghetto' (Delaney & Bonnie)

¶Bach, 'Sanctus' (from *Mass in B minor*) (BBC Chorus/NPO/Klemperer)

¶'Dear Mary' (Steve Miller Band)

¶Dylan Thomas, 'Fern Hill' (Dylan Thomas)

¶LUXURY: Painting equipment.

¶BOOK: *The Oxford Book of English Verse*

21 March 1970
1013 Judy Hashman
World badminton singles champion

¶Gilbert & Sullivan, 'Three Little Maids from School' (from *The Mikado*) (Jean Hindmarsh/Beryl Dixon/Jennifer Toye/NPO/Godfrey)

¶Romberg, 'Serenade' (from *The Student Prince*) (Mario Lanza)

¶Rodgers & Hammerstein, 'Edelweiss' (from *The Sound of Music*) (Julie Andrews/Christopher Plummer/children)

¶'Whither Thou Goest' (Perry Como)

¶'Madeira, M'Dear' (from *At the Drop of a Hat*) (Michael Flanders/Donald Swann)

¶'O Little Town of Bethlehem' (Mormon Tabernacle Choir/New York Philharmonic/Bernstein)

¶'The Bowery Grenadiers' (Mitch Miller and his Orchestra)

*¶Lerner & Loewe, 'Camelot' (from *Camelot*) (Richard Burton)

¶LUXURY: A stamp album.

¶BOOK: An anthology of medieval English prose and verse.

28 March 1970
1014 Nyree Dawn Porter
Actress

¶'Aquarius' (from *Hair*) (Ronald Dyson/company)

¶Debussy, 'La plus que lente' (Peter Frankl *piano*)

¶'Irene' (Nana Mouskouri/Harry Belafonte)

¶Beethoven, Sonata No. 8 in C minor (opus 13) (Pathétique) (Stephen Bishop *piano*)

¶'Lilacs Out of the Dead Land' (Manos Hadjidakis)

*¶John Aubrey, *Brief Lives* (excerpt) (Roy Dotrice)

¶Debussy, Prelude No. 8, Book 1 (La fille aux cheveux de lin) (Peter Frankl *piano*)

¶'Let the Sunshine In' (from *Hair*) (Paul Nicholas/Annabel Leventen/Marsha Hunt/tribe)

¶LUXURY: An umbrella.

¶BOOK: James Thurber, *The Thurber Carnival*

4 April 1970
1015 Sheridan Russell
Cellist and medical social worker

*¶Bach, Brandenburg Concerto No. 4 in G major (BWV 1049) (Bush Chamber Players/Busch)

¶Stravinsky, Symphony of Psalms (choirs/Suisse Romande Orchestra/Ansermet)

¶Brahms, Sextet No. 2 in G for Strings (opus 36) (Jascha Heifetz and Israel Baker *violins*/William Primrose and Virginia Majewski *violas*/Gregor Piatigorsky and Gabor Rejto *cellos*)

¶Schubert, String Quintet in C (D. 956) (Isaac Stern and Alexander Schneider *violins*/Milton Katims *viola*/Pablo Casals and Paul Tortelier *cellos*)

¶Bach, Suite No. 3 in C major (BWV 1009) (Pablo Casals *cello*)

¶Fauré, 'Après un rêve' (Pablo Casals *cello*/Nicolai Mednikov *piano*)

¶Beethoven, Piano Trio in D (opus 70, no. 1) (Geister) (Trio Santoliquido)

¶Mozart, Oboe Quartet in F (K. 370) (Léon Goossens/Léner Quartet)

¶LUXURY: A cello.

¶BOOK: Thomas à Kempis, *Imitation of Christ*

11 April 1970
1016 Deryck Guyler
Character actor

*¶'Crooked Blues' (King Oliver's Creole Jazz Band)

¶'Barnyard Blues' (Original Dixieland Jazz Band)

¶Porter, 'Miss Otis Regrets' (Mills Brothers)

¶'Home Again' (from *ITMA*) (Tommy Handley/Deryck Guyler)

¶'September Song' (from *September Affair*) (Walter Huston)

¶Bach, 'Aria' (from Suite No. 3 for Orchestra) (Jacques Loussier Trio)

¶'Jimmy's Blues' (Original New Orleans All Stars)

¶'We Shall Overcome' (Pete Seeger)

¶LUXURY: A Roman legionary's helmet in the British Museum.

¶BOOK: *Hannibal*, by Colonel Dodge, in series 'Great Captains of the Past.'

18 April 1970
1017 James Lockhart
Music Director of the Welsh
National Opera Company
¶ Wagner, 'Wotan's Farewell'
(from *Die Walküre*) (Ferdinand
Frantz/Vienna Philharmonic/
Furtwängler)
¶ Mozart, Quintet in G minor
for Strings (K. 516) (Amadeus
String Quartet/Cecil Aronowitz
viola)
¶ Brahms, Symphony No. 1 in
C minor (opus 68) (Columbia
Symphony/Walter)
¶ R. Strauss, *Der Rosenkavalier*
(final duet) (Sena Jurinac/Hilde
Gueden/Vienna Philharmonic/
Kleiber)
*¶ Verdi, 'Triumphal March'
(from *Aida*) (NBC Symphony/
Toscanini)
¶ 'Number Twelve Train' (Josh
White)
¶ Beethoven, Sonata No. 29 in B
flat major (opus 106)
(Hammerklavier) (Artur
Schnabel *piano*)
¶ Elgar, 'The Sun Goes Down'
(from *The Kingdom*, opus 51)
(Margaret Price/LPO/Boult)
¶ LUXURY: A piano.
¶ BOOK: The works of John
Donne.

25 April 1970
1018 Sir Gavin de Beer
Scientist
¶ Pierné, 'Entry of the Little
Fauns' (from *Cydalise and the
Satyr*) (Pro Arte Orchestra/
Vinter)
¶ Debussy, 'La Mer' (Orchestre
de la Suisse Romande/
Ansermet)
*¶ Villa-Lobos, Bachianas
Brasileiras No. 5 (Bidú Sayão/8
cellos/Villa-Lobos)
¶ Rachmaninov, Piano
Concerto No. 2 in C minor
(opus 18) (Sviatoslav Richter/
Warsaw National
Philharmonic/Wislocki)
¶ Delius, 'Serenade' (from
Hassan) (RPO/Beecham)
¶ Falla, *The Three-Cornered Hat*
(Orchestre de la Suisse
Romande/Ansermet)

¶ Mussorgsky, 'Farewell, and
Death of Boris' (from *Boris
Godunov*) (Feodor Chaliapin)
¶ Wagner, 'Ride of the
Valkyries' (from *Die Walküre*)
(Vienna Philharmonic/Solti)
¶ LUXURY: A typewriter.
¶ BOOK: Cecil Taur, *Small Talk
at Wrayland*

2 May 1970
1019 Gina Cigna
Opera singer
¶ Purcell, 'When I am Laid in
Earth' (from *Dido and Aeneas*)
(Janet Baker/English Chamber
Orchestra/Lewis)
¶ Monteverdi, *L'Orfeo*
(prologue) (Maria Duchenc/
Berlin Radio Chamber
Orchestra/Koch)
*¶ Beethoven, Symphony No. 9
in D minor (opus 125) (Robert
Shaw Chorale/NBC Symphony/
Toscanini)
¶ Vivaldi, 'Gloria' (Friederike
Sailer/Pro Musica Choir and
Orchestra, Stuttgart/Couraud)
¶ Wagner, 'Forest Murmurs'
(from *Siegfried*) (Berlin
Philharmonic/von Karajan)
¶ Gershwin, 'Summertime'
(from *Porgy and Bess*)
(Leontyne Price/RCA Victor
Symphony/Henderson)
¶ Dukas, 'The Sorcerer's
Apprentice' (Israel
Philharmonic/Solti)
¶ Ravel, 'Bolero' (LSO/
Monteux)
¶ LUXURY: A piano.
¶ BOOK: Anatole France, *Le
crime de Sylvestre Bonnard*

9 May 1970
1020 Carol Channing
Actress and singer
*¶ 'Sometimes I Feel Like a
Motherless Child' (Marian
Anderson)
¶ 'Heartbreak Hotel' (Elvis
Presley)
¶ 'Civil War' (from *Beyond the
Fringe*) (Alan Bennett/Peter
Cook/Jonathan Miller/Dudley
Moore)
¶ 'Born on the Bayou'
(Creedence Clearwater Revival)

¶ Mussorgsky/Rimsky-
Korsakov, 'Night on the Bare
Mountain' (LSO/Stokowski)
¶ 'Moanin' Low' (from *The First
Little Show*) (Libby Holman)
¶ 'Ma pomme' (Maurice
Chevalier)
¶ Styne, 'Rose's Turn' (from
Gypsy) (Ethel Merman)
¶ LUXURY: Writing and painting
materials.
¶ BOOK: Konstantin
Stanislavsky, *My Life in Art*

16 May 1970
1021 Graham Usher
Ballet dancer
¶ Rubinstein, Romance in E flat
(Capitol Symphony/Dragon)
¶ R. Strauss, *Salome* (closing
passage) (Birgit Nilsson/Vienna
Philharmonic/Solti)
*¶ 'Fly Me to the Moon'
(Discotheque Orchestra)
¶ Franck, Symphonic
Variations (Moura Lympany
piano/RPO/Silvestri)
¶ Oscar Wilde, 'Lady Bracknell
Interviews John Worthing'
(from *The Importance of Being
Earnest*, Act 1) (John Gielgud/
Edith Evans)
¶ Puccini, *Tosca* (Act 1 duet)
(Leontyne Price/Giuseppe di
Stefano/Vienna Philharmonic/
von Karajan)
¶ Hérold, arranged Lanchbery,
La fille mal gardée (Royal Opera
House Orchestra, Covent
Garden/Lanchbery)
¶ 'Hello Dolly' (from *Hello
Dolly*) (Carol Channing)
¶ LUXURY: *The Nike of
Samothrace (Winged Victory)*, in
the Louvre.
¶ BOOK: The works of Beatrix
Potter.

23 May 1970
1022 Andy Stewart
Scottish entertainer
¶ Mozart, *The Magic Flute*
(overture) (Hallé Orchestra/
Barbirolli)
¶ 'The Birth of the Blues' (from
film) (Frank Sinatra)
¶ 'Torna a Sorrento' (Beniamino
Gigli)
¶ Mendelssohn, Violin Concerto
in E minor (Fritz Kreisler/
LPO/Ronald)

¶ Rodgers & Hammerstein, 'If I Loved You' (from *Carousel*) (Gordon Macrae)
¶ 'When I Fall in Love' (Nat 'King' Cole)
¶ Mozart, Porgi amor (from *The Marriage of Figaro*) (Joan Hammond/Hallé Orchestra/ Heward)
*¶ Crimond, 'The Twenty-Third Psalm' (Glasgow Orpheus Choir/Roberton)
¶ LUXURY: Writing materials.
¶ BOOK: The works of Robert Burns, together with a biography of him.

30 May 1970
1023 Keith Michell
Actor, singer and painter
¶ Paganini, Caprice No. 24 (John Williams *guitar*)
¶ Menotti, To this we've come (from *The Consul*) (Patricia Neway/Orchestra/Engel)
¶ Rodrigo, Concierto de Aranjuez (Laurindo Almeida *guitar*/Modern Jazz Quartet)
¶ Stravinsky, *Oedipus Rex* (Cologne Radio Symphony and Chorus/Stravinsky)
¶ Bach, Toccata (from Toccata, Adagio and Fugue for Organ in C (BWV 564) (Jacques Loussier Trio)
¶ Gesualdo, Madrigal for Five Voices (from Book 5) (vocal ensemble/Denis Stevens)
¶ Ravel, *Daphnis and Chloe* (Royal Opera House Chorus, Covent Garden/LSO/Monteux)
*¶ Bach, Brandenburg Concerto No. 4 in G major (BWV 1049) (Pro Arte Chamber Orchestra, Munich/Redel)
¶ LUXURY: Painting equipment.
¶ BOOK: The *I Ching*

6 June 1970
1024 Monica Dickens
(2nd appearance)
Novelist
¶ Clarke, 'Trumpet Voluntary' (Nicholas Danby *organ*)
¶ 'Scarborough Fair' (Simon & Garfunkel)
¶ Mozart, Bassoon Concerto in B flat (K 191) (George Zukerman/Württemberg Chamber Orchestra/Fäerber)

¶ Ellis, 'This is My Lovely Day (from *Bless the Bride*) (Georges Guetary/Lizbeth Webb)
¶ 'A Visit to America' (Dylan Thomas)
¶ 'Plaisir d'amour' (Suzi Delair)
¶ Bach, 'Sleepers Wake' (Cantata No. 140) (St Thomas's Church Choir, Leipzig/ Mauersberger)
¶ 'Far, Far from Wipers' (from film *Oh, What a Lovely War*) (Richard Howard)
¶ LUXURY: Writing materials.
¶ BOOK: *Roget's Thesaurus* (*No favourite disc chosen.*)

13 June 1970
1025 Barbara Windsor
Actress and comedienne
¶ Beethoven, 'Für Elise' (Wilhelm Kempff *piano*)
¶ 'Do It Again' (from *Mayfair and Montmartre*) (Judy Garland)
¶ 'The Best is Yet to Come' (Frank Sinatra/Count Basie)
*¶ Norman, 'Fings Ain't Wot They Used to Be' (from *Fings Ain't Wot They Used to Be*) (original cast of Theatre Workshop production)
¶ 'Not an Asp' (from *Pieces of Eight*) (Kenneth Williams/Peter Brett)
¶ 'Every Little Movement Has a Meaning of Its Own' (Marie Lloyd)
¶ Wagner, *Götterdämmerung* (excerpt) (Gottlob Frick/Vienna Philharmonic/Solti)
¶ 'Après l'amour' (Charles Aznavour)
¶ LUXURY: Hair pieces.
¶ BOOK: A history of Great Britain.

20 June 1970
1026 Ida Haendel
Violinist
*¶ Brahms, Symphor.y No. 4 (Berlin Philharmonic/ Furtwängler)
¶ Puccini, 'Che gelida manina' (from *La bohème*) (Beniamino Gigli)
¶ Wieniawski, Violin Concerto in D minor (Ida Haendel/ Prague Symphony/Smetacek)
¶ 'Kol Nidrei' (Richard Tucker)
¶ Beethoven, Trio No. 3 in D minor (Isaac Stern Trio)

¶ Brahms, Violin Concerto (Ida Haendel/LSO/Celibidache)
¶ 'There's a Hole in the Bucket' (Harry Belafonte/Odetta)
¶ Enesco, Sonata No. 3 (George Enesco *violin*/Dinu Lipatti *piano*)
¶ LUXURY: Writing materials.
¶ BOOK: A survival manual.

27 June 1970
1027 Vidal Sassoon
'A barber for women'
¶ 'Diminuendo and Crescendo in Blue' (Duke Ellington and his Orchestra)
*¶ Sibelius, Symphony No. 2 in D (Philharmonia Orchestra/von Karajan)
¶ 'Respect' (Aretha Franklin)
¶ Mozart, Piano Concerto No. 21 in C (K. 467) (Daniel Barenboim *piano and conducting*/English Chamber Orchestra)
¶ Delerue, 'Black Orpheus' (from film) (Georges Delerue and his Orchestra)
¶ Mascagni, *Cavalleria rusticana* (excerpt) (Franco Corelli/Rome Opera House Orchestra and Chorus/Santini)
¶ 'Laila Laila' (Topol)
¶ 'Walk on By' (Isaac Hayes)
¶ LUXURY: A piece of sculpture by Baracal.
¶ BOOK: Blank paper, pens and a thesaurus.

4 July 1970
1028 Robin Knox-Johnston
Solo round-the-world yachtsman
¶ 'Swinging Safari' (Bert Kaempfert and his Orchestra)
¶ Gilbert & Sullivan, 'A Wand'ring Minstrel I' (from *The Mikado*) (Philip Potter/ D'Oyly Carte Opera Chorus/ RPO/Sargent)
¶ Beethoven, Symphony No. 5 in C minor (opus 67) (Philharmonia Orchestra/ Klemperer)
¶ 'Stranger on the Shore' (Acker Bilk *clarinet*/Leon Young String Chorale)

¶Gilbert & Sullivan, 'Tan-Tan-Ta-Ra' (from *The Pirates of Penzance*) (D'Oyly Carte Opera Company/RPO/Godfrey)
¶Lennon & McCartney, 'All You Need is Love' (The Beatles)
¶Bach, 'Jesu, Joy of Man's Desiring' (from Cantata No. 147) (Temple Church Choir/Thalben-Ball *organ*)
*¶Elgar, 'Land of Hope and Glory' (from *Coronation Ode*) (RAF Central Band)
¶LUXURY: Writing materials.
¶BOOK: H. G. Wells, *The Outline of History, Being a Plain History of Life and Mankind*

11 July 1970
1029 Barbara Cartland
Novelist, journalist, biographer and campaigner
*¶'April in Paris' (from *Walk a Little Faster*) (Frank Sinatra)
¶Lerner & Loewe, 'Say a Prayer for Me Tonight' (from film *Gigi*) (Leslie Caron)
¶'Harrow School Song' (from *Forty Years On*) (West End cast)
¶'I'm in Love' (Mrs Gerald Legge – daughter of Barbara Cartland)
¶Rodgers & Hammerstein, 'Climb Every Mountain' (from *The Sound of Music*) (Sammy Davis Jnr)
¶'Keep Young and Beautiful' (Roy Fox and his Orchestra)
¶'If You are but a Dream' (Frank Sinatra)
¶'If I Ruled the World' (from *Pickwick*) (Harry Secombe)
¶LUXURY: Make-up.
¶BOOK: Barbara Cartland, *The Knave of Hearts*

18 July 1970
1030 John Piper
Artist
*¶Mozart, Sinfonia Concertante in E flat major (K. 364) (Norbert Brainin *violin*/Peter Schidlof *viola*/Netherlands Chamber Orchestra/Zinman)
¶Stravinsky, *Apollon Musagète* (Academy of St Martin-in-the-Fields/Marriner)

¶Gershwin, 'I'd Rather Charleston' (from *Lady be Good*) (Fred & Adele Astaire)
¶Britten, *The Turn of the Screw* (excerpt) (David Hemmings/Olive Dyer/Peter Pears/Arda Mandikian/English Opera Group Orchestra/Britten)
¶Mozart, *Don Giovanni* (opening of Act 1) (Giuseppe Taddei/Philharmonia Orchestra/Giulini)
¶Debussy, Etude No. 12 (Pour les accords) (Charles Rosen *piano*)
¶'A Cottage for Sale' (Earl Hines Trio)
¶Schubert, Octet in F major (Melos Ensemble)
¶LUXURY: A pillow.
¶BOOK: James Joyce, *Ulysses*

25 July 1970
1031 Joan Hammond (2nd appearance)
Singer
¶Puccini, 'Entrance of Butterfly' (from *Madam Butterfly*) (Joan Hammond/Philharmonia Orchestra/Susskind)
*¶Saint-Saëns, Piano Concerto No. 5 in F (Jeanne Marie Darré/French National Radio Orchestra/Fourestier)
¶Massenet, 'Meditation' (from *Thaïs*) (Roger Anbre *violin*/Bernard Galais *harp*/Paris Opera Orchestra/Dervaux)
¶Hagemann, 'At the Well' (Joan Hammond/Ivor Newton *piano*)
¶Rachmaninov, Piano Concerto No. 2 in C minor (Julius Katchen/LSO/Solti)
¶Beethoven, Symphony No. 6 in F major (Pastoral) (Amsterdam Concertgebouw/Sawallisch)
¶Puccini, 'O mio babbino caro' (from *Gianni Schicchi*) (Joan Hammond/Hallé Orchestra/Heward)
¶Elgar, 'Pomp and Circumstance' March No. 1 in D major (LSO/Sargent)
¶LUXURY: A toothbrush.
¶BOOK: *The Oxford English Dictionary*

1 August 1970
1032 Terry-Thomas (2nd appearance)
Actor and comedian
*¶'Honeysuckle Rose' (Django Reinhardt *guitar*/Stephane Grappelli *violin*/Quintet of the Hot Club of France)
¶Rodgers & Hart, 'Where or When?' (from *Babes in Arms*) (Hutch)
¶Schubert, 'Heidenröslein' (Richard Tauber/Percy Kahn *piano*)
¶Granados, Spanish Dance No. 5, in E minor (Andaluza) (Andrés Segovia *guitar*)
¶Sarasate, Spanish Dance No. 6 (Zapateado) (Antonio *dancer*/Symphony Orchestra/Currás)
¶'Alice is at It Again' (Noël Coward)
¶'A New-Fangled Tango' (Lena Horne)
¶Chopin/Sargent, 'Mazurka' (from Ballet *Les sylphides*) (Royal Opera House Orchestra, Covent Garden/Sargent)
¶LUXURY: Brandy.
¶BOOK: Terry-Thomas, *Filling the Gap*

8 August 1970
1033 David Davis
Broadcaster for children
*¶Mozart, Horn Concerto No. 4 in E flat (K. 495) (Dennis Brain/Philharmonia Orchestra/von Karajan)
¶Kreisler, 'Liebeslied' (Sergei Rachmaninov *piano*)
¶Elgar, *The Music Makers* (LPO and Choir/Boult)
¶Walton, Symphony No. 1 (NPO/Sargent)
¶Delius, 'Brigg Fair' (RPO/Beecham)
¶Trad. arranged Canteloube, 'L'Aio de Rotso' (from *Songs of the Auvergne*) (Netania Davrath/Orchestra/de la Roche)
¶Quilter, 'Go Lovely Rose' (Hubert Eisdell)
¶Coward, 'The Party's Over Now' (from *Words and Music*) (Noël Coward)
¶LUXURY: Pipes and tobacco.
¶BOOK: Sir Thomas Browne, *Religio Medici*

15 August 1970
1034 Erich Leinsdorf
Conductor

¶ Bach, Partita in C minor (BWV 826) (Wanda Landowska *harpsichord*)

¶ Beethoven, Quartet No. 7 in F (opus 59, no. 1) (Rasoumovsky) (Amadeus String Quartet)

¶ Schönberg, Quartet No. 2 in F sharp minor (Juilliard String Quartet)

¶ Mozart, String Quintet in G minor (K. 516) (Heinz-Otto Graf *viola*/Heutling String Quartet)

¶ Bach, Brandenburg Concerto No. 6 in B flat major (BWV 1051) (Württemberg Chamber Orchestra/Fäerber)

¶ Beethoven, Quartet No. 12 in E flat major (opus 127) (Hungarian Quartet)

¶ Schubert, 'The Linden Tree' (Richard Tauber)

¶ Bach, Prelude and Fugue in E flat (BWV 552) (St. Anne) (Helmut Walcha *organ*)

¶ LUXURY: Insect repellent.

¶ BOOK: Goethe's *Faust*

22 August 1970
1035 Freya Stark
Explorer, traveller and writer

¶ Chopin, Nocturne No. 1 in G minor (opus 37) (Artur Rubinstein *piano*)

¶ Chopin, Fantasie-Impromptu in C sharp minor (Artur Rubinstein *piano*)

¶ Beethoven, Sonata No. 14 in C sharp minor (opus 27, no. 2) (Moonlight) (Artur Schnabel *piano*)

¶ Beethoven, Sonata No. 23 in F minor (opus 57) (Appassionata) (Artur Schnabel *piano*)

¶ Mozart, 'Pamina's Aria' (from *The Magic Flute*, Act 2) (Gundula Janowitz/ Philharmonia Orchestra and chorus/Klemperer)

¶ Debussy, *Prélude à l'après-midi d'un faune* (NPO/Boulez)

¶ Verdi, *Falstaff* (excerpt) Rosalind Elias/Ilva Ligabue/ Giulietta Simionato/Mirella Freni/RCA Italiana Opera Orchestra/Solti)

*¶ 'Agnus Dei' (Choir of Benedictine Abbey of St Martin, Beuron)

¶ LUXURY: A bath with a hot water system.

¶ BOOK: *Encyclopaedia Britannica* (1911 edition).

29 August 1970
1036 Dick Emery
Comedian

¶ Flotow, 'M'appari tutt'amor' (from *Marta*) (Enrico Caruso)

¶ Gardiner, 'Shepherd Fennel's Dance' (New Symphony Orchestra/Collins)

*¶ 'Love was Young' (Robert Goulet)

¶ Lennon & McCartney, 'And I Love Her' (Boston Pops Orchestra/Fiedler)

¶ 'It was a Very Good Year' (Frank Sinatra)

¶ 'The Reading of the Will' (from *You Don't Have to be Jewish*) (Jack Gilford/Lou Jacobi/company)

¶ Puccini, 'E lucevan le stelle' (from *Tosca*) (Beniamino Gigli)

¶ Impressions of Humphrey Bogart, James Cagney and James Stewart (Sammy Davis Jnr)

¶ LUXURY: A bed.

¶ BOOK: Charles Dickens, *A Christmas Carol*

5 September 1970
1037 Ellen Pollock
Actress

¶ 'Scarborough Fair' (Simon & Garfunkel)

¶ Bach/Stokowski, Toccata and Fugue in D minor (Stokowski Symphony)

¶ 'Cinderella Rockefella' (Esther & Abi Ofarim)

*¶ Beethoven, Symphony No. 3 in E flat major (Eroica) (Boston Symphony/Leinsdorf)

¶ 'People' (from *Funny Girl*) (Barbra Streisand)

¶ Brahms, 'Weigenlied' (opus 49, no. 4) (Lotte Lehmann)

¶ 'Everybody's Talking' (from film *Midnight Cowboy*) (Nilsson)

¶ Liszt, 'Le Grand Galop Chromatique' (György Cziffra *piano*)

¶ LUXURY: A painting by her husband, James Gunn, of their son Michael.

¶ BOOK: The plays of George Bernard Shaw.

12 September 1970
1038 Helen Watts
Contralto

¶ Bach, 'Et Ressurexit' (from *Mass in B minor*) (Munich Bach Choir and Orchestra/Richter)

¶ Mahler, Symphony No. 3 in D minor (LSO/Solti)

¶ Bach, Double Concerto in D minor (BWV 1043) (Igor & David Oistrakh *violins*/RPO/ Goossens)

*¶ Bach, 'Betracht Meine Seel'' (from *St John Passion*) (Max Van Egmond/Concentus Musicus, Vienna/Gillesberger)

¶ Delius, 'Idyll' (Heather Harper/John Shirley-Quirk/ RPO/Davies)

¶ Stravinsky, *The Rite of Spring* (Orchestre de la Suisse Romande/Ansermet)

¶ Berlioz, *Béatrice et Bénédict* (duet) (Helen Watts/April Cantelo/LSO/Colin Davis)

¶ Handel, *Zadok the Priest* (from Coronation Service of HM Queen Elizabeth II)

¶ LUXURY: Velásquez, *The Maids of Honour*, in the Prado.

¶ BOOK: An illustrated book on gardening.

19 September 1970
1039 Sir Alan (A. P.) Herbert (2nd appearance)
Poet, playwright, novelist and politician

¶ Offenbach, 'O God of Love' (from *La belle Hélène*) (Columbia Light Opera Company)

¶ Lehár, 'Girls were Made to Love and Kiss' (from *Paganini*) (Richard Tauber)

¶ Puccini, *La bohème* (end of Act 1) (Renata Tebaldi/Giacinto Prandelli/Santa Cecilia Orchestra, Rome/Erede)

¶ 'A Nice Cup of Tea in the Morning' (from *Home and Beauty*) (Binnie Hale)

¶ Arne, 'Rule Britannia' (from *Alfred*) (Royal Choral Society/ Philharmonia Orchestra/ Sargent)

*¶ Davies, 'Solemn Melody' (Temple Church Choir/ Thalben-Ball *organ*)

¶Wagner, 'The Prize Song' (from *Die Meistersinger*) (Walter Widdop/orchestra/Sargent)
¶Ellis/Herbert 'England is a Lovely Place' (from *Tough at the Top*) (Maria D'Attili/George Tozzi)
¶LUXURY: A pair of field glasses.
¶BOOKS: His favourite novels by Charles Dickens.

26 September 1970
1040 Harry Carpenter
Boxing commentator
¶Chabrier, 'España' (RPO/Beecham)
¶'The Elements' (Tom Lehrer)
¶'O Come, All Ye Faithful' (King's College Chapel Choir/Willcocks)
¶'One for My Baby' (Frank Sinatra)
¶Bach, Brandenburg Concerto No. 5 in D major (BWV 1050) (Berlin Philharmonic/von Karajan)
¶Puccini, *Tosca* (Act 3 duet) (Maria Callas/Giuseppe di Stefano/La Scala Orchestra, Milan/de Sabata)
¶Elgar, 'Pomp and Circumstance' March No. 1 in D major (LSO/Sargent)
*¶Beethoven, Symphony No. 9 in D minor (opus 125) (Berlin Philharmonic/von Karajan)
¶LUXURY: A guitar.
¶BOOK: *Encyclopaedia Britannica*

3 October 1970
1041 Carrie Tubb
Soprano
¶Wagner, *Götterdämmerung* (closing scene) (Kirsten Flagstad/Philharmonia Orchestra/Furtwängler)
¶Wagner, 'Liebestod' (from *Tristan und Isolde*) (Frida Lieder)
¶Handel, 'And the Glory of the Lord' (from *Messiah*) (1926 Handel Festival Choir and Orchestra/Wood)
¶Puccini, 'In questa reggia' (from *Turandot*) (Eva Turner/Orchestra/Stanford Robinson)
*¶Delius, 'The Walk to the Paradise Garden' (from *A Village Romeo and Juliet*) (Hallé Orchestra/Barbirolli)

¶'Blow the Wind Southerly' (Kathleen Ferrier)
¶Monckton, 'The Dancing Lesson' (from The Quaker Girl) (Carrie Tubb)
¶R. Strauss, *Der Rosenkavalier* (final trio) (Lotte Lehmann/Elisabeth Schumann/Maria Olszewska/Vienna Philharmonic/Heger)
¶LUXURY: A parasol.
¶BOOK: *The Oxford Dictionary of Quotations*

10 October 1970
1042 Lynn Redgrave
Actress
¶'Once in Royal David's City' (King's College Chapel Choir/Ord)
¶Loesser, 'A Bushel and a Peck' (from *Guys and Dolls*) (Vivian Blaine)
¶Vivaldi, 'Spring' (from *The Four Seasons*) (Virtuosi di Roma/Fasano)
¶'If You're Going to San Francisco' (Petula Clark)
¶Delerue, 'Brouillard' (from film *Jules et Jim*) (George Delerue and His Orchestra)
¶Medley of songs (Noël Coward)
*¶Lennon & McCartney, 'Penny Lane' (The Beatles)
¶R. Strauss, 'Also Sprach Zarathustra' (Berlin Philharmonic/Böhm)
¶LUXURY: An excerpt from the BBC recording of *Just William* (John Clark/Tony Stockman).
¶BOOK: Penelope Mortimer, *The Pumpkin Eater*

17 October 1970
1043 Sari Barabas
Opera and operetta singer
¶Bach, Toccata and Fugue in D minor (BWV 565) (Nicholas Danby *organ*)
¶Kreisler, 'Liebesfreud' (Henryk Szeryng *violin*)
¶J. Strauss, *Die Fledermaus* (Excerpt) (Sari Barabas/Anneliese Rothenberger/Rudolf Schock/Horst Günther/Herman Prey/Gustav Neidlinger/chorus/North West German Radio Symphony/Schüchter)

*¶R. Strauss, 'The Singer's Aria' from *Der Rosenkavalier*) (Franz Klarwein/Munich State Opera Orchestra/Krauss)
¶Rossini, *Le Comte Ory* (Act 2 excerpt) (Sari Barabas/Monica Sinclair/Juan Oncina/Dermot Troy/Michel Roux/Ian Wallace/Glyndebourne Festival Orchestra and Chorus/Gui)
¶Rubinstein, 'Melody in F' (Jack Byfield and his Orchestra)
¶'Blue Gardenia' (Nat 'King' Cole)
¶J. Strauss/Tiomkin (arr.), 'Tales from the Vienna Woods' (from film *The Great Waltz*) (Sari Barabas/Walter Cassell)
¶LUXURY: Knitting needles and wool.
¶BOOKS: The books of Leo Slezak.

24 October 1970
1044 John Lill
Pianist
¶Beethoven, Violin Concerto in D major (Jascha Heifetz/NBC Symphony/Toscanini)
¶Mozart, Sonata in B flat major (K. 570) (Emil Gilels *piano*)
¶Brahms, Piano Concerto in D minor (Claudio Arrau/Philharmonia Orchestra/Giulini)
¶'Tales of Old Dartmoor' (The Goons)
¶J. Strauss, 'The Blue Danube' (Josef Lhévinne *piano*)
¶Elgar, Cello Concerto in E minor (Jacqueline du Pré/LSO/Barbirolli)
¶Prokofiev, Symphony No. 6 in E flat minor (Moscow Radio Symphony/Rozhdestvensky)
*¶Beethoven, Symphony No. 9 in D minor (opus 125) (NBC Symphony/Toscanini)
¶LUXURY: A piano
¶BOOK: *Modern Chess Openings*

31 October 1970
1045 Joan Whittington
Red Cross worker
¶J. Strauss, 'The Blue Danube' (Vienna Philharmonic/Boskovsky)
¶Dylan, 'Blowin' in the Wind' (The Seekers)

176

¶ Schubert, Symphony No. 8 in B minor (Unfinished) (Vienna Philharmonic/Münchinger)
¶ 'Lilli Marlene' (Vera Lynn)
¶ 'Yellow Bird' (Lord Busta and the Caribbean Royals)
¶ Gilbert & Sullivan, 'Taken from the County Jail' (from *The Mikado*) (Martyn Green/D'Oyly Carte Opera Company/Godfrey)
¶ Bach/Gounod, 'Ave Maria' (Gracie Fields)
*¶ Elgar, 'Pomp and Circumstance' March No. 1 in D Major (from the last night of the 1969 Proms) (BBC Symphony/Colin Davis)
¶ LUXURY: A radio receiver.
¶ BOOK: A law study course.

7 November 1970
1046 Vilem Tausky
Conductor
¶ Brahms, Piano Concerto No. 2 in B flat (Vladimir Horowitz/NBC Symphony/Toscanini)
¶ Bruckner, Symphony No. 9 in D minor (Berlin Philharmonic/von Karajan)
¶ Mussorgsky, 'I Have Attained the Highest Power' (from *Boris Godunov*) (Feodor Chaliapin)
¶ Fall, 'Madame Pompadour's Waltz' (from *Madame Pompadour*) (Margit Schramm)
¶ Shakespeare, 'John of Gaunt's Speech' (from *Richard II*) (Leo McKern)
¶ Britten, *Albert Herring* (excerpt) (April Cantelo/Sheila Amit/Anne Pashley/Stephen Terry/English Chamber Orchestra/Britten)
*¶ Janáček, *Glagolitic Mass* (Czech Philharmonic Orchestra and Chorus/Ančerl)
¶ Boulez, 'Pli selon pli' (BBC Symphony/Boulez)
¶ LUXURY: A watch.
¶ BOOK: An encyclopaedia.

14 November 1970
1047 Margaret Powell
Writer and broadcaster from 'below stairs'
*¶ Verdi, 'Sempre libera' (from *La traviata*) (Amelita Galli Curci)
¶ Verdi, 'Anvil Chorus' (from *Il trovatore*) (La Scala Chorus and Orchestra Milan/Serafin)
¶ Weber, 'Invitation to the Dance' (Philadelphia Orchestra/Stokowski)
¶ 'Valencia' (Edmundo Ros and his Orchestra)
¶ Offenbach, *Orpheus in the Underworld* (overture) (Sadler's Wells Theatre Orchestra/Faris)
¶ 'Solitude' (Paul Robeson)
¶ Halvorsen, 'Entry of the Boyards' (Boston Promenade Orchestra/Fiedler)
¶ Bach, Suite No. 3 in D major (BWV 1068) (Nathan Milstein *violin*/Leon Pommers *piano*)
¶ LUXURY: A Tahitian language course.
¶ BOOK: Edward Gibbon, *The History of the Decline and Fall of the Roman Empire*

21 November 1970
1048 David Hughes (2nd appearance)
Singer
¶ Bizet, *Carmen* (prelude) (Paris Opera Orchestra/Prêtre)
¶ Godard, 'Angels Guard Thee' (from *Jocelyn*) (John McCormack/Fritz Kreisler *violin*/Vincent O'Brien *piano*)
¶ 'Suo-Gân' (traditional Welsh song) (Philharmonia Orchestra/Weldon)
¶ Mozart, 'Placido è il mar' (from *Idomeneo*) (Glyndebourne Festival Orchestra and Chorus/Pritchard)
¶ Massenet, *Werther* (Act 3 excerpt) (Tito Schipa)
¶ R. Strauss, *Der Rosenkavalier* (final trio) (Elisabeth Schwarzkopf/Teresa Stich-Randall/Christa Ludwig/Philharmonia Orchestra/von Karajan)
¶ Verdi, *Otello* (excerpt) (James McCracken/Gwyneth Jones/NPO/Barbirolli)

*¶ Verdi, *Requiem* (excerpt) (NPO and Chorus/Barbirolli)
¶ LUXURY: Golf clubs and balls.
¶ BOOK: Henry Thoreau, *Walden*

28 November 1970
1049 Diana Rigg
Actress
¶ Albinoni/Giazotto, Adagio in G minor (Eduard Kaufmann *organ*/Lucerne Festival Strings/Baumgartner)
¶ 'In a Silent Way' (Miles Davis *trumpet*/Ensemble)
¶ Wolf-Ferrari, *The Jewels of the Madonna* (intermezzo) (Philharmonia Orchestra/Mackerras)
¶ Mozart, Concerto in C for Flute and Harp (K. 299) (Hubert Barwahser *flute*/Osian Ellis *harp*/LSO/Colin Davis)
¶ 'At a Secret Beach' (Laikes Ensemble/Theodorakis)
¶ Nielsen, Symphony No. 5 (NPO/Horenstein)
¶ 'What a Wonderful World' (Louis Armstrong)
*¶ Satie, 'Trois gymnopédies' (Aldo Ciccolini *piano*)
¶ LUXURY: Vegetable garden from Stratford-upon-Avon.
¶ BOOK: Primary instruction in all languages.

5 December 1970
1050 Wally Herbert
Polar explorer
*¶ Vivaldi, 'Spring' (from *The Four Seasons*) (Ruggiero Ricci *violin* and *directing* the Stradivarius Chamber Orchestra)
¶ 'Brownskin Sugarplum' (Blind Boy Fuller)
¶ Mozart, Piano Concerto No. 20 in D minor (K. 466) (Clara Haskil/Lamoureux Orchestra/Markevitch)
¶ Bach, Concerto in D minor for Violin, Oboe and Strings (BWV 1060) (Otto Buchner *violin*/Edgar Shann *oboe*/Munich Bach Orchestra/Münchinger)
¶ 'Besame Mucho' (Los Paraguayos)
¶ Bach, 'Bourrée' (from *English Suite No. 2*) (Swingle Singers)

¶Brahms, Symphony No. 4 in E minor (opus 98) Berlin Philharmonic/von Karajan)
¶Bach, 'Air' (from Suite No. 3 in D major, BWV 1068) (Stuttgart Chamber Orchestra/Münchinger)
¶LUXURY: Not required.
¶BOOK: An anthology of poetry.

12 December 1970
1051 Arthur Lowe
Actor
¶Tosti, 'Parted' (Peter Dawson)
¶'Love is the Sweetest Thing' (Al Bowlly/Ray Noble and his Orchestra)
¶'At Last' (Glenn Miller and his Orchestra)
¶Litolff, Concerto symphonique No. 4 in D minor (scherzo) (Clifford Curzon *piano*/LPO/Boult)
¶Berlin, 'It's a Lovely Day Today' (from *Call Me Madam*) (Shani Wallis/Jeff Warren)
¶Bach, Concerto in C minor (Paul Badura-Skoda and Jörg Demus *pianos*/Vienna State Opera Orchestra/Redel)
*¶Debussy, 'La Mer' (NPO/Boulez)
¶'Who Do You Think You are Kidding, Mr Hitler?' (from TV series *Dad's Army*) (Bud Flanagan)
¶LUXURY: Claret.
¶BOOK: A book on tropical plants.

19 December 1970
1052 Ivan Mauger
World speedway champion
*¶'Pokarekare' (St Joseph Maori Girls' Choir)
¶'The Lonely Bull' (Herb Alpert and the Tijuana Brass)
¶'Distant Drums' (Jim Reeves)
¶'Chitty Chitty Bang Bang' (from film) (Dick van Dyke)
¶Bart, 'Consider Yourself' (from *Oliver!*) (Mark Lester/Jack Wild)
¶'I Don't Believe in If Anymore' (Roger Whittaker)
¶'Ring of Fire' (Johnny Cash)
¶'Tijuana Taxi' (Herb Alpert and the Tijuana Brass)
¶LUXURY: A box of family photographs.
¶BOOK: A survival manual.

26 December 1970
1053 Quentin Poole
Head chorister of King's College Chapel Choir, Cambridge (aged 13)
¶Holst, 'Mars' (from *The Planets*) (NPO/Boult)
¶Purcell, 'Remember Not, Lord, Our Offences' (King's College Chapel Choir/Willcocks)
¶Bach, Sonata No. 2, in E flat, for Flute and Harpsichord (BWV 1031) (Maxence Larrieu *flute*/Rafael Puyana *harpsichord*)
¶Vaughan Williams, A Sea Symphony (LSO and Chorus/Previn)
¶Mozart, Flute Concerto in D (K 314) (Hubert Barwahser/Vienna Symphony/Pritchard)
¶Vaughan Williams, 'Oxford Elegy' (John Westbrook *speaking*/King's College Chapel Choir/Jacques Orchestra/Willcocks)
¶'Deep Purple' (The Scholars/Carrington)
*¶Walton, 'Mariner Man' (from *Façade*) (Cleo Laine/Annie Ross/Ensemble/Dankworth)
¶LUXURY: A flute and music.
¶BOOK: His favourite detective novels by Agatha Christie.

2 January 1971
1054 Sacha Distel
Vocalist, guitarist and composer
¶Weill/Brecht, 'Mack the Knife' (from *The Threepenny Opera*) (Louis Armstrong)
*¶'Parker's Mood' (Charlie Parker *alto saxophone* and His All Stars)
¶Ravel, 'La valse' (LSO/Monteux)
¶'Israel' (Miles Davis *trumpet* and his Orchestra)
¶'Georgia on My Mind' (Ray Charles *vocal* and *piano* and his Orchestra/Burns)
¶'People' (from *Funny Girl*) (Dionne Warwick)
¶'To Wait for Love' (Sacha Distel)
¶'Only the Lonely' (Frank Sinatra)
¶LUXURY: A guitar.
¶BOOK: An illustrated English dictionary.

9 January 1971
1055 James Fitton RA
Painter
¶Puccini, *La bohème* (Act 4 excerpt) (Robert Merrill/Jussi Björling/John Reardon/Giorgio Tozzi/Lucine Amara/Victoria de los Angeles/RCA Victor Symphony/Beecham)
¶Mozart, Sinfonia Concertante in E flat (K. 364) (Igor Oistrakh *violin*/David Oistrakh *viola*/Moscow State Philharmonic/Kondrashin)
¶Chopin, Nocturne No. 1 in E minor (opus 72) (Artur Rubinstein *piano*)
¶Stravinsky, *The Firebird* (Columbia Symphony/Stravinsky)
¶Mozart, Quartet No. 1 in D (K. 285) for Flute and Strings (Jean-Pierre Rampal/Pasquier Trio)
*¶Bach, 'Thou that Sitteth at the Right Hand of God the Father' (from *Mass in B minor*) (Kathleen Ferrier/LPO/Boult)
¶'St James' Infirmary' (Louis Armstrong and his Savoy Ballroom Five)
¶Albinoni/Giazotto, Adagio in G minor (Paris Conservatoire Orchestra/Lombard)
¶LUXURY: Painting equipment.
¶BOOK: An encyclopaedia.

16 January 1971
1056 Robert Bolt
Playwright and screenwriter
¶Verdi, *I vespri Siciliani* (Act 5 aria) (Joan Sutherland/Paris Conservatoire Orchestra/Santi)
¶'Way Down Yonder in New Orleans' (Dutch Swing College Band)
*¶Mozart, Clarinet Quintet in A (K. 581) (Karl Leister/members of the Berlin Philharmonic)
¶'Underneath the Arches' (Flanagan & Allen)
¶Handel, *Zadok the Priest* (King's College Chapel Choir/English Chamber Orchestra/Willcocks)
¶Bach, Double Concerto in D minor (BWV 1043) (Alice Harnoncourt and Walter Pfeiffer *violins*/Concentus Musicus of Vienna/Nikolaus Harnoncourt)

¶ Britten, *Missa Brevis* (St John's College Choir, Cambridge/Guest)
¶ Sousa, 'Stars and Stripes Forever' (BMC, Fairey & Fodens massed bands/Mortimer)
¶ LUXURY: Writing materials.
¶ BOOKS: His favourite novels of P. G. Wodehouse.

23 January 1971
1057 Madame (Lilian) Stiles-Allen
Soprano and teacher
¶ Vaughan Williams, 'Serenade to Music' (16 soloists/BBC Symphony/Wood)
¶ Gershwin, 'Rhapsody in Blue' (Leonard Bernstein *piano and conducting*/Columbia Symphony)
¶ 'Lazy Afternoon' (Julie Andrews)
¶ Schubert, Symphony No. 8 in B minor (Unfinished) Philharmonia Orchestra/Giulini)
¶ Puccini, 'Vissi d'arte' (from *Tosca*) (Madame Stiles-Allen)
¶ Schubert, 'Ständchen' (Dietrich Fischer-Dieskau/Gerald Moore *piano*)
*¶ Wagner, 'Liebestod' (from *Tristan und Isolde*) (Kirsten Flagstad/Philharmonia Orchestra/Furtwängler)
¶ Handel, 'Hallelujah Chorus' (from *Messiah*) (Sheffield Choir/orchestra/Henry Coward)
¶ LUXURY: A piano.
¶ BOOK: Ernest Holmes, *The Science of Mind*

30 January 1971
1058 Laurie Lee
Poet and writer
¶ 'Stevedore Stomp' (Duke Ellington and his Orchestra)
¶ 'Seguidillas' (La Nina de los Peines *flamenco singer*/Nino Ricardo *guitar*)
¶ 'Bells of Bethlehem' (Victoria de los Angeles/Renata Tarrago *guitar*)
¶ Dowland, 'Lachrimae Antiquae' (Julian Bream *lute*)
¶ Chopin, Nocturne No. 1 in B flat (opus 9, no. 1) (Artur Rubinstein *piano*)

¶ Harrison, 'Isn't It a Pity?' (George Harrison)
*¶ Beethoven, String Quartet No. 15 in A minor (opus 132) (Amadeus String Quartet)
¶ Bach, 'Chaconne' (from Sonata No. 4, in D minor (BWV 1004) (Yehudi Menuhin *violin*)
¶ LUXURY: Materials for making wine or beer.
¶ BOOK: *The Atlantic Book of British and American Poetry*, compiled by Edith Sitwell.

6 February 1971
1059 Alan Keith
Actor and broadcaster
¶ 'Je tire ma révérence' (Jean Sablon)
¶ Elgar, Violin Concerto in B minor (Yehudi Menuhin/LSO/Elgar)
¶ Berlioz, Symphonie fantastique (LSO/Colin Davis)
¶ Rodgers & Hammerstein, 'Surrey with the Fringe on Top' (from *Oklahoma*) (Gordon Macrae/Shirley Jones/Charlotte Greenwood/Orchestra/Blackton)
¶ Parry/Blake, 'Jerusalem' (Royal Choral Society/Philharmonia Orchestra/Sargent)
¶ Mozart, 'La ci darem la mano' (from *Don Giovanni*) (Irmgard Seefried/Dietrich Fischer-Dieskau/Berlin Radio Symphony Orchestra/Fricsay)
*¶ Beethoven, Symphony No. 5 in C minor (opus 67) (Berlin Philharmonic/von Karajan)
¶ Allegri, 'Miserere' (Roy Goodman *treble*/King's College Chapel Choir/Willcocks)
¶ LUXURY: Model-making tools.
¶ BOOK: *The Oxford Book of English Verse*

13 February 1971
1060 Harvey Smith
Showjumper
¶ 'The North Star March' (Hammond's Sauce Works Band)
¶ Lennon & McCartney, 'The Fool on the Hill' (Shirley Bassey)
¶ 'We'll Keep a Welcome' (Harry Secombe)

¶ 'Quando, Quando, Quando' (Marino Marini and his Quartet)
¶ Lerner & Loewe, 'On the Street Where You Live' (from *My Fair Lady*) (Welsh Guards Band)
*¶ Jarre, 'Lara's Theme' (from film *Dr Zhivago*) (MGM Studio Orchestra/Jarre)
¶ Romberg, 'Serenade' (from *The Student Prince*) (Mario Lanza)
¶ 'On Ilkley Moor Bah't 'At' (Muriel George/Ernest Butcher/piano)
¶ LUXURY: A radio receiver.
¶ BOOK: A selection to sample.

20 February 1971
1061 Wendy Craig
Actress
¶ Grainger, 'Mock Morris' (Philharmonia Orchestra/Weldon)
¶ Butterworth, 'A Shropshire Lad' (Hallé Orchestra/Barbirolli)
¶ Betjeman, 'Middlesex' (John Betjeman)
¶ Elgar, Serenade for Strings in E minor (Academy of St Martin-in-the-Fields/Marriner)
¶ Chabrier, 'Marche joyeuse' (Paris Conservatoire Orchestra/Dervaux)
¶ Glazunov, Violin Concerto in A minor (Ida Haendel/Prague Symphony/Smetacek)
¶ 'Petronella' (Jimmy Shand and his Band)
*¶ Cimarosa, arranged Benjamin, Oboe Concerto in C (Heinz Holliger/Bamberg Symphony/Maag)
¶ LUXURY: Toothbrushes.
¶ BOOK: The complete works of Oscar Wilde.

27 February 1971
1062 Ravi Shankar
Musician
*¶ 'Jamunaketeer' (Abdul Karin Khan)
¶ Novacek, 'Perpetuum Mobile' (Yehudi Menuhin *violin*/Paris Symphony/Monteux)
¶ Scarlatti, Sonata in D minor (George Malcolm *harpsichord*)

¶Mozart, Concerto in C for Flute, Harp and Orchestra (K. 299) (Aurèle Nicolet/Rose Stein *harp*/Munich Bach Orchestra/ Richter)
¶'Scarborough Fair' (Simon & Garfunkel)
¶'Worried Dream' (B. B. King)
¶'Fiesta en Sevilla' (Paco Peña)
¶Harrison, 'My Sweet Lord' (George Harrison)
¶LUXURY: Perfume.
¶BOOK: The Poems of Rabindranath Tagore.

6 March 1971
1063 Ludovic Kennedy
Writer and broadcaster
¶Beethoven, Leonora Overture No. 3 (Berlin Philharmonic/ Kempe)
¶'Manhattan' (from *Garrick Gaieties*) (Ella Fitzgerald)
¶'Scotland the Brave' (Scots Guards Massed Pipe Band)
*¶Adam, *Giselle* (LSO/ Fistoulari)
¶'Annie Laurie' (Maxine Sullivan)
¶Bach, Concerto in the Italian Style (BWV 971) (Jacques Loussier Trio)
¶Wagner, 'Liebestod' (from *Tristan und Isolde*) (Kirsten Flagstad/Philharmonia Orchestra/Furtwängler)
¶'Climax Rag' (Chris Barber and his Band)
¶LUXURY: Tartar sauce.
¶BOOK: The poems of George Herbert and John Donne.

13 March 1971
1064 Patrick Cargill
Actor
¶J. Strauss, 'Tales from the Vienna Woods' (Vienna Philharmonic/Boskovsky)
¶'Is that All There Is?' (Peggy Lee)
¶Alford, 'Colonel Bogey' (from film *The Bridge on the River Kwai*) (Mitch Miller and his Orchestra)
¶Coward, 'I'll See You Again' (from *Bitter Sweet*) (Vanessa Lee/Roberto Cardinali)
¶Chaplin, 'This is My Song' (from film *A Countess from Hong Kong*)

¶'The Blood Donor' (from radio series *Hancock's Half Hour*) (Tony Hancock/Patrick Cargill)
¶'Meditation' (Frank Sinatra)
*¶'We'll Meet Again' (The Inkspots)
¶LUXURY: His Bentley car.
¶BOOK: The *Spotlight* casting directory.

20 March 1971
1065 Sir Louis Gluckstein
President of the Royal Albert Hall
*¶Bach, Double Concerto in D minor (BWV 1043) (Jascha Heifetz *violin* [playing both parts]/RCA Victor Chamber Orchestra/Waxman)
¶Mendelssohn, Symphony No. 4 in A major (Italian) (Orchestre de la Suisse Romande/ Ansermet)
¶Elgar, 'Nimrod' (from *Enigma Variations*) (LPO/Boult)
¶Gilbert & Sullivan, 'Sentry's Song' (from *Iolanthe*) (Owen Brannigan/Pro Arte Orchestra/ Sargent)
¶Bruch, Violin Concerto in G minor (Jascha Heifetz/NPO/ Sargent)
¶Brahms, Piano Concerto No. 1 in D minor (Artur Rubinstein/ Boston Symphony/Leinsdorf)
¶Wagner, 'Liebestod' (from *Tristan und Isolde*) (Kirsten Flagstad/Philharmonia Orchestra/Furtwängler)
¶Handel, *Zadok the Priest* (from Coronation Service of HM Queen Elizabeth II)
¶LUXURY: A four-poster bed.
¶BOOK: *The Oxford Dictionary of Quotations*

27 March 1971
1066 Clodagh Rogers
Pop singer
¶'Resurrection Shuffle' (Ashton, Gardner & Dyke)
*¶'Watching and Waiting' (The Moody Blues)
¶'Mental Journey' (Trini Lopez)
¶'By the Time I Get to Phoenix' (Glen Campbell)
¶Lennon & McCartney, 'Martha My Dear' (The Beatles)
¶'Snowbird' (Anne Murray)

¶'Just a Little More Line' (Moonshine)
¶R. Strauss, 'Also Sprach Zarathustra' (Berlin Philharmonic/Böhm)
¶LUXURY: Prawn cocktails.
¶BOOK: Mario Puzo, *The Godfather*

3 April 1971
1067 Peter Daubeny
Theatrical producer
¶Coward, 'I'll Follow My Secret Heart' (from *Conversation Piece*) (Yvonne Printemps)
¶'Lilacs Out of the Dead Land' (Manos Hadjidakis)
¶Puccini, 'Vissi d'arte' (from *Tosca*) (Maria Callas/Paris Conservatoire Orchestra/ Prêtre)
¶Tchaikovsky, Symphony No. 5 in E minor (USSR Symphony/Svetlanov)
¶Bolling, Theme from film *Borsalino* (Claude Bolling *piano* and conducting his orchestra)
¶'Ev'ry Time We Say Goodbye' (from *Seven Lively Arts*) (Ella Fitzgerald)
*¶Sibelius, Symphony No. 1 in E minor (BBC Symphony/ Sargent)
¶Coward, 'London Pride' (Noël Coward)
¶LUXURY: A picture of his family.
¶BOOK: His own book, *My World of Theatre*

10 April 1971
1068 Geoff Boycott
Cricketer
¶'I Say a Little Prayer' (Dionne Warwick)
¶'Twelfth of Never' (Johnny Mathis)
¶'If I Had a Hammer' (Trini Lopez)
¶Rachmaninov, 'Rhapsody on a Theme of Paganini' (Julius Katchen *piano*/LPO/Boult)
¶Lennon & McCartney, 'Yesterday' (The Beatles)
¶Bernstein/Sondheim, 'Somewhere' (from *West Side Story*) (Reri Grist)
¶Tchaikovsky, 'Dance of the Sugar Plum Fairy' (from *The Nutcracker Suite*) (Berlin Philharmonic/von Karajan)

*¶ 'My Way' (Frank Sinatra)
¶ LUXURY: A telephone line to a sports newspaper.
¶ BOOK: A set of *Wisdens*.

17 April 1971
1069 Mrs Mills
Pianist and entertainer
¶ 'I Love You and Don't You Forget It' (Perry Como)
¶ Jarre, 'Somewhere My Love (Lara's theme)' (from film *Dr Zhivago*) (Mike Sammes Singers)
¶ 'My Very Good Friend, the Milkman' (Fats Waller and his Rhythm)
¶ 'The Sewing Machine' (from film *The Perils of Pauline*) (Betty Hutton)
¶ 'Moonlight and Roses' (Victor Silvester and his Ballroom Orchestra)
*¶ 'Charmaine' (Mantovani and his Orchestra)
¶ 'Theme from *Match of the Day*' (from TV series)
¶ Suppé, *Poet and Peasant* (overture) (Hallé Orchestra/ Barbirolli)
¶ LUXURY: A family photograph.
¶ BOOK: A cookery encyclopaedia.

24 April 1971
1070 Jonathan Miller
Revue artist, doctor of medicine, writer and theatre and film director
¶ 'Sambre et Meuse' (Batteries et Musique de la Garde République)
¶ Schubert, 'Der Hirt auf dem Felsen' (opus 129) (Margaret Ritchie/Gervase de Peyer *clarinet*/George Malcolm *piano*)
¶ Purcell, 'Sound the Trumpet' (from *Come Ye Sons of Art*) (Alfred Deller/John Whitworth L'oiseau Lyre Ensemble/Lewis)
¶ 'Immortal, Invisible, God Only Wise' (St John's College Choir, Cambridge/Guest)
¶ Scarlatti, Sonata in E major (Wanda Landowska *harpsichord*)
¶ Bach, *Goldberg Variations* (BWV 988) (Charles Rosen *piano*)

*¶ Beethoven, String Quartet No. 13 in B flat major (opus 130) (Amadeus String Quartet)
¶ 'Goodnight Irene' (Huddie 'Leadbelly' Ledbetter)
¶ LUXURY: A razor.
¶ BOOK: John Livingstone Lowe, *The Road to Xanadu*

1 May 1971
1071 Billie Whitelaw
Actress
¶ 'Singin' in the Rain' (from film) (Gene Kelly)
*¶ Bruckner, Symphony No. 7 in E major (Vienna Philharmonic/ Solti)
¶ Bernstein/Sondheim, 'America' (from *West Side Story*) (Chita Rivera/company)
¶ Sibelius, Symphony No. 5 in E flat major (Philharmonia Orchestra/von Karajan)
¶ 'Raindrops Keep Fallin' on My Head' (from film *Butch Cassidy and the Sundance Kid*) (Sacha Distel)
¶ 'Sanctus' and 'Benedictus' (from *Missa Luba*) (Les Troubadours du Roi Baudouin)
¶ Porter, 'I Concentrate on You' (from film *Broadway Melody of 1940*) (Frank Sinatra)
¶ Mahler, Symphony No. 8 in E flat major (soloists/choirs/ Vienna Festival Orchestra/ Mitroupoulos)
¶ LUXURY: Make-up.
¶ BOOK: A cookery book.

8 May 1971
1072 Reginald Foort
Organist
¶ Rimsky-Korsakov, *Scheherazade* (RPO/Beecham)
¶ Beethoven, Violin Concerto in D (Fritz Kreisler/LPO/ Barbirolli)
*¶ 'Lullaby of Broadway' (from film *Golddiggers of 1935*) (Joe Loss and his Orchestra)
¶ Puccini, 'Che gelida manina' (from *La bohème*) (John Heddle Nash)
¶ 'Dancing Tambourine' (George Wright *organ*)
¶ Elgar, 'Nimrod' (from *Enigma Variations*) (LSO/Monteux)
¶ Mozart, Symphony No. 40 in G minor (K. 550) (RPO/ Beecham)

¶ Handel, 'Hallelujah Chorus' (from *Messiah*) (Huddersfield Choral Society/Royal Liverpool Philharmonic/Sargent)
¶ LUXURY: An organ.
¶ BOOK: Back numbers of *The Reader's Digest*.

15 May 1971
1073 John Braine
Writer
¶ 'The Stranger Song' (Leonard Cohen)
¶ 'Plaisir d'amour' (Joan Baez)
¶ 'Roses of Picardy' (Alfred Piccaver)
¶ 'Feed the Birds' (from film *Mary Poppins*) (Julie Andrews/ chorus)
¶ 'Perfectly Marvellous' (from *Cabaret*) (Judi Dench)
¶ 'Goodnight Irene' (Huddie 'Leadbelly' Ledbetter)
*¶ Seeger, 'Where Have All the Flowers Gone?' (Vera Lynn)
¶ Elgar, 'Pomp and Circumstance' March No. 1 in D major (recorded at a 'Last Night of the Proms') (BBC Symphony/Davis)
¶ LUXURY: René Magritte, *The Empire of Light*.
¶ BOOK: The collected poems of John Betjeman.

22 May 1971
1074 Joyce Grenfell (2nd appearance)
Writer and entertainer
¶ Bach, 'Adagio' (from Toccata, Adagio and Fugue in C (BWV 564)) (Myra Hess *piano*)
¶ Handel, Cantata No. 1, 'Ah crudel nel pianto mio' (Janet Baker/English Chamber Orchestra/Leppard)
¶ Mozart, Piano Concerto No. 24 in C minor (K. 491) (Solomon/Philharmonia Orchestra/Menges)
¶ 'She Moved Through the Fair' (Mary O'Hara)
¶ Bach, French Suite No. 5 in G (BWV 816) (Myra Hess *piano*)
¶ Mozart, Rondo in A minor (K. 511) (Vladimir Ashkenazy *piano*)
¶ 'You Make Me feel So Young' (Frank Sinatra)

*¶Bach, Brandenburg Concerto No. 6 in B flat major (BWV 1051) (English Chamber Orchestra/Britten)
¶LUXURY: Writing and drawing materials.
¶BOOK: Mary Baker Eddy, *Science and Health, with Key to the Scriptures*

19 May 1971
1075 Ronnie Corbett
Comedian
¶'By Cool Siloam's Shady Rill' (Glasgow Orpheus Choir/Roberton)
*¶Handel, 'I Know that My Redeemer Liveth' (from *Messiah*) (Isobel Baillie/Hallé Orchestra/Heward)
¶Coward, 'I'll See You Again' (from *Bitter Sweet*) and 'Dance Little Lady' (from *This Year of Grace*) (Noël Coward)
¶'I Found a Million-Dollar Baby' (Mel Torme)
¶Rodgers & Hart, 'I Wish I Were in Love Again' (from *Babes in Arms*) (Frank Sinatra)
¶*Gentlemen Prefer Blondes* (overture) (from film) (orchestra/Ainsworth)
¶'It's the Talk of the Town' (Anthony Newley)
¶'Upa, Neguinho' (Sergio Mendes and Brasil 66)
¶LUXURY: Golf clubs and balls.
¶BOOK: A handbook on tropical vegetation.

5 June 1971
1076 Vernon Bartlett
Broadcaster and writer on foreign affairs
¶Beethoven, Symphony No. 6 in F major (Pastoral) (Philharmonia Orchestra/Klemperer)
*¶Beethoven, Symphony No. 3 in E flat major (Eroica) (LPO/Boult)
¶Dvořák, Symphony No. 9 in E minor (Berlin Philharmonic/Kempe)
¶Chopin, Étude in C minor (opus 10, no. 12) (Vladimir Horowitz *piano*)
¶Lerner & Loewe, 'With a Little Bit of Luck' (from *My Fair Lady*) (Stanley Holloway)

¶Granados, Spanish Dance No. 5 in E minor (Andrés Segovia *guitar*)
¶Mozart, *Eine Kleine Nachtmusik* (Columbia Symphony/Walter)
¶Maderna, Serenata No. 2 (English Chamber Orchestra/Maderna)
¶LUXURIES: Writing materials and playing cards.
¶BOOK: An encyclopaedia.

12 June 1971
1077 Elizabeth Ryan
Tennis champion
¶Schubert, 'An die Musik' (Gerald Moore *piano*)
¶'Greensleeves' (massed bands)
¶Parry/Blake, 'Jerusalem' (Kirsten Flagstad/LPO/Boult)
¶Beethoven, Piano Concerto No. 5 in E flat major (Emperor) (Gina Bachauer/LSO/Skrowaczewski)
¶'Lovely Hula Hands' (Alfred Apaka)
¶Coward, 'I'll See You Again' (from *Bitter Sweet*) (Vanessa Lee/Roberto Cardinali)
¶'Abide with Me' (Clara Butt)
*¶Korngold, 'Gluck, das mir verlieb' (from *Die Tote Stadt*) (Richard Tauber/Lotte Lehmann)
¶LUXURY: A piano.
¶BOOK: *The Oxford Book of English Verse*

19 June 1971
1078 Clive Dunn
Comedian, actor and amateur painter
¶Lennon & McCartney, 'Something' (The Beatles)
¶'Common Entrance' (Peter Sellers)
¶Borodin/Wright & Forrest (arr.), 'And This is My Beloved' (from *Kismet*) (Doretta Morrow/Alfred Drake/Richard Kiley/Henry Calvin)
¶Schönberg, Piano Concerto (opus 42) (Alfred Brendel/South-west Germany Radio Symphony/Gielen)
¶'Grandad' (Clive Dunn)
*¶'Little Green Apples' (Dionne Warwick)

¶Delibes, 'Bell Song' (from *Lakmé*) (Joan Sutherland/Monte Carlo Opera Orchestra/Bonynge)
¶Mozart, Symphony No. 40 in G minor (K. 550) (NPO/Giulini)
¶LUXURY: Soap.
¶BOOK: An encyclopaedia.

26 June 1971
1079 Maurice Woodruff
Clairvoyant
¶'I Know Now' (from *Robert and Elizabeth*) (Keith Michell/June Bronhill)
¶'Mr Wonderful' (from *Mr Wonderful*) (Peggy Lee)
*¶'Psalm 91' (Laurence Olivier)
¶Lai/Sigman, 'Where Do I Begin?' (from film *Love Story*) (Shirley Bassey)
¶Novello, 'My Dearest Dear' (from *The Dancing Years*) (Anne Rogers)
¶'Stella by Starlight' (Sergio Franchi)
¶'On Mother Kelly's Doorstep' (Danny La Rue)
¶Puccini, 'Che gelida manina' (from *La bohème*) (David Hughes/City of Birmingham Symphony/Frémaux)
¶LUXURY: Writing materials.
¶BOOK: *The Golden Treasury*, compiled by Francis Palgrave.

3 July 1971
1080 Michael Crawford
Comedy actor
¶'Gloria' (from *Missa Luba*) (Les Troubadours du Roi Baudouin)
¶'For All We Know' (Billie Holiday)
*¶'Singin' in the Rain' (from film) (Gene Kelly)
¶Donovan, 'Catch the Wind' (Donovan)
¶Barry 'Theme from *The Lion in Winter*' (from film) (soundtrack)
¶Legrand, 'Theme from *Les parapluies de Cherbourg*' (from film) (soundtrack)
¶'When I Grow Too Old to Dream' (Evelyn Laye)
¶Brahms, Symphony No. 2 in D major (opus 73) (Vienna Philharmonic/Barbirolli)
¶LUXURY: A cherry tree.
¶BOOK: *A Book of Beauty*, compiled by John Hadfield.

10 July 1971
1081 Laurence Whistler
Glass engraver and writer
*¶ Mozart, Piano Concerto No. 20 in D minor (K. 466) (Walter Gieseking/Philharmonia Orchestra/Rosbaud)
¶ 'Underneath the Arches' (Flanagan & Allen)
¶ Purcell, 'When I am Laid in Earth' (from *Dido and Aeneas*) (Kirsten Flagstad)
¶ Dylan Thomas, *Under Milk Wood* (excerpt) (Hugh Griffith/Rachel Thomas)
¶ 'La mer' (Charles Trenet)
¶ Messiaen, Turangalîla Symphony (Toronto Symphony/Ozawa)
¶ Beethoven, Septet in E flat (opus 20) (NBC Symphony/Toscanini)
¶ 'Classicold Musee' (Stanley Unwin)
¶ LUXURY: A magnifying glass.
¶ BOOK: *Come Hither*, compiled by Walter De la Mare.

17 July 1971
1082 John Cleese
Writer and performer
¶ 'Love Story' (Peggy Lee)
¶ 'Tarzan' (Paul Jones)
*¶ Elgar, 'Nimrod' (from *Enigma Variations*) (Royal Albert Hall Orchestra/Elgar)
¶ 'Raindrops Keep Fallin' on My Head' (from film *Butch Cassidy and the Sundance Kid*) (B. J. Thomas)
¶ 'Simon Smith and His Amazing Dancing Bear' (The Alan Price Set)
¶ Tchaikovsky, Romeo and Juliet Fantasy Overture (Vienna Philharmonic/Maazel)
¶ 'Show Me a Rose' (Groucho Marx)
¶ Legrand, 'Theme from the film *Les parapluies de Cherbourg*' (Michel Legrand and his Orchestra)
¶ LUXURIES: A life-sized *papier mâché* model of Margaret Thatcher, and a baseball bat.
¶ BOOK: Vincent Price's cookery book.

24 July 1971
1083 James Laver
Writer on costume and the psychology of taste
¶ Mozart, 'Sanctus' (from *Requiem*) (Munich Bach Choir and Orchestra/Richter)
*¶ Beethoven, Symphony No. 3 in E flat major (Eroica) (RPO/Sargent)
¶ 'The Rose of Tralee' (John McCormack)
¶ Porter, 'How Could We be Wrong?' (from *Nymph Errant*) (Gertrude Lawrence)
¶ 'Quand je suis chez toi' (Maurice Chevalier/Yvonne Vallée)
¶ 'The Bonnie Earl of Moray' (Rory & Alex McEwan)
¶ Sibelius, 'Finlandia' (Hallé Orchestra/Barbirolli)
¶ R. Strauss, 'Scene between Baron Ochs and Anina' (from *Der Rosenkavalier*) (Otto Edelmann/Kirsten Meyer/Philharmonia/von Karajan)
¶ LUXURY: A Buddhist altar in the British Museum.
¶ BOOK: *The Oxford Book of English Verse*

31 July 1971
1084 Lorin Maazel
Conductor
¶ Mahler, Symphony No. 4 in G major (New York Philharmonic/Walter)
¶ Bach, *Goldberg Variations* (BWV 988) (Wanda Landowska *harpsichord*)
¶ Bach, Sonata No. 3 in A minor (BWV 1003) (Nathan Milstein *violin*)
¶ R. Strauss, 'Don Quixote' (Vienna Philharmonic/Maazel)
¶ Debussy, 'La danse de Puck' (*Prelude No. 10, Book 1*) (Walter Gieseking *piano*)
¶ Wagner, 'Siegfried Idyll' (NBC Symphony/Toscanini)
*¶ Schubert, Quartet No. 14 in D minor (Death and the Maiden) (Budapest String Quartet)
¶ Verdi, *Falstaff* (Act 3 fugue) (NBC Symphony/Toscanini)
¶ LUXURY: A chess set and chess book.
¶ BOOK: The works of Epictetus.

7 August 1971
1085 Ian McKellen
Actor
*¶ Chopin, Étude in C sharp minor (opus 25, no. 7) (Vladimir Horowitz *piano*)
¶ Elgar, Cello Concerto in E minor (opus 85) (Jacqueline du Pré/LSO/Barbirolli)
¶ 'Leanin' on a Lamp Post' (George Formby)
¶ Sibelius, Symphony No. 2 in D major (BBC Symphony/Sargent)
¶ Styne, 'Rose's Turn' (from *Gypsy*) (Ethel Merman)
¶ Vivaldi, 'Winter' (from *The Four Seasons*) (Felix Ayo *violin* I Musici)
¶ 'Honeysuckle Rose' (Lena Horne)
¶ Mahler, Symphony No. 8 in E flat major (LSO/Bernstein)
¶ LUXURY: Writing materials
¶ BOOK: The novels of Jane Austen.

14 August 1971
1086 Richard Gordon
Writer
¶ Handel, *Alcina* (overture) (Boyd Neel Orchestra/Neel)
*¶ 'A Small Town in Germany' (Jock Strapp Ensemble)
¶ Rodgers & Hammerstein, 'It Might as Well be Spring' (from film *State Fair*) (Margaret Whiting/Paul Weston's Orchestra)
¶ 'Po Ataru' (Maori Concert Party)
¶ Tchaikovsky, 'Capriccio Italien' (opus 45) (Belgian National Radio Orchestra/André)
¶ 'Lord of the Dance' (Donald Swann)
¶ Gilbert & Sullivan, 'Duke of Plaza-Toro's Song' (from *The Gondoliers*) (Martyn Green/D'Oyly Carte Opera Orchestra/Godrey)
¶ Mozart, Symphony No. 40 in G minor (K. 550) (NPO/Giulini)
¶ LUXURY: A pin.
¶ BOOK: *The Michelin Guide to France*

21 August 1971
1087 Mrs Sylva Stuart Watson
Licensee of the Theatre Royal, Haymarket
¶Glazunov, *The Seasons* (opus 67) (Orchestre de la Suisse Romande/Ansermet)
¶'Evensong' (King's College Chapel Choir, Cambridge/Ord)
¶Gay, 'Oh, Polly, You Might Have Toy'd and Kissed' (from *The Beggar's Opera*) (Constance Willis/Audrey Mildmay/Roy Henderson/Glyndebourne Festival Orchestra/Mudie)
¶Delius, 'The Walk to the Paradise Garden' (from *A Village Romeo and Juliet*) (LSO/Barbirolli)
¶Elgar, Cockaigne Overture 'In London Town' (opus 40) (Philharmonia Orchestra/Barbirolli)
¶'Hippo Encore' (Michael Flanders/Donald Swann)
¶Mendelssohn, 'The Wedding March' (from *A Midsummer Night's Dream*) (BBC Symphony and Chorus/Sargent)
*¶Bach, 'Gigue' (from French Suite No. 5 in G major (BWV 816)) (George Malcolm *harpsichord*)
¶LUXURY: 40 yards of flowered chintz, a needle and cotton.
¶BOOKS: Volumes on astronomy and astrology.

28 August 1971
1088 Artur Rubinstein
Concert pianist
¶Brahms, Piano Quartet in A (opus 26) (Jörg Demus/Eduard Drolc *violin*/Stefano Passaggio *viola*/Georg Donderer *cello*)
¶Beethoven, String Quartet in F (opus 59, no. 1) (Rasoumovsky) (Guarneri Quartet)
¶Schubert, 'Die Wetterfahne' (from *Winterreise*, opus 89) (Dietrich Fischer-Dieskau/Gerald Moore *piano*)
¶Bartók, Concerto for Orchestra (Philadelphia Orchestra/Ormandy)
¶Mozart, Piano Concerto in C minor (K. 491) (Solomon/Philharmonia Orchestra/Menges)

¶Chopin, Nocturne in E flat major (opus 9, no. 2) Artur Rubinstein *piano*)
*¶Schubert, String Quintet in C (opus 163) (Amadeus String Quartet/William Pleeth *cello*)
¶Schubert, Sonata in B flat (opus posth.) (Artur Rubinstein *piano*)
¶LUXURY: A revolver.
¶BOOK: Any one from his library.

4 September 1971
1089 Glenda Jackson
Actress
¶Bach, Double Concerto in D minor (BWV 1043) (Igor & David Oistrakh *violins*/RPO/Goossens)
¶Beethoven, Piano Concerto No. 5 in E flat major (Emperor) (Wilhelm Kempff/Berlin Philharmonic/Leitner)
¶Stravinsky, *The Firebird* (Philharmonia Orchestra/Giulini)
¶Dvořák, Cello Concerto in B minor (Pierre Fournier/Berlin Philharmonic/Szell)
¶Vaughan Williams, Symphony No. 5 in D (Philharmonia Orchestra/Barbirolli)
¶Shostakovich, Symphony No. 5 in D (opus 47) (New York Philharmonic/Bernstein)
*¶Beethoven, Symphony No. 9 in D minor (opus 125) (Philharmonia Orchestra/Klemperer)
¶Rogers, Hart, 'It Never Entered My Head' (from *Higher and Higher*) (Ella Fitzgerald)
¶LUXURY: Queen Mary's dolls' house.
¶BOOK: Jane Austen, *Persuasion*

11 September 1971
1090 David Shepherd
Painter
¶Sibelius, Symphony No. 1 in E minor (LSO/Collins)
¶'Tuxedo Junction' (Syd Lawrence and his Orchestra)
¶Puccini, 'Love Duet' (from *Madam Butterfly*) (Maria Callas/Nicolai Gedda/La Scala Orchestra, Milan/von Karajan)
¶'Mother, What'll I do Now?' (George Formby)

¶R. Strauss, 'Death and Transfiguration' (opus 24) (Vienna Philharmonic/von Karajan)
¶Delius, 'The Walk to the Paradise Garden' (from *A Village Romeo and Juliet*) (RPO/Beecham)
¶Stereo recordings of a steam locomotive
*¶Mahler, Symphony No. 8 in E flat major (soloists/choirs/LSO and Chorus/Bernstein)
¶LUXURIES: The 'Black Prince' steam locomotive, canvases and oil paints.
¶BOOK: A volume on elementary calculus

18 September 1971
1091 Kenneth Allsop
Writer, journalist and broadcaster
¶'Muggles' (Louis Armstrong *trumpet* and his Orchestra)
¶'Yesterdays' (Billie Holiday)
¶Bach, Suite No. 2 in B minor (BWV 1067) (Prades Festival Orchestra/Casals)
¶'Joe Hill' (Joan Baez)
¶Lennon & McCartney, 'Hey Jude' (The Beatles)
¶'Let the Sunshine In' (from *Hair*) (original cast)
¶Dylan, 'Rainy Day Women Nos. 12 and 35' (Bob Dylan)
*¶Mahler, Symphony No. 2 in C minor (Resurrection) (LSO and Chorus/Solti)
¶LUXURY: A pair of binoculars.
¶BOOK: A do-it-yourself manual.

25 September 1971
1092 Mollie Lee
'Woman's Hour' broadcaster
¶'The Cuckoo' (Alfred Deller/Desmond Dupré *lute*)
¶Shakespeare, *The Merchant of Venice* (excerpt) (Marlowe Society/professional players)
¶'La Marseillaise' (Chorus of the Jeunesses Musicales de France/Band of the Gardiens de la Paix, Paris/Dondeyne)
*¶Tchaikovsky, *Eugene Onegin* (excerpt) (Bolshoi Opera Orchestra and Chorus/Rostropovich)

¶ Saint-Saëns, Sonata No. 1 in D minor (opus 75) (André Pascal *violin*/Isidore Phillipp *piano*)
¶ 'Dishonoured' (The Goons)
¶ 'Non, je ne regrette rien' (Edith Piaf)
¶ Lennon & McCartney, 'Eleanor Rigby' (The Beatles)
¶ LUXURY: A typewriter and paper
¶ BOOK: Marcel Proust, *À la recherche du temps perdu*

2 October 1971
1093 Caterina Valente
International entertainer
*¶ Rodrigo, Concierto de Aranjuez for Guitar and Orchestra (John Williams/Philadelphia Orchestra/Ormandy)
¶ Bizet, 'Seguidilla' (from *Carmen*) (Leontyne Price/Franco Corelli/Vienna Philharmonic/von Karajan)
¶ 'Spinning Wheel' (Blood, Sweat and Tears)
¶ Rachmaninov, 'Vocalise' (opus 34, no. 14) (Philadelphia Orchestra/Ormandy)
¶ Gershwin, 'Someone to Watch Over Me' (from *Oh, Kay!*) (Ella Fitzgerald)
¶ Ramirez, 'Gloria' (from *Misa Criolla*) (Los Fronterizos/Socorro Basilica Choir/Ensemble/Ramirez)
¶ 'Mornin' Reverend' (Thad Jones–Mel Lewis Jazz Orchestra)
¶ 'Don't Worry About Me' (Django Reinhardt *guitar*/Stephane Grappelli *violin*/Quintet of the Hot Club of France)
¶ LUXURY: An English pub.
¶ BOOKS: Selected novels by James Mitchener.

9 October 1971
1094 Sir Sacheverell Sitwell
Writer and poet
¶ Mozart, Piano concerto in C major (K. 415) (Daniel Barenboim *piano and conducting*/English Chamber Orchestra)

¶ Schumann, 'Warum' (Fantasiestucke, Opus 12, No. 3) (Ignace Jan Paderewski *piano*)
¶ Schumann/Liszt, 'Frühlingsnacht' (Josef Lhévinne *piano*)
*¶ Bizet, *Carmen* (Act 3 chorus) (French National Radio Orchestra and Chorus/Beecham)
¶ Verdi, *Un ballo in maschera* (Act 1 chorus) (Robert Shaw Chorale/NBC Symphony/Toscanini)
¶ Liszt, 'Bénédiction de Dieu dans la solitude' (Aldo Ciccolini *piano*)
¶ Meyerbeer/Liszt (arr.), 'Valse Infernale' (from *Robert le diable*) (Earl Wild *piano*)
¶ Bach, *Goldberg Variations* (BWV 988) (Wanda Landowska *harpsichord*)
¶ LUXURY: A refrigerator.
¶ BOOKS: Leo Tolstoy, *War and Peace* and *Anna Karenina*.

16 October 1971
1095 Ivy Benson
Danceband leader
¶ 'Fantail' (Count Basie and his Orchestra)
¶ Lerner & Loewe, 'If Ever I Should Leave You' (from *Camelot*) (Aretha Franklin)
¶ Gershwin, 'Lady be Good' (from *Lady be Good*) (Benny Goodman Trio)
¶ Dylan, 'Blowin' in the Wind' (Stan Getz *tenor saxophone*/orchestra)
¶ Verdi, 'Và pensiero, sull'alli dorate' (from *Nabucco*) (Choir and Orchestra of Munich State Theatre/Kulka)
*¶ 'Oh, Happy Day' (Edwin Hawkins Singers)
¶ Beethoven, Piano Concerto No. 5 in E flat major (Emperor) (Claudio Arrau/Amsterdam Concertgebouw/Haitink)
¶ Lennon & McCartney, 'Can't Buy Me Love' (The Beatles)
¶ LUXURY: A piano.
¶ BOOK: Phyllis Thompson, *London Sparrow*

23 October 1971
1096 Dame Sibyl Hathaway
Dame of Sark
*¶ Mahler, Symphony No. 5 in C sharp minor (NPO/Barbirolli)
¶ Gershwin, 'Rhapsody in Blue' (Leonard Pennario *piano*/Hollywood Bowl Symphony/Slatkin)
¶ Dvořák, 'Songs My Mother Taught Me' (Florence Easton)
¶ Ponchielli, 'Dance of the Hours' (from *La Gioconda*) (Philharmonia Orchestra/von Karajan)
¶ Debussy, Prelude No. 1, Book 8, 'La fille aux cheveux de lin' (Walter Gieseking *piano*)
¶ Pierń, 'Aubade' (Léon Goossens *oboe*/Gerald Moore *piano*)
¶ Coward, 'Matelot' (from *Sigh No More*) (Noël Coward)
¶ Mendelssohn, 'Oh, for the Wings of a Dove' (Ernest Lough/G. Thalben-Ball *organ*/Temple Church Choir, London)
¶ LUXURY: Canvas and tapestry tools.
¶ BOOK: Sir Keith Feiling, *History of England*

30 October 1971
1097 C. A. Joyce
Worker in the prison service and in approved schools
¶ 'Roses of Picardy' (Stuart Burrows/Eurfryn Jones *piano*)
*¶ 'Nobody Knows de Trouble I've Seen' (Paul Robeson)
¶ Drigo, 'Serenade' (Boston Pops Orchestra/Fiedler)
¶ 'For You' (Donald Peers)
¶ Kern & Hammerstein, 'Look for the Silver Lining' (from *Sally*) (Vera Lynn)
¶ 'The British Grenadiers' (HM Grenadier Guards Band)
¶ Bach/Hess, 'Jesu, Joy of Man's Desiring' (from Cantata 147) (Dinu Lipatti *piano*)
¶ Sibelius, 'Finlandia' (Philharmonia Orchestra/von Karajan
¶ LUXURY: A self-portrait painted by his wife.
¶ BOOKS: His favourites among Georgette Heyer's novels.

6 November 1971
1098 Lieutenant-Colonel Sir Vivian Dunn
Ex-Principal Director of Music of the Royal Marines
*¶ Elgar, 'Praise to the Holiest in the Height' (from *The Dream of Gerontius*) (Richard Lewis/ Marjorie Thomas/Huddersfield Choral Society/Royal Liverpool Philharmonic/Sargent)
¶ Bach arranged Wood, Partita No. 3 in E (BWV 1006) (New Queen's Hall Orchestra/Wood)
¶ 'Wild Cat' (Joe Venuti *violin*/ Eddie Lang *guitar*)
¶ 'The Preobrajensky March' (HM Royal Marines Band)
¶ 'A Life on the Ocean Wave' (HM Royal Marines Band)
¶ Farnon, 'À la claire fontaine' (Light Music Society Orchestra/ Dunn)
¶ Holst, 'Jupiter' (from *The Planets*) (BBC Symphony/ Boult)
¶ Walton, 'Crown Imperial' (HM Royal Marines Band)
¶ LUXURIES: A piano, music manuscript paper, pencils and a rubber.
¶ BOOK: The autobiography of Sir Winston Churchill.

13 November 1971
1099 Nicolette Milnes-Walker
Lone sailor
¶ Ireland, 'Sea Fever' (John Shirley-Quirk/Viola Tunnard *piano*)
¶ Bach, Brandenburg Concerto No. 5 in D major (BWV 1050) (Stuttgart Chamber Orchestra/ Münchinger)
¶ 'Stranger on the Shore' (Acker Bilk)
¶ J. Strauss, 'The Blue Danube Waltz' (Vienna Philharmonic/ Boskovsky)
¶ Mozart, Clarinet Concerto in A major (K. 622) (Gervase de Peyer/LSO/Maag)
¶ Lennon & McCartney, 'With a Little Help from My Friends' (The Beatles)
*¶ Walton, *Belshazzar's Feast* (London Philharmonic Choir/ Philharmonic Promenade Orchestra/Boult)

¶ Beethoven, Symphony No. 9 in D minor (opus 125) (Berlin Philharmonic Orchestra and Chorus/von Karajan)
¶ LUXURY: Hot water and bath oil.
¶ BOOK: J. R. R. Tolkien, *The Lord of the Rings*

20 November 1971
1100 Alfred Brendel
Concert pianist
¶ Gesualdo, 5 part madrigal, 'In Van Dunque, O Crudele'(Hilverson Vocal Ensemble/Voorberg)
*¶ Bach, Prelude No. 24 in B minor (from *The Well-Tempered Clavier*, Book 1) (Edwin Fischer *piano*)
¶ Mozart, Quintet in E flat major (K. 614) (Cecil Aronowitz *viola*/Amadeus String Quartet)
¶ Beethoven, Quartet in C sharp minor (opus 131) (Busch Quartet)
¶ Schubert, String Quintet in C major (opus 163) Isaac Stern and Alexander Schneider *violins*/Milton Katims *viola*/ Pablo Casals and Paul Tortelier *cellos*)
¶ Chopin, Prelude in F sharp minor, (opus 28, no. 8) (Alfred Cortot *piano*)
¶ Wagner, *Tristan und Isolde* (opening of Act 2) (Philharmonia Orchestra/ Furtwängler)
¶ Mahler, Symphony No. 9 in D (Columbia Symphony/ Walter)
¶ LUXURY: A Bavarian rococo church.
¶ BOOK: Schubert's *Lieder*.

27 November 1971
1101 Steve Race (2nd appearance)
Broadcaster and musician
¶ Elgar, Cockaigne Overture (In London Town) (LSO/Davis)
¶ Monteverdi, 'O Rosetta che Rosetta' (Gerald English/ Robert Tear/English Chamber Orchestra/Leppard)

¶ Weill/Brecht, 'Mack the Knife' (from *The Threepenny Opera*) (Clark Terry *trumpet*/ Oscar Peterson Trio)
¶ Vaughan Williams, 'Serenade to Music' (16 soloists/LPO/ Boult)
¶ 'The Sea Gulls' (Panos Gavalas)
¶ Elgar, Violin Concerto in B minor (opus 61) (Jascha Heifetz/LSO/Sargent)
¶ Gershwin, 'Lady be Good' (from *Lady be Good*) (Ella Fitzgerald)
*¶ Wagner, 'Liebestod' (from *Tristan und Isolde*) (Kirsten Flagstad/Philharmonia Orchestra/Furtwängler)
¶ LUXURY: A pair of binoculars.
¶ BOOK: *The Dictionary of Musical Themes*

1 December 1971
1102 Graham Kerr
Cookery expert
¶ 'Kamate! Kamate!' (Maori Chorus of New Zealand Opera Company)
*¶ Slade, 'We Said We Wouldn't Look Back' (from *Salad Days*) (John Warner/Eleanor Drew/ Edward Rubach and Robert Docker *pianos*)
¶ Puccini, 'Love Duet' (from *Madam Butterfly*) (Victoria de los Angeles/Giuseppe di Stefano/Rome Opera House/ Gavazzeni)
¶ Rachmaninov, Piano Concerto No. 2 in C minor (Moura Lympany/RPO/ Sargent)
¶ 'Papier Mâché' (Dionne Warwick)
¶ 'Kalinka' (Red Army Ensemble)
¶ 'Sweet Inspiration' (Cilla Black)
¶ Elgar, 'Pomp and Circumstance' March No. 1 in D major (from last night of 1969 Proms) (BBC Symphony/ Davis)
¶ LUXURY: Wine.
¶ BOOK: An encyclopaedia of ancient civilisations.

11 December 1971
1103 Barbara Mullen (2nd appearance)
Actress

¶ Theme from film 'The Big Country' (Orchestra/Morross)
¶ 'Jonah and the Whale' (Louis Armstrong *trumpet* and *vocal* and the All-Stars)
¶ Bach arranged Hess, 'Jesu, Joy of Man's Desiring (from Cantata No. 147) (Myra Hess *piano*)
¶ 'Raindrops Keep Fallin' on My Head' (from film *Butch Cassidy and the Sundance Kid*) (B. J. Thomas)
¶ Mozart/de los Rios, Symphony No. 40 in G minor (K. 550) (Manuel de Falla Orchestra/de los Rios)
¶ Grieg, 'Solveig's Song' (from *Peer Gynt Suite No. 2*, opus 55) (Erna Spoorenberg/Hague Philharmonic/Van Otterloo)
¶ 'Jig-a-Jig' (East of Eden)
*¶ 'Adeste Fideles' (St John's College Choir, Cambridge/ Guest)
¶ LUXURY: A dart board and darts of different weights.
¶ BOOK: An illustrated herbal.

18 December 1971
1104 Julia Trevelyan Oman
Designer

¶ Bizet, Symphony in C (French National Radio Orchestra/ Beecham)
¶ Verdi, *Falstaff* (excerpt from Act 3) (Juan Oncina/Graziella Sciutta/Vienna Philharmonic/ Bernstein)
¶ 'Poet and Singer' (Rudolf Aue)
¶ John Aubrey, *Brief Lives* (excerpt) (Roy Dotrice)
¶ Mozart, Piano Concerto No. 23 in A major (K 488) (Clifford Curzon/LSO/Kertesz)
¶ Simon, 'Old Friends' (Simon & Garfunkel)
¶ Tchaikovsky, *Eugene Onegin* (excerpt) (Ivan Petrov/Bolshoi Theatre Orchestra/Khaikin)
*¶ Elgar, 'Nimrod' (from *Enigma Variations*) (NPO/Barbirolli)
¶ LUXURY: Seeds.
¶ BOOK: Roy Strong & Julia Trevelyan Oman, *Elizabeth R*

25 December 1971
1105 David Frost (2nd appearance)
Interviewer and tycoon

¶ 'The Impossible Dream' (from *Man of La Mancha*) (Roberta Flack)
*¶ Sibelius, 'Finlandia' (LPO/ Hermann)
¶ 'Go Tell It on the Mountain' (Ella Mitchell)
¶ 'Brigt mich Pünkt lich zum Altar' (Get Me to the Church on Time) (from *My Fair Lady*) (Willy Millowitsch)
¶ Handel, 'Largo' (from the opera *Serse*) (Philadelphia Orchestra/Ormandy)
¶ 'Blueberry Hill' (Louis Armstrong and his All Stars)
¶ Bobby Kennedy, interviewed by David Frost
¶ 'Meeting with Roosevelt' (speech, 24 August 1941) (Sir Winston Churchill)
¶ 'I Have a Dream' (speech, 28 June 1963) (Dr Martin Luther King)
¶ 'Love's Been Good to Me' (Frank Sinatra)
¶ Puccini, 'Chi il bel sogno di Doretta' (from *La rondine*) (Leontyne Price/Rome Opera House Orchestra/Fabritiis)
¶ *The Frost Report on Everything* (excerpt) (David Frost/Ronnie Barker/John Cleese/Ronnie Corbett)
¶ 'Why Did I Choose You?' (from the musical *The Yearling*) (Barbra Streisand)
¶ 'The Lord's Prayer' (Billy Graham Los Angeles Crusade Choir)
¶ 'My Way' (Sammy Davis Jnr)
¶ *(Extra records allowed for this extended edition.)*
¶ LUXURY: Paper and felt-tipped pens.
¶ BOOK: A set of *Hansard*.

1 January 1972
1106 Gwen Berryman
Actress

*¶ Clarke, 'Trumpet Voluntary' (Gordon Webb/LPO/Boult)
¶ Bizet, 'The Flower Song' (from *Carmen*) (John Heddle Nash/Royal Liverpool Philharmonic/Sargent)
¶ Handel, 'I Know that My Redeemer Liveth' (from *Messiah*) (Elizabeth Harwood/ RPO/Sargent)
¶ Saint-Saëns, 'The Swan' (from *Carnival of the Animals*) (Robert Cordier *cello*/Paris Conservatoire/Prêtre)
¶ Gounod, 'The Jewel Song' (from *Faust*) (Victoria de los Angeles/Paris Opera Orchestra/ Cluytens)
¶ Mozart, Horn Concerto No. 1 in D (K. 412) (Dennis Brain/ Philharmonia Orchestra/von Karajan)
¶ Mozart, 'Letter Duet' (from *The Marriage of Figaro*, Act 3) (Mirella Freni/Jessye Norman/ BBC Symphony/Colin Davis)
¶ *The Archers* (excerpt) (Harry Oakes/Gwen Berryman) 'When We are Married' (from *The Belle of New York*) and 'Barwick Green' (*The Archers* signature tune) (New Concert Orchestra/ Wilbur)
¶ LUXURY: Writing materials.
¶ BOOK: An illustrated cookery book.

8 January 1972
1107 Isaac Stern
Concert violinist

¶ Brahms, Symphony No. 4 in E Minor (Philadelphia Orchestra/Stokowski)
¶ Schubert, Sonata No. 5 in A (opus 162) (Fritz Kreisler *violin*/ Sergei Rachmaninov *piano*)
¶ Beethoven, 'Florestan's Aria' (from *Fidelio*) (Helge Roswaenge/Berlin State Opera Orchestra/Seidler-Winkler)
¶ Bruch, 'Scottish Fantasy' (opus 46) (Jascha Heifetz *violin*/ NPO/Sargent)
¶ Brahms, String Quintet No. 2 in G (opus 111) (Isaac Stern and Alexander Schneider *violins*/ Milton Katims and Milton Thomas *violas*/Paul Tortelier *cello*)
¶ Chopin, Mazurka No. 10 in B flat (opus 17, no. 1) (Artur Rubinstein *piano*)
¶ Scriabin, Sonata No. 9 (opus 68) (Vladimir Horowitz *piano*) *(Only seven records were chosen and played: no favourite disc.)*

¶ LUXURY: A refrigerator.
¶ BOOK: *Encyclopaedia Britannica* (12th edition, pre-1914)

15 January 1972
1108 Christopher Plummer
Actor
¶ Rachmaninov, Piano Concerto No. 3 in D minor (opus 30) (Sergei Rachmaninov/Philadelphia Orchestra/Ormandy)
¶ 'Monsieur Lenoble' (Edith Piaf)
¶ 'The Music that Makes Me Dance' (from *Funny Girl*) (Barbra Streisand)
¶ Sibelius, Symphony No. 4 in A minor (Berlin Philharmonic/von Karajan)
¶ Tchaikovsky, Piano Concerto No. 1 in B flat minor (opus 23) (Vladimir Horowitz/NBC Symphony/Toscanini)
¶ Giordano, 'Amor ti vieta' (from *Fedora*) (Jussi Björling/Orchestra/Grevillius)
¶ Shostakovich, Symphony No. 5 in D minor (opus 47) (New York Philharmonic/Bernstein)
*¶ Mahler completed by Deryck Cooke, Symphony No. 10 in F sharp (Philadelphia Orchestra/Ormandy)
¶ LUXURY: A jeroboam of Taittinger champagne.
¶ BOOK: A. A. Milne, *Winnie the Pooh*

22 January 1972
1109 Richard Ingrams
Editor of *Private Eye*
¶ Beethoven, Cello Sonata No. 3 in A (opus 69) (Pablo Casals/Rudolf Serkin *piano*)
¶ Mozart, Quintet in G minor (K. 516) (Cecil Aronowitz *viola*/Amadeus String Quartet)
¶ Brahms, 'Variations on a Theme of Haydn' (opus 56a) (Suisse Romande Orchestra/Ansermet)
¶ R. Strauss, 'September' (from *Four Last Songs*) (Lisa della Casa/Vienna Philharmonic/Böhm)

¶ 'Harold Macmillan sings "She Didn't Say Yes, She Didn't Say No"' (from *Private Eye's Blue Record*)
¶ Schubert, Quintet in C major (opus 163) (Isaac Stern and Alexander Schneider *violins*/Milton Katims *viola*/Pablo Casals and Paul Tortelier *cellos*)
¶ Elgar, Violin Concerto in B minor (opus 61) (Yehudi Menuhin/LSO/Elgar)
*¶ Bach, 'Gloria' (from *Mass in B minor*, BWV 232) (RIAS Chorus/Berlin Radio Symphony/Maazel)
¶ LUXURY: A piano.
¶ BOOK: 'Teach Yourself Piano Tuning'.

29 January 1972
1110 Stuart Burrows
Tenor
¶ 'Cwm Rhondda' (Morriston Orpheus Choir)
¶ 'Addio, sogni di gloria' (Giuseppe di Stefano)
*¶ Mendelssohn, 'Oh, for the Wings of a Dove' (Ernest Lough/G. Thalben-Ball *organ*/Temple Church Choir, London)
¶ Donizetti, 'Mad Scene' (from *Lucia de Lammermoor*) (Joan Sutherland/Paris Conservatoire Orchestra/Santi)
¶ Mozart, *The Magic Flute* (excerpt from Act 1) (Dietrich Fischer-Dieskau/Stuart Burrows/Vienna Philharmonic/Solti)
¶ Bach, 'Et Incarnatus Est' (from *Mass in B minor*, BWV 232) (BBC Chorus/NPO/Klemperer)
¶ Verdi, 'Và pensiero sull'ali dorate' (from *Nabucco*) (La Scala Chorus and Orchestra/Serafin)
¶ 'I'll Walk with God' (Mario Lanza)
¶ LUXURY: Soap.
¶ BOOK: The complete works of Oscar Wilde.

5 February 1972
1111 David Hockney
Artist
¶ Beethoven/Liszt (arr.), Symphony No. 5 in C minor (opus 67) (Glenn Gould *piano*)
¶ Satie, 'La belle excentrique' (Aldo Ciccolini *piano*)
¶ Wagner, 'Sach's Last Song' (from *Die Meistersinger*, Act 3) (Theo Adam/Dresden State Orchestra/von Karajan)
¶ Poulenc, *Les biches* (Paris Conservatoire Orchestra/Désormière)
¶ 'San Francisco' (from film) (Jeanette MacDonald)
¶ Giordano, *Fedora* (opening) (Monte Carlo Opera Orchestra/Gardelli)
¶ 'I'm Through with Love' (from film *Some Like It Hot*) (Marilyn Monroe)
*¶ Wagner, 'Liebestod' (from *Tristan und Isolde*) (Birgit Nilsson/Vienna Philharmonic/Solti)
¶ LUXURY: Paper, pencils and a battery-operated pencil sharpener.
¶ BOOK: Floyd Carter, *Route 69*

12 February 1972
1112 Alice Delysia
Revue and musical comedy actress
*¶ O. Straus, 'C'est la saison d'amour' (from *Les trois valses*) (Yvonne Printemps)
¶ Mussorgsky, 'The Death of Boris' (from *Boris Godunov*) (Feodor Chaliapin/Royal Opera House Chorus and Orchestra/Bellezza)
¶ Saint-Saëns, 'The Swan' (from *Carnival of the Animals*) (Robert Cordier *cello*/Paris Conservatoire Orchestra/Prêtre)
¶ Coward, 'Poor Little Rich Girl' (from *On with the Dance*) (Noël Coward)
¶ Puccini, 'Vissi d'arte' (from *Tosca*) (Geraldine Farrar)
¶ Bizet, 'The Flower Song' (from *Carmen*) (Enrico Caruso/Orchestra/Rogers)
¶ Berlioz, Symphonie fantastique (opus 14) (French National Radio Orchestra/Beecham)

¶ 'If You Could Care' (from *As You Were*) (Alice Delysia)
¶ LUXURY: A bed.
¶ BOOK: Victor Hugo, *Les misérables*

19 February 1972
1113 Michael Parkinson
Television interviewer
*¶ 'Singin' in the Rain' (from film) (Gene Kelly)
¶ Handel, *Messiah* (excerpt) (Huddersfield Choral Society/ Royal Liverpool Philharmonic/ Sargent)
¶ 'Here's that Rainy Day' (Stan Getz *tenor saxophone* and his Quartet)
¶ Rodgers & Hart, 'I Wish I Were in Love Again' (from *Babes in Arms*) (Frank Sinatra)
¶ Coward, 'Mad About the Boy' (from *Words and Music*) (Blossom Dearie)
¶ 'How High the Moon' (Stan Kenton and his Orchestra)
¶ Lerner & Loewe, 'If Ever I Would Leave You' (from *Camelot*) (Robert Goulet)
¶ 'As Time Goes By' (Billie Holiday/Teddy Wilson *piano*)
¶ LUXURY: A typewriter and paper.
¶ BOOK: Ernest Hemingway, *Death in the Afternoon*

26 February 1972
1114 Hammond Innes
Novelist
¶ Gershwin, 'Bess, You is My Woman Now' (from *Porgy and Bess*) (Lawrence Winters/ Camilla Williams)
¶ Chopin, Étude No. 4 in C sharp minor (Shura Cherkassky *piano*)
*¶ 'God Rest Ye Merry, Gentlemen' (King's College Chapel Choir/Ord)
¶ Weill/Brecht, 'Pirate Jenny' (from *The Threepenny Opera*) (Lotte Lenya)
¶ Bach, Violin Concerto No. 2 in E major (BWV 1042) (David Oistrakh/Philadelphia Orchestra/Ormandy)
¶ 'Sailors' Hornpipe' (J. B. Robertson *bagpipes*)
¶ 'Earthquake!' (Yma Sumac)
¶ 'Helen of Kirconnell' (John Laurie)

¶ LUXURY: *The Guinness Book of Records*
¶ BOOK: Stanley Elliott Morrison, *The European Discovery of North America*

4 March 1972
1115 Raymond Leppard
Musician
*¶ Bach, 'Et Resurrexit' (from *Mass in B minor*, BWV 232) (Munich Bach Choir and Orchestra/Richter)
¶ Verdi, 'Fugue' (from *Falstaff*, Act 3) (Soloists/NBC Symphony/Toscanini)
¶ Wolf, Italian Serenade in G major (Budapest String Quartet)
¶ Elgar, 'Where Corals Lie' (from *Sea Pictures*, opus 37) (Janet Baker/LSO/Barbirolli)
¶ Wagner, 'Liebestod' (from *Tristan und Isolde*) (Kirsten Flagstad/Philharmonia Orchestra/Furtwängler)
¶ Eudora Welty, 'Why I Live at the P.O.' (Eudora Welty *speaking*)
¶ Boulez, 'Bel édifice et les pressentiments' (from *Le marteau sans maître*) (Jeanne Deroubaix/ensemble/Boulez)
¶ Monteverdi, 'Chiome d'oro' (from the 7th Book of Madrigals) (Gerald English/ Hugues Cuenod/Robert Masters and Sydney Humphreys *violins*/Bath Festival Ensemble/Leppard)
¶ LUXURIES: Gin, dry Martini and lemons.
¶ BOOK: Homer's *Iliad* and *Odyssey*.

11 March 1972
1116 David Storey
Playwright and novelist
¶ 'Anniversary Song' (from film *The Jolson Story*) (Anne Shelton)
¶ Mendelssohn, Symphony No. 4 in A (Italian) (LSO/Previn)
¶ Prokofiev, Symphony No. 5 in B flat (opus 100) (Moscow Radio Symphony/ Rozhdestvensky)

¶ Stravinsky, *A Lyke-Wake Dirge* (from Cantata (1952)) (Adrienne Albert/Alexander Young/Gregg Smith Singers/ Columbia Chamber Ensemble/ Stravinsky)
¶ Lennon & McCartney, 'A Day in the Life' (The Beatles)
¶ Dvořák, 'Scherzo capriccioso' (opus 66) (Hallé Orchestra/ Barbirolli)
¶ Lennon, 'God' (John Lennon)
*¶ Beethoven, Quartet in F major (opus 135) (Amadeus String Quartet)
¶ LUXURY: Wood and stone carving tools.
¶ BOOK: The collected poetry of W. B. Yeats.

18 March 1972
1117 Elizabeth Harwood
Soprano
*¶ Handel, 'For Unto Us a Child is Born' (from *Messiah*) (Ambrosian Singers/English Chamber Orchestra/Mackerras)
¶ Rossini, *Le Comte Ory* (Act 2 trio) (Juan Oncina/Sari Barabas/Cora Canne-Meijer/ Glyndebourne Festival Orchestra/Gui)
¶ R. Strauss, 'Im Abendrot' (from *Four Last Songs*) (Elisabeth Schwarzkopf/ Philharmonia Orchestra/ Ackermann)
¶ Handel, 'Heart, the Seat of Soft Delight' (from *Acis and Galatea*) (Joan Sutherland/ Philomusica of London/Boult)
¶ 'Girl of My Dreams' (Erroll Garner *piano*)
¶ Mozart, *Don Giovanni* (Act 1 trio) (Eberhard Wächter/ Giuseppe Taddei/Gottlob Frick/Philharmonia Orchestra/ Giulini)
¶ Bach, *Christmas Oratorio* (Part 1, BWV 248) (Lubecker Kantorei/Stuttgart Chamber Orchestra/Münchinger)
¶ Mozart, *The Marriage of Figaro* (Act 2 finale) (soloists/ Vienna Philharmonic/von Karajan)
¶ LUXURY: A Constable landscape.
¶ BOOK: A survival manual.

25 March 1972
1118 Robertson Hare (3rd appearance)
Character actor
¶ Lerner & Loewe, 'I Could Have Danced All Night' (from *My Fair Lady*) (Julie Andrews)
¶ Wagner, 'Ride of the Valkyries' (from *Die Walküre*) (Vienna Philharmonic/Solti)
¶ 'Alice' (Noël Coward)
¶ 'Transatlantic Lullaby' (from *The Gate Revue*) (Turner Layton)
¶ Novello/Melville, 'Vitality' (from *Gay's the Word*) (Cicely Courtneidge)
¶ 'Sunset' (Royal Marines Massed Bands)
¶ 'Louise' (from film *Innocents in Paris*) (Maurice Chevalier)
*¶ 'John Brown's Body' (Paul Robeson)
¶ LUXURY: Scotch whisky.
¶ BOOK: Robertson Hare, *Yours Indubitably*

1 April 1972
1119 John Noakes
Children's television presenter
*¶ Newley/Bricusse, 'Who Can I Turn To?' (from *The Roar of the Greasepaint, the Smell of the Crowd*) (Shirley Bassey)
¶ 'The Last of the Texas Rangers' (Lew Stone and his Band)
¶ Lerner & Loewe, 'Gigi' (from film) (Louis Jourdan)
¶ Bernstein/Sondheim, 'Somewhere' (from *West Side Story*) (Reri Grist)
¶ 'Unforgettable' (Nat 'King' Cole)
¶ 'Our Language of Love' (from *Irma La Douce*) (Elizabeth Seal/Keith Michell)
¶ Gershwin, 'Rhapsody in Blue' (Julius Katchen *piano*/LSO/Kertesz)
¶ 'They Didn't Believe Me' (from the sound track of *Oh, What a Lovely War*) (Rita Williams Singers/Orchestra/Ralston)
¶ LUXURY: A 12th-century Gloucester brass candlestick in the Victoria and Albert Museum.
¶ BOOK: Emlyn Williams, *The Corn is Green*

8 April 1972
1120 Sir Geoffrey Jackson
Diplomat
¶ 'Begone Dull Care' (Georgian Singers)
¶ 'When Day is Done' (Django Reinhardt *guitar*/Quintet of the Hot Club of France)
¶ Schubert, 'An die Musik' (D. 547) (Dietrich Fischer-Dieskau/Gerald Moore *piano*)
¶ 'The Girl from Ipanema' (Los Machucambos)
¶ Villa-Lobos, Bachianas Brasileiras No. 2 (Cleveland Pops Orchestra/Lane)
¶ Bach, Toccata and Fugue in D minor (Father Sebastian Wolff *organ*)
*¶ Ramirez, 'Gloria' (from *Misa Criolla*) (Los Fronterizos)
¶ Brahms, Intermezzo in C major (opus 119, no. 3) (Clifford Curzon *piano*)
¶ LUXURY: A Spanish guitar.
¶ BOOK: J. R. R. Tolkien, *The Lord of the Rings*

15 April 1972
1121 Wendy Hiller
Actress
¶ 'Hail Smiling Morn' (Grimethorpe Colliery Band)
¶ Schubert, Symphony No. 8 in B minor (Unfinished) (Philharmonia Orchestra/Klemperer)
¶ Delius, 'In a Summer Garden' (RPO/Beecham)
¶ Quilter, 'Now Sleeps the Crimson Petal' (Kathleen Ferrier/Phyllis Spurr *piano*)
*¶ Shakespeare, 'When in disgrace with Fortune and Men's Eyes' (Sonnet 29) (John Gielgud)
¶ Elgar, Violin Concerto in B minor (opus 61) (Yehudi Menuhin/LSO/Elgar)
¶ Chopin, Prelude No. 4 in E minor) (Artur Rubinstein *piano*)
¶ 'The Flowers o' the Forest' (Barbara Dickson)
¶ LUXURY: Sir Stanley Spencer, *Cookham Resurrection*
¶ BOOK: James Woodforde, *The Diary of a Country Parson 1758–1802*

22 April 1972
1122 Leonide Massine
Dancer and choreographer
¶ Mozart, Symphony No. 40 in G minor (K. 550) (Vienna Philharmonic/Furtwängler)
*¶ Mussorgsky, 'I Have Attained the Highest Power' (from *Boris Godunov*) (Feodor Chaliapin)
¶ Stravinsky, *The Rite of Spring* (Paris Conservatoire Orchestra/Monteux)
¶ Hindemith, *Nobilissima Visione* (Philharmonia Orchestra/Hindemith)
¶ Bach, *St John's Passion* (closing passage) (soloists/Munich Bach Choir and Orchestra/Richter)
¶ Wagner, *Parsifal* (prelude) (Bayreuth Festival Orchestra/Knappertsbusch)
¶ Beethoven, Symphony No. 7 in A major (opus 92) (NBC Symphony/Toscanini)
¶ Verdi, *Falstaff* (opening) (Geraint Evans/RCA Italiana Opera Orchestra/Solti)
¶ LUXURY: Not required.
¶ BOOK: Leonide Massine, *The Theory of Choreography*

29 April 1972
1123 Elizabeth Jane Howard
Novelist
¶ Mozart, Concerto No. 14 in E flat major for Piano and Orchestra (K. 449) (Rudolf Serkin/Columbia Symphony/Schneider)
¶ Chopin, Mazurka in A minor (Ignace Jan Paderewski *piano*)
¶ Bach, 'Ich habe genug' (Gérard Souzay/German Bach Soloists/Winschermann)
¶ C. P. E. Bach, Concerto in D minor (George Malcolm *harpsichord*/Bath Festival Orchestra/Menuhin)
¶ Brahms, 'Variations and Fugue on a Theme by Handel' (Walter Klien *piano*)
¶ R. Strauss, 'Zerbinetta's Aria' (from *Ariadne auf Naxos*) (Rita Streich/Philharmonia Orchestra/von Karajan)
¶ Scarlatti, Sonata in A major (L. 238) (Nina Milkina *piano*)
*¶ Bach, Toccata and Fugue in D minor (Geraint Jones *organ*)
¶ LUXURY: Writing materials.
¶ BOOK: An encyclopaedia.

6 May 1972
1124 David Bryant
World bowls champion
¶Addinsell, 'Warsaw Concerto' (from film *Dangerous Moonlight*) (Boston Pops Orchestra/ Fiedler)
¶'The Deadwood Stage' (from film *Calamity Jane*) (Doris Day)
¶'A String of Pearls' (Glenn Miller and his Orchestra)
¶Debussy, 'Clair de lune' (from *Suite bergamasque*) (Philadelphia Orchestra/ Ormandy)
*¶'Gone Fishin'' (Bing Crosby/ Louis Armstrong)
¶Carmichael, 'Stardust' (Hoagy Carmichael)
¶Bart, 'Where is Love?' (from *Oliver!*) (Keith Hamshere/ Orchestra/Dods)
¶'When I'm Cleaning Windows' (George Formby)
¶LUXURY: Golf clubs and balls.
¶BOOK: An encyclopaedia of gardening.

13 May 1972
1125 Joan Bakewell
Television interviewer
¶Bach, Double Concerto in D minor (BWV 1043) (Henryk Szeryng and Peter Rybar *violins*/Collegium Musicum Winterthur/Szeryng)
¶Berlioz, 'Women's Chorus' (from *Les troyens*, Act 2) (Royal Opera House Orchestra and Chorus, Covent Garden/Colin Davis)
¶Brahms, String Sextet No. 1 in B flat (opus 18) (Isaac Stern and Alexander Schneider *violins*/Milton Katims and Milton Thomas *violas*/Pablo Casals and Madeline Foley *cellos*)
¶Dylan, 'Mr Tambourine Man' (Bob Dylan)
¶Harrison, 'Here Comes the Sun' (The Beatles)
¶Verdi, *Don Carlos* (Act 1 duet) (Mario Flippeschi/Tito Gobbi/ Rome Opera House Orchestra/ Santini)
¶'Frank Mills' (from *Hair*) (Sonja Kristina)

*¶Boito, *Mefistofele* (prologue) (Nicola Moscona/Robert Shaw Chorale/Columbus Boys' Choir/NBC Symphony/ Toscanini)
¶LUXURY: A yellow Lamborghini.
¶BOOK: The collected works of James Joyce.

20 May 1972
1126 Geoffrey Parsons
Accompanist
¶Mozart, 'Ch'io mi scordi di te?' (concert aria) (Teresa Berganza/LSO/Pritchard)
¶'In the Bleak Midwinter' (Stephen Varcoe/King's College Chapel Choir/Willcocks)
*¶Elgar, 'The Farewell of the Angel' (from *The Dream of Gerontius*, opus 38) (Janet Baker/Hallé Orchestra/ Barbirolli)
¶Ovalle, 'Azulão' (Victoria de los Angeles/Sinfonia of London/Frühbeck de Burgos)
¶Wagner, 'Liebestod' (from *Tristan und Isolde*) (Kirsten Flagstad/Philharmonia Orchestra/Furtwängler)
¶J. Strauss, 'The Blue Danube Waltz' (Josef Lhévinne *piano*)
¶R. Strauss, 'Im Abendrot' (from *Four Last Songs*) (Elisabeth Schwarzkopf/Berlin Radio Symphony/Szell)
¶Rossini, *Le Comte Ory* (Act 1 finale) (soloists/Glyndebourne Festival Orchestra and Chorus/ Gui)
¶LUXURY: Crystal rock specimens.
¶BOOK: J. R. R. Tolkien, *The Lord of the Rings*

27 May 1972
1127 Tony Bennett
Vocalist
¶'The Kid from Red Bank' (Count Basie and his Orchestra)
¶'Take the "A" Train' (Duke Ellington and his Orchestra)
¶'You Make Me Feel So Young' (Frank Sinatra)
¶'Smile' (Tony Bennett)
*¶'Song of the Islands' (Louis Armstrong and his All Stars)
¶'Deep Purple' (Sarah Vaughan)

¶Rodgers, Hart, 'My Heart Stood Still' (from *A Connecticut Yankee*) (Art Tatum *piano*)
¶Ravel, *Daphnis and Chloe Suite No. 2* (Cleveland Orchestra/Boulez)
¶LUXURY: Painting equipment.
¶BOOK: The complete works of Leonardo da Vinci.

3 June 1972
1128 Alec Robertson (2nd appearance)
Writer, broadcaster and critic
¶Bach, Sonata No. 2 in A for Violin and Harpsichord (BWV 1015) (Henryk Szeryng *violin*/Helmut Walcha *harpsichord*)
¶Beethoven, String Quartet No. 13 in B flat (opus 130) (Quartetto Italiano)
¶Bartók, Sonata for Two Pianos and Percussion (Bracha Eden and Alexander Tamir *pianos*/ James Holland and Tristan Fry *percussion*)
¶Schubert, 'An mein Klavier' (D. 342) (Elisabeth Schumann/ Gerald Moore *piano*)
¶Cilèa, 'Io son l'umile ancella' (from *Adriana Lecouvreur*, Act 1) (Renata Tebaldi/Academia Santa Cecilia, Rome/Erede)
¶Elgar, Introduction and Allegro for Strings (opus 47) (Allegri String Quartet/Sinfonia of London/Barbirolli)
¶Tchaikovsky, 'Panorama' (from *The Sleeping Beauty*, Act 3) (Paris Conservatoire Orchestra/Fistoulari)
*¶Fauré, 'In Paradisum' (from *Requiem*, opus 48) (King's College Chapel Choir, Cambridge/NPO/Willcocks)
¶LUXURY: A piano.
¶BOOK: Bach's 48 preludes and fugues.

10 June 1972
1129 Professor Francis Camps
Emeritus Professor of Forensic Medicine
*¶Gershwin, 'Rhapsody in Blue' (George Gershwin *piano*/Paul Whiteman and his Concert Orchestra)
¶'Falling in Love Again' (from the film *The Blue Angel*) (Marlene Dietrich)

¶'Our Language of Love' (from *Irma La Douce*) (Elizabeth Seal)
¶Coward, 'Mad Dogs and Englishmen' (from *Words and Music*) (Noël Coward)
¶'The Blood Donor' (from radio series *Hancock's Half Hour*) (Tony Hancock/company)
¶'I Hold Your Hand in Mine' (Tom Lehrer)
¶'Sospan Fach' (Treorchy Male Choir)
¶Rodgers & Hammerstein, 'My Favourite Things' (from *The Sound of Music*) (Julie Andrews)
¶LUXURY: A tape recorder.
¶BOOK: *The Oxford English Dictionary*

17 June 1972
1130 Judi Dench
Actress
¶Bach, 'Gladly Would I Take' (from *St Matthew Passion*) (William Parsons/Jacques Orchestra/Jacques)
¶'The Lark in the Clear Air' (Dara Carroll *treble*)
¶Shakespeare, 'Deposition Speech' (from *Richard II*) (John Gielgud)
¶'Bonnie Lass O'Fyvie' (John Mearns)
¶Weill/Brecht, 'Pirate Jenny' (from *The Threepenny Opera*) (Lotte Lenya)
*¶Elgar, Cello Concerto in E minor (opus 85) (Jacqueline du Pré/LSO/Barbirolli)
¶Kern & Fields, 'The Way You Look Tonight' (from film *Swing Time*) (Edward Woodward)
¶Purcell, 'March (from Music for the Funeral of Queen Mary) (Geraint Jones Orchestra/Jones)
¶LUXURY: Basil Brush films and projector.
¶BOOK: *The Book of Kells*

24 June 1972
1131 Jean Plaidy
Historical novelist
¶Weber, 'Invitation to the Dance' (opus 65) (Vienna Philharmonic/Boskovsky)
*¶Beethoven, Symphony No. 7 in A major (opus 92) (Philharmonia Orchestra/Klemperer)

¶Beethoven, Symphony No. 5 in C minor (opus 67) (Vienna Philharmonic/Schmidt-Isserstedt)
¶Shakespeare, 'Polonius's Speech to Laertes' (from *Hamlet*) (George Howe)
¶Bizet, *Carmen* (prelude to Act 4) (Orchestra of German Opera, Berlin/Maazel)
¶Tchaikovsky, 'Pas de deux' (from *Swan Lake*, opus 20) (Suisse Romande Orchestra/Ansermet)
¶Rimsky-Korsakov, *Scheherazade* (opus 35) (RPO/Kempe)
¶Handel, *Water Music Suite* (English Chamber Orchestra/Leppard)
¶LUXURIES: A typewriter, paper and a hostess gown.
¶BOOK: *The Dictionary of National Biography*
*Unable to decide between these two favourite records

1 July 1972
1132 Charles Groves
Conductor
¶Oldham, 'Alleluia on a Plainsong Melody' (King's College Chapel Choir/Willcocks)
¶Schubert, Symphony No. 9 in C (Great) (Berlin Philharmonic/Furtwängler)
¶Massenet, 'Dream Song' (from *Manon*) (John Heddle Nash/Orchestra)
¶Beethoven, Symphony No. 9 in D minor (opus 125) (Vienna Philharmonic/Schmidt-Isserstedt)
¶Dylan Thomas, 'Polly Garter's Song' (from *Under Milk Wood*) (Diana Maddox)
*¶Wagner, 'Siegmund's Spring Song' (from *Die Walküre*) (Jon Vickers/LSO/Leinsdorf)
¶Messiaen, 'Quartet for the End of Time' (Erich Gruenberg *violin*/ Gervase de Peyer *clarinet*/William Pleeth *cello*/ Michel Béroff *piano*)
¶R. Strauss, 'Ein Heldenleben' (RPO/Beecham)
¶LUXURY: Cigars.
¶BOOK: An anthology of English poetry.

8 July 1972
1133 Henry Cecil
Novelist and playwright
*¶Beethoven, String Quartet in B flat (opus 130) (Amadeus String Quartet)
¶Dylan Thomas, *Under Milk Wood* (opening) (Richard Burton)
¶Shostakovich, Piano Quintet (opus 57) (Quintetto Chigiano)
¶'Oh Look at Me' (from *Salad Days*) (John Warner/Eleanor Drew)
¶Bach, *The Art of Fugue* (BWV 1080) (Philomusica of London/Malcolm)
¶Beethoven, Violin Sonata No. 8 in G (opus 30, no. 3) (David Oistrakh/Lev Oborin *piano*)
¶Flies, 'Wiegenlied' (Elisabeth Schumann/Orchestra/Collingwood)
¶Bach, Double Concerto in D minor (BWV 1043) (Igor & David Oistrakh *violins*/RPO/Goossens)
¶LUXURY: Aspirin.
¶BOOK: *Fowler's Modern English Usage*

15 July 1972
1134 Joe Henderson
Pianist, entertainer and songwriter
¶Riddle, 'Orange' (from *Tone Poems of Colour*) (Orchestra/Frank Sinatra)
¶'Amazing Grace' (Royal Scots Dragoon Guards Pipes, Drums and Military Band)
¶'After You've Gone' (Benny Goodman Trio)
¶'Put Your Arms Around Me, Honey' (Joe Henderson and his Friends)
*¶Butterworth, 'A Shropshire Lad' (LPO/Boult)
¶'Theme from *Shaft*' (from film) (Isaac Hayes)
¶'L'il Darling' (Count Basie and his Orchestra)
¶'It was a Very Good Year' (Frank Sinatra)
¶LUXURY: A radio receiver.
¶BOOK: Van Loon's *The Story of Mankind*

22 July 1972
1135 Marcel Marceau
Mime artist

¶ Mozart, Piano Concerto No. 21 in C (K. 467) (Geza Anda *piano* and directing the Camerata Academica of the Salzburg Mozarteum)
¶ Mussorgsky, 'The Death of Boris' (from *Boris Godunov*) (Feodor Chaliapin/Royal Opera House Chorus and Orchestra/ Bellezza)
¶ 'No Matter How You Pray' (Mahalia Jackson)
¶ Mozart, Clarinet Concerto in A (K. 622) (John McCaw/NPO/ Leppard)
¶ 'Les amants d'un jour' (Edith Piaf)
¶ Guillou, 'Icare' (Jean Guillou *organ*)
¶ 'High Society' (New Orleans Jazzmen)
*¶ Verdi, 'Dies Irae' (from *Requiem*) (Moscow State Academy Chorus/Moscow Philharmonic/Markevitch)
¶ LUXURY: Painting equipment.
¶ BOOK: Not chosen.

29 July 1972
1136 Sir Arthur Bliss (2nd appearance)
Composer and Master of the Queen's Musick

¶ Recording of the call of the laughing kookaburra
¶ 'The Elements' (Tom Lehrer)
*¶ Bliss, 'Fair is My Love' (from Serenade for Baritone and Orchestra) (John Shirley-Quirk/ LSO/Priestman)
¶ 'Raga Bhimpalasi' (Ravi Shankar *sitar*)
¶ Recording of sounds of wolves
¶ Bliss, 'Meditations on a theme by John Blow' (City of Birmingham Symphony/ Rignold)
¶ Borodin, 'In the Steppes of Central Asia' (Bournemouth Symphony/Silvestri)
¶ Bliss/Theocritus, 'The Song of the Reapers' (from *Pastoral*) (Bruckner-Mahler Choir of London/LCO/Morris)
¶ LUXURY: A pair of field glasses.
¶ BOOK: Johann David Wyss, *The Swiss Family Robinson*

5 August 1972
1137 Edward Ardizzone RA
Water-colourist and illustrator

¶ Brahms, Piano Concerto No. 2 in B flat (opus 83) (Sviatoslav Richter/CSO/Leinsdorf)
¶ Mozart, Symphony No. 41 in C major (K. 551) (Jupiter) (RPO/Beecham)
*¶ Beethoven, Piano Concerto No. 5 in E flat major (Emperor) (Rudolf Serkin/New York Philharmonic/Bernstein)
¶ Rossini, *La Cenerentola* (overture) (Philharmonia Orchestra/Giulini)
¶ Schubert, 'Die Forelle' (D. 550) (Dietrich Fischer-Dieskau/ Gerald Moore *piano*)
¶ Gluck, *Orfeo ed Euridice* (overture) (Virtuosi di Roma/ Collegium Musicum Italicum/ Fasano)
¶ Vivaldi, 'Spring' (from *The Four Seasons*) (Academy of St Martin-in-the-Fields/Marriner)
¶ Bach, Brandenburg Concerto No. 1 in F major (BWV 1046) (I Musici)
¶ LUXURIES: Malt whisky and drawing paper.
¶ BOOK: Charles Dickens, *The Pickwick Papers*

12 August 1972
1138 Stephane Grappelli
Jazz violinist

¶ Beethoven, Symphony No. 6 in F major (Pastoral) (Berlin Philharmonic/von Karajan)
¶ Debussy, *Prélude à l'après-midi d'un faune* (French National Radio Orchestra/Münch)
¶ 'In a Mist' (Bix Beiderbecke *piano*)
¶ 'I Can't Believe that You're in Love with Me' (Louis Armstrong and his Orchestra)
¶ Dvořák, 'Humoresque' (Art Tatum *piano*)
¶ 'My One and Only Love' (Art Tatum–Ben Webster Quartet)
¶ 'Body and Soul' (John Coltrane *tenor saxophone*/ ensemble)
*¶ 'Gary' (Stephane Grappelli *violin*/Marc Hemmeler *piano*/Jack Sewing *bass*/Kenny Clarke *drums*)
¶ LUXURY: The Koh-i-noor diamond.
¶ BOOK: An atlas.

19 August 1972
1139 Professor Barry Cunliffe
Archaeologist

¶ Janáček, 'Sinfonietta' (Pro Arte Orchestra/Mackerras)
¶ Wagner, 'Siegfried's Funeral March' (from *Götterdämmerung*) (Berlin Philharmonic/von Karajan)
*¶ Mozart, Clarinet Concerto in A (K. 622) (John McCaw/NPO/ Leppard)
¶ Cohen, 'Sister of Mercy' (Leonard Cohen)
¶ Brahms, Symphony No. 1 in C minor (opus 68) (Philharmonia Orchestra/ Klemperer)
¶ 'If You Want to be a Bird' (from film *Easy Rider*) (Holy Modal Rounders)
¶ 'Antara' (Los Calchakis)
¶ Beethoven/Carlos, Symphony No. 9 in D minor (opus 125) (4th movement, from film *A Clockwork Orange*) (Walter Carlos *moog synthesizer*)
¶ LUXURY: A still.
¶ BOOK: A book on plant genetics.

26 August 1972
1140 Jimmy Tarbuck
Comedian

¶ Bart, 'Consider Yourself' (from *Oliver!*) (Max Bygraves)
¶ 'Alfie' (from film) (Cilla Black)
¶ 'Paradise' (Frankie Vaughan)
*¶ 'The Girls I Like' (Max Miller)
¶ Lennon & McCartney, 'This Boy' (The Beatles)
¶ 'I'll Never Fall in Love Again' (Tom Jones)
¶ 'Up on the Roof' (Kenny Lynch)
¶ Harrison, 'My Sweet Lord' (George Harrison)
¶ LUXURY: Golf clubs and balls.
¶ BOOK: *Encyclopaedia Britannica*

2 September 1972
1141 David Franklin
Broadcaster

*¶ Bach, Brandenburg Concerto No. 3 in G (BWV 1048) (I Musici)
¶ Ravel, Trois Beaux Oiseaux de Paradis (from Trois Chansons – 1915) (Robert Shaw Chorale)

¶ Mozart, Quintet in A for Clarinet and Strings (K. 581) (Jack Brymer *clarinet*/Allegri Quartet)

¶ Wagner, 'Träume' (from 5 Gedichte von Mathilde Wesendonck) (Kirsten Flagstad/Vienna Philharmonic/Knappertsbusch)

¶ Handel, 'Love in Her Eyes Sits Playing' (from *Acis and Galatea*) (John Heddle Nash)

¶ Tallis, 40-part Motet 'Spem in Alium' (Cambridge University Musical Society/King's College Chapel Choir/Willcocks)

¶ Brahms, 'Sonntag' (opus 47, no. 3) Alexander Kipnis/Gerald Moore *piano*)

¶ Handel, 'Arrival of the Queen of Sheba' (from *Solomon*) (RPO/Groves)

¶ LUXURY: A padded deckchair.

¶ BOOK: *Fowler's Modern English Usage*

9 September 1972
1142 Anthony Lawrence
BBC Far East correspondent
*¶ Bach, Brandenburg Concerto No. 4 in G major (BWV 1049) (English Chamber Orchestra/Britten)

¶ Chopin, Nocturne No. 2 in D flat (opus 27) (Artur Rubinstein piano)

¶ 'These Foolish Things' (from *Spread It Abroad*) (Turner Layton)

¶ 'Yunan Province' (Lee Lynn)

¶ Weill/Brecht, 'Pirate Jenny' (from *The Threepenny Opera*) (members of original Berlin cast)

¶ Schubert, 'Die Forelle' (Elisabeth Schumann/George Reeves *piano*)

¶ 'Onward Christian Soldiers' (York Celebration Choir/Dunn)

¶ 'The Man Who Broke the Bank at Monte Carlo' and 'I've Got a Lovely Bunch of Coconuts' (street piano)

¶ LUXURY: Two armchairs.

¶ BOOK: Marcel Proust, *À la recherche du temps perdu*

16 September 1972
1143 Margaret Lockwood (2nd appearance)
Actress
*¶ Beethoven, 'Für Elise' (Alfred Brendel *piano*)

¶ 'Unforgettable' (Nat 'King' Cole)

¶ Mendelssohn, *A Midsummer Night's Dream* (overture) (LSO/Maag)

¶ 'Volare' (Marino Marini and his Quartet)

¶ Chopin, Prelude No. 7 in A major (opus 28, no. 7) (John Ogdon *piano*)

¶ 'Eton Boating Song' (Eton College Musical Society)

¶ J. Strauss, 'Tales from the Vienna Woods' (Vienna Philharmonic/Boskovsky)

¶ 'Scarborough Fair' (Simon & Garfunkel)

¶ LUXURY: A piano.

¶ BOOK: *Encyclopaedia Britannica*

23 September 1972
1144 John Reed
Principal Comedian, D'Oyly Carte Opera Company
*¶ Rachmaninov, Piano Concerto No. 2 in C minor (opus 18) (Vladimir Ashkenazy/Moscow Philharmonic/Kondrashin)

¶ 'The Last Rose of Summer' (Ada Alsop/Boyd Neel String Orchestra)

¶ Barber, Adagio for Strings (opus 11) (Philadelphia Orchestra Strings/Ormandy)

¶ Sullivan/Mackerras, *Pineapple Poll* (opening dance) (RPO/Mackerras)

¶ Offenbach, 'Oh Little Cloud' (from *La vie parisienne*) (Cynthia Moray/Eric Shilling/Sadler's Wells Orchestra/Faris)

¶ 'The Stripper' (David Rose and his Orchestra)

¶ 'Man of La Mancha' (from *Man of La Mancha*) (Richard Kiley/Irving Jacobson)

¶ 'Come Dance the Syrtaki' (Stelios Zafirou and his Bouzoukia)

¶ LUXURY: Painting equipment.

¶ BOOK: A do-it-yourself manual.

30 September 1972
1145 Terence Cuneo
Painter
¶ 'Welcome to My World' (Jim Reeves)

¶ 'I Wish You Love' (Peter Nero *piano*)

¶ Recording of a French locomotive

*¶ Rachmaninov, Piano Concerto No. 2 in C minor (opus 18) (Benno Moiseiwitsch/LPO/Goehr)

¶ Jarre, 'Theme from *Lawrence of Arabia*' (from film) (LPO/Jarre)

¶ Dylan, 'Go 'Way from My Window' (Joan Baez)

¶ 'Not Goin' Home Anymore' (from film *Butch Cassidy and the Sundance Kid*) (soundtrack)

¶ 'I'd Like to Teach the World to Sing' (The New Seekers)

¶ LUXURY: Painting equipment.

¶ BOOK: Harvey Allen, *Anthony Adverse*

7 October 1972
1146 Michael Aspel
Broadcaster
¶ 'I'm the Guy Who Found the Lost Chord' (Jimmy Durante)

¶ Arnold, 'Allegro Risoluto' (from *English Dances*) (LPO/Boult)

¶ Rodgers & Hart, 'Slaughter on Tenth Avenue' (from *On Your Toes*) (Paul Whiteman and his Concert Orchestra)

¶ 'Puppet Man' (The Fifth Dimension)

¶ Mussorgsky/Ravel (arr.), 'The Great Gate at Kiev' (from *Pictures at an Exhibition*) (Philharmonia Orchestra/Maazel)

¶ 'That's My Kick' (Erroll Garner *piano*)

¶ 'Drinking Water' (Frank Sinatra)

*¶ Ravel, *Ma mère l'oye* (Detroit Symphony/Paray)

¶ LUXURY: A piano.

¶ BOOK: A history of the world.

14 October 1972
1147 Christopher Gable
Actor

¶ Prokofiev, *Romeo and Juliet* (Orchestre de la Suisse Romande/Ansermet)

¶ Bellini, 'Casta diva' (from *Norma*) (Joan Sutherland/Royal Opera House Chorus and Orchestra, Covent Garden/Molinari-Pradelli)

¶ Ravel, 'Beach Scene' (from *Daphnis and Chloe*) (Orchestre de la Suisse Romande/Choir/Ansermet)

¶ 'I'm the Greatest Star' (from *Funny Girl*) (Barbra Streisand)

¶ Delius, 'A Song of Summer' (LSO/Barbirolli)

¶ Mahler, 'Wenn Dein Mütterlein' (from *Kindertotenlieder*) (Dietrich Fischer-Dieskau/Berlin Philharmonic/Böhm)

¶ 'Nathan La Franeer' (Joni Mitchell)

*¶ Mahler, 'Abschied' (from *Das Lied von der Erde*) (Kathleen Ferrier/Vienna Philharmonic/Walter)

¶ LUXURY: A still.

¶ BOOK: J. R. R. Tolkien, *The Lord of the Rings*

21 October 1972
1148 Jackie Charlton
Footballer

¶ Newman, 'How the West was Won' (from film) (soundtrack)

¶ Gershwin, 'A Foggy Day' (from film *A Damsel in Distress*) (Frank Sinatra)

¶ Verdi, 'Grand March' (from *Aida*) (Combined BMC, Fairey and Foden Motor Works Bands/Mortimer)

¶ Arlen & Harburg, 'Over the Rainbow' (from film *The Wizard of Oz*) (Judy Garland)

¶ 'Pandora' (Jim Shepherd *cornet*/John Foster & Sons and Black Dyke Mills Bands)

¶ 'Little Green Apples' (Roger Miller)

¶ World Cup Final 1966 (last minute of extra time)

*¶ Elgar, 'Pomp and Circumstance' March No. 1 in D major (opus 39) (recorded at last night of 1969 Proms) (BBC Symphony/Colin Davis)

¶ LUXURY: A spy-glass.

¶ BOOKS: Mark Twain, *The Adventures of Tom Sawyer* and *The Adventures of Huckleberry Finn*.

28 October 1972
1149 Imogen Holst
Musician, conductor and writer

*¶ Purcell, 'Rondo' (from *The Fairy Queen*) (English Chamber Orchestra/Britten)

¶ Trad., 'The Sprig o' Thyme' (Joseph Taylor)

¶ 'Bristol Surprise Major' (Bells of St Mary's, Debenham, Suffolk)

¶ 'Chaiti-Dhun' (Vilayat & Bismillah Khan *sitar and shehnai*)

¶ Wilbye, Madrigal 'Sweet Honeysucking Bees' (Wilbye Consort/Pears)

¶ Holst, 'Saturn' (from *The Planets*, opus 32) (LSO/Holst)

¶ Britten, 'The Autumn Wind' (from Songs from the Chinese) (Peter Pears/Julian Bream *guitar*)

¶ Bach, Brandenburg Concerto No. 2 in F major (BWV 1047) (English Chamber Orchestra/Britten)

¶ LUXURY: A miniature spy-glass.

¶ BOOK: Reverend Francis Kilvert, *Diary 1870–1879*

4 November 1972
1150 Dennis Wheatley
Novelist and thriller writer

¶ 'The Man Who Broke the Bank at Monte Carlo' (Charles Coburn)

¶ 'Tipperary' (Chelsea Pensioners)

¶ 'If You were the Only Girl in the World' (from *The Bing Boys are Here*) (Violet Loraine/George Robey)

¶ Elgar, 'Pomp and Circumstance' March No. 1 in D major (opus 39) (recorded at last night of 1969 proms) (BBC Symphony/Colin Davis)

¶ Lehár, *The Merry Widow* (waltz) (Sadler's Wells Opera Company and Orchestra/Reid)

¶ 'Washington Post' (Band of the Blues and Royals)

¶ 'La Marseillaise' (Paris Opera Chorus)

*¶ Coward, 'I'll See You Again' (from *Bitter Sweet*) (Peggy Wood/George Metaxa)

¶ LUXURY: His stamp collection.

¶ BOOK: *Encyclopaedia Britannica*

11 November 1972
1151 Maggie Smith
Actress

¶ Mozart, Clarinet Quintet in A major (Gervase de Peyer/Melos Ensemble)

¶ 'Kathleen Mavourneen' (John McCormack)

¶ 'Raindrops Keep Fallin' on My Head' (from film *Butch Cassidy and the Sundance Kid*)

*¶ Shakespeare, 'Let Me not to the Marriage of True Minds' (Sonnet 116) (John Gielgud)

¶ Ovalles 'Azulão' (Salli Terri/Laurindo Almeida *guitar*)

¶ 'La vie en rose' (Edith Piaf)

¶ 'A Bar on the Piccola Marina' (Noël Coward)

¶ Bach, Concerto in D minor for violin, oboe and orchestra (BWV 1060) (Yehudi Menuhin *violin and conducting*/Léon Goossens *oboe*/Bath Festival Chamber Orchestra)

¶ LUXURIES: Sun-barrier cream and a straw hat.

¶ BOOK: *Encyclopaedia Britannica*

18 November 1972
1152 Beverly Sills
Opera singer

¶ R. Strauss, *Der Rosenkavalier* (final trio) (Lotte Lehmann/Elisabeth Schumann/Maria Olszewska/Vienna Philharmonic/Heger)

¶ 'When the World was Young' (Frank Sinatra)

¶ Rossini, 'Una voce poco fà' (from *The Barber of Seville*) (Amelita Galli-Curci)

¶ Handel, 'Da tempeste il legno infranto' (from *Julius Caesar*) (Beverly Wolff/Beverly Sills/New York City Opera Chorus and Orchestra/Rudel)

¶ Wagner, 'Liebestod' (from *Tristan und Isolde*) (Birgit Nilsson/Philharmonia Orchestra/Ludwig)

¶'Fascination' (André Previn *piano*/Orchestra/Williams)
¶Wagner, *Lohengrin* (Act 3 prelude) (Vienna Philharmonic/ Kempe)
*¶R. Strauss, *Salome* (final scene) (Ljuba Welitsch/ Metropolitan Opera Association Orchestra/Reiner)
¶LUXURY: A telephone.
¶BOOK: Margaret Mitchell, *Gone with the Wind*.

25 November 1972
1153 Group Captain Peter Townsend
Writer and traveller
*¶'L'ame des poètes' (Charles Trenet)
¶Gounod, 'Ballet Music' (from *Faust*) (Paris Opera Orchestra/ Cluytens)
¶Lloyd-Webber/Rice, 'Jesus Christ Superstar' (from *Jesus Christ Superstar*) (London cast)
¶Crimond, 'The Twenty-Third Psalm' (Glasgow Orpheus Choir/Roberton)
¶Porter, 'Calypso' (from film *High Society*) (Lous Armstrong *vocal* and his Band)
¶'N'kosi Sikelela' (New Church Mission Choir)
¶Beethoven, Piano Concerto No. 5 in E flat major (Emperor) (Rudolf Serkin/Pittsburgh Symphony/Steinberg)
¶Rossini, *The Barber of Seville* (overture) (Philharmonia Orchestra/von Karajan)
¶LUXURY: Seeds.
¶BOOK: Daniel Defoe, *Robinson Crusoe*

2 December 1972
1154 Adelaide Hall
Singer and Actress
¶'He Ain't Heavy, He's My Brother' (Malcolm Roberts)
*¶Malotte, 'The Lord's Prayer' (Mahalia Jackson)
¶'You're a Lady' (Peter Skellern)
¶'That Old Feeling' (from film *Vogues of 1938*) (Adelaide Hall)
¶Borodin/Wright & Forrest (arr.), 'And This is My Beloved' (from *Kismet*) (Moira Anderson)

¶'The Great Wall of Harpenden' (Eric Morecambe/ Ernie Wise)
¶Aznavour, 'Yesterday When I was Young' (Shirley Bassey)
¶Porter, 'Let's Do It' (from *Paris*) (Noël Coward)
¶LUXURY: Crochet needles and wool.
¶BOOK: A history of the United States.

9 December 1972
1155 Johnny Speight
Television writer
¶ 'My Very Good Friend, the Milkman' (Fats Waller *piano* and *vocal* and his Rhythm)
¶'Saturday Night (is the Loneliest Night of the Week)' (Frank Sinatra)
*¶'My Way' (Frank Sinatra)
¶'Cool Blues' (Charlie Parker Quartet)
¶Rodgers, Hart, 'Thou Swell' (from *A Connecticut Yankee*) (Joe Williams/Count Basie and his Orchestra)
¶'Hello Dolly' (from *Hello Dolly*) (Louis Armstrong *vocal* and *trumpet* and the All Stars)
¶Berlin, 'White Christmas' (from film *Holiday Inn*) (Charlie Parker *alto saxophone*/ Ensemble)
¶Rodgers, Hart, 'Have You Met Miss Jones?' (from *I'd Rather be Right*) (Stan Getz *tenor saxophone*/Ensemble)
¶LUXURY: Golf clubs and balls.
¶BOOK: The prefaces of George Bernard Shaw.

16 December 1972
1156 Tom Harrisson (2nd appearance)
Naturalist and anthropologist
¶Walton, *Façade* (Dame Edith Sitwell *speaker*/English Opera Group/Collins)
*¶English birds, recorded by Ludwig Koch
¶'Postscript to the Epic of Dunkirk' (J. B. Priestley)
¶Weill/Brecht , 'Mack the Knife' (from *The Threepenny Opera*) (Lotte Lenya)
¶'Music from Bali' (Gamelan Orchestra)

¶'I'm Gonna Sit Right Down and Write Myself a Letter' (Fats Waller *piano* and *vocal* and his Rhythm)
¶'Mr Gallagher and Mr Sheen' (Bing Crosby/Johnny Mercer)
¶Bach, *Goldberg Variations* (BWV 988) (Wilhelm Kempff *piano*)
¶LUXURY: A snorkel.
¶BOOK: The *I Ching*

23 December 1972
1157 Elsie & Doris Waters (2nd appearance)
Comediennes
¶(E) Stravinsky, *The Firebird* (Columbia Symphony/ Stravinsky)
¶(D) 'Right, Said Fred' (Bernard Cribbins)
¶(E) Debussy/Hartman, Prelude No. 8, Book 1, 'La fille aux cheveux de lin' (Yehudi Menuhin *violin*/Gerald Moore *piano*)
¶(D) Coward, 'I'll Follow My Secret Heart' (from *Conversation Piece*) (Yvonne Printemps)
¶(E) Sousa, 'Stars and Stripes Forever' (Black Dyke Mills Band/Newsome)
¶(D) 'A Walk in the Black Forest' (Horst Jankowski and his Orchestra)
¶(E) 'A Gal in Calico' (from film *The Time, the Place, the Girl*) (Bing Crosby)
¶(D) Bourgeois/Vaughan Williams, 'The Old Hundredth' (from Coronation Service of HM Queen Elizabeth II)
¶LUXURIES: (D) a piano; (E) sheet music.
¶BOOKS: (D) her favourite novels of Charlotte Brontë; (E) an anthology of poetry.
(*No favourite disc was chosen*)

30 December 1972
1158 Noel Rawsthorne
Organist
*¶Bach, 'Osanna in Excelsis'
(from *Mass in B minor*, BWV
232) (Munich Bach Choir and
Orchestra/Richter)
¶Bartók, Piano Concerto No. 3
(Annie Fischer/LSO/
Markevitch)
¶J. Strauss, 'Adele's Laughing
Song' (from *Die Fledermaus*)
(Florence Foster Jenkins/
Cosme McMoon *piano*)
¶R. Strauss, 'Also Sprach
Zarathustra' (Vienna
Philharmonic/von Karajan)
¶Bach, 'Have Mercy, Lord, on
Me' (from *St Matthew Passion*)
(Kathleen Ferrier/Jacques
Orchestra/Jacques)
¶Mozart Opera' (from *Caught
in the Act*) (Victor Borge)
¶Arlen & Harburg, 'Over the
Rainbow' (from film *The
Wizard of Oz*) (Art Tatum
piano)
¶'On This Day Earth Shall
Ring' (Liverpool Cathedral
Choir)
¶LUXURY: A harpsichord.
¶BOOK: A survival manual.

6 January 1973
1159 Tony Britton
Actor
*¶Mozart, Symphony No. 39 in
E flat (K. 543) (Vienna
Philharmonic/Kertesz)
¶Bruckner, Symphony No. 4 in
E flat (Romantic) (Amsterdam
Concertgebouw/Haitink)
¶Vaughan Williams, 'Fantasia
on a Theme by Thomas Tallis'
(Sinfonia of London/Barbirolli)
¶Shakespeare, 'When Icicles
Hang' (from *Love's Labour's
Lost*) (Robert Donat)
¶Porter, 'You're Sensational'
(from film *High Society*) (Frank
Sinatra)
¶Tchaikovsky, 'Waltz of the
Flowers' (from *The Nutcracker
Suite*) (Vienna Philharmonic/
von Karajan)
¶Dvořák, Symphony No. 9 in E
minor (From the New World)
(Vienna Philharmonic/Kubelik)

¶Bach, Brandenburg Concerto
No. 4 in G major (BWV 1049)
(Vienna State Opera Chamber
Orchestra/Prohaska)
¶LUXURIES: Scotch and
champagne.
¶BOOKS: Language courses in
Italian, French and German.

13 January 1973
1160 Mike Yarwood
Impersonator
¶Chaplin, 'Theme from
Limelight' (from film) (Frank
Chacksfield and his Orchestra)
¶Berlin, 'White Christmas'
(from film *Holiday Inn*) (Bing
Crosby)
¶'Reach Out for Me'
(orchestra/Burt Bacharach)
¶'People' (from *Funny Girl*)
(Barbra Streisand)
¶Bach/Gounod, 'Ave Maria'
(Beniamino Gigli)
¶'How High the Moon' (Erroll
Garner *piano*)
¶Mitchell, 'Both Sides Now'
(Andy Williams)
*¶Elgar, 'Pomp and
Circumstance' March No. 1 in
D major (opus 39) (recorded at
last night of 1969 Proms) (BBC
Symphony/Colin Davis)
¶LUXURY: A daily newspaper.
¶BOOK: A volume of colour
reproductions of paintings.

20 January 1973
1161 Denise Robins
Romantic novelist
¶Bach, Suite No. 3 in D (BWV
1068) (Academy of St Martin-
in-the-Fields/Marriner)
*¶Wagner, *Die Walküre* (Act 1)
(Lauritz Melchior/NBC
Symphony/Toscanini)
¶Rachmaninov, 'Rhapsody on
a Theme of Paganini' (opus 43)
(Vladimir Ashkenazy *piano*/
LSO/Previn)
¶Granados, 'The Lover and the
Nightingale' (Victoria de los
Angeles/Philharmonia
Orchestra/Fistoulari)
¶Tchaikovsky, Romeo and
Juliet Fantasy Overture (Vienna
Philharmonic/Maazel)

¶Schumann, 'Im
wunderschönen Monat Mai'
(from *Dichterliebe*) (Dietrich
Fischer-Dieskau/Jörg Demus
piano)
¶Chopin, Fantasie-Impromptu
in C sharp minor (opus 66)
(Artur Rubinstein *piano*)
¶Bach, 'Sheep May Safely
Graze' (from Cantata No. 208)
(Phyllis Sellick and Cyril Smith
pianos)
¶LUXURY: Family photographs.
¶BOOK: *Encyclopaedia
Britannica*

27 January 1973
1162 Robert Nesbitt
**Theatrical director and
producer**
¶Prokofiev, *Romeo and Juliet*
(Bolshoi Theatre Orchestra/
Rozhdestvensky)
¶'Fascination Medley' (Pete
Fountain *clarinet*)
¶Porter, 'You're the Top' (from
Anything Goes (Ella Fitzgerald)
¶Rimsky-Korsakov, *Sadko*
(Musical Picture for Orchestra)
(Suisse Romande Orchestra/
Ansermet)
¶Coward, 'Mad Dogs and
Englishmen' (from *Words and
Music*) (Noël Coward)
¶'One Mint Julep' (Count Basie
Orchestra)
*¶Beethoven, Piano Concerto
No. 1 in C major (opus 15)
(Christoph Eschenbach/Berlin
Philharmonic/von Karajan)
¶'Ta Evghenika Pedia' (Manos
Hadjidakis)
¶LUXURY: 1966 Moët Chandon.
¶BOOK: *Encyclopaedia
Britannica*

3 February 1973
1163 Anthony Smith
Writer and traveller
¶Schubert, Quintet in A (opus
114) (Artur Schnabel *piano*/Pro
Arte Quartet)
*¶'Iranian Love Song' (vocal
with violin)
¶'Ose Yie' (Ghanaian war
chant) (De Paur Chorus)
¶'Petite fleur' (Monty Sunshine
clarinet/Chris Barber's Jazz
Band)

¶ 'Crazy Kid' (from *King Kong*) (original cast)
¶ Recording of the calls of a whale
¶ 'The Wild Colonial Boy' (Clancy Brothers)
¶ R. Strauss, 'Also Sprach Zarathustra' (Berlin Philharmonic/Böhm)
¶ LUXURY: Sketching materials.
¶ BOOK: An atlas.

10 February 1973
1164 Rita Hunter
Operatic soprano
¶ Wagner, *Lohengrin* (prelude) (Vienna Philharmonic/Kempe)
¶ Offenbach, 'So Gleam with Desire' (from *The Tales of Hoffmann*) (Bruce Dargavel/RPO/Beecham)
¶ Wagner, 'Love Duet' (from *Tristan und Isolde*) (Kirsten Flagstad/Ludwig Suthaus/Philharmonia Orchestra/Furtwängler)
¶ Mozart, 'Deh! Vieni alla finestra' (from *Don Giovanni*) (Ezio Pinza/New York Metropolitan Opera Orchestra/Cleva)
¶ Wagner, 'Zu neuen thaten' (from *Götterdämmerung*) (Rita Hunter/Alberto Remedios/LPO/Mackerras)
*¶ Verdi, 'Ingemisco' (from *Requiem*) (Beniamino Gigli/Rome Opera House Orchestra/Serafin)
¶ Wagner, 'Wotan's Farewell' (from *Die Walküre*) (George London/Vienna Philharmonic/Knappertsbusch)
¶ 'Cabaret' (from *Cabaret*) (Jill Haworth)
¶ LUXURY: Oil painting equipment.
¶ BOOK: An anthology of poetry.

17 February 1973
1165 John Le Mesurier
Actor
¶ 'Take the "A" Train' (Duke Ellington and his Famous Orchestra)
¶ 'Spring is Here' (from *Spring is Here*) (Bill Evans Trio)
¶ 'Setting Fire to the Policeman' (Peter Sellers)
¶ 'Come Rain or Come Shine' (from *St Louis Woman*) (Judy Garland)

¶ 'Easy Living' (Bob Burns *clarinet*/Alan Clare Trio)
¶ 'What's New?' (Annie Ross)
¶ 'After You, Who?' (from *The Gay Divorce*) (Fred Astaire)
*¶ Bach, Double Concerto in D minor (BWV 1043) (David & Igor Oistrakh *violins*/RPO/Goossens)
¶ LUXURY: A small distillery.
¶ BOOK: Samuel Pepys' *Diary*

24 February 1973
1166 Leslie Thomas
Writer
¶ 'Morning Has Broken' (Cat Stevens)
*¶ Mozart, Horn Concerto No. 1 in D major (Dennis Brain/Philharmonia Orchestra/von Karajan)
¶ Rimsky-Korsakov, *Scheherazade* (RPO/Beecham)
¶ 'Didn't We, Girl?' (Richard Harris)
¶ Litolff, Concerto Symphonique No. 4 (Clifford Curzon *piano*/LPO/Boult)
¶ Denver, 'Take Me Home, Country Roads' (John Denver)
¶ 'Autumn Rendezvous' (Françoise Hardy)
¶ Lennon & McCartney, 'Penny Lane' (The Beatles)
¶ LUXURY: A sand iron and golf balls.
¶ BOOK: Leslie Thomas, *The Virgin Soldiers*

3 March 1973
1167 Alexander Gibson
Conductor
¶ Purcell, 'When I am Laid in Earth' (from *Dido and Aeneas*) (Janet Baker/English Chamber Orchestra/Lewis)
¶ Mozart, March in D major (K. 249) (RPO/Beecham)
¶ Puccini, *Madam Butterfly* (opening) (Rome Opera House Orchestra/Barbirolli)
¶ Bartók, 'Music for Strings, Percussion and Celesta' (National Youth Orchestra of Great Britain/Boulez)
¶ Villa-Lobos, Prelude No. 3 in A minor (Julian Bream *guitar*)
¶ Sibelius, *Karelia* (overture, opus 10) (Scottish National Orchestra/Gibson)

¶ Schubert, Impromptu in G flat (opus 90, no. 3) (Clifford Curzon *piano*)
*¶ Wagner, 'Liebestod' (from *Tristan und Isolde*) (Helga Dernesch/Berlin Philharmonic/von Karajan)
¶ LUXURY: A piano.
¶ BOOK: Gustav Kobbe, *Complete Opera Book*

10 March 1973
1168 Dame Veronica Wedgwood OM
Historian
*¶ Beethoven, 'Leonora Overture' (No. 3) (Philharmonia Orchestra/Klemperer)
¶ Mozart, 'La ci darem la mano' (from *Don Giovanni*) (Enzio Pinza/Elisabeth Rethberg)
¶ Mozart, *Eine Kleine Nachtmusik* (K. 525) (Academy of St Martin-in-the-Fields/Marriner)
¶ Massenet, 'Obéissons quand leur voix appelle' (from *Manon*) (Victoria de los Angeles/Paris Opéra Comique Orchestra/Monteux)
¶ Verdi, 'Sul fil d'un suffio' (from *Falstaff*) (Rita Streich/Berlin Opera Orchestra/Peters)
¶ Verdi, 'Tu che le vanita' from *Don Carlos*) (Montserrat Caballé/Royal Opera House Orchestra, Covent Garden/Giulini)
¶ Oscar Wilde, *The Importance of Being Earnest (Act 1)* (Edith Evans/John Gielgud)
¶ Schubert, 'Das Wandern' (from *Die Schöne Müllerin*) (Dietrich Fischer-Dieskau/Gerald Moore *piano*)
¶ LUXURY: A pair of binoculars.
¶ BOOK: A volume containing reproductions of the work of Venetian painters.

17 March 1973
1169 George Melly
Writer, film critic and blues singer
¶ Lennon & McCartney, 'Sergeant Pepper's Lonely Hearts Club Band' (The Beatles)
¶ 'Auntie Maggie's Remedy' (George Formby)

¶ 'Potato Head Blues' (Louis Armstrong *cornet* and His Hot Seven)

¶ Vivaldi, 'Spring' (from *The Four Seasons*) (Robert Michelucci *violin*/I Musici)

¶ Kern, 'Yesterdays' (from *Roberta*) (Billie Holiday)

¶ 'At the Ball' (Douglas Byng)

¶ 'Winin' Boy Blues' (Jelly Roll Morton's New Orleans Jazzmen)

*¶ 'Hustlin' Dan' (Bessie Smith)

¶ LUXURY: A piano.

¶ BOOK: Marcel Proust, *À la recherche du temps perdu*

24 March 1973
1170 Cathleen Nesbitt
Actress

¶ Rodgers & Hammerstein, 'Oh, What a Beautiful Morning' (from *Oklahoma*) (Alfred Drake)

¶ 'La Seine' (Jacqueline François)

¶ Weill/Brecht, 'Alabama Song' (from *The Rise and Fall of the City of Mahagonny*) (Lotte Lenya)

*¶ Brahms, Symphony No. 1 in C minor (Boston Symphony/Münch)

¶ Tchaikovsky, *The Sleeping Beauty* (Vienna Philharmonic/von Karajan)

¶ Chopin, Nocturne in G minor (opus 37, No. 1) (Artur Rubinstein *piano*)

¶ Lerner & Loewe, 'The Rain in Spain' (from *My Fair Lady*) (Rex Harrison/Julie Andrews)

¶ Mozart, Horn Concerto No. 1 in D major (Dennis Brain/Philharmonia Orchestra/von Karajan)

¶ LUXURY: A duvet.

¶ BOOK: The works of Montaigne.

31 March 1973
1171 Christopher Serpell
BBC diplomatic correspondent

¶ Handel, 'Worthy is the Lamb' (from *Messiah*) (Huddersfield Choral Society/Royal Liverpool Philharmonic/Sargent)

¶ Beethoven, Symphony No. 6 in F major (Pastoral) (Philadelphia Orchestra/Walter)

¶ Puccini, 'Amaro sol per te' (from *Tosca*) (Maria Callas/Giuseppe di Stefano/La Scala Orchestra/Sabata)

¶ 'Scalinatella' (Roberto Murolo)

¶ Mozart, 'Che grido indiavolato' (from *Don Giovanni*) (Nicolai Ghiaurov/Franz Crass/Walter Berry/NPO/Klemperer)

¶ 'The House of the Rising Sun' (Josh White)

*¶ Bach, Prelude and Fugue No. 17 in A flat (Wanda Landowska *harpsichord*)

¶ Machaut, 'Sanctus' (from *Notre Dame Mass*) (London Ambrosian Singers/Vienna Renaissance Players/McCarthy)

¶ LUXURY: Equipment for wine-making and brewing.

¶ BOOK: Samuel Pepys' *Diary*

7 April 1973
1172 Florence de Jong
Cinema organist and pianist

¶ Widor, Organ Symphony No. 5 (toccata) (Simon Preston)

¶ Kalman, 'Tanzen macht' ich' (from *The Gypsy Princess*) (Vienna Volksoper Orchestra/Grüber)

¶ Wagner, 'Siegfried Idyll' (San Francisco Symphony/Monteux)

¶ Puccini, 'O Mimi, tu più non torni' (from *La bohème*) (Jussi Björling/Robert Merrill/RCA Victor Symphony/Beecham)

¶ 'Brazil' (from film *The Eddy Duchin Story*) (Carmen Cavallaro *piano*/orchestra/Stoloff)

¶ Borodin/Wright & Forrest (arr.), 'And This is My Beloved' (from *Kismet*) (Doretta Morrow)

¶ Addinsell, 'Warsaw Concerto' (from film *Dangerous Moonlight*) (Florence de Jong *organ*/Ena Baga *piano*)

*¶ 'The Good Old, Bad Old Days' (from *The Good Old, Bad Old Days*) (Anthony Newley)

¶ LUXURY: An accordion.

¶ BOOK: A book of Giles cartoons.

14 April 1973
1173 Harry Loman
Stage-door keeper and ex-music hall artist

¶ 'They Didn't Believe Me' (Mario Lanza)

¶ 'The Galloping Major' (Stanley Holloway)

¶ 'Hello, Who's Your Lady Friend?' (Leslie Sarony)

¶ Carmichael, 'Stardust' (Hoagy Carmichael)

*¶ 'Thanks for the Memory' (from film *Big Broadcast of 1938*) (Shirley Ross/Bob Hope)

¶ 'I Do Like to be Beside the Seaside' (Bernard Bedford)

¶ 'We'll Keep a Welcome' (Harry Secombe)

¶ 'We'll Meet Again' (Vera Lynn)

¶ LUXURY: A pack of cards.

¶ BOOK: Charles Dickens, *A Tale of Two Cities*

21 April 1973
1174 Chris Bonington
Mountaineer, writer and photographer

¶ Bizet/Hammerstein, 'Dat's Love' (from film *Carmen Jones*) (Marilyn Horne)

¶ Bach/Duarte, Suite No. 3 in C (John Williams *guitar*)

¶ 'Queen of Hearts' (Joan Baez)

¶ Bach, Suite No. 2 in B minor (BWV 1067) (Claude Monteux *flute*/LSO/Pierre Monteux)

¶ 'Brown Boy' (David Campbell)

¶ 'Moon Shadow' (Cat Stevens)

¶ 'Hey, That's No Way to Say Goodbye' (Judy Collins)

*¶ Handel, Harp Concerto in B flat (opus 4) (Nicanor Zabaleta/Berlin Radio Symphony/Fricsay)

¶ LUXURY: A radio receiver.

¶ BOOK: Sir Winston Churchill, *Marlborough: His Life and Times*

28 April 1973
1175 Edith Coates
Opera singer
¶ Britten, 'Young Person's Guide to the Orchestra (Variations on a Theme of Purcell)' (LSO/Britten)
*¶ Wagner, 'Liebestod' (from *Tristan und Isolde*) (Kirsten Flagstad/Philharmonia Orchestra/Furtwängler)
¶ Mendelssohn, *A Midsummer Night's Dream* (Amsterdam Concertgebouw/Haitink)
¶ Mozart, *The Magic Flute* (overture) (Vienna Philharmonic/Solti)
¶ R. Strauss, *Der Rosenkavalier* (waltz) (Vienna Philharmonic/ Kleiber)
¶ Elgar, Introduction and Allegro for Strings (Sinfonia of London/Allegri String Quartet/ Barbirolli)
¶ Janáček, Sinfonietta (Pro Arte Orchestra/Mackerras)
¶ Bernstein, *Candide (overture)* (soundtrack/Krachmalnick)
¶ LUXURY: Brandy.
¶ BOOK: Her favourite novels of Jean Plaidy.

5 May 1973
1176 Norman Thelwell
Artist and cartoonist
¶ Grieg, 'Morning' (from *Peer Gynt Suite No. 1*) (RPO/ Beecham)
¶ 'Three Coins in the Fountain' (from film) (Frank Sinatra)
¶ 'Island in the Sun' (Harry Belafonte)
*¶ Chopin, Nocturne in F sharp (opus 15, No. 2) (Artur Rubinstein *piano*)
¶ Gilbert & Sullivan, 'When a Felon's Not Engaged on His Employment' (from *The Pirates of Penzance*) (Richard Watson/ D'Oyly Carte Opera Company/ Godfrey)
¶ Vaughan Williams, 'Fantasia on Greensleeves' (LSO/Boult)
¶ Beethoven, Piano Sonata No. 14 in C sharp minor (Moonlight) (Wilhelm Kempff)
¶ Borodin, 'Polovtsian Dances' (from *Prince Igor*) (Philharmonia Orchestra/von Karajan)

¶ LUXURY: Drawing and painting equipment.
¶ BOOK: Johann David Wyss, *Swiss Family Robinson*

12 May 1973
1177 John Huston
Film director
*¶ 'Shenandoah' (Salli Terri)
¶ 'St Louis Blues' (Bessie Smith)
¶ Gershwin, 'Summertime' (from *Porgy and Bess*) (Ethel Waters)
¶ Foster, 'Jeannie with the Light Brown Hair' (John McCormack)
¶ Lennon & McCartney, 'Yellow Submarine' (from film) (The Beatles)
¶ 'My Lady Greensleeves' (John Faulkner)
¶ 'Loch Lomond' (Maxine Sullivan)
¶ Weill, 'September Song' (from *Knickerbocker Holiday*) (Walter Huston)
¶ LUXURY: Havana cigars.
¶ BOOK: *The Dialogues of Plato*

19 May 1973
1178 Joseph Cooper
Pianist, lecturer and broadcaster
¶ Haydn, Trumpet Concerto (Alan Stringer/Academy of St Martin-in-the-Fields/Marriner)
¶ Elgar, Symphony No. 1 in A flat major (LPO/Boult)
¶ Bach, Double Concerto in D minor (BWV 1043) (Yehudi Menuhin and Georges Enesco *violins*/Paris Symphony/ Monteux)
¶ Delius, 'On Hearing the First Cuckoo in Spring' (RPO/ Beecham)
*¶ Rachmaninov, 'Rhapsody on a Theme of Paganini' (Vladimir Ashkenazy *piano*/LSO/Previn)
¶ R. Strauss, 'Herr Gott . . . Wiedersehen' (from *Arabella*, Act 1) (Lisa della Casa/Vienna Philharmonic/Solti)
¶ Schumann, 'Fantasia in C' (opus 17) (Sviatoslav Richter *piano*)
¶ Beethoven, Piano Concerto No. 4 in G major (opus 58) (Emil Gilels/Cleveland Orchestra/Szell)

¶ LUXURY: A dummy piano keyboard.
¶ BOOK: *Come Hither*, compiled by Walter de la Mare.

2 June 1973
1179 Baroness Summerskill CH
Doctor of medicine and politician
¶ J. Strauss, *Die Fledermaus* (overture) (Vienna Philharmonic/von Karajan)
¶ Gilbert & Sullivan, 'Three Little Maids from School' (from *The Mikado*) (Margaret Mitchell/Joyce Wright/Joan Gillingham/D'Oyly Carte Opera Company/Godfrey)
*¶ 'I'll Walk Beside You' (Walter Glynne)
¶ 'Little Old Lady' (Gracie Fields)
¶ Beethoven, Symphony No. 5 in C minor (opus 67) (Philharmonic Promenade Orchestra/Boult)
¶ Chopin, Waltz No. 9 in A flat major (opus 69, No. 1) (Artur Rubinstein *piano*)
¶ Elgar, 'Pomp and Circumstance' March No. 1 in D major (Philharmonia Orchestra/Barbirolli)
¶ G. B. Shaw, *St Joan* (excerpt) (Sybil Thorndike)
¶ LUXURY: A four-poster bed.
¶ BOOK: *Brewer's Dictionary of Phrase and Fable*

9 June 1973
1180 Joe Bugner
Heavyweight boxer
¶ 'Theme from *Shaft*' (from film) (Isaac Hayes)
*¶ 'Where's the Girl?' (Walker Brothers)
¶ 'Get Down' (Gilbert O'Sullivan)
¶ 'Till' (Tom Jones)
¶ 'Tie a Yellow Ribbon Round the Old Oak Tree' (Dawn)
¶ 'In My Room' (Walker Brothers)
¶ 'By the time I Get to Phoenix' (Anne Murray/Glen Campbell)
¶ Lennon & McCartney, 'The Long and Winding Road' (The Beatles)
¶ LUXURY: A chess set.
¶ BOOK: Henri Charrière, *Papillon*

16 June 1973
1181 Basil Dean
Theatre and film producer and director
¶ 'Daisy (A Bicycle Built for Two)' (Florrie Forde)
¶ Anon. Shakespeare, 'When That I was but a Little Tiny Boy' (from *Twelfth Night*) (Maurice Bevan/Elizabethan Consort of Viols/Taylor Consort of Recorders)
¶ Stravinsky, 'The Shrovetide Fair' (from *Petrushka*) (Orchestre de la Suisse Romande/Ansermet)
¶ Delius, 'Serenade' (from *Hassan*) (RPO/Beecham)
¶ Mozart, 'Tamino's Aria' (from *The Magic Flute*) (Helge Roswaenge/Berlin Philharmonic/Beecham)
¶ 'Smile When You Say Goodbye' (Gracie Fields)
*¶ R. Strauss, *Der Rosenkavalier* (final trio) (Elisabeth Schumann/Lotte Lehmann/ Maria Olszewska/Vienna Philharmonic/Heger)
¶ Delius, 'The Golden Road to Samarkand' (from *Hassan*) (LPO/Beecham)
¶ LUXURY: Whisky.
¶ BOOK: An anthology of poetry.

23 June 1973
1182 Georgie Fame
Musician and singer
¶ 'What's Going On?' (Donny Hathaway)
¶ 'Whitburn' (Carlton Main Frickley Colliery Band)
¶ 'Diminuendo and Crescendo in Blue' (Duke Ellington and his Orchestra)
¶ 'Midnight Special' (Jimmy Smith *organ*/Stanley Turrentine *saxophone*)
¶ 'Kennedy and Krushchev' (Mighty Sparrow)
¶ 'One-Room Country Shack' (Mose Allison Trio)
*¶ 'This is for Us to Share' (John McLaughlin *guitar*/group)
¶ 'Let the Good Times Roll' (Louis Jordan and his Tympany Five)
¶ LUXURY: A saxophone.
¶ BOOK: A history of mankind.

30 June 1973
1183 Brenda Bruce
Actress
¶ Bach/Loussier, Concerto in the Italian Style (BWV 971) (Jacques Loussier Trio)
*¶ Delius, *Florida Suite* (RPO/ Beecham)
¶ Beethoven, Sonata No. 26 in E flat major (opus 81a) (Les Adieux) (Benno Moiseiwitsch *piano*)
¶ Vaughan Williams, 'Wither's Rocking Hymn' (Westminster Abbey Choir/Guest)
¶ Prokofiev, 'Tybalt's Death' (from *Romeo and Juliet*) (Czech Philharmonic/Ančerl)
¶ Corrette, Concerto in D minor for Organ, Flute and Strings (Helmuth Rilling *organ*/ Württemberg Chamber Orchestra/Faerber)
¶ Shakespeare, 'Seven Ages of Man' (from *As You Like It*, Act 2) (John Gielgud)
¶ Woolfenden, *The Revenger's Tragedy* (incidental music) (RSC Wind Band/Woolfenden)
¶ LUXURY: Writing materials.
¶ BOOK: *Bhagavad-Gita*, edited by Christopher Isherwood.

7 July 1973
1184 Wilfred Van Wyck
Concert agent and promoter
¶ Franck, Symphony in D minor (Czech Philharmonic/Barbirolli)
¶ R. Strauss, Violin Sonata in E flat (opus 18) (Sidney Weiss/ Jeanne Weiss *piano*)
¶ Chopin, Berceuse in D flat (opus 57) (Josef Hofmann *piano*)
¶ 'I Hear You Calling Me' (John McCormack/Edwin Schneider *piano*)
¶ Rachmaninov, Étude-Tableau in E flat minor (opus 39, No. 5) (Vladimir Horowitz *piano*)
¶ Liszt, Fantasy and Fugue on 'Ad Nos, Ad Salutarem Undam' (Pierre Cochereau *organ*)
¶ Falla, 'Seguidilla Murciana' (from 7 *Canciones populares espanoles*) (Victoria de los Angeles)
*¶ Brahms, Ballade in B (opus 10, No. 4) (Artur Rubinstein *piano*)
¶ LUXURY: A radio receiver.
¶ BOOK: The short stories of Somerset Maugham.

14 July 1973
1185 Colonel Sir Michael Ansell
Leading figure in the world of showjumping
¶ 'Regimental March of the King's Royal Rifle Corps' (Royal Military School of Music)
¶ 'The Keel Row' and 'D'ye Ken John Peel' (Royal Horse Guards Band)
¶ 'Thanks for the Buggy Ride' (Percival Mackey's Band)
¶ 'Lilli Marlene' (Lale Andersen)
¶ Rodgers & Hammerstein, 'Shall We Dance?' (from *The King and I*) (Gertrude Lawrence/Yul Brynner)
¶ Rodgers & Hammerstein, 'Climb Every Mountain' (from *The Sound of Music*) (Peggy Wood)
¶ 'Sunset' (HM Royal Marines Band)
*¶ 'Fare Ye Well, Inniskilling' (Royal Corps of Transport Band)
¶ LUXURY: Knitting wool and needles.
¶ BOOK: Blank paper and a typewriter.

21 July 1973
1186 Andrew Lloyd Webber
Composer
¶ 'Teddy Bear' (Elvis Presley)
¶ ''Til I Kissed You' (Everly Brothers)
¶ Prokofiev, *Cinderella* (Moscow Radio Symphony/ Rozhdestvensky)
¶ 'Disillusion Me' (Gary Bond)
*¶ Shostakovich, Cello Concerto in E flat (Mstislav Rostropovich/Philadelphia Orchestra/Ormandy)
¶ 'Mona Lisas and Mad Hatters' (Elton John)
¶ Lerner & Loewe, 'I'm an Ordinary Man' (from *My Fair Lady*) (Rex Harrison)
¶ 'Satisfaction' (The Rolling Stones)
¶ LUXURY: Wine.
¶ BOOK: *The Oxford Rhyming Dictionary*

28 July 1973
1187 Ruskin Spear RA
Painter
¶ 'Song of the Plains' (Red Army Ensemble)
*¶ Bach, Chromatic Fantasia and Fugue in D minor (George Malcolm *piano*)
¶ 'Sugar' (Fred Elizalde *piano* and his orchestra)
¶ 'Dr Rock' (Roger Ruskin Spear/ensemble)
¶ 'The Intro and the Outro' (Bonzo Dog Band)
¶ Ravel, 'Jeux d'eau' (Walter Gieseking *piano*)
¶ Ravel, String Quartet in F major (Galimir String Quartet)
¶ Dvořák, Symphony No. 9 in E minor (LSO/Kertesz)
¶ LUXURY: A radio receiver.
¶ BOOK: Aldous Huxley, *Ends and Means*
¶ PAINTING: William Hogarth, *The Grahame Children* (1724)

4 August 1973
1188 Colin Welland
Actor and playwright
¶ Gilbert & Sullivan, *The Yeomen of the Guard* (overture) (Royal Liverpool Philharmonic/ Groves)
¶ Wood, 'Tom Bowling' (from *Fantasia on British Sea Songs*) (BBC Symphony/Davies)
¶ 'Peterloo' (John Howarth/ Oldham Tinkers)
¶ Simon, 'Bridge over Troubled Waters' (Simon & Garfunkel)
¶ 'Barney Brallaghan' (JSD Band)
*¶ 'Londonderry Air' (Philharmonia Orchestra/ Weldon)
¶ 'Co–Co' (Sweet)
¶ 'Onward Christian Soldiers' (Salvation Army Band and chorus)
¶ LUXURY: A bed.
¶ BOOK: The complete *Oxford English Dictionary*

11 August 1973
1189 Gervase de Peyer
Clarinetist and conductor
¶ Stravinsky, Symphony in Three Movements (LSO/Davis)
¶ Mozart, String Quintet in C minor (Cecil Aronowitz *viola*/ Amadeus String Quartet)

¶ Bartók, Music for Strings, Percussion and Celesta (LSO/ Solti)
¶ Verdi, 'O fatidica foresta' (from *Giovanna d'Arco*) (Montserrat Caballé/LSO/ Levine)
¶ Delius, *Fennimore and Gerda* (intermezzo) (RPO/Beecham)
¶ Janáček, *Mládi* (sextet for wind instruments) (Melos Ensemble)
¶ Sibelius, Symphony No. 4 in A minor (Philharmonia Orchestra/von Karajan)
*¶ Verdi, 'Libera me' (from *Requiem*) (Martina Arroyo/LSO and Chorus/Bernstein)
¶ LUXURY: Grape vines.
¶ BOOK: *The Penguin Book of Quotations*

18 August 1973
1190 June Whitfield
Comedy actress
¶ 'Bond Street' (orchestra/ Bacharach)
¶ 'Wing Commander Hancock, Test Pilot' (from radio series *Hancock's Half Hour*) (Tony Hancock/Kenneth Williams)
¶ Gershwin, 'A Foggy Day' (from film *A Damsel in Distress*) (Frank Sinatra)
¶ Styne, 'Everything's Coming Up Roses' (from *Gypsy*) (Ethel Merman)
¶ 'Solving the Riddle' (Billy May's Brass)
¶ 'Moonlight Becomes You' (from film *The Road to Morocco*) (Bing Crosby)
¶ 'Moonlight Serenade' (Glenn Miller and his Orchestra)
*¶ Porter, 'Well, Did You Evah?' (from film *High Society*) (Frank Sinatra/Bing Crosby)
¶ LUXURY: A tape recorder.
¶ BOOK: A do-it-yourself manual.

25 August 1973
1191 Bert Foord
Forecaster from the London Weather Centre
¶ Puccini, 'Che gelida manina' (from *La bohème*) (Beniamino Gigli/La Scala Orchestra/ Berrettoni)
*¶ Borodin, 'Polovtsian Dances' (from *Prince Igor*) (LSO and Chorus/Solti)
¶ Verdi, 'Celeste Aida' (from *Aida*) (Enrico Caruso)
¶ Chopin, Waltz in D flat major (opus 64, no. 1) (Peter Katin *piano*)
¶ Grieg, 'In the Hall of the Mountain King' (from *Peer Gynt*) (Beecham Choral Society/RPO/Beecham)
¶ Rodgers & Hammerstein, 'Bali Ha'i' (from *South Pacific*) (Juanita Hall)
¶ Dukas, 'The Sorcerer's Apprentice' (Orchestra of Paris/ Jacquillat)
¶ Handel, 'The Arrival of the Queen of Sheba' (from *Solomon*) (Academy of St Martin-in-the-Fields/Marriner)
¶ LUXURY: Golf clubs and balls.
¶ BOOK: The short stories of P. G. Wodehouse.

1 September 1973
1192 Earl Wild
Concert pianist
*¶ Beethoven, Symphony No. 4 in B flat major (opus 60) (NBC Symphony/Toscanini)
¶ Tchaikovsky, 'Manfred' Symphony in B minor (opus 58) (LSO/Markevitch)
¶ 'Great Balls of Fire' (Mae West)
¶ R. Strauss, *Die Frau Ohne Schatten* (final scene) (Christel Goltz/Paul Schoeffler/Vienna State Opera Chorus/Vienna Philharmonic/Böhm)
¶ Elgar, *Enigma Variations* (No. 12) (NBC Symphony/ Toscanini)
¶ 'Hello Dolly' (from *Hello Dolly*) (Carol Channing)
¶ Saint-Saëns, 'Bacchanale' (from *Samson and Delilah*) (New York Philharmonic/Bernstein)

¶ Massenet, 'J'aurais sur ma poitrine' (from *Werther*, Act 2) (Nicolai Gedda/French National Radio Orchestra/Prêtre)

¶ LUXURY: The Bernini columns from the Vatican.

¶ BOOK: The transcript of the Watergate hearings.

8 September 1973
1193 Joyce Carey
Actress

*¶ Elgar, Introduction and Allegro for Strings (opus 47) (English Chamber Orchestra/Britten)

¶ 'The Second Time Around' (Frank Sinatra)

¶ Mendelssohn, *A Midsummer Night's Dream* (overture) (Bavarian Radio Symphony/Kubelik)

¶ Coward, 'London Pride' (Noël Coward)

¶ Addinsell, 'Invitation Waltz' (from *Ring Round the Moon*) (Semprini *piano* and his Orchestra)

¶ Delius, 'The Walk to the Paradise Garden' (from *A Village Romeo and Juliet*) (LSO/Barbirolli)

¶ Purcell, 'When I am Laid in Earth' (from *Dido and Aeneas*) (Kirsten Flagstad/Mermaid Orchestra/Jones)

¶ Rachmaninov, Piano Concerto No. 2 in C minor (Benno Moiseiwitsch/Philharmonia Orchestra/Rignold)

¶ LUXURY: A box of oddments from her dressing-table.

¶ BOOK: *The Oxford Book of English Verse*

15 September 1973
1194 Bill Sowerbutts
Gardening expert

*¶ Berlioz, *Les francs juges* (overture) (RPO/Beecham)

¶ Verdi, 'Và pensiero, sull'ali dorate' (from *Nabucco*) (Rome Opera House Orchestra and Chorus/Morelli)

¶ Beethoven, 'Für Elise' (Alfred Brendel *piano*)

¶ Beethoven, Symphony No. 9 in D minor (opus 125) (Vienna Philharmonic/Schmidt-Isserstedt)

¶ J. Strauss, 'The Nun's Chorus' and 'Laura's Song' (from *Casanova*) (Elisabeth Schwarzkopf/Philharmonia Chorus and Orchestra/Ackermann)

¶ Bach/Gounod, 'Ave Maria' (Kirkintilloch Junior Choir)

¶ Rossini, 'Une voce poco fa' (from *The Barber of Seville*) (Maria Callas/Philharmonia Orchestra/Galliera)

¶ Beethoven, Symphony No. 3 in E flat major (Eroica) (Berlin Philharmonic/von Karajan)

¶ LUXURIES: Tobacco seeds and a brewing vat.

¶ BOOK: An English dictionary.

22 September 1973
1195 Leontyne Price
Singer

*¶ Rachmaninov, Piano Concerto No. 2 in C minor (Alexis Weissenberg/Berlin Philharmonic/von Karajan)

¶ 'Spanish Harlem' (Aretha Franklin)

¶ 'I Can Make It Through the Days but Oh Those Lonely Nights' (Ray Charles)

¶ Bizet, 'Card Scene' (from *Carmen*) (Leontyne Price/Monique Linval/Geneviève Macaux/Vienna Philharmonic/von Karajan)

¶ Verdi, 'Sempre libera' (from *La traviata*) (Leontyne Price/Ryland Davis/LSO/Cleva)

¶ Beethoven, Piano Concerto No. 5 in E flat major (Emperor) (Vladimir Horowitz/RCA Victor Symphony/Reiner)

¶ Verdi, 'Dies Irae' (from *Requiem*) (Robert Shaw Chorale/NBC Symphony/Toscanini)

¶ 'My Melancholy Baby' (Leontyne Price/André Previn *piano*)

¶ LUXURY: Soap.

¶ BOOK: Mildred Newman, *How to be Your Own Best Friend*

29 September 1973
1196 Ian Hendry
Actor

¶ 'Lights Out' (Scottish Regiments Massed Pipes and Drums)

¶ 'You're Nobody Till Somebody Loves You' (Dean Martin)

¶ 'A String of Pearls' (Glenn Miller and his Orchestra)

¶ 'The Driving Instructor' (Bob Newhart)

*¶ 'Sally' (Gracie Fields)

¶ 'Girl of My Dreams' (Erroll Garner Trio)

¶ 'What a Wonderful World' (Louis Armstrong)

¶ 'There, I've Said It Again' (Nat 'King' Cole)

¶ LUXURY: Brandy.

¶ BOOK: The timetable of passing steamers.

6 October 1973
1197 Mary Peters
Athlete

¶ 'Green, Green Grass of Home' (Tom Jones)

¶ 'Danny Boy' (Brendan O'Dowda)

¶ 'Tokyo Melody' (Helmut Zacharias)

¶ 'Mexico' (Long John Baldry)

¶ 'Strangers in the Night' (Frank Sinatra)

¶ Jarre, 'Lara's Theme' (from film *Dr Zhivago*) (MGM Studio Orchestra/Jarre)

¶ 'Stranger on the Shore' (Acker Bilk *clarinet*/Leon Young String Chorale)

*¶ 'Raindrops Keep Fallin' on My Head' (from film *Butch Cassidy and the Sundance Kid*) (B. J. Thomas)

¶ LUXURIES: A comb, manicure set, etc.

¶ BOOK: Norman Vincent Peale, *The Power of Positive Thinking*

13 October 1973
1198 Edward Robey
Barrister and ex-London magistrate

¶ Beethoven, 'Mir ist so wunderbar' (from *Fidelio*) (Christa Ludwig/Ingeborg Hallstein/Gerhard Unger/ Gotlob Frick/Philharmonia Orchestra/Klemperer)

¶ Elgar, Violin Concerto in B minor (Yehudi Menuhin/LSO/ Elgar)

¶ Wagner, 'Ich bin's, ich bin's, Süssester Freund!' (from *Tristan und Isolde*) (Kirsten Flagstad/Philharmonia Orchestra/Furtwängler)

¶ R. Strauss, 'Don Quixote' (excerpt) (Pierre Fournier *cello*/ Cleveland Orchestra/Szell)

¶ Verdi, *Falstaff* (Act 2, Scene 1 duet) (Giuseppe Valdengo/ Frank Guarrera/NBC Symphony/Toscanini)

¶ Mahler, Symphony No. 9 in D (Columbia Symphony/Walter)

¶ Debussy, *Pelléas et Mélisande* (Act 3, Scene 1) (Camille Maurane/Erna Spoorenberg/ Orchestre de la Suisse Romande/Ansermet)

*¶ Wagner, 'Selig wie die Sonne' (from *Die Meistersinger*) (Ferdinand Frantz/Rudolf Schock/Gerhard Unger/ Elisabeth Grümmer/Marga Höffgen/Berlin Philharmonic/ Kempe)

¶ LUXURY: German white wine.

¶ BOOK: *Grove's Dictionary of Music and Musicians*

20 October 1973
1199 Peter Rogers
Film producer

¶ Massenet, 'Meditation' (from *Thaïs*) (Roger André *violin*/ Paris Opéra Orchestra/ Dervaux)

¶ Gluck, 'Dance of the Blessed Spirits' (from *Orfeo ed Euridice*) (Sergei Rachmaninov *piano*)

¶ Liszt, Consolation No. 3 in D flat (Tamás Vásáry *piano*)

¶ Bizet, *L'arlésienne Suite* (Orchestre de la Suisse Romande/Ansermet)

¶ Scriabin, Étude in C sharp minor (opus 2, No. 1) (Vladimir Horowitz *piano*)

¶ Albinoni/Giazotto, Adagio in G minor for Organ and Strings (Eduard Kaufmann *organ*/ Lucerne Festival Strings/ Baumgartner)

¶ Franck, Prelude, Fugue and Variations (opus 18) (Simon Preston *organ*)

*¶ Fauré, 'Sanctus' (from *Requiem*) (Choeurs Elisabeth Brasseur/Paris Conservatoire Orchestra/Cluytens)

¶ LUXURY: A ninth record: Massenet's 'Élégie'.

¶ BOOK: A bound volume of *Punch* from the 1960s.

27 October 1973
1200 Professor Sir Alister Hardy FRS
Zoologist

¶ 'The Honeysuckle and the Bee' (Ellaline Terriss/Seymour Hicks/orchestra)

¶ O. Straus, 'A Waltz Dream' (from *A Waltz Dream*) (June Bronhill/David Hughes)

¶ 'Blaydon Races' (Owen Brannigan/Max Harris and his Orchestra)

¶ 'Santa Lucia' (Beniamino Gigli)

¶ Boughton, 'The Faery Song' (from *The Immortal Hour*) (Osian Ellis *baritone* and *harp*)

¶ 'What Shall We Do with a Drunken Sailor?' (Shantymen)

*¶ Coward, 'I'll See You Again' (from *Bitter Sweet*) (Peggy Wood/George Metaxa)

¶ Grieg, 'Anitra's Dance' (from *Peer Gynt*, opus 23, no. 16) (LSO/Fjeldstad)

¶ LUXURIES: Writing and water-colour materials.

¶ BOOK: William Wordsworth, *The Prelude* (original version of 1805).

3 November 1973
1201 Arnold Ridley
Actor and playwright

*¶ Wagner, *Tannhäuser* (overture) (Vienna Philharmonic/Solti)

¶ 'I Hear You Calling Me' (John McCormack/Edwin Schneider *piano*)

¶ 'Un peu d'amour' (Palm Court Trio)

¶ Coward, 'If Love were All' (from *Bitter Sweet*) (Ivy St Helier)

¶ 'Parlez moi d'amour' (Lucienne Boyer)

¶ Chopin, Nocturne No. 18 in E major (opus 62, no. 2) (Benno Moiseiwitsch *piano*)

¶ 'Roses of Picardy' (Alfred Piccaver)

¶ Elgar, 'Pomp and Circumstance' March No. 1 in D major (opus 39) (recorded at last night of 1969 Proms) (BBC Symphony/Colin Davis)

¶ LUXURY: A wine-making kit.

¶ BOOK: A vintage copy of *Bradshaw's Railway Timetable*.

10 November 1973
1202 Trevor Philpott
Reporter

¶ 'Relaxin' at the Touro' (Muggsy Spanier's Ragtime Band)

¶ 'Introducing Tobacco to Civilisation' (Bob Newhart)

¶ 'Fever' (Peggy Lee)

¶ 'See Amid the Winter's Snow' (Westminster Abbey Choir/ McKie)

¶ Granados, Spanish Dance No. 5 (Campoli *violin*/Eric Gritton *piano*)

¶ 'Over the Gate' (Bernard Miles)

¶ 'Bird on the Wire' (Esther Ofarim)

*¶ 'Dusk' (Duke Ellington and his Famous Orchestra)

¶ LUXURIES: *The Oxford World Atlas* and Ordnance Survey maps of the British Isles.

¶ BOOK: An anthology of world poetry, compiled by Van Doren.

17 November 1973
1203 Vic Feather
Retired TUC General Secretary

¶ Ketelbey, 'In a Monastery Garden' (RPO/Rogers)

¶ Arnold, 'Peterloo' overture (City of Birmingham Symphony/Arnold)

*¶ Tchaikovsky, *Swan Lake* (LSO/Monteux)

¶ 'Non, je ne regrette rien' (Edith Piaf)

¶Mendelssohn, 'The Hebrides Overture' (Hallé Orchestra/Barbirolli)
¶Handel, *Water Music Suite* (RPO/Sargent)
¶Gershwin, 'Bess, You is My Woman Now' (from *Porgy and Bess*) (Leontyne Price/William Warfield/RCA Victor Symphony/Henderson)
¶Mozart, *Eine Kleine Nachtmusik* (Berlin Philharmonic/von Karajan)
¶LUXURY: Jacob Epstein, *Madonna and Child*
¶BOOK: An anthology of poetry.

24 November 1973
1204 Barry Humphries
Actor, comedian and writer
¶'The Floral Dance' (Peter Dawson)
¶Gershwin, 'My Ship' (from *Lady in the Dark*) (Gertrude Lawrence)
¶'On Mother Kelly's Doorstep' (Randolph Sutton)
*¶Grainger (arr.), 'Shallow Brown' (John Shirley-Quirk/Ambrosian Singers/English Chamber Orchestra/Britten)
¶Boughton, 'The Faery Song' (from *The Immortal Hour*) (Webster Booth/John Cockerill *harp*)
¶Korngold, 'Glück, das mir verblieb' (from *Die Tote Stadt*) (Lotte Lehmann/Richard Tauber/Orchestra/Szell)
¶'Show Me a Rose' (Groucho Marx)
¶Honegger, Symphony No. 2 for Strings and Trumpet (Suisse Romande Orchestra/Ansermet)
¶LUXURY: Painting equipment.
¶BOOK: The works of Max Beerbohm.

1 December 1973
1205 Marghanita Laski
Novelist, critic and journalist
¶'The Blues I Love to Play' (Garland Wilson *piano*)
¶'Cherry Ripe' (Jennifer Vyvyan/Ernest Lush *piano*)
¶Du Bellay, 'Heureux qui comme Ulysse' (Gérard Philipe)
¶Beethoven, Quartet No. 13 in B flat major (opus 130) (Amadeus String Quartet)

*¶'Vespers of Christmas Eve, Psalmus 109' (Gregorian chant) (Choir of Monks of Benedictine Abbey of St Martin, Beuron)
¶Couperin, 'The Lamentations of Jeremiah, 3rd Lesson' (from *Leçons des ténèbres*) (Alfred Deller/Wilfred Brown/Desmond Dupré *viola da gamba*/Harry Gabb *organ*)
¶Stanford, 'Magnificat in G' (Richard White/King's College Chapel Choir/Ord)
¶Verdi, 'Dies Irae' (from *Requiem*) (Robert Shaw Chorale/NBC Symphony/Toscanini)
¶LUXURY: A gold bracelet called 'The Lion of Judah'.
¶BOOK: *The Oxford English Dictionary*

8 December 1973
1206 Gareth Edwards
Rugby footballer: captain of Wales
*¶Simon, 'Bridge Over Troubled Waters' (Simon & Garfunkel)
¶'Delilah' (Tom Jones)
¶'March of the Men of Harlech' (Morriston Orpheus Choir/Welsh Guards Band)
¶J. Strauss, 'Blue Danube Waltz' (Vienna Philharmonic/Boskovsky)
¶'My Way' (Frank Sinatra)
¶Lennon & McCartney, 'Paperback Writer' (The Beatles)
¶'Rave On' (Buddy Holly)
¶Tchaikovsky, '1812 Overture' (LPO/Welsh Guards Band/Mackerras)
¶LUXURY: A cornet.
¶BOOK: The works of Dylan Thomas.

15 December 1973
1207 Alexander Young
Singer
¶Mendelssohn, Octet in E flat major (Vienna Octet)
¶Mozart, Symphony No. 40 in G minor (Berlin Philharmonic/von Karajan)

*¶Mozart, 'Crudel! Perchè finora' (from *The Marriage of Figaro*) (Dietrich Fischer–Dieskau/Edith Mathis/Deutsche Oper Orchestra, Berlin/Böhm)
¶Stravinsky, *The Rake's Progress* (final scene) (Alexander Young/RPO/Stravinsky)
¶Bach, 'Erbarme dich, Mein Gott' (from *St Matthew Passion*) (Helen Watts/Philomusica of London/Dart)
¶Handel, Concerto Grosso No. 8 in C minor (opus 6) (English Chamber Orchestra/Leppard)
¶Berlioz, 'Ardente flamme' (from *The Damnation of Faust*) (Janet Baker/Orchestra of Paris/Prêtre)
¶Mahler, Symphony No. 5 in C sharp minor (Amsterdam Concertgebouw/Haitink)
¶LUXURY: A radio-controlled model aircraft.
¶BOOK: *Grove's Dictionary of Music and Musicians*

22 December 1973
1208 John Mills
Actor
¶'And the Angels Sing' (Bing Crosby)
¶Tchaikovsky, 'Romeo and Juliet Fantasy Overture' (Berlin Philharmonic/von Karajan)
¶Coward, 'Some Day I'll Find You' (from *Private Lives*) (Noël Coward)
¶Rachmaninov, Piano Concerto No. 2 in C minor (Vladimir Ashkenazy/LSO/Previn)
¶Beethoven, Piano Sonata No. 14 in C sharp minor (Moonlight) (Rudolf Serkin)
¶Elgar, 'Nimrod' (from *Enigma Variations*) (LSO/Boult)
¶Gershwin, 'Rhapsody in Blue' (André Previn *piano and conducting*/LSO)
*¶Elgar, 'Pomp and Circumstance' March No. 1 in D major (opus 39) (recorded at last night of 1969 Proms) (BBC Symphony/Colin Davis)
¶LUXURY: A piano.
¶BOOK: A book on zoology.

29 December 1973
1209 Marion Stein (Mrs Jeremy Thorpe)
Musician
*¶ Bach, *St Matthew Passion* (final chorus) (Philharmonia Choir and Orchestra/ Klemperer)
¶ Mozart, Piano Concerto No. 20 in D minor (K. 466) (Artur Schnabel/Philharmonia Orchestra/Susskind)
¶ Mahler, 'Abshied' (from *Das Lied von der Erde*) (Kathleen Ferrier/Vienna Philharmonic/ Walter)
¶ Verdi, *Falstaff* (Act 1 finale) (soloists/RCA Italiana Opera Orchestra/Solti)
¶ Schubert, 'Frühlingstraum' (from *Die Winterreise*) (Peter Pears/Benjamin Britten *piano*)
¶ Beethoven, Sonata in G minor for Cello and Piano (opus 5, no. 2) (Sviatoslav Richter *piano*/ Mstislav Rostropovich *cello*)
¶ Berg, 'Three Fragments' (from *Wozzeck*) (LSO/Dorati)
¶ Britten, Spring Symphony (Peter Pears/Royal Opera House Orchestra and Chorus, Covent Garden/Emanuel School Boys' Chorus/Britten)
¶ LUXURY: The score of Mozart's *The Magic Flute*.
¶ BOOK: Goethe's *Faust*

5 January 1974
1210 Dr Jacob Bronowski
Scientist and broadcaster
¶ Schubert, 'Wasserflut' (from *Die Winterreise*) (Richard Tauber/Mischa Spoliansky *piano*)
¶ 'The Four-Loom Weaver' (Ewan McColl)
*¶ Mozart, 'Se vuol ballare' (from *The Marriage of Figaro*) (Giuseppe Taddei/ Philharmonia Orchestra/ Giulini)
¶ Weill/Brecht, 'Seeräuberjenny' (from *The Threepenny Opera*) (Lotte Lenya/Lewis–Ruth Band/ Mackeben)
¶ 'The Wild West' (Tom Lehrer)

¶ Britten, 'Not in the Hands of Boys . . .' (from *War Requiem*) (Peter Pears/LSO/Melos Ensemble/Britten)
¶ Fricker, String Quartet No. 2 (Amadeus String Quartet)
¶ 'Falling in Love Again' (from film *The Blue Angel*) (Marlene Dietrich)
¶ LUXURY: An antique chess set.
¶ BOOK: A volume on chess championship play.

12 January 1974
1211 Sir Terence Rattigan
Playwright
*¶ 'Forty Years On' (Harrow School Boys)
¶ Puccini, 'O soave fanciulla' (from *La bohème*) (Licia Albanese/Jan Peerce/NBC Symphony/Toscanini)
¶ 'Stormy Weather' (Duke Ellington and his Famous Orchestra)
¶ Tchaikovsky, *Swan Lake* (Orchestre de la Suisse Romande/Ansermet)
¶ Oscar Wilde, 'Lady Bracknell Interviews John Worthing' (from *The Importance of Being Earnest*, Act 1) (Edith Evans/ John Gielgud)
¶ 'Saturday Night at the Rose and Crown' (from *The Girl Who Came to Supper*) (Tessie O'Shea)
¶ 'You and I' (from film *Goodbye Mr Chips*) (Shirley Bassey)
¶ Puccini, 'Vissi d'arte' (from *Tosca*) (Renata Tebaldi/Santa Cecilia Orchestra, Rome/ Molinari-Pradelli)
¶ LUXURY: Dom Perignon champagne.
¶ BOOK: Edward Gibbon, *The History of the Decline and Fall of the Roman Empire*

19 January 1974
1212 Bernard Haitink
Conductor
¶ Mozart, Quintet in G minor (K. 516) (Cecil Aronowitz *viola*/ Amadeus String Quartet)
¶ Beethoven, String Quartet in C sharp (opus 131) (Amadeus String Quartet)

¶ Beethoven, String Quartet in A minor (opus 132) (Amadeus String Quartet)
¶ Schubert, String Quintet in C (D. 856) (William Pleeth *cello*/ Amadeus String Quartet)
¶ Wagner, Act 2 (from *Tristan und Isolde*) (Kirsten Flagstad/ Ludwig Suthaus/Philharmonia Orchestra/Furtwängler)
*¶ Mozart, 'Signore! Cos'è quel stupore?' (from *The Marriage of Figaro*) (Hilde Gueden/Lisa della Casa/Alfred Poell/Vienna Philharmonic/Kleiber)
¶ Wagner, *Götterdämmerung* (closing scene) (Helga Dernesch/Berlin Philharmonic/ von Karajan)
¶ LUXURY: A Dutch winter landscape by Bruegel.
¶ BOOK: The poetry of Roland Holst.
(Act 2 of Tristan und Isolde *counted as two records.)*

26 January 1974
1213 John Brooke-Little
Richmond Herald of Arms
¶ Perosi, 'Tu es Petrus' (Sistine Chapel Choir/Perosi)
*¶ Mozart, Piano Concerto No. 21 in C major (K. 467) (Geza Anda *piano* and directing the Camerata Academica of Salzburg Mozarteum)
¶ Bizet/Guirand, 'Agnus Dei' (Beniamino Gigli/Berlin State Opera Orchestra and Chorus/ Seidler-Winkler)
¶ 'Land of My Fathers' (Investiture Choir/BBC Welsh Orchestra/Kneller Hall Trumpeters)
¶ Tchaikovsky, Symphony No. 4 in F minor (RPO/Beecham)
¶ Mawby, 'Haec Dies' (Westminster Cathedral Choir/ strings)
¶ Donizetti, 'Una furtiva lacrima' (from *L'elisir d'amore*) (Beniamino Gigli/orchestra/ Barbirolli)
¶ Chopin, Sonata in B flat minor (opus 35) (Sergei Rachmaninov *piano*)
¶ LUXURY: A four-poster bed.
¶ BOOK: Burke's *Landed Gentry*

2 February 1974
1214 Fay Compton (2nd appearance)
Actress
¶ Delius, 'Love's Philosophy' (John Heddle Nash/Gerald Moore *piano*)
¶ Debussy, 'Claire de lune' (from *Suite bergamasque*) (Walter Gieseking *piano*)
¶ Grieg, Piano Concerto in A minor (Wilhelm Backhaus/New Symphony Orchestra/Barbirolli)
*¶ Rossini, 'Duetto Buffo di due Gatti' (Cat Duet) (Victoria de los Angeles/Elisabeth Schwarzkopf/Gerald Moore *piano*)
¶ 'What Would I Be?' (Val Doonican)
¶ Sibelius, 'The Swan of Tuonela' (Second of Four Legends for Orchestra) (Louis Rosenblatt *cor anglais*/Philadelphia Orchestra/Ormandy)
¶ 'My Way' (Frank Sinatra)
¶ O'Neill, 'The Call' (from *Mary Rose*) (Court Symphony/O'Neill)
¶ LUXURY: An electric blanket.
¶ BOOK: A selection of her favourite novels of Charles Dickens.

9 February 1974
1215 Brian Inglis
Writer, journalist and broadcaster
¶ 'Music, Maestro, Please' (from *These Foolish Things*) (Flanagan & Allen)
¶ R. Strauss, 'Till Eulenspiegel' (Philharmonia Orchestra/Klemperer)
¶ 'Lilli Marlene' (Lale Andersen)
¶ Tchaikovsky, Symphony No. 4 in F minor (RPO/Beecham)
¶ 'Les sabots d'hélène' (Georges Brassens)
¶ Bellini, 'O rendetemi la speme' (from *I puritani*) (Mirella Freni/Rome Opera House Orchestra/Ferraris)
¶ 'Easy Does It' (Eartha Kitt)
*¶ Brahms, Symphony No. 3 in F (NBC Symphony/Toscanini)
¶ LUXURY: A typewriter and paper.
¶ BOOK: James Stephens, *The Crock of Gold*

16 February 1974
1216 Roy Fox
Dance band leader
¶ Weill/Brecht, 'Mack the Knife' (from *The Threepenny Opera*) (Louis Armstrong and his Orchestra)
¶ Debussy/Stokowski, 'Clair de lune' (from *Suite bergamasque*) (Stokowski conducting his Symphony Orchestra)
¶ 'Mississippi Mud' (Paul Whiteman's Rhythm Boys)
¶ 'A Love Story' (from *Intermezzo*) (Liberace *piano*)
¶ 'The Birth of the Blues' (Sammy Davis Jnr)
¶ Gershwin, 'Rhapsody in Blue' (Roy Bargy *piano*/Paul Whiteman and his Concert Orchestra)
¶ Chopin, Nocturne in E flat major (opus 9, no. 2) (Wolfgang Schneiderhan *violin*/Albert Hirsh *piano*)
*¶ 'Whispering' (Roy Fox and his Orchestra)
¶ LUXURY: A radio receiver.
¶ BOOK: A volume of crossword puzzles.

23 February 1974
1217 Eddie Waring
Television commentator
¶ 'Deep Harmony' (Black Dyke Mills Band)
¶ Porter, 'I Love Paris' (from film *Can-Can*) (Mantovani and his Orchestra)
¶ 'On the Road to Mandalay' (Peter Dawson/Hubert Greenslade *piano*)
¶ 'Yellow Bird' (Bert Kaempfert and his Orchestra)
*¶ Crimond, 'The Twenty-Third Psalm' (Glasgow Orpheus Choir/Roberton)
¶ Gilbert & Sullivan, 'For He is an Englishman' (from *HMS Pinafore*) (Jeffrey Skitch/D'Oyly Carte Opera Chorus/New Symphony Orchestra/Godfrey)
¶ 'Snowbird' (Perry Como)
¶ 'L'entente cordiale' (Scots Guards Band)
¶ LUXURY: A couch.
¶ BOOK: A vintage *Bradshaw's Railway Timetable.*

2 March 1974
1218 Maureen O'Sullivan
Actress
¶ 'Macushla' (John McCormack)
¶ 'Bye, Bye, Blackbird' (Russ Morgan Orchestra)
¶ 'The Best Things in Life are Free' (from *Good News*) (Ted Lewis and his Orchestra)
¶ 'Tiene mi niña el balcon' (flamenco) (Manolo Vargas/Bernardo el de los Lobitos)
¶ 'Love Letters in the Sand' (from film *Bernardine*) (Pat Boone)
¶ Lennon & McCartney, 'Dear Prudence' (The Beatles)
¶ Theodorakis, 'Zorba's Dance' (from film *Zorba the Greek*) (soundtrack/Theodorakis)
*¶ Rachmaninov, Symphony No. 2 in E minor (LSO/Previn)
¶ LUXURY: Tranquillizers.
¶ BOOK: A volume on animal communication.

9 March 1974
1219 Eileen Fowler
Physical exercise instructor
¶ 'Tie a Yellow Ribbon Round the Old Oak Tree' (Dawn)
¶ Grieg, Piano Concerto in A minor (Artur Rubinstein/RCA Victor Symphony/Wallenstein)
¶ Khatchaturian, *Masquerade Suite* (RCA Victor Symphony/Kondrashin)
¶ Mendelssohn, 'Oh, for the Wings of a Dove' (Ernest Lough/G. Thalben-Ball *organ*/Temple Church Choir, London)
¶ 'Strangers in the Night' (Frank Sinatra)
¶ Puccini, 'Egli, col cuore grosso' (from *Madam Butterfly*) (Renata Scotto/Rome Opera House Orchestra/Barbirolli)
¶ 'Song of the Plains' (Red Army Ensemble)
*¶ 'Dive and Shake Exercise' (from *Slim to Rhythm*) (Eileen Fowler)
¶ LUXURY: Writing materials.
¶ BOOK: Thor Heyerdahl, *The Kon-Tiki Expedition*

16 March 1974
1220 Brian Johnston
Broadcaster
¶ 'Eton Boating Song' (Eton College Musical Society)
¶ 'All the Things You Are' (Hutch)
¶ Novello, 'We'll Gather Lilacs' (from *Perchance to Dream*) (Vanessa Lee/Bruce Trent)
*¶ 'Double Damask' (Cicely Courtneidge/Ivor McLaren/Lawrence Green)
¶ 'Strolling' (Bud Flanagan)
¶ Elgar, 'Nimrod' (from *Enigma Variations*) (Philharmonia Orchestra/Sargent)
¶ 'Tie a Yellow Ribbon Round the Old Oak Tree' (Dawn)
¶ 'End of the Party' (Barry Alexander/Design)
¶ LUXURY: An automatic bowling machine and cricket balls.
¶ BOOK: John Fisher, *Funny Way to be a Hero*

23 March 1974
1221 Edward Woodward
Actor
¶ Barry, 'The Lion in Winter' (from film) (soundtrack/Barry)
*¶ Holst, 'Venus' (from *The Planets*) (NPO/Boult)
¶ Schubert, Symphony No. 8 in B minor (Unfinished) (RPO/Sargent)
¶ 'The Very Thought of You' (Nat 'King' Cole)
¶ Byrd, *Mass for Five Voices* (King's College Chapel Choir/Willcocks)
¶ Tchaikovsky, '1812 Overture' (LSO/Previn)
¶ Rimsky-Korsakov, 'The Sea and Sinbad's Ship' (from *Scheherazade*) (LSO/Previn)
¶ 'Cabaret' (from *Cabaret*) (Judi Dench)
¶ LUXURY: A bed.
¶ BOOK: Jerome K. Jerome, *Three Men in a Boat*

30 March 1974
1222 Philip Hope-Wallace
Drama and music critic
¶ Handel, 'Where'er You Walk' (from *Semele*) (Richard Lewis/LSO/Sargent)
¶ Schumann, 'Carnaval' (opus 9) (Claudio Arrau *piano*)

¶ Schubert, Piano Quintet in A major (Clifford Curzon/Members of the Vienna Octet)
¶ Leoncavallo, *Pagliacci* (prologue) (Robert Merrill/Santa Cecilia Orchestra, Rome/Gardelli)
¶ Zeller, 'Sei Nicht Bös' (from *Der Obersteiger*) (Elisabeth Schwarzkopf/Philharmonia Orchestra/Ackermann)
¶ 'La mer' (Charles Trenet)
¶ R. Strauss, 'Wiegenlied' (Lisa della Casa/Arpád Sándor *piano*)
*¶ Verdi, 'Dies Irae' and 'Salve Me' (from *Requiem*) (Philharmonia Chorus and Orchestra/Giulini)
¶ LUXURY: An ivory chess set.
¶ BOOK: Goethe's *Faust*

6 April 1974
1223 John & Roy Boulting
Film-makers
¶ (J) 'My Way' (Frank Sinatra)
*¶ (R) Mozart, String Quintet in G minor (Walter Trampler *viola*/Budapest String Quartet)
¶ (J) 'The Love that I Have' (from *Violette*) (Virginia McKenna)
¶ (R) Elgar, Cello Concerto in E minor (Pablo Casals/BBC Symphony/Boult)
*¶ (J) Bach/Hess, 'Jesu, Joy of Man's Desiring' (Myra Hess *piano*)
¶ (R) 'Tangerine' (Shelly Manne *drums*/André Previn *piano*/Leroy Vinnegar *bass*)
¶ (J) Franck, Symphony in D minor (French National Radio Orchestra/Beecham)
¶ (R) Sibelius, Symphony No. 2 in D major (Hallé Orchestra/Barbirolli)
¶ LUXURIES: (R) a piano; (J) wine.
¶ BOOKS: (R) Leo Tolstoy, *War and Peace*; (J) Lewis Carroll, *Alice in Wonderland*.

13 April 1974
1224 Dr Thor Heyerdahl
Anthropologist and leader of the Kon Tiki expedition
¶ Halvorsen, 'March of the Boyars' (Philadelphia Orchestra/Ormandy)
¶ 'Happy Trumpeter' (Bert Kaempfert and his Orchestra)

*¶ Beethoven, Symphony No. 5 in C minor (opus 67) (Berlin Philharmonic/von Karajan)
¶ 'Valdres March' (Eastman Wind Ensemble/Fennell)
¶ Mozart, *Eine Kleine Nachtmusik* (Columbia Symphony/Walter)
¶ Grieg, 'Morning' (from *Peer Gynt Suite*) (Philadelphia Orchestra/Ormandy)
¶ Benjamin, 'Jamaican Rumba' (Cleveland Pops Orchestra/Lane)
¶ Schubert, Symphony No. 8 in B minor (Unfinished) (Berlin Philharmonic/von Karajan)
¶ LUXURY: A wood-carving kit.
¶ BOOK: Blank paper.

20 April 1974
1225 Patricia Routledge
Actress and singer
¶ Bach, Oboe d'amore Concerto in A major (BWV 1055) (Helmut Winschermann/Frankfurt Bach Orchestra/Egel)
¶ Lerner & Loewe, 'How Can I Wait?' (from *Paint Your Wagon*) (Julie Andrews)
¶ Shostakovich, Symphony No. 5 in D minor (Moscow Philharmonic Symphony/Kondrashin)
¶ 'The Laughing Policeman' (Charles Penrose)
¶ Cavalli, *La Calisto* (duet) (Janet Baker/James Bowman/LPO/Leppard)
¶ Mozart, Oboe Quartet in F major (K. 370) (Ian Wilson/Gabrieli Quartet)
*¶ Elgar, 'Go, in the Name of Angels' (from *The Dream of Gerontius*) (Dennis Noble/Huddersfield Choral Society/Royal Liverpool Philharmonic/Sargent)
¶ Bach, 'Vergnügte Ruh, Beliebte' (Cantata No. 170) (Janet Baker/Academy of St Martin-in-the-Fields/Marriner)
¶ LUXURY: Varieties of tea and a tea-making outfit.
¶ BOOK: An anthology of poetry.

28 April 1974
1226 David Dimbleby
Reporter and interviewer

*¶ Bach, Concerto in D minor for Violin, Oboe and Strings (BWV 1060) (Otto Buchner *violin*/Edgar Shann *oboe*/Munich Bach Orchestra/Richter)

¶ Purcell, 'Frost Scene' (from *King Arthur*) (Trevor Anthony/Philomusica of London/Lewis)

¶ Lotti, 'Pur Dicesti' (Nellie Melba)

¶ 'The Lying in State of HM King George VI' (Richard Dimbleby *commentator*)

¶ Bach, 'Ich folge dir gleichfalls' (from *St John Passion*) (soloist of Vienna Sängerknaben/Chorus Viennensis/Concentus Musicus, Vienna/Gillesberger)

¶ 'Lonely Road' (from film *Song of Freedom*) (Paul Robeson)

¶ Verdi, 'Dies Irae' (from *Requiem*) (Philharmonia Chorus and Orchestra/Giulini)

¶ Mozart, Piano Concerto No. 24 in C minor (K. 491) (Solomon/Philharmonia Orchestra/Menges)

¶ LUXURY: Havana cigars.

¶ BOOK: *The Oxford English Dictionary*

4 May 1974
1227 Arthur Marshall
Broadcaster

¶ Elgar, 'Cockaigne Overture' (In London Town) (LPO/Boult)

*¶ Bach, 'Credo' (from *Mass in B minor*, BWV 232) (BBC Chorus/NPO/Klemperer)

¶ Novello, 'Highwayman Love' (from *Perchance to Dream*) (Olive Gilbert)

¶ Franck, 'Panis Angelicus' (from Mass in A) (Elisabeth Schwarzkopf/Chorus/Orchestra/Organ/Mackerras)

¶ Liszt, Hungarian Rhapsody No. 2 (Viennese Seven Singing Sisters)

¶ Borodin, 'Polovtsian Dances' (from *Prince Igor*) (Philharmonia Orchestra/von Karajan)

¶ Berlin, 'Doing What comes Naturally' (from *Annie Get Your Gun*) (Ethel Merman)

¶ Schumann, Piano Concerto in A minor (Dinu Lipatti/Philharmonia Orchestra/von Karajan)

¶ LUXURY: Nougat.

¶ BOOK: A bound volume of his favourite novels of P. G. Wodehouse.

11 May 1974
1228 Antoinette Sibley
Prima ballerina

*¶ Stravinsky, *The Rite of Spring* (Columbia Symphony/Stravinsky)

¶ 'You're My World' (Dionne Warwick)

¶ Puccini, 'Il mio mistero' (from *Turandot*) (Birgit Nilsson/Jussi Björling/Rome Opera House Orchestra/Leinsdorf)

¶ 'The Blood Donor' (from radio series *Hancock's Half Hour*) (Tony Hancock/company)

¶ Villa-Lobos, Bachianas Brasileiras No. 5 (Galina Vishnevskaya/Bolshoi Theatre Orchestra/Khaikin)

¶ e. e. cummings, 'what if a much of a which of a wind' (e. e. cummings)

¶ 'My Way' (Frank Sinatra)

¶ 'Rock Around the Clock' (Bill Haley and his Comets)

¶ LUXURY: A bed.

¶ BOOK: *Snoopy Dog* by Charles Schulz

18 May 1974
1229 T. C. Fairbairn
Centenarian impresario

¶ Puccini, Un bel di vedremo (One Fine Day) (from *Madam Butterfly*) (Madam Stiles Allen)

¶ Gounod, 'Jewel Song' (from *Faust*) (Miriam Licette/Orchestra/Beecham)

¶ Wagner, 'Forging Song' (from *Siegfried*) (Lauritz Melchior/Sinfonia of London/Heger)

¶ Puccini, 'Che gelida manina' (from *La bohème*) (Beniamino Gigli)

*¶ Wagner, 'Prize Song' (from *Die Meistersinger*) (Walter Widdop/Orchestra/Sargent)

¶ Wagner, 'Prelude' and 'Bridal Chorus' (from *Lohengrin*) (Bayreuth Festival Chorus and Orchestra/Tietjen)

¶ Verdi, 'Celeste Aida' (from *Aida*) (Placido Domingo/German Opera Orchestra, Berlin/Santi)

¶ Verdi, 'Triumphal March' (from *Aida*) (NBC Symphony/Toscanini)

¶ LUXURY: A tape recorder.

¶ BOOK: The complete works of John Milton.

25 May 1974
1230 James Stewart
Actor

¶ 'On the Road to Mandalay' (Kenneth McKellar)

¶ 'Bye, Bye Blues' (Bert Lown and his Orchestra)

¶ Gershwin, 'I've Got a Crush on You' (from *Treasure Girl*) (Betty Grable/Jack Lemmon)

¶ 'I Hadn't Anyone Till You' (Ray Noble and his Orchestra)

¶ 'There, I've Said It Again' (Vaughan Monroe and his Orchestra)

¶ 'Don't Cry, Joe' (Gordon Jenkins Orchestra)

¶ 'Moonlight Serenade' (Glenn Miller Orchestra)

*¶ 'Dream' (The Pied Pipers)

¶ LUXURY: A piano.

¶ BOOK: Brubeck musical arrangements.

1 June 1974
1231 Leslie Mitchell
Broadcaster

¶ Chopin, Nocturne No. 12 in G major (opus 37, no. 2) (Benno Moiseiwitsch *piano*)

¶ Debussy, *Prélude à l'après midi d'un faune* (Orchestre de la Suisse Romande/Ansermet)

*¶ Delius, 'Summer Night on the River' (RPO/Beecham)

¶ Gay, 'If the Heart of a Man' (from *The Beggar's Opera*) (Frederick Ranalow/Orchestra/Austin)

¶ Falla, 'Nights in the Gardens of Spain' (Artur Rubinstein *piano*/Philadelphia Orchestra/Ormandy)

¶ Elgar, 'Nimrod' (from *Enigma Variations*) (NBC Symphony/Toscanini)

¶ Lumbye, 'Champagne Galop' (Copenhagen Symphony/Friisholm)

¶'Jonah and the Whale' (Louis Armstrong *vocal* and *trumpet* and the All Stars/the Sy Oliver Choir)
¶ LUXURY: A silver-gilt patch box containing a miniature singing bird.
¶ BOOK: A biography of Leonardo da Vinci.

8 June 1974
1232 Susan Hill
Writer
*¶Bach, 'Gloria' (from *Mass in B minor*, BWV 232) (Vienna Singakademie Chorus/Stuttgart Chamber Orchestra/Münchinger)
¶Bach, Concerto in D minor for Oboe, Violin and Orchestra (BWV 1060) (Arthur Grumiaux *violin*/Heinz Holliger *oboe*/NPO/de Waart)
¶Elgar, 'Where Corals Lie' (from *Sea Pictures*) (Janet Baker/LSO/Barbirolli)
¶Tippett, Concerto for Double String Orchestra (Academy of St Martin-in-the-Fields/Marriner)
¶Elgar, Cello Concerto in E minor (Paul Tortelier/LPO/Boult)
¶T. S. Eliot, 'Preludes 1917' (Ian Richardson)
¶Schumann, 'Im wunderschönen Monat Mai' (from *Dichterliebe*) (Peter Pears/Benjamin Britten *piano*)
¶'Praise My Soul, the King of Heaven' (Coventry Cathedral Boys' Choir)
¶LUXURIES: A triple folding screen and personal photographs.
¶ BOOK: Nancy Mitford, *The Pursuit of Love*

15 June 1974
1233 Mark Lubbock
Composer and conductor
¶Lecocq/Jacob, *Mam'zelle Angot* (RPO/Irving)
*¶Wagner, 'Hans Sachs' Monologue' (from *Die Meistersinger*) (Paul Schoeffler/Vienna Philharmonic/Knappertsbusch)

¶Litolff, Concerto Symphonique No. 4 (scherzo, opus 102) (Irene Scharrer *piano*/LSO/Wood)
¶R. Strauss, 'Zerbinetta's Aria' (from *Ariadne auf Naxos*) (Maria Ivogün/Berlin State Opera Orchestra/Blech)
¶Mozart, 'Wie, Wie, Wie' (from *The Magic Flute*) (soloists/Berlin Philharmonic/Böhm)
¶J. Strauss, *A Night in Venice* (Act 1 finale) (Nicolai Gedda/Philharmonia Orchestra/Ackermann)
¶'So Long, Mom' (Tom Lehrer)
¶Lubbock, 'A Smuggler's Song' (Owen Brannigan/Ernest Lush *piano*)
¶LUXURY: Gin.
¶ BOOK: Sheridan Le Fanu, *The House by the Churchyard*

22 June 1974
1234 Max Wall
Entertainer
¶'A Cup of Coffee, a Sandwich and You' (from *Charlot's Revue of 1926*) (Nick Lucas)
¶'I See a Tree' (Peter Dawson)
¶'Truckin'' (Fats Waller and his Rhythm)
¶'Hora Staccato' (Larry Adler *harmonica*/Orchestra/Gamley)
¶Lehár, 'Patiently smiling' (from *The Land of Smiles*) (Richard Tauber)
¶'The Canoe Song' (from film *Sanders of the River*) (Paul Robeson)
*¶Gretchaninov, 'The Creed' (Choir of the Russian Church of the Metropolitan of Paris/Afonsky)
¶'Alfie' (from film) (Cilla Black)
¶LUXURY: A guitar.
¶BOOKS: His favourite novels of Charles Dickens

29 June 1974
1235 Osian Ellis
Harpist
¶'Watching the Wheat' (Brychan Powell/Orchestra of Wales/Ffrangcon Thomas)
¶Beethoven, Symphony No. 9 in D minor (opus 125) (LSO/Giulini)
¶Porter, 'Just One of Those Things' (from *Jubilee*) (Frank Cordell and his Orchestra)

¶R. Strauss, *Der Rosenkavalier* (final duet) (Christa Ludwig/Teresa Stich-Randall/Philharmonia Orchestra/von Karajan)
¶Ravel, *Daphnis and Chloe* (Royal Opera House Chorus, Covent Garden/LSO/Monteux)
¶Bach, Double Concerto in D minor (BWV 1043) (David & Igor Oistrakh *violins*/RPO/Goossens)
¶Britten, 'Deo Gratias' (from *Ceremony of Carols*) (King's College Chapel Choir/Osian Ellis *harp*/Willcocks)
*¶Britten, 'Mad Woman's Prayer' (from *Curlew River*) (Peter Pears/Bruce Webb/instrumental ensemble/Britten)
¶LUXURY: An electronic pipe organ.
¶ BOOK: A collection of Welsh poetry.

6 July 1974
1236 Richard Walker
Angler
¶Bellini, 'Ite sul colle' (from *Norma*) (Nicola Rossi-Lemeni/Royal Opera House Chorus, Covent Garden/Philharmonia Orchestra/Braithwaite)
¶'Over the Gate' (Bernard Miles)
¶Rimsky-Korsakov, 'Chanson hindoue' (from *Sadko*) (Dusan Georgevic/Suisse Romande Orchestra/Erede)
¶'A Satisfied Mind' (Joan Baez)
¶Puccini, Che gelida manina (Your Tiny Hand is Frozen) (from *La bohème*) (Charles Craig/RPO/Tausky)
¶Seeger, 'Where Have All the Flowers Gone?' (Marlene Dietrich)
¶'The Holy City' (Frederick Harvey/Fredric Bayco *organ*)
*¶Puccini, 'Nessun dorma' (from *Turandot*) (Flaviano Labo/Santa Cecilia Orchestra, Rome/Previtali)
¶LUXURY: Benvenuto Cellini's golden salt cellar.
¶ BOOK: Rudyard Kipling, *Puck of Pook's Hill*

13 July 1974
1237 Sheridan Morley
Biographer and critic
¶ 'Once in Love with Amy' (from *Where's Charley?*) (Ray Bolger)
¶ 'There are Those' (from *The Happiest Millionaire*) (Geraldine Page/Gladys Cooper/Tommy Steele/Orchestra/Elliott)
¶ Arden, Ornadel, 'Jonah and the Whale' (Robert Morley)
¶ 'As Time Goes By' (from film *Casablanca*) (Dooley Wilson/ Elliott Carpenter *piano*)
*¶ *Noël Coward at Las Vegas* (medley) (Noël Coward)
¶ Shakespeare, 'Caliban's Speech: Be Not Afear'd' (from *The Tempest*) (John Gielgud)
¶ 'The Ravens' (Peter Cook/ Dudley Moore)
¶ Lloyd Webber/Rice, 'Joseph's Final Song' (from *Joseph and the Amazing Technicolor Dream Coat*) (Gary Bond/original London cast)
¶ LUXURY: A radio receiver.
¶ BOOK: The short stories of Somerset Maugham.

20 July 1974
1238 Sir Keith Falkner
Singer and ex-Director of the Royal College of Music
¶ 'Jesu Dulcis Memoria' and 'Psalm No. 139' (Jonathan Burgess/Dara Carroll/New College Choir, Oxford/ Lumsden)
¶ Schubert, 'Der Krähe' (from *Die Winterreise*) (Heinrich Rehkemper)
¶ Schubert, Symphony No. 9 in C (Great) (LPO/Boult)
¶ Britten, 'The Ride to Rome' (from *The Rape of Lucretia*) (Peter Pears/English Chamber Orchestra/Britten)
¶ Verdi, 'Willow Song' (from *Otello*) (Gwyneth Jones/Royal Opera House Orchestra, Covent Garden/Downes)
¶ Brahms, 'Variations on a Theme of Paganini' (John Lill *piano*)

¶ Messiaen, 'Quartet for the End of Time' (Erich Gruenberg *violin*/Gervase de Peyer *clarinet*/ William Pleeth *cello*/Michel Béroff *piano*)
*¶ Bach, 'Kyrie Eleison' (from *Mass in B minor*, BWV 232) (BBC Chorus/NPO/ Klemperer)
¶ LUXURY: Colin Cowdrey's bowling machine.
¶ BOOKS: His favourite novels of Anthony Trollope.

27 July 1974
1239 Valerie Singleton
Television interviewer and reporter
¶ 'What's Going On?' (Marvin Gaye)
¶ Elgar, Cello Concerto in E minor (Jacqueline du Pré/LSO/ Barbirolli)
¶ Brahms, Symphony No. 4 in E minor (RPO/Kempe)
¶ 'Sergeant Stamoulis' (John Kalatzis)
¶ Bach, Concerto in D minor for Oboe, Violin and Orchestra (Léon Goossens *oboe*/Yehudi Menuhin *violin and conducting*/ Bath Festival Orchestra)
¶ J. Strauss, 'Blue Danube Waltz' (Vienna Philharmonic/ Boskovsky)
¶ Rodgers & Hammerstein, 'There is Nothin' Like a Dame' (from *South Pacific*) (Ray Walston/Ken Darby Singers/ Orchestra/Newman)
*¶ Beethoven, Violin Concerto in D (Yehudi Menuhin/Vienna Philharmonic/Silvestri)
¶ LUXURY: A small photographic darkroom.
¶ BOOK: H. G. Wells, *The Outline of History, Being a Plain History of Life and Mankind*

3 August 1974
1240 Roland Culver
Actor
*¶ Brahms, Piano Concerto No. 2 in B flat (Vladimir Ashkenazy/ LSO/Mehta)
¶ Bellini, 'Casta Diva' (from *Norma*) (Joan Sutherland/Royal Opera House Orchestra and Chorus, Covent Garden/ Molinari-Pradelli)

¶ Rodgers & Hammerstein, 'Oh, What a Beautiful Morning' (from *Oklahoma*) (Alfred Drake)
¶ Verdi, 'Si pel ciel marmoreo giuro' (from *Otello*) (Enrico Caruso/Titta Ruffo)
¶ 'Mr Gallagher and Mr Sheen' (Bing Crosby/Johnny Mercer)
¶ Mozart, Piano Concerto No. 9 in E flat (K. 271) (Vladimir Ashkenazy/LSO/Kertesz)
¶ Rodgers & Hammerstein, 'A Wonderful Guy' (from *South Pacific*) (Mary Martin)
¶ 'Stop Yer Tickling, Jock' (Sir Harry Lauder)
¶ LUXURY: Painting equipment.
¶ BOOK: *The Oxford Book of English Verse*

10 August 1974
1241 Michael Levey
Director of the National Gallery
¶ Handel, 'Let the Bright Seraphim' (from *Samson*) (Isobel Baillie/Hallé Orchestra/ Braithwaite)
¶ Mozart, Clarinet Concerto in A (K. 622) (Jack Brymer/LSO/ Davis)
¶ R. Strauss, 'Presentation of the Silver Rose' (from *Der Rosenkavalier*) (Maria Olszewska/Vienna Philharmonic/Heger)
¶ Bellini, *Norma* (Act 1 finale) (Joan Sutherland/Marilyn Horne/LSO and Chorus/ Bonynge)
¶ Wagner, 'Siegfried's Journey to the Rhine' (from *Götterdämmerung*) (Berlin Philharmonic/von Karajan)
¶ Tchaikovsky, 'M. Triquet's Song' (from *Eugene Onegin*) (Vitali Vlassov/Bolshoi Opera Chorus and Orchestra/ Rostropovich)
*¶ Mozart, 'Bei Männern' (from *The Magic Flute*) (Hilde Gueden/Walter Berry/Vienna Philharmonic/Böhm)
¶ Weber, 'Mermaid's Song' (from *Oberon*) (Arleen Auger/ Bavarian Radio Orchestra/ Kubelik)
¶ LUXURY: A kaleidoscope.
¶ BOOK: Brigid Brophy, *The Adventures of God in Search of the Black Girl*

17 August 1974
1242 Dodie Smith
Playwright and novelist
¶ Tchaikovsky, 'Barcarolle' (opus 37, no. 6) (Philippe Entremont *piano*)
¶ Schumann, 'Im wunderschönen Monat Mai' (from *Dichterliebe*) (Dietrich Fischer-Dieskau/Jörg Demus *piano*)
*¶ Beethoven, Quarter in B flat major (opus 130) (Amadeus String Quartet)
¶ Beethoven, Quartet in C major (opus 59) (Amadeus String Quartet)
¶ Brahms, Clarinet Quintet in B minor (opus 115) (Alfred Boskovsky/members of the Vienna Octet)
¶ Fauré, 'Une sainte en son auréole' (from *La Bonne chanson*, opus 61) (Gérard Souzay/Dalton Baldwin *piano*)
¶ Joplin, 'The Entertainer' (Joshua Rifkin *piano*)
¶ Lennon & McCartney, 'Being for the Benefit of Mr Kite' (The Beatles)
¶ LUXURY: Sketching materials.
¶ BOOK: Marcel Proust, *À la recherche du temps perdu*

24 August 1974
1243 Dandy Nichols
Actress
¶ Mendelssohn, *A Midsummer Night's Dream* (BBC Symphony/Sargent)
¶ Carmichael, 'Stardust' (Bing Crosby)
¶ 'Mood Indigo' (Duke Ellington and his Orchestra)
¶ Coward, 'Nina' (from *Sigh No More*) (Noël Coward)
*¶ Beethoven, Symphony No. 7 in A major (opus 92) (Berlin Philharmonic/von Karajan)
¶ *Frankie Howerd at the Establishment* (Frankie Howerd)
¶ Shakespeare, 'What Must the King Do Now?' (from *Richard II*, Act 3, Scene 3) (John Gielgud)
¶ 'The Holly and the Ivy' (King's College Chapel Choir/Willcocks)
¶ LUXURY: A pack of cards.
¶ BOOK: The plays of George Bernard Shaw.

31 August 1974
1244 Phyllis Barclay-Smith
Ornithologist
*¶ Chopin, Nocturne in E flat (opus 9, no. 2) (Artur Rubinstein *piano*)
¶ Schubert/Liszt, 'Die Forelle' (Jorge Bolet *piano*)
¶ Puccini, 'O soave fanciulla' (from *La bohème*) (Victoria de los Angeles/Jussi Björling/RCA Victor Symphony/Beecham)
¶ Beethoven, Symphony No. 9 in D minor (opus 125) (LSO/Giulini)
¶ Recordings of birdsong: mistle thrush, song thrush, blackbird
¶ 'The Aspen' (Magyari Imre/instrumental ensemble)
¶ Wagner, 'The Ride of the Valkyries' (from *Die Walküre*) (Philharmonia Orchestra/Klemperer)
¶ 'Follow the Wind to Cousin' (Regius Hoareau/The Nightshades)
¶ LUXURY: A pair of field glasses.
¶ BOOK: Charles Dickens, *The Pickwick Papers*

7 September 1974
1245 Graham Hill (2nd appearance)
Racing driver
¶ Lennon & McCartney, 'Penny Lane' (The Beatles)
¶ Lerner & Loewe, 'Wand'ring Star' (from *Paint Your Wagon*) (Lee Marvin)
¶ Parry/Blake, 'Jerusalem' (Royal Choral Society/Philharmonia Orchestra/Sargent)
¶ 'Spanish Eyes' (Al Martino)
¶ Mozart, Clarinet Concerto in A (K. 622) (Gervase de Peyer/LSO/Maag)
¶ 'Grand Prix' (from film) (soundtrack/Jarre)
¶ 'The Driving Instructor' (Bob Newhart)
*¶ Elgar, 'Land of Hope and Glory' (from *Coronation Ode*) (recorded at last night of 1969 Proms) (BBC Symphony/Prom audience/Davis)
¶ LUXURY: David Wynne, *The Dancers*.
¶ BOOK: A family photograph album.

14 September 1974
1246 Denholm Elliott
Actor
¶ Handel, *Water Music Suite* (Berlin Philharmonic/von Karajan)
¶ Rodrigo, 'Concierto de Aranjuez' (Siegfried Behrend *guitar*/Berlin Philharmonic/Peters)
¶ 'Don't Let It Bother You' (Fats Waller and his rhythm)
¶ Rachmaninov, Piano Concerto No. 2 in C minor (Sviatoslav Richter/Warsaw Philharmonic/Wislocki)
¶ Rodgers & Hart, 'The Lady is a Tramp' (from *Babes in Arms*) (Shirley Bassey)
¶ J. Strauss, 'The Blue Danube' (Vienna Symphony/Stolz)
¶ 'Chicago' (Coleman Hawkins/The Ramblers)
*¶ Taverner, Kyrie a 4 (Leroy) (King's College Chapel Choir/Willcocks)
¶ LUXURY: A still.
¶ BOOK: A survival manual.

21 September 1974
1247 Frank Swinnerton (2nd appearance)
Novelist, biographer and critic
¶ 'The First Noel' (King's College Chapel Choir/Willcocks)
¶ 'The Wee Cooper o' Fife' (Ian Wallace)
¶ Rossini, *William Tell* (overture) (New Queen's Hall Orchestra/Wood)
¶ 'A Little of What You Fancy Does You Good' (Marie Lloyd)
¶ Berlioz, Symphonie fantastique (LSO/Davis)
¶ Bizet, 'Au fond du temple saint' (from *Les pêcheurs de perles*) (Jussi Björling/Robert Merrill/RCA Victor Symphony/Cellini)
*¶ Beethoven, Symphony No. 6 in F major (Pastoral) (Philharmonia Orchestra/Klemperer)
¶ Sullivan/Mackerras, *Pineapple Poll* Ballet (RPO/Mackerras)
¶ LUXURY: Gin and vermouth.
¶ BOOK: James Woodforde , *The Diary of a Country Parson 1758–1802*

28 September 1974
1248 David Munrow
Musician

¶ Tallis, 40-part motet (Spem In Alium) (Clerkes of Oxenford)
¶ 'La pitita' (Luis Abanto Morales)
¶ Bach, 'Agnus Dei' (from *Mass in B minor*, BWV 232) (Alfred Deller/Leonhardt Baroque Ensemble)
¶ Elgar, Symphonic Study: *Falstaff* (LSO/Collins)
¶ Bernstein/Sondheim, 'I Feel Pretty' (from *West Side Story*) (Natalie Wood [Marni Nixon])
¶ 'At the Jazz Band Ball' (Bix Beiderbecke and his Gang)
¶ 'Love Song' (Daian Luca *pan pipes*/Orchestra Lautaru Barbu)
*¶ Handel, 'He was Despised' (from *Messiah*) (James Bowman/ Academy of St Martin-in-the-Fields/Willcocks)
¶ LUXURY: A piano.
¶ BOOK: *Men and Animals*, a book in Italian.

5 October 1974
1249 Cyril Ray
Writer and wine expert

¶ Offenbach, *La perichole* (waltz) (Les Musiciens de l'Opéra, Paris/Gabon)
*¶ Mozart, 'Voi che sapete' (from *The Marriage of Figaro*) (Fiorenza Cossotto/ Philharmonia Orchestra/ Giulini)
¶ 'Il tamburo della banda d'affori' (march) (Macario/ orchestra/Rizza)
¶ Delibes, *Coppélia* (Philharmonia Orchestra/ Irving)
¶ O. Straus, 'La Ronde Waltz' (from film *La Ronde*) (Vienna State Orchestra/Stolz)
¶ Albinoni, Oboe Concerto in B flat major (Sydney Sutcliffe/ Virtuosi of England/Davison)
¶ R. Strauss, *Der Rosenkavalier* (waltz) (Dresden State Orchestra/Kempe)
¶ Purcell, 'When I am Laid in Earth' (from *Dido and Aeneas*) (Kirsten Flagstad/Mermaid Orchestra/Jones)
¶ LUXURY: An airmail edition of *The Times*.
¶ BOOK: R. S. Surtees, *Mr Sponge's Sporting Tour*

12 October 1974
1250 William Hardcastle
Radio and television journalist

¶ Sousa, 'The Liberty Bell March' (US Navy Band)
¶ 'Brother, Can You Spare a Dime' (Al Bowlly/Lew Stone and his Orchestra)
¶ 'Sentimental Journey' (Les Brown and his Band of Renown)
¶ 'C'est si bon' (from *Latin Quarter 1950*) (Jean Sablon)
¶ Kristopherson, 'Me and Bobby McGee' (Janis Joplin)
¶ 'Avalon' (Benny Goodman Quartet)
¶ Mancini, 'The Days of Wine and Roses' (Henry Mancini and his Orchestra)
*¶ 'Keep Your Feet Still, Geordie Hinny' (The Shiremoor Marras)
¶ LUXURY: A tobacco plant.
¶ BOOK: A P. G. Wodehouse omnibus.

19 October 1974
1251 Polly James
Actress

¶ Shostakovich, Symphony No. 5 in D minor (USSR Symphony/Maxim Shostakovich)
¶ Satie, *Trois gymnopédies* (Frank Glazer *piano*)
¶ 'Sing as We Go' (from film) (Gracie Fields)
*¶ Puccini, 'Che gelida manina' (from *La bohème*) (Jussi Björling/Orchestra/Grevillius)
¶ Ravel, 'Pavane pour une infante défunte' (NPO/Giulini)
¶ 'Magic to Do' (from *Pippin*) (Ben Vereen/company)
¶ 'The Streams of Lovely Nancy' (Martin Best Consort)
¶ Coward, 'The Boy Actor' (from *Cowardy Custard*) (John Moffatt)
¶ LUXURY: A group photograph of friends.
¶ BOOK: Elizabeth Longford, *Victoria RI*

26 October 1974
1252 Dr Magnus Pyke
Scientist, writer and broadcaster

¶ Grieg, 'Anitra's Dance' (from *Peer Gynt Suite*) (LPO/ Pritchard)
¶ 'The Irish Jubilee' (Pat Harrington)
¶ Delibes, *Coppélia* (Suisse Romande Orchestra/Bonynge)
¶ 'The Mountains of Mourne' (Kenneth McKellar)
*¶ Mozart, Clarinet Quintet in A major (K. 581) (Gervase de Peyer/Melos Ensemble)
¶ Crimond, 'The Twenty-Third Psalm' (Temple Church Choir/ Thalben-Ball)
¶ 'Part of the Union' (The Strawbs)
¶ 'House of the King' (Focus)
¶ LUXURY: Writing materials.
¶ BOOK: *The Oxford Book of English Verse*

2 November 1974
1253 Alan Ayckbourn
Playwright

¶ Britten, 'The Young Person's Guide to the Orchestra' (LSO/ Britten)
*¶ Bach, Concerto in C minor for Violin, Oboe and Orchestra (Isaac Stern *violin*/Harold Gomberg *oboe*/New York Philharmonic/Bernstein)
¶ 'Flamenco Sketches' (Miles Davis *trumpet*/ensemble)
¶ Prokofiev, *Cinderella* (finale) (Prague Radio Symphony/ Meylan)
¶ Rodgers & Hart, 'Where or When?' (from *Babes in Arms*) (Peggy Lee/Benny Goodman and his Sextet)
¶ 'Welscher Tanz Wascha Mesa' (Konrad Ragossnig *lute*/ Ulsamer Collegium)
¶ 'Eclipse' (Pink Floyd)
¶ Saint-Saëns, 'Agnus Dei' (from *Requiem*) (soloists/ Contrepoint Choral Ensemble/ French National Radio Orchestra/Gaussens)
¶ LUXURY: A mellotron.
¶ BOOK: Moss Hart, *Act One*

9 November 1974
1254 Elisabeth Frink
Sculptor
¶ Vivaldi, 'Spring' (from *The Four Seasons*) (Luigi Ferro *violin*/Virtuosi di Roma/Fasano)
¶ 'Mounsiers Almaine' (Julian Bream *lute*)
¶ Kodály, Duo for Violin and Cello (opus 7) (Vilmos Tátrai *violin*/Ede Banda *cello*)
¶ Beethoven, Triple Concerto in C major (David Oistrakh *violin*/Sviatoslav Richter *piano*/Mstislav Rostropovich *cello*/Berlin Philharmonic/von Karajan)
¶ Granados, Spanish Dance No. 5 (John Williams *guitar*)
¶ Albinoni, Concerto in B flat for Trumpet and Orchestra (Maurice André/ Saar Radio Chamber Orchestra/Ristenpart)
¶ Bartók, Violin Concerto No. 2 (Yehudi Menuhin/NPO/Dorati)
*¶ Bach, Brandenburg Concerto No. 1 in F major (BWV 1046) (Emanuel Hurwitz *violin*/Peter Graeme *oboe*/English Chamber Orchestra/Britten)
¶ LUXURIES: Drawing and writing materials.
¶ BOOK: The collected stories of Albert Camus.

16 November 1974
1255 Robin Ray
Broadcaster
¶ 'Once in Royal David's City' (King's College Chapel Choir/Willcocks)
¶ Ravel, Piano Concerto for the Left Hand (Julius Katchen/LSO/Kertesz)
¶ 'Miss Otis Regrets' (José Feliciano)
¶ 'Take a Pew' (from *Beyond the Fringe*) (Alan Bennett)
*¶ Rachmaninov, Symphony No. 2 in E minor (LPO/Weller)
¶ 'Fly Me to the Moon' (Johnny Mathis)
¶ Puccini, 'Mi sento assai meglio' (from *La bohème*) (Victoria de los Angeles/Jussi Björling/Robert Merrill/RCA Victor Symphony/Beecham)

¶ Chopin, Ballade No. 4 in F minor (opus 52) (Artur Rubinstein *piano*)
¶ LUXURY: A piano.
¶ BOOK: Auguste Escoffier, *Ma cuisine*

23 November 1974
1256 Bruce Tulloh
Long-distance runner
¶ 'Muskrat Ramble' (Louis Armstrong and his All Stars)
¶ Sibelius, Symphony No. 2 in D (Hallé Orchestra/Barbirolli)
¶ Lennon & McCartney, 'Penny Lane' (The Beatles)
¶ Mendelssohn, Violin Concerto in E minor (Yehudi Menuhin/LSO/Frühbeck de Burgos)
¶ 'My Elusive Dreams' (Nancy Sinatra/Lee Hazlewood)
¶ 'River Deep, Mountain High' (Ike & Tina Turner)
¶ Rodrigo, Concierto de Aranjuez (Julian Bream *guitar*/Melos Chamber Orchestra/Davis)
*¶ 'A felicidade' (from film *Black Orpheus*) (Antonio Carlos Jobim)
¶ LUXURY: A harmonica.
¶ BOOK: Jane Austen, *Pride and Prejudice*

30 November 1974
1257 Oliver Reed
Actor
¶ Rodgers & Hammerstein, 'Soliloquy' (from *Carousel*) (Gordon Macrae)
¶ Mozart, Piano Concerto No. 21 in C (Daniel Barenboim/English Chamber Orchestra)
*¶ Debussy, 'Jardins sous la pluie' (Walter Gieseking *piano*)
¶ 'In the Heat of the Night' (Ray Charles/Quincy Jones Orchestra)
¶ 'Ecstasy' (Ben E. King)
¶ 'The Lady Came from Baltimore' (Tim Hardin)
¶ 'Singin' in the Rain' (from film) (Gene Kelly)
¶ 'The First Nowell' (King's College Chapel Choir/Willcocks)
¶ LUXURY: An inflatable rubber woman.
¶ BOOK: A. A. Milne, *Winnie the Pooh*

7 December 1974
1258 P. J. Kavanagh
Poet, novelist and broadcaster
¶ 'Biddy Mulligan' (Jimmy O'Dea/Harry O'Donovan)
*¶ Bach, Partita No. 2 in D minor (BWV 1004) (Arthur Grumiaux *violin*)
¶ Weill, *Knickerbocker Holiday* (from *September Affair*) (Walter Huston)
¶ 'At Dawning' (Paul Robeson)
¶ Mozart, *Cosi fan tutte* (Act 1 trio) (Elisabeth Schwarzkopf/Christa Ludwig/Walter Berry/Philharmonia Orchestra/Böhm)
¶ Rodgers & Hart, 'Do It the Hard Way' (from *Pal Joey*) (Kenneth Remo)
¶ Beethoven, Piano Sonata No. 23 in F minor (Daniel Barenboim)
¶ Balinese gamelan music (Gamelan Orchestra)
¶ LUXURY: A pair of shoes.
¶ BOOK: The collected poems of Edward Thomas.

14 December 1974
1259 Betty Kenward
Social editor and writer of *Jennifer's Diary*
¶ Coward, 'I'll See You Again' (from *Bitter Sweet*) (Noël Coward)
¶ 'Underneath the Arches' (Flanagan & Allen)
¶ 'The Birth of the Blues' (from *George White's Scandals of 1926*) (Carroll Gibbons and his Boy Friends)
¶ Rodgers & Hammerstein, 'The Sound of Music' (from *The Sound of Music*) (Mary Martin)
¶ Tchaikovsky, *Swan Lake* (Act 2 *pas de deux*) (Yehudi Menuhin *violin*/Philharmonia Orchestra/Kurtz)
¶ Lerner & Loewe, 'I Could Have Danced All Night' (from *My Fair Lady*) (Julie Andrews)
*¶ J. Strauss, 'The Blue Danube' (Vienna Philharmonic/Boskovsky)
¶ Elgar, 'Land of Hope and Glory' (from *Coronation Ode*) (Clara Butt)
¶ LUXURY: A radio receiver.
¶ BOOK: *Debrett's Peerage*

21 December 1974
1260 Angela Baddeley
Actress
*¶Wagner, 'Liebestod' (from *Tristan und Isolde*) (Birgit Nilsson/Vienna Philharmonic/Solti)
¶Mozart, *Cosi fan tutte* (overture) (RPO/Colin Davis)
¶Chopin, Waltz No. 6 in D flat (opus 64, no. 1) Artur Rubinstein *piano*)
¶Gershwin, 'Lady be Good' (from *Lady be Good*) (William Kent)
¶Verdi, 'Willow Song' (from *Otello*) (Joan Sutherland/Royal Opera House Orchestra, Covent Garden/Molinari-Pradelli)
¶Porter, 'Now You Has Jazz' (from film *High Society*) (Bing Crosby/Louis Armstrong)
¶J. Strauss, *Die Fledermaus* (Act 2 finale) (Sadler's Wells Opera Company and Orchestra/Tausky)
¶Beethoven, Sonata No. 14 in C sharp minor (opus 27, no. 2) (Moonlight) (Wilhelm Backhaus *piano*)
¶LUXURY: Portrait of her husband, Glen Byam Shaw, by Glen Philpott.
¶BOOK: Lewis Carroll, *Alice in Wonderland*

28 December 1974
1261 Percy Press
Punch & Judy showman
*¶Mendelssohn, *A Midsummer Night's Dream* (overture) (Bavarian Radio Symphony/Kubelik)
¶*Max at the Met* (Max Miller)
¶'My Blue Heaven' (Whispering Jack Smith and the Whispering Orchestra)
¶'The Punch and Judy Show' (Gracie Fields)
¶'Because' (Webster Booth)
¶Gilbert & Sullivan, 'The Flowers that Bloom in the Spring' (from *The Mikado*) (Peter Pratt/Thomas Round/chorus/New Symphony Orchestra/Godfrey)
¶Slaughter, *Maria Marten or Murder in the Red Barn* (excerpt) (Tod Slaughter/theatre company)

¶'Sussex by the Sea' (HM Royal Marines Band)
¶LUXURY: A pair of binoculars.
¶BOOK: Jerome K. Jerome, *Three Men in a Boat*

4 January 1975
1262 Alan Civil
French horn player
¶'Old Comrades' (military band)
¶Gilbert & Sullivan, 'None Shall Part Us from Each Other' (from *Iolanthe*) (Margaret Mitchell/Alan Styler/D'Oyly Carte Opera Company/Godfrey)
¶Thomas, *Raymond* (overture) (Guckenheimer Sour Kraut Band)
¶Britten, Serenade for Tenor, Horn and Strings (Peter Pears/Dennis Brain *horn*/Boyd Neel Orchestra/Britten)
¶Waldteufel, 'Skaters' Waltz' (from *Les Patineurs*) (Philharmonia Orchestra/von Karajan)
¶Bach, 'Cum Sancto Spiritu' (from *Mass in B minor*, BWV 232) (BBC Chorus/NPO/Klemperer)
*¶Beethoven, Symphony No. 9 in D minor (opus 125) (Philharmonia Orchestra/Klemperer)
¶Mozart, Serenade for Thirteen Wind Instruments (K. 361) (London Wind Quintet/ensemble/Klemperer)
¶LUXURY: Something to improve the taste of coconut milk.
¶BOOK: The score of Stockhausen's *Gruppen*.

11 January 1975
1263 Rt Hon. James Prior MP
Politician and farmer
¶Franck, Symphonic Variations for Piano and Orchestra (Moura Lympany/Philharmonia Orchestra/Susskind)
¶'Dear Lord and Father of Mankind' (King's College Chapel Choir/Willcocks)
¶Rodgers & Hammerstein, 'People Will Say We're in Love' (from *Oklahoma*) (Joan Roberts)

¶Beethoven, 'Prisoners' Chorus' (from *Fidelio*) (Philharmonia Chorus and Orchestra/Klemperer)
¶Bernstein/Sondheim, 'Tonight' (from *West Side Story*) (Natalie Wood [Marni Nixon])
*¶Elgar, Symphony No. 1 in A flat major (Philharmonia Orchestra/Barbirolli)
¶Rodgers & Hammerstein, 'My Favourite Things' (from *The Sound of Music*) (Julie Andrews)
¶Beethoven, Symphony No. 9 in D minor (opus 125) (Vienna Singverein/Berlin Philharmonic/von Karajan)
¶LUXURY: A radio receiver.
¶BOOK: Sir Winston Churchill, *A History of the English-Speaking Peoples*

18 January 1975
1264 Charles Mackerras (2nd appearance)
Conductor
¶Mozart, Symphony No. 38 in D major (K. 504) (Prague) (LPO/Mackerras)
¶Mozart, Clarinet Quintet in A major (K. 581) (Thea King/Aeolian String Quartet)
¶Dvořák, Cello Concerto in B minor (opus 104) (Mstislav Rostropovich/Czech Philharmonic/Talich)
*¶Verdi, *Otello* (Act 2 finale) (Herva Nelli/Ramon Vinay/Giuseppe Valdengo/Nan Merriman/NBC Symphony/Toscanini)
¶Janáček, *The Makropoulos Affair* (Act 1 prelude) (Pro Arte Orchestra/Mackerras)
¶Wagner, 'Magic Fire Music' (from *Die Walküre*) (Vienna Philharmonic/Furtwängler)
¶Mahler, Symphony No. 7 in B minor (CSO/Solti)
¶Handel, 'Hallelujah Chorus' (from *Messiah*) (Ambrosian Singers/English Chamber Orchestra/Mackerras)
¶LUXURY: Wine.
¶BOOK: The Bible in German.

25 January 1975
1265 Bernard Hailstone
Portrait painter

¶ Sibelius, 'Finlandia' (Berlin Philharmonic/von Karajan)
¶ Elgar, Cello Concerto in E minor (Jacqueline du Pré/LSO/Barbirolli)
¶ Grieg, Piano Concerto in A minor (Radu Lupu/LSO/Previn)
¶ 'Chopsticks' (Victor Borge)
¶ Handel, *Music for the Royal Fireworks* (wind ensemble/Mackerras)
¶ Delius, 'A Song Before Sunrise' (RPO/Beecham)
*¶ Bach, Brandenburg Concerto No. 1 in F major (BWV 1046) (Bath Festival Orchestra/Menuhin)
¶ Prokofiev, Ballet *Romeo and Juliet* (Cleveland Orchestra/Maazel)
¶ LUXURY: A radio receiver with solar batteries.
¶ BOOK: Ouspensky, *In Search of the Miraculous*

1 February 1975
1266 Celia Johnson
(3rd appearance)
Actress

¶ Bach, Brandenburg Concerto No. 6 in B flat major (BWV 1051) (Bath Festival Chamber Orchestra/Yehudi Menuhin)
¶ Haydn, Symphony No. 88 in G major (NPO/Klemperer)
¶ Coward, 'Sail Away' (from *Sail Away*) (Noël Coward)
¶ Mozart, Clarinet Concerto in A (K. 622) (Jack Brymer/Academy of St Martin-in-the-Fields/Marriner)
¶ 'O Come All Ye Faithful' (King's College Chapel Choir/Willcocks)
¶ Prokofiev, Ballet *Romeo and Juliet* (Minneapolis Symphony/Skrowaczewski)
¶ Bach, *St Matthew Passion* (final chorus) (Stuttgart Hymnus Boys' Choir and Chamber Orchestra/Münchinger)
*¶ Beethoven, Violin Concerto in D major (David Oistrakh/French National Radio Orchestra/Cluytens)
¶ LUXURY: A Rolls-Royce.
¶ BOOKS: Novels by Anthony Trollope.

8 February 1975
1267 Lord Longford
Writer, publisher and politician

¶ 'Eton Boating Song' (Eton College Musical Society)
¶ Coward, 'Dance Little Lady' (from *This Year of Grace*) (Noël Coward)
¶ W. B. Yeats, 'Easter 1916' (C. Day Lewis)
¶ 'Westward, Look, the Land is Bright' (broadcast speech, 27 April 1941) (Sir Winston Churchill)
¶ *The Gospel According to St Matthew* (chapter 25) (Barbara Jefford)
¶ Bach/Gounod, 'Ave Maria' (Joan Hammond)
¶ 'O Come All Ye Faithful' (BBC Singers/Academy of the BBC/Heath)
*¶ 'Psalm 51' (King's College Chapel Choir/Willcocks)
¶ LUXURY: Golf clubs and balls.
¶ BOOK: Thomas à Kempis, *Imitation of Christ*

15 February 1975
1268 Emlyn Williams
(3rd appearance)
Playwright and actor

¶ Grieg, 'In the Hall of the Mountain King' (from *Peer Gynt*) (Beecham Choral Society/RPO/Beecham)
¶ 'Watching the Wheat' (Portardulais Male Choir/Noel Davies)
¶ Pierné, 'Entry of the Little Fauns' (from *Cydalise and the Satyr*) (Pro Arte Orchestra/Vinter)
¶ 'Shadows on the Grass' (Irene Handl/Peter Sellers)
¶ Coward, 'London Pride' (Gracie Fields)
¶ Butterworth, 'A Shropshire Lad' (LPO/Boult)
¶ 'Lilacs Out of the Dead Land' (Manos Hadjidakis)
*¶ 'Elizabethan Serenade' (Ron Goodwin and his Orchestra)
¶ LUXURY: A typewriter, pen and paper.
¶ BOOK: A dictionary.

22 February 1975
1269 Valerie Masterson
Soprano

*¶ Franck, Symphony in D minor (Paris Orchestra/von Karajan)
¶ Simon, 'Bridge Over Troubled Water' (Simon & Garfunkel)
¶ Gilbert & Sullivan, *The Mikado* (Act 1) (D'Oyly Carte Opera Company/New Symphony Orchestra/Godfrey)
¶ 'I'm a Little Teapot' (children's choir)
¶ Charpentier, 'Depuis le jour' (from *Louise*) (Ninon Vallin)
¶ Beethoven, Violin Concerto in D (David Oistrakh/Stockholm Festival Orchestra/Ehrling)
¶ Debussy, 'La danse de Puck' (*Prelude*, Book 1, No. 11) (Walter Gieseking *piano*)
¶ Verdi, 'Sempre libera' (from *La traviata*) (Maria Callas/EIAR Symphony Orchestra, Turin/Santini)
¶ LUXURY: A chestful of beauty products.
¶ BOOK: A survival manual.

1 March 1975
1270 John Conteh
World light-heavyweight boxing champion

*¶ 'Bless the Beasts and the Children' (Shirley Bassey)
¶ 'Samba pa ti' (Santana)
¶ McCartney, 'Band on the Run' (Paul McCartney and Wings)
¶ Gershwin, 'Rhapsody in Blue' (André Previn *piano and conducting*/LSO)
¶ John/Taupin, 'Bennie and the Jets' (Elton John)
¶ 'The Great Deception' (Van Morrison)
¶ Bowie, 'Space Oddity' (David Bowie)
¶ Lennon & McCartney, 'A Day in the Life' (The Beatles)
¶ LUXURY: An electric guitar with solar batteries.
¶ BOOK: A work on botany.

8 March 1975
1271 Jilly Cooper
Writer and journalist

¶ Gershwin, 'Our Love is Here to Stay' (from film *An American in Paris*) (Gene Kelly)
¶ 'I'm in the Mood for Love' (Freddy Gardner *saxophone*)
¶ Brahms, Piano Concerto No. 1 in D minor (Rudolf Serkin/ Cleveland Orchestra/Szell)
¶ Haydn, Trumpet Concerto in E flat (John Wilbraham/ Academy of St Martin-in-the-Fields/Marriner)
¶ Verdi, 'Dies Irae' (from *Requiem*) (Philharmonia Chorus and Orchestra/Giulini)
*¶ Beethoven, 'Mir ist so wunderbar' (from *Fidelio*) (Gwyneth Jones/Edith Mathis/ Franz Crass/Peter Schreier/ Dresden State Orchestra/ Böhm)
¶ 'Where are You Going to, My Pretty Maid?' (Cynthia Glover/ John Lawrenson)
¶ Mozart, *The Marriage of Figaro* (Act 2 quartet) (Georges Bacquier/Elisabeth Söderström/Reri Grist/Geraint Evans/NPO/Klemperer)
¶ LUXURY: A large notebook and pencils.
¶ BOOKS: Anthony Powell, *A Dance to the Music of Time* sequence of novels (12 vols.).

15 March 1975
1272 Duncan Grant
Painter

¶ Bach, 'Gavotte' (from Partita in E (BWV 1006)) (Andrés Segovia *guitar*)
¶ Purcell, 'When I am Laid in Earth' (from *Dido and Aeneas*) (Kirsten Flagstad/Mermaid Orchestra/Jones)
¶ Handel, Suite No. 5 in E major (Wanda Landowska *harpsichord*)
¶ Beethoven, Trio in B flat (opus 97) (Alfred Cortot *piano*/ Jacques Thibaud *violin*/Pablo Casals *cello*)
¶ 'A Paradigm of Love' (Paul Roche)
¶ Charpentier, 'Depuis le jour' (from *Louise*) (Mary Garden/ Orchestra/Bourdon)

*¶ Monteverdi, *L'incoronazione di Poppea* (final duet) (Magda Laszlo/Richard Lewis/RPO/ Pritchard)
¶ Stravinsky, 'Sanctus' (from *Mass*) (Christ Church Cathedral Choir, Oxford/London Sinfonietta/Preston)
¶ LUXURY: Artist's materials.
¶ BOOKS: The novels of Jane Austen.

22 March 1975
1273 Eric Thompson
Actor, director and children's television performer

*¶ 'Oh Happy Day' (Edwin Hawkins Singers)
¶ 'Romance' (from film *Jeux interdits*) (Narciso Yepes *guitar*)
¶ 'Everybody's Talking' (from film *Midnight Cowboy*) (Nilsson)
¶ Verdi, 'D'amor sull'ali rosee' (from *Il trovatore*) (Zinka Milanov/RCA Victor Symphony/Cellini)
¶ Weill, 'September Song' (from *Knickerbocker Holiday*) (Walter Huston)
¶ 'Unsquare Dance' (Dave Brubeck Quartet)
¶ Schubert, Piano Quintet in A major (Clifford Curzon *piano*/ members of the Vienna Octet)
¶ 'Frank Mills' (from *Hair*) (Shelley Plimpton)
¶ LUXURY: A set of drums.
¶ BOOK: A volume of *Pogo* comic strips by Walt Kelly.

29 March 1975
1274 Stanley Dangerfield
International dog show judge

¶ 'My Way' (Brook Benton)
¶ 'Because' (Percy Faith Strings)
¶ 'How Much is that Doggie in the Window?' (Baja Marimba Band)
¶ 'He Touched Me' (from the musical *Drat! The Cat*) (Barbra Streisand/Don Costa and his Orchestra)
¶ 'Your Feet's Too Big' (Fats Waller and his Rhythm)
¶ 'The Most Beautiful Girl' (Charlie Rich)
*¶ 'Introducing Tobacco to Civilisation' (Bob Newhart)
¶ 'Lazy River' (Mills Brothers/ Count Basie and his Orchestra)

¶ LUXURY: The mermaid statue in Copenhagen harbour.
¶ BOOK: Axel Munthe, *The Story of San Michele*

5 April 1975
1275 Lionel Blair
Dancer, choreographer and director

*¶ Styne, *Gypsy* (overture) (orchestra/Rosenstock)
¶ 'That Face' (Fred Astaire/ Buddy Bregman and his Orchestra)
¶ Rodgers & Hart, 'Slaughter on Tenth Avenue' (from *On Your Toes*) (MGM Studio Orchestra/Hayton)
¶ 'Change Partners' (from film *Carefree*) (Sammy Davis Jnr)
¶ Tchaikovsky, Romeo and Juliet, Fantasy Overture (David Rose and his Orchestra)
¶ 'Come Rain or Come Shine' (from *St Louis Woman*) (Judy Garland)
¶ 'Let There be Love' (Nat 'King' Cole)
¶ 'Real Live girl' (Jack Jones)
¶ LUXURY: An oyster knife.
¶ BOOK: The biggest crossword book in the world, plus pencils.

12 April 1975
1276 Sir John Betjeman (2nd appearance)
Poet Laureate

¶ Bach, Suite No. 2 in B minor (BWV 1068) (Richard Adeney *flute*/English Chamber Orchestra/Leppard)
¶ Porter, 'Let's Do It' (from *Paris*) (Ella Fitzgerald)
*¶ Handel, 'Ombra mai fù' (from *Xerxes*) (Janet Baker/English Chamber Orchestra/Leppard)
¶ 'Ducker' (Harrow School Choir)
¶ Shakespeare, 'Seven Ages of Man' (from *As You Like It*, Act 2) (John Gielgud)
¶ *Max at the Met* (Max Miller)
¶ Stanford, 'Magnificat in G' (King's College Chapel Choir/ Ord)
¶ 'Flora MacDonald' (Douglas Byng)
¶ LUXURY: Champagne.
¶ BOOK: *The Golden Treasury*, compiled by Francis Palgrave.

19 April 1975
1277 Patricia Hayes
Actress
¶ 'My Blue Heaven' (Gracie Fields)
¶ 'It Doesn't Matter Anymore' (Buddy Holly)
¶ 'Boy Meets Girl' (from radio series *Take It from Here*) (Dick Bentley/June Whitfield/Jimmy Edwards)
¶ Lennon & McCartney, 'Eleanor Rigby' (The Beatles)
*¶ Chopin, Nocturne No. 8 in D flat (opus 27, no. 2) (Dinu Lipatti *piano*)
¶ Puccini, 'Si, mi chiamano Mimi' (from *La bohème*, Act 1) (Victoria de los Angeles/RCA Victor Symphony/Beecham)
¶ Joplin, 'The Entertainer' (Swingle II)
¶ Beethoven, 'Mir ist so wunderbar' (from *Fidelio*) (Ingeborg Hallstein/Christa Ludwig/Gottlob Frick/Gerhard Unger/Philharmonia Orchestra/Klemperer)
¶ LUXURY: A four-poster bed with accessories.
¶ BOOK: Sigrid Undset, *Kristin Lauransdatter*.

26 April 1975
1278 John Hillaby
Naturalist and writer
¶ Prokofiev, Symphony No. 5 (New York Philharmonic/Bernstein)
¶ Haydn, String Quartet No. 44 in B flat (opus 50, no. 1) (Vienna Konzerthaus Quartet)
¶ 'Royal Tutsi Drums' (Royal Kalinga Drummers of the Mwami of Ruanda)
¶ Tallis, *Lamentations of Jeremiah* (no. 1) (Renaissance Singers/Howard)
¶ Prokofiev, Piano Concerto No. 2 (John Browning/Boston Symphony/Leinsdorf)
¶ Mozart/Wilbraham, 'Queen of the Night's Aria' (from *The Magic Flute*, Act 1) (John Wilbraham *trumpet*/London Festival Orchestra/Camarata)
¶ 'Pat-a-Cake' (Don Carlos's Singing Dogs)
*¶ Verdi, 'Dies Irae' (from *Requiem*) (Rome Opera House Orchestra and Chorus/Serafin)

¶ LUXURY: John Hillaby, *Journey Through Europe*
¶ BOOK: John Hillaby, *Journey Through Britain*

3 May 1975
1279 Matt Munro
Singer and entertainer
¶ Porter, 'Did You Evah?' (from film *High Society*) (Frank Sinatra/Bing Crosby)
¶ Addinsell, 'Warsaw Concerto' (from film *Dangerous Moonlight*) (Leo Litwin *piano*/Boston Pops Orchestra/Fiedler)
¶ 'Prisoner of Love' (Perry Como)
¶ 'For All We Know' (Dinah Washington)
*¶ Bach, 'Air on the G String' (from Suite No. 3 in D major) (Swingle Singers)
¶ 'Passing Strangers' (Sarah Vaughan/Billy Eckstein)
¶ 'The Blood Donor' (from radio series *Hancock's Half Hour*) (Tony Hancock/June Whitfield/Patric Cargill)
¶ Wagner, *Tannhäuser* (overture) (Vienna Philharmonic/Solti)
¶ LUXURY: A video recorder, TV set and tapes.
¶ BOOK: Harold Robbins, *The Adventurers*

10 May 1975
1280 Ben Travers
Writer of farces
¶ Wagner, *Lohengrin* (Act 3 prelude) (Berlin Philharmonic/Jochum)
¶ Gilbert & Sullivan, 'This Heart of Mine' (from *Ruddigore*) (Leonard Osborn/Martyn Green/Margaret Mitchell/D'Oyly Carte Opera Orchestra/Godfrey)
¶ R. Strauss, 'Letter Scene' (from *Der Rosenkavalier*) (Alexander Kipnis/Else Ruziczka/Berlin State Opera Orchestra/Orthmann)
¶ Schumann, 'Aufschwung' (from *Fantasiestücke*, opus 12) (Artur Rubinstein *piano*)
¶ 'I'm Gonna Sit Right Down and Write Myself a Letter' (Fats Waller and his Rhythm)

*¶ 'My Love Parade' (from film *Love Parade*) (Maurice Chevalier)
¶ 'The 1932 Derby' (Tom Walls *actor and owner of winner*)
¶ Tchaikovsky, Symphony No. 5 in E minor (Berlin Philharmonic/von Karajan)
¶ LUXURIES: His pipe and favourite tobacco, and a pack of cards.
¶ BOOK: The complete works of Robert Browning.

17 May 1975
1281 John Arlott (2nd appearance)
Writer and cricket commentator
¶ Rubinstein, 'Melody in F' (opus 3, no. 1) (Philippe Entremont *piano*)
¶ 'Mercy Pourin' Down' (Edric Connor)
¶ 'Kalinka' (Don Cossack Choir)
*¶ Dylan Thomas, 'Fern Hill' (Dylan Thomas)
¶ Finzi, 'To Lizbie Browne' (from *Earth and Air and Rain*) (John Carol Case/Howard Ferguson *piano*)
¶ 'Buttercup Joe' (The Yetties)
¶ 'Go Down, You Red, Red Roses' (Burl Ives)
¶ 'The Boar's Head Carol' (Elizabethan Singers)
¶ LUXURY: Champagne.
¶ BOOK: Laurence Sterne, *Tristram Shandy*

24 May 1975
1282 Gordon Jackson
Actor
¶ Hamilton, 'Scottish Dances' (opus 32) (Scottish National Orchestra/Gibson)
*¶ Mozart, Piano Concerto No. 27 in B flat major (K. 595) (Daniel Barenboim *piano and conducting*/English Chamber Orchestra)
¶ Debussy, *Pelléas et Mélisande* (Act 3 excerpt) (Elisabeth Söderström/George Shirley/Royal Opera House Orchestra, Covent Garden/Boulez)
¶ Chopin, Polonaise No. 5 in F sharp minor (opus 44) (Artur Rubinstein *piano*)

¶ Walton, Violin Concerto (Jascha Heifetz/Philharmonia Orchestra/Walton)
¶ Wolf, 'Und steht ihr früh' (Dietrich Fischer-Dieskau/Jörg Demus *piano*)
¶ 'The Edwardians' (Theme from TV series *Upstairs, Downstairs*) (Ray Martin and his Orchestra)
¶ Wagner, *Das Rheingold* (finale) (Eberhard Wächter/Vienna Philharmonic/Solti)
¶ LUXURY: A dummy piano keyboard.
¶ BOOK: William Robinson, *The English Flower Garden*

31 May 1975
1283 Tom Hustler
Photographer
¶ 'The Harry Lime Theme' (from film *The Third Man*) (Anton Karas *zither*)
*¶ 'Making Whoopee' (from *Whoopee*) (Frank Sinatra)
¶ 'Skin' (Allan Sherman)
¶ J. Strauss, 'Annen Polka' (Vienna Philharmonic/von Karajan)
¶ 'Home Town' (from *London Rhapsody*) (Flanagan & Allen)
¶ 'Big Spender' (from *Sweet Charity*) (Juliet Prowse/London cast)
¶ Wilson, 'It's Never Too Late to Fall in Love' (from *The Boy Friend*) (Jacqueline Clarke/Geoffrey Hibbert)
¶ 'Spanish Flea' (Herb Alpert and the Tijuana Brass)
¶ LUXURY: A mouth organ.
¶ BOOK: A large leatherbound blank ledger and pen.

7 June 1975
1284 Norman St John-Stevas MP
Writer, politician and broadcaster
¶ Peel, 'The Early Morning' (No. 4 of The Country Lover) (Elisabeth Schumann/Leo Rosenck *piano*)
¶ Verdi, 'Và, pensiero, sull'ali dorate' (from *Nabucco*) (Royal Opera House Chorus and Orchestra, Covent Garden/Gardelli)

¶ Bellini, 'Casta diva' (from *Norma*) (Joan Sutherland/LSO/Bonynge)
¶ Lerner & Loewe, 'I Remember It Well' (from film *Gigi*) (Maurice Chevalier/Hermione Gingold)
¶ Gounod, 'Papal March' (Orchestra of St Gabriel, Radio Vatican/Vitalini)
*¶ Mozart, 'Dove sono' (from *The Marriage of Figaro*) (Margaret Price/English Chamber Orchestra/Lockhart
¶ Elgar, 'Praise to the Holiest' (from *The Dream of Gerontius*) (Ambrosian Singers/Hallé Orchestra/Barbirolli)
¶ 'Non, je ne regrette rien' (Edith Piaf)
¶ LUXURY: An emerald, his birthstone.
¶ BOOK: The collected sermons of John Henry Cardinal Newman.

14 June 1975
1285 Sammy Cahn
Songwriter and entertainer
*¶ 'Li'l Darlin'' (Count Basie and his Orchestra)
¶ Gershwin, 'Embraceable You' (from *Girl Crazy*) (Frank Sinatra)
¶ Porter, 'Why Shouldn't I?' (from musical *Jubilee*) (Jeri Southern/Billy May and his Orchestra)
¶ 'Didn't We?' (Des O'Connor)
¶ Lennon & McCartney, 'Here, There and Everywhere' (Petula Clark)
¶ Arlen/Mercer, 'That Old Black Rhythm' (from film *Starspangled Rhythm*) (Johnny Mercer)
¶ Berlin, 'I Got Lost in His Arms' (from *Annie Get Your Gun*) (Peggy Lee)
¶ 'Here's That Rainy Day' (Andy Williams)
¶ LUXURY: A typewriter.
¶ BOOK: A rhyming dictionary.

21 June 1975
1286 Sir Maurice Yonge
Marine biologist
¶ Verdi, *La traviata* (Act 2 duet) (Victoria de los Angeles/Mario Serena/Rome Opera House Orchestra/Serafin)
*¶ Mozart, Piano Concerto No. 21 in C (K. 467) (Artur Rubinstein/RCA Victor Symphony Orchestra/Wallenstein)
¶ Beethoven, 'Prisoners' Chorus' (from *Fidelio*) (Philharmonia Orchestra and Chorus/Klemperer)
¶ Bruch, Violin Concerto No. 1 in G minor (Igor Oistrakh/RPO/David Oistrakh)
¶ Bellini, 'Casta diva' (from *Norma*) (Maria Callas/Orchestra of La Scala, Milan/Serafin)
¶ Mozart, Bassoon Concerto in B flat major (K. 191) (Gwydion Brooke/RPO/Beecham)
¶ 'El Paso' (Marty Robbins)
¶ Verdi, 'Ella giammai m'amo' (from *Don Carlos*) (Nicolai Ghiaurov/Royal Opera House Orchestra, Covent Garden/Solti)
¶ LUXURY: A low-power binocular dissecting microscope.
¶ BOOK: Edward Gibbon, *The History of the Decline and Fall of the Roman Empire*

28 June 1975
1287 David Hemmings
Actor
¶ 'When I Look in Your Eyes' (from film *Dr Doolittle*) (Rex Harrison)
¶ Prokofiev, Ballet *Romeo and Juliet* (LSO/Previn)
¶ *Woody Allen at Mr Kelly's, Chicago* (Woody Allen)
¶ Weiss, 'Prelude' (Andrés Segovia *guitar*)
¶ 'Love Song' (Elton John/Leslie Duncan)
¶ Styne, 'Mr Goldstone' (from *Gypsy*) (Ethel Merman)
¶ 'Macarthur Park' (Richard Harris)
*¶ Britten, 'The Young Person's Guide to the Orchestra' (Philharmonia Orchestra/Giulini)
¶ LUXURY: A set of architectural pens with ink and paper.
¶ BOOKS: Paul Klee, *The Seeing Eye* and *The Nature of Nature*.

5 July 1975
1288 Helen Bradley
Painter

*¶Satie, *Trois gymnopédies* (no. 1) (Frank Glazer *piano*)
¶'A Perfect Day' (Stuart Burrows/John Constable *piano*)
¶Debussy, Estampes No. 3 (Jardins sous la pluie) (Walter Gieseking *piano*)
¶'All in the April Evening' (Glasgow Orpheus Choir/Roberton)
¶'Celebrating a Bountiful Year' (solo on ancient Chinese harp)
¶Bizet, 'Serenade' (from *The Fair Maid of Perth*) (John Heddle Nash)
¶Stockhausen, 'Kontakte' (electronics/Sands)
¶Elgar, 'Nimrod' (from *Enigma Variations*) (Philharmonia Orchestra/Barbirolli)
¶LUXURY: A soap that kills mosquitoes.
¶BOOK: A great tome on the Law.

12 July 1975
1289 Dave Allen
Comedian

¶Albéniz, 'Asturias' (from Suite Espanola, opus 47, no. 5) (John Williams *guitar*)
¶J. Strauss the Elder, 'Radetzky March' (Johann Strauss Orchestra of Vienna/Boskovsky)
¶Bizet, 'Au fond du temple saint' (from *Les pêcheurs de perles*) (Jussi Björling/Robert Merrill/RCA Victor Symphony/Cellini)
¶Bernstein/Sondheim, *West Side Story* (Medley) (Buddy Rich *drums* and his Orchestra)
¶Beethoven, Symphony No. 6 in F major (Pastoral) (Berlin Philharmonic/von Karajan)
¶'I Don't Want to Play in Your Yard' (Peggy Lee)
¶Haydn, Harpsichord Concerto in D major (George Malcolm/Academy of St Martin-in-the-Fields/Marriner)
*¶Pachelbel, Canon in D major (Jean-François Paillard Orchestra/André)
¶LUXURY: A painting by Van Hook of two children walking down a path.
¶BOOK: Oscar Wilde, *The Ballad of Reading Gaol*

19 July 1975
1290 James Herriot
Writer and veterinary surgeon

¶Schubert, Trio in B flat major (Yehudi Menuhin *violin*/Hephzibah Menuhin piano/Maurice Gendron *cello*)
¶'Mood Indigo' (Louis Armstrong *vocal and trumpet*/Duke Ellington Piano Ensemble)
¶Franck, 'Panis Angelicus' (from Mass in A) (Beniamino Gigli/Berlin State Opera Orchestra/Seidler-Winkler)
¶Granados, 'The Maiden and the Nightingale' (Artur Rubinstein *piano*)
¶'The Story of My Life' (Michael Holliday)
*¶Elgar, Violin Concerto in B minor (Jascha Heifetz/LSO/Sargent)
¶'A Friend with a Dog' (Bob Newhart)
¶Mozart, 'Porgi amor' (from *The Marriage of Figaro*) (Gundula Janowitz/Orchestra of German Opera House, Berlin/Böhm)
¶LUXURY: A violin.
¶BOOK: The most modern publication on veterinary medicine.

26 July 1975
1291 Anthony Dowell
Dancer

¶'Love Comes Easy' (The Stylistics)
¶Ravel, Piano Concerto in G major (Martha Argerich/Berlin Philharmonic/Abbado)
*¶Britten, *The Prince of the Pagodas* (Royal Opera House Orchestra, Covent Garden/Britten)
¶Mendelssohn, *A Midsummer Night's Dream* (scherzo) (Vienna Philharmonic/Monteux)
¶Puccini, *Manon Lescaut* (Act 1 duet) (Maria Callas/Giuseppe di Stefano/Orchestra of La Scala, Milan/Serafin)
¶'Starting Here, Starting Now' (from the musical) (Barbra Streisand/Don Costa and his Orchestra)
¶*Round the Horne* (excerpt from radio series) (Kenneth Horne/Bill Pertwee/Hugh Paddick)

¶Elgar, *Enigma Variations* (LSO/Boult)
¶LUXURY: A radio receiver.
¶BOOK: Kenneth Grahame, *The Wind in the Willows*

2 August 1975
1292 C. P. Snow
Novelist

¶Saint-Saëns, Sonata No. 1 in D minor for Violin and Piano (Flora Elphège/Jean Martin)
*¶Shakespeare, *Henry IV Part II* (Act 3, Scene 2) (various artists)
¶'Hebridian Boat Song' (John Laurie/Robert King)
¶'The Twenty-Third Psalm' (Laurence Olivier)
¶Gay, 'Were I Laid on Greenland's Coast' (from *The Beggar's Opera*) (Elsie Morrison/John Cameron/Pro Arte Orchestra/Sargent)
¶Prokofiev, *War and Peace* (excerpt) (soloists/Chorus and Orchestra of Bolshoi Theatre/Melik-Pashayev)
¶Rodgers & Hammerstein, 'The Farmer and the Cowman' (from *Oklahoma*) (Gordon Macrae/company)
¶Beethoven, Symphony No. 9 in D minor (opus 125) (Berlin Philharmonic/von Karajan)
¶LUXURY: Writing materials.
¶A Russian grammar.

9 August 1975
1293 Jean Simmons
Actress

¶'Love's Old Sweet Song' (Turner Layton)
¶Sondheim, 'I am Still Here' (from *Follies*) (Nancy Walker)
¶Monteverdi, *Orpheus* (aria) (Helmut Krebs)
¶Copland, *El salón México* (New York Philharmonic/Bernstein)
¶Legrand, 'What are You Doing the Rest of Your Life?' (Michel Legrand *piano*)
¶Bach, 'Have Mercy, Lord, on Me' (from *St Matthew Passion*) (Kathleen Ferrier)
¶McKuen, 'A Cat Named Sloopy' (Rod McKuen)

¶ 'Wish You were Here' (from *Wish You were Here*) (Cleo Laine)
¶ LUXURY: A teapot and tea.
¶ BOOK: Enid Bagnold's autobiography.

16 August 1975
1294 Robert Robinson
Broadcaster, journalist and writer
¶ Mozart, Clarinet Concerto in A (Rudolf Jettel/Pro Musica Orchestra, Vienna/Emmer)
¶ Weill/Brecht, 'Lust' (from *The Seven Deadly Sins of the Middle Class*) (Lotte Lenya)
*¶ James Joyce, 'Anna Livia Plurabelle' (from *Finnegan's Wake*) (James Joyce)
¶ Donizetti, *Don Pasquale* (Act 3 duet) (Juan Oncina/Lina Aimaro/Vienna State Opera Orchestra/Quadri)
¶ 'Back Buchanan Street' (Jackie & Bridie)
¶ Mozart, Piano Concerto No. 20 in D minor (K. 466) (Ingrid Haebler/LSO/Galliera)
¶ Mozart, 'Catalogue Aria' (from *Don Giovanni*) (Geraint Evans)
¶ T. S. Eliot, *The Love Song of J. Alfred Prufrock* (T. S. Eliot)
¶ LUXURY: White burgundy.
¶ BOOK: Charles Dickens, *The Pickwick Papers*

23 August 1975
1295 The Marquess of Bath
Owner of Longleat
¶ 'Memories are Made of This' (Dean Martin)
¶ Mozart, Piano Concerto No. 21 in C major (Daniel Barenboim *piano and conducting*/English Chamber Orchestra)
¶ 'Les trois cloches' (Edith Piaf/Les Compagnons de la Chanson)
¶ Verdi, *Il trovatore* (Act 4 aria) (Joan Hammond/LSO/Susskind)
¶ 'Good Luck Charm' (Elvis Presley)
*¶ Tchaikovsky, 'Dance of the Maidens' (from *The Sleeping Beauty*) (Philharmonia Orchestra/von Karajan)
¶ 'Scarlet Ribbons' (Harry Belafonte)

¶ 'Walk Tall' (Val Doonican)
¶ LUXURY: Whisky.
¶ BOOK: Bagwan Shri Rajnish, *The Book of Secrets*

30 August 1975
1296 Jimmy Jewel
Comedian and actor
¶ 'Young at Heart' (Frank Sinatra)
¶ Gershwin, 'Born in a Trunk' (from film *A Star is Born*) (Judy Garland)
¶ 'Louise' (from film *Innocents in Paris*) (Maurice Chevalier)
¶ Gershwin, 'Rhapsody in Blue' (George Gershwin *piano*/Paul Whiteman and his Concert Orchestra)
¶ Jarre, 'Lara's Theme' (from film *Dr Zhivago*) (MGM Studio Orchestra/Jarre)
¶ 'Let Me Sing and I'm Happy' (Al Jolson)
¶ 'Singin' in the Rain' (from film) (Gene Kelly)
*¶ 'My Way' (Frank Sinatra)
¶ LUXURY: A Rolls-Royce Corniche.
¶ BOOK: Nevil Shute, *Beyond the Blackstamp*

6 September 1975
1297 Alec Waugh
Novelist
¶ 'Gilbert the Filbert' (from *The Passing Show*) (Basil Hallam)
¶ 'Let the Great Big World Keep Turning' (from the revue *The Bing Girls are there*) (Billy Cotton/Kathie Kay/Pete Moore and his Orchestra)
¶ Sibelius, 'Valse triste' (Philadelphia Orchestra/Ormandy)
*¶ Turner, 'Romance' (V. C. Clinton Baddeley)
¶ Coward, *Private Lives* (Act 1) (Gertrude Lawrence/Noël Coward)
¶ 'These Foolish Things' (from *Spread It Abroad*) (Hutch)
¶ Porter, 'I Get a Kick Out of You' (from *Anything Goes*) (Ethel Merman)
¶ 'Franklin D. Roosevelt Jones' (from *The Little Dog Laughed*) (Judy Garland)
¶ LUXURY: Wine.
¶ BOOK: *The Golden Treasury*, compiled by Francis Palgrave.

13 September 1975
1298 Esther Rantzen
Broadcaster
¶ Porter, 'Well, Did You Evah?' (from film *High Society*) (Frank Sinatra/Bing Crosby)
¶ 'Coventry Carol' (King's College Chapel Choir/Willcocks)
¶ Mozart, Symphony No. 40 in G minor (K. 550) (Berlin Philharmonic/Böhm)
¶ 'If I were a Rich Man' (from *Fiddler on the Roof*) (Topol)
*¶ Brahms, Concerto for Violin and Cello and Orchestra in A minor (David Oistrakh *violin*/Mstislav Rostropovich *cello*/Cleveland Orchestra/Szell)
¶ Bizet/Hammerstein, 'Recipe for Picking a Man' (from *Carmen Jones*) (Dorothy Dandridge)
¶ Bach, Brandenburg Concerto No. 1 in F major (BWV 1046) (Stuttgart Chamber Orchestra/Münchinger)
¶ Mahler, Symphony No. 2 in C minor (Elly Ameling/Amsterdam Concertgebouw/Haitink)
¶ LUXURY: Bath salts and a warm waterfall or spring.
¶ BOOK: Jane Austen, *Emma*

20 September 1975
1299 Bevis Hillier
Art historian, writer and collector
¶ Mozart, Piano Concerto No. 24 in C minor (K. 491) (Louis Kentner/Philharmonia Orchestra/Blech)
¶ Wolf, 'Und Steht Ihr Früh' (Dietrich Fischer-Dieskau/Gerald Moore *piano*)
¶ Schubert, Sonatina No. 2 in A minor (Josef Suk *violin*/Rudolf Buchbinder *piano*)
¶ Somervell, 'Loveliest of Trees' (from *A Shropshire Lad*) (John McCormack/Gerald Moore *piano*)
¶ Brahms, Sonata No. 2 in E flat major (Jacques Lancelot *clarinet*/Annie d'Arco *piano*)
¶ 'Poetry in Motion' (Johnny Tillotson)

*¶ Mozart, Piano Concerto No. 23 in A major (K. 488) (Daniel Barenboim *piano and conducting*/English Chamber Orchestra)
¶ Prokofiev, Piano Concerto No. 1 in D flat major (Gary Graffman/Cleveland Orchestra/Szell)
¶ LUXURY: A Japanese bonsai tree.
¶ BOOK: A street map of London.

27 September 1975
1300 Rt Hon. the Lord Carrington
Politician and administrator
¶ Tchaikovsky, 'The Letter Song' (from *Eugene Onegin*) (Leontyne Price)
¶ Schubert, Trio in B flat major (Yehudi Menuhin *violin*/Maurice Gendron *cello*/Hephzibah Menuhin *piano*)
¶ 'Smoke Gets in Your Eyes' (from *Roberta*) (Irene Dunne)
¶ Brahms, Symphony No. 1 in C minor (Philharmonia Orchestra/Klemperer)
¶ Mozart, 'Non temer' (from *Idomeneo*) (Teresa Berganza/LSO/Pritchard)
¶ Puccini, 'Tre sbirri, una carrozza' (from *Tosca*) (Tito Gobbi/Orchestra of La Scala, Milan/de Sabata)
¶ Ravel, *Daphnis and Chloe Suite No. 2* (Amsterdam Concertgebouw/Haitink)
*¶ Elgar, Violin Concerto in B minor (Yehudi Menuhin/LSO/Elgar)
¶ LUXURY: His favourite armchair.
¶ BOOKS: Lewis Carroll, *Alice in Wonderland* and *Through the Looking Glass*.

4 October 1975
1301 Paul Jennings
Writer and humorist
¶ 'How to Do Your Own Gilbert and Sullivan' (Anna Russell/John Coveart *piano*)
¶ Elgar, *Enigma Variations* (Philharmonia Orchestra/Barbirolli)

¶ Bach, Double Concerto in D minor (BWV 1043) (Yehudi Menuhin and Christian Ferras *violins*/Festival Chamber Orchestra/Menuhin)
¶ Byrd, *Four-Part Mass* (King's College Chapel Choir/Willcocks)
¶ Mozart, Horn Concerto No. 2 in E flat major (Dennis Brain/Philharmonia Orchestra/von Karajan)
¶ Purcell, 'Sound the Trumpet' (from 'Come Ye Sons of Art' – Ode for Queen Mary's Birthday 1694) (Alfred Deller/John Whitworth/L'Oiseau-Lyre Orchestra/Lewis)
¶ T. S. Eliot, 'The Dry Salvages' (T. S. Eliot)
¶ Beethoven, 'Credo' (from *Missa Solemnis*) (soloists/NPO and Chorus/Klemperer)
¶ LUXURY: A steam locomotive from the Hythe, New Romney and Dymchurch Railway, and rails.
¶ BOOK: *The Ontological Argument from St Anselm to Contemporary Philosophers*

11 October 1975
1302 Doris Hare
Actress
*¶ Vaughan Williams, 'Fantasia on Greensleeves' (LSO/Boult)
¶ 'Watching the Wheat' (Thomas L. Thomas)
¶ Coward, 'Mad Dogs and Englishmen' (from *Words and Music*) (Noël Coward)
¶ 'These Foolish Things' (from *Spread It Abroad*) (Jean Sablon)
¶ Coward, 'I'll See You Again' (from *Bitter Sweet*) (Evelyn Laye)
¶ 'Big Best Shoes' (from *Valmouth*) (Cleo Laine)
¶ Porter, 'Now You Has Jazz' (from film *High Society*) (Bing Crosby/Louis Armstrong)
¶ Debussy, *Prélude à l'après-midi d'un faune* (RPO/Beecham)
¶ LUXURY: A piano.
¶ BOOK: *The Oxford Dictionary of Quotations*

18 October 1975
1303 Lord (John Julius) Norwich
Writer and film-maker for television
*¶ Beethoven, 'Mir ist so wunderbar' (quartet) (from *Fidelio*) (soloists/Berlin Philharmonic/von Karajan)
¶ Schubert, String Quintet in C (opus 163) (Richard Harand *second cello*/Vienna Philharmonic Quartet)
¶ Wagner, 'Prelude' and 'Liebestod' (from *Tristan und Isolde*) (New York Philharmonic/Boulez)
¶ Mozart, 'Il mio tesoro' (from *Don Giovanni*) (Leopold Simoneau/Vienna Symphony and Chamber Choir/Morat)
¶ Coward, 'Useful Phrases' (from *Sail Away*) (Noël Coward)
¶ R. Strauss, 'Beim Schlafengehen' (from *Four Last Songs*) (Lisa della Casa)
¶ Chopin, Waltz in A flat (opus 34, no. 1) (Dinu Lipatti *piano*)
¶ Verdi, 'Và, pensiero, sull'ali dorate' (from *Nabucco*) (NBC Symphony and Chorus/Toscanini)
¶ LUXURY: Writing materials.
¶ BOOK: Edward Gibbon, *The History of the Decline and Fall of the Roman Empire*

25 October 1975
1304 Stanley Holloway (3rd appearance)
Actor and entertainer
¶ Templeton, 'Bach Goes to Town' (Arthur Young *novachord*)
¶ Coleridge-Taylor/Longfellow, 'Farewell, Said He, Minnehaha' (from *Hiawatha*) (Royal Choral Society/Philharmonia/Sargent)
¶ Stanford, 'The Old Superb' (from Songs of the Sea, No. 5) (Peter Dawson)
¶ Lerner & Loewe, 'Wouldn't It be Loverly?' (from *My Fair Lady*) (André Previn and his Quartet)
¶ Elgar, 'Chanson du matin' (LPO/Boult)

*¶ Borodin/Wright & Forrest, 'And This is My Beloved' (from *Kismet*) (Doretta Morrow/Orchestra/Adrian)

¶ Ravel, 'Pavane pour une infante défunte' (Cleveland Orchestra/Szell)

¶ Mendelssohn, *A Midsummer Night's Dream* (Benno Moiseiwitsch *piano*)

¶ LUXURY: A manicure and pedicure set.

¶ BOOK: A book on the musical plays of the last century.

1 November 1975
1305 William Frankel
Editor of *The Jewish Chronicle*
¶ 'Prayer on the Evening of Atonement' (Josef Rosenblatt)

¶ Mendelssohn, 'Hebrides Overture' (RPO/Sargent)

¶ Beethoven, Romance in F (Yehudi Menuhin *violin*/Berlin Philharmonic/Furtwängler)

¶ 'Ballad of Davy Crockett' (from film *Davy Crockett*) (Fess Parker)

*¶ Bach, 'Laudamus Te' (from *Mass in B minor*, BWV 232) (Christa Ludwig/Berlin Philharmonic/von Karajan)

¶ Verdi, 'Dies Irae' (from *Requiem*) (Philharmonia Chorus and Orchestra/Giulini)

¶ Lerner & Loewe, 'The Rain in Spain' (from *My Fair Lady*) (Julie Andrews/Rex Harrison/Robert Coote/Orchestra/Allers)

¶ Bloch, *Sacred Service* (LPO and Choir/Bloch)

¶ LUXURY: A carpentry set.

¶ BOOK: The current *Wisden*.

8 November 1975
1306 Rumer Godden
Novelist
¶ Schumann, Fantasiestucke opus 12, No. 3 (Warum) (Artur Rubinstein *piano*)

¶ 'Sangdans Under Saharay-Festern' (Bengali folk song)

¶ Saint-Saëns, 'The Swan' (from *Carnival of the Animals*) (Reginald Kilbey *cello*/Jack Byfield *piano*)

¶ Ravel, 'Gaspard de la nuit' (Vladimir Ashkenazy *piano*)

¶ Franck, 'Panis Angelicus' (Beniamino Gigli/Berlin State Opera Orchestra/Seidler-Winkler)

¶ Bruch, Violin Concerto No. 1 in G minor (Jascha Heifetz/New Symphony Orchestra/Sargent)

¶ Puccini, 'Vissi d'arte' (from *Tosca*) (Maria Callas/Orchestra of La Scala, Milan/de Sabata)

*¶ Liszt, 'Benediction of God in Solitude' (from *Harmonies poétiques et religieuses*, no. 3) (Claudio Arrau *piano*)

¶ LUXURY: Her four-poster bed.

¶ BOOK: *Another World than This*, compiled by Vita Sackville-West and Harold Nicolson.

15 November 1975
1307 Vince Hill
Singer and entertainer
¶ Rodrigo, Concierto de Aranjuez (John Williams *guitar*/Philadelphia Orchestra/Ormandy)

¶ Aubrey, *Brief Lives* (excerpt) (Roy Dotrice)

¶ Delius, 'On Hearing the First Cuckoo in Spring' (RPO/Beecham)

¶ Bizet, 'Au fond du temple saint' (from *Le pêcheurs de perles*) (Jussi Björling/Robert Merrill/RCA Victor Symphony/Cellini)

¶ Wonder, 'He's Mister Know-It-All' (Stevie Wonder)

*¶ Respighi, *Fountains of Rome* (Philadelphia Orchestra/Ormandy)

¶ Trad. arr. Canteloube, 'Baïlèro' (from *Songs of the Auvergne*) (Victoria de los Angeles/Lamoureux Orchestra/Jacquillat)

¶ Vaughan Williams, Symphony No. 4 in F minor (LSO/Previn)

¶ LUXURY: One of Turner's seascapes.

¶ BOOK: A giant do-it-yourself book.

22 November 1975
1308 Graham Thomas
Gardens consultant to the National Trust
*¶ Byrd, *Mass for Five Voices* (King's College Chapel Choir/Willcocks)

¶ Bach, *Mass in B minor* (BWV 232) (Nicolai Gedda/Vienna Singverein/Vienna Philharmonic/von Karajan)

¶ Brahms, Piano Concerto No. 1 in D minor (Clifford Curzon/LSO/Szell)

¶ Bach, Prelude and Fugue No. 7 in E flat (BWV 852) (Maurice Cole *piano*)

¶ Beethoven, Sonata No. 29 in B flat major, opus 106 (Hammerklavier) (Solomon *piano*)

¶ Bateson, 'Sister Awake, Close Not Your Eyes' (Purcell Consort of Voices/Burgess)

¶ Brahms, 'Die schöne Magelone' (Dietrich Fischer-Dieskau/Sviatoslav Richter *piano*)

¶ Vaughan Williams, 'Serenade to Music' (16 soloists/LPO/Boult)

¶ LUXURY: Paints, pencils and paper.

¶ BOOK: The collected works of Hilaire Belloc.

29 November 1975
1309 Ron Moody
Actor, comedian and writer
*¶ 'Sparky's Magic Piano' (Henry Blair, Verne Smith *voices*/Ray Turner *piano*/the Sonovox Talking Piano)

¶ Beethoven, Sonata No. 8 in C minor, opus 13 (Pathétique) (Daniel Barenboim *piano*)

¶ Prokofiev, *Love of Three Oranges* (march) (LPO/Boult)

¶ Puccini, 'Nessun dorma' (from *Turandot*) (Jussi Björling/Rome Opera House Orchestra/Leinsdorf)

¶ 'Kalinka' (Red Army Ensemble)

¶ 'Rinkety Tink' (Ron Moody)

¶ Chopin, Fantasie-Impromptu in C sharp minor, opus 66 (Hollywood Bowl Symphony/Dragon)

¶ 'Foggy Mountain Breakdown' (Flatt & Scruggs)

¶ LUXURY: Oil painting materials.

¶ BOOK: Bertrand Russell, *A History of Western Philosophy*

6 December 1975
1310 Frederick Forsyth
Writer

¶ Coates, 'The Dam Busters March' (from film *The Dam Busters*) (Concert orchestra/Coates)

¶ 'The Harry Lime Theme' (from film *The Third Man*) (Anton Karas *zither*)

¶ Dvořák, Symphony No. 9 in E minor (New World) (Vienna Philharmonic/Kertesz)

¶ 'Non, je ne regrette rien' (Edith Piaf)

¶ Sibelius, 'Finlandia' (Hallé Orchestra/Barbirolli)

¶ 'Manolete' (25th Jaen Infantry Regimental Band/Sánchez-Curto)

*¶ Simon, 'The Sound of Silence' (Simon & Garfunkel)

¶ 'Londonderry Air' (Philadelphia Orchestra/Ormandy)

¶ LUXURY: A competition bow with a quiver full of arrows.

¶ BOOK: Charles Baudelaire, *Les fleurs du mal*

13 December 1975
1311 Margaret Price
Soprano

¶ Chopin, Waltz No. 9 in A flat (opus 69, no. 1) (Dinu Lipatti *piano*)

¶ R. Strauss, 'Morgen' (Elisabeth Schumann/Orchestra/Collingwood)

¶ Tchaikovsky, 'Polonaise' (from *Eugene Onegin*) (USSR Symphony/Rostropovich)

¶ Falla, 'Dance at the Wedding' ([from *La vida breve*) (Paris Conservatoire/de Burgos)

¶ Keats, 'La belle dame sans merci' (Ralph Richardson)

¶ Kern & Hammerstein, 'Can't Help Lovin' Dat Man' (from *Show Boat*) (Ella Fitzgerald)

¶ Mozart, 'Ch'io mi secordi di te' (concert aria) (Margaret Price/James Lockhart *piano*)

*¶ Wagner, 'Liebestod' (from *Tristan und Isolde*) (Kirsten Flagstad/Philharmonia/Furtwängler)

¶ LUXURY: Perfume.

¶ BOOK: Tredavic's *Pacific Cookbook*

27 December 1975
1312 Bing Crosby
Vocalist and entertainer

*¶ 'South Rampart Street Parade' (Bob Crosby and his Bobcats)

¶ Debussy, 'Clair de lune' (from *Suite bergamasque*) (LSO/Black)

¶ 'And the Angels Sing' (Benny Goodman *clarinet* and his Orchestra)

¶ 'Moonlight Serenade' (Glenn Miller and his Orchestra)

¶ Liszt, Liebestraum No. 3 (Philadelphia Orchestra/Ormandy)

¶ Porter, 'Begin the Beguine' (from *Jubilee*) (Artie Shaw and his Orchestra)

¶ Rimsky-Korsakov, 'Song of India' (from *Sadko*) (Tommy Dorsey and his Orchestra)

¶ Mascagni, *Cavalleria rusticana* (intermezzo) (La Scala Orchestra/von Karajan)

¶ LUXURY: A guitar.

¶ BOOK: *Roget's Thesaurus*

3 January 1976
1313 Julia Foster
Actress

¶ Bach, Violin Concerto in G minor (Pinchas Zukerman/English Chamber Orchestra/Barenboim)

¶ King, 'Tapestry' (Carole King)

¶ Berlin, 'Top Hat, White Tie and Tails' (from film *Top Hat*) (Fred Astaire)

¶ Porter, 'I Get a Kick Out of You' (from *Anything Goes*) (Stephane Grappelli and Yehudi Menuhin *Violins*)

¶ Adam, *Giselle* (Paris Conservatoire Orchestra/Martinon)

¶ Legrand, 'I Will Wait for You' (from film *Les parapluies de Cherbourg*) (Michel Legrand *piano*)

¶ 'The Ying Tong Song' (The Goons)

*¶ 'And I Love You So' (Bobby Goldsboro)

¶ LUXURY: A tapestry frame and materials.

¶ BOOK: *The Oxford Dictionary of Quotations*

10 January 1976
1314 Sherrill Milnes
Baritone

¶ Handel, 'All We Like Sheep' (from *Messiah*) (Luton Choral Society/RPO/Beecham)

¶ Bach, Suite No. 3 in D major (BWV 1068) (Swingle Singers)

¶ Verdi, 'E gettata la mia sorte' (from *Attila*) (Sherrill Milnes/RPO/Gardelli)

¶ Prokofiev, 'The Battle on the Ice' (from *Alexander Nevsky*) (Sherrill Milnes/CSO/Reiner)

¶ R. Strauss, 'Don Juan' (Opus 20) (CSO/Reiner)

*¶ Beethoven, Symphony No. 9 in D minor (opus 125) (CSO/Reiner)

¶ Brahms, *German Requiem* (Montsarrat Caballé/Sherrill Milnes/Boston Symphony/Leinsdorf)

¶ 'Life is Just a Bowl of Cherries' (from *George White's Scandals of 1931*) (The Hi-Los)

¶ LUXURY: Herrings in sour cream.

¶ BOOK: *Twenty-five Years of New Yorker Cartoons*

17 January 1976
1315 Noel Streatfeild
Writer

¶ Wolf-Ferrari, 'Serenade' (from *The Jewels of the Madonna*) (Paris Conservatoire Orchestra/Santi)

¶ Boughton, 'Faery Song' (from *The Immortal Hour*) (Webster Booth)

¶ Coward, 'I'll See You Again' (from *Bitter Sweet*) (Peggy Wood/George Metaxa)

*¶ 'The Old Hundredth' (recorded at Coronation Service of HM Queen Elizabeth II)

¶ Tchaikovsky, Symphony No. 5 in E minor (USSR Symphony/Svetlanov)

¶ Tallis, 'Glory to Thee, My God' (The Templars)

¶ Saint-Saëns, 'The Swan' (from *Carnival of the Animals*) (City of Birmingham Symphony/Frémaux)

¶ Recording of the bells of St Paul's Cathedral, London

¶ LUXURY: A gardening kit.

¶ BOOK: John Galsworthy, *The Forsyte Saga*

24 January 1976
1316 Gavin Lyall
Thriller writer
¶ 'When the Saints Go Marching In' (Bunk Johnson *trumpet* and his New Orleans Band)
¶ 'John Henry' (Josh White)
¶ Loesser, 'The Oldest Established Permanent Floating Crap Game in New York' (from *Guys and Dolls*) (Sam Levene/ Stubby Kaye/Johnny Silver)
¶ Dvořák, Symphony No. 9 in E minor (New World) (Berlin Philharmonic/Kubelik)
¶ Templeton, 'Bach Goes to Town' (Benny Goodman *clarinet* and his Orchestra)
¶ 'Tiger Rag' (Benny Goodman Trio)
¶ Mercer Ellington, 'Things Ain't Wot They Used to Be' (Johnny Hodges *alto saxophone* and his Orchestra)
*¶ 'March of the Bob Cats' (Bob Crosby and his Bob Cats)
¶ LUXURY: A pack of cards.
¶ BOOK: James Jones, *From Here to Eternity*

31 January 1976
1317 Ronnie Scott
Saxophonist and jazz club impresario
¶ 'The Look of Love' (Stan Getz *tenor saxophone*/Orchestra/ Ogerman)
¶ Puccini, 'Si, mi chiamano Mimi' (from *La bohème*, Act 1) (Elisabeth Schwarzkopf/Philharmonia Orchestra/Rescigno)
¶ 'Invitation' (Joe Henderson *tenor saxophone*/Don Friedman *piano*/Ron Carter *bass*/Jack Dejohnette *drums*)
*¶ Ravel, 'Lever du jour' (from *Daphnis and Chloe Suite No. 2*) (Orchestre de la Suisse Romande/Ansermet)
¶ Borodin, 'Stranger in Paradise' (from *Kismet*) (Charles McPherson Quartet)
¶ 'In a Sentimental Mood' (John Coltrane *saxophone*/Duke Ellington and his Orchestra)
¶ Ponce, 'Scherzino Mexicano' (John Williams *guitar*)
¶ 'For All We Know' (Billie Holiday)
¶ LUXURY: His saxophone.

¶ BOOK: Kenneth Grahame, *The Wind in the Willows*

7 February 1976
1318 Lynn Seymour
Ballerina
¶ Beethoven, String Quartet No. 13 in B flat (opus 130) (Quartetto Italiano)
¶ Bartók, Sonata for Two Pianos and Percussion (Dezso Ránki and Zoltán Kocsis *pianos*/Ferenc Petz and József Marton *percussion*)
¶ Lennon & McCartney, 'I am the Walrus' (Spooky Tooth)
¶ Mozart, Piano Concerto No. 21 in C (K. 467) (Geza Anda *piano* and *conducting* the Camerata Academica of the Salzburg Mozarteum)
¶ Lennon & McCartney, 'Eleanor Rigby' (The Beatles)
¶ 'Kozmic Blues' (Janis Joplin)
¶ 'Let It Grow' (Eric Clapton)
*¶ Mahler, 'Abschied' (from *Das Lied von der Erde*) (Christa Ludwig/NPO/Klemperer)
¶ LUXURIES: An elegant dress and champagne.
¶ BOOK: Kenneth Clark, *Civilisation*

14 February 1976
1319 Luciano Pavarotti
Operatic tenor
*¶ Mozart, Symphony No. 40 in G minor (K. 550) (LSO/Giulini)
¶ Goldmark, 'Magiche Note' (from *The Queen of Sheba*) (Enrico Caruso)
¶ Gluck, 'Che faro senza Euridice' (from *Orfeo ed Euridice*) (Tito Schipa)
¶ Donizetti, 'Pour mon âme il faut partir' (from *The Daughter of the Regiment*) (Joan Sutherland/Luciano Pavarotti/ Royal Opera House Orchestra, Covent Garden/Bonynge)
¶ Donizetti, 'Era d'amor l'immagine', (from *Maria Stuarda*) (Luciano Pavarotti/ Teatro Communale Orchestra/ Bonynge)
¶ Beethoven, Symphony No. 6 in F (opus 68) (CPO/Solti)
¶ Mussorgsky, orchestrated Ravel, 'Ballet of the Unhatched Chicks' (from *Pictures from an Exhibition*) (Los Angeles Philharmonic/Mehta)

¶ Verdi, 'Dies Irae' (from *Requiem*) (Philharmonia Orchestra and Chorus/Giulini)
¶ LUXURY: A bicycle.
¶ BOOK: Dante's *Divine Comedy*

21 February 1976
1320 Tim Rice
Lyricist
¶ Gershwin, 'Nice Work if You Can Get It' (from film *A Damsel in Distress*) (Billie Holiday)
¶ 'Runaway' (Del Shannon)
¶ 'Travellin' Light' (Cliff Richard/The Shadows)
¶ Mendelssohn, Symphony No. 3 in A minor (Berlin Philharmonic/ von Karajan)
¶ 'New Orleans' (Elvis Presley)
¶ Lerner & Loewe, 'You Did It' (from *My Fair Lady*) (Rex Harrison)
¶ Puccini, 'Musetta's Waltz' (from *La bohème*) (Elisabeth Harwood/Berlin Philharmonic/ von Karajan)
*¶ 'Stand by Your Man' (Tammy Wynette)
¶ LUXURY: A fully equipped cricket bag.
¶ BOOK: The collected works of Lewis Carroll.

28 February 1976
1321 Sir Robert Mark
Commissioner of the Metropolitan Police
¶ Anon, Minuet in G (from Little Note Book for Anna Magdalena Bach) (Kornel Zempléni *piano*)
¶ Mozart, 'Bei Männern, welche Liebe fühlen' (from *The Magic Flute*) (Pilar Lorengar/Herman Prey/Vienna Philharmonic/ Solti)
¶ 'Coburg March' (HM Life Guards Band)
¶ 'The Supreme Sacrifice' (George Baker/Men of Queen Mary's Hospital for Limbless Men)
¶ 'Be Prepared' (Tom Lehrer)
*¶ Smetana, 'Ma Vlast' (Boston Symphony/Kubelik)
¶ Chopin, Fantaisie-Impromptu in C sharp minor (opus 66) (Artur Rubinstein *piano*)
¶ 'Sunset' (HM Royal Marines Band)

¶ LUXURIES: A large bug-proof sleeping bag, and a television set that does not work.
¶ BOOK: Collected works of Lewis Carroll.

6 March 1976
1322 Vincent Brome
Writer
¶ Wagner, *Tannhäuser* (overture) (Vienna Philharmonic/Solti)
¶ Tchaikovsky, Romeo and Juliet Fantasy Overture (Vienna Philharmonic/Maazel)
*¶ Mozart, *The Marriage of Figaro* (overture) (BBC Symphony/Colin Davis)
¶ Saint-Saëns, Piano Concerto No. 2 in G minor (Artur Rubinstein/Philadelphia Orchestra/Ormandy)
¶ Beethoven, Quartet No. 16 in F (opus 135) (Hungarian String Quartet)
¶ Dylan Thomas, 'Do Not Go Gentle into That Good Night' (Dylan Thomas)
¶ Joplin, 'The Ragtime Dance' (Joshua Rifkin *piano*)
¶ 'Bertrand Russell on George Bernard Shaw' (Bertrand Russell)
¶ LUXURY: An inflatable rubber woman.
¶ BOOK: Bertrand Russell, *A History of Western Philosophy*

13 March 1976
1323 Noel Barber
Writer and foreign correspondent
¶ 'Songs of the Islands' (Waikiki Beach Boys)
¶ Shostakovich, 'The Song of the Forests' (Ivan Petrov/Moscow State Boys' Chorus/RSFSR Academic Russian Choir/Moscow Philharmonic/Yurlov)
¶ 'Kalinka' (Gabor Radics Family Orchestra)
¶ Bizet, 'Au fond du temple saint' (from *Les pêcheurs de perles*) (Ernest Blanc/Nicolai Gedda/Opéra-Comique Orchestra, Paris/Dervaux)
*¶ Beethoven, Piano Trio in B flat, opus 97 (Archduke) (Alfred Cortot *piano*/Jacques Thibaud *violin*/Pablo Casals *cello*)

¶ Mahler, Symphony No. 5 in C sharp minor (Amsterdam Concertgebouw/Haitink)
¶ 'Kumbaya' (The Seekers)
¶ R. Strauss, 'Also Sprach Zarathustra' (CSO/Solti)
¶ LUXURY: A piano.
¶ BOOK: *The Oxford Dictionary of Quotations*

20 March 1976
1324 Rosina Harrison
Former lady's maid to Lady Astor
*¶ 'Bless This House' (Webster Booth)
¶ Lemare, 'Andantino' (Fredric Bayco *(organ)*
¶ Mendelssohn, 'Hear My Prayer' (Ernest Lough/Temple Church Choir, London)
¶ Puccini, 'O mio babbino caro' (from *Gianni Schicchi*) (Joan Hammond)
¶ J. Strauss, 'The Blue Danube' (Stokowski Symphony)
¶ *Chu Chin Chow* (selection) (Gaumont British Orchestra/Levy)
¶ 'Taita Inty' (Yma Sumac)
¶ Sinding, 'Rustle of Spring' (Cyril Scott *piano*)
¶ LUXURY: A picture called *Summer Arrangements* by Nikolsky.
¶ BOOK: Charles Dickens, *Oliver Twist*, bound with one or two other Dickens novels.

27 March 1976
1325 Paul Theroux
Novelist and travel writer
¶ 'Shuckin' the Corn' (Flatt & Scruggs)
¶ cummings, 'what if a much of a which of a wind' (e. e. cummings)
¶ 'Aaage Bhi Hame Na Tu' (Asha Bhosle)
¶ Mozart, Clarinet Quintet in A (K. 581) (Gervase de Peyer/Melos Ensemble)
¶ 'Alabamy Bound' (Fletcher Henderson and his Band)
¶ Sousa, *'Washington Post* March' (Band of HM Coldstream Guards)
¶ 'Malaika' (Fadhili William/The Black Shadows)

*¶ Bach, 'Vergnügte Ruh' (Cantata No. 170) (Alfred Deller/Leonhardt Baroque Ensemble)
¶ LUXURY: Champagne.
¶ BOOK: An anthology of English poetry from 1400.

3 April 1976
1326 Charlotte Rampling
Actress
*¶ Beethoven, Piano Concerto No. 5 in E flat major (Emperor) (Ashkenazy/CSO/Solti)
¶ Lennon & McCartney, 'A Day in the Life' (The Beatles)
¶ Tchaikovsky, *The Sleeping Beauty* (waltz) (LSO/Monteux)
¶ 'Don't be Cruel' (Elvis Presley)
¶ R. Strauss, 'Also Sprach Zarathustra' (Berlin Philharmonic/Böhm)
¶ 'Day by Day' (from *Godspell*) (Julie Covington)
¶ Mozart, 'Wie stark ist nicht' (from *The Magic Flute*) (Fritz Wunderlich/Berlin Philharmonic/Böhm)
¶ 'All by Myself' (Eric Carmen)
¶ LUXURY: A ballet picture by Degas.
¶ BOOK: Frank Herbert, *Dune*

10 April 1976
1327 John Pardoe MP
Politician
¶ 'In the Bleak Mid-Winter' (King's College Chapel Choir/Willcocks)
¶ Bach, 'Frohe hirten' (from *Christmas Oratorio*) (Fritz Wunderlich/Paul Meisen *flute*)
¶ Mahler, Symphony No. 1 in D (LSO/Solti)
¶ 'Padstow May Day Song' (crowd in Padstow)
¶ Causley, 'The Seasons in North Cornwall' (Charles Causley)
¶ Handel, 'Since by Man Came Death' (from *Messiah*) (King's College Chapel Choir/Academy of St Martin-in-the-Fields/Willcocks)
*¶ Beethoven, Symphony No. 9 in D minor (opus 125) (soloists/chorus/Berlin Philharmonic/von Karajan)
¶ Mozart, *The Magic Flute* (Act 2 duet) (Hermann Prey/Renata Holm/Vienna Philharmonic/Solti)

¶ LUXURY: A piano.
¶ BOOK: Bertrand Russell, *A History of Western Philosophy*

17 April 1976
1328 Dr Christian Barnard
Heart surgeon
*¶ 'Spanish Eyes' (Bert Kaempfert Orchestra)
¶ 'A Rose Has to Die' (Ryders)
¶ 'I Can't Stop Loving You' (Ray Charles)
¶ 'Rocky' (Austin Roberts)
¶ Jarre, 'Lara's Theme' (from film *Dr Zhivago*) (MGM Studio Orchestra/Jarre)
¶ 'I Found a Million-Dollar Baby' (Nat 'King' Cole)
¶ 'A Kiss to Build a Dream On' (Louis Armstrong *vocal* and *trumpet* and the All Stars)
¶ Lennon & McCartney, 'When I'm Sixty-Four' (The Beatles)
¶ LUXURY: Michelangelo's statue, *David*.
¶ BOOK: Hermann Bessmann, *The Best of Bessmann*

24 April 1976
1329 Glynis Johns
Actress
¶ 'A Piece of Ground' (Miriam Makeba)
¶ Gretchianinov, 'The Creed' (Choir of the Russian Church of the Metropolitan of Paris/Afonsky)
¶ Rossini/Respighi, *La boutique fantasque* (LSO/Ansermet)
¶ Gilbert & Sullivan, 'The Sun Whose Rays' (from *The Mikado*) (Jean Hindmarsh/D'Oyly Carte Opera Orchestra/Godfrey)
¶ 'Les trois cloches' (Edith Piaf/Les Compagnons de la Chanson)
¶ 'Son of a Preacher Man' (Dusty Springfield)
¶ Sondheim, 'Send in the Clowns' (from *A Little Night Music*) (Glynis Johns)
*¶ Sibelius, 'Finlandia' (opus 26) (Hallé Orchestra/Barbirolli)
¶ LUXURY: Michelangelo's statue, *David*.
¶ BOOK: The *I Ching*.

1 May 1976
1330 Sir William Gladstone
Chief Scout
¶ Bach, Brandenburg Concerto No. 5 in D major (BWV 1050) (Bath Festival Chamber Orchestra/Menuhin)
¶ Handel, *Scipio* (march) (RPO/Groves)
¶ Mozart, Horn Concerto No. 3 in E flat (Dennis Brain/Philharmonia Orchestra/von Karajan)
¶ Sor, 'Sonata' (opus 15, no. 2) (Rey de la Torre *guitar*)
¶ Beethoven, Symphony No. 8 in F major (opus 93) (Berlin Philharmonic/von Karajan)
*¶ Brahms, Symphony No. 1 in C minor (LPO/Boult)
¶ Elgar, 'Sanctus Fortis' (from *The Dream of Gerontius*) (Richard Lewis/Hallé Orchestra/Barbirolli)
¶ Britten, 'Kyrie' (from *Noye's Fludde*) (Aldeburgh Festival Children's Chorus/English Chamber Orchestra/del Mar)
¶ LUXURY: J. B. Pine, *The Chinese Temple at Virginia Water*
¶ BOOK: Edward Gibbon, *The History of the Decline and Fall of the Roman Empire*

8 May 1976
1331 John Napier
Anatomist and anthropologist
¶ 'Who?' (from *Sunny*) (Binnie Hale/Jack Buchanan)
*¶ 'Falling in Love Again' (from film *The Blue Angel*) (Marlene Dietrich)
¶ 'Once in Royal David's City' (King's College Chapel Choir/Willcocks)
¶ Rodgers & Hammerstein, 'Oklahoma' (from *Oklahoma*) (Howard Keel/original London cast)
¶ 'Les lavandières du Portugal' (Franck Pourcel and his Strings)
¶ 'You Need Hands' (Max Bygraves)
¶ Steffe/Howe, 'Battle Hymn of the Republic' (Mormon Tabernacle Choir/Philadelphia Orchestra/Ormandy)

¶ Stravinsky, *The Rite of Spring* (Columbia Symphony/Stravinsky)
¶ LUXURY: A Charles I silver tankard.
¶ BOOK: Erskine Childers, *The Riddle of the Sands*

15 May 1976
1332 John Laurie
Actor
¶ Beethoven, Leonora Overture No. 3 (CSO/Solti)
¶ Debussy, Quartet in G minor (opus 10) Guarneri Quartet)
*¶ Elgar, *The Music Makers* (Janet Baker/LPO and Choir/Boult)
¶ R. Strauss, 'Don Quixote' (Paul Tortelier *cello*/Dresden State Orchestra/Kempe)
¶ Crimond, 'The Twenty-Third Psalm' (Glasgow Orpheus Choir/Roberton)
¶ Robert Burns, 'My Love is Like a Red, Red Rose' (John Laurie)
¶ Wagner, *Tristan und Isolde* (prelude) (Bayreuth Festival Orchestra/Böhm)
¶ Dvořák, 'Songs My Mother Taught Me' (from *Gypsy Songs*, opus 55) (Joan Hammond/Ivor Newton *piano*)
¶ LUXURY: A big reading glass with light.
¶ BOOK: *The Oxford English Dictionary*

22 May 1976
1333 Tony Grieg
Cricketer
¶ 'There'll Always be an England' (Vera Lynn/Tony Osborne and his Orchestra)
¶ 'Scotland the Brave' (Kenneth McKellar)
¶ 'I'll Never Find Another You' (The Seekers)
¶ 'Happiness' (Ken Dodd)
¶ 'Welcome Home' (Peters & Lee)
¶ 'Ag Pleez Deddy' (from *Wait a Minim!*) (Jeremy Taylor)
*¶ 'Husbands and Wives' (Neil Diamond)
¶ 'I Do, I Do, I Do' (Abba)
¶ LUXURY: A bed.
¶ BOOK: A copy of *Wisden*.

29 May 1976
1334 Douglas Fairbanks Jr
Actor
¶ Lerner & Loewe, 'Camelot' (from *Camelot*) (Richard Burton)
¶ Gershwin, 'Summertime' (from *Porgy and Bess*) (June McMechen)
¶ 'In the Beginning . . .' (Genesis 1) (Laurence Olivier)
¶ Styne, 'People' (from *Funny Girl*) (Barbra Streisand)
*¶ Chopin, Fantaisie-Impromptu in C sharp minor (opus 66) (Artur Rubinstein *piano*)
¶ 'My Blue Heaven' (Bing Crosby)
¶ Lennon & McCartney, 'Strawberry fields Forever' (The Beatles)
¶ Porter, 'Night and Day' (from *Anything Goes*) (André Kostelanetz Orchestra)
¶ LUXURY: Writing materials.
¶ BOOK: Daniel Defoe, *Robinson Crusoe*

5 June 1976
1335 Eric Simms
Naturalist and broadcaster
¶ Schubert, 'Heidenröslein' (opus 3, no. 3) (Elisabeth Schumann)
*¶ Beethoven, Symphony No. 7 in A major (opus 92) (Berlin Philharmonic/von Karajan)
¶ Dvořák, Symphony No. 9 in E minor (LSO/Kertesz)
¶ Recording of birdsong: a blackbird in London
¶ Mozart, Clarinet Concerto in A (K. 622) (Gervase de Peyer/LSO/Maag)
¶ Bruch, Violin Concerto No. 1 in G minor (Nathan Milstein/Philharmonia Orchestra/Barzin)
¶ Monteverdi, 'Magnificat' (from *Vespers of 1610*) (Spandauer Kantorei Instrumental Ensemble/Rilling)
¶ Rachmaninov, Piano Concerto No. 2 in C minor (Vladimir Ashkenazy/Moscow Philharmonic/Kondrashin)
¶ LUXURY: Tape-recording equipment.
¶ BOOK: Gilbert White, *The Natural History of Selborne*

12 June 1976
1336 Malcolm Williamson
Master of the Queen's Musick
¶ Britten, 'Les illuminations' (Peter Pears/NPO/Goossens)
¶ Vaughan Williams, Symphony No. 9 in E minor (LPO/Boult)
¶ Williamson, Violin Concerto (Yehudi Menuhin/LPO/Boult)
¶ Messiaen, 'Communion' (from *Messe de la Pentecôte*) (Olivier Messiaen *organ*)
¶ Stravinsky, Symphony of Psalms (Orchestre de la Suisse Romande/Ansermet)
*¶ Mozart, Symphony No. 40 in G minor (K. 550) (English Chamber Orchestra/Britten)
¶ Williamson, 'My Bed is a Boat' (from *From a Child's Garden*) (April Cantelo/Michael Williamson *piano*/Nash Ensemble)
¶ Brahms, Symphony No. 2 in D (LPO/Boult)
¶ LUXURY: A puppet theatre.
¶ BOOK: The lyric dramas of Strindberg.

19 June 1976
1337 Len Deighton
Writer
¶ Beethoven, 'Für Elise' (John Ogdon *piano*)
¶ 'Stars Fell on Alabama' (Jack Teagarden *vocal* and *trombone*/Louis Armstrong and the All-Stars)
¶ 'There Ain't No Easy Run' (Johnny Cash)
¶ 'I'll Make a Man of You' (from *The Passing Show of 1914*) (Gwendoline Brogden)
¶ Ravel, 'La valse' (Suisse Romande Orchestra/Ansermet)
¶ Mozart, Piano Concerto No. 11 in F (K. 413) (Ingrid Haebler/LSO/Colin Davis)
¶ 'Cracklin' Rosie' (Neil Diamond)
*¶ Mahler, *Lieder Eines Fahrenden Gesellen* (Janet Baker/Hallé Orchestra/Barbirolli)
¶ LUXURY: A fully equipped darkroom.
¶ BOOK: *The Art of Modern French Cooking*

26 June 1976
1338 Philip Jones
Trumpet player
¶ Purcell, *The Fairy Queen* (overture) (English Chamber Orchestra/Britten)
*¶ Beethoven, 'Er Sterbe' (from *Fidelio*, Act 2) (Christa Ludwig/Jon Vickers/Gottlob Frick/Walter Berry/Philharmonia Orchestra/Klemperer)
¶ Schubert, Symphony No. 3 in D (RPO/Beecham)
¶ R. Strauss, Horn Concerto No. 1 in E flat (Dennis Brain/Philharmonia Orchestra/Sawallish)
¶ Betjeman, 'Business Women' (Sir John Betjeman/ensemble/Parker)
¶ Mozart, Piano Concerto No. 17 in G (K. 453) (Daniel Barenboim *piano and conducting*/English Chamber Orchestra)
¶ Elgar, Introduction and Allegro for Strings (LPO/Boult)
¶ 'The Cuckoo' (Philip Jones Brass Ensemble)
¶ LUXURY: Champagne.
¶ BOOK: *Grove's Dictionary of Music and Musicians*

3 July 1976
1339 The Most Reverend and Rt Hon. Stuart Blanch
The Archbishop of York
¶ 'Fiddler on the Roof' (from *Fiddler on the Roof*) (Topol/company)
¶ Pachelbel, Canon in D (Jean-François Paillard Chamber Orchestra)
¶ *New English Bible*: John 1:1–14 (Lockward West)
¶ 'Dirty Old Town' (The Spinners)
¶ Mozart, Flute Concerto in G (K. 313) (Claude Monteux/Academy of St Martin-in-the-Fields/Marriner)
¶ 'Slow Train' (from *At the Drop of Another Hat*) (Michael Flanders/Donald Swann)
*¶ Mozart, Brandenburg Concerto No. 2 in F major (BWV 1047) (Yehudi Menuhin *violin and conducting*/Bath Festival Chamber Orchestra)

¶ Handel, 'I Know that My Redeemer Liveth' (from *Messiah*) (Isobel Baillie/Hallé/Heward)
¶ LUXURY: A flute.
¶ BOOK: George MacDonald, *Diary of an Old Soul*

10 July 1976
1340 Alan Pascoe
Hurdler
¶ 'Still Love You' (Rod Stewart)
*¶ Denver, 'Looking for Space' (John Denver)
¶ Lennon & McCartney, 'Hey Jude' (The Beatles)
¶ Wonder, 'You are the Sunshine of My Life' (Stevie Wonder)
¶ Lennon & McCartney, 'Lucy in the Sky with Diamonds' (Elton John)
¶ 'Brown Sugar' (The Rolling Stones)
¶ Tchaikovsky, '1812 Overture' (opus 49) (LSO/Previn)
¶ 'Home Thoughts from Abroad' (Clifford T. Ward)
¶ LUXURY: A diary and a pencil.
¶ BOOK: The Reader's Digest *Gardeners' Yearbook*

17 July 1976
1341 Philip Larkin
Poet
¶ 'Dallas Blues' (Louis Armstrong *vocal* and *trumpet*/Luis Russell and his Orchestra)
¶ 'Dollia' (Louis Killen)
¶ Tallis, 'Spem in Alium' (40 part motet) (King's College Chapel Choir/Cambridge University Musical Society/Willcocks)
*¶ 'I'm Down in the Dumps' (Bessie Smith)
¶ 'The Coventry Carol' (St George's Canzona)
¶ Elgar, Symphony No. 1 in A flat (LPO/Boult)
¶ 'These Foolish Things' (from *Spread It Abroad*) (Billie Holiday)
¶ Handel, 'Praise the Lord' (from *Solomon*) (Beecham Choral Society/RPO/Beecham)
¶ LUXURY: A typewriter and an unlimited supply of paper.
¶ BOOK: The plays of George Bernard Shaw.

24 July 1976
1342 Mel Torme
Singer and songwriter
¶ 'Westwood Walk' (Gerry Mulligan and his Ten-Tette)
¶ Grainger, 'My Robin is to the Greenwood Gone' (Eastman-Rochester Pops Orchestra/Fennell)
¶ Chopin, Prelude No. 7 in A major (Jimmy Lunceford and his Orchestra)
¶ 'The Christmas Song' (Nat 'King' Cole)
*¶ Delius, 'On Hearing the First Cuckoo in Spring' (RPO/Beecham)
¶ 'The Carioca' (from film *Flying Down to Rio*) (Artie Shaw and his Orchestra)
¶ 'Reminiscing in Tempo' (Duke Ellington and his Orchestra)
¶ 'Dusk' (Light Music Society Orchestra/Dunn)
¶ LUXURY: An air conditioner with solar batteries.
¶ BOOK: *The* New York Times *Film Directory*

31 July 1976
1343 George Guest
Organist and Director of the Choir of St John's College, Cambridge
¶ 'Cyfri'r Geifr (Counting the Goats)' (Sian Emlyn)
¶ Elgar, Cello Concerto in E minor (opus 85) (Paul Tortelier/LPO/Boult)
¶ 'Salve Regina' (Monks of the Abbey of Solesmes)
¶ 'On a Clear Day' (Cleo Laine)
¶ Haydn, Trumpet Concerto in E flat (John Wilbraham/Academy of St Martin-in-the-Fields/Marriner)
¶ Owen, 'To Our Lady of Sorrows' (Janet Price/Anthony Saunders *piano*)
¶ 'Cymylau' (Sidan)
*¶ Fauré, 'In Paradisum' (from *Requiem*) (St John's College Choir, Cambridge/Academy of St Martin-in-the-Fields/Guest)
¶ LUXURY: A clavichord with a tuning fork and key.
¶ BOOK: The complete works of Saunders Lewis.

7 August 1976
1344 Melvyn Bragg
Writer and broadcaster
¶ Tchaikovsky, Violin Concerto in D (opus 35) (Jascha Heifetz/LPO/Barbirolli)
¶ Harrison, 'My Sweet Lord' (George Harrison)
¶ Bridge, 'Go not, Happy Day' (Kathleen Ferrier/Frederick Stone *piano*)
¶ Bartók, Music for Strings, Percussion and Celesta (Philharmonia Hungarica/Dorati)
¶ 'Black, Brown and White' (Big Bill Broonzy *vocal* and *guitar*)
¶ Beethoven. Piano Sonata No. 26 in E flat (Les Adieux) (Daniel Barenboim)
¶ Goss, 'The Twenty-Third Psalm' (King's College Chapel Choir/Willcocks)
*¶ Mozart, 'Pa, pa, pa . . .' (from *The Magic Flute*, Act 3) (Dietrich Fischer–Dieskau/Lisa Otto/Berlin Philharmonic/Böhm)
¶ LUXURY: Champagne.
¶ BOOK: Leo Tolstoy, *Anna Karenina*

14 August 1976
1345 James Galway
Flautist
*¶ Mozart, *The Magic Flute* (overture) (Vienna Philharmonic/von Karajan)
¶ Starr, 'Octopuses Garden' (The Beatles)
¶ Bach, Brandenburg Concerto No. 2 in F major (BWV 1047) (Marcel Moyse *flute*/Adolf Busch Chamber Orchestra)
¶ 'Oh, Marie' (Joseph Schmidt)
¶ J. Strauss, 'The Blue Danube' (Berlin Philharmonic/von Karajan)
¶ 'Atom Heart Mother' (Pink Floyd)
¶ Chopin, Ballade No. 4 in F minor (opus 52) (Vladimir Horowitz *piano*)
¶ Mendelssohn, Violin Concerto in E minor (Jascha Heifetz/Boston Symphony/Münch)
¶ LUXURY: His golden flute.
¶ BOOK: A volume of poetry from around the world.

21 August 1976
1346 Penelope Keith
Actress

¶ 'You are My Sunshine' (Trini Lopez)

*¶ Elgar, Introduction and Allegro for Strings (LPO/Boult)

¶ 'Here's That Rainy Day' (Frank Sinatra)

¶ Bernstein, *Candide* (overture) (New York Philharmonic/ Bernstein)

¶ Styne, 'Some People' (from *Gypsy*) (Angela Lansbury)

¶ Coward, 'Useful Phrases' (from *Sail Away*) (Noël Coward)

¶ Satie, *Trois gymnopédies* (Aldo Ciccolini *piano*)

¶ Lennon & McCartney, 'All You Need is Love' (The Beatles)

¶ LUXURY: Lapsang soochong tea.

¶ BOOK: Marcel Proust, *À la recherche du temps perdu*

28 August 1976
1347 Tolchard Evans
Song writer and composer of light music

¶ Dukas, 'The Sorcerer's Apprentice' (City of Birmingham Symphony/ Frémaux)

¶ Chopin, Fantaisie-Impromptu in C sharp minor (opus 66) (Semprini *piano*)

¶ 'Lily of Laguna' (George Mitchell Minstrels)

¶ Sousa/Horowitz, 'Stars and Stripes Forever' (Vladimir Horowitz *piano*)

¶ 'Misery Farm' (Tommy Handley)

¶ 'Dreaming' (Debroy Somers Band)

¶ 'Fourth Form at St Michael's' (Will Hay and his Scholars)

*¶ Evans, 'Lady of Spain' (Capitol Symphony/Dragon)

¶ LUXURY: Manuscript paper and pens.

¶ BOOK: Voltaire, *Candide*

4 September 1976
1348 George Cole
Actor

¶ Benatzky, 'Goodbye' (from *White Horse Inn*) (Andy Cole)

¶ 'We Could Use a Little Rain' (Rogue)

¶ Wagner, 'Ride of the Valkyries' (from *Die Walküre*) (LSO/Stokowski)

¶ Weinberger, Polka from *Schwanda the Bagpiper* (Philadelphia Orchestra/ Ormandy)

¶ 'A Man of Our Time' (James Clarke and Sounds)

¶ 'El presidente' (Herb Alpert and his Tijuana Brass)

*¶ Sibelius, Symphony No. 2 in D (Hallé Orchestra/Barbirolli)

¶ Handel, 'Hallelujah Chorus' (from *Messiah*) (RPO and Chorus/Beecham)

¶ LUXURY: Havana cigars.

¶ BOOK: The form book.

12 September 1976
1349 Michael Bond
Writer and creator of Paddington Bear

¶ 'What a Wonderful World' (Louis Armstrong)

*¶ 'La vie en rose' (Edith Piaf)

¶ 'Kyra Giorgaina (George's Wife)' (Yiannis Kalatzis/Litsa Diamanti/Orchestra/Katsaros)

¶ Puccini, 'O soave fanciulla' (from *La bohème*) (Bidú Sayão/ Richard Tucker/Metropolitan Opera Orchestra/Antonicelli)

¶ 'The Driving Instructor' (Bob Newhart)

¶ 'Mama' (Sanganas Five)

¶ 'Dream a Little Dream of Me' (Ella Fitzgerald/Count Basie and his Orchestra)

¶ Beethoven, Symphony No. 9 in D minor (opus 125) (Chorus and Orchestra of 1951 Bayreuth Festival/Furtwängler)

¶ LUXURY: A grapevine.

¶ BOOK: An album of personal photographs.

18 September 1976
1350 David Wilkie
Swimmer

¶ Wonder, 'Heaven is Ten Zillion Light Years Away' (Stevie Wonder)

¶ 'Hot Stuff' (The Rolling Stones)

¶ 'Give Me Strength' (Eric Clapton)

¶ 'Love is the Drug' (Roxy Music)

¶ 'Out with the Boys' (Mandrill)

¶ Lennon, 'Instant Karma' (John Lennon/Plastic Ono Band)

¶ 'Tragic Magic' (Traffic)

*¶ 'John McLaughlin' (Miles Davis *trumpet*/ensemble)

¶ LUXURY: Painting materials.

¶ BOOK: An English/Spanish dictionary.

25 September 1976
1351 Peter Quennell
Writer and editor of *History Today*

¶ Gluck, 'Dance of the Blessed Spirits' (from *Orfeo ed Euridice*) (James Galway *flute*/National Philharmonic/Gerhardt)

¶ Mozart, 'E un certo balsana' (from *Don Giovanni*) (Mirella Freni/Royal Opera House Orchestra, Covent Garden/ Colin Davis)

¶ Michael Drayton, 'Since There's No Help, Come Let Us Kiss and Part' (Anthony Quayle)

¶ Gershwin, 'Rhapsody in Blue' (George Gershwin *piano*/Paul Whiteman and his Concert Orchestra)

¶ Dvořák, Slavonic Dance in E minor (opus 72, no. 2) (Cleveland Orchestra/Szell)

¶ Shakespeare, *The Merchant of Venice* (Act 5, Scene 1) (John Gielgud)

¶ Matthew Arnold, 'Dover Beach' (John Neville)

*¶ Albinoni/Giazotto, Adagio in G minor for Strings and Organ (Wolfgang Meyer *organ*/Berlin Philharmonic/von Karajan)

¶ LUXURY: Champagne.

¶ BOOK: François-René Vicomte de Chateaubriand, *Memoires d'outre-tombe*

2 October 1976
1352 Frank Muir (2nd appearance)
Writer and broadcaster
¶ Vaughan Williams, 'The Lark Ascending' (Hugh Bean *violin/* NPO/Boult)
¶ Vivaldi, 'Summer' (from *The Four Seasons*) (Pinchas Zukerman *violin and conducting/* English Chamber Orchestra)
¶ 'Sega la mode' (Kersley Vinay/Orchestre Typique de la Police)
¶ Betjeman, *A Shropshire Lad* (John Betjeman/ensemble/ Parker)
¶ 'Sunday Morning' (Coleman Hawkins Quintet)
*¶ Mozart, Piano Concerto No. 27 in B flat (K. 595) (Alfred Brendel *piano/* Academy of St Martin-in-the-Fields/Marriner)
¶ Lennon & McCartney, 'Let It Be' (The Beatles)
¶ Elgar, 'Pomp and Circumstance' March No. 1 in D major (opus 39) (RPO/del Mar)
¶ LUXURY: A navel brush.
¶ BOOK: J. L. Carr, *The Harpole Report*

9 October 1976
1353 Alan Bates
Actor
¶ 'I'm Free' (from *Tommy*) (Roger Daltry/The Who)
¶ Chopin, Fantaisie-Impromptu in C sharp minor (opus 66) (John Ogdon *piano*)
¶ Fauré, 'Après un rêve' (Pablo Casals *cello/* Nikolai Mednikov *piano*)
*¶ Pergolesi, Flute Concerto No. 1 in G (Jean-Pierre Rampal/ Stuttgart Chamber Orchestra/ Münchinger)
¶ 'I Got Life' (from *Hair*) (Nina Simone)
¶ Bach, Brandenburg Concerto No. 3 in G major (BWV 1048) (Yehudi Menuhin *violin and conducting/* Bath Festival Chamber Orchestra)
¶ Bernstein/Sondheim, 'Something's Coming' (from *West Side Story*) (Larry Kert)

¶ Boccherini, Cello Concerto in B flat (Jacqueline du Pré/English Chamber Orchestra/Barenboim)
¶ LUXURY: A flute.
¶ BOOK: A comprehensive anthology of poetry.

16 October 1976
1354 Anthony Powell
Writer
¶ 'If You were the Only Girl in the World' (from *The Bing Boys are Here*) (Violet Loraine/ George Robey)
¶ Gay, 'Were I Laid on Greenland's Coast' (from *The Beggar's Opera*) (Elsie Morison/ John Cameron/Pro Arte Orchestra/Sargent)
¶ Verdi, 'La donna e mobile' (from *Rigoletto*) (Luciano Pavarotti/LSO/Bonynge)
¶ J. Strauss, 'Tales from the Vienna Woods' (Vienna Philharmonic/Boskovsky)
¶ Borodin, 'Polovtsian Dances' (from *Prince Igor*) (Berlin Philharmonic/von Karajan)
*¶ Lambert, Rio Grande (soloists/chorus/Hallé Orchestra/Lambert)
¶ Milhaud, *La création du monde* (Orchestre du Théâtre des Champs-Elysées/Milhaud)
¶ Debussy, 'Iberia' (from *Images for Orchestra*, no. 2) (Orchestre de la Suisse Romande/Ansermet)
¶ LUXURY: One bottle of red wine every day.
¶ BOOK: Mikhail Lermontov, *A Hero of Our Time*

23 October 1976
1355 Norman Bailey
Baritone
¶ Wagner, 'Siegfried Idyll' (Philharmonia Orchestra/ Klemperer)
¶ Beethoven, Symphony No. 9 in D minor (opus 125) LSO and Chorus/Giulini)
¶ Mancini, 'Moon River (from film *Breakfast at Tiffany's*) (Henry Mancini and his Orchestra)
¶ Debussy, 'Clair de lune' (from *Suite bergamasque*) (Orchestre de la Suisse Romande/ Ansermet)
¶ 'My Way' (Frank Sinatra)

¶ Rachmaninov, Piano Concerto No. 2 in C minor (Vladimir Ashkenazy/Moscow Philharmonic/Kondrashin)
¶ 'Year of Sunday' (Seals & Croft)
*¶ Wagner, 'Verachtet mir die Meister nicht' (from *Die Meistersinger*) (Norman Bailey/ Vienna Philharmonic/Solti)
¶ LUXURY: A pocket calculator.
¶ BOOK: Baha'i Allah & Abdul Baha'i, *The Baha'i Revelation*

30 October 1976
1356 Lt-Colonel John Blashford-Snell
Soldier and explorer
¶ Theodorakis, 'Zorba's Dance' (from film *Zorba the Greek*) (soundtrack/Theodorakis)
¶ 'Theme from *Lawrence of Arabia*' (from film) (Ron Goodwin and his Orchestra)
¶ 'He Played His Ukelele as the Ship Went Down' (Ambrose and his Orchestra)
¶ 'Hurrah for the CRE' (Corps of Royal Engineers Band)
¶ 'Sky Bird' (Neil Diamond)
¶ Dvořák, Symphony No. 9 in E minor (New World) (LSO/ Kertesz)
¶ 'Amazing Grace' (Pipes and Drums of the Royal Scots Dragoon Guards)
*¶ Elgar, 'Pomp and Circumstance' March No. 1 in D major (opus 39) (recorded at last night of 1969 Proms) (BBC Chorus/BBC Symphony/Colin Davis)
¶ LUXURY: Malt whisky.
¶ BOOK: The complete works of Rudyard Kipling.

6 November 1976
1357 Anthony Quayle (2nd appearance)
Actor
¶ 'There's a Long, Long Trail' (John McCormack)
¶ 'Underneath the Arches' (Flanagan & Allen)
*¶ Mendelssohn, *A Midsummer Night's Dream* (Philharmonia Orchestra/Klemperer)
¶ Mozart, Symphony No. 40 in G minor (K. 550) (Berlin Philharmonic/Böhm)
¶ 'Australia' (Uffa Fox)

¶Rodgers and Hart,
'Manhattan' (from *Garrick Gaieties*) (Ella Fitzgerald/
Orchestra/Buddy Bregman)
¶Recording of the song of the humpback whale
¶Beethoven, Romance in F (opus 50) (David Oistrakh *violin*/RPO/Goossens)
¶LUXURY: A magnifying glass.
¶BOOK: The complete works of Edward Lear.

13 November 1976
1358 Christopher Milne
Bookseller and the original Christopher Robin
¶'Blessed be the God and Father' (Parish Church of St Peter's Choir, Leeds)
¶Mendelssohn, 'I Waited for the Lord' (from 'Hymn of Praise') (Worcester Cathedral Choir)
¶Rossini, String Sonata No. 1 in G major (Academy of St Martin-in-the-Fields/Marriner)
¶Mascagni, 'Easter Hymn' (from *Cavalleria Rusticana*) (Maria Callas/La Scala Orchestra and Chorus/Serafin)
¶Schubert, Symphony No. 9 in C (Great) (LPO/Boult)
¶'In Dulci Jubilo' (King's College Chapel Choir/Willcocks)
¶Beethoven, Symphony No. 8 in F major (opus 93) (Berlin Philharmonic/von Karajan)
*¶Brahms, Symphony No. 2 in D (Berlin Philharmonic/Abbado)
¶LUXURY: Writing materials.
¶BOOK: Richard Jefferies, *Bevis: The Story of a Boy*

20 November 1976
1359 Anna Moffo
Opera singer
¶Mozart, Horn concerto No. 1 in D (K. 412) (Dennis Brain/Philharmonia Orchestra/von Karajan)
¶'Three Coins in a Fountain' (from film) (Frank Sinatra)
¶Verdi, 'Nannetta's Aria' (from *Falstaff*) (Anna Moffo/Philharmonia Orchestra/von Karajan)

¶Tchaikovsky, Romeo and Juliet Fantasy Overture (NBC Symphony/Toscanini)
¶Puccini, 'O saro la più bella' (from *Manon Lescaut*, Act 2) (Leontyne Price/Placido Domingo/NPO/Santi)
*¶Ravel, *Daphnis and Chloe* (LSO/Monteux)
¶'C Minor Complex' (Lennie Tristano *piano*)
¶Styne, 'People' (from *Funny Girl*) (Barbra Streisand)
¶LUXURY: A piano.
¶BOOK: Dante's *Divine Comedy*

27 November 1976
1360 Eric Idle
Comedian and scriptwriter
*¶Haydn, Cello Concerto in C (Mstislav Rostropovich/English Chamber Orchestra/Britten)
¶'Marie' (Randy Newman)
¶'Carey' (Joni Mitchell)
¶Mozart, Symphony No. 29 in A (K. 201) (Berlin Philharmonic/von Karajan)
¶'I Don't Want to Talk About It' (Rod Stewart)
¶'It's All Over Now' (Ry Cooder)
¶'Dear One' (George Harrison)
¶Elgar, 'Nimrod' (from *Enigma Variations*) (LSO/Colin Davis)
¶LUXURY: An acoustic guitar with spare strings.
¶BOOK: A compendium of world philosophy.

4 December 1976
1361 Igor Kipnis
Harpsichordist
¶Brahms, Sonata No. 3 in F minor (Percy Grainger *piano*)
¶Chopin, Ballade No. 4 in F minor (opus 52) (Solomon *piano*)
¶Moszkowski, 'Etincelles' (Vladimir Horowitz *piano*)
*¶Mozart, Symphony No. 35 in D (K. 385) (Haffner) (New York Philharmonic/Toscanini)
¶Ravel, *L'Enfant et les sortilèges* (excerpt) (soloists/French National Radio Orchestra/Bour)
¶Wagner, 'Schlafend ein Wonniges Weib' (from *Götterdämmerung*) (Lauritz Melchior/Berlin State Opera Orchestra/Blech)

¶Rachmaninov, 'O Cease Thy Singing, Maiden Fair' (Alexander Kipnis [his father]/Delius Dougherty *piano*)
¶Bach, Concerto in the Italian Style in F (BWV 971) (Igor Kipnis *harpsichord*)
¶LUXURY: A clavichord.
¶BOOK: Dylan Thomas, *Under Milk Wood*

11 December 1976
1362 Gemma Jones
Actress and singer
¶Chopin, Nocturne No. 2 in E flat (opus 9, no. 2) (Alexis Weissenberg *piano*)
¶'Fred Fannakapan' (Gracie Fields)
¶'Away in a Manger' (Mark Tinkler/St John's College Choir, Cambridge/Guest)
¶'A Whiter Shade of Pale' (Procol Harum)
¶Orff, 'Veni Veni Venias' (from *Carmina Burana*) (Deutsche Oper Choir and Orchestra, Berlin/Jochum)
¶Dylan, 'Lay, Lady, Lay' (Bob Dylan)
*¶Wagner, 'Siegfried Idyll' (Vienna Philharmonic/Solti)
¶'Killing Me Softly with His Song' (Roberta Flack)
¶LUXURY: A deeply upholstered armchair.
¶BOOK: *The Oxford Book of English Verse*

18 December 1976
1363 Sir Denys Lasdun
Architect
¶Monteverdi, *L'incoronazione di Poppea* (Act 2, closing duet) (Magda Laszlo/Richard Lewis/RPO/Pritchard)
¶Bach, Suite No. 2 in B minor (BWV 1067) (English Chamber Orchestra/Leppard)
¶Schubert, String Quintet in C (D. 956) (William Pleeth *cello*/Amadeus String Quartet)
¶Beethoven, Grosse Fugue in B flat (opus 133) (Hungarian Quartet)
¶Beethoven, Symphony No. 7 in A major (opus 92) (Vienna Philharmonic/Schmidt-Isserstedt)

¶ Schœnberg, Wind Quintet (opus 26) (Westwood Wind Quintet)
¶ 'I Don't Know' (Johnny Shines)
*¶ Mozart, Symphony No. 40 in G minor (K. 550) (English Chamber Orchestra/Britten)
¶ LUXURY: A telescope.
¶ BOOK: A book about the night sky.

25 December 1976
1364 Charlie Cairoli
Clown
*¶ 'Darling, je vous aime beaucoup' (Nat 'King' Cole)
¶ 'Kalinka' (Red Army Ensemble)
¶ J. Strauss, 'Nun's Chorus' (from Casanova) (Joan Sutherland/Ambrosian Light Opera Chorus/NPO/Bonynge)
¶ Coates, 'Calling all workers' (Symphony Orchestra/Coates)
¶ Adam, 'Amis, écoutez l'histoire' (from Le postillon de Longjumeau, Act 1) (Nicolai Gedda/French National Radio Orchestra/Prêtre)
¶ 'Lily the Pink' (Scaffold)
¶ Beethoven, Sonata No. 14 in C sharp minor (opus 27, no. 2) (Moonlight) (Daniel Barenboim piano)
¶ R. Strauss, 'Also Sprach Zarathustra' (Berlin Philharmonic/Böhm)
¶ LUXURY: Champagne.
¶ BOOK: A survival manual.

1 January 1977
1365 Kenneth McKellar (2nd appearance)
Singer
¶ 'Bern-Lotschber-Simplon' (Lander Capella Tuona Se Bois)
¶ Bach, 'Sanctus' (from Mass in B minor, BWV 232) (Vienna Singverein/Berlin Philharmonic/von Karajan)
¶ Quilter, 'O Mistress Mine' (from Twelfth Night) (Kenneth McKellar/Johnny Evans piano)
¶ William McGonagall, 'The Tay Bridge Disaster' (John Laurie)
¶ 'My Love is Like a Red, Red Rose' (Jimmy Shand and his Band)
¶ 'A Call from Long Island' (from You Don't Have to be Jewish) (Betty Walker/Arlene Golonka)

¶ 'Core' ngrato' (Beniamino Gigli/Royal Opera House Orchestra, Covent Garden/Zamboni)
*¶ R. Strauss, 'Frühling' (from Four Last Songs) (Gundula Janowitz/Berlin Philharmonic/von Karajan)
¶ LUXURY: A bicycle.
¶ BOOK: 'The Complete Book of World Cookery'.

8 January 1977
1366 Robert Dougall
Former BBC newsreader
¶ Rossini/Respighi, Ballet La Boutique fantasque (RPO/Sargent)
¶ Kern, 'Smoke Gets in Your Eyes' (from Roberta) (Irene Dunne)
¶ Holst, The Perfect Fool (LPO/Boult)
¶ 'La mer' (Charles Trenet)
¶ Purcell, 'Come Ye Sons of Art' (Ode for Queen Mary's Birthday 1694) (Alfred Deller/John Whitworth/L'Oiseau Lyre Orchestral Ensemble/Lewis)
¶ 'Your Feet's Too Big' (Fats Waller and his Rhythm)
*¶ Recording of birdsong: nightingale
¶ Cricket commentary by Howard Marshall
¶ LUXURY: A pair of field glasses.
¶ BOOK: A volume on tropical flora and fauna.

15 January 1977
1367 James Blades
Percussionist
*¶ Britten, 'All People that on Earth Do Dwell' (from St Nicolas Cantata, opus 42) (Aldeburgh Festival Choir and Orchestra/Britten)
¶ Beethoven, 'Coriolan Overture' (opus 62) (Berlin Philharmonic/von Karajan)
¶ 'Space Man' (Lionel Hampton and Jess Stacey pianos)
¶ Stravinsky, L'histoire du soldat (suite) (Israel Baker violin/ensemble/Stravinsky)
¶ The chimes of Big Ben
¶ Britten, 'Timpani Piece for Jimmy' (James Blade timpani/Joan Blades piano)

¶ Mozart, Piano Concerto No. 22 in E flat (K. 482) (Géza Anda piano and conducting/Camerata Academica of the Salzburg Mozarteum)
¶ Walton, Belshazzar's Feast (LSO and Chorus/Previn)
¶ LUXURY: A telescope.
¶ BOOK: Grove's Dictionary of Music and Musicians

22 January 1977
1368 Michael Holroyd
Biographer
¶ 'Dinner for One Please, James' (Hutch)
¶ Wagner, 'The Ride of the Valkyries' (from Die Walküre) (LSO/Stokowski)
¶ Berwald, String Quartet No. 3 in E flat (Bentheim Quartet)
¶ Britten, 'Variations on a Theme of Frank Bridge' (English Chamber Orchestra/Britten)
*¶ Beethoven, String Quartet No. 16 in F (opus 135) (Budapest Quartet)
¶ Prokofiev, Piano Sonata No. 8 in B flat (Sviatoslav Richter)
¶ Schubert, String Quintet in C (D. 956) (William Pleeth cello/Amadeus String Quartet)
¶ Samuel Beckett, Malone Dies (excerpt) (Jack Emery)
¶ LUXURY: A water bed.
¶ BOOK: Hugh Kingsmill, The High Hill of the Muses

29 January 1977
1369 Roy Dotrice
Actor
¶ Dowland, 'Mignarda' (Henry Noel's Galliard) (Juliam Bream lute)
¶ McTell, 'The Streets of London' (Ralph McTell)
¶ 'Angelus Autem Domini' (Benedictine monks of the Abbey Saint Maurice and Saint Maur of Clairvaux)
¶ 'Only the Lonely' (Frank Sinatra)
¶ Mahler, Symphony No. 8 in E flat (CSO/Solti)
¶ Bach, Suite No. 3 in D major (BWV 1068) (Jean-Christian Michel clarinet/Monique Thus organ/Michel Seck bass/Roger Rostan percussion)

¶Butterworth, *A Shropshire Lad* (Academy of St Martin-in-the-Fields/Marriner)
*¶Dylan Thomas, 'Do Not Go Gentle into That Good Night' (Dylan Thomas)
¶LUXURY: An evening dress suit.
¶BOOK: Isaac Walton, *The Compleat Angler*

5 February 1977
1370 Barry Tuckwell
Horn player
¶Prokofiev, Sinfonia Concertante (Mstislav Rostropovich *cello*/RPO/Sargent)
¶Brahms, Serenade No. 1 in D (opus 11) (LSO/Kertesz)
¶Schœnberg, String Trio (opus 45) (members of Juilliard Quartet)
*¶Beethoven, String Quartet No. 14 in C sharp minor (opus 131) (Busch Quartet)
¶Schubert, Symphony No. 9 in C (Great) (LSO/Krips)
¶Schumann, Fantasia in C (opus 17) (Vladimir Ashkenazy *piano*)
¶Sibelius, Symphony No. 4 in A minor (Finnish Radio Symphony/Berglund)
¶R. Strauss, 'September' (from *Four Last Songs*) (Lisa della Casa/Vienna Philharmonic/Böhm)
¶LUXURY: A family photograph album.
¶BOOK: Jonathan Swift, *Gulliver's Travels*

12 February 1977
1371 John Curry
World champion figure skater
¶Debussy, *Prélude à l'après-midi d'un faune* (Berlin Philharmonic/von Karajan)
¶R. Strauss, 'September' (from *Four Last Songs*) (Lisa della Casa/Vienna Philharmonic/Böhm)
¶'Cuddle Up' (The Beach Boys)
¶Tchaikovsky, Symphony No. 6 in B minor (Pathétique) (Moscow Radio Symphony/Rozhdestvensky)
¶Albinoni, Trumpet Concerto in B flat (Maurice André/Vienna soloists)

¶Styne, 'Some People' (from *Gypsy*) (Angela Lansbury)
¶Mahler, *Das Lied von der Erde* (James King/Amsterdam Concertgebouw/Haitink)
*¶Vivaldi, Concerto in A minor for Two Violins (opus 3, no. 8) (David & Igor Oistrakh/RPO/David Oistrakh)
¶LUXURY: Pencils, paints and paper.
¶BOOK: A transcript of the Erhard Seminar Training (est) course.

19 February 1977
1372 Egon Ronay
Food and wine expert and restaurant critic
¶Debussy, 'Clair de lune' (from *Suite bergamasque*) (Walter Gieseking *piano*)
¶Bartók, 'Evening in Transylvania' (from *Hungarian Sketches*) (Budapest Symphony/Erdelyi)
¶Beethoven, Symphony No. 2 in D (Berlin Philharmonic/von Karajan)
¶Bach, Brandenburg Concerto No. 4 in G major (BWV 1049) (Bath Festival Chamber Orchestra/Menuhin)
¶Respighi, 'L'ottobrata' (from *Feste Romane*) (Philadelphia Orchestra/Ormandy)
*¶Kodály, 'Variations on a Hungarian Folksong (The Peacock)' (Hungarian Radio and Television Symphony/Lehel)
¶Prokofiev, 'Dance of the Knights' (from Ballet *Romeo and Juliet*) (Boston Symphony/Leinsdorf)
¶Khachaturian, Piano Concerto in D flat major (Mindru Katz/LPO/Boult)
¶LUXURY: Champagne.
¶BOOK: Leo Tolstoy, *War and Peace*

26 February 1977
1373 Merle Park
Prima ballerina
¶Sibelius, 'Finlandia' (opus 26) (Hallé Orchestra/Barbirolli)
¶'Kwela Joe' (Specks Rampura)
¶Chopin, Ballade No. 2 in F (opus 38) (Artur Rubinstein *piano*)

*¶R. Strauss, 'Im Abendrot' (from *Four Last Songs*) (Elisabeth Schwarzkopf/Berlin Radio Symphony/Szell)
¶Lloyd Webber/Rice, 'Don't Cry for Me, Argentina' (from *Evita*) (Julie Covington/LPO/Bowles)
¶Dvořák, Symphony No. 9 in E minor (New World) (Berlin Philharmonic/Kubelik)
¶Mendelssohn, 'Hear My Prayer' (Paul Dutton/Leeds Parish Church Choir/Hunt)
¶Fauré, 'In Paradisum' (from *Requiem*, opus 48) (King's College Chapel Choir/NPO/Willcocks)
¶LUXURY: A piano.
¶BOOK: *Fowler's Modern English Usage*

5 March 1977
1374 Oliver Ford
Decorator and garden designer
¶'Aquarius' (from *Hair*) (Button-Down Brass)
¶'RAF March Past' (RAF Central Band)
¶Puccini, 'In questa reggia' (from *Turandot*, Act 2) (Eva Turner)
¶'Little Old Lady' (from *The Show is On*) (Turner Layton)
¶Newley/Bricusse, 'What Kind of Fool am I?' (from *Stop the World, I Want to Get Off*) (Anthony Newley)
¶Parry/Blake, 'Jerusalem' (Royal Choral Society/LPO/Davis)
¶'The Test Pilot' (extract) (from radio series *Hancock's Half Hour*) (Tony Hancock/Kenneth Williams)
*¶Elgar, 'Pomp and Circumstance' March No. 1 in D major (opus 39) (recorded at last night of the 1969 Proms) (BBC Symphony and Chorus/Davis)
¶LUXURY: An orchid collection.
¶BOOK: A book on tropical flora and fauna.

12 March 1977
1375 James Bolam
Actor
*¶Beethoven, Violin Concerto in
D (opus 61) (David Oistrakh/
French National Radio
Orchestra/Cluytens)
¶ 'Heartbreak Hotel' (Elvis
Presley)
¶Berlin, 'They Say It's
Wonderful' (from *Annie Get
Your Gun*) (Ethel Merman)
¶Mozart, Clarinet Concerto in
A (K. 622) (Alfred Prinz/
Vienna Philharmonic/
Münchinger)
¶Speech at the Oxford Union
(Gerard Hoffnung)
¶ 'The Call of the Faraway Hills'
(from film *Shane*) (United
Artists Studio Orchestra)
¶Loesser, 'Fugue for Tinhorns'
(from *Guys and Dolls*) (original
New York cast)
¶Simon, 'Seven o'clock News/
Silent Night' (Simon &
Garfunkel)
¶LUXURY: Selected cases of
French wine.
¶BOOK: J. R. R. Tolkien, *The
Lord of the Rings*

19 March 1977
1376 Jacqueline du Pré
Cellist
¶Schubert, String Quintet in C
(D. 956) (William Pleeth *cello*/
Amadeus String Quartet)
¶Brahms, Sonata in F major
(opus 99) (Jacqueline du Pré
cello/Daniel Barenboim *piano*)
¶Mozart, 'La bella tua Zerlina'
(from *Don Giovanni*, Act 1)
(Helen Donath/Roger Soyer/
English Chamber Orchestra/
Barenboim)
¶Chopin, Polonaise No. 3 in A
(opus 40, no. 1) (Artur
Rubinstein *piano*)
*¶Schubert, Piano Quintet in A
(Trout) (Itzhak Perlman *violin*/
Pinchas Zukerman *viola*/
Jacqueline du Pré *cello*/Zubin
Mehta *double bass*/Daniel
Barenboim *piano*)
¶ 'Phonetic Pronunciation'
(Victor Borge)
¶Schubert, Impromptu in B flat
(opus 142, no. 3) (Clifford
Curzon *piano*)

¶Mozart, Piano Concerto No.
27 in B flat (K. 595) (Daniel
Barenboim *piano and
conducting*/English Chamber
Orchestra)
¶LUXURY: Pencils and paper.
¶BOOK: *Roget's Thesaurus*

26 March 1977
1377 Mary Martin
Actress and singer
¶Rodgers & Hammerstein,
'Some Enchanted Evening'
(from *South Pacific*) (Ezio
Pinza)
¶ 'Andamento' (Os Ritimistas
Brasileiros)
¶Novello, 'Some Day My Heart
Will Awake' (from *King's
Rhapsody*) (Vanessa Lee)
¶Coward, 'This is a Changing
World' (from *Pacific 1860*)
(Noël Coward)
¶ 'O del mio amato ben' (Dino
Borgioli/Ivor Newton *piano*)
¶McCartney, 'Let 'Em In'
(Wings)
¶ 'Blow the Wind Southerly'
(Kathleen Ferrier)
*¶ 'I've Gotta Crow' (from *Peter
Pan*) (Mary Martin/Heller
Halliday)
¶LUXURY: Scissors, needles and
thread.
¶BOOK: *Around the Year with
Emmet Fox*

2 April 1977
1378 Brigadier Peter
Young
**Military historian and founder
of the Sealed Knot Society**
¶Recording of a Hoolock
gibbon, London Zoo
*¶Meyerbeer, *Les huguenots*
(chorale) (recorded at the
Trooping of the Colour)
(Household Cavalry Bands/
Brigade of Guards Massed
Bands, Pipes and Drums)
¶ 'Lilli Marlene' (Lale
Andersen)
¶Handel, *Water Music Suite*
(no. 1) (English Chamber
Orchestra/Leppard)
¶Mozart, 'Pa, pa, pa,
Papagena' (from *The Magic
Flute*) (Lisa Otto/Dietrich
Fischer-Dieskau/Berlin
Philharmonic/Böhm)

¶Gay, 'Were I Laid on
Greenland's Coast' (from *The
Beggar's Opera*) (Carmen
Prietto/Dennis Noble/Argo
Chamber Ensemble/Austin)
¶Gluck, 'What is Life?' (from
Orfeo ed Euridice) (Kathleen
Ferrier/LSO/Sargent)
¶Ravel, 'Bolero' (Paris
Orchestra/Martinon)
¶LUXURY: A ton of treasure,
dated about 1642.
¶BOOK: A large blank book with
pencils.

9 April 1977
1379 Rod Hull
**Comedian, scriptwriter and
Emu-owner**
¶Vaughan Williams, *The Wasps*
(overture) (LPO/Boult)
¶Arnold, English Dance No. 5
(Philharmonia Orchestra/
Arnold)
¶Bart, 'Who Will Buy?' (from
Oliver!) (Mark Lester/
ensemble)
¶Vaughan Williams,
Symphony No. 5 in D major
(LPO/Boult)
¶Recording of the song of a
skylark
¶Elgar, 'Chanson du matin'
(opus 15, no. 2) (LSO/Elgar)
¶ 'Lovin' You' (Minnie
Riperton)
¶Hely-Hutchinson, Carol
Symphony (Pro Arte Orchestra/
Rose)
¶LUXURY: A pianola and a
supply of piano rolls.
¶BOOK: The *Boys' Own* annual
for 1926.

16 April 1977
1380 Yehudi Menuhin
(2nd appearance)
Violinist
¶J. Strauss, 'Kaiser-Waltzer'
(Vienna Philharmonic/
Boskovsky)
¶Schubert, Symphony No. 9 in
D (Great) (Berlin Philharmonic/
Furtwängler)
*¶Mozart, 'Ach, ich fühls' (from
The Magic Flute, Act 2) Irmgard
Seefried/Vienna Philharmonic/
von Karajan)
¶Bartók, Viola Concerto
(Yehudi Menuhin/NPO/
Dorati)

¶Beethoven, String Quartet No. 13 in B flat (opus 130) (Budapest String Quartet)
¶Bach, *St Matthew Passion* (final chorus) (Amsterdam Toonkunst Choir/Amsterdam Concertgebouw/Mengelberg)
¶Britten, *Les Illuminations* (opus 18) (Peter Pears/English Chamber Orchestra/Britten)
¶Purcell, 'When I am Laid in Earth' (from *Dido and Aeneas*) (Kirsten Flagstad/Mermaid Orchestra/Geraint Jones)
¶LUXURY: An album of photographs of his wife.
¶BOOK: The collected works of John Donne.

23 April 1977
1381 Magnus Magnusson
Writer and broadcaster
¶Orff, *Carmina Burana* (Deutsche Oper Chorus and Orchestra, Berlin/Jochum)
¶Mozart, Concerto in A major for Clarinet and Orchestra (K. 622) (Alfred Prinz/Vienna Philharmonic/Böhm)
*¶'Ar Vas Alda' (Fostbraedur Male Choir/Thorarinsson)
¶Albinoni/Giazotto, Adagio in G minor for Organ and Strings (Douglas Hass/Württemberg Chamber Orchestra/Faerber)
¶Trad. arr. Canteloube, 'Baïlèro' (from *Songs of the Auvergne*) (Victoria de los Angeles/Lamoureux Orchestra/Jacquillat)
¶Shostakovich, Symphony No. 9 in E flat (opus 70) (Czech Philharmonic/Neumann)
¶'All in the April Evening' (Glasgow Orpheus Choir/Roberton)
¶Rodrigo, Concierto de Aranjuez (Julian Bream *guitar*/Melos Chamber Orchestra/Colin Davis)
¶LUXURY: His pipe.
¶BOOK: Kenneth Grahame, *The Wind in the Willows*

30 April 1977
1382 David Niven
Actor and writer
¶'You are the Sunshine of My Life' (Blue Mink)
¶'Amazing Grace' (Royal Scots Dragoon Guards Pipes, Drums and Military Band)
¶'Never Can Say Goodbye' (Gloria Gaynor)
¶Verdi, 'Celeste Aida' (from *Aida*) (Jussi Björling/Rome Opera Orchestra/Perlea)
¶'Rock Your Baby' (George McCrae)
¶Delibes, 'Bell Song' (from *Lakmé*, Act 2) (Maria Callas/Philharmonia Orchestra/Serafin)
¶Rodgers & Hammerstein, 'There is Nothin' Like a Dame' (from *South Pacific*) (Men's Chorus/Orchestra/Dell'Isola)
*¶Shakespeare, 'Once more unto the breach' (from *Henry V*, Act 2, Scene 3) (Laurence Olivier)
¶LUXURY: A double bed.
¶BOOK: A British Army survival manual.

7 May 1977
1383 Lord Home of the Hirsel
Ex-Prime Minister
¶'Roaming in the Gloaming' (Sir Harry Lauder)
¶'Alec Bedser Calypso (England *v* Australia 1953)' (Lord Kitchener)
¶Mozart, 'Bei Männern, welche Liebe fühlen' (from *The Magic Flute*) (Maria Stader/Dietrich Fischer-Dieskau/Berlin Radio Symphony/Fricsay)
¶Gluck, 'What is Life?' (Che faro senza Euridice?) (from *Orfeo ed Euridice*) (Kathleen Ferrier/LSO/Sargent)
¶Slade, 'I Sit in the Sun' (from *Salad Days*) (Eleanor Drew/Edward Rubach, Robert Docker *pianos*)
¶Handel, *Water Music Suite* (Academy of St Martin-in-the-Fields/Marriner)
¶Handel, *Zadok the Priest* (King's College Chapel Choir/English Chamber Orchestra/Willcocks)

*¶Crimond, 'The Twenty-Third Psalm' (Glasgow Orpheus Choir/Roberton)
¶LUXURY: A pair of field glasses.
¶BOOK: A comprehensive book on birds.

14 May 1977
1384 Peggy Lee
Singer
¶Satie/Camarata, *Trois gymnopédies* (Camarata Contemporary Chamber Group)
¶'The Shadow of Your Smile' (from film *The Sandpiper*) (soundtrack/Armbuster)
¶Respighi, *The Pines of Rome* (Orchestre de la Suisse Romande/Ansermet)
¶Bach, 'Wachet auf' (from Cantata No. 140) (Peter Schreier/Leipzig Orchestra/Mauersberger)
*¶Delius, 'The Walk to the Paradise Garden' (from *A Village Romeo and Juliet*) (LSO/Barbirolli)
¶Delibes, 'The Maids of Cadiz' (Miles Davis *trumpet*)
¶Lennon & McCartney, 'The Long and Winding Road' (The Beatles)
¶Brahms, Symphony No. 3 in F major (LSO/Boult)
¶LUXURY: A huge picture of all her loved ones.
¶BOOK: *Letters of the Scattered Brotherhood*, edited by Mary Strong.

21 May 1977
1385 P. L. Travers
Writer and creator of 'Mary Poppins'
¶William Blake, 'The Little Black Boy' (from *Songs of Innocence*) (Ralph Richardson)
¶George W. Russell ('A.E.'), 'The Outcast' (John Hewitt)
¶W. B. Yeats, 'The Lake Isle of Innisfree' (W. B. Yeats)
¶Gerard Manley Hopkins, 'God's Grandeur' (Cyril Cusack)
¶Robert Louis Stevenson, 'The Cow' (Mary O'Farrell)
¶Robert Frost, 'Choose Something Like a Star' (Robert Frost)

¶ T. S. Eliot, 'Little Gidding' (from *The Four Quartets*) (Alec Guinness)

*¶ Shakespeare, 'Fear No More the Heat o' the Sun' (from *Cymbeline*, Act 4, Scene 2) (John Stride/Alan Bates)

¶ LUXURY: Her little marble Buddha.

¶ BOOK: A very thick blank book and a pen.

28 May 1977
1386 Marisa Robles
Harpist

¶ Britten, Simple Symphony (English Chamber Orchestra/Britten)

¶ Beethoven, 'O namenlose Freude' (from *Fidelio*, Act 2) (Christa Ludwig/Jon Vickers/Philharmonia Orchestra and Chorus/Klemperer)

¶ Mozart, 'Voi che sapete' (from *The Marriage of Figaro*, Act 1) Teresa Berganza/NPO/Klemperer)

¶ Bartók, *Rumanian Dances* (Suisse Romande Orchestra/Ansermet)

¶ Chopin, Prelude No. 7 in A (Alfred Cortot *piano*)

*¶ Vivaldi, 'Spring' (from *The Four Seasons*) (Alan Loveday *violin*/Academy of St Martin-in-the-Fields/Marriner)

¶ Rachmaninov, Piano Concerto No. 2 in C minor (Moura Lympany/RPO/Sargent)

¶ Brahms, Violin Concerto in D (David Oistrakh/French National Radio Orchestra/Klemperer)

¶ LUXURY: Oils and a comb.

¶ BOOKS: A. A. Milne, *Now We are Six* and *When We were Very Young*

4 June 1977
1387 Sir Oliver Millar
Surveyor of the Queen's Pictures

¶ Gilbert & Sullivan, 'If You're Anxious for to Shine' (from *Patience*) (George Baker)

¶ Britten (arr.), 'The Plough Boy' (Peter Pears/Benjamin Britten *piano*)

¶ 'Lillibulero' (Band of HM Coldstream Guards)

¶ Mozart, Piano Concerto No. 21 in C major (K. 467) (Daniel Barenboim *piano and conducting*/English Chamber Orchestra)

¶ Purcell, 'I Attempt from Love's Sickness to Fly' (from *The Indian Queen*) (Alfred Deller *soloist and conductor*/King's Musick)

*¶ Mozart, 'Sull'aria' (from *The Marriage of Figaro*, Act 3) (Lisa della Casa/Hilde Gueden/Vienna Philharmonic/Erich Kleiber)

¶ Haydn, Symphony No. 100 in G (Military) (Philharmonia Hungarica/Dorati)

¶ Britten, *The Little Sweep* (final chorus) (Alleyn's School Choir/English Opera Group Orchestra/Britten)

¶ LUXURY: His sketchbook, pencil, pen and ink.

¶ BOOK: Jane Austen, *Emma*

11 June 1977
1388 Mirella Freni
Soprano

¶ Beethoven, Symphony No. 7 in A major (opus 92) (New York Philharmonic/Toscanini)

¶ Donizetti, *Anna Bolena* (aria) (Maria Callas/Philharmonia Orchestra/Rescigno)

¶ Lennon & McCartney, 'Michelle' (The Beatles)

¶ Mussorgsky, 'The Death of Boris' (from *Boris Godunov*, Act 4) (Nicolai Ghiaurov/Vienna State Opera Chorus/Vienna Philharmonic/von Karajan)

*¶ R. Strauss, 'Im Abendrot' (from *Four Last Songs*) (Elisabeth Schwarzkopf/Berlin Radio Symphony/Szell)

¶ Tchaikovsky, Piano Concerto No. 1 in B flat minor (Alexis Weissenberg/Paris Orchestra/von Karajan)

¶ 'Volver a Los 17' (Inti Illimani)

¶ Puccini, 'Un bel di vedremo' (from *Madam Butterfly*, Act 2) (Mirella Freni/Vienna Philharmonic/von Karajan)

¶ LUXURY: Painting equipment.

¶ BOOK: Margaret Mitchell, *Gone with the Wind* (in Italian).

18 June 1977
1389 Derek Randall
Cricketer

¶ 'Here Come the Aussies' (Australian Cricket Team 1972)

¶ 'Happy to be on an Island in the Sun' (Demis Roussos)

¶ 'Carolina Moon' (Connie Francis)

¶ 'When Irish Eyes are Smiling' (Bing Crosby)

¶ 'Catch a Falling Star' (Perry Como)

¶ 'Sailing' (Rod Stewart)

*¶ 'The Sun Has got His Hat On' (BBC Dance Orchestra/Hall)

¶ 'The Bumper Song' (The Bumpers)

¶ LUXURY: A bath with warm water.

¶ BOOK: *The Guinness Book of Records*

25 June 1977
1390 Jack Parnell
Bandleader and drummer

¶ 'Daybreak Express' (Duke Ellington and his Orchestra)

¶ 'Sing, Sing, Sing' (Benny Goodman and his Orchestra)

¶ 'Every Tub' (Count Basie and his Orchestra)

¶ Delius, 'Summer Night on the River' (LPO/Beecham)

¶ Ravel, *L'Enfant et les sortilèges* (soloists/French National Radio Orchestra/Bour)

¶ Ravel, *Le tombeau de Couperin* (New York Philharmonic/Boulez)

¶ Bach, Concerto in the Italian Style (BWV 971) (George Malcolm *harpsichord*)

*¶ 'Morning Star' (Hubert Laws *flute*/orchestra/Sebesky)

¶ LUXURY: A very deep, flock-cushioned armchair.

¶ BOOK: A selection of stories by W. W. Jacobs.

2 July 1977
1391 'Miss Read'
Novelist

¶ Mozart, Piano Concerto No. 23 in A (K. 488) (Dennis Matthews/Philharmonia Orchestra/Schwarz)

¶ 'Slow Train' (from *At the Drop of Another Hat*) (Michael Flanders/Donald Swann)

¶ Clarke, 'Trumpet Voluntary' (Alex Harris/Hallé Orchestra/Harty)

¶ Dohnanyi, Rhapsody No. 3 in C major (opus 11) (Joseph Cooper *piano*)

¶ Toye, 'The Haunted Ballroom' (Orchestra Raymonde/Walter)

¶ Gluck, 'What is Life?' (Che faro senza Euridice?) (from *Orfeo ed Euridice*) (Kathleen Ferrier/LSO/Sargent)

¶ 'Thank You, Mister Bach' (BBC Dance Orchestra/Hall)

*¶ Oscar Wilde, *The Importance of Being Earnest* (Act 1) (John Gielgud/Edith Evans)

¶ LUXURY: Exercise books and ballpoint pens.

¶ BOOK: James Woodforde, *The Diary of a Country Parson 1758–1802*

9 July 1977
1392 Clare Francis
Sailor and journalist

*¶ Debussy, 'La Mer' (NPO/Boulez)

¶ Prokofiev, 'Dance of the Knights' (from Ballet *Romeo and Juliet*) (Cleveland Orchestra/Maazel)

¶ 'The Peanut Vendor' (Original Trinidad Steel Band)

¶ 'C'est à Hambourg' (Edith Piaf)

¶ Leoncavallo, 'Vesti la giubba' (from *Pagliacci*, Act 1) (Placido Domingo/LSO/Santi)

¶ Brahms, Symphony No. 4 in E minor (Berlin Philharmonic/von Karajan)

¶ 'Doina de Jale' (Theme from TV series *The Light of Experience*) (Gheorge Zamfir *pan pipes*/ensemble)

¶ Widor, Symphony No. 5 in F minor (toccata) (Fernando Germani *organ*)

¶ LUXURY: A fresh-water shower.

¶ BOOK: A volume on physics.

16 July 1977
1393 Shirley Conran
Designer and writer

¶ 'I'm a Woman' (Peggy Lee)

¶ 'I Can't Get Started' (Bunny Berigan *trumpet* and his Orchestra)

¶ 'Muskrat Ramble' (Louis Armstrong and his Hot Five)

¶ Lennon & McCartney, 'When I'm Sixty-Four' (The Beatles)

¶ 'Career Opportunities' (The Clash)

¶ Mozart, Symphony No. 40 in G minor (K. 550) (English Chamber Orchestra/Barenboim)

*¶ Beethoven, Symphony No. 7 in A major (opus 92) (Berlin Philharmonic/von Karajan)

¶ 'My Old Flame' (Billie Holiday)

¶ LUXURY: Oil painting equipment.

¶ BOOK: *Light on Yoga*, with introduction by Yehudi Menuhin.

23 July 1977
1394 Arthur C. Clarke
Science fiction writer

*¶ Elgar, Violin Concerto in B minor (Yehudi Menuhin/LSO/Elgar)

¶ Grieg, Piano Concerto in A minor (opus 16) (Solomon/Philharmonia Orchestra/Menges)

¶ Vaughan Williams, Sinfonia Antartica (LPO and Choir/Boult)

¶ Rachmaninov, Piano Concerto No. 3 in D minor (Sergei Rachmaninov/Philadelphia Orchestra/Ormandy)

¶ R. Strauss, 'Also Sprach Zarathustra' (Berlin Philharmonic/Böhm)

¶ Sibelius, Symphony No. 2 in D (Philharmonia Orchestra/von Karajan)

¶ Beethoven, Symphony No. 9 in D minor (opus 125) (Vienna Singverein/Berlin Philharmonic/von Karajan)

¶ Bach/Stokowski, Toccata and Fugue in D minor (BWV 565) (Czech Philharmonic/Stokowski)

¶ LUXURY: A solar-powered short-wave radio.

¶ BOOK: *The Golden Treasury*, compiled by Francis Palgrave.

30 July 1977
1395 Billy Connolly
Entertainer

¶ 'Bridgton' (Frankie Miller)

¶ 'Save the Last Dance for Me' (The Drifters)

¶ Lennon, 'Imagine' (John Lennon)

¶ Lennon & McCartney, 'Across the Universe' (The Beatles)

¶ 'The Postman's Knock' (Albion Dance Band)

¶ 'You are My Flower' (Nitty Gritty Dirt Band)

¶ John/Taupin, 'Sorry Seems to be the Hardest Word' (Elton John)

*¶ 'At the Ball That's All' (Laurel & Hardy)

¶ LUXURY: An electrical device to heat shaving foam.

¶ BOOK: Joseph Heller, *Catch 22*

6 August 1977
1396 Jessica Mitford
Writer

¶ 'After the Ball' (Florrie Forde)

¶ 'Sex Appeal Sarah' (Douglas Bynge)

¶ 'Louise' (from film *Innocents in Paris*) (Maurice Chevalier)

*¶ 'Die Moorsoldaten' (Ernst Busch/chorus)

¶ 'The Red Flag' (Centenary Choir/Bush)

¶ 'Lullaby of Broadway' (from film *The Golddiggers of 1935*) (Wini Shaw/chorus)

¶ Berlin, 'Cheek to Cheek' (from film *Top Hat*) (Fred Astaire)

¶ 'You're Gonna Lose Your Girl' (Carroll Gibbons/Savoy Hotel Orphans)

¶ LUXURY: A supply of Gentlemen's Relish.

¶ BOOK: Rose Macaulay, *Orphan Island*

13 August 1977
1397 A. L. Rowse
Historian, biographer and poet

¶ Bach, Brandenburg Concerto No. 5 in D major (BWV 1050) (Stuttgart Chamber Orchestra/Münchinger)

*¶ Byrd, 'Agnus Dei' (from *Mass for Five Voices*) (Christ Church Cathedral Choir, Oxford/Preston)

¶Duparc, 'L'invitation au voyage' (Maggie Teyte/LPO/ Howerd)
¶Beethoven, Sonata No. 30 in E (opus 109) (Artur Schnabel *piano*)
¶Tchaikovsky, 'Polonaise' (from *Eugene Onegin*) (New York Philharmonic/Bernstein)
¶Elgar, Cello Concerto in E minor (Pablo Casals/BBC Symphony/Boult)
¶T. S. Eliot, 'Death by Water' (from *The Wasteland*) (T. S. Eliot)
¶'This was Their Finest Hour' (speech, 18 June 1940) (Sir Winston Churchill)
¶LUXURY: Georges Seurat, *Sunday on the Island of La Grande Jatte*
¶BOOK: Marcel Proust, *À la recherche du temps perdu*

20 August 1977
1398 Deborah Kerr (2nd appearance)
Actress
*¶Dvořák, Symphony No. 9 in E minor (New World) (Vienna Philharmonic/Kertesz)
¶'She' (Gram Parsons)
¶Lennon & McCartney, 'The Fool on the Hill' (Sergio Mendes and Brasil 77)
¶'Historia de un amor' (Lucho Gatica/Jose Sabre Marroquin and his Orchestra)
¶Fauré, 'Sanctus' (from *Requiem*) (King's College Chapel Choir/NPO/Willcocks)
¶'Fiesta en Sevilla' (Paco Peña *guitar*)
¶'Gentle on My Mind' (Glen Campbell)
¶Bach, Toccata and Fugue in D minor (BWV 565) (Nicholas Danby *organ*)
¶LUXURY: Wool and a crochet hook.
¶BOOK: *The Oxford English Dictionary*

27 August 1977
1399 Dannie Abse
Poet
¶Beethoven, Sonata No. 7 in D (opus 10, no. 3) (Alfred Brendel *piano*)
¶Schubert, String quintet in C (D. 956) (William Pleeth *cello*/ Amadeus String Quartet)

¶Weil, 'Surabaya Johnny' (from *Happy End*) (Lotte Lenya)
¶Mozart, Clarinet Quintet in A (K. 581) (Gervase de Peyer/ Amadeus String Quartet)
¶Mozart, Piano Concerto No. 9 in E flat (K. 271) (Daniel Barenboim *piano and conducting*/English Chamber Orchestra)
¶Bach, Violin Concerto No. 2 in E (BWV 1042) (Isaac Stern/ New York Philharmonic/ Bernstein)
*¶Mozart, String Quintet in G minor (K. 516) (Cecil Aronowitz *viola*/Amadeus String Quartet)
¶Beethoven, String Quartet No. 12 in E flat (opus 127) (Budapest Quartet)
¶LUXURY: A bed.
¶BOOK: The collected poetry of W. H. Auden.

3 September 1977
1400 Dame Daphne du Maurier
Writer
¶Grieg, Piano Concerto in A minor (Géza Anda/Berlin Philharmonic/Kubelik)
¶Rachmaninov, 'Rhapsody on a Theme of Paganini' (opus 43) (Julius Katchen (*piano*/LPO/ Boult)
¶Debussy, 'Claire de lune' (from *Suite bergamasque*) (Eileen Joyce *piano*)
¶Ravel, 'Pavane pour une infante défunte' (LSO/ Monteux)
¶Vaughan Williams, 'Fantasia on Greensleeves' (Sinfonia of London/Barbirolli)
¶Aznavour, 'She' (Charles Aznavour)
*¶Khachaturian, *Spartacus* (Vienna Philharmonic/ Khachaturian)
¶'Sailing' (ship's company and band of HMS *Ark Royal*)
¶LUXURY: Whisky and ginger ale.
¶BOOKS: Jane Austen, *Mansfield Park*, *Pride and Prejudice* and *Sense and Sensibility*

10 September 1977
1401 Robin Richmond
Organist and entertainer
¶'The Chimes of Swing' (David Carroll and his Orchestra)
¶Bonnet, 'Étude de concert' (Nicolas Kynaston *organ*)
¶Lehár, 'Meine Lippen, sie küssen so heiss' (from *Giuditta*) (Anneliese Rothenberger)
*¶Delius, 'The Walk to the Paradise Gardens' (from *A Village Romeo and Juliet*) (Hallé Orchestra/Barbirolli)
¶Speech at the Oxford Union (Gerard Hoffnung)
¶'Running Wild' (Benny Goodman Quartet)
¶'I'll Follow My Secret Heart' (from *Conversation Piece*) (Buddy Cole *cinema organ*)
¶Grofé 'Mardi Gras' (from *Mississippi Suite*) (Hollywood Bowl Symphony/Slatkin)
¶LUXURY: The Royal Albert Hall organ.
¶BOOK: Collected Giles cartoons.

17 September 1977
1402 Michael Croft
Founder and director of the National Youth Theatre
¶'Get Out of Town' and 'Night and Day' (Hutch)
¶Tchaikovsky, Piano Concerto No. 1 in B flat minor (Solomon/ Hallé Orchestra/Harty)
¶Grieg, Piano Concerto in A minor (opus 16) (Moura Lympany/Philharmonia Orchestra/Menges)
¶Coward, 'Any Little Fish' and 'I'll See You Again' (Noël Coward)
¶'One for My Baby' (Frank Sinatra)
*¶John/Taupin, 'Candle in the Wind' (Elton John)
¶'As Time Goes By' (from film *Casablanca*) (Harry Nilsson/ Gordon Jenkins and his Orchestra)
¶Ravel, 'Bolero' (Boston Pops Orchestra/Fiedler)
¶LUXURY: A still for making whisky.
¶BOOK: The collected poetry of Rudyard Kipling.

24 September 1977
1403 Mike Brearley
Cricketer

¶ Brahms, Clarinet Sonata in E flat (opus 120, no. 2) (Gervase de Peyer/Daniel Barenboim *piano*)

¶ Johnson/Shakespeare, 'Where the Bee Sucks' (Alfred Deller/Deller Consort)

¶ Bach, 'Contrapunctus XII' (from *The Art of Fugue*, BWV 1080) (Lionel Rogg *organ*)

*¶ Beethoven, String Quartet in C sharp minor opus 131 (Amadeus String Quartet)

¶ Haydn, *Mass in D minor* (King's College Chapel Choir/LSO/Willcocks)

¶ Mozart, *Don Giovanni* (Act 2, Scene 8 sextet) (soloists/Royal Opera House Orchestra, Covent Garden/Colin Davis)

¶ Carmichael, 'Georgia on My Mind' (Ray Charles)

¶ Bach, 'Gottes Zeit (Actus Tragicus)' (Cantata No. 106) (Bach Guild Choir and Orchestra/Prohaska)

¶ LUXURY: Golf clubs and balls.

¶ BOOK: A large anthology of English poetry.

1 October 1977
1404 Louis Frémaux
Conductor

¶ Massenet, *Le Cid* (ballet music) (City of Birmingham Symphony/Frémaux)

¶ 'Le chant des partisans' (Germaine Sablon)

¶ 'March of the Foreign Legion' (Foreign Legion Band)

¶ Gilles, 'Introit' (from *Requiem*) (Philippe Caillard Chorus/Jean-François Paillard Instrumental Ensemble/Frémaux)

¶ Berlioz, 'Marche au supplice' (from Symphonie fantastique) (Monte Carlo Opera Orchestra/Frémaux)

¶ Bizet, 'Love Duet' (from *Les pêcheurs de perles*, Act 2, Scene 3) (Martha Angelici/Henri Legay/Orchestra of Théâtre National de l'Opéra-Comique/Cluytens)

*¶ Britten, 'Fanfare' (from *Les Illuminations*, opus 18) Peter Pears/English Chamber Orchestra/Britten)

¶ Berlioz, 'Rex Tremendae' (from *Grande messe des morts*) (City of Birmingham Orchestra and Chorus/Frémaux)

¶ LUXURY: Manuscript paper and pens.

¶ BOOK: Pierre Louys, *Les chansons de Bilitis*

8 October 1977
1405 Molly Weir
Actress

¶ Gossec, 'Tambourin' (James Galway *flute*/National Philharmonic/Gerhardt)

¶ Donizetti, 'Mad Scene' (from *Lucia di Lammermoor*) (Joan Sutherland/Paris Conservatoire Orchestra/Santi)

¶ Lerner & Loewe, 'Just You Wait' (from *My Fair Lady*) (Audrey Hepburn [Marni Nixon])

¶ Bruch, 'Scottish Fantasia' (opus 46) (David Oistrakh *violin*/LSO/Horenstein)

¶ 'Just A-Wearying' for You' (Paul Robeson)

¶ Rossini, 'Duetto buffo di due gatti' (Victoria de los Angeles/Elisabeth Schwarzkopf/Gerald Moore *piano*)

¶ Gluck, 'Che faro senza Euridice' (from *Orfeo ed Euridice*) (Teresa Berganza/Royal Opera House Orchestra, Covent Garden/Gibson)

*¶ 'All in The April Evening' (Glasgow Orpheus Choir/Roberton)

¶ LUXURY: A typewriter, spare ribbons and paper.

¶ BOOK: Compton Mackenzie, *The Four Winds of Love*

15 October 1977
1406 Barry Sheene
World champion of 500cc motorcycle racing

¶ Bacharach, 'Do You Know the Way to San José?' (Dionne Warwick)

¶ 'Crackerbox Palace' (George Harrison)

¶ 'New Kid in Town' (The Eagles)

¶ 'Don't Let the Sun Catch You Crying' (José Feliciano)

¶ 'Nights on Broadway' (Candi Staton)

¶ 'In the Mood' (Glenn Miller and his Orchestra)

¶ 'Sunshine After the Rain' (Elkie Brooks)

*¶ 'If You Should Leave Me Now' (Chicago)

¶ LUXURY: An effigy of Denis Healey and a supply of pins.

¶ BOOK: A study book of six languages.

22 October 1977
1407 Claire Rayner
Novelist, journalist and broadcaster

¶ Mendelssohn, 'Song Without Words' (opus 62, no. 6) (Daniel Barenboim *piano*)

¶ 'With My Little Wigger Wagger' (Arthur Elwood)

¶ Sondheim, 'Another Hundred People' (from *Company*) (Pamela Myers)

*¶ Lalo, Symphonie espagnole in D minor (opus 21) (Henryk Szeryng *violin*/CSO/Hendl)

¶ Shakespeare, *Hamlet* (Act 1, Scene 2) (from film) (Laurence Olivier/Philharmonia Orchestra/Mathieson)

¶ Porter, 'Just One of Those Things' (from *Jubilee*) (Ella Fitzgerald)

¶ 'Honeysuckle Rose' (Django Reinhardt *guitar*/Stephane Grappelli *violin*/Quintet of the Hot Club of France)

¶ Rodrigo, Concierto de Aranjuez (John Williams *guitar*/Philadelphia Orchestra/Ormandy)

¶ LUXURY: A bath with hot water, soap and towels.

¶ BOOK: A guide to boat-building.

29 October 1977
1408 Wayne Sleep
Dancer and entertainer

¶ Beethoven, 'Choral Fantasia' (Alfred Brendel *piano*/LPO and Choir/Haitink)

¶ Lennon & McCartney, 'All You Need is Love' (The Beatles)

¶ Handel, 'O Thou That Tellest' (from *Messiah*) (James Bowman/King's College Chapel Choir/Academy of St Martin-in-the-Fields/Willcocks)
¶ Stravinsky, *The Firebird* (Columbia Symphony/Stravinsky)
¶ 'As Time Goes By' (from film *Casablanca*) (Harry Nilsson)
¶ Verdi, 'Dies Irae' (from *Requiem*) (Philharmonia Orchestra and Chorus/Giulini)
*¶ 'La belle histoire d'amour' (Edith Piaf)
¶ Coates, 'By the Sleepy Lagoon' (Glenn Miller and his Orchestra)
¶ LUXURY: Poppy seeds.
¶ BOOK: An atlas of the stars.

5 November 1977
1409 Richard Adams
Novelist
¶ Palestrina, *Missa Papae Marcelli* (King's College Chapel Choir/Willcocks)
¶ Weelkes, 'As Vesta was from Latmos Hill descending' (Purcell Consort of Voices/Burgess)
¶ Bach, Goldberg Variations (aria, BWV 988) (Helmut Walcha *harpsichord*)
¶ Haydn, String Quartet in E flat (opus 64, no. 6) (Amadeus String Quartet)
*¶ Mozart, 'Non so più' (from *The Marriage of Figaro*) (Yvonne Minton/BBC Symphony/Davis)
¶ Beethoven, Symphony No. 4 in B flat major (opus 60) (CSO/Solti)
¶ Schubert, Trio No. 1 in B flat (D. 898) (Yehudi Menuhin *violin*/Hephzibah Menuhin *piano*/Maurice Gendron *cello*)
¶ R. Strauss, 'Du wirst mich Befreien' (from *Ariadne auf Naxos*) (Gundula Janowitz/Dresden State Opera/Kempe)
¶ LUXURY: Leonardo da Vinci's painting of the Annunciation.
¶ BOOK: Marcel Proust, *À la recherche du temps perdu*

12 November 1977
1410 Professor Alan Gemmell
Botanist, biologist and gardener
¶ 'My Love is Like a Red, Red Rose' (Kenneth McKellar)
¶ Sibelius, 'Finlandia' (Hallé Orchestra/Barbirolli)
¶ 'Manhattan' (from *Garrick Gaieties*) (Ella Fitzgerald)
¶ 'June in January' (from film *Here is My Heart*) (Bing Crosby)
¶ T. S. Eliot, *Murder in the Cathedral* (excerpt) (Robert Donat)
*¶ Mendelssohn, 'The Hebrides Overture' (Berlin Philharmonic/von Karajan)
¶ Gershwin, 'Lady be Good' (from *Lady be Good*) (Yehudi Menuhin and Stephane Grappelli *violins*/Alan Clare Trio)
¶ 'O Come All Ye Faithful' (Black Dyke Mills Band/Huddersfield Choral Society/Newsome)
¶ LUXURY: Paper and pencils.
¶ BOOK: A book on elementary calculus.

19 November 1977
1411 Peter Ustinov (3rd appearance)
Writer and actor
¶ Berlioz, 'Le spectre de la rose' (from *Les nuits d'été*) (Janet Baker/NPO/Barbirolli)
¶ Prokofiev, Violin Concerto No. 2 in G minor (Henryk Szeryng/LSO/Rozhdestvensky)
¶ Mahler, 'Oft denk'ich' (from *Kindertotenlieder*) (Kathleen Ferrier/Vienna Philharmonic/Walter)
¶ Beethoven, Piano Concerto No. 3 in C minor (Wilhelm Kempff/Berlin Philharmonic/Leitner)
*¶ Mozart, 'In diesen heil'gen Hallen' (from *The Magic Flute*) (Martti Talvela/Vienna Philharmonic/Solti)
¶ Speech on the Budget, 1909 (H. H. Asquith)
¶ 'Los Dorados de Pancho Villa' (Trio Mexico)

¶ Mussorgsky, 'Where are You, Little Star?' (Mascia Predit/Italian Radio Orchestra/Markevich)
¶ LUXURY: A bath with solar-heated water.
¶ BOOK: A blank book with pencils.

26 November 1977
1412 Winston Graham
Novelist
¶ Schubert, Impromptu in A flat (opus 142, no. 2) (Alfred Brendel *piano*)
¶ Rachmaninov, Piano Concerto No. 2 in C minor (Benno Moiseiwitsch/Philharmonia Orchestra/Rignold)
¶ Beethoven, Piano Concerto No. 3 in C minor (Artur Rubinstein/Boston Symphony/Leinsdorf)
¶ Speech at the Oxford Union (Gerard Hoffnung)
¶ 'Recurdos de Ypacarai' (Trio Los Paraguayos)
¶ 'Kisses Sweeter than wine' (Jimmie Rodgers)
*¶ Vivaldi, *The Four Seasons* (opus 8) (Pinchas Zukerman *violin and conducting*/English Chamber Orchestra)
¶ Saint-Saëns, 'The Nightingale and the Rose' (Rita Streich/Berlin Radio Symphony/Gaebel)
¶ LUXURY: Many exercise books and ballpoint pens.
¶ BOOK: Benham's *Book of Quotations*

3 December 1977
1413 Grace Bumbry
Opera singer
¶ 'Teach Me Tonight' (Erroll Garner *piano*)
*¶ Schubert, Impromptu in G flat (opus 90, no. 3) (Dinu Lipatti *piano*)
¶ Bellini, 'Casta diva' (from *Norma*, Act 1) (Maria Callas/La Scala Orchestra/Serafin)
¶ 'Feelings' (Shirley Bassey)
¶ Chopin, Scherzo No. 3 in C sharp minor (opus 39) (Aleksander Slobodyanik *piano*)
¶ 'Grande, grande, grande' (Mina)
¶ 'It's Impossible' (Perry Como)

¶Massenet, 'Pleurez, mes yeux' (from *Le Cid*, Act 3) (Grace Bumbry/New York Opera Orchestra/Queler)
¶LUXURY: Perfume.
¶BOOK: *The Letters of Giuseppe Verdi*, edited by Charles Osborne.

10 December 1977
1414 Phil Drabble
Countryman and naturalist
¶Song of a curlew (recorded by Ludwig Koch)
¶Seeger, 'Little Boxes' (Pete Seeger)
¶'Misalliance' (Michael Flanders/Donald Swan)
¶'Cinderella Rockefella' (Esther & Abi Ofarim)
¶'What Have They Done to the Rain?' (Judith Durham/The Seekers)
¶Porter, 'Let's Do It' (from *Paris*) (Noël Coward)
¶'Wish You Were Here' (The King's Singers)
*¶Recording of the song of the blackbird
¶LUXURY: A set of bird-ringing tools, including rings.
¶BOOK: A shorthand instruction book with paper and pens.

17 December 1977
1415 Dennis Potter
Television playwright
¶'Immortal, Invisible, God Only Wise' (Treorchy Male Choir)
*¶'Sons of the Brave' (GUS [Footwear] Band)
¶'You Couldn't be Cuter' (Al Bowlly/Lew Stone and his Band)
¶'Twelfth Street Rag' (Duke Ellington and his Orchestra)
¶'Somebody Stole My Gal' (Reginald Dixon *cinema organ*)
¶'The Clouds Will Soon Roll By' (Elsie Carlisle/Ambrose and his Orchestra)
¶'Eadie was a Lady' (Al Bowlly/Nat Gonella/Lew Stone and his Band)
¶'Roses of Picardy' (Gracie Fields)
¶LUXURY: Edward Hopper's painting, *Gas*
¶BOOK: The collected essays of William Hazlitt.

24 December 1977
1416 Sir Alec Guinness (2nd appearance)
Actor
¶Seeger, 'Little Boxes' (Pete Seeger)
¶Poulenc, Organ Concerto in G minor (Maurice Duruflé/French National Radio Orchestra/Prêtre)
¶'Por ti mi corazon' (John Williams *guitar*)
¶Haydn, Symphony No. 85 in B flat major (Philharmonia Hungarica/Dorati)
¶Mahler, Symphony No. 5 in C sharp minor (CSO/Solti)
¶Satie, 'Trois morceaux en forme de poire' (Aldo Ciccolini *piano*)
*¶Beethoven, Sonata No. 32 in C minor (opus 111) (Daniel Barenboim *piano*)
¶'Te Lucis Ante Terminum' (Compline hymn) (Monks of Abbey Saint-Pierre de Solesmes)
¶LUXURY: A leather wallet containing photographs of his family and dog.
¶BOOK: *The Oxford Anthology of 20th-Century Verse*

31 December 1977
1417 Dorothy Edwards
Children's writer
¶Smetana, 'The Moldau' (from *Ma Vlast*) (Boston Symphony/Kubelik)
¶'St Louis Blues' (Bing Crosby/Duke Ellington Orchestra)
¶Mendelssohn, *A Midsummer Night's Dream* (scherzo) (RPO/Vonk)
¶Dorothy Edwards, 'My Naughty Little Sister' (Kaye Webb)
¶Beethoven, Piano Concerto No. 4 in G major (opus 58) (Clifford Curzon/Vienna Philharmonic/Knappertsbusch)
¶de Plata, 'Fandangos' (Manitas de Plata *guitar*)
¶Sibelius, 'The Swan of Tuonela' (Hallé Orchestra/Barbirolli)
*¶Handel, 'Hallelujah Chorus' (from *Messiah*) (LSO and Chorus/Boult)
¶LUXURY: A typewriter and paper.
¶BOOK: *The Oxford Book of English Verse*

7 January 1978
1418 Franco Zeffirelli
Director and designer of plays, operas and films
*¶Bizet, 'Les tringles des sistres tintaient' (from *Carmen*, Act 2) (Maria Callas/Paris Opera Orchestra/Prêtre)
¶Beethoven, Symphony No. 9 in D minor (opus 125) (Berlin Philharmonic/von Karajan)
¶Donizetti, 'Spargi d'amaro pianto' (mad scene from *Lucia di Lammermoor*, Act 3) (Joan Sutherland/Santa Cecilia Orchestra, Rome/Pritchard)
¶'Only You' (The Platters)
¶Shakespeare, 'Once More Unto the Breach' (from *Henry V*, Act 3) (Laurence Olivier)
¶'Salve Regina' (Choir of Benedictine Abbey of Santo Domingo de Silas)
¶'Let's Twist Again' (Chubby Checker)
¶Rossini, *The Barber of Seville* (overture) (NBC Symphony/Toscanini)
¶LUXURY: Perfume.
¶BOOK: Leo Tolstoy, *War and Peace*

14 January 1978
1419 Omar Sharif
Actor
*¶'All the Way' (Frank Sinatra)
¶'Wasted' (Donna Summer)
¶'Nevertheless I'm in Love with You' (Liza Minnelli)
¶'Wish You Were Here' (Pink Floyd)
¶'La vie en rose' (Edith Piaf)
¶'Let the Music Play' (Barry White)
¶'Seul sur son étoile' (Gilbert Bécaud)
¶Styne, 'Don't Rain on My Parade' (from *Funny Girl*) (Barbra Streisand)
¶LUXURY: Several decks of cards.
¶BOOK: Antoine de Saint-Exupéry, *The Little Prince*

21 January 1978
1420 Alan Coren
Humorous writer and editor of
Punch
¶ 'Lovesick Blues' (Emmett
Miller and his Georgia
Crackers)
*¶ Bach, Double Concerto in D
minor (BWV 1043) (David &
Igor Oistrakh *violins*/RPO/
Goossens)
¶ 'Margie' (Bix Beiderbecke and
his Gang)
¶ 'The 2000-Year-Old Man'
(Carl Reiner/Mel Brooks)
¶ 'Fräulein Annie' (Marlene
Dietrich)
¶ Beethoven, Sonata No. 29 in B
flat (opus 106) (Alfred Brendel
piano)
¶ Porter, 'Get Out of Town'
(from *Leave It to Me*) (Ella
Fitzgerald)
¶ 'Tittle Tattle Rag' (Instant
Sunshine)
¶ LUXURY: A typewriter and
paper.
¶ BOOK: *The Oxford English
Dictionary*

28 January 1978
1421 Raymond Mander &
Joe Mitchenson
Writers and theatre historians
*¶ Wagner, 'The Ride of the
Valkyries' (from *Die Walküre*)
(Vienna Philharmonic/Solti)
¶ George Bernard Shaw, *The
Apple Cart* (interlude) (Noël
Coward/Margaret Leighton)
¶ Offenbach, 'Fly Duet' (from
Orpheus in the Underworld)
(June Bronhili/Eric Shilling/
Sadler's Wells Opera
Orchestra/Faris)
¶ Tchaikovsky, *Swan Lake*
(National Philharmonic/
Bonynge)
¶ 'Cabaret' (from *Cabaret*) (Judi
Dench)
¶ Yvonne Arnaud introducing
and playing Bach's Organ
Fugue (BWV 578) on the piano
¶ Shakespeare, 'Advice to the
Players' (from *Hamlet*, Act 3,
Scene 2) (John Gielgud)
¶ Monckton, *The Arcadians*
(overture) (Gilbert Vinter and
his Orchestra)

¶ LUXURIES: (JM) a couch for
sunbathing and some coconut
oil; (RM) an ultra-sensitive
receiver to hear voices from the
past.
¶ BOOKS: (JM) photograph
albums of all his friends; (RM) a
complete set of *Who's Who in the
Theatre*.

4 February 1978
1422 Spike Milligan
(2nd appearance)
Comedian, actor and writer
¶ Respighi, *Feste Romane* (NBC
Symphony/Toscanini)
¶ 'Women of Ireland' (from film
Barry Lyndon) (The Chieftains)
¶ Debussy, 'En bâteau' (from
Petite Suite) (John Ogdon and
Brenda Lucas *pianos*)
*¶ Lennon & McCartney,
'Yesterday' (The Beatles)
¶ Shostakovich, Symphony No.
6 in B minor (Leningrad
Philharmonic/Mravinsky)
¶ 'The Shadow of Your Smile'
(from film *The Sandpiper*)
(Frank Sinatra)
¶ Grieg, *Shepherd's Boy* (from
Lyric Suite) (LSO/Black)
¶ 'Theme from *The Snow Goose*'
(from film) (LSO/Welch)
¶ LUXURY: A Barclaycard.
¶ BOOK: Alvin Toffler, *Future
Shock*

11 February 1978
1423 Amadeus String
Quartet
**(Norbert Brainin, Siegmund
Nissel, Peter Schidlof, Martin
Lovett)**
¶ (NB) Beethoven, Symphony
No. 7 in A major (opus 92)
(New York Philharmonic/
Toscanini)
¶ (SN) Mozart, 'Voi che sapete'
(from *Marriage of Figaro*, Act 2)
(Teresa Berganza/LSO/
Pritchard)
¶ (PS) Mozart, 'Ach, ich fühls'
(from *The Magic Flute*, Act 2)
(Tiana Lemnitz/Berlin
Philharmonic/Beecham)

¶ (ML) Schumann, Cello
Concerto in A minor (opus 129)
(Pablo Casals/Prades Festival
Orchestra/Ormandy)
¶ (NB) Schubert, String Quintet
in C major (opus 163) (William
Pleeth *cello*/Amadeus String
Quartet)
¶ (SN) Schubert, 'Nur wer die
Sehnsucht kennt' (*Mignon III*,
D. 877) (Janet Baker/Gerald
Moore *piano*)
¶ (PS) J. Strauss, 'Csárdás'
(from *Die Fledermaus*) (Hilde
Gueden/Vienna Philharmonic/
Krauss)
¶ (ML) Bach, 'Et Resurrexit'
(from *Mass in B minor*, BWV
232) (Munich Bach Choir and
Orchestra/Richter)
¶ LUXURIES: (ML) a projector,
screen and eight films; (PS) his
viola and bow; (SN) a transistor
radio; (NB) paper and pencils.
¶ BOOKS: (ML) Marcel Proust, *À
la recherche du temps perdu*; (PS)
a book on instrument-making;
(SN) Dante's *Divine Comedy* (in
Italian) and an Italian
dictionary; (NB) Leo Tolstoy,
War and Peace.

18 February 1978
1424 The Rt Hon.
Margaret Thatcher
Leader of the Opposition
*¶ Beethoven, Piano Concerto
No. 5 in E flat major (Emperor)
(Alfred Brendel/LPO/Haitink)
¶ Dvořák, arr. Boddington,
'Going Home' (based on the
Largo from Symphony No. 5 in
E minor, (New World)) (GUS
[Footwear] Band/Boddington)
¶ Verdi, 'Grand March' (from
Aida, Act 2) (Rome Opera
House Orchestra/Mehta)
¶ 'Introducing Tobacco to
Civilisation' (Bob Newhart)
¶ Kern, 'Smoke Gets in Your
Eyes' (from *Roberta*) (Irene
Dunne)
¶ Beethoven, 'Be Not Afraid'
(from *Elijah*) (Gwyneth Jones/
NPO/Frühbeck de Burgos)
¶ Saint-Preux, Andante for
Trumpet (Pierre Thibaud/
orchestra/Saint-Preux)

¶Mascagni, 'Easter Hymn' (from *Cavalleria rusticana*) (Royal Opera House Orchestra and Chorus, Covent Garden/Gardelli)

¶LUXURY: A photograph album of her children.

¶BOOK: Michael Allaby, *The Survival Handbook*

25 February 1978
1425 Professor J. H. Plumb
Historian

¶Handel, Zadok the Priest (Coronation anthem) (King's College Chapel Choir/English Chamber Orchestra/Willcocks)

¶Handel, 'O Fatal Day' (from *Saul*) (James Bowman/English Chamber Orchestra/Mackerras)

¶Chopin, Nocturne No. 4 in F (opus 15, no. 1) (Vladimir Ashkenazy *piano*)

¶Mozart, Sinfonia Concertante in E flat (K. 364) (Alan Loveday *violin*/Stephen Shingles *viola*/Academy of St Martin-in-the-fields/Marriner)

*¶Beethoven, Piano Concerto No. 4 in G major (opus 58) (Solomon/Philharmonia Orchestra/Cluytens)

¶Schubert, String Quartet No. 13 in A minor (D. 804) (Amadeus String Quartet)

¶'Mood Indigo' (Duke Ellington and his Orchestra)

¶'Petite fleur' (Sidney Bechet *soprano saxophone* and his All-Stars)

¶LUXURY: A dozen cases of Château Latour '61.

¶BOOK: Voltaire's correspondence.

4 March 1978
1426 Paco Peña
Flamenco guitarist

¶'Fiesta por Bulerias' (La Peria de Cadiz)

¶Beethoven, 'Agnus Dei' (from *Missa Solemnis*) (Elisabeth Schwarzkopf/Christa Ludwig/Nicolai Gedda/Nicola Zaccaria/Vienna Singverein/Berlin Philharmonic/von Karajan)

¶'Hier encore' (Yesterday when I was young) (Charles Aznavour)

*¶Bach, Prelude, Fugue and Allegro in E flat major (BWV 998) (John Williams *guitar*)

¶Brahms, Violin Concerto In D (Itzhak Perlman/CSO/Giulini)

¶Chopin, Waltz No. 7 in C sharp minor (opus 62, no. 2) (Dinu Lipatti *piano*)

¶'Killing Me Softly with His Song' (Cleo Laine/John Williams *guitar*)

¶'Ya vienen los reyes' (Choir of Los Pedroches, Cordoba)

¶LUXURY: A painting of his family by Aurelio.

¶BOOK: The collected poetry of Frederico Garcia Lorca.

11 March 1978
1427 The Rt Rev. and Rt Hon. Gerald Ellison
Bishop of London

*¶Elgar, Symphony No. 1 in A flat (LPO/Boult)

¶Handel, Suite No. 5 in E (Wanda Landowska *harpsichord*)

¶Gilbert & Sullivan, *Patience* (Act 1 finale) (soloists/D'Oyly Carte Opera Chorus and Orchestra/Godfrey)

¶'Thank You Very Much' (Scaffold)

¶R. Strauss, 'Zueignung' (opus 10, no. 1) (Gérard Souzay/Dalton Baldwin *piano*)

¶Boëllmann, Variations for Cello and Orchestra (Anthony Pini/Royal Symphony/Batten)

¶Tchaikovsky, 'Tatiana's Letter Scene' (from *Eugene Onegin*) (Galina Vishnevskaya/Bolshoi Opera Orchestra/Rostropovich)

¶Beethoven, 'Agnus Dei' (from *Missa Solemnis*) (Vienna Singverein/Berlin Philharmonic/von Karajan)

¶LUXURY: A trombone.

¶BOOK: George Bernard Shaw, *Music Criticisms 1888–89*

18 March 1978
1428 George MacDonald Fraser
Writer

¶'The Smugglers' Song' (Peter Dawson)

¶'John Peel' (march of the Border Regiment) (Royal Military School of Music, Kneller Hall)

¶'My Very Good Friend, the Milkman' (Fats Waller and his Rhythm)

¶Weill/Brecht, 'Kanonensong' (from *The Threepenny Opera*) (Willy Trenck-Trebitsch/Kurt Gerron/Lewis-Ruth Band/Mackeben)

¶'Cock o' the North' (3rd Battalion Gordon Highlanders Pipes and Drums)

¶'Sword for Your Supper' (from film *The Three Musketeers*) (Michel Legrand and his Orchestra)

¶'Give Me the Bus Fare to Laxey' (Mike Williams and Laury Kermode *harmonicas*)

*¶Korngold, 'Theme from *The Adventures of Robin Hood*' (from film) (National Philharmonic/Gerhardt)

¶LUXURY: A typewriter, ribbons and paper.

¶BOOK: *The Oxford English Dictionary*

25 March 1978
1429 David Wall
Ballet dancer

¶Trad. arranged Canteloube, 'Baïlèro' (from *Songs of the Auvergne*) (Victoria de los Angeles/Lamoureux Orchestra/Jacquillat)

¶Puccini, 'Chi il bel sogno di Doretta' (from *La Rondine*) (Leontyne Price/Rome Opera House Orchestra/Fabritiis)

¶'Voodoo Chile' (Jimi Hendrix Experience)

¶Mahler, 'Von der Schönheit' (from *Das Lied von der Erde*) (Kathleen Ferrier/Vienna Philharmonic/Walter)

*¶Sibelius, Kullervo Symphony (opus 7) (Helsinki University Male Voice Choir/Bournemouth Symphony/Berglund)

¶ Rachmaninov, 'The Isle of the Dead' (opus 29) (LSO/Previn)
¶ Poulenc, Concerto in G minor for Organ, Strings and Timpani (Maurice Duruflé *organ*/French National Radio Orchestra/Prêtre)
¶ John/Taupin, 'Candle in the Wind' (Elton John)
¶ LUXURY: A carbonated-drink maker and a supply of flavourings.
¶ BOOK: A large, comprehensive book on Claude Monet.

1 April 1978
1430 Felicity Kendal
Actress
¶ Marcello, Oboe Concerto in D minor (Heinz Holliger/Dresden State Orchestra/Negri)
*¶ Beethoven, Violin Concerto in D major (opus 61) (Pinchas Zukerman/CSO/Barenboim)
¶ Hamlisch, 'One' (from *A Chorus Line*) (Broadway cast)
¶ Cimarosa, Oboe Concerto in G (Pierre Pierlot/I Solisti Veneti/Scimone)
¶ Sanz, 'Pavanas' (Julian Bream *guitar*)
¶ Schubert, Symphony No. 8 in B minor (Unfinished) (Berlin Philharmonic/von Karajan)
¶ Albinoni/Giazotto, Adagio in G minor for Organ and Strings (Maria Teresa Garatti *organ*/I Musici)
¶ 'Misty Roses' (Tim Hardin)
¶ LUXURY: Perfume.
¶ BOOK: The plays of George Bernard Shaw.

8 April 1978
1431 Les Dawson
Comedian
*¶ Ravel, 'Pavane pour une infante défunte' (Suisse Romande Orchestra/Ansermet)
¶ 'Matchstick Men and Matchstick Cats and Dogs' (Brian & Michael)
¶ 'Non, je ne regrette rien' (Edith Piaf)
¶ 'Passing Strangers' (Sarah Vaughan/Billy Eckstine/Orchestra/Mooney)
¶ 'You Make Me Feel Brand New' (The Stylistics)
¶ 'The Day I Drank a Glass of Water' (W. C. Fields)

¶ Lloyd Webber/Rice, 'Don't Cry for Me, Argentina' (from *Evita*) (Julie Covington/LPO/Bowles)
¶ Chopin, Étude in C minor (opus 10, no. 12) (Sviatoslav Richter *piano*)
¶ LUXURY: A piece of Georgian furniture.
¶ BOOK: Nevil Shute, *Trustee from the Toolroom*

15 April 1978
1432 Sir John Glubb (Glubb Pasha)
Writer and former Commander of the Arab Legion
¶ 'Wings' (march past of the Royal Engineers) (Royal Engineers Band)
¶ Sinding, 'Rustle of Spring' (Joseph Cooper *piano*)
¶ Gilbert & Sullivan, 'I Have a Song to Sing-o' (from *The Yeomen of the Guard*) (John Reed/Elizabeth Harwood/RPO/Sargent)
¶ Verdi, Ai nostri monti (Home to Our Mountains) (from *Il trovatore*) (Charles Craig/Patricia Johnson/Sadlers Wells Orchestra/Moores)
¶ 'Sweet Lass of Richmond Hill' (Kenneth McKellar)
¶ Gluck, 'Che faro senza Euridice?' (What is Life?) (from *Orfeo ed Euridice*) (Kathleen Ferrier/LSO/Sargent)
*¶ Mozart, 'Serenade in G' (*Eine Kleine Nachtmusik*) (English Chamber Orchestra/Barenboim)
¶ Bach, 'Jesu, Joy of Man's Desiring' (from Cantata 147) (Harry Secombe)
¶ LUXURY: Paper and ballpoint pens.
¶ BOOK: *Other Men's Flowers*, compiled by Lord Wavell.

22 April 1978
1433 Robert Hardy
Actor
¶ Schubert, Symphony No. 2 in B flat major (Berlin Philharmonic/Böhm)
¶ 'Two Ladies in de Shade of de Banana Tree' (from *The House of Flowers*) (Pearl Bailey)

¶ Trad. arranged Canteloube, 'Obal, din lou limouzi' (from *Songs of the Auvergne*) (Victoria de los Angeles/Lamoureux Orchestra/Jacquillat)
¶ Brahms, Double Concerto in A minor (opus 102) (David Oistrakh *violin*/Mstislav Rostropovich *cello*/Cleveland Orchestra/Szell)
¶ Paganini, *Twenty-Four Caprices* (no. 9) (Itzhak Perlman *violin*)
¶ Sibelius, Symphony No. 7 in C minor (RPO/Beecham)
*¶ Beethoven, String Quartet No. 13 in B flat major (opus 130) (Amadeus String Quartet)
¶ LUXURY: A Greek sculpture of a female head.
¶ BOOK: A French dictionary.

29 April 1978
1434 Itzhak Perlman
Violinist
¶ Schubert, 'Das Fischermädchen' (from *Schwanengesang*) (Dietrich Fischer-Dieskau/Gerald Moore *piano*)
¶ Sinding, Suite in A minor (opus 10) (Jascha Heifetz *violin*/Los Angeles Philharmonic/Wallenstein)
¶ Lennon & McCartney, 'I'm Looking Through You' (The Beatles)
¶ Beethoven, String Quartet No. 13 in B flat major (opus 130) (Juilliard Quartet)
¶ Mozart, 'Dies Bildnis ist Bezau Bernd schön' (from *The Magic Flute*, Act 1) (Fritz Wunderlich/Berlin Philharmonic/Böhm)
*¶ Bach, 'Ich habe genug' (Cantata No. 82) (Dietrich Fischer-Dieskau/Munich Bach Choir and Orchestra/Richter)
¶ Brahms, *Geistliches Wiegenlied* (opus 91, no. 2) (Marian Anderson/William Primrose *viola*/Franz Rupp *piano*)
¶ Elgar, Cello Concerto in E minor (Jacqueline du Pré/Philadelphia Orchestra/Barenboim)
¶ LUXURY: His violin, strings and case.
¶ BOOKS: Fyodor Dostoevsky, *The Brothers Karamazov*, and the Sherlock Holmes stories by A. Conan Doyle.

6 May 1978
1435 Charles Aznavour
Entertainer, actor and song-writer
*¶ 'Kalinka' (Red Army Ensemble)
¶ 'God Rest Ye Merry, Gentlemen' (Bing Crosby)
¶ 'Le fanion de la légion' (Edith Piaf)
¶ Prokofiev, *Lieutenant Kijé* (LSO/Previn)
¶ 'John and Marsha' (Stan Freberg)
¶ Weill, 'September Song' (from *Knickerbocker Holiday*) (Walter Huston)
¶ 'My Yiddishe Momme' (Sophie Tucker)
¶ Lennon & McCartney, 'Eleanor Rigby' (The Beatles)
¶ LUXURY: A tape recorder.
¶ BOOK: A French dictionary.

13 May 1978
1436 Sir Lennox Berkeley
Composer
¶ Mozart, Piano Concerto No. 21 in C (K. 467) (Murray Perahia *piano and conducting*/English Chamber Orchestra)
¶ Bach, 'Am Abend aber desselbigen Sabbats' (Cantata No. 42) (Alexander Young/Teresa Stich-Randall/Vienna Radio Orchestra/Scherchen)
¶ Beethoven, Quartet No. 16 in F (opus 135) (Juilliard Quartet)
¶ Verdi, 'Labbra di fouco' (from *Falstaff*, Act 1) (Graziella Sciutta/Juan Oncina/Vienna Philharmonic/Bernstein)
¶ Debussy, *Prélude à l'après-midi d'un faune* (New York Philharmonic/Bernstein)
*¶ Martin, Petite symphonie concertante (Suisse Romande Orchestra/Ansermet)
¶ Britten, *The Turn of the Screw* (excerpt) (David Hemmings/Peter Pears/English Opera Group Orchestra/Britten)
¶ Ravel, *Valses nobles et sentimentales* (no. 3) (Vlado Perlemuter *piano*)
¶ LUXURY: A painting of a restaurant on the banks of the Marne, by Renoir.
¶ BOOK: *The New Oxford Book of English Verse*

20 May 1978
1437 The Rt Hon. Lord Shinwell
Politician
¶ Balfe, 'I Dreamt I Dwelt in Marble Halls' (from *The Bohemian Girl*) (Joan Sutherland/LSO/Bonynge)
¶ Mascagni, *Cavalleria rusticana* (intermezzo) (La Scala Orchestra, Milan/von Karajan)
¶ 'Maybe It's Because I'm a Londoner' (Bud Flanagan)
*¶ 'I Belong to Glasgow' (Will Fyffe)
¶ 'Mother Machree' (John McCormack)
¶ Wagner, 'Prize song' (from *Die Meistersinger*) (James McCracken/Vienna Opera Orchestra/Bernet)
¶ 'Blaydon Races' (Owen Brannigan)
¶ Beethoven, Symphony No. 9 in D minor (opus 125) (Philharmonia Chorus and Orchestra/Klemperer)
¶ LUXURY: Whisky.
¶ BOOK: *The Oxford Dictionary of Quotations*

27 May 1978
1438 Anna Raeburn
Problem-page editor, and broadcaster
¶ Albinoni/Giazotto, Adagio in G minor for Organ and Strings (Wolfgang Meyer *organ*/Berlin Philharmonic/von Karajan)
¶ 'Ballad for Americans' (Paul Robeson)
¶ Satie/Camerata, *Trois gymnopédies* (no. 1) (Camarata Contemporary Chamber Group)
¶ 'Heart Like a Wheel' (Linda Ronstadt)
¶ 'Christ is Risen' (from the Easter Mass) (Russian Orthodox Church choir)
*¶ 'Amazing Grace' (Aretha Franklin)
¶ 'Birdland' (Weather Report)
¶ 'Life in the Fast Lane' (The Eagles)
¶ LUXURY: Indian tea.
¶ BOOK: Agnes Smedley, *Daughter of the Earth*

3 June 1978
1439 Victoria de los Angeles
Soprano
¶ Debussy, 'Reflets dans l'eau' (*Images*, no. 1) (Arturo Benedetti Michelangeli *piano*)
¶ Wagner, 'Liebestod' (from *Tristan und Isolde*) (Kirsten Flagstad/Philharmonia Orchestra/Furtwängler)
¶ Pablo Neruda, 'Let the Railsplitter Awake' (Paul Robeson)
¶ Bizet, 'Les tringles des sistres tintaient' (from *Carmen*) (Conchita Supervia/Andrée Vavon/Andrée Bernadet/Orchestra/Cloëz)
¶ Mozart, Violin Concerto No. 3 in G major (K. 216) (Isaac Stern/Cleveland Orchestra/Szell)
¶ Debussy, 'C'est le dernier soir' (from *Pelléas et Mélisande*, Act 4) (Irène Joachim/Jacques Jansen/Paris Conservatoire Orchestra/Désormière)
*¶ Mahler, Symphony No. 5 in C sharp minor (CSO/Solti)
¶ Sound effects: birds, animals, crowds, traffic, etc.
¶ LUXURY: *The Nike of Samothrace ('Winged Victory')*, in the Louvre.
¶ BOOK: The poetry of Rainier Maria Rilke in Spanish and German.

10 June 1978
1440 Derek Jacobi
Actor
*¶ Coward, 'There are Bad Times Just Around the Corner' (from *The Globe Revue*) (Noël Coward)
¶ Hérold/Lanchbery, 'Clog Dance' (from Ballet *La Fille mal gardée*) (Royal Opera House Orchestra, Covent Garden/Lanchbery)
¶ Congreve, *The Way of the World* (excerpt) (Edith Evans/John Gielgud)
¶ Shakespeare/Dankworth, 'Shall I Compare Thee' (Cleo Laine/John Dankworth and his Orchestra)
¶ 'The Impossible Dream' (from *Man of La Mancha*) (Roberta Flack)

¶Chopin, Fantaisie-Impromptu in C sharp minor (opus 66) (Artur Rubinstein *piano*)
¶Heuberger, 'Im chambre separée' (from *Der Opernball*) (Elisabeth Schwarzkopf/Philharmonia Orchestra/Ackermann)
¶Aznavour, 'Yesterday When I was Young' (Charles Aznavour)
¶LUXURY: A king-size water bed.
¶BOOK: The complete works of Lord Byron.

17 June 1978
1441 Sir Clifford Curzon
Pianist
¶Ketelbey, 'In a Monastery Garden' (Albert Ketelbey and his Concert Orchestra)
*¶Mozart, Piano Concerto No. 21 in C (K. 467) (Artur Schnabel/LSO/Sargent)
¶Liszt, 'Gnomenreigen' (Clifford Curzon *piano*)
¶Brahms, 'Feldeinsamkeit' (opus 86, no. 2) (Elena Gerhardt/Coenraad van Bos *piano*)
¶Schumann, *Fantaisiestücke* (opus 12) (Ignace Jan Paderewski *piano*)
¶Couperin, 'Passacaglia' (from *Livres de clavecin*) (Wanda Landowska *harpsichord*)
¶Schubert, Sonata No. 20 in A (D. 959) (Artur Schnabel *piano*)
¶Wagner, 'Liebestod' (from *Tristan und Isolde*) (Kirsten Flagstad/Philharmonia Orchestra/Furtwängler)
¶LUXURY: A pill to put him to sleep for ever.
¶BOOK: George Eliot, *Middlemarch*

24 June 1978
1442 Dr Catherine Gavin
Novelist and historian
¶Clarke, 'Trumpet Voluntary' (John Wilbraham/Academy of St Martin-in-the-Fields/Marriner)
¶'Cock o' the North' (Gordon Highlanders Military Band, Pipes and Drums)

¶Gluck, 'Che faro' (from *Orfeo ed Euridice*) (Kathleen Ferrier/Netherlands Opera Orchestra/Bruck)
¶'How Deep is the Ocean' (Bing Crosby)
¶Puccini, 'One Fine Day' (from *Madam Butterfly*) (Joan Hammond/City of Birmingham Symphony/Heward)
¶'Non, je ne regrette rien' (Edith Piaf)
¶Rachmaninov, 'Mazurka' (from *A Life for the Tsar*) (Monte Carlo Opera Orchestra/Frémaux)
*¶de Lisle, 'La Marseillaise' (Paris Police Band)
¶LUXURY: Camille Pissarro, *On the Banks of the Marne*
¶BOOK: The letters of Queen Victoria.

1 July 1978
1443 Mel Brooks
Actor, writer and film director
¶Porter, 'Begin the Beguine' (from *Jubilee*) (Artie Shaw and his Orchestra)
¶Beethoven, Symphony No. 5 in C minor (opus 67) (NBC Symphony/Toscanini)
*¶'Can't We Talk It Over?' (Bing Crosby)
¶Chopin, Prelude No. 4 in E minor (opus 28, no. 4) (Artur Rubinstein *piano*)
¶'In the Wee Small Hours of the Morning' (Frank Sinatra)
¶Bach, Brandenburg Concerto No. 3 in G major (BWV 1048) (Bath Festival Chamber Orchestra/Menuhin)
¶'In Love in Vain' (Dick Haymes/Helen Forrest)
¶'Springtime for Hitler' (from film *The Producers*) (soundtrack)
¶LUXURY: Several cases of Château-Lafite Rothschild 1945.
¶BOOK: Stendhal, *The Charterhouse of Parma*

8 July 1978
1444 Jane Grigson
Cookery writer
¶Schubert, 'Der Hirt auf dem Felsen' (Christa Ludwig/Gervase de Peyer *clarinet*/Geoffrey Parsons *piano*)
¶Bach, 'Sanctus' (from *Mass in B minor*, BWV 232) (BBC Chorus/NPO/Klemperer)
*¶Grigson, 'Hollowed Stone' (Geoffrey Grigson)
¶'Cool Waters' (Nellie Lutcher)
¶'Quand au temple' (Guy Beart)
¶Schumann, 'Träumerei' (from *Kinderscenen*, opus 15) (Vladimir Horowitz *piano*)
¶Mozart, 'Bei Männern' (from *The Magic Flute*, Act 1) (Gundula Janowitz/Walter Berry/Philharmonia Orchestra/Klemperer)
¶Britten, 'Nocturne' (from Serenade for Tenor, Horn and Strings) (Peter Pears/Dennis Brain/New Symphony Orchestra/Goossens)
¶LUXURY: A typewriter and paper.
¶BOOK: Geoffrey Grigson, *Notes from an Odd Country*

15 July 1978
1445 Rita Streich
Soprano
¶Mendelssohn, 'Auf Flügeln des Gesanges' (Rita Streich/Geoffrey Parsons *piano*)
¶'The Lord's Prayer' (Russian Orthodox Cathedral Choir, Paris)
*¶Mozart, Symphony No. 36 in C major (Linz) (K. 425) (Berlin Philharmonic/von Karajan)
¶Handel, 'Art Thou Troubled?' (from *Rodelinda*) (Kathleen Ferrier/LSO/Sargent)
¶Debussy, *Pelléas et Mélisande* (Act 1) (Erna Spoorenberg/Suisse Romande Orchestra/Ansermet)
¶Rodrigo, Concierto de Aranjuez (John Williams *guitar*/English Chamber Orchestra/Barenboim)
¶Byrd, 'Earle of Oxford's March' (Philip Jones Brass Ensemble)

¶Saint-Saëns, 'Le rossignol et la rose' (Rita Streich/Berlin Radio Symphony/Gaebel)
¶LUXURY: Painting equipment.
¶BOOK: Malford, *The Nonsense of Dying*

22 July 1978
1446 Patricia Batty Shaw
Chairwoman of the National Federation of Women's Institutes
¶Lerner & Loewe, 'Thank Heaven for Little Girls' (from film *Gigi*) (Maurice Chevalier)
¶'Get Out and Get Under' (from *Hullo Ragtime*) (Gerald Kirby)
¶Mendelssohn, 'The Hebrides Overture' (RPO/Sargent)
¶'Tiroler Knappentanz' (Schlernhexen)
¶Mozart, Sonata No. 11 in A major (K. 331) (Conrad Hansen *piano*)
¶Britten, *Noye's Fludde* (Opening) (East Suffolk children's chorus/English Opera Group Orchestra/del Mar)
¶Bach, Concerto in the Italian Style (BWV 971) (Alicia de Larrocha *piano*)
*¶Sibelius, 'Finlandia' (Hallé Orchestra/Barbirolli)
¶LUXURY: A selection of herbs.
¶BOOK: Kenneth Clark, *Civilisation*

29 July 1978
1447 Barbara Pym
Novelist
¶R. Strauss, *Der Rosenkavalier* (first Waltz sequence) (Amsterdam Concertgebouw/Jochum)
¶Chopin, Variations on 'Là ci darem le mano' (opus 2) (Claudio Arrau *piano*/LPO/Inbal)
¶Puccini, 'Vissi d'arte' (from *Tosca*) (Maria Callas/Paris Conservatoire Orchestra/Prêtre)
¶Larkin, 'An Arundel Tomb' (Philip Larkin)
¶Messiaen, 'Les enfants de Dieu' (from *La nativité du Seigneur*) (Simon Preston *organ*)
¶Theodorakis, 'Sto Periyiali To Krypho' (Grigoris Bithikotsis)

¶J. Strauss, 'Csárdás' (from *Die Fledermaus*) (Vienna Philharmonic/Boskovsky)
*¶'In the Bleak Midwinter' (King's College Chapel Choir/Willcocks)
¶LUXURY: German white wine.
¶BOOK: Henry James, *The Golden Bowl*

5 August 1978
1448 Simon Rattle
Conductor
¶Ravel, L'Enfant et les sortilèges (soloists/French National Radio Orchestra and Chorus/Bour)
¶Verdi, *Falstaff* (Act 1 opening scene) (Tito Gobbi/Philharmonia Orchestra/von Karajan)
¶Bach, Cello Suite No. 5 in C minor (BWV 1011) (Pablo Casals)
¶Janáček, *The Cunning Little Vixen* (excerpt) (Helena Tattermuschová/Prague National Theatre Orchestra/Gregor)
¶Szymanowski, 'Christe Cum Sit' (from *Stabat Mater*) (Stefania Woytowicz/Krystyana Szczepanska/Andrzej Hiolski/Warsaw National Philharmonic Orchestra and Chorus/Rowicki)
*¶Beethoven, String Quartet in B flat (opus 130) (Amadeus String Quartet)
¶Mahler, 'Abshied' (from *Das Lied von der Erde*) (Kathleen Ferrier/Vienna Philharmonic/Walter)
¶'The Duke' (Dave Brubeck Quartet)
¶LUXURY: German white wine.
¶BOOK: The *I Ching*

12 August 1978
1449 Janet Suzman
Actress
*¶Mozart, 'Porgi amor' (from *The Marriage of Figaro*, Act 2) (Elisabeth Schwarzkopf/Philharmonia Orchestra/Giulini)
¶Tchaikovsky, Violin Concerto in D (Pinchas Zukerman/LSO/Dorati)

¶Mozart, Piano Concerto No. 23 in A (K. 488) (Daniel Barenboim *piano and conducting*/English Chamber Orchestra)
¶'St Louis Blues' (Bessie Smith/Louis Armstrong *cornet*/Fred Longshaw *harmonium*)
¶Bach, Cello Suite No. 2 in D minor (BWV 1008) (Pablo Casals)
¶Beethoven, Piano Trio No. 5 in E flat (opus 70, no. 2) (Jacqueline du Pré *cello*/Pinchas Zukerman *violin*/Daniel Barenboim *piano*)
¶'Lord Bless Africa' (African choir)
¶Donizetti, 'Spargi d'amaro pianto' (mad scene from *Lucia di Lammermoor*, Act 2) (Joan Sutherland/Royal Opera House Orchestra, Covent Garden/Bonynge)
¶LUXURY: A mink-lined hammock.
¶BOOK: No book – instead, an enormous basket of cosmetics.

19 August 1978
1450 Fred Trueman
Cricketer
¶Tchaikovsky, '1812 Overture' (opus 49) (Grenadier Guards Band/LSO/Alwyn)
¶'Tables and Chairs' (Yorkshire County Cricket Club)
¶'Blue Hawaii' (from film) (Ray Coniff Singers and Orchestra)
¶Berlin, 'White Christmas' (from film *Holiday Inn*) (Bing Crosby)
¶Bizet, *Carmen Suite No. 1* (prelude) (French National Radio Orchestra/Beecham)
¶'And I Love You So' (Shirley Bassey)
¶'Unforgettable' (Nat 'King' Cole)
*¶Dvořák, Symphony No. 9 in E minor (New World) (LSO/Kertesz)
¶LUXURY: A pair of high-powered binoculars.
¶BOOK: Harold Macmillan's memoirs.

26 August 1978
1451 The Rt Hon. Denis Healey MP
Chancellor of the Exchequer

¶ Betjeman, *A Shropshire Lad* (John Betjeman/ensemble/ Parker)

¶ Templeton, 'Bach Goes to Town' (George Malcolm *harpsichord*)

¶ 'Catari! Catari! (Core'ngrato)' (Tino Rossi)

¶ Handel, 'I Know that My Redeemer Liveth' (from *Messiah*) (Heather Harper/ LSO/Colin Davis)

¶ Trad. arranged Canteloube, 'Baïlèro' (from *Songs of the Auvergne*) (Netania Davrath/ Orchestra/Pierre de la Roche)

¶ Weill, 'Kleine Dreigroschenmusik' (London Sinfonietta/Atherton)

*¶ Mozart, 'Soave sia il vento' (from *Così fan tutte*, Act 1 trio) (Elisabeth Schwarzkopf/Christa Ludwig/Walter Berry/ Philharmonia Orchestra/Böhm)

¶ Beethoven, Piano Concerto No. 5 in E flat major (Emperor) (Artur Schnabel/CSO/Stock)

¶ LUXURY: Oil painting equipment.

¶ BOOK: The complete poetry of W. B. Yeats.

2 September 1978
1452 Gian Carlo Menotti
Composer

¶ Lassus, 'Missa Bell' Amfitrit' Altera' (Christ Church Cathedral Choir, Oxford/ Preston)

¶ Bach, Prelude and Fugue No. 21 in B flat minor (from *The Well-Tempered Clavier, Book 1*) (Glenn Gould *piano*)

¶ Schubert, Quintet in C (D. 956) (Bernard Greenhouse *cello*/ Juilliard Quartet)

¶ Debussy, *Pelléas et Mélisande* (Act 1 interlude) (Suisse Romande Orchestra/Ansermet)

¶ Barber, *Vanessa* (Act 4 quintet) (soloists/Metropolitan Opera Orchestra/Mitropoulos)

¶ Palestrina, 'Veni Sponsa Christi' (motet) (St John's College Choir, Cambridge/ Guest)

¶ Wagner, *Tristan und Isolde* (excerpt from Act 2) (Kirsten Flagstad/Ludwig Suthaus/ Philharmonia Orchestra/ Furtwängler)

¶ Mozart, 'Non so più' (from *The Marriage of Figaro*, Act 1) (Teresa Berganza/English Chamber Orchestra/ Barenboim)

¶ *(Mr Menotti refused to select only one disc.)*

¶ LUXURY: Tarot cards.

¶ BOOK: A book on philosophy by Kant or Wittgenstein.

9 September 1978
1453 Tennessee Williams
Playwright

*¶ 'Danny Boy' (Harry Belafonte)

¶ Nevin, 'Oh, That We Two Were Maying' (Alma Gluck/ Louise Homer)

¶ Lennon & McCartney, 'A Day in the Life' (The Beatles)

¶ 'If I Didn't Care' (The Inkspots)

¶ 'Love Me Tender' (Elvis Presley)

¶ 'The Shadow of Your Smile' (from film *The Sandpiper*) (Sarah Vaughan)

¶ 'Quiereme mucho' (Yours) (Tito Schipa)

¶ 'Me and My Shadow' (Judy Garland)

¶ LUXURY: A typewriter and paper.

¶ BOOK: The collected poetry of Hart Crane.

16 September 1978
1454 Cathy Berberian
Singer

¶ 'The Drums Roll' (Chorus and Orchestra of Bulgarian Republic Ensemble/Koutev)

¶ Puccini, 'Sono andati' (from *La bohème*) (Licia Albanese/ NBC Symphony/Toscanini)

¶ Stravinsky, 'The Sacrifice (from *The Rite of Spring*) (Paris Conservatoire Orchestra/ Monteux)

¶ R. Strauss, *Der Rosenkavalier* (final trio) (Elisabeth Schwarzkopf/Teresa Stich-Randall/Christa Ludwig/ Philharmonia Orchestra/von Karajan)

¶ Monteverdi, 'Non Havea Febo Ancora' (from *Madrigali Amorosi*) (Deller Consort/ Baroque String Ensemble/ Deller)

¶ Puccini, 'Vissi d'arte' (from *Tosca*) (Maria Callas/La Scala Orchestra/Sabata)

*¶ Berio, 'Sinfonia' (Swingle Singers/New York Philharmonic/Berio)

¶ Lennon & McCartney, 'Eleanor Rigby' (The Beatles)

¶ LUXURY: A big box of spices.

¶ BOOK: A survival manual.

23 September 1978
1455 Alan Jay Lerner
Lyricist

¶ 'Without a Song' (from *Great Day*) (Frank Sinatra)

¶ 'The Very Thought of You' (Al Bowlly/Ray Noble and his Orchestra)

¶ R. Strauss, 'Baron Ochs' Waltz' (from *Der Rosenkavalier*) (Manfred Jungwirth/Vienna Philharmonic/Solti)

¶ Porter, 'Just One of Those Things' (from *Jubilee*) (Frank Sinatra)

¶ Mahler, Symphony No. 5 in C sharp minor (New York Philharmonic/Bernstein)

*¶ Weill/Brecht, 'Mack the Knife' (from *The Threepenny Opera*) (Louis Armstrong and his Allstars)

¶ Beethoven, Symphony No. 9 in D minor (opus 125) (CSO and Chorus/Solti)

¶ 'Ain't Misbehavin'' (Fats Waller and his Rhythm)

¶ LUXURY: A piano with his wife's picture attached.

¶ BOOK: Mark Twain, *Huckleberry Finn*

30 September 1978
1456 Alec Clifton-Taylor
Architectural historian

¶ Beethoven, Symphony No. 4 in B flat major (opus 60) (Berlin Philharmonic/von Karajan)

¶ Mozart, Piano Concerto No. 24 in C minor (K. 491) (Clifford Curzon/LSO/Kertesz)

*¶ Brahms, Intermezzo in C (opus 119, no. 3) (Julius Katchen *piano*)

¶Elgar, Cello Concerto in E minor (Pablo Casals/BBC Symphony/Boult)
¶Coward, 'Alice is at It Again' (Noël Coward)
¶Fauré, Impromptu in F minor (opus 31, no. 2) (Joseph Cooper *piano*)
¶Brahms, Violin Concerto in D (Yehudi Menuhin/Berlin Philharmonic/Kempe)
¶Arne, Symphony No. 2 in F (Bournemouth Sinfonietta/ Montgomery)
¶LUXURY: A divan bed with a waterproof cover.
¶BOOK: A set of the Shell county guides.

7 October 1978
1457 Christopher Fry
Playwright
¶Schubert, Trio No. 1 in B flat (Alfred Cortot *piano*/Jacques Thibaud *violin*/Pablo Casals *cello*)
¶'Dinah' (Savoy Orpheans)
¶Handel/Beecham, *The Faithful Shepherd* (RPO/ Beecham)
¶Tippett, Concerto for Double String Orchestra (LPO/ Handley)
¶'Singin' in the Rain' (from film) (Gene Kelly)
*¶Britten, Spring Symphony (Wandsworth School Boys' Choir/Royal Opera House Orchestra and Chorus, Covent Garden/Britten)
¶Beethoven, Quartet No. 13 in B flat (opus 130) (Juillard Quartet)
¶Stravinsky, Symphony of Psalms (English Bach Festival Chorus/LSO/Bernstein)
¶LUXURY: An adjustable rocking chair.
¶BOOK: *The Oxford Dictionary of Quotations*

14 October 1978
1458 Noel Edmonds
Disc jockey and television presenter
¶Vaughan Williams, Symphony No. 3 (LSO/Previn)
¶*Round the Horne* (excerpt) (Kenneth Horne/Kenneth Williams *company*)

¶'Born to Run' (Bruce Springsteen)
¶'Armstrong' (John Stewart)
¶Parry/Blake, 'Jerusalem' (BBC Symphony and Chorus/ Davis)
¶'Done Too Soon' (Neil Diamond)
¶Dowland, 'Sir John Souche's Galliard' (Julian Bream *lute*)
*¶Croce, 'Time in a Bottle' (Jim Croce)
¶LUXURY: A motorway service station.
¶BOOK: *Roget's Thesaurus*

21 October 1978
1459 Colin Wilson
Writer
¶Wagner, 'Schwules Gedunst (Storm Music)' (from *Das Rheingold*) (Eberhard Wächter/ Vienna Philharmonic/Solti)
¶'Et la fête continue' (Yves Montand)
¶'Something's Gotta Give' (from film *Daddy Longlegs*) (Fred Astaire)
*¶Beethoven, String Quartet in F major (opus 135) (Amadeus String Quartet)
¶Coates, 'Covent Garden' (from *London Suite*) (Philharmonic Promenade Orchestra/Coates)
¶'Jazz Me Blues' (Bix Beiderbecke and his Gang)
¶Weill/Brecht, *The Rise and Fall of the City of the Mahagonny* (excerpt) (Lotte Lenya/Berlin Radio Orchestra/Bruckner-Ruggeberg)
¶Bécaud, *Opera d'Aran* (Alvino Misciano/Paris Conservatoire Orchestra/Prêtre)
¶LUXURY: A supply of Beaujolais.
¶BOOK: Charles Montagu Doughty, *Travels in Arabia Deserta*

28 October 1978
1460 Jule Styne
Composer and songwriter
¶Styne, 'People' (from *Funny Girl*) (Barbra Streisand)
*¶Mozart, Piano Concerto No. 2 in D minor (K. 466) (Vladimir Ashkenazy/LSO/Schmidt-Isserstedt)
¶Styne, 'Let It Snow' (Ella Fitzgerald)

¶Styne, 'Three Coins in the Fountain' (from film) (Frank Sinatra)
¶Gershwin, Piano Concerto in F (André Previn *piano and conducting*/LSO)
¶Styne, 'Guess I'll Hang My Tears Out to Dry' (from *Glad to See You*) (Frank Sinatra)
¶Styne, 'Don't Rain on My Parade' (from *Funny Girl*) (Barbra Streisand)
¶Styne, 'All I Need is the Girl' (from *Gypsy*) (Frank Sinatra/ Duke Ellington and his Orchestra)
¶LUXURY: A picture of all his family.
¶BOOK: Anna Sewell, *Black Beauty*

4 November 1978
1461 John Wain
Poet, novelist and biographer
¶'Your Feet's Too Big' (Fats Waller)
*¶Mozart, 'Voi che sapete' (from *The Marriage of Figaro*, Act 2) (Sena Jurinac/Vienna Philharmonic/von Karajan)
¶R. Strauss, *Till Eulenspiegel* (Dresden State Orchestra/ Kempe)
¶'St Louis Blues' (Django Reinhardt and Louis Gaste *guitars*/Eugene d'Hellemmes *bass*)
¶'Lazy River' (Louis Armstrong and his Allstars)
¶'Darktown Strutters' Ball' (Art Hodes and his Blue Note Jazz Men)
¶'Sloop John B' (London Welsh Male Voice Choir)
¶'Irish Girl' (Emma Kirkby)
¶LUXURY: His canoe.
¶BOOK: James Boswell, *The Life of Samuel Johnson*

11 November 1978
1462 Michael Crawford (2nd appearance)
Actor
*¶'Gloria' (from *Missa Luba*) (Les Troubadours du Roi Baudouin)
¶'For All We Know' (Billie Holiday)
¶'Cavatina' (from film *The Deer Hunter*) (John Williams *guitar*)

¶Simon, 'The Right Thing to Do' (Carly Simon)
¶'Singin' in the Rain' (from film) (Gene Kelly)
¶'When I Grow Too Old to Dream' (from film *The Night is Young*) (Evelyn Laye)
¶'Clouds Suite' (David Gates)
¶Hamlisch, 'I Hope I Get It' (from *A Chorus Line*) (New York Shakespeare Festival cast/Pippin)
¶LUXURY: An inflatable woman and a puncture repair kit.
¶BOOK: John Seymour, *Self-Sufficiency*

18 November 1978
1463 David Bellamy
Botanist and television presenter
*¶'The Better Land' (Clara Butt)
¶Ibert, 'Divertissement' (Paris Conservatoire Orchestra/Martinon)
¶Recording of small children playing nursery games
¶Orff, 'Veris Leta Facies' (from *Carmina Burana*) (Brighton Festival Chorus/Southend Boys' Choir/RPO/Dorati)
¶Dawn chorus (recorded by Ludwig Koch)
¶Delibes, 'Galop Finale' (from *Coppélia*) (Suisse Romande Orchestra/Ansermet)
¶Schubert, 'Ave Maria' (from soundtrack of film *Fantasia*) (Philadelphia Orchestra and Chorus/Stokowski)
¶'Je sais comment' (Edith Piaf)
¶LUXURY: Linen sheets.
¶BOOK: J. R. R. Tolkien, *The Lord of the Rings*

25 November 1978
1464 Joan Fontaine
Actress
¶Elgar, Violin Concerto in B minor (opus 61) (Yehudi Menuhin/LSO/Elgar)
¶Weill, 'September Song' (from *Knickerbocker Holiday*) (Walter Huston)
*¶Grieg, Piano Concerto in A minor (Artur Rubinstein/RCA Victor Symphony/Wallenstein)
¶'Comedy of Errors' (famous radio 'bloopers', collected by Kermit Schafer)

¶'Autumn Leaves' (Nat 'King' Cole)
¶Mozart, 'Madamina, il catalogo e questo' (from *Don Giovanni*) (Donald Gramm/English Chamber Orchestra/Bonynge)
¶An analysis of 'The Ring of the Nibelung' (Anna Russell/John Coveart *piano*)
¶Rachmaninov, Piano Concerto No. 3 in D minor (Moura Lympany/New Symphony Orchestra/Collins)
¶LUXURY: The Taj Mahal.
¶BOOK: A single-volume encyclopaedia.

2 December 1978
1465 Vladimir Ashkenazy
Pianist
¶Rachmaninov, Symphony No. 2 in E minor (opus 27) (LSO/Previn)
*¶Mozart, Piano Concerto No. 27 in B flat (K. 595) (Daniel Barenboim *piano and conducting*/English Chamber Orchestra)
¶Schubert, String Quintet in C (D. 956) (Richard Harand *cello*/Vienna Philharmonic Quartet)
¶Brahms, Symphony No. 4 in E minor (opus 98) (Berlin Philharmonic/von Karajan)
¶Schumann, 'Du Ring an meinen Finger' (from *Frauenliebe und Leben*, no. 4) (Elly Ameling/Dalton Baldwin *piano*)
¶Beethoven, String Quartet No. 15 in A minor (opus 132) (Juilliard Quartet)
¶Sibelius, Symphony No. 2 in D (opus 43) (LSO/Collins)
¶Bach, *St Matthew Passion* (final chorus) (Vienna Singverein/Berlin Philharmonic/von Karajan)
¶LUXURY: A well-programmed robot.
¶BOOK: A blank book and pens.

9 December 1978
1466 Barry John
Rugby player
¶Simon, 'Bridge Over Troubled Water' (Simon & Garfunkel)
¶'Art Gallery' (Peter Cook/Dudley Moore)

¶'Beautiful Noise' (Neil Diamond)
¶'The Scottish Trip' (Max Boyce)
¶J. Strauss, 'The Blue Danube' (Vienna Philharmonic/Boskovsky)
*¶'Myfanwy' (Treorchy Male Voice Choir)
¶Denver, 'Take Me Home, Country Roads' (Olivia Newton-John)
¶'My Way' (Frank Sinatra)
¶LUXURY: A collection of assorted balls.
¶BOOK: A. Conan Doyle, *The Complete Penguin Sherlock Holmes*

16 December 1978
1467 Dinsdale Landen
Actor
¶'Muskrat Ramble' (Sidney Bechet *soprano saxophone* and the Blue Note Jazzmen)
*¶Fauré, 'Sanctus' (from *Requiem*) (King's College Chapel Choir/Willcocks)
¶'Singin' in the Rain' (from film) (Gene Kelly)
¶Sibelius, Violin Concerto in D minor (opus 47) (David Oistrakh/Moscow Radio Symphony/Rozhdestvensky)
¶Gershwin, ''S Wonderful' (from film *An American in Paris*) (Gene Kelly/Georges Guetary)
¶Berlioz, Symphonie fantastique (Amsterdam Concertgebouw/Colin Davis)
¶Fauré, 'Pavane' (French National Radio Orchestra/Beecham)
¶Beethoven, Symphony No. 6 in F major (Pastoral) (Berlin Philharmonic/von Karajan)
¶LUXURY: Champagne.
¶BOOK: Charles Dickens, *Great Expectations*

23 December 1978
1468 Sir Robert Helpmann (2nd appearance)
Dancer, choreographer, actor and director
¶Sibelius, Symphony No. 1 in E minor (New York Philharmonic/Bernstein)
¶Sondheim, 'Send in the Clowns' (from *A Little Night Music*) (Sarah Vaughan)

¶ 'This Masquerade' (George Benson)

¶ Tchaikovsky, Piano Concerto No. 1 in B flat (Vladimir Ashkenazy/LSO/Maazel)

*¶ Trad. arranged Canteloube, 'Baïlèro' (from *Songs of the Auvergne*) (Victoria de los Angeles/Lamoureux Orchestra/Jacquillat)

¶ 'By the Time I Get to Phoenix' (Glen Campbell)

¶ 'Say Goodbye to Hollywood' (Bette Midler)

¶ Tchaikovsky, 'Fantasy Overture, Hamlet' (USSR Symphony/Svetlanov)

¶ LUXURY: Toothbrushes and toothpaste.

¶ BOOK: A volume on boat-building for beginners.

30 December 1978
1469 Norman Parkinson
Photographer

¶ 'Norman, is that You?' (Curvin Merchant)

¶ 'I Can't Get Started' (Bunny Berigan *trumpet* and his Orchestra)

¶ 'A Sleepin' Bee' (from *A House of Flowers*) (Pearl Bailey)

¶ Ives, Symphony No. 2 (New York Philharmonic/Bernstein)

¶ 'The Vatican Rag' (Tom Lehrer)

¶ 'La vie en rose' (Grace Jones)

*¶ 'Fanfare' (Trumpeters of the Royal Military School of Music, Kneller Hall/Jaeger)

¶ Shakespeare, 'Fear No More the Heat o' the Sun' (from *Cymbeline*, Act 4, Scene 2) (John Gielgud)

¶ LUXURY: A life-size bronze statue of an Ama-Indian woman, by Cornelius Zitman.

¶ BOOK: Cyril Connolly, *The Unquiet Grave*

6 January 1979
1470 Robert Powell
Actor

¶ Janáček, 'Sinfonietta' (Czech Philharmonic/Ančerl)

¶ Gershwin, 'Summertime' (from *Porgy and Bess*) (Miles Davis *trumpet*/Gil Evans and his Orchestra)

¶ John Keats, 'When I Have Fears' (Ralph Richardson)

*¶ Mahler, Symphony No. 5 in C sharp minor (Amsterdam Concertgebouw/Haitink)

¶ Dylan, 'Don't Think Twice, It's All Right' (Bob Dylan)

¶ Stravinsky, *L'histoire du soldat* (suite) (Israel Baker *violin*/instrumental ensemble/Stravinsky)

¶ 'Samba de Orfeu' (from film *Black Orpheus*) (soundtrack)

¶ Lloyd-Webber, 'Variations on a Theme of Paganini' (Julian Lloyd Webber *cello*/instrumental ensemble)

¶ LUXURY: A typewriter and paper.

¶ BOOK: *Fowler's Modern English Usage*

13 January 1979
1471 Allan Prior
Novelist and television scriptwriter

¶ 'Why am I Always the Bridesmaid?' (Lily Morris)

¶ Kern & Hammerstein, 'Make Believe' (from *Show Boat*) (Allan Jones)

¶ 'Gone fishin'' (Bing Crosby/Louis Armstrong)

¶ 'You'll Never Know' (from film *Hello Frisco Hello*) (Anne Shelton/Ambrose and his Orchestra)

¶ 'Johnny Todd' (Theme from TV series *Z Cars*) (James Ellis)

¶ 'In Other Words' (Frank Sinatra/Count Basie and his Orchestra)

¶ 'Canals (Just the Two of Us)' (Maddy Prior/Ensemble/Close)

*¶ 'Never Been Kissed in the Same Place Twice' (Maddy Prior)

¶ LUXURY: A looking-glass.

¶ BOOK: Robert Louis Stevenson, *Treasure Island*

20 January 1979
1472 Elia Kazan
Stage and screen director

¶ 'The North Star' (Zoe Fitonsi)

¶ 'Royal Garden Blues' (Charlie Christian *guitar*/Benny Goodman Septet)

¶ 'Come as You Are' (Marika Ninou)

¶ 'A Streetcar Named Desire' (Theme from film) (Elmer Bernstein and his Orchestra)

¶ 'Do Your Duty' (Bessie Smith)

¶ 'I Can't Get No Satisfaction' (The Rolling Stones)

¶ Mozart, 'La ci darem la mano' (from *Don Giovanni*, Act 1) (Eberhard Wächter/Graziella Sciutti/Philharmonia Orchestra/Giulini)

*¶ Beethoven, String Quartet in A minor (opus 132) (Quartetto Italiano)

¶ LUXURY: 20 tons of pine needles.

¶ BOOK: Homer's *Iliad*

27 January 1979
1473 Benjamin Luxon
Baritone

¶ 'The Newquay Fisherman's Song' (Holman-Climax Male Voice Choir)

¶ Dylan Thomas, *Under Milk Wood* (excerpt) (BBC Radio cast)

¶ Britten, 'Dawn' (from 'Four Sea Interludes', *Peter Grimes*) (LSO/Previn)

¶ Schubert, String Quintet in C (D. 956) (William Pleeth *cello*/Amadeus String Quartet)

¶ Verdi, 'Piango su voi' (from *Simon Boccanegra*) (Lawrence Tibbett/Giovanni Martinelli/Rose Bampton/Robert Nicolson/Metropolitan Opera Orchestra and Chorus/Pelletier)

*¶ Elgar, 'Proficiscere Anima Christiana' (from *The Dream of Gerontius*) (Benjamin Luxon/Scottish National Orchestra/Gibson)

¶ Tallis, 40-part motet 'Spem in Alium' (Cambridge University Musical Society/King's College Chapel Choir/Willcocks)

¶ 'Mock Mozart' (Peter Ustinov)

¶ LUXURY: A piano and music.

¶ BOOK: The collected stories of Idris Shah.

3 February 1979
1474 Robert Stephens
Actor

¶ Soundtrack of the film *Casablanca* (Humphrey Bogart/Ingrid Bergman/Dooley Wilson)

¶ Lehár, 'I'm Off to Chez Maxime' (from *The Merry Widow*) (Jeremy Brett)

*¶ Shakespeare, 'Speak the Speech, I Pray You' (from *Hamlet*, Act 3, Scene 2) (Laurence Olivier)
¶ 'Science Fiction: Double Feature' (from *The Rocky Horror Show*) (Patricia Quinn)
¶ Coward, 'I'll See You Again' (from *Bitter Sweet*) (Noël Coward)
¶ 'The Trail of the Lonesome Pine' (from film *Way Out West*) (Laurel & Hardy)
¶ Mascagni, *Cavalleria rusticana* (prelude) (Rome Opera Orchestra/Varviso)
¶ Lehár, 'Girls were Made to Love and Kiss' (from *Paganini*) (Richard Tauber)
¶ LUXURY: A tobacco plant.
¶ BOOK: The collected works of Raymond Chandler.

10 February 1979
1475 Norris McWhirter
Writer, broadcaster and editor of *The Guinness Book of Records*
¶ 'Amazing Grace' (Royal Scots Dragoon Guards Pipes, Drums and Military Band)
*¶ Elgar, 'Pomp and Circumstance' March No. 1 in D major (Opus 39) (HM Royal Marines Band)
¶ 'Czechoslovak National Anthem'
¶ 'Singing the Blues' (Tommy Steele)
¶ 'I Love a Lassie' (Sir Harry Lauder)
¶ *Requiem* (traditional) (Mikhail Storogenka/Russian Orthodox Cathedral Choir, Paris/Spassky)
¶ 'Hark the Herald Angels Sing' (Marlborough College Choir/Christopher Rathbone *organ*/Wilkinson)
¶ Lehár, 'You are My Heart's Delight' (from *The Land of Smiles*) (Richard Tauber)
¶ LUXURY: A roll of cloth.
¶ BOOK: *The National Dictionary of Biography*

17 February 1979
1476 Sir Arthur Bryant (2nd appearance)
Historian
¶ 'If Time is Up' (Harrow School boys)
¶ Gay, 'Were I Laid on Greenland's Coast' (from *The Beggar's Opera*) (Dennis Noble/Argo Chamber Ensemble/Austin)
¶ Gilbert & Sullivan, 'When the Buds are Blossoming' (from *Ruddigore*) (Glyndebourne Festival Chorus/Pro Arte Orchestra/Sargent)
*¶ Mozart, *The Magic Flute* (Act 2 prelude) (Vienna Philharmonic/Solti)
¶ Bach, Brandenburg Concerto No. 1 in F major (BWV 1046) (Stuttgart Chamber Orchestra/Münchinger)
¶ Elgar, Symphony No. 1 in A flat major (Philharmonia Orchestra/Barbirolli)
¶ 'O Little Town of Bethlehem' (King's College Chapel Choir/Willcocks)
¶ Holst, 'Jupiter' (from *The Planets*) (LSO/Previn)
¶ LUXURY: A painting of a little princess, by Velázquez.
¶ BOOK: James Boswell, *The Life of Samuel Johnson*

24 February 1979
1477 Nana Mouskouri
Singer
¶ 'Come Rain or Come Shine' (Judy Garland)
¶ Simon, 'Old Friends' (Simon & Garfunkel)
¶ 'When the Fires Light Up' (from *Lilacs out of the Dead Land*) (Manos Hadjidakis)
¶ Brel, 'Le plat pays' (Jacques Brel)
¶ Bellini, 'Casta diva' (from *Norma*) (Maria Callas/La Scala Orchestra/Serafin)
¶ 'Blow the Wind Southerly' (Kathleen Ferrier)
*¶ Dylan, 'Girl from the North Country' (Bob Dylan)
¶ 'Mon Dieu' (Edith Piaf)
¶ LUXURY: A telephone.
¶ BOOK: Antoine de Saint-Exupéry, *The Little Prince*

3 March 1979
1478 Lauren Bacall
Actress
¶ Gershwin, 'Isn't It a Pity?' (from *Pardon My English*) (Ella Fitzgerald)
¶ Rachmaninov, Piano Concerto No. 2 in C minor (Sergei Rachmaninov/Philadelphia Orchestra/Stokowski)
*¶ Shakespeare, 'My Mistress' Eyes' (Sonnet 130) (John Gielgud)
¶ Moszkowski, Étude in A flat (Vladimir Horowitz *piano*)
¶ Brahms, Violin Concerto in D (Isaac Stern/Philadelphia Orchestra/Ormandy)
¶ Coward, 'Has Anybody Seen Our Ship?' (from *Red Peppers*) (Noël Coward/Gertrude Lawrence)
¶ 'When the World was Young' (Nat 'King' Cole)
¶ Puccini, 'O soave fanciulla' (from *La bohème*, Act 1) (Placido Domingo/Monserrat Caballé/LPO/Solti)
¶ LUXURY: Suntan lotion.
¶ BOOK: The collected short stories of John Cheever.

10 March 1979
1479 David Attenborough (2nd appearance)
Naturalist and zoologist
¶ Handel, 'The Lord is My Light' (Chandos Anthem No. 10) (Ian Partridge/King's College Chapel Choir/Academy of St Martin-in-the-Fields/Willcocks)
¶ Beethoven, Symphony No. 2 in D (Academy of St Martin-in-the-Fields/Marriner)
¶ Bach/Busoni (arr.), Chaconne from Partita No. 2 in D minor for Solo Violin (BWV 1004) (Arturo Benedetti Michelangeli *piano*)
¶ Mozart, 'Soave sia il vento' (from *Cosi fan tutte*) (Monserrat Caballé/Janet Baker/Richard Van Allen/Royal Opera House Orchestra, Covent Garden/Colin Davis)
¶ Stravinsky, *The Firebird* (Columbia Symphony/Stravinsky)

¶ Zelenka, Trio Sonata No. 1 in F (Sachka Gavriloff *violin*/Heinz Holliger and Maurice Bourgue *oboes*/Klaus Thunemann *bassoon*/Lucio Buccarella *double bass*/Christiane Jaccottet *harpsichord*)
¶ Britten, Spring Symphony (opus 44) (Royal Opera House Orchestra and Chorus, Covent Garden/Britten)
*¶ Mozart, String Quintet in G minor (K. 516) (Cecil Aronowitz *viola*/Amadeus String Quartet)
¶ LUXURY: A pair of binoculars.
¶ BOOK: Lord & Baines, *Shifts and Expedients of Camp Life*

17 March 1979
1480 Ileana Cotrubas
Soprano
¶ Gluck, 'Dance of the Blessed Spirits' (from *Orfeo ed Euridice*) (Jean-Pierre Rampal *flute*/I Solisti Veneti/Scimone)
¶ Bach, Suite No. 3 in D major (BWV 1068) (NPO/Klemperer)
¶ Mozart, Symphony No. 39 in E flat (K. 543) (Berlin Philharmonic/Böhm)
¶ Debussy, *Pelléas et Mélisande* (prelude) (Suisse Romande Orchestra/Ansermet)
*¶ Verdi, Dies Irae' (from *Requiem*) (Carlo Bergonzi/Boston Symphony/Leinsdorf)
¶ Chopin, Waltz No. 4 in F (opus 34, no. 3) (Dinu Lipatti *piano*)
¶ Schumann, Symphony No. 4 in D minor (Berlin Philharmonic/Furtwängler)
¶ Schubert, Impromptu No. 2 in E flat (D. 946) (Alfred Brendel *piano*)
¶ LUXURY: The Sistine Chapel in the Vatican.
¶ BOOK: A history of the whole world.

24 March 1979
1481 Ray Reardon
World champion snooker player
¶ 'Ramona' (The Bachelors)
¶ 'A Song for All Nations' (Morriston Orpheus Choir)
¶ 'The Blood Donor' (from radio series *Hancock's Half Hour*) (Tony Hancock)

¶ Theodorakis, 'Zorba's Dance' (from film *Zorba the Greek*) (London Festival Orchestra/Black)
¶ 'You Always Hurt the One You Love' (Spike Jones and his City Slickers)
¶ Lai, 'Theme from *Love Story*' (from film) (Mantovani and his Orchestra)
¶ 'Land of My Fathers' (Tredegar Orpheus Male Voice Choir/Davies)
*¶ Beethoven, Symphony No. 5 in C minor (opus 67) (LSO/Solti)
¶ LUXURY: Golf clubs and balls.
¶ BOOK: Alastair Maclean, *Where Eagles Dare*

31 March 1979
1482 Burl Ives
Actor and folk singer
*¶ Mozart, Horn Concerto No. 4 in E flat (K. 495) (Dennis Brain/Philharmonia Orchestra/von Karajan)
¶ Handel, 'Silent Worship' (from *Ptolemy*) (Derek Barsham)
¶ 'Ravishing Ruby' (Tom T. Hall)
¶ Franck, 'Panis Angelicus' (John McCormack)
¶ Verdi, 'Caro nome' (from *Rigoletto*, Act 1) (Joan Sutherland/Royal Opera House Orchestra, Covent Garden/Molinari-Pradelli)
¶ 'Closing Hour Blues' (Meade Lux Lewis *piano*)
¶ Coward, 'A Bar on the Piccola Marina' (Noël Coward)
¶ Bach/Hess, 'Jesu, Joy of Man's Desiring' (Myra Hess *piano*)
¶ LUXURY: Tobermory whisky.
¶ BOOK: The *I Ching*

7 April 1979
1483 Sir Adrian Boult
(2nd appearance)
Conductor
*¶ Mozart, Symphony No. 40 in G minor (K. 550) (Berlin State Opera Orchestra/Strauss)
¶ Rubbra, Symphony No. 2 in D (NPO/Handley)
¶ Bliss, 'Meditations on a Theme of John Blow' (City of Birmingham Symphony/Rignold)

¶ Finzi, 'When I Set Out for Lyonesse' (from *Earth and Air and Rain*) (John Carol Case/Howard Ferguson *piano*)
¶ Simpson, Symphony No. 3 (LSO/Horenstein)
¶ Howells, 'Hymnus Paradisi' (Heather Harper/Robert Tear/Bach Choir/NPO/Willcocks)
¶ Silver Jubilee Message to the Empire (HM King George V)
¶ Parry, 'I was Glad When They Said Unto Me' (King's College Chapel Choir/NPO/Ledger)
¶ LUXURY: Several panama hats stuffed with barley sugar.
¶ BOOK: John Bunyan, *Pilgrim's Progress*

14 April 1979
1484 Sir Edmund Hillary
Explorer and first man to climb Everest
¶ 'Red River Valley' (Pete Seeger)
¶ 'There's a Bridle Hangin' on the Wall' (Carson Robison and his Pioneers)
*¶ Dylan, 'Blowin' in the Wind' (Peter, Paul & Mary)
¶ Denver, 'Leaving on a Jet Plane' (Peter, Paul & Mary)
¶ 'Now is the Hour' (Vera Lynn/Tony Osborne and his Orchestra)
¶ Simon, 'Bridge Over Troubled Water' (Simon & Garfunkel)
¶ 'Song of Bangladesh' (Joan Baez)
¶ 'To Bobby' (Joan Baez)
¶ LUXURY: A painting he has of the Kathmandu valley.
¶ BOOK: J. R. R. Tolkien, *The Lord of the Rings*

21 April 1979
1485 Patricia Highsmith
Crime writer
¶ Mozart, Piano Concerto No. 23 in A (K. 488) (Geza Anda *piano*/Camerata Academica of Salzburg Mozarteum)
*¶ Rachmaninov, Piano Concerto No. 2 in C minor (Sergei Rachmaninov/Philadelphia Orchestra/Stokowski)
¶ Bach, 'Heute Noch' (from Cantata No. 211) (Elly Ameling/Collegium Aureum/Leonhardt)

254

¶ Bach, 'Wir setzen uns mit Tränen nieder' (from *St Matthew Passion*) (Vienna Singverein/Berlin Philharmonic/von Karajan)
¶ Rodgers & Hart, 'In Our Little Den of Iniquity' (from *Pal Joey*) (Vivienne Segal/Harold Lang)
¶ Mahler, Symphony No. 6 in A minor (Berlin Philharmonic/von Karajan)
¶ Albéniz, 'Rondena' (from *Iberia*) (Michel Block *piano*)
¶ 'Lullaby of Birdland' (George Shearing *piano* and his orchestra)
¶ LUXURY: Writing materials.
¶ BOOK: Herman Melville, *Moby Dick*

28 April 1979
1486 Edward Fox
Actor
¶ 'My Very Good Friend, the Milkman' (Fats Waller and his Rhythm)
¶ John Keats, 'La belle dame sans merci' (Robert Donat)
¶ Schubert, 'Du Bist Die Ruh'' (Elisabeth Schumann/Karl Alwin *piano*)
¶ Coward, 'The Stately Homes of England' (from *Operetta*) (Noël Coward)
¶ R. Strauss, *Der Rosenkavalier* (final duet) (Maria Olszewska/Elisabeth Schumann/Vienna Philharmonic/Heger)
¶ Beethoven, Sonata No. 32 in C minor (opus 111) (Artur Schnabel *piano*)
¶ 'These are Great Days' (speech to boys of Harrow School, 29 October 1941) (Sir Winston Churchill)
*¶ Bach/Hess, 'Jesu, Joy of Man's Desiring' (Dinu Lipatti *piano*)
¶ LUXURY: 'Limes' toilet water by Floris.
¶ BOOKS: Evelyn Waugh, *Officers and Gentlemen*, *Men at Arms* and *Unconditional Surrender*

5 May 1979
1487 James Cameron
Journalist
¶ 'Difficulties and Repairs' (Listen and Learn Japanese)

¶ Granados, Spanish Dance No. 5 (Playera) (John Williams *guitar*)
¶ Bach, 'Gavotte' (from Partita in E) (BWV 1006) (Andrés Segovia *guitar*)
¶ 'Sirba lui pompieru si am mindra mitifica' (Gheorghe Zamfir *pan pipes*)
¶ '43rd Ward' (Win Stracke)
*¶ Dylan Thomas, *Under Milk Wood* (excerpt) (Richard Burton)
¶ 'We Shall Overcome' (Pete Seeger)
¶ Sousa, *'Washington Post March'* (United States Navy Band)
¶ LUXURY: Malt whisky.
¶ BOOK: Laurence Sterne, *Tristram Shandy*

12 May 1979
1488 Peter Blake
Artist
¶ Lennon & McCartney, 'Sergeant Pepper's Lonely Hearts Club Band' (The Beatles)
¶ 'Lucille' (The Everly Brothers)
¶ *Max at the Met* (Max Miller)
¶ 'A Little Bit More' (Dr Hook and the Medicine Men)
¶ 'Pony Express' (Danny and the Juniors)
¶ 'Whoops-a-Daisy' (Humphrey Ocean and the Hardy Annuals)
¶ 'Don't Ask Me' (Ian Dury and the Blockheads)
*¶ James Joyce, 'Molly Bloom's Soliloquy' (from *Ulysses*) (Siobham McKenna)
¶ LUXURY: Cement and tools to build a folly.
¶ BOOK: James Joyce, *Ulysses*

19 May 1979
1489 Alec McCowen
Actor
¶ 'Goodnight Vienna' (from film) (Jack Buchanan)
¶ Rachmaninov, Suite No. 2 for Two Pianos (André Previn/Vladimir Ashkenazy)
¶ Coward, 'Touring Days' (from *Cowardy Custard*) (John Moffat/Patricia Routledge)
¶ 'After You' (Lena Horne)
¶ Porter, 'Just One of Those Things' (from *Jubilee*) (Frank Sinatra)

¶ 'Losing My Mind' (from *Follies*) (Dorothy Collins)
*¶ Styne, *Gypsy* (overture) (Broadway Orchestra/Rosenstock)
¶ Elgar, Symphony No. 2 in E flat (Hallé Orchestra/Barbirolli)
¶ LUXURY: Painting equipment.
¶ BOOK: George Meredith, *The Egoist*

26 May 1979
1490 Jack Brymer
Clarinetist
¶ Berlioz, *Le corsaire* (overture) (RPO/Beecham)
*¶ Mozart, String Quintet No. 3 in G minor (K. 516) (Arthur Grumiaux and Arpad Gerecz *violins*/Georges Janzer and Max Lesuer *violas*/Eva Czako *cello*)
¶ Sibelius, Violin Concerto in D minor (Isaac Stern/RPO/Beecham)
¶ Chopin, Nocturne No. 8 in D flat (opus 27, no. 2) (Solomon *piano*)
¶ Mozart, 'L'ho perduta' (from *The Marriage of Figaro*) (Margaret Price/NPO/Klemperer)
¶ 'Have You Met Miss Jones?' (from *I'd Rather be Right*) (Oscar Peterson Trio)
¶ Beethoven, String Quartet in C sharp minor (opus 131) (Amadeus String Quartet)
¶ R. Strauss, *Don Quixote* (Opus 35) (Paul Tortelier *cello*/RPO/Beecham)
¶ LUXURY: A piano.
¶ BOOKS: Two or three novels by Charles Dickens.

2 June 1979
1491 Sir Robert Mayer (2nd appearance)
Founder of 'Youth and Music' and of the Robert Mayer Concerts for Children
¶ Beethoven, Sonata in F (opus 24) (Adolf Busch *violin*/Rudolf Serkin *piano*)
¶ Wagner, 'Selig, wie die Sonne' (from *Die Meistersinger*) (Elisabeth Schumann/Lauritz Melchior/Gladys Parr/Ben Williams/Friedrich Schorr/LSO/Barbirolli)

¶Lehár, 'Da geh' ich zu Maxim' (from *The Merry Widow*) (Eberhard Wächter/ Philharmonia Orchestra/von Matacic)

¶Verdi, 'Dies Irae' (from *Requiem*) (La Scala Orchestra and Chorus/de Sabata)

¶Schubert, Sonata in B flat (D. 960) (Artur Schnabel *piano*)

¶Bartók, Concerto for Orchestra (Jeunesses Musicales World Orchestra/Abbado)

*¶Schubert, 'An die Musik' (Lotte Lehmann/Paul Ulanowsky *piano*)

¶Mozart, Sinfonia Concertante in E flat (K. 364) (Jascha Heifetz *violin*/William Primrose *viola*/Victor Symphony/ Orchestra/Solomon)

¶LUXURY: Seedless grapes.

¶BOOK: His visitors' book.

9 June 1979
1492 Ian Carmichael (2nd appearance)
Actor

¶Holst, *The Planets* (Vienna Philharmonic/von Karajan)

¶Richard Rodney Bennett, 'Theme from *Murder on the Orient Express*' (from film) (Royal Opera House Orchestra, Covent Garden/Dods)

¶Chopin, Waltz in C sharp minor (opus 64, no. 2) (Artur Rubinstein *piano*)

*¶Khachaturian, 'Adagio' (from *Spartacus*) (Vienna Philharmonic/Khachaturian)

¶'On the Alamo' (Tommy Dorsey and his Orchestra)

¶'Theme from *Boeing, Boeing*' (from film) (soundtrack)

¶Duet of Guy and Madeleine from film *Les parapluies de Cherbourg* (Nino Castelnuovo/ Ellen Farner/orchestra/ Legrand)

¶'Doin' Basie's Thing' (Count Basie and his Orchestra)

¶LUXURY: Paper and pencils.

¶BOOK: Leo Tolstoy, *War and Peace*

16 June 1979
1493 Irene Thomas
Broadcaster and former 'Brain of Britain'

¶Vecchi, 'Fa una canzone' (Robert Shaw Chorale)

¶Green, 'Sunset' (HM Royal Marines Band/Vivian Dunn)

¶Heuberger, 'Im chambre separée' (from *Der Opernball*) (Elisabeth Schwarzkopf/ Philharmonia Orchestra/ Ackermann)

¶'Begilior Gwyneth Gwyn' (Thomas L. Thomas)

¶Steffe/Howe, 'The Battle Hymn of the Republic' (Val Doonican/ George Mitchell Choir)

¶'The Field' (Yuri Guliov)

¶Tallis, 40-part motet, 'Spem in Alium' (Cambridge University Musical Society/ King's College Chapel Choir/ Willcocks)

*¶Mozart, 'Soave sia il vento' (from *Cosi fan tutte*, Act 1) (Christa Ludwig/Elisabeth Schwarzkopf/Walter Berry/ Philharmonia Orchestra/Böhm)

¶LUXURY: A teddy bear stuffed with tea bags.

¶BOOK: The score of Beethoven's opera *Fidelio*.

23 June 1979
1494 Ed McBain (alias Evan Hunter)
Writer and creator of The 8th Precinct

¶'Sing, Sing, Sing' (Benny Goodman's Orchestra)

¶'Artistry Jumps' (Stan Kenton and his Orchestra)

¶Stravinsky, *The Rite of Spring* (Columbia Symphony/ Stravinsky)

¶'Ode to Billie Joe' (Bobbie Gentry)

¶Messaien, 'Prière du Christ montant vers Son Père' (from *L'ascension*) (LSO/Stokowski)

¶'When Joanna Loved Me' (Tony Bennett)

¶Lennon & McCartney, 'Something' (The Beatles)

*¶Rachmaninov, Piano Concerto No. 3 in D minor (Lazar Berman/LSO/Abbado)

¶LUXURY: Whisky.

¶BOOK: Evan Hunter, *Streets of Gold*

30 June 1979
1495 Tito Gobbi (2nd appearance)
Baritone

*¶'La montanara' (Tito Gobbi)

¶Tchaikovsky, Piano Concerto No. 1 in B flat minor (opus 25) (Vladimir Horowitz/NBC Symphony/Toscanini)

¶Gruber, 'Stille Nacht, Heilige Nacht' (Bielefelder Kinderchoir/Oberschelp)

¶Bizet, *Carmen* (prelude) (Paris Opera Orchestra/Prêtre)

¶Verdi, 'Và pensiero, sull'ali dorate' (from *Nabucco*) (Ambrosian Opera Chorus/ NPO/Muti)

¶J. Strauss, 'The Blue Danube' (Vienna Philharmonic/ Boskovsky)

¶Rossini, *William Tell* (overture) (NBC Symphony/ Toscanini)

¶Respighi, *Feste Romane* (NBC Symphony/Toscanini)

¶LUXURY: A bar of gold.

¶BOOK: Leslie Greenwood, *Flowers of the World*

7 July 1979
1496 Glen Tetley
Choreographer

¶Ravel, *L'Enfant et les sortilèges* (soloists/French National Radio Orchestra/Bour)

¶'I Get Along Without You Very Well' (Billie Holiday)

¶Haydn, *The Seven Last Words of Christ* (String Quartets Nos. 50–56) (Amadeus String Quartet)

¶'You Make Me Feel Like a Natural Woman' (Aretha Franklin)

¶Beethoven, String Quartet No. 14 in C sharp minor (opus 131) (Quartetto Italiano)

¶Rossini, 'Assisa a'pie d'un salice' (from *Otello*) (Frederica von Stade/Rotterdam Philharmonic/de Waart)

¶'I Am, I Said' (Neil Diamond)

*¶Monteverdi, 'Laudamus Te' (from *Selva Morale*) (Instrumental and Vocal Ensemble of Lausanne/Corboz)

¶LUXURY: A South American hammock.

¶BOOK: Colette, *Earthly Paradise*

14 July 1979
1497 C. Northcote Parkinson
Writer, historian and discoverer of 'Parkinson's Law'

¶ 'Sumer is Icumen In' (Alfred Deller Consort)

¶ Gay, 'Fill Every Glass' (from *The Beggar's Opera*, Act 2) (Alexander Young/Pro Arte Orchestra/Sargent)

¶ 'Spanish Ladies' (Uffa Fox/Ron Goodwin and his Orchestra)

¶ 'This Heart of Mine' (Fred Astaire)

¶ Walton, 'Agincourt Song' (from film *Henry V*) (Philharmonia Chorus and Orchestra/Walton)

*¶ 'The Old Hundredth' (from Coronation Service of HM Queen Elizabeth II)

¶ 'Never on Sunday' (from film) (Manos Hadjidakis *piano*)

¶ Lerner & Loewe, 'I Remember It Well' (from film *Gigi*) (Maurice Chevalier/Hermione Gingold)

¶ LUXURY: A radio receiver.

¶ BOOK: Edward Gibbon, *The History of the Decline and Fall of the Roman Empire*

21 July 1979
1498 Dick Clements & Ian La Frenais
Scriptwriters

¶ (DC) 'L'il Darlin'' (Count Basie and his Orchestra)

¶ (IL) 'I'll be Around' (Billie Holiday)

*¶ (DC) 'You Make Me Feel Like a Natural Woman' (Aretha Franklin)

*¶ (IL) 'Born Under a Bad Sign' (Albert King)

¶ Lennon & McCartney, 'Penny Lane' (The Beatles)

¶ (IL) 'All Along the Watchtower' (Jimi Hendrix)

¶ (DC) Mendelssohn, 'Be Not Afraid' (from *Elijah*) (RPO and Choral Society/Sargent)

¶ (IL) 'Hotel California' (The Eagles)

¶ LUXURIES: (DC) a pack of cards; (IL) a guitar.

¶ BOOKS: (DC) A. A. Milne, *Winnie the Pooh*; (IL) 'Teach Yourself the Guitar'.

28 July 1979
1499 Moura Lympany (2nd appearance)
Concert pianist

*¶ Mendelssohn, Piano Concerto No. 1 in G minor (Moura Lympany/Philharmonia Orchestra/Kubelik)

¶ Rachmaninov, Prelude No. 16 in G (opus 32, no. 5) (Moura Lympany *piano*)

¶ Khachaturian, Piano Concerto in D flat (Moura Lympany/LPO/Fistoulari)

¶ Rawsthorne, Piano Concerto No. 1 (Moura Lympany/Philharmonia Orchestra/Menges)

¶ Mozart, Piano Concerto No. 21 in C (K. 467) (Moura Lympany/Philharmonia Orchestra/Menges)

¶ Chopin, Prelude in E minor (opus 28, no. 4) (Moura Lympany *piano*)

¶ Schubert, Piano Quintet in A (Trout) (Moura Lympany/members of the LSO)

¶ Rachmaninov, Piano Concerto No. 3 in D minor (Moura Lympany/New Symphony Orchestra/Collins)

¶ LUXURY: Wine from her own vineyard.

¶ BOOK: A book about growing flowers and vegetables on a desert island.

4 August 1979
1500 Sir Ralph Richardson (2nd appearance)
Actor

¶ 'Tea for Two' (from *No, No, Nanette*) (Binnie Hale/Seymour Beard)

¶ Beethoven, Piano Sonata No. 12 in A flat (Opus 26) (Artur Schnabel)

¶ 'A-Tisket, A-Tasket' (Ella Fitzgerald/Chick Webb Orchestra)

¶ Gilbert & Sullivan, 'There Grew a Little Flower' (from *Ruddigore*) (Christine Palmer/Donald Adams/RPO/Sargent)

¶ Chopin, Nocturne No. 19 in E minor (opus 72) (Vladimir de Pachmann *piano*)

¶ Chopin, Nocturne No. 17 in B (Opus 62, no. 1) (Jan Smeterling *piano*)

¶ 'The Cruise of the USS *Codfish*' (Bob Newhart)

*¶ Mozart, Clarinet Concerto in A (K. 622) (Jack Brymer/RPO/Beecham)

¶ LUXURY: His pipe and a supply of tobacco.

¶ BOOKS: Three novels by Henry James.

11 August 1979
1501 The Countess of Longford (Elizabeth Longford)
Historian and biographer

¶ Gibbons, 'The Cries of London' (Alfred Deller Consort)

¶ Liszt, Hungarian Rhapsody No. 2 in C minor (LPO/Boskovsky)

¶ 'England Arise' (Socialist Singers/Glasgow YCL Choir/Bush)

¶ Prince Albert, 'Der Ungeliebte' (Susan Longfield/Jennifer Partridge *piano*)

¶ Beethoven, 'Wellington's Victory' (LSO/Dorati)

*¶ Handel/Harty, 'Air' (from *Water Music Suite*) (RPO/Weldon)

¶ Gerard Manley Hopkins, 'Starlight Night' (Margaret Rawlings)

¶ Mozart, 'A Fowler Bold' (from *The Magic Flute*) (Dennis Noble/Hallé Orchestra/Braithwaite)

¶ LUXURY: A tapestry set.

¶ BOOK: Sir Thomas More, *Utopia*

18 August 1979
1502 Boris Christoff
Bass

¶ Weber, 'Casting the Magic Bullet' (from *Der Freischütz*) (Municipal Opera Chorus, Berlin/Berlin Philharmonic/Keilberth)

*¶ Bellini, 'Prendi, l'anel ti dono' (from *La sonnambula*) (Tito Schipa/Toti Dal Monte)

¶ Rimsky-Korsakov, 'Song of the Viking Guest' (from *Sadko*) (Boris Christoff/Philharmonia Orchestra/Dobrowen)

¶ Verdi, 'Dormiro sol nel manto mio regal' (from *Don Carlos*) (Boris Christoff/Philharmonia Orchestra/Semkow)

¶ Leoncavallo, 'Vesti la giubba' (from *Pagliacci*) (Enrico Caruso)

¶ Chesnokov, 'Zhertva Verchernyaya' (Boris Christoff/Alexander Nevsky Cathedral Choir, Sofia/Konstantinov)

¶ Vivaldi, 'Spring' (from *The Four Seasons*) (Berlin Philharmonic/von Karajan)

¶ Mussorgsky, *Boris Godunov* (Act 4 final scene) (Boris Christoff/French National Radio Orchestra/Dobrowen)

¶ LUXURY: Refused to choose one.

¶ BOOK: The poetry of Yuarroros.

25 August 1979
1503 Barry Norman
Writer, journalist and broadcaster

¶ Vaughan Williams, 'Fantasia on Greensleeves' (LSO/Boult)

¶ Shakespeare/Walton, 'Once More Unto the Breach' (from film *Henry V*) (Laurence Olivier/Philharmonia Orchestra/Mathieson)

¶ Lennon & McCartney, 'When I'm Sixty-Four' (The Beatles)

¶ 'The Lion in Winter' (from film) (John Barry Orchestra)

¶ Prokofiev, *Lieutenant Kijé* (suite) (LSO/Previn)

*¶ Beethoven, Symphony No. 5 in C minor (opus 67) (Philharmonia Orchestra/Klemperer)

¶ Shakespeare/Young, 'It was a Lover and His Lass' (Cleo Laine/Keith Christie Quintet)

¶ Mozart, Symphony No. 41 in C (K. 551) (Jupiter) (Berlin Philharmonic/von Karajan)

¶ LUXURIES: Typewriter, paper and a desk with cricket balls in the drawers.

¶ BOOK: P. G. Wodehouse, *The World of Jeeves*

1 September 1979
1504 Peter Barkworth
Actor

*¶ Elgar, Symphony No. 1 in A flat (LPO/Solti)

¶ Rossini, 'Cujus Animam' (from *Stabat Mater*) (Josef Traxel/Berlin Symphony/Forster)

¶ Brahms, 'Variations on a Theme of Paganini' (Agustin Anievas *piano*)

¶ Beethoven, Symphony No. 3 in E flat major (Eroica) (Berlin Philharmonic/Kempe)

¶ R. Strauss, *Der Rosenkavalier* (Act 3 trio) (Christa Ludwig/Elisabeth Schwarzkopf/Teresa Stich-Randall/Philharmonia Orchestra/von Karajan)

¶ Hérold, 'Clog Dance' (from Ballet *La fille mal gardée*) (Royal Opera House Orchestra, Covent Garden/Lanchbery)

¶ Hamlisch, *A Chorus Line* (finale) (original cast)

¶ Schubert, String Quintet in C (opus 163) (Benar Heifetz *cello*/Budapest String Quartet)

¶ LUXURY: A beautifully bound blank book and supply of ballpoint pens.

¶ BOOK: His diaries to date.

8 September 1979
1505 June Mendoza
Portrait painter

¶ Paganini, Violin Concerto No. 1 in D (Itzhak Perlman/RPO/Foster)

¶ Ravel, Piano Concerto in G (Julius Katchen/LSO/Kertesz)

¶ Bach, Cello Suite No. 3 in C (BWV 1009) (Pablo Casals)

¶ Berlioz, 'Lacrymosa' (from *Requiem*) (Wandsworth School Boys' Choir/LSO and Choir/Davis)

¶ Schubert, Piano Quintet in A (Trout) (Clifford Curzon *piano*/members of the Vienna Octet)

¶ Blacher, 'Orchestral Variations on a Theme by Paganini' (Berlin Radio Symphony/Fricsay)

¶ Gershwin, 'My Man's gone Now' (from *Porgy and Bess*) (Cleo Laine)

*¶ Britten, Spring Symphony (finale) (LSO and Chorus/Previn)

¶ LUXURY: Canvases, brushes and paint.

¶ BOOK: *The Penguin Chronology of the Modern World*

15 September 1979
1506 Richard Buckle
Writer, ballet critic and exhibition designer

¶ Liszt, 'O quand je dors' (Dietrich Fischer-Dieskau/Jörg Demus *piano*)

¶ Wagner, *Götterdämmerung* (Act 3 excerpt) (Alberto Remedios/English National Opera Orchestra/Goodall)

¶ Mozart, 'Soave sia il vento' (from *Cosi fan tutte*, Act 1) (Sena Jurinac/Blanche Thebom/Mario Borriello/Glyndebourne Festival Orchestra/Busch)

¶ Verdi, 'Willow song' (from *Otello*, Act 4) (Monserrat Caballé/Barcelona Symphony/Cillario)

*¶ Schubert, Piano Quintet in A (Trout) (Alfred Brendel/Cleveland Quartet)

¶ Bach, 'Herz und Mund' (Cantata No. 147) (King's College Chapel Choir/Academy of St Martin-in-the-Fields/Willcocks)

¶ Scarlatti, Sonata in F (L. 474) (Wanda Landowska *harpsichord*)

¶ Stravinsky, *Les noces* (Paris Opera Orchestra and Chorus/Boulez)

¶ LUXURY: Paper and pencils.

¶ BOOK: Thomas Hardy, *Tess of the D'Urbervilles*

22 September 1979
1507 Ted Allbeury
Thriller writer

¶ 'Twelfth Street Rag' (Harry Roy and his Band)

*¶ 'Love is the Sweetest Thing' (Al Bowlly/Ray Noble and his Orchestra)

¶ 'La chanson des rues' (Jean Sablon)

¶ 'I Breathe on Windows' (from *Over She Goes*) (Adele Dixon)

¶ 'Moonlight Serenade' (Glenn Miller Orchestra)

¶ 'Let's Say Goodnight Till the Morning' (from *Sunny*) (Jack Buchanan/Elsie Randolph)
¶ 'Sag' Beim Abschied Leise Servus' (Peter Alexander)
¶ Kalman, 'Tausend Kleine Engles Singen' (from *The Gypsy Princess*) (Anneliese Rothenberger/Nicolai Gedda/Graunke Symphony/Mattes)
¶ LUXURY: Writing pads and 4B pencils.
¶ BOOK: Cyril Connolly, *The Unquiet Grave*

29 September 1979
1508 Pam Ayres
Poet-comedienne
¶ 'Battle of New Orleans' (Lonnie Donegan)
*¶ 'The New St George' (John & Chris Leslie)
¶ 'Non, je ne regrette rien' (Edith Piaf)
¶ 'Mountain of the Women' (The Gaels)
¶ 'A Weekend in New England' (Randy Edelman)
¶ 'Misalliance' (from *At the Drop of a Hat*) (Michael Flanders/Donald Swann)
¶ 'The Hard-Knock Life' (from *Annie*) (Ann-Marie Gwatkins/chorus)
¶ '21st Speech' (Fred Dagg)
¶ LUXURY: A large basket full of sugared almonds.
¶ BOOK: Frederick Forsyth, *The Day of the Jackal*

6 October 1979
1509 Wilfred Thesiger
The last in the tradition of the individual explorer
*¶ Fauré, 'Pié Jesu' (from *Requiem*) (Robert Chilcott/King's College Chapel Choir/Willcocks)
¶ 'The Birth of Christ' (Music of the Ethiopian Coptic Church)
¶ 'Highland Laddie' (2nd Battalion Scots Guards Pipes and Drums)
¶ Granados, 'La maja y el ruisenor' (from *Goyescas*) (Victoria de los Angeles/Philharmonia Orchestra/Fistoulari)
¶ 'Music of the Rashaida' (Rashaida desert nomads)

¶ Mussorgsky, 'The Death of Boris' (from *Boris Godunov*, Act 4) (Feodor Chaliapin/Royal Opera House Orchestra and Chorus, Covent Garden/Bellezza)
¶ Walter de la Mare, 'Arabia' (Robert Harris)
¶ T. S. Eliot, 'What the Thunder Said' (from *The Wasteland*) (Alec Guinness)
¶ LUXURY: A supply of acid drops.
¶ BOOK: Edward Gibbon, *The History of the Decline and Fall of the Roman Empire*

13 October 1979
1510 Josephine Barstow
Soprano
¶ Samuel Taylor Coleridge, 'Kubla Khan' (John Neville)
¶ Verdi, 'Sanctus' (from *Requiem*) (Philharmonia Chorus and Orchestra/Giulini)
¶ Gluck, 'Dance of the Blessed Spirits' (from *Orfeo ed Euridice*) (Virtuosi di Roma/Fasano)
¶ Beethoven, 'Gott! Welch' Dunkel hier!' (from *Fidelio*, Act 2) (Jon Vickers/Philharmonia Orchestra/Klemperer)
¶ Mozart, 'Soave sia il vento' (from *Cosi fan tutte*, Act 1) (Kiri Te Kanawa/Frederica von Stade/Jules Bastin/Strasbourg Philharmonic/Lombard)
¶ Elgar, Cello Concerto in E minor (Jacqueline du Pré/LSO/Barbirolli)
¶ Janáček, *Katya Kabanova* (overture) (Vienna Philharmonic/Mackerras)
*¶ Beethoven, Symphony No. 9 in D minor (opus 125) (Philharmonia Orchestra/von Karajan)
¶ LUXURY: Michelangelo's *David*
¶ BOOKS: Thomas Hardy, *Tess of the D'Urbervilles*, *Jude the Obscure* and *The Woodlanders*.

20 October 1979
1511 Rex Harrison
Actor
*¶ 'A Lull at Dawn' (Barney Bigard and his Orchestra)
¶ 'Clarinade' (Benny Goodman and his Orchestra)
¶ 'Clarinet Lament' (Barney Bigard *clarinet*/Duke Ellington Orchestra)
¶ 'Slipped Disc' (Benny Goodman Sextet)
¶ 'My Melancholy Baby' (Benny Goodman Quartet)
¶ 'Bach Goes to Town' (Benny Goodman and his Orchestra)
¶ Weber, Clarinet Concerto No. 1 in F minor (Benny Goodman/CSO/Martinon)
¶ Mozart, Clarinet Concerto in A (K. 622) (Benny Goodman/Boston Symphony/Münch)
¶ LUXURY: Painting equipment for oils and watercolours.
¶ BOOK: Bertrand Russell, *A History of Western Philosophy*

27 October 1979
1512 Roald Dahl
Writer of short stories, children's books and screenplays
¶ Dylan Thomas, 'Fern Hill' (Dylan Thomas)
¶ Puccini, 'Che gelida manina' (from *La bohème*) (Enrico Caruso)
¶ Beethoven, Violin Concerto in D (Yehudi Menuhin/NPO/Klemperer)
*¶ Bach, 'Agnus Dei' (from *Mass in B minor*, BWV 232) (Vienna Singverein/Berlin Philharmonic/von Karajan)
¶ Beethoven, Symphony No. 9 in D minor (opus 125) (Berlin Philharmonic/von Karajan)
¶ Fauré, 'Sanctus' (from *Requiem*) (King's College Chapel Choir/NPO/Willcocks)
¶ Bach, Suite No. 3 in D major (BWV 1068) (Berlin Philharmonic/von Karajan)
¶ Mozart, Sonata in A (K. 331) (Alfred Brendel *piano*)
¶ LUXURIES: A still, grapevine cuttings and tobacco seeds.
¶ BOOK: *The New Oxford Book of English Verse*, compiled by Dame Helen Gardner.

3 November 1979
1513 Sian Phillips
Actress

¶ Oscar Wilde, 'Lady Bracknell Interviews John Worthing' (from *The Importance of Being Earnest*, Act 1) (John Gielgud/Edith Evans)

¶ 'Y Fedwin Arian' (Llanelli Male Voice Choir)

¶ Wonder, 'You are the Sunshine of My Life' (Stevie Wonder)

¶ Handel, 'Arm, Arm Ye Brave' (from *Judas Maccabaeus*) (John Shirley-Quirk/Wandsworth School Choir/English Chamber Orchestra/Mackerras)

¶ Gershwin, 'I Got Rhythm' (from *Girl Crazy*) (Ethel Merman)

¶ Verdi, 'Si pel ciel marmoreo giuro' (from *Otello*) (Titta Ruffo/Enrico Caruso)

¶ A. E. Housman, 'When First My May to Fair I Took' (from *Last Poems*) (James Mason)

*¶ Vivaldi, 'Summer' (from *The Four Seasons*) (Berlin Philharmonic/von Karajan)

¶ LUXURY: A solar-powered refrigerator full of champagne.

¶ BOOK: Robert Baden-Powell, *Scouting for Boys*

10 November 1979
1514 Marti Caine
Entertainer

¶ 'Birdland' (Manhattan Transfer)

¶ 'Dance, Ballerina, Dance' (Bing Crosby)

¶ 'Tonight' (Elton John)

¶ 'Some Cats Know' (Peggy Lee)

¶ 'England's Carol' (Modern Jazz Quartet)

¶ 'Q' (Brothers Johnson)

¶ 'Snowfall' (Singers Unlimited)

*¶ 'Coming Home' (Marshall Hain)

¶ LUXURY: A bath with solar-heated water and bubble bath.

¶ BOOK: Robert Heinlein, *Glory Road*

17 November 1979
1515 Michael Palin
Actor and scriptwriter

¶ 'Things Ain't Wot They Used T'Be' (Duke Ellington and his Orchestra)

¶ 'Tales of Men's Shirts' (The Goons)

¶ 'Londonderry Air' (Black Dyke Mills Band/Brand)

¶ 'You're a Heartbreaker' (Elvis Presley)

¶ 'And When They Ask Us (They Didn't Believe Me)' (from film *O What a Lovely War*) (Rita Williams Singers)

¶ 'Lullaby of Broadway' (from film *Golddiggers of 1935*) (Winifred Shaw/Dick Powell)

¶ Lennon & McCartney, 'The Things We Said Today' (The Beatles)

*¶ Elgar, 'Nimrod' (from *Enigma Variations*) (LSO/Davis)

¶ LUXURY: A bed with a feather-filled pillow.

¶ BOOK: William Makepeace Thackeray, *Vanity Fair*

24 November 1979
1516 Peter Shaffer
Playwright

¶ Handel, 'Ode for the Birthday of Queen Anne' (James Bowman/Academy of Ancient Music /Preston)

¶ Haydn, Symphony No. 53 in D (Academy of St Martin-in-the-Fields/Marriner)

*¶ Mozart, Piano Concerto No. 9 in E flat (K. 271) (Myra Hess/Perpignan Festival Orchestra/Casals)

¶ Mendelssohn, Octet in E flat (Vienna Octet)

¶ Stravinsky, Symphony of Psalms (Toronto Festival Singers/CBC Symphony/Stravinsky)

¶ Schumann, Piano Concerto in A minor (Dinu Lipatti/Philharmonia Orchestra/von Karajan)

¶ J. Strauss, 'Brüderlein und Schwesterlein' (from *Die Fledermaus*, Act 2) (Hilde Gueden/Julius Patzak/Vienna State Opera Chorus/Vienna Philharmonic/Krauss)

¶ Mozart, 'Che del ciel' (from *La clemenza di Tito*, Act 2) (Royal Opera House Orchestra and Chorus, Covent Garden/Davis)

¶ LUXURY: Claude Monet, *Dawn on the Seine*

¶ BOOK: Edward Gibbon, *The History of the Decline and Fall of the Roman Empire*

1 December 1979
1517 Charles Causley
Poet

*¶ Anon., *The Play of Daniel* (overture) (Ensemble Hortus Musicus/Mustonen)

¶ Dibdin, 'Tom Bowling' (Robert Tear/Andre Previn *piano*)

¶ Porter, 'Just One of Those Things' (from *Jubilee*) (Garland Wilson *piano*)

¶ Percy Shelley, 'Ozymandias' (John Gielgud)

¶ Mozart, Concerto in E flat for Two Pianos and Orchestra (K. 365) (Alfred Brendel/Walter Klien/Vienna Volksoper Orchestra/Angerer)

¶ 'The Cutty Wren' (Ian Campbell Folk Group)

¶ Coward, 'Imagine the Duchess's Feelings' (Noël Coward/Carroll Gibbons *piano*)

¶ Janáček, 'Sinfonietta' (Czech Philharmonic/Ančerl)

¶ LUXURY: A piano.

¶ BOOK: James Boswell, *The Life of Samuel Johnson*

8 December 1979
1518 Elisabeth Söderström
Soprano

¶ 'Sailing' (Rod Stewart)

¶ Grieg, 'Landkjenning' (opus 31) (Stockholm Student Singers)

¶ *Starting Finnish* (excerpt) (Finnish language course)

¶ 'Je ne veux pas faire l'amour' (Anna Russell/Eugene Rankin *piano*)

*¶ Shostakovich, *The Age of Gold* (polka) (Bolshoi Theatre Orchestra/Maxim Shostakovich)

¶ 'Regency Rake' (New Dance Orchestra)

¶ 'Denis' (Blondie)

¶Franck, 'Symphonic Variations' (Clifford Curzon *piano*/LPO/Boult)
¶LUXURY: Her own bed.
¶BOOK: Simone de Beauvoir, *The Second Sex*

15 December 1979
1519 Norman Mailer
Writer
¶Elgar, 'Pomp and Circumstance' March No. 1 in D major (opus 39) (LPO/Boult)
¶'Arf a Pint o' Ale' (Gus Elen)
¶Gershwin, 'Nice Work if You Can Get It' (from film *A Damsel in Distress*) (Sonny Stitt *tenor saxophone* and his Quartet)
¶Kern, 'The Way You Look Tonight' (from film *Swing Time*) (Sonny Rollins *tenor saxophone*/Thelonious Monk *piano*/Tommy Potter *bass*/Art Taylor *drums*)
¶''Round Midnight' (Miles Davis Quintet)
¶'Lilli Marlene' (Lale Andersen)
*¶'Imagination' (Carmen McRae)
¶Beethoven, Symphony No. 3 in E flat major (Eroica) (CSO/Solti)
¶A stick of the best marijuana.
¶BOOK: Jorge Luis Borges, *Labyrinths*

22 December 1979
1520 Sir Osbert Lancaster (2nd appearance)
Cartoonist, theatre designer and writer
¶Gluck, 'Che faro senza Euridice?' (from *Orfeo ed Euridice*) (Kathleen Ferrier/Netherlands Opera Orchestra/Bruck)
¶Weill/Brecht, 'Alabama Song' (from *The Rise and Fall of the City of Mahagonny*) (Lotte Lenya)
¶'Spring' (Douglas Byng)
¶Verdi, 'Và pensiero, sull'ali dorate' (from *Nabucco*) (La Scala Chorus and Orchestra/Abbado)
¶Coward, *Private Lives* (Act 1 love scene) (Noël Coward/Gertrude Lawrence)

¶Poulenc, *Les mamelles de Tirésias* (excerpt) (Chorus and Orchestra of Opéra-Comique, Paris/Cluytens)
¶Stravinsky, *Apollon Musagetes* (Orchestra de la Suisse Romande/Ansermet)
*¶Bach, 'Ein' feste burg ist unser Gott' (Cantata No. 80) (South German Madrigal Choir/Consortium Musicum/Gonnenwein)
¶LUXURY: A live sturgeon to provide caviar.
¶BOOK: Edward Gibbon, *The History of the Decline and Fall of the Roman Empire*

29 December 1979
1521 Kyung-Wha Chung
Violinist
¶Sinding, Suite in A minor (Jascha Heifetz *violin*/Los Angeles Philharmonic/Wallenstein)
¶Schumann, Piano Trio in D minor (Jacques Thibaud *violin*/Alfred Cortot *piano*/Pablo Casals *cello*)
¶Mozart, Sonata in F for Piano and Violin (K. 376) (Clara Haskil *piano*/Arthur Grumiaux *violin*)
¶'A Little Jazz Exercise' (Oscar Peterson *piano*)
¶R. Strauss, 'Don Quixote' (Gregor Piatigorsky *cello*/Boston Symphony/Münch)
¶Beethoven, String Quartet No. 13 in B flat (opus 130) (Budapest Quartet)
¶Porter, 'Let's Do It' (from *Paris*) (Ella Fitzgerald)
*¶Bach, Cello Suite No. 5 in C minor (BWV 1011) (Pablo Casals)
¶LUXURY: Mixed flower seeds.
¶BOOK: Hermann Hesse, *Siddhartha*

5 January 1980
1522 Reginald Goodall
Conductor
¶'Alleluia' (from *Mass for Third Sunday After Easter*) (Monks of the Abbey of St Pierre de Solesmes/Gajard)
*¶Bach, Prelude and Fugue No. 1 in C (BWV 846) (Sviatoslav Richter *piano*)

¶Bach, 'Kyrie Eleison' (from *Mass in B minor*, BWV 232) (BBC Chorus/NPO/Klemperer)
¶Bach, Cello Suite No. 1 in G (BWV 1007) (Pablo Casals)
¶Beethoven, Symphony No. 9 in D minor (opus 125) (Bruno Kittel Chorus/Berlin Philharmonic/Furtwängler)
¶Wagner, 'Ihn selbst am Kreuze' (from *Parsifal*, Act 3) (Ludwig Weber/Wolfgang Windgassen/Bayreuth Festival Orchestra and Chorus/Knappertsbusch)
¶Tchaikovsky, Symphony No. 6 in B minor (Berlin Philharmonic/Furtwängler)
¶Debussy, *Prélude à l'après-midi d'un faune* (Berlin Philharmonic/von Karajan)
¶LUXURY: An English garden.
¶BOOK: John Milton, *Paradise Lost*

12 January 1980
1523 Sir Peter Parker
Industrialist and Chairman of British Rail
¶De Lisle, arr. Berlioz, 'La Marseillaise' (Andréa Guiot/Claude Calès/Paris Opera Chorus and Orchestra/Jacquillat)
*¶Mozart, Oboe Quartet in F (K. 370) (Léon Goossens/members of the Léner String Quartet)
¶Britten, 'Nocturne' (from Serenade for Tenor, Horn and Strings) (Peter Pears/Barry Tuckwell/LSO/Britten)
¶Albinoni/Giazotto, Adagio in G minor for Organ and Strings (SAAR Chamber Orchestra/Ristenpart)
¶O. Straus, *Mariette* (Act 2, final scene) (Sacha Guitry/Yvonne Printemps)
¶'Better than Anything' (Al Jarreau)
¶William Blake, 'The Crystal Cabinet' (Ralph Richardson)
¶Beethoven, Symphony No. 7 in A major (opus 92) (Philharmonic Promenade Orchestra/Boult)
¶LUXURY: His gold pass giving him the freedom of the railways.
¶BOOK: The collected works of William Blake.

19 January 1980
1524 Dizzy Gillespie
Jazz trumpeter

¶ 'Rockin' Chair' (Roy Eldridge *trumpet*/Gene Krupa Band)
¶ 'Body and Soul' (Art Tatum *piano*)
¶ 'Lament' (Miles Davis *trumpet*/Gil Evans Orchestra)
¶ 'Deep Purple' (Sarah Vaughan)
¶ 'Daahoud' (Clifford Brown Ensemble)
¶ 'You Don't Know What Love Is' (Billy Eckstine/Eddie Fraser Bebop Band)
*¶ 'Parker's Mood' (Charlie Parker All Stars)
¶ 'Passion Flower' (Ella Fitzgerald/Duke Ellington Orchestra)
¶ LUXURY: His trumpet.
¶ BOOK: His Baha'i prayer book.

26 January 1980
1525 Sir Cecil Beaton
Photographer, designer and writer

¶ Lehár, 'Ich seh' Schon' (from *The Merry Widow*, Act 2) (Teresa Stratas/Werner Hollweg/Berlin Philharmonic/von Karajan)
¶ Chopin/Douglas, *Les sylphides* (prelude) (Berlin Philharmonic/von Karajan)
¶ Berlin, 'Cheek to Cheek' (from film *Top Hat*) (Fred Astaire)
¶ Poulenc, 'Adagietto' (from *Les biches*) (Paris Conservatoire Orchestra/Désormière)
¶ Lerner & Loewe, 'Gigi' (from film) (Louis Jourdan)
¶ Weill/Brecht, 'Mack the Knife' (from *The Threepenny Opera*) (Boston Symphony/Leinsdorf)
¶ Mahler, 'Die zwei blauen Augen' (from *Lieder Eines fahrenden Gesellen*) (Janet Baker/Hallé Orchestra/Barbirolli)
*¶ Beethoven, Symphony No. 1 in C (opus 21) (NBC Symphony/Toscanini)
¶ LUXURY: A cashmere shawl.
¶ BOOK: One of his scrapbooks.

2 February 1980
1526 Otto Preminger
Film producer and director
(who chose only music from his own films)

*¶ 'Laura' (from film) (Frank Sinatra/Orchestra/Stordahl)
¶ 'Frankie Machine' (from film *The Man with the Golden Arm*) (Orchestra/Elmer Bernstein)
¶ Bizet/Hammerstein, 'Beat Out That Rhythm on a Drum' (from film *Carmen Jones*) (Marilyn Horne/Orchestra/Gilbert)
¶ 'The Moon is Blue' (from film) (Sally Sweetland/Sauter-Finegan Orchestra)
¶ 'Almost Cried' (from film *Anatomy of a Murder*) (Duke Ellington and his Orchestra)
¶ 'Advise and Consent' (from film) (Orchestra/Fielding)
¶ Gershwin, 'A Woman is a Sometime Thing' (from *Porgy and Bess*) (Robert McFerrin/Orchestra/Prévin)
¶ 'Fight for Survival' (from film *Exodus*) (Sinfonia of London/Gold)
¶ LUXURY: A beautiful watch.
¶ BOOK: His autobiography.

9 February 1980
1527 Claudio Abbado
Conductor

¶ Beethoven, Symphony No. 9 in D minor (opus 125) (Berlin Philharmonic/Furtwängler)
¶ Debussy, 'Fêtes' (from *Nocturnes*) (Boston Symphony/Monteux)
*¶ Bach, 'Kommt, ihr Tochter' (from *St Matthew Passion*) (Philharmonia Orchestra and Chorus/Klemperer)
¶ Schubert, Quintet in C (Isaac Stern and Alexander Schneider *violins*/Milton Katims *viola*/Pablo Casals and Paul Tortelier *cellos*)
¶ Bruckner, Symphony No. 7 in E (Berlin Philharmonic/Furtwängler)
¶ Mozart, *The Magic Flute* (overture) (Columbia Symphony/Walter)
¶ Mahler, Symphony No. 9 in D (Vienna Philharmonic/Walter)

¶ Wagner, 'Liebestod' (from *Tristan und Isolde*) (Kirsten Flagstad/Philharmonia Orchestra/Furtwängler)
¶ LUXURY: Writing materials.
¶ BOOK: Dante's *The Divine Comedy*

16 February 1980
1528 Timothy West
Actor-manager

¶ 'Ain't No Use' (Sarah Vaughan)
¶ R. Strauss, 'Beim Schlafengehen' (from *Four Last Songs*) (Elisabeth Schwarzkopf/Berlin Radio Symphony/Szell)
¶ Mendelssohn, Octet in E flat (opus 20) (Academy of St Martin-in-the-Fields Chamber Ensemble/Marriner)
¶ 'Don't Tell Mama' (from *Cabaret*) (Judi Dench/Barry Dennen)
¶ Mozart, 'Der Vogelfänger bin ich Ja' (from *The Magic Flute*) (Walter Berry/Philharmonia Orchestra/Klemperer)
*¶ Beethoven, Bagatelle in B flat (opus 119, no. 11) (Alfred Brendel *piano*)
¶ Bach, 'Gloria' (from *Mass in B minor*, BWV 232) (Herta Töpper/Munich Bach Choir and Orchestra/Richter)
¶ Haydn, Symphony No. 94 in G (Surprise) (RPO/Beecham)
¶ LUXURY: A typewriter, desk and paper.
¶ BOOK: Sir Thomas Malory, *Le morte d'Arthur*

23 February 1980
1529 Fay Weldon
Novelist and playwright

¶ Schumann, Piano Concerto in A minor (Fanny Davies/RPO/Ansermet)
¶ O. Strauss, 'La ronde de l'amour' (from film *La ronde*) (Anton Walbrook/Vienna Bohemian Orchestra)
¶ 'Liverpool Lullaby' (Judy Collins)
¶ Handel, 'Angels Ever Bright and Fair' (from *Theodora*) (Isobel Baillie)
¶ 'Never Let Your Braces Dangle' (Harry Champion)

¶ Sainte-Marie, 'Little Wheel, Spin and Spin' (Buffy Sainte-Marie)
¶ Arlen & Harburg, 'Over the Rainbow' (from film *The Wizard of Oz*) (Judy Garland)
¶ ''Tis the Gift to be Simple' (Carolyn Hester)
¶ LUXURY: Shiny white paper and felt-tipped pens.
¶ BOOK: Kennedy's *Latin Primer*

1 March 1980
1530 Susannah York
Actress
¶ 'A Good Man is Hard to Find' (Bessie Smith)
*¶ Bach, Concerto in D minor for Violin, Oboe and String Orchestra (BWV 1060) (Yehudi Menuhin *violin and conducting*/Léon Goossens *oboe*/Bath Festival Chamber Orchestra)
¶ Porter, 'Miss Otis Regrets' (José Feliciano)
¶ 'Desperado' (The Eagles)
¶ Mozart, Clarinet Quintet in A (K. 581) (members of the Vienna Octet)
¶ Kristopherson, 'Me and Bobby McGhee' (Janis Joplin/Full Tilt Boogie Band)
¶ Beethoven, Symphony No. 3 in E flat major (Eroica) (Berlin Philharmonic/von Karajan)
¶ Theodorakis, 'Tou Pikramenou' (from *Seven Songs of Lorca*) (Maria Farandouri/John Williams *guitar*)
¶ LUXURY: Paper and pens to correct a manuscript by Nicholas Humphrey.
¶ BOOK: *Italian Touring Atlas of the World*

8 March 1980
1531 Kiri Te Kanawa
Soprano
¶ Albinoni/Giazotto, Adagio in G minor for Organ and Strings (Saar Chamber Orchestra/Ristenpart)
*¶ Mozart, Flute Concerto No. 1 in G (K. 313) (Richard Adeney/English Chamber Orchestra/Leppard)
¶ R. Strauss, 'Tod und Verklärung' (Vienna Philharmonic/Furtwängler)

¶ Berlioz, 'Villanelle' (from *Les nuits d'été*, no. 1) (Janet Baker/NPO/Barbirolli)
¶ Ramirez, 'Kyrie' (from *Misa Criolla*) (Los Fronterizos/Cantoria of Basilica del Socorro/Ramirez)
¶ 'The *Ring of the Nibelung*: An Analysis' (Anna Russell)
¶ 'Women of Ireland' (from film *Barry Lyndon*) (The Chieftains)
¶ 'What a Wonderful World' (Louis Armstrong)
¶ LUXURY: A collection of cooking knives.
¶ BOOK: Leo Tolstoy, *War and Peace* (in French) plus a French/English dictionary.

15 March 1980
1532 Geoffrey Household
Novelist
¶ Schubert, Symphony No. 8 in B minor (CSO/Giulini)
¶ Mussorgsky, 'The Old Castle' (from *Pictures at an Exhibition*) (Andrés Segovia *guitar*)
¶ 'What is This Thing Called Love?' (from *Wake Up and Dream*) (Gerry Grey and his Orchestra)
¶ 'Organ Grinder Blues' (Ethel Waters/Clarence Williams *piano*)
¶ 'Az Az Szep' (Andor Körössy and his Budapest Gypsy Orchestra)
¶ Ravel, 'Pavane pour une infante défunte' (LSO/Monteux)
*¶ Beethoven, Symphony No. 5 in C minor (opus 67) (Berlin Philharmonic/von Karajan)
¶ 'Christ is Born' (monks of Greek Orthodox church)
¶ LUXURY: Claret.
¶ BOOK: Lyrics from Elizabethan songbooks bound together with Lyrics from Elizabethan dramatists.

22 March 1980
1533 Frances Perry
Writer, lecturer and broadcaster on gardening
¶ Gounod, 'Soldier Chorus' (from *Faust*) (Treorchy Male Choir/Jones)
*¶ Sousa, 'The Stars and Stripes Forever' (Royal Military School of Music Band and Trumpeters/Sharpe)

¶ 'The Biggest Aspidistra in the World' (Gracie Fields)
¶ J. Strauss, 'The Blue Danube' (Vienna Philharmonic/Boskovsky)
¶ Galapagos sea-lions (recorded by her son)
¶ Grieg, 'Morning' (from *Peer Gynt Suite No. 1*) (RPO/Beecham)
¶ German, 'The Yeomen of England' (from *Merrie England*) (Peter Glossop)
¶ 'The Floral Dance' (Peter Dawson)
¶ LUXURY: A lamp with solar batteries.
¶ BOOK: A survival manual.

29 March 1980
1534 Donald Pleasence
Actor
¶ 'I Will Survive' (Gloria Gaynor)
¶ Bach, French Suite No. 4 in E flat (BWV 815) (Glenn Gould *piano*)
¶ Lennon & McCartney, 'A Day in the Life' (The Beatles)
¶ 'Blues in A minor' (Modern Jazz Quartet)
¶ Elgar, Violin Concerto in B minor (Yehudi Menuhin/NPO/Boult)
¶ Rodrigo, Concierto de Aranjuez (Miles Davis *trumpet*/Gil Evans Orchestra)
¶ 'Scouse the Mouse' (Ringo Starr)
*¶ Verdi, 'Dies Irae' (from *Requiem*) (Vienna State Opera Chorus/Vienna Philharmonic/Solti)
¶ LUXURY: Writing materials.
¶ BOOKS: Fyodor Dostoevsky, *The Brothers Karamazov* and *Crime and Punishment*

5 April 1980
1535 Commissioner Catherine Bramwell Booth of the Salvation Army
¶ Beethoven, Sonata No. 14 in C sharp minor (Moonlight) (Wilhelm Kempff *piano*)
¶ Bruch, Violin Concerto No. 1 in G minor (Yehudi Menuhin/LSO/Boult)

¶Mozart, Horn Concerto No. 1 in D (K. 412) (Dennis Brain/Philharmonia Orchestra/von Karajan)

¶Mendelssohn, 'Hear My Prayer' (Ernest Lough/G. Thalben-Ball *organ*/Temple Church Choir, London)

¶Mendelssohn, 'Frühlingslied' (from *Songs Without Words*, opus 62, no. 6) (Daniel Barenboim *piano*)

¶Saint-Saëns, 'Le cygne' (from *Carnival of the Animals*) (Jacqueline du Pré *cello*/Osian Ellis *harp*)

¶'The Fount' (Portsmouth Citadel Band/Nobes)

*¶Handel, 'Hallelujah Chorus' (from *Messiah*) (Huddersfield Choral Society/Royal Liverpool Philharmonic/Sargent)

¶LUXURY: A strong, wooden armchair.

¶BOOK: The Salvation Army songbook.

12 April 1980
1536 Leonard Rossiter
Actor

¶'Bach Goes to Town' (Benny Goodman and his Orchestra)

¶Mozart, *Eine Kleine Nachtmusik* (K. 525) (Berlin Philharmonic/von Karajan)

¶Schubert, 'Was bedeutet die Bewegung' (Elisabeth Schwarzkopf/Geoffrey Parsons *piano*)

¶Bach, 'Sheep May Safely Graze' (Cyril Smith & Phyllis Sellick *pianos*)

*¶Max at the Met (Max Miller)

¶Willson, 'Ya Got Trouble' (from *The Music Man*) (Robert Preston)

¶Beethoven, Symphony No. 5 in C minor (opus 67) (Vienna Philharmonic/Schmidt-Isserstedt)

¶Lerner & Loewe, 'I've Grown Accustomed to Her Face' (from *My Fair Lady*) (Rex Harrison)

¶LUXURY: Moselle wine.

¶BOOKS: Three early novels by P. G. Wodehouse.

19 April 1980
1537 Erich Segal
Scholar, athlete and novelist

*¶'A Fifth of Beethoven' (Walter Murphy Band)

¶'Fight Fiercely, Harvard' (Tom Lehrer)

¶Vivaldi, 'Summer' (from *The Four Seasons*) (Itzhak Perlman *violin and conducting*/LPO)

¶Milhaud, *Le boeuf sur le toit* (LSO/Dorati)

¶Aznavour, 'Our Love, My Love' (Charles Aznavour)

¶Mozart, Horn Concerto No. 2 in E flat (K. 417) (Alan Civil/Academy of St Martin-in-the-Fields/Marriner)

¶Bruch, 'Kol Nidrei' (Pablo Casals *cello*/LSO/Ronald)

¶Gay, 'Fill Every Glass' and 'Let Us Take the Road' (from *The Beggar's Opera*) (Alexander Young/Pro Arte Orchestra and Chorus/Sargent)

¶LUXURY: A stop watch.

¶BOOK: Homer's *Odyssey*

16 April 1980
1538 Salvatore Accardo
Violinist

¶Verdi, 'Dies Irae' (from *Requiem*) (Robert Shaw Chorale/NBC Symphony/Toscanini)

¶Brahms, Violin Concerto in D (David Oistrakh/Dresden State Orchestra/Konwitschny)

¶Schubert, Quartet No. 14 in D minor (Busch Quartet)

¶Kreisler, 'Liebeslied' (Fritz Kreisler *violin*/Franz Rupp *piano*)

¶Brahms, 'Variations on a theme of Paganini' (Arturo Benedetti Michelangeli *piano*)

¶Sarasate, 'Zigeunerweisen' (Jascha Heifetz *violin*/RCA Victor Symphony/Steinberg)

¶Schubert, Quintet in C (Isaac Stern and Alexander Schneider *violins*/Milton Katims *viola*/Pablo Casals and Paul Tortelier *cellos*)

*¶Gluck, 'Che faro senza Euridice' (from *Orfeo ed Euridice*) (Tito Schipa)

¶LUXURY: His violin.

¶BOOK: Homer's *Odyssey*

3 May 1980
1539 Lindsay Anderson
Film and theatre director

¶'Scotland the Brave' (Gordon Highlanders Military Band and Pipe and Drum Corps/Ford)

¶Bushes and Briars' (Baccholian Singers of London)

¶Tchaikovsky, Serenade in C for String Orchestra (LSO/Barbirolli)

¶'She Wore a Yellow Ribbon' (Kingsway Marching Band and Chorus/Civil)

¶Price, 'Poor People' (from film *O Lucky Man*) (Alan Price)

*¶Bach, Brandenburg Concerto No. 6 in B flat major (BWV 1051) (LPO/Boult)

¶'The Day Thou Gavest' (Leeds Parish Church Choir/Hunt)

¶Weill/Brecht, 'Die Ballade von der Unzulänglichkeit Menschlichen Strebens' (from *The Threepenny Opera*) (Bertolt Brecht/Lewis–Ruth Band)

¶LUXURY: A box of mixed seeds and a watering can.

¶BOOK: Roger Martin du Gard, *Les Thibault*

10 May 1980
1540 Natalie Wood
Screen actress

¶Schubert, 'Ständchen' (from *Schwanengesang* No. 4) (Dietrich Fischer-Dieskau/Gerald Moore *piano*)

¶'Kalinka' (Red Army Ensemble)

¶'Greensleeves' (Ambrosian Children's Choir and Players)

¶Beethoven, Sonata No. 14 in C sharp minor (Moonlight) (Alfred Brendel *piano*)

¶Dylan, 'Just Like a Woman' (Bob Dylan)

*¶Maclean, 'American Pie' (Don Maclean)

¶'We've Got Tonite' (Bob Seger/Silver Bullet Band)

¶Lennon, 'Imagine' (John Lennon/Plastic Ono Band)

¶LUXURY: A piano.

¶BOOK: The poetry of e. e. cummings.

17 May 1980
1541 The Rt Hon. Lord Denning
Master of the Rolls

*¶Vaughan Williams, 'Fantasia on Greensleeves' (LSO/Boult)
¶'Colonel Bogey' (Royal Marines Band, Portsmouth/Mason)
¶'He Who Would Valiant Be' (Worcester Cathedral Choir and Festival Choral Society/Hunt)
¶Rodgers & Hammerstein, 'I Whistle a Happy Tune' (from *The King and I*) (Valerie Hobson)
¶'Roses of Picardy' (Webster Booth/Fred Hartley's Quintet)
¶Steffe/Howe, 'Battle Hymn of the Republic' (Robert Shaw Chorale/RCA Victor Symphony/Shaw)
¶Gilbert & Sullivan, 'Judge's Song' (from *Trial by Jury*) (Leo Sheffield/D'Oyly Carte Opera Company Orchestra/Norris)
¶Elgar, 'Pomp and Circumstance' March No. 1 in D major (opus 39) (LPO/Boult)
¶LUXURY: Indian tea and a means of boiling water.
¶BOOK: *The Golden Treasury*, compiled by Francis Palgrave.

25 May 1980
1542 Earl Hines (2nd appearance)
Jazz pianist

¶'Chant of the Weed' (Don Redman and his Orchestra)
¶'Have You Met Miss Jones?' (from *I'd Rather be Right*) (Sam Browne/Jack Hylton and his Orchestra)
¶'Sleep' (Fred Waring and his Pennsylvanians)
¶'East of the Sun' (Tommy Dorsey and his Orchestra)
¶'It Isn't Fair' (Bill Farrell)
¶'It Happens to be Me' (Ben Webster *tenor sax*/ensemble)
*¶'Trust in Me' (Dinah Washington/Quincy Jones and his Orchestra)
¶'Satin Doll' (Duke Ellington and his Orchestra)
¶LUXURY: Physical culture equipment.
¶BOOK: Stanley Dance, *The World of Duke Ellington*

31 May 1980
1543 Robert Tear
Tenor

¶J. S. Bach, *Christmas Oratorio* (King's College Chapel Choir/Academy of St Martin-in-the-Fields/Ledger)
¶Haydn, 'Und Gott schuf grosse Walfische' (from *The Creation*) (José van Dam/Philharmonia Orchestra/Frühbeck de Burgos)
¶Mozart, 'Don Giovanni, a cenar teco' (from *Don Giovanni*, Act 2) (Luigi Roni/Ingvar Wixell/Royal Opera House Orchestra, Covent Garden/Davis)
¶Beethoven, Piano Concerto No. 5 in E flat major (Emperor) (Daniel Barenboim/NPO/Klemperer)
¶Schubert, Fantasia in F minor (opus 103) (Alfred Brendel and Evelyne Crochet *pianos*)
¶Verdi, 'Sanctus' (from *Requiem*) Philharmonia Chorus and Orchestra/Giulini)
¶Wagner, 'March to Valhalla' (from *Das Rheingold*, Act 1, Scene 4) (Vienna Philharmonic/Solti)
*¶Tippett, Concerto for Double String Orchestra (Academy of St Martin-in-the-Fields/Marriner)
¶LUXURY: Postcard reproductions of his favourite paintings with his favourite poems on the backs.
¶BOOK: Alan Watts, *The Wisdom of Insecurity*

7 June 1980
1544 Freddie Jones
Actor

¶Gershwin, 'Rhapsody in Blue' (Gervase de Peyer *clarinet*/André Previn *piano and conducting*/LSO)
¶Debussy, 'La fille aux cheveux de lin' (*Prelude*, Book 1, No. 8) (Arturo Benedetti Michelangeli *piano*)
¶Bach, Brandenburg Concerto No. 5 in D major (BWV 1050) (Berlin Philharmonic/von Karajan)
¶'A Nightingale Sang in Berkeley Square' (Hutch)

¶Vaughan Williams, *The Wasps* (overture) (LPO/Boult)
¶Brahms, Symphony No. 4 in E minor (Berlin Philharmonic/von Karajan)
¶Wagner, *Die Meistersinger* (overture) (Hallé Orchestra/Barbirolli)
¶Kern & Hammerstein, 'Make Believe' (from *Show Boat*) (Kathryn Grayson/Howard Keel)
*On second thoughts, he would reject all of the above in favour of one of the late quartets of Beethoven.
¶LUXURY: A Liebig condenser for distilling gin.
¶BOOK: Kenneth Grahame, *The Wind in the Willows*

14 June 1980
1545 Clive James
Critic and television personality

¶Scarlatti, 'Ahi che sara di me?' (from *Floro e Tirsi Cantata*) (Elsie Morison/Jennifer Vyvyan/Thurston Dart *harpsichord*/Desmond Dupré *viola da gamba*)
¶Mozart, 'Non so più' (from *The Marriage of Figaro*) (Teresa Berganza/LSO/Pritchard)
¶Charpentier, 'Depuis le jour' (from *Louise*, Act 3) (Maria Callas/French National Radio Orchestra/Prêtre)
¶R. Strauss, *Der Rosenkavalier* (Act 3 trio) (Elisabeth Schwarzkopf/Christa Ludwig/Teresa Stich-Randall/Philharmonia Orchestra/von Karajan)
¶Hahn, 'En Sourdine' (Maggie Teyte/Gerald Moore *piano*)
¶'Pennies from Heaven' (from film) (Billie Holiday)
*¶'Baby Love' (Diana Ross/The Supremes)
¶'If I Had My Time Again' (Julie Covington)
¶LUXURY: The game, Space Invaders.
¶BOOK: A book by Willi Messerschmidt on how to build your own single-seater long-range monoplane out of palm fronds and coconut fibre.

21 June 1980
1546 General Sir John Hackett
Soldier, scholar and writer
¶Mozart, 'Non so più' (from *The Marriage of Figaro*) (Elly Ameling/English Chamber Orchestra/de Waart)
¶'Some of These Days' (Sophie Tucker)
¶Brahms, Violin Concerto in D (Jascha Heifetz/CSO/Reiner)
¶'The Birth of the Blues' (Layton & Johnstone)
*¶Beethoven, String Quartet No. 13 in B flat (opus 130) (Quartetto Italiano)
¶Schumann, 'Im wunderschönen Monat Mai' (from *Dichterliebe*) (Dietrich Fischer-Dieskau/Jörg Demus *piano*)
¶Schubert, Piano Quintet in A (Trout) (Paul Badura-Skoda/Barylli Quartet)
¶Wagner, 'Brünnhilde's Immolation' (from *Götterdämmerung*) (Kirsten Flagstad/Philharmonia Orchestra/Furtwängler)
¶LUXURY: Six dozen bottles of Château La Tour 1962.
¶BOOK: *1001 Gems of English Poetry* (1868 edition).

28 June 1980
1547 Barbara Woodhouse
Dog trainer
¶Ketelbey, 'In a Monastery Garden' (Albert Ketelbey and his Concert Orchestra)
¶'Charmaine' (Mantovani and his Orchestra)
¶'Whispering' (Victor Silvester Orchestra)
¶'Will You Remember?' (from film *Maytime*) (Jeanette MacDonald/Nelson Eddy)
¶'Stranger on the Shore' (Acker Bilk *clarinet*)
¶'My Blue Heaven' and 'Bye Bye Blackbird' (Turner Layton)
*¶'Skye Boat Song' (Adrian Brett *flute*)
¶'Sweet Talkin' Rag' (theme from her television programme)
¶LUXURY: Her mother's ormolu clock.
¶BOOK: Her autobiography, *Talking to Animals*

5 July 1980
1548 V. S. Naipaul
Writer
¶'Poorbi-Dhun' (Bismillah Khan)
¶Tchaikovsky, Serenade in C for String Orchestra (waltz) (Berlin Philharmonic/von Karajan)
¶Kern, 'Smoke Gets in Your Eyes' (from *Roberta*) (Dinah Shore)
¶'Lilli Marlene' (Lale Andersen)
¶Bach, Brandenburg Concerto No. 5 in D major (BWV 1050) (Bach Festival Chamber Orchestra/Menuhin)
¶Mahler, Symphony No. 4 in G (Frederica von Stade/Vienna Philharmonic/Abbado)
*¶Beethoven, Piano Sonata No. 32 in C minor (opus 111) (Alfred Brendel)
¶Raga: 'Des Malhar' (Ustad Ali Akbar Khan *sarod*/Shankar Gohosh *tabla*)
¶LUXURY: The icon, *The Enlightened Buddha*
¶BOOK: *Teach Yourself Mathematics*

12 July 1980
1549 Tom Lehrer
Composer and singer of cynical songs
¶Gilbert & Sullivan, 'The Entry of the Peers' (from *Iolanthe*) (D'Oyly Carte Opera Chorus and Orchestra/Sargent)
¶Coward, 'Nina' (from *Sigh No More*) (Noël Coward)
¶Loesser, 'Luck be a Lady' (from *Guys and Dolls*) (Robert Alda)
¶'Vanilla Ice Cream' (from *She Loves Me*) (Barbara Cook)
¶Bernstein, 'Bon Voyage' (from *Candide*) (William Ovis)
¶'Sail Away' (from *Sail Away*) (Randy Newman)
¶Sondheim, 'Send in the Clowns' (from *A Little Night Music*) (Glynis Johns)
*¶R. Strauss, *Der Rosenkavalier* (Act 3 duet) (Christa Ludwig/Teresa Stich-Randall/Philharmonia Orchestra/von Karajan)
¶LUXURY: A piano and a tuning tool.
¶BOOK: *The Oxford English Dictionary*

19 July 1980
1550 Daley Thompson
World champion decathlete
¶'Abraham, Martin and John' (Marvin Gaye)
¶King, 'You've Got a Friend' (James Taylor)
¶'Sho'nuff, Must be Love' (Heatwave)
¶'Together' (O. C. Smith)
¶'For the Good Times' (Al Green)
¶'The Best Days of My Life' (Rod Stewart)
*¶'Unchained Melody' (George Benson)
¶'Three Times a Lady' (The Commodores)
¶LUXURY: A guitar and an instruction book.
¶BOOKS: A few of John Wyndham's novels.

26 July 1980
1551 David Scott Blackhall
Blind broadcaster, writer and poet
¶'Non, je ne regrette rien' (Edith Piaf)
¶'Home' (Layton & Johnstone)
¶'The Whiffenpoof Song' (Bing Crosby)
*¶Gershwin, 'Our Love is Here to Stay' (Yehudi Menuhin and Stephane Grappelli *violins*/Alan Clare Trio)
¶'Lollipops' (Mario de Pietro *banjo*)
¶'The Click Song' (Miriam Makeba)
¶Chopin, Nocturne in E flat (opus 9, no. 2) (Moura Lympany *piano*)
¶Bach/Gounod, 'Ave Maria' (Pierre Fournier *cello*/Lamar Crowson *piano*)
¶LUXURY: Perkins' Brailler and Braille paper.
¶BOOKS: *The Oxford Book of English Verse* and *The Oxford Book of 20th-Century Verse*, both in Braille.

2 August 1980
1552 Gregory Peck
Actor

*¶ Beethoven, Symphony No. 7 in A major (opus 92) (Los Angeles Philharmonic/Mehta)

¶ Verdi, *La traviata* (Act 1 prelude) (RPO/Ceccato)

¶ 'Satin Doll' (Duke Ellington and his Orchestra)

¶ Mozart, Symphony No. 40 in G minor (K. 550) (Vienna Philharmonic/Böhm)

¶ Puccini, 'Che gelida manina' (from *La bohème*, Act 1) (Luciano Pavarotti/Berlin Philharmonic/von Karajan)

¶ Beethoven, Violin Concerto in D (Isaac Stern/New York Philharmonic/Bernstein)

¶ Chopin, Fantaisie-Impromptu in C sharp minor (opus 66) (Artur Rubinstein *piano*)

¶ 'New York, New York' (from film *New York, New York*) (Frank Sinatra/Orchestra/Falcone)

¶ LUXURY: Some cases of Château Lafite-Rothschild 1967.

¶ BOOK: Carl Sandburg, *Abraham Lincoln*

9 August 1980
1553 William Trevor
Writer

¶ Schubert, String Quartet in C (William Pleeth *cello*/Amadeus String Quartet)

¶ Purcell, 'Sound the Trumpet' (from *Come Ye Sons of Art*) (from *Ode for the Birthday of Queen Mary*) (Alfred & Mark Deller/Oriana Concert Orchestra/A. Deller)

¶ Bach, Concerto in C minor for Two Harpsichords and String Orchestra (BWV 1060) (Andrew Davis and Raymond Leppard *harpsichords*/English Chamber Orchestra/Leppard)

¶ Mozart, Piano Concerto No. 24 in C minor (Murray Perahia *piano and conducting*/English Chamber Orchestra)

¶ 'The Mouse Problem' (from *Monty Python's Flying Circus*) (John Cleese/Michael Palin)

¶ Schubert, Impromptu in B flat (opus 142, no. 3) (Ingrid Haebler *piano*)

*¶ Brahms, Clarinet Quintet in B minor (Alfred Boskovsky/members of the Vienna Octet)

¶ Byrd, 'Ave Verum Corpus' (motet) (King's College Chapel Choir/Willcocks)

¶ LUXURY: Grapevines.

¶ BOOK: Samuel Butler, *Lives of the Saints*

16 August 1980
1554 Stephen Sondheim
Composer and lyricist

¶ Ravel, *Valses nobles et sentimentales* (no. 7) (Orchestre de la Suisse Romande/Ansermet)

¶ Bartók, Concerto for Orchestra (Pittsburgh Symphony/Reiner)

*¶ Gershwin, *Porgy and Bess* (last act trio) (Lawrence Winters and others/Engel)

¶ Brahms, Piano Concerto No. 2 in B flat (Vladimir Horowitz/NBC Symphony/Toscanini)

¶ Sondheim, 'Poems' (from *Pacific Overtures*) (Isao Sato/Sab Shimono)

¶ Ravel, Piano Concerto in D for the Left Hand (Robert Casadesus/Philadelphia Orchestra/Ormandy)

¶ Stravinsky, Symphony of Psalms (English Bach Festival Chorus/LSO/Bernstein)

¶ Sondheim, 'The Ballad of Sweeney Todd' (from *Sweeney Todd*) (Len Cariou/Broadway cast)

¶ LUXURY: A piano.

¶ BOOK: The collected works of E. B. White.

23 August 1980
1555 Tristan Jones
Sailor and writer

¶ Gilbert & Sullivan, 'A Wandering Minstrel I' (from *The Mikado*) (Richard Lewis/PRO Arte Orchestra/Sargent)

¶ Lennon & McCartney, 'Hello Goodbye' (The Beatles)

¶ Mussorgsky/Stokowski, 'Night on the Bare Mountain' (LSO/Stokowski)

¶ 'Love Will Keep Us Together' (Dionne Warwick)

*¶ Tchaikovsky, '1812 Overture' (LSO/HM Grenadier Guards Band/Alwyn)

¶ 'Lullaby of Broadway' (from film *Golddiggers of 1935*) (Ella Fitzgerald)

¶ Handel, 'Hallelujah Chorus' (from *Messiah*) (RPO and Chorus/Beecham)

¶ 'Hearts of Oak' (HM Royal Marines Band, Portsmouth/Lambert)

¶ LUXURY: A 12-foot-by-8-foot Union Jack.

¶ BOOK: John Goswell, *Modern Wooden Yacht Construction*

30 August 1980
1556 Renata Scotto
Soprano

¶ Schumann, Arabesque in C (opus 18) (Vladimir Horowitz *piano*)

¶ Giordano, 'Amor ti vieta' (from *Fedora*, Act 2) (Aureliano Pertile)

¶ Chopin, Nocturne in E flat (opus 9, no. 2) (Vladimir Horowitz *piano*)

¶ Wagner, 'Liebestod' (from *Tristan und Isolde*) (Kirsten Flagstad/Philharmonia Orchestra/Furtwängler)

¶ Lennon & McCartney, 'Yesterday' (The Beatles)

*¶ Puccini, 'Sola, perduta, abbandonata' (from *Manon Lescaut*, Act 2) (Renata Scotto/LSO/Gavazzeni)

¶ Schumann, 'Träumerei' (*Kinderscenen*, no. 7) (Vladimir Horowitz *piano*)

¶ Cilèa, 'Poveri fiori' (from *Adrienne Lecouvreur*, Act 4) (Renata Scotto/NPO/Levine)

¶ LUXURY: A Silver Shadow Rolls-Royce.

¶ BOOK: Dante's *Divine Comedy*

6 September 1980
1557 The Earl of Snowdon
Photographer

¶ 'The Green Cockatoo' (Roberto Inglez and his Orchestra)

¶ Coward, 'London Pride' (Noël Coward)

¶ Porter, 'Night and Day' (from *The Gay Divorce*) (Al Bowlly/Carroll Gibbons and his Savoy Orpheans)

¶ 'See What the Boys in the Back Room Will Have' (from film *Destry Rides Again*) (Marlene Dietrich)
¶ Bernstein/Sondheim, *West Side Story* (prologue) (soundtrack/Green)
*¶ Tchaikovsky, *Swan Lake* (Act 1 waltz) (National Philharmonic/Bonynge)
¶ Beethoven, Symphony No. 9 in D minor (opus 125) (LSO and Chorus/Stokowski)
¶ 'Land of My Fathers' (Treorchy Male Choir/Jones)
¶ LUXURY: Oil paints, brushes and canvas.
¶ BOOK: Sir Banister Fletcher, *A History of Architecture on the Comparative Method*

13 September 1980
1558 Antal Dorati (2nd appearance)
Conductor
*¶ Mendelssohn, 'Rondo Capriccioso' (opus 14) (Ilse von Alpenheim *piano*(his wife))
¶ Haydn, 'Winter' (from *The Seasons*) (Ileana Cotrubas/ Werner Krenn/Hans Sotin Brighton Festival Chorus/RPO/ Dorati)
¶ Bartók, Concerto for Orchestra (Hungarian State Symphony/Dorati)
¶ Beethoven, 'O namen-, namenlose freude!' (from *Fidelio*, Act 2) (Martha Mödl/ Wolfgang Windgassen/Vienna Philharmonic/Furtwängler)
¶ Mozart, String Quartet No. 21 in D (K. 575) (Quartetto Italiano)
¶ Brahms, Clarinet Quintet in B minor (opus 115) (Karl Leister/ Amadeus String Quartet)
¶ Schubert, 'Täuschung' (from *Winterreise*, no. 19) (Dietrich Fischer-Dieskau/Gerald Moore *piano*)
¶ Shakespeare, 'Now is the Winter of Our Discontent' (from *Richard III*, Act 1) (Laurence Olivier)
¶ LUXURY: An Italian landscape drawing from his collection.
¶ BOOK: Yokoi, *The Golden Man*

20 September 1980
1559 Michael Powell (2nd appearance) & Emeric Pressburger
Film makers
¶ (EP) Bach, Prelude and Fugue No. 1 in C (BWV 846) (Sviatoslav Richer *piano*)
¶ (MP) 'Disc Jockey' (Mike Nichols/Elaine May)
¶ (EP) Beethoven, Violin Sonata in A (opus 47) (Georg Kulenkampff/Georg Solti *piano*)
¶ (MP) Thomas, 'Do Not Go Gentle into that Good Night' (Dylan Thomas)
*¶ (EP) R. Strauss, *Der Rosenkavalier* (Act 3, final duet) (Teresa Stich-Randall/Christa Ludwig/Philharmonia Orchestra/von Karajan)
¶ (MP) Mussorgsky, 'On the Dnieper' (Galina Vishnevskaya/ USSR State Symphony/ Markevitch)
¶ (EP) Bach, Partita No. 2 in D minor (BWV 1004) (Yehudi Menuhin *violin*)
*¶ (MP) Offenbach, 'Barcarolle' (from *The Tales of Hoffmann*, Act 2) (RPO/Sadler's Wells Chorus/Beecham)
¶ LUXURIES: (EP) a cask of brandy; (MP) a blank ship's logbook.
¶ BOOKS: (EP) Saul Bellow, *Herzog*; (MP) the essays of Montaigne.

27 September 1980
1560 Andrea Newman
Novelist and television writer
¶ Widor, Symphony No. 5 in F minor (toccata) (Nicolas Kynaston *organ*)
¶ Vaughan Williams, Symphony No. 6 in E minor (LSO/Previn)
¶ Puccini, 'In sistiamo' (from *Tosca*, Act 2) (Maria Callas/Tito Gobbi/La Scala Orchestra/de Sabata)
¶ Wagner, 'Liebestod' (from *Tristan und Isolde*) (Birgit Nilsson/Bayreuth Festival Orchestra/Böhm)
¶ 'Here's That Rainy Day' (Frank Sinatra)
¶ Legrand, 'What are You doing the Rest of Your Life?' (from film *Les parapluies de Cherbourg*) (Barbra Streisand)

¶ Thomas, 'Fern Hill' (Dylan Thomas)
*¶ R. Strauss, 'Im Abendrot' (from *Four Last Songs*) (Elisabeth Schwarzkopf/Berlin Radio Symphony/Szell)
¶ LUXURY: Krug 1959 champagne.
¶ BOOK: Rosamund Lehmann, *The Weather in the Streets*

4 October 1980
1561 Ronald Lockley
Naturalist and writer
¶ 'The Twelve Days of Christmas' (St John's College Choir, Cambridge/Guest)
¶ Grieg, 'Solveig's Song' (from *Peer Gynt*) (Ilse Hollweg/RPO/ Beecham)
¶ Chopin/Douglas, 'Mazurka' (from *Les Sylphides*) (Paris Conservatoire Orchestra/Maag)
*¶ Debussy, *Prélude à l'après-midi d'un faune* (RPO/Beecham)
¶ J. Strauss, 'The Blue Danube' (Berlin Philharmonic/von Karajan)
¶ Fauré, 'Après un rêve' (Kiri Te Kanawa/Richard Amner *piano*)
¶ 'David of the White Rock' (Harry Secombe/Welsh Festival Chorus and Orchestra/Knight)
¶ 'The Foggy, Foggy Dew' (Peter Pears/Osian Ellis *harp*)
¶ LUXURY: A telescope.
¶ BOOK: Gilbert White, *The Natural History of Selborne*

11 October 1980
1562 Sir John Tooley
General Administrator of the Royal Opera House, Covent Garden
¶ Tippett, Concerto for Double String Orchestra (Academy of St Martin-in-the-Fields/ Marriner)
¶ Wagner, 'Selig, Sind wie die Sonne' (from *Die Meistersinger*, Act 3) (Elisabeth Grummer/ Marga Höffgen/Rudolf Schock/ Gerhard Unger/Ferdinand Frantz/Berlin Philharmonic/ Kempe)
¶ Schubert, Octet in F (Melos Ensemble)

¶Berlioz, *Les troyens* (Act 4, love duet) (Josephine Veasey/ Jon Vickers/Royal Opera House Orchestra and Chorus, Covent Garden/Davis)
¶Verdi, 'Ella giammai m'amo' (from *Don Carlos*, Act 4) (Boris Christoff/Philharmonia Orchestra/von Karajan)
¶Haydn, Symphony No. 88 in G (Amsterdam Concertgebouw/ Davis)
¶Schumann, 'Mein schöner Stern' (opus 101, no. 4) (Peter Schreier/Norman Shetler *piano*)
*¶Mozart, *The Marriage of Figaro* (Act 2 finale) (soloists/ Vienna Opera Chorus/Vienna Philharmonic/Kleiber)
¶LUXURY: Sugared apricots from the Shilling Coffee Company.
¶BOOK: *The Oxford Book of English Verse*

18 October 1980
1563 Brian Glover
Actor, playwright and ex-wrestler
¶Handel, 'Sarabande' (from film *Barry Lyndon*) (NPO/ Rosenman)
*¶Dylan, 'Like a Rolling Stone' (Bob Dylan)
¶'The Lark in the Morning' (Maddy Prior/Steeleye Span)
¶'Non, je ne regrette rien' (Edith Piaf)
¶Prokofiev, Ballet, *Romeo and Juliet* (Cleveland Orchestra/ Maazel)
¶Bach, Brandenburg Concerto No. 3 in G major (BWV 1048) (LPO/Boult)
¶'Too Young' (Nat 'King' Cole)
¶'Lay Me Low' (John Tams/ Albion Band)
¶LUXURY: An MGTD 2952 car.
¶BOOK: John Scarne, *Card Games*

25 October 1980
1564 Catherine Gaskin
Novelist
¶Tchaikovsky, Symphony No. 6 in B minor (Berlin Philharmonic/von Karajan)
¶Chopin, Scherzo No. 2 in B flat minor (opus 31) (Artur Rubinstein *piano*)

¶Mozart, Sinfonia Concertante in E flat for Violin and Viola (K. 364) (Alan Loveday *violin*/ Stephen Shingles *viola*/ Academy of St Martin-in-the-Fields/Marriner)
¶Brahms, Piano Concerto No. 1 in D minor (Artur Rubinstein/ Boston Symphony/Leinsdorf)
¶Bach, Orchestral Suite No. 2 in B minor (BWV 1067) (Berlin Philharmonic/von Karajan)
¶Copland, 'A Lincoln Portrait' (Henry Fonda *narrator*/LSO/ Copland)
¶Schubert, Symphony No. 9 in C (Great) (LPO/Boult)
*¶Beethoven, String Quartet No. 14 in C sharp minor (opus 131) (Amadeus String Quartet)
¶LUXURY: A piano, plus a stool packed with music and books on music.
¶BOOK: Will & Eriol Durant, *The Story of Civilization*

1 November 1980
1565 Derek Tangye
Writer
¶Puccini, 'Io de'sospiri' (from *Tosca*, Act 3) (Alvaro Cordova/ La Scala Orchestra/Sabata)
¶Debussy, 'Reflets dans l'eau' (from *Images*) (Walter Gieseking *piano*)
¶Bizet, 'Galop' (from *Jeux d'enfants*) (Orchestre de la Suisse Romande/Ansermet)
¶Foster, 'Jeannie with the Light Brown Hair' (Carroll Gibbons and his String Quintet)
*¶Rachmaninov, Symphony No. 2 in E minor (LSO/Previn)
¶Haydn, String Quartet in D (opus 76, no. 5) (Amadeus String Quartet)
¶Grieg, *Holberg Suite* (prelude) (Northern Sinfonia/Tortelier)
¶Ellis, 'This is My Lovely Day' (from *Bless the Bride*) (Lizbeth Webb)
¶LUXURY: An astronomical telescope.
¶BOOK: Marcel Proust, *À la recherche du temps perdu*

8 November 1980
1566 Mark Elder
Musical Director of the English National Opera
¶Mozart, Piano Concerto No. 17 in G (K. 453) (Alfred Brendel/Academy of St Martin-in-the-Fields/Marriner)
¶Gibbons, 'Almighty and Everlasting God' (Clerkes of Oxenford)
¶Verdi, 'Torno all'assalto' (from *Falstaff*, Act 1) (Luigi Alva/Anna Moffo/Philharmonia Orchestra/von Karajan)
¶Dvořák, *Overture: In Nature's Realm* (Czech Philharmonic/ Ančerl)
*¶Berlin, 'I Used to be Colour Blind' (from film *Carefree*) (Fred Astaire)
¶R. Strauss, 'Ein Heldenleben' (Dresden Staatskapelle/Kempe)
¶Wagner, 'Wie Klug! Wie Gut' (from *Die Meistersinger*, Act 2) (Elisabeth Grummer/Gottlob Frick/Berlin Philharmonic/ Kempe)
¶Schubert, String Quintet in C (Isaac Stern and Alexander Schneider *violins*/Milton Katims *viola*/Pablo Casals and Paul Tortelier *cellos*)
¶LUXURY: His wife's sherry trifle in a solar-powered freezer.
¶BOOK: Leo Tolstoy, *War and Peace*

15 November 1980
1567 Jacquetta Hawkes
Writer and archaeologist
¶'Smoking in a Hot Bath' (J. B. Priestley)
*¶Mozart, Clarinet Concerto in A (K. 622) (Gervase de Peyer/ LSO/Maag)
¶Beethoven, Sonata No. 9 in A for Violin and Piano (Kreutzer) opus 47 (Itzhak Perlman *violin*/ Vladimir Ashkenazy *piano*)
¶Mozart, String Quintet in G minor (K. 516) (Cecil Aronowitz *viola*/Amadeus String Quartet)
¶Handel, *Water Music Suite* (RPO/Weldon)
¶Loesser, 'Fugue for Tinhorns' (from *Guys and Dolls*) (Stubby Kaye/Johnny Silver/Isabel Bigley/Douglas Deane)

¶ Elgar, Cello Concerto in E minor (opus 85) (Jacqueline de Pré/Philadelphia Orchestra/Barenboim)
¶ 'Balham – Gateway to the South' (Peter Sellers)
¶ LUXURY: A supply of red and white wines.
¶ BOOK: The works of Goethe in English.

22 November 1980
1568 Tom Conti
Actor
¶ Handel, 'Where'er You Walk' (from *Semele*) (Kenneth McKellar/Royal Opera House Orchestra, Covent Garden/Boult)
¶ Mozart, Piano Concerto No. 23 in A (K. 488) (Annie Fischer/Philharmonia Orchestra/Boult)
¶ Seguiriyas y Bulerias' (Paco Aguilera/Antonio González *guitars*)
¶ 'Alfie' (Cilla Black)
¶ Bach, Partita No. 1 in B flat (BWV 825) (Glenn Gould *piano*)
*¶ Verdi, 'Dies Irae' (from *Requiem*) (Philharmonia Chorus and Orchestra/Giulini)
¶ Elgar, 'Sea Slumber' (from *Sea Pictures*) (Janet Baker/LSO/Barbirolli)
¶ Giordani, 'Caro mio ben' (Beniamino Gigli)
¶ LUXURY: A piano, and a stool containing music.
¶ BOOK: A. S. Neill, *Summerhill*

29 November 1980
1569 Alan Minter
Boxer
¶ 'Sweet Lorraine' (Nat 'King' Cole)
¶ 'Brown Girl in the Ring' (Boney M)
¶ Joel, 'Just the Way You Are' (Billy Joel)
¶ 'He was Beautiful (Cavatina)' (Iris Williams)
¶ 'Wide-Eyed and Legless' (Andy Fairweather-Low)
*¶ 'My Way' (Frank Sinatra)
¶ 'Prize Fighter' (Jigsaw)
¶ Elgar, 'Pomp and Circumstance' March No. 1 in D major (opus 39) (BBC Chorus and Symphony/Colin Davis)
¶ LUXURY: A solar-powered transistor radio.
¶ BOOK: A survival manual.

6 December 1980
1570 José Carreras
Operatic tenor
¶ Leoncavallo, 'Vesti la giubba' (from *Pagliacci*) (Enrico Caruso)
¶ Rossini, 'La danza' (Mario Lanza)
*¶ Puccini, 'Che gelida manina' (from *La bohème*, Act 1) (Giuseppe di Stefano/La Scala Orchestra/Votto)
¶ Verdi, 'Ingemisco' (from *Requiem*) (Jussi Björling/Vienna Philharmonic/Reiner)
¶ Mozart, 'Dies Bildnis ist bezaubernd schön (from *The Magic Flute*) (Fritz Wunderlich/Hamburg Opera Orchestra/Rother)
¶ Bellini, 'Col sorriso d'innocenza' (from *Il pirata*, Act 2) (Montserrat Caballé/Italian Radio Orchestra/Gavazzeni)
¶ Mahler, Symphony No. 6 in A minor (Berlin Philharmonic/von Karajan)
¶ Puccini, 'Non la sospiri nostra cassetta' (from *Tosca*, Act 1) (Maria Callas/Giuseppe di Stefano/La Scala Orchestra/Sabata)
¶ LUXURY: Velázquez, *Les Hilanderas* (The Spinners)
¶ BOOK: The poems of Rabindranath Tagore.

13 December 1980
1571 Neville Marriner
Conductor
¶ Mendelssohn, 'What Have I to Do With Thee?' (from *Elijah*) (Isobel Baillie/Harold Williams/Royal Liverpool Philharmonic/Sargent)
¶ Elgar, Violin Concerto in B minor (Albert Sammons/New Queen's Hall Orchestra/Wood)
¶ Berlioz, *Romeo and Juliet* (LSO/Monteux)
*¶ 'There is No Rose' (King's College Chapel Choir/Willcocks)
¶ Ravel, 'Asie' (from *Schéhérazade*) (Janet Baker/NPO/Barbirolli)
¶ Schumann, Symphony No. 4 in D minor (Cleveland Orchestra/Szell)

¶ Schönberg, 'Verklarte Nacht' (Alvin Dinkin *viola*/Kurt Reher *cello*/Hollywood String Quartet)
¶ Walton, Violin Concerto (Jascha Heifetz/Philharmonia Orchestra/Walton)
¶ LUXURY: His violin.
¶ BOOK: David Attenborough, *Life on Earth*

20 December 1980
1572 Arthur Askey (4th appearance)
Comedian
*¶ Tchaikovsky, 'Romeo and Juliet Fantasy Overture' (LSO/Previn)
¶ Sinding, 'Rustle of Spring' (third of six pieces, opus 32) (Semprini *piano*)
¶ Lennon & McCartney, 'Yesterday' (The Beatles)
¶ 'Music, Maestro, Please' (Jack Hylton and his Orchestra)
¶ 'Brahn Boots' (Stanley Holloway)
¶ A mixture of several pieces of pop music that he would be glad to leave behind
¶ Grieg, 'Last Spring' (second of Two Elegiac Melodies) (Northern Sinfonia/Tortelier)
¶ Rodgers & Hammerstein, 'There is Nothin' Like a Dame' (from *South Pacific*) (Broadway cast)
¶ LUXURY: A piano.
¶ BOOK: *The Guinness Book of Records*

27 December 1980
1573 Placido Domingo
Tenor
¶ Chapí, 'La revoltosa' (Orchestra of Camara de Madrid/Argenta)
¶ Halévy, 'Rachel, quand du seigneur' (from *La juive*, Act 4) (Enrico Caruso)
¶ Puccini, *Manon Lescaut* (Act 3 intermezzo) (Berlin Philharmonic/von Karajan)
¶ Trad., 'El Cant Dels Ocells' (Pablo Casals *cello and conducting*/Prades Festival Orchestra)
¶ Puccini, 'In questa reggia' (from *Turandot*, Act 2) (Birgit Nilsson/Rome Opera House Orchestra/Molinari-Pradelli)

*¶Verdi, *Otello* (Act 1 opening) (Roman Vinay/NBC Symphony/Toscanini)

¶Beethoven, Piano Concerto No. 3 in C minor (Maurizio Pollini/Vienna Philharmonic/Böhm)

¶Beethoven, Symphony No. 5 in C minor (opus 67) (Vienna Philharmonic/Kleiber)

¶LUXURY: A video cassette recorder and a cassette of his own performances.

¶BOOK: Miguel de Cervantes, *Don Quixote*

3 January 1981
1574 Robin Cousins
World champion ice skater
¶'Handful of Keys' (Fats Waller and his Rhythm)

¶*Thunderbirds* Theme (Thunderbirds are Go)' (from TV series)

¶'Help Me Make It Through the Night' (Gladys Knight and the Pips)

¶Stravinsky, *The Firebird* (Columbia Symphony/Stravinsky)

¶'The World is a Concerto' (Barbra Streisand)

¶John/Taupin, 'Sorry Seems to be the Hardest Word' (Elton John)

¶'Rumour Has It' (Donna Summer)

*¶Bizet/Shchedrin, *Carmen Ballet* (Strings and percussion of Bolshoi Theatre Orchestra/Rozhdestvensky)

¶LUXURY: Marzipan.

¶BOOK: James Clavell, *Shogun*

10 January 1981
1575 John Fowles
Writer
¶'Bulerias' (Enrique 'El Culata'/Nino Ricardo)

¶Couperin, 'Les barricades mystérieuses' (from Suite No. 6 in B flat major for Harpsichord) (Robert Veyron-Lacroix)

¶'Pendem Devla Drabora' (Maria Ion)

¶Vivaldi, Concerto in B (opus 10, no. 2) (Concentus Musicus of Vienna)

¶Berlin, 'This Year's Kisses' (from film *On the Avenue*) (Billie Holiday)

¶'As I Roved Out on a May Morning' (from *Seventeen Come Sunday*) (Sarah Makem)

¶'At the Window' (Jimmy Yancey *piano*)

¶Bach, Trio Sonata in G (BWV 1039) (Franz Brüggen and Leopold Stastny *flutes*/Nikolaus Harnoncourt *cello*/Herbert Tachezi *harpsichord*)

*(Mr Fowles chose Bach's Goldberg Variations as his favourite but did not include it among his eight records as he felt it should be played in its entirety.)

¶LUXURY: A pair of field glasses.

¶BOOK: Dictionary of National Biography.

17 January 1981
1576 HRH Princess Margaret, Countess of Snowdon
¶Sousa, 'King Cotton' (Band of HM Royal Marines/Dunn)

¶'Scotland the Brave' (Royal Highland Fuseliers)

¶'Sixteen Tons' (Tennessee Ernie Ford)

¶Brahms, Symphony No. 2 in D (NBC Symphony/Toscanini)

¶Arne, 'Rule Britannia' (from *Alfred*) (Elizabeth Bainbridge/BBC Symphony/Davis)

*¶Tchaikovsky, *Swan Lake* (LSO/Previn)

¶'Rock, Rock, Rock' (Carl Ravazza/Sid Phillips and his Band)

¶'Cwm Rhondda (Guide Me, O Thou Great Redeemer)' (Pendyrus Male Choir)

¶LUXURY: A piano.

¶BOOK: Leo Tolstoy, *War and Peace*

24 January 1981
1577 Joan Plowright
Actress
¶Sibelius, 'The Swan of Tuonela' (Eric Fletcher *cor anglais*/Hallé Orchestra/Barbirolli)

*¶Beethoven, Symphony No. 6 in F major (Pastoral) (Philharmonia Orchestra/Klemperer)

¶Walton, 'Popular Song' (from *Façade Suite No. 2*) (Royal Opera House Orchestra, Covent Garden/Fistoulari)

¶'The House That Mac Built' (Peter Sellers)

¶'Why Should I Care?' (from *The Entertainer*) (Laurence Olivier)

¶Bernstein/Sondheim, 'I Feel Pretty' (from *West Side Story*) (Johnny Green and his Orchestra)

¶Simon, 'The Sounds of Silence' (Simon & Garfunkel)

¶Bizet, 'Bohemian Dance' (from *Carmen Suite No. 2*) (New York Philharmonic/Bernstein)

¶LUXURY: A piano.

¶BOOK: Three Aldous Huxley novels bound together.

31 January 1981
1578 Jeffrey Archer
Writer
*¶Lennon & McCartney, 'Help!' (from film) (The Beatles)

¶'Brother Bill' (Bing Crosby/Louis Armstrong)

¶Beethoven, Symphony No. 9 in D minor (opus 125) (Berlin Philharmonic/von Karajan)

¶'A Bar on the Piccola Marina' (Noël Coward)

¶John/Taupin, 'Candle in the Wind' (Elton John)

¶Incidental music to *Much Ado About Nothing* (National Theatre Players)

¶'It's Hard to be Humble' (Mac Davis)

¶'Hosanna to the Son of David' (Choir of St John's College, Cambridge/Guest)

¶LUXURY: A plasticine model of Roy Plomley and one pin.

¶BOOK: Fred Ulmann, *Reunion*

7 February 1981
1579 Mary O'Hara
Irish Singer
¶Ó Riada, 'Caithréim' (from film *Mise Éire*) (Radio Eireann Symphony/Ó Riada)

¶'All My Trials' (Joan Baez)

¶Purcell, 'Sound the Trumpet' (from *Come Ye Sons of Art*) (Alfred Deller/John Whitworth/L'Oiseau Lyre Ensemble/Lewis)

¶Orff, 'In Trutina Mentis Dubia' (from *Carmina Burana*) (Gundula Janowitz/Choir and Orchestra of Deutsche Oper, Berlin/Jochum)

*¶Bach, Double Concerto in D minor (BWV 1043) (Igor & David Oistrakh *violins*/RPO/Goossens)

¶'Sometimes When We Touch' (Dan Hill)

¶Handel, Harp Concerto in B flat (opus 4, no. 6) (Osian Ellis *harp*/Philomusica of London/Jones)

¶Mahler, 'Abschied' (from *Das Lied von der Erde*) (Janet Baker/Amsterdam Concertgebouw/Haitink)

¶LUXURY: Tennis practice wall with rackets and balls.

¶BOOK: J. R. R. Tolkien, *The Lord of the Rings*

14 February 1981
1580 David Broome
Showjumper

¶'Amazing Grace' (Pipes and Drums and Military Band of Royal Scots Dragoon Guards)

¶'My Way' (Frank Sinatra)

¶J. Strauss, 'The Blue Danube' (Berlin Philharmonic/von Karajan)

¶'Wooden Heart' (Elvis Presley)

¶Jarre, 'Lara's Theme' (from film *Dr Zhivago*) (MGM Studio Orchestra/Jarre)

*¶'Hymns and Arias' (Max Boyce)

¶Rodgers & Hammerstein, 'You'll Never Walk Alone' (from *Carousel*) (Harry Secombe)

¶'We Will Make Love' (Russ Hamilton)

¶LUXURY: Wine.

¶BOOK: The collected speeches of Sir Winston Churchill.

21 February 1981
1581 Frederic Raphael
Writer

¶Beethoven, Violin Concerto in D (Nathan Milstein/Pittsburgh Symphony/Steinberg)

¶'Milord' (Edith Piaf)

¶Haydn, Piano Trio in F (Beaux Arts Trio)

¶Vivaldi, Concerto in D for Lute and Strings (Julian Bream/Julian Bream Consort)

¶Monteverdi, 'Vespro della Beata Vergine' (Philip Jones Brass Ensemble/Monteverdi Choir and Orchestra/Gardiner)

¶Bach, Concerto in D minor for Violin and Oboe (Itzhak Perlman *violin*/Neil Black *oboe*/English Chamber Orchestra/Barenboim)

¶Theodorakis, 'Boat on the Beach' (Maria Farandouri/Georg Kapernaros)

*¶Dvořák, Cello Concerto in B minor (Paul Tortelier/LSO/Previn)

¶LUXURY: Canvases, paints and brushes.

¶BOOK: A bilingual edition of the poetry of Giorgos Seferis.

28 February 1981
1582 Carla Lane
Television comedy writer

¶Shostakovich, Symphony No. 5 in D minor (USSR State Symphony/Shostakovich)

¶'Shine On, You Crazy Diamond' (Pink Floyd)

*¶Tchaikovsky, Violin Concerto in D (Salvatore Accardo/BBC Symphony/Davis)

¶Vivaldi, 'Summer' (from *The Four Seasons*) (Berlin Philharmonic/von Karajan)

¶Albinoni/Giazotto, Adagio for Organ and Strings (Alastair Ross *organ*/Richard Hickox Orchestra)

¶Donizetti, 'O! La belle campagne' (from *Ne m'oubliez pas*) (Margreta Elkins/Geoffrey Mitchell Choir/Philharmonia Orchestra/Judd)

¶Berlioz, Symphonie fantastique (Berlin Philharmonic/von Karajan)

¶'Red Sails in the Sunset' (Ambrose and his Orchestra)

¶LUXURY: French shampoo.

¶BOOK: A dictionary of quotations.

7 March 1981
1583 Daniel Massey
Actor

¶Tchaikovsky, Symphony No. 2 in C minor (Amsterdam Concertgebouw/Haitink)

¶Ravel, Piano Concerto in G (Arturo Benedetti Michelangeli/Philharmonia Orchestra/Gracis)

¶Schubert, Symphony No. 9 in C (Great) (Amsterdam Concertgebouw/Haitink)

¶Sibelius, 'The Death of Melisande' (from *Pelléas and Mélisande*) (RPO/Beecham)

¶'Red Top' (Erroll Garner *piano*)

¶Mozart, 'Soave sia il vento' (from *Cosi fan tutte*) (Elizabeth Schwarzkopf/Christa Ludwig/Walter Berry/Philharmonia Orchestra/Böhm)

¶'Come Rain or Come Shine' (Frank Sinatra)

*¶Beethoven, Violin Concerto in D (David Oistrakh/French National Radio Orchestra/Cluytens)

¶LUXURY: Wine.

¶BOOK: James Agate, *Ego*

14 March 1981
1584 Peter Nichols
Playwright

¶'I'm A Ding Dong Daddy from Dumas' (Benny Goodman Quartet)

¶Coward, 'Why Do the Wrong People Travel?' (from *Sail Away*) (Elaine Stritch)

¶Mozart, Horn Concerto No. 3 in E flat (K447) (Alan Civil/Philharmonia Orchestra/Klemperer)

¶'At Least You Can Say You Have Seen It' (Barry Humphries)

¶'Carolina Shout' (Fats Waller)

¶'The Latin-American Way' (from *Privates on Parade*) (Dennis Quilley)

*¶Handel, 'He Trusted in God' (from *Messiah*) (LSO and Chorus/Colin Davis)

¶'Solitude' (Duke Ellington and his Orchestra)

¶LUXURY: A vibraphone.

¶BOOK: *The Collected Essays, Journalism and Letters of George Orwell*

21 March 1981
1585 Russell Harty
Television interviewer

¶ Walton, *Henry V Suite* (overture) (Philharmonia Orchestra/Walton)

¶ 'When I'm Cleaning Windows' (George Formby)

¶ Berlioz, 'Villanelle' (from *Les nuits d'été*) (Janet Baker/NPO/ Barbirolli)

*¶ 'In the Bleak Midwinter' (King's College Chapel Choir/ Willcocks)

¶ Prokofiev, 'Dance with Mandolins' (from ballet *Romeo and Juliet*) (LSO/Previn)

¶ 'My Way' (Paul Phoenix/ Jeremy Carpenter/Boys of St Paul's Cathedral Choir/Rose)

¶ 'If You Were the Only Girl in the World' (from *The Bing Boys are Here*) (Violet Loraine/ George Robey)

¶ 'The National Anthem' (Cambridge University Musical Society/NPO/Ledger)

¶ LUXURY: A flagpole with a Union Jack.

¶ BOOK: Whittaker, *A History of Craven*.

28 March 1981
1586 Patricia Ruanne
Ballerina

¶ Stravinsky, *The Rite of Spring* (LSO/Abbado)

¶ Wagner/Liszt (arr.), 'Liebestod' (from *Tristan und Isolde*) (Michele Campanella *piano*)

¶ Nielson, Symphony No. 5 (NPO/Horenstein)

¶ Puccini, 'Che gelida manina' (from *La bohème*) (Luciano Pavarotti/Berlin Philharmonic/ von Karajan)

¶ Kabalevsky, Piano Concerto No. 3 in D (Youth) (Vladimir Fetsman/Moscow Philharmonic/Mansurov)

¶ Saint-Saëns, Symphony No. 3 in C minor (Gaston Litaize *organ*/CSO/Barenboim)

¶ Bruch, Violin Concerto No. 1 in G minor (Yehudi Menuhin/ LSO/Boult)

*¶ Prokofiev, ballet *Romeo and Juliet* (LSO/Previn)

¶ LUXURY: Sunglasses.

¶ BOOK: J. R. R. Tolkien, *The Lord of the Rings*

4 April 1981
1587 Gary Glitter
Pop singer

¶ 'In the Mood' (Glenn Miller Orchestra)

¶ Lennon, 'Starting Over' (John Lennon)

¶ 'Busted' (Ray Charles)

¶ Beethoven, Violin Concerto in D (Yehudi Menuhin/NPO/ Klemperer)

¶ 'Falling in Love Again' (from film *The Blue Angel*) (Marlene Dietrich)

¶ 'Bona Performers' (from radio series *Round the Horne*) (Kenneth Horne/Kenneth Williams/Hugh Paddick)

*¶ 'All Shook Up' (Elvis Presley)

¶ 'Rock and Roll, I Gave You the Best Years of My Life' (Gary Glitter)

¶ LUXURY: Elastoplast.

¶ BOOK: *The Times Concise Atlas*

11 April 1981
1588 Sir Fitzroy Maclean (2nd appearance)
Writer and traveller

¶ 'The Barren Rocks of Aden' (Regimental Band and Pipes and Drums of the Black Watch)

¶ Tchaikovsky, *Swan Lake* (waltz) (Orchestre de la Suisse Romande/Ansermet)

¶ 'As Time Goes By' (from film *Casablanca*) (Russell Scott *organ*)

¶ 'Lilli Marlene' (Lale Andersen)

¶ Haydn, Trumpet Concerto in E flat (Maurice André/LSO/ Lopez-Cobos)

¶ Mozart, 'Voi che sapete' (from *The Marriage of Figaro*) (Fiorenza Cossotto/ Philharmonia Orchestra/ Giulini)

¶ 'The Road to the Isles' (from *Songs of the Hebrides*) (Archie Mactaggart/Cameron MacKichan)

*¶ Beethoven, Piano Concerto No. 5 in E flat major (Emperor) (Vladimir Ashkenazy/CSO/ Solti)

¶ LUXURY: Writing materials.

¶ BOOK: Leo Tolstoy, *War and Peace* (in Russian).

18 April 1981
1589 Princess Grace of Monaco

¶ Berlin, 'You're Easy to Dance With' (from film *Holiday Inn*) (Fred Astaire)

¶ 'You Make Me Feel So Young' (Frank Sinatra)

¶ Ellis, 'On the Amazon' (from *Mr Cinders*) (Don MacLean)

*¶ Chopin, Berceuse in D flat (opus 57) (Artur Rubinstein *piano*)

¶ Shakespeare, 'The Proud Horse' (from *Venus and Adonis*) (Princess Grace of Monaco/ Richard Pasco)

¶ Bach, Sonata No. 1 in G (BWV 1027) for Viola da Gamba and Harpsichord (Leonard Rose *viola da gamba*/ Glenn Gould *harpsichord*)

¶ Haydn, Symphony No. 101 in D (The Clock) (Academy of St Martin-in-the-Fields/Marriner)

¶ Khachaturian, 'Sabre Dance' (from *Gayaneh*) (Vienna Philharmonic/Khachaturian)

¶ LUXURY: Two pillows.

¶ BOOK: The plays of George Kelly.

25 April 1981
1590 Stewart Granger (2nd appearance)
Actor

¶ Tchaikovsky, Piano Concerto No. 1 in B flat minor (Artur Rubinstein/Boston Symphony/ Leinsdorf)

¶ Gretchaninov, 'Glory to Thee, O Lord' (Feodor Chaliapin)

¶ Bath, 'Cornish Rhapsody' (from film *Love Story*) (Leo Litwin *piano*/LSO/Bath)

¶ Paganini, Violin Concerto No. 1 in D (Yehudi Menuhin/RPO/ Erede)

¶ Lennon & McCartney, 'Yesterday' (The Beatles)

*¶ Beethoven, Piano Concerto No. 5 in E flat major (Emperor) (Artur Rubinstein/LPO/ Barenboim)

¶ 'Les trois cloches' (Edith Piaf/ Les Compagnons de la Chanson)

¶ 'My Way' (Frank Sinatra)

¶ LUXURY: A miniature statuette in gold of Sir Winston Churchill.

¶ BOOK: The collected works of Ernest Hemingway.

2 May 1981
1591 Sir Frederick Ashton (2nd appearance)
Choreographer

¶ Liszt, 'Valse oubliée' No. 1 (Vladimir Horowitz *piano*)
¶ Franck, 'Symphonic Variations' (Moura Lympany *piano*/Philharmonia Orchestra/ Susskind)
¶ Satie, orchestrated Debussy, *Trois gymnopédies* (no. 1) (Royal Opera House Orchestra, Covent Garden/Lanchbery)
¶ Schubert, String Quintet in C (D. 956) (William Pleeth *cello*/ Amadeus String Quartet)
¶ 'La vie en rose' (Edith Piaf)
¶ Poulenc, Ballet *Les biches* (Paris Conservatoire Orchestra/ Prêtre)
¶ Elgar, 'Nimrod' (from *Enigma Variations*) (LSO/Boult)
*¶ Mozart, Piano Concerto No. 21 in C (K. 467) (Géza Anda *piano and conducting*/Salzburg Mozarteum Camerata Academica)
¶ LUXURY: Two packs of playing cards.
¶ BOOK: Marcel Proust, *À la recherche du temps perdu* in French, plus a French/English dictionary.

9 May 1981
1592 Buddy Rich
Bandleader and drummer

¶ 'Tiger Rag' (Ray Noble and his Orchestra)
¶ 'The Good Life' (Tony Bennett)
¶ 'Willow, Weep for Me' (Ella Fitzgerald)
¶ Gershwin, 'I Loves You, Porgy' (from *Porgy and Bess*) (Miles Davis *trumpet*/Gil Evans Orchestra)
¶ 'In the Wee Small Hours of the Morning' (Frank Sinatra)
¶ 'Mission to Moscow' (Benny Goodman Band)
*¶ 'The Girl on the Rock' (from *Seven Dreams*) (Soloists/Ralph Brewster Singers/Orchestra/ Gordon Jenkins)
¶ 'The Kid from Red Bank' (Count Basie Band)
¶ LUXURY: A Ferrari.
¶ BOOK: *The Story of O*

16 May 1981
1593 Sir John Gielgud (2nd appearance)
Actor

*¶ Bach, Double Concerto in D minor (BWV 1043) (Fritz Kreisler and Efrem Zimbalist *violins*/string quartet)
¶ Purcell, 'When I am Laid in Earth' (from *Dido and Aeneas*) (Janet Baker/Aldeburgh Festival Strings/Bedford)
¶ Delius, 'The Walk to the Paradise Garden' (from *A Village Romeo and Juliet*) (RPO/ Beecham)
¶ Mahler, 'Abschied' (from *Das Lied von der Erde*) (Kathleen Ferrier/Vienna Philharmonic/ Walter)
¶ Brahms, 'An Jeder Hand die Finger' (from *Neue Liebeslieder*, opus 65) (Irmgard Seefried)
¶ William Blake, 'The Chimney Sweeper' and 'The Sick Rose' (Ralph Richardson)
¶ Mozart, Clarinet Concerto in A (K. 622) (Jack Brymer/RPO/ Beecham)
¶ Fauré, 'In Paradisum' (from *Requiem*) (King's College Chapel Choir/NPO/Willcocks)
¶ LUXURY: None chosen.
¶ BOOK: Marcel Proust, *À la recherche du temps perdu*

23 May 1981
1594 Edmund Rubbra
Composer

¶ Monteverdi, 'Amor' (from *Lamento della Ninfa*) (Marie-Blanche de Polignac/Paul Devenue/Hugues Cuenod/Doda Conrad/unknown *cello*/Nadia Boulanger *piano*)
¶ Tallis, 40-Part Motet, 'Spem in Alium' (Cambridge University Musical Society/ Willcocks)
¶ Fauré, 'In Paradisum' (from Requiem) (King's College Chapel Choir/NPO/Willcocks)
¶ Stravinsky, Symphony of Psalms (Choir of Christ Church Cathedral, Oxford/Philip Jones Brass Ensemble/Preston)
¶ 'Te Deum' (Benedictine monks of the Abbey Saint-Maurice & Saint-Maur of Clervaux)

¶ Byrd, 'Kyrie' (from *Mass for Five Voices*) (King's College Chapel Choir/Willcocks)
¶ 'Tabhair Dom Do Lamh (Give Me Your Hand)' (The Chieftains)
*¶ Schubert, Symphony No. 9 in C (Great) (LPO/Boult)
¶ LUXURY: Music manuscript paper and pencils.
¶ BOOK: A. A. Milne, *Winnie the Pooh* and *The House at Pooh Corner*

30 May 1981
1595 Eric Shilling
Opera Singer

¶ 'Why Can't We Have the Sea in London?' (Billy Williams)
*¶ Mozart, 'Deh vieni, non tardar' (from *The Marriage of Figaro*) (Elly Ameling/English Chamber Orchestra/de Waart)
¶ Verdi, 'Bella figlia dell'amore' (from *Rigoletto*) (Marcella Sembrich/Gina Severina/Enrico Caruso/Antonio Scotti)
¶ Arne, 'One Night with Friends' (from *The Cooper*) (Eric Shilling/Ann Dowdall/ Duncan Robertson/orchestra/ Hopkins)
¶ J. Strauss, 'Brüderlein und Schwesterlein' (from *Die Fledermaus*) (Sadler's Wells Opera Chorus and Orchestra/ Tausky)
¶ Offenbach, 'Fly Duet' (from *Orpheus in the Underworld*) (June Bronhill/Eric Shilling/ Sadler's Wells Opera Chorus and Orchestra/Faris)
¶ Bach, 'Erbarme dich, Mein Gott' (from *St Matthew Passion*) (Janet Baker/Munich Bach Orchestra/Richter)
¶ Schubert, String Quintet in C (D. 956) (William Pleeth *cello*/ Amadeus String Quartet)
¶ LUXURY: An astronomical telescope.
¶ BOOK: *Collins' Albatross Book of Verse*

6 June 1981
1596 The Rt Hon. William Whitelaw
Home Secretary

¶ 'Highland Laddie' (HM Scots Guards Band/Howe)

¶ Bizet, 'Les voici' (from *Carmen*) (French National Radio Chorus and Orchestra/Beecham)

¶ J. Strauss, 'The Blue Danube' (Vienna Philharmonic/Boskovsky)

*¶ Berlin, 'White Christmas' (from film *Holiday Inn*) (Bing Crosby)

¶ 'D'Ye Ken John Peel' (Owen Brannigan/Hendon Grammar School Choir/Pro Arte Orchestra/Mackerras)

¶ Crimond, 'The Twenty-Third Psalm' (Glasgow Orpheus Choir/Roberton)

¶ 'Run, Rabbit, Run' (Flanagan & Allen)

¶ 'The Duke of Perth' (Jimmy Shand, Jr and his Band)

¶ LUXURY: A bath with a hot water system.

¶ BOOK: Bernard Darwin, *The World that Fred Made*

13 June 1981
1597 Richard Leakey
Anthropologist

¶ Mozart, Violin Concerto No. 5 in A (K. 219) (Yehudi Menuhin *violin and conducting*/Bath Festival Chamber Orchestra)

¶ 'Kenyan National Anthem' (chorus)

¶ Rodgers & Hammerstein, *South Pacific* (overture) (soundtrack)

¶ Jarre, 'Theme from *Lawrence of Arabia*' (from film) (LPO/Jarre)

¶ Jarre, 'Lara's Theme' (from film *Dr Zhivago*) (MGM Studio Orchestra/Jarre)

¶ Sibelius, 'Finlandia' (Helsinki Philharmonic/Panula)

¶ 'Matondoni Wedding' (people of Lamu, Kenya/Fanshawe)

*¶ Solo Whale (recorded by Frank Watlington)

¶ LUXURY: A pillow.

¶ BOOK: *Touch the Earth* (speeches of American Indians when negotiating treaties).

20 June 1981
1598 Giuseppe di Stefano
Tenor

¶ 'Mutetti di lu paliu' (Giuseppe di Stefano/RCA Victor Symphony/Cellini)

¶ Verdi, 'Ingemisco' (from *Requiem*) (Giuseppe di Stefano/NBC Symphony/Toscanini)

¶ Sousa/Horowitz (arr.), 'Stars and Stripes Forever' (Vladimir Horowitz *piano*)

¶ Mahler, Symphony No. 5 (NPO/Barbirolli)

*¶ Bellini, 'Qui la voce sua soave' (from *I puritani*) (Maria Callas/Philharmonia Orchestra and Chorus/Rescigno)

¶ Vivaldi, 'Autumn' (from *The Four Seasons*) (LPO/Perlman)

¶ 'This is All I Ask' (Nat 'King' Cole)

¶ 'People' (from *Funny Girl*) (Barbra Streisand)

¶ LUXURY: A roulette wheel.

¶ BOOK: Ariana Stassinopoulos, *Maria*

27 June 1981
1599 Morris West
Novelist

*¶ Mozart, Sinfonia Concertante in E flat major (K. 364) (Isaac Stern *violin*/Pinchas Zukerman *viola*/English Chamber Orchestra/Barenboim)

¶ 'Les amants de Paris' (Edith Piaf)

¶ Lerner & Loewe, 'If Ever I Would Leave You' (from *Camelot*) (Robert Goulet)

¶ 'Santa Lucia Luntana' (Aurelio Fierro/Neapolitan Song Orchestra/Campanino)

¶ Bruch, Violin Concerto No. 1 in G minor (Yehudi Menuhin/LSO/Boult)

¶ Lloyd Webber/Black, 'Tell Me on a Sunday' (Marti Webb/LPO/Rabinowitz)

¶ Puccini, 'Nessun dorma' (from *Turandot*) (Luciano Pavarotti/LPO/Mehta)

¶ Sondheim, 'Send in the Clowns' (from *A Little Night Music*) (Glynis Johns)

¶ LUXURY: Pencils and paper.

¶ BOOK: John Donne, *Meditations upon Our Humane Condition*

4 July 1981
1600 Gloria Swanson
Actress

¶ 'I Love You So Much I Hate You' (from film *Perfect Understanding*) (Gloria Swanson)

¶ 'Très moutarde' (New Orleans Ragtime Orchestra)

¶ Gershwin, 'Rhapsody in Blue' (George Gershwin *piano*/Paul Whiteman and his Concert Orchestra)

¶ 'Wonderful One' (Mel Torme)

*¶ Puccini, 'Un bel di vedremo' (from *Madam Butterfly*) (Rosa Ponselle)

¶ J. Strauss, 'Kaiserwalzer' (Berlin Philharmonic/von Karajan)

¶ Thomas, 'Connais-tu le pays?' (from *Mignon*) (Frederica von Stade/LPO/Pritchard)

¶ 'Love (Your Spell is Everywhere)' (from film *The Trespasser*) (Gloria Swanson)

¶ LUXURY: A telephone.

¶ BOOK: Kahlil Gibran, *The Prophet*

11 July 1981
1601 Gillian Lynne
Director and choreographer

¶ 'Top of the World' (Diana Ross)

¶ Prokofiev, 'Balcony Scene' (from Ballet, *Romeo and Juliet*) (LSO/Previn)

¶ Woolfenden, 'You Spotted Snakes' (from *A Midsummer Night's Dream*) (Martin Best)

¶ Walton, 'The Magician and the Transformation' (from *The Quest*) (LSO/Walton)

¶ Tippett, 'Ritual Dances' (from *The Midsummer Marriage*) (Royal Opera House Orchestra, Covent Garden/Pritchard)

¶ 'Shine Like You Should' (Melissa Manchester)

¶ Lloyd Webber/Eliot, 'Jellicle Ball' (from *Cats*) (original London cast)

*¶ Tippett, Concerto for Double String Orchestra (Academy of St Martin-in-the-Fields/Marriner)

¶ LUXURY: Eyelash curlers.

¶ BOOK: A French Language course.

18 July 1981
1602 Carl Sagan
Astronomer and author
¶ 'Symphony to the Powers B' (Vangelis)
¶ Pachelbel, Canon in D for 3 violins and continuo (Academy of St Martin-in-the-Fields/Marriner)
¶ 'Fly, Night Bird' (Roy Buchanan *guitar*/synthesizers)
¶ Shostakovich, Symphony No. 11 in G minor (Houston Symphony/Stokowski)
¶ 'Depicting Cranes in Their Nests' (Goro Yamaguchi *Shakuhaci*)
¶ 'Alpha' (Vangelis)
*¶ Bach, Partita No. 3 in E (Arthur Grumiaux *violin*)
¶ 'Iziel Je Delyo Hajdutin' (Valya Balkanska *vocal*/bagpipes)
¶ LUXURY: A reflecting telescope.
¶ BOOK: A Boy Scout handbook.

25 July 1981
1603 Roger Moore
Actor
*¶ 'Theme from *New York, New York*' (from film) (Frank Sinatra)
¶ Puccini, 'Quando me'n vo' (from *La bohème*) (Renata Tebaldi/NPO/Bonynge)
¶ 'Ready to Take a Chance Again' (Barry Manilow)
¶ Verdi, *La traviata* (prelude) (NPO/Bonynge)
¶ 'The Cruise' (Bob Newhart)
¶ 'Fill the World with Love' (from film *Goodbye Mr Chips*) (Petula Clarke/Peter O'Toole)
¶ Tarrega, 'Recuerdos de la Alhambra' (Liona Boyd *guitar*)
¶ 'I Hold Your Hand in Mine' (Tom Lehrer *vocal/piano*)
¶ LUXURY: A video recorder with cassettes of his family.
¶ BOOK: James Clavell, *Noble House*

1 August 1981
1604 Julian Lloyd Webber
Cellist
¶ 'Take Good Care of My Baby' (Bobby Vee)
¶ Shostakovich, Cello Concerto in E flat (Mstislav Rostropovich/Philadelphia Orchestra/Ormandy)
¶ Mozart, String Quintet in G minor (K. 516) (William Primrose *viola*/Griller String Quartet)
¶ Delius, 'La calinda' (from *Koanga*) (Hallé Orchestra/Barbirolli)
¶ Beethoven, Symphony No. 8 in F major (opus 93) (NBC Symphony/Toscanini)
¶ 'Nocturne' (Django Reinhardt *guitar*/Stephane Grapelli *violin*)
*¶ Elgar, Cello Concerto in E minor (Beatrice Harrison/New Symphony Orchestra/Elgar)
¶ Britten, Suite No. 3 for Cello (Julian Lloyd Webber)
¶ LUXURY: His cello.
¶ BOOK: The history of Orient Football Club.

8 August 1981
1605 Terry Hands
Theatre producer and director
¶ Dvořák, Cello Concerto in B minor (opus 104) (Pierre Fournier/Berlin Philharmonic/Szell)
¶ Lennon & McCartney, 'Michelle' (The Beatles)
¶ Anon, 'The Play of Daniel' (New York Pro Musica/Greenberg)
*¶ Haydn, String Quartet in C (opus 54, no. 2) (Amadeus String Quartet)
¶ Verdi, 'Dio! Mi potevi scagliar' (from *Otello*) (Placido Domingo/NPO/Levine)
¶ Rodrigo, Concierto de Aranjuez (John Williams *guitar*/English Chamber Orchestra/Barenboim)
¶ T. S. Eliot, *Murder in the Cathedral* (excerpt) (Susan Fleetwood/Royal Shakespeare Company)
¶ Elgar, Cello Concerto in E minor (Jacqueline du Pré/LSO/Barbirolli)
¶ LUXURY: A cello.
¶ BOOK: An English dictionary.

15 August 1981
1606 Sebastian Coe
World champion athlete
¶ 'History of a Boy Scout' (Dave Brubeck Quartet)
¶ 'A Sunday Afternoon at Home' (from radio series *Hancock's Half Hour*) (Tony Hancock/company)
¶ Puccini, *Tosca* (excerpt from Act 1) (Katia Ricciarelli/José Carreras/Berlin Philharmonic/von Karajan)
¶ 'Georgia on My Mind' (Billie Holiday and her Orchestra)
¶ 'Just a Closer Walk with Thee' (Lawson-Haggart Greats of Jazz)
¶ 'Olympic Anthem', 1980
¶ 'Love for Sale' (from *The New Yorkers*) (Sidney Bechet *soprano saxophone* and his Quartet)
*¶ Gershwin, 'A Foggy day' (from film *A Damsel in Distress*) (Ella Fitzgerald/Louis Armstrong *vocal and trumpet*/Oscar Peterson Trio/Buddy Rich *drums*)
¶ LUXURY: A comfortable bed.
¶ BOOK: *The Penguin Dorothy Parker*

22 August 1981
1607 Paul Eddington
Actor
*¶ Bach, *St Matthew Passion* (nos. 45 & 46) (Peter Schreier/Anton Diakov/Vienna Singverein/Berlin Philharmonic/von Karajan)
¶ Britten, 'Dawn' (from 'Four Sea Interludes' in *Peter Grimes*) (Royal Opera House Orchestra, Covent Garden/Britten)
¶ Butterworth, 'The Banks of Green Willow' (LPO/Boult)
¶ Vivaldi, 'Winter' (from *The Four Seasons*) (English Chamber Orchestra/Szeryng *violin* and conductor)
¶ Elgar, Cello Concerto in E minor (Pablo Casals/BBC Symphony/Boult)
¶ Chopin, Nocturne in F minor (opus 55, no. 1) (Artur Rubinstein *piano*)
¶ Verdi, 'Macchia e qui tuttora!' (from *Macbeth*) (Maria Callas/Philharmonia Orchestra/Rescigno)

¶Mozart, Piano Concerto No. 27 in B flat minor (K. 595) (Daniel Barenboim *piano and conducting*/English Chamber Orchestra)
¶LUXURY: Ivon Hitchin, *Boathouse at Dawn*
¶BOOK: Somerville and Ross, *Experiences of an Irish RM*

29 August 1981
1608 Frank Oz
Puppeteer and voice of 'Miss Piggy' in The Muppet Show
*¶'Don't Get Around Much Anymore' (Mose Allison)
¶'God Rest You Merry, Gentlemen' (Bing Crosby)
¶'What a Waste' (from *Wonderful Town*) (George Gaynes/Warren Galjour/Albert Linville Orchestra/Lehman Engel)
¶'Bill Bailey, Won't You Please Come Home' (from film *The Five Pennies*) (Louis Armstrong *vocal*/Orchestra)
¶'Lost Mind' (Mose Allison)
¶'Racing in the Street' (Bruce Springsteen)
¶'Antmusic' (Adam and the Ants)
¶'New Parchman' (Mose Allison)
¶LUXURY: Clean sheets.
¶BOOK: The complete works of Emily Dickinson.

5 September 1981
1609 Alan Jones
Racing driver
¶J. Strauss, 'The Blue Danube' (Berlin Philharmonic/von Karajan)
¶Tchaikovsky, 'Romeo and Juliet Fantasy Overture' (Philharmonia Orchestra/Muti)
¶Lightfoot, 'Summer Side of Life' (Gordon Lightfoot)
¶'Highway 61' (Mississippi Fred McDowell)
¶'Nashville Wimmin' (Waylon Jennings)
¶'Rhiannon' (Fleetwood Mac)
¶'Sultans of Swing' (Dire Straits)
*¶'Reminiscing' (Little River Band)
¶LUXURY: Australian lager.
¶BOOK: Wilbur Smith, *Eagle in the Sky*

12 September 1981
1610 Jessye Norman
Singer
¶Brahms, 'Alto Rhapsody' (opus 53) (Marian Anderson/RCA Victor Symphony/Shaw)
¶Bach, Cello Suite No. 3 in C (BWV 1009) (Pierre Fournier)
¶Beethoven, *Fidelio* (Act 1 quartet) (Martha Mödl/Sena Jurinac/Rudolf Shock/Gottlob Frick/Vienna Philharmonic/Furtwängler)
¶'I Have a Dream' (speech, 27 August 1963) (Martin Luther King)
¶'Could Love You for Ever' (from *The Lunatic, the Lover and the Poet*) (Isla Blair/Derek Jacobi)
*¶Wagner, 'Love Duet' (from *Tristan und Isolde*) (Kirsten Flagstad/Lauritz Melchior/Metropolitan Opera Orchestra/Leinsdorf)
¶Debussy, 'Golliwog's Cakewalk' (from *Children's Corner Suite*) (Arturo Benedetti Michelangeli *piano*)
¶Mozart, *The Marriage of Figaro* (Act 2 finale) (soloists/BBC Symphony/Davis)
¶LUXURY: Perrier water.
¶BOOK: The diaries of Virginia Woolf.

19 September 1981
1611 Malcolm Muggeridge (2nd appearance)
Writer
*¶Mozart, 'Exultate Jubilate' (K. 165) (Kiri Te Kanawa/LSO and Chorus/Davis)
¶Albinoni/Giazotto, Adagio in G minor (SAAR Chamber Orchestra/Ristenpart)
¶Dvořák, Cello Concerto in B minor (Pablo Casals/Czech Philharmonic/Szell)
¶R. Strauss, 'September' (from *Four Last Songs*) (Lisa della Casa/Vienna Philharmonic/Böhm)
¶Beethoven, Violin Concerto in D major (opus 61) (Yehudi Menuhin/Vienna Philharmonic/Silvestri)
¶Elgar, Serenade in E minor for Strings (Academy of St Martin-in-the-Fields/Marriner)

¶Beethoven, Trio in B flat, Opus 97 (Archduke) (Pinchas Zukerman *violin*/Jacqueline du Pré *cello*/Daniel Barenboim *piano*)
¶Gretchaninov, 'The Creed' (Choir of the Russian Church of the Metropolitan of Paris/Afonsky)
¶LUXURY: A beehive.
¶BOOK: As many of the writings of Samuel Johnson as possible.

26 September 1981
1612 James Mason (2nd appearance)
Actor
¶Rodrigo, Concierto de Aranjuez (Narciso Yepes *guitar*/National Orchestra of Spain/Argenta)
¶'My Home' (Pipes and Drums and Military Band of Royal Scots Dragoon Guards)
¶Beethoven, Piano Sonata in C minor (Pathétique) (Sviatoslav Richter)
¶Beethoven, Symphony No. 9 in D minor (opus 125) (Berlin Philharmonic/von Karajan)
¶'Come Rain or Come Shine' (Judy Garland)
¶Mozart, Flute Concerto No. 2 in D major (K. 314) (James Galway/Festival Strings of Lucerne/Rudolf Baumgartner)
¶Orff, *Carmina Burana* (Choir and Orchestra of German Opera, Berlin/Jochum)
*¶'My Man' (Billie Holiday)
¶LUXURY: A guitar.
¶BOOK: Vladimir Nabokov, *Ada*

3 October 1981
1613 Beaux Arts Trio (Isidore Cohen, Menahem Pressler, Bernard Greenhouse)
¶Beethoven, Symphony No. 7 in A major (opus 92) (NBC Symphony/Toscanini)
¶Beethoven, Piano Concerto No. 4 in G major (opus 58) (Artur Schnabel/LPO/Sargent)
¶Schumann, Cello Concerto in A minor (Gregor Piatigorsky/LPO/Barbirolli)
¶Beethoven, String Quartet No. 8 in E minor (opus 59, no. 2) (Rasoumovsky) (Juilliard Quartet)

¶Ravel, Piano Trio in A minor (Beaux Arts Trio)
¶Schubert, Piano Trio No. 1 in B flat (Alfred Cortot *piano*/Jacques Thibaud *violin*/Pablo Casals *cello*)
¶Mahler, *Das Lied von der Erde* (Kathleen Ferrier/Vienna Philharmonic/Walter)
¶Schubert, String Quintet in C (D. 956) (Bernard Greenhouse *cello*/Juilliard Quartet)
¶LUXURIES: (IC) a violin; (MP) a piano; (BG) a supply of violin and piano strings to set up a trading post.
¶BOOKS: (IC) a gardening manual; (MP) reproductions of great paintings; (BG) Chapman's book on handling small boats.

10 October 1981
1614 Montserrat Caballé
Singer
¶Wagner, 'Entrance of Brünnhilde' (from *Die Walküre*) (Birgit Nilsson/LSO/Leinsdorf)
¶Halévy, 'Rachel, quand du seigneur' (from *La juive*) (Richard Tucker/NPO/de Almeida)
¶Mozart, 'Die Bildnis' (from *The Magic Flute*) (Fritz Wunderlich/Berlin Philharmonic/Böhm)
¶Bellini, 'Lanello mio . . .' (from *La sonnambula*) (Maria Callas/La Scala Orchestra/Votto)
¶Wagner, 'Winterstürme' (from *Die Walküre*) (Lauritz Melchior/Vienna Philharmonic/Walter)
¶R. Strauss, 'Im Abendrot' (from *Four Last Songs*) (Elisabeth Schwarzkopf/Philharmonia Orchestra/Ackermann)
¶Chopin, Ballade No. 1 in G minor (opus 23) (Arturo Benedetti Michelangeli *piano*)
¶Mendelssohn, 'O Rest in the Lord' (from *Elijah*) (Kathleen Ferrier/Boyd Neel Orchestra)
¶LUXURY: A box to put her records in.
¶BOOK: *The Bible* will suffice. (*No favourite disc chosen*)

17 October 1981
1615 Elspeth Huxley
Writer
¶Porter, 'Anything Goes' (from *Anything Goes*) (Cole Porter *piano*)
¶Dvořák, Symphony No. 9 in E minor (New World) (Berlin Philharmonic/Kubelik)
¶Gershwin, 'Rhapsody in Blue' (George Gershwin *piano*/Paul Whiteman and his Concert Orchestra)
*¶Grieg, Piano Concerto in A minor (Clifford Curzon/LSO/Fjeldstad)
¶'La mer' (Charles Trenet)
¶Holst, 'Jupiter' (from *The Planets*) (LPO/Boult)
¶'The Flame Trees of Thika' (theme of TV series)
¶Beethoven, Symphony No. 6 in F major (Pastoral) (Philharmonia Orchestra/Klemperer)
¶LUXURY: A camera and film, plus developing and printing equipment.
¶BOOK: One of P. G. Wodehouse's Blanding novels.

24 October 1981
1616 Joseph Cotten
Actor
*¶Brahms, Symphony No. 1 in C minor (Berlin Philharmonic/von Karajan)
¶'Dixie' (Goldman Band)
¶Weill, 'September Song' (from *Knickerbocker Holiday*) (Walter Huston)
¶Porter, 'I Get a Kick Out of You' (from *Anything Goes*) (Ethel Merman)
¶Bach/Stokowski, Little Fugue in G minor (Boston Pops Orchestra/Fiedler)
¶Titheradge, 'Double Damask' (comedy sketch from *Clowns in Clover*) (Cicely Courtneidge/Ivor McLaren/Lawrence Green)
¶'This Could be the Start of Something Big' (Peter Duchin and his Orchestra)
¶'Cocktails for Two' (Spike Jones and his City Slickers)
¶LUXURY: Book on boat building.
¶BOOK: A gardening manual.

31 October 1981
1617 Patrick Lichfield (Thomas Patrick John Anson, 5th Earl of Lichfield)
Photographer
¶'I'm Gonna Sit Right Down and Write Myself a Letter' (Fats Waller *vocal and piano*)
*¶'As Time Goes by' (from film *Casablanca*) (Dooley Wilson)
¶Bach, 'Sheep May Safely Graze' (from Cantata No. 208) (Cyril Smith & Phyllis Sellick *pianos*)
¶Dylan, 'Just Like a Woman' (Bob Dylan)
¶'Banana Boat' (Stan Freberg *vocal*/Peter Leeds *speaking*/Billy May and his Music)
¶'A Whiter Shade of Pale' (Procol Harum)
¶McLean, 'Vincent' (Don McLean)
¶Holst, 'I Vow To Thee, My Country' (choirs, congregation and organ of St Paul's Cathedral)
¶LUXURY: An astronomical telescope.
¶BOOK: A book with blank cork pages.

7 November 1981
1618 Professor Glyn Daniel
Archaeologist
¶Vaughan Williams, 'Rhosymedre' (Philip Ledger *organ*)
¶Britten, *Missa Brevis* (Choir of St John's College, Cambridge/Guest)
*¶Bach, Partita No. 1 in B flat (Jacques Loussier Trio)
¶Orr, Symphony in One Movement (Scottish National Orchestra/Gibson)
¶Bach/Pick-Mangiagalli, Violin Sonata No. 6 in E (BWV 1006) (Boston Symphony/Koussevitzky)
¶Poulenc, Organ Concerto in G minor (Maurice Duruflé/French National Radio Orchestra/Prêtre)
¶'Blow the Wind Southerly' (Kathleen Ferrier)
¶Allegri, 'Miserere' (Psalm 51) (Ray Goodman *treble*/King's College Chapel Choir/Willcocks)

¶ LUXURY: Wine.
¶ BOOK: *Brewer's Dictionary of Phrase and Fable*

14 November 1981
1619 James Clavell
Novelist and film-maker
*¶ 'The Impossible Dream' (from *Man of La Mancha*) (Keith Michell)
¶ 'Eternal Father, Strong to Save' (Holman–Climax Male Voice and Mabe Ladies Choirs)
¶ 'Rainflower' and 'Easty' (Jade Warrior)
¶ Lennon & McCartney, 'A Hard Day's Night' (from film) (The Beatles)
¶ Lerner & Loewe, 'If Ever I Should Leave You' (from *Camelot*) (Robert Goulet)
¶ Lloyd Webber/Rice, 'Don't Cry for Me, Argentina' (from *Evita*) (Julie Covington/LPO/Bowles)
¶ 'Greensleeves' (Perry Como)
¶ Rodgers & Hammerstein, 'Some Enchanted Evening' (from *South Pacific*) (Frank Sinatra/Rosemary Clooney)
¶ LUXURY: None wanted.
¶ BOOK: The Koran.

21 November 1981
1620 Diana Dors (2nd appearance)
Actress
¶ 'The Best is Yet To Come' (Tony Bennett)
¶ 'Tomorrow' (from *Annie*) (Ann-Marie Gwatkin)
¶ Lane/Lerner, 'Come Back To Me' (from *On A Clear Day You Can See For Ever*) (Peggy Lee)
¶ Sibelius, Symphony No. 2 in D (Bournemouth Symphony/Parvo Berglund)
¶ Bacharach/David, 'The Look of Love' (Johnny Mathis)
¶ Ravel, *Pavane Pour Une Infante Defunte* (Concertgebouw Orchestra of Amsterdam/Haitink)
¶ Sibelius, *Valse Triste* (Berlin Philharmonic/von Karajan)
¶ Hamlish/Bergman, 'The Way We Were' (from film) (Gladys Knight and the Pips)
¶ LUXURY: Chocolates.
¶ BOOK: Her own autobiography.

28 November 1981
1621 Group Captain Sir Douglas Bader
Celebrated wartime flyer
¶ Sieczynsky, 'Wien, du Stadt meiner Träume' (Richard Tauber/Odeon Künstlerorchester)
¶ 'The King of Borneo' (Frank Crumit)
¶ 'Underneath the Arches' (Flanagan & Allen)
¶ 'Charmaine' (Mantovani and his Orchestra)
¶ 'Paddy McGinty's Goat' (Val Doonican)
¶ 'Lilli Marlene' (Vera Lynn)
¶ Coward, 'I Wonder What Happened to Him' (Noël Coward)
¶ 'I'd Like to Teach The World to Sing' (The New Seekers)
*¶ (As his favourite disc, Sir Douglas chose a selection of Bing Crosby, but did not include this among his eight records.)
¶ LUXURY: A sand iron and golf balls.
¶ BOOK: The complete works of Alfred, Lord Tennyson.

5 December 1981
1622 Alan Howard
Actor
*¶ Beethoven, Sonata No. 15 in D, opus 28, (Pastoral) (Daniel Barenboim *piano*)
¶ Mozart, 'Der Hölle Rache' (from *The Magic Flute*) (Lucia Popp/Philharmonia Orchestra/Klemperer)
¶ Haydn, String Quartet in B flat (opus 76, no. 4) (Sunrise) (Aeolian Quartet)
¶ Samuel Taylor Coleridge, *The Ancient Mariner* (Ralph Richardson)
¶ Woolfenden, 'Coronation March' from *The Revenger's Tragedy* (Royal Shakespeare Company Wind Band/Woolfenden)
¶ Schubert, String Quartet No. 14 in D minor (D. 810) (Amadeus String Quartet)
¶ Haydn, *Mass in D minor* (King's College Chapel Choir/LSO/Willcocks)

¶ Mozart, String Quintet No. 6 in E flat (K. 614) (Arthur Grumiaux *violin*/Arpad Gérecz *violin*/Georges Janzer *viola*/Max Lesuer *viola*/Eva Czako *cello*)
¶ LUXURY: A piano.
¶ BOOK: A piano manual.

12 December 1981
1623 Jack Higgins (Harry Paterson)
Thriller writer
¶ 'Laura' (from film) (Oscar Peterson *piano*)
¶ 'Moonlight on the Highway' (Al Bowlly/Lew Stone and his Band)
¶ 'Gone with the Wind' (from film) (Dave Brubeck Quartet)
¶ 'As Time Goes By' (from film *Casablanca*) (Dooley Wilson)
¶ 'Misa Criolla' (Los Fronterizos/Cantoria de la Basilica del Socorro/Ramirez)
¶ 'Eagle Falls In Love' (from film *The Eagle Has Landed*) (Instrumental group/Lalo Schifrin)
*¶ Rachmaninov, Piano Concerto No. 4 in G minor (Rafael Orozco/RPO/de Waart)
¶ Gershwin, 'A Foggy Day' (from film *A Damsel in Distress*) (Fred Astaire)
¶ LUXURY: Writing materials.
¶ BOOK: T. S. Eliot, *The Four Quartets*

19 December 1981
1624 Helene Hanff
Writer
¶ Bach/Stokowski, Toccata and Fugue in D minor (Philadelphia Orchestra/Stokowski)
¶ Handel, 'Comfort Ye' (from *Messiah*) (Philip Langridge/Academy of St Martin-in-the-Fields/Marriner)
¶ Barber, Knoxville: 'Summer of 1915' (Leontyne Price/NPO/Schippers)
¶ Vaughan Williams, 'Serenade to Music' (16 Soloists/LPO/Boult)
¶ Bax, 'Coronation March' (LSO/Sargent)
¶ Sondheim, 'The Miller's Son' (from *A Little Night Music*) (D. Jamin-Bartlett)

*¶Bach, 'In Tears of Grief' (from *St Matthew Passion*) (Bach Choir/Thames Chamber Orchestra/Willcocks)
¶Stravinsky, Ballet *The Firebird* (closing passage) (CSO/Giulini)
¶LUXURY: A Scrabble set.
¶BOOK: Louis de Rouvroy, Duc de Saint-Simon, *Memoirs*

26 December 1981
1625 Lord Harewood (2nd appearance)
Managing Director of the English National Opera
¶Haydn, String Quartet No. 75 in G (opus 76, no. 1) (Amadeus String Quartet)
¶Wagner, 'Selig, wie die Sonne' (from *Die Meistersinger*) (Elisabeth Schumann/Gladys Parr/Lauritz Melchior/Ben Williams/Fredrich Schorr/LSO/Barbirolli)
¶Beethoven, Piano Trio No. 4 in D (opus 70, no. 1) (Daniel Barenboim *piano*/Pinchas Zukerman *violin*/Jacqueline du Pré *cello*)
¶Bellini, 'Qui la voce sua soave' (from *I puritani*) (Maria Callas/La Scala Orchestra and Chorus/Serafin)
¶Verdi, 'Ma lassu di vedremo' (from *Don Carlos*) (Montserrat Caballé/Placido Domingo/Royal Opera House Orchestra, Covent Garden/Giulini)
¶Janáček, *Katya Kabanová* (prelude) (Vienna Philharmonic/Mackerras)
¶Britten, 'Now Until the Break of Day' (from *A Midsummer Night's Dream*) (Elizabeth Harwood/Alfred Deller/LSO/Britten)
*¶Schubert, Piano Sonata in A (D. 959) (Alfred Brendel)
¶LUXURY: A typewriter, table and paper.
¶BOOK: An anthology of poetry.

2 January 1982
1626 Trevor Brooking
Footballer
¶'The Tracks of My Tears' (Smoky Robinson and the Miracles)
¶'Higher and Higher' (Jackie Wilson)

¶John/Taupin, 'Don't Let the Sun Go Down on Me' (Elton John)
¶'How Sweet It is (To be Loved by You)' (Junior Walker and the All Stars)
¶Lennon & McCartney, 'Let It Be' (The Beatles)
¶'Arthur's Theme (Best That You Can Do)' (from film *Arthur*) (Christopher Cross)
¶'Endless Love' (Diana Ross/Lionel Ritchie)
*¶'What Kind of Fool' (Barbra Streisand/Barry Gibb)
¶LUXURY: Golf clubs and balls.
¶BOOK: Crossword puzzles and pencils.

9 January 1982
1627 Martin Gilbert
Historian and biographer
¶'There'll Always be an England' (Jack Payne and his Band)
¶Handel, 'Honour and Arms' (from *Samson*) (Benjamin Luxon/London Voices/English Chamber Orchestra/Leppard)
*¶Flotow, 'M'appari' (from *Martha*) (Beniamino Gigli)
¶Vivaldi, 'Winter' (from *The Four Seasons*) (Itzhak Perlman *violin and conducting*/LPO)
¶Steffe/Howe, 'Battle Hymn of the Republic' (Thomas Pyle/Robert Shaw Chorale/RCA Victor Symphony/Shaw)
¶'Super Trooper' (Abba)
¶'Bialystok is My Home' (Polish Army Central Artistic Ensemble)
¶Parry/Blake, 'Jerusalem' (Janet Baker/Philip Ledger *organ*)
¶LUXURY: Drawings of his two children.
¶BOOKS: The document volumes of his Churchill biography.

16 January 1982
1628 Angela Rippon
Broadcaster and writer
*¶Holst, 'Jupiter' (from *The Planets*) (LSO/Sargent)
¶Villa-Lobos, Bachianas Brasileiras No. 5 (Victoria de los Angeles/8 cellos/Villa-Lobos)

¶'If' (Jack Jones)
¶Rezniček, *Donna Diana* (overture) (Vienna Philharmonic/Boskovsky)
¶'Superbird' (Neil Sedaka)
¶Bizet, 'Au fond du temple saint' (from *Les pêcheurs de perles*) (Jussi Björling/Robert Merrill/RCA Victor Symphony/Cellini)
¶'Bona Law' (from radio series *Round the Horne*) (Kenneth Horne/Kenneth Williams/Hugh Paddick)
¶Mendelssohn, Violin Concerto in E minor (Yehudi Menuhin/Philharmonia Orchestra/Kurtz)
¶LUXURY: Water colours, brushes and paper.
¶BOOK: Jane Austen, *Pride and Prejudice*

23 January 1982
1629 Frankie Howerd (2nd appearance)
Comedian
¶'Knees Up, Mother Brown' (audience of the Metropolitan, Edgware Road, London)
¶Chopin, Nocturne in C minor (opus 48, no. 1) (Artur Rubinstein *piano*)
¶Beethoven, Symphony No. 9 in D minor (opus 125) (Philharmonia Orchestra and Chorus/Klemperer)
¶'Autumn Leaves' (Nat 'King' Cole)
¶Puccini, 'Love and Music' (from *Tosca*) (Joan Hammond/Philharmonia Orchestra/Curiel)
¶Sondheim, 'Send in the Clowns' (from *A Little Night Music*) (Cleo Laine)
¶J. Strauss, 'Brüderlein und Schwesterlein' (from *Die Fledermaus*) (Vienna State Opera Chorus/Vienna Philharmonic/von Karajan)
*¶Parry/Blake, 'Jerusalem' (Coventry Cathedral Boys' Choir)
¶LUXURY: A Little cross given to him by his mother.
¶BOOK: Charles Dickens, *David Copperfield*

30 January 1982
1630 Paul McCartney
Composer, musician and ex-Beatle
¶ 'Heartbreak Hotel' (Elvis Presley)
¶ 'Sweet Little Sixteen' (Chuck Berry)
¶ Britten, 'Courtly Dances' (from *Gloriana*) (Julian Bream Consort)
¶ 'Be-Bop-a-Lula' (Gene Vincent)
*¶ Lennon, 'Beautiful Boy' (John Lennon)
¶ 'Searchin'' (The Coasters)
¶ 'Tutti-Frutti' (Little Richard)
¶ 'Walking in the Park with Eloise' (Country Hams)
¶ LUXURY: A guitar.
¶ BOOK: *Linda's pictures*, by his wife.

6 February 1982
1631 Professor J. K. Galbraith
Writer, economist and ex-US ambassador
¶ 'Skye Boat Song' (Glendaurel Highland Pipe Band)
¶ 'California, Here I Come' (Ray Noble and his Orchestra)
¶ 'Fair Harvard' (Harvard Glee Club)
¶ Gershwin, 'I Got Plenty of Nuttin'' (from *Porgy and Bess*) (Robert McFerrin)
¶ 'Happy Days are Here Again' (Jack Hylton and his Orchestra)
*¶ Rodgers & Hammerstein, 'Oh, What a Beautiful Morning' (from *Oklahoma*) (Alfred Drake)
¶ Lerner & Loewe, 'Get Me to the Church on Time' (from *My Fair Lady*) (Stanley Holloway)
¶ J. Strauss, 'Tales from the Vienna Woods' (New York Philharmonic/Bernstein)
¶ LUXURY: A typewriter and paper.
¶ BOOK: A personal anthology.

13 February 1982
1632 Sir Christopher Leaver
Lord Mayor of London
¶ Chopin, 'Grand Fantasy on Polish Airs' (opus 13) (Alexis Weissenberg *piano*/Paris Conservatoire Orchestra/ Skrowaczewski)
¶ Gluck, 'Che faro senza Euridice?' (from *Orfeo ed Euridice*) (Kathleen Ferrier/ Netherlands Opera Orchestra/ Bruck)
*¶ Beethoven, Triple Concerto in C (Sviatoslav Richter *piano*/ David Oistrakh *violin*/Mstislav Rostropovich *cello*/Berlin Philharmonic/von Karajan)
¶ Mozart, Piano Concerto No. 25 in C (K. 503) (Alfred Brendel/Academy of St Martin-in-the-Fields/Marriner)
¶ Berlioz, Les francs juges (overture) (LSO/Davis)
¶ Elgar, Cello Concerto in E minor (Jacqueline du Pré/LSO/ Barbirolli)
¶ Mozart, 'Ave Verum Corpus' (K. 618) (St Paul's Cathedral Choir/Philharmonia String Orchestra/Bower)
¶ Bruckner, Symphony No. 4 in E flat (Romantic) (Berlin Philharmonic/von Karajan)
¶ LUXURY: The contents of his wine cellar.
¶ BOOK: *Grove's Dictionary of Music and Musicians*

20 February 1982
1633 Petula Clark (2nd appearance)
Singer and actress
¶ 'Black Coffee' (Peggy Lee)
¶ 'Straphangin'' (Brecker Brothers)
¶ 'Lengths' (Peter Cook/Dudley Moore)
*¶ R. Strauss, 'Ein Heldenleben' (Cleveland Orchestra/Maazel)
¶ 'Lazy Afternoon' (Freddie Hubbard Ensemble)
¶ 'What a Fool Believes' (Doobie Brothers)
¶ Rodgers & Hammerstein, 'So Long, Farewell' (from *The Sound of Music*) (children from Apollo Victoria cast)

¶ LUXURY: A piano.
¶ BOOK: The short stories of John Steinbeck.

27 February 1982
1634 John Osborne (2nd appearance)
Playwright
¶ 'Doctor Jazz' (Jelly Roll Morton and his Red Hot Peppers)
¶ 'The Entertainer' (Bunk Johnson and his Band)
¶ 'Just A-Wearyin' for You' (Paul Robeson)
¶ Handel, 'Oh, What Art can Teach' (from *Ode for St Cecilia's Day*) (Theresa Stich-Randall/ LCO/Bernard)
¶ 'Yankee Doodle Boy' (from film *Yankee Doodle Dandy*) (James Cagney)
¶ Elgar, Cello Concerto in E minor (Pablo Casals/BBC Symphony/Boult)
¶ Mozart, 'Fin ch'han dal vino' (from *Don Giovanni*) (Eberhard Wächter/Philharmonia Orchestra/Giulini)
*¶ Vaughan Williams, 'The Lark Ascending' (Hugh Bean *violin*/ NPO/Boult)
¶ LUXURY: A piano and an instruction book.
¶ BOOK: Jeremy Taylor, *Holy Living and Holy Dying*

6 March 1982
1635 Dame Eva Turner (3rd appearance)
Prima donna
¶ Schubert, 'An die Musik' (Lotte Lehmann/Paul Ulanowsky *piano*)
*¶ Refice, 'Umbra di nube' (Claudia Muzio)
¶ Verdi, 'O Don Fatale' (from *Don Carlo*) (Ebe Stignani)
¶ Vaughan Williams, 'Serenade to Music' (16 soloists/BBC Symphony/Wood)
¶ Rossini, *La scala di seta* (overture) (LPO/Beecham)
¶ Puccini, 'Nessun dorma' (from *Turandot*) (Placido Domingo/Deutsche Oper Orchestra, Berlin/Santi)

¶Mozart, Sinfonia Concertante (K. 364) (Isaac Stern *violin*/Pinchas Zukerman *viola*/New York Philharmonic/Mehta)
¶Verdi, 'Dies Irae' (from *Requiem*) (Rome Opera House Chorus and Orchestra/Serafin)
¶LUXURY: A pair of castanets.
¶BOOK: Dante's *Inferno* in Italian.

13 March 1982
1636 George Chisholm (2nd appearance)
Jazz trombonist
¶'Autumn Leaves' (Nat 'King' Cole)
¶Bach, orchestrated Gerhardt, Flute Sonata No. 4 in C major (BWV 1033) (James Galway/National Philharmonic/Gerhardt)
¶'Thanks a Million' (Louis Armstrong and his Orchestra)
¶Massenet, 'Élégie' (Art Tatum *piano*)
¶'Blue Turning Grey Over You' (George Chisholm Quartet)
*¶'I Guess I'll Have to Change My Plan' (Jack Teagarden/Bobby Hackett and his Band)
¶Mozart, Horn Concerto No. 2 in E flat (K. 417) (Dennis Brain/Philharmonia Orchestra/Susskind)
¶'The Look of Love' (Urbie Green/20 other trombonists)
¶LUXURY: An engraved glass and a supply of bitter lemon.
¶BOOK: Books by P. G. Wodehouse and Spike Milligan bound together.

20 March 1982
1637 Bernard Miles (Lord Miles) (2nd appearance)
Actor, producer and founder of the Mermaid Theatre, London
¶Schubert, 'Die Forelle' (Gérard Souzay/Dalton Baldwin *piano*)
¶Grieg, 'Med en Vandlilje' (Kirsten Flagstad/Gerald Moore *piano*)
¶Mascagni, 'Voi lo sapete' (from *Cavalleria rusticana*) (Eva Turner/Orchestra/Beecham)
¶'Sally' (Gracie Fields)

¶'West End Blues' (Louis Armstrong *vocal* and *trumpet* and His Hot Five)
¶Miles, 'The Race for the Rhinegold Stakes' (Bernard Miles)
¶Coward, 'I'll See You Again' (from *Bitter Sweet*) (Art Tatum *piano*)
*¶Mozart, Piano Concerto No. 24 in C minor (K. 491) (Walter Gieseking/Philharmonia Orchestra/von Karajan)
¶LUXURY: A box of notebooks, pencils and sharpeners.
¶BOOK: Homer's *Odyssey*, translated by W. H. D. Rouse.

27 March 1982
1638 Sir William Walton (2nd appearance)
Composer
¶S. S. Wesley, 'The Wilderness' (St John's College Choir, Cambridge/Guest)
¶Mozart, Piano Concerto No. 23 in A (K. 488) (Daniel Barenboim *piano and conducting*/English Chamber Orchestra)
¶Walton, 'Old Sir Faulk' (Kiri Te Kanawa/Richard Amner *piano*)
*¶Walton, Violin Concerto (Jascha Heifetz/Philharmonia Orchestra/Walton)
¶Sibelius, Symphony No. 5 in E flat (Berlin Philharmonic/von Karajan)
¶Puccini, 'E lucevan le stelle' (from *Tosca*) (Placido Domingo/Philharmonia Orchestra/Levine)
¶Henze, 'A l'acqua de liffuntanelle' (from *Five Neapolitan Songs*) (Dietrich Fischer-Diskau/Berlin Philharmonic/Kraus)
¶Walton, *Belshazzar's Feast* (LSO and Chorus/Previn)
¶LUXURY: A funicular for hills.
¶BOOK: Russell Page, *The Education of a Gardener*

3 April 1982
1639 Richard Armstrong
Conductor and Music Director of the Welsh National Opera
¶'Deus In Adjutorium' (Gregorian chant) (Chorus of monks of L'Abbaye Saint-Pierre de Solesmes)
¶Beethoven, String Quartet No. 8 in E minor (opus 59, no. 2) (Rasoumovsky) (Amadeus String Quartet)
¶Tallis, 40-part motet, 'Spem in Alium' (King's College Chapel Choir/Willcocks)
¶Tippett, Piano Sonata No. 1 (Margaret Kitchin)
¶Janáček, String Quartet No. 2 (Intimate Letters) (Janáček Quartet)
¶R. Strauss, 'September' (from *Four Last Songs*) (Elisabeth Söderström/Welsh National Opera Orchestra/Armstrong)
¶Tippett, Symphony No. 2 (LSO/Davis)
*¶Wagner, 'Tristan's Monologue' (from *Tristan und Isolde*, Act 3) (John Mitchinson/Welsh National Opera Orchestra/Goodall)
¶LUXURY: A piano.
¶BOOK: The scores of Beethoven's piano sonatas.

10 April 1982
1640 Julia McKenzie
Actress and singer
¶Sondheim, *Company* (opening) (Larry Kert/London company)
¶Mozart, 'Porgi amor qualche ristoro' (from *The Marriage of Figaro*, Act 2) (Jessye Norman/BBC Symphony/Colin Davis)
¶Gershwin, 'Bess, You is My Woman Now' (from *Porgy and Bess*) (Robert McFerrin/Adele Addison)
¶Ravel, 'Lever du jour' (from *Daphnis and Chloe Suite No. 2*) (LSO/Previn)
¶'Them There Eyes' (Barbara Cook)
¶Elgar, 'Soul, Take Me Away' (from *The Dream of Gerontius*) (Richard Lewis/Royal Liverpool Philharmonic/Sargent)

*¶ 'Skylark' (Hoagy Carmichael *vocal*/Johnny Mandel and his Orchestra)
¶ Porter, 'Blow, Gabriel, Blow' (from *Anything Goes*) (Ethel Merman)
¶ LUXURY: Painting equipment.
¶ BOOK: Moss Hart, *Act One*

17 April 1982
1641 Brian Aldiss
Novelist, short story writer and critic
¶ Borodin, Symphony No. 2 in B minor (Philharmonia Orchestra/Malko)
¶ 'The Waiter and the Porter and the Upstairs Maid' (from film *Birth of the Blues*) (Bing Crosby/Jack Teagarden/Mary Martin)
¶ 'Kazi Vaske' (Bronislav Simorovic/Danica Obrenic/Belgrade Radio Light Orchestra)
*¶ Schubert, Sonata in A (D. 574) (David Oistrakh *violin*/Lev Oborin *piano*)
¶ 'Kansas City Breakdown' (Bennie Moten and his Kansas City Orchestra)
¶ Mascagni, 'Easter Hymn' (from *Cavalleria rusticana*) (Victoria de los Angeles/Rome Opera House Chorus and Orchestra/Santini)
¶ Holst, 'Saturn' (from *The Planets*) (Berlin Philharmonic/von Karajan)
¶ Lehrer, 'Vatican Rag' (Tom Lehrer)
¶ LUXURY: A time machine.
¶ BOOK: Samuel Johnson, *Rasselas*, bound together with some of his *Lives of the Poets* and extracts from James Boswell.

24 April 1982
1642 Dorothy Dunnett
Novelist
¶ Bach, Brandenburg Concerto No. 3 in G major (BWV 1048) (English Chamber Orchestra/Leppard)
¶ Handel, 'Come Unto Him' (from *Messiah*) (Isobel Baillie)
¶ Saint-Saëns, Piano Concerto No. 2 in G minor (Aldo Ciccolini/Paris Orchestra/Baudo)

¶ R. Strauss, *Der Rosenkavalier* (final duet) (Anne Howells/Teresa Cahill/Scottish National Orchestra/Gibson)
*¶ Beethoven, Symphony No. 7 in A major (opus 92) (LSO/Davis)
¶ Boccherini, Concerto in G for Cello and Strings (Moray Welsh/Scottish Baroque Ensemble)
¶ Rodrigo, Concierto de Aranjuez (John Williams *guitar*/English Chamber Orchestra/Barenboim)
¶ Dvořák, Symphony No. 3 in E flat (LSO/Kertesz)
¶ LUXURY: A guitar.
¶ BOOK: Edward Gibbon, *The History of the Decline and Fall of the Roman Empire*

1 May 1982
1643 Jenny Agutter
Actress
¶ 'Baroque and Blue' (Claude Bolling *piano*/Jean-Pierre Rampal *flute*)
¶ 'Peggy Sue' (Buddy Holly and the Crickets)
¶ Beethoven, Symphony No. 6 in F major (Pastoral) (Berlin Philharmonic/von Karajan)
¶ Dylan, 'I Want You' (Bob Dylan)
*¶ Vaughan Williams, 'Fantasia on a Theme by Thomas Tallis' (Sinfonia of London/Barbirolli)
¶ 'Bourée' (Jethro Tull)
¶ 'As' (Stevie Wonder)
¶ Lennon & McCartney, 'Blackbird' (The Beatles)
¶ LUXURY: An Oriental rug.
¶ BOOF: *The Oxford Book of 20th-Century English Verse*

8 May 1982
1644 Lucia Popp
Lyric soprano
¶ Bach, Violin Concerto No. 2 in E (David Oistrakh/Vienna SO/Igor Oistrakh)
¶ Schubert, Piano Trio in E flat (D. 929) (Adolf Busch and Hermann Busch *violins*/Rudolf Serkin *piano*)
¶ Humperdinck, *Hansel und Gretel* (Act 3, Scene 2) (Elisabeth Schwarzkopf/Elisabeth Grümmer/Philharmonia Orchestra/von Karajan)

¶ Elgar, 'Pleading' (Mary Thomas/Daphne Ibbott *piano*)
¶ Dowland, 'Me, Me and None but Me' (from *The Third Booke of Songs 1603*) (Consort of Musicke/Rooley)
¶ Mozart, Clarinet Quintet in A (K. 581) (Benny Goodman/Boston Symphony String Quartet)
¶ Brahms, Symphony No. 2 in D (Philharmonia Orchestra/Klemperer)
*¶ 'The Teddy Bears' Picnic' (Henry Hall and BBC Dance Orchestra/Rosing)
¶ LUXURY: Her teddy bear.
¶ BOOK: Thomas Mann, *The Magic Mountain*

15 May 1982
1645 Julian Symons
Crime writer, biographer and critic
¶ 'Yes! We Have No Bananas' (The Two Gilberts)
*¶ W. H. Auden, 'The Quarry' (Prunella Scales/Peter Orr)
¶ Thomas, 'If I Were Tickled by the Rub of Love' (Dylan Thomas)
¶ Fuller, 'The Middle of a War' (Roy Fuller)
¶ 'That Lovely Weekend' (Anne Shelton/Ambrose and his Orchestra)
¶ Weill/Brecht, 'Mack the Knife' (from *The Threepenny Opera*) (Scott Merrill)
¶ 'Murder He Says' (from film *Happy Go Lucky*) (Betty Hutton)
¶ MacNeice, 'Sunlight on the Garden' (Louis MacNeice)
¶ LUXURY: A couch.
¶ BOOK: Charles Dickens, *Bleak House*

22 May 1982
1646 Marti Webb
Actress and singer
¶ Tchaikovsky, Piano Concerto No. 1 in B flat minor (Sviatoslav Richter/Vienna Symphony/von Karajan)
¶ Rossini, 'Una voce poco fa' (from *The Barber of Seville*) (Maria Callas/Philharmonia Orchestra/Galliera)

¶ Saint-Saëns, 'The Swan' (from *Carnival of the Animals*) (Julian Lloyd Webber *cello*/Yitkin Seow *piano*)
¶ 'Oh Happy Day' (Edwin Hawkins Singers)
¶ 'Layla' (Derek and the Dominos)
¶ Simon, 'Bridge Over Troubled Water' (Simon & Garfunkel)
¶ 'Space Oddity' (David Bowie)
*¶ 'The Dreaded Batter Pudding Hurler of Bexhill-on-Sea' (The Goons)
¶ LUXURY: A piano.
¶ BOOK: An illustrated dictionary.

29 May 1982
1647 Desmond Hawkins
Writer, critic, broadcaster and founder of the BBC Natural History Unit.
¶ Beethoven, Cello Sonata No. 3 in A (opus 69) (Jacqueline du Pré/Stephen Bishop *piano*)
¶ Thomas, 'Polly Perkins' (Dylan Thomas)
¶ Handel, 'Where'er You Walk' (from *Semele*) (John McCormack)
¶ 'The Prickerty Bush' (Marjorie Westbury/John Rudge)
¶ Curlew (recorded by Ludwig Koch)
¶ Bellini, 'Casta diva' (from *Norma*) (Joan Sutherland/L.S. Chorus and Orchestra/Bonynge)
¶ Donizetti, 'Cheti, cheti, immantinente' (from *Don Pasquale*) (Fernando Corena/Tom Krause/Vienna Opera Orchestra/Kertesz)
*¶ Schubert, Octet in F major (D. 805) (Melos Ensemble)
¶ LUXURY: A pair of binoculars.
¶ BOOK: Roger Tory Peterson's field guide to the birds of the island.

5 June 1982
1648 Delia Smith
Cookery expert
¶ Simon, 'The Sounds of Silence' (Simon & Garfunkel)
¶ Britten, Missa Brevis in D (George Malcolm *organ*/Westminster Cathedral Boys' Choir)
¶ Albinoni/Giazotto, Adagio in G minor for Organ and Strings (Douglas Haas/Württemberg Chamber Orchestra/Faerber)
¶ 'Forever Afternoon' (from *Days of Future Passed*) (The Moody Blues/London Festival Orchestra/Knight)
¶ Fauré, 'Pavane' (NPO/Willcocks)
*¶ 'Lief' (Rhos Male Choir)
¶ 'Rivers of Babylon' (Boney M)
¶ Bach, 'Oh, Sacred Head' (from *St Matthew Passion*) (Chorus of Deutsche Oper, Berlin/Berlin Philharmonic/von Karajan)
¶ LUXURY: Writing materials.
¶ BOOK: The autobiography of St Thérèse of Lisieux.

12 June 1982
1649 Sir Anton Dolin
(2nd appearance)
Dancer and choreographer
¶ Lehár, 'You are My Heart's Delight' (from *The Land of Smiles*) (Richard Tauber/Berlin State Opera Orchestra/Lehár)
¶ 'Farewell' (from *The Maid of the Mountains*) (José Collins)
¶ Ravel, *Daphnis and Chloe* (Royal Opera House Chorus, Covent Garden/LSO/Monteux)
¶ Coward, *Private Lives* (Act 1) (Noël Coward/Gertrude Lawrence)
¶ Verdi, *La Traviata* (Act 3) (Maria Callas/Cetra Chorus/EIAR Radio Symphony, Turin/Santini)
*¶ 'They Don't Make Them Like That Anymore' (from *Phil the Fluter*) (Evelyn Laye/company)
¶ 'Miss Otis Regrets' (Ella Fitzgerald/Buddy Bregman and his Orchestra)
¶ 'Ebony and Ivory' (Paul McCartney/Stevie Wonder)
¶ LUXURY: An electric razor.
¶ BOOK: Anton Dolin, *Friends and Memories*

19 June 1982
1650 Eric Newby
Writer and traveller
¶ Beethoven, Piano Concerto No. 5 in E flat major (Emperor) (Artur Schnabel/LSO/Sargent)
¶ 'Thanks for the Memory' (from film *The Big Broadcast of 1938*) (Shirley Ross/Bob Hope)
¶ Tchaikovsky, Symphony No. 6 in B minor (Berlin Philharmonic/Furtwängler)
¶ Bach, Toccata and Fugue in D minor (BWV 565) (Helmut Walcha *organ*)
¶ Lennon & McCartney, 'When I'm Sixty-Four' (The Beatles)
¶ 'The Flies Crawled Up the Window' (from film *Jack's the Boy*) (Jack Hulbert)
¶ Mozart, 'Porgi amor qualche ristoro' (from *The Marriage of Figaro*, Act 2) (Victoria de los Angeles/Rome Opera House Orchestra/Morelli)
*¶ Joplin, 'Solace' (Joshua Rifkin *piano*)
¶ LUXURY: Whisky.
¶ BOOK: *Dictionary of National Biography*

26 June 1982
1651 Joss Ackland
Actor
¶ 'Mr Bojangles' (Nina Simone)
¶ Sibelius, Violin Concerto in D minor (Ivry Gitlis/Pro Musica Symphony/Horenstein)
¶ 'Green Door' (Jim Lowe)
¶ Willson, 'Ya Got Trouble' (from *The Music Man*) (Robert Preston/company)
*¶ 'Bailero' (from *Songs of the Auvergne*) (Victoria de los Angeles/Lamoureux Orchestra/Jacquillat)
¶ Sondheim, 'Someone in a Tree' (from *Pacific Overtures*) (James Dybas/company)
¶ 'My Cup Runneth Over' (from *I Do, I Do*) (Mary Martin/Robert Preston)
¶ 'The Party's Over' (from *Bells are Ringing*) (Judy Holliday)
¶ LUXURY: A video player with cassettes of old movies.
¶ BOOK: A dictionary.

3 July 1982
1652 John Mortimer QC (2nd appearance)
Playwright, novelist and barrister

*¶ Mozart, 'Soave sia il vento' (from *Cosi fan tutte*, Act 1) (Kiri Te Kanawa/Frederica von Stade/Jules Bastin/Strasbourg Philharmonic/Lombard)

¶ 'Fancy Our Meeting' (from *That's a Good Girl*) (Jack Buchanan/Elsie Randolph)

¶ Elgar, Cello Concerto in E minor (Jacqueline du Pré/LSO/Barbirolli)

¶ Puccini, 'O soave fanciulla' (from *La bohème*, Act 1) (Luciano Pavarotti/Mirella Freni/Berlin Philharmonic/von Karajan)

¶ Dylan, 'Just Like a Woman' (Bob Dylan)

¶ Puccini, 'Io de' sospiri' (from *Tosca*, Act 3) (David Sellar *treble*/Paris Conservatoire Orchestra/Prêtre)

¶ Verdi, 'Veglia, o donna, questo fiore' (from *Rigoletto*) (Piero Cappucilli/Ileana Cotrubas/Vienna Philharmonic/Giulini)

¶ Mozart, 'Qual tremole insolito' (from *Don Giovanni*, Act 2) (Ruggero Raimondi/Paris Opera Chorus and Orchestra/Maazel)

¶ LUXURY: A bath.

¶ BOOK: *The Oxford Book of English Verse*

10 July 1982
1653 Captain Jacques Cousteau
Oceanographer and marine explorer

¶ 'Ma Méditerranée' (Harry Pagani)

*¶ Bach, Chromatic Fantasia and Fugue in D minor (BWV 903) (Reine Gianoli *piano*)

¶ Gershwin, 'Summertime' (from *Porgy and Bess*) (Ella Fitzgerald)

¶ Partch, 'Daphne of the Dunes' (Harry Partch/instrumentalists)

¶ Liszt, 'St Francis of Assisi Preaching' (Wilhelm Kempff *piano*)

¶ Villa-Lobos, Bachianas Brasilieras No. 5 (Salli Terri/Laurindo Ameida *guitar*)

¶ Paganini, Caprice No. 24 in A minor (Yehudi Menuhin *violin*)

¶ 'Out of the Darkness' (Craig Degree/Graham Nash/David Crosby)

¶ LUXURY: A stone from the stomach of a fossilised dinosaur.

¶ BOOK: Michel de Montaigne, *Essais*

17 July 1982
1654 Pamela Stephenson
Actress and comedienne

¶ 'Love is the Greatest Thing' (Mae West)

¶ 'Balham – Gateway to the South' (Peter Sellers)

¶ 'The Good Time Girl' (from *Over Here*) (Patty Andrews/company)

¶ Bellini, 'Ah, non giunge' (from *La sonnambula*) (Luisa Tetrazzini)

¶ 'Tickle Me' (Randy Newman)

¶ 'Brain Damage' (Pink Floyd)

¶ 'Cat Handcuffs' (Steve Martin)

*¶ 'Legong Kraton' (Gong Kebyar of the Banjar of Belaluan Sadmerta, Bali)

¶ LUXURY: A television set with a satellite link-up.

¶ BOOK: *Dama Pada*, a Buddhist scripture.

24 July 1982
1655 Lyall Watson
Marine biologist, archaeologist and writer

¶ 'Aguara Trumpets of the Alur People'

¶ Tallis, 40-part Motet, 'Spem in Alium' (Clerkes of Oxenford/Wulstan)

¶ 'Comin' Home, Baby' (Herbie Mann *flute*/Ensemble)

¶ Mussorgsky, orchestrated Ravel, *Pictures at an Exhibition* (New York Philharmonic/Bernstein)

¶ 'Buddy Brown's Blues' (Lightnin' Hopkins)

¶ Barber, 'Summer Music' (New York Woodwind Quintet)

¶ Mozart, Symphony No. 41 in C (K 551) (Jupiter) (English Chamber Orchestra/Barenboim)

*¶ The call of a Burchell's coucal (recorded in Johannesburg, South Africa)

¶ LUXURY: A film projector and 20 western films.

¶ BOOK: *Pear's Cyclopaedia*

31 July 1982
1656 George Martin
Record producer

¶ Rodgers & Hart, 'Good Mornin'' (from film *Babes in Arms*) (Judy Garland/Mickey Rooney)

¶ Debussy, *Prélude à l'après-midi d'un faune* (Peter Lloyd *flute*/LSO/Previn)

¶ 'A Song of Patriotic Prejudice' (from *At the Drop of Another Hat*) (Michael Flanders/Donald Swann)

¶ Cimarosa, Concerto in C major for Oboe and Strings (Heinz Holliger/Bamberg Symphony/Maag)

¶ Lennon & McCartney, 'Here, There and Everywhere' (The Beatles)

¶ 'Any Old Iron' (Peter Sellers)

¶ Lennon & McCartney, 'In My Life' (The Beatles)

*¶ Bach, *St Matthew Passion* (opening) (Berlin Philharmonic/von Karajan)

¶ LUXURY: A clavichord.

¶ BOOK: A manual on practical engineering.

7 August 1982
1657 Dame Janet Baker (2nd appearance)
Mezzo-soprano

*¶ Scarlatti, Sonata in A minor (K. 54) (Richard Lester *harpsichord*)

¶ Bach, Toccata and Fugue in D minor (BWV 565) (Peter Hurford *organ*)

¶ Handel, *Water Music Suite* No. 3 (Academy of St Martin-in-the-Fields/Marriner)

¶ Beethoven, Piano Concerto No. 5 in E flat major (Emperor) (Vladimir Ashkenazy/CSO/Solti)

¶ Schubert, Symphony No. 9 in C (Great) (CSO/Giulini)

¶ Cavalli, 'Vivi a'nostri amori' (from *La Calisto*, Act 2) (James Bowman/Janet Baker/LPO/Leppard)

¶Vaughan Williams, Symphony No. 5 in D (Philharmonia Orchestra/ Barbirolli)
¶Mozart, *Cosi fan tutte* (overture) (Royal Opera House Orchestra, Covent Garden/ Colin Davis)
¶LUXURY: Pencils and papers.
¶BOOK: Jane Austen, *Persuasion*, bound with Lord David Cecil's biography of her.

14 August 1982
1658 Donald Sinden (2nd appearance)
Actor
¶'Vienna, City of My Dreams' (Richard Tauber)
*¶Beethoven, Symphony No. 6 in F major (Pastoral) (Vienna Philharmonic/Furtwängler)
¶Bach, Double Concerto in D minor (BWV 1043) (David & Igor Oistrakh *violins*/RPO/ Goossens)
¶Wide, 'Namner du Sverige' (Jussi Björling/Orchestra/ Grevillius)
¶'Let the Grass Grow' (from *Free as Air*) (Roy Godfrey/ Howard Goorney/Michael Aldridge/Orchestra/Martell)
¶Verdi, 'Dies Irae' (from *Requiem*) (Nicolai Gedda/ Nicolai Ghiaurov/Elisabeth Schwarzkopf/Christa Ludwig/ Philharmonia Chorus and Orchestra/Giulini)
¶Speech at the Oxford Union (Gerard Hoffnung)
¶'The Old Hundredth' (from the Coronation Service of HM Queen Elizabeth II)
¶LUXURY: His favourite picture in the Walker Art Gallery, Liverpool.
¶BOOK: Sir Banister Fletcher, *A History of Architecture on the Comparative Method*

21 August 1982
1659 Carl Davis
Composer and conductor
¶Buxtehude, 'Aperite Mihi Portas Justitiae' (cantata) (Elsa Sigfuss/Holger Nørgaard/Else Marie Brunn and Julius Koppel *violins*/Torben Anton Svendsen *cello*/Mogens Woldike *harpsichord*)

¶Beethoven, String Quartet No. 13 in B flat (opus 130) (Hungarian String Quartet)
¶Beethoven, Symphony No. 7 in A major (opus 92) (New York Philharmonic/Toscanini)
*¶Mozart, 'Hm, hm, hm!' (Act 1 quintet from *The Magic Flute*) (Helge Rosvaenge/Gerhard Hüsch/Elfriede Marherr/Hilde Scheppan/Rut Berglund/Berlin Philharmonic/Beecham)
¶Bernstein/Sondheim, 'Somewhere' (from *West Side Story*) (Reri Grist/ensemble)
¶Stravinsky, 'Dance of the Adolescents' (from Ballet *The Rite of Spring*) (Columbia Symphony/Stravinsky)
¶'My Man' (Billie Holiday)
¶'Song of Australia' (Dame Edna Everage/LSO/Carl Davis)
¶LUXURY: Shampoo.
¶BOOK: The short stories of Anton Chekhov.

28 August 1982
1660 The Duke and Duchess of Devonshire
(Recorded at Chatsworth House in Derbyshire, one of England's most celebrated stately homes.)
¶a = Duchess b = Duke
¶(a) 'Heart of Stone' (Fred Astaire)
¶(b) Sousa, 'King Cotton' (HM Grenadier Guards Band)
*¶(a) Porter, 'You're the Top' (from *Anything Goes*) (Ethel Merman)
*¶(b) Beethoven, Leonora Overture No. 3 (Philharmonia Orchestra/Klemperer)
¶(a) 'Holy, Holy, Holy' (Leontyne Price)
¶(b) 'When Somebody Thinks You're Wonderful' (Fats Waller *vocals and piano* and His Rhythm)
¶(a) Rossini/Respighi, Ballet *La boutique fantasque* (RPO/Dorati)
¶(b) 'Underneath the Arches' (Flanagan & Allen)
¶LUXURIES: (a) new potatoes; (b) after shave.
¶BOOKS: (a) the Beatrix Potter books bound together; (b) *Chambers' Biographical Dictionary*.

4 September 1982
1661 Claire Bloom (2nd appearance)
Actress
¶Beethoven, Piano Concerto No. 5 in E flat major (Emperor) (Maurizio Pollini/Vienna Philharmonic/Böhm)
*¶Mozart, 'Soave sia il vento' (from *Cosi fan tutte*, Act 1) (Gundula Janowitz/Brigitte Fassbänder/Rolando Panerai/ Vienna Philharmonic/Böhm)
¶Debussy, 'Reflets dan l'eau' (from *Images*) (Arturo Benedetti Michelangeli *piano*)
¶Britten/Shakespeare, 'I Know A Bank Whereon the Wild Thyme Grows' (from *A Midsummer Night's Dream*) (Alfred Deller/LSO/Britten)
¶Mozart, Symphony No. 31 in D (K 297) (Paris) (Berlin Philharmonic/Böhm)
¶R. Strauss, 'September' (from *Four Last Songs*) (Elisabeth Schwarzkopf/Berlin Radio Symphony/Szell)
¶Ponchielli, 'Suicidio!' (from *La Gioconda*, Act 4) (Maria Callas/La Scala Orchestra/ Votto)
¶Poulenc, 'Hotel' (from *Banalités*) (Pierre Bernac)
¶LUXURY: Coffee and an espresso machine.
¶BOOK: Marcel Proust, *À la recherche du temps perdu*

11 September 1982
1662 James Loughran
Principal Conductor of the Hallé Orchestra
¶'Pascha Nostrum' (monks of the Abbey of St Pierre de Solesmes/Gajard)
¶Walton, Violin Concerto (Jascha Heifetz/Cincinnati Symphony/Goossens)
¶J. Strauss, 'Entrance March' (from *The Gypsy Baron*) (Dutch street organ)
¶Schubert, Trio in B flat (Alfred Cortot *piano*/Jacques Thibaud *violin*/Pablo Casals *cello*)
¶'Puirt-a-Beul' (mouth music) (Norman Kennedy)

*¶ Beethoven, 'Mir ist so wunderbar' (from *Fidelio*, Act 1) (Christa Ludwig/Philharmonia Orchestra/Klemperer)

¶ Dvořák, Serenade in E for Strings (English Chamber Orchestra/Kubelik)

¶ Handel, arranged Beecham, 'Love in Bath' (RPO/Beecham)

¶ LUXURY: Drawing and painting equipment.

¶ BOOK: A comprehensive world airways timetable.

18 September 1982
1663 Carlo Curley
Organist

¶ Ives, 'Variations on America' (E. Power Biggs *organ*)

*¶ Brahms, 'Wie lieblich sind Deine Wohnungen' (from *German Requiem*) (Dietrich Fischer-Dieskau/Philharmonia Chorus and Orchestra/Klemperer)

¶ Hawthorne, 'Whispering Hope' (Robert White/National Philharmonic/Mace)

¶ Brahms, Symphony No. 4 in E minor (opus 98) (CSO/Levine)

¶ Prokofiev, *Love of Three Oranges* (march, opus 33a) (Artur Rubinstein *piano*)

¶ Bach, Concerto in D minor for Two violins and Orchestra (BWV 1043) (Jascha Heifetz playing both solo parts/RCA Chamber Orchestra/Waxman)

¶ Guilmant, 'Introduction et variations sur un ancien noël polonais' (Odile Pierre *organ*)

¶ Wagner, 'The Ride of the Valkyries' (from *Die Walküre*) (Sir George Thalben-Ball *organ*)

¶ LUXURY: Small portable Danish pipe organ.

¶ BOOK: A cookery book by Julia Childs.

25 September 1982
1664 Wilbur Smith
Writer of adventure novels

¶ 'My Way' (Frank Sinatra)

¶ 'Take Five' (Dave Brubeck Quartet)

*¶ Beethoven, Symphony No. 3 in E flat major (Eroica) (Berlin Philharmonic/von Karajan)

¶ 'You're My Best Friend' (Don Williams)

¶ Berlin, 'Cheek to Cheek' (from film *Top Hat*) (Oscar Peterson Trio)

¶ Lloyd Webber/Rice, 'Don't Cry for Me, Argentina' (from *Evita*) (Gheorghi Zamfir *pan flute*/Orchestra/van Hoof)

¶ Gershwin, 'Rhapsody in Blue' (George Gershwin *piano*/Paul Whiteman and his Concert Orchestra)

¶ 'Ramblin' Rose' (Nat 'King' Cole)

¶ LUXURY: A brass bedstead and a feather mattress.

¶ BOOK: The complete *Oxford English Dictionary*.

2 October 1982
1665 David Lloyd Jones
Artistic Director of Opera North

¶ Berlioz, *Béatrice et Bénédict* (overture) (LSO/Colin Davis)

¶ Bach, *Christmas Oratorio* (Elly Ameling/Brigitte Fassbänder/Horst R. Laubenthal/Hermann Prey/Bavarian Radio Chorus and Symphony/Jochum)

¶ Verdi, 'Ave Maria' (from *Otello*) (Margaret Price/Vienna Philharmonic/Solti)

¶ Tchaikovsky, *The Nutcracker Suite* (LSO/Dorati)

¶ Elgar, *Falstaff: Symphonic Study* (LPO/Boult)

¶ Debussy, Sonata No. 2 for Flute, Viola and Harp (Melos Ensemble)

¶ Tippett, 'Ritual Dances' (from *The Midsummer Marriage*) (Royal Opera House Orchestra, Covent Garden/Pritchard)

*¶ Schubert, Symphony No. 9 in C (Great) (New York Philharmonic/Walter)

¶ LUXURY: None required.

¶ BOOK: Edmond and Jules Goncourt, *Journal*

9 October 1982
1666 Nicholas Busch, John Kuchmy, Martin Parry and Marie Wilson
Members of the London Philharmonic Orchestra

¶ (NB) R. Strauss, 'Frühling' (from *Four Last Songs*) (Lucia Popp/LPO/Tennstedt)

¶ (JK) Grieg, Sonata No. 3 in C minor (Fritz Kreisler *violin*/Sergei Rachmaninov *piano*)

¶ (MP) Bach, Brandenburg Concerto No. 5 in D major (BWV 1050) (Marcel Moyse *flute*/Adolf Busch *violin*/Rudolf Serkin *piano*/Adolf Busch Chamber Orchestra)

¶ (MW) Bach, 'Credo' (from *Mass in B minor*, BWV 232) (Agnes Giebel/Janet Baker/BBC Chorus/NPO/Klemperer)

¶ (NB) 'Space Oddity' (David Bowie)

¶ (JK) Brahms, Symphony No. 1 in C minor (LPO/Boult)

¶ (MP) Mahler, Symphony No. 5 in C sharp minor (LPO/Tennstedt)

¶ (MW) Fauré, 'Pavane' (Edinburgh Festival Chorus/Paris Orchestra/Barenboim)

¶ LUXURIES: (NB) razor and shaving soap; (JK) a video machine with a tape of Laurel & Hardy's *A Chump at Oxford*; (MP) wine; (MW) her violin.

¶ BOOKS: (NB) *The memoirs of Hector Berlioz*; (JK) Charles Dickens, *A Christmas Carol*; (MP) Hugh Johnson, *A World Atlas of Wine*; (MW) a cookery book.

16 October 1982
1667 Geoffrey Grigson
Poet, critic and writer on art, natural history and travel

¶ Haydn, 'Serenade' (from Quartet in F, opus 3, no. 5) (Janáček Quartet)

¶ Britten, Serenade for Tenor, Horn and Strings (Peter Pears/Dennis Brain *horn*/Boyd Neel String Orchestra/Britten)

¶ Purcell, 'Dido's Lament' (from *Dido and Aeneas*, Act 3) (Victoria de los Angeles/English Chamber Orchestra/Barbirolli)

*¶Haydn, 'She Never Told Her Love' (Peter Pears/Benjamin Britten *piano*)
¶Haydn, String Quartet in D (opus 76, no. 5) (Tatrai Quartet)
¶Bizet, *Jeux d'enfants* (Paris Conservatoire Orchestra/Martinon)
¶Britten, 'Death be not Proud' (Peter Pears/Zorian String Quartet/Britten)
¶Verdi, 'Và pensero, sull'ali dorate' (from *Nabucco*) (La Scala Chorus and Orchestra/Abbado)
¶LUXURY: Pâté de foie gras.
¶BOOK: *The Oxford English Dictionary*

23 October 1982
1668 Mike Harding
Comedian
¶Delius, 'Brigg Fair' (Hallé Orchestra/Barbirolli)
¶'The Dreaded Batter Pudding Hurler of Bexhill-on-Sea' (The Goons)
¶'Sweet Little Sixteen' (Chuck Berry)
¶Parry/Blake, 'Jerusalem' (Black Dyke Mills Band)
¶'The John Maclean March' (Dick Gaughan)
¶'Next' (Alex Harvey Band)
*¶'2000-Year-Old Man' (Carl Reiner/Mel Brooks)
¶'Pennies from Heaven' (from 1936 film) (Stephane Grappelli *violin*/Diz Disley Trio)
¶LUXURY: A set of one-inch Ordnance Survey maps, together with a set of the books about the fells by A. W. Wainwright.
¶BOOK: *The New Oxford Book of English Verse*

31 October 1982
1669 The Rt Hon. George Thomas
Speaker of the House of Commons
¶Handel, 'Hallelujah Chorus' (from *Messiah*) (Mastreechter Staar Choir, The Netherlands/Jean Wolfs *organ*/Koekelkoren)
¶'Myfanwy' (1000 Welsh male voices at the Royal Albert Hall)
¶'A Valley Called the Rhondda' (Treorchy Male Choir)

¶Handel, 'Largo' (from *Xerxes*) (William Davies *organ*)
¶'God Bless the Prince of Wales' (Investiture Choir/BBC Welsh Orchestra/Bohana)
¶Vivaldi, *The Four Seasons* (Itzhak Perlman *violin and conducting*/LPO)
¶'We'll Keep a Welcome' (Treorchy Male Choir)
¶'What a Friend We Have in Jesus' (Leontyne Price/Choir of men and boys of St Thomas Episcopal Church, New York)
¶LUXURY: Writing materials.
¶BOOK: The Methodist hymn book.

6 November 1982
1670 Thomas Allen
Baritone
¶Parry, 'I was Glad' (King's College Chapel Choir/Trumpeters of Kneller Hall School of Music/Ledger)
¶Mahler, Symphony No. 5 in C sharp minor (Amsterdam Concertgebouw/Haitink)
¶Elgar, *The Dream of Gerontius* (excerpt) (Helen Watts/Nicolai Gedda/Robert Lloyd/London Philharmonic Choir/John Alldis Choir/NPO/Boult)
¶Brahms, 'Vier Ernste Gesänge' (no. 3) (Alexander Kipnis/Gerald Moore *piano*)
*¶Beethoven, Concerto in C for Violin, Cello and Piano (David Oistrakh *violin*/Mstislav Rostropovich *cello*/Karl Richter *piano*/Berlin Philharmonic/von Karajan)
¶Shakespeare, 'St Crispin's Day Speech' (from *Henry V*) (Laurence Olivier)
¶Delius, 'The Walk to the Paradise Garden' (from *A Village Romeo and Juliet*) (LSO/Barbirolli)
¶Mozart, Clarinet Concerto in A (K. 622) (Jack Brymer/RPO/Beecham)
¶LUXURY: Golf clubs and balls.
¶BOOK: Charlotte Brontë, *Jane Eyre*

13 November 1982
1671 Rosamund Lehmann
Novelist
¶Liza Lehmann, 'Ah! Moon of My Delight' (from *In a Persian Garden*) (Hubert Eisdell)
¶Puccini, 'Si, mi chiamano Mimi' (in English) (from *La bohème*, Act 1) (Joan Cross)
¶Gounod, 'Envoi des fleurs' (Vanni-Marcoux/Lucien Petitjean *piano*)
¶'These Foolish Things' (from *Spread It Abroad*) (Hutch)
¶Schubert, Impromptu in A flat (opus 90, no. 4) (Clifford Curzon *piano*)
¶Britten, 'Variations on a Theme of Frank Bridge' (English Chamber Orchestra/Britten)
¶R. Strauss, 'Frühling' (from *Four Last Songs*) (Elisabeth Schwarzkopf/Berlin Radio Symphony/Szell)
*¶Burgon, 'Nunc Dimittis' (from television serial *Tinker, Tailor, Soldier, Spy*) (Paul Phoenix *treble*/James Watson *trumpet*/John Scott *organ*/Ensemble/Rose)
¶LUXURY: Writing materials.
¶BOOK: *The Letters of the Marquise de Sévigné*

20 November 1982
1672 P. D. James
Writer of detective fiction
¶Fauré, 'Agnus Dei' (from *Requiem*) (King's College Chapel Choir/NPO/Willcocks)
¶Dowland, 'Come Again Sweet Love' (Janet Baker/Gerald Moore *piano*)
¶Oscar Wilde, 'Lady Bracknell Interviews John Worthing' (from *The Importance of Being Earnest*, Act 1) (Edith Evans/John Gielgud)
¶Elgar, *The Dream of Gerontius* (Ambrosian Singers/Sheffield Philharmonic Chorus/Hallé Orchestra/Barbirolli)
¶Coward, 'Mad Dogs and Englishmen' (from *Words and Music*) (Noël Coward)
*¶Bach, *St Matthew Passion* (first chorus) (Philharmonia Choir and Orchestra/Klemperer)
¶Dibdin, 'Tom Bowling' (Robert Tear/André Previn *piano*)

¶Telemann, Concerto in D for Trumpet, Two Oboes and Strings (John Wilbraham *trumpet*/Academy of St Martin-in-the-Fields/Marriner)
¶LUXURY: Claret.
¶BOOK: George Eliot, *Middlemarch*

27 November 1982
1673 Helen Mirren
Actress
¶Bruch, Violin Concerto No. 1 in G minor (Kyung Wha Chung/RPO/Kempe)
*¶'Pass the Dutchie' (Musical Youth)
¶Albinoni/Giazotto, Adagio in G minor (Maria Teresa Garatti *organ*/I Musici)
¶'Doctor Brownie's Famous Cure' (Sonny Terry/Brownie McGhee)
¶Lyubimov, 'Psalm 1 (Blazhen Muzh)' (male chamber choir/Milkov)
¶Donizetti, 'Mad Scene' (from *Lucia di Lammermoor*) (Joan Sutherland/Paris Conservatoire Orchestra/Santi)
¶'Raga Bhairavi' (Suryanarayana *vina*/tanpura/mridangam)
¶'Falling in Love Again' (from film *The Blue Angel*) (Billie Holiday)
¶LUXURY: Silk underwear.
¶BOOK: The *Bhagavad-Gita*

4 December 1982
1674 Alan Price
Composer, singer and pianist
¶'In Party Mood' (West End Celebrity Orchestra)
¶Carmichael, 'Stardust' (Willie Nelson)
¶'House of the Rising Sun' (Alan Price/The Animals)
¶'I Heard It Through the Grapevine' (Marvin Gaye)
¶'Body and Soul' (Art Tatum *piano*)
¶Beethoven, Symphony No. 6 in F major (Pastoral) (Los Angeles Philharmonic/Giulini)
¶'I'll Drown in My Own Tears' (Ray Charles)
*¶'I Ain't Got Nobody' (Louis Prima)

¶LUXURY: A piano.
¶BOOK: Kenneth Grahame, *The Wind in the Willows*

18 December 1982
1675 György Ligeti
Composer
¶Gesualdo, 'Beltá poi che t'assenti' (five-part madrigal) (Quintetto Vocale Italiano)
¶Monteverdi, 'Alle danze' (from *Madrigal Book 9*) (Robert Tear/Alexander Oliver/Stafford Dean/Raymond Leppard *harpsichord*/Joy Hall *cello*)
¶Mozart, String Quintet in C (K. 515) (Cecil Aronowitz *viola*/Amadeus String Quartet)
*¶Schubert, String Quintet in C (D. 956) (William Pleeth *cello*/Amadeus String Quartet)
¶Verdi, *Simon Boccanegra* (Act 3 duet) (Piero Cappucilli/Nicolai Ghiaurov/Orchestra of La Scala Opera House, Milan/Abbado)
¶Brahms, 'Variations and Fugue on a Theme of Handel' (Rudolf Serkin *piano*)
¶Wolf, 'Geh' geliebter, geh jetzt' (Elisabeth Schwarzkopf/Gerald Moore *piano*)
¶Bartók, 'Bánat' (from *27 Choruses*) (Györ Music High School Female Choir/Szabo)
¶LUXURY: Hieronymus Bosch, *Garden of Earthly Delights*, in the Prado, Madrid.
¶BOOKS: Louis Carroll, *Alice in Wonderland* and *Through the Looking Glass*.

25 December 1982
1676 Mary Ellis (2nd appearance)
Singer and actress
¶Mozart, Horn Concerto No. 2 in E flat (K. 417) (Alan Civil/Philharmonia Orchestra/Klemperer)
¶R. Strauss, 'Zerbinetta's Aria' (from *Ariadne auf Naxos*) (Rita Streich/Philharmonia Orchestra/von Karajan)
¶Brahms, Symphony No. 1 in C minor (Berlin Philharmonic/von Karajan)
¶Schubert, 'Du bist die Ruh' (Dietrich Fischer-Dieskau/Gerald Moore *piano*)

¶Bruch, Violin Concerto No. 1 in G minor (Igor Oistrakh/RPO/David Oistrakh)
¶Shakespeare/Walton, 'St Crispin's Day Speech' (from film *Henry V*) (Laurence Olivier/Philharmonia Orchestra/Walton)
¶Mozart, 'Dove sono' (from *The Marriage of Figaro*, Act 3) (Kiri Te Kanawa/LPO/Solti)
*¶Ramirez, 'Gloria' (from *Misa Criolla*) (Basilica del Socorro Choir/Ramirez)
¶LUXURY: Writing materials.
¶BOOK: An encyclopaedia.

1 January 1983
1677 Rachel Billington
Novelist
¶'Tantum Ergo' (Benedictine nuns of St Cecilia's Abbey, Ryde, Isle of Wight)
¶Dylan, 'Mr Tambourine Man' (Bob Dylan)
¶Rachmaninov, Symphony No. 2 in E minor (LSO/Previn)
*¶Mozart, Concerto in E flat for Two Pianos (K. 365) (Alfred Brendel/Imogen Cooper/Academy of St Martin-in-the-Fields/Marriner)
¶Tchaikovsky, 'Gremin's Aria' (from *Eugene Onegin*, Act 3, Scene 1) (Nicolai Ghiaurov/Royal Opera House Orchestra, Covent Garden/Solti)
¶Wagner, 'Siegfried's Funeral March' (from *Götterdämmerung*, Act 3) (Vienna Philharmonic/Solti)
¶Schubert, *Rosamunde* (entr'acte no. 3) (Amsterdam Concertgebouw/Haitink)
¶Mozart, 'Ruhe Sanft, Mein holdes leben' (from *Zaïde*, Act 1) (Edith Mathis/Berlin State Orchestra/Klee)
¶LUXURY: Writing materials.
¶BOOK: Leo Tolstoy, *Anna Karenina* (in Russian).

8 January 1983
1678 Steve Davis
Snooker champion
¶'Blue Side of Midnight' (Narada Michael Walden)
¶Ravel, 'Bolero' (New York Philharmonic/Bernstein)
¶Wonder, 'Ribbon in the Sky' (Stevie Wonder)

¶ 'Ima Suri Dondai' (Christian Vander)
¶ 'The Falcon' (Earl Klugh *guitar*/Bob James *keyboards*/ensemble)
¶ 'I C'n Hear That' (George Duke)
¶ 'Octopus Medley' (Gentle Giant)
*¶ 'I Need You Now' (George Duke)
¶ LUXURY: A snooker table.
¶ BOOK: Tom Sharpe, *The Throwback* and *Wilt*.

15 January 1983
1679 Baroness Maria von Trapp
Writer, Lecturer and musician, on whose life The Sound of Music **was based**
¶ Mozart, *Eine Kleine Nachtmusik* (K. 525) (Berlin Philharmonic/Böhm)
¶ Schubert, 'An die Musik' (D. 547) (Lotte Lehmann/Orchestra/Gurlitt)
¶ Mozart, 'O Isis und Osiris' (from *The Magic Flute*) (Richard Mayr)
¶ Mozart, Symphony No. 41 in C (K. 551) (Jupiter) (NPO/Giulini)
¶ Schubert, 'Der Neugierige' (from *Die Schöne Müllerin*) (Lotte Lehmann/Paul Ulanowsky *piano*)
¶ Mozart, 'In Diesen Heil'gen Hallen' (from *The Magic Flute*, Act 2) (Richard Mayr)
¶ Schubert, 'Ungeduld' (from *Die Schöne Müllerin*) (Lotte Lehmann/Paul Ulanowsky *piano*)
*¶ Bach, Brandenburg Concerto No. 1 in F major (BWV 1046) (Berlin Philharmonic/von Karajan)
¶ LUXURY: A 17th-century statue of madonna and child, once in her family's possession.
¶ BOOK: True funny stories told by well-known people, in German; title forgotten.

22 January 1983
1680 Gwyneth Jones
Soprano
¶ Beethoven, Symphony No. 9 in D minor (opus 125) (Vienna Philharmonic/Bernstein)
¶ 'Der Fröhliche Wanderer' (Obernkirchen Children's Choir)
¶ Humperdinck, 'The Evening Prayer' (from *Hansel und Gretel*) (Elisabeth Schwarzkopf/Elisabeth Grümmer/Philharmonia Orchestra/von Karajan)
¶ Mozart, Piano Concerto No. 21 in C major (K. 467) (Géza Anda *piano and conducting*/Camerata Academica of Salzburg Mozarteum)
*¶ Monteverdi, *L'incoronazione di Poppea* (Act 2, Scene 7) (Elisabeth Söderström/Helen Donath/Concentus Musicus, Vienna/Harnoncourt)
¶ Wagner, 'Ewig war Ich' (from *Siegfried*, Act 3) (Gwyneth Jones/Bayreuth Festival Orchestra/Boulez)
¶ Bach, *St Matthew Passion* (final chorus) (Netherlands Radio Chorus/Amsterdam Concertgebouw/Jochum)
¶ R. Strauss, *Der Rosenkavalier* (final duet) (Lucia Popp/Gwyneth Jones/Vienna Philharmonic/Bernstein)
¶ LUXURY: A piano, with bath salts, etc, inside the stool.
¶ BOOK: Kahil Gibran, *The Prophet*

29 January 1983
1681 Tim Severin
Explorer and writer
¶ Beethoven, Trio in B flat, opus 97 (Archduke) (Pinchas Zukerman *violin*/Jacqueline du Pré *cello*/Daniel Barenboim *piano*)
¶ Porter, 'You're the Top' (from *Anything Goes*) (Ella Fitzgerald)
¶ Davey, 'Water Under the Keel' (from *The Brendan Voyage*) (Liam O'Flynn *Uillean Pipes*/Orchestra/Kelehan)
¶ Lerner & Loewe, 'Wouldn't It be Loverly?' (from *My Fair Lady*) (Audrey Hepburn [Marni Nixon]/Orchestra/Previn)

¶ Mozart, *Don Giovanni* (overture) (National Theatre Orchestra, Prague/Böhm)
*¶ 'Non, je ne regrette rien' (Edith Piaf)
¶ 'L'homme à la moto' (Edith Piaf)
¶ McCartney, 'Mull of Kintyre' (Paul McCartney/Wings)
¶ LUXURY: A herb garden.
¶ BOOK: James Morris, *Pax Britannica*

5 February 1983
1682 Beryl Reid (2nd appearance)
Actress and comedienne
¶ 'Monte Carlo or Bust' (from the film) (Jimmy Durante/Ron Goodwin and his Orchestra)
¶ 'So Close to Me' (Julio Iglesias)
¶ Thackeray, 'Leopold Alcox' (Jake Thackeray)
¶ Aznavour, 'The Old-Fashioned Way' (Charles Aznavour)
¶ Speech at the Oxford Union (Gerard Hoffnung)
*¶ Handel, 'Let the Bright Seraphim' (from *Samson*) (Isobel Baillie/Hallé Orchestra/Braithwaite)
¶ Elgar, Cello Concerto in E minor (Jacqueline du Pré/LSO/Barbirolli)
¶ Lloyd Webber/Eliot, 'Memory' (from *Cats*) (Elaine Page)
¶ LUXURY: A pure silk garment for floating about in.
¶ BOOK: Kathleen Winsor, *Forever Amber*

12 February 1983
1683 Zandra Rhodes
Fashion designer
¶ 'Twelfth Street Rag' (Pee Wee Hunt and his Orchestra)
¶ 'Sparky's Magic Piano' (Verne Smith *narrator*/Henry Blair/Ray Turner *piano*/the Sonovox Talking Piano)
¶ Lennon & McCartney, 'Strawberry Fields Forever' (The Beatles)
¶ 'Us and Them' (Pink Floyd)
¶ Villa-Lobos, Bachianas Brasileiras No. 5 (Mady Mesplé/8 cellos of the Paris Orchestra/Capolongo)

*¶ Ravel, 'Bolero' (Paris Orchestra/Martinon)
¶ 'The Maharajah of Magador' (The Squadronaires)
¶ Handel, 'For Unto Us a Child is Born' (from *Messiah*) (London Symphony Choir and Orchestra/Colin Davis)
¶ LUXURY: Sketchbook, pens and pencils.
¶ BOOK: Mrs Beeton's *Household Management*

19 February 1983
1684 James Ivory
Film director
*¶ Mozart, 'The Three Ladies Find Tamino' (from *The Magic Flute*, Act 1) (Fritz Wunderlich/ Berlin Philharmonic/Böhm)
¶ Bach, Prelude and Fugue No. 21 in B flat (Helmut Walcha *harpsichord*)
¶ Bach, 'Auf das Fest' (from *St Matthew Passion*, BWV 244) (Peter Schreier/Vienna Singverein/Berlin Philharmonic/von Karajan)
¶ 'Raga Shree Kalyan-Tritaal' (Kumar Gandharva/company)
¶ Gershwin, *Three Preludes*(1926) (William Bolcom *piano*)
¶ R. Strauss, 'Frühling' (from *Four Last Songs*) (Elisabeth Schwarzkopf/Philharmonia Orchestra/Ackermann)
¶ Glass, 'Façades' (Philip Glass/ company)
¶ Mozart, 'Soave sia il vento' (from *Cosi fan tutte*, Act 1) (Elisabeth Schwarzkopf/Christa Ludwig/Walter Berry/ Philharmonia Orchestra/Böhm)
¶ LUXURY: A shower with hot water.
¶ BOOK: Marcel Proust, *À la recherche du temps perdu*

26 February 1983
1685 Tom Keating
Painter, restorer and authority on the techniques of painters of the past
¶ Mahler, Symphony No. 1 in D (LSO/Solti)
¶ Gershwin, 'Love Walked In' (from film *Goldwyn Follies*) (Hutch)

¶ Kern & Hammerstein, 'All the Things You Are' (from film *Very Warm for May*) (Richard Tauber)
¶ Dvořák, Cello Concerto in B minor (Pablo Casals/Czech Philharmonic/Szell)
¶ Schubert, Symphony No. 8 in B minor (Unfinished/Böhm)
¶ 'Black Moonlight' (from film *Too Much Harmony*) (Bing Crosby)
*¶ Sibelius, Symphony No. 2 in D (Berlin Philharmonic/von Karajan)
¶ 'I Can't Give You Anything but Love' (from *Blackbirds of 1928*) (Louis Armstrong and his All Stars)
¶ LUXURY: A mattock.
¶ BOOK: Giorgio Vasari, *Lives of the Painters*

5 March 1983
1686 Kenneth MacMillan
Choreographer
*¶ Romberg, 'Students' Chorus' (from *The Student Prince*) (Joan Sutherland/Ambrosian Light Opera Chorus/NPO/Bonynge)
¶ Poulenc, 'Domine Deus' (from *Gloria*) (French National Radio Chorus and Orchestra/ Pretre)
¶ 'Misty' (Sarah Vaughan)
¶ Mahler, 'Der Einsame In Herbst' (from *Das Lied von der Erde*) (Kathleen Ferrier/Vienna Philharmonic/Walter)
¶ Britten, 'Four Sea Interludes' (from *Peter Grimes*) (Royal Opera House Orchestra, Covent Garden/Britten)
¶ Fauré, *Requiem*(St John's College Choir, Cambridge/ Academy of St Martin-in-the-Fields/George Guest)
¶ 'If Love Were All' (from *Bitter Sweet*) (Julie Andrews/Henri Renee and his Orchestra)
¶ Elgar, Cello Concerto in E minor (Jacqueline du Pré/LSO/ Barbirolli)
¶ LUXURY: 'Godiva' chocolates from Belgium.
¶ BOOK: A. E. Ellis, *The Rack*

12 March 1983
1687 Douglas Reeman
(*a.k.a.* Alexander Kent)
Novelist
¶ Gilbert & Sullivan, 'When I was a Lad' (from *HMS Pinafore*) (George Baker/ Glyndebourne Festival Chorus/ Pro Arte Orchestra/Sargent)
¶ Beethoven, Violin Concerto in D (Yehudi Menuhin/NPO/ Klemperer)
¶ Mendelssohn, 'The Hebrides Overture' (Scottish National Orchestra/Gibson)
¶ 'Lilli Marlene' (Marlene Dietrich)
*¶ Eliot, 'The Song of the Jellicles' (from *Old Possum's Book of Practical Cats*) (T. S. Eliot)
¶ Boyce, Symphony No. 1 in B flat (English Chamber Orchestra/Hurwitz)
¶ Stanford, 'The Old Superb' (Frederick Harvey/HM Royal Marines Band/Vivian Dunn)
¶ Grieg, 'Morning' (from *Peer Gynt Suite*) (RPO/Beecham)
¶ LUXURY: An orchid-growing kit.
¶ BOOK: *The Admiralty Seamanship Manual*

19 March 1983
1688 Michael Wood
Director and Chief Surgeon of East African Flying Doctor Service
¶ Brahms, Rhapsody in B minor (opus 79, no. 1) (Julius Katchen *piano*)
¶ Mendelssohn, 'I Waited for the Lord' (from *Hymn of Praise*) (Winchester Cathedral Choir/ Harry Bramma *organ*/Hunt)
*¶ Bach, Toccata and Fugue in D minor (BWV 565) (Helmut Walcha *organ*)
¶ Bach, 'Commend Thy Way' (from *St Matthew Passion*, BWV 244) (Philharmonia Choir and Orchestra/Klemperer)
¶ Liszt, 'Canzonetta del Salvator Rosa' (from *Années de pèlerinage*) (Alfred Brendel *piano*)
¶ Mahler, Symphony No. 2 in C minor (Philharmonia Orchestra/ Klemperer)

¶Vangelis, 'Chariots of Fire' (from film) (Vangelis)
¶Beethoven, Symphony No. 3 in E flat major (Eroica) (Berlin Philharmonic/von Karajan)
¶LUXURY: A pair of field glasses.
¶BOOK: Wavell, *Other Men's Flowers*

26 March 1983
1689 Jan Morris
Writer and traveller
*¶Bach, 'Badinerie' (from Suite No. 2 in B minor) (Gareth Morris *flute*/NPO/Klemperer)
¶'Sunset' (from the ceremony of Beating the Retreat) (HM Royal Marines Band)
¶Mozart, String Quartet in C (K. 465) (Amadeus String Quartet)
¶Mendelssohn, Symphony No. 4 in A (Italian) (NPO/Muti)
¶'Tea for Two' (from *No, No, Nanette*) (Thelonious Monk *piano*/Oscar Pettiford *bass*/Art Blakey*drums*)
¶'Dacw 'Nghariad I Lawr Yn Y Berllan' (Buddug Lloyd Roberts)
¶'I'r Gad' (Dafydd Iwan)
¶Bach, 'Jesu, Joy of Man's Desiring' (from Cantata No. 147) (Munich Bach Choir and Orchestra/Richter)
¶LUXURY: An astronomical telescope, with Messier's *Catalogue of Nebulae*.
¶BOOK: Her own book on Venice.

2 April 1983
1690 James Fox
Actor
¶'Dead Man Blues' (Jelly Roll Morton and his Red Hot Peppers)
¶Chopin, Nocturne in B (opus 9, no. 3) (Stefan Askenase *piano*)
¶Thomas, 'A Child's Christmas in Wales' (Dylan Thomas)
¶'And I am Telling You I'm Not Going' (from musical *Dreamgirls*) (Jennifer Holliday/Orchestra/Segovia)
¶Dylan, 'Mr Tambourine Man' (The Byrds)
¶'Oft in the Stilly Night' (Bolsterstone Male Voice Choir)

¶Beethoven, Symphony No. 6 in F major (Pastoral) (Vienna Philharmonic/Böhm)
*¶Dylan, 'I Believe in You' (Bob Dylan)
¶LUXURY: Water-colour equipment.
¶BOOK: Colour reproductions of the works of Michelangelo and other Renaissance artists.

9 April 1983
1691 Ruggiero Ricci
Violinist
*¶Bach, Prelude and Fugue No. 1 in C (BWV 846) (Wanda Landowska *harpsichord*)
¶Mozart, Sonata in F for Violin and Piano (K. 377) (David Oistrakh *violin*/Paul Badura-Skoda *piano*)
¶R. Strauss, 'Don Quixote' (Gregor Piatigorsky *cello*/Boston Symphony/Münch)
¶Glinka, 'Doubt' (Jennie Tourel/George Ricci *cello*)
¶Bruch, Violin Concerto No. 2 in D minor (Jascha Heifetz/RCA Victor Symphony/Solomon)
¶Mozart, 'Adagio' (Ruggiero Ricci *violin*/Leon Pommers *piano*)
¶Tchaikovsky, Piano Concerto No. 1 in B flat minor (Martha Argerich/Bavarian Radio Symphony/Kondrashin)
¶Rossini, *William Tell*(overture) (Spike Jones and his City Slickers)
¶LUXURY: The Plowden Guarneri violin.
¶BOOK: The letters of Beethoven.

16 April 1983
1692 Geoffrey Moorhouse
Foreign correspondent, writer and traveller
¶Allegri, 'Miserere' (Roy Goodman *treble*/King's College Chapel Choir/Willcocks)
¶Fifth test match: England *v* Australia 1948 (extract) (commentary by John Arlott)
*¶Mozart, 'Notte e giorno faticar' (from *Don Giovanni*, Act 1) (Gabriel Bacquier/LPO/Solti)

¶Bach, Fugue in G minor (BWV 578) (Helmut Walcha *organ*)
¶'Kafi-Holi' (Ravi Shankar *sitar*/Chatur Lal *tabladrums*/N.C. Mullick *tanpura*)
¶Simon, 'The Sound of Silence' (Simon & Garfunkel)
¶'Kyrie Eleison' (St Alexander Nevsky Cathedral Choir, Paris)
¶'The Old 93rd Caber Feidh' and 'The Badge of Scotland' (Pipes and Drums of 1st Battalion of the Argyll and Sutherland Highlanders)
¶LUXURY: A recording of curlews, and Indian spices.
¶BOOK: *Dictionary of National Biography*

23 April 1983
1693 Max Boyce
Entertainer
*¶MacColl, 'The First Time Ever I Saw Your Face' (Roberta Flack)
¶'Carrickfergus' (The Dubliners)
¶Comedy sketch from radio programme *Gala Performance*(Al Read)
¶'Land of My Fathers' (Hen Wlad by Nhadau) (Cardiff Arms Park crowd)
¶'Three Little Birds' (Bob Marley/The Wailers)
¶'Hiraeth' (Einir Wyn Owen)
¶Puccini, 'Nessun dorma' (from *Turandot*, Act 3) (Luciano Pavarotti/LPO/Mehta)
¶Handel, 'Pastoral Symphony' (from *Messiah*) (LSO/Colin Davis)
¶LUXURY: Oil painting equipment.
¶BOOK: Laurie Lee, *I Can't Stay Long*

30 April 1983
1694 A. N. Wilson
Novelist
¶'A Nightingale Sang in Berkeley Square' (from *New Faces*) (Barbara Cartland/Mike Sammes Singers/RPO/Fahey)
¶Schubert, Impromptu in G flat (opus 90, no. 3) (Dinu Lipatti *piano*)
¶'Eternal Father Strong to Save' (Royal Naval College Chapel Choir/Clarke)

¶ Haydn/Piati, 'Tempo di minuetto' (from Duo No. 6 in C) (Pablo Casals *cello*)
¶ Donizetti, 'Se tradirmi tu portrai' (from *Lucia di Lammermoor*, Act 2) (Maria Callas/Tito Gobbi/Maggio Musicale Fiorentino Orchestra/ Morisini)
¶ Lawes, *Comus*(incidental music to John Milton's masque) (Robert Tear/instrumental ensemble/Leppard)
¶ Belloc, 'The Winged Horse' (Hilaire Belloc)
*¶ Elgar, 'Profisciere Anima Christiana' (from *The Dream of Gerontius*) (Kim Borg/Sheffield Philharmonic Chorus/ Ambrosian Singers/Hallé Orchestra and Choir/Barbirolli)
¶ LUXURY: A bed and blankets.
¶ BOOK: *The Golden Treasury*, compiled by Francis Palgrave.

7 May 1983
1695 Arthur English
Actor and comedian
¶ Gershwin, 'Born in a Trunk' (from film *A Star is Born*) (Judy Garland)
¶ 'Underneath the Arches' (Flanagan & Allen)
¶ Chopin/Douglas, *Les Sylphides* (waltz) (National Philharmonic/ Bonynge)
¶ 'La vie en rose' (Mantovani and his Orchestra)
¶ Grieg, 'In the Hall of the Mountain King' (from *Peer Gynt Suite*) (LPO/Pritchard)
¶ 'Morning Has Broken' (Trinity Boys' Choir)
¶ J. Strauss, 'Mein Herr Marquis' (from *Die Fledermaus*) (Elisabeth Schumann/ Orchestra/Alwin)
*¶ Tchaikovsky, '1812 Overture' (Minneapolis Symphony/ University of Minnesota Brass Band/Dorati)
¶ LUXURY: A weekend in Paris.
¶ BOOK: John Julius Norwich, *Britain's Heritage*

14 May 1983
1696 Judge Alan King-Hamilton
Retired Old Bailey judge
¶ Gilbert & Sullivan, *Yeomen of the Guard* (Act 1 finale) (D'Oyly Carte Opera Company/RPO/ Sargent)
¶ Grieg, Piano Concerto in A minor (Clifford Curzon/LSO/ Fjeldstad)
¶ Puccini, 'Un bel di vedremo' (from *Madam Butterfly*, Act 2) (Victoria de los Angeles/Rome Opera House Orchestra and Chorus/Santini)
¶ Widor, 'Toccata' (from Symphony No. 5 in F minor) (Marie-Claire Alain *organ*)
¶ Rodgers & Hammerstein, 'The Lonely Goatherd' (from *The Sound of Music*) (Julie Andrews/chorus)
¶ Rachmaninov, Piano Concerto No. 2 in C minor (Vladimir Ashkenazy/LSO/ Previn)
¶ Mascagni, *Cavalleria rusticana* (intermezzo) (Berlin Philharmonic/von Karajan)
*¶ Beethoven, Symphony No. 5 in C minor (opus 67) (Berlin Philharmonic/von Karajan)
¶ LUXURY: A television set.
¶ BOOK: *Barclay's World of Cricket*, edited by Jim Swanton and John Woodcock.

21 May 1983
1697 Terry Wogan
Broadcaster
¶ Carmichael, 'Stardust' (Nat 'King' Cole)
*¶ Rimsky-Korsakov, 'The Young Prince and the Young Princess' (from *Scheherazade*) (Rodney Friend *violin*/LPO/ Haitink)
¶ 'Carrickfergus' (The Chieftains)
¶ 'The Cobbler's Song' (from *Chu Chin Chow*) (Paul Robeson)
¶ 'Heartbreak Hotel' (Elvis Presley)
¶ Mascagni, 'Easter Hymn' (from *Cavalleria rusticana*) (Victoria de los Angeles/Rome Opera House Orchestra and Chorus/Santini)

¶ Rodgers & Hart, 'My Funny Valentine' (from film *Babes in Arms*) (Frank Sinatra)
¶ Rodgers & Hammerstein, 'You'll Never Walk Alone' (from *Carousel*) (Shirley Jones)
¶ LUXURY: Vodka.
¶ BOOK: His favourite P. G. Wodehouse novels bound together, plus *At Swim-Two-Birds* by Myles na Gopaleen.

28 June 1983
1698 Sinead Cusack
Actress
¶ 'Carrickfergus' (The Clancy Brothers/Tommy Makem)
*¶ Bruch, Violin Concerto No. 1 in G minor (Kyung Wha Chung/RPO/Kempe)
¶ Prokofiev, 'Arrival of Guests' (from Ballet *Romeo and Juliet*) (LSO/Previn)
¶ Debussy, Sonata for Flute, Viola and Harp (Melos Ensemble)
¶ 'Bundle of Sorrow, Bundle of Joy' (Kate and Anna McGarrigle)
¶ Saint-Saëns, 'Le cygne' (from *Carnival of the Animals*) (Jacqueline du Pré *cello*/Osian Ellis *harp*)
¶ 'Demewer but Dangerous' (from Royal Shakespeare Company production of *The Swan Down Gloves*) (Jonathan Hyde/Sinead Cusack)
¶ Fauré, 'Pie Jesu' (from *Requiem*) (Victoria de los Angeles/Elisabeth Brasseur Choir/Paris Conservatoire Orchestra/Cluytens)
¶ LUXURY: Writing materials.
¶ BOOK: Her favourite books by John le Carré, bound together.

4 June 1983
1699 Raymond Briggs
Artist, writer and cartoonist
¶ 'Better Get It in Your Soul' (Charles Mingus *bass*/ensemble)
¶ 'Big Fat Alice's Blues' (Duke Ellington and his Orchestra)
¶ 'Hong Kong Blues' (Hoagy Carmichael *vocal and piano*)
¶ 'Far More Drums' (Dave Brubeck *piano*/Joe Morello *drums*)
*¶ 'The Boogie Rocks' (Albert Ammons Rhythm Kings)

¶ 'Dancy Dancy' (John Handy Quintet)

¶ 'I Want a Little Girl' (Clark Terry *trumpet*/Bob Brookmeyer Quintet)

¶ 'Blue Connotation' (Ornette Coleman Quartet)

¶ LUXURY: A billiard table with snooker balls and cues.

¶ BOOK: The complete works of Beachcomber.

11 June 1983
1700 Sir Peter Pears (2nd appearance)
Tenor

¶ 'The Foggy, Foggy Dew' (Peter Pears/Osian Ellis *harp*)

¶ Grainger (arr.), 'Shepherd's Hey' (English Chamber Orchestra/Britten)

¶ Schubert, 'Im Dorfe' (from *Winterreise*) (Peter Pears/ Benjamin Britten *piano*)

¶ Rosseter, 'Sweet Come Again' (Peter Pears/Julian Bream *lute*)

¶ Britten, 'Dawn' (from 'Four Sea Interludes' in *Peter Grimes*) (Royal Opera House Orchestra, Covent Garden/Britten)

¶ Dibdin, 'Tom Bowling' (Peter Pears/Benjamin Britten *piano*)

¶ Britten, String Quartet No. 3 (opus 94) (Amadeus Quartet)

*¶ 'The Sprig of Thyme' (Peter Pears/Benjamin Britten *piano*)

¶ LUXURY: A painting from his collection.

¶ BOOK: The commonplace book of E. M. Forster.

18 June 1983
1701 Fleur Cowles
Writer, painter, editor and traveller

*¶ Mussorgsky, 'Promenade' and 'Tuileries' (from *Pictures at an Exhibition*) (Gina Bachauer *piano*)

¶ Porter, 'True Love' (from film *High Society*) (Grace Kelly/Bing Crosby)

¶ Valencia, 'Dolencias' (theme from TV series *The Flight of the Condor*)

¶ Saint-Saëns, *Carnival of the Animals* (Cyril Smith & Phyllis Sellick *pianos*/instrumental ensemble)

¶ Granados, Danza espanola No. 5 in E minor (Andaluza) (Andrés Segovia *guitar*)

¶ 'The Girl from Ipanema' (Astrud Gilberto/Stan Getz *tenor saxophone*/João Gilberto *vocal and guitar*/Antonio Carlos Jobim *piano*)

¶ Puccini, 'Sola, perduta, abbandonata' (from *Manon Lescaut*, Act 4) (Montserrat Caballé/NPO/Bartoletti)

¶ Bernstein, Psalm No. 131 (from *Chichester Psalms*) (Camerata Singers/New York Philharmonic/Bernstein)

¶ LUXURY: Painting equipment.

¶ BOOK: Some blank paper and pens to write one herself.

25 June 1983
1702 Peter Maxwell Davies
Composer

¶ Beethoven, Grosse Fugue (opus 133) (Lindsay String Quartet)

¶ Ravel, 'The Frogs' (from *L'Enfant et les sortilèges*) (Nadine Sautereau/Yvon Le Marc'Hadour/Marguerite Legouhy/French National Radio Orchestra and Chorus/ Bour)

¶ Schœnberg, 'Farben' (from Five Pieces for Orchestra, opus 16) (BBC Symphony/Boulez)

¶ Carter, Concerto for Orchestra (New York Philharmonic/Bernstein)

¶ Bartók, String Quartet No. 5 (Hungarian String Quartet)

¶ Monteverdi, 'Pur ti miro' (from *L'incoronazione di Poppea*, Act 3) (Helen Donath/ Elisabeth Söderström/ Concentus Musicus, Vienna/ Harnoncourt)

¶ Sibelius, Symphony No. 7 in C (Hallé Orchestra/Barbirolli)

*¶ Byrd, 'Agnus Dei' (from *Mass for Four Voices*) (Christ Church Cathedral Choir, Oxford/ Preston)

¶ LUXURY: Music manuscript paper and pencils.

¶ BOOK: James Joyce, *Ulysses*

Index

References are to programme numbers

Dragon, Carmen, 535
Drake, Charlie, 418
Dresdel, Sonia, 66
Driberg, Tom, 28
Duckmanton, Talbot, 829
Duckworth, Canon Noel, 565
Dukes, Sir Paul, 742
du Maurier, Dame Daphne, 1400
Dunn, Clive, 1078
Dunn, Lieutenant-Colonel Sir Vivian, 1098
Dunnett, Dorothy, 1642
du Pré, Jacqueline, 1376
Durbridge, Francis, 923
Durrell, Gerald, 556
Dyall, Valentine, 258

Eddington, Paul, 1607
Edgar, Joan, 49
Edmonds, Noel, 1458
Edrich, W.J., 87
Edwards, Dorothy, 1417
Edwards, Gareth, 1206
Edwards, Jimmy, 98, 532
Edwards, Percy, 339
Elder, Mark, 1566
Ellington, Ray, 438
Elliott, Denholm, 1246
Elliott, G.H., 414
Elliott, Rev. Canon W.H., 9
Ellis, Mary, 205, 1676
Ellis, Osian, 1235
Ellis, Vivian, 102
Ellison, Rt Rev. Gerald, 1427
Elton, Lord, 21
Emery, Dick, 1036
Emett, Rowland, 653
Emney, Fred, 128
Engelmann, Franklin, 603
English, Arthur, 1695
Epstein, Brian, 730
Evans, Dame Edith, 702
Evans, Admiral Sir Edward, 25
Evans, Geraint, 662
Evans, Tolchard, 1347

Fabian, Ex-Detective Superintendent Robert, 270
Fairbairn, T.C., 1229
Fairbanks, Douglas Jr, 1334
Faith, Adam, 541
Falkner, Sir Keith, 1238
Fame, Georgie, 1182
Farnon, Robert, 441
Farr, Tommy, 235
Farrar, David, 349
Feather, Vic, 1203
Feldman, Marty, 934
Fettes, Peter, 46
Feuillère, Edwige, 930

Ffrangcon-Davies, Gwen, 617
Fiedler, Arthur, 743
Field, Xenia, 866
Fielding, Fenella, 865
Fields, Gracie, 91, 576
Finch, Peter, 313
Fingleton, Jack, 557
Fisher, James, 362
Fisher, Norman, 451
Fitton, James, 1055
Fitzgibbon, Maggie, 953
Flagstad, Kirsten, 134
Flanagan, Bud, 327
Flanders, Michael, 376, 789
Fleming, Ian, 665
Fleming, Peter, 83
Fletcher, Cyril, 428
Foldes, Andor, 469
Fontaine, Joan, 1464
Fonteyn, Dame Margot, 750
Foord, Bert, 1191
Foort, Reginald, 1072
Forbes, Bryan, 823
Ford, Oliver, 1374
Formby, George, 113
Forsyth, Bruce, 605
Forsyth, Frederick, 1310
Foster, Julia, 1313
Fowler, Eileen, 1219
Fowles, John, 1575
Fox, Edward, 1486
Fox, James, 1690
Fox, Roy, 1216
Fox, Uffa, 445
Foyle, Christina, 594
Francis, Clare, 1392
Francis, Dick, 855
Francis, Sir Frank, 800
Frankau, Pamela, 41
Frankel, William, 1305
Franklin, David, 1141
Fraser, Lady Antonia, 971
Fraser, Bill, 799
Freeman, John, 487
Frémaux, Louis, 1404
Freni, Mirella, 1388
Freud, Clement, 850
Frink, Elisabeth, 1254
Frost, David, 647, 1105
Fry, Christopher, 1457
Fuller, Rosalinde, 905

Gable, Christopher, 1147
Galbraith, Professor J.K., 1631
Gallico, Paul, 573
Galway, James, 1345
Gamlin, Lionel, 242
Gander, L. Marsland, 960
Gaskin, Catherine, 1564
Gavin, Dr Catherine, 1442
Gedda, Nicolai, 968
Gemmell, Professor Alan, 1410
Genn, Leo, 191

Geraldo, 380
Gerhardt, Elena, 412
Gibbons, Carroll, 119
Gibson, Alexander, 1167
Gibson, Wing Commander Guy, 43
Gielgud, Sir John, 581, 1593
Gielgud, Val, 622
Gilbert, Martin, 1627
Gillard, Frank, 1108
Gillespie, Dizzy, 1524
Gilliat, Sidney, 590
Gingold, Hermione, 127, 982
Giulini, Carlo Maria, 929
Gladstone, Sir William, 1330
Glendenning, Raymond, 589
Glitter, Gary, 1587
Glover, Brian, 1563
Glubb, Sir John (Glubb Pasha), 1432
Gluckstein, Sir Louis, 1065
Gobbi, Tito, 394, 1495
Godden, Rumer, 1306
Godfrey, Isidore, 1007
Godwin, Dame Anne, 933
Gollancz, Victor, 525
Gonella, Nat, 820
Goodall, Reginald, 1522
Goodwin, Dennis, 263
Goolden, Richard, 64, 846
Goossens, Léon, 478
Goossens, Sidonie, 256
Gordon, Richard, 1086
Gore-Booth, Sir Paul, 944
Goring, Marius, 354
Grace, Princess of Monaco, 1589
Graham, Winston, 1412
Grainer, Ron, 682
Granger, Stewart, 63, 1590
Grant, Duncan, 1272
Grappelli, Stephane, 1138
Gray, Dulcie, 148
Greco, Juliette, 660
Green, Hughie, 578
Greenhouse, Bernard, 1613
Greenslade, Bill, 165
Greenwood, Joan, 147
Gregg, Hubert, 803
Gregson, John, 253
Grenfell, Joyce, 99, 1074
Grenfell, Stephen, 714
Grey, Anthony, 993
Grey, Beryl, 377
Grey Walter, Dr W., 549
Grieg, Tony, 1333
Griffith, Hugh, 852
Grigson, Geoffrey, 1667
Grigson, Jane, 1444
Grinham, Judy, 429

Grisewood, Freddy, 45, 517
Groves, Charles, 1132
Grunwald, Anatole, 747
Gubbins, Nathaniel, 18
Guest, George, 1343
Guinness, Sir Alec, 498, 1416
Gunn, James, 577
Guthrie, Tyrone, 435
Guyler, Deryck, 1016

Hackett, General Sir John, 1546
Haendel, Ida, 1026
Hailstone, Bernard, 1265
Haitink, Bernard, 1212
Hale, Binnie, 156
Hale, Lionel, 369
Hale, Sonnie, 163
Hall, Adelaide, 1154
Hall, Dr Elsie, 966
Hall, Henry, 144, 920
Hall, Peter, 779
Hammond, Joan, 78, 1031
Hammond, Kay, 76
Hampshire, Susan, 901
Hancock, Sheila, 753
Hancock, Tony, 346
Handl, Irene, 586
Hands, Terry, 1605
Hanff, Helene, 1624
Hansford-Johnson, Pamela, 620
Hanson, John, 785
Harben, Philip, 251
Hardcastle, William, 1250
Harding, Gilbert, 138
Harding, Mike, 1668
Hardwicke, Sir Cedric, 222
Hardy, Professor Sir Alister, 1200
Hardy, Robert, 1433
Hare, Doris, 1302
Hare, Robertson, 70, 459, 1118
Harewood, Earl of, 788, 1625
Harker, Gordon, 164
Harmer, Cyril, 980
Harper, Gerald, 849
Harper, Heather, 950
Harris, Robert, 225
Harris, Rolf, 856
Harrison, Kathleen, 114
Harrison, Michael, 48
Harrison, Rex, 1511
Harrison, Rosina, 1324
Harrisson, Tom, 34, 1156
Hartnell, William, 770
Harty, Russell, 1586
Harvey, Laurence, 265
Harvey, Len, 281
Harwood, Elizabeth, 1117
Hashman, Judy, 1013
Hastings, Macdonald, 769